THE WORLD BANK
Its First Half Century

Devesh Kapur

John P. Lewis

Richard Webb

Editors

BROOKINGS INSTITUTION PRESS
Washington, D.C.

Copyright © 1997
THE BROOKINGS INSTITUTION
1775 Massachusetts Avenue, N.W., Washington, D.C. 20036

Library of Congress Cataloging-in-Publication data:

Kapur, Devesh, 1959–
The World Bank : its first half century / Devesh Kapur, John P. Lewis, and Richard Webb.
p.   cm.
Includes bibliographical references and index.
ISBN 0-8157-5230-X (set). — ISBN 0-8157-5234-2 (v. 1). — ISBN 0-8157-5236-9 (v. 2)
1. World Bank—History. I. Lewis, John Prior. II. Webb, Richard Charles, 1937–   .
HG3881.5.W57L49   1997
332.1'532'05—dc21   97-21093
                                                                                CIP

9 8 7 6 5 4 3 2 1

The paper used in this publication meets the minimum requirements of the
American National Standard for Information Sciences—Permanence of Paper for
Printed Library Materials, ANSI Z39.48-1984.

Composition by Princeton Editorial Associates
Scottsdale, Arizona, and Roosevelt, New Jersey

Printed by R. R. Donnelley and Sons Co.
Crawfordsville, Indiana

THE BROOKINGS INSTITUTION

The Brookings Institution is an independent organization devoted to nonpartisan research, education, and publication in economics, government, foreign policy, and the social sciences generally. Its principal purposes are to aid in the development of sound public policies and to promote public understanding of issues of national importance.

The Institution was founded on December 8, 1927, to merge the activities of the Institute for Government Research, founded in 1916, the Institute of Economics, founded in 1922, and the Robert Brookings Graduate School of Economics and Government, founded in 1924.

The Board of Trustees is responsible for the general administration of the Institution, while the immediate direction of the policies, program, and staff is vested in the President, assisted by an advisory committee of the officers and staff. The by-laws of the Institution state: "It is the function of the Trustees to make possible the conduct of scientific research, and publication, under the most favorable conditions, and to safeguard the independence of the research staff in the pursuit of their studies and in the publication of the results of such studies. It is not a part of their function to determine, control, or influence the conduct of particular investigations or the conclusions reached."

The President bears final responsibility for the decision to publish a manuscript as a Brookings book. In reaching his judgment on the competence, accuracy, and objectivity of each study, the President is advised by the director of the appropriate research program and weighs the views of a panel of expert outside readers who report to him in confidence on the quality of the work. Publication of a work signifies that it is deemed a competent treatment worthy of public consideration but does not imply endorsement of conclusions or recommendations.

The Institution maintains its position of neutrality on issues of public policy in order to safeguard the intellectual freedom of the staff. Hence interpretations or conclusions in Brookings publications should be understood to be solely those of the authors and should not be attributed to the Institution, to its trustees, officers, or other staff members, or to the organizations that support its research.

Foreword

IN 1973, in connection with the World Bank's first twenty-five years, Edward Mason and Robert Asher wrote *The World Bank since Bretton Woods,* the first major authorized but independent history of the institution. Some years later, the Bank's retired senior executive, William Diamond, proposed that an overall history of the Bank's first half century be prepared by authors who, like Mason and Asher, would have full access to the Bank's people and papers but would write free of institutional control. It was decided the study should be seated administratively at an external organization, and, as a matter of fresh choice, not tradition, the Bank and the Brookings Institution agreed that, like the study by Mason and Asher, the new project would be based at Brookings.

Again there were to be two authors, but this time one should come from the North, the other from the South. In 1989 John Lewis of Princeton University in the United States and Richard Webb of Peru were recruited. Both had long known the Bank but neither had worked for it at great length. Webb had been on the research staff for five years in the 1970s before returning to Peru as governor of its central bank; Lewis, a veteran of USAID and OECD/DAC, had worked for and with the Bank in various consulting capacities. As research associate to the project, Brookings employed Devesh Kapur, an Indian national then pursuing a Ph.D. in public and international affairs at Princeton's Woodrow Wilson School. By mid-1993 Kapur had become so indispensable and so engaged in the writing that, by common consent, he was graduated to coauthorship.

For two components of this project the authors sought and gratefully accepted reenforcement. The record of the Bank's subsidiary, the International Finance

vii

Corporation, was important but substantially separate from that of the mother institution. Jonas Haralz of Iceland, a World Bank economist earlier in his career and the Nordic executive director on the Bank board in the late 1980s, was well qualified to address the IFC. Robert Wade, originally of New Zealand, later of the Institute of Development Studies in the United Kingdom, and currently of Brown University in the United States, wrote the chapter on the Bank's relationship with the environment.

From the beginning all parties to the project—the authors, the Bank, Brookings, and the international advisory committee recruited to help guide the venture— agreed that along with the main volume of history for which the authors themselves would be responsible, the work should include a second volume (edited by the authors of the first volume) consisting of views of the Bank from various external perspectives. The perspectives—a dozen in number—are those of close observers of the Bank's work and relations with its major shareholders, its interaction with financial markets and its Bretton Woods sister institution, the International Monetary Fund, its standing with the profession of development economics, and country and regional experiences with borrowers.

Brookings extends its thanks to the World Bank for the freedom and accessibility it has afforded the authors and adds its gratitude to all those whose help the authors acknowledge in the preface.

Brookings gratefully acknowledges funding for the project, which was provided in part by The Ford Foundation, The World Bank, The John D. and Catherine T. MacArthur Foundation, Deutsche Bank AG, The Japan Foundation, Japan Center for International Finance, The Life Insurance Association of Japan, The Federation of Bankers Association of Japan, Nikko Securities Company, Ltd., Nomura Securities Company, Ltd., Yamaichi Securities Company, Ltd., Daiwa Securities Company, Ltd., F. L. Smidth & Company A/S (Denmark), Haldor Topsoe A/S (Denmark), Landsvirkjun, The National Power Company (Iceland), Reykjavik Hot Water System (Iceland), Swedish Bankers Association, A/S Veidekke (Norway), Central Bank of Norway, Statkraft SF (Norway), Asea Brown Boveri AS, and Robert S. McNamara.

The views expressed in this book are those of the authors and should not be ascribed to the organizations acknowledged above or to the trustees, officers, or staff members of the Brookings Institution or the World Bank.

MICHAEL H. ARMACOST
President

July 1997
Washington, D.C.

Preface

THE FOREWORD has outlined the general development of the World Bank history project and the focus and organization of the two volumes. We wish here to elaborate a bit. It may be useful to know the division of labor in volume 1. John Lewis was the principal drafter of chapters 8–10, 17, and 18; Richard Webb of chapters 2–7; and Devesh Kapur of chapters 11, 12, and 14–16. Kapur and Lewis collaborated on chapter 1. Robert Wade was chosen to write a chapter on the subject of the bank and environmental protection, not only because of his record as a policy analyst but also because he undertook the assignment without having a position on the issues. He wrote well and covered the subject thoroughly, but the chapter was long and the physical balance of the two volumes was better if we included it in volume 2. Its location there satisfies the concept of volume 2 well enough, but it should be read as an integral component of volume 1, analogous to the chapters on agriculture, poverty, and the social sectors.

Half the contributed chapters of volume 2 focus on the World Bank's relations with particular member countries. Volume 1 grapples even more with these relations. It was clear as we progressed that the Bank's overall experience and performance had to be illustrated by its transactions with individual borrowing countries. We could not possibly discuss the relations with each of them, but neither could we convey the texture of the experience without digging into country cases. We have done so fairly widely, selecting countries arbitrarily if not randomly. The result is a richer view of the record, but a lumpy one. In volume 1, along with fairly intensive discussions of Bank relations with fifteen or so borrowing countries during various portions of the fifty years covered in the story, we have one long chapter on the most challenging geographic region (sub-Saharan Africa) and another on a region (Latin America) that was involved in a particularly traumatic episode (the debt crisis). As a result, treatment of other areas—China is a major example—is thinner than we would have preferred.

We must record one particular regret. The biggest hole in the study's coverage is the Bank's experience since 1990 in eastern Europe and the former Soviet Union. That we would face a problem in this regard was evident when the subject surged into prominence well after our plan for these volumes, and related allocations of time and assignments, had become firm. Although we recruited a highly qualified author to write a chapter on the subject for volume 2, the deadline for submission was not met. By then it was altogether too late to contrive any substitute for the missing material. We apologize to our readers.

We acknowledge some of the volume 2 authors—among them S. Guhan, Catherine Gwin, Jacques Polak, and Nicholas Stern—whose final drafts were completed long before volume 1 was finished.

The principal authors are most grateful to the World Bank for the combination of access and independence they have been afforded. It is hard to think of another instance in which a public or private institution has made its personnel, present and past, as well as its documents and files (recent as well as earlier, most of them nonpublic, many still explicitly confidential) so freely accessible to a group of outsiders and then exercised virtually no control over the conclusions of the research and the resulting publication.

This is by no means to say that Bank people approved our work in all instances. Many objected to the drafts we presented and wrote dissenting commentaries that were enlightening. But there was no instance in which the Bank sought to overrule one of our interpretations.

From the beginning the Brookings Institution also afforded us a very large measure of autonomy. What it and the Bank regretted was the length of time the study consumed. Like our two principal sponsors, we started out expecting the entire exercise to occupy four or five years instead of the more than seven that it finally consumed, and there were extra costs, opportunity and otherwise, to seeing it through. But there was no good way to anticipate how long a thorough job would take. Although not disagreeing much with the conclusions of Edward Mason and Robert Asher's *The World Bank since Bretton Woods*, which was published in 1973, we needed to address various issues that had their roots at the Bank's inception. That meant twice as much time to cover. And in its second quarter century the Bank had become more complex: its emphases had changed, and its membership, clientele, and staff and the variety of its portfolio, as well as the span of its external relations, had grown exponentially. Moreover, a researcher needed to be careful. As we pursued the rare opportunity to look into the recesses of the institution, it often took several trial drafts to get our narrative straight.

In one respect our exceptional access to internal Bank sources skewed the selection of subject matter and references. Historians of the Bank are bound to deal in some measure with the political, economic, geographic, and cultural contexts in which the institution has operated. Some senior Bank personnel urged more attention to these aspects, and some academic readers would have preferred further citation of the nonofficial studies that bear upon many facets of the present work. As members of the nonofficial research community ourselves, we sympathized with such views. Yet if one really respects these studies, it is clear that no history of the World Bank can pretend to be an adequate review of issues involving general development and development policy. Besides, our comparative advantage was to tell outsiders some of the content of internal Bank thinking and debate that they cannot readily obtain elsewhere.

Our research method has been commonplace: we conducted hundreds of interviews; read countless memoranda, minutes, reports, and other materials; traveled to developing countries to investigate Bank operations on site; and cross-referenced readers' seminars and comments. Bank staff members' support for the project was uneven. Some did not welcome intrusions on their work or thought the time was inappropriate for investigative reporting or simply lacked interest. Some forgot the research was under way. But these were far outnumbered by the many who were curious and responsive and volunteered their help.

We do have some complaints. Although we benefited greatly from the Bank's extensive and admirably managed archives, we suffered, as will other researchers, from the institution's lack of a clear policy about ownership of officers' personal files. Some senior executives of the Bank have, upon retirement, taken with them large quantities of papers that by rights, it seems to us, should remain with the institution. We were fortunate (and grateful) to gain access to some of these files. But the policy should be clarified. In addition, in its internal correspondence the Bank uses the classification "confidential" rather freely. This is understandable for facilitating operations, although greater restraint would be appropriate. What is less excusable is that there has been no regular regime for declassifying papers after a specified time has passed or some other marker has been reached.

In our work we have been counseled by two worthy committees. The first was a formal advisory committee formed at the start of the project that had three meetings and continued to comment on drafts and correspond with the authors. It consisted of Abdlatif Al-Hamad, Rodrigo Botero, Robert Cassen, William Diamond, Crauford Goodwin, Catherine Gwin, Gerald Helleiner, Takashi Hosomi, the late Philip Ndegwa, Widjojo Nitisastro, I. G. Patel, Helga Steeg, and John Williamson. The second ("guidance and closure") group was formed by Brookings to assist us in the final stages. It met quarterly during the later years of the project and consisted of William Diamond and Gerald Helleiner together with Jonas Haralz and Mervyn Weiner. We extend many thanks to the members of both committees.

At Brookings, we are grateful to former president Bruce MacLaury and former Foreign Policy Studies director John Steinbruner. For editorial work, we thank the staff of the Brookings Institution Press, Sam Allen, and Princeton Editorial Associates, and for verification, Christopher Dall, Maya Dragicevic, Gary Gordon, and Alexander Ratz. The volumes were typeset and indexed by Princeton Editorial Associates. In and around the Bank we are indebted to Jochen Kraske, before and after he became Bank historian, and to the godfather of the project, William Diamond, who has never lost concerned interest in it. The regional and joint Bank-Fund libraries, the Offices of the Secretary and General Counsel, the Operations Evaluation Department, and the Bank's archives under Charles Ziegler are among the units to which we owe particular thanks.

We would especially like to thank the staff at the Executive Director's Library (now renamed the Board Resources Center) under Kenlee Ray: Michael Dompas, Andrea Nash, and Herve Tien-Sing Young. We are also most grateful to Charles McCaskill for his help in steering us through the maze of data on the Bank's operations and William Silverman on personnel data. Concetta DeNaro and William Katzenstein (both in the Planning and Budget Department) also assisted our access to data.

We much appreciate the counsel of our predecessor, Robert Asher. It is impossible to name all the people of the Bank, of various vintages, who have helped. But we must list those who were exceptionally generous with their time and attention: Warren Baum, Robert Calderisi, Barber Conable, Richard Demuth, Stephen Eccles, Nicholas Hope, S. Shahid Husain, Benjamin King, Burke Knapp, David Knox, Robert McNamara, Barbara Opper, Guy Pierre Pfeffermann, Eugene Rotberg, Ibrahim Shihata, Ernest Stern, Willi Wapenhans, Christopher Willoughby, and Peter Wright.

We also gratefully acknowledge the help of these other past or present Bank personnel and executive directors: Yoshiaki Abe, James Adams, Bilsel Alisbah, Gerald Alter, Robert Ayres, Jean Baneth, Bernard Bell, Munir Benjenk, Hans Binswanger, Nancy Birdsall, Shirley Boskey, Pieter Bottelier, Mark Bowyer, Aron Broches, Shahid Javed Burki, Sven Burmester, Elkyn Chaparro, Roger Chaufournier, Russell Cheetham, S.H. Choi, Armeane Choksi, Lief Christoffersen, Anthony Churchill, A.W. Clausen, Kevin Cleaver, Roberto Cuca, P. N. Damry, Stephen Denning, Kemal Dervis, Dennis De Tray, Shantayanan Devarajan, Ashok Dhareshwar, Graham Donaldson, Robert Drysdale, Stanley Fischer, Edward Fried, Marie Gallup, Michael Gillette, Joseph Goldberg, Melvin Goldman, Mohan Gopalan Gopal, Julian Grenfell, Enzo Grilli, Ann Hamilton, Marianne Hang, Randolph Harris, James Harrison, John Holsen, David Hopper, Ishrat Husain, Gregory Ingram, Paul Isenman, Ruth Jacoby, Bimal Jalan, Frederick Jasperson, Edward V. K. Jaycox, William Jones, Charlotte Jones-Carroll, Andrew Kamarck, Ravi Kanbur, Robert Kaplan, Shiv Kapur, Martin Karcher, Gautam Kasi, Basil Kavalsky, James Kearns, Timothy King, Ciao Koch-Weser, K. P. Krishnan, Anne

Krueger, Olivier Lafourcade, Luis Landau, Kenneth Lay, Mark Leiserson, Enrique Lerdau, Robert Liebenthal, Johannes Linn, Richard Lynn, Dirk Mattheisen, Oey Meesook, Paul Meo, Marisela Montoliu, Ricardo Moran, Gobind Nankani, Binod Nayak, Julio Nogues, Lester Nurick, Michel Petit, Robert Picciotto, Lewis Preston, V. S. Raghavan, V. Rajagopalan, Luis Ramirez, D. C. Rao, Martin Ravallion, Christopher Redford, Helena Ribe, Peter Richardson, Ronald Ridker, Andres Rigo, William Ryrie, Francisco Sagasti, Joanne Salop, Hugh Scott, Marcelo Selowsky, Alexander Shakow, John Shilling, Gerardo Sicat, Richard Skolnik, Parita Soebsaeng, Davidson Sommers, Rainer Steckhan, Ashok Subramanian, Sachi Takeda, Wilfred Thalwitz, Rene Vandendries, Adriaan Verspoor, Paulo Vicira Da Cunha, Frank Vogl, Harry Walters, Dennis Whittle, D. Joseph Wood, Ngaire Woods, Hans Wyss, Lorene Yap, Montague Yudelman, and Manuel Zymelman.

Among the non-Bank people consulted, we acknowledge, in particular, Edward Bernstein, David Cole, Vijay Jagannadakan, Alexander Kafka, Gustav Papanek, Judith Tendler, and Paul Volcker.

The project has had a very small staff to whom the authors are greatly indebted and who have served mostly in series: as secretary–office manager–research assistant: Polly Buechel, Laura Powell, Deborah Jaffe, Alison Bishop, Seiko Kyan, and Kurt Lindblom; as research assistants: Karen Semkow, Chris Watkins, David Brindley, Esther Benjamin, and Sachiko Kataoka.

Despite all the help, final responsibility for the outcome lies with the authors.

Contents of Volume Two

Contents of Volume One

ONE

The World Bank as a Development-Promoting Institution

The Editors

AMID the celebrations for the fiftieth anniversary of the Bretton Woods Conference in 1994, a group of nongovernmental organizations proclaimed, "Fifty years is enough." The World Bank was under fire. International organizations with prominent and contested missions have ways of inviting that predicament; some also handle it well. But a good guess is that fifty years is not enough.

From its inception the World Bank has put a premium on confidentiality. Though it has recently become more open with much of its information, the Bank has rarely invited study of the institution as an institution (as opposed to outside participation by consultants and others in its substantive analyses and assessments). Once before, at the twenty-fifth anniversary of the World Bank Group, Edward Mason and Robert Asher, of Harvard University and the Brookings Institution, respectively, were invited to study the Bank. Their research produced *The World Bank since Bretton Woods*.[1] When we were invited to prepare a study to coincide with the Bank's fiftieth anniversary, we (along with an international advisory board) decided that a multiplicity of perspectives offered in a complementary volume would contribute much to the main text. This volume of essays from development thinkers and practitioners around the world is the result. Each of the chapters offers a unique view of the Bank. Taken together, these outside perspectives in volume 2 fill out the account found in volume 1.

Five of the chapters presented here address relations between the World Bank and individual countries; all of them address the World Bank's contribution to development.

1. Edward S. Mason and Robert E. Asher, *The World Bank since Bretton Woods* (Brookings, 1973).

1

Borrower Country Cases: Korea, Mexico, and Côte d'Ivoire

For a development bank, the bottom line is developmental contribution, client by client. The task of development is formidable. It takes decades; setbacks muddy the picture. More than an analysis of gross national product (GNP) is involved. Growth should be shared, indigence abated, natural resources and culture preserved, and rules should be more predictable and participatory. Though it began with a primary focus on project promotion and selected inputs to GNP growth, the Bank has steadily broadened its own terms of reference.

The World Bank can help in the drive to development but only to a degree—largely determined by a country's circumstances. Compared with the needs of large nations such as India, Brazil, Indonesia, or China, Bank loans are merely a drop in the ocean of need. Even a nation of medium economic size such as Colombia, Kenya, the Philippines, Morocco, or Malaysia must invest twenty or fifty times more than it is allowed to borrow from the Bank each year. In the smaller nations such as Guinea-Bissau, Honduras, or Chad, Bank disbursements of foreign exchange (before netting out repayments), in good years, cover some 10 to 15 percent of imports.

In slaying the developmental giant, the Bank must emulate David, with influence as its sling. Far more than it can ever admit, its business is persuasion—teaching, backing "the good guys," plotting with other donors, and occasionally (when cold war politics called for it, or when a country is needed to right its international finances) playing hardball reform through loan conditionalities. In the development context, Albert Hirschman described this as "reform-mongering." Eugene Black, president of the Bank from 1949 through 1962, called it the "diplomacy of development."[2]

Pity the auditor—and the historian. The official books keep track of loans and expenses, yet few records convey the full business of the Bank. Letters and memorandums in the files provide glimpses, though presidential and vice presidential files tend to leave the Bank with their originators. Oral histories provide further glimpses, but memories weaken and are fallible. Even perfect records and excellent memories fall short of the mark. We know little about the workings of influence on decisions, or even of government measures on economies. Our ignorance is there to see in the vagaries of development fashion.

Can the clients fill in the missing record? Are they not the best judges of the Bank's developmental contribution? Can they at least provide us with a fuller account of the Bank's doings (above all as influencer and educator) in their countries? If bias is unavoidable, a borrower's point of view might at least offset the material, biased in favor of the Bank, that is the principal and usual source for accounts and judgments about the institution. Indeed, even criticism is largely the Bank's self-criticism, or based on it.

---

2. Eugene R. Black, *The Diplomacy of International Development* (Harvard University Press, 1960).

In chapter 2, Mahn-Je Kim, former deputy prime minister and minister of economic planning for South Korea, provides an insider's perspective on Korea's relations with the Bank. What influence did the Bank exert in Korea? Although the government borrowed heavily from the Bank in the 1970s and 1980s (accounting for nearly half of Korea's external public borrowing during this period), perhaps attesting to the value placed on the Bank's technical project advice and intellectual support, Kim is subdued on that score. He is more forthcoming in crediting Bank help in "selling" the country's economic leadership to its own people. The effect of the Bank's recommendations was also greater externally, through the Bank's efforts in the consultative group for Korea, in promoting Korea to the outside world. Yet in the end Kim attributes his country's success to a cultural phenomenon: Confucianism. He believes the quality of a government dominates the way it implements policies.

Three studies of borrowing countries are presented in this volume: Korea, Mexico, and Ivory Coast. Of these three nations, only Mexico sent a representative to the Bretton Woods Conference, and Mexico's relations with the Bank are most extensive. Tapping into this rich history, Carlos M. Urzúa finds that the Bank's relations with Mexico fall into two distinct periods: before and after the debt crisis. From its first lending in 1959 until the early 1980s, the Bank maintained a stable, low-key relationship with Mexico, contributing modestly through resources and advice. Later—during the 1970s, with the government awash in oil revenues and private capital and with the quality of its economic policy deteriorating—the Bank lent vigorously. But with regard to policy, the Bank was little more than a bystander, except in poverty-oriented sectors. That seeming idleness came to an end in August 1982, when Mexico announced that it was unable to service its external debt. At that point, the Bank became both financier and intimate policy adviser to the Mexican government as the nation went through a wrenching structural adjustment.

The resolution of the debt crisis did not signal the end of Mexico's problems. Urzúa criticizes the undiscerning support the Bank gave the Mexican reforms in the early 1990s. He contends that the Bank became too close a policy adviser and influence to remain an effective critic. Complacent with economic policies and closely identified with the incumbent administration, the Bank was overconfident about Mexico, and this contributed to the peso crisis of December 1994.

Like Korea, Côte d'Ivoire began borrowing from the Bank in 1968. Unlike Korea, and more like many of its Sub-Saharan African partners, Côte d'Ivoire fell prey to radical swings in its fortunes. In chapter 4 Jacques Pégatiénan and Bakary Ouayogode (former head of the government's research establishment) examine the painful story of the stark decline of a country that, as late as the early 1980s, was one of Africa's brightest economic stars. Pégatiénan and Ouayogode's view interweaves the perspective of the academic with that of the practitioner.

The authors place the blame for Côte d'Ivoire's decline on its late president, Felix Houphouët-Boigny, and on France, arguing that the Bank was too deferential to both in the face of failing economic policies. Bolstered by his country's early success, Houphouët-Boigny—backed by France—became obstinate and failed to recognize and adapt to changes in the world economy. Oddly enough, many critics accuse the Bank of heavy-handedness with its weaker African clients and of turning a deaf ear to its non-Western members. When the Bank began asserting strong pressure on Côte d'Ivoire's leaders at the end of the 1980s, the damage was, for the most part, irrevocable.

Taken together, these chapters cast light on the myriad factors that affect Bank-country relations and the dilemmas inherent in conducting them. The Bank's primary role—and one bolstered by accumulated experience—has been that of lender and adviser to governments—more specifically, central governments. As such, the Bank has been most effective in countries with strong leadership committed to economic development. Yet, as evidenced by the Korean case, the Bank's assistance is less needed in such instances.

This dilemma is equally true within countries. In meting out its resources, should the Bank invest in the sector or region where its potential influence would be greatest because of the receptivity of a particular ministry or regional government? Or should it go where borrower management is most dynamic, thereby ensuring successful implementation? Alternatively, should the Bank direct its energies where the need for change appears greatest? Unfortunately, the three criteria rarely coincide. When differences arise between borrowing governments and the Bank, whose priorities should prevail? Borrowing governments argue that their priorities reflect national interests and should therefore be paramount. Yet what constitutes "national interests" is often a matter of heated debate and can be a cover for much more parochial concerns.

The Bank's shifting intellectual advice (for example, its support for Côte d'Ivoire's public enterprises in the 1970s, which it pressed to privatize in the 1980s), produces its own difficulties. Is the Bank being inconsistent, at the peril of its borrowers; or is this a reflection of its intellectual flexibility and willingness to learn? Another tension arises when borrowers face financial emergencies, as in Côte d'Ivoire and Mexico, which renders it difficult to reconcile the Bank's long-term developmental mission with shorter-term considerations.

Too often the Bank is attributed powers that it does not possess. These chapters illustrate the Bank's limited capacity for leverage over governments. But we also see that the institution's leverage and power of persuasion shift with a borrowing country's economic success. The Bank's broad range of activities allows for a greater horizon of opportunities to influence, with inevitable trade-offs and compromises. External players also enter this playing field, as is evident in Côte d'Ivoire and Mexico, where the interests of large shareholders (namely, France and the United States) intrude on relationships between the Bank and borrowing countries.

The Korean case challenges several elements of conventional wisdom. The Bank supported Korea's massive investments in industrial development in an economy strongly controlled by the government. Indeed, much of the Bank's lending went for physical infrastructure, whereas governance issues such as weak beneficiary participation, excessive military spending, and self-reliance (dictated by security concerns) received short shrift from the Bank.

The three countries examined here also challenge the Bank's more recent promotion of participation and openness as a crucial ingredient of *economic* development. All three had more or less authoritarian regimes; however, performance varied widely both across countries and over time. In Korea and Mexico, the lack of openness helped forge trust between the Bank and national officials, whereas in Côte d'Ivoire, it had the opposite effect.

Sub-Saharan Africa

The plan for this volume had been for Carol Lancaster to collaborate with her longtime friend, Philip Ndegwa, the distinguished Kenyan former civil servant and business executive, on a joint chapter on the Bank in Sub-Saharan Africa. With Lancaster appointed deputy administrator for the United States Agency for International Development in 1993 and Ndegwa heavily engaged in Nairobi, the collaboration was not yet fully realized when Philip Ndegwa died suddenly in January 1996. We are retaining his voice by publishing (in slightly edited form) the extensive commentary he provided in 1994 on an early draft of chapter 5.

Lancaster, from the point of view of a political scientist, focuses on the politics of the Bank's structural adjustment lending (SAL) in Africa. Her sketch of the early days of development in postindependence Sub-Saharan Africa amplifies chapters on this subject in volume 1. In the SAL era, whose rationale for Africa was laid out in the 1981 Berg Report, the Bank is seen as exchanging conditioned program loans for "agreed economic policy reforms."[3]

Reforms were needed to repair the domestic macroeconomic policy errors that, although aggravated from outside, were the principal source of unmanageable payment deficits. As Africa's lead donor for structural adjustment (albeit with a shared role for France and the International Monetary Fund in francophone Africa), the Bank's task was to persuade both borrowing countries and other external interveners to implement coherent adjustment programs.

Lancaster draws a sharp contrast regarding the Bank's comparative success with the two sets of addressees. Many African borrowers asserted that they were treated abrasively, subjected to stereotypical reform formulas, and had dubious reforms pressed on them. In contrast, Lancaster finds a high degree of Bank success in holding substantive sway over donors. But she also recognizes the cost. By the early

---

3. World Bank, *Accelerated Growth in Sub-Saharan Africa: An Agenda for Action* (Washington: World Bank, 1981). This report is commonly named after Elliot Berg, coordinator of the African Strategy Review Group, which produced the study.

1990s, the Bank found itself increasingly insecure with being far out front in Africa with an adjustment policy lead falling short of its earlier billing.

In his comments on Lancaster's draft, Ndegwa reminisces about Robert McNamara's 1969 visit to Kenya when Ndegwa was permanent secretary for agriculture and about Bank arrogance and the African appetite for constructive, politically feasible structural adjustment. He concludes with some penetrating observations about key African personalities and about some Bank personnel.

The U.S. Role

Arguably, the international community was not about to commit as much access to power as it did to the new Bretton Woods institutions unless the new bodies were controlled by the economically (and militarily) weightier countries. Moreover, in the aftermath of World War II (especially after the Soviet Union withdrew from Bretton Woods), politicoeconomic weight was so overwhelmingly centered in the United States that there was no way America could have avoided dominating the new International Bank for Reconstruction and Development (IBRD). The task of the historian is to determine how much and in what capacity the United States came to dominate the Bank. As the Bank's largest donor and often most vocal partner, the United States has received considerable treatment in volume 1 of this history.

As a chronicler of the U.S. role in the Bank, Catherine Gwin takes the obligations and responsibilities of the United States seriously. In chapter 6 she carefully and critically examines U.S. performance. As leading owner of the Bank, could the United States have been less (and less characteristically) overbearing? Has U.S. leadership—constructive at the beginning, when it played a heavy hand in drafting the rules of the house—declined? The United States gained benefits from the Bank, which increased American leverage over programs and events, especially in the developing world. But has the Bank been a good foreign policy bargain? Most of the U.S. administrations during the Bank's first fifty years insisted they were acting in behalf of global welfare, especially that of developing countries. But did the United States take its role in the Bank seriously enough? In what ways, apart from the political, does the United States exert influence on the Bank?

Gwin's review of the Bank's launch and subsequent evolution up to the McNamara accession in April 1968 does not differ notably from various discussions in volume 1. Her analysis becomes more distinctive with respect to the 1970s. Gwin provides a vivid picture of the turbulence of Bank–U.S. interaction (centering particularly on the actions and voice of U.S. treasury secretary William Simon) in the early 1970s and the first oil shock. Gwin was a senior member of the Carter administration's bilateral aid team, and her chapter has an almost confessional quality about that administration's failure to achieve better relations with the Bank.

She underplays the seismic force (unexpected by Bank players and watchers) that Robert McNamara brought to the institution. In due course, this bulldozed a reluctant Republican administration into renominating him. In the late 1970s Bank management, while continuing to expand the scale of Bank operations at an unprecedented rate, jousted with its largest owner, particularly over the issue of human rights. But the Bank remained in accord with the United States over antipoverty and policy strategy.

Gwin's chapter is notable for several of its emphases. First, as a donor member, the United States is important not just because of its size: its government is nonparliamentary and its power divided. The U.S. Congress thus has had an endlessly complex and prominent role to play vis-à-vis the Bank, and not just because the Bank is headquartered in Washington, D.C. Gwin captures this in a colorful and informative way. But her contention that relations between the Bank and the U.S. Treasury Department have been equally exceptional can be challenged. Such relations would be similar even if the United States were a parliamentary democracy and Treasury were a ministry of finance.

In addition, as relative U.S. material inputs to the IBRD and the International Development Association (IDA) diminished during the 1980s, the executive branch reasserted its leadership. The American voice, represented partially by default by Treasury undersecretary David Mulford, became harsher and shriller than in earlier years.

Gwin also provides a careful and balanced review of cases in the 1970s and 1980s in which the United States was widely alleged to use political muscle—not just its votes in the Bank's board room—to influence institutional decisions. These included both substantive choices (for example, concerning investments in oil production and distribution) and those, positive and negative, with respect to borrower regimes (such as Chile and Vietnam).

Finally, in the eyes of the editors, Gwin can be charged with one count of *under*emphasis. She does not dwell as much as she might on the casualness of the process by which the United States has wielded its prerogative (thus far successfully asserted) to select the World Bank president. The most influential (McNamara) was also the most accidental. For however long the United States has the de facto entitlement, it is likely to treat the office with less respect than it deserves as long as, in the eyes of most Americans (official and otherwise), the United States is so vastly more important than the World Bank. This estimate is a frustration the Bank in varying degrees encounters in dealing with other member countries. It surfaces again in Bank relations with Japan.

Japan: Borrower and Donor

No other country has progressed through as many stages in its dealings with the World Bank as has Japan. Starting as a project and sectoral borrower and a recipient of technical assistance, Japan moved swiftly to become a major market for Bank loans and a leading aid donor. It surmounted frictions that delayed its becoming the Bank's second-largest shareholder. It struggled with the problem of winning representation in the Bank's anglophone staff, but, in the 1990s, participated more and more in debates over Bank development doctrines.

Toyoo Gyohten, as Japan's vice minister of finance, rose to the top of the Japanese career service, dealing with development and multilateral matters. Having declined offers of senior positions in the World Bank and the Asian Development Bank, Gyohten was preparing to become chairman of the board of the (commercial) Bank of Tokyo as this World Bank history was being shaped. He was ideally cast in intellect as well as by experience to review the Japan–World Bank story.

Gyohten makes a sweeping job of it in chapter 7. He reviews the circumstances under which Japan joined the Bretton Woods institutions before it joined the United Nations and was bumped from the Export-Import Bank of the United States to the World Bank as a project borrower. He goes on to discuss Japan's rapid graduation from its dozen years of heavy borrowing from the Bank (1955–66), then to the mode for Bank borrowing from Japan that President McNamara entered into with the Japanese Ministry of Finance, through which the Bank became a mentor of Japan's financial market development.

The review details Japan's polite struggle to win a larger shareholding to match heavier contributions to the Bank Group. One of the innovations, in response to the country's burgeoning payments balance in the 1990s, was the 1990 Policy and Human Resources Development Fund, the Bank's largest bilateral trust fund and virtually the only one that remains untied. Gyohten also refers to cofinancing as a positive-sum venture for the World Bank and the Japanese government.

Gyohten writes as a student of developmental political economy as well. Countries that are currently developing, he argues, should find Japanese experience between the world wars (not just since World War II) illuminating. He provides an extensive examination of the Bank's *East Asian Miracle* study as an attempt to reconcile the more interventionist East Asian mode of developmental policy with Bank orthodoxy. Gyohten compares the intellectual environments from which the two views arose.[4]

In the final section Gyohten becomes unabashedly prescriptive. Speaking for Japan's policy elite, he addresses an extensive set of recommendations (critical but supportive, on balance) to the World Bank and another list to his Japanese compatriots. Gyohten's analysis reflects Japanese frustration with the Bank. However, despite Japan's major role in the Asian Development Bank, that institution strikingly resembles the World Bank.

---

4. World Bank, *The East Asian Miracle: Economic Growth and Public Policy* (Oxford University Press, 1993).

Project Lending in South Asia and East Africa

What is often called the Bank's bread-and-butter work—the financing of economic and social infrastructure projects—is the subject matter of two chapters in this volume. Each takes a regional focus. S. Guhan, emeritus fellow at the Madras Institute for Development Studies in India, has written on project lending in South Asia; and Alex Duncan, program director of the Food Studies Group at Oxford University, examines the equivalent experience in East Africa.

Project lending is mandated in the Bank's Charter. Its Articles steer the Bank toward "productive" and "specific project" loans, restricting non-project lending to "exceptional circumstances."[5] For the fledgling institution, the injunction proved a convenient shield against political pressures and an attractive selling point when it came to marketing bonds to cautious postwar investors. Project lending took a firm hold and came to be seen as the Bank's métier. From the late 1940s to the early 1980s, more than 90 percent of Bank lending to developing countries consisted of project loans. Even during the 1980s—when the Bank sought to increase its influence on macroeconomic policies and then responded to debt problems with a spate of non–project-based structural adjustment loans—the greater part of its lending commitments (some two-thirds) continued to be in the form of project loans.

If the Bank's financing were packaged as projects, most of its advisory and tutelary assistance was also delivered in the course of and along with such lending. Any Bank lending was, to begin with, conditioned on country "creditworthiness," which was equated with sound credit and fiscal and monetary behavior and with export policies that promised a capacity to pay. "Policy dialogues" on such matters were thus a major and continuous order of business in Bank-client relations.

But project loans were particularly suited to the transfer of technical expertise, especially engineering and managerial skills related to specific productive activities. Rolling up their sleeves to work with local and sectoral authorities, Bank officials used projects as opportunities for how-to demonstrations and for discussions of international experience and best practice with respect to the choice, design, preparation, implementation, and subsequent upkeep of investment projects. Even more broadly, the appraisal and negotiation of project loans became a way of persuading borrowers of ways to improve sector-wide policies and institutions. Project lending thus became the vehicle and the lever for the Bank's wider developmental agenda. Seeking projects to finance, the Bank looked beyond rates of return, output priorities, and productive bottlenecks, scouting for opportunities to influence development policies and practices in particular sectors.

The reader should not be surprised, therefore, that the two chapters on the World Bank as project lender focus as much on policies and institutions as on investment projects in the narrower sense. The question of this larger developmen-

5. Articles of Agreement of the International Bank for Reconstruction and Development, Article I (I); and Article III, Section 4 (vii).

tal influence is especially pursued by Guhan in chapter 8, who notes: "As a development lender, the Bank has been interested in extending the benefits of its project lending beyond the successful completion of the project itself to improvements in implementation capacity, long-term sustainability of projects, diffusion and replication of the learning experience in project execution, institution building, and sectoral policy reforms." Tracing project lending sector by sector and country by country, Guhan repeatedly asks whether the Bank succeeded in projecting itself beyond the investment project itself to influence the broader development context.

The converse influence—from the policy and institutional environment to project performance—also concerns both authors. But it arises most forcefully in Duncan's discussion of East Africa. In chapter 9, he argues that a pronounced deterioration in project performance was largely the result of a worsening in that environment.

Regarding project performance, both chapters conclude on a critical note. In his summary Duncan states: "Projects alone have proven not to be the key to Africa's development in the way that for perhaps twenty of the years under review the Bank assumed they were." The failure, he argues, was less one of project design than of weakness and neglect of policies and institutions. As a result, "the Bank has found itself impelled . . . upstream from project-specific concerns, to involve itself closely with budgetary processes, and with the planning and management of public institutions at the heart of government." Likewise, Guhan concludes, "the Bank's project lending in South Asia has fallen short of the expectations, and often the claims, placed on it by the Bank."

What is perhaps most remarkable about these criticisms is that, written and circulated (as drafts) in the early 1990s, they were not at all remarkable. Similar and even more severe criticism was becoming common currency within the Bank. To some extent, the Bank was carrying on a tradition: few institutions have practiced self-evaluation to a similar extent, or with a comparable degree of openness. But the process became intensified during the 1990s as the Bank responded to bad news from project audits and to an escalation of external pressures. The severely self-critical Wapenhans Report of 1992 drew much attention.[6] Indeed, though both Guhan and Duncan provide considered, independent critiques based on direct experience of Bank project work, their views are reinforced by the substantial body of self-evaluation the Bank conducted. This is especially the case with Duncan, who shares the generalized picture of East African project failure drawn by internal reports and who is more concerned with the explanation of that result than with speculation about the complex and multiple effects of long-lived projects.

Has there been a rush to judgment? Certainly, cycles of self-criticism, innovation, and rededication have been a constant source of energy for the Bank. Yet

6. World Bank, "Effective Implementation: Key to Development Impact." Working Paper R92-195 (Washington: November 3, 1992). Willi Wapenhans served as chairman of the Portfolio Management Task Force that produced this study.

project evaluation is an imperfect exercise. This is all the more true when judgments are essentially projections, made early in the productive life of a project—as is the Bank's usual practice—and when project objectives include noninvestment externalities, such as training and policy influence.[7]

Thirty years ago Albert Hirschman studied the behavior of development projects and picked a number of World Bank investments for the purpose. He did so even though, as he wrote:

> exclusive reliance on World Bank projects could of course be criticized on the grounds that the resulting sample was likely to be highly biased because the Bank insists on very high standards and picks only the best ventures available. Fortunately (at least for my research!) I found, upon looking more closely, that not one of the projects I had selected had been free from serious problems. It quickly became apparent to me that all projects are problem-ridden; the only valid distinction appears to be between those that are more or less successful in overcoming their troubles and those that are not.[8]

With his determined "bias for hope," Hirschman found it difficult to arrive at definite judgments about projects. But his plea for "modesty with respect to generalized evaluation and quantification" and his suggestion that such effort would be better spent exploring the twists and turns of project experience were probably not possible for an official institution, particularly one specifically charged with project investment.[9] Yet the reviews carried out by Guhan and Duncan suggest that much could be learned by more examinations of project behavior in the Hirschman style.

European Funding

How the World Bank funds its operations, project and otherwise, is often overlooked or (what is worse) misunderstood. Of its four sources of funds—paid-in capital, retained earnings, prepayment of loans, and borrowings on world markets —borrowings represent the greatest portion. As such, the Bank's lending capacity is directly related to its ability to borrow. The intricacies of this story are detailed in volume 1 (chapters 14–16). In chapter 10 in this volume, Hilmar Kopper, chairman of Deutsche Bank, the Bank's largest European commercial bank partner, focuses on IBRD borrowing in one of its principal markets: Europe.

7. The principal basis for Bank evaluations, used in turn by non-Bank authors and critics, has been a project rate of return estimated by the Operations Evaluation Department (OED) as part of its Project Performance Audit Report (PPAR). The PPAR is carried out when project implementation (construction and setting up) and corresponding loan disbursements are completed. For the great majority of projects the PPAR rate of return estimate is the last evaluation carried out by the Bank, so it is at this moment of project birth that most projects are defined by the Bank as a "success" or "failure."

8. Albert O. Hirschman, *Development Projects Observed* (Brookings, 1967), pp. 1–3.

9. Ibid., p. 188.

Although the Bank initially kept out of war-torn European markets, it quickly branched out of the United States and into England and Switzerland in 1951. With a striking lack of partisanship, the Bank has sought the highest return and maximum efficiency by diversifying markets, currencies, and types of placement and maturities. (The Bank entered the Swiss market when rates there were lower than in the United States, even though Switzerland became an official member only in 1992.)

Capital market restrictions and higher interest rates in nearly all European countries kept the IBRD's European borrowings confined mainly to Germany (dominated by Deutsche Bank) and Switzerland (under the cartel of the three largest commercial banks—Swiss Bank Corporation, Crédit Suisse, and Union Bank of Switzerland) for nearly three decades. The Bank forged its way into European capitals through aggressive marketing and lobbying (similar to its initial efforts in the United States). As European countries gradually liberalized, their central banks subscribed to the Bank's nonmarket borrowings before allowing market borrowings. The Bank's overall volume and share in Europe rose almost continuously during this three-decade period, from roughly 10 percent in the 1950s to nearly 25 percent in the 1960s and (with brief interruptions following the two oil shocks) to about 40 percent in the 1970s.

Just as the markets were diversifying, so too were the Bank's borrowings. A combination of factors—rapid capital market liberalization, the advent of swaps, an explosion in financial product innovation (including the rapid growth of Eurobond markets in the 1970s), and tax privileges (hard fought for by the Bank)—led to a substantial broadening of the Bank's European funding base in the 1980s. Eurobond markets alone accounted for almost one-fifth of the IBRD's borrowings in the 1980s.

Charting the Bank's trajectory of increasingly diverse market activity not only in Europe but also throughout the world, the more recent appearance of "global" bonds (which allow the Bank to borrow simultaneously in principal capital markets worldwide) seems a metadiversification. No longer is the Bank confined to specific geographical market segments. Moreover, changes in the IBRD's currency policies at the end of the 1980s, along with stagnating IBRD borrowings, indicate that the Bank's European borrowings are not likely to expand as quickly as they had in the institution's first fifty years.

The International Monetary Fund

Of all the outside "looks" at the Bank represented by the chapters in this volume, perhaps none is as inherently intriguing as that of the view from across the street: from the International Monetary Fund. In chapter 11, Jacques Polak, the author of *The World Bank and the IMF,* writes as a former official and director of the Fund's research department (1958–79) and former IMF executive director for the Netherlands (1981–86). He has also served as an occasional consultant to the Bank. Polak's identification with the IMF is even greater than that suggested by his length of service: his name is attached to what has long been the Fund's core analytical framework, the Polak model.

This is worthy of interest for two reasons. One is that the two institutions are known to have an intimate relationship based on the circumstances of their birth— John Maynard Keynes dubbed them the "twin sisters"—and on their overlapping purposes and operational contact, all enhanced by physical proximity. Another is IMF secretiveness, which makes any informed and reasonably open statement from a (former) senior Fund official, and bearing on a major aspect of the Fund's work, an unusual occurrence.

Polak centers his chapter on the sensitive issue of turf. As could be expected from a former Bretton Woods delegate, he provides a rich historical account of the way in which the separation and overlap of tasks has evolved over fifty years. He traces that evolution from the respective charters through the institutional responses to a changing world economy to the more circumstantial contributions of some individuals. Both organizations moved from being "world" institutions to a more restricted role as lenders to less developed countries. Both encroached on the other's original turf—the Fund becoming a concessional lender to poor countries, the Bank moving to provide (more openly than in the past) balance of payments support. The relationship is marked by an ongoing liveliness, up to more recent developments—a concordat reached in 1989 and the pending issue of a hypothetical merger, a proposal that draws a resounding "no" from the author. Polak has preferred not to mention what to many must appear to be the most surprising turn of events: the Fund's recent reassurances that poverty alleviation—including the mitigation of possible short-term adverse effects of reform and adjustment programs on "the poor and vulnerable"—is among its fundamental objectives.[10]

Though much is brought to light, there is one aspect of the relationship between the Bank and the Fund that is discreetly downplayed in this chapter: their common owner(s) have been continually responsible for many, if not most, key decisions. Principal ownership has shifted over the decades—from the United States, to the Group of Five, and now perhaps to the Group of Seven. It remains for a later historian to unravel the extent to which national interests, in contrast to institutional autonomy (and interests), have determined the major turns of events recounted by Polak.

The U.S. interest, for instance, is necessary to understand the conflicting versions that are given with regard to the cause célèbre incident over Argentina in

10. Address by Michel Camdessus, Managing Director of the International Monetary Fund, at the UN World Summit for Social Development, Copenhagen, Denmark, March 7, 1995, p. 1.

1988, an incident Polak uses to illustrate Bank-Fund conflict. That year the Bank broke with precedent, approving a large package of balance-of-payments support for Argentina despite IMF disapproval. Polak's account of the reasons for and the effects of that decision should be contrasted with those given by Bank president Barber Conable and Shahid Husain, the Bank's vice president for Latin America and the Caribbean. Polak sees a strictly institutional interest and an operational "failure"; Husain cites political motivations (such as fear of a coup d'état) and claims success on that score. A fuller, though not necessarily complete, account of this complex decision, including political motivations, is given in chapter 10 of volume 1.

Intellectual Contribution

Admirers and critics of the World Bank commonly agree on a surprising view of the institution: the principal function of each loan is to serve as an ideological Trojan horse. It is the critic who will term this ideological and having pejorative intent. The admirer will make the same point using different language, speaking of the Bank as not a mere bank but a "developmental agency," citing the technical assistance, training, and advice that it provides, as well as its contributions to development research. Both critic and admirer see loans as levers and packaging for the transmission of those ideas.

As historians who are both its admirers and its critics, we share this sense of the importance of the Bank's nonfinancial role. More concretely, we subscribe to the view (as does the Bank itself) that ideas and expertise have been at the heart of the Bank's mission. That view is evident in many of the chapters of volume 1 of this history.[11] It also helps explain why the Bank does not suffer criticism gladly with regard to its intellectual leadership.

Nicholas Stern (with Francisco Ferreira) provides another (and more focused) examination of the Bank as a source and as a transmitter of thinking on economic development in his essay on the Bank's intellectual activity. In chapter 12 Stern is an observer who wears two hats. As a university economist, he looks for originality and scientific power in the Bank's work as a creative center of development studies. As an institutional historian, Stern examines the way in which ideas about develop-ment have been part of the Bank's practical, operational life—including that large part of "operations" that consists of doctrinal persuasion.

As it turns out, Stern the academic gets short shrift. Despite the Bank's early start as a development practitioner (its first development loans in the late 1940s antedated the birth of development as a field in university curricula) and the early

---

11. Especially the accounts of poverty and the Bank's evolving mission (chapters 2 to 7), of its policy-based lending (chapters 9 and 10), and of its lending for agriculture and rural development (chapter 8).

association of eminent development economists with the Bank (notably Paul Rosenstein-Rodan and Albert Hirschman), and despite its massive budgetary presence in development research during the 1970s and 1980s, Stern is unable to cite any significant, pioneering scientific contribution. Loosening the criteria, Stern does speak of the Bank's "intellectual leadership" with respect to structural adjustment during the 1980s: It "became a prominent champion" and "was seen to be leading the charge." But, Stern admits, the Bank's analytical role was not pathbreaking, the underlying theories and views "were not new"; indeed, they had "long lain at the heart of the whole subject of economics." Similarly, Stern recalls the Bank's role as a champion for equity and poverty under McNamara, but points out that here, too, it was adopting the ideas of others.

It is Stern the institutional historian who bears the burden of the account of the Bank as intellectual actor. In that capacity he examines a broad range of Bank activity and economic work in project design and evaluation, in judging creditworthiness, in recommending development policies to borrowers, and in acting more generally as an educator and champion of particular economic doctrines. On this ground, and though his account is more detailed, Stern covers many topics that are discussed in the first volume of this history. The reader might find that much of the interest of Stern's chapter lies in contrasting his perspectives on those topics with those provided in volume 1.

The Bank and the Environment

Robert Wade's closing essay for this volume is much more than an account of a particularly contentious issue in the Bank's history. For one, the clash between the environmental movement and the Bank, beginning in the early 1980s, became, in itself, a major piece of the institution's "modern history." For another, behind the arguments and counterarguments regarding the environmental impact of specific Bank projects and the adequacy or inadequacy of the Bank's environmental procedures, two fundamental matters of governance were at stake. One concerned the social priorities that should guide the institution: what weight should be attached to particular human values—environmental preservation and protection from forcible resettlement—as distinct from the discounted present value of additional production. The second point of contention was the right to a voice in decision-making, along with the related matter of access to information—were decisions to remain the province of G-7 ministries of finance and the Bank's senior, career officials, or would shouting, prying, emotional, generally self-appointed "voices of the people"—for the most part western NGOs—to be admitted into the discourse? In both cases the answer was a compromise. The struggle over the environment changed the Bank. The 1990s institution is more open to a broader social agenda and more directly responsive to NGOs, project beneficiaries, the media, and other voices and constituencies. The process of accommodation leaned heavily on semantic innovation: terms such as "sustainable development," "participation," and "stakeholders" became part of the Bank's 1990s language.

The choice of author for this assignment was particularly difficult. The topic demanded objectivity on the issues at stake, knowledge of the Bank, and a sense for the mechanics of decision-making. Wade's chapter provides a detailed and closely documented examination of the Bank's bureaucratic processes that is unmatched elsewhere in this two-volume history.

TWO

The Republic of Korea's Successful Economic Development and the World Bank

Mahn-Je Kim

THE SUCCESSFUL economic development of the Republic of Korea (ROK) over the past few decades can be attributed to many factors, persons, and institutions. The World Bank, which was founded a few years before the official birth of Korea in August 1948, is one of those major institutions to which the Korean economy owes much of its success.

The Republic of Korea officially joined the Bank in 1955. In 1961 Korea became a member of the International Development Association (IDA), the Bank's affiliated institution established in 1960, and in 1964 Korea joined the International Finance Corporation (IFC), the financial subsidiary of the Bank. Korea received its first loan from the World Bank in 1962. It is largely accepted that the Korean economy started its rapid industrialization in the early 1960s. The active working relationship with the Bank begun during this period created the opportunity for the Bank to play an influential role in Korea's economic development.

The objective of this chapter is to describe and evaluate the part the World Bank has played in the course of Korea's economic modernization. In doing so, it is useful to briefly review the effects of foreign aid on the Korean economy in the earlier

I appreciate the valuable and detailed comments by Dr. R. Webb, Dr. R. J. Goodman, and Dr. D. Kapur. Dr. D. W. Nam, former prime minister of the Republic of Korea; Mr. S. K. Lee, former vice minister of the Economic Planning Board; and Dr. S. W. Nam, vice president of the Korea Development Institute, also provided valuable information for this chapter. I also would like to acknowledge the assistance of Dr. T. Kwack. The views expressed or implied here are of course my personal ones. None of the individuals listed above shares my responsibility for any remaining deficiencies.

phase of the Republic's economic development before discussing the financial aspects of the Bank's role in Korea's industrialization. Among the institutions and nations that provided public loans to Korea, the Bank was the most important in terms of both the amount and number of loans. The Bank also helped Korea critically in accessing other sources of foreign capital financing, and its project loans and other financial assistance not only provided Korea with needed foreign currency capital, but also facilitated the transmission of important management techniques. Equally important has been the role of the Bank in Korea's policymaking. Through various missions to Korea, publication of reports on the Korean economy, personnel exchange programs, and informal contacts and discussions with Korean government officials and researchers the Bank has influenced Korea's economic policymaking. In concluding the chapter an attempt is made to identify factors that explain why relations between the Republic of Korea and the World Bank have been so successful, and to identify Korean social, political, and cultural characteristics that help to account for that success.

Provision of Financial Resources by the World Bank

The very first systematic foreign assistance to Korea was given in September 1945 by the U.S. military government on the Korean peninsula, an occupied area at the time.[1] Under the first assistance program, called Government and Relief in Occupied Area (GARIOA), a total of $502.5 million was provided to Korea over the period 1945 to 1949. The program's main purpose was to provide fiscal resources and relief goods to the poverty-stricken occupied area on a short-term basis. The long-term strategy of the United States was to build a strong, independent, and democratic nation on the Korean peninsula that could serve as a balancing factor in the East Asian region and as a showcase of free democracy to be emulated by other Asian nations.[2] This long-term perspective was not fully reflected in the GARIOA program mainly because it was assumed that the peninsula, which was divided at the thirty-eighth parallel, would soon be unified and that long-term plans could then be worked out. The short-term perspective of the program was well reflected by the items imported: between 80 and 90 percent of the items were consumer goods for relief purposes.

In 1948 the Republic of Korea was formally launched and the Economic Cooperation Administration (ECA) took over management of U.S. aid to Korea. By

1. This section draws heavily on Edward S. Mason and others, *The Economic and Social Modernization of the Republic of Korea* (Harvard University Press, 1980), chapter 6; and on Korea Development Institute, *A Forty-Year History of Korean Public Finance,* vol. 6 (Seoul: KDI, 1991), chapter 4.

2. See William A. Brown and Redvers Opie, *American Foreign Assistance* (Brookings, 1953), pp. 372–73.

this time the possibility of unifying the Korean peninsula had faded, so the ECA concluded that assistance should be directed toward development projects rather than immediate relief. The ECA's plan, however, was frustrated by the outbreak of the Korean War in mid-1950 and ECA aid was concentrated on immediate relief rather than on reconstruction or long-term development.

Wartime aid was organized by the Civil Relief in Korea (CRIK) plan under the United Nations flag. In December 1950 the United Nations Korean Reconstruction Agency (UNKRA) was created to assist in the reconstruction of a unified democratic nation on the Korean peninsula. The plan was to be funded by voluntary contributions of United Nations members. These two U.N. aid plans were funded mostly by the United States. The CRIK plan supplied a total of $218 million between 1950 and 1956, and UNKRA supplied $120 million between 1951 and 1960.

A more formal economic cooperation or development assistance program by the United States began with the establishment of the Foreign Operations Administration (FOA) in 1955, at the suggestion of the Tasca Mission's report to U.S. President Dwight D. Eisenhower.[3] Almost simultaneously, the Office of the Economic Coordinator (OEC) was opened in Seoul. In 1959 this organization became the U.S. Operations Mission to Korea (USOM/K), later changed to USAID/Korea. This organization played an important role in the post–Korean War period until the end of the 1960s.

The Korean economy depended heavily on foreign grant aid during the 1953–61 period.[4] Most efforts were concentrated on reconstruction of the economy, but rapid and sustained growth had not yet begun. Aid from CRIK and UNKRA rapidly declined; major aid was provided through the International Cooperation Administration. In 1956, the import of surplus agricultural products under U.S. Public Law 480 began. A total of $2,580 million was provided during this period as economic aid. The inflow of grant aid peaked in 1957 and then rapidly declined. By the end of the 1950s U.S. foreign aid policy had switched from the focus on grants to one on loans. The first public loan agreement with the United States was signed in 1959.[5]

During the 1953–61 period some 70 percent of the ROK's total imports were financed through foreign aid. This amounted to about 70 percent of Korea's total investment during the period. But in spite of such a heavy input of foreign re-

3. Henry J. Tasca, on a special mission for President Eisenhower, visited Korea for about six weeks in the spring of 1953. His so-called Tasca Report of July 1953 proposed replacing multinational UN-managed aid with an assistance system managed solely by the United States. FOA was the organization designed to take over the assistance operations managed by the UN. It was later known as the International Cooperation Administration (ICA).

4. For a more detailed discussion of grant aid during this period, see KDI, *Forty-Year History*, vol. 6, pp. 129–35.

5. Ibid.

sources the economy was recovering rather slowly. During this time U.S. officials seemed to have little confidence in the future of the Korean economy. Domestic politics was rather unstable, and political leaders and high-ranking government officials had little experience with policymaking for economic development. Both aid officials and domestic policy authorities were focused on short-term macro-economic stabilization problems. Thus aid resources were largely spent on import-ing consumer goods for the stabilization of domestic inflation. U.S. aid during the period was composed of project aid and program aid. Program aid was 80 percent of total aid, and 50 percent of that aid was in surplus agricultural products. Other aid was mainly in petroleum products and fertilizers. Project aid was heavily allocated to transportation, electricity, and a few key manufacturing industries.

In addition to economic aid, $1,561 million was provided to Korea as military aid.[6] Military expenses are usually classified as consumption. However, many posi-tive effects resulted from military aid to Korea, especially during the 1950s. U.S. military assistance contributed significantly to training military personnel to be-come able managers, administrators, and technicians. A substantial portion of military investment, such as the construction of military roads, bridges, and other infrastructure, could be productively used by the private sector.

There was an important negative element related to aid grants, however. In general, grant aid tends to make a receiving party more dependent on the aid. Although concrete evidence is difficult to identify, it has been argued that post–Korean War foreign aid to the ROK contributed to orienting domestic policy to short-run maximization of the availability of disposable resources.[7] Korean officials by that time were more concerned with getting the aid amount increased or at least not decreased and did not pay due attention to using resources more productively from a long-term perspective. (Once an economy, a household, or an individual becomes accustomed to an easy solution, it tends to cling to the easy way.) The Korean economy during the 1953–61 period invested approximately 12 percent of GNP, 71 percent of which was financed through net foreign savings, most of it grant aid.[8] Of course, Koreans were poor at the time and could not save much. But at the same time the authorities were not doing enough to maximize domestic savings mobilization.

To the U.S. aid authorities, in spite of the substantial amount of aid poured into Korea, the economy was not making satisfactory progress. Growth rates were below 5 percent and inflation was accelerating. In 1957 a strong and comprehen-

6. See Mason and others, *Economic and Social Modernization*, p. 182, table 35.
7. See D. C. Cole and P. N. Lyman, *Korean Development: The Interplay of Politics and Economics* (Harvard University Press, 1971), p. 170; and A. O. Krueger, *The Development Role of the Foreign Sector and Aid: Studies in the Modernization of the Republic of Korea, 1945–1975* (Cambridge, Mass.: Council on East Asian Studies, Harvard University, 1979), pp. 79–80.
8. Bank of Korea, *National Accounts* (1987).

sive stabilization plan, suggested by U.S. aid authorities, was implemented to curb inflation and encourage private sector investment. This program succeeded in stabilizing inflationary pressure, but economic growth slowed down in the late 1950s.

It is difficult to determine whether the assistance to Korea in the post–Korean War period was a success or a failure. The survival of multitudes of Koreans depended on U.S. assistance. But many specialists, including U.S. officials who were involved with the Korean economy in the 1950s, commented that the money spent in Korea did not produce satisfactory returns.[9]

Several reasons for that unsatisfactory performance may be identified. One is that the two parties—the Korean government and the U.S. aid authorities—did not get along very well. Korean president Syngman Rhee was a stubborn diplomat and did not yield to U.S. pressure. On the other hand, U.S. authorities were often suspicious of the Korean government's policy actions and wanted to maintain some control over Korea's allocative decisions. This lack of mutual trust is a critical point that distinguishes U.S.-Korean relations in the 1950s from Korea–World Bank relations in the 1970s and 1980s. Under such circumstances even policy advice given with good intentions may not be welcomed. The advising party may also not supply the best policy advice. Lack of trust results in difficulties in communication. Without an efficient information flow, it is difficult to work out the best development plan or policies.

Another important element that prevented a satisfactory economic performance was the excessive reliance on an import substitution industrialization strategy. Many factors explain this choice. The Korean government insisted on an over-valued domestic currency. Undervalued foreign currency was rationed by the government among the importers. This was an important source of governmental power over the business sector. U.S. aid authorities advised depreciating the Korean currency, but having the hard currency at hand, the government was reluctant to implement measures that would weaken the power of its allocating hand. This situation illustrates one of the greatest weaknesses of grant aid and public loans: the aid money simply strengthens the hand of the government, thus causing various economic distortions. Even if the market is not perfect, when money is rationed entirely by government discretion the most probable result is excess inefficiency and inequity. In Korea, when the exports by private firms later became the major source of foreign currency, direct government intervention with resource allocation became relatively less problematic. But with exchange rates distorted as they were in the 1950s and early 1960s, the industrial sector naturally favored import substitution projects. Import substitution firms operated inefficiently because their profitability depended heavily on their privileged access to undervalued foreign currency and on the general restriction of imports.

9. See, for example, Mason and others, *Economic and Social Modernization*, pp. 204–05.

Another fundamental source of inefficiency was the regime's lack of ability in economic planning and development management. The government's limited experience and knowledge of economic policymaking hampered economic growth. These weaknesses, along with ineffective, corrupt political leadership, prevented Korea from pursuing a reasonably efficient growth path.[10]

Transition to New Economic Cooperation

When the military government led by President Park Chung Hee took power in 1961, various macroeconomic variables were performing poorly. The new regime emphasized long-term development to get out of the vicious cycle of poverty. The fiscal stabilization plan introduced in 1957 was abolished in 1961 and an aggressive investment policy was pursued, which resulted in severe inflation during 1963–64. Moreover, the economy was suffering from a severe shortage of food grain because of a bad crop in 1962, and foreign exchange was running out. Deteriorating economic conditions weakened the position of the military government at the negotiation table with U.S. aid authorities. When the United States asked Korea to tighten fiscal management and to depreciate the Korean currency by as much as 50 percent, Korea had to accept the suggestions to secure the required food grain supply. The Korean government began to realize that such a dependent relationship could not continue. At the same time, domestic financial needs grew and became more diversified, and Korea felt the need for development financing. The military government's desire for development naturally transferred its economic focus from short-term macroeconomic stabilization to longer-term industrialization.

Such changes in perspectives and financial needs influenced the attitudes of both the U.S. and the Korean governments toward economic assistance. Koreans no longer insisted on getting only grant aid. For example, before President Park held a summit talk with U.S. president Lyndon B. Johnson in 1965, Korean leaders debated whether Korea should ask for more grant aid or accept a development loan of $150 million; the conclusion was to take the loan offer. On their part, U.S. aid authorities in the mid-1960s began to emphasize such basic issues as research and statistics, economic planning and policymaking, and the design of various market systems. In the mid-1960s a larger portion of grant aid to Korea supported research projects on economic systems and policy issues.

Korean leaders, realizing that the inflow of grant aid could not be maintained and that money was needed for investment, sought alternative sources of finance to

10. I am not arguing here that the economy should be planned and managed by the government. I do not believe either that laissez-faire is the best solution. I believe appropriate government intervention can be very helpful especially in the earlier stages of industrialization. The Korean government in the 1950s, however, did not understand the basic market mechanisms and often chose a wrong set of policies.

implement development. In January 1960 the Foreign Capital Inducement Law was promulgated to attract investment capital to Korea. The law was revised in 1962 and again in 1966 to strengthen its appeal. The first direct investment project, a joint Korean-U.S. project for nylon fiber manufacturing, was approved in 1962 by the Korean government.

Under pressure from and through the intermediation of the United States, economic talks between Korea and Japan were promoted, in spite of strong resistance by Korean students and opposition leaders. In the 1950s and 1960s, Japan was no better friend than North Korea in the eyes of the South Korean public, so it was politically risky for the Korean military government—still a stranger to the public—to promote reconciliation with Japan. Nevertheless, the talks finally succeeded in 1965. Under the terms of the agreement, Japan was to provide the ROK with $300 million in grants and $200 million in public loans over the 1965–75 period.[11] Both the ROK government and the United States understood, however, that an array of economic relations with Japan, extending beyond financial assistance, would be essential for Korea's economic development.

The Korean government also sought to develop more practical relations with international development organizations. In addition to becoming a member of the IDA in 1961 and the IFC in 1964, Korea signed a standby agreement with the International Monetary Fund (IMF) in 1965. In 1966 the ROK government persuaded the World Bank to organize the International Economic Consultative Organization for Korea (IECOK), whose members were donor countries. In promoting the organization of IECOK, both the World Bank and the U.S. Agency for International Development (USAID) played active roles.[12] This organization, which lasted until 1984, played an important role in facilitating Korea's foreign borrowing.

At the time of these changes in the mid-1960s Korea was having its first round of success in exporting labor-intensive light manufacturing products, which signaled auspicious development for the Korean economy. Pursuing more aggressive development policies requiring larger financial resources, the regime sought diverse sources of finance on both political and strategic grounds. Rapid increases in the demand for development investment funds later justified the need for diversification of financial sources on economic grounds.

From the mid-1960s on the inflow of foreign capital increased dramatically. Although the inflow of grants continued until the mid-1970s, their relative importance declined. In particular, the composition of U.S. aid changed drastically from grants to development loans. In 1963 nongrant aid was 17 percent of total U.S. aid amounting to $252 million; in 1970 the nongrant share was 59 percent of total U.S.

11. Charles R. Frank, Jr., Kwang Suk Kim, and Larry E. Westphal, *Foreign Trade Regimes and Economic Development: South Korea* (New York: National Bureau of Economic Research, 1975), p. 106.

12. R. J. Goodman, commenting on this section, notes that credit should be given to the United States for pressing the Bank to form such a group.

aid of $182 million. In 1975 only $0.9 million of a total of $277 million was provided in grants.[13]

The dominant form of capital inflow, however, was in loans (borrowing) rather than direct investment. In 1965 only 17 percent of the total $121 million of net nongrant capital inflow was in direct investment. In 1970 a total of $61 million, or 13 percent, of the total $481 million in net nongrant capital inflow was direct investment. In 1974 the total net nongrant capital inflow jumped to $1,311 million, but the direct investment amount increased to only $140 million dollars, its share dropping further to 11 percent.[14] Thus although its quantity increased, direct foreign investment did not quickly become a major substitute for public transfers (see table 2-1). These changes meant that the Korean government's relationship with the U.S. aid authorities became less important, whereas its relationships with international financial institutions, especially the World Bank, became increasingly important.

To say that foreign capital played a critical role in Korea's successful economic development is to state the obvious.[15] Capital was the binding factor; it was much more important than some growth accounting studies of the Korean record suggest. If the input of factors had been evaluated at their correct shadow prices, the results of growth accounting would have changed substantially in favor of capital. In addition, technical progress was closely connected with capital, either through direct investment or through the import of capital goods in which advanced technologies were embodied. Moreover, a substantial portion of total factor productivity can be explained by changes in the country's industrial structure. In Korea, rapid structural changes were promoted at least in part by the discretionary allocation of public investment by the government. And investment in primary education in the 1950s, which required substantial aid funds, is believed to have played a critical role in labor-intensive industrialization in the 1960s.[16] Investment in higher education proved to be helpful in alleviating shortages of technicians and engineers during development of heavy industry and the chemical industry in the 1970s. Initial investment in educational hardware such as school buildings and laboratories played an essential role in directing more material and nonmaterial resources to education.

In the 1950s the investment-to-GNP ratio was around 13 percent, and most investment was financed by foreign savings. During the First Five-Year Economic Development Plan (1961–66) the ratio was about 16 percent. The ratio jumped to almost 26 percent during the Second Five-Year Plan (1967–71), with almost one-

13. Mason and others, *Economic and Social Modernization*, p. 199, table 41.

14. See KDI, *Forty-Year History*, vol. 6, p. 13.

15. For example, Kim and Park suggest that the average growth rate of 7.1 percent during the 1972–83 period was accounted for by a 3.5 percent labor input, 2.1 percent capital input, and 1.5 percent total factor productivity growth. See Kwang Suk Kim and Joon-Kyung Park, *Sources of Economic Growth in Korea: 1963–1982* (Seoul: KDI, 1985), pp. 61–62, table 4-6.

16. See Yung Bon Kim, "Education and Economic Growth," in Chong Kee Park, ed., *Human Resources and Social Development in Korea* (Seoul: KDI, 1980), pp. 243–52.

Table 2-1. *Foreign Capital Inflow (Arrival)*[a]: *1945–91*

Year	Grants	Public loan (from the Bank)		Commercial loan	FDI	Total
(Million dollars)						
1945–49	525.4	0.0	(–)	0.0	0.0	525.4
1950–53	520.7	0.0	(–)	0.0	0.0	520.7
1954–61	2,106.7	5.6	(–)	0.0	0.0	2,112.3
1962–66	805.1	136.0	(14.0)	196.5	25.1	1,162.7
1967–71	508.1	902.9	(245.8)	1,514.9	151.7	3,077.6
1972–76	142.9	1,881.2	(976.0)	2,610.6	417.7	5,042.8
1977–81	60.8	5,734.1	(2,213.5)	7,469.9	532.5	13,797.3
1982–86	12.5	6,699.5	(3,092.5)	5,334.0	1,100.5	13,146.5
1987–91	0.0	3,338.5	(835.3)	3,435.6	4,402.5	11,176.6
(Percent)						
1945–49	100.0	0.0	(–)[b]	0.0	0.0	100.0
1950–53	100.0	0.0	(–)	0.0	0.0	100.0
1954–61	99.7	0.3	(0.0)	0.0	0.0	100.0
1962–66	69.2	11.7	(10.3)	16.9	2.2	100.0
1967–71	16.5	29.3	(27.2)	49.2	4.9	100.0
1972–76	2.8	37.3	(51.9)	51.8	8.3	100.0
1977–81	0.4	41.6	(38.6)	54.1	3.9	100.0
1982–86	0.1	51.0	(46.2)	40.6	8.4	100.0
1987–91	0.0	29.9	(25.0)	30.7	39.4	100.0

Source: Korea Development Institute (1991), table 5-3, p. 13; Bank of Korea (1992).

a. Includes government-guaranteed loans. Short-term capital and financial transactions are not included.

b. Ratios of the loans from the Bank to total public loan amounts.

third of total investment financed by foreign savings. But as a result of recession in the early 1970s the ratio remained at 26 percent during the Third Five-Year Plan (1972–76). During the Fourth Five-Year Plan (1977–81), however, the ratio increased to 32 percent. In the 1980s the ratio remained above 30 percent. A substantial portion of such high investment was financed by foreign savings in the 1960s and in the 1970s; in the early 1960s, almost half of the total investment was financed by foreign savings. During the Second Plan period, about one-third of the total investment was financed by foreign savings. In the third and fourth plan periods—until the early 1980s—from 10 to 20 percent of investment was due to foreign savings.[17]

The inflow of foreign capital is outlined in table 2-1. As indicated, in the late 1940s and in the 1950s nearly all foreign saving was in the form of grants. The first borrowing, as noted, was the Development Loan Fund (DLF) loan of $2.2 million in 1959. Until the first half of the 1960s almost 70 percent of the foreign financial resources made available to Korea were grants; public and commercial loan shares were 12 percent and 17 percent, respectively. The total amount of foreign capital

17. Calculations are from Bank of Korea, *National Accounts* (1987).

inflow, however, decreased significantly compared with the inflow during the post–Korean War period in the 1950s, a result mainly of a rapid decrease in grants. During the Second Five-Year Plan the share of grants dropped to 17 percent, and the main source of foreign financing became commercial borrowing, which accounted for about half of the total. The share of public loans jumped to 29 percent, and that of direct foreign investment more than doubled to 5 percent from 2 percent. Supporting aggressive investment during the 1967–71 period, the total amount of foreign capital inflow almost tripled from what it had been in the 1962–66 period. During the Third Five-Year Plan, the share of public loans increased to 37 percent, the share of grants was reduced to 3 percent, and the share of direct investment increased to 8 percent. The total amount of capital inflow increased rapidly during the Fourth and Fifth Five-Year plans, reflecting mainly emergency borrowing during Korea's balance of payment crisis in the early 1980s. Since then the share of direct foreign investment has increased dramatically.

It can be concluded from table 2-1 that the share of public loans in total foreign capital has been high during all periods of Korea's rapid economic growth, except during the early 1960s. The World Bank was the most important provider of such public loans during these periods.

Financial Relations with the World Bank

Particularly in the 1970s and early 1980s, the money borrowed from the Bank amounted to almost half of the total public loans. Thus the Bank helped finance a significant portion of investment funds during Korea's high-growth decades.

The yearly amounts and composition of the loans from the Bank are summarized in table 2-2. During the years 1963 to 1990, a total of $7,264.8 million was provided by the Bank in the form of public loans. About 26 percent of the total, or $1,920 million, was allocated to the transportation sector. It is noteworthy that transportation-related loans were distributed rather evenly over the whole period after 1963. The next largest share of the loans went to development finance institutions, mainly to the Korea Development Finance Corporation (KDFC). This institution, established in 1967 by the Bank's subsidiary International Finance Corporation, supplied funds to various industrial investment projects. Loans to development finance institutions, to industry, and to small-scale industry, taken together, indicate an allocation of $1,969.5 million, or about 27 percent of total Bank loans, to industrial sectors. Most loans for industrial investment were received in the 1970s and the early 1980s.

About 9 percent of the total was allocated for agricultural and rural development projects, mostly during the 1970s. The amount was not insignificant, and the impact of such loans on agricultural productivity was substantial. Many argue that Korean agricultural policy was a failure on the grounds that the sector still depends

Table 2-2. *World Bank Loans by Year and Sector*
Millions of U.S. dollars

Fiscal Year	Agricultural and rural development	Industry	Small-scale industry	Energy (power)	Transportation	Development finance	Water supply, sewage	Urbanization	Population, health, and nutrition	Education	Nonproject loans	Total
1963	–	–	–	–	14.0 (14.0)	–	–	–	–	–	–	14.0
1968	–	–	–	–	11.0 (11.0)	5.0	–	–	–	–	–	16.0
1969	45.0	–	–	–	3.5 (3.5)	20.0	–	–	–	14.8 (14.8)	–	83.3
1970	–	–	–	–	55.0 (15.0)	–	–	–	–	–	–	55.0
1971	7.0 (7.0)	–	–	–	54.5	30.0	–	–	–	–	–	91.5
1972	58.5 (25.5)	–	–	–	–	–	–	–	–	–	–	58.5
1973	–	–	–	–	120.0	40.0	–	–	–	43.0 (20.0)	–	203.0
1974	20.0	25.0	–	–	47.0	–	–	–	–	–	–	92.0
1975	–	–	–	–	100.0	60.0	–	15.0	–	22.5	100.0	297.5
1976	75.0	–	–	–	90.0	85.0	–	–	–	–	75.0	325.0
1977	144.0	80.0	–	–	67.0	152.5	–	–	–	–	–	443.5
1978	131.0	–	–	–	120.0	165.0	–	–	–	23.0	–	439.0
1979	–	29.0	–	–	143.0	100.0	125.0	–	–	–	–	397.0
1980	50.0	–	–	115.0	94.0	90.0	–	65.0	30.0	100.0	–	544.0
1981	50.0	–	–	–	–	250.0	–	90.0	–	–	–	390.0
1982	50.0	50.0	–	–	–	30.0	90.0	–	–	–	250.0	470.0
1983	–	–	70.0	–	247.0	255.0	–	100.0	–	–	–	672.0
1984	–	–	–	–	230.0	–	78.5	60.0	–	100.0	300.0	768.5
1985	25.0	50.0	111.0	–	–	222.0	95.0	53.0	–	–	–	556.0
1986	–	–	–	230.0	208.0	–	38.0	150.0	–	–	–	626.0
1987	–	–	–	–	–	–	–	200.0	–	–	–	200.0
1988	–	50.0	–	–	116.0	–	–	30.0	–	–	–	196.0
1989	–	–	–	–	200.0	–	–	–	–	16.4	–	216.4
1990	–	–	–	–	–	–	34.0	–	–	76.6	–	110.6
Total	655.0	284.0	181.0	345.0	1,920.0	1,504.5	460.5	763.0	30.0	396.3	725.0	7,268.4

Source: World Bank.
Note: Figures in parentheses are International Development Association loan amounts.

critically on government grain management programs and the absolute protection of the domestic rice market.[18] As for the cause of such failure, there is no consensus. Some argue that too little investment was made in that sector; others argue that continued protection delayed structural adjustment in the sector. If money supplied by the Bank had not been earmarked for the agricultural sector, that money possibly would have been redirected to other, more urgent, sectors. It is hard to judge which was the better path, but the rapid rise in productivity in rice farming provided important groundwork on which a consistent and stable industrialization could be pursued.

As noted, the KDFC was the main channel through which the Bank supplied financial resources to Korean industries. The Bank also supplied various managerial and operational techniques to the KDFC. In particular, industrial project evaluation techniques acquired from the Bank contributed greatly to improvements in the quality of development financing services. The Bank also initiated and supported several technology-related projects, among them the Korea Technology Development Corporation (KTDC).

The Bank was especially interested in promoting small- and medium-scale industries. In the mid-1970s, when a drive to develop heavy industry and the chemical industry was in full swing, the Korean government was unable to pay attention to small- and medium-scale industries, and they were not given due priority. However, those industries led the export-oriented rapid growth in the 1960s and exported a great deal even in the 1970s. These industries also created relatively more employment than did capital-intensive heavy industry and the chemical industry. From the late 1970s the Bank directed loans toward small- and medium-scale industries through the Small and Medium Industry Bank and the Citizen's National Bank, helping to improve management of these institutions.

Although the Bank's direct financial investment was not insignificant for the Korean economy, the Bank's indirect role in Korea's foreign borrowing for development was more important. The International Development Consultative Organization for Korea was a key instrument through which the Bank exercised influence on donor institutions and countries. In IECOK meetings the Korean government usually presented an outline of a five-year plan and projects to be carried out to achieve the plan's goals, as well as estimates of financial requirements. Donor countries and institutions got information about the Korean economy that usually evoked confidence in the economy. The Bank's affirmative evaluation of the Korean economy and its decision to supply large loans to Korea provided a guarantee to other potential lenders, including commercial lenders. Thus although Korea had no proven credibility in international financial markets, it did not face serious difficulties in financing its development projects.

The influence and positive role of the World Bank in attracting foreign currency for Korea's capital financing was illustrated when the Pusan and Muckho harbor

18. The grain manangement program provides a price support system for rice and barley.

project, initially financed by the Bank, suffered cost overruns in the mid-1970s.[19] The Bank could not make additional loans to make up the cost overruns, but the project could not be left unfinished. Lee Sun Ki, then assistant deputy minister of Korea's Economic Planning Board, negotiated a $75 million loan for the project from the Saudi Fund for Development, but Saudi Fund officials were not willing to accept the guarantee of the Korean government and asked for an endorsement and cosignature by the World Bank. Because of the urgency of the project and the lengthy procedure for obtaining Bank endorsement of a loan, Lee flew from Jeddah, Saudi Arabia, to World Bank offices in Washington, explained the situation to Bank vice president I. P. M. Gargill, and was able to return to Jeddah with the Bank's Korean division chief, David Loos, to sign the contract. Loos's cosignature was by no means a Bank endorsement, but the loan was made. The money was more than enough to complete the harbor project; leftover money was used to construct the Taegu-Masan highway.

The role of the World Bank in Korea's financing was so important that Bank officials visiting Seoul were treated extremely well by Korean officials, including President Park. For example, Ray Goodman, then Asia-Pacific director of the Bank, was invited to have lunch with President Park whenever Goodman visited Seoul; this was exceptional treatment. Beyond such tactical considerations, many Korean leaders were also eager to learn from World Bank economists. President Park in particular was a pragmatic person; he thought that there was no better tutor in economic development policy than the Asia-Pacific director of the Bank. It is known that President Park and Goodman came to like each other very much. It is said that Mr. Goodman often told Korean friends that he had never met a leader of a developing country who was so sincerely devoted to the economic enhancement of his nation. Good personal relations between Korean leaders and influential Bank officials played valuable roles in making the developmental experiment in Korea a successful model.

Finally, projects financed by the World Bank were chosen and managed very carefully. The Bank's project appraisal techniques were transferred to Korea through its project selection practices. Cost-benefit analysis, introduced to the Economic Planning Board in 1970,[20] was intensively used in the evaluation of heavy industry and chemical projects in the 1970s. In this process a few World Bank–trained economists at the Korea Development Institute (KDI) played a critical role. This technique was later disseminated among development financing institutions, mostly through the KDFC. Cost-benefit analysis was not a perfect technique, but its careful application in investment decisionmaking enhanced the efficient use of foreign capital borrowed from the Bank. In addition, the Bank-financed projects were managed so carefully and honestly that the quality of the output, in general,

19. This episode is based on the author's interview with S. K. Lee.
20. See S. H. Jo, *A Study on the Development of a Manual for the Analysis of Investment Projects* (Seoul: Sogang University, 1971).

was considerably higher. Korean officials, fully understanding that Korea would have to depend on the Bank for continued economic development, did their best to meet the standards and requirements specified in the loan documents. Such sincerity in carrying out Bank-financed projects contributed greatly to the development of friendly relations between Korean and Bank officials. Through such practices, Koreans also mastered basic project management techniques.

The U.S. Role in Korea's Economic Policymaking

The American military administration in the 1940s and U.S. aid authorities in the subsequent two decades played critical roles in laying the foundations for the development of the Korean economy, at least in its earlier stages of industrialization. In the 1940s U.S. influence was absolute in designing the educational system and in promoting agricultural land reforms, both of which had significant and lasting influence on Korea's economic and social development. In the 1950s and 1960s the U.S. aid authorities contributed greatly to building the economic infrastructure in many areas. They were closely involved in financial and tax reforms. Basic economic statistics such as national income accounting and input-output tables were compiled by the U.S. authorities from early years.

In the 1950s U.S. aid authorities were mainly concerned with short-term stabilization issues. As representatives of the country that was providing Korea with substantial grants, and as trained economists, the U.S. officials more or less assumed the role of guardians or supervisors of the Korean policymakers. Korean officials were not happy about their role, especially in the late 1950s when the strong stabilization policy of 1957 was overshadowing the economy. Relations between Korean and U.S. officials, which were based more on game players' strategies and tactics than on mutual trust, became uncomfortable.

Leaders of the Korean military government, especially President Park, were welcomed by U.S. officials for their straightforwardness, at least in the early years of the military regime. But when the military government abolished the fiscal stabilization plan in 1962 and adopted the aggressive investment policy that led to high inflation in 1963–64, U.S. officials reacted by practically forcing strong stabilization measures and a 50 percent depreciation to control inflation; the measures were taken rather reluctantly by the Korean government. Nevertheless, these measures brought important benefits to the Korean economy. Although the First Five-Year Economic Development Plan (1962–66) was closer to an import substitution plan than to an export-oriented plan, following the depreciation exports in simple manufactured products surged. The experience of an unexpected export surge in the mid-1960s played an important role in Korea's turn toward an aggressive export promotion strategy in the late 1960s and thereafter, and reminded Korean leaders of the need for independence from foreign (particularly U.S.)

influence. Thus the diversification of foreign financial sources was eagerly promoted. The interest rate reform of 1965 can be interpreted as another measure to reduce dependency on foreign sources of investment financing.[21]

The Second Five-Year Economic Development Plan was made with the very extensive and practical help of the U.S. Agency for International Development (USAID). Several well-known American economists and USAID economists participated in a joint task force with Korean officials to set the basic targets, investment policies, and strategies for the plan.[22] It was the last major contribution of the U.S. aid authorities in the development of Korean economic policy. The World Bank, whose relations with Korea were becoming significant at that time, was skeptical about the ambitious targets of the plan, and the IMF expressed concern about the possibility of inflation, but the economy outperformed the targets and later the Bank became supportive of Korean development policies in general.

In the early 1960s USAID performed another important task for the future development of Korea; it financed research projects on such pending economic and social issues as financial systems and policies, grain market systems, land ownership systems, and tax systems. These were performed mainly by young Korean scholars returning from abroad. Some of the research results were immediately used in economic policy reforms and planning. The young economists became both healthy critics of economic policies and later able advisers and sometimes government technocrats. USAID also supported the establishment of the Korea Institute of Science and Technology (KIST) in 1966 and the Korea Development Institute (KDI) in 1971. The KDI has played a central role in economic policy analysis since its opening and has served as a major Korean counterpart or contact point in relations between the Korean government and the World Bank. As noted earlier, however, toward the end of the 1960s the role of USAID in Korea was fading very rapidly.

Although the Korean economy was performing impressively, Korean leaders were seriously lacking in experience with and knowledge of economic policymaking and were eager to find good sources of policy advice. In the early years of the military regime, senior economic professors in Korean universities, trained mostly in Japanese universities, were invited to advise the president. Several years later, however, the president began to realize that U.S.-educated mainstream economists were more appropriate for practical economic policy advice. World Bank economists were welcomed by Korean government leaders, including the president.

21. Official deposit rates were raised to approximately 30 percent in the hope that domestic savings would be effectively mobilized through official financial institutions.

22. One by-product of the task force. Irma Adelman, ed., *Practical Approaches to Development Planning: Korea's Second Five-Year Plan* (Johns Hopkins University Press, 1969).

The World Bank Role in Korean Economic Policymaking

The Korean government's relations with the World Bank were quite different from those with the U.S. government. Relations with the United States were nation to nation—donor and receiver. In Korean perceptions, the United States attempted to assert some control over Korean affairs, whereas Koreans eagerly sought independence. In Korean–World Bank relations, the question of dependency was much less relevant. That the Bank provided Korea largely with loans, not grants, probably made Korean officials psychologically more comfortable with Bank personnel than with U.S. aid officials.

Another important area of difference was that the Bank had relatively less interest in macroeconomic issues than in specific sectoral issues. The United States intervened heavily in Korean macroeconomic management, especially in the late 1950s and early 1960s.[23] Whereas proud Korean junior and middle-level officials could be hurt by the impression that foreigners were intervening in the major economic management of their country, criticism on specific sectoral issues could be accepted as friendly advice. Largely because of these factors, Korean relations with the Bank were much smoother than with the U.S. government, at least in regard to economic policy. However, the causal direction of mutual influence in Korean–World Bank relations is not obviously identifiable.

Until the mid-1960s Korean–World Bank policy discussions and consultations were not very active. Although skeptical about the targets of the Second Five-Year Plan, the Bank was impressed by Korea's initial economic success in the mid-1960s. Nevertheless, Korea was still viewed as a newcomer to the scene. In the eyes of the Bank as well as of many Korean scholars, the ambitious Seoul-Pusan highway project was premature. Yet during the Second Five-Year Plan, the economy grew more than targeted, and the demand for inland surface transportation increased rapidly, more than justifying the construction of the controversial highway project.

In the late 1960s, as the Bank became more interested in the Korean economy, the issue of structural deepening was attracting attention domestically. Rapid structural transformations had already taken place during the first phase of economic development. The agrarian economy of the early 1960s had become considerably industrialized by the end of the decade. The growing manufacturing sector, however, was dominated by light industry and was labor intensive. Korea was exporting a lot of manufactured goods, but the balance of payments was chronically in deficit due to imports of materials and capital goods. Still, the government and the business sector were confident about the capability of the economy.

23. In the 1970s and 1980s, the Korean government was doing much better in macroeconomic management than in the 1950s and early 1960s. In addition, the IMF, under the standby agreement, was specializing in macroeconomic issues in Seoul.

President Park held a deep-rooted belief that both the economy and the nation should eventually become self-reliant. To Park, economic growth had a double role: it would enhance the material well-being of the Korean people and it would build up the power of the nation. A minimum level of income should be attained first; then the structure of the economy should be corrected, to become as self-sufficient as possible. A self-reliant defense capacity would be another important early step and would have structural implications. Self-reliance meant a "balanced," in contrast to a specialized, industrial structure. It also meant that some key items should be produced domestically. One of them was rice, the staple grain of the Korean people. Other key items could be produced by heavy industry and the chemical industry, which manufacture both the plow and the sword.

Industrial Structural Deepening

Discussions regarding the need for structural deepening were enriched and encouraged by supportive comments from the World Bank, although initially the Bank officials viewed Korea's interest in heavy industry and the chemical industry as premature. Korea did not have sufficient funds to invest in risky and capital-demanding projects and, in addition, its level of technology was negligible. However, Bank officials were eventually persuaded by Koreans; the Bank saw Koreans as trustworthy and reliable and recognized the potential of a Korean economy that was outperforming its targets. World Bank country reports published in the late 1960s and early 1970s noted that the Korean economy, with its light manufacturing industries, was approaching maturation of import substitution and needed a massive expansion of the capital goods sector in order to achieve structural balance.[24] The Bank recommended protecting the intermediate and capital goods industries to achieve deepening in industrial structure. Because the easy import substitution stage was already over, the Bank commented that Korean growth could not be sustained by exporting only products of light manufacturing industries.

Encouraged by such comments from the Bank, the Korean government became even more confident about pursuing structural deepening. The term "industrial structural deepening" became a frequently used phrase in policy discussions until the end of the 1970s.

The self-reliance argument of President Park was reinforced and justified by economists in Korea and at the Bank, who made at least five points in its favor. The first justification was based on the Chenery-Syrquin normal pattern argument.[25] As Bank reports noted, Korea's capital goods sector was at that time underdeveloped, so it would be natural to direct more resources to boost the growth of the sector.

24. World Bank, *Current Economic Positions and Prospects of the Republic of Korea* (1969); *The Economic Situation and Prospects of the Republic of Korea* (1971).

25. See Hollis Chenery and Moises Syrquin, *Patterns of Development, 1950–1970* (Oxford University Press for the World Bank, 1975).

The basic metal and petrochemical industries were also seen as underdeveloped. The second point concerned income elasticity. Light manufacturing products are largely necessities; therefore the growth rate of world demand for such items would be less than or at most equal to the growth rate of world income. To Korea, the world income growth rate was far too low to justify tying the future export growth rate to it. Korea saw the income elasticities of heavy industry and chemical products as much higher than those of light manufacturing items. A third point focused on the latecomers' case. Light manufacturing products based on simple technologies could easily be emulated by other developing Asian countries, which would erode the competitive edge of Korean exports. To remain competitive in the world market relative to latecomers, Korea had to move to a higher stage of industrialization. Structural deepening, according to this argument, should not only take place in import substitution for domestic demand but also be extended to export substitution so that the export structure could be enhanced. The fourth point centered on the domestic content of exports. In spite of the rapid growth of exports, Korea's current account balance persistently recorded deficits—a result of importing intermediate materials and capital goods for export manufacturing. In other words, Korean exports in general had very little domestic content, which meant that the value-added ratio of export production was very low. Closely related was the fifth point, concerning technology intensity. Because Korea was not abundantly endowed with natural resources, the most promising way to increase domestic value-added production would be to raise the overall technological intensity of the economy. Thus more investment was needed in industries that would adopt advanced technology. Many, including some Bank economists, argued that the Korean economy needed skill- or technology-intensive, rather than capital-intensive, structural deepening.

Domestic economists, including government officials and World Bank economists on the Korean country desk, agreed on most of the above arguments. Because Koreans shared the same ideas with economists at the Bank, the confidence level of Korean policymakers in the direction of industrial structural policies was increased. With such theoretical and moral support, heavy industry and the chemical industry were promoted and supported with the full strength of the Korean economy from the start of the 1970s.

Heavy Industry and the Chemical Industry

From the early stage of industrialization President Park had been interested in heavy industry and the chemical industry. Although few key industries had been targeted for import substitution programs during the First Five-Year Plan, during the Second some major investments were made in heavy industry and the chemical industry. Under the Third Five-Year Plan, 50 percent of manufacturing investments were allocated to heavy industry. In the late 1960s, when structural deepening was actively discussed, several major projects in heavy industry and the chemical industry were already in the planning or preparation stages; these included Pohang Steel, Changwon Heavy Machinery Complex, and Ulsan Petrochemicals. The formal declaration of the heavy industry and chemical industry strategy was made in 1973, when the economy was already moving in that direction. At that time World Bank reports consistently expressed support for this industrialization strategy. The Bank emphasized import substitution in capital goods and other intermediate goods via the needed protection and intervention. One Bank report warned of the probability of higher production costs during the transition period because of the use of more expensive domestically produced capital goods and other intermediate goods, which would probably be of lower quality than imported goods. The same report, however, stressed the inevitability of following that strategy: "Korea has little choice but to brave the uncertainties of deepening the industrial structure if it is to stay on a fairly rapid course of development of which it seems capable."[26]

Around the mid-1970s, the Bank began to express concern about the drive for heavy industry and the chemical industry.[27] It cautioned Korea about the overly ambitious scale and export targets of the drive and recommended scaling down and simultaneously supporting the traditional light industries and small and medium-size firms. The Bank also emphasized the necessity of building institutions, securing adequate technology, training manpower, and investing in infrastructure. But overall the Bank was supportive of the Korean strategy for heavy industry and the chemical industry. To efficiently achieve the intermediate goals of that strategy, the Bank recommended government intervention, exercise of leadership, and comprehensive planning.

The agendas agreed on at the policy table were not always honestly implemented in the field, nor were government plans to deepen the industrial structure implemented exactly as intended. The plans were not perfect, but they were consistent and relatively well organized. Those plans, however, could not fully incorporate the unpredictable dynamics of various noneconomic factors. Even in terms of economic variables, long-term dynamic repercussions could not be easily captured.

Implementation of policies for heavy industry and the chemical industry affected large business conglomerates most directly, and their reactions in turn affected critically the actual results of the policies. In particular, policies for these industries were promoted on the premise that the government would intervene in the private sector in a highly selective manner.

The selection process resulted in many problems. Projects of heavy industry and the chemical industry were essentially high risk, given the inexperience of Korean firms. The government, however, bore most of the risk. Abundant funds, supplied by or through the government, were an important source of attraction. Under

26. World Bank, *The Economic Situation and Prospects of the Republic of Korea* (1971), para. ix.

27. World Bank, *Growth and Prospects in the Korean Economy* (1977).

chronic inflation, the low–interest rate funds could produce large capital gains when invested in some types of real property. In the late 1960s and early 1970s, many large corporations enjoyed enormous capital gains from the inflation of land prices.[28] On the positive side, this prospect encouraged risk taking by guaranteeing substantial scrap value for factory sites or for office buildings even if the project totally failed. On the negative side, it provided some room to relax and enjoy inefficiency. In other words, a firm that was operating less efficiently than its competitor could survive if it owned a piece of rapidly appreciating land as one of its business assets. Such inefficiency could be converted to excessive scale. The firm that had larger sites eventually won if the other conditions were equal. Thus every businessman wanted to have as much cheap money as possible, even if the money was earmarked for a project.

A more important problem affecting the promotion of the heavy industry and the chemical industry was excessive competition among large business conglomerates. The extreme rivalry among the large Korean business groups is not easily understood, but nevertheless it has been the reality. Excessive competition resulted in excessive and extensive expansion. Large-scale projects characterized firm-level plans. To justify such large projects in a limited domestic market, huge export targets were projected. These projects were evaluated by the government and for some time by the Korea Development Institute, but the actual decisions on important projects were made at the political level. Among the strategic weaknesses in promoting selective intervention policies were the morbid competition under a distorted incentive structure and the dominance of political factors in picking so-called winners.

Toward the end of the 1970s, concerns over such excessive scales and overly ambitious export targets increased among domestic economists and government officials as well as at the World Bank. Other problems also began to be revealed. The costs of learning by doing—a trial-and-error process—were much higher than expected. Much of the knowledge and skills accumulated through experience could not be learned from textbooks or manuals. Managerial ability at both the firm and government levels was seriously deficient. Institutional deficiency, rigidity, and inefficiency created other problems. Moreover, the excessive competition among business groups intent on building their own self-sufficient empires resulted in investment overlaps and further inefficiency. The integrated facilities at the Changwon machinery complex, for example, were not used as intensively as intended.

In spite of these problems, the aggregate targets set by the government for heavy industry and the chemical industry were successfully achieved. Investment resources were massively directed to these industrial sectors, and their shares of production and exports increased dramatically. The growth rate of the whole

28. The introduction of a real estate speculation control tax in 1967 reflected the seriousness of the issue.

economy, driven by the aggressive capital investments in heavy industry and chemicals, was maintained at a very high level throughout the 1970s.

The economy nevertheless began to show symptoms of overheating around the end of the decade. To control mounting inflationary pressures, a comprehensive stabilization policy was implemented in 1979. However, other destabilizing events followed. President Park was assassinated in 1979, the Kwang-ju incident occurred and the second international oil crisis shocked the economy. The sudden worsening of the economic environment revealed, and in some cases exaggerated, the problems of policies for heavy industry and the chemical industry. Even before these events took place, several large projects had to be delayed, scaled down, or canceled.

In sum, both Korean policymakers and World Bank economists agreed on the desirability of promoting heavy industry and the chemical industry through highly selective government intervention and import substitution under tariff protection. Even at the end of the 1970s, when the problems of the drive to promote these heavy industries began to be revealed, the Bank supported the basic direction of structural deepening through selective government intervention. It even recommended further government intervention to remedy some of the revealed symptoms. Moreover, neoclassical market economists at the Bank refrained from monitoring interventionist Korean officials. On the contrary, the Bank and the Korean government encouraged each other to pursue the industrialization strategy. But the Bank cannot be blamed for the strategy's excesses. The flexibility of the World Bank economists should be emphasized. They were typical neoclassical market economists, and they contributed greatly to the indoctrination of Korean officials with the ideals of the market economic system. The Bank's economists in general were not dogmatic and knew how to harmonize textbook principles with real-world constraints.

Structural Adjustment in the 1980s

In many ways the 1980s were a period of structural adjustment for the Korean economy. The rapid growth and change of the two preceding decades had prevented Koreans from carefully investigating and coping with the economic problems that had arisen. Then in 1980 the galloping economy slowed to a halt, and the first negative rate of growth since 1953 was recorded. At the same time, mainly as a result of the oil crisis, inflation peaked at almost 40 percent, as measured by the wholesale price index—the second highest rate since the Korean War truce. The current account balance registered a huge deficit, and the external debt was rapidly accumulating. The heavy industry and chemical sectors, which had become leaders of the Korean economy, severely faltered.

The dead weight of numerous troubled industries in these sectors was burdensome to the economy. Moreover, throughout the 1970s credit expansion had remained excessive to finance not only projects in those sectors, but also projects for regional and agricultural development. The foreign exchange rate had been fixed since the mid-1970s to keep down the cost of imported capital goods and other intermediate goods for heavy industry and the chemical industry. At the same time, chronic inflationary pressures made it difficult to depreciate the won for fear that such an action might trigger a severe inflationary spiral. The adverse effects of the distorted foreign exchange rate policy on exports were largely offset by various export incentives. Such macroeconomic mismanagement began to be criticized openly by Korean and World Bank economists. Political turmoil also contributed to the macroeconomic difficulties at the beginning of the 1980s.

Not all the evils that appeared in the early 1980s could be attributed to domestic factors. The second oil price shock hit Korea's economy hard. The world economy was slowing down, and protectionism was beginning to prevail among the advanced countries, the principal markets for Korean exports. Extremely high interest rates in the international capital markets seriously burdened the heavy borrowers.

Under such difficult conditions the sickness that had been dormant in many of Korea's heavy industries and chemical industries became apparent. Many industrial units in these sectors were seen to be underused. Some units were producing items that nobody wanted to buy; and in general units in these sectors were producing low-quality products at high production costs, mainly because of lack of experience. In addition, a rise in interest rates and depreciation of the won severely hit the heavily indebted import-substituting industries. However, some of the difficulties of heavy industry and the chemical industry exposed during that period were substantially exaggerated. If macroeconomic conditions had not been so severe, some of them eventually would have become mature competitive business units.

As the problems of heavy industry and the chemical industry drive became more visible, open criticisms of the government's industrial policies of protection and intervention mounted and the arguments for liberalization and exposure to international competition gained wider support. It is ironic that at that time the government was practicing extreme intervention, even commanding private firms to manufacture only a specified line of products. Government officials and economists in research institutions preached the virtues of market mechanisms and the positive effects of being exposed to international competition. The technocrats, particularly Kim Jae-Ik, who served as senior secretary to the president on economic matters, convinced President Chun Doo Hwan of the superiority of the market mechanism in achieving efficiency in resource allocation and of the importance of removing the entrenched inflationary expectation that prevailed in the early 1980s. World Bank economists, too, became skeptical about the effectiveness of the interventionist industrial policies.

Industrial Restructuring

Faced with these conditions, the new government led by President Chun initiated drastic restructuring processes. Some restructuring programs had already been initiated, but in the early 1980s extensive and direct restructuring was enforced in several problem industries.

One of the most important restructuring cases was that of the automobile industry. The government selected two firms to specialize in producing passenger cars and one firm to specialize in commercial vehicles—a government fiat not easily conceivable in a market economy. However, the World Bank suggested that the government suspend its support of the automobile manufacturing firms and that the industry give up the manufacture of finished automobiles and specialize in producing exportable automotive parts and components. The Korea Development Institute and the Korea Institute for Economics and Technology (KIET) also studied the issue.[29] A KIET report pointed out the structural weakness of the Korean automobile industry. It noted that it would be very difficult to improve the product quality to the exportable level, and even the low-quality products would be produced at very high costs.[30] It also observed that the Korean automobile firms did not have marketing and service networks in major potential markets and that such networks were essential in exporting automobiles and extremely costly to set up. The report concluded that Korea would have a greater comparative advantage in manufacturing automotive parts and components and recommended that Korea forgo the national manufacture of finished automobiles. It also suggested that exposure to world competition should be increased, thus allowing the market to select the appropriate areas of automotive specialization for Korea, a line of reasoning that was widely accepted at that time.

As the Bank had suggested, government assistance was removed from the restructured automobile firms. Other suggestions were not followed. The restructured automobile firms invested heavily in their own products. One result was that Hyundai, which was 100 percent domestically owned, succeeded in shipping finished automobiles to North American markets in the mid-1980s.

It is difficult to identify the factors that enabled Korean automobile manufacturers to succeed. For one thing, the government's restructuring of the industry and continued tariff protection reduced excessive competition in the domestic market. At the same time, the unexpected removal of government assistance, which was originally intended to discourage the industry, contributed to activating the firms to live up to their potential. It was made clear that the firms must stand on their own feet in order to survive. This convinced them that the protection of the domestic market would not last permanently. Thus the success of the automobile industry in Korea was achieved by private initiative. That success cannot be attributed to market conditions alone; although improvements in economic condi-

29. Some of the studies were reported in Korea Institute for Economics and Technology (KIET), *Problems and Policy Directions of the Automobile Industry*, Special Analysis 3 (Seoul, 1982); Y. B. Kim, *Policy Direction for the Development of the Automobile Industry* (Seoul: KDI, 1981); and C. H. Lee, *Automobile Industry in Korea* (Seoul: KDI, 1980).

30. KIET, *Problems and Policy Directions*.

tions in both domestic and world markets contributed to the success of the private ventures. Korean automobiles nonetheless faced severe competition at the export frontiers. Yet it was not market competition that stimulated the industry to grow strong enough to venture into the world market. Rather, an environment was provided in which the creativity and responsibility of the private sector could be maximized. Neither World Bank economists nor Korean economists correctly evaluated the problem and the possibilities; thus they provided unrealistic policy recommendations. What if the government had taken their advice to an extreme and intervened further to prevent the "waste" of investment resources in the "hopeless" automobile assembly lines?

Another example of restructuring can be found in the production of heavy equipment for thermal power generation—one of those industries cited for excessive scale and overly ambitious targets. Four companies were initially licensed, with each company's capacity far exceeding total domestic demand. One reason for the excessive capacity was that the government's energy policy unexpectedly switched emphasis from thermal to nuclear power generation. This change can be attributed to inconsistency in long-term planning and to the difficulties, in project evaluation, of forecasting demand and other relevant variables. At the time the World Bank was supplying a loan to one of the thermal projects; the major switch in energy policy was made right after the loan was approved. Restructuring merged the four companies into two. After several years of losses and difficulties, the break-even point was finally reached in 1986, mainly as a result of drastically improved domestic and international economic environments. The capacity utilization rate was as high as 90 percent, with a substantial portion of the products being sold in international markets. The opportunity cost of that restructuring project, however, was enormous; precious capital was not used efficiently. One would be warranted in concluding that the heavy electrical machinery project was a success only because it eventually reached the break-even point or produced exportable products.

Although both the automobile industry and the heavy machinery industry eventually achieved success, it is clear that such outcomes do not justify the interventionist industrial policies that were followed. But neither do these outcomes refute the usefulness of government intervention in promoting industrial development. The science of economics always seeks to pursue the optimal path, but it is not easy to follow an unknown optimal path closely in designing economic development policies. To achieve a reasonably good performance, both intervention and market mechanisms must be used. World Bank economists, in concert with Korean technocrats and economists working mostly at government research institutions, helped keep Korean government actions from going to extremes. During the drive for heavy industry and the chemical industry, however, the checking role appears to have been overdone; it was performed at a level that was too conservative. The restructuring process, on the other hand, showed a well-balanced harmony of intervention and free competition. During the restructuring period economists at Korean research institutions and at the Bank for the most part took a balanced position.

Other Structural Policies and Macroeconomic Adjustment

The effectiveness of interventionist industrial policies in a dynamic situation has been a controversial topic. In an uncertain world, it cannot be theoretically determined; it is an empirical question. Most economists knew that not all the economic difficulties experienced in Korea in the late 1970s and the early 1980s were attributable to excessively interventionist policies, and when they looked at the many structural difficulties in heavy industry and the chemical industry, they tended to favor noninterventionist, market-determined resource allocation. As a result, the pendulum began to swing to the other side, and the government promoted liberalization in various fields.

Within Korea, five government-owned commercial banks were privatized. The government had used its hold on commercial banks to intervene deeply in the credit rationing of those banks in the 1970s. Administrative price controls were reduced drastically. A new fair trade and antimonopoly law was enacted to prevent unfair business practices and collusion among firms. Korea's more important reforms were enacted in the area of external transactions. Active liberalization of the domestic market under a preannounced schedule, including removal of tariff and nontariff protections, was promoted. At the same time, targeting of strategic industries was discontinued. The industry-specific support system, which involved preferential interest rates, industry-oriented financial facilities, and industry-specific tax incentives, was phased out in the early 1980s. In other words, the government intentionally and voluntarily abandoned its cherished instruments for controlling the private sector.

To cope with the current account deficit and the accumulating debt accompanied by high inflation, the government formulated a drastic macroeconomic adjustment program. The strategy was straightforward and honest; it called for lower growth targets, depreciation, fiscal stringency, and a tight credit policy. Impressively enough, the rate of increase in the money supply (M2) was reduced to about 15 percent in 1983, which was about 60 percent of the 1981–82 expansion.[31] Taxes were raised and government expenditures were almost frozen, reducing the debt-to-GNP ratio drastically. The real exchange rate was raised substantially.

As the most visible and important result of such adjustments, inflation as measured by the wholesale price index increase rate was abruptly reduced to 0.1 percent in 1983 and to –1.5 to 0.9 percent during the 1984–87 period. Balance of payments was rapidly stabilized. Thanks to the so-called three lows (low oil

31. Bank of Korea, *Economic Statistics Yearbook* (1992), p. 3.

prices, low interest rates, and a low yen-dollar rate) and the macroeconomic adjustment efforts in the early 1980s, the Korean economy recorded an extraordinary performance in the mid-1980s.

These macroeconomic adjustments seemed more successful than the industrial restructuring of the early 1980s, although such comparison cannot be made on a scientific basis. But industrial restructuring and the well-conceived and superbly performed macroeconomic adjustment were mutually complementary and brought about the remarkable performance in the mid- and late 1980s.

Regarding the macroeconomic adjustments of the 1980s, the World Bank was more or less an impressed onlooker rather than a contributing participant in policy discussions. Perhaps that was a result of the Bank's focus on microeconomic resource allocation issues.[32]

Social Development Policy

In the 1960s, the World Bank praised Korea for achieving equitable income distribution as well as high growth. It was not concerned about equity issues in Korea in the early stages of industrialization. The Bank was committed, however, to rural and agricultural development in Korea, and it provided substantial loans to be invested in projects in these sectors, especially during the 1970s. At the same time, the Korean government began to feel the need for rural development measures and launched the Saemaul campaign toward that end. Other social development policies also attracted the attention of policymakers; studies on major social development programs were pursued, and some programs were implemented in the 1970s. Although significant resources were allocated to social development projects at that time, this fact was lost in the clamor over the drive for heavy industry and the chemical industry. On balance, the 1970s was a decade in which the drive for growth and efficiency resulted in rapidly worsening income distribution, particularly during the second half of the decade.

In the early 1980s the enhancement of equity and acceleration of social development were highly emphasized policy goals. These goals were suggested as an antithesis to the previous regime's policy focus on high growth and efficiency and paralleled the emphasis on liberalization in the 1980s. As a gesture to emphasize the social side of development, the official name of the five-year plans, beginning with the fifth plan (1982–86), was changed to "Economic and Social Development Plan" from "Economic Development Plan."

Social development objectives were not pursued as effectively in the early 1980s as the government's rhetoric promised. The stabilization objective was more important, and the resultant stringent fiscal policy did not provide much room for the social development budget. During the second half of the 1980s the equity goals of

32. The World Bank and the Korea Development Institute carried out an ex-post research project on Korea's experience in structural adjustment.

the government were emphasized more strongly, but again, largely because of financial constraints, they were not pursued aggressively. Income distribution, however, appeared to have improved in the 1980s mainly as a result of price stabilization.[33]

The World Bank also began to emphasize social development in Korea in the early 1980s. As shown in table 2-2, the Bank provided substantial loans for social development projects, mostly during the 1980s.

Other Dimensions of Cooperation

Trained economists were scarce in Korea in the 1960s. Government officials in charge of drafting economic policies did not have even the basic concepts of modern economics. Economists working at the U.S. Agency for International Development and on advisory missions in Korea were valuable sources of knowledge that was essential for economic policymaking and institutional reforms. In addition, the research department of the Bank of Korea was an important source of policy ideas and information, and the bank was heavily involved in formulating early long-term development plans.

The establishment of the Korea Development Institute in 1971 was an important turning point in the number of economists in Korea. Numerous U.S.-trained economists, some of whom had been working at the World Bank, were brought to Korea. At a time when there was a shortage of economists, the various World Bank missions and Bank economists visiting Korea were valuable resources. KDI economists, having good connections with the Bank, multiplied the usefulness of such Bank economists.

At the same time, the training of domestic policy economists was sponsored by the Bank through its Economic Development Institute. Whereas USAID sponsored rather formal training of Korean economists at American universities, the EDI program was oriented more toward development policy and short-term training. Thanks to these programs and to the Korean government's programs to support the training of officials abroad, the government had abundant foreign-trained economists in the late 1970s and the 1980s. The number of economic professionals

33. See Hakchung Choo, "Income Distribution and Distributive Equity in Korea," paper presented at the USCD/KDI Joint Symposium on Micro-Social Issues in South Korea, La Jolla, Calif., June 26–27, 1992. There has been some controversy regarding the reliability of the official income distribution statistics, which show a clear trend of improving distribution in recent years. Soonwon Kwon, "Korea: Income and Wealth Distribution and Government Initiatives to Reduce Disparities," Korea Development Institute Working Paper 9008 (June 1990); and D. Kim and K. S. Ahn, *Korea's Income Distribution, Its Determinants and People's Consciousness about [the] Distribution Problem* (Seoul: Jungang University Press, 1987), among others, using different data sets or different assumptions, show a worsening trend of income distribution. I chose to rely on the official statistics.

outside the government also skyrocketed during the 1980s. In the early 1980s, the KDI even began providing training programs for policymakers in other developing countries; some of the programs have been presented in conjunction with the Bank's EDI.

It is not easy to identify the effects on Korean economic development of the Bank's training programs. However, the short-term, policy-oriented EDI program was especially appropriate for Korean officials in that it provided practical knowledge and opportunities to develop personal connections with the Bank staff and officials from other countries. Such opportunities enabled middle-level Korean government officials to gain international perspectives. Many of the middle-level officials trained by EDI were promoted to ministerial rank or became presidential secretaries in various fields.

Factors in Korea's Success

Korea is one of the most successful among those countries that have benefited from World Bank support. Korea is widely considered as a role model by many developing countries and was treated as such in development economics textbooks that were published in the 1970s or 1980s. Learning missions from communist and socialist countries seeking economic reform and development swarmed into Seoul. What has made Korea such an outstanding success among so many member countries of the World Bank?

To begin with, Korean government leaders in the 1960s and 1970s had a strong and, in a sense, single-minded desire for national economic enhancement. They did not, however, have any idea how to achieve that goal, at least in the earlier stages of development. Korea's strong demand for advice on economic development policy created a close and smooth relationship between Korean officials and Bank economists; thus the advice of Bank missions was highly regarded and well taken. At the same time, because of that intimate relationship, the real problems of the Korean government, which were not easily captured by analyses of published statistics or expressed in formal interviews, could easily be transmitted to the Bank's analysts. Yet it is important to note that Korean leaders did not take the advice of the Bank's economists blindly. They digested that advice and used it in modifying and developing their own policies. A country must establish its own well-defined goals and a basic system to pursue and manage them, regardless of the availability of capable policy consultants.

The Confucian culture and tradition of Korean society was the most critical factor in formulating and bringing about the success of the Korean approach to economic development. Centralization of power and decisionmaking in almost all organizations, from the national level to the household level, has been a natural phenomenon in that culture. Without the Confucian culture's respect for seniors and for authority, the two dictatorial regimes that governed Korea for almost three decades—decades during which the Korean economy witnessed its miracles—could have survived only at a much higher social cost and through cruel and systematic oppression.

The Confucian culture also explains much of the Korean's drive for higher education. Moreover, the Confucian philosophy is relatively mundane in that it values worldly achievement in a way that religions more oriented to life after death do not, with a possible exception of Protestantism. Therefore hard work, accumulation of wealth, and pursuit of status are a natural and commendable pattern of Korean life.

Yet Korea's Confucian tradition has elements that have been detrimental to economic development. It has valued empty formalities too much. It has respected scholars, government officials, and other professionals but despised those in manufacturing and commerce.[34] However, that part of the tradition was considerably weakened during the period of drastic social changes in the 1940s and the 1950s. With the traditional structure of social status thus radically broken, wealth became the new standard of status, and the pursuit of it became more attractive.

Personal factors were also important in determining the course of Korea's modern economic history. President Park's influence on Korea's industrialization was especially critical. Park was a humble man with outstanding leadership abilities; he was very smart and austere. His aspirations for economic development and the buildup of national power were exceptional. His stern personality and tight control of the information network kept the dictatorial regime relatively uncorrupted.

With its extremely centralized power structure, the government had relatively few restrictions in choosing among various policy alternatives. It was rarely forced to adopt a populist policy that might conflict with goals of efficiency. In the early 1970s, however, Park had to take various pacifying measures to gain support for the extension of his presidency, which would have been impossible under normal Korean procedures. In particular, a substantial amount of public money was spent on the development of rural areas, the locus of the regime's main support. Such policies, however, were not totally out of line with the pursuit of the economic development of the nation. Thus the Korean economic policy was not seriously distracted from its long-term development goals.

This is not to say that the regime was indifferent to political popularity. With neither strong support from the people nor legal orthodoxy, it could not have remained in power for an extended time. Park's strategy to gain support was to achieve successful economic development; high economic growth became his

34. For an interesting discussion of the relationship between religious background and entrepreneurship in Korea, see Leroy P. Jones and I. Sakong, *Government, Business, and Entrepreneurship in Economic Development: The Korean Case* (Harvard University Press, 1980), pp. 221–23.

trademark. The World Bank played a critical role in this achievement, praising Korea's success. Such recognition from the Bank—the world's most authoritative international development organization—positively influenced Korea's international relations, but was even more important domestically. It provided a powerful and persuasive justification to the Korean public for the existence of a dictatorial government devoted to economic development. Park's exceptional aspiration for development and his humble personality, together with the domestic political advantage of World Bank recognition, contributed critically to the development of a special relationship between the Korean government and the World Bank.

During his regime, Park was the source of all power in Korea, and high-ranking government officials and major business leaders were attentive to even minor movements in the Blue House, the official residence of the president. But it was not only the leadership that was effective in pursuing economic growth; the government's staff was able and efficient, and Korea's bureaucracy was orderly and powerful. In general, junior staff members were obedient to their superiors—as a result of the Confucian tradition. Reinforced by the military influence in government organizations, a submissive supervisor-subordinate relationship was almost absolute. In such a system, once a decision was made at the top, implementation could be accomplished efficiently.

Both the Confucian tradition and the civil service examination system ensured that only persons of the best quality could get government jobs. Such officials were highly motivated, hard working, and fast learning. During the high-growth decades, government officials in the major policymaking ministries worked especially hard. Ambitious young officials were eager to absorb advanced knowledge in their specialized fields, to master English, and to acquire academic degrees, all of which not only improved the quality of their analytical work but also enabled them to communicate smoothly with foreigners, including the members of the World Bank staff. Contributing to such learning and communication were the professional U.S. economists at the Korea Development Institute as well as various overseas training programs for government officials, including those conducted by the Bank's Economic Development Institute.

At an early stage of modern Korea's development, the government created a powerful ministry, the Economic Planning Board, which would take the responsibility for drafting economic development plans and related policies, managing the macroeconomy, allocating the government's budget among various projects and programs, and resolving possible conflicts among ministries. With its concentrated power and information, this ministry, headed by the deputy prime minister, managed the development of the Korean economy effectively. Generally the officials working for the Board possessed the best intellectual ability, training, and motivation. The Board was directly supported by the research efforts of the KDI, whose staff included some thirty to forty full-time professional economists specializing in various policy fields. The Board was the counterpart of the World Bank in

Korean–World Bank relations. The structure of the bureaucracy was thus oriented toward economic development and allowed the government to focus on economic policy issues.

Another source of the power of the administration was the high degree of compliance by the people with government policy. Such a behavioral pattern can be partly explained by the Confucian tradition. A public accustomed to oppressive regimes could account, in part, for the extended existence of the Park administration. A powerful and efficient administration that designed and implemented development policies effectively was an essential complement to a leader devoted to economic development.

It should also be said that the Park regime was relatively little tainted by economic corruption. The regime was not particularly of very high moral standard, nor was everybody in the power circle honest and clean. Dictatorship itself can be regarded as immoral. And in general, to maintain a dictatorial regime for a prolonged period, a ruling group often resorts to inappropriate actions. But in terms of material well-being, President Park was strict with himself and his family. Moreover, a wide range of societal leaders was closely watched by well-organized and even threatening intelligence networks. Foreign exchange was especially tightly controlled. Investment funds, and in particular capital borrowed from abroad, rarely leaked out of the system. Money borrowed from the World Bank in conjunction with specific projects was especially well managed and honestly invested, in part because the Korean officials were well aware that maintaining credible relations with the Bank was essential to securing its continued support.

During Korea's industrialization and rapid economic growth, the most critically binding factor was the continuing flow of foreign capital. It was the World Bank that took care of the bottlenecks by directly lending to Korea and by endorsing the economy in international capital markets. At the same time, the Bank helped Korean officials to develop and implement sound and efficient development policies. Sometimes the Bank's economic policy advice was general, but in most cases it was specific and pertinent.

Valuable materials and advice provided by the Bank, such as foreign capital and policy ideas, were efficiently and honestly used by Korean political leaders, technocrats, and civil servants. But most critical to the remarkably successful development of the Korean economy was the special and mutually trusting character of the relationship that developed between the Korean government and the World Bank.

Korea now has started the process of transforming itself from being a taker into being a giver. The process cannot be rapid, but the direction cannot be reversed. Korean public sentiment for repaying the benefit received from richer friends during the hard days, by helping other countries now in difficult situations, is rapidly spreading. Private campaigns to help starving people in Africa and South Asia are harvesting great success. Although the amount is small, government aid money has been included in the budget. Currently Korea faces some balance-of-payment difficulties, but it will probably join the givers shortly.

THREE

Five Decades of Relations between the World Bank and Mexico

Carlos M. Urzúa

FORTY–FOUR countries from Latin America and the Caribbean were represented at Bretton Woods in July 1944. Yet, while they constituted a near majority, these countries came away with less than 5 percent of total subscriptions in the new International Bank for Reconstruction and Development (IBRD). Aside from the obvious fact that the rich donors wanted to have control, the meager quota can also be explained by the decision to link capital shares in the IBRD to members' quotas in the International Monetary Fund (IMF). This ruling, opposed by the Latin American countries, was an attempt to ensure that all countries accepted that their liabilities to the IBRD should be proportionate to their assets in the IMF.

Of course, the Latin American representatives were fully aware that their economies were then marginal at best. They also knew that the IBRD was initially

I am thankful to the many individuals who contributed to making this a better chapter: in Mexico City, former Mexican presidents Luis Echeverría, José López Portillo, and Miguel de la Madrid, together with Francisco Suárez Dávila, and several other persons who wish to remain anonymous; in Washington, Gary Gordon, Karin Lissakers, John Williamson, and eighteen World Bank staff members; and in Oxford, Ngaire Woods. I am also grateful to Gladstone Bonnick and coworkers at the Operations Evaluation Department of the World Bank for sharing with me their outstanding work on World Bank–Mexico relations.

John Lewis's incisive criticism of an earlier version of this chapter was quite helpful. I also very much appreciate the help given to me by Richard Webb during the entire project, together with his sharp and extensive comments on several versions of the chapter. Last but not least, I am most thankful to Devesh Kapur for quite valuable discussions on the Bank, for his extensive comments on this chapter, and for sharing with me some of his work on the relations between Mexico and the World Bank during the mid-1980s. None of these individuals is responsible for any errors, omissions, or misinterpretations made by me.

meant to aid the European economies ravaged by World War II. In any case, judging by the candid remembrances of some, the Latin Americans were simply exhilarated at the chance to participate at Bretton Woods, not to mention the opportunity of debating strategy with world-renowned economists such as Lionel Robbins, Joan Robinson, and John Maynard Keynes.[1]

And debate they did. Mexico, for instance, submitted to the IBRD committee at Bretton Woods (led by Keynes) an amendment to the Articles of Agreement that explicitly put the IBRD's dual tasks of reconstruction and development on the same footing.[2] It was one of the few amendments accepted by Keynes. The modification of Article III reads: "The resources and the facilities of the Bank shall be used exclusively for the benefit of members with equitable consideration to projects for development and projects for reconstruction alike."[3] Mexico also succeeded in persuading the delegates to accept silver as a possible medium to store foreign reserves (a dear point for Mexico, an important silver producer).[4]

Such relative success at the conference creating the World Bank, as the IBRD and its younger affiliates came to be known, has been mostly but not always maintained in the five decades since. Indeed, as of 1994, Mexico became the largest borrower in the history of the IBRD.[5] (If other World Bank institutions are included, the largest borrower continues to be India.) In addition, the economic reforms undertaken by Mexico in the late 1980s and early 1990s were used by the Bank as a model for the rest of the developing world.

Of course, Mexico fell from its pedestal during the disastrous peso crisis of 1994. In fact, the Bank has often misread Mexico. For instance, in a lecture given in 1961, almost at the end of his term as president of the World Bank, Eugene Black noted that Russia, Mexico, and Japan (in that order!) "have yet to achieve high consumption economies, but could conceivably achieve them in the foreseeable future."[6]

1. See, for the case of Mexico, Daniel Cosío Villegas, *Memorias* (Mexico City: Joaquín Mortiz, 1976), pp. 216–21; Eduardo Suárez, *Comentarios y recuerdos, 1926–1946* (Mexico City: Editorial Porrúa, 1977), pp. 273–83; and Víctor L. Urquidi, "Bretton Woods: Un recorrido por el primer cincuentenario," *Comercio Exterior,* vol. 44, no. 40 (October 1994), pp. 838–47.

2. *Proceedings and Documents of the United Nations Monetary and Financial Conference* (Bretton Woods, New Hampshire: 1944), vol. II, document 306. See also Urquidi, "Bretton Woods," for a detailed account of this amendment.

3. International Bank for Reconstruction and Development, *Articles of Agreement* (Washington: World Bank, 1991), p. 5.

4. Suárez, *Comentarios y recuerdos,* p. 281.

5. See World Bank, *Annual Report, 1994* (Washington: World Bank, 1994), appendix 6. Since the Bank calculates its cumulative lending without correcting for the loss in the value of the dollar over the years, and hence biases the ranking toward the most recent heavy borrowers, this claim is questionable.

6. Eugene R. Black, *The Diplomacy of Economic Development* (Cambridge: Harvard University Press, 1960), p. 2.

It is my purpose to review the more than five decades of relations between Mexico and the World Bank with a critical eye, paying close attention to the peaks and troughs in the relationship. I should note, in passing, that the interested reader may supplement the reading of this chapter with the excellent survey of this topic made by the Bank's own staff.[7] The present work complements that survey by covering a wider period and providing a different perspective.

The chapter does not cover each decade equally. In particular, since the heyday of the relationship can be traced back only to the late 1980s, almost half of the chapter is dedicated to a review of the post-1988 period, which begins with the Salinas administration. Furthermore, a long section is dedicated to the economic crisis that erupted in December 1994.

Also, this chapter is ordered according to different Mexican presidential regimes, rather than World Bank presidential periods. Since Mexico still has what could be described as an autocratic political regime, the Mexican president in office at the time necessarily set the tone, overtly or not, for relations with the Bank.

For readers unfamiliar with Mexico, it is worth remembering that embarrassing domestic facts are often better explained in the words of an outsider. The economist Angus Maddison correctly and succinctly described the Mexican political cal system as follows:

> Enormous power is concentrated in the presidency. . . . The president can veto any legislation, and the veto cannot be overridden. This concentration of power is limited by a regular six-year alternation and ineligibility for reelection. . . . There are no overt checks and balances in this system, and the legislature has no control over budgetary policy. The party and the presidency also wield considerable power of patronage. . . .[8]

The First Two Decades

When the World Bank and the International Monetary Fund effectively got under way in the summer of 1946, Mexico was set to start a new paradigm for development. Its import substitution strategy would prove to be quite successful over the next quarter-century in terms of both high rates of growth and intensive industrialization.

Since that economic paradigm did not clash with the basic tenets then held by the Bank, the relationship was acceptably good for the first two decades. After all,

7. World Bank, *OED Study of Bank/Mexico Relations, 1948–1992*, Report No. 12923 (World Bank, April 1994). Readers in Spanish can also benefit from the work of Francisco Suárez Dávila, "La política financiera internacional de México: Relaciones con el Banco Mundial y el FMI," *Comercio Exterior*, vol. 44, no. 40 (October 1994), pp. 853–64.

8. Angus Maddison and Associates, *The Political Economy of Poverty, Equity and Growth: Brazil and Mexico* (New York: Oxford University Press, 1992), p. 115.

it was in all respects a marriage of convenience. On the one hand, Mexico in 1946 finally concluded a series of defaults and debt rescheduling agreements with foreign creditors—episodes that had been recurring since the Great Depression.[9] Consequently, Mexico was keenly aware of the fact that it would not have access to private capital markets for a while, and that all foreign credit would have to come from official sources (more than fifteen years had to pass before Mexico was able to sell bonds again to private foreign investors). On the other hand, during its first two decades of existence the World Bank directed most of its energies to lending for infrastructure, and Mexico, as a large country growing rapidly in the first phase of industrialization, was fertile ground for such aid.

The Urgency for Industrialization

Using the traditional taxonomy in Mexican economic history, the administration of Miguel Alemán (1946–52) constituted the last part of the so-called inflationary development period, characterized by high rates of growth and high variability of the inflation rate.[10] This era is typically traced back to the administration of Lázaro Cárdenas (1934–40) and continued during that of Manuel Ávila Camacho (1940–46). Yet it seems slightly odd to lump together those three administrations on the basis of two indicators only, growth and inflation.

For one, the conservative Alemán administration contrasted sharply from an ideological point of view with the Cárdenas administration. While Cárdenas nationalized the oil industry in 1938, Alemán tried to attract foreign investment to the manufacturing sector; while Cárdenas engaged in a massive land redistribution, the last economic reform truly descendant of the Mexican Revolution (1910–20), Alemán tacitly sided with the rich landowners who remained after the agrarian reform.

The Alemán administration also contrasted, albeit more subtly, with the Ávila Camacho administration. Although both came from the more conservative end of the political spectrum, Ávila Camacho's economic policies were mostly a response to the turbulence of World War II. During his term, the increase in the domestic production of manufactured goods, accompanied by a hefty increase in agricultural exports, mostly occurred because a world production gap had been caused by the drop in the manufacturing of nonwar goods by the industrialized countries. Even the raising of tariffs during the period seems to have been adopted more for fiscal reasons, as an expeditious way to increase tax revenue, than for industry protection.

9. See Jan Bazant, *Historia de la deuda exterior de México, 1823–1946* (Mexico City: El Colegio de México, 1968).

10. A general reference on this period is Enrique Cárdenas, *La hacienda pública y la política económica, 1929–1958* (Mexico City: El Colegio de México and Fondo de Cultura Económica, 1994). For a concise reference in English see Maddison, *The Political Economy of Poverty, Equity and Growth.*

Under Alemán, however, the new economic paradigm of inward development was fully assumed and forcefully pursued. In a way, it was natural to follow that strategy, given the abrupt changes the economy endured during the first years of his administration. After the war ended, the flow of foreign manufactured goods to Mexico increased sharply, not only because the industrialized countries switched out of war production but also because the Mexican economy was growing and the fixed exchange rate was becoming increasingly overvalued.

As a consequence, from mid-1947 to mid-1948 the Alemán administration had to impose a series of quotas and tariff increases. Furthermore, in 1947, the Mexican central bank, Banco de México, had to request for the first time an exchange transaction of $22.5 million with the IMF to support the Mexican peso. Mexico also received some help from a stabilization agreement with the U.S. Treasury.

Nevertheless, all those measures were unable to stem the deterioration of the current account, and in July 1948 the peso had to be devalued. The devaluation in itself was not surprising; after all, Argentina, Colombia, France, Spain, and Uruguay had to devalue their currencies in the same year. What surprised (and irked) the IMF was that Mexico let the peso freely fluctuate for almost a year, from July 1948, when the parity was at 4.85 pesos per dollar, to June 1949, when the parity was finally set at 8.65, a move in plain violation of the fixed exchange rate regime advocated worldwide in those years. As a response, the IMF rejected a petition in May 1948 for a second exchange transaction.[11]

Another source of friction, with both the IMF and the U.S. Treasury, was that the new parity set by Banco de México was substantially lower than the ten pesos per dollar that the two institutions were suggesting to Mexico. This devaluation episode, incidentally, marked the first time in which the U.S. Treasury–IMF duo (the Bad and the Ugly, as some Mexicans think) jointly participated (or colluded) in a Mexican crisis. The same behavior has been repeated since.

In the short term, the devaluation had positive effects: In 1950, the rate of real GDP growth reached 9.9 percent, the inflation rate was kept at 6.7 percent, and the current account deficit turned into a healthy surplus. Growth continued to be healthy until the end of the Alemán administration, but the relatively high inflation that the country had to endure in 1951–52 had already consumed most of the comparative advantage of the peso when a new administration arrived at the end of 1952.

Interestingly, the Mexican devaluation episode prompted Jacques Polak, at the IMF, to write the paper "Depreciation to Meet a Situation of Over-Investment" that would become the first in a series of IMF studies on the absorption approach to balance of payments adjustment. In that unpublished paper, dated September 1948, Polak wanted to show that "devaluation cannot be effective in correcting a large and persistent balance of payments deficit that is the result of overinvest-

11. J. K. Horsefield, *The International Monetary Fund, 1945–1965* (IMF, 1969), p. 228.

ment."[12] Perhaps in response to that warning, the Mexican government not only devalued, but also turned a fiscal deficit in 1948 into a surplus over the next three years.

THE FIRST IBRD LOAN TO MEXICO. It was in this economic environment that the first World Bank loan to Mexico was made in January 1949. The loan, for electric power development, was contracted by the Comisión Federal de Electricidad (CFE), a public utility founded by the state in 1937. It is noteworthy that electric power loans were to constitute the vast majority of the Bank's loans to Mexico for the next decade, with the exceptions of a loan for railway development, to be reviewed later, and a failed loan made in 1950 for the private industrial sector (of which only 5 percent was ever disbursed). Consequently, until 1972 electric power loans accounted for more than 50 percent of the Bank's total exposure in Mexico; at that point, disputes between the Bank and Mexico on electric tariffs made the Bank cease its lending to that sector for more than a decade.

ECONOMIC ASSESSMENTS OF MEXICO BY THE BANK. Although the World Bank wrote an economic report on Mexico as early as August 1948, the first serious attempt by the Bank to evaluate the Mexican economy was made in February 1951 at the petition of Nacional Financiera (NAFIN), the main state development bank of Mexico.[13] As a result, a Combined Working Party of four economists from Mexico (Raúl Ortiz Mena and Víctor L. Urquidi) and the World Bank (Albert Waterston and Jonas H. Haralz) was convened to report on the long-term prospects of the economy. The wording "Combined Working Party" was carefully chosen, since the Mexican government did not want to convey the impression that it was mostly a report by the Bank, even though Haralz and Waterston were indeed the main contributors.

The report, published two years later, concluded both that Mexico was ready to absorb foreign loans and that there was a need for fiscal caution. Furthermore, the report was mildly enthusiastic about Mexico's import substitution strategy: "There is no doubt that tariffs have stimulated some branches of industry. . . . [Import restrictions] had important effects in promoting industrial development."[14] This last point was in line with the import substitution strategy given academic credence by Raúl Prebisch at the United Nations' Economic Commission for Latin America (ECLA). His work, which was fervently received across Latin America, justified import substitution and a drive for industrialization by claiming that developing countries faced deteriorating barter terms of trade—that is, the price of primary

12. See Margaret Garritsen de Vries, *Balance of Payments Adjustment, 1945 to 1986: The IMF Experience* (Washington: International Monetary Fund, 1987), p. 18.

13. Until the end of the 1980s the name of this development bank was lengthier: Nacional Financiera S. A. (NAFINSA). To avoid confusion, I always use the current, shorter name.

14. *The Economic Development of Mexico: Report of the Combined Mexican Working Party* (Baltimore: Johns Hopkins University Press, 1953), p. 80.

products exported by developing countries was falling over time relative to the price of the manufactures produced in the industrialized world.[15]

It is worth stressing that the report by the Combined Working Party was the best economic study ever made of a Latin American country until that point. In particular, its detailed statistical analysis was so broad that it included estimates for capital-output ratios. At that time, the use of such indicators was uncommon in economic studies of developed countries.

Toward a More Stable Path of Growth

The Adolfo Ruiz Cortines administration (1952–58) brought a new stage of high growth coupled with abating inflation. This is apparent in table 3-1, which presents the main economic indicators of the past eight Mexican administrations, a period that overlaps with the Bank's own existence. Incidentally, as the table shows, annual World Bank commitments to Mexico during the Ruiz Cortines administration averaged a meager 0.2 percent of GDP, the lowest level of the postwar era.

The economic successes of the era were not easily obtained, however. As noted earlier, the exchange rate adjustment of 1949 turned out to be inadequate by mid-1951, and by mid-1952 Mexico was suffering from a problem that would become endemic later: capital flight. The speculation against the peso continued intermittently until April 1954, when the central bank devalued the currency without warning and without consulting the IMF. A chagrined IMF was left to note in its next Annual Report that: "On the proposal of the Government of Mexico, in which the Fund [sic] concurred, the par value of the Mexican peso was changed on April 19, 1954 from 8.65 pesos to 12.50 pesos per U.S. dollar."[16] After the devaluation, Mexico once again requested help from the "duo": an IMF standby arrangement for $50 million (only $22.5 million was drawn) and a currency support agreement with the U.S. Treasury.

The 1954 devaluation turned out to be highly controversial among Mexican economists. On one side, analysts believed it would "undermine confidence in the future stability of the peso."[17] On the other, which included the majority, the

15. See Raúl Prebisch, *The Economic Development of Latin America and Its Principal Problems* (New York: United Nations ECLA, 1950). An independent study along the same lines was also undertaken by Hans W. Singer, "The Distribution of Gains between Investing and Borrowing Countries," *American Economic Review*, vol. 40 (May 1950), pp. 473–85. A recent appraisal of the Prebisch-Singer hypothesis is given in John T. Cuddington and Carlos M. Urzúa, "Trends and Cycles in the Net Barter Terms of Trade: A New Approach," *Economic Journal*, vol. 99 (June 1989), pp. 426–42.

16. International Monetary Fund, *Annual Report, 1954* (Washington: International Monetary Fund, 1954), p. 84.

17. Dwight S. Brothers and Leopoldo Solís M., *Mexican Financial Development* (Austin: University of Texas Press, 1966), p. 86.

Table 3-1. *Performance of the Mexican Economy, 1946–94*
Average annual percent changes, unless otherwise noted

	Real GDP growth[a]	Inflation rate[b]	Real wages growth[c]	Gross national savings/GDP[d]	Public sector deficit/GDP[e]	Current account deficit/GDP[f]	Public foreign debt/GDP[g]	Percentage of poor people[h]	World Bank commitments/GDP[i]
Alemán (1946–52)	5.8	9.6	6.0	11.8	-0.1	-1.6	8.5	n.a.	0.4
Ruiz Cortines (1952–58)	6.4	6.7	1.7	15.8	-0.7	-2.9	6.5	n.a.	0.2
López Mateos (1958–64)	6.4	2.2	10.0	16.5	-0.8	-2.3	7.7	77.5	0.3
Díaz Ordaz (1964–70)	6.2	3.6	5.2	19.0	-1.9	-2.6	11.5	72.6	0.3
Echeverría (1970–76)	6.0	15.2	4.1	18.9	-6.4	-3.7	15.7	58.0	0.4
López Portillo (1976–82)	6.6	35.7	-3.8	21.7	-9.7	-5.1	34.2	48.5	0.5
De la Madrid (1982–88)	0.2	86.7	-8.6	21.5	-11.9	1.7	67.1	58.5	1.0
Salinas (1988–94)	3.0	15.9	-4.3	17.7	-2.8	-5.6	30.7	66.0	0.7

Sources: See notes below.

a. Growth of real GDP is given in 1980 pesos. For 1947–59, the rate is estimated using data in Banco de México, *Indicadores económicos*, various editions. For 1960–94, the source is INEGI, Banco de datos.

b. For 1947–69, the rate is based on a wholesale price index for Mexico City, and for 1970–94 on the national consumer price index. The source is Banco de México, *Indicadores económicos*.

c. Growth of the general minimum wage (national average) is deflated by the price index described in note b. The source for the minimum wage is Comisión Nacional de los Salarios Mínimos.

d. Gross domestic savings minus net transfers from abroad were estimated by the author. For 1947–79, the source is Banco de México, *Indicadores económicos*, and for 1980–93 INEGI, Banco de datos.

e. For 1947–52, the estimated proportion is based on INEGI, *Estadísticas históricas de México* (Aguascalientes, Mexico: INEGI, 1990). For 1953–85, the data are from Pedro Aspe, *Economic Transformation: The Mexican Way* (Cambridge, Mass.: MIT Press, 1993), table 2.3. For 1986–94 the source is Secretaría de Hacienda y Crédito Público, *Estadísticas de finanzas públicas*, several issues. The figures do not include the revenue from privatizations, and all include the deficit of financial intermediaries.

f. Figures for 1947–49 are based on *The Economic Development of Mexico: Report of the Combined Mexican Working Party* (Baltimore: Johns Hopkins University Press, 1953), table 122. For 1950–94 the source is Banco de México, *Indicadores económicos*. The conversion from dollars to pesos was made by the author using the end-of-the-period exchange rate.

g. The first figure is based on the estimate for 1951 given in *The Economic Development of Mexico*, table 151. For 1953–64 the source is Nacional Financiera, *Informe anual*. For 1965–94 the figures for total long-term public debt are from Secretaría de Hacienda y Crédito Público. The conversion from dollars to pesos was made using the end-of-the period exchange rate.

h. Poor and extremely poor individuals are estimated for years 1963, 1968, 1977 (imputed due to lack of data for the Echeverría period), 1981, 1984, and 1992. The first five figures are taken from Enrique Hernández Laos, *Crecimiento económico y pobreza en México* (Mexico City: UNAM, 1992), table 3.2. The last estimate is due to Julio Boltvinik (personal communication).

i. Average of annual commitments as percentage of GDP is given (after converting the commitments to pesos using the end-of-the-period exchange rate). The source is World Bank, data bank.

n.a. Not available.

devaluation was viewed as a success: after a typical J-curve effect that worsened the trade balance in 1954, the current account balance was restored the next year. Furthermore, GDP growth rates were very high during the first three years after the devaluation (10 percent, 8.5 percent, and 6.8 percent), and there was only a short-lived increase in inflation during 1955.

As noted in later sections, the mechanics of this devaluation, engineered by the then director of Banco de México, Rodrigo Gómez, differ sharply from how devaluations were orchestrated in the later decades. Part of its success was due to the care taken by the government in supplementing the devaluation with other measures: (i) the control of money aggregates, (ii) a comprehensive law for import licensing and fiscal subsidies in the case of imported capital goods, and (iii) an increase in export taxes to capture part of the exporters' windfall, which would bolster the government's fiscal position.

A LOAN FOR RAILWAY TRANSPORTATION. Four months after the devaluation, the World Bank lent Mexico $61 million, the largest project investment loan ever made by the Bank to that point. (During the next three years, Mexico did not receive any new loans.) The money was loaned to Ferrocarril Sud-Pacífico for railway transportation development. Interestingly, the loan agreement stated that "the labor force should be reduced to and maintained at the minimum necessary for efficient operations."[18] That clause notwithstanding, it actually took four decades before the government decided, in 1992, to substantially reduce the railway work force. And three years later, in 1995, when the government announced that the railways would be privatized, one of the most contentious points in the privatization process continued to be the size of the work force.

MEXICO APPROACHES THE BANK FOR OIL FINANCING. After Cárdenas nationalized the oil industry in 1938, oil exploration, production, and refining, together with the production of petrochemicals, were left to a single state company: Petróleos Mexicanos (PEMEX).

PEMEX had lackluster production for several years after the nationalization: by the end of the Second World War, owing to a lack of foreign funds for much needed investment, as well as limited local knowledge, poor administration, and even boycotts by the major oil producers (the "seven sisters"), oil production dropped to less than one-fourth of the highest production level attained before nationalization. The Mexican government contributed to the difficulties by keeping domestic energy prices artificially low and imposing very high taxes on all PEMEX activities (not just oil exploration and production). These policies weakened PEMEX's financial position to such a degree that, in most years, the state monopoly lacked money for new oil exploration.

18. Cited in World Bank, "Transport Sector," background paper in electronic form for the *OED Study of Bank/Mexico Relations* (Washington: World Bank, January 1993), pp. 21–22.

In 1943, when Mexico, like other Latin American countries, decided to support the Allies in the war (and a year after the indemnification process to U.S. oil companies for the 1938 expropriation), PEMEX was able to get from the U.S. Export-Import Bank (Eximbank) a $10 million credit for the construction of the Azcapotzalco oil refinery. In 1949, however, when the Mexican government requested a second oil credit from the Eximbank it got no response. Apparently, the U.S. State Department had vetoed the request on the grounds that the Mexican government could tap private U.S. capital for that purpose.[19]

Whether the U.S. State Department's policy was concerned with a similar policy espoused by the World Bank is unclear. What is known is that Mexican authorities approached the Bank in the mid-1950s looking for oil exploration loans. Months after the 1954 devaluation, President Black received a memo from J. Burke Knapp, who two years later became vice-president of the Bank, establishing that Antonio J. Bermúdez, then the managing director of PEMEX, had inquired about the possibility of Bank financing for oil exploration in Mexico.[20] Black replied that "he thought that the sector was more appropriate for development by the private sector and declined to hold out any hope for Bank support for Mexico's industry, it being in the public sector and a monopoly at that."[21] At the time almost all Bank lending to Mexico had gone to a state electric utility, which was also a monopoly, the CFE. Until the mid-1970s, the Bank as a matter of policy did not lend for oil and gas exploration and development.

In retrospect, that episode represented a missed opportunity not only for Mexico but also for the Bank and the United States. For the former, it would have opened a big new market for the Bank's loans worldwide and the Bank would have been able to monitor PEMEX finances, a sore point with the Mexican government for many years to come. The United States lost because it failed to support more oil production in the Americas, a shortsightedness that ended up being costly after the Organization of Petroleum Exporting Countries (OPEC) embargo in the 1970s.

The First Half of the "Stabilizing Development" Period

It may sound paradoxical to some readers that, for the entire twentieth century, the best performance of the Mexican economy was attained under the decidedly interventionist government of Adolfo López Mateos (1958–64). As can be appreciated from table 3-1, during his six-year term the average annual rate of real GDP growth was 6.4 percent, the average inflation rate was just 2.2 percent, and real wages rose at an annual average of 10 percent a year! No wonder that the

19. Antonio J. Bermúdez, *Doce años al servicio de la industria petrolera mexicana, 1947–1958* (Naucalpan de Juárez, Mexico: Comaval), pp. 254–60.
20. Carlos M. Urzúa, interview with Gladstone Bonnick, November 11, 1994.
21. World Bank, *OED Study of Bank/Mexico Relations*, p. 34.

period 1958-70 was christened, before a World Bank–IMF audience, as one of "stabilizing development" (*desarrollo estabilizador*) by one of its architects, Finance Minister Antonio Ortiz Mena.[22]

The López Mateos administration enacted several policies that go against current orthodoxy. The government intervened in most nonmanufacturing sectors; there were widespread price controls; real minimum wages kept increasing; a very high level of nontariff protection prevailed (four out of five imports required a license); and some key industries were nationalized.

Although the United States was not particularly happy with López Mateos's nationalization policies, Mexico in those years was hardly a major worry; in January 1959, Cuba saw a communist revolution. In response, the United States hurriedly announced in August of that year its support for a pan-American regional bank—an idea that had been repeatedly urged throughout the Americas since the end of the nineteenth century. Mexico, for instance, had proposed a continental quasi–central bank in the 1930s.[23] As a result of the U.S. proposal, the Inter-American Development ment Bank (IDB) was officially created in October 1960. Kennedy's Alliance for Progress came onto the scene the next year.

The creation of the IDB as well as the changed political context in Latin America and the Caribbean also spurred the World Bank to rethink its relationship with Mexico, as suggested by the sharp jump in annual lending commitments between 1955 and 1962: $0, $0, $0, $45 million, $0, $25 million, and $160.5 million (in successive fiscal years). Indeed, in the 1990s, competition from the IDB is of considerable concern to World Bank staff.

A CLASH. At the end of the 1950s, the Bank started to pressure Mexico to realign public tariffs, especially electricity rates, which it blamed for the country's chronic (albeit small, see table 3-1) public deficits. The discussion reached its climax in August 1959, in a meeting between Mexican President López Mateos and World Bank President Black. The former resented a petition for electricity rate increases "which he saw as bringing undue pressure on Mexico for the purpose of advancing the interests of [a foreign] company since he understood that the Bank's policy would be to make no further loans to Mexico for any purpose until the rate issue was resolved."[24] An increase in electricity tariffs was agreed only in 1961, a year after López Mateos ordered the nationalization of the sector.

NATIONALIZATION OF THE ELECTRICITY SECTOR. The Mexican government nationalized all privately owned electricity utilities (mostly U.S. and Canadian) in

22. Antonio Ortiz Mena, "Stabilizing Development: A Decade of Economic Strategy in Mexico," paper presented at the 1969 annual meeting of the World Bank and the IMF. Published in Spanish as "Desarrollo estabilizador: Una década de estrategia económica en México," *Trimestre Económico*, vol. 37 (1970), pp. 417–50.

23. See Sidney Dell, *The Inter-American Development Bank: A Study in Development Financing* (New York: Praeger, 1972), p. 4.

24. World Bank, *OED Study of Bank/Mexico Relations*, p. 93.

1960. This nationalization lead to the CFE becoming the national power utility, except for a small public utility, Compañía de Luz y Fuerza del Centro, which to the constant chagrin of the Bank, remains separate because the government has avoided a confrontation with its strong labor union. Interestingly, after the nationalization, not only was there no apparent effect on World Bank lending for electric power development but, as noted by an internal Bank document, the repeated request by the Bank for the integration of the power sector amounted, under the circumstances, "to a tacit support for the Government's nationalization policies."[25] The Mexican incident, however, appears to be an exception to the Bank's implicit opposition in the case of other Latin American countries.[26]

THE FIRST LOAN FOR IRRIGATION. For many years, and for several reasons, the bulk of government spending on agriculture was allocated to irrigation.[27] Thus, it is no surprise that the first nonindustrial loan made by the Bank to Mexico, in 1961, was targeted to that end; fourteen others would follow over the next two decades. The majority of these irrigation investments were biased, however, toward the northern states and toward nonrepresentative farmers holding relatively large extensions of land. This selective lending behavior in the agricultural sector had dire consequences in the 1960s.

Irrigation, the draining of wetlands, and hydroelectric dams were for many years three of the most preferred giant projects of the Mexican government. Since many of these ventures have adverse environmental impacts, one could then ask if the Bank blundered while collaborating with Mexico.[28]

The biggest blunder, however, actually came from the IDB when it financed, in the early 1960s, what would become an extreme example of bad planning: Plan Chontalpa. In 1961, the Mexican government, partially due to the ephemeral pan-American feelings of the times, proposed to the newly created IDB the financing of a project, in the southeastern state of Tabasco, to make agriculturally productive several tens of thousand hectares of humid tropical land. It took Mexico and the IDB five years to start the project, but when they did, they did so with zest: forty thousand hectares were deforested, with all the wood burned in situ, and five

25. World Bank, "Mexico, Power Sector," background paper in electronic form for the *OED Study of Bank/Mexico Relations*, p. 18.

26. As recounted by an influential Latin American historian, a few years after the Mexican nationalization the Bank appeared too protective regarding the interests of the U.S. company Electric Bond & Share in Guatemala (1966) and Colombia (1967), a company that, incidentally, had on its board of directors none other than Eugene Black (who had retired by then as the Bank's president). See Eduardo Galeano, *Open Veins of Latin America: Five Centuries of the Pillage of a Continent,* trans. Cedric Belfrage (New York: Monthly Review Press, 1973), pp. 256–57.

27. A general reference on this subject is Miguel Wionczek, "The Roots of the Mexican Agricultural Crisis: Water Resources Development Policies (1920–1970)," *Development and Change,* vol. 13 (July 1982), pp. 365–99.

28. For a general reference on Mexican environmental policies, see Enrique Leff, *Medio ambiente y desarrollo en México* (Mexico City: Unam and M. A. Porrúa, 1990).

thousand families were relocated (with a little help from the army). All to no avail: the agricultural yields were so disappointing that two years later the land was used mostly for cattle raising.

To be fair, there appears to be no blatant example of a similar lack of concern for the Mexican environment on the part of the World Bank; indeed there is evidence of a few cases where the Bank showed more respect for the environment than the Mexican government itself. In sum, the Bank's remark on the subject seems quite fair: Mexico and the Bank "were developing environmental awareness and expertise during the same period."[29] To which one might add: "and at roughly the same pace."

The End of the "Stabilizing Development" Period

During the Díaz Ordaz administration (1964–70), the economy continued on its stabilizing development path (see table 3-1). As years passed, however, more and more signals of the unsustainability of the strategy surfaced: a continuous deterioration of the current account; a decline of the agricultural sector; a slowing down of labor productivity growth; and, finally, increasing political repression by the government. An example of the latter was the killing of hundreds of students in October 1968, a crime known as the Matanza de Tlatelolco (Tlatelolco massacre).

In retrospect, the most serious economic problem faced by the Díaz Ordaz government was the debacle in agriculture, which soon became a major, permanent drag on the economy. During the López Mateos administration, the gross product of the agricultural sector grew a healthy 33.5 percent in six years; during the Díaz Ordaz period, it only grew 6.1 percent. Many factors contributed to the decline—the increasing density of the rural population arising from a high population growth rate and an overvalued exchange rate that penalized agriculture and rewarded the urban sector. But the lack of good planning in the sector should be singled out. By biasing lending and investment toward the rich, capital-intensive private lands in northern Mexico, leaving aside the majority of communal land (*ejidos*) where most of the rural population lived, the government (and implicitly the Bank) contributed to that decline. This pattern of investment should be contrasted with the strategy so successful in countries like Japan and Taiwan, where "the pursuit of unimodal strategies for modernizing the small farm units progressively, by means of divisible, yield increasing innovations that are neutral to scale [achieved] widespread increases in rural incomes and well-being."[30]

Regarding World Bank financing to Mexico, the number and volume of the loans rose substantially during the Díaz Ordaz government. In 1970, the last year

29. World Bank, *OED Study of Bank/Mexico Relations*, p. 43.
30. Bruce F. Johnston, "The Design and Redesign of Strategies for Agricultural Development: Mexico's Experience Revisited," in Clark W. Reynolds and Carlos Tello, eds., *U.S.–Mexico Relations: Economic and Social Aspects* (Palo Alto: Stanford University Press, 1983), p. 225.

of the administration, Mexico's share of total IBRD disbursements reached the staggering figure of 14.2 percent, a percentage surpassed only one other time (in 1990). Yet, most of the Bank projects simply perpetuated ones initiated by earlier Mexican administrations. The only outstanding difference was that the Bank was giving greater attention to the troubled agricultural sector.

THE FIRST AGRICULTURAL CREDIT. Already in 1954, Banco de México had created two agricultural trust funds, known jointly as Fideicomisos Instituidos en Relación con la Agricultura (FIRA), with the purpose of promoting, under the aegis of the central bank, the agricultural sector. Until 1965, however, the funds managed by FIRA were relatively meager. In that year, the World Bank made its first loan for agricultural credit to Mexico. To manage this and subsequent loans by the Bank and the IDB, the central bank added a third trust fund, Fondo Especial de Financiamiento, to FIRA in 1965. Since then, FIRA has managed, with some success, the several billion dollars lent by the Bank and the IDB.

In its agricultural credit lending, the Bank deliberately eschewed the channeling of funds through the government-owned main rural bank, Banco Nacional de Crédito Rural (BANRURAL), which was, and continues to be, quite inefficient in its operations.[31] By circumventing BANRURAL, however, the World Bank implicitly contributed to the "bimodal" pattern of investment mentioned earlier: since FIRA loans were made through commercial banks, in contrast with BANRURAL loans, which were lent directly, the World Bank loans were being distributed only among low-risk large private farmers.

AN ICONOCLASTIC AGRICULTURAL SECTOR STUDY. Buried as an annex in the 1966 seven-volume Bank report on the Mexican economy is a remarkable study on the agricultural sector.[32] The second part of it was made by Wolf Ladejinsky, a noted expert on agrarian reforms (having worked on countries as diverse as India, Japan, and Taiwan). Although the study was not publicly acknowledged by the Mexican government, it became an underground classic among government officials with an interest in the agricultural sector.

Ladejinsky's work was full of recommendations to improve the productivity of the *ejidatario* (a member of an *ejido*). In one, he suggested that "the ejidatario should be given a status which, with freeing him completely to transfer the land as he wishes, would permit him to make various adjustments, including the transfer of his interest in a particular holding to other ejidatarios, thereby realizing the accrued value of his land. . . ."[33] This recommendation coincides with one tenet of the land reform undertaken twenty-five years later.

31. World Bank, "Study of Relations between the World Bank and Mexico: The Agricultural Sector," background paper in electronic form for the *OED Study of Bank/Mexico Relations*, p. 8.
32. World Bank, *Current Economic Position and Prospects of Mexico*, vol. IV, annex VII (Washington: World Bank, 1966).
33. Ibid., pp. 94–95.

Relations between McNamara's Bank and Mexico

As Robert McNamara was stepping into the World Bank presidency in 1968, Mexico was two years short of embarking on a new development paradigm that would stress the need for poverty alleviation and other social policies. This new paradigm roughly matched McNamara's own views.[34] Reading McNamara's famous 1973 Nairobi speech, when he asserted that at least half of the Bank's loans to agriculture should be targeted to rural poverty, one cannot help but notice its remarkable similarity to the views held by the Mexican government in the 1970s. Naturally, this ideological concurrence helped to build up a better relationship between Mexico and the Bank.

The new, closer relationship also depended on the main actors during those years: McNamara and Mexican presidents Luis Echeverría (1970–76) and José López Portillo (1976–82). All of them had strong personalities, with a penchant for centralized decisionmaking, and personal relations between both sides were quite good. When I asked Echeverría about McNamara, he simply said "a first-rate person." López Portillo described McNamara as "quite capable and objective, with an authentic social emotion," and then he added with a smile, "it was as if he were expiating some Vietnam sins."[35]

The relationship between the Bank and Mexico was also colored by economic conditions. A briefing paper to McNamara prepared for his 1969 visit to Mexico remarked: "there is little more that we can expect to achieve in the way of institution-building or influence over policy; . . . the Mexicans naturally prefer the Bank's money to its advice; . . . they can reasonably claim to have made a pretty good job of economic development." Consequently, the briefing paper noted, "Mexico is the last country in the world in which the overt exercise of leverage can be expected to pay off."[36]

"Shared Development" Period

"Shared development" was the name chosen by the Echeverría cabinet to distinguish their policies from those adopted during the "stabilizing development" period, since the high growth rates attained in the 1960s were thought to have had several adverse effects on poverty, income distribution, and the rural sector, as well as on political cohesion.

Among all the policies it considered, the new administration made the need for increasing social expenditures a priority, paid for by a more progressive and effec-

34. See, for instance, Robert S. McNamara, *Address to the University of Notre Dame* (Washington, D.C.: IBRD, 1969).

35. Carlos M. Urzúa, interview with Luis Echeverría, February 16, 1995; and interview with José López Portillo, February 28, 1995.

36. World Bank, *OED Study of Bank/Mexico Relations,* pp. 48, 94.

tive tax system. Soon, however, the proposed tax reform ran into strong opposition from the private sector.[37] Consequently, in lieu of increases in government revenue, the administration ended up relying more heavily on foreign borrowing and budget deficits (see table 3-1).

The key year in the Echeverría administration was 1973. In that year the conservative wing of the cabinet, represented by Finance Minister Hugo B. Margain, lost the ideological battle over social expenditures and was considerably weakened. Furthermore, by 1973 it was evident that no sizable increases in tax revenues were forthcoming. As a result, in that year alone, the foreign public debt rose from $5 billion to $7 billion. Even that increase, however, was soon overwhelmed by the events of the remaining years of the Echeverría administration: from 1974 to 1976, foreign public debt almost tripled to $19.6 billion. In percentage terms, the fivefold increase was much bigger than the increase to be registered during the López Portillo administration (about threefold).

World Bank financing to Mexico also greatly expanded during Echeverría's term: there were more Bank loans during those six years than during all past administrations put together. The average annual IBRD's share in Mexico's long-term debt reached almost 17 percent, while Mexico's average share in total IBRD loans was above 10 percent.

This new, closer involvement by the Bank was already agreed upon when Echeverría met McNamara in 1972. In that meeting, Echeverría described a new rural development program, Programa de Caminos de Mano de Obra, just initiated by his administration. The highly labor-intensive program involved the construction of local roads joining small towns (500–2,500 inhabitants) and became a great success among the participants (peasants from the same communities).[38] According to Echeverría, McNamara was very enthusiastic about it, and, although the Bank never participated in the project, both decided to focus a great deal of their future joint efforts on programs to address poverty and income inequality.[39]

As shown in the second to the last column of table 3-1, during the Echeverría administration, poverty, represented by the percentage of people unable to afford a given basket of goods, had its steepest decline.[40] How much of that was due to the Bank-Mexico effort would be difficult to assess; but the Bank projects over the

37. A review of tax reforms in Mexico, from 1970 to 1994, is given in Carlos M. Urzúa, "An Appraisal of Recent Tax Reforms in Mexico," forthcoming in Gary McMahon, Guillermo Perry, and John Whalley, eds., *Tax Reform and Structural Change* (London: Macmillan, 1995).

38. See the survey in Marielle P. L. Martínez, *Los caminos de mano de obra como factores de cambio socioeconómico*, Cuadernos del CES, No. 27 (Mexico City: El Colegio de México, 1980).

39. Carlos M. Urzúa, interview with Luis Echeverría, February 16, 1995.

40. As is well known, the poverty statistics derived from income and expenditure surveys, as the ones in table 3-1, could be contaminated by potential measurement errors. See Nora Lustig and Ann Mitchell, "Poverty in Mexico: The Effects of Adjusting Survey Data for Under-Reporting," *Estudios Económicos,* vol. 10, no. 1 (January 1995), pp. 3–28.

period were interesting and diverse, as the next sections will show, and the most innovative relationship between the Bank and Mexico was attained during those years. This was despite the fact that the financing consisted of old-fashioned sectoral loans, rather than the newer structural adjustment loans developed by the Bank.

LOANS FOR RURAL DEVELOPMENT. To operationalize its new emphasis on rural poverty, the Mexican government launched a rural development program in 1973 known as Programa de Inversiones Públicas para el Desarrollo Rural, later known as Programa Integral para el Desarrollo Rural.[41] The Bank joined the program, which lasted a decade and cost more than $2 billion, contributing over $400 million in three loans (1975, 1977, and 1982). While all parties were initially satisfied with the program, the Bank later classified it as unsatisfactory because of cost overruns.

The principal goal of the program was to channel loans to poor rural areas for the financing of small investments at the community level ("microregions"), emphasizing the decentralization of its administration. The government had already experimented with the direct participation of the beneficiaries in a program. The novelty this time was that Mexico joined forces with the World Bank, the IDB, and the International Fund for Agricultural Development (IFAD). This caused some problems in the implementation of the project, for the Mexican government had to face loan requirements from three different organizations. As told in a Bank's report: "[T]he Bank's requirements for public works bids went beyond Mexican law, and the Bank showed insufficient flexibility in regulations governing bidding, force account administration and poverty definition." But there is an added footnote: "That the Bank was not the worst offender was illustrated by the remarks that the IDB at one point (unsuccessfully) tried to require drastic reforms of the existing agrarian legislation . . . while IFAD proposed such objectionable legal paragraphs that its own Board adopted the Mexican position."[42]

A TRY AT TOURISM. From 1972 to 1978, the World Bank made five loans to the tourism sector, to finance studies on Mexico's tourist potential and tourism projects themselves (including a resort that would become famous, Ixtapa-Zihuatenejo). Following the Bank's advice, the Mexican government created a tourism trust fund in 1974, managed by Nacional Financiera, to coordinate development of the industry. Although the Bank has always pointed to this fact with some pride, it is fair to note that Mexico had already created other tourism trust funds (the first in 1969), although on a smaller scale.

41. This program was preceded by a similar one initiated in the state of Durango by the Díaz Ordaz administration in 1968. A general reference on rural development programs in Mexico is Eric J. Miller, *Desarrollo integral del medio rural: Un experimento en México* (Mexico City: Fondo de Cultura Económica, 1976).

42. "Study of Relations between the World Bank and Mexico: The Agricultural Sector," background paper for the *OED Study of Bank/Mexico Relations*, chapter 2, p. 7, and footnote 9.

NO MORE LOANS FOR POWER DEVELOPMENT. From 1972 to 1989, the Bank stopped its lending for electric power development. The issue of electric tariffs, which had been an irritant at the end of the 1950s, resurfaced in the early 1970s. Increasingly, electric tariffs were allowed to lag behind inflation, as the government attempted to check the price-inflationary spiral (a pattern that would be repeated several times over the next two decades). This led to the government transferring ever larger sums of money to the sector, a situation that proved unsustainable by the mid-1980s. The Bank resumed its lending to the electric power sector in 1989–90, when two loans, totaling over $900 million, were made to Mexico after the government adjusted its tariffs.

THE FIRST LOAN TO THE STEEL SECTOR. The World Bank made its first loan to Mexico for investment in a state-owned industrial complex in September 1973, after three years of difficult negotiations, to the tune of $70 million (the IDB lent $54 million). The stories behind both the creation of the complex, named Siderúrgica Lázaro Cárdenas–Las Truchas S. A. (SICARTSA), and the Bank's own involvement deserve some attention.[43]

Since 1957, the iron deposits found in Las Truchas, at the border of the southwestern states of Michoacán and Guerrero, were large enough for the Mexican government to plan a steel complex there. More than a decade passed before the project came to fruition. In 1968, Díaz Ordaz officially announced the creation of Siderúrgica Las Truchas, to be headed by former President Cárdenas, whose home state was Michoacán and who had lobbied for the project for many years.

Coincidentally or not, the announcement was made two weeks after the Matanza de Tlatelolco, and many interpreted the measure as Díaz Ordaz's way of appeasing the left wing of his party, represented by Cárdenas. The project did not flourish, however, until the Echeverría administration and after Cárdenas's death (hence the name change at Echeverría's suggestion). It then became the government's most ambitious industrial project, to the dismay of both the Mexican private sector and the U.S. steel industry.

Given the controversial nature of the project, why did the Bank agree to finance it? First, as with rural poverty projects, there was a coincidental match in the needs of both Mexico and the Bank: the latter was looking to expand its financing from infrastructure to industry in the early 1970s. Second, once the Bank started talks with Mexico, it was unable to back away without appearing too protective of U.S. interests. As told by the Bank itself, "Early press accounts in the [United States] had warned of impending competition in the steel sector that U.S. firms faced from low wage based production by SICARTSA. The Mexicans were concerned that such fears would bias the Bank's evaluation of the project, on the assumption that the Bank was overly influenced by U.S. interests."[44]

---

43. What follows draws mostly on the work of Nelson Minello and Arístides Rivera, *Siderúrgica Lázaro Cárdenas Las Truchas: Historia de una empresa* (Mexico City: El Colegio de México, 1982).

44. World Bank, "The Bank and the Mexican Industrial Sector," background paper in electronic form for the *OED Study of Bank/Mexico Relations,* p. 61.

So the project sailed on. The first stage (there were to be four) was completed in November 1976, days before Echeverría left office, at a final cost of about $1 billion. The second stage was postponed for several years by President López Portillo, even though the World Bank and the IDB had already committed money. It was finished near the end of his term. To finish, SICARTSA experienced losses during the rest of the 1970s (partially as a result of a drop in the worldwide demand for steel rods), was moderately profitable in the early 1980s, and was privatized in 1991 at a price substantially below its original cost.

TWO SOLID PLANS. Among other Mexico–World Bank projects during the period, two interesting studies are worth noting. The first, a resounding success according to all sides, represented a joint research venture among the United Nations Development Program, the World Bank, and the Mexican government on the devising of a national water plan. The venture, which started in 1972, resulted in the Plan Nacional Hidráulico of 1975, a landmark water plan that guided the next two decades of work in that sector.

The second research project was a four-volume 1971 study on the transport sector made by the Bank, which had a lasting impact on the design of Mexican transport policy, and on future Bank loans for highway development.[45] That study correctly raised an issue that was to become a source of much friction: lack of an adequate system of road user charges to the detriment of both government finances and the railways. The latter had to compete with trucks subsidized by low diesel prices and almost nonexistent road charges. This friction between the Bank and the Mexican government lasted two decades, until the Salinas government deregulated the transport sector.

Oil Boom

As the gap between government revenue and government expenditures increased, and as some of that difference was monetized, the problem of chronic government budget deficits coupled with relatively high inflation resurfaced in the final years of the Echeverría administration.

The exchange rate, fixed since 1954 at 12.5 pesos per dollar, had become overvalued by the early 1970s, and a sizable trade deficit, as well as speculative capital flight, soon developed (see table 3-1). Three months before Echeverría left office, the peso was devalued. The event initiated a six-year cycle of devaluations, as well as an unwritten rule that was to prevail for almost two decades: an outgoing president had to clean house before the arrival of his successor.

Together with the devaluation, a three-year Extended Fund Facility agreement for about $1 billion was signed with the IMF in October 1976, effective at the beginning of 1977, and, as usual, the U.S. Treasury provided a stabilization fund.

45. World Bank, *The Transport Sector of Mexico* (Washington: World Bank, 1971).

However, the macroeconomic adjustment in 1977, the first calendar year of the López Portillo administration, was modest, partly because the government took a tough stance when it negotiated with the IMF. The government deficit declined from 9.1 percent to 6.3 percent of GDP, and because the contractive stance was mild, annual growth was still 3.4 percent. In any event, the IMF agreement soon became irrelevant after a new actor jumped to center stage in 1978: oil exports.

OIL VEINS ARE THE DEVIL'S GIFT.[46] For many years, the Mexican oil sector was in a sorry state. By the mid-1960s, the country was unable to export oil, for the first time since the industry's nationalization in 1938. Furthermore, the country became a net importer of oil by 1971, and the twenty-four million barrels of oil imported in 1973 easily exceeded any of the export figures ever attained by PEMEX.

The government was alarmed by the state of affairs and took steps to meet the problem. The Echeverría government had set up a commission to initiate more intensive oil exploration, emphasizing geographic diversification. The search paid off in 1973: new oil reserves were discovered in the southern states of Chiapas and Tabasco.

The discoveries were kept secret for a while, since Mexico did not want the United States to pressure it for fast oil exploitation (those were the years of the OPEC embargoes). But weeks after López Portillo took office in late 1976, it was publicly announced that proven oil reserves had gone up from 6.3 billion barrels to over 11 billion. And that was just the beginning; by the end of 1978, reserves had risen to over forty billion oil barrels, and by 1982 to over seventy-two billion. "We were the fifteenth oil producing country in the world," said López Portillo in his September 1980 presidential address, "today we are the fifth. We had the eighteenth largest oil reserves, today we have the sixth."[47]

Hand in hand with the oil boom came recklessness. Mexico was growing at more than 8 percent in real terms by the end of the 1970s, and López Portillo kept reminding the population that Mexico's problem was not to generate wealth but to administer it wisely. Unfortunately, neither Mexico nor he ever took that refrain seriously. Mexico's failure did not mimic the so-called Dutch disease, where the manufacturing sector in the Netherlands had suffered indirectly from the exploitation of a natural resource. Mexico's disease was less sophisticated: bad spending habits and overborrowing (compare the figures in table 3-1). Regarding the former, government economists adopted a grossly procyclical policy of heavy government spending.[48] The overborrowing side of the story is even more interesting.

---

46. Free translation of a verse by the venerated Mexican poet Ramón López Velarde (1888–1921).

47. Instituto Nacional de Estadística, Geografía e Informática, *Estadísticas Históricas de México* (Aguascalientes: INEGI, 1990), vol. 1, p. 465. Author's translation.

48. See Carlos M. Urzúa, *El Déficit del Sector Público y la Política Fiscal en México* (Santiago, Chile: Comisión Económica para América Latina y el Caribe, 1991).

COMMERCIAL BANKS AS LOAN PUSHERS.[49] Soon after the oil discoveries, Mexico became the darling of foreign commercial banks. For bankers busy recycling petrodollars in the late 1970s, Mexico was a tailor-made borrower. As a result, fierce competition ensued: during the best years, 1979-80, Mexico got spreads (margins over the London interbank offer rate, LIBOR), which were supposed to reflect country risk, that would have been the envy of prime multinationals and even the Kingdom of Sweden.[50]

As one would expect, not only public debt but also private debt increased sharply during the oil boom. In fact, the private sector's foreign debt grew at a faster pace than the public sector's: from $6.5 billion at the end of 1976 to over $27 billion at the end of 1982 (including the debt of the banks nationalized in September 1982). This is an important fact because, at least in the Bretton Woods literature on the Mexican debt crisis, it is never pointed out that the oil disease infected not only the government but also the private sector. Actually, the most important industrial group in Mexico at the time, Alfa, went bust almost a year before the government did and had to be rescued with public funds.

During the oil boom, Mexico could call the shots with the IMF, the United States, and the foreign commercial banks. But, because of a genuine appreciation for what it had done years earlier, the World Bank was treated more cordially during the boom period. As recounted by López Portillo, the Mexican government appreciated the Bank's sectoral expertise and wanted to continue borrowing from it. After McNamara complained personally to him about the lack of good individual projects in Mexico, as opposed to the global plans that the Mexican government kept (and keeps) churning out, López Portillo created a special commission to propose projects to the Bank.[51]

That acquiescence notwithstanding, the World Bank's lending to Mexico mirrored commercial banking practices. The terms on several Bank loans seem to have been substantially relaxed; a good instance of the latter was the way in which the Bank ended up agreeing, after so many years of refusing, to channel agricultural loans through BANRURAL, though doubts persisted about the agency's efficiency and transparency.

49. For the orthodox or incredulous reader alarmed by the possibility that a banker can become a loan pusher, see the lecture of William Darity, Jr., and Bobbie L. Horn, *The Loan Pushers: The Role of Commercial Banks in the International Debt Crisis* (Cambridge, Mass.: Ballinger Publishing Company, 1988). As noted by Karin Lissakers, *Banks, Borrowers, and the Establishment: A Revisionist Account of the International Debt Crisis* (New York: Basic Books, 1991), pp. 114–36, one reason for the overlending was that the banks were taking advantage of tax loopholes in the United States and other industrialized countries.

50. For a general review of the spreads charged to less developed countries before the debt crisis, and a theory that tries to account for their sudden changes, see Carlos M. Urzúa, "Lending to Sovereign Borrowers: Snapshots of the Eurocurrency Market Using a Thomian Camera," *International Economic Review*, vol. 31, no. 2 (May 1990), pp. 469–89.

51. Carlos M. Urzúa, interview with José López Portillo, February 28, 1995.

Furthermore, most of the projects were a continuation of programs initiated earlier. Aside from a loan at the end of the López Portillo administration for pollution control (the first environmental loan to Mexico), and some overtures on the Mexican urban sector, the World Bank's projects simply continued financing projects that had been jointly pursued during the first half of the 1970s.

ONE MISJUDGMENT AFTER ANOTHER. The World Bank began to monitor the new surge in Mexican oil production in its 1972 annual report on the Mexican economy. It concluded that "hydrocarbon imports were likely to represent an increasingly large share of merchandise imports in times to come and to account for a growing proportion of foreign exchange resources."[52] This was a reasonable statement, since the Bank did not necessarily know about the new oil reserves discovered by PEMEX at roughly the same time. Similar underestimations pervaded the economic reports of the next few years, however, after the discoveries had been confirmed. This is shown by the following extract from the World Bank's own evaluation report:

> The 1974 Economic Report . . . continued to forecast oil imports despite the confirmed Chiapas-Tabasco discoveries, assuming that an increase in oil production would take time to become effective. This proved quite unrealistic since Mexico's output rose rapidly and Mexico became a net oil exporter as early as 1975. . . . The 1976 Report was again too conservative regarding oil exports "given the lead time needed for capital investment to achieve full production." This proved wrong since exports of crude oil rose tenfold in 1975-80. . . . For the first time, the 1977 Bank Economic Mission included energy specialists. . . . The mission forecast proved again too pessimistic for exports of crude. . . . Staff analysis in the end proved only correct for total output of crude and domestic consumption in 1982.[53]

But just as the Bank consistently underestimated PEMEX capacity for increasing oil production, it also consistently underestimated, together with the Mexican government, the danger for Mexico of having an economy too dependent on oil. Again, to quote the Bank's own evaluation study,

> The 1979 Economic Report came out rather in support of the oil based strategy of accelerated growth arguing that vast oil reserves had considerably increased Mexico's "flexibility of maneuver" particularly regarding acute social problems. . . . In 1981, another Economic Mission did not accept PEMEX's imposed ceiling in exports of crude oil (1.5 million barrels/day) for 1982 and subsequent years although the ceiling eventually proved right. . . . It would thus appear that throughout the 1970s and the 1980s, Bank economic reports have consistently and logically aimed at evaluating in macroeconomic terms the effects of oil resources on the Mexican economy. But such evaluations have generally been poorly performed.[54]

Two possible reasons for the Bank's failure to assess correctly the advantages and risks of the oil boom might be its lack of expertise in that sector and the secrecy

52. World Bank, "The Oil Sector," background paper in electronic form for the *OED Study of Bank/Mexico Relations* (Washington, March 1993), p. 44.
53. World Bank, "The Oil Sector," p. 44.
54. Ibid., "The Oil Sector," pp. 45–46.

with which the Mexican authorities treated all information on PEMEX assets. What is certainly true is that the Bank missed two more opportunities to help Mexico in managing the oil boom: in mid-1977, Mexican authorities quietly approached the Bank looking for oil financing, but to no avail. By coincidence, as in the 1954 request, Bank vice-president Knapp was the person to receive the request and return the denial. Furthermore, since by January 1979 the Bank had approved its new Accelerated Program for Petroleum Production, which sanctioned oil loans for the first time, two months later an economic advisor to López Portillo let it be known to Ardito Barleta, the vice-president for Latin America, that Mexico wanted to participate in the program. Once again, the request was denied, but this time the reasons were that a full-fledged appraisal of the oil situation in Mexico was beyond the Bank's capabilities and that the Bank was going to give priority to poor oil-importing countries.

Beginning of the Debt Crisis

Just as McNamara was stepping down in July 1981 as president of the World Bank, Mexico was also stepping down, albeit more quietly, as the prime developing country in the Eurocredit market. Lending terms for Mexico, and the rest of the developing world, were hardened in the early 1980s, when a financial crunch, caused mostly by a contractive U.S. monetary policy, spread around the world.

To compound the problem, oil prices declined in 1981, and the Mexican current account deficit was becoming unsustainable with an overvalued exchange currency. In that year alone, Mexico's total external debt increased by $24 billion, of which more than one-third was short term (with a maturity of less than a year). The new money was needed to cover the swelling trade deficit and to honor repayments of foreign debt, which were climbing with world interest rates. Furthermore, an estimated $11.8 billion left Mexico as capital flight in that same year.[55] The relationship between foreign debt and capital flight would aggravate the problem.[56]

By early 1982, the Mexican economy was heading to bankruptcy. In February of that year, the government attempted to regain control of the economy by twice devaluing the peso (with a cumulative devaluation of about 67 percent). But since the government did not follow up with a credible fiscal adjustment, the economy continued to head toward financial insolvency.

Foreign debt repayments were becoming so high that the government attempted to arrange in the Eurocredit market for a trio of medium-term "jumbo" loans through PEMEX ($2 billion), Nacional Financiera ($1.2 billion), and the Mexican government ($2.5 billion). Mexico's perceived creditworthiness had

55. Figures taken from José Ángel Gurría, *La política de la deuda externa* (Mexico City: Fondo de Cultura Económica, 1993), tables 3, 4.

56. For a paper on that relationship see Manuel Pastor, Jr., "Capital Flight from Latin America," *World Development*, vol. 18, no. 1 (January 1990), pp. 1–18.

deteriorated so badly by then, however, that few banks were willing to participate in the syndication of the last jumbo loan (July 1982), even though the terms were extremely favorable to the lenders.

A month later, on August 6, foreign reserves fell to about $100 million, while the country's financial obligations in just the first half of that month were seven times higher. That day, the Mexican government decided that a debt moratorium was the only avenue left.[57] On August 13, it announced, to the dismay of many foreign private investors, that the dollar-denominated deposits in the Mexican bank system would be only partially honored: investors would be paid back in pesos at an artificially low exchange rate, while the central bank retired from the foreign exchange market. The "mex-dollars" were suddenly converted to what could be called "U.S. pesos." This is a good example of what is known as "political risk" in the textbooks on international finance.

That same day, a Friday, Finance Minister Jesús Silva-Herzog, who had been appointed barely five months earlier, started a series of meetings in Washington asking for financial help from official sources. He had interviews with the IMF managing director Jacques de Larosière, the chairman of the Federal Reserve Board Paul Volcker, and the U.S. Treasury secretary Donald Regan. After a long weekend, he was able to return to Mexico with a financial rescue package. He then returned to Washington to meet, on August 20, with 115 representatives of Mexico's main foreign commercial creditors, from whom he asked for a ninety-day debt moratorium. Mexico had no other choice since its debt obligations for the rest of the year had climbed to over $11 billion, while reserves were almost nil.

That date, August 20, 1982, has been singled out as the beginning of the developing-country debt crisis, even though several African, Central American, and Eastern European countries had already begun a series of debt renegotiations. Furthermore, soon after Mexico declared a moratorium, many other countries followed suit. In 1983 alone, twenty developing countries, ranging from Argentina to Yugoslavia, held debt renegotiations with their commercial banks.

The economic and political dealings that took place while Silva-Herzog was bargaining in Washington are fascinating, and have been told in a number of good books.[58] For the purposes of this chapter, it suffices to note three interesting outcomes of the bargaining game, which curiously enough, would be played out again in the next Mexican financial crisis a dozen years later.

First, as in all its economic emergencies since 1947, Mexico obtained some financial help from the United States. This time, however, one billion dollars were lent against future oil purchases (another billion came from the Commodity Credit Corporation), a contract that caused an uproar in Mexico where the nationalized oil

57. See Gurría, *La política de la deuda externa*, p. 29.

58. A reference in English is the delightful book by Joseph Kraft, *The Mexican Rescue* (New York: Group of Thirty, 1984). For a reference in Spanish see Gurría, *La política de la deuda externa*.

industry was almost sacred. Furthermore, the loan had harsh terms: the oil price was set too low, and the U.S. Treasury wanted $100 million as a commission for the transaction. When López Portillo heard about the latter, he ordered Silva-Herzog to return home to initiate a unilateral debt moratorium. Almost immediately, however, the U.S. Treasury officials changed their minds and offered to halve the commission. In the end, the U.S. loan had an implicit interest rate of about 38 percent![59] The U.S. officials also tried to impose, according to López Portillo, political conditions, such as requiring Mexico "to act as a strikebreaker against OPEC by unilaterally lowering its oil prices, and to sever our diplomatic relations with Cuba."[60]

A second interesting outcome of the bargaining game was that, unlike previous crises, the financial obligations were so large, and the United States so adamant about their repayment, that Mexico had to look for help from other industrialized countries as well. By the end of August, Mexico had obtained a $1.85 billion loan from the other central banks that were members of the Bank for International Settlements.

The last noteworthy outcome was that, in December 1982, an IMF three-year Extended Fund Facility agreement was signed for about $4 billion. An interesting part of the agreement was that the loan was conditioned on the commercial banks lending $5 billion to Mexico. By early 1983, the banks did just that, and later in that year they also rescheduled Mexico's commercial debt, involving obligations from late 1982 to the end of 1984. The new period of repayment was extended to eight years.

And the World Bank?

The Mexican debt crisis took the World Bank by surprise, as it did most other observers. Already in 1981, the Bank was courting Mexico as a prospective donor to the International Development Association, since its growing affluence had led to preliminary negotiations on "graduating" Mexico, along with several other countries. In that regard, McNamara personally approached López Portillo to tell him that Mexico did not need World Bank financing anymore, since it was "taking off," to which the Mexican president answered that "if one were to use that aerodynamical simile, then Mexico needs the most fuel at this point."[61]

When the new Bank's president, A. W. (Tom) Clausen, visited Mexico in March 1982 his briefings and conversations dwelled only marginally on prospective liquidity problems. In his meetings with Mexican officials, he had mainly endorsed the position that Mexico could continue to envisage very high growth rates in the near future. There was no sense of an impending crisis. Naturally, after Silva-

---

59. See Gurría, *La política de la deuda externa*, p. 31.
60. Carlos M. Urzúa, interview with José López Portillo, February 28, 1995.
61. Ibid.

Herzog's announcement of a moratorium just five months later, Clausen felt "rather caught with his pants down."[62]

Several reasons may be adduced for the Bank's failure to predict the impending crisis. First, the Bank had little influence on, and even scarce knowledge of, Mexico. This is illustrated by the limited nature of the Bank's contacts with Mexico, which were closely regulated by the government. The regulation extended not only to noneconomic ministries but to PEMEX and the private sector. Second, the Bank lacked in the early 1980s a data base that incorporated short-term debt, which, as noted earlier, had become substantial in the case of Mexico. Finally, the view that the Mexican economy was poised to implode was inconsistent with the volume of the Bank's lending to Mexico (1980–82), and this could have led to the suppression of any pessimistic assessment. The last point is illustrated by the following episode.

INTERNAL DISSENT. Not everybody at the World Bank had been so optimistic about Mexico's prospects. A junior staff member had been quite critical since early 1981 of the growth strategy being followed by Mexico. His dissent was even more remarkable given that not only inside the Bretton Woods institutions, but also inside Mexico, very few Cassandras were warning about an impending crisis at such an early point.[63]

The staff member was part of a World Bank economic mission to Mexico in February 1980 and was responsible for the quantitative macroeconomic work. After having studied the data, he concluded that the Mexican economic strategy would almost inevitably lead to a crisis. The rest of the mission members disagreed with his alarmist assessment, however, feeling that the debt problem could be managed. Drafts of the team's report were discussed with Mexican officials at the end of 1980 and in mid-1981, and the final report appeared in August 1981.[64]

Despite the refusal from the rest of the team to consider his views seriously, he wrote a minority economic report in the form of a memorandum to files. Although the leaders of the mission were willing to keep his main point in the final report, as a possible scenario if everything started to go wrong, it was relegated to an annex. Then, on July 14, 1981, a Mexican delegation went to Washington to review, among other things, the Bank's report. It was headed by Carlos Salinas de Gortari, then a brash young man in his early thirties who, as a director-general, was the right-hand man of Budget and Planning Minister Miguel de la Madrid. During the meeting, Salinas launched a sharp attack against the staff member's bleak assessment of the Mexican economy. In the Bank's own historical study of its relations with Mexico,

62. Devesh Kapur and Richard Webb, interview with a World Bank staff member, January 19, 1993.

63. Among the honorable exceptions on the Mexican side is the great poet and engineer, who in his spare time is also an excellent economist, Gabriel Zaid, *El progreso improductivo* (Mexico City: Siglo XXI Editores, 1979).

64. World Bank, *Mexico: Development Strategy—Prospects and Problems,* Report No. 3605-ME (Washington: World Bank, 1981).

one finds this candid note: "Bank staff recall that [Salinas] had been critical of a Bank report that suggested that the public expenditure expansion financed by debt and money creation would lead to inflation."[65] Another member of the Mexican delegation has confirmed this quote.

What could be the explanation for Salinas's bitter criticism of the report? One reason could be ideological, since at that time Salinas was, at least on the surface, a leftist economist. But a more likely explanation has to do with politics: the report happened to come out in the middle of a battle between his boss Miguel de la Madrid and Finance Minister David Ibarra. Both wanted to become the next presidential candidate of the official party, and Ibarra had endorsed the Bank's document from the beginning. This conjecture is reinforced by the fact that Salinas's explosive behavior at the World Bank prompted a letter from Ibarra to Clausen, on September 11, 1981, in which Ibarra praised the entire report. Two weeks later, on September 25, Miguel de la Madrid was chosen by López Portillo as the party's next presidential candidate. By March 1982, Ibarra had left the Finance Ministry.

The sad end of the story is that the staff member's career in the World Bank subsequently stagnated. After Salinas's criticism, his supervisors in the Mexico division had wanted to sack him, but he fought back, with the aid of a lawyer, and was reluctantly retained by the Bank. He was nonetheless treated as an outcast for several years after the incident.

Toward Closer Relations

On December 1, 1982, fifteen weeks after the eruption of the debt crisis, Miguel de la Madrid became Mexico's president for the next six years. He inherited an economy in shambles and under an IMF Extended Fund Facility agreement that required deep cuts in government spending. It is not surprising that in 1983 the economy suffered its worst recession in half a century (a drop in real GDP of 4.2 percent).

De la Madrid's administration is very difficult to evaluate. Not only did most of the main developments of the debt crisis take place during his term, but there were natural disasters as well, and a substantial deterioration of Mexico's terms of trade. As a result of all these factors, and some bad economic policies, the performance of the economy was extremely poor during these years (see table 3-1).

For the purposes of this chapter, the de la Madrid years are the key to understanding why the relationship between the World Bank and Mexico evolved as it did during the 1980s. To start, it should be noted that most of the breakthroughs in the relationship, to be recounted shortly, were made with de la Madrid and not his

65. World Bank, *OED Study of Bank/Mexico Relations*, p. 75.

successor Carlos Salinas. Although the Mexican reforms of the past decade are almost solely associated with Salinas, it was de la Madrid who, for good or for bad, unlocked the key doors. He made the initial decisions on all major fronts.

De la Madrid had been very interested in the World Bank since the mid-1960s, when he was a young middle-level government official.[66] As a subdirector of credit in the Finance Ministry from 1965 to 1970, he had the opportunity to appreciate the quality of the Bank's sector work. A few years later, he met McNamara and came to respect his intelligence and leadership—qualities that he did not find in President Clausen, whom he met twice in Washington, or Barber Conable, who succeeded Clausen in 1986. In sum, de la Madrid was the first of a new breed of Mexican politicians: he did postgraduate work at Harvard, and neither he nor his circle was afraid of, or even suspicious about, a close relationship with the Bank.

World Bank Starts to Move In

After the debt moratorium in August 1982, major management changes occurred in the Bank's Latin American division.[67] Since the new officers were to play an important role in the relationship that developed between 1983 and 1987, it is convenient to record their names: Rainer B. Steckhan, director for the region that included Mexico; Pieter P. Bottelier, the division chief for Mexico; and Frederick E. Berger, lead economist for Mexico. (The latter, a Danish-Uruguayan economist, died of a brain tumor in 1988.)

Bottelier made the first attempt to forge a new relationship between the Bank and Mexico. In a memorandum written in late 1983, he proposed to the Mexican government that the World Bank could have a high-quality macroeconomic dialogue with Mexico and might even construct a few policy loans around that dialogue. These loans were called, in the jargon of the Mexico division of the Bank, "development policy loans," although since 1980 they have been officially known as "structural adjustment loans."

The memorandum became the subject of enormous debate within the de la Madrid cabinet. Many resisted a prominent policy dialogue with the Bank, including the Bank's most important borrower, Nacional Financiera. Gustavo Petricioli, its then director, submitted a response to Finance Minister Silva-Herzog explaining that the World Bank wanted inadmissible prerogatives. This note was then confidentially shown to Bottelier by officials in the Finance Ministry as an explanation for why the Bank's proposal had to be rejected.

Meanwhile the debt crisis in Mexico had spilled over to other countries, and the banking community began to push the international agencies to assume a more prominent role to protect their own backs and to get out of further lending. Thus,

---

66. Carlos M. Urzúa, interview with Miguel de la Madrid, March 3, 1995.

67. This section has benefited greatly from the unpublished article by Devesh Kapur, "The World Bank and the Mexican Reforms after 1982" (Washington: Brookings, 1994).

the World Bank and the IMF were slowly becoming the escorts, so to speak, of the banking community. Silva-Herzog saw that very well and overruled Petricioli, deciding to accept the Bank's proposal at the end of 1983. This marked the beginning of what gradually evolved into a closer relationship.

A WATERSHED AGREEMENT. The Bank first attempted to focus its new policy dialogue with Mexico on interest rates. At that time, the Bank's lending portfolio to Mexico consisted principally of credit operations. The portfolio had fifteen lines of credit to many different on-lending institutions, each of which had different loan covenants, reflecting the somewhat ad hoc manner in which these project loans had been negotiated.

Most of the loans went through Nacional Financiera, which on-lent directly to firms and served as the lead agency for on-lending to banks. Nominal interest rates charged by Nacional Financiera on its loans had fallen below the inflation rate in Mexico, becoming negative in real terms. That often violated loan covenants that prohibited negative real interest rates.

Thus, as its first major project, the Bank proposed to the Mexican government that they negotiate an umbrella interest rate agreement that would substitute for the covenants of the fifteen individual loan agreements. The proposal was a novelty at that time, and within the Bank there was considerable skepticism that the Mexican government would accept the idea. Nonetheless, the proposal was sent in early 1984, and, much to the Bank's surprise, it had a negotiated legal document by May. This agreement became known as the General Interest Rate Agreement (GIRA), which substituted for the preceding covenants, and set out a three-year timetable, sector by sector, on how the rates would be adjusted every three months to an inflation proxy (with an exemption for most loans in the rural sector).

The GIRA was a watershed in the relations between the Bank and Mexico. The agreement covered not only Bank loans but also loans from external donors, including, to its chagrin, the IDB. It was the first time that the Bank had succeeded in initiating a policy dialogue on a broader front. The Mexican Finance Ministry was also quite bold in accepting the agreement, for the harmonization of loan rates across so many governmental agencies implied an enormous amount of work, including political lobbying.

Partially because of the political difficulties, the Mexican government had failed to comply with the GIRA agreement by the end of 1984. A decision had been taken internally by the Bank that the agreement was a make-or-break point, and the Bank decided to suspend disbursements. The Mexican government was orally advised that they should not submit any disbursement applications under any of the fifteen loans. Since these loans amounted to more than half of the total ongoing Bank loans, the Bank's hard line was no minor thing for the Mexican government. However, to everybody's relief, the adjustments were made within a few weeks, and the agreement sailed through.

Cartagena Meeting

In June 1984, there was a meeting in Cartagena, Colombia, where most of the foreign and finance ministers in Latin America openly discussed possible avenues to cope with the debt overhang (a first meeting had been held in Quito months earlier). The international press covered the event heavily, and for the first time the specter of a Latin American debtor's cartel started to haunt bankers around the world.

The coalition never prospered, however, since a debtor's cartel poses many incentive problems; each country is tempted to distinguish itself from the rest. Yet, it is puzzling that so few countries dared to declare a moratorium on their *own*, since, as noted by Kaletsky in his classical work, the costs of a conciliatory default "may not be as daunting as is often supposed. On the contrary, these penalties could be surprisingly moderate. . . . A bank attempting to invoke the modest legal sanctions available might do more harm to itself than to the defaulter."[68]

Furthermore, from a legal point of view, the principle that a country could be entitled to a partial default, if it were able to prove an unforeseen change of circumstances, is quite persuasive. This was precisely the case during the debt crisis, given that the sharp increases in the world real interest rates at the beginning of the 1980s were certainly unanticipated by the developing countries when they contracted the debt.[69]

In reality, however, few Latin American countries dared to challenge the banks in the1980s. One was Costa Rica, which perfectly showed how a small country could benefit from simply (and quietly) stopping debt payments. Several larger countries, like Peru (since 1984) and Brazil (1987), also staged temporary face-downs with creditors. Why not Mexico? After all, it is so close to the United States, and their economies are so intertwined, that any U.S. retaliation against Mexico would seem self-destructive.

Why not Mexico? I asked former president de la Madrid. He answered that since the country had suffered so much by being shut out of the international credit markets for decades after the defaults in the 1930s, it would have been an "historical irresponsibility" to have made the same mistake again.[70] Yet, those were other times, and the investors were individuals, not banks. Furthermore, although Mexico behaved in the 1980s more "correctly" than, say, Brazil, few people would dare to claim now that such a distinctive behavior made any difference at all once international lending was resumed in the 1990s.

Clearly, there are other explanations for Mexico not having chosen to default, two of which have the advantage of being quite simple. The first is the human factor. Fortunately for the bankers, the Mexican officials with decisionmaking

68. Anatole Kaletsky, *The Costs of Default* (New York: Twentieth Century Fund, 1985), p. 65.

69. For a cogent defense of that point, see George T. Kanaginis, "Default on Developing Country Debt: Is It Justified by International Law?" *Economics and Politics,* vol. 3, no. 3 (November 1991), pp. 239–63.

70. Carlos M. Urzúa, interview with Miguel de la Madrid, March 3, 1995.

power during the debt crisis were uncharacteristically cautious. President de la Madrid was a conservative at heart, both ideologically and temperamentally, and Finance Minister Silva-Herzog was never known as a politician willing to take risks. Finally, the chief foreign debt negotiator for several years, José Ángel Gurría, was an economist who became known for his nonconfrontational style, and, perhaps because of that, as the archetypical Latin pal of the New York bankers. They were so comfortable with him that the Mexican government had to renew his appointment for a dozen years, until the end of 1994, when he was promoted to foreign minister.

The second is a systemic factor. The semi-authoritarian regime in Mexico has always had enormous control over the population, and the country is extremely unbalanced in terms of income distribution and political power. Those two characteristics of the Mexican political system played a role in the debt crisis as well: few members of the elite would back a Mexican default because they knew that the lower classes would bear most of the debt burden and that as individuals they *did* run the risk of being the subject of retaliation in case of a Mexican default. After all, they had more than $50 billion deposited in the United States and other foreign countries.

Beginning of Full-Blown Relations

As noted earlier, a procedure that was helpful in strengthening the relationship between the World Bank and Mexico was the "country strategy implementation" meetings begun in late 1983. These meetings, held alternately in Washington and Mexico every six months, provided a forum for consultation. During the meetings, the Bank would produce, first, a ten-page paper on the macroeconomic situation; second, a paper that reviewed the project implementation of the existing portfolio; and, finally, a "forward-looking" paper. The consultation based on this routine became an established pattern that continued until the early 1990s.

Trade Liberalization Saga

Based on the themes developed in those short papers, and emboldened by the success of GIRA, the World Bank began in early 1984 to propose a trade policy loan that would significantly liberalize the Mexican economy.[71] This was the heyday of Anne Krueger, then the Bank's vice-president for economic research and well known in academic circles as a forceful proponent, some would say "a zealot," of free trade. As such, there was ready acceptance within the Bank of this approach to Mexico. It took more than a year, however, before this momentum translated into a loan, as the negotiations proved very difficult. The biggest handicap was the weight of history: in Mexico, the World Bank was (and still is) identified with Washington.

71. See also Kapur, "The World Bank and the Mexican Reforms after 1982."

Of course, some compensating factors worked in favor of the trade policy loan. An obvious one was that some Mexican government officials had begun to look at liberalizing the economy as a way to lower inflationary pressures, which were steep by late 1984. Another factor could have been, according to some World Bank officials, Silva-Herzog's awareness that without the trade loan he would have even greater difficulties rescheduling Mexico's debt with its commercial bank creditors. In 1985, Mexico was negotiating what was then the largest financial deal in world history, a deal that involved its entire commercial bank debt. And Silva-Herzog knew that to get the roughly five hundred participating banks to underwrite this new program, Mexico needed the participation of the multilateral institutions.

But Mexico's decision to proceed with a radical trade reform was too complex to be explained by these two factors alone. The following incident exemplifies neatly the delicacies involved.[72] In April 1985, a Bank manager gave a copy of a so-called policy matrix for the proposed loan to Finance Undersecretary Francisco Suárez Dávila. The matrix set out what Mexico would have to do regarding trade liberalization, and how much of the $500 million loan Mexico would receive in each tranch. A few days later, he was called into the office of the Bank's vice-president for Latin America, David Knox, who had just received a complaint from Senior Vice-President Ernest Stern, who apparently had been summoned by Clausen, who had been called by Donald Regan, who in turn had been called by Volcker! The policy matrix caused such a furor, since it appeared to dictate terms to Mexico, that the Mexican government angrily decided to pull out all stops.

When I asked former president de la Madrid about the political maneuvering that swirled around the trade reform, he asserted immediately that the economic cabinet members largely agreed regarding the issue. In fact, he said, the trade minister at the time, Héctor Hernández, supposedly the most vocal opponent of the trade policy loan, had been de la Madrid's main collaborator in 1979–80 when de la Madrid as budget and planning minister had pushed for Mexico's entrance to the General Agreement on Tariffs and Trade (GATT), a suggestion eventually rejected by López Portillo.

During 1984–85, differences among the economic cabinet members were more "a matter of rhythm rather than of substance," said de la Madrid.[73] Some cabinet members were afraid that, after liberalizing the economy, the current account would deteriorate rapidly, at a time when there was an acute shortage of fresh foreign credit. This explained, he said, the piecemeal approach to liberalization that took place in 1983 and 1984.

But how did the group dynamics within the cabinet evolve to the point where President de la Madrid ended up accepting the trade reform in mid-1985? He did

72. Devesh Kapur and Richard Webb, interview with a World Bank staff member, January 19, 1993.

73. Carlos M. Urzúa, interview with Miguel de la Madrid, March 3, 1995.

not say, but perhaps there was a shift in the balance. One guess is that the most powerful cabinet member, Budget and Planning Minister Carlos Salinas de Gortari, President de la Madrid's right-hand man, became more involved and tilted the balance.

For a while, Salinas had kept his distance from the trade debate, partly because he was not yet a neoliberal. But if so, why did he change his mind? The influence of two new players, who suddenly gained prominence in the Mexican government, may be responsible. The main one was Pedro Aspe, who Salinas promoted in 1985 to his undersecretary; the other was Aspe's former professor Francisco Gil Díaz, a conservative economist who was head of economic research at the central bank.

Whatever the political impetus, the fact is that on July 23, 1985, the Mexican government ended the import-substitution strategy that had guided its economy for decades. The trade reform, which was downplayed as another component of a general stabilization plan, was implicitly justified as an anti-inflation measure. The reform was, however, quite dramatic: it called for over 60 percent of the controlled-good categories to be removed from import licensing and simultaneously increased tariffs to provide roughly equivalent protection. The trade measures took place after the government devalued the currency by 20 percent.

As a bonus, the Mexican government started to dismantle other parts of the import substitution framework: fiscal incentives and implicit subsidies to domestic firms. The dismantling was done mostly in the manufacturing sector, where, according to a World Bank study, in 1980 total government subsidies "were worth more than 10 percent of value added in the sector, of which 1.8 percent were fiscal incentives, 0.9 percent were credit subsidies, 1.6 percent were straight subsidies, and 5.8 percent were the implicit subsidy due to underpricing of inputs supplied from public corporations."[74] The last step in this trade liberalization saga was concluded when Mexico acceded to GATT in August 1986.

An Earthquake and a Debt Plan

The economic adjustment initiated at the end of 1982 was able to stabilize the economy by 1984. It was, however, a Pyrrhic victory, gained at a considerable cost in terms of output and employment. Thus, the government was rather distressed when it saw that by early 1985 the macroeconomic indicators had again worsened.

When the economy picked up in 1984, imports grew as well, and soon the government faced a foreign credit constraint, made more critical by the hemorrhage of debt repayments and a drop in oil prices. Furthermore, domestic prices grew with the economy, and the surge of inflation led to a corresponding surge of capital flight induced by an overvalued exchange rate. It is no surprise that, by mid-1985, the Mexican government was unable to meet IMF fiscal targets, and hence the Fund agreement was canceled.

74. Maddison, *The Political Economy of Poverty, Equity and Growth*, p. 180.

Then, on September 19, 1985, came the proverbial straw that broke the camel's back: an earthquake (with another one following the next day). It was a shock of enormous dimensions: roughly 10,000 people perished, and 85,000 families lost their homes. But Mexico was also shocked by what the earthquake exposed about Mexico's inner-city shantytowns, and the Mexico City inhabitants, while on the streets, released, for the first time in many years, all their contained grievances against a corrupt and incompetent government.

After the tragedy, the World Bank intervened in a felicitous way (as opposed to the IMF that initially showed very little empathy). More than $90 million from other Bank projects were immediately shifted to earthquake reconstruction. Six months later, the Mexican government also received a Bank loan for $400 million to help with rehabilitation and reconstruction. The Bank's opportune intervention was helped by the fact that, months before the earthquake, Mexico and the Bank had signed the first of a series of low-income housing loans to be managed by the Fondo Nacional de Habitaciones Populares, a fund that on-lent to local developers (with a remarkable success, since the production of housing units increased twenty times from 1982 to 1986).

THE BAKER PLAN. On October 8, 1985, barely two weeks after the earthquake, U.S. Treasury Secretary James A. Baker unveiled a new plan to cope with the debt crisis. The Baker Plan called for the provision of fresh money to the fifteen most indebted countries, with twenty billion dollars coming from commercial banks and roughly another nine billion from multilateral institutions. The new loans were conditioned on deep structural reforms in the recipient countries, such as trade liberalization and privatization of public enterprises.

The announcement of the plan was widely celebrated in Washington circles. But, even from the beginning, it failed to address the issue of how the commercial banks were going to be forced to participate. Less than a year later, it was considered a failure by most debtor countries. That has led many countries to ask whether the Baker Plan was simply a response to a possible Latin American radicalization on the debt issue. In Washington, the typical answer is a resounding no! And predictably in Latin America, one gets precisely the opposite response.

Several academics who have studied the case side with the latter view.[75] In mid-1985, the new Peruvian president Alan García had imposed a 10 percent ceiling on the proportion of export earnings that would be used to repay the debt. By early August, Fidel Castro had held a well-attended meeting on the Latin American debt problem in Havana, Cuba. In that meeting, Castro, with his sense of political opportunity and baroque rhetoric that are still his mark, vociferously

75. See, for instance, Lissakers, *Banks, Borrowers, and the Establishment;* and Diana Tussie, "The Coordination of the Latin American Debtors: Is There a Logic behind the Story?" in Stephany Griffith-Jones, ed., *Managing World Debt* (New York: St. Martin's Press, 1988), pp. 282–307.

called for a Latin American debt moratorium.[76] Certainly, those two factors were more than enough to crisp the nerves of more than one U.S. official. Indeed, the author of a highly respected book on the debt crisis quotes a U.S. Treasury Department official as saying that the Baker Plan had been "pasted together quickly in breakfast meetings" as a response to the new radical proposals.[77]

A New Slump

In 1986, the average annual price of oil dropped more than 50 percent compared with a year earlier. That external shock sent the Mexican terms of trade reeling to its lowest level ever registered. Furthermore, the consolidated government deficit reached 20 percent of GDP in that year, partly because of the drop in oil revenues, but two other factors also contributed.

First, the domestic debt burden had become by 1986 a problem even more pressing than the foreign debt overhang. Because of its lack of external financing, the government ran up its domestic debt after 1982, so much so that by 1986 interest payments on the domestic debt had climbed up to over 12 percent of GDP, about 40 percent of total public revenues from tax and sales.

The second factor was political. The government not only refused to adjust other spending items to cope with the fall in revenue, but it even increased slightly current and capital expenditures before the national elections in mid-1986. That policy was engineered mostly by Budget and Planning Minister Salinas. He had become by then the most powerful member of the de la Madrid cabinet, and his main rival, Silva-Herzog, soon was to leave his post as finance minister, apparently because of economic and political differences with de la Madrid and Salinas.

Silva-Herzog was succeeded by Gustavo Petricioli, who as a director of Nacional Financiera had had some frictions with the World Bank but in his new post would become quite friendly with the Bank. Meanwhile, a new multiyear debt rescheduling package was being structured. Mexico was meant to be a principal "beneficiary" of the Baker Plan, and soon after that initiative was announced, Mexico started a round of negotiations with the multilateral institutions and the commercial banks to reschedule its existing debt and to renew the flow of credit.

After difficult negotiations, the first accord was reached with the IMF in July 1986, when Mexico signed a standby agreement for $1.7 billion. The main bone of contention was how to measure the fiscal deficit for the purposes of setting the fiscal targets in the agreement. Mexico contended, following an argument put

76. Fidel Castro, *La impagable deuda externa de América Latina y del Tercer Mundo: Cómo puede y debe ser cancelada y la urgente necesidad del nuevo orden económico internacional* (Havana: Editora Política, 1985).

77. Lissakers, *Banks, Borrowers, and the Establishment,* p. 229. At the time, Karin Lissakers was a professor at Columbia University; she is currently serving as the U.S. Executive Director of the IMF.

forward by Brazil, that the targets should be set in terms of the so-called operational deficit, or the inflation-adjusted government deficit (about 7 percent of GDP in that year), as opposed to the nominal deficit (about 20 percent). After initially opposing it strenuously, the IMF finally went along with Mexico's proposal. Shortly thereafter, the World Bank announced a $2.3 billion lending program in 1986–87.

The Bank and the Mexican Debt Issue

The Federal Reserve, the U.S. Treasury, and the IMF were the main official interlocutors with Mexico during the first part of the debt crisis.[78] That the IMF played a role and the Bank did not was natural given that, in the initial stages, most people saw the problem as a temporary liquidity issue.

AN OPPORTUNITY FOR THE BANK. As noted, the Baker Plan gave an explicit role to the multilateral institutions. Until the plan, the Bank had been left in the cold while the debt crisis unfolded, criticized externally for its seeming passivity and internally for wasting an opportunity to use its expertise.

Since Mexico was the first major country where a new role for the World Bank was to be tested, Senior Vice-President Ernest Stern used all his influence to make it a success. Stern was heavily involved in the negotiations between Mexico and the commercial banks, as well as in the Bank's guarantee negotiations with Mexico. A process was initiated whereby Stern would inform Finance Minister Petricioli of the status of each project and the steps required to expedite the flow of funds. To move the funds, the Mexico division at the Bank was allowed to cut through the normal bureaucratic processes at the Bank.

By the end of September 1986, after a series of nasty clashes between Mexico and the commercial banks, a new debt package was completed.[79] It involved the rescheduling of around $52 billion of public debt, of which almost $44 billion was given a lengthier maturity (twenty years) and a lower spread over LIBOR ($^{13}\!/_{16}$ percent). Furthermore, the banks agreed to provide $6 billion in new money and to lend another $1.7 billion in case of adverse external developments.

LACK OF DEBT INITIATIVES FROM THE WORLD BANK. In a quite detailed study on the Bank's intellectual contribution to the understanding and solution of the debt crisis sponsored by the London School of Economics, the authors concluded that "the Bank was overoptimistic before 1982, sometimes disseminating assessments and advice which they would directly contradict later, with the benefit of hindsight. And it also seems that during the crisis, it was a slow follower in the debate on possible remedies."[80]

---

78. See also Kapur, "The World Bank and the Mexican Reforms after 1982."

79. A detailed account of the negotiations with the commercial banks is given in Gurría, *La política de la deuda externa*, pp. 75–79.

80. Beatriz Armendáriz de Aghion and Francisco Ferreira, "The World Bank and the Analysis of the International Debt Crisis," Discussion Paper No. 51 (Development Economics Research Programme, London School of Economics, November 1993), p. 3.

Most observers outside the World Bank would agree with this sober statement. But the Bank itself has been more self-congratulatory about its role in the debt crisis. A pamphlet circulated by the Bank purports to show that "the World Bank played an important role in the way Latin America dealt with the debt crisis."[81]

And, in fact, the Bank has a point. As opposed to the IMF, the Bank is a more open organization, made of members with a wide range of economic and political beliefs. This was illustrated quite neatly in the case of the debt crisis. That problem was viewed very differently by different members of the Bank staff, even at the top level. Among the ones that opposed, and discouraged, any nonofficial view on the debt problem were Clausen, Stern, and Krueger. Stern, for instance, once chastised Guy Pfeffermann, then chief economist for Latin America, for publishing in 1986 a well-regarded book on the impact of the debt crisis on poverty in Latin America.[82] Krueger, after leaving the Bank to return to academia, and when almost all observers were pushing for some kind of debt relief, still opposed it with such statements as: "It can even be argued that, in countries where fiscal discipline is lax, relaxation of the debt-service burden would simply result in increases in other expenditures or a retardation in the rate of reforms."[83] The claim, by the way, is at odds with what actually happened.

A different view was held by another group in the Bank, which included the vice-president for operations policy Shahid Husain, the vice-president for Latin America David Knox (the former replaced the latter in 1987), and some of the staff in the Mexico division at the Bank. By 1985, this group became convinced that mere debt rescheduling was not enough, and that debt reduction had to become part of the solution. No one at the Bank dared to put those words on paper, however. There was a belief that the World Bank could not be an active agent on debt reduction and simultaneously remain a preferred creditor in the capital markets.

Initial work on debt reduction came from the Mexico division, which contacted Donald Lessard, a finance professor, to explore ways in which the World Bank could contribute to effective debt reduction through some form of financial engineering. The working papers and strategic sketches that resulted actually preceded the Baker speech in 1985. But since the Mexico division was afraid the papers might leak, they had little effect in the rest of the Bank.

Other papers were also produced internally, such as Fred Jasperson's, who worked for Pfeffermann. Furthermore, by the end of 1986, there was a change in the official attitude of the Bank itself, albeit in an unassuming and quiet way: in December the Bank appears to have put the words "debt relief" in print for the first

81. Sebastian Edwards, *The Evolving Role of the World Bank: The Latin American Debt Crisis* (Washington: World Bank, undated), p. 2.

82. Guy Pfeffermann, *Poverty in Latin America: The Impact of Depression* (Washington: World Bank, 1986).

83. Anne O. Krueger, "Resolving the Debt Crisis and Restoring Developing Countries' Creditworthiness," *Carnegie-Rochester Conference Series on Public Policy*, vol. 30 (Spring 1989), p. 105.

time. It was on the last page of an economic report on Bolivia.[84] By that time, the idea that debt reduction could be optimal, if the debt overhang was too taxing, had been given academic credence by Harvard Professor Jeffrey Sachs and others.[85]

GURRÍA BORROWS AN IDEA. Lessard's pieces were shown confidentially to Mexican officials, who grew exasperated by the schizophrenic attitude of an institution that was officially ignoring any possibility of debt reduction, but was clearly taking the issue seriously.

The exasperation did not last long. One day the Mexico division staff learned that Mexico's chief debt negotiator, Gurría, who had access to all the debt reduction papers, had taken them to New York and shopped around for an agent willing to do a debt reduction scheme for Mexico. He found none other than J. P. Morgan & Co., which during the entire century had been ready to do all kinds of financial deals with Mexico, even in the revolutionary times.[86] The new debt reduction strategy replaced the one preferred by the government up to that point: it featured debt-for-equity swaps. The conversion scheme was initiated and had its largest success (swaps actually represented half of the foreign investment in 1986), but soon afterwards enthusiasm for it abated, owing to fears of the effects of the monetary redemption that accompanied the swaps.

The J. P. Morgan deal proved unsuccessful. Mexico tried to implement it through a bond auction to be held in February 1988, expecting to redeem about $20 billion of commercial bank debt at an average discount of 50 percent, by offering, in exchange, zero coupon bonds with a maturity of twenty years and a spread of 1.625 percent over LIBOR, fully guaranteed (by zero coupon bonds that Mexico bought from the U.S. Treasury). However, the accepted bids only amounted to $3.7 billion, at an average discount of only 30.2 percent.

A Heterodox Stabilization Plan

By December 1987, faced with the traumatic experience of an annual inflation rate exceeding 150 percent (never experienced in Mexico before), the government launched a new stabilization program known as the Pacto de Solidaridad Económica, the Economic Solidarity Pact. It involved heterodox policies, wage and price controls, and (as opposed to other stabilization plans tried earlier in Argentina and Brazil) some orthodox policies, such as stringent fiscal and monetary stances. In the middle was the exchange rate, which was pegged to the dollar in March 1988 as a

84. World Bank, *Updating Economic Memorandum on Bolivia,* Report No. 6455-BO (Washington: World Bank, December 1986), p. 44.

85. See Jeffrey Sachs, "Managing the LDC Debt Crisis," *Brookings Papers on Economic Activity,* 2:1986, pp. 397–431.

86. See Emilio Zebadúa, *Banqueros y revolucionarios: La soberanía financiera de México, 1914–1929* (Mexico City: El Colegio de México and Fondo de Cultura Económica, 1994).

nominal anchor. Given the semi-authoritarian cum corporatist character of the Mexican political system, the package won ready acceptance from the private sector, the workers, and the peasants.

The pact also involved a practice that was becoming increasingly orthodox: further trade liberalization to gain more control over domestic prices. By the end of 1987 the average tariff was lowered to just 10 percent (from 22 percent in 1986) and the weighted average to about 6 percent (from 13 percent). At that point, Mexico became more open than almost any industrialized country. It should be noted that the pact was similar to the Argentinian and Brazilian pacts tried a few years back.

The pact brought down inflation to 52 percent in 1988 and 20 percent in 1989, without a drop in output (the economy actually grew 1.2 percent in 1988). Given its success, the government has since renewed the pact. In November 1991, a new Pacto de Estabilidad y Crecimiento Económico, the Pact for Stability and Economic Growth, allowed for readjustments in energy prices, increased minimum wages, slowed down the peso crawling peg, and decreased the value-added tax rates.

The World Bank played no role in devising the 1987 pact. As noted by its own staff, "the Bank was essentially caught unprepared for the comprehensive Mexican homemade heterodox approach by dint of having focused too narrowly on trade liberalization. . . . At first, Bank reaction to the novelty of the Mexican approach was slightly skeptical due mainly to unfamiliarity with aspects like incomes policy."[87]

The Heyday of the Relations

During Carlos Salinas de Gortari's mandate (1988–94), the government made the most drastic economic reforms in recent Mexican history. They ranged from a large-scale privatization program, to a plan to attack extreme poverty; from a free trade agreement with the United States and Canada, to a land counterreform.

A masterly politician, Salinas so impressed his foreign peers that he was reportedly filmed by World Bank staff during a speech, for it was thought that he could be of great help in spreading the gospel of neoliberalism in other countries. His influence even reached the United States, where he received many awards and, after leaving office, was for a while the U.S. candidate to head the new World Trade Organization in 1995.

Readers unfamiliar with Mexico might be puzzled about how Salinas managed to effect so many reforms and command so much recognition. It seems less surprising, however, after allowing for the sui generis Mexican political system. For more than six decades, the dominant party, Partido Revolucionario Institucional (PRI), had delivered a model autocracy. But in July 1988, the PRI hegemony was

87. World Bank, *OED Study of Bank/Mexico Relations,* p. 98.

suddenly in danger during a presidential election. Its candidate, Salinas, handicapped by the dismal performance of the economy during the de la Madrid
administration (see again table 3-1), and his own poor public image, had to compete for the presidency against a popular Cuauhtémoc Cárdenas, the son of re-
vered former president Lázaro Cárdenas.

In an election marred by dubious electoral practices by the PRI, Salinas was
proclaimed the winner after the computerized voting system suffered a convenient
"breakdown" for several hours. When Salinas took office on December 1, 1988,
many Mexicans questioned his legitimacy. To the credit of Salinas's political skills,
he gained more and more recognition from some of the skeptics as his administration went on.

Brady Plan

On March 10, 1989, Treasury Secretary Nicholas Brady disclosed a new U.S.
debt plan that explicitly incorporated, for the first time, the goal of debt and debt
service relief. How much relief he had in mind is unclear, but it was certainly much
lower than what Mexico and other debtor countries ended up requesting. There
has been much speculation about the reasons for that change in the U.S. debt
strategy, but the new initiative was, almost certainly, a response to a constellation of
events happening in Latin America.

First, since the 1988 electoral results in Mexico pointed to a resurgence of a
nationalistic left, an event probably not welcome in the United States, the election
results could have prompted the U.S. government to help Salinas to gain more
legitimacy. Second, in February 1989, one month before the Brady Plan was
announced, a team of Mexican government officials, headed by the new finance
minister, Aspe, let the U.S. Treasury know that Mexico was going to demand a
significant debt reduction in the next round of debt rescheduling. Third, also in
February, a series of riots in Venezuela left about three hundred dead after that
government, following typical IMF advice, took a series of unpopular adjustment
measures. Fourth, in 1988, the Japanese government appeared ready to underwrite
a new initiative, the Miyazawa Plan, which proposed the securitization of the debt,
with the IMF as a guarantor; hence it was somewhat the predecessor of the Brady
Plan. And fifth, the commercial banks' health had substantially improved by then,
and they were able to write down part of their debt. Whatever the rationale for the
Brady Plan, Mexico was its first beneficiary. Tentative negotiations with the commercial banks and the multilateral institutions started in April 1989 and were
formally on track after Mexico signed in May 1989 an IMF three-year EFF
agreement for $4.1 billion, part of which was explicitly targeted for debt reduction.

The core of the Brady Plan was the use of financial mechanisms to support debt
and debt service reduction by exchanging old commercial debt for new securities,
the so-called Brady bonds, using loans from multilateral and official creditors as

guarantees. Since there were supposed to be several financial alternatives to allow for some flexibility, the procedure was labeled the "menu approach to debt reduction."

Negotiations between the banks and the Mexican government lasted longer than anyone thought and were colored by sharp remarks among the negotiators.[88] Just the design of the menu took from April 19 to July 23, with the low point of the negotiations coming on July 20, when President Salinas ordered the Mexican negotiators to return to Mexico for good. However, the U.S. Treasury immediately backed off (similarly to what happened in 1982 with López Portillo) and called for another round of negotiations on July 22; it turned out to be the final session. It was mediated by Brady himself, Treasury Undersecretary David Mulford (the intellectual author of the Brady Plan), and the chairman of the Federal Reserve Bank of New York, Gerald Corrigan. Despite their stated neutrality, it was obvious that they were occasionally unhappy with the Mexican negotiating stance, something that Mulford suddenly let be known with an expletive against the "number-people" on the Mexican team.[89]

The menu contained three options for the banks: exchange their existing Mexican debt for thirty-year bonds with a 35 percent lower face value, yielding $13\frac{3}{16}$ percent over LIBOR; accept thirty-year bonds with the same face value as the existing debt but with a fixed interest rate of 6.25 percent; or provide, over the next four years, fresh loans to Mexico equivalent to 25 percent of the existing exposure. The debt relief dishes were spiced with an oil recapture clause that gave the banks, beginning July 1996, extra income if the price of oil were to rise above $14 (real terms) per barrel.[90] It took another six months, from September 1989 to February 1990, to get all the banks to submit their choices. The deal was closed on March 28, 1990. The first option was chosen by banks holding 42 percent of the $48.5 billion of eligible commercial bank debt; the second, by banks holding 47 percent of the debt; and the third, by those banks holding the balance.

After Mexico, more than a dozen other highly indebted countries used the Brady agreement. According to a careful study sponsored by the Organization for Economic Cooperation and Development (OECD), the effects of the plan differed considerably from country to country: Costa Rica benefited greatly, Mexico also gained from the deal; the Philippines and Uruguay benefited very little.[91] The agreement did help to reduce the commercial banks' exposure in the developing world, mainly at the expense of the multilateral institutions.

ROLE OF THE WORLD BANK. The Bank's main financial contribution to the Mexican component of the Brady deal was made through a $1.26 billion loan for

88. See Gurría, *La política de la deuda externa,* pp. 105–66, for a very detailed account.

89. Ibid., p. 147.

90. See Stijn Claessens and Sweder van Wijnbergen, "The 1990 Mexico and Venezuela Recapture Clauses: An Application of Average Price Options," *Journal of Banking and Finance,* vol. 17 (June 1993), pp. 733–45.

91. See Jean-Claude Berthélemy and Anne Vourc'h, *Debt Relief and Growth* (Paris: OECD, 1994), pp. 58–59.

interest support. The Bank also provided $750 million of set-asides from existing loans. Together with the IMF and World Bank loans, Japan also lent about two billion dollars, bringing the total guarantees for the new Mexican bonds to $7.1 billion.

The Bank also played an important advisory role to the Mexican government on the design of the different options to be presented to the commercial banks. One has only to look at the memoranda in the Bank files for the year 1989, especially the ones relating to the vice-presidency for development economics (then headed by former MIT professor Stanley Fischer), to realize the enormous effort the Bank made to advise the Mexican government. It is worth reproducing some of those comments:

> Bank staff helped Mexican authorities to evaluate debt-service relief implied by the different options in the menu offered to commercial banks including the pricing of the oil recapture clause. . . . The Bank also advised Mexico during negotiations with the commercial Bank Advisory Committee, initially favoring a more demanding posture vis a vis commercial banks than the one Mexico finally took. Particularly, Bank projections of Mexico's external financing needs played an important role in validating Mexico's request for debt-service relief.[92]

Another Bank claim, made repeatedly by its staff, is quite doubtful, however. Several published documents assert that the debt relief obtained through the Brady Plan was the main reason for the (mild) recovery of the Mexican economy during the next few years.[93] It is difficult to sustain this claim in view of other positive factors that were simultaneously present during the rest of the Salinas administration (1990–94). First, world interest rates, as represented by LIBOR, dropped from an average of 9.1 percent in 1990 to 3.9 percent in 1994. Second, the income accruing from the Mexican privatization process was extremely large, reaching 4.1 percent of GDP in 1991 and 4.2 percent in 1992. And, finally, by 1992 the Mexican economy had started reaping benefits, in the form of a sharp increase in foreign investment, from a possible North American Free Trade Agreement (see below).

Of course, the Bank is entitled to advertise its work, but selective self-congratulation is less acceptable. The large number of staff papers on the Brady deal contrasts with the lack of published work on the trade reform of 1985 and the social and environmental programs in which the Bank actively participated during the Salinas administration.

Privatization Process

At the end of the López Portillo administration, the Mexican federal government owned 1,155 enterprises. When de la Madrid left office, that number had

92. World Bank, "Review of Mexican External Debt," background paper in electronic form for the *OED Study of Bank/Mexico Relations*, p. 11.

93. See, for instance, Banco Mundial, *América Latina y el Caribe: Diez años después de la crisis de la deuda* (Washington: World Bank, 1993), p. 48; and Sweder van Wijnbergen, "The Mexican Debt Deal," *Economic Policy*, vol. 6, no. 12 (April 1991), pp. 13–56.

declined to 618, though most of the enterprises sold (or liquidated) were small. By the end of the Salinas administration, the number had further declined to 252, and the enterprises sold included all the commercial banks, the phone monopoly, and the two main airlines.

For a while, the Mexican privatization process, among the largest in the world both in number and value of the public enterprises sold, received resounding applause from the multilateral institutions, especially the World Bank, and the industrialized world. More recently, however, a backlash has set in, so that one can now find even in the U.S. press opinions like the following: "The privatization of state-owned companies—supposedly Salinas's crowning achievement—degenerated into a piñata for the cronies of powerful officials, beginning with the friends of the President."[94] The truth, as usual, lies between the extremes.

It may be too early to take full stock of Mexico's privatization process. The sheer number of enterprises sold, together with the lack of information for hundreds of them, makes the accounting a daunting job. Accordingly, the following remarks are somewhat limited and general:

(1) Generally speaking, the sale process was accomplished swiftly and with limited instances of corruption. Whether the same good marks can be given to the privatization outcomes is an issue that needs some qualification, as noted below.

(2) The privatization drive obeyed fiscal considerations more than efficiency goals. Using the privatization revenue, the government was able to decrease domestic debt from 20 percent of GDP in 1988 to barely 8.5 percent in 1993. This was a good use of the sales receipts, because the economy was burdened by a huge domestic debt in the second half of the 1980s, a debt run up to pay for its foreign debt. Thus, efficiency, although given lip service by the Mexican bureaucrats, was never the main issue. Budgetary pressures account for both the speed of privatization and the government's frequent disregard for efficiency considerations.[95]

(3) Just as in many other Mexican government ventures, the selling process was sometimes marred by irregularities. They ranged from selling to the nonhighest bidder (for example, the Cananea copper mine) to dubious financial engineering (such as illegally declaring dozens of enterprises bankrupt right before their privatization).[96] The latter hoax was particularly expedient: with a single stroke, the government could make the enterprises more palatable to private buyers, not only

94. Andrew A. Reding, "It Isn't the Peso. It's the Presidency," *New York Times Magazine*, April 9, 1995, p. 55.

95. Some of the many efficiency issues involved in a privatization process are reviewed by Raúl E. Sáez and Carlos M. Urzúa, "Privatisation and Fiscal Reform in Eastern Europe: Some Lessons from Latin America," forthcoming in Gary McMahon, ed., *Economic Lessons for Eastern Europe from Latin America* (London: Macmillan, 1995).

96. Francisco Valdés Ugalde, "From Bank Nationalization to State Reform: Business and the New Mexican Order," in Maria Lorena Cook, Kevin J. Middlebrook, and Juan Molinar Horcasitas, eds., *The Politics of Economic Restructuring: State-Society Relations and Regime Change in Mexico* (University of California–San Diego, 1994), pp. 219–42.

by boosting the deals' financials but also by disposing of such nuisances as syndicates and possible past misconduct by the bureaucrats formerly in charge.

(4) It is common to point to the commercial banks as successful examples of privatized companies. From mid-1991 to mid-1992, the government sold all eighteen commercial banks to the Mexican private sector in a deal that, judging solely by the revenue obtained by the government, was a resounding success; the receipts exceeded the initial value expected by the government by more than 50 percent.

Yet, it is unclear that bank consumers benefited from the sale: by September 1994, still three months away from the financial collapse (reviewed below), past-due loans, as a percentage of total loans, were at an historical high of almost 10 percent. This was partly due to the high interest margins charged by what became a protected oligopolistic banking sector. After privatization, the difference between the lending and borrowing rates grew dramatically. As a consequence, net earnings grew as well. To give an idea of the magnitude of the profit margins, in 1992 the average pretax profits of the three largest Mexican banks were larger than those of the three largest French banks ($752 million versus $738 million), while the average return on assets was almost eight times as large (2.2 percent versus 0.3 percent).[97]

The problems of oligopolistic practices and poor asset quality were compounded by negligent regulation by the government. Examples include inadequate reserve requirements on the banks and a bank president who lent $700 million to his own enterprises prior to the collapse of the institution. These lapses occurred despite the fact that a $500 million World Bank loan disbursed to Mexico in 1989 was meant to be partially used to improve prudential regulation and supervision in the financial sector.

It is true that the absence of these problems during the period of government ownership could be attributed partly to the banks being forced to finance the government, rather than the private sector. Yet, deregulation of the sector, which relaxed the requirement of forced lending as well as lending rates, started in 1988—three years before the banking sector was privatized, a period during which the nationalized banks continued to be managed reasonably well.

An antistatist reader might ask, but what about the quality of the banking services? Surprisingly, the privatized banks have performed better, at least regarding the provision of innovative services, than when they were government owned. After the nationalization, the banks developed several new products, ranging from NOW-type accounts to such services as factoring. As an extensive study on the subject concludes, the government "used nationalization to strengthen the banks, in order to perform a market oriented role in the economy. . . . The banks became profitable and introduced many new products and services."[98]

97. Figures calculated by the author using data from *The Banker*, July (vol. 143, no. 809, p. 99) and August 1993 (vol. 143, no. 810, p. 43).

98. Dianne Stewart, "Changes in the Pattern of Ownership, Structure and Operations of the Mexican Banks: 1982–1991," Working Paper No. 26 (London: Department of Economics, SOAS, University of London, 1992), p. 34.

(5) But the bad ex post performance of the privatized banking sector pales in comparison with the performance of other privatized enterprises. Three cases taken from a cross-country privatization study sponsored by the World Bank and conducted from 1990 to 1992 are illustrative. The study included two airlines, Aeroméxico and Mexicana, as well as the phone monopoly, Teléfonos de México (TELMEX).[99] Very simply, the first two firms were technically bankrupt by mid-1995, even though they were financially healthy when sold by the government in 1989. A more subtle case is the monopoly TELMEX. In the study sponsored by the Bank, a key question is raised: who won and who lost from the sale? The author of the study answered candidly:

> The government gained . . . other winners were employees, domestic shareholders, and buyers. . . . Foreign buyers have gained 27 percent of 1991 sales, so there has been substantial leakage of benefits abroad. . . . Consumers were the only losers. They lost mainly because of the price increases. It is important to emphasize, however, that this welfare loss to consumers is not net of any gain from improved quality, which could be substantial.[100]

Moreover, foreign buyers not only gained 27 percent (of 1991 sales) but also won *most* among the groups of winners. Furthermore, Mexican consumers lost more than 60 percent (of 1991 sales)! Finally, regarding the issue of higher quality, it is interesting to note that from 1990 (the year of its privatization) to 1994 TELMEX led the number of complaints received by the Mexican consumer protection agency: 70 percent of all complaints.

(6) A final troubling aspect of the privatizations was their effect on equity. In reviewing the privatizations covered in the above mentioned study, then chief economist of the World Bank Lawrence H. Summers argued, "there will probably still be some privatizations that will make some people very rich, and the ethical defense of that wealth will be difficult to achieve . . . [b]ut if, as I believe, issues of income distribution are best approached through concern for the poor rather than envy of the wealthy, these results will not prove to be such a serious problem."[101]

To place Summers's argument in perspective, consider the following: according to the magazine *Forbes,* the number of billionaires in Mexico rose from two in 1991, to seven in 1992, to thirteen in 1993, to twenty-four in 1994.[102] By then Mexico had more billionaires than the United Kingdom and Italy. Admittedly, part

99. Pankaj Tandon, "Mexico," in Ahmed Galal and Mary Shirley, eds., *Does Privatization Deliver? Highlights from a World Bank Conference* (Washington: World Bank, 1994), pp. 59–69.

100. Tandon, "Mexico," p. 68.

101. Lawrence H. Summers, "A Changing Course toward Privatization," in Galal and Shirley, eds., *Does Privatization Deliver?,* p. 17.

102. *Forbes,* "The Billionaires," July 18, 1994, pp. 134–219.

of the reason was that the peso was grossly overvalued in 1994; a year later, "only" ten of the twenty-four remained on *Forbes's* list. Still, how did Mexico create a net increase of eleven billionaires during 1993, a year in which the economy was virtually stagnant? One simple reason is that most of those "entrepreneurs" were earning rents from oligopolistic privatized industries and unregulated privatized monopolies.[103]

PRONASOL: A Program against Extreme Poverty

Salinas's doctoral dissertation in political economy written in the late 1970s was entitled "Public Investment, Political Participation, and System Support."[104] Clearly, he had a long-standing interest in how economic patronage could build political support. Not surprisingly, this interest would be reflected in his programs, especially that against extreme poverty, Programa Nacional de Solidaridad (PRONASOL), the National Solidarity Program, which was initiated soon after he took office and lasted until mid-1995 (when a new program with a less centralist overtone was launched).

From the beginning, PRONASOL was supposed to be a grassroots poverty alleviation program. Among its key elements were (i) the direct targeting of poor communities by the federal government, bypassing state and local governments; (ii) the use of a corps of local leaders; (iii) an emphasis on beneficiary participation; and (iv) the provision of soft loans to small enterprises. In one way or another, the first three of those elements were present in Salinas's doctoral thesis on how to build system support.

The World Bank publicly embraced PRONASOL. In private, however, Bank staff were more cautious: "The co-existence of the hefty subsidies and grants-in-aid under Solidarity with policies to liberalize and deregulate urban development and housing markets may prove contradictory at the local level. It is, however, consistent with the Mexican tradition of identifying each president with a particular social interest program which generally operates apart from the long-term development policy."[105] In any event, by early 1991 the Bank had already made an important contribution to PRONASOL, when it approved a loan for $350 million as part of a $1.4 billion program to attack extreme poverty in the four poorest Mexican states: Chiapas, Guerrero, Hidalgo, and Oaxaca.

103. For instance, Carlos Slim, the sixth richest man in the world in 1994, is the largest stockholder of TELMEX.

104. Carlos Salinas de Gortari, *Political Participation, Public Investment, and System Support: Study of Three Rural Communities in Central Mexico*, Ph.D. dissertation, Harvard University, 1978. The Spanish version appeared as *Producción y participación política en el campo* (Mexico City: Fondo de Cultura Económica, 1982).

105. World Bank, "Overview of the Urban Sector Story," background paper in electronic form for the *OED Study of Bank/Mexico Relations*, p. 4.

Empirically, the obvious question is whether PRONASOL succeeded in poverty alleviation. Interestingly, there has been almost no study of this question, though there is a considerable literature on the electoral effect of the program in 1994. From the few available studies of poverty, three discouraging findings emerge: first, political and administrative criteria were more important than extreme poverty in explaining the statewide allocation of funds; second, in Chiapas many of the poor viewed the program as a government imposition that forced them to provide unpaid labor for projects that would not directly benefit them; and third, regional distribution was not responsive to comparative need as indicated by World Bank guidelines.[106]

Clearly, more evidence on the impact of the program is needed, especially given the sharp increase in the percentage of poor people during the Salinas administration (see table 3-1). In particular, it can be argued that the World Bank, as a main endorser of PRONASOL, should fully appraise its success, or lack of it. Furthermore, whatever the Bank ultimately finds, the research should be made public by the Mexican government to quell suspicions (most likely erroneous) that PRONASOL was solely a pork barrel program devised by Salinas to get votes for his party.

North American Free Trade Agreement

At the beginning of his administration, President Salinas was reluctant to consider the possibility of a free trade agreement with the United States and Canada, even though members of his cabinet, especially the new trade minister, Jaime Serra Puche, urged him to do so. It is said that the Mexican government started to consider an agreement seriously only in 1989 when it looked very possible that Eastern Europe could draw an increasingly larger share of foreign investment from the West (a possibility that did not materialize).

Once it decided to go for an agreement, the Mexican government allocated a lot of effort, as well as money, lobbying during the formulation of the trade agreement and getting it passed. After some strong opposition in the United States and Canada, and almost none in Mexico, the final text of the North American Free Trade Agreement (NAFTA) was signed at the end of 1992 and took effect the first day of January 1994.

There is no evidence to indicate that the World Bank ever sponsored the agreement or participated in its design. Perhaps regional trade is not the Bank's cup

106. See, respectively, Adalberto García Rocha and Alejandro Guevara, "Impacto socioeconómico del Programa Nacional de Solidaridad en el estado de Zacatecas" (Mexico City: El Colegio de México, 1992); Carlos Marín, "Estudio del propio Consejo Consultivo del Pronasol: Solidaridad hundió más en la desesperanza a los ocho municipios del estallido zapatista," *Proceso*, January 9, 1995, pp. 28–33; and Sara Lovera, "Efecto relativo del Pronasol en el combate a la pobreza extrema," *Jornada*, October 30, 1994, p. 25.

of tea, or it would have been awkward for the Bank staff to help Mexico, or any other participant, in the trade negotiations. Nevertheless, the Bank made sixteen sectoral studies on how NAFTA would affect the Mexican economy. Most remain unpublished and are not particularly enlightening. The only one published was on the agricultural sector; it attempts to show that the impact of NAFTA on poor, corn-producing rural workers would be relatively mild.[107]

Land Counterreform

At the end of 1991, Salinas called for an amendment to the Mexican constitution that would modify the land tenure system inherited from the Mexican Revolution. The system had rested, since the Agrarian Reform Act of 1915, on the principle of communal lands (*ejidos* and *comunidades agrarias*) owned by the state and lent to the peasants. The core of Salinas's counterreform was to change property rights and make it possible for the peasants to trade the communal land, which accounted for about 60 percent of total arable land in central and southern Mexico. Before, the *ejidatarios* were able only to bequeath to their descendants their rights in an *ejido;* they could not (in principle) rent the land. By transferring the property rights to the peasants, the government hoped to induce the more productive *ejidatarios* to hold more land and benefit from increasing returns to scale. The reform also attempted to send a message to the private agricultural and cattle-raising sectors that the expropriation risk with which they had had to cope for many decades was gone.

As noted earlier, the Bank has had a long-standing interest in the Mexican land tenure system, going back to Ladejinsky's work in 1966. Yet, Mexican officials deny that the Bank played an important role in the counterreform, and only a few Bank documents refer to it even tangentially. Consider, for instance, the following statement: "Whether [the land counterreform] will ease or exacerbate the problem of rural poverty remains to be seen. The Bank has only recently begun to show an interest in this subject that goes beyond micro-economic efficiency. However, in deference to Mexican political sensitivities, the Bank (as well as the IDB) are keeping a low profile with respect to reforms in this field, while furnishing advice and technical collaboration when so requested."[108] It should be noted in passing that the skepticism of the Bank regarding the land reform was warranted: the impact of the reform has not been significant.

107. Santiago Levy and Sweder van Wijnbergen, "El maíz y el Acuerdo de Libre Comercio entre México y Estados Unidos," *Trimestre Económico*, vol. 58, no. 232 (October 1991), pp. 823–62.

108. World Bank, "Study of Relations between the World Bank and Mexico: The Agricultural Sector," background paper in electronic form for the *OED Study of Bank/Mexico Relations*, pp. 23–24.

OTHER WORLD BANK INVOLVEMENT. During the Salinas administration, the Bank had up to fifty-five people in Mexico at one point plowing through the government's list of reforms with Mexican officials. The Bank's main contribution was to give other perspectives by providing the officials with intellectual partners for discussions. There is no space to go over the list of sectoral reforms undertaken jointly by the Mexican government and the Bank during the Salinas government, but very briefly one reform that the Bank tenaciously pursued for almost a quarter of a century was the deregulation of the transport sector. Starting with its 1971 report on the transport sector in Mexico, the Bank had always been quite critical of the way in which the Mexican government had regulated entry into the trucking industry and controlled freight rates. The Bank won the argument in 1989, when the Mexican government relaxed entry conditions into the trucking industry, and a year later abolished the regulation of freight rates.

A Lackluster Performance

Despite Mexico's much lauded stabilization efforts from 1987 onward, plus the financial relief that was to have resulted from the Brady Plan, the resources that accrued from privatization, and the many structural reforms touted by the World Bank, a tantalizing puzzle remained: the Mexican economy continued to grow anemically.

This is illustrated quite dramatically in table 3-2, which presents a ranking of the last eight administrations in terms of key economic indicators. Comparatively speaking, the Salinas administration did very poorly. The performance of the economy during that period was the worst, except for that during the de la Madrid administration (which can be partially explained by the poor policies followed during the last two years of the López Portillo administration). Furthermore, it is precisely during those two periods that the Bank had some influence on the macroeconomic policies followed by the Mexican government.

Given such a dismal performance, by early 1994 the Bank was already distancing itself from the economic reforms adopted in Mexico. In a 1992 article entitled "Mexico's Growing Intimacy with the World Bank," the *Financial Times* was quoting the Mexican debt negotiator Gurría as saying that World Bank economists "and Mexican officials often spend weekends together brainstorming on policy issues. Many are the graduates of the same U.S. universities, and friends."[109] But two years later, the same newspaper was reporting that the Bank "is worried about Mexico's slow economic growth and low savings rate, which it believes makes its economy over-dependent on foreign capital."[110]

109. Damian Fraser, "Mexico's Growing Intimacy with the World Bank," *Financial Times,* March 3, 1992, p. 7.
110. Damian Fraser, "Trying Hard but Could Do Better, Says World Bank," *Financial Times,* February 22, 1994, p. 6.

Table 3-2. Rankings of Economic Performance, 1946–94

	World Bank influence in macro policy	Real GDP growth	Inflation rate	Growth of real wages	Gross national savings/GDP	Public sector deficit/GDP	Current account deficit/GDP	Public foreign debt/GDP	Percentage of poor households
Alemán	Minimal	6	4	2	8	1	2	3	n.a.
Ruiz Cortines	Minimal	2	3	5	7	2	5	1	n.a.
López Mateos	Minimal	2	1	1	6	3	3	2	6
Díaz Ordaz	Minimal	4	2	3	3	4	4	4	5
Echeverría	Minimal	5	5	4	4	6	6	5	2
López Portillo	Minimal	1	7	6	1	7	7	7	1
De la Madrid	High	8	8	8	2	8	1	8	3
Salinas	High	7	6	7	5	5	8	6	4

Sources: See table 3-1.

A New Financial Crisis

On December 1, 1994, Ernesto Zedillo took office as the new president of Mexico. Twenty days later the Mexican financial markets were in trouble. Three months after that, the Mexican economy was heading toward its largest recession since 1932. The factors behind this collapse were so many and sometimes so bizarre that the following brief synopsis can seem occasionally like the script of an operetta.

Promise of Foreign Investment

To understand what happened next to the Mexican economy, it is necessary to pause over a key worldwide development that started in the late 1980s: the renaissance of private, nonbank foreign investment. From Mexico to India, from China to even Cuba, the phrase "foreign investment" began flowing from the lips of policy makers with a fervor of alchemists close to a major discovery. Equally remarkable is that, unlike what happened in the 1970s, the developing world welcomed foreign capital in all forms, from foreign direct investment to portfolio investment in stock markets. Furthermore, the sharp increase in demand for capital was partially fulfilled by the suppliers: about three-fourths of the long-term investment to the developing world is now private, although the growth in private capital flows to less developed countries has recently subsided (from 55 percent of annual growth in 1993 to 9 percent in 1994).

However, as optimism about Latin American economic prospects rapidly transformed into euphoria, Mexico came to depend too heavily on sales of short-term government bonds to foreigners. By the end of 1993, this type of debt to foreigners accounted for over $21 billion, with 70 percent of it coming from sales of peso-denominated treasury bills, Cetes. During 1994, though, foreign (and domestic) investors started to change the composition of their bond portfolio toward the so-called Tesobonos, bonds denominated in Mexican pesos but pegged to the prevailing peso-dollar exchange rate as a way to protect against exchange risk. When Salinas left office at the end of November 1994, Tesobonos accounted for about 70 percent of the roughly $24 billion owed to foreign short-term bond holders. These highly speculative and volatile forms of investment can represent a high risk for an economy that grows too dependent on them. This rather obvious fact was painfully evident during the 1994–95 Mexican financial crisis.

A Rebellion and Two Assassinations

On January 1, 1994, the precise day when NAFTA went into effect and eleven months from the end of the Salinas administration, a peasant uprising began in the southern highlands of the state of Chiapas. That day, hundreds of masked natives of Maya descent, the poorest of the poor, boldly occupied several cities to demand better economic and social conditions. The Chiapas uprising was a public relations debacle for the Salinas administration. The charismatic leadership of the Ejército Zapatista de Liberación Nacional (EZLN), under Subcomandante Marcos, fired the imagination of a segment of the Mexican population.[111]

But the shocks to the Mexican political system did not stop there. Almost three months after the uprising, on March 23, Luis Donaldo Colosio, the PRI presidential candidate in the upcoming elections, was assassinated. The murder was alleged to have been committed by a lonely and deranged man, although other hypotheses point to a conspiracy. After Colosio's death, Salinas hurriedly handpicked Ernesto Zedillo, a Ph.D. in economics from Yale with no charisma and little political background, as the new PRI candidate.

Helped by a still growing economy, Zedillo won the presidential election on August 21 with 50.2 percent of the valid votes. That magnitude was large enough to appease most of the opposition, and the renewed stability was only slightly shaken when a month later, on September 28, José Francisco Ruiz Massieu, the new PRI secretary and a self-described political reformer, was assassinated. But the worst was to come, and the next and decisive blow to the system would be financial.

Beginning of the Financial Crisis

As political events unfolded, foreign reserves, which had attained a respectable peak of about $29 billion by the end of February 1994 (the EZLN uprising in January notwithstanding), started a toboggan ride down. After the killing of Colosio in March, the reserves suffered a fast and continuous depletion of more than $10 billion in less than a month, forcing Mexico to ask for help from the U.S. Treasury, which opened a six billion dollar line of credit to prop up the peso. To compound the problem, an unexpected rise in U.S. interest rates took place over 1994: the average of the three-month T-bill rate went from 3.02 percent to 5.64 percent between January and December.

Given those factors, the central bank had lost $13 billion by July. That figure included several billion dollars used in active interventions when the number of pesos per dollar in the foreign exchange market exceeded a certain threshold. (The peso had been allowed to float inside an exchange rate band whose ceiling and floor were daily adjusted by a preannounced depreciation rate.)

The situation appeared to improve after the presidential elections in August, and the reserves did not change much immediately after the killing of Ruiz Massieu at the end of September. However, after the prosecutor of the case resigned in November 23, alleging the complicity of PRI bosses in the killing, a new drop of several billion dollars ensued in the next few days. Thus, when Zedillo came to

111. A good reference in English to the armed movement is Alma Guillermoprieto, "The Shadow War," *New York Review of Books,* March 2, 1995, pp. 34–43.

office at the beginning of December, foreign reserves were at about $10 billion, almost one-third of its peak nine months earlier. The stage was ready for a final run on the peso. And the new government did not wait long to provide a reason for it.

Immediately after taking office, President Zedillo sent signals that he was considering a military option in the case of the EZLN rebellion. As a response, the rebels started a swift advance that allowed them by December 18 to take possession of dozens of villages. Predictably, the next day Zedillo got the news from the new finance minister Jaime Serra Puche that the prospect of further trouble in Chiapas had prompted investors to move about one billion dollars out of Mexico in a single day, that the peso had reached the exchange rate band ceiling, and that the stock market had gone down more than 4 percent.

That same night, at 10:00 p.m., a meeting was convened for the signing of an "addendum" to the Pacto para el Bienestar, la Estabilidad y el Crecimiento, the Pact for Welfare, Stability and Growth, the last of the series of economic pacts that, as noted earlier, had been renewed from time to time since the late 1980s. In that meeting, Serra told the private sector representatives that the government was considering stopping central bank intervention in the exchange market, allowing the peso to fall an estimated 15 percent. But, after an arduous debate that lasted hours, it was agreed instead on widening the exchange rate band by increasing its ceiling by 15 percent. The next day, foreign reserves fell by about $3 billion. As a consequence, a new pact meeting had to be held a day later to announce that the central bank would let the peso freely float.

Another Pact and a Rescue Plan

A new pact, Acuerdo de Unidad para Superar la Emergencia Económica, the Unity Agreement to Overcome the Economic Emergency, was unveiled on January 3, 1995. This pact involved the free flotation of the peso and a cut in government spending. It also contemplated the future privatization of railroads and ports and the opening of the banking system to complete foreign ownership. Weeks later, the privatization of PEMEX's secondary petrochemical production and gas distribution was also announced.

The plan also included the provision of a line of credit of $18 billion extended by the U.S. Treasury ($9 billion), the Canadian government (about $1 billion), other members of the Bank for International Settlements ($5 billion), and some foreign commercial banks ($3 billion). Most of the credit was to be used to finance the repayments of Tesobonos, of which the amount outstanding was then about $29 billion.

On the next Monday, January 9, after the Banco de México increased short-term interest rates on domestic bonds to 50 percent, the Mexican stock market suffered a 6.7 percent loss, and the central bank had to ask the intervention of the central banks in United States and Canada to support the peso. But the consequent gain of 7.7 percent in the peso value was quickly lost a day later when there was a decline of 8.1 percent. During that same day, the exchanges in Argentina and Brazil had losses of more than 9 percent. This was the most dramatic example of what was becoming known as the "tequila effect." This picturesque term was first coined in South America, after the Argentinean and Brazilian financial markets started to suffer the indirect consequences of the devaluation in Mexico. Since both of these countries had been using the dollar exchange rate as a nominal anchor to control inflation, private investors in the industrialized world saw them as the next trouble spots.[112]

It only took a week after Zedillo's announcement of the new pact for everybody to realize that the Mexican economy was not going to survive without either a moratorium or a larger injection of dollars. Thus, U.S. President Bill Clinton was forced on January 12 to announce the possibility of a new package of U.S. loan guarantees for as much as $40 billion. But in less than a week, Clinton faced a revolt from both Republicans and Democrats against the package. On January 30, the Mexican stock market then plunged again to its lowest level in more than a year, and the peso dropped to 6.35 pesos to the dollar, a devaluation of about 85 percent from before the crisis. On the same day, several U.S. senators made known that the aid package would not pass the Senate, despite the announcement that it had the bipartisan backing of three former presidents, six former secretaries of state, five former secretaries of the Treasury, and six former secretaries of commerce. At 11:30 that night, President Clinton changed plans.

A New Package, and Some New Mistakes

On January 31, Clinton, bypassing the U.S. Congress, announced a new $51 billion rescue plan for Mexico. The plan extended the U.S. Treasury line of credit to $20 billion, by means of the Exchange Rate Stabilization Fund. It also included a $10 billion increase in the IMF standby agreement announced a week earlier, for a new total of $17.8 billion. Also, the pledge made on January 3 by the Bank for International Settlements was doubled to $10 billion, and the $3 billion promised by the commercial banks was reaffirmed.

The $20 billion pledge was controversial in the U.S. Congress. After all, it committed four-fifths of the entire U.S. Exchange Rate Stabilization Fund. But the $10 billion increase in the IMF standby agreement was even more contentious

---

112. It is also interesting to record that the "tequila effect" not only affected financial markets in the Americas but also the market for neoliberal economists: "Shame of the Technocrats," read the January 16 cover of *Newsweek* (international ed.). That phrase probably sounded quite strange to the many academics who just a few years earlier had been celebrating the arrival of economics Ph.D.s to Latin American cabinets. See, for instance, the witty paper by John Williamson, "In Search of a Manual for Technopols," in John Williamson, ed., *The Political Economy of Policy Reform* (Washington: Institute for International Economics, 1994), pp. 11–28.

among IMF members, given that the initial proposal of $7.8 billion was already a record. Although the IMF board accepted the increase the day after Clinton's announcement, some European nations abstained from approving the increase, as a silent protest against not being consulted. Since the IMF credit could not, in principle, be larger than $7.2 billion, roughly the dollar equivalent of 300 percent of the Mexican quota in special drawing rights, the European representatives expressed concern that the United States was dangerously bending the institutional rules. In the end, the IMF directors pulled out of the hat an "exceptional clause" that allowed the extra amount. A few days later, the Group of Seven industrialized countries publicly endorsed the plan.

Predictably enough, the day after Clinton's announcement, the Mexican stock market bounced back by more than 10 percent, although foreign reserves were just about $3.5 billion, and the amount of Tesobonos still circulating was nearly $24 billion (roughly $14 billion in the hands of foreigners). With the bailout, everything suddenly seemed to go right: the World Bank announced it would lend $2 billion to Mexico during 1995 to strengthen its financial system, advise on the new rally of privatizations, and support poverty alleviation programs, and the IMF disbursed $7.8 billion from its line of credit.

A Chain of Mishaps

Soon after negotiations with the United States over the terms of the financial rescue plan, President Zedillo went on national television to announce that he had ordered the arrest of the EZLN leaders, after disclosing their presumed identities. The move did not succeed: the rebels hid in the jungle, and more than one hundred thousand Mexicans immediately took to the streets in repudiation of the government while chanting "All of us are Marcos."

By mid-February, Zedillo was backing away from his verbal attacks on the EZLN, and the initial euphoria in the Mexican markets was abating. At last, on February 21, the three-week-long bargaining session between Mexican and U.S. officials on the terms of the bailout plan was concluded. The foremost condition, in Mexican eyes, was that which required foreign buyers of Mexican oil to send payments to a special account in the Federal Reserve Bank of New York in case Mexico were to stop repayments of the loan. Although the use of Mexican oil as collateral went back to 1982, the novelty in 1995 was that *all* the oil revenue had to be deposited in the United States, regardless of whether or not there was a breach of contract. Other loan conditions called for Mexico to follow a stringent monetary policy, to realize a fiscal budgetary surplus in 1995, and to publish some key economic indicators, including the main items of the central bank's balance sheet, weekly; before, the central bank revealed only the amount of foreign reserves and only thrice a year.

ON HOW NOT TO PLAY POKER. The financial bailout was regarded in the United States as a defense of the neoliberal economic policies that Mexico and other Latin American countries had espoused in the 1990s. According to the director of the Washington-based Institute for International Economics, a Mexican financial collapse would have tempted other countries to revert "to the discredited managed-economy policies of the past . . . [which] would of course be extremely adverse to the interest of the U.S."[113] Yet, the terms of the agreement were greeted with great resentment and skepticism in Mexico: on the day of the announcement, the peso fell 4 percent against the dollar, the interest rate on domestic bonds rose 2.5 percent, and the stock market lost 4.9 percent of its value.

Why did the Mexican government show so much docility while negotiating the loan terms? As in other instances, the answer seems to lie in the poker players. Responding to several economists (inside and outside Mexico) who wanted the government unilaterally to extend the maturity of the Tesobonos so that they could be repaid over a much longer period, Zedillo publicly declared that a debt moratorium would only hurt Mexico. At one point he claimed, based on unknown arguments, that a moratorium could cause a drop in GDP of up to 30 percent.

Two New Pacts

Paralleling the rapid decline of Mexico's economic fortunes was that of the principal architect of these policies, Carlos Salinas. Following the arrest of his brother Raúl on February 28, who was accused of masterminding the murder of PRI Secretary Ruiz Massieu, Salinas launched a hunger strike and soon had to go into an exile.

Naturally, the turbulence of the Salinas family saga seized the economy as well. By March 9, the peso had fallen to 7.5 pesos per dollar, a devaluation of 120 percent since Zedillo came to office. That night, the Mexican government finally disclosed the long-awaited adjustment plan negotiated with the U.S. Treasury and the IMF. Perhaps the only true novelty of the pact was its Orwellian doublespeak: Programa de Acción para Reforzar el Acuerdo de Unidad para Superar la Emergencia Económica—the Action Program to Reinforce the Unity Agreement to Overcome the Economic Emergency. Its content was very much as expected, since the agreement with the U.S. Treasury already had as conditions some new measures, while the rest were typical of most IMF stabilization programs.

As the U.S. Treasury and IMF credits were religiously used to pay back the debt in Tesobonos, the financial markets settled down for the next six months. Better than expected export performance, coupled with substantial import compression, also helped; they allowed Mexico to effect a trade surplus by the first quarter of 1995. Finally, the initiation of a peace dialogue between the government and the EZLN in April calmed nerves.

By October, however, the markets suffered a new upset, although by then practically all the Tesobonos had been paid. Thus, the government was forced to

113. C. Fred Bergsten, quoted in *Time* (international ed.), March 6, 1995, p. 14.

announce a new pact at the end of that month in the hope of reviving the economy through tax deductions and fiscal incentives to enterprises hiring more workers. At the root of the new turmoil was the cold fact that the economy had in 1995 its largest recession in memory, with an annual drop in real GDP of 6.9 percent. The adjustment, it was now clear, had been too severe.[114] To end with the saddest note of the drama, around one and a half million workers lost their jobs in the formal sector during 1995.

AND THE WORLD BANK? The main contribution of the World Bank during the crisis was to help, with the IDB, to capitalize the Fondo Bancario de Protección al Ahorro (FOBAPROA), an insurance banking fund created in 1990, which served as the conduit for an emergency capitalization program for the banking sector, called Programa de Capitalización Temporal. The FOBAPROA was urgently needed since the commercial banks faced a sharp increase in nonperforming assets, due to both bad lending practices and sharp hikes in interest rates; as such, the government had to rescue the entire financial sector.

The Bank contributed not only by extending a loan of more than $1 billion but also by helping to diagnose the health of the financial system and to reform the accounting standards and prudential regulations for banks. As noted earlier, the Bank had already provided to the Mexican government a financial sector adjustment loan in June 1989 that lasted until June 1993, with obviously inadequate results.

AND THE CASSANDRAS? Contrary to the crisis of 1982 recounted earlier, the new crisis did not take all people by surprise. As far back as 1992, several academics were warning about the current account deficit, which that year had reached an historic high of 7 percent of GDP. In fact, by the end of 1992 the deficit was very likely unsustainable without a change in macroeconomic policies.[115]

The political opposition also supplied a few Cassandras. For instance, the two main opponents to Zedillo in the presidential race, Cuauhtémoc Cárdenas and Diego Fernández de Cevallos, both warned about the risk of an overvalued exchange rate. In Cárdenas's first economic speech as a candidate, he was so close to forecasting what happened fifteen months later that, as one observer noted, he failed only to give the precise day and hour of the crisis.[116] Similarly, Fernández de Cevallos's economic plan hung on the premise that a peso correction would be unavoidable after Salinas left office.

On the other hand, both the IMF and the U.S. government failed to acknowledge the gravity of the situation. The IMF's review of the Mexican economy in

114. See Carlos M. Urzúa, "Monetary Policy and the Exchange Rate," paper presented at the conference "Mexico: Assessing Neo-Liberal Reform," held at the University of London, London, December 1, 1995.

115. See Urzúa, "Monetary Policy and the Exchange Rate."

116. Adolfo Aguilar Zínser, ¡Vamos a ganar! La pugna de Cuauhtémoc Cárdenas por el poder (Mexico City: Oceano, 1995), pp. 360–64.

February 1994 does not contain any hint of a possible financial crisis, or even of the eventual need to adjust the exchange rate. This failure, from an organization designed to anticipate problems in countries' external accounts, is quite worrisome. The U.S. government failed, according to a critic of the Clinton administration, to recognize the seriousness of the problem even after receiving a series of signals and warnings. Already by March 1994, the U.S. Treasury had had to open a line of credit for Mexico. Furthermore, the Central Intelligence Agency was sending warnings about the Mexican economic situation by the spring of 1994. There were even internal U.S. Treasury documents on the subject being circulated a bit later.[117]

Interestingly, the World Bank *did* have some misgivings about the Mexican economic situation as early as the beginning of 1993. This is shown in an aide memoire written after a mission that took place in January 1993:

> The high [Mexican] current account deficit would be less of a concern if it could be traced primarily to a rise in domestic investment, rather than to a fall in domestic savings. . . . The economy is now dependent on high levels of foreign capital inflows, which are subject to often rapid shifts in expectations. . . . Whether it will be possible to work out of this situation with little cost is not clear. . . . All this suggests that the Government should consider allowing further exchange rate flexibility, which could be best achieved through a widening of the band.[118]

Given the varied perceptions that individuals and institutions held about the Mexican economy from 1992 to 1994, were there factors that misled observers? One factor could have been Salinas's undeniable political skills, which caused such euphoria in some foreign circles. Another could have been the way in which the Mexican government hid information, even from its own citizens, a dramatic example being the concealment of the deficit of financial intermediaries (with Nacional Financiera the prime example) in 1993 and 1994. By that means, the government was able to overspend on the back of its citizens, especially during the election year (1994). Finally, foreign observers may have overestimated the independence of the central bank, perhaps taking too seriously the fact that the Banco de México became nominally autonomous in April 1994.

Concluding Remarks

As interesting as the most recent economic events in Mexico are, relations between the World Bank and Mexico have evolved over the last five decades and gone through several stages. As is apparent from the chapter, the first stage took place during the twenty-five-year period from 1946 to the end of the 1960s.

117. A. M. Rosenthal, "Cover-Up Chronology," *New York Times*, April 4, 1995, p. A25.
118. World Bank, "Aide Memoire: Mexico Private Sector Assessment Study," unpublished paper (Washington: World Bank, 1993), pp. 3–4.

Regarding that period, Mason and Asher claim, in their classic book on the Bank written in the early 1970s: "In a country like Mexico, which has made excellent economic progress and has received substantial assistance from the Bank, some believe that the progress was due almost exclusively to Mexico's firm adherence to policies it considered appropriate rather than to the regular flow of loans and advice."[119] This is true, except for the assertion that Mexico received "substantial assistance from the Bank." As noted earlier, almost all of the Bank's sectoral loans were used for just two purposes: electrical power development and irrigation projects. And although the World Bank did produce several high-quality reports on the Mexican economy, the fact is that the Bank had little influence on the economic policies undertaken during the period.

The second stage in the relationship developed during the first part of the 1970s. The similarity of views on economic issues, such as the need to attack rural poverty, between McNamara's Bank and the Echeverría government led to a series of interesting and diverse joint projects. Those fruitful relations could have continued under the López Portillo administration had oil not come onto the scene. Once the Mexican government started to borrow from private commercial banks in the Eurodollar market, a new phase in the relationship developed—one in which the government, out of a genuine regard for the Bank, continued to pursue several sectoral projects jointly, but also one in which the role of the Bank as a policy interlocutor became almost negligible.

After the debt crisis of 1982, a new, much closer association developed. During the de la Madrid administration, particularly from 1984 to 1988, the World Bank continuously widened its policy dialogue with Mexico. This was a consequence of the introduction of structural adjustment loans and Mexico's need for fresh loans. During this period, the Bank was a key factor in several reforms made by the Mexican government, including the important trade liberalization of 1985. Furthermore, in the second half of the 1980s, the World Bank shed its passive role regarding the developing-country debt crisis and became an active player in devising debt reduction mechanisms later used by the government.

The apogee of the relationship occurred during the Salinas administration. During those years, the Mexican government and the World Bank engaged in an open policy dialogue on almost all major economic issues, with dozens of Bank staff working in Mexico at various points. The level of the Bank's involvement in several reforms of the period was quite high, although the outcomes were varied. Examples range from a successful collaboration during the negotiations to secure debt and debt service reductions from private banks, to an association in the controversial PRONASOL, to a joint effort to improve the prudential regulation of the financial sector.

119. Edward S. Mason and Robert E. Asher, *The World Bank since Bretton Woods* (Brookings, 1973), p. 648.

The final phase of the relationship between the World Bank and Mexico came with the financial crisis at the end of 1994. The resources needed to overcome that crisis pushed the IMF and the U.S. Treasury to the fore and in 1995 the role of the World Bank was reduced to the channeling of funds to save the Mexican financial system. Given the amount of funds required to do so (more than 5 percent of GDP was spent in 1995), it is likely that a good part of the Bank's loans will be allocated to that end in the next few years.

Finally, what will the next century bring to the relationship between the World Bank and Mexico? It is difficult to say, given that Mexico will be an entirely different country. Not only will the economic crisis have brought significant policy changes by then, but the authoritarianism that has ruled Mexico for so many decades will likely disappear. The nature of the new political system will be the most important determinant in future Bank-Mexico relations. This probably means that the days of fast, sweeping economic reforms is gone and that the Bank will be dealing with a more diverse set of political and social groups. Despite the challenges such pluralism will pose, there is strong evidence that the new political reality in Mexico represents a step forward: as the Mexican history has repeatedly shown, it is risky to leave all important decisions in the hands of just a few.

FOUR

The World Bank and Côte d'Ivoire

Jacques Pégatiénan and Bakary Ouayogode

WHEN the World Bank began its intervention in independent Côte d'Ivoire, in June 1968, most international opinion subscribed to the view that Black Africa, politically independent since the early 1960s, was off to a bad start on its journey toward economic development. Only one country, Côte d'Ivoire, appeared to escape this gloomy verdict, to such an extent that its achievement, which long remained unparalleled, was termed the "Ivorian miracle." In the mid-1970s, at the time of Ivorian economic prosperity and ten years after it first criticized the policies of the young Black African independent nations, the World Bank made an in-depth study of Côte d'Ivoire and concluded that the nation's success, far from being attributable to good luck, as some had suggested, was actually the result of the prudent policies of a government that stubbornly and consistently was able to extract the greatest benefits from market opportunities.[1]

The Bank was unrestrained in its optimism about this exemplary economy's future, which was expected to show great promise once certain structural problems created by past successes had been attended to. But to everyone's surprise, the crisis that began in Sub-Saharan Africa in the early 1980s did not spare the showcase country. Indeed, Côte d'Ivoire has been so affected by this prolonged crisis that it can be wondered if there is hope for recovery. Given the Bank's reputation, it is somewhat surprising that it should have been so mistaken about the

1. Bastiaan A. den Tuinder and World Bank, *Ivory Coast, the Challenge of Success: Report of a Mission Sent to the Ivory Coast by the World Bank* (Johns Hopkins University Press, 1978).

strength of the Ivorian economy. This chapter traces the stages of Ivorian economic decline and evaluates the impact that relations between the World Bank and the government of Côte d'Ivoire have had on these developments.

Overview and Characteristics of the Ivorian Economy

The Ivorian economy is dominated by agriculture; coffee and cocoa are its principal exports. For almost two decades after independence Côte d'Ivoire enjoyed vigorous and sustained economic growth, until 1978.[2] From 1969 to 1973 annual real economic growth was strong (7.2 percent), inflation weak (4.0 percent); the balance of payments showed a slight excess, which represented 0.3 percent of the gross domestic product (GDP), and the state budget (minus public enterprises) had a surplus equaling 6.1 percent of GDP. The economy's savings rate was higher than its investment rate, with most of the excess accruing to the private sector.

In 1974–75 real economic growth (6.5 percent) was barely affected by the first oil price shock resulting from a ban on oil exports imposed by Arab producers. Subsequent domestic inflation occurred because of a simultaneous increase in coffee and cocoa quotations. However, the balance of payments deteriorated, posting a deficit of 0.07 percent of GDP, compared with the previous period's surplus. The state budget showed a deficit equal to 4.7 percent of GDP. Total investment exceeded savings, but the savings shortfall was all in the public sector: the public deficit equaled 10.2 percent of GDP, whereas the excess of private savings over investment represented 9.1 percent of GDP.

In 1976–77 the economy revived with an unparalleled real growth rate (16 percent) and inflation rate (16 percent), caused by a surge of coffee and cocoa on the world market. The excess in the balance of payments amounted to 1.3 percent of GDP, and the government budget surplus stood at 0.4 percent. The most striking characteristic of this spurt was that the investment rate went from 6.0 percent in 1974–75 to 11.0 percent in 1976–77, financed in part by the exceptional revenues of the Stabilization Fund, but especially by external public borrowing, which went from 5.2 percent of GDP in 1974–75 to 11.0 percent in 1976–77. In effect, the financial surplus of the Stabilization Fund served as security for the debt expansion. The private sector again saved more than it invested, the surplus representing 10.22 percent of GDP. The ability of the country to attract sufficient capital to finance its current account deficit would decline after 1977.

The 1976–77 boom in raw materials was brief. Export markets began to deteriorate in 1978, and in 1979 the inflationary effects of the second oil price shock aggravated the decline in the terms of trade. By 1980 servicing the debt that

2. Data here and in the two following paragraphs are from Hiey Jacques Pégatiénan, "The Sources of Economic Growth in Côte d'Ivoire: Preliminary Results," National University of Côte d'Ivoire, Abidjan, Faculty of Economic Sciences and CIRES, 1992.

Table 4-1. *Côte d'Ivoire's Macroeconomic Evolution, 1970–90*
Percent

Indicator	Pre-adjustment, 1970–79	Adjustment period, 1980–87	Post-adjustment, 1988–90
Central government fiscal balance	–4.7	–7.3	–12.7
Current account balance (percent of GDP in current U.S. dollars)	–6.9	–9.2	–10.0
Real GDP growth rate	6.8	0.9	–1.9
Gross domestic savings (percent of GDP in current prices)	27.4	20.5	14.2
Gross domestic investment (percent of GDP in current prices)	24.1	18.4	11.8
Annual inflation rate (Consumer Price Index)	11.7	6.3	7.0
Total external debt (percent of GDP)	30.7	101.4	141.4
Net foreign assets in months of imports (Central Bank)	1.2	–4.0	–5.6

Source: World Bank, "World Bank Structural and Sectoral Adjustment Operations: The Second OED Overview," Report 10870, June 30, 1992, annex 3, statistical tables.

had been contracted during the boom years had become extremely painful. The government turned toward the international financial institutions.

Between 1981 and 1986 several adjustment programs supported by the International Monetary Fund (IMF) and the World Bank were put into place in Côte d'Ivoire. Although the nation's internal and external imbalances were somewhat relieved, by 1983 economic growth had not revived. The sharper reduction of the imbalance in 1984 and 1985 can be credited to a marked reduction in public spending and an improvement in international prices. But the amelioration was brief; in 1987 commodity prices deteriorated further, to the point of causing the government to suspend payments on its debt in May 1987. Since that time the state's financial crisis has kept the economy on the brink of paralysis. The economy's internal problems (a declining real growth rate and a large and widening budget deficit) and external problems (growing balance of payments deficits and rising debt) have persisted since the beginning of the adjustment period (see table 4-1). Even inflation has remained at roughly the same rate.

The Ivorian economy can be summarized by six structural characteristics. First, the state has been a lever for investment. Until the crisis at the end of the 1970s, massive public investment acted as a magnet for private investment and foreign capital, owing to a constant improvement of the physical infrastructure, which helped to increase the return on private investment. Unfortunately, public investment became less and less productive and generated decreasing hard currency, yet became increasingly costly. It also led to the country's becoming massively indebted.

Second, the cost of living is high in Côte d'Ivoire because of high production and transaction costs, which make Ivorian products less competitive both internally and externally. The principal reasons for the high cost of living are high fiscal rates (a value-added tax and a tax on services), which affect both production and external commerce; overvaluation of the CFA franc; and massive use of European workers who cost three times more than they would in Europe.[3] European workers represent about 3 percent of the modern work force, but receive about 40 percent of the Ivorian wage bill in the modern, private nonagricultural sector.

Third, the massive presence of Europeans and European technical assistance has imposed external consumption and architectural norms on the country. Furthermore, the management requirements that this foreign presence raises exceed the current capacities of the Ivorians. This situation has increased production and transaction costs.

A fourth characteristic is that Côte d'Ivoire devotes about 40 percent of its budget to education—a world record. However, it is also a country where technical and financial control of the system of production is concentrated in the hands of expatriates, with adverse cost effects. The economic inefficiency of educational investment constitutes an important problem.

Fifth, the country lacks an efficient mechanism for internalizing foreign technology aimed at reducing production and transaction costs. In this context, opening the economy to constant external technological progress and massive use of high-cost foreign production methods weakens its competitiveness and makes it difficult for Ivorian nationals to master the process of growth.

The sixth characteristic is that institutional mechanisms for planning, control of public spending, and public investment selection are neither transparent nor rigorous. The main reason for this defect almost certainly has been the total absence of a counterweight at the level of political decisionmaking.

Overview of World Bank Intervention

The financial weight of the World Bank in Côte d'Ivoire can be measured in relation to the country's gross domestic product and volume of investment, on the one hand, and in relation to France, the privileged partner of Côte d'Ivoire, on the other. It was only in 1974 that the volume of the Bank's intervention became important. Between 1976 and 1980 the uneven evolution of Bank commitments most likely reflected hesitation on the part of the government, or the Bank itself, at a time when the country had contracted many debts, but when the government was financially secure enough to avoid implementing the Bank's recommendations. After 1981 the financial support of the Bank was considerably reinforced, with

3. World Bank, "Ivory Coast Industrial Sector: Back to Office Report," December 27, 1979.

Table 4-2. *Evolution of World Bank Lending in Côte d'Ivoire, 1954–91*
Millions of U.S. dollars, unless otherwise specified

Sector	1954–80		1981–91		Total	
	Dollars	Percent	Dollars	Percent	Dollars	Percent
Agriculture and forestry	161.9	28.0	135.8	6.3	297.7	10.9
Mines and industry	116.3	20.1	131.5	6.1	247.8	9.1
Infrastructure, water and wastes, and environment	257.8	44.6	432.4	20.1	690.2	25.2
Education and health	42.2	7.3	24.4	1.1	66.6	2.4
Structural and sectoral adjustment	. . .[a]	. . .[a]	1,432.2	66.4	1,432.2	52.4
Total	578.2	21.1	2,156.3	78.9	2,734.5	100.0

Source: Authors' calculations based on World Bank data.
a. Not applicable.

important interruptions in 1984 and 1988 when no lending occurred. In the first case, the interruption seems to have reflected an improved economic situation following the Bank's first structural adjustment loan (SAL) to the country; in the second, the absence of lending represented deep discord between the Bank and the government over the appropriate—indeed, even acceptable—macroeconomic framework.

The measure of Côte d'Ivoire's borrowings from the World Bank is also a measure of the banking risk the Bank has accepted. Both the borrowing and the risk-taking became serious in Côte d'Ivoire's period of crisis after 1980. Of the Bank's total lending up to 1994, only 21 percent occurred in the period before 1980.

The Bank's annual input over the 1969–90 period represented on the average 1.22 times that of the French government, Côte d'Ivoire's principal bilateral partner. But this average hides large shifts; thus, before adjustment, the Bank's input represented only 0.77 times that of France, whereas with structural adjustment the ratio of Bank transfers to those from France rose to 1.84.[4]

As to areas of intervention, before the period of adjustment in the 1980s the bulk of the Bank's financing (about 45 percent) was directed to the infrastructure sector; agriculture and forestry took second place (28 percent), and industry was third (20 percent) (see table 4-2). The social sector (education and health) was obviously not a priority for the Bank, whereas for the Côte d'Ivoire it always maintained a high priority. With adjustment, Bank financing went more toward policy-based adjustment lending (66.4 percent) than individual projects. Yet even during adjustment 20 percent of the Bank's financing continued to be aimed at infrastructure. Agriculture, however, lost importance as the preferred sector for

4. Authors' calculations based on UN Development Programme data.

individual projects (6 percent). In the cumulative totals of Bank financing in Côte d'Ivoire, one quarter of overall lending has gone to infrastructure and about half of the total to structural adjustment.

To the extent that loan allocations are an indication of the Bank's policies, while at the same time reflecting creditworthiness considerations, it is clear that during the country's period of prosperity before 1980 the Bank actively participated in the promotion of public investment as the vehicle for Ivorian growth. Furthermore, the importance of agriculture in the Bank's portfolio indicated that the government's agricultural policy was accepted by the Bank. Because that policy was largely implemented by state enterprises, it is evident that the Bank actively contributed to the rise of public enterprise and the consolidation of state intervention. From 1980, at the time of crisis, the Bank abruptly seemed to change its institutional mind, indicting public investment and public enterprise as the major internal causes of the country's economic and financial disarray. This change in doctrine has been one of the points of contention in the ongoing dialogue between the Bank and the Ivorian government.

World Bank intervention in Côte d'Ivoire dates back to 1954, during the colonial era. Côte d'Ivoire joined the Bank on March 11, 1963, and the Bank's first report on the Ivorian economy was made public on April 30, 1963. The Bank's regional office in Abidjan opened in April 1965, and the first loan in the independence era was granted on June 21, 1968. The dialogue between the Bank and the Côte d'Ivoire government became livelier in the early 1970s. Its evolution thereafter can be divided into six phases: the first ended around 1976, the second spread over the 1977–80 period, the third covered 1981–86, the fourth lasted from 1987 to November 1990, the fifth began with the nomination of the first prime minister of independent Côte d'Ivoire, on November 30, 1990, and the sixth began at the end of 1993 with the death of President Felix Houphouët-Boigny, a change of prime ministers, and the long anticipated and long resisted devaluation of the CFA franc.

During the country's early period, when it was widely celebrated for what it could produce through capitalism and the clever implementation of appropriate and sustained economic policies, the Bank approved the financing of thirty or more Ivorian projects, while voicing policy advice. But before the Bank made its first loan to independent Côte d'Ivoire in 1968, it was already skeptical of the extreme optimism that President Houphouët-Boigny and his collaborators shared about the country's creditworthiness and potential for development. Specifically, the Bank was worried by the government's preoccupation with urban infrastructure in its public investments (notably in Abidjan), and by the very optimistic projections of future growth rates (on the scale of 6 percent) made in the 1965–69 five-year plan.[5] In regard to the latter, the Bank noted that "considering the formidable obstacles to rapid growth, it seemed unrealistic for Ivory Coast to base its development plan-

5. Letter of Mr. Jentgen, November 25, 1962, in World Bank, Côte d'Ivoire country files, 1960–82, Abidjan (hereafter cited as World Bank, Côte d'Ivoire country files).

ning, now in process, on the expectation that a 6 percent rate of economic growth could be realized."[6]

The Bank's refusal, in November 1965, to finance the Kossou hydroelectric dam in the Bandama Valley because of the project's potentially weak economic profitability, "seriously strained relations" between the Bank and the government of Côte d'Ivoire.[7] Thereafter the Bank perceived in the government's attitude toward the Bank a "coolness and disinterest, if not to say rudeness, which found its climax in the way Mr. Knapp was received by the Minister of Finance."[8] Reciprocally, the Bank's attitude was interpreted by President Houphouët-Boigny as disinterest on the part of the Bank in Côte d'Ivoire's development. In 1968 Houphouët-Boigny was to write to World Bank president Robert S. McNamara that "it is with attention and profound interest that I have personally followed the state of our relations with the World Bank Group. I must say that after several years of inaction, your institutions have recently become interested in my country's fate."[9]

After the Bank granted its first loan to Côte d'Ivoire in 1968, to finance a road in the east of the country linking Abengourou to Agnibilékrou, relations became more relaxed, especially with a visit by McNamara. But this did not prevent the Bank from continuing to criticize the government for the size of its development program and the mechanisms employed to allocate public resources. For the first time, on September 15, 1970, the Bank formally addressed its comments to President Houphouët-Boigny, who interpreted them as strong criticism of his bold economic policies. It was noted that although "formulated in moderate terms, the World Bank's letter constitutes a firm warning before the implementation of our plan."[10] The next year, when the Bank cited problems of financial disequilibria and over-leveraging, these criticisms received so little attention from the government that the Bank wondered about its own readiness and capacity to penalize future disregard of its advice; the question was raised of "whether the Bank would be ready to employ sanctions of whatever kind should the government persist in a policy of overextending itself."[11] At the same time, the Bank recognized that it was difficult to apply sanctions against a winning country, too often vindicated by events: "It was not easy to take a firm line with a country whose performance hitherto had been good."[12]

6. Minutes of a staff Economic Committee meeting on the economy of the Ivory Coast, February 25, 1963, in World Bank, Côte d'Ivoire country files.

7. Mr. El Emary, note to files, February 20, 1967, in World Bank, Côte d'Ivoire country files.

8. Note to files, June 1966, in World Bank, Côte d'Ivoire country files.

9. Felix Houphouët-Boigny to Robert S. McNamara, November 21, 1968, in World Bank, Côte d'Ivoire country files.

10. Xavier de la Renaudière to Roger Chaufournier, October 15, 1975, in World Bank, Côte d'Ivoire country files.

11. Minutes of an Economic Committee review of an Ivory Coast Country Program Paper, June 28, 1971, in World Bank, Côte d'Ivoire country files.

12. Ibid.

In 1972 the Bank perceived what it regarded as greater realism on the part of the government in its approach to the country's economic problems.[13] After the first oil price shock in 1974, however, the government seemed to renounce budgetary discipline, realistic investment programs, and a prudent use of public resources. During this period the Bank's recommendations concerned the problems and dangers that could be created by the speed of investment growth in relation to the availability of local taxes and savings, on the one hand, and to the need for drastic reductions in public spending on the other.[14] But the Bank noted its general inability to influence President Houphouët-Boigny's decisions on the nature, dimensions, and programming of any project. It also observed that there existed within the heart of the Ivorian administration a combination of great assurance and stubborn optimism that was attributable both to past successes and to the many previous gloomy and erroneous predictions by foreign observers.[15] Caught between the obstinate Ivorian administration and the economic problems Côte d'-Ivoire was exposed to, the Bank did not give up. But the tone of the alarm bells it continued to sound seemed slightly less confident and categorical than in the past:

> Total external debt has already increased from $424 million in 1970 to $1,529 million at the end of 1975, and with an annual growth rate of 30 percent per year, public debt is probably the fastest growing economic indicator in the country. This development presents serious dangers, and debt service already plays a major role in the deterioration of the balance of payments. . . . We are not excessively worried about these facts and trends. Ivory Coast has on many occasions proved to be capable of solving its problems and adapting to complex and difficult situations. We believe, nevertheless, that public investments envisaged for the next five year period (1976–80) have to be carefully selected and rationed to give priority to those that are most profitable.[16]

The Bank also noted that the ministers it was obliged to go through were not able to influence the president, who was the sole decision maker. It was observed that "the Minister [of Planning] is well aware of the overall problems and the need for determining the real priorities, but has not been able to convince the President, who seems to have a low regard for so-called experts and a firm belief that oil hidden under Ivorian territory will be found in the not-too-distant future."[17]

13. Cornelius Jansen to Roger Chaufournier, April 20, 1972, in World Bank, Côte d'Ivoire country files.
14. Luc de Wulf, IMF, to B. den Tuinder, International Bank for Reconstruction and Development (IBRD), April 15, 1975, in World Bank, Côte d'Ivoire country files; Burke Knapp to Robert McNamara, July 2, 1975, in World Bank, Côte d'Ivoire country files.
15. Luis de Azcarate to Roger Chaufournier, July 30, 1975, in World Bank, Côte d'Ivoire country files.
16. Burke Knapp to Felix Houphouët-Boigny, November 3, 1976, in World Bank, Côte d'Ivoire country files.
17. Bastiaan den Tuinder to Peter Eigen, December 9, 1976, in World Bank, Côte d'Ivoire country files.

In 1976 what had become the Bank's predictable macroeconomic diagnoses and recommendations were dismissed by the Ivorian economic administration as lacking technical rigor. Objecting to a Bank report, Minister of Finance Konan Bédié wrote that "finally, this document, extremely rich in information and analyses, does not to our eyes represent, in its composition as in certain details of its form, the rigor that would seem useful for it to have, given the authority that is given to the Bank's work."[18] As though to verify the validity of its criticisms, the Bank began a systematic study of the Ivorian economy that reflected the embarrassment it felt at advising change to a country whose policies recent events seemed to have vindicated. This 1978 study for the first time gathered in one place the analyses and recommendations the Bank had made since the beginning of its dialogue with the government of Côte d'Ivoire.[19]

Convinced of the correctness of its past policy choices as well as of its future prospects, the government did not at the time grant the attention that the criticisms and recommendations of the Bank warranted. The government was offended by the criticisms because the macroeconomic disequilibria were not worrisome in the short term; the country at the time disposed of sufficient means to enable it to mask obvious imbalances. Moreover, the financial weight of the Bank in the country's economy was not great enough to influence the course of events. In any case, the Bank's mode of intervention at the time—that is, support for individual projects and specific sectors—gave it little power to demand macroeconomic policy changes. Côte d'Ivoire and its government already had performed exceptionally well within a Black Africa that was arguably on the wrong path.

Despite the cold welcome its criticisms received, the Bank was convinced of the validity of its role as an independent economic adviser—the more so because in the Bank's opinion the large French technical assistance program, while competent, was biased by its own professional interests against pinpointing in a timely way problems created by the policies of its employer, the government.

In the face of the government's obstinacy, the Bank seemed resigned to letting Côte d'Ivoire incur the costs implicit in a bold and imprudent public investment policy. No other course seemed feasible in view of the surge in the coffee and cocoa market in 1976–77, which considerably improved the country's balance of payments, and of the discovery of oil in Côte d'Ivoire. These developments gave new hope to the country and new ambitions to President Houphouët-Boigny.

In the euphoria of the new financial rewards, Côte d'Ivoire did indeed become bolder; it initiated major public investment programs that had not been screened against rigorous economic criteria. This new laxness was aggravated by the govern-

18. Letter from Minister of Finance Konan Bédié to Robert S. McNamara objecting to the publication of the Basic Economic Report, December 16, 1976, in World Bank, Côte d'Ivoire country files.

19. See den Tuinder and World Bank, *Ivory Coast*.

ment's easy access to short-term supplier credits. The Bank contented itself with drawing the government's attention to the need to curb its expansive budgeting, which could only augment the country's debt burden.[20] The Bank also noted that despite the lack of economic rigor in the investment planning by public enterprises, the government was approving their external borrowings, even when the borrowers' projects promised to generate few financial resources.[21]

The unprecedented atmosphere of prosperity in the late 1970s made the administration slack, especially in industrial and commercial policy. The government was considerably weakened after 1975 by institutional changes associated with a ministerial reshuffling in 1976, and by corruption linked in part to the granting of import and export quotas for coffee, cocoa, and rice.[22]

At the end of 1979 and through 1980 the country began to feel the adverse effects of a drop in coffee and cocoa prices, as well as the effects of a second oil price shock, as it was more a consumer than a producer of oil. The Bank and the government differed over both the causes of this crisis and the necessary remedies. For a long time the Ivorian government chose to emphasize the external origins of the troubles, blaming speculation in raw materials on international markets. Yet the government did finally recognize the role played by poor internal management in public enterprises, among others. For its part, the Bank was consistent in its emphasis on Côte d'Ivoire's internal structural problems, and on the need for improved financial balance, external as well as internal. Among sectoral matters, the dialogue on agricultural policy was particularly difficult, with the government arguing that there was no need to change its policy course, and viewing the sectoral problems as mainly external.

The role and reform of the Stabilization Fund was a particular bone of contention between the Bank and the government. The Fund fixed the prices of principal export products—among them coffee and cocoa—for producers, and for a long time producer prices stayed below the international price received by the Stabilization Fund, which also acted as the vendor of Ivorian products on the international market. The difference between the international and producer prices was public revenue, transferred in part to the state budget and in part used to finance public investments. The management of the Stabilization Fund was under the exclusive authority of the president.

The Bank realized that the structural and institutional reforms it advocated—particularly those that would reduce the role of the state and alter the process of resource allocation—were neither easily accepted nor effectively implemented.[23] For its part, the government was neither convinced of the benefit of radical reforms

20. World Bank, "Country Program Paper: Ivory Coast," November 16, 1977.

21. World Bank, Ivory Coast economic memorandum, May 30, 1979.

22. World Bank, "Ivory Coast Industrial Sector: Back to Office Report," December 27, 1979.

23. World Bank, "Steering the Ivorian Economy toward Sustained Recovery," July 15, 1989.

nor prepared to cope with the social and political problems they might generate. (As will be seen, an example would arise in 1984 when the country's second structural adjustment loan would seek to simulate a devaluation of the CFA franc by simultaneously increasing import customs duties and export subsidies. Neither the administration nor the private sector could be persuaded of the efficacy of such a de facto devaluation.)

From 1980 onward, the Bank made changes in the development model whose virtues it had previously extolled and whose implementation it had supported financially. It now advocated state divestiture, privatization, and the liberalization of a commerce already considered open—all of which represented for the Ivorian administration new fads that might pass with the change of seasons. The new doctrines were seen as applicable everywhere, regardless of a given country's specific needs. In short, Ivorian government lenders saw the Bank as being driven by an ideological agenda.[24]

The Bank's change in tone precisely at the time when it became an indispensable source on the international financial market upset the Ivorian administration. Needing new money, the administration found itself obliged to accept policies in whose purpose it did not fully believe. Until 1983 the government could escape the Bank's requirements, and its remaining financial means still allowed for a margin of negotiation; but by 1987 this option had practically disappeared.[25]

Vigorous economic growth over a period of twenty years had fashioned the mentality and behavior of the Ivorians; for a long time they believed that their relatively easily acquired prosperity would be without limit or end. The thought of abruptly abandoning a model that seemed to foster growth caused fear and distress. The government's misgivings about the importance of the Bank-advocated reforms were all the more understandable in that the reforms were proposed toward the end of the long reign of President Houphouët-Boigny, whose tenure represented prosperity and stability to both Ivorians and the outside world.

At the end of 1986 there was still hope that Côte d'Ivoire would come out of its crisis, but shifts in the international market forced the government to suspend servicing of its external debt in May 1987. The political uncertainties of a centralized Ivorian administration, completely dependent on a leader with a glorious past, compounded the difficulty of understanding and accepting the radical changes that were needed in economic policies. Although President Houphouët-Boigny was not as strong as he once had been, it was difficult to imagine replacing him.

Within the administration there was disillusionment about the Bank—a disillusionment all the greater because despite its criticisms, the Bank had always shown optimism in its analyses and recommendations. Although such confidence had been warranted in regard to individual and sectoral projects, it appeared that

24. Opinion of a director of public investments, Côte d'Ivoire.
25. Opinion of a former minister of state, Côte d'Ivoire.

more prudence in ascertaining the impact of structural and institutional reforms would have been advisable. A crisis of mutual confidence set in: Côte d'Ivoire found it hard to accept measures it considered too austere; the Bank found itself battling the technical ministries' indecision and a lack of will for radical change at the top of the government. For the Bank the realization that its advice was going unheeded was bitter. The Bank's position was that the government understood the measures that needed to be taken, but that it refused to enforce them.[26]

During this particularly difficult time, Côte d'Ivoire's dialogue with the Bank was further complicated by the actions of the Direction et Contrôle des Grands Travaux (DCGTX), a parallel administration dominated and directed by French expatriates. Historically, the DCGTX was not always as powerful as it became after 1987. At the beginning, under the protection of the Ministry of Public Works, it was charged strictly with control over the technical aspects (such as architecture and execution) of state infrastructure works. It acquired importance through a weakening of the technical ministries after the cabinet reshuffling in 1976, which saw the departure of four important ministers—those for economy and finance, planning, agriculture, and foreign affairs. Subsequently there was a merging of ministries. Planning, for example, disappeared as an autonomous ministry, merging with the Ministry of Economy and Finance. This merger led to heavy centralization of the country's economic administration. Through this redistribution of roles and powers in the regular bureaucracy the DCGTX gained its importance, allegedly to limit the poor financial management that had become commonplace. Henceforth placed under the direct stewardship of the president, the DCGTX attained the height of its power when in March 1987 the technical ministries were entirely removed from the making of project studies.

The DCGTX had the reputation of being fiercely opposed to many viewpoints of the Bank.[27] In the Bank as in the regular administration, it was generally agreed that the parallel administration played a negative role in the dialogue between the Bank and the government until 1991, when new agreements with the Bretton Woods institutions were signed.[28] At that time the DCGTX was officially removed from negotiations with the Bank; it had been quite unqualified to handle the country's macroeconomic problems, especially without the help of the technical ministries.

In summary, the paralysis in Bank-Ivorian relations reflected the weakening of the technical ministries to the advantage of the DCGTX, frequent institutional changes after 1986, and excessive centralization of the decisionmaking power in the hands of a leader who could not easily see new internal and external developments with a fresh eye.[29]

26. World Bank, "Steering the Ivorian Economy."
27. Ibid.; World Bank, "Country Strategy Paper, Ivory Coast: Comments and Suggestions," September 19, 1988.
28. Opinion of a former minister of state, Côte d'Ivoire.
29. World Bank, "Steering the Ivorian Economy."

Throughout this period the Bank noted that Ivorian economic leaders gave no importance to the links among the budget deficit, inflation, and the current account deficit.[30] On this matter there was disagreement. The government was not convinced of the compulsory link between the budget deficit and inflation.[31] Nor was it convinced of the supposed negative link between public investment and private investment.[32] On the contrary, it held that even when not cost effective, public investment created opportunities for profitable private investment.[33] There was also Bank-Ivorian disagreement on the availability of financing for public investment. Objectively, Côte d'Ivoire no longer had the means to finance its investments, and foreign backers who were approached to provide financing were skeptical of the viability of the government's current economic policy. The Bank-government dialogue also labored over the allegedly excessive volume of public spending (chiefly the wage bill for the public staff), and the weak competitiveness of Ivorian products resulting from the overvaluation of the CFA franc and the absence of a credible macroeconomic framework.[34] The absence of any new Bank financing in Côte d'Ivoire in 1988 is attributable to the failure to resolve these problems.

On the government side, an attempt to break the stagnation was made at the end of 1989 through the creation of an Interministerial Coordination Committee charged with stabilization and economic recovery. The committee was presided over by the Ivorian governor of the Banque Centrale des Etats de l'Afrique de l'Ouest (BCEAO), Allassane Dramane Ouattara, who on November 30, 1990, was to become prime minister of Côte d'Ivoire. The Bretton Woods institutions were certainly not without a role in this unprecedented institutional and political change. Both the creation of the post itself and the prime minister's technical credentials spoke to the gravity of the economic and political problems that had developed.

With the creation of the Interministerial Committee, the tone of the Bank's dialogue with Côte d'Ivoire took a remarkably warm turn, although the country's economic and financial situation remained basically unchanged.[35] This shift was associated with the signing, in September 1991, of three new sectoral adjustment loans. The reforms

30. World Bank, "Côte d'Ivoire Industrial Sector Work and Bank Support for the Interministerial Commission on Factor Cost," September 6, 1988.

31. Opinion of a former minister of state, Côte d'Ivoire.

32. The way that public investment can "crowd in" private investment is a reality for Côte d'Ivoire, as well as for many other countries. Pégatiénan, in an ongoing study on the impact of devaluation on the Ivorian economy, estimates that a 10 percent increase in the volume of total public investment induces a 4.3 percent rise in the volume of private investment. At the present time it is not possible to show that public investment has a financial "crowding out" effect, or to determine whether the "crowding in" dominates over financial "crowding out."

33. Opinion of a former minister of state, Côte d'Ivoire.

34. Bank documents, 1988.

35. Opinion of a director of public investments, Côte d'Ivoire.

contained in these loans were the spearhead of a medium-term economic program that was supposed to lead to the recovery of economic growth by 1995.

As late as December 1993, however, the Ivorian economy did not show any signs of revival. By then the prime minister had exhausted his capabilities and faced enormous political difficulties. Furthermore, President Houphouët-Boigny fell ill and died on December 7, 1993. In accordance with article 11 of the constitution, Henri Konan Bédié, president of the National Assembly, succeeded Houphouët-Boigny. The prime minister resigned and was replaced by Daniel Kablan Duncan. Completing these rapid changes was the devaluation of the CFA franc by 50 percent on January 11, 1994.

The Institutional Actors

It will illuminate this analysis to establish more fully the roles of the two principal institutional actors, the World Bank and the government of Côte d'Ivoire, as well as the role of the government of France, the other main official intervener in Ivorian affairs. In doing so, attention is given to how each of the principal actors has been seen by the other.

The World Bank

It is important to note that the Bank is a moneylender whose role in Côte d'Ivoire long remained secondary. Its financial input has generally been less prominent than that of bilateral lenders and donors. However, in the context of structural adjustment, agreement with the Bank and the International Monetary Fund became a precondition for all financial contributions from other moneylenders belonging to the Paris and the London clubs (except at times for contributions from France itself, which has tended to act on its own counsel). Thus the Bank's credentialing role has remained as important as its role as lender in its own right. The projects in which the Bank has participated have been judged by the outside world to be healthy and viable. Such judgments would increase the country's financial credibility and ease the future mobilization of external funding—although in the past in many instances Côte d'Ivoire could have done without the Bank's assistance (as in cases involving palm oil and rubber). Nevertheless, when relations between President Houphouët-Boigny and his ministers soured and decisions were concentrated more tightly in the president's hands, the Bank's approval was an instrument ministers used to convince the president of the value of a project.

The Bank generally has been perceived as a flexible institution, disposed to resolve the problems it encounters.[36] This has helped it to free administrative and financial deadlock. The government's directors of public investment have ap-

36. An opinion expressed to us by all those spoken to in the current and former Côte d'Ivoire administrations.

preciated the Bank's contributions to the programming process for choosing public investments and deciding their geographic locations and designs.[37] Furthermore, the intense dialogue with the Bank since the early 1980s has allowed administration executives to improve their analytical competence.[38]

But there have also been numerous complaints about the Bank's role from the government side. The most widespread is that Bank staff members give the impression of always knowing more about technical matters than those out in the field. Occasionally such lack of modesty causes setbacks that hamper the proper execution of projects.[39] Moreover, Ivorian agents in the field live with the cultural and political constraints of the country; they perceive that the Bank is unaware of these constraints, whether because of the youth of its staff or the latter's ignorance of the Ivorian terrain. Even when it has recognized the constraints, the Bank has not been particularly sensitive to them, in part because noneconomic variables are not addressed by orthodox neoclassical economic tools.[40] In many cases, especially since the advent of the economic crisis in the 1980s, the Bank has been seen to bypass the technical echelons of the administration to deal directly with the president or the prime minister.[41] The Bank has argued that with the weakening of the economic administration since the disappearance of the Ministry of Planning it has been necessary to go straight to the president or the prime minister when urgent decisions have been needed. Although possibly justified, the Bank's behavior has emphasized a weakness in the administration that the latter itself had denounced.

The Ivorian Regime

That public investment has played a decisive role in the growth of Côte d'Ivoire has already been emphasized. The effects of such investment have rested as much on the choice of investments as on their overall quantity. Thus the Bank's perception of the quality of Ivorian development promotion has depended heavily on its view of the government's resource-allocation machinery. According to the Bank, a program of public investment as ambitious as that of the Ivorian government requires an administration strong and structured enough to select, program, execute, and control investment projects in an orderly and coherent manner. The degree to which the government has met this standard changed sharply in the later 1970s. Before 1977 the Ministry of Planning was the administrative structure responsible for the entire sequence of the public investment activity. It also ensured coordination with such other technical ministries as Agriculture, Public

---

37. Opinion of the current and former directors of public investments, Côte d'Ivoire.

38. Opinion of the current director of public investments, Côte d'Ivoire.

39. Opinion of a former director of the Agricultural Development Bank, Côte d'Ivoire.

40. For an example of political constraints and Bank responses, see note 97 and related text, and World Bank, "Basic Economic Mission, Ivory Coast," May 29, 1975.

41. Opinion of the director of public investments, Côte d'Ivoire.

Table 4-3. *World Bank Evaluation of Project Performance, Various Periods*
Percent satisfactory

Country or region	Before 1974	1974–79	1980–91	All years
Côte d'Ivoire	91.7	68.2	62.5	73.8
	(12)[a]	(22)	(8)	(42)
Africa region of the Bank	79.2	58.5	67.5	67
	(245)	(364)	(246)	(855)
All regions	85.1	73.3	71.1	76

Source: World Bank data.
a. Numbers in parentheses are the total number of projects evaluated.

Works, and Finance.[42] The process of planning, selecting, and programming public investment, orchestrated by the Ministry of Planning, was informed by a series of technical and economic studies. The agencies charged with these studies, such as the Bureau National d'Etudes Techniques et de Développement (BNETD), had mandates that encompassed physical infrastructure (roads, bridges, dams) and multisectoral projects such as development of the Valley of Bandama and of the Southwest region (the Port of San Pedro), as well as more limited sectoral projects such as those in agriculture. Foreign consulting firms were also very active.

At that time projects tended to form a coherent whole rather than a string of isolated ventures. The arbitration of the Ministry of Planning was something of a constraint on other ministries. The selection procedures for investment projects were not transparent or formal to the extent that all persons, whether or not they were members of the Ivorian administration, might evaluate them. The Bank, however, admired the efficiency with which the projects were conceived, programmed, and executed during these years. The satisfaction the Bank felt in successive periods about the efficiency with which its Ivorian projects were executed is indicated in table 4-3. Before 1974 the performance of Côte d'Ivoire, with a 92 percent success rate, exceeded that of all countries in the Africa region of the Bank by 16 percent, and that of the Bank's worldwide projects by 8 percent. Between 1974 and 1979 the Ivorian performance remained 17 percent higher than that of the African continent, but equaled only 93 percent of that of the institution's projects worldwide.

Despite the strength of the technical administration, public investment projects often were programmed or executed without the necessary inputs of technical and economic expertise. Moreover, the transparency of the decisionmaking process for public investments was diminished by the existence of parallel decisionmaking circuits.[43] The latter phenomenon particularly affected the efficiency of public enterprises.[44] The stewardship of the administrators of public enterprises was not, in general, discharged properly. The general manager of a public enterprise could

42. Opinion of a former minister of agriculture, Côte d'Ivoire.
43. Opinion of a former director of public investments, Côte d'Ivoire.
44. World Bank, "Ivory Coast Public Enterprise Sector Review," July 15, 1981.

not only program unauthorized investments, but also borrow on the international financial market without interference from the central government's representatives. A Bank document noted that "the public enterprises exercised a good deal of independence from the government and prepared investment programs based on inadequate financing plans."[45] Nevertheless, public enterprises could obtain the state's guarantee of their foreign borrowings. The enterprises themselves did not generate sufficient financial resources, so the bulk of their financing came from loans or public subsidies.[46]

The state's guarantee generally signified that the state would service the debts. The weakness of the legal links of public enterprises to the central administration favored such an outcome. The general managers of such enterprises, who were nominated by presidential decree, did not feel obliged to follow the recommendations of departmental administrators, who were nominated by simple ministerial decree.[47]

After the cabinet reshuffling of 1976, when four important ministers were removed from the government, the duties of the Ministry of Planning, which had coordinated the economic development and social policies of the government, were merged with the more traditional duties of the Ministry of Economy and Finance, as noted earlier. The purely financial tradition of the Ministry of Economy and Finance apparently came to dominate, and dim, the more economics-oriented approach of the Ministry of Planning; furthermore, the role of coordination was no longer clearly defined and facilitated by a well-identified administrative structure. According to the Bank,

> since 1975 the capability of the government to effectively implement industrial policies appears to have declined, [because] the combining of the Ministry of Finance and Planning under a single minister has apparently led to considerable bureaucratic inertia, [and] corruption is generally considered to have become much more widespread and more serious, particularly in customs, but also in the Ministry of Commerce . . . private interests are said to be taking an increasing percentage of the time of an increasing number of government officials.[48]

This situation persisted until 1986–87, when a much weaker Ministry of Planning reappeared.

After the submergence of the Planning Ministry, the formal economic administration weakened in favor of the parallel administration constituted by the Direction et Contrôle de Grands Travaux, described above. The concentration of

45. World Bank, Ivory Coast economic memorandum, May 30, 1979.

46. World Bank, "Country Program Paper: Ivory Coast," June 20, 1980; World Bank, Ivory Coast economic memorandum, May 30, 1979.

47. Opinion of the director of public investments, Côte d'Ivoire.

48. World Bank, "Ivory Coast Industrial Sector: Back to Office Report," December 27, 1979.

functions within the DCGTX underlined the government's desire to rely on the technical efficiency of that group while relegating the technical ministries to the consideration of broader policy frameworks. The separation of the technical and the political within a government tends to be feasible only if the methods of communication between these two compartments of the administration are clearly defined and known to all. In post-1977 Côte d'Ivoire this was far from being the case.

The Direction et Contrôle de Grands Travaux very quickly moved beyond its purely technical domain into defining general policy goals. This expansion, often unintended, sometimes arrogant, was in any case encouraged by the prestige and authority directly mandated to DCGTX by the president. The role of the parallel administration certainly permitted the realization of substantial cost savings in some public investment projects. However, the central administration found itself weakened. It did not profit from the expertise and experience acquired by DCGTX over the years because the French expatriates held a monopoly over the technical information circuits and decision centers. This problem was aggravated by the conflictual relationships between DCGTX and the technical ministries themselves, which were confined to purely routine tasks.

The World Bank took note of these shifting roles and the problems they created: "The weakening of the technical ministries has been linked to the increasing prominence of DCGTX, an institution run by expatriates and directly controlled by the Presidency. The lack of a clear delineation of responsibilities between the technical ministries and DCGTX, as well as the adversarial relationship and personal animosities that have developed between them, have led to a general state of paralysis, with increasing recourse to the President's arbitration."[49] The Bank saw a significant deterioration in Côte d'Ivoire's project performance during this period of weakened official economic administration (see table 4-3).

The official administration's weakening was aggravated when, after a first adjustment phase, the country faced an accelerated drop in the prices of raw materials. The Bank was constrained to conduct its dialogue on the subject with DCGTX instead of with the technical ministries, whose capacity for analysis and assessment had all but been taken away.[50]

Important public investment choices had always been the personal decisions of the president, as the Bank observed: "Any decision of consequence, especially in the field of economic policy, is taken by the President himself."[51] Moreover, all stages of major public investment projects, from concept through implementation, were subject to the same presidential control. According to a Bank document, "no high official will dare question [the president] on the nature, size or timing of any

49. World Bank, "Steering the Ivorian Economy."
50. Ibid.
51. World Bank, "Country Program Paper: Ivory Coast," November 16, 1977.

proposed project, especially if it has special presidential backing as most of the larger ones do."[52] Decisions were often based on Houphouët-Boigny's personal intuition—intuition that was at least partly responsible for the overdesign and sometimes inappropriate location of physical infrastructure. Some favored infrastructure projects proved useful, even if overdesigned, as was the case with the Houphouët-Boigny Bridge, which quickly became too narrow for the traffic between the business district and Treichville. But other favored projects, such as the Kossou Dam and sugar factories, were outright failures.[53]

Along with personal intuitions, the vagaries of public investment choice could be attributed to tolerance of decisionmaking circuits that bypassed formal administrative procedures. The president always found the financial resources for his projects even though stubbornly refusing, with remarkable consistency, to submit the allocation of Stabilization Fund revenues to transparent procedures. The Bank for a long time was completely unsuccessful in engaging in dialogue on this issue:

> We have argued thus far without success for a system in which a given share, 75 percent, of expected [Stabilization Fund] revenues would be included in the investment budget, with shortfalls or surpluses carried over to the next year and, where necessary, foreign exchange reserves or foreign borrowing could make up possible shortfalls in a given year. . . . Those problems are compounded by the ad hoc manner in which allocations to the investment programs from the [Stabilization] funds are approved. These allocations, because they do not undergo normal procedures, are frequently used for projects in which political rather than economic judgments are more important.[54]

The advent of relatively weak technical ministries after 1977, and especially after the mid-1980s, partly explains the central administration's inability to make routine decisions, a problem compounded by the distance between the president and his ministers. That this situation motivated the Bank to try to deal more directly with the president or the prime minister did not improve the Bank's relations with the regular bureaucracy. It is arguable that rather than trying to repair relations with the bureaucracy the Bank should have worked harder and earlier on its relations with the president himself, who, under the de facto circumstances in Côte d'Ivoire, and whatever the bureaucratic structure, should have been the Bank's primary interlocutor. The Bank knew this full well, but often seemed to forget it.

France

The opening of Côte d'Ivoire toward the West has been a fundamental part of the country's politicoeconomic strategy. But this opening has not been the same to all industrialized countries. France, the former colonizer, has occupied the place of

52. Luis de Azcarate to Roger Chaufournier, July 30, 1975, in World Bank, Côte d'Ivoire country files, Abidjan.
53. World Bank, Ivory Coast economic memorandum, May 30, 1979.
54. Bank documentation, 1980.

choice in all aspects of the nation's economic and political life. Indeed, the close-ness of the link has exceeded what might be extrapolated from the history of the two countries or their common language.

It has been observed above that for a long time the low volume of the Bank's contribution made it a secondary partner of Côte d'Ivoire, far behind France. Côte d'Ivoire also had constant recourse to massive French technical assistance in all branches of public administration, including secondary and higher education. Technical personnel were either employees of the French government or agents recruited by private or parastatal research and consultancy groups to staff specific Ivorian government contracts. A limited number of these groups systematically divided among themselves the placement of agents in such key technical ministries as Planning, Agriculture, and Economy and Finance. Consultancy groups also benefited from the positioning of their representatives at the heart of the Ivorian administration, where they could win public contracts for studies ordered by the government in support of its economic-development and public-investment plan-ning. Such contracting was easy because it was directed by technical-assistance expatriates employed at the Ministry of Economy and Finance. Thus the use of foreign research and consultancy groups was systematic and routine. There was lively competition among the several relevant French groups for the award of study contracts, but there was little uncertainty about the nationality of recipients.

Traditionally all technical advisers to the Ivorian administration, to the president as well as to each ministry, had been French. But from the mid-1980s onward the country's waning financial resources forced the government to accept advisers of other nationalities in some ministries.

In the private sector, until recently, business was under the financial and techni-cal control of the French—a phenomenon reinforced with the dismantling of state corporations after 1980. When bad management became widespread during the crisis, expatriates took back the management responsibilities that had been given to Ivorians a few years earlier.

The persistence of massive French technical assistance has reflected a lasting conviction on the part of the highest Ivorian authorities that rapid "Ivorization" would be costly. As a World Bank document noted, "he [the president] personally did not intend to replace Frenchmen by Africans merely for the sake of having African ministers or advisers, until he thought they were good enough for the job."[55] The pattern of reinforcing Ivorian nationals named to lead state corporations with one or more expatriates became routine. In many cases these expatriates held the real power. The pattern was even more pronounced in the private sector.

The sustained presence of expatriate technical assistance met a specific need of the Ivorian leaders, namely, to cope with the generational conflict that existed

55. J. H. Williams, note to files on the first visit of a World Bank president to Côte d'Ivoire, June 24, 1960, in World Bank, Côte d'Ivoire country files.

between the older Ivorian executives and the younger, more technically skilled native officials who were challenging them. The presence of an expatriate especially suited the self-serving older executive, who was preoccupied with parallel activities that his decisionmaking post in the administration facilitated. Such a senior executive could count on the loyalty of the expatriate to whom he could entrust important technical matters. A corresponding wedge of distrust intruded between the older executive and the young Ivorian professional, who, possessing more prestigious diplomas, was determined to meet the challenge posed by the expatriate against whom he had measured himself in the French grandes écoles and universities.

In this context in which the executive delved little into the technical dimensions of issues for which he was responsible, the expatriate sought to make himself indispensable and thereby to preserve his financial interests. The latter were enormous; as the Bank observed: "As a rule of thumb, expatriate managers or professionals (for example, engineers) were said to cost about three times their cost in France. A typical annual cost of CFA 18 million (about $90,000) was mentioned."[56] Keeping oneself indispensable was made easier by the expatriates' control of technical information. The consequence was to give the technical assistant a superiority complex with respect to the chief executive he was advising as well as to other administration managers.[57]

Although Côte d'Ivoire's development strategy was widely praised before the adjustment crisis, it lagged badly in reducing dependence on the French. Quite naturally, French technical assistance was designed (subject to its other goals) to preserve and develop French interests in the country. Ivorian development is based on the production of agricultural commodities for industry and export, and its success has depended on agronomic research. Such research remained essentially French until the end of the 1980s. The market and feasibility studies for agricultural projects were performed by French consultancy groups to the advantage of French enterprises, which generally received the contracts to carry out the projects. With agronomic materials and cultivation techniques under the control of French researchers, such projects had a high probability of success.

Feasibility studies were generally financed through the Assistance and Cooperation Fund, whereas the work carried out by contracting enterprises was typically financed by the Central Fund for Economic Cooperation; both organizations were financial arms of the French government.[58] The remainder of foreign exchange needed for their projects could be obtained from multilateral lenders such as the World Bank. As already indicated, the prestige accorded participation of the Bank in financing could be used to demonstrate to other lenders, notably private ones,

56. World Bank, "Ivory Coast Industrial Sector: Back to Office Report," December 27, 1979.
57. Opinion of the director of public investments.
58. Description given by a former minister of agriculture, Côte d'Ivoire.

the technical quality of a project's design and the country's financial credibility. The Bank recognized these links: "It is clear that the Ivory Coast's ease of access to commercial capital markets is of critical importance to its development. This is an important reason for the close relationship that has developed between the Ivory Coast and ourselves, since the Ivorians are aware of the degree to which sources of commercial and export guaranties agencies consult with us."[59]

Given the control of French technical assistance over the process of project identification and project study in the government, on the one hand, and the system for allocating public works contracts, on the other, it is that clear the Bank's financial assistance tended to contribute positively to the prosperity of French enterprises already established in the host country, as well as to French external trade. As long as the Bank's intervention was within this framework there would be few tensions in the dialogue between the Bank and the Ivorian administration, which, as late as 1990, was too often represented in technical meetings and loan negotiations by expatriates who were more persuasive and eloquent than Ivorians.

For a long time the Ministry of Economy and Finance contained a division charged with international cooperation and headed by an expatriate. The preference this division gave to the reports of the French Central Fund for Economic Cooperation over those of all other external lenders long suggested that French enterprises were sheltered from all foreign competition.[60] To this day Côte d'Ivoire's reputation in this regard has not improved significantly; the development of the government's current privatization program illustrates the point. Other Francophone economic actors—Canada, for example—have not been able to penetrate the Ivorian market despite making interesting offers in such sectors as energy and the drug industry.

Nevertheless, with the economic and financial crisis of the 1980s the external environment changed and the Bank's role widened considerably. It embraced economic policy as a whole. In particular, the Bank received a mandate from most of the moneylenders, bilateral, multilateral, and private, henceforth to demand changes in the government's macroeconomic policies. Some of these policy changes ran afoul of French interests.

As financial constraints forced the Ivorian government to reduce French technical assistance, the role and decisionmaking power of the Direction et Contrôle des Grands Travaux were strengthened to the point of supplanting the technical ministries and becoming the Bank's sole interlocutor during negotiations on structural adjustment loans. A DCGTX delegation that excluded nearly all high-level Ivorian officials represented the Ivorian government in the adjustment loan negotiations of 1989–90.[61] It would seem that DCGTX played for French interests the same role

59. World Bank, "Country Program Paper: Ivory Coast," June 20, 1980.
60. Opinion of the director of public investments, Côte d'Ivoire.
61. Information from a former director of public investments who headed the official Côte d'Ivoire delegations in negotiations with the Bank.

that French technical assistance had when the latter was all-powerful within the technical ministries. This was all the more likely once DCGTX took over the letting of contracts in 1987.

Three-Cornered Relations

The interplay among the government, the French, and the Bank has been critical to many aspects of the Ivorian economy. Its effects in four striking examples—training, economic doctrine, agricultural research, and the CFA franc exchange rate—can be cited.

Many expatriates posted in public enterprises and charged with the execution of projects had much decisionmaking discretion as well as important financial interests to defend. This motivated an underemphasis on training Ivorian locals, while the expatriates held onto their monopoly on technical information. The lack of appropriate candidates who might benefit from such training has constantly been evoked as an explanation for project shortfalls. Yet institutional mechanisms for planning and promoting the transfer of knowledge from expatriates to Ivorians have been inadequate.

The World Bank itself, despite protestations to the contrary, has not seemed particularly well placed to accomplish the training task.[62] Although as early as 1977 a World Bank country program paper asserted that "at the sector and project level our influence has been directed towards project design, institution building, Ivorization and training," subsequent evidence of achievements in these areas has been scant.[63] The failure of training at the project level has limited the Bank's net input to the country. Once a project ended and the experts left, the project's results could not be repeated by the Ivorians.

Seen through French lenses, the Bank's more recent economic ideology has seemed not only hostile but inconsistent. Thus there is a question as to why the Bank is trying to dismantle a public sector that it once financially supported and felt was efficient in executing projects in which it participated. Part of Côte d'Ivoire's French-schooled resistance to the Bank's economic prescriptions has been cultural. An example is seen in the Ivorian view of the Bank's emphasis on the harmonization of effective rates of protection. As in France, the Ivorian official working in the economic administration does not have a doctorate; rather, he has professional training from a specialized school or an engineering diploma in one of a variety of disciplines. He does not base his decisions on neoclassical theory. Effective rates of protection and other analytical criteria invoked by Bank employees in promoting new industrial and commercial policies do not particularly interest him. The intel-

62. Comments of David Knox, former World Bank regional vice president for Africa, July 18, 1992.

63. World Bank, "Country Program Paper: Ivory Coast," November 16, 1977.

lect of the Bank's Ph.D. economists is apt to be undervalued by their Ivorian interlocutors, and their approach, however scientific, to Ivorians seems very academic.

The important case of agronomic research, however, illustrates that reform can
be blocked as much by excessive Bank deference to the French as by French-
Ivorian solidarity. Ivorian agronomic research rested for a long time on an essentially French technical and human apparatus. When the Bank wanted to support the
Ivorian government's will to reorganize this sector and make it key to the medium-
and long-term economic future of the country, the intransigence of the French
technical assistants caused the Bank to hastily retreat, to the despair of the Ivorians,
who were unable to break the stalemate.[64] The Ivorians were told to sort out their
problem with France before seeking any assistance from the Bank. The Bank
proved it could be more royalist than the king.

French influence has also been strong in regard to the Ivorian currency problem. Although the Bank has recognized that the drop in competitiveness has been
a major problem for the Ivorian economy, the nominal devaluation of the CFA
franc—the currency common to all African countries in the franc zone—was never
part of the adjustment measures aimed at restoring the macroeconomic equilibrium of the country. Such devaluation was made institutionally impossible by the
rule of unanimity within the West African Monetary Union. But even without this
obstacle, the Ivorian government was fiercely opposed to the nominal devaluation
of the CFA franc. This opposition was a major stumbling block in the dialogue
between the Bank and the Ivorian government, and on this issue France backed
the Ivorian stance.

The positions of France and Côte d'Ivoire on the maintenance of the CFA
franc's parity were supported by the positive effects of the franc zone on the
monetary policies of Côte d'Ivoire, and on its economic performance during pros-
perous years. Even though Ivorian imports were probably more expensive because
they mainly came from France, Côte d'Ivoire had a very low inflation rate (around
5 to 6 percent a year over a thirty-year period), in contrast to African countries
having nonconvertible currencies.[65] This modest inflation was the result of financial
discipline imposed by the Central Bank of West African States, which since 1975
had limited the budget deficit that could be monetized by the Central Bank to
20 percent of the fiscal revenues of the previous year (the percentages had been
even lower before 1975). Furthermore, the one-hundred-percent convertibility of
the CFA franc and freedom of transfer within the franc zone considerably eased
foreign private investment in the country, especially by French investors. These are
believed to have been important advantages for Côte d'Ivoire's economic growth.

64. Opinion of a former director of scientific affairs at the Ministry of Scientific Research,
Côte d'Ivoire, who negotiated financing designed to reinforce agronomic research.
65. Alexander J. Yeats, "Do African Countries Pay More for Imports? Yes," World Bank
Working Paper 265 (September 1989).

The question of overvaluation of the CFA franc and its devaluation remained taboo until January 13, 1994, when its devaluation by 50 percent was decided upon at a summit meeting of heads of state in Dakar, Senegal. Before that date no top Ivorian civil servant could engage in technical discussions on this topic. The problem was always reduced to its purely political dimensions.[66] The political costs of devaluation were judged to be too high in comparison with the economic benefits that might be gained from such an operation. During the period preceding the devaluation the Bank was forced to adopt a low profile on the topic, if not eliminating the subject from its dialogue with the government, at least approaching it only with the greatest circumspection.

The echoes emanating from the meeting of heads of state in Dakar in 1994 emphasized the intense opposition to monetary adjustment of certain African countries—Gabon, for example—and also emphasized the firm positive commitment of Côte d'Ivoire. According to the African press, France pushed Francophone Africa into devaluing the CFA Franc, even though the large majority of African countries did not want to. France's attitude was generally interpreted as desertion of its African partners; many in Côte d'Ivoire have thought that the death of President Houphouët-Boigny facilitated desertion by France. Whether there was desertion or not, the decision to devalue the CFA franc was timely and necessary; it should have been done much sooner. However, there remains the danger that the devaluation, insufficiently prepared for by African countries, will not produce the anticipated benefits.

In summary, Côte d'Ivoire's special relationship with France created for a long time a wall between the World Bank and the Ivorian economic administration. It harmed relations between the two partners, and because of different interpretations by the Bank and France of what was in Côte d'Ivoire's best interests, often sent contradictory messages to Ivorian decision makers.[67] Yet French cooperation was beneficial for the Ivorian side, for Côte d'Ivoire would not be what it is today had it not been for French technical assistance; and France has also benefited from the relationship.

Ivorian-Bank Issues

Many questions have arisen between the government of Côte d'Ivoire and the World Bank: macroeconomic and structural adjustment matters, as well as sectoral ones such as agricultural pricing, relations between public and private investments, the state's engagement in privatization, industrial and commercial policy, and the government's social policies. This section addresses these issues in greater detail,

66. Point of view of a director of public investments.
67. Comments of David Knox.

and examines the challenges currently facing the two parties—overexposure for the Bank, economic breakdown for the country.

Macroeconomics

The combination of investment programs that were too ambitious, insufficient local savings, and financial management methods lacking any economic foundation could only lead to serious internal and external public disequilibria for Côte d'Ivoire. From the beginning of its dialogue with Côte d'Ivoire the Bank brought the government's attention to, and reproached the government for, the increasing macroeconomic disequilibria resulting from the budget deficit, the balance of payments deficit, and leveraging. The origin of the internal disequilibria lay in the pace of public investment, which was hard to restrict to what could be funded through the country's own resources, given Côte d'Ivoire's ability to mobilize external finances. In the Bank's view, "the government clearly wants too many things done in too short a time. . . . Some of the objectives are a high rate of growth in each sector and each region, a better distribution of income, and better living conditions and better opportunities for everybody. Expressed in terms of invest-ments, this adds up to a heavy investment program, and it is obvious that setting priorities and phasing in of the program have become major issues."[68]

The Ivorian government's will to go fast and far did not dwindle even with the deterioration of the economic situation at the end of the 1970s. The first reform that the Bank hoped to see was a psychological one: acceptance of a smaller scale and slower pace of public investment in order to reduce the budget deficit and increase public savings. The Bank also wanted to see the government, in paring down to a deficit-reducing level of public investment, eliminate low-return projects. A Bank document stated that "the Bank's net lending program of $25 million per annum [was a] level of assistance [that] would depend on the government's willing-ness to reduce its commitment to projects of low economic value . . . and to increase public savings . . . partly by gaining access to private savings presently outside the tax net."[69]

The Ivorian government's expansionist budget policy created a surplus in the demand for goods and services. If part of the excess demand for foreign exchange was attributable to exuberant public investments, it was driven even more by the degree to which Ivorian current-account spending absorbed foreign inputs of labor and services. The Bank observed that

> the Ivorian economy has historically relied heavily on foreign services. Ivorization may bring some relief eventually, but inflated profits and salaries of expatriates, as well as

68. World Bank, "Basic Economic Mission, Ivory Coast," May 29, 1975.
69. Minutes of an Economic Committee review of an Ivory Coast Country Program Paper, June 28, 1971, in World Bank, Côte d'Ivoire country files.

higher interest payments on debts, will make the situation worse, and the current account balance will therefore be increasingly negative. It is not at all clear that the foreign capital can be found at reasonable terms to compensate for this deficit. It is therefore essential that the government development policy give priority to areas of activity which contribute to reducing the current account deficit. Careful estimate of future capital requirement and the potential availability of capital from abroad from existing and new sources are needed.[70]

After the first structural adjustment program the Bank insisted on a sustained reduction in macroeconomic disequilibria: "Imperative need to further reduce external and internal imbalances in the short term, and the necessity to rapidly restore conditions for sustained growth beyond."[71] Toward the end of the 1980s the weight of the debt became unbearable. According to the Bank, "In 1988, the Bank disbursed US$113 million, while receiving US$133 million in amortization and US$156 million in interest, implying negative net disbursements of US$20 million, and negative net transfers of US$176 million (about 2 percent of GDP). This situation is considered intolerable by the Ivorian authorities. . . . The year 1989 started with IBRD debt outstanding and disbursed of US$1.7 billion, around 20 percent of Côte d'Ivoire overall debt. . . . Interest repayments will be US$151 million and principal repayments will be US$128 million."[72] At the end of the 1980s, Côte d'Ivoire had lost almost all its financial credibility.

The country's financial situation had become so difficult that interruptions had been threatened in the Bank's disbursements to Côte d'Ivoire between December 1983 and March 1984, as they were again in 1988 and in 1989, as noted earlier. In regard to the latter interruption, the Bank commented, "In November 1988 and again in May 1989 payment arrears had reached 75 days and the Bank was about to stop all disbursements when payment was made upon the personal intervention of President Houphouet Boigny. . . . Unless the flow is reversed, it is unlikely that Côte d'Ivoire can continue to service Bank debt any longer."[73]

The deterioration in the country's financial credibility was certainly the most striking development in the history of the country and of its relations with the Bank. In 1968 Côte d'Ivoire had been the first developing country to obtain a credit on the Eurodollar market. A predominant portion of the country's foreign debt was owed to private creditors. Côte d'Ivoire had only occasionally availed itself of International Development Association (IDA) credits in the 1970s, which at the time was seen as an indication of its economic success and of the great confidence the country inspired in international financial circles. Since 1991, however, Côte d'Ivoire has been readmitted to IDA.

70. World Bank, "Basic Economic Mission, Ivory Coast," May 29, 1975.
71. World Bank, "Country Program Paper: Ivory Coast," December 1984.
72. World Bank, "Steering the Ivorian Economy."
73. Ibid.

As late as 1979, a year before the beginning of the economic and financial crisis, internal Bank evaluations had still been optimistic about the ability of the Ivorian government to maintain financial credibility and to pursue development without great difficulty. The reforms required by the SAP to reduce the volume of investment and slow external borrowing, as well as to streamline and strengthen investment programming procedures, were meant to slow the decline of the country's creditworthiness. But moderate reforms were not enough. Côte d'Ivoire could not escape the need for more radical restructuring. In the Bank's view, "the deterioration of the terms of trade, the debt overhang and the loss of competitiveness due to the overvaluation of the CFA leave Côte d'Ivoire with no option but to adjust."[74]

Despite the fall of Côte d'Ivoire's financial credibility and prestige abroad, the government continued to object to the Bank's proposed macroeconomic and institutional reforms. The implementation of economic policies can only be effective if the administration that puts them into effect is convinced of the utility of the measures. In the past, the differences between the Bank and the government over budget policies and the selection criteria for public investments were not as great as those that now emerged over basic economic policies. But the situation had now completely changed. The country no longer possessed sufficient financial resources to execute the policies of its choice.

The protection system put into place by the country's existing industrial and commercial policy created an anti-export environment. Thus the removal of export disincentives was a priority for structural reform of the kind urged by the Bank. Furthermore, the imperative to develop the export zone in Côte d'Ivoire and to broaden the range of export products would require substantial improvement in internal and external competitiveness. The reduction of state intervention and promotion of the private sector also appeared to be new directions for exploration.

The structural and institutional reforms proposed for the industrial sector were intended to unleash the market, reestablish competitiveness, and improve public management. They included the following: general revision of customs tariffs, replacement of quantitative restrictions by import surcharges, introduction of a system of subsidies to value-added exports, revision of investment codes, and reform of the institutional framework of industrial promotion in favor of small and mid-level enterprises.[75] None of these reforms was put into effect. The Bank saw two reasons for this failure: first, a "hasty preparation of these measures by the Bank. . . . [The] intention to proceed with an implicit devaluation lacked credibility;

74. World Bank, "Country Strategy Paper, Ivory Coast: Comments and Suggestions," September 19, 1988.

75. World Bank memorandum, "Second Structural Adjustment Loan. Reform of the System of Industrial Incentives. Report and Recommendation of the World Bank's Supervisory Mission," February–March 1984.

[and] second, frequent institutional changes (cabinet reshufflings) [that led] to the weakening of the technical ministries."[76]

There was also a profound disagreement between the government and the Bank on agricultural price policy and commercialization (see the section on agricultural pricing). The government was not convinced of the need to change agricultural prices to reflect a world market that, according to official speeches, was mostly affected by speculation. The government maintained that farmers' revenues should not be left at the mercy of world market fluctuations.[77]

Beyond the sectoral reforms recommended, the Bank put pressure on the government to reform the macroeconomic framework to more clearly define the economic responsibilities of the technical ministries and more vigorously coordinate government action at a central level. In the Bank's view, "the lack of an institution or individual responsible for macroeconomic coordination and management, together with the duplication of responsibilities, has made it difficult for the Bank to carry out its policy dialogue."[78] For the Bank, establishment of an adequate macroeconomic framework by Côte d'Ivoire had become the first priority: "It was indicated to the government that the precondition for negotiating an ASAL [agricultural structural adjustment loan] is an adequate macroeconomic framework and an agreement with the IMF."[79] It was the lack of such a framework that led to an interruption of Bank assistance in 1988.[80]

As already noted, one reason for the gap in Bank assistance was the weakening of the technical ministries, notably the Ministry of Planning. But there was also an absence within the administration of executives in sufficient quantity and of sufficient quality to confront the size and complexity of the reform task. This situation was explained less by a real scarcity than by the departure of existing executives when the Ministry of Planning was dismantled in 1976. Furthermore, even when there were executives in the country, as was again the case by the early 1980s, the budget constraints of structural adjustment made it impossible for the government to recruit them. A poorly coordinated economic administration during the first decade of structural adjustment probably contributed, in the Bank's view, to the slowness with which Ivorian civil servants perceived the linkage between inflation and the balance of payments deficit.

Finally, one of the most important points of substantive disagreement between the government and the Bank—a disagreement that existed at both the sectoral and macroeconomic levels—was over the importance of market forces in deter-

76. World Bank, "Retrospective Evaluation Report on the Côte d'Ivoire Program: 2nd and 3rd Structural Adjustment Loans," April 13, 1990.
77. World Bank, "Côte d'Ivoire Agricultural Sector Adjustment Operation," April 5, 1989.
78. World Bank, "Steering the Ivorian Economy."
79. World Bank, "Côte d'Ivoire Agricultural Sector Adjustment Operation."
80. World Bank, "Steering the Ivorian Economy."

mining the government's economic policy in general and the agricultural pricing policy in particular. Ivorian leaders had developed a great mistrust of the international market and of the signals given by that market. As the Bank put it, "He [the president] distrusts world markets, and, since he has often [been] proven right in the past, is reluctant to adapt policies to a changing external environment."[81]

All of these policy disagreements between the Bank and the government made the government reluctant to accept measures proposed by the Bank, and the latter more cautious. The Bank saw the government as lacking the political will to reform and as hoping, even as it distrusted the international market, that the market would take a turn for the better. The government was obliged to implement a bare minimum of recovery measures to maintain some access to Bank resources. For its part, the Bank counseled itself that only in "the unlikely event that Côte d'Ivoire is ready to adopt more radical policies . . . [should] the Bank . . . be ready to increase the level of its assistance"; but such a shift on the part of the government appeared improbable: "He [the president] is likely to move slowly and, if so, only under the force of circumstance and in limited areas rather than undertaking radical changes."[82]

Agricultural Pricing

Fixing the farmgate price for coffee and cocoa was the privileged instrument of the government's agricultural policy. As noted, this producer price was generally maintained at a lower level than the price paid on the international market; the difference between the prices went to the Stabilization Fund, which then transferred this revenue to the state budget to finance public investment. The difference also served as an implicit levy on the farmer's work. It is generally recognized that the rate of implicit tax imposed by the Ivorian government was very reasonable. The farmer received incentives to increase his effort and produce more.

The Bank had long approved of this agricultural pricing policy, considering Côte d'Ivoire to be one of the few African countries to encourage farmers to increase production by rewarding producer prices. Thus the Bank encouraged the government's policy through its financing of many projects for developing agricultural exports.

For the 1983–84 agricultural season, Côte d'Ivoire and the Bank agreed on the need to increase the farmgate price of coffee and cocoa up to 400 FCFA per kilogram, a price level hitherto unequaled. This occurred in the midst of the structural adjustment period, when it was believed that the world market had become favorable again and would remain so for a long time. But there was disagreement between the Bank and the government after 1987 when the Bank

81. Ibid.
82. Ibid.

proposed a decrease in the producer price for the same agricultural products. The Bank's initiative was interpreted as a change in attitude toward the agricultural pricing policy that had been in effect—a change perceived both as abrupt and as surprising, coming as it did from a moneylender until then firmly supportive of the government's encouragement of the Ivorian farmer.

Was there an attitude or policy change by the Bank? The Bank's attitude can be interpreted as having changed if considered in the context of the impact of the agricultural price-fixing mechanism on the budget deficit. The Bank modified its position because after 1987 the downward tendency of coffee and cocoa prices on the international market had appeared to be worsening and lasting for a long time. This unfavorable tendency was unprecedented. The already catastrophic financial situation of the Stabilization Fund did not permit the government to continue paying the producer a price higher than the international one. Such action would have contributed to a budget deficit already deemed too high.

When considered in the context of the need to link the international price to the farmer through the intermediary of the price to the producer, it is clear that the Bank's attitude was consistent over time. The government, however, was inconsistent. It was quick to pay the international price to the producer when it was high, but it obstinately refused to do so when the international price dropped. These differing perspectives have been summarized by a Bank official:

> I certainly heard many times in the Bank in the 1970s that Côte d'Ivoire was almost unique in Africa in paying decent farmgate prices instead of taxing its farmers to death. To the Bank, that was letting market forces work by passing through to the farmer world market prices with the corollary that when world prices fell sharply so too should farmgate prices. For the government, however, the perception was probably different: a policy of encouraging agricultural production with the corollary that one kept farmgate prices up even when world prices fell. If that is the scenario, and it probably is, no wonder the government felt aggrieved when the Bank criticised its agricultural pricing in the 1980s. The Bank would see itself as consistent, the Ivoirians would see it as inconsistent.[83]

Social protection of the farmer was the reason for the government's asymmetrical behavior.

Although the Bank's argument in favor of a link between the farmgate price and the international price was consistent, the Bank's position in regard to the Stabilization Fund was not. In the past the Bank had not questioned the stabilizing function of the prices put into effect by the government. It recognized the efficiency of that function because the incentives given to the farmers were judged appropriate. The high level of international prices during the 1960s and 1970s made the stabilization function itself appear unnecessary in the Bank's eyes. But during the period of low international prices the Bank judged the stabilization function to be inappropriate and strongly recommended that the Stabilization Fund be suppressed: "The price

83. Comments of David Knox.

stabilization function would be abandoned along with the institution responsible for stabilization [the Stabilization Fund]. A variable export tax would be introduced to permit [the] government to capture some of the benefits of windfall increases in export prices. This tax would fall to zero when prices reached a preestablished (low) level."[84]

The Bank's rejection of the stabilization function was even more asymmetrical because, as the Bank recognized, it had greatly contributed to reinforcing state intervention in the commercialization of agricultural exports. In essence, the Bank had helped to build the Stabilization Fund; it was therefore going back on its word. It can be said that the Bank must take responsibility for having supported a policy that gave Ivorian farmers and the governing body habits that are today difficult to abandon.

Public and Private Investments

Broadly, over the years, the Bank approved the Ivorian government's development policy. Public investment in infrastructure favored both the use of natural resources and private investment. By facilitating the productive activity of private entities, particularly rural ones, public investment had become the vehicle for economic growth for two decades. On this point the views of the Bank and the government converged, with the limited difference that the government believed that even if public investment was not profitable to begin with, it could nevertheless be constructive if and as it encouraged profitable private activities.

Because this policy was effective for twenty years and enabled the country to realize remarkable growth rates, the government stuck with it even when it no longer possessed the necessary resources. The Bank, however, changed its position and opposed any increase in the volume of public investment, especially in view of the laxity of the government's selection criteria for public investment. Moreover, during the adjustment period financial constraints made it impossible for the government to continue to finance investment spending through borrowing, especially if such borrowing were not to be productive. To the Bank, it was unrealistic to believe that public investment could continue to be the principal vehicle for economic growth. For the government, it was difficult to accept the change in Bank policy. The emphasis on disciplined investment spending that circumstances and the Bank came to demand was not sudden. Throughout its dialogue with the government, the Bank had drawn the government's attention to the negative effects of soft, noneconomic investment criteria and the need to abandon them.

State Engagement in Privatization

When the government of Côte d'Ivoire was asked to disengage from the economy to allow more participation by the private sector, more than just the role of public

84. World Bank, "Côte d'Ivoire Agricultural Sector Adjustment Operation."

investment was involved: the entire economic philosophy of the Ivorian government was on the line. The Ivorian government had always thought that at this stage of the country's development there could be no private domestic sector without the state's intervention. The creation of public enterprises and the participation of the state in an enterprise's capital had the avowed objective of temporarily filling the void created by the nonexistence of local entrepreneurs. The government planned to withdraw in favor of the Ivorian private citizen in the future. The pursuit of this last objective had justified the creation of the Société Nationale de Financement (SONAFI) (which was dissolved at the end of the 1980s).[85]

It was generally recognized that the poor economic and financial management of most public enterprises helped create or accentuate the budget deficit of the public sector and the weight of the public debt. Consequently a streamlining of the public sector was seen to be beneficial even if it created financial and social problems for many families. However, the systematic dismantling of public enterprises and their sale to the private sector was also seen as tantamount to increasing foreign technical and financial control over the country's economy, because Ivorians had been insolvent since the beginning of the 1980s.[86] Such a change in control was precisely what the government's policy sought to avoid, despite the reform's outward orientation. In proposing reforms in the early 1980s the Bank had also understood this: "Where state participation is deemed not necessary, offer them [the public enterprises] to private purchasers. One restraining consideration preventing the acceleration of actions in this direction is the realization that any such moves on a large scale in the near future would require sales to foreign purchasers since Ivorians lack the capital and entrepreneurial expertise to participate on a large scale."[87]

Ivorians believe that a new dogmatism on the part of the Bank was introduced with such privatization proposals, for no one remembered the Bank warning the Ivorian government against the creation of too many public enterprises. On the contrary, the Bank's strategy had consisted in actively supporting the consolidation of the public sector.[88] It would be financed through plans for palm oil, rubber, and cotton projects, not to mention the improvement of cocoa plantations and a reforestation program.[89] These programs and development plans were put into effect and directed within the framework of public enterprises or mixed-economy institutions. The Bank's subsequent evaluation of them had even recognized that the management of these agencies, through the projects it financed, was generally good. Through the financing granted to these public and mixed institutions, the

85. Opinion of a former minister of state, Côte d'Ivoire.
86. Opinion of a former minister of state.
87. World Bank, "Country Program Paper: Ivory Coast," June 20, 1980.
88. World Bank, "Côte d'Ivoire Agricultural Sector Adjustment Operation."
89. Opinion expressed to the authors by all administrative executives who were approached.

Bank therefore had directly and efficiently contributed to the development of public enterprise in Côte d'Ivoire. For these reasons the Bank's change in policy has been perceived as dogmatic.

The Bank has viewed its position as more pragmatic than dogmatic.[90] It would not seem to be pragmatic, however, if it results in total foreign control of Ivorian enterprises and fails to guarantee that the price of goods and services will decrease and thus lighten the burden on families who might be affected by unemployment.

Industrial and Trade Policy

The Bank's position on industrial and commercial policy has also been the subject of misunderstanding. Côte d'Ivoire was long considered an open country that knew how to take advantage of favorable external factors to develop its economy. The Bank was especially impressed that the government had created an environment favorable to private local and foreign investments; the terms of the investment code favored enterprises that agreed to invest in the sectors and activities judged priority areas. The export-oriented policy of the early 1970s was also hailed as beneficial; at that time large textile establishments were developed and systematically directed toward exports. The Bank praised the government for practicing a policy of openness to the outside rather than a policy of closing in on the local market.

However, the Bank felt that rates of protection in Côte d'Ivoire were too high and too diversified. According to the Bank, the country needed to reduce industrial protection and make it uniform at the rate of 40 percent, and replace all quantitative barriers to imports with equivalent tariffs. It was also strongly suggested that the country further liberalize external trade.

To reduce the anti-export bias of Côte d'Ivoire's industrial and commercial policy, the Bank thus recommended in 1984 a de facto nominal (or simulated) devaluation of the CFA franc by raising the level of customs import duties while simultaneously instituting an export subsidy, as noted earlier. Manipulation of the nominal exchange rate of the CFA franc was institutionally impossible.

It is difficult not to agree with the Bank about the necessity for improving the external and internal competitiveness of Ivorian industrial products, for as long as the country imports, it must export in order to pay for its imports. Because traditional agricultural exports could not be increased owing to overproduction on the international market, this profit loss would have to be compensated for by an increase in industrial exports. Stressing industrial exports and seeking to increase their range, in particular in the direction of nontraditional exports, has therefore not been a question of ideology or dogmatism but of good economic sense.

The bone of contention, however, has been how to increase industrial exports. The Bank had no alternative but to recommend a devaluation. The intrinsic value of this solution cannot be doubted. But the Côte d'Ivoire government and local

90. Comments of David Knox.

businesses had to be convinced; devaluation by itself would not be enough to develop nontraditional exports. Opponents also argued that the government was not able to pay export subsidies.

The mechanism of simulated devaluation did not function because, in reality, the Ivorian government never accepted it. Nor did the government release sufficient funds to pay for export subsidies—perhaps because it never wanted to do so. The revenues drawn from the higher tariffs should have paid for the export subsidies; to succeed, the operation would have required a good system of duty and tax collection. But Côte d'Ivoire's institutional problems in regard to tax collection in general and custom duties in particular explain why the government could not implement the devaluation mechanism. The Bank understands well the problems of governance in Côte d'Ivoire; but in this instance the Bank wrongly minimized the institutional problems involved. The failure of the simulated devaluation, which seemed to have worked reasonably well in some other countries, tarnished the Bank's prestige and credibility in the eyes of the Ivorian government and the private sector.

The principal objectives of "real adjustment," attempted in Côte d'Ivoire from the beginning of the 1980s, were to reduce the budget deficit and to restore the internal and external competitiveness of the economy (the trade-weighted real exchange rate appreciated by around 30 percent between 1986 and 1991). The instruments utilized were budgetary and monetary restrictions, on the one hand, and tariff increases, on the other. These instruments did not achieve the goals of reducing the cost of labor in the public and private sectors and reducing the cost of imported inputs on which production depends. "Real adjustment," therefore, could not ameliorate internal and external economic competitiveness.

Côte d'Ivoire and the assembly of African countries of the franc zone finally accepted devaluation of the CFA franc in 1994, after more than ten years of hemming and hawing, and setbacks, as noted earlier. Devaluation is a powerful alternative to "real adjustment" because its principal objectives are to reduce local production costs compared to those outside, and to increase the relative price of tradeable goods in comparison with nontradeable goods and services.

In summary, the advent of Côte d'Ivoire's financial crisis in the late 1970s greatly strengthened the Bank's hold on the economy. At a time when the Bank's intervention was determined only by the profitability of individual and sectoral projects, government disagreements with the Bank could not have irreversible consequences. With the onset of adjustment, the reform of an array of policies that would condition the Bank's financial assistance effected a shift in the country's entire economic philosophy. This new context has given the Bank enormous power over Côte d'Ivoire's economic and social policies; its control is all the greater because the country's financial resources are so limited.[91]

91. Opinion of a director of public investments, Côte d'Ivoire.

Social Policy

Although foreign factors of production have occupied too great a place in the Ivorian economy, without them Côte d'Ivoire's performance would have been impossible. The Ivorization of the economy has been the most important problem the government has had to face. The problem has been exacerbated by the economy's high growth rate, which aroused great hopes among Ivorians who legitimately desired a larger share of the economic pie. Yet the success of Ivorization will determine the future development of the Ivorian economy.[92] To attain this fundamental objective, the government put into effect elitist human resource development policies that raised important equity problems for groups of individuals and regions. The government must be credited with many remarkable social policies, but these achievements have been costly to society as a whole. The government's social objectives have also weighed heavily in its dialogue on adjustment with the Bank.

Throughout the period of Côte d'Ivoire's economic prosperity President Houphouët-Boigny told Ivorians that despite his aversion to socialism, he had promoted bold social policies. Côte d'Ivoire had thus become one of the champions of economic liberalism in Africa. The country's policies for housing, health, and education, among other examples, support the president's assertion.

Housing policy has routinely affected the lives of citizens. The Houphouët-Boigny government favored access to affordable housing and private ownership of such housing through the actions of public real estate companies, such as the Société de Gestion et de Financement de l'Habitat (SOGEFIHA), and mixed companies, such as the Société Ivoirienne de Construction et de Gestion Immobilières (SICOGI). Many individuals were thus able to own their homes. However, these housing programs created equity problems. They favored salaried urban civil servants and employees of the private sector; so-called affordable housing was thus concentrated in the hands of those who had money or enjoyed influential political connections. It was not the most needy who mainly benefited.

In the health sector there were also bold social initiatives. Medical care in hospitals and public health centers was provided free of charge to all patients until the mid-1980s. Here too there was a problem of equity, because of the uneven distribution of the health infrastructure and medical or paramedical personnel. These were concentrated in urban centers, notably in Abidjan, whereas the majority of the population lived in the villages and had little or no access to the new facilities.

Education has been the most important aspect of the government's social policy. Although education weighs heavily on a family's spending, in Africa's system of extended families access to education affects a family's revenue only in the mid and longer terms. Educational subsidies crystallized President Houphouët-Boigny's social ambitions for Ivorian youth. Such subsidies had been anticipated as early as

92. Den Tuinder and World Bank, *Ivory Coast.*

1946, when approximately 150 young Ivorians (boys and girls) were dispatched to France to learn various trades and to receive technical training in high schools and secondary schools. At that time Côte d'Ivoire was a colony that had no such institutions, and the idea of political independence had not yet crossed anyone's mind. To mark the historical nature of this venture and show their gratitude to the government for its financial support, members of the group created an association named the Compagnons de l'Aventure de 1946. At the time of independence in 1960 these young diploma holders and their predecessors (who had been educated by the colonial administration at the William Ponty de Gorée School in Senegal, and among whom were President Houphouët-Boigny and most of his political companions) formed a core group of Ivorian executives who occupied the first positions of responsibility alongside the French in the country's public and private administration.

After independence the government had the clear policy of favoring secondary and higher education over primary education, which had already been well developed under the colonial administration.[93] The government implemented that policy by investing heavily in the construction of high schools and municipal schools throughout the country and by establishing a new national university. (A maximum of 7,000 university students was anticipated for 1963, but by 1994 more than 30,000 students were enrolled, on three campuses.) In secondary education and the university the classical French tradition, which excluded technical disciplines and the engineering sciences, was followed; the government also followed French tradition by separately constructing high schools, municipal schools, and écoles supérieures for technical learning and engineering sciences.

After the 1960s Côte d'Ivoire devoted more than 40 percent of the total state budget to education and training. Secondary and higher education, both general and technical, received especially generous subsidies. Not only was no tuition charged, but room and board for students admitted as boarders was free. Furthermore, all students who had obtained their baccalaureate (the high school graduation certificate) were admitted to the university and automatically received a monthly stipend. For a long time the Ivorian government offered its students some of the most generous study grants in Francophone Black Africa; only oil-rich Gabon could afford to be more generous. Housing and food services were also generously subsidized, and health care was free.

State subsidies for instructors were also generous; the separation in the early 1970s of their nominal salaries from those of public officials put them into the category of the country's best-paid civil servants, on an equal footing with military officers and magistrates. The fact that the Ivorian elementary school teacher was better paid than the young civil service medical doctor illustrates the financial

93. Note of Leonard Rist, November 24, 1961, in World Bank, Côte d'Ivoire country files.

privilege attached to a teaching career. Moreover, teachers in public secondary schools and higher education had the added benefit, until 1987–88, of free housing. To bridge the country's deficit in teachers in the face of a rapidly increasing demand for education, the government called upon foreigners, both French citizens and non-Ivorian Africans. They were attracted by even greater financial rewards than those bestowed on their Ivorian counterparts, and therefore responded in massive numbers. The spectacular development of training in the 1960s and 1970s was the result of the government's education subsidies.

Among the brilliant policies of the Ivorian government, combining both social and economic elements, was the regionalization of public investment. This policy was exemplified by the development of cotton and sugarcane culture in the savannah regions of the center and north of the country. Regionalization was also applied through the celebration of the national holiday of August 7 (later changed to December 7) outside of Abidjan every other year, in a different administrative region of the country. On the occasion of this revolving national holiday, physical infrastructure projects (such roads, bridges, and dams) and social infrastructure projects (such elementary, secondary, and municipal schools, health centers, and sports equipment) were granted to the host region or built by the government. The financial crisis ended this practice in 1979. Also noteworthy was an electrification program in villages and rural centers carried out through the Energie Electrique de Côte d'Ivoire, a "mixed" company charged with the production and distribution of electrical energy. The development of cotton and sugarcane culture, the social initiatives linked to the revolving national holiday, and village electrification were partially financed by discretionary transfers from the Stabilization Fund, whose revenues came from the export of coffee and cocoa produced in the richest areas of the south of the country.

The beautification of Abidjan—the first Ivorian city seen by outside visitors— was another element of the nation's social policy. Whether the visitor comes from Africa or elsewhere, Abidjan surprises, for beyond the natural beauty of the site the city was constructed in a planned and orderly fashion. But it has also drawn heavy criticism because of the proliferation of peripheral neighborhoods (Marcory-sans-fil and Abobo-derrière-rails, for example) and "spontaneous" housing, which coexist alongside the affluence of the business area (Abidjan-Plateau) and the residential zones (Cocody, Riviera, and Deux Plateaux).

In the beginning, the government was not overly concerned with the impact of its economic and social policies on the distribution of income. Its strategy consisted of attaining the highest possible level of economic growth and hoping that the benefits would later be spread over the largest possible number of citizens. But has the strategy really benefited the majority of citizens? The government's policies have been expensive and their distribution unequal; they have worsened the poverty of the poorest Ivorians. In regard to these distributional inequalities the Bank was inclined to be more pro-interventionist than the government, commenting that "in Bank reports on the economy of Ivory Coast, we have stated repeatedly that the government should come to grips with the social aspects of its development policies and programs, including income distribution among groups and regions and the related problems of employment, population growth and ivorization."[94] Nevertheless, the Bank did not see Côte d'Ivoire's income distribution problem as particularly severe: "Although there still exists considerable inequalities, the personal and regional distribution of income on the Ivory Coast compared favorably with [that of] other underdeveloped countries in and outside Africa."[95]

The Bank's opinion on Ivorian income distribution should be only partially accepted. Within Ivorian borders everyone was intuitively convinced that the distribution of income was very unequal. The political and administrative elites had easy access to financial and material advantages in an environment that had never in Ivorian memory penalized a voracious leader. Heavy-handed "rent" collection became an effective political instrument at the time of democratic pluralism, after February 1990.[96] In retrospect, however, it seems possible that an aggressive imposition of elite privileges was used to squelch political dissent during the earlier era of single-party rule.

To comprehend the cost of Côte d'Ivoire's social policies it must be remembered that education alone accounted for 40 percent of the state's annual budget during the period of prosperity. The generous subsidies granted to secondary and post-secondary students, as well as the financial and material advantages given to teachers, contributed substantially to the country's budget deficit. Among the structural characteristics of public spending was the prominent share of salaries and social benefits, which represented approximately 75 percent to 80 percent of the Education Ministry's total budget. Thus the ministry was left with few resources with which to operate, and could not always properly realize its assigned objectives.

The country also supported the supplemental costs linked to the overdesign and the architectural extravagance of the school and university infrastructure, in particular the big engineering schools located in Yamoussoukro. It has been common knowledge at the World Bank and in Côte d'Ivoire that the cost of these institutions was too high. Each cost tens of billions of CFA francs, and would serve only a few hundred students; such a high per-student cost was typical of the Ivorian government's pronounced taste for grandiose public works.

Extravagance of that kind might have been acceptable if the cost of the government's education policy had reaped a high return on its investment. However, it is apparent that the return was relatively low—proof of this was that expatriates effectively continued their control of private business. Foreign control even seems

94. World Bank, "Basic Economic Mission, Ivory Coast," May 29, 1975.

95. Bastiaan den Tuinder to Xavier de la Renaudière, in a back-to-office report of a basic economic mission, September 17, 1975, in World Bank, Côte d'Ivoire country files.

96. Those toward whom justice had been tolerant could show their gratitude by not openly voting against the president's ruling party in free elections.

to have been reinforced, in the period following the crisis, in the enterprises that managed to survive. There has been an obvious gap between the education provided by the system and the qualifications required for the private jobs available, a discrepancy resulting from the educational system's inability to adapt to the changing job market. The government has been aware of this problem for a long time; in 1977 it created the Usher Assouan Commission to reform the education system. Yet the commission's conclusions have remained unheeded, for unknown reasons.[97]

The spatial distribution of the government's social spending contributed to the increased poverty of the most underprivileged groups in the country. Rural regions received a relatively small share of the elementary and secondary school infrastructure; and as discussed above, health infrastructure and medical and paramedical personnel were concentrated in urban zones to the detriment of villages. Moreover, the government's health policy favored curative medicine, as opposed to preventive care. Because the villages and rural zones harbor the majority of the population as well as the poorest people, such allocations of social spending accentuated poverty by reducing the access of underprivileged groups to social services. Unequal allocation probably increased the absolute number of poor people.

The government's particular choices for social policy had another negative impact on poverty. By clearly opting for the development of secondary and university schooling as a priority, the government chose to offer a promising future only to the minority of young Ivorians who were fortunate enough to obtain secondary-level schooling.

It is obvious that the government's social objectives slowed down the adjustment process in Côte d'Ivoire from 1981 onward; in particular, they prevented the government from taking the necessary radical measures to reduce the budget deficit and reorient the structure of social spending. Yet Côte d'Ivoire waited a long time before initiating the reform of its elitist human resource policy. The public accepted the liquidation of numerous public enterprises in the 1980s and the resultant rise in unemployment. But an intended reduction in the salaries of civil servants in the central government (forecast for 1990), and a change in the status of teachers to that of general public officials, which would have entailed a substantial salary reduction, led to social unrest. That unrest, in turn, gave birth to the multiparty system in Côte d'Ivoire.

The Bank was concerned with the negative impact of the government's choices in matters of education and health policy—a concern expressed in a 1980 paper:

97. Reform of the Ivorian educational system is absolutely essential, because the system has related poorly to the physical and cultural environment of Côte d'Ivoire. As an essentially agricultural country Côte d'Ivoire has great need for scientists, technicians, and engineers. Yet the schools breed in young Ivorians an aversion to manual work and technical jobs and a preference for office careers in urban surroundings; agricultural and rural cultural values are generally absent from Ivorian schools. Furthermore, the Ivorian school serves as a vehicle for Western and urban values, synonymous with a certain desirable modernism; the essentially rural African values are rejected. If schools continue to neglect agricultural jobs, the productivity of agriculture will not improve and the progress of the country's economy as a whole will slow down.

"Since government has consistently overdesigned schools, hospitals and other facilities, a reduction in unit costs such as we have frequently recommended, could free resources for programs to reach larger portions of the population."[98] Yet a World Bank sectoral adjustment loan for the development of human resources was negotiated only in 1991, ten years after the initiation of reform policies. That delay prompts a question: What was the weight of social objectives in the Bank's adjustment policy?

The reduction of school and university subsidies, as stipulated in the sectoral adjustment loan for human resources, led in 1992 to unrest at the national university, which made the political and social climate tense. The government had delayed reducing the subsidies because of their adverse impact on the student population, for with the advent of the multiparty system the students had acquired considerable political strength.

It must be wondered why the Bank was so patient with the reform of the government's social and economic policies. The answer probably lies in the Ivorian government's obstinacy—an obstinacy aroused and encouraged by the fact that events had often proved it right—as well as in the Bank's optimism and flexibility.

The Bank thought that the structural problems it had discerned in the 1970s could be resolved under the favorable conditions created by the strong rise in cocoa and coffee prices after 1975 (it is easier to resolve problems when resources are available). At the same time, the Bank overestimated its ability to persuade the government. Similarly, it overestimated the government's creativity and ability to put into effect appropriate policies, and to change policies when they were no longer suited to the situation. It noted that "the Ivory Coast has shown considerable foresight in managing its problems to date, and it is to be expected to continue to follow a prudent policy in the future."[99] As late as mid-1979 the Bank believed that the few reforms proposed within the framework of its routine consultant mission would suffice to enable Côte d'Ivoire to strengthen the high growth rate of the past and to maintain its prior exceptional financial credibility: "The Ivory Coast should be able to continue its strong growth record of the past while retaining its high creditworthiness rating. . . . The Ivory Coast's current public investment program and its external borrowing requirements are a reasonable path to sustained growth with an acceptable level of risk."[100]

In 1980 the Bank even predicted that the country's credit would be completely restored by around 1990.[101] The Bank clearly was mistaken about the outlook for the price of cocoa, as it was about the fluidity of the Ivorian government's economic policy when faced with changed circumstances. The Bank must have known that Côte d'Ivoire could not quickly develop nontraditional exports capable of compen-

98. World Bank, "Country Program Paper: Ivory Coast," June 20, 1980.
99. World Bank, Ivory Coast economic memorandum, May 30, 1979.
100. Ibid.
101. World Bank, "Country Program Paper: Ivory Coast," June 20, 1980.

sating for the currency losses brought about by the decline in earnings from cocoa exports. It should also have understood the government's obstinate will to maintain its policies and force the course of external events as it had always done with internal events.

Despite its blighted hopes (notably, the failure of the simulated devaluation of the CFA franc) the Bank's optimism revived somewhat with the conception of a medium-term economic program in 1987 (covering the period 1989 to 1995). The anticipated results of this program were based on two assumptions: first, that the private sector would henceforth dominate economic activity; and second, that the institutional changes under consideration in the adjustment loans would soon free private initiative in the export sector.[102]

Given the Bank's experience with the government's obstinacy, it can be wondered how, more recently, the Bank expected to convince the government to take the radical measures it previously had refused to take. If the obstinacy had been politically based, how could the Bank neglect the political obstacles?

The answer may be that the Bank relied too much on official reports of public opinion. In the Bank's view, "the need for strong recovery measures [was] well understood by the population."[103] Even the central government was seduced by flattering reports by regional authorities on the state of mind of the general populace. But what actually preoccupied the population in the hard light of day at the beginning of 1990 was not the necessity of the adjustment measures, but the unequal distribution of the sacrifices different social groups would have to make. Most Ivorians were convinced that their share of the sacrifice was going to be greater than that of those who had had preferred access to financial resources during times of prosperity.

The Challenge to the Bank: Overexposure

From 1981 to 1991 the World Bank invested US$1,432.2 million to finance adjustment programs, or 52.4 percent of all its economic assistance to Côte d'Ivoire over twenty-three years (see table 4-2). It is prudent for a bank to take such a financial risk only if it is convinced of the soundness of its client's economic and financial health. But in 1989, only two years after the official publication of the relatively optimistic medium-term economic program for Côte d'Ivoire, the Bank estimated that the country's economic future had become uncertain and that the country's financial credibility had become precarious. In the Bank's view, "this high exposure, together with Côte d'Ivoire's uncertain economic prospects and precarious creditworthiness, [put] the Bank in a very delicate position."[104]

102. World Bank, "The Côte d'Ivoire in Transition: from Structural Adjustment to Self-Sustained Growth," Report 6051 (Washington, March 9, 1987).
103. World Bank, "Country Program Paper: Ivory Coast," December 1984.
104. World Bank, "Steering the Ivorian Economy."

The fear was justified, for payment arrears to the Bank were accumulating and risked blocking Bank activities in the country.[105] A persistent opinion, in the Bank as well as within the Ivorian government, has been that Côte d'Ivoire will probably be unable to resume servicing all of its outside debt in general and its Bank debt in particular.[106]

Given the importance of the Bank's portfolio in the country (a little more than $2 billion U.S.) the institution had to be more cautious. The Bank recognized that "our lending strategy must be extremely prudent" and that "the Bank should avoid a rapid rise in its exposure."[107] The Bank also had to do everything possible to enable Côte d'Ivoire to find the road to recovery, in hope of being reimbursed one day: "In this context [the Bank's West and Central Africa Department] has endeavored to resuscitate the dialogue on economic policy reform . . . and discuss possible loan conditionality."[108] But it also recognized that "trying to quickly reduce our exposure through highly negative net transfers would seriously jeopardize our preferred creditor status."[109] Côte d'Ivoire had suddenly become, financially, a high-risk country.

It also became a high-risk country politically, because of the concentration of decisionmaking power in the hands of the president. Undeniably, President Houphouët-Boigny had been a charismatic leader whose history of economic accomplishments had confirmed his economic and political wisdom. But his advanced age brought inertia to the management of the economy, even though in November 1990, in an ad hoc constitutional reform, the creation of the post of prime minister prevented governance from coming to a complete stop. However, solutions for the fundamental problems could not be achieved without the president. Thus the focus was brought back to the central problem of the Bank and Côte d'Ivoire—that is, to the dialogue with a partner who did not want to, or could not, change. The Bank's disillusionment was a measure of the excessiveness of its previous optimism about Côte d'Ivoire; it finally recognized that prospects were not as positive as it had hoped.

A question therefore arises: Why did the Bank increase its financial risk by continuing substantial support for a reform policy judged relatively weak, and a government obstinately attached to its positions? The Bank's flexibility has certainly been the natural corollary of its optimism, but this flexibility, appreciated by Ivorians, has appeared at times to be a weakness of the Bank in regard to the Ivorian president.[110] The Bank had earlier approved the liberal economic gradualism and the constructive economic program of President Houphouët-

105. Ibid.
106. An opinion prompted by our conversation with a World Bank official.
107. World Bank, "Steering the Ivorian Economy."
108. World Bank, "Côte d'Ivoire Agricultural Sector Adjustment Operation."
109. World Bank, "Steering the Ivorian Economy."
110. Comments of David Knox.

Boigny; despite the latter's excesses, the Bank wanted to support the program and the president at all costs. This may explain the institution's weakness with regard to Côte d'Ivoire.

The Challenge to the Government: Disarray

Côte d'Ivoire's current financial difficulties have brought to the forefront the structural and institutional problems that have been eroding the country's economy for a long time. These problems were brought to the attention of the Ivorian government by the World Bank, but the government chose to underestimate or hide them. Now that the abscess is open, it is important to build the political consensus that the creation of lasting solutions requires. These solutions cannot be discovered as long as Ivorians of all political opinions, in a multiparty environment, do not agree on a blueprint for a future society.

Ivorians do not have a plan for tomorrow's society. Their earlier plan was based exclusively on the well-being easily acquired by elites who were fortunate enough to attend school and to occupy administrative and political posts, and whose influence and prestige were highly valued. But this well-being was acquired as a result of a tax levied on the hard and relentless work of the farmers. The government was unable to breed in Ivorians, especially the elites, respect for the public and general interest, which in times of trouble would have given them the will to fight collectively against the economic and financial crisis. There is today in Côte d'Ivoire a social crisis that is distressing for everyone, both those who govern, and those who are governed.[111] The message that was retained and followed by the young generation of Ivorians over the last thirty years exemplified neither frugality nor saving. It encouraged even less the rigorous management of public resources. Thus the values most needed today are lacking.

Although acquiring an important stock of human resources at great cost, the government of Côte d'Ivoire was unable to create within the country the capacity for a coherent medium- and long-term program, which, in difficult situations such as the country has experienced for more than ten years, is the only recourse. New ideas and project proposals have had difficulty emerging and finding expression. They have been inhibited by a pronounced taste for repeating a past that is insufficient for preparing for the future.[112] The absence of a plan for a future society that would place emphasis on respect for the general and national interest, and the present economic administration's lack of concerted thought about a medium- and long-term macroeconomic framework, have complicated and will continue to complicate the dialogue with the Bank, for the Bank tries systematically to place itself within such a framework.[113]

111. A view prompted by our conversation with the director of public investments, Côte d'Ivoire.

112. Opinion of a former minister of agriculture, Côte d'Ivoire.

113. Opinion of a former minister of agriculture, Côte d'Ivoire.

What Went Wrong? Two Interpretations

The story of the relationship between the World Bank and Côte d'Ivoire since the early 1970s is a sad one, running from a sunny start to substantial stalemate during the years of financial crisis at the end of the reign of a national patriarch. Here we try to address more deeply, and hypothetically, the question of what went wrong. We offer two answers—political and social constraints on the one hand, and structural problems on the other. They are not opposed. We tend to accept both, but the first, the more conventional, will be more widely credited.

Political and Social Constraints

In terms of their underlying macroanalyses of Côte d'Ivoire, the Ivorian government and the World Bank have been on the same wavelength in recent years: the country must recover its internal and external balances, by a demand-stabilizing fiscal adjustment and by relative price changes in favor of tradeables that would narrow the balance-of-payments gap. Where the two parties have differed is over the choice of instruments to achieve these goals.

The Bank endorses the view that Côte d'Ivoire's main problems remain those of the budget deficit, the effective real exchange rate, and the lack of private investment.[114] There is no mention of any other real structural problem. According to this view, Côte d'Ivoire would find itself in a much better situation today if it had adopted measures designed to raise its fiscal revenues and cut salaries in the public sector in order to cut public spending. Moreover, out of concern for equity in relation to the private sector, and for peasants in particular, Côte d'Ivoire should earlier have devalued the CFA franc to improve the economy's competitiveness. This package of measures is considered "real adjustment." Its implementation would have stimulated private investment, thereby stimulating Côte d'Ivoire's economic growth. The country's political and social constraints explain why such "real adjustment" was not chosen by the government. But the disinclination of economists to engage the sociopolitical constraints has made the debate over adjustment artificial.

The fiscal adjustments implemented by the government essentially have addressed spending and only marginally addressed the matter of receipts.[115] To be sure, one of the first prime minister's first objectives was to recover overdue taxes. But even if it is assumed that the tax on private and foreign enterprises could be

114. Lionel Demery, "Fettered Adjustment: the Case of Côte d'Ivoire in the 1980s," April 1993.

115. Shantayanan Devarajan, "Comments on 'Côte d'Ivoire: The Failure of Structural Adjustment,' by Christophe Chamley," in Paul Mosley, Jane Harrigan, and John Toye, eds., *AID and Power: The World Bank and Policy Based Lending*, vol. 2 (London: Routledge, 1991), pp. 305–308.

recovered, it is hardly likely that the taxes on private property would be similarly enforced. Arguably, the protection granted to the political class (which is also the propertied class) and to those who gravitate around it partially explains why taxes, particularly those long overdue, are not being paid. This is why adjustment efforts have focused on public investment spending rather than on revenues.

Civil servants' salaries today represent too heavy a burden for the treasury. The government can reduce the wage bill either by dismissing some civil servants or by keeping them all but at reduced nominal salaries. The second approach was tried in the early 1980s; it affected a minority of employees in the public sector and in the para-public sector, whose wages were realigned with those of general civil service employees. The change went smoothly because of the small number of people involved and because the main union to which the workers belonged (the Union Générale de Travailleurs de Côte d'Ivoire) was aligned with the party in power. The same approach was tried in 1990, but without success because of the political turmoil that then threatened the regime itself, and which led to the establishment of the multiparty system—the most important by-product of the upheaval.

The difference in success between these two attempts to reduce the wage bill can be explained by the determination to apply the measure, during the second episode, to all 120,000 civil servants at once. It can also be explained by the political power of the teaching trade unions (at all levels), which represented a large percentage of those civil servants. Because of its financial problems the government would have liked to cut civil service salaries, but it hesitated to do so because of the political costs. It would have been out of character for the president to have imposed such a burden on public employees.

This was a costly inhibition for the country, because it left public investment to bear the bulk of the financial adjustment burden. As perceived by Côte d'Ivoire's government, the political cost outweighed the economic cost. It seems to us that the best way to reduce that political cost would be to create a national consensus on a new plan for society, a plan that would be managed by stable institutions whose mandate would be recognized by all. But to this day such a consensus has not been on the agenda.

In Côte d'Ivoire until the beginning of 1994, however, the worst obstacle to orthodox adjustment reform was the adamant opposition of the government (with the government of France standing behind it) to devaluation of the CFA franc. For some years the Bank had deplored this stance, even if its protests were muted. With the death of President Houphouët-Boigny and French approval of a 50 percent devaluation of the CFA franc at the beginning of 1994, the obstacles to orthodox adjustment, although by no means eliminated, on the domestic side appeared to be dramatically reduced. The question of how complete an adjustment may be in prospect, however, brings us to a second hypothesis on what went wrong.

Structural Problems in the Economy

During the recession created or intensified by the drop in public investment, the desired cuts in imports and in domestic inflation in fact occurred; these have been the main achievements of the monetary stabilization policies. But Côte d'Ivoire's nonagricultural exports did not increase to compensate for the losses of foreign exchange in the coffee and cocoa trade. Thus the weakness of industrial exports prevented the restoration of growth and of debt servicing. Evidently correcting the internal disequilibrium, in particular the primary fiscal disequilibrium, does not automatically create propitious conditions for correcting the external disequilibrium. More specifically, perhaps the devaluation of the CFA franc, considered the sine qua non for growth in economic activity in Côte d'Ivoire, will not necessarily unleash such growth.[116]

The effective real exchange rate is the most important relative price for the economy, and any policy that moves it to a competitive level is welcome. However, such a manipulation alone (or even coupled with the traditional measures that come with it) is unlikely to be sufficient to create the desired behavior at the entrepreneurial level and to modify concretely the composition of Côte d'Ivoire's production in a way required by the current economic situation. The structural change required today is to produce less coffee and cocoa for export and more industrial exports, including those associated with the two primary products. It is essential that Côte d'Ivoire substitute tradeable goods for nontradeables, as recommended by the adjustment model used by the Bretton Woods institutions. It is our opinion that Côte d'Ivoire should go beyond such an adjustment; the country should especially seek to substitute industrial exports for the primary exports of coffee and cocoa. Such a substitution would protect the country from fluctuations in raw material prices. As long as the decline in the price for raw materials continues, a devaluation of the CFA franc is unlikely to solve Côte d'Ivoire's growth and debt problems because it cannot instantaneously increase the elasticity of technical transformation of industrial exports.

The excessive reliance of Côte d'Ivoire's economy on coffee and cocoa underlies the rigidity of the system of production, the fragility of the country's financial system, and the structure of government fiscal revenues. With the exception of Gilles Duruflé, those who recognize this fundamental structural problem rarely indicate the nature of the transformation required to make the economy more flexible.[117] Considering the diversification already achieved in agriculture, it is difficult to see where nontraditional agricultural exports, capable of compensating

---

116. Demery, "Fettered Adjustment"; Devarajan, "Comments on 'Côte d'Ivoire.'"

117. Gilles Duruflé, *L'Ajustement Structurel en Afrique: Sénégal, Côte d'Ivoire, Madagascar* (Paris: Editions Karthala, 1988); Christophe Chamley, "Côte d'Ivoire: The Failure of Structural Adjustment," in Paul Mosley, Jane Harrigan, and John Toye, eds., *AID and Power: The World Bank and Policy Based Lending*, vol. 2 (London: Routledge, 1991), pp. 287–305.

for losses in foreign exchange from unfavorable coffee and cocoa sales, could come from. Only diversified industrial exports would fill this void. To this end, industrial enterprises must develop a culture of industrial exportation—that is to say, put themselves in the psychological and technical disposition necessary for a battle against stronger adversaries in international markets. Unfortunately, such an aggressive commercial culture is seriously lacking. The maintenance of a competitive effective real exchange rate could contribute to a culture of industrial exportation, but cannot create it.

To rely on relative price adjustments as the World Bank does, when the real Ivorian constraints are structural, is to be dogmatic. However, once dogmatism is rejected, it must be recognized that in practice the country cannot wait for years for structural change to effectively bring about a more flexible system of production. The Bank quite pragmatically should use the correction of relative tradeable-goods prices as a way to win time, rather than viewing it as a measure that might definitively uproot the structural malfunctions of the Ivorian economy. While such a holding operation is under way, steps designed to build a culture of industrial exportation should be pursued. Otherwise need for the correction of relative prices (by devaluations, for example) will become increasingly frequent and increasingly costly.

It is useful to examine, as Devarajan has done, the reasons for the country's economic growth during the period of prosperity before the adjustment crisis.[118] The massive presence of the government and the distortions associated with that presence are not new phenomena. The investment code and industrial protection have been in place since 1959; minimum wage laws date to before the 1960s; and throughout the period of prosperity public enterprises proliferated. The fixed parity of the CFA franc with the French franc was the primary distortion; it was in effect from 1946. Despite the government's presence and the distortions it created, Côte d'Ivoire's economy achieved a growth rate of approximately 7 percent in real terms over a twenty-year period (1960–80). What, then, was the engine of this exemplary growth?

The answer is public investment, which opened up the agricultural sector and integrated it with domestic and external markets, and which developed the physical infrastructure (particularly Abidjan's port) and popularized improved agricultural techniques. This led to the spectacular development of an industry- and export-oriented agriculture. In our opinion, the mutual reinforcement of relative prices and productive public investment was the key to the growth of the country's agriculture. Relative prices alone, even if appropriate, could not have produced such a result. The elimination of structural constraints—namely, communication and knowledge barriers to peasants' access to modern agricultural methods—allowed remunerative agricultural prices to have a significant impact on agricultural production. Public investment in physical infrastructure was an essential facilitator of

118. See Devarajan, "Comments on 'Côte d'Ivoire.'"

agricultural dynamism, from which other sectors and private economic agents later benefitted. Because public investment is governmentally determined, it can be said that the persevering determination of a shrewd and creative government in eliminating the real constraints on modernized agriculture has been the key to the country's rapid economic growth.

By reducing public investment to the current low level, macroeconomic adjustment therefore has broken the engine of Côte d'Ivoire's economic growth. For this type of adjustment to succeed, the structure of the economy should have been less dependent on government activity and protection. In our opinion, the significant drop in private investment, which was accustomed to relying on government activity and protection, is explained chiefly by the collapse of public investment.[119]

The World Bank had always wanted the Côte d'Ivoire government to cut its public investment program, arguing that the program was too ambitious to be sustained over a long period. Thus the recent reduction, forced by the government's diminished financial means, is what the Bank had been seeking. But it has not paid off. Although the government deficit has narrowed, private investment, on which all hope rested, is now collapsing in an unprecedented fashion. The country is still waiting for the cut in government size to stimulate private investment.

A less ambitious, more selective and timely restraint on public investment might have worked better. But the government was too slow off the mark. For a long time it chose to ignore the Bank's advice to moderate its ambitious and imprudent investment policy. From the beginning of the 1960s the Bank had emphasized the risk that such a policy would become bogged down in untenable debt. History will show that the Bank was the first international institution to warn the government about the disastrous consequences of its policy, and the Bank was right to keep sounding the alarm right up to the eve of the crisis.

Although the government began to realize in 1978 that the boom in raw materials in 1976 and 1977 was not yielding permanent revenue gains, and as a consequence delayed or canceled certain public investment projects, formal adjustment only began in 1981. This was too late to heed the Bank's persistent warnings and advice. By then the country's economic disease was too advanced to permit an easy and swift recovery. And it is true that, by the standards of orthodox adjustment therapy, the reform agenda adopted was less than optimal. Disagreements within the government led to delays, and, arguably, the reforms were wrongly sequenced. If the regime had been able to cut the number of salaried workers in the state sector, relax labor market regulations, and devalue the CFA franc *before* public investment was reduced, the system's increased flexibility might have accommodated a countervailing rise in private investment.

But about such a rise we are skeptical. The outlook for investment in enhanced industrial export capacity was dim unless there was a change in the mentality and

119. See Pégatiénan, "Sources of Economic Growth."

behavior of industrial enterprises that had become dependent on protected domestic markets. Price flexibility does not directly address the structural constraints imposed by the lack of a culture of industrial exportation. Instead of promoting it, the reforms on which the government and the Bank focused postulated that such a culture already existed.

Conclusions

In Côte d'Ivoire the World Bank addressed a country long admired for its economic success, with strong, enduring leadership and a strong, possessive patron. Did the Bank's intervention affect the country's life and political changes? Before the crisis, the Bank had little opportunity to influence the political life in a direction that was not desired by the government, because the government could do without Bank assistance without serious consequences. Furthermore, during the period of economic prosperity the country functioned in a political atmosphere bound by unity of thought and action (at least in appearance) between the government and the population. All government decisions were generally implemented without any real chance of being modified by the populace. The Bank itself recognized the autocratic nature of the political regime in place. "The PDCI [Partie Democratique de la Côte d'Ivoire], the single ruling party, includes most elements of the country's political life. Dissent, to the extent that it exists, is underground."[120]

By financially supporting, in a decisive manner, the government's action, the Bank helped to consolidate a political regime. The Bank's reinforcement of the political regime was facilitated by the regime's liberal economic stance. Moreover, the Bank has admitted that by financing the activities of public enterprises it contributed to reinforcement of those distortions associated with the state's intervention that it is fighting today.[121] It must also accept that through the same financing it actively supported and strengthened political monolithism instead of true democracy.

With regard to the political changes during the latter years of the Houphouët-Boigny regime, the Bretton Woods institutions probably influenced not only the creation but also the choice of the prime minister in November 1990. The first to hold this position had the advantage of being well regarded because of his experience at the International Monetary Fund, as the former director for the Africa region. Such experience was reassuring in view of the economic reforms that had to be undertaken. The Bank and the government, in 1991 and 1992, negotiated three sectoral adjustment loans aimed at improving the competitiveness of the economy, developing human resources, and making the financial sector healthier. If the

---

120. World Bank, "Country Program Paper: Ivory Coast," November 16, 1977.
121. World Bank, "Côte d'Ivoire Agricultural Sector Adjustment Operation."

extent of financing designed to support the structural and institutional measures contained in this reform program reflected the confidence the Bank had in the prime minister's actions, it can be said that the Bank certainly has influenced the short-term economic future of the ruling political regime.

About the attitude of France to the "real adjustment" recommended by the Bank it is possible to speculate. That attitude can be interpreted as a protest against the harshness of the Bank's posture, or as resistance to a liberal policy seen to go against French economic and political interests in Côte d'Ivoire, or as a combination of these elements. Whatever its motivation, France's attitude clearly has tempered the Bank's forthrightness; the Bank has displayed a certain weakness vis-à-vis Côte d'Ivoire.

It can be argued that the direct pressures the Bretton Woods institutions placed on the Francophone African governments by slowing down Bank and IMF financial transfers eventually paid off in that the CFA franc finally was strongly devalued. In view of the opposition of these African governments as a whole, however, it is certain that this historic decision would not have been made without the turnaround of France. Similarly, the reform undoubtedly was facilitated by Côte d'Ivoire's shift on the matter just before President Houphouët-Boigny fell ill in mid-1993.

Can the Bank intervene in sectors that are of strategic importance to France? Côte d'Ivoire has been a beacon for the Bank's liberal policies. The country has presented an example of what needed to be done in certain key sectors such as agriculture. Thus, with a focus on tropical tree crops, the Bank has been prepared to assist the country in exploiting the economic potential it has been able to accumulate throughout the years. However, it is possible that in the future the Bank will not provide Côte d'Ivoire with all the assistance the country may desire when dealing with sectors that conflict with France's economic and political strategy, even though that assistance might be essential for effective realization of Ivorian economic potential. This may apply not just in matters of currency, but also in the development of a trained work force and to scientific research, each of which is a highly strategic activity without which economic and political sovereignty cannot be effectively exerted. Given its economic and political weight, Côte d'Ivoire is an essential focal point for France's influence in Francophone Africa, and France continues to resist the intrusion of other actors into these strategic sectors.

Can the Bank support Côte d'Ivoire against French wishes? Bank deference to France might force the Bank to suspend its pressure on the Ivorian government. The ultimate sanction the Bank can exert on the government is the interruption of its programs in Côte d'Ivoire. But this pressure would not be constraining as long as France would be ready to pay enough Ivorian bills. As recently as January 12, 1994, when France decided to push African countries to accept devaluation, pressures emanating from the Bank were not very constraining.

Now that the Ivorian economy has become more competitive the government again faces challenges, one of which is reinforcement of the monopoly of French capital in the Ivorian economy. The reinforcement of French financial and economic presence is France's reward for the role it played in settling President Houphouët-Boigny's succession in favor of Henri Konan Bédié. In essence, on December 8, 1993, it was the French role that guaranteed that article 11 of the constitution would be applied quickly and fully.

In accepting French monopoly, Côte d'Ivoire has chosen to remain in an expensive economic zone. At the same time, French influence in the country has been strengthened by the uncertainties of the present transitional period and by the political imponderables of the 1995 general elections. The dialogue between the Bank and Côte d'Ivoire, intensified by the CFA franc's devaluation and the accompanying measures, will always involve France.

We can conclude that thirteen years after the beginning of the adjustment policy, the main objective of that policy—renewed economic growth—had not yet been reached. The fundamental structural problem of Côte d'Ivoire's economy is not directly addressed by the proposed adjustment measures, and those measures that were implemented by the government broke the engine of economic growth. The primary measures contained in the "real adjustment" proposed by the Bank involve a political price too high for the government to pay. The political context of the end of an era in Côte d'Ivoire has not lent itself to full-scale adjustment. Furthermore, intervention by France has postponed those reforms that, without uprooting Côte d'Ivoire's structural economic deficiencies, could help to move the economy in the right direction. Côte d'Ivoire has chosen for a long time not to follow the Bank on a few essential aspects of its reform policy. In this complex situation the Bank's freedom of action in regard to Côte d'Ivoire and its protector, France, is quite restricted.

Côte d'Ivoire remains a strategic country for France, even if President Konan Bédié does not possess the stature of the late President Houphouët-Boigny. It would therefore not be surprising if France intervenes more often than before in the dialogue between the World Bank and Côte d'Ivoire.

FIVE

The World Bank in Africa since 1980: The Politics of Structural Adjustment Lending

Carol Lancaster

THERE is no region of the world where the World Bank is more visible and more influential than in Sub-Saharan Africa.[1] The Bank is one of the largest and most active providers of foreign aid in a region where most aid-giving governments and international institutions have programs. Foreign aid in Africa has become a major source of domestic investment and an important lever used by aid donors to encourage recipient governments to undertake economic and political reforms. The Bank has taken a lead role in promoting economic reforms by African governments and coordination among aid donors in supporting those reforms.

The role of the World Bank in Africa has not always been so prominent. During the first two decades of its lending in the region, the Bank remained a relatively

Editors' Note: A valued member of the World Bank History Project's advisory committee was Philip Ndegwa, formerly a leading Kenyan official and economist. In 1992 Mr. Ndegwa and Professor Lancaster, whose work on African development had long overlapped, agreed to collaborate on a general chapter on the World Bank's experience in Africa. But Ndegwa was running Kenya's national airline, and in early 1993 Lancaster became absorbed in her new role as deputy administrator of the U.S. Agency for International Development. Although the coauthors could not get together, Ndegwa did send Lancaster extensive comments on an early draft of the chapter. When he very sadly and unexpectedly passed away in January 1996, Lancaster, his family, and we all agreed that his comments (very lightly edited) should be appended to the Lancaster chapter, both for their intrinsic worth and in affectionate tribute to this fine colleague.

1. The focus of this chapter is Sub-Saharan Africa. I will use the terms *Africa* and *Sub-Saharan Africa* interchangeably.

small and conservative donor, providing aid primarily for projects in such areas as infrastructure, energy, and education. It was only with the second oil price increase in 1979 and the ensuing balance of payments crisis that World Bank lending in Africa expanded rapidly and the emphasis in that lending shifted from projects to programs of structural adjustment.

The visibility of its lending in Africa over the last decade and a half and the breadth and depth of the reforms it has advocated have made the Bank the object of considerable controversy and criticism, both in Africa and abroad. Objections have been raised about the nature and pace of the reforms it has promoted and the way its staff has pushed those reforms. More fundamentally, some Africans and outside experts have criticized the Bank's apparent degree of influence over policy-making in Africa as a new form of colonialism, threatening the very sovereignty of African regimes.

These criticisms often overlook the very real constraints on the Bank's influence in Africa, which derive from the nature of the institution itself and its imperatives to lend and from the diversity of other donors operating in the region, whose varying interests do not always coincide with the goals of the Bank.

The Bank has been well aware of both the potential costs of its high profile in Africa and the limitations on its influence there, and it has taken measures to address these two problems. These aspects of the World Bank in Africa over the past decade are relatively little known but are key parts of its activities and a major focus of this chapter.

The Early Years: 1963–79

The World Bank made its first loan to an African government, Ethiopia, in 1950, to finance road rehabilitation. At that time, there were only two African members of the World Bank. In the ensuing years, the number of African member states rose rapidly as independence swept the continent: in 1957 there were still only two African members in the Bank, but by 1971 African membership had grown to forty.[2] With African countries joining at a rapid pace, the Bank struggled initially to familiarize itself with the problems and personalities of the region. The first step in dealing with a new member was to send out an economic mission. Once the economies were analyzed, it still took some time to propose and appraise projects. Unlike India, Pakistan, and the Latin American countries, the African countries lacked the administrative capacity to navigate projects through the Bank's rigorous project pipeline. The Bank was thereby called upon to provide technical assistance, not always evident in lending statistics.

2. Edward S. Mason and Robert E. Asher, *The World Bank since Bretton Woods* (Brookings, 1973), p. 65.

Lending to countries of Sub-Saharan Africa grew steadily, reaching $2.186 billion by fiscal year 1970.[3] During the 1960s, World Bank lending in Africa concentrated on transportation and power development. Loans for these purposes reflected the then prevailing Western views on the role of foreign aid in development: it was to finance the foreign exchange costs of investments in physical and human infrastructure that were necessary to encourage private investment and growth.

As views on development and the role of foreign aid in supporting it shifted during the 1970s, so did the nature of World Bank lending in Africa. Lending to the region in the 1970s focused on agriculture and rural development (35 percent of total project lending for 1975–79), while transportation projects remained a large portion of total lending and education projects roughly equaled power projects (see table 5-1). During this decade, overall Bank lending in Africa rose steadily, from a total of 123 projects funded during the 1960s to 583 during the 1970s. The terms of lending softened as well, as lending by the International Bank for Reconstruction and Development (IBRD) decreased and highly concessional lending from the International Development Association (IDA) rose (see table 5-2).

During the 1960s and 1970s, World Bank lending in Africa, although increasing, was still a relatively small proportion—between 10 and 20 percent—of total flows of aid to the region. The Bank's presence and influence remained limited. However, those Africans involved with the Bank and the International Monetary Fund —the ministers of finance who were among the governors of the institution— organized themselves early. In 1964, African representatives met at each annual meeting, discussed issues of common concern, and presented their views in a letter to the management of the Bank. The first memo of this group to the then president of the World Bank, George Woods, and to the managing director of the IMF, urged that special attention be given to the needs and priorities of African members, especially in the agricultural and social sectors; that resources of the Bank's soft loan window—IDA—be expanded; that the Bank find ways to refinance suppliers' credits (permitting Africans to borrow further from suppliers); that the Bank reduce the interest charged for its loans; and that it finance local currency costs of its projects. Behind most of the Africans' proposals were the goals of increasing the size and flexibility of Bank lending and reducing the costs to borrowers.[4]

In a point-by-point reply to this first memorandum from its African members, the president of the World Bank and the managing director of the IMF politely rejected most of the Africans' requests.[5] This exchange set the pattern for the next few years, in which African governors urged the Bank to lend more and on more

3. World Bank, *Annual Report,* 1970.
4. "Memorandum on African Problems" from African Caucus to George D. Woods, president, World Bank, IDA, and IFC, and Pierre-Paul Schweitzer, managing director, IMF, September 11, 1964.
5. Response by Woods and Schweitzer to "Memorandum on African Problems," September 1964.

Table 5-1. *Average Annual IBRD and IDA Commitments to Sub-Saharan Africa, by Sector, Fiscal Years 1960–94*
Percent

Type of lending and sector	1960–64	1965–69	1970–74	1975–79	1980–84	1985–89	1990–94
Project lending sector							
Agriculture	17	13	24	35	31	29	18
Education	1	12	11	8	7	7	10
Energy	0	0	0	0	5	1	5
Finance	0	1	4	6	6	2	2
Industrial	0	0	0	5	3	2	2
Mining	15	4	2	2	1	0	0
Other nonsector	0	0	0	1	5	3	2
Population	0	0	0	0	1	5	10
Power	46	10	14	6	11	7	8
Public sector management	0	5	0	0	0	0	1
Telecommunications	1	3	4	2	2	3	3
Tourism	0	0	0	1	0	0	0
Transportation	20	52	38	25	21	22	20
Urban development	0	0	0	3	3	10	8
Water supply	0	1	2	6	4	6	8
Total	100	100	100	100	100[a]	100[a]	100[a]
Adjustment lending sector							
Agriculture	0	0	0	0	22	7	13
Education	0	0	0	0	0	1	11
Finance	0	0	0	0	4	26	21
Industrial	0	0	0	0	0	3	4
Mining	0	0	0	0	4	0	0
Other nonsector	0	0	0	37	70	58	46
Population	0	0	0	0	0	0	2
Power	0	0	0	0	0	0	1
Public sector management	0	0	100	63	0	5	2
Water supply	0	0	0	0	0	0	0
Total	0	0	100	100	100	100	100

Source: LCI Database.
a. Includes lending for which no sector classification was available.

favorable terms to Africa and the Bank management responded by citing what they had done and planned to do in regard to African priorities but acceded to few of the actual demands.

With the election of Robert McNamara as president of the Bank in 1968, the tone of the responses to the annual memorandum from the African governors— now organized in an African caucus—became more forthcoming and in agreement with a number of the recommendations made by the Africans. McNamara, for

Table 5-2. *Bank Group Financial Role in Sub-Saharan Africa, Selected Years, 1970–90*

Millions of 1990 U.S. dollars

Debt category	1970	1975	1980	1985	1990
IBRD/IDA commitments, nonadjustment lending	1,090	2,050	2,180	1,800	2,600
IBRD/IDA commitments, adjustment lending	0	130	180	230	1,260
Total IBRD/IDA commitments	1,090	2,180	2,360	2,030	3,860
Percentage IBRD	64	60	35	46	16
Total IBRD/IDA disbursements	544	1,086.4	1,168.6	2,172.6	2,852.0
IDA disbursement as percentage of ODA disbursement	6	6	6	8	12
ODA disbursements	4,400	8,200	10,866.5	15,086.5	17,407.5
Total external debt as percentage of GNP	. . .	. . .	28	56	107
Debt outstanding and disbursed as percentage of GNP	13	15	18	39	107
Total debt service as percentage of exports	61	58	79	178	316

Source: World Bank LCI Database; World Debt Tables, 1981, 1982, 1983, 1985, 1989, 1992; OECD Development Co-Operation Annual Reports, 1975, 1978, 1986, 1989, 1994.

example, committed the Bank to triple its lending rate to Africa over the coming five years, to set up additional permanent missions in Africa, to lend to development finance banks, and to give greater emphasis in Bank operations to agriculture and education. The Bank management was more sympathetic under McNamara's leadership both because McNamara himself quickly became a development enthusiast and because Africa remained the region of the developing world with the most poor countries and the most difficult development challenges. But more practically, McNamara's goal of rapidly expanding Bank lending worldwide required increased lending in Africa. And to do so with a minimum of second thoughts and haggling on the part of Africans, the Bank management had to establish more responsive and harmonious relationships with its African member governments. Being more sympathetic to their views and requests was one way of doing so.

During the 1970s, the types of projects broadened to include rural development and more social sector activities, consistent with the growing focus by the Bank and other donors on alleviating poverty and meeting basic human needs. The principal group of Africans concerned with the role of the Bank in Africa remained the government ministers, particularly ministers of finance and planning responsible for overseeing relations with the Bank. But that was soon to change.

The Bank in Africa in the 1980s

As the 1980s began, many of the countries of Sub-Saharan Africa faced the most severe economic crisis in their two decades of independence. The second oil shock plus inflation in the West had resulted in rapidly rising prices for their imports of petroleum and manufactured goods. Meanwhile, prices had collapsed during the latter half of the 1970s for many metals, tropical beverages, uranium, and other raw materials, causing African countries' earnings from exports to drop, sometimes dramatically. And by the mid-1980s, the fall in oil prices caused a balance of payments crisis for the petroleum-exporting countries of Africa, which had earlier benefited from the surge in oil prices.

A number of African governments, hoping that their balance of payments crisis was transitory, borrowed commercially to fill the gap.[6] When commercial lending to Africa dried up after 1982, a number of governments—now unable to service their foreign debts—called for debt rescheduling. Some imposed controls on allocations of foreign exchange, hoping to reduce their import bill. And many turned to their traditional sources of foreign aid and to the World Bank for extra assistance.

Few believed that the increases in petroleum prices were temporary. Non-petroleum-producing countries would have to adjust their economies to export more and import less if they were to close the gap in their balance of payments. This was one of the origins of the new thrust in Bank lending, termed *structural adjustment.* Lending would involve a transfer of resources to an African government (a "program" rather than a "project loan," which could be used to finance imports) in support of, or—as many saw it—in exchange for agreed economic policy reforms, including trade liberalization, increases in prices for agricultural goods (especially export crops), reform of financial systems, and a host of other changes in economic policies and institutions.[7] At the same time, the IMF was

6. Guaranteed commercial bank debt as a percentage of total long-term debt for all Sub-Saharan African countries rose from 2.3 percent in 1970 to 19.1 percent by 1980, but then retreated to 15.3 percent by 1986. Nigeria's share in commercial debt (which jumped from 3.2 percent in 1970 to 49.0 percent in 1980) was a large factor in this marked rise, but other countries also borrowed heavily from commercial banks during this period, including Côte d'Ivoire and Kenya. World Bank, *World Debt Tables, 1994–95,* vol. 2 (Washington: World Bank, 1994).

7. The first adjustment loan to Senegal in 1980, for instance, spelled out six realms of economic reform. Public finance reforms called for eliminating the overall budget deficit and increasing the ratio of public savings covering public investment initially to 15 percent, and thereafter to 25 percent, in addition to repaying arrears and freezing expenditures. In its investment program, the government agreed to raise the share of directly productive investment in its total investment program from 43 percent to 55 percent and to improve its project selection. Some parastatals were to be privatized, and those remaining were to have greater autonomy. A de facto devaluation of 15 percent (subsidies on nontraditional exports,

conditioning its rapidly expanded lending to African governments on their adoption of "stabilization" programs, which were intended to reduce inflation and close the gap in the balance of payments. These programs normally included an exchange rate devaluation, restrictions on domestic credit, and reductions in the fiscal deficit. They often overlapped with structural adjustment programs supported by the Bank. Indeed, they were often coordinated with those of the Bank and vice versa.

In an effort to persuade the Bank and other aid donors to expand their assistance to Africa, the African governors at the annual Bank-Fund meeting in Belgrade in 1979 asked the Bank to prepare a special paper on their economic crisis, to define the role of the international community in solving this crisis, and to produce a "special program of action" within the Bank to assist the region, both with its own resources and by mobilizing those of others. This study, published in 1981 and entitled *Accelerated Growth in Sub-Saharan Africa: An Agenda for Action,* certainly called attention to the deepening economic problems facing Africa and recommended a doubling in aid to the region. But far more important, it argued strongly that economic policy reform was critical to any economic recovery in Africa. The "Berg report," as the study came to be known (the principal author was Elliot Berg), provided a rationale for structural adjustment lending in Africa. It argued in particular that domestic policy deficiencies and administrative constraints impeded economic progress, and it called for policy reform in trade, exchange rates, and the agricultural sector, as well as increased efficiency in the public sector's use of resources. Implicit in this argument, and soon to be explicit in analyses of African economic problems by the Bank and other institutions, was the conclusion that state-led development had been a failure. The role of the state needed to be diminished in favor of free markets and the private sector if healthy economic growth were ever to be achieved in the region.

The Bank's report produced a storm of criticism in Africa and among many individuals and institutions working in Africa, including Western academics, private voluntary organizations, and international institutions such as UNICEF. There were complaints about high-handedness on the part of the Bank for publicly criticizing the policies of African governments and infringing on the sovereignty of African countries if assistance was conditioned on policy reform. There were also criticisms that the policy prescriptions themselves were inappropriate, that the state still had a key role to play in development in Africa, that the amount and pace

---

extra duties on imports) would be implemented in order to reform prices and producers' incentives. As for agricultural institutions, the government agreed to conduct a number of studies on a new cooperative structure and to reform agricultural credit. Ceilings on commercial debt were to be placed to reign in external debt, and in monetary policy, monthly credit ceilings were set. See World Bank, "Program Performance Audit Report: Senegal—Structural Adjustment Loan and Credit," Operations Evaluation Department, Report 5637, May 9, 1985 (SecM85-624), pp. 2–4.

of proposed reforms were unrealistic, and that the kinds of economic reforms proposed would be especially costly to the poor, who stood to lose jobs, subsidies, social services, and real income. Africans also saw the Berg report's criticisms of state intervention in the economy as an indirect criticism of the Lagos Plan of Action, which was signed by all African heads of state at the Organization of African Unity (OAU) meeting in 1980. Some argued that the real source of economic problems in Africa was an unfavorable and unjust world economy, which should be the major focus of reform efforts.

In contrast to the widespread criticisms of the Berg report in Africa and elsewhere, a number of Western governments welcomed the report. It fitted their analyses of the causes of the region's economic problems, and its emphasis on freeing up markets coincided with their own ideological preferences. (Conservative governments had taken office in the United States, the United Kingdom, and Germany at the beginning of the 1980s.) All of these governments were happy for the World Bank to take the lead in promoting economic reform in Africa. As a multilateral institution, the Bank would probably have fewer problems in pressing for economic change—clearly an intrusive posture—than Western governments. Africans would always be suspect of their economic and political motivations, and their relationships with African governments could be damaged by a too enthusiastic advocacy of painful economic policy changes.

During the 1980s, overall lending by the Bank to African governments expanded rapidly, and the proportion of lending for adjustment expanded even more rapidly (see tables 4-1, 4-2, and 4-3). The types of loans in support of adjustment diversified. In addition to structural adjustment loans, which tended to be relatively large loans for a broad set of macroeconomic reforms, the Bank began to make loans in support of economic reforms in particular sectors. A third type of loan—a mix of adjustment lending and project lending—made its appearance later in the 1980s. By fiscal year 1990, $1.362 billion, or 34.4 percent, of Bank lending to Sub-Saharan Africa was in support of some form of adjustment lending.[8]

Mitigating the Political Costs of Adjustment Lending

Almost from the beginning of the 1980s, senior Bank officials recognized that there would be two challenges in the institution's taking the lead in adjustment lending in Africa. One was dealing with criticisms and resistance by Africans. The other was making sure that other aid donors supported the Bank's approach. Without a measure of acceptance by Africans, the Bank's ability to lend in the region would be limited; and without support from other major donors, its efforts to promote difficult policy reforms would be undercut.

8. World Bank, "Adjustment in Sub-Saharan Africa: Selected Findings from OED Evaluations," June 30, 1993, Report 2155, p. 19.

Dealing with the Africans

The first and most important challenge involved the Africans. Three aspects of Bank-supported structural adjustment in Africa lay behind the criticisms and resistance of Africans: these programs were highly intrusive; they were also often politically painful and even risky; and they were frequently complex and controversial.

REASONS FOR RESISTANCE. Adjustment programs were intrusive in that they brought costs as well as benefits (aid-financed projects normally appeared to bring only benefits), and they affected an entire society or large segments of it. A currency devaluation could significantly raise import prices, for example, which effectively reduced the real income of those directly or indirectly reliant on imports. An increase in food prices would benefit the large numbers of farmers producing food for sale but would also hurt urban dwellers who had to purchase food. Trade liberalization could drive uncompetitive enterprises out of business and expand unemployment.

In addition, Africans were sensitive to the appearance (and reality) of having their policy choices dictated by outside powers or institutions. This sensitivity was heightened by the experience of colonialism, which most of them had escaped no more than two decades earlier. Finally, the sensitivity to Bank intrusiveness was exacerbated by what many Africans regarded as the high-handed and often arrogant style of some Bank staff. One story, widely recounted in Africa, captures this view. Early in the 1980s, the World Bank regional vice president for Eastern Africa paid a visit to Tanzania. The purpose of the visit was to persuade the Tanzanians to eliminate arrears in their payments to the Bank. (According to the then governor of the Central Bank of Tanzania, the failure to repay was a result of a bureaucratic mistake rather than intentional.) In a meeting with Tanzanian President Julius Nyerere (who was apparently unaware of the arrears), the Bank vice president declared that he "had come for his check." This greatly offended Nyerere, who demanded that his aides pay the Bank immediately regardless of the costs, asked the Bank vice president whether the issue of arrears was all he had to talk to a country's president about (the issue being more appropriately raised at the ministerial level), and stood up and left the meeting. Relations between Tanzania and the Bank remained cool for some years after this incident, and the Tanzanian government resisted the adoption of a structural adjustment program.

More generally, criticisms by African officials of the Bank's style often included complaints about the tendency of Bank staff to preach to Africans and at times to appear to be giving instructions to them. (These criticisms were also echoed by various officials of bilateral aid agencies based in African countries.)

More substantive criticisms of the Bank in Africa, particularly in the early days of structural adjustment, included the tendency to apply similar advice to all countries despite their very different political and social characteristics and to require more reforms in a shorter period of time than African governments were capable of implementing. This latter criticism appears to have been indirectly acknowledged by the Bank, as in recent years it has tried to reduce the number of reforms it requests in adjustment programs.

Finally, Africans have been critical of the Bank and of foreign governments alike for not seriously addressing their debt problems. Many African countries are among the most heavily indebted in the world, and much of their debt is owed to the IMF and the World Bank. Africans have argued that structural adjustment—however extensive—is unlikely to contribute to a brighter economic future for their countries as long as their debt burdens remain so great.

Structural adjustment reforms are often politically painful and even risky. They almost always create losers as well as winners, with the losses often experienced almost immediately and the benefits gained over the longer term. While the winners may be expected to act eventually as a constituency in support of reforms, it is hardly surprising that the losers are frequently critical of and resistant to the reforms. In Africa, the political equation of winners and losers has been an especially problematical one. There the losers tended to be the political elites who were the same individuals charged with implementing the reforms. They typically lost their access to cheap imports, economic rents (and the ability to dispense patronage), subsidies of various kinds, and, sometimes, their jobs. The benefits of the reforms typically accrued to the least politically influential group: the small farmers who received higher prices for their products. In contrast to other parts of the developing world, there were few competitive private entrepreneurs who would benefit from reforms; most of the limited private sector was dependent on government protection or largesse to survive, and this tended to diminish as structural adjustment measures were implemented. Thus a politically significant constituency for reform was typically very limited in Africa, as farmers had little voice in the many one-party states and authoritarian regimes of the 1980s. The extreme danger in Africa was that economic reforms would provoke political violence and instability. In fact, this occurred relatively rarely, but it remained a concern among Bank staff and others.

A third element in the challenge of promoting economic reform in Africa was the nature of the reforms themselves. The economic impact claimed for the reforms by the Bank and its supporters was often challenged by Africans and others. Critics often claimed that exchange rate adjustment frequently failed to decrease outlays on imports and increase receipts from exports: indeed, it could widen the gap in the balance of payments as a result of inelasticities in the demand for imports and the response of highly competitive export markets. Another common objection to the reforms was that open markets in states with small and poorly developed markets like those of Africa were seldom free of imperfections that could limit economic growth just as much as the widely acknowledged imperfections of African governments. Further, a common criticism has been that the economic reforms urged by the Bank and other donors harm the poor in particular.

These criticisms were more strident at the beginning of the 1980s, but they have never really abated despite responses from Bank staff and others that they are inaccurate or unfair. Perhaps the only argument that will convince the critics of reform that they are wrong will be several cases of definitive structural adjustment successes in Africa, and these have not yet occurred.

A final criticism, related to the nature and pace of the reforms, is that they are often complex and numerous and overtax the limited abilities of African governments to implement them effectively. For example, changes involving privatization of state-owned enterprises require the government to undertake a complicated and interrelated series of activities (such as evaluation of assets, preparation of assets for sale, the selling process and its management) within a limited period. African ministries tend to have very capable individuals in the few senior positions, but mid-level bureaucrats are often poorly trained and lack authority to make significant decisions. Thus responsibility for implementing reforms tends to land on the desks of the few very busy senior officials or gets stalled at middle levels of the government. Similarly, large numbers of reforms to be implemented over a relatively short period often prove to be beyond the abilities of governments to carry out. These criticisms have been widely acknowledged by officials inside and outside the Bank as having a degree of validity. Yet the policy framework papers drafted by the International Monetary Fund, World Bank staff, and African government officials continue to include large numbers of economic changes to be implemented over a three-year period. There appears to be a political dynamic at work in which each office and institution wishes to make sure "its" reforms are included in the overall package, a phenomenon commented on by a number of observers of the Bank in the past.[9]

In light of all these challenges to the effective implementation of economic reforms in Africa, the Bank recognized that it would have to push reforms in the face of African reluctance and, in so doing, possibly provoke real resistance to or even repudiation of Bank structural adjustment lending. Vociferous and public criticisms of the Bank and repudiation of its adjustment lending by one or more major African countries would probably strengthen resistance by other critics of Bank-sponsored reforms inside and outside African governments and, in the end, limit the ability of the Bank to lend for adjustment in the region. Yet it appears that the Bank very much wished to avoid such limitations.

PRESSURES FOR BORROWING AND LENDING. It must be asked why African governments, desperate for foreign aid even with unwelcome conditions, would reject Bank advice and adjustment lending. There were, in fact, already several

---

9. An internal Bank report observed "a bias for complexity—perhaps caused by the urge to include as many novel features as possible to secure a favorable management and Board response." ("Effective Implementation: Key to Development Impact," R92-195, September 22, 1992, p. iiii.) The comment was made about projects but is equally applicable to adjustment loans.

examples. Tanzania and other governments (such as Zaire, Zambia, Zimbabwe, Ethiopia, and Sudan) at times threatened to reject Bank adjustment aid or for a time actually did so. African political leaders had in the past at times rejected aid when it appeared too costly or threatened their sovereignty; for example, Guinea under Sékou Touré in the early 1960s repudiated Russian and then Western aid. One African government after another broke diplomatic relations with Israel in the early 1970s (and lost the small but valued aid from that country) or with Taiwan earlier (and lost aid from that country with no guarantee that similar amounts of aid from China would be forthcoming). A few African governments, taking a public stand on principle, could set a pattern others might feel compelled to follow.

It must also be asked why an institution like the World Bank, with so many demands for its resources throughout the world, would worry about being unable to lend to a significant number of African governments. There are several reasons why the Bank did not want to see its adjustment lending operations significantly restricted in Sub-Saharan Africa. First, at least since the McNamara presidency, there has been pressure within the Bank—on individual staff, divisions, and regions —to fulfill notional lending quotas by country and region. This pressure to lend has been especially strong when and where the Bank has sought to expand its lending rapidly. The force behind this "lending imperative" (which is often present in aid agencies) is that failure to obligate available funds within an anticipated period suggests to governments contributing funds to the Bank that they are providing more than is really needed. Should there be a shortfall in lending, contributing governments would be likely to reduce the amount of their contributions to the Bank in successive replenishment periods.[10]

Analysts of the Bank have remarked on the pressure on Bank staff to lend, and staff members frequently acknowledge that pressure in private conversations. A critical report on the problems of implementation in the Bank's lending portfolio made its own, somewhat elliptical reference to this problem: "In the eyes of Borrowers and co-lenders as well as staff, the emphasis on timely loan approval (described by some assistance agencies as the 'approval culture') and the often active Bank role in [loan] preparation, may connote a promotional—rather than objective—approach to appraisal."[11]

Pressure to lend was likely to have been especially strongly felt in the Africa region, where the Bank had taken a visible and active role in calling attention to the need for additional assistance to support adjustment programs. Moreover, the institution knew from its own large pipeline of unspent project moneys (a sign that

10. This imperative to lend is obviously stronger in areas drawing on IDA funds, which are highly concessional and are dependent on replenishment by donor governments every three years. Lending programs involving the relatively hard IBRD terms rely on borrowings by the Bank from world money markets and are not as subject to scrutiny or pressure to lend as those associated with IDA. Nearly all lending in Africa is drawn from IDA funds.

11. "Effective Implementation," p. iii.

African governments were having trouble spending existing levels of project assistance) that significantly increased assistance could be programmed only as fast-dispersing, balance of payments financing.

There were other reasons why the Bank was anxious to avoid rejection of its adjustment programs by major African governments. The institution had claimed a visible and active leadership role in promoting adjustment lending in Africa. Its reputation in the region and internationally was riding on making a success of adjustment lending in Africa. If significant numbers of African governments began to reject Bank adjustment programs, its leadership role would be undercut and its reputation damaged. It would also lose the leadership position it had claimed with donor governments in adjustment lending.

Not only does there appear to have been an eagerness to lend for adjustment in Africa, but the Bank was also reluctant to terminate adjustment lending or cancel adjustment programs even when borrowing governments failed to comply with loan conditions. There were several cancellations of adjustment programs for nonperformance, but often these canceled programs were followed by new adjustment loans with many of the same conditions as the previous loan. Outside observers have sometimes argued that the Bank has been subject to pressures by its major contributors to continue lending even when governments were clearly unwilling to abide by conditions. There is some evidence of these pressures, particularly in Francophone Africa. But the Bank has also lent where major member governments objected (for example, in Ethiopia under Mengistu) and has canceled programs where major member states continued to lend (for example, in Zaire).

The real reasons for continuing to lend for adjustment despite noncompliance by recipients appear to come from within the Bank itself. Bank management often hesitates to withdraw from a country where the Bank has put in considerable effort and funding: there is a hope that things will soon improve (there is a culture of optimism in the Bank, often reflected in its reports and projections), or there is concern that if a government does decide to implement an adjustment program, the Bank will not easily regain influence with that government. (These arguments are similar to those often made in bilateral aid agencies against terminating programs.) One senior Bank official put it this way in commenting on Bank programs in two of its poorer adjustment performers:

> Excessive optimism about the external environment . . . about government commitment to policy change, and about the extent of supply responses has characterized Bank operations for a long time. . . . I think the Bank has a particularly difficult time in saying no when it faces a government that is expressing a willingness, and indeed eagerness, to promote reform. . . . After all, we all like to believe in the power of ideas and in our own power of persuasion. . . . I would submit as a general proposition that the Bank tends to give greater weight to the risks of non-involvement (either on the grounds that it would undermine the standing of the reformers in the country, would result in a loss of the Bank's "seat at the table," or would result in serious loss of economic momentum, in loss

of complementary financing, or in avoidable human suffering) than to the risks associated with lending (both risks to the country and risks to the Bank itself).[12]

In its concerns about fully obligating its resources, keeping harmonious relationships with its borrowers, and maintaining its influence and leadership, the Bank begins to resemble aid-giving governments: it has interests and goals beyond those strictly concerned with development that constrain its ability to pursue development goals alone.

The amount of criticism of the Bank provoked by the Berg report, particularly from Africans, surprised senior Bank management. By the early 1980s, the Economic Commission for Africa (ECA) was beginning to voice criticisms of the Berg report and structural adjustment lending. The ECA appeared to be particularly concerned that the Bank's approach to dealing with Africa's growing economic crisis (through policy reform) would eclipse the Lagos Plan of Action, which involved a broad set of actions to be undertaken largely by governments. The intent of the plan was to stimulate development through economic integration, which would create large, protected markets that were expected to boost trade and investment in Africa—in effect, an import substitution policy for the entire continent. Berg and the Bank sought to dismantle barriers to trade in Africa and to reduce the role of the state in development, which was quite the opposite approach from the Lagos Plan, despite diplomatic statements by the Bank at various times during the 1980s acknowledging the plan and expressing its support for economic cooperation in Africa.

BUILDING SUPPORT FOR STRUCTURAL ADJUSTMENT. To deal with the criticisms of its structural adjustment lending, the Bank commissioned an "African Perceptions" study. The study, completed in 1983, was based on interviews held with a variety of individuals in several countries of the region. It contained a number of sharp criticisms of the Bank and recommendations for addressing those criticisms.[13] The criticisms included the limited role and low quality of the Bank's resident missions in Africa, the arrogant and insensitive behavior of Bank staff, their inadequate knowledge of Africa and the demands they make on the time of senior African officials, the tendency on the part of the Bank to impose expatriate consultants on Africans when local Africans could easily act as consultants, and the ineffective public relations activities of the Bank in Africa. These criticisms caused senior Bank management considerable discomfort, and they were anxious that the report not be circulated widely and that its contents—which they saw as potentially

12. Johannes Linn, "Africa Operational Issues" memo, April 2, 1989.
13. The methodology of this study was highly controversial (relying on interviews with a limited sample of people) and its criticisms of the Bank were so incendiary that it had very limited circulation among Bank staff (summaries of its findings were circulated). Even today the text of the study is unavailable to researchers from the Brookings World Bank History Project. Descriptions here of the contents of this report are based on summaries in Bank documents and interviews with one of the drafters of the report.

quite damaging to the Bank's image—not find their way into the public media. But its message was taken seriously, and Bank management held discussions to evaluate its charges.

Bank management also began to take action to deal with the growing criticisms of the institution coming from Africans and others. An internal task force was set up to develop a public affairs strategy, which would include targeting major countries for special efforts at "telling the Bank's story"; strengthening contacts between influential Africans and Bank staff; sponsoring local events to provide better information on the Bank's activities and achievements; inspiring articles on the Bank in newspapers and journals; and developing lists of influential people to invite to Bank activities who would not only help inform the Bank better about their particular countries but would also, it was hoped, present the Bank in a sympathetic light to other Africans.

A host of other activities were undertaken during the 1980s aimed at building consensus on the need for adjustment and support for the Bank in Africa. The number of resident missions was expanded to include nearly every African country with an adjustment program, and the level of Bank representation was upgraded. The Bank tripled the number of mid- and high-level African officials in courses on development and economic reform offered by its Economic Development Institute in Washington between 1983 and 1987 (totaling over 4,000 for the five-year period). It increased its use of African consultants on Bank studies and other work, and senior Bank staff visiting African countries made greater efforts to meet with prominent individuals and groups (for example, the unions or the "hajjis").[14] A particularly important initiative occurred in 1988, when the Bank launched its Council of African Advisers, made up of fifteen prominent Africans, to meet with senior Bank staff twice a year to discuss and advise on Bank activities in their region. This group was seen as valuable for its advice and support of Bank activities in Africa and was described by a senior Bank official as "an important instrument for the management of the Africa region."

The Bank also took other actions. Like the Fund, the Bank began to seek out and strengthen allies in borrowing governments who supported adjustment programs. (These individuals were frequently but not always ministers of finance.) The Bank understood that without some influential allies in African governments, the prospects for the adoption and implementation of reforms were limited and persuasion or threats by the Bank were of little avail. The Bank began to use the drafting of country strategy statements with African officials as a basis for educating and building consensus within African governments on needed reforms. In 1984 the Bank created a Special Project Preparation Facility to help African governments develop reform programs and investment projects suitable for external financing, through workshops, seminars, and visits abroad for Africans from the

14. Those Moslems who have made the Hajj to Mecca. These individuals tend to be respected and influential in their communities.

public and private sector, including local nongovernmental organizations. This facility was intended to help build support for economic reforms inside and outside African governments. In 1989 the Bank vice president for Africa characterized it as having provided the Bank "the opportunity to make a greater impact, exercise more flexibility, and permit greater advocacy than the objectives and scope of our operations by themselves allow"; it had helped "move governments toward policy or institutional change in areas in which they might otherwise be hesitant to embark."[15]

The most important Bank initiative during the 1980s to build consensus around adjustment programs was the African Long-Term Perspective Study, launched in 1986 and published in 1989. This study was an effort by the Bank to write a comprehensive report on African economies and to identify actions needed to promote future growth. It became a consensus-building document, with background papers contributed by Africans and drafts discussed in conferences and seminars in Africa, Europe, and North America and by the Council of African Advisers. What in the end it lacked in sharpness of focus it gained in breadth. The Bank vice president for Africa described it to the Bank's board of directors as "perhaps the most striking example of how the Bank has taken the lead in developing a coherent, long term strategy to tackle the region's problems."

None of these initiatives by the Bank satisfied or silenced the ECA, whose criticism of Bank adjustment lending grew in stridency during the 1980s. By the middle of the decade, the ECA decided to develop an alternative strategy to adjustment in Africa. A document was drafted and discussed by African planning ministers in Malawi in 1987. Coinciding with the discussion in Malawi, the Bank issued a short report of its own on progress toward adjustment in Africa. Bank staff deny that the timing of this (apparently) hastily drafted report had anything to do with the ECA conference. But the ECA and many other observers saw the timing of the report as a tactic to draw attention away from the ECA report. Thereafter, Bank President Barber Conable asked Adebayo Adedeji, UN undersecretary-general and executive secretary of the ECA, to come to Washington to gain consensus on development approaches in Africa. No consensus was gained; indeed, Bank managers complained that "the ECA continues to criticize the adjustment process and the work of the Bank and Fund in a strident and counterproductive way." The ECA published its report in 1989. The Bank did not see the report as a real alternative to adjustment, and apparently key Africans shared that view. The African representatives to IDA treated it as a "non-event," and at the OAU meeting in Addis Ababa in 1989 not only was there "no enthusiastic support" for the report, but the Nigerian representative declared that there was no alternative to adjustment.

15. Memo from Vice President Edward V. K. Jaycox to Senior Vice President Moeen Qureshi, October 30, 1989, reviewing the performance of the Fund over the past five years.

The weakness of the ECA report, the efforts by the Bank during the 1980s to build consensus among influential Africans for adjustment, and the fact that the Bank had money to lend and the ECA did not explain the failure of the ECA to create a groundswell of resistance to adjustment in Africa and to the Bank's lending activities in support of adjustment there.

Despite the ECA's failure to create an alternative to the Bank, senior Bank staff continued to worry about the lack of consensus among Africans on the need for adjustment. In 1988 Vice President Edward V. K. Jaycox commented to the Bank's board of directors:

> We do not claim that there has been some great religious conversion in Africa that has moved these countries to this state of enlightenment [support for adjustment]. Quite simply, this has happened out of desperation. There is no question about it. . . . In almost every case, a country has gone right to the edge or even fallen over the edge, before it has undertaken an adequate structural adjustment program.[16]

However, in the same presentation, Jaycox complained that "the Bank has become *too important* in Africa. . . . What we do or do not do in Africa now matters too much—because when we give emphasis to something, everyone else tends to march over the horizon in the same direction."[17] The implication of Jaycox's statements is that the Bank had had a great success in its search for influence in Africa and at the same time had failed in some measure by not being able to convince African governments of the salience of adjustment before their economic problems reached crisis proportions.

Dealing with the Donors

The second major challenge facing the Bank in the 1980s, as it claimed a leadership role in promoting structural adjustment in Africa, was coordinating other aid donors: governments and multilateral institutions. There were three parts to this challenge: ensuring that the size of adjustment lending was adequate to encourage African governments to adopt needed reforms; persuading other donors to support the general goals of adjustment lending as well as the specific program goals in individual African countries—and to make that support known to the officials of those countries; and maintaining the Bank's position as the lead agency overall (though not necessarily in individual African countries) in promoting structural adjustment. These concerns of the Bank related to three groups of aid donors and institutions: governments, particularly that of France; other multilaterals, principally the IMF and the African Development Bank and Fund; and the UN, including the secretariat and United Nations Development Program (UNDP).

16. Vice President Edward V. K. Jaycox, statement to the World Bank Board, SECM88-1381, December 7, 1988, p. 4.
17. Ibid., p. 1.

The World Bank developed a number of mechanisms and approaches for coordinating donors: it took the direct approach, making its concerns known to governments and multilateral institutions in the field and in capitals or at their headquarters; it encouraged aid donors to engage in cofinancing of Bank reform programs; it created the Special Program for Africa in the 1980s; and it expanded the use of consultative groups. Some of the approaches recounted below will give a flavor of how the Bank met this challenge and did so with remarkable success.

GOVERNMENTS. The most important support for the Bank's efforts to promote adjustment in Africa came from developed country governments, above all the United States, the United Kingdom, Germany, Japan, and France. For the most part, the United States, the United Kingdom, Germany, and Japan supported the overall goals of adjustment, although for diplomatic, commercial, and occasionally developmental reasons, one or another of these governments criticized or opposed Bank programs in particular countries. But the most difficult problem in coordinating donor governments was with the French. The government of France had long regarded the Bretton Woods twins as *institutions anglo-saxones* (especially the Bank, which has always been headed by an American). In the 1960s, concerned with losing its predominant influence (vis-à-vis other aid donors, especially the United States) in these countries, it did not welcome a significant Bank presence in its former colonial territories. It also feared that the Bank and other donors would undertake activities that did not fit the needs of the countries and France would have to bear the cost of any mistakes.

The Sahelian drought of the 1970s and the spreading balance of payments crisis of the 1980s proved beyond the willingness of the French government to finance alone, and so it chose to accept and even seek aid from other sources, including the Bank. However, its relations with the Bank about adjustment programs were sometimes unsettled. While many of the development experts within the French government recognized the need for policy reforms by Francophone African governments, the political and diplomatic advisors (particularly in the president's office) were primarily concerned with maintaining harmonious political relationships with African leaders. And when leaders strongly objected to Bank programs and took those objections to the French president (as they did on occasion), the French government would at times respond by supporting the Africans rather than the Bank.

The issue that most divided the Bank and the French in Africa was devaluation of the CFA franc. Fourteen Francophone African countries participated in a monetary union with France, with their currency—the CFA franc—tied to the French franc at a fixed rate.[18] It was clear from the beginning of the 1980s that the

18. The CFA franc–zone countries include Benin, Burkina Faso, Cameroon, Central African Republic, Chad, Comoros, Congo, Côte d'Ivoire, Equatorial Guinea (the only non-Francophone member), Gabon, Mali, Niger, Senegal, and Togo.

CFA franc was overvalued, and the Bank believed that this overvaluation was aggravating the balance of payments gaps of these countries (by encouraging imports that were relatively cheap and discouraging exports, which became less and less profitable at world prices). By the end of the 1980s, the overvaluation of the CFA franc had, in the Bank's view, become so great that it blocked any chance of economic progress in the region. Some in the French government shared this view, especially toward the end of the 1980s. Others argued that devaluation would only make matters worse because of unfavorable elasticities of supply and demand of African imports and exports (an argument Africans had often made against devaluation at the beginning of the 1980s). French officials also argued that a devaluation would break the fiscal discipline policies imposed on African governments through their membership in the franc zone, discourage trade and investment in the region, and provoke economically disruptive speculation against the CFA in the future. Most Francophone Africans who followed these issues (that is, political elites) opposed devaluation on the same grounds and also gained considerable benefits from maintaining an overvalued currency. But behind these economic arguments was a major political concern on the part of both African leaders and the French: the CFA franc had become an important symbol of France's engagement in Africa. A devaluation of the franc might well be seen as a sign of lessening French interest and engagement in the region (there were already signs of this in other quarters). Neither side wanted to give such a signal. And the French in particular were reluctant to support a devaluation of the CFA franc without African support, even though maintaining the value of the currency was reportedly costing the French treasury upwards of $1 billion a year by the end of the 1980s.[19]

The issue of a CFA devaluation became so sensitive with the government of France that Bank staff were reluctant to talk about it even in private. One senior manager in the Africa department was removed in the late 1980s, reportedly at French insistence, for talking about the need for a devaluation privately to African officials.

The focus of the CFA problem was on Côte d'Ivoire, although the issue came up often with regard to Senegal, Cameroon, and other of the larger Francophone African countries. By the end of the 1970s, the problem of an overvalued CFA franc had already been recognized by Bank staff. But Côte d'Ivoire had long been one of the few successful examples of African development based on relatively free markets. The Bank therefore continued to lend there (on the hard terms of IBRD

---

19. Nicolas van de Walle notes that "France handed out 20 billion French francs to support the CFA franc's parity in 1988 alone." See Nicolas van de Walle, "The Decline of the Franc Zone: Monetary Politics in Francophone Africa," *African Affairs*, vol. 90 (July 1991), p. 393. The French, of course, benefited from their support of the CFA franc, their aid, and other support for their former African territories. French commercial interests often enjoyed preferential access and treatment, and France maintained its special influence in these countries.

loans because of the relatively high levels of per capita income). During the 1980s, the country benefited from Bank project lending as well as three structural adjustment loans. Despite these loans, there was little sign of economic recovery, and indeed per capita income dropped by 25 percent between 1986 and 1990. By 1987 Bank staff were warning that continued lending there was risky unless the government could deal with the problem of CFA overvaluation.

There were essentially two ways of dealing with the CFA problem: to devalue the currency or to deflate the domestic economy. By pushing down domestic prices and incomes, the demand for imports would fall and resources would be freed up to produce increased exports. It was this approach that the government of Côte d'Ivoire attempted at the end of the 1980s. One key element in domestic deflation had to be a reduction in nominal salaries of civil service employees, as these salaries had remained high since independence and constituted a major portion of the government's budget. Both the Bank and the Fund urged the government to decrease salaries, and future lending from these institutions was certainly conditioned on these and other actions to make the economy "more competitive." However, an effort to decrease salaries in 1989 led to riots and almost toppled the government.

In the wake of the riots, President Felix Houphouët-Boigny asked Allassane Ouattara (from Burkina Faso) to become prime minister and undertake an economic reform program. Ouattara was then governor of the Banque Centrale des Etats de l'Afrique de l'Ouest, the central financial institution for six West African countries in the CFA franc zone, and had previously been director of the Africa region of the IMF. He was highly regarded by the management of the Bank and Fund. Upon taking office, he argued that the Bank, which was threatening to cut off disbursements of several sectoral adjustment programs, should continue those disbursements while he developed a medium-term plan for restoring the competitiveness of the Ivorian economy. The French government supported him within the Bank. The French were concerned that a cutoff of disbursements by the Bank would create a net negative resource flow to the Bank, making it very difficult for the Ivorians to service their debts to that institution (there were already problems with arrears in repayments to the Bank) and causing the country to lose its international credit rating. At one point, the French promised the Bank that they would make good on repayments to the institution if disbursements, or, as they put it, "the rhythm of lending," continued. (They in fact did lend to a number of Francophone African governments the funds needed to service their debts to the Bank on several occasions.)

By 1991 little progress had been made on the Ivorian agreement on a medium-term plan. Ouattara found that he was politically unable to implement the tough policies that would force a domestic deflation, and he would not agree to a plan he did not believe he could implement. He appealed to the Bank once again to continue its adjustment lending (even without adjustment) until he could come up with a politically feasible way to deflate the economy. Despite supportive pressures from the French, the Bank agreed only to appraise several new sectoral adjustment programs but refused to implement them without an acceptable medium-term plan. It was clear to all that competitiveness would not be restored by deflation in any of the CFA countries, and the Bank would not continue adjustment lending without improved competitiveness. The institution's lending to Côte d'Ivoire and other CFA countries began to shrink, putting additional pressure on those countries and the French to address the devaluation issue head-on. It was undoubtedly one of the factors that contributed to a decision in late 1993 by the French and the Africans to devalue the CFA franc against the French franc in January 1994.[20] After the devaluation, the Bank provided $325 million in economic recovery loans and credits to CFA countries in fiscal year 1994.

The Bank was willing to intervene with other governments that did not support adjustment programs or had programs of their own that threatened to undercut adjustment reforms. Informal approaches occurred in individual African countries, typically involving a group of aid donors urging a recalcitrant government to drop inappropriate projects or programs. One circuitous effort to bring pressure on President Mobutu Sese Seko of Zaire to implement agreed reforms took place in 1989. Bank vice president Jaycox came away from a discussion with President Mobutu with the impression that the only thing that would persuade the president to abide by agreed fiscal guidelines was credible pressure from his major bilateral patrons. As a result, Bank president Conable called Brent Scowcroft, director of the U.S. National Security Council, just before a meeting between President George Bush and President Mobutu in Japan to ask that Bush "send a clear message" to Mobutu to respect existing agreements. A similar approach was also planned with the Belgian and French governments. (Bush did not raise the issue with Mobutu, but Scowcroft promised that the United States would do so in a later démarche.)[21]

MULTILATERALS. The second most important institution with which to coordinate appears to have been the IMF. Outside observers of the Bank and the Fund would be hard pressed to detect significant differences between them in their approaches to stabilization and adjustment reforms. But Bank files suggest that periodically, at senior levels of Bank management, there was real frustration with the Fund's approach to economic reform. There were problems. First, the Fund's mission was different from that of the Bank. Stabilization—closing the balance of payments gap—could be achieved through relatively short-term demand management approaches: reductions in the levels of credit, devaluation, increased taxation,

20. Another key factor in the timing of the devaluation may have been the death in December 1993 of President Houphouët-Boigny of Côte d'Ivoire. Closer than any other African officials to French leaders, he had been adamantly opposed to any devaluation.

21. Office memorandum from E. V. K. Jaycox to Moeen Qureshi, senior vice president, Operations, March 22, 1989, with written note from Barber Conable attached.

and reductions in government expenditures. These were tried repeatedly in Africa during the early 1980s and were effective—for a time. But they did not address the more difficult and longer-term need to stimulate new growth. Indeed, many thought they had just the opposite effect of depressing economic activity, imports, investment, and future growth prospects. The Bank recognized the need for stabilization but was concerned that it not be implemented in a way that blocked growth. Much of the frustration with the Fund centered on the policy commitments in the policy framework papers that each adjusting government was supposed to draft and negotiate with the Fund and the Bank. (The reality, according to Bank and Fund staff, was that the Fund wrote the first draft and negotiated it with the Bank and the government.) At one point, the Bank vice president for Africa complained to a top Bank manager:

> We have been having what seems to us as inordinate troubles in agreeing on growth-oriented PFPs with the IMF . . . pressure [from the Fund] has arisen to use the additional [adjustment] resources to avoid rescheduling rather than get investment up and avoid further consumption declines. . . . The idea of beefing up imports to get higher levels of investment without further contraction in per capita consumption which will lead to higher growth and eventually be sustainable is a relatively foreign concept to most of our Fund colleagues.[22]

Other complaints concerned Bank staff's being left out of key meetings with African government officials on monetary, fiscal, and macroeconomic issues. Given the different missions, styles, and institutional cultures of these two institutions, it is perhaps remarkable, despite their proximity and intercommunication, that their differences during the 1980s were not greater. But the coordination obviously took work.

One other multilateral institution posed a potential challenge to the Bank in the late 1980s: the European Development Fund (EDF) of the European Commission, which decided to initiate its own sizable program of concessional adjustment assistance in Africa. If the EDF (the largest single source of aid in a number of African countries but seldom an influential one) decided to compete with the Bank in the area of adjustment lending, offering Africans alternatives to Bank programs, the influence of the Bank would be undercut and Africans would undoubtedly play off one institution against the other, much as they did with the United States and the Soviet Union during the cold war. Bank senior management immediately recognized the potential threat to its programs posed by the EDF's initiative, as did officials of the European Commission. In a memo from a senior official of the commission to a senior Bank official, the commission urged:

> We [the Bank and the EDF] should set up rapid and efficient measures for intensified coordination and for resolving any divergent views that may arise. . . . The role of the

22. Memorandum from Jaycox to Qureshi, June 14, 1988.

Bretton Woods institutions is very important in this, and the Commission can join you in these efforts, it being understood that we do not wish to open up parallel paths.[23]

The EC signaled that although it would follow the Bank's lead in countries where there were adjustment programs with few problems, it would, on a case-by-case basis, become active in "seeking a joint position" with the government and would seek to help "states to reach agreement with the World Bank."[24] Relations with the EC appear to have been well coordinated thus far vis-à-vis African reforms.

A final multilateral development institution with which the Bank made some effort to coordinate was the African Development Bank and Fund (AfDBF). For most of the 1980s, the AfDBF did not engage in adjustment lending. It was not staffed to do so, and an attempt to lend for adjustment would have put the institution's management in a particularly difficult position. It would probably have found itself under cross-pressures from its African members (who had the majority of the votes in the board) to avoid imposing difficult conditions and its developed country members (who contributed the bulk of the institutions's funds) to impose strict conditions or follow those of the World Bank. However, there was at least one case in which the AfDBF announced its intention to make a series of loans to the government of Zaire, with a size and purpose that threatened to undercut World Bank pressures on Mobutu to implement reforms. (The Bank made known to the AfDBF its displeasure with these proposed projects.)[25] And the World Bank may have been concerned about the AfDBF's possible support for the ECA in criticizing adjustment in Africa. In a letter from World Bank President Conable to AfDBF president N'Diaye in April 1989, Conable stressed the need for consensus among donors (a term World Bank staff often used to mean agreement on structural adjustment) and worried that "there seems to be a continuing divergence of views within some UN agencies. This is leading to a great deal of confusion and contradictions—and Africa is paying the price."[26] The AfDBF was careful throughout this period to avoid actions or words of its own that undercut the World Bank.

UN BODIES. The third group of institutions the Bank had to be concerned with was the UN, including the Secretariat and the United Nations Development Program. In the case of the UNDP, the main point of intersection was in whether an individual country had a Bank-organized consultative group or a UNDP-organized-roundtable, both comprising the country's principal aid donors and representatives of the government. These groups met periodically to discuss reform programs and coordinate donor responses. In 1980 there were three UNDP roundtables and three Bank consultative groups in Africa. By 1992 there were five and nine,

23. Memo from vice president, European Commission, to Bank senior vice president Qureshi, March, 1990.

24. Ibid.

25. Memorandum from Paul Isenman (World Bank) to Moeen Qureshi, senior vice president, Operations, World Bank, April 14, 1988.

26. Letter from President Conable to President N'Diaye, April 6, 1989.

respectively.[27] The clear preference of Africans (as well as the Bank and most bilateral donors) was the consultative group, since the Bank was far better positioned than the UNDP to legitimize a government's reform program and mobilize resources to support it. (The UNDP mainly provided limited amounts of technical assistance to developing country governments and was widely regarded as weak by developed and less developed country governments alike.)

At one point in the early 1980s, there was concern in the World Bank that the UN Secretariat might undertake an initiative directly involving the mobilization of aid resources for Africa. The economic problems of Africa were beginning to catch the world's attention, and a UN initiative that would actually produce additional resources under UN control had long been attractive to Africans and other developing countries. Those resources would inevitably carry far fewer conditions than any provided by the Bretton Woods institutions. (For these same reasons, a number of developed country governments—in particular the United States—had long resisted attempts to create or expand UN aid programs.) At the end of 1983, the secretary-general of the UN cabled the president of the World Bank to express his increasing concern about the deteriorating economic and social conditions in Africa and his intent to mobilize a concerted international effort to help Africa address the crisis and its long-term development needs.

An effort by the UN to mobilize resources for Africa presented the Bank with two challenges. First, it would probably further weaken donor contributions to the replenishment of the International Development Association, which had only recently failed to reach a $12 billion target level set earlier; as a result, the Bank had made a special appeal to the United States to increase its contribution. Second, a UN initiative, especially if the UN itself or one of its agencies would disburse moneys, would dilute the Bank's lead in mobilizing and influencing the allocation of adjustment resources in Africa. As a result, Bank president Clausen sent a very diplomatic letter to the UN secretary-general underlining his concern for African development, describing the Bank's important activities in this area and arguing that the efforts of the two institutions in Africa must complement each other. A much more candid snapshot of what Bank management was thinking about the UN initiative was captured in an internal memo from the vice president for external affairs to the two regional vice presidents for Africa, informing them of the impending visit of the UN director-general for development and international economic cooperation:

It is not clear whether these speeches and Mr. Ripert's visit herald a formal U.N. sponsored effort to raise funds for Africa. Mr. Ripert implied that this was not the case,

27. Numbers for 1980 are from A. J. Barry, *Aid Co-Ordination and Aid Effectiveness: A Review of Country and Regional Experience* (Paris: OECD, 1988), pp. 15, 21. The 1990 figures are from office memorandum from Timothy Thahane to executive directors and alternates, January 11, 1993, pp. 2–4.

but in case he is so inclined, he should be discouraged. If any institution can raise additional funds for Africa, it is the Bank, either through special IDA contributions or, possibly, through a special effort on Africa. . . . If and when such an effort takes off, political help from the Secretary-General would be very welcome indeed.[28]

The UN later sponsored a special session on Africa in 1986, which called attention to Africa's economic and social crisis but did not attempt to raise additional monies through the UN itself to address that crisis.

It is worth examining two mechanisms the Bank used to coordinate donors in promoting adjustment in Africa. One was the consultative groups, already referred to, and the other was the special program of action created by the Bank in 1988 and described by Vice President Jaycox as best epitomizing "the Bank's leadership and catalytic role."

The consultative group mechanism has been part of the international development scene for several decades. The Bank was, however, able to use it in an especially effective manner to support adjustment in Africa, both to provide African governments with an incentive to undertake reforms and to mobilize donor support for those reforms. The Bank was unwilling to call a consultative group for a particular country until that country's government came up with an acceptable adjustment program or it had performed adequately on previous programs. However, once an acceptable performance and program were turned in, the Bank would lobby donors before the consultative group to come up with resource commitments adequate to cover estimated needs, usually for the coming year or so. The actual group meetings themselves were usually set pieces with all the important business having been accomplished before the meeting.

The special program of action was a mechanism for coordinating donors to the collectivity of Sub-Saharan countries. It was created by the Bank to bring major aid donors together to keep them informed and engaged in supporting adjustment in Africa (and better able to defend that engagement with their own parliaments and peoples), to discuss the general direction of adjustment in the region and issues associated with it, to include in these discussions considerations of African debt (which had become a major problem for many countries), and, most important, to commit themselves to provide agreed levels of financing over a three-year period to support adjustment.

The efforts by the Bank during the 1980s to assume a leadership role in promoting adjustment in Africa and in coordinating donors to support both its leadership and adjustment in the region were remarkably successful. However, by the early 1990s, there were still no definitive adjustment successes in Africa (although there were some encouraging gains in export levels and capacity utilization in countries implementing reforms), and many countries continued to struggle with slow growth, low savings, and inadequate levels of private investment. These

28. Memo from M. P. Benjenk to Knox and Wapenhans, January 17, 1984.

contradictory developments contributed to a growing unease at the senior level of Bank management of the Africa region, which reacted in two ways. It made an effort to share more widely the responsibilities of leadership in promoting reforms in Africa through the creation of the Global Commission on Africa. And it began to examine seriously why economic reforms had been so slow to produce investment and growth, in the process raising the issue of "governance."

After the publication of the Long-term Perspective Study and following a recommendation contained in that study, the government of the Netherlands hosted a high-level conference on aid coordination for Africa in July 1990. The conference was cochaired by the president of Botswana, the Netherlands's minister for development cooperation, and Robert McNamara. Out of the conference came the creation of the Global Coalition for Africa (GCA), which would involve the Bank, aid donors, and Africans to build support for Africa in the international community and to monitor development progress in Africa. But there was another reason for the Bank's active support for creating the GCA; it was growing increasingly uncomfortable with the visibility and influence it had gained and the risks associated with its large financial exposure in a region that was still suffering from slow growth at best. Reflecting these sentiments, Vice President Jaycox explained why he was particularly interested in the establishment of the GCA:

> The World Bank's reputation is on the line in Africa. We have become too important and there is a default situation on the part of African countries themselves in terms of their economic management and also on the part of the international community in general which has preferred to reduce its exposure in Africa and leave the Bank to shoulder the burden. Speaking frankly, there is a tendency to let the Bank do more and more of what needs to be done and also take the risks, which are very high. Half of IDA, for example, is now allocated to Africa. If we do not succeed in Africa, therefore, it seems to me that the very rationale for IDA may well be undermined . . . the importance of the Global Coalition for Africa [is] to ensure that the burden and the risks that are associated with external support for African development are shared in a realistic way.[29]

The GCA was duly established; it has held a number of meetings on a variety of issues and has sponsored an array of research projects. It produces an annual report on economic conditions in Africa. But it does not appear to have done much to shift the burden of external support for Africa to other sources of financing.

The other Bank response to Africa's troubled development experience was to begin to examine the issue of governance in Sub-Saharan Africa. Problems of governance—the lack of transparency, accountability, and predictability in many African countries—had been mentioned briefly in the Long-term Perspective Study, reportedly at the urging of the Council of African Advisers. The Bank and others outside the institution began to link the many inept, corrupt, and authori-

29. Vice President Jaycox, statement to the board, November 19, 1990, SecM90-1504, November 30, 1990, p. 11.

tarian governments in Africa with the failure of growth in the region, even where economic reforms had been implemented. Where there was no rule of law or there was political insecurity or instability, private investors, domestic or foreign, would not risk their resources in investments and economic recovery would not take place.

The growing focus on governance in Africa by Bank senior management in 1990 coincided with an increasing emphasis by bilateral aid donors, especially the United States, on the need for African authoritarian regimes to democratize. In part, it was argued that democracy was essential for healthy long-run growth. And, in part, it was argued that democracy, like human rights, was a worthy end in itself. These arguments hit a responsive chord within many African countries, where deepening economic crisis and the example of democratization in Eastern Europe had stimulated hopes and demands for similar changes. Indeed, such changes came about in Benin in 1990, followed by several other countries.

The World Bank, it should be noted, proceeded cautiously into the area of governance. The senior management of the Africa region thought it the key to long-term growth in the region but was unsure how African governments would react to the Bank's pushing governance. In 1990, senior Bank managers, including the president, gave speeches signaling the importance the Bank was putting on good governance. But they were very careful to talk about governance as "accountability, transparency and the rule of law," of reducing corruption and unpredictability on the part of governments (no fingers were pointed at specific governments). They did not push any particular types of political organization— like democracy—even though it is hard to envision a transparent, accountable government observing the rule of law without being a democracy.

The Bank proceeded cautiously because it was approaching one of the most politically sensitive issues for any government: the way it organizes itself and its functions. Too direct and open an attack on these essentially political issues— particularly in the case of individual countries—could well provoke the repudiation by key borrowing governments the Bank had earlier avoided. But also constraining the Bank were its Articles of Agreement, which specifically state that "the Bank and its officers shall not interfere in the political affairs of any member; nor shall they be influenced in their decisions by the political character of the member or members concerned. Only economic considerations shall be relevant to their decisions."[30]

However, an interpretation of these articles' relation to governance issues by the Bank's legal counsel left some ambiguity and thus discretion to Bank managers:

> The Bank should not allow political factors or events (no matter how appealing they may seem to be) to influence its decisions unless it deems them as having direct and obvious economic effects relevant to its work. . . . The staff have to establish the case for the

30. Article 4, sec. 10.

significant direct economic effect in a clear and uncontroversial manner. . . . Reform policies cannot be effective in the absence of a system which translates them into workable rules and makes sure they are complied with. . . . While popular participation and democratization are indeed important goals which developing countries are generally trying to achieve, it is not clear how these goals may, in the abstract, become an operational concern for the Bank . . . to insist, as a general proposition that each borrowing country should have a Western-style democratic form of government cannot in my view be reconciled with the Articles' requirement that neither the Bank nor its officers should be influenced by the political character of its members or interfere in their political affairs.[31]

What this opinion implies is that Bank staff cannot openly advocate a particular form of government nor can the Bank condition its assistance on the existence of such a form of government. But if a borrowing government behaves in a manner that undercuts the economic objectives of Bank lending or makes it impossible for that government to fulfill its obligations under Bank loan agreements, then the Bank staff may be justified in urging changes that will make its lending more effective, or it may terminate that lending altogether.

In at least two cases, Bank staff tested the limits of the institution's ability to press individual African governments for improved governance. The first involved the government of Kenya, which was widely seen as increasingly authoritarian and corrupt. On a number of occasions, senior Bank officials urged Kenyan president Moi to "broaden political consensus" in his country—a proxy for political liberalization and reform. Bank staff also raised the need for political reform at the consultative group meeting on Kenya in 1991. In each documented case, Bank staff were careful to cite the views of other donors urging these changes and the likelihood that other donors would withhold their aid unless a movement toward greater political pluralism was apparent. Thus, while the Bank has been quite clever in using the bilaterals to protect its visibility and exposure in Africa—both politically and for resources—the bilaterals have used the World Bank (and IMF) to push their views and preferences on governance issues. Nevertheless, the very fact that Bank officials cited other donors on these issues suggested that the Bank itself was in agreement with them.

The Bank took a similar position at the consultative group meeting for Malawi:

As the Government knows, . . . donors believe that there is a major problem—so major in fact that a number of donors have already flagged that unless something extraordinary happens, they will not be in a position to pledge additional balance of payments support, as a result of concerns about the governance issues, including release or trial of detainees, conditions in the prisons, freedom of speech, freedom of the press, and freedom of association. Donors are pressing these concerns, not only because they believe that they are central to progress on issues like poverty alleviation, but also because they feel that human rights issues underlie the sustainability of the reform program.[32]

31. Memorandum from Ibrahim F. I. Shihata, vice president and general counsel, to Barber Conable, November 9, 1990, pp. 40, 42, 51–52.

32. IBRD, "Consultative Group for Malawi, Paris, May 11–13, 1992, Chairman's Report of Proceedings," MAI92-2, August 12, 1992, p. 21.

It appears that after taking a relatively forward position on governance issues in these two meetings, Bank staff backed away from pushing the issue aggressively with individual governments. This may be a result of reported criticisms of the Bank staff's actions by members of the Bank's board, or major donors may have been uncomfortable with conditioning lending on political reforms once an election (however marred) had taken place (in Kenya). In any case, the Bank appears to have decided to restrict its role in promoting improved governance in Africa to reforms of the civil service, public administration, and legal system.

Conclusion

The story of the World Bank in Africa is one of an institution seeking and achieving leadership, prominence, and influence on an important and controversial issue: the need for painful, complex, and often politically risky economic reforms. It achieved that goal during the 1980s only to find that economic reforms, to be successful, often needed to be supported by political reforms. As the Bank vice president and general counsel observed, "The Bank's increasing concern with issues of governance in its borrowing members seems to have come as a logical last step in its gradually expanding involvement in policy reform through adjustment lending, which has been extended to social sectors."[33]

But the Bank was limited in its ability to promote political reforms. And so, by the beginning of the 1990s, it remained in a highly exposed position in Africa, with a large outstanding portfolio of loans to countries of the region, continuing problems of slow growth in most countries, the absence of a definitive adjustment success, and a spreading problem of political violence and state collapse in the region, further undermining the economic health and prospects of affected countries (as well as their ability to repay loans from the Bank). Although economic reforms had been widely implemented and some real economic progress had been achieved, the goal of achieving sustainable, healthy growth throughout the region seemed still a long way off.

Appendix: A View from Africa

Philip Ndegwa

The main points on World Bank structural adjustment programs in Sub-Saharan Africa are well covered in this chapter. The literature on the subject, however, is vast, although some of it is not entirely useful. The chapter is interesting and for me very informative in some sections, especially the story on the CFA franc. Inciden-

---

33. Memo from Shihata to Conable, p. 2.

tally, the cost to France of the overvalued CFA franc—which it said was estimated at about $1 billion a year—does not, of course, tell the whole story. Specifically, the French were getting much in return—materially, financially, and influence-wise.

In the introduction to the chapter Ms. Lancaster could refer to some of the activities and events when the World Bank was starting its programs in Sub-Saharan Africa, soon after or just before political independence. It would be useful, for example, to mention the economic missions the Bank organized. In that regard, I remember, as a young economist, having interesting discussions with Professor Edward Mason and others when the reports on the East African countries were being prepared. Some of those reports were quite useful in some ways: for example, what was more effective in developing agriculture—gradual improvement or revolution?

Views from Africa, especially from African governments, have not been adequately articulated. While there is a lot from the World Bank—nearly a major report every year during the 1980s—much of that has taken the form of preaching to Africans, and, in some cases, giving instructions in indirect ways. Let me also say that the Lagos Plan deserved more attention than it received in Washington circles. I agree that technically it needed more action; but the spirit behind the plan needed commendation and support. Incidentally, some think that the main purpose of the Berg report was to discredit the Lagos plan, in addition to promoting an alternative ideological framework.[34]

Reference also can be made to the UN Development Decades. I do not think that the first UN Development Decade strategy influenced the World Bank, but I suspect that the second one had some impact. Those were the years when the environmental movement got into high gear, leading to the Stockholm conference and other activities and programs.

With regard to relations and respective roles in Africa between the World Bank, the UN, and other agencies, it is useful to distinguish between rhetoric and actual programs involving mobilization of resources. In that connection, during the 1980s most of the UN organizations merely talked, except perhaps for the UNDP. Even UNICEF's role was largely in the form of mobilization of public reaction—and in that regard its slogan "adjustment with a human face" was clearly useful. It can also be recalled that the World Bank brought in the UNDP through publication of their joint assessment report on adjustment measures in Africa. This was criticized by many and in my view was premature. The report's use of statistics was distorted.

Incidentally, when McNamara came to Kenya in 1969 I was permanent secretary for the Ministry of Agriculture, with Bruce McKenzie as minister. We took

34. Under the direction of Elliot Berg, the World Bank African Strategy Review Group prepared a study that became known as the "Berg report." See World Bank, *Accelerated Development in Sub-Saharan Africa: An Agenda for Action,* Report 3358, Office of the Senior Vice President, Operations (R81-211) (1981).

McNamara to various parts of the country and he was quick to develop impressions. Most interestingly, McNamara had a kind of mechanical approach to development. When we discussed rural development and what the World Bank could do to accelerate it, we said, "Give us five years." He seemed to jump to the view that within five years major improvements would have been achieved. I rather shared his enthusiasm and impatience to do things, some of which appeared very obvious. Alas, the process takes much longer than that, even when what needs to be done appears very obvious and when the resources needed are available.

It should be stressed that discussions between the World Bank and African countries are hardly ever conducted on what is now called "a level playing field." By and large, African countries are in desperate need of resources and therefore there is pressure to agree quickly to World Bank demands. More often than not, they do not have adequate capacity, in terms of technically competent and experienced persons, to negotiate effectively with World Bank officials. It is not unfair to say that Africa has been, for many years, something on which to cut one's teeth in both the World Bank and the IMF (the African Department in the IMF was at one time, and perhaps still is, the largest and the one that used to gather in many young graduates).

An important point is that Africa consists of many small countries. This in turn creates some difficulties in understanding each country and its people fully, which then leads to the temptation to generalize and use standard approaches. This was certainly true after the second oil price crisis. Obviously, there is much to be said about this particular aspect. On one score, in the early years of structural adjustment, the World Bank was rather naive and unrealistic. In the case of Kenya's first structural adjustment loan, a great variety of conditions in the program were to be met within a very short time frame. Some of them—such as population planning, land tenure reforms, and export promotion—could not have been achieved within the time specified. When I went to the Central Bank and discovered what had happened, I told the Kenyan officials involved in the negotiations that they should never have signed the loan document. I also mentioned to the World Bank officials that they did not seem to understand the complexities involved in economic planning and in the political and economic management of countries.

This chapter appears to suggest that African officials were against structural adjustment. I believe this is not the case. However, African countries were very unhappy, and still are very unhappy, that external factors, including external debt, were not being addressed. This chapter should include a careful discussion of the debt problem. However, it appears that the Bank has not yet mustered enough courage to discuss the matter frankly with major creditors. Clearly, no economic recovery and growth in Sub-Saharan Africa will take place unless there is a satisfactory solution to the debt problem.

In the actual designing of structural adjustment programs, many African countries were happy to agree to the World Bank (and IMF) conditions if resources were going to be made immediately available. There is a great deal of education to be undertaken—on both sides. Two related points: first, the World Bank now recognizes the importance of "ownership" of structural adjustment programs, but it needs to encourage that in a deliberate fashion; second, unless much more attention is given to the social dimension of adjustment, much faster progress will not be achieved—indeed, some reversals can be expected. Even in Kenya we have had to work very hard to get general political agreement that the process should continue.

The assessment of the impact of structural adjustment in Sub-Saharan Africa is an important subject and is also technically complicated if it is to be done properly. This is partly because the impact and influence of other factors, especially external ones, must be taken into account. Isolating some of those factors may not be very easy. Sectoral assessments are therefore easier than whole-economy assessments. This is not to say that some macroeconomic assessment should not be attempted, but one should be aware of the danger of giving all credit to structural adjustment programs. The quality of political leadership is very important in the degree to which it inspires people to accept sacrifices and hardships. Obviously, so is management capacity, alas, too weak now in many cases. Incidentally, the turnaround in recent months in Kenya's foreign exchange position and the value of the shilling is a very interesting and supportive case.

I could say more about the impact of these adjustment programs. Some of their contributions have been nonmaterial: educating politicians and the general populace about the importance of interactions of various factors in the development process, such as the contribution of the exchange rate in promotion of exports (including tourism); the senselessness of having too many extension officers without supporting facilities; the meaning of government deficits; and the end of the era of soft options.

A sensitive point: in Africa, at least, personalities have been a factor that cannot be ignored. In that connection, Conable was much better than Clausen in communicating with African presidents, perhaps because he had been a politician himself. I remember separate meetings between our president and Clausen and Conable. With Clausen, all the time was wasted discussing liberalizing movement of maize. I felt sad. With Conable, it was a jovial meeting, where we discussed decontrol of prices, population planning, government finances, corruption, and the like. This was a much more useful meeting for both sides.

It is important to refer to Hollis Chenery and his activities in the Development Policy Department of the World Bank. During that time many development specialists came to be involved in World Bank activities, at the Institute for Development Studies, Sussex, for example. Some important publications resulted from those activities, including Chenery's *Redistribution with Growth*. Some of those economists were also involved in International Labor Organization employment missions. As noted, those were the years of "basic needs" and related issues. Kim Jaycox, energetic, enthusiastic, and courageous, has been a major positive factor for Sub-Saharan Africa. He has been more politically aware than some of his officers. At lower levels, I remember a truly distressing situation because the World Bank "man" in Nairobi was arrogant, did not know his job, and saw himself as "ambassador" of a great institution that must be listened to. The situation and environment were changed quickly when we got a better "man."[35]

It is true that the World Bank has been careful in avoiding taking dangerous or risky positions on the subject of governance. However, bilateral agencies have not been so cautious: they seem to think that political reforms can be programmed in the same way as economic reforms. This idea is dangerous because while target dates for interest rates, exchange rates, and perhaps also government deficits can be set, various developments in political reform programs must simply evolve. This is clearly illustrated by the Kenyan situation. Bilateral agencies, which appear to have expected the opposition parties to have remained as strong and vigorous after elections, are now saying that the weakness of the Kenyan opposition parties is due to obstacles and pressures created by the Kenya African National Union (KANU). This is not true. It was naive in the first place to have expected the opposition parties to be strong, especially when they were so divided during the elections and, even to this day, have no credible development agenda. Therefore, while the Bank has been quite clever in using bilateral agencies to protect its visibility and exposure in Africa—politically and resource-wise—bilaterals have used the Bank (and IMF) to push forward their views and preferences. This is clearly evident now. In consultative group meetings for Kenya, bilaterals are now raising, in loud voices, patently political matters. The situation is not made any easier by their interpretations of democracy in Western terms and styles. In my view, the World Bank will have to do something to ensure that consultative group meetings continue to be useful mechanisms for objective exchange of ideas on development policies and programs. Additionally, it would be good to discuss how the United States could be made to pay more intelligent attention to Africa.

Bokassa, Idi Amin, and other "awkward" African leaders have done a great deal of harm not only to their own countries but to Africa as a whole. As one often notices, as far as Africa is concerned, the negative is highlighted in the West. Bokassa, Idi Amin, and others seemed to give justification to the view held by outsiders that Africans cannot manage their affairs properly without strong supervision from outside. So the harm done by awkward leaders has not only affected their countries but Africa as a while—economically, socially, and in undermining confidence in Africa and African leaders.

A further point: the tragic situations in countries such as Uganda, Somalia, Liberia, and now Rwanda—all principally because of poor leadership—indicate to

35. Some of these general comments are covered in greater detail in Philip Ndegwa and Reginald Herbold Green, *Africa to 2000 and Beyond: Imperative Political and Economic Agenda* (Nairobi: East African Educational Publishers, 1994).

many Africans (and friends of Africa) how weak and ineffective African institutions are in dealing with their situations. Actually, some of the country situations have contributed toward the weakening of continental institutions, by dividing citizens within countries into those in support of the ruling regime and those opposed to it.

I do not think that one could make a generalized statement that African states are "suspended from above." Certainly that is not true in Kenya, Tanzania, or Zimbabwe—or also in the young country of Eritrea. I do not think the Bank has generally been "anti-state." More interesting and relevant is the fact that the Bank has been experimenting and learning. The Bank encouraged, very directly, the establishment of parastatals in Kenya, in order to provide better emoluments, fewer civil service procedures in the management of direct production sectors. Later on, as you know, the same Bank vigorously encouraged privatization. I am certain the Bank feels it has been learning within Africa. In recent years, moreover, it has been influenced by powerful members who have been advocating "market" systems.

SIX

U.S. Relations with the World Bank, 1945–1992

Catherine Gwin

THROUGHOUT the history of the International Bank for Reconstruction and Development (the World Bank), the United States has been the largest shareholder and most influential member country. U.S. support for, pressures on, and criticisms of the Bank have been central to its growth and the evolution of its policies, programs, and practices. The United States, in turn, has benefited substantially in both foreign policy and economic terms from the Bank's promotion of development. The benefits have been especially significant during the past two decades as U.S. bilateral development aid has dwindled.

Underlying this half century of U.S.–World Bank relations has been a fundamental ambivalence on the part of the United States toward both development assistance and multilateral cooperation. On the one hand U.S. support for foreign aid generally and the Bank specifically has been guided by the view that promoting economic growth and development in other parts of the world is in the national interest and that multilateral cooperation is a particularly effective way of both leveraging and allocating resources for development. U.S. policy toward the Bank, led by the Treasury Department, has consistently emphasized these points. On the other hand the United States has viewed all multilateral organizations, including the World Bank, as instruments of foreign policy to be used in support of specific U.S. aims and objectives. Thus while it has supported the Bank for its capacity as a multilateral institution to leverage funds and influence borrowing countries' economic development policies, the United States has been uneasy with both the autonomy on which the Bank's development role depends and the power sharing that accompanies burden sharing. And the United States is often impatient with the processes of consensus building on which multilateral cooperation rests.

This ambivalence, a preoccupation with containing communism, and the change in the relative U.S. power in the world explain much of the evolution in U.S. relations with the World Bank over the past fifty years. In addition, the U.S. Congress, unlike the legislators in other Bank member countries, has been a major influence on policy. Within the context of changing foreign policy concerns, congressional involvement has significantly affected the tenor and style of U.S. participation in the Bank. Having led in the establishment, early financial growth, and encouragement of the Bank's program expansion, the United States was by the 1970s at odds within itself over issues of foreign policy and foreign aid and frequently at odds with the Bank over its rate of growth and specific aspects of its operations. The development constituency, which had never been strong, was shattered, with groups on both the Left and the Right increasingly vocal in their criticisms of the Bank. After a supportive Carter administration was unable to knit the constituency together anew, the first Reagan administration added, for the first time, an executive branch voice to the chorus of multilateral aid opponents. The debt crisis in the south and the collapse of communism in eastern Europe led to renewed U.S. interest in the Bank. Simultaneously, pressure from nongovernmental organizations caused the U.S. government to push for increased Bank attention to the environment. However, renewed attention to the Bank was accompanied through the 1980s and into the early 1990s by both a continuing decrease in the U.S. share of Bank funding and a unilateral (at times dogmatic) assertiveness on matters of Bank policy, a combination that antagonized other member countries.

U.S. Leadership in Launching the Bank

Well before the end of World War II the United States began to plan for the economic recovery that would follow the peace. The aim of the postwar planning was to design a system of international economic cooperation that would avoid a repetition of the beggar-thy-neighbor trade and currency practices of the interwar period and instead encourage economic stability, full employment, and rising levels of income through the growth of international trade and investment.

Both the International Monetary Fund (IMF) and the International Bank for Reconstruction and Development were the results of that planning effort. In contrast to the Fund, which was the outcome of intense negotiation between the United States and Britain, the Bank was largely an American creation.[1] The United States proposed its basic design and led the effort to get it off the ground. From

1. The U.S. role was acknowledged by John Maynard Keynes in his opening remarks at the Bretton Woods Conference when he observed that the international bank draft document being considered was due "primarily to the initiative and ability of the United States Treasury." Edward S. Mason and Robert E. Asher, *The World Bank since Bretton Woods* (Brookings, 1973), p. 13.

1945 through 1960 it provided much of the Bank's top management and staff, the active support needed for its early institutional growth and policy expansion, and, through the U.S. market, most of the capital for lending. The result was a strong and enduring American imprint on all aspects of the Bank, including its structure, general policy direction, and forms of lending. Although this early history has been much written about, a number of points are worth repeating because they indicate the underlying U.S. perspective on the Bank and have proved central to the Bank's operations.

The White Plan

Work on a plan for an international bank began within the U.S. government in 1941.[2] In the interwar period many countries that had borrowed heavily from private banks defaulted on their commercial obligations. The international bank, designed largely by Harry Dexter White, adviser to the U.S. Treasury, was meant to overcome that legacy by facilitating an international flow of private investment and by encouraging countries to use financing effectively. Convinced that private investors could not be relied on to provide the net flow of dollars that would be needed for postwar reconstruction and development, he conceived of the Bank as an institution that would guarantee foreign securities and when necessary lend directly to governments. "The primary aim of such an agency should be to encourage private capital to go abroad for productive investment by sharing the risks of private investors in large ventures."[3] The initial capital of the Bank was set at $10 billion, an amount thought adequate for this catalytic task.[4] Participation by other countries in the Bank's design was minimal. John Maynard Keynes is reputed to have said that the United States got it wrong, that the International Monetary Fund should have been a bank and the Bank a fund. He also observed that the draft Bank document, "stripped, as it had long since been, of all exciting features," was "an uninspiring

---

2. This section on the founding of the Bank draws heavily on several histories, including Mason and Asher, *World Bank since Bretton Woods;* Richard N. Gardner, *Sterling-Dollar Diplomacy in Current Perspective* (Columbia University Press, 1980); and Robert W. Oliver, *Early Plans for a World Bank,* Princeton Studies in International Finance no. 29, Princeton University, 1971.

3. Harry Dexter White, quoted in Mason and Asher, *World Bank since Bretton Woods,* p. 18. The same point was stressed by American economist Alvin H. Hansen, who proposed in 1944 an international development and investment bank. According to Hansen, in the absence of basic developmental projects financed by public funds, private investments in many cases could not be undertaken. See "World Institutions for Stability and Expansion," *Foreign Affairs,* vol. 22 (January 1944), pp. 248–55.

4. Consideration was also given to establishing an international development corporation and commodity price stabilization mechanism, but these elements as well as a larger capital base for the Bank were rejected in discussions within the U.S. government before the plan for the Bank was presented to other countries.

one . . . dressed, with an eye to Congress, to look as orthodox as possible."[5] Nevertheless, most countries, including the United Kingdom, refrained from taking much initiative on the plan because they did not expect to be in a position after the war to make significant contributions.

The Bank that emerged from the planning effort "was not created neutral."[6] U.S. views regarding how the world economy should be organized, how resources should be allocated, and how investment decisions should be reached were enshrined in the Charter and the operational policies of the Bank. This included the decision that the Bank should not lend directly to private enterprises. Two other early decisions reflected strong U.S. preferences for close oversight of the Bank by national representatives: the choice of a permanent site for the headquarters of the Bank and the definition of the role of the executive directors.[7] Britain, joined by many other countries, urged that the Bank be located outside the United States, but once it became clear that the United States would not agree, they sought at least to locate the headquarters in New York rather than Washington. As Keynes said, this was necessary to keep the institutions "clear of 'the politics of Congress and the nationalistic whispering gallery of the Embassies and Legations.'"[8] But the United States was strongly committed to Washington. The aim of Treasury Secretary Henry Morgenthau in the postwar planning effort was "to move the financial center of the world from London and Wall Street to the United States Treasury, and to create a new concept among nations in international finance." The new institutions were to be "instrumentalities of sovereign governments and not of private financial interests."[9]

This same perspective shaped the U.S. position on the role of the Bank's directors. In debating the duties of the executive directors, Britain (supported by some Commonwealth and European countries) sought again to minimize the influence of national governments. It argued that the directors should be officials resident in their home countries who would visit the Bank at regular intervals to deal with matters of high policy and leave the day-to-day affairs of the organization to management and staff. In contrast, the United States, which was committing the most money, insisted that the directors serve full time and exercise more initiative and control over operations and policy. Keynes made a strong and bitter speech on this matter and finally refused to vote for the U.S. formula. But the U.S. view prevailed.

The arrangement, and especially the function of the first U.S. executive director, Emilio Collado, led to a power struggle between the first few Bank presidents and

5. Quoted in Mason and Asher, *World Bank since Bretton Woods,* p. 12.

6. C. Fred Bergsten, working paper of the Study Group on International Financial Institutions, Council on Foreign Relations, New York, 1980, p. 4. Cited with permission of the author.

7. Gardner, *Sterling-Dollar Diplomacy,* pp. 258–59.

8 . Quoted ibid., p. 258.

9 . Quoted ibid., p. 76.

the board—notwithstanding that the presidents were American citizens closely tied to the U.S. government. According to Davidson Sommers, an early member of the Bank's staff, "in the beginning [there] was the Board. . . . They, not too harmoniously but very effectively, assumed the initiative in organizing and running the affairs of the Bank. . . . [But] what was really important was the very predominant position of the American Director on the Board and the role that he played." Although no loans were actually made until 1947, it was "the normal thing for an applicant for a loan to stop on his way to the Bank and get the support of the U.S. Director."[10] Interestingly, Collado was an appointee from the State Department, not, as later became the rule, from Treasury.

The situation produced a great deal of tension and led to the early resignation of the Bank's first president, Eugene Meyer, out of frustration with his position vis-à-vis the U.S. director.

> Partly because of disputes between member nations, most particularly the United States and Britain, and partly because of distrust on Wall Street, he had not been able to sell a single bond or issue any development loans. He had also found himself embroiled in a debilitating conflict with his own board of executive directors, in particular the U.S. executive director. . . . "Pete" Collado had spent his entire professional life in the Roosevelt administration, working with such liberal personalities as Harry Dexter White at the Treasury Department and Alger Hiss in the State Department. Meyer consequently considered him a brash young New Dealer, and they didn't get along. Collado and the executive directors from other nations believed Meyer should run the Bank according to policy voted upon by the board. They were eager to issue as many loans as possible, and quickly. When Meyer refused one day to approve an early loan to Chile, Collado pounded the table, demanding that the loan be approved. Meyer calmly refused, saying the Bank was not a relief agency. But such constant disputes with Collado took their toll on the seventy-one-year-old Meyer, and in December 1946 he resigned. He told his secretary, "I could stay and fight these bastards, and probably win in the end, but I'm too old for that."[11]

In consultation with other members of the executive board, the United States approached several prominent bankers to succeed Meyer, including Graham F. Towers, governor of the Bank of Canada. But Towers declined, saying that a U.S. citizen had to lead the Bank if its credibility on Wall Street was to be established. The United States then turned to John J. McCloy, a Wall Street lawyer. "Some of McCloy's Wall Street colleagues saw in his possible appointment an opportunity to take control of the World Bank away from the New Deal crowd represented by 'Morgenthau and those clucks.'"[12] But despite Wall Street's enthusiasm, McCloy

10. Davidson Sommers, Address to Professional Staff Meeting on "The Early Days of the Bank," Washington, May 5, 1960, pp. 5, 7.
11. Kai Bird, *The Chairman: John J. McCloy, The Making of the American Establishment* (Simon and Schuster, 1992), p. 283.
12. Ibid., p. 285. Their enthusiasm may have been heightened by the fact that the Republicans won a resounding victory in the November 1946 elections.

initially turned down the offer on the grounds that the Bank's Articles of Agreement placed a preponderance of power in the hands of the directors. This would make the intervention of politics into lending decisions inevitable and, as a result, make it difficult to sell Bank loans.

McCloy changed his decision only after the United States and the rest of the board accepted conditions defining his role and after he was satisfied that the only potential buyers of Bank bonds, the New York commercial banks and insurance companies, were likely to cooperate. His conditions were that first, the United States would not interfere in loan negotiations; in particular, loan applicants would be directed to the Bank's management and not given a prior indication of the U.S. position. Second, the Bank president would have a free hand in administrative matters, including the hiring and firing of staff. Third, McCloy would nominate the U.S. executive director. Although the conditions were rejected by U.S. government officials, President Truman overruled his advisers and told McCloy that the United States would accept them.[13] Collado was subsequently replaced by Eugene Black who, on McCloy's insistence, simultaneously took charge of the Bank's bond operations.[14]

In the summer of 1949 McCloy resigned to assume the position of high commissioner in Germany and urged that Black be appointed to succeed him. Given his assertive style, McCloy's tenure had created substantial tensions with the Board, especially with the non-American members, who objected to the American "monopoly" in the Bank. Although Black did much to relieve the tensions, he also continued the practice of nominating the U.S. director and continued to rely heavily on and work closely with both the U.S. government and its director.

The decisions on the Bank's location and the role of its directors, which were to have profound effects on its operations, facilitating daily interaction between the Bank and the U.S. government and frequent political intrusion into Bank decision-making by all member governments, reflected U.S. ambivalence toward multilateral cooperation. But these features also contributed to broad-based and strong support for the Bank in Congress and with the public.

Congressional Approval

When the legislation authorizing U.S. participation in the Bank and the IMF was submitted to Congress, the House voted 345–18 in favor and the Senate 61–16.[15] The administration based its advocacy for U.S. membership on the importance of the two institutions ensuring the stability of the postwar economy. Treasury Secretary Morgenthau told Congress that the Bretton Woods plan was "the first practical test of our willingness to cooperate in the work of world reconstruction

13. Sommers, "Early Days of the Bank," p. 10.
14. Bird, *The Chairman*, p. 286.
15. Jonathan E. Sanford, *U.S. Foreign Policy and Multilateral Development Banks* (Boulder, Colo.: Westview Press, 1982), p. 44.

[and] one very important step towards the orderly, expanding foreign trade on which our agriculture and industry depends." Assistant Secretary of State Dean Acheson told Congress that the proposal represented a chance to avoid the disaster of international warfare "by acting in common with the other nations of the world to put aside the implements of economic warfare and make possible an expansion of production and consumption and trade." Assistant Treasury Secretary Harry Dexter White emphasized further that the plan was necessary for international economic peace, economic prosperity, and the revitalization of markets for U.S. goods.[16]

In its deliberations Congress made two changes in the legislation submitted by the administration. The first called for the creation of a National Advisory Committee on International Monetary and Financial Problems. This was to be a cabinet-level committee chaired by the secretary of the Treasury and composed of heads of other departments. It was "to coordinate the policies and operations of the representatives of the United States."[17] In a second change, Congress required that the executive branch obtain prior authorization on major decisions regarding U.S. participation in the Fund and Bank.

A minority report issued by a small group of conservative senators denounced the Bretton Woods Act for starting the United States "on a permanent policy of foreign lending and investment by Americans in huge sums, sponsored and to a large extent guaranteed by the Federal Government."[18] For the most part, however, the Bretton Woods initiative received strong support from a wide range of national groups and from a bipartisan majority of Congress and swiftly "moved through the Congress on soaring hopes for a better world."[19]

The "Dollar Bank"

With that broad-based endorsement the U.S. government undertook actively to help sell the World Bank to the U.S. financial market.[20] This task dominated the administrations of the first three Bank presidents and largely determined the shape of Bank lending in its first decade.

The original U.S. capital subscription was $3,175 million or 34.9 percent of the $9,100 million total.[21] Its overall contribution to the financial start-up of the Bank was far greater, however. Of the Bank's total initial capitalization of $10 billion, 20 percent was to be paid in and 80 percent held in reserve by member countries.

16. Ibid., p. 43.
17. Mason and Asher, *World Bank since Bretton Woods*, p. 34.
18. Sanford, *U.S. Foreign Policy*, p. 43.
19. Gardner, *Sterling-Dollar Diplomacy*, p. 142.
20. The phrase "a dollar bank" and this summary are drawn largely from Mason and Asher, *World Bank since Bretton Woods*, pp. 105–49.
21. Ibid., p. 779.

Of the 20 percent paid in, 10 percent was to be in gold or dollars and 90 percent in the currency of each member country. During the Bank's first ten years, except for Canada's payment of part of its subscription in U.S. dollars and a few small payments from other countries, the U.S. subscription was the only fully usable subscription. Not until other currencies became convertible and economies recovered did this situation change. Also during the initial ten years, 85 percent of World Bank bonds were denominated in U.S. dollars and most were sold in the U.S. market. For related reasons, the only portion of the 80 percent "callable" reserves considered a significant guarantee to investors was the U.S. share. This became evident in 1958 when the spread between the volume of outstanding debt and the amount of the U.S. guarantee narrowed to only about $700 million, and the U.S. bond market rating services sounded the alarm. In effect, until well into the 1960s, Bank borrowing was limited by the amount of the U.S. share of the guarantee reserve.

It had been expected that the Bank would operate by guaranteeing securities issued by others rather than by issuing bonds of its own. But in 1946 U.S. efforts to enlist the interest of banking and insurance groups made clear that large investors would prefer to hold Bank securities rather than the securities of foreign governments backed by guarantees from the Bank.[22] Two obstacles confronted early efforts to sell Bank securities, however. The Bank did not fit under existing state banking laws and regulations, and, as a legacy of the interwar period, investment in foreign securities was considered risky. The U.S. government actively confronted both obstacles. The U.S. executive director took the lead in campaigning for the necessary changes in state legislation, and other officials helped the Bank's president to inform the investment community about the Bank's nature and policies.[23] These efforts quickly paid off: by the mid-1950s, Bank issues had achieved an AAA rating in the U.S. market and had begun to attract interest from non-American investors. In addition, until the early 1960s the Treasury Department gave its required consent for the issue of dollar-denominated Bank securities as a matter of course.

In this early period, Bank lending policies were conditioned by the necessity of finding U.S. investors who were willing to buy the Bank's securities and accept its guarantee. The management's view that the Bank's credit standing depended on the character of its loans led to an early emphasis on financing capital infrastructure and little lending in the social sectors.[24] By the start of the 1960s, however, the

22. Ibid., pp. 43–44.

23. To gain investors' support, Bank president John McCloy, his chosen vice president, Robert L. Garner, a fellow U.S. banker and businessman, and U.S. executive director Eugene Black spent much of the spring of 1947 on the road, giving speeches at bankers' conventions and lobbying various state legislatures.

24. This point is drawn from quotations from several World Bank oral histories cited in Mason and Asher, *World Bank since Bretton Woods.*

Table 6-1. *World Bank Medium- and Long-Term Borrowings, by Country before Swaps and by Currency after Swaps, Fiscal Years 1971–91*
Millions of U.S. dollars

	Country					Currency				
Year	France	Germany	Japan	United Kingdom	United States	French franc	German mark	Japanese yen[a]	U.K. pound	U.S. dollar
1971	3	296	229	0	400	0	296	219	0	775
1972	6	347	160	37	425	31	342	150	24	796
1973	5	387	614	25	0	0	371	606	0	440
1974	6	235	471	25	0	0	220	461	0	659
1975	5	526	129	5	500	0	512	121	0	2,515
1976	4	707	197	19	1,275	0	850	0	0	2,152
1977	4	1,412	20	13	1,250	0	1,394	7	0	2,181
1978	4	1,149	582	5	1,360	0	1,120	646	0	2,099
1979	6	1,033	1,191	63	0	0	1,016	1,176	0	666
1980	9	1,993	1,288	5	0	0	2,256	1,266	0	694
1981	12	1,326	971	237	0	0	1,522	1,091	216	1,611
1982	7	738	1,337	266	1,687	0	1,229	1,341	311	2,602
1983	7	1,134	1,267	8	2,041	0	1,519	1,326	321	2,036
1984	11	1,382	1,579	152	0	0	1,838	1,700	421	1,170
1985	8	1,500	1,890	146	911	0	1,927	2,199	323	1,870
1986	147	1,609	2,036	136	429	−6	2,080	1,946	131	1,478
1987	9	1,392	1,461	20	1,107	0	1,897	3,383	73	1,757
1988	192	404	4,711	5	2,404	177	1,524	5,431	596	2,849
1989	7	716	3,782	64	−822	161	657	3,754	8	5,522
1990	14	1,709	2,274	0	449	178	3,372	2,618	0	5,232
1991	5	919	611	0	114	11	3,094	1,262	4	4,519

Source: World Bank annual reports.
a. Numbers in the data for Japan are elevated because of refinancing. Refinancing data for 1987–89 are available and must be subtracted from totals.

lending policy was less constrained by the attitudes of U.S. investors, in part because investor confidence had by then been established by the cautious policies Bank management had pursued and in part because investors had a better understanding of the Bank's role in promoting economic growth and development. Meanwhile, the relative importance of the U.S. market as a source of Bank borrowing began to decline (even though in absolute terms the volume of sales of dollar securities continued to increase). From 1956 to 1962–63 the Bank not only saw the release of capital subscriptions from its major European contributors but also succeeded in tapping non-U.S. markets for more of its capital. In the mid-1960s, confronted with a balance of payments deficit, the U.S. Treasury for the first time briefly denied the Bank access to its capital market and most Bank funds had to be raised elsewhere. And by the late 1960s more than half the Bank's dollar borrowings were being bought by investors outside the United States.

At the end of the decade, incoming Bank President Robert McNamara, with U.S. encouragement, accelerated this trend in portfolio diversification. His aim was not only to escape the effects of U.S. macroeconomic policy on the Bank, but also to lay the foundation for a sharp rise in Bank borrowing sufficient to enable lending to double. The change in medium- and long-term borrowing is shown in table 6-1. With U.S. support having helped build a strong financial position, portfolio diversification was not a difficult task. But it was one of a number of early signals of changing U.S. relations with the Bank that followed the shift in the Bank's focus from postwar reconstruction to development and accompanied the gradual decline of U.S. predominance in the postwar world economy.

The Shift to Development

As it quickly became clear that needed postwar reconstruction would exceed the resources of the newly created World Bank, the United States initiated the Marshall Plan as a separate recovery program for Europe and helped the Bank turn its attention to its second objective, development. But with the Bank's shift to the problems of development, the support of the United States, which remained dominant, became more hesitant and more conditional than at the outset.

In 1947 Britain withdrew its troops from the civil war raging in Greece, an act that precipitated the Truman Doctrine. The world, Truman said, faced a stark choice between two ways of life: communism and democracy. In this unfolding context, U.S. policy toward World Bank lending took on new political ramifications. In the face of mounting Communist party pressures in Europe, John McCloy and other leading Americans insisted that European recovery required assistance so massive that it surpassed the Bank's capacity. The effort, they argued, would have to be financed by the American taxpayer through a bilateral economic recovery program, first publicly proposed by Secretary of State George Marshall. While still president of the Bank, McCloy lobbied vigorously for what came to be known as the Marshall Plan, explaining that Bank lending was constrained by the need to sell its securities in the financial markets. He also resisted U.S. pressure to have the Bank fund food aid to Western Europe as a temporary measure until Marshall Plan aid arrived. The Bank, McCloy insisted, was no substitute, even in the interim, for massive bilateral, politically motivated aid.[25]

Following the launching of the Marshall Plan, McCloy turned the Bank's attention to the less developed countries, beginning with Latin America. However, as constituted the Bank was ill prepared to assume a major role in development financing. Its financial resources were too small, and many of the world's poorest countries could not afford its near-market rates. Moreover, the Articles of Agreement prohibited lending directly to private enterprises. As a result of these and

---

25. Bird, *The Chairman*, pp. 292–93.

other constraints, Bank lending to developing countries increased only slowly. Pressure to resolve these problems led ultimately to the establishment of the Bank's two affiliates, the International Finance Corporation (IFC) in 1956 and the International Development Association (IDA) in 1960, but only after the United States dropped its opposition and agreed to support them. In both cases the U.S. endorsement was given grudgingly, as much in response to foreign policy considerations as to the challenges of development.

An IFC and an IDA linked to the World Bank were proposed in 1951 by a U.S. advisory group appointed by President Truman to recommend ways to achieve the objectives of the Point Four Program. Point Four in Truman's 1949 inaugural address had called for a new program to make the benefits of scientific advances and industrial progress available to underdeveloped areas. A leading purpose of the new program was to strengthen key countries in the third world, particularly those surrounding the emerging Soviet bloc, and to dissuade others from aligning with the Soviets. Emphasizing the link between U.S. security interests and economic development in the third world, the program marked a historic turn in U.S. relations with developing countries and the beginnings of substantial U.S. foreign aid commitments to non-European countries.

In making its recommendations, the advisory group emphasized the need for some form of international machinery "for employing the techniques which lay between pure loans and pure grants," and it urged that the United States not undertake the development assistance task on its own.[26] It proposed that the United States take the lead in establishing both an IFC and an IDA affiliated with the World Bank, the IFC to mobilize capital for direct lending to the private sector and IDA to provide concessional loans to poor countries using funds contributed by governments. These recommendations elicited no immediate U.S. government response, however. The United States was at war in Korea, it was faced with a growing budget deficit, and it was not yet convinced that more was needed to stimulate development, despite mounting pressure from developing countries within the United Nations for larger amounts of development funds on softer terms.

Frustrated by their inability to afford World Bank loans at market rates and emboldened by the perceived largesse of the Marshall Plan, developing countries had begun arguing in the late 1940s and early 1950s for the establishment of a new UN development agency that would provide technical and financial assistance on concessional terms and that would operate under the UN rule of one country, one vote, rather than under the Bank and its system of weighted voting. The United States strongly opposed a series of such proposals, but in 1954 abruptly endorsed the idea of the IFC as a political concession.[27] Concerned with the escalating cold

26. James H. Weaver, *The International Development Association* (Praeger, 1965), p. 31.

27. Bronislaw E. Matecki, *Establishment of the International Finance Corporation and United States Policy* (Praeger, 1957), p. 149.

war and Soviet attempts to exploit the UN debate between developed and developing countries, the United States determined that some response was necessary.
"The State Department urged that the United States must make at least a gesture;
and, this having been decided in principle, the government looked around for the
cheapest thing to do, and the cheapest thing to do was the IFC."[28] In the request to
Congress for support, President Eisenhower emphasized the IFC's potential contribution to "prosperity, expanded trade, and 'the peace and solidarity of the free
world.'"[29] The proposal passed in both the House and Senate with little debate and
a wide margin of support.[30]

Establishment of the IFC did not, however, stem developing countries' demands for a new concessional aid agency, to which the United States remained
opposed until Congress broke the stalemate. In 1958 the Senate endorsed a
proposal of one of its members, Mike Monroney of Oklahoma, for an international
development agency linked to the World Bank that would use surplus unconver-
tible currency held by rich nations to fund projects in developing countries. As
presented, Monroney's plan would have been costless but largely ineffectual. However, the favorable domestic response the Senator's proposal received, combined
with the growing pressure from developing countries for a Special UN Fund for
Economic Development (SUNFED), finally convinced the United States, in consultation with the World Bank's president, to present the executive board with a
plan for the International Development Association. The plan for what became the
Bank's concessional or soft loan window was accepted and submitted to governments for approval in January 1960.

The fact that many developing countries were quickly reaching the limits of
their creditworthiness in Bank terms contributed to the U.S. decision to launch
IDA. This problem had already led to the start-up in 1958 of the U.S. Development
Loan Fund, a large bilateral concessional capital transfer operation, and to collaboration between Bank President Eugene Black and Undersecretary of State
Douglas Dillon on the launching of the India aid consortium, the first effort of its
kind. In presenting the IDA proposal to Congress, Treasury Secretary Robert
Anderson noted that "it showed the rich countries' commitment" to helping to
meet the development needs of the poor nations and would help them "advance
their economic life under free institutions."[31] For the United States it also provided
a way to get other developed countries to begin to share more of what had come to
be seen as the aid burden. As in the case of the IFC, the International Development Association received strong support from a broad range of national groups,

28. Ibid.
29. Quoted in Sanford, *U.S. Foreign Policy*, p. 46.
30. Congress formally authorized U.S. membership in the IFC in August 1955 and
approved an initial U.S. capital subscription of $35 million out of a total capital base of
$100 million.
31. Quoted in Sanford, *U.S. Foreign Policy*, p. 47.

and legislation authorizing U.S. participation passed both houses of Congress by comfortable margins. As had been recommended in the advisory board report a decade earlier, the United States assumed a substantial (42 percent) share of the initial IDA contribution and took the lead in mobilizing the support of other countries.

The End of an Era

With the establishment of IDA, the start-up phase of what came to be known as the World Bank was complete. Having led in this launching, the United States over the next decade encouraged the Bank to expand its lending to low-income countries, become more involved in addressing the need for increases in agricultural productivity and other major emerging development problems, and take the lead in approaching politically sensitive matters such as trade and industrial liberalization in India. Although disagreements arose between the U.S. government and the World Bank in the 1960s that tested the Bank's autonomy, for the most part relations were good. The United States was still by far the dominant member country. Its bilateral aid program remained for a time the larger and more innovative force in the enterprise of development assistance, and in many cases it worked closely with the Bank in the field. The professional development community, which emerged largely in the United States, also gave intellectual support to the strategy of development advanced by the United States and the Bank.

The support for the buildup of the Bank's development financing formed part of a U.S. turn to long-term economic development assistance in the 1950s and early 1960s. Although the early geographic focus of economic aid to the third world was a few countries in East Asia, by 1960 assistance had been expanded. The poverty-ridden countries of South Asia, America's near neighbors in Latin America, and later the emerging independent states of Africa all became recipients under a program of assistance that was building in the late Eisenhower years and was expanded after President Kennedy took office in 1961.

The Soviet Union had by then developed nuclear weapons, launched Sputnik, and extended its diplomatic reach into Africa, Asia, and America's neighbor, Cuba. Out of concern that the developing countries would succumb to the influence of communist ideology and the offers of support from the Soviet Union, the Kennedy administration took steps to strengthen U.S. foreign assistance. It consolidated existing aid programs into the Agency for International Development (AID), created the Peace Corps and the Alliance for Progress, and emphasized the need for the transfer of large financial resources by both bilateral and multilateral institutions. The rationale for this new aid was based on the conviction that deterrence of the Soviet military threat, while a necessary keystone of U.S. foreign policy, was not in itself adequate. It was an essential American interest that the countries of the developing world achieve economic growth and social stability within a democratic framework, not only to limit the Soviet orbit of interest but also to avoid the evolution of those nations into authoritarian systems that would be anti-American and anti-Western. These goals were believed to require a program of economic development aid to foster self-sustaining growth; and to be effective, programs of assistance needed to be institutionally divorced from the foreign policy apparatus.[32]

Development activists in later years have looked back on this as a time of "high expectations . . . both in the United States and in the Third World . . . [and] the only time when a true national consensus in favor of active development cooperation with the Third World prevailed." The consensus "brought together those motivated by security concerns . . . [and] those motivated by humanitarianism and a belief in the United States' interest in a rapidly expanding . . . world economy."[33] But the consensus proved short-lived.

In the context of the Kennedy administration's expanded foreign assistance policy, the United States took the lead in the first replenishment negotiations for IDA, calling for support of the Bank president's request for a fivefold, $1.5 billion three-year funding increase and seeking a reduction in the U.S. share from its initial 42.34 percent to 33.3 percent. In the face of resistance from other donors, however, it settled for a smaller replenishment (of $750 million) and only a token reduction in the share (41.89 percent). The IDA 2 negotiations were far more troubled, however.[34] IDA, as distinct from the World Bank itself, required the use of tax dollars and, with the second replenishment, became the lightening rod of U.S. World Bank policy.

George Woods became president of the Bank in 1963, taking over from Eugene Black. Woods was also a New York banker, but unlike his predecessor, he did not retain control over the appointment of the U.S. executive director, nor were relations between him and the U.S. government as close and as congenial as Black's had been. The change in relations had partly to do with personality.[35] But it had far more to do with changing U.S. economic fortunes and domestic policy concerns. The change was evident in the role the United States took in the IDA 2 negotiations. Although it had taken the lead in promoting the first IDA replenishment, when negotiations began on IDA 2, the United States was committed to reducing its outflow of dollars, resisting inflation, and maintaining the integrity (preventing a devaluation) of the dollar.[36]

32. For a discussion of the evolution of these views see, for example, Congressional Research Service, "Soviet Policy and United States Response in the Third World," March 1981, p. 5.

33. Robert J. Berg and David F. Gordon, eds., *Cooperation for International Development: The United States and the Third World in the 1990s* (London: Lynne Rienner, 1989), pp. 1–2.

34. Mason and Asher, *World Bank since Bretton Woods,* p. 411.

35. According to Robert W. Oliver in his forthcoming biography of George Woods, "everyone remembered Eugene Black as a warm person who entertained Congressmen, but George Woods entertained little." *The Anguish of George Woods,* chap. 8, p. 29.

36. Paul A. Volcker and Toyoo Gyohten, *Changing Fortunes: The World's Money and the Threat to American Leadership* (Times Books, 1992), chap. 2.

Henry Fowler, secretary of the Treasury, urged Woods to lead the IDA 2 negotiations if he wanted to expand the agency. Woods proposed a $1 billion replenishment, which the United States favored. Concerned with avoiding a negative effect on its own balance of payments, however, the United States pressed hard in the negotiations for special balance of payments safeguards and a significant reduction in its IDA share, an objective that was to be emphasized in all subsequent replenishments. The United States did not gain agreement on either the "tied" or burden-sharing arrangements it sought, but it did achieve special "end of the queue" treatment for its contribution.

Even with that concession, however, congressional debate on IDA 2 questioned so large an increase at a time when government was cutting domestic programs and raising taxes. The debate delayed approval of U.S. participation, leaving other countries to advance funding to avoid a temporary suspension in IDA lending. In 1966 in response to the difficulty that foreign aid in general and the IDA negotiations in particular had begun to face in the United States, Woods hired a retired U.S. senator, A. Willis Robertson, to serve as consultant and lobbyist. By the time the IDA 2 negotiations were completed and brought to Congress for approval, Robert McNamara had become Bank president. The difficulty he faced in getting IDA 2 approved led him to take the further step of assigning to a senior Bank staff member, William Clark, the responsibility of building and maintaining better communications with Congress.[37] In sum, with the second replenishment, a pattern of U.S. demands for concessions and delays in authorizing or appropriating its IDA contributions had emerged. By the end of the 1960s the era of innovative and active U.S. leadership in development had begun to wane.

Policy Evolution and Erosion of Support

Three main objectives guided U.S. policy toward the Bank in the 1950s and early 1960s. The first was to build a strong organization as a means of promoting the stability and growth of a free and open world economy. The second was to ease the burden on the United States of providing economic assistance to other countries by leveraging funds from the private market and, with their recovery from World War II, from other industrialized countries. The third was to support countries of importance to the United States. Although these were to remain major objectives, during the 1970s U.S. support for and leadership in the Bank faltered.

37. Bank Vice President Burke Knapp suggested at the time that it would also be useful to have the Department of State designate the U.S. alternate executive director as a way to keep the department informed of Bank policies and operations. But after the removal of Emilio Collado as the first director, the Treasury Department had gained increasing control of the U.S. multilateral development bank policy process, usually collaborating but at times disagreeing with the State Department on the handling of individual country cases as well as broad policy toward the Bank.

The United States had launched the Bank in a foreign policy environment different from the one that emerged in the early 1970s. Three changes proved to have a major bearing on relations between the United States and the Bank.

The first was the relative decline of the United States in the world economy. By 1973 the U.S. share of world GDP had shrunk to 26 percent from a level of nearly 35 percent two decades earlier.[38] Western Europe and Japan grew more rapidly through the 1960s than did the United States, which also experienced a shift from persistent balance of payments surpluses, with resultant dollar shortages in the rest of the world, to frequent deficits. The postwar economic boom had also given way to concerns about domestic poverty, unemployment, and race inequalities. The 1971 dollar devaluation and general deterioration in the country's economic situation turned attention to the costs of U.S. international economic policy. As spelled out by a Treasury official in 1972,

> There is a . . . sharply heightened feeling in the United States today that the economic interests of our country have not been given sufficient weight in international policy making. What follows from this is that financial and other burdens traditionally accepted without question by the United States can no longer be automatically accepted on that basis. The new international economic environment is radically different from the familiar "post-war" period that must now be regarded as definitively ended. Now, the United States is compelled to weigh its actions in terms of the benefits and the burdens that will result.[39]

A second change for the country was the Vietnam War and the shattering of the foreign aid constituency. The prolonged and divisive war provoked domestic dissent and uncertainty about the U.S. role in the world. One observer commented, "virtually all the familiar geopolitical moorings of U.S. foreign policy have become unhitched. What for years seemed axiomatic now seems dubious, if not false. John F. Kennedy may be the last President who could, without creating a credibility gap, maintain that 'we in this country . . . are—by destiny rather than choice—the watchmen on the walls of world freedom.'"[40] The policy of containment that had shaped U.S. activities in the developing world in the 1950s and early 1960s "was progressively abandoned in the late 1960s and 1970s, less because of a national consensus that the Soviet threat had declined than because of a sense that the Vietnam experience demonstrated that such a policy, when severely tested, was excessively expensive and not necessarily effective."[41] Moreover, the Agency for International Development, which had been heavily involved in Vietnam, was

38. Angus Maddison, *The World Economy in the 20th Century* (Paris: OECD, 1989), p. 113.

39. Deputy Treasury Secretary Charles E. Walker, quoted in National Advisory Council on International Monetary and Financial Policies, *Annual Report* (Washington, 1972), p. 12.

40. Robert E. Asher, *Development Assistance in the Seventies: Alternatives for the United States* (Brookings, 1970), p. 19.

41. Congressional Research Service, "Soviet Policy and United States Response," p. 1.

seriously discredited. Although it maintained considerable programmatic energy into the mid-1970s, both it and foreign assistance generally lost their solid constituency.

Changes in perspectives on development further shattered the coalition of support for foreign aid, including support for the World Bank. In the early 1970s, development experts and public interest development groups began to criticize the prevailing trickle-down theory of development. Despite McNamara's efforts to broaden the lending policy of the Bank, the institution came under attack for supporting regimes that were persistent violators of human rights and for not doing enough to aid the poor. Constituency groups, which had given nearly automatic support to U.S. funding of the Bank, became at best conditional proponents. The problem was worsened by the rapid growth of lending under the dynamic leadership of McNamara, which stimulated a considerable increase in public and congressional attention to Bank policies and practices.

A final change was the onset of congressional activism in foreign policy. The creation of IDA, with its requirement for regular replenishments, brought Congress into the making of U.S. policy toward the Bank in a significant way. Before the early 1970s Congress's role was a relatively passive one, certainly as compared to its involvement with the bilateral aid program. It had strongly supported the launching of the Bank and the establishment of the two early Bank affiliates. But for the most part, early congressional action consisted of approving administration requests for U.S. membership in the Bank and providing funding for it. Although individual members raised particular concerns from time to time in private exchanges with the executive branch or Bank management, their public statements usually supported administration policy. This pattern began to change in the 1960s when support for foreign aid waned and Congress dragged its feet on the first and second IDA replenishments. It was the changes of the late 1960s and early 1970s, however, that led to an increasing activism on the part of Congress. Since then, Congress has used its power of the purse to direct and restrict U.S. participation in the Bank in many specific ways.[42]

The development that contributed most to Congress's more active role was the growth in the Bank's lending program and the corresponding increase of administration funding requests, especially for IDA. According to the Bank's annual reports, appropriations for all multilateral development banks rose in nominal terms from $700 million in fiscal year 1970 to $2.3 billion in fiscal year 1980. This increase attracted the attention of Congress, the press, and the development policy constituency in the United States. Although the Bank regularly fared better in Congress from the 1970s on than did other multilateral agencies or the bilateral aid program, the increases in appropriation requests provoked much greater scrutiny

42. For a detailed discussion of Congress's role in U.S. World Bank policymaking, see Jonathan E. Sanford, "U.S. Policy toward the Multilateral Development Banks: The Role of Congress," *George Washington Journal of International Law and Economics*, vol. 22 (1988), pp. 1–115.

and heightened criticism of policies and practices. Although most of the criticism came from traditional opponents of foreign aid, from the 1970s on, prodevelopment groups, including mainly church groups and private voluntary organizations, began to lobby in opposition to an ever widening range of specific features of Bank operations. Previously the active bulwarks of support, these groups became provisional proponents willing to endorse U.S. contributions to the Bank only if certain reforms were made in its policies and practices.

Foreign aid has never been popular in Congress. Although objections were muted in the years just after World War II, Congress quickly became dissatisfied with it and distrustful of multilateral institutions. No one ever ran for Congress on a pro-aid platform nor got elected for supporting the World Bank. As a consequence, most members of Congress were uninterested and uninformed about the Bank's operations. Even on key committees there has been much misunderstanding of what the Bank did and how it operated.[43] Executive branch leadership and active constituency groups provided the initial energy and pressure to sustain support; but with both in decline by the 1970s, the increased appropriation requests became attractive targets.

Two other forces, unrelated to the Bank's performance, were at work as well. The Vietnam War not only shattered the consensus on foreign policy but also ended the period of congressional quiescence on foreign affairs. Many members of Congress deeply objected to the escalation of U.S. involvement in the war and to the Johnson and Nixon administrations' attempts to use bilateral and multilateral aid in support of the war effort. As a consequence, Congress sought a greater role in directing foreign policy, which included more detailed oversight of U.S. participation in the Bank.

At the same time, there was a breakdown of discipline and effective leadership in Congress that made it infinitely more difficult to maneuver unpopular aid requests through the labyrinthine authorization and appropriation procedures. No fewer than five committees came to have significant jurisdiction over policy toward the Bank. This arrangement provided multiple entry points for interested groups with specific policy agendas, and it created the opportunity for strategically placed members of Congress and specific issues to gain disproportionate weight in the policy process. As long as Congress was passive in making Bank policy, its basic dislike of foreign aid and multilateral institutions and its cumbersome legislative procedures were of limited significance. But as it became less deferential on matters of foreign affairs, these factors became formative influences on U.S. policy toward and participation in the Bank.

A number of studies written in the late 1960s and early 1970s urged the United States to increase its reliance on multilateral assistance as a way to counter growing "aid fatigue" and improve the effectiveness of development

43. For a discussion of this problem see Lars Schoultz, "Politics, Economics, and U.S. Participation in Multilateral Development Banks," *International Organization*, vol. 36 (summer 1982), pp. 537–74.

assistance.[44] Although multilateral aid had increased fourfold under the Kennedy administration, it accounted for less than 10 percent of total U.S. foreign assistance at the end of the 1960s. The proposals for a shift in favor of multilateral aid were based on several rationales. Because waning public support for foreign aid would not allow the United States to continue to increase its foreign aid program, the multilateral development banks offered the best means of leveraging funds for developing countries. By relying on multilateral institutions to promote effective development policies, the United States could depoliticize foreign assistance and avoid strains in its relations with developing countries that resulted from bilateral policy interference. Finally, the multilateral development banks could promote more coordination and fewer unproductive and costly overlaps in international aid efforts.[45] The recommendation was picked up by the incoming Nixon administration, and in a message submitted to Congress in September 1970, President Nixon proposed a sweeping reorganization of the U.S. bilateral aid program and greater reliance on multilateral aid. The United States, he said, "should channel an increasing share of its development assistance through multilateral institutions as readily as practicable. . . . Our remaining bilateral assistance should be provided largely within a framework established by the international institutions."[46]

However, the relative increase in U.S. multilateral development bank contributions occurred in the mid-1960s and, in real terms, has held fairly steady since then (table 6-2). Thus its relative share of total U.S. foreign aid has reflected more the ebb and flow of bilateral aid levels, not any real increase in the proportion of U.S. aid flows through multilateral institutions in the 1970s or thereafter.

In fact, a substantial deterioration occurred in U.S. relations with the World Bank during the 1970s. This change was marked by frequent open conflict between the two over a variety of issues, repeated failures on the part of the United States to deliver on its share of replenishments within the same period as other member countries, and, by the end of the decade, the breakdown of the bipartisanship in U.S. Bank policy that had prevailed since the signing of the Bretton Woods Act.

The Early 1970s

The early l970s marked a turning point that began with a souring of relations between the Bank and the U.S. Treasury. As one indication of trouble, in early 1972

44. See, for example, Rudolph A. Petersen, "U.S. Foreign Assistance in the 1970s: A New Approach," Task Force on International Development, Washington, 1970; Dexter Perkins, "Development Assistance in the New Administration: Report of the President's General Advisory Committee on Foreign Assistance Programs," Agency for International Development, Washington, 1968; and Lester Pearson, *Partners in Development: Report of the Commission on International Development* (Praeger, 1969).

45. Asher, *Development Assistance in the Seventies*, esp. pp. 119–24.

46. Richard M. Nixon, message to Congress, October 15, 1970. Quoted in Sanford, *U.S. Foreign Policy*, p. 58.

Table 6-2. *U.S. Foreign Aid, by Major Programs, 1946–89*
Billions of constant 1989 dollars

Year	Development assistance	Food aid	Other economic aid	Multilateral development banks	Economic support fund	Military aid	Total
1946	...	...	17.6	4.6	...	...	22.2
1947	...	...	39.6	...	...	1.0	40.6
1948	...	...	15.1	...	...	1.7	16.8
1949	33.3	...	8.2	...	...	1.6	43.1
1950	19.3	...	6.0	...	...	6.3	31.6
1951	12.5	...	3.9	...	0.8	21.2	38.4
1952	8.9	0.4	1.7	...	1.0	21.9	33.9
1953	7.4	...	1.4	...	2.1	13.3	24.2
1954	3.4	0.3	0.5	...	7.4	11.4	23.0
1955	2.8	2.5	0.1	...	6.0	7.9	19.3
1956	1.7	4.0	0.2	...	5.3	10.8	22.0
1957	2.3	5.1	0.2	0.2	5.0	8.6	21.4
1958	3.7	3.4	0.1	...	3.4	6.6	17.2
1959	4.5	3.5	0.1	...	3.6	9.5	21.2
1960	4.4	4.0	0.1	0.3	3.4	9.2	21.4
1961	5.2	4.6	0.1	0.3	3.4	8.5	22.1
1962	7.2	5.6	1.1	0.7	3.2	8.2	26.0
1963	7.1	5.6	1.1	0.5	2.4	7.9	24.6
1964	7.0	5.8	0.7	0.4	1.8	4.6	20.3
1965	6.4	5.1	1.0	1.2	1.8	4.9	20.4
1966	6.5	5.7	0.7	1.3	3.3	7.8	25.3
1967	5.8	3.4	0.6	1.3	2.7	8.5	22.2
1968	5.4	4.5	0.6	1.4	2.1	9.1	23.1
1969	4.0	3.8	0.6	1.6	1.4	10.1	21.5
1970	4.2	3.5	0.5	1.5	1.5	8.9	20.1
1971	3.7	3.6	0.5	0.6	1.7	12.8	22.8
1972	4.0	3.4	1.4	0.4	1.7	14.0	24.9
1973	3.6	2.9	0.6	2.0	1.6	14.1	24.8
1974	2.8	2.4	0.8	2.0	1.6	11.2	20.8
1975	2.9	2.9	0.6	1.7	2.7	4.4	15.2
1976	2.5	2.7	0.5	0.1	2.3	5.2	13.3
1976TQ	0.8	0.4	0.2	0.7	1.8	1.3	5.2
1977	2.7	2.3	0.5	1.8	3.3	4.1	14.7
1978	3.3	2.2	0.4	2.0	3.9	4.2	16.0
1979	3.0	2.1	0.6	2.7	3.2	11.0	22.6
1980	2.8	2.2	0.9	2.2	3.3	3.2	14.6
1981	2.7	2.1	0.8	1.3	3.0	4.6	14.5
1982	2.6	1.7	0.7	1.6	3.5	5.5	15.6
1983	2.7	1.7	0.6	1.8	3.6	6.9	17.3
1984	2.9	1.8	0.6	1.6	3.7	7.7	18.3
1985	3.2	2.3	0.7	1.8	6.0	6.6	20.6
1986	2.9	1.8	0.6	1.3	5.4	6.4	18.4
1987	2.3	1.5	0.7	1.6	3.8	5.5	15.4
1988 (est.)	2.3	1.6	0.7	1.5	3.3	5.6	15.0
1989 (req.)	2.2	1.4	0.6	1.5	3.3	5.6	14.6
Total	218.9	113.8	114.8	45.4	123.3	349.4	965.6

Source: Stanely J. Heginbotham and Larry Q. Knowles, *An Overview of U.S. Foreign Aid Programs* (Congressional Research Services, 1988), p. 17.

the United States gave "belated and grudging" support to Robert McNamara for a second term as World Bank president.[47] According to the press, McNamara was not the first choice of Republican President Nixon. Names of former Republican cabinet members were proposed, but the international development constituency came out strongly in McNamara's support, and European member states hinted that if the U.S. nominee were not McNamara, they might advance a European alternative.[48] According to a retrospective analysis of these years by the Bank's vice president for external affairs during his term, McNamara "had irritated many important leaders in the Nixon administration. They had thought that, as an American, McNamara should be responsive to policy nudges, but over and over again he proved to be unnudgeable."[49] The grudging support for his nomination was a harbinger of difficulties that beset his relations with the United States until Jimmy Carter's election to the presidency.

Also in 1971 at the initiative of the executive branch, the United States cast its first "no" vote on a World Bank loan. The proposed loan was to Guyana and was opposed by the United States as part of a policy condemning expropriation of U.S. private property. Although this was not the first credit the United States had opposed, it was the first time that it chose to cast an opposing vote on the Bank's executive board and thereby put its disagreement with the Bank on the record.

Two years later, in negotiations for the fourth IDA replenishment, the United States was for the first time the main donor country seeking to limit the increase in contributions. It made the World Bank and other countries take over its role of conciliator, soliciting contributions and arranging compromises. Moreover, it demanded and got a number of concessions. On the list of U.S. conditions for the replenishment were the establishment of an independent audit process for Bank operations, removal of the maintenance of value obligation that required member countries to maintain the foreign exchange values of their IDA contributions, and a commitment for a future leveling off of IDA replenishments in real terms. The United States also demanded a commitment for a reduction in the differences between U.S. official and World Bank salaries and due consideration of the U.S. position in response to the expropriation of U.S. private property in Peru. In addition, it demanded and received a substantial reduction in its share of IDA funding and agreement on stretching out its contribution over four years rather than the regular three. These arrangements allowed the United States to hold its annual payment to the same level in current dollars as in IDA 3, while other countries made sizable increases in their contributions.

In asserting the U.S. position on IDA 4, the Nixon administration clearly had one eye on mounting deficits and signs of inflation in the U.S. economy and one eye

47. William Clark, "Robert McNamara at the World Bank," *Foreign Affairs*, vol. 60 (fall 1981), p. 176.

48. See, for example, Stephen S. Rosenfeld, "Robert S. McNamara and the Wiser Use of Power," *World Opinion*, July 3, 1973, pp. 19–20.

49. Clark, "Robert McNamara," p. 176.

on Congress, which was becoming increasingly restless over various aspects of the administration's Bank policy. However, the major breakpoint in U.S. policy focused not on IDA but the Bank itself, and it was brought on not by Congress but by the executive branch, which voiced strong opposition to continued growth in lending. At the outset of the first oil shock in 1973–74, the United States expressed skepticism about continued expansion of regular Bank lending and opposed initial efforts by McNamara to enlist development funds from oil producers with capital surpluses. In early 1974 he sought agreement from those countries on establishing an OPEC fund for development whose operations would be carried out by existing World Bank staff and whose votes would be divided equally into three groups: OPEC, developed, and developing countries. "But he had reckoned without the determination of the Americans . . . to break the OPEC cartel and not to collaborate with it in any way. In the face of U.S. opposition the proposals sank without trace."[50] Recycling of petrodollars, the United States held, was a function best left to the commercial banks.

The success of OPEC in manipulating a fourfold increase in oil prices emboldened developing countries in the mid-1970s to intensify demands for a new international economic order. Acting in concert, they demanded a greater share of the benefits from international economic cooperation and a greater voice in the system. In staunchly opposing these demands the United States insisted on the need for developing countries to put their national economic policies in order and emphasized the importance of the Bretton Woods institutions in assisting development. In a speech written for the special session of the UN General Assembly in September 1975, which was intended to be responsive to but not supportive of the developing countries' demands, Secretary of State Henry Kissinger offered a number of initiatives, including two new facilities to be linked to the World Bank and U.S. support for expansion of both the IFC and the Bank.[51] Although these were initiatives that would have had a relatively small impact on the U.S. budget, the political strategy of the State Department was constrained by strong Treasury opposition to continued growth in World Bank lending.

In a dispute that came to a head at the annual meeting of the Bank in 1976, the Ford administration's Treasury secretary, William Simon, countered McNamara's call for increased Bank lending and an attendant general increase in the Bank's capital. Simon supported IDA but opposed the rate of the Bank's growth in both

50. Ibid., p. 178. This 1974 attempt had a parallel in 1980–82 following the second oil shock when the incoming Reagan administration rejected an initiative to create an energy affiliate, as discussed later.

51. Kissinger was concerned that, following OPEC's actions, other third world countries would try to form cartels in strategic commodities. Therefore one of his initiatives was for a resource development bank. McNamara, as indicated in minutes of the meetings of his president's council, took Kissinger's proposal as a signal that the United States would support Bank lending in the mining and production of minerals, but this was not to prove so.

borrowing and lending. In contrast to McNamara's emphasis on the need for increased lending in the wake of the oil price hikes, declining global growth, and mounting third world debt, Simon called for a concerted attack on inflation at home and abroad and insisted that the time had come for deficit countries to slow their borrowing and for less developed countries to adjust their economic policies to allow for greater reliance on market forces. In his statement at the annual meeting Simon foreshadowed several issues that figured prominently in the policy of the Reagan administration.

> In considering how the present system might be improved to the mutual benefit of all nations, we should be guided by the following principles:
> —Development by definition is a long-term process. . . . Foreign aid can help, but such aid can only complement and supplement those policies developing countries adopt, which in the end will be decisive.
> —The role of the private sector is critical. There is no substitute for a vigorous private sector mobilizing the resources and energies of the people of the developing countries.
> —A market-oriented system is not perfect, but it is better than any alternative system. . . .
> —A basic focus must be on increasing savings and making the institutional and policy improvements which will enable the financial markets to channel those savings into activities that enhance the opportunities for people to live better lives.[52]

Simon contended that the larger role McNamara sought for the Bank would result in some nations borrowing beyond their capacity to repay and would weaken the Bank's standing in the capital markets. He insisted, therefore, that Bank lending should be temporarily frozen at current levels. In IDA 5 negotiations the United States also expressed an unwillingness to see its annual payments increase. After other countries countered by insisting that it maintain a reasonable proportional share, negotiations concluded with an agreement on a smaller replenishment than had been proposed by the Bank. Thus the long-standing U.S. goal of burden sharing had come to have the effect of holding down rather than increasing IDA contributions.

In the view of senior Treasury officials, the Bank was out of control. According to the U.S. executive director, they were concerned that the rapid growth in lending, which had resulted in massive undispersed commitments, was mortgaging the Bank's future borrowing capacity and that Bank management was not responsive to donor criticism. Treasury also raised questions about the bankability of new projects undertaken as part of the Bank's emphasis on alleviating poverty and about the Bank's support for widening the role of governments in the development process.[53] To

52. Statement by William E. Simon, *Summary Proceedings of the 1976 Annual Meetings of the Boards of Governors* (Manila: IBRD, 1976), p. 190.

53. Charles A. Cooper, working paper for the Study Group on International Financial Institutions, Council on Foreign Relations, New York, March 1980. Cited with permission of the author. See also National Advisory Council on International Monetary and Financial Policy, *Annual Report to the President and to the Congress, July 1, 1975–June 30, 1976* (Washington, 1977).

others in the Bank and on the executive board, however, U.S. opposition to the rapid growth of the Bank appeared to reflect two quite different concerns. First, with U.S. bilateral aid shrinking, a growing Bank might displace the U.S. economic, and therefore political, leverage in developing countries. Second, with the increase in Bank borrowing in non-U.S. markets, the United States would lose its influence over how and where Bank funds were spent. Opposition to an increase in the capital subscription of Japan, which would have eroded the U.S. veto, was taken as an indication of the latter concern.[54]

One effect of a policy less supportive of the Bank was that the United States fell behind in its contributions to the Bank and IDA. The delay eroded U.S. relations with other member countries, a problem the Carter administration sought to remedy later in the decade. But it had to contend with, and itself contributed to, the worst period in relations between the World Bank and Congress.

The Proliferation of Legislative Restrictions

By the time President Carter came to office, Congress had established a practice of tying directives to its approval of World Bank funding bills. These restrictions proliferated rapidly in the second half of the 1970s because of the personalities in key congressional positions, the growing criticism of the Bank from both liberal and conservative members of Congress, and the mismanagement of legislative relations by Carter administration officials.

The Foreign Operations Subcommittee of the House Appropriations Committee, which essentially held the House purse strings on foreign aid, was chaired from 1955 to 1977 by Otto Passman of Louisiana. Passman "voted against every foreign aid authorization after the 1947 Greek-Turkey loan and he gave the program a skeptical treatment during the twenty-two years he chaired the panel."[55] In 1977 Clarence Long of Maryland took over as chair. Although he was more supportive of the goals and purposes of the U.S. foreign aid program, he was generally critical of the World Bank. His criticism focused particularly on what he viewed as the Bank's failure to help the poor, but many have claimed that the death of his son in Vietnam made him a staunch and unrelenting critic of Robert McNamara and his tenure in office. The rise in congressional opposition to the Bank was not limited to Long and the subcommittee, however. It was fed by public interest groups on both the Left and the Right and by increased coverage of the Bank in the media as each replenishment required larger funding bills.

Paradoxically, one effect of Congress's increased attention was to bring development issues more into focus in the formation of policy toward the Bank. In the 1950s and 1960s, when bilateral aid was the dominant force in development

54. John Lewis and Richard Webb interview with Robert S. McNamara, May 10, 1991, transcript, p. 7.
55. Sanford, *U.S. Foreign Policy*, p. 120.

assistance, the United States interacted closely with the Bank in the field, and U.S. policy toward the Bank was mediated, to a considerable extent, by coordinated actions of the Bank and USAID within countries. This interaction was especially intense in South Asia when the United States was giving large amounts of aid to India and Pakistan and in Latin America during the Alliance for Progress. Although the agencies continued to interact, by the mid-1970s USAID had become a less innovative force in development. U.S. relations with the Bank were left largely to the Treasury and State departments, which brought little development interest or expertise to policymaking. With no place in the executive branch to consider the development policies and performance of the Bank, the development community turned to Congress, which from the 1970s on showed more concern and interest in the effectiveness of development assistance programs than did the bureaucracy.

Congress's initiative in 1973 to set "new directions" for the U.S. aid program was a clear example of this interest.[56] Although the new directions legislation did not succeed in shoring up waning public support for foreign aid, it did set guidelines for the executive branch in the uses of aid dollars appropriated by Congress. In subsequent years Congress gave increasing attention to new directions issues in its deliberation of Bank funding bills. Thus in the late 1970s and throughout the 1980s, Congress held hearings, requested studies, and at times mandated that the United States use its voice and vote in the Bank to strengthen the development impact of Bank lending, particularly in alleviating poverty.

The interest of some members of Congress in development was not sufficient, however, to withstand the general waning of support for foreign aid and growing attacks on the Bank from both traditional opponents and proponents of foreign aid. As a result, the effort of securing money for the Bank came to dominate policymaking.

Congressional reluctance to appropriate funds for the Bank mounted. This reluctance led, first, to delays in voting the full amount of funding requested by the executive branch, and the United States failed repeatedly to deliver its shares of negotiated replenishments on time. One of the most dramatic instances of this was the 1974 defeat of the IDA 4 funding bill in the House. Although Congress had held up approval of the first three IDA funding requests, the IDA 4 bill was the first to be defeated. The action was taken in a burst of anger over the economy and was actually less an indication of Congress's attitude toward the Bank than of a general discontent in the wake of Watergate, oil price hikes, and stagflation. Although the action was successfully overturned in a later vote after heavy administration lobbying, the defeat clearly demonstrated a new vulnerability of Bank funding requests. In subsequent years Congress not only delayed making appropriations but also, from time to time, appropriated less, sometimes far less, than the amounts requested by the executive branch and less than what was required to meet pledges

56. Foreign Assistance Act of 1973, P.L. 93-189.

made by the United States in international negotiations. As a consequence, the United States became the only donor to fall into arrears to the Bank.

In this environment, "particularism . . . found fertile soil."[57] In effect, Congress became the staging ground for criticisms of the Bank that multiplied as funding requests grew larger. More and more, committee chairs had to cater to members' particularistic views to obtain the support necessary to move authorization and appropriation bills. Vocal minorities exacted concessions on an array of narrow, short-run issues, or committee bills were altered by floor amendments proposed with little regard for their ultimate impact on the operations of the Bank. In the absence of a strong constituency that could be mobilized by the floor leadership to counter particularistic amendments, an extensive body of legislation built up that required the United States to go to the Bank and seek numerous specific concessions.

Many of the issues that were built into legislation were brought to Congress by outside groups, but not all. One of the first issue-specific legislative actions was the Gonzalez amendment of 1972, which required the United States to oppose World Bank loans to countries that had expropriated U.S. private investments without proper compensation.[58] In the 1960s Congress had passed legislation barring U.S. bilateral aid to countries that confiscated U.S. investments (the 1962 Hickenlooper amendment) and requiring the United States to vote against Inter-American Development Bank loans to them. The 1972 legislation extended the restriction to loans of all multilateral development banks. The World Bank, at U.S. urging, had adopted operational guidelines in response to expropriations, and the administration had sought to discourage expropriations through a variety of diplomatic efforts, but the Gonzalez amendment overruled a reluctance within the bureaucracy to adopt a formal, blanket statement of opposition.[59]

Although expropriation policy was the specific issue, support for the amendment was driven by a broader concern with Congress's role in the oversight of U.S. aid policy. Having increased its control over the bilateral aid program through various legislative restrictions and earmarkings, Congress was unwilling to see its directives circumvented by the relative increase in multilateral aid that the administration sought at the start of the 1970s. As a House Appropriations Committee report stated in 1972,

> The Committee is deeply concerned over the trend to direct an increasing amount of U.S. foreign assistance through the multilateral institutions while at the same time decreasing the bilateral aid program. . . . The same degree of detailed examination which is possible in the bilateral foreign assistance programs is not possible in the multilateral

57. Bergsten, working paper, p. 14.

58. The amendment added section 21 to the 1959 Inter-American Development Bank Act, section 11 to the 1960 International Development Association Act, and section 18 to the 1966 Asian Development Bank Act.

59. Sanford, *U.S. Foreign Policy;* and Jessica Pernitz Einhorn, *Expropriation Politics* (Lexington, Mass.: Lexington Books, 1974).

assistance programs. The Congress does not know when, where or how the budget requests will be disbursed by these multilateral organizations because they do not justify their requests by specific project.[60]

This broader concern was repeatedly voiced in subsequent years, with attention focused on the inadequacy of executive branch consultation with Congress, the need for more information from the Bank, and the need for more independent and more transparent evaluation and audit procedures. At Congress's request the General Accounting Office undertook several assessments of the management of U.S. Bank policy and the evaluation and audit procedures.[61] On the basis of a 1978 report, Congress passed legislation directing the United States to establish an independent review mechanism. But the reforms that followed did little to quiet the charge that the executive branch was using support for the multilateral development banks as a way around congressional restrictions on bilateral aid and that the Bank was unresponsive to Congress's requests for more information and more transparency. A Senate report said in 1978, "for more than five years the Committee has pressed the banks to open their doors and encourage both their supporters and the media to make informed judgments as to how well and how efficiently they are carrying out their international mandate. It is apparent that our exhortations have fallen on deaf ears."[62] Criticism was even more strongly worded in a House minority report that same year: "By making our contributions through multi-lateral institutions, Congress has lost the ability to have control over how American tax dollars are spent and who will receive them. . . . The fact that the administration wants to put even more of these tax dollars into multilateral aid programs will remove even further the oversight capability of the Congress."[63] And in 1979, under the leadership of Clarence Long, the House Appropriations Committee issued an investigative report that strongly criticized the ability of the United States to influence the Bank, the inadequacy of audit and evaluation systems, the limited flow of information to Congress and the public, and the Bank's record on lending to the poor.[64]

In addition to congressional oversight and Bank transparency, five other issues dominated congressional debate through the 1970s and into the 1980s (there were

60. House Committee on Appropriations, *Foreign Assistance and Related Programs Appropriation Bill, 1972*, report 92-711, 92nd Cong. 1st sess. (1971), p. 33.

61. See, for example, General Accounting Office, "More Effective United States Participation Needed in World Bank and International Development Association," 1973; and General Accounting Office, "Effectiveness of the World Bank's Independent Review and Evaluation System," 1978.

62. Senate Committee on Appropriations, *Foreign Assistance and Related Programs Appropriation Bill, 1978*, report 95-352, 95th Cong. 1st sess. (July 1977), p. 124.

63. House Committee on Appropriations, *Foreign Assistance and Related Programs Appropriation Bill, 1978*, report 95-417, 95th Cong. 1st sess. (June 1977), pp. 72–73.

64. Although the executive branch countered most of the charges, the report was picked up in the press and darkened the Bank's image with both Congress and the public at large.

many more). Through successive pieces of legislation, these matters became demands that the government was instructed to pursue within the Bank.

MANAGEMENT AND PERSONNEL PRACTICES. Congress's attitude that the Bank was excessively closed and arrogant was inflamed by the high Bank staff salaries and the difficulties Congress encountered in getting information on them. Whether or not the issue was deliberately fanned by those opposed to foreign aid, and particularly multilateral aid, it seriously undermined Hill support for the Bank. A Senate subcommittee report commented in 1975, "many who are said to be dedicated servants of the poor receive unseemly compensation for their service."[65] A year later Congress indicated that future IDA appropriations would be affected by progress on reducing salaries, and the following year it adopted legislation directing the administration to seek to keep Bank and IMF salaries and benefits at levels comparable to those paid by private employers and the U.S. government. Subsequently, the Bank and the IMF agreed to personnel guidelines that closely followed a U.S. proposal to set salary schedules by reference to a basket of compensation packages of civil servants of several member governments and the U.S. private sector.[66] This action reduced the level of controversy for a time, but it did not eliminate the salary issue. In 1989 Congress recommended that the Treasury make known to the Bank its "extreme displeasure" with a salary increase and "the damaging impact such a large increase has on support for the World Bank in Congress."[67]

LENDING TO SPECIFIC COUNTRIES. Before the mid-1970s, Congress voiced little concern over World Bank country allocations, with the notable exception of lending to countries that expropriated U.S. private property. After the mid-1970s, however, Congress frequently expressed opposition to loans to particular countries. India was an early target of criticism, and support in Congress for IDA replenishments was undermined by India's large share of IDA resources, which exceeded 40 percent at its peak. Legislation targeted particularly at India instructed the U.S. representative in the Bank to consider whether a recipient country had detonated a nuclear device or refused to sign the Treaty on Nonproliferation of Nuclear Weapons. And in response to congressional pressure the administration made the reduction of India's share a condition of IDA negotiations. More controversial and more strident was a late 1970s effort, led by Representative Bill Young, to stop lending to Vietnam and five other socialist countries. Young and other conservative

65. Senate Committee on Appropriations, *Foreign Assistance and Related Programs Appropriation Bill, 1975,* report 94-39, 94th Cong. 1st sess. (March 1975), p. 142.

66. U.S. civil service salary scales were lower than those of some other developed countries and salaries were capped for much of the time after 1968, which added to resentment of rising salaries in an international institution just blocks away from the Treasury Department and other offices.

67. Senate Committee on Appropriations, *Foreign Operations, Export Financing, and Related Programs Appropriation Bill, 1990,* report 101-131, 101st Cong. 1st sess. (September 1989), p. 72.

members of Congress strongly objected to what they viewed as the Bank's support of socialist regimes and statist solutions to development problems. Young believed that indirect U.S. aid to Vietnam through multilateral development banks was especially objectionable, and his opposition led to a major dispute over a proposed earmarking of U.S. contributions to the Bank.

PROTECTION OF U.S. PRODUCERS. From 1976 through the 1980s, Congress also objected to Bank lending to increase the production of commodities that could compete with U.S. commodities. In 1977 Congress adopted legislation requiring U.S. executive directors at each of the multilateral development banks to oppose loans for the production of palm oil, citrus crops, and sugar.[68] In 1978, Congress mandated U.S. directors' opposition to all loans for the production of export commodities, including mineral commodities, that were in surplus in world markets and that could cause substantial injury to U.S. producers.[69] Proposed but not passed was a more stringent amendment to the 1987 Omnibus Trade Act that sought to prohibit the United States from participating in future funding agreements for multilateral development banks that made loans for the production of agricultural and mineral commodities in surplus in the world market. And in 1989 Congress extended its legislative restrictions by mandating the U.S. executive director to vote against loans that would subsidize development of export industries in countries engaging in dumping or other unfair practices against the United States.

AID TO THE POOR. Consistent with the new directions policy, Congress also mandated that the United States pressure the Bank to increase the share of its assistance going to the poor and expand its emphasis on projects designed to meet basic human needs. Despite recognition of the efforts made under the leadership of Robert McNamara, both supporters and opponents of the Bank expressed a strong sense of frustration over the lack of assistance to the poor in the late 1970s, charges leveled mostly by liberal and conservative development groups. In the 1980s Congress forced renewed U.S. emphasis on alleviating poverty when it requested studies on the effects on poverty of structural adjustment and urged the administration to make attention to poverty alleviation a condition of its continuing support for IDA.

HUMAN RIGHTS. In 1975 an effort by Representative Tom Harkin led to a provision requiring the U.S. representative to the Inter-American and African Development banks to vote against loans to any country whose government violated its citizens' human rights. In 1976, although it lacked legislation covering World Bank lending, members of Congress nonetheless sought to persuade the administration to vote against Bank loans to Chile because of its human rights violations. But the Ford administration, wary of the effects of introducing human rights

68. For a review of the congressional debate and legislation, see House Committee on Foreign Affairs, *Congress and Foreign Policy, 1977* (1978).

69. For a review of the congressional debate and legislation, see House Committee on Foreign Affairs, *Congress and Foreign Policy, 1978* (1979), esp. pp. 88–92.

criteria into Bank lending decisions and convinced that it could not rally enough votes of other member countries to prevent the loans to Chile, voted in favor. In response, key members of Congress decided to enact new human rights legislation in the subsequent Congress, and a legislative battle ensued with the Carter administration.

The Failed Efforts of the Carter Administration

The Carter administration entered office committed to expanding U.S. development assistance, eliminating the arrearages that had built up in its payments to the multilateral development banks, and making the banks the keystone of U.S. development policy. Its support for the banks was clearly reflected by Michael Blumenthal in his confirmation hearings for Treasury secretary:

> I would hope that to the largest extent possible, whatever we do as a country with regard to economic assistance be handled through multilateral organizations where we can be one of a group of countries who work together and contribute to the solution of these problems.
>
> I think that the time for a large national program or a bilateral program for economic aid is probably past, except in certain exceptional circumstances. I expect our work in these international organizations to be very intense and very active.[70]

A report issued in the administration's first year further set the tone of its development assistance policy by calling for efforts to improve conditions in poor countries through economic and technical assistance, funds for meeting basic human needs, and increased multilateral lending.[71] This orientation was reiterated by President Carter in summit statements and in the congressional testimonies of Treasury and State Department officials. The administration immediately tried to win support for IDA funding and for the general capital increase that the Ford administration had opposed.

The Carter administration was beleaguered, however, by deteriorating economic conditions at home and abroad and, late in its term, by a consuming concern with the Iran hostage taking and Soviet expansionism in Afghanistan. As a result, despite its encouragement of the multilateral development banks and its close relations with McNamara, it was unable to build a political constituency for its development bank policies.[72] A concerted effort succeeded in convincing Congress

---

70. Testimony of W. Michael Blumenthal, *Nomination of W. Michael Blumenthal,* Hearings before the Senate Committee on Finance, 95th Cong. 1st sess. (GPO, 1977), quoted in Sanford, *U.S. Foreign Policy,* p. 68.

71. Mark F. McGuire and Vernon W. Ruttan, "Lost Directions: U.S. Foreign Assistance Policy since New Directions," *Journal of Developing Areas,* vol. 24 (January 1990), p. 137.

72. For example, McNamara was invited to participate in National Security Council meetings in the White House that dealt with gaining support for IDA 5 and the general capital increase that the Ford administration had opposed.

to appropriate in a single package funds for the last payment of IDA 4 and the first of IDA 5. This action put the United States back on the same schedule as other donors, but it also meant that the IDA appropriation crossed the $1 billion mark for the first time. To sweeten the package, the Carter administration took on the contentious issue of World Bank salaries that had first been raised in the early 1970s. While indicating that it supported both the IDA funding and the general capital increase for the Bank, the administration informed the Bank and its board that it would not take a formal position on refunding until the compensation issue was resolved. Thus in 1978 the United States made a proposal to the Joint Committee on Compensation of the Bank and the Fund that, after much debate, became the basis of an across-the-board salary cut and the guideline for future salary increases. The U.S. formula did not, however, resolve the salary issue, which remained a major irritant in relations between the United States and the Bank and one of a growing number of matters emphasized by an increasingly hostile Congress.

VIETNAM AND THE DISPUTE OVER EARMARKING. Congress and the Carter administration came into their greatest conflict in a dispute over Bank lending to Vietnam and an attempt by members of Congress to earmark U.S. contributions. The opposition was led by an alliance of liberal human rights activists and conservative opponents of foreign aid.

In its early days the Carter administration spoke of human rights as a centerpiece of its foreign policy. But like previous administrations, it sought to limit proposed legislation to a requirement that the United States use its voice to advance human rights concerns in countries that were borrowers of the Bank rather than use its vote to oppose loans to countries defined by the United States as violators of basic rights. Although human rights activists in Congress were willing to give the Carter administration the flexibility it sought, a coalition of the most active rights proponents in the House and conservative opponents of the development banks won passage of a provision that mandated the United States to vote "no" on loans, those except for meeting basic human needs, to any country with a poor human rights record.

In the midst of this debate an even more restrictive amendment was proposed by Representative Bill Young that sought to prohibit U.S. funds from being used for multilateral development bank loans to various socialist countries, including Vietnam and Uganda. Such earmarking had become a common practice with the bilateral aid program, but until the debate over supporting human rights, Congressional activism on MDB issues had mainly taken the form of cuts in appropriations and instructions to Treasury to use the U.S. voice and vote in the Bank to advance certain positions. Had the Young amendment become law, the Bank would have had to refuse the U.S. contribution because its charter prohibited it from accepting earmarked funds. To break congressional deadlock and to avoid having its total foreign aid request put into a continuing resolution with funding levels far short of what was being sought, the Carter administration struck a compromise with Young. In a letter to Congress, President Carter promised that the U.S. directors would vote against all MDB loans to the countries in question.[73] His promise did not, however, end the earmarking debate.

In 1978, over a U.S. objection, the Bank board approved a $60 million IDA loan to Vietnam for agricultural development. In response, the House of Representatives approved an amendment to its fiscal year 1979 appropriation bill that prohibited U.S. funds from being used for loans to Vietnam and several other countries. This action "served to place moderate members opposed to earmarking in the uncomfortable position of having to go on record opposing a measure to halt aid to Vietnam." Although the amendment was ultimately defeated in House-Senate conference, Young introduced a similar one in 1979 that led to heated debate on the Senate floor between conservatives in favor and moderate Democrats who supported the administration's stand against earmarking. Again the amendment went to conference, where it gave rise to "the most acrimonious foreign aid debate of the 1970s."[74]

At that point, McNamara took the unusual step of meeting with twelve members of Congress to assure them that a lending freeze had been imposed on Vietnam. But Young refused to back down until McNamara sent a letter to Congress stating that because of "a very serious question" about Vietnam's commitment to a rational development policy, there would be no new IDA loans to the country in the coming year.[75] Although the McNamara letter temporarily ended the earmarking conflict, the debate over aid to Vietnam reduced congressional support for the Bank to an all-time low and contributed significantly to shattering the tradition of bipartisanship on MDB policy.

BIPARTISANSHIP SHATTERED. Until the late 1970s, partisan divisions were not a major factor in congressional deliberations of U.S. Bank policy.[76] Democratic members of the House tended to vote in larger majorities for Bank bills than did their Republican counterparts, but the differences were not dramatic. Many members from both parties often voted in favor or against administration funding requests and a majority of Republicans often supported World Bank legislation.

73. Letter from Jimmy Carter to Clarence D. Long, chairman of the Subcommittee on Foreign Operations and Related Agencies, House Committee on Appropriations, October 6, 1977. *Congressional Record*, vol. 123 (October 18, 1977), p. 34093.

74. Schoultz, "Politics, Economics, and U.S. Participation," pp. 568–69.

75. Letter from Robert S. McNamara to Clarence Long, chairman of the Subcommittee on Foreign Operations and Related Agencies, House Committee on Appropriations, November 1, 1979. Reproduced in *Congressional Record* (December 3, 1979), p. 34415. Reference to a second letter from McNamara apologizing to Treasury Secretary G. William Miller for not going through usual channels is in Bartram S. Brown, *The United States and the Politicization of the World Bank* (London: Kegan Paul, 1992), p. 189. No subsequent loans have been made to Vietnam.

76. Discussion of the politicization of MDB legislative action draws heavily on Catherine Gwin, interview with Jonathan Sanford, Congressional Research Service, May 14, 1991.

Beginning in 1978, however, a series of highly critical minority reports were issued as part of the annual House Appropriations subcommittee report on foreign assistance. Then in 1980 Republicans made it clear that they were prepared to oppose enactment of the large development bank funding bill proposed by the outgoing Carter administration. That same year the Republican presidential platform statement strongly emphasized bilateral rather than multilateral aid. Furthermore, in 1978 and again in 1980 legislative decisions on multilateral development banks became issues of electoral politics. Some Democratic incumbents were attacked by their opponents for allegedly supporting aid to Vietnam when they voted against the MDB earmarking amendments. Because the attacks appeared about the same time and in the same words in different parts of the country, the Democrats concluded that the Republican national electoral organizations had orchestrated the effort.[77] In response, Representative David Obey demanded that the incoming Reagan administration issue a statement opposing such attacks, and the House Democratic leadership told the new administration that it would have to mobilize more Republican support for future MDB legislation if the Democrats were to join in.[78] The Democrats held to this on a major funding bill that the Reagan administration, in its early days, had to bring to Congress as a piece of unfinished business of the Carter administration.

At the end of the decade the Carter administration entered into negotiations for both a sixth replenishment of IDA and a further capital increase for the World Bank. As it had done in 1977, it sought major concessions that it hoped would help win congressional approval for the refunding agreements. In the negotiation for a capital increase, the United States pressed to lower to 7.5 percent the amount of the increase that was to be paid in. It also insisted on further reducing the U.S. capital share and, in opposition to all other member countries, refused to accept the obligation to maintain the value of its commitments to the Bank against foreign exchange fluctuations. In the IDA 6 negotiations the United States made additional

77. See, for example, the remarks of Congressman David Obey stating that he had been so attacked, in *Foreign Assistance and Related Programs Appropriations for 1982*, pt. 4, Hearings before the House Committee on Appropriations, 97th Cong. 1st sess. (GPO, 1981), pp. 186–88.

78. House Committee on Foreign Affairs, *Congress and Foreign Policy, 1981* (GPO, 1982), p. 50. A letter from President Reagan did not, however, end the Republican party's attack on Democratic supporters of the World Bank and IMF up for reelection. In 1983 Phil Gramm proposed that the U.S. executive director to the IMF be directed to oppose any use of IMF credit to "communist dictatorships." His motion passed in the House 242–185, and two weeks later the National Republican Congressional Committee began distributing press releases in the districts of 21 Democrats who voted against the Gramm amendment, charging them with voting in favor of communism. The Republican administration having sought the quota increase, House Democrats demanded and received a letter from President Reagan expressing his strong appreciation for their support of the IMF legislation and their opposition to the amendment. See Juan Williams and Hobart Rowen, "Reagan Thanks Democrats for IMF Bill Votes," *Washington Post*, October 25, 1983, p. A4.

demands. Although it endorsed an increase, it again insisted on a smaller share and an increase in the roster of donors. Allowing for inflation, its pledge was thus the same as it had been for IDA 5. In addition, it demanded that the Bank increase lending for energy production and poverty alleviation projects, introducing into the IDA negotiations policy issues that other member countries viewed as in the purview of the board. The outcome was a substantial broadening of burden sharing but also a further fraying of U.S. relations with Bank management and other member countries.

Even with these concessions, lack of enthusiasm in Congress for the negotiated funding package and inept handling by the administration of the request to Congress delayed action on the replenishments. As a result the Carter administration left office recommending, but not having attained, adoption of the largest MDB package ever put before Congress, including $12 billion for the Bank and IDA combined. It also left U.S. policy toward MDBs in shambles. Despite its pro-Bank orientation, the administration had sought to achieve a multiplicity of objectives that it could not reconcile into a coherent and compelling strategy. Instead, in an effort to patch together the necessary margin of support for continued U.S. contributions to the Bank, the administration firmly established a practice of tying policy demands to replenishment agreements. In the aftermath of its election defeat, the Carter administration reached agreement with the incoming Reagan administration on a mutually acceptable, but not strong, nominee for McNamara's successor as president of the Bank; but it had to leave an unfinished agenda to a new administration, key members of which were openly critical of multilateral assistance.[79]

Retrenchment and Reassessment under Reagan

The Reagan administration came into office in January 1981 critical of the World Bank and other multilateral institutions on both ideological and political grounds and in favor of reduced U.S. support for them. This position represented a breakpoint in U.S. policy toward the Bank in two regards: previous Bank policy goals had been largely bipartisan in character, and disputes on specific issues notwithstanding, all previous administrations had supported the Bank as an important instrument of U.S. policy.

The 1980 Republican platform statement described America as dangerously adrift in a perilous world.

79. The Carter administration also initiated monetary and fiscal actions (continued by the Reagan administration) aimed at bringing down double-digit inflation that had a far more devastating immediate effect on developing economies than aid transfers helped them. For a discussion of these effects, see John P. Lewis, "Can We Escape the Path of Mutual Injury?" in John P. Lewis and Valeriana Kallab, eds., *U.S. Foreign Policy and the Third World Agenda, 1983* (Praeger for Overseas Development Council, 1983), pp. 7–48.

Our country moves agonizingly, aimlessly, almost helplessly into one of the most dangerous and disorderly periods in history. . . . At home, our economy careens, whiplashed from one extreme to another. . . . Overseas, conditions already perilous, deteriorate. The Soviet Union for the first time is acquiring the means to obliterate or cripple our land-based missile system and blackmail us into submission. Marxist tyrannies spread more rapidly through the Third World and Latin America. Our alliances are frayed in Europe and elsewhere. Our energy supplies become even more dependent on uncertain foreign suppliers. In the ultimate humiliation, militant terrorists in Iran continue to toy with the lives of Americans.

The platform promised dramatic changes in U.S. foreign policy, including a return to bilateral assistance programs "whenever possible." Bilateral programs, it stated, "provide the best assurance that aid programs will be fully accountable to the American taxpayer, and wholly consistent with our foreign policy interests." It also criticized the Carter administration for diminishing the role of military assistance and foreign arms sales and pledged to "reform and rebuild" the military assistance programs.[80]

Immediately following the 1980 election, the new administration signaled its intentions not only to emphasize bilateral over multilateral programs and security over development assistance but also to seek a substantial reduction in foreign aid. This position was set out by the director of the Office of Management and Budget, David Stockman, in a planning memo leaked to the press on January 27, 1981, which called for a "foreign aid retrenchment." In his own account of the memo, Stockman described its rationale and objectives:

> The Gramm-Stockman budget plan had called for deep cuts in foreign economic aid on the basis of pure ideological principle. Both Gramm and I believed that the organs of international aid and so-called Third World development . . . were infested with socialist error. The international aid bureaucracy was turning Third World countries into quagmires of self-imposed inefficiency and burying them beneath mountainous external debts they would never be able to pay.[81]

Stockman also maintained that if Congress was to be persuaded to make cuts in domestic programs to achieve a balanced budget, aid increases of the size that had been proposed by the Carter administration would be out of the question. The memo proposed, therefore, to cut U.S. bilateral and multilateral aid by 45 percent, which would have amounted to a $13 billion reduction for 1982–86. The proposal would have revoked the U.S. pledge to contribute $3.2 billion to IDA 6 and reopened negotiations with other IDA donors to cut contributions in half. It would also have terminated all future U.S. contributions to IDA and the other multilateral

---

80. "1980 Republican Platform Text," *Congressional Quarterly Almanac,* vol. 36 (Washington: Congressional Quarterly, 1980), pp. 58-B, 83-B.

81. David A. Stockman, *The Triumph of Politics: How the Reagan Revolution Failed* (Harper and Row, 1986), pp. 116–19.

development bank soft loan windows, frozen contributions to all UN agencies, held bilateral development assistance to no more than 3 percent growth while increasing the relative share of military assistance, and phased out both the Peace Corps and the P.L. 480 food credit sales program.

Strong State Department pressure blocked OMB and Treasury Department inclinations to renege on the Bank and IDA commitments that had been negotiated by the Carter administration. However, in agreeing to meet the commitments, the Reagan administration moved to advance its own policy perspectives. In its request to Congress for funds for IDA 6, it proposed a schedule of appropriations—$500 million in year one, $800 million in year two, and $1.8 billion in the third year—that it knew Congress would not accept without stretching out the U.S. payment over four years.[82] The administration also made clear in its statements to Congress that its support for IDA 6 and a general capital increase should not be taken as a signal of future funding policies. It would, it announced, undertake a broad reassessment that would establish policy guidelines and a budgetary framework for U.S. participation in the multilateral development banks in the 1980s. Representative Jack Kemp, a staunch critic of foreign aid and IDA, then led the effort to line up support for the administration's 1981 World Bank request, organizing conservative Republican votes for IDA in exchange for Democratic support for bilateral military assistance.

The assessment that was subsequently undertaken was led by the Treasury Department.[83] It entailed an account of the role of the multilateral development banks in the international economic system, a review of criticisms of the banks over the years, and an evaluation of the ability of the United States to achieve its objectives through the banks. It also outlined a plan to improve MDB policy effectiveness and provided specific U.S. funding and policy recommendations. Although it discussed nineteen criticisms leveled against the banks, ranging from excessive salaries to support for statist development approaches to emphasis on loan quantity instead of quality, its tone was positive. To the surprise of many, the assessment approved the overall performance of the MDBs and noted the benefits to the United States of participation in them.

The main policy conclusions were not, however, wholly consistent with the body of the report. There were three core recommendations. First, U.S. support for the MDBs should be designed to foster greater adherence to open markets and greater emphasis on the private sector as the main vehicle for growth. Second, the United States should work to ensure that loan allocations were made conditional on policy reforms in recipient countries. Finally, the United States should reduce its expenditures on the banks. This third recommendation, the report suggested, should be

82. Although other donors objected to this unilateral move, they adhered to the rds over and above their regular three-year schedule and later agreed to provide additional funds to enable IDA to continue its regular operations during the fourth year.

83. Department of the Treasury, *United States Participation in the Multilateral Development Banks in the 1980s* (1982).

accomplished in two ways. The United States should develop a plan to reduce and eventually phase out new paid-in capital for the hard loan windows of all MDBs. And it should reduce, in real terms, its future participation in all MDB soft loan windows, especially IDA. In other words, countries should be encouraged not only to adopt more market-based policies but also to rely more on private sector financing than on World Bank and other public sector financing.

The international debt crisis that burst onto the international stage not long after the Treasury assessment was completed required the Reagan administration to revise its views on graduating countries out of the ranks of World Bank borrowers. But it did not dampen the administration's criticism of the MDBs nor its own pressure for more focus on the private sector. In September 1983 President Reagan addressed the annual meeting of the World Bank and reiterated the policy directives contained in the Treasury report.

> The societies that achieved the most spectacular, broad-based economic progress in the shortest period of time have not been the biggest in size, nor the richest in resources and certainly not the most rigidly controlled. What has united them all was their belief in the magic of the marketplace. Millions of individuals making their own decisions in the marketplace will always allocate resources better than any centralized government planning process.[84]

He also expressed the willingness of the United States to support the replenishment and capital increase agreements negotiated by the previous administration. But he made it clear that U.S. policy toward multilateral development banks was now set on a new course, one based on sharp criticism of the operations of the banks and an ideological opposition to centralized direction of development.

In effect, the Reagan administration did what the Carter administration failed to do: it identified strategic program objectives for U.S. participation in the Bank. One outcome was that the United States dropped its previous opposition to the Bank management's proposal for a new kind of policy-based, structural adjustment lending. The administration came to view this new lending as an important way to advance market-oriented reforms. However, because the administration's objectives were stated in highly ideological terms and aimed at reducing U.S. funding for the Bank, the United States was often at odds with the Bank and other members of the board during the 1980s design and implementation of lending policy.

During the IDA 7 replenishment talks in 1983, the United States insisted on holding its pledge to an amount less than it contributed to IDA 6. This position, advanced by the Treasury Department, was supported by President Reagan against the recommendations of the Department of State and the National Security Council. Although other countries expressed willingness to discuss a $12 billion to $16 billion replenishment if the United States carried an appropriate share, the Reagan ad-

---

84. Opening remarks by President Ronald Reagan, *Summary Proceedings of 1983 Annual Meetings of the Boards of Governors* (Washington: IBRD, 1983), p. 2.

ministration indicated that the maximum it would agree to was a $750 million annual payment and a 25 percent share. The result was a total replenishment of only $9 billion, 25 percent lower than the IDA 6 level. One of the Bank's reasons for recommending a large replenishment was to accommodate the entry of its new client, China. A key element of the administration's stance, however, was that India and China should rely more on commercial borrowing.

In 1985 the administration declined to participate in the new IDA Special Facility for Africa. The Bank and other donors had designed the Facility as a temporary mechanism to channel additional resources to African governments that agreed to implement specific policy reforms after the reduction in U.S. funding had resulted in holding down the size of the IDA 7 replenishment. Also in 1985 President Reagan stated in a budget message to Congress that although the administration intended to honor existing commitments to IDA and other MDB concessional windows, in light of severe fiscal pressures it was "not budgeting at this time for the future replenishments of these particular institutions."[85] But Congress, which after a brief interlude had returned to a Democratic majority in both chambers, did not concur. It opposed putting a five-year ceiling on IDA refunding. Congress also authorized $225 million for the IDA-related Special Facility for Sub-Saharan Africa, which the administration had opposed. At the time of the IDA 7 negotiations, the administration had explained that Congress would not exceed the funding ceiling. However, congressional staff indicated in interviews with me that legislative support for the Special Africa Facility was mobilized in explicit contradiction to that claim. And even though the administration never requested appropriation of the special Africa funds, Congress stipulated that some $140 million be allocated in subsequent legislation. Then before negotiations for the next IDA replenishment began, James Baker replaced Donald Regan as Treasury secretary, and the administration rediscovered the importance of the World Bank as an instrument in the deepening debt of less developed countries.

THE DEBT CRISIS AND RENEWED INTEREST IN THE BANK. In August 1982 Mexico suspended payment on its international debt. For more than five years analyses had been warning of impending trouble, but they were the minority view and neither the U.S. government nor the World Bank had forecast the extent of the crisis that ensued throughout the developing world.[86] The initial reactions of U.S.

85. Quoted in Hobart Rowen, "U.S. May End Support of IDA Programs," *Washington Post,* February 5, 1985, p. C1.

86. For early indications of impending problems, see *Multinational Corporations and Foreign Policy,* pt. 15, Hearings before the Subcommittee on Multinational Corporations of the Senate Committee on Foreign Relations, 94th Cong. 1st sess. (GPO, July–October 1975); and *The Wittaveen Facility and the OPEC Financial Surpluses,* Hearings before the Senate Subcommittee on Foreign Economic Policy, 95th Cong. 1st sess. (GPO, September–October 1977). For a review of the unfolding of the international debt crisis see Karin Lissakers, *Banks, Borrowers, and the Establishment* (Basic Books, 1991).

officials to the financial crisis in Mexico has been described as a "dialogue of the deaf."[87] After months of deliberation a bridging loan was arranged, followed by longer-term rescheduling negotiations in conjunction with an IMF stabilization loan. With active U.S. support, the IMF pressed commercial banks to keep lending to Mexico and, subsequently, to others. The IMF and the World Bank also increased their own lending by limited amounts.

In 1982 the United States considered the crisis a problem of short-term liquidity that would recede when the prolonged worldwide recession ended. In 1983, as debtor after debtor experienced continuing difficulties, the Reagan administration reluctantly supported a quota increase for the IMF to enable it to play a catalytic role in mobilizing new lending by commercial banks. The objective of the increase was to avoid the collapse of the international banking system and, to that end, to buy time to allow for renewed growth in the debtor countries. But, consistent with its insistence on the short-term nature of the problem confronting the less developed countries, the administration continued until 1987–88 to oppose a general capital increase for the World Bank.

With an easing of the global recession in late 1983 and 1984, the official U.S. view was that recovery from the "liquidity" problem would follow. The administration also maintained that existing resources were adequate and opposed raising a tightly set ceiling on World Bank policy-based lending. Yet, even after rescheduling, most severely indebted developing countries continued to experience difficulties in servicing their debts, and few showed any resumption of growth. By early 1985 most analysts had concluded that the countries required serious policy reforms and access to more financial resources or debt relief than they were getting.

Faced with the deepening financial crisis in the developing countries and mounting criticism of its policy, the United States revised its policy in the fall of 1985. Although it still considered the debt crisis a short-term liquidity problem, the administration conceded that a more concerted effort was required. In a speech at the World Bank–IMF annual meeting Treasury Secretary James Baker called for new money and a greater role for the Bank. By all accounts the Baker initiative was designed hastily and with little consultation with international financial institutions, other creditor governments, or debtor countries. Nonetheless, the plan included a lead role for the World Bank. Its main elements were a $9 billion increase over planned amounts in World Bank and Inter-American Development Bank lending to fifteen heavily indebted countries, a $20 billion net increase in lending by private banks over three years, and further policy reforms by debtor countries. Combined with previously planned financing, the proposed increase was expected to amount to $20 billion in net new lending by the MDBs after repayments of loans coming due. According to Baker, these steps would help debtor countries adjust and grow their way out of debt.

87. Joseph Kraft, *The Mexican Rescue* (New York: Group of Thirty, 1984), p. 11.

At least three considerations converged in the redesign of the U.S. debt strategy. First, as commercial banks virtually halted new lending, severe recessions in the debtor countries caused a noticeable decrease in U.S. exports. Second, because the limited size and scope of U.S. bilateral aid precluded substantial funding of the heavily indebted countries and because there were strong pressures from Congress not to bail out the banks, the international financial institutions had to play the lead role in helping to renew growth. Finally, the administration had become convinced that the World Bank's new form of structural adjustment lending could be used as a way to respond to the debt crisis and to advance market liberalizing and private sector policy reforms at the same time. Thus for the next four years the United States encouraged multilateral banks to support policy reforms and pushed them to take the lead in providing new monies themselves and in coordinating the activities of commercial banks. Nonetheless, the Baker plan foundered, as many predicted it would, because of inadequate financing. The private banks failed to provide the full amount of their targeted lending and official capital flows decreased because of negative net IMF flows and decreases in bilateral (mainly export credit agency) flows that were not offset by increased MDB lending.[88]

In mid-December 1988, President-elect George Bush called for a reassessment of the prevailing U.S. international debt strategy. And in March 1989, at the start of the Bush administration, Treasury Secretary Nicholas Brady proposed a successor debt plan that introduced the element of voluntary debt reduction. In offering this proposal the administration adopted what had by then become the prevailing view. The case for debt reduction had been building in academic and other analytic circles for several years.[89] It was being promoted by members of Congress who argued that the United States and other developed countries should do more to help relieve the debt burden of developing countries. The Baker plan, some members argued, only provided a way for the World Bank to bail out the commercial banks; it did not do enough to help countries reduce their debt and restore investment and growth.[90] Also, by the time of Brady's speech, debt reduction was being publicly espoused by some in the banking community and by the managing director of the IMF.[91] The major banks had by that time built reserves and taken

88. William R. Cline, "The Baker Plan and Brady Reformulation: An Evaluation," in Richard O'Brien and Ingred Iversen, eds., *Finance and International Economics*, vol. 3 (Oxford University Press for American Express Bank Review, 1989).

89. See, for example, Rudiger Dornbusch, ed., *Alternative Solutions to Developing-Country Debt Problems* (Washington: American Enterprise Institute, 1989).

90. Debate on debt-related issues held up approval on the U.S. contribution to the Bank's general capital increase for over a year in 1988–89. See Richard Lawrence, "World Bank Contribution Hinges on Congressional Compromise," *Journal of Commerce*, August 12, 1988, pp. 1A, 10A; and Hobart Rowen, "David Obey's World Bank Crusade," *Washington Post*, November 12, 1989, pp. H1, H4.

91. See, for example, Third World Debt Panel of the Economic Policy Council of the United Nations Association of the United States of America, "Third World Debt: A Re-examination of Long-Term Management" (New York, September 7, 1988).

other steps that had left them in strengthened positions and removed securing the international banking system as a primary concern.

The Brady proposal, like the Baker plan, insisted on policy reform in the indebted countries as a condition of external support, but it also called for two innovations. First, instead of focusing on new lending, it encouraged multilateral institutions to use their funds to support voluntary write-offs of commercial bank debt. The target was 20 percent, or $70 billion, of the $350 billion debt outstanding. The Brady initiative also proposed that the IMF no longer withhold its own lending to countries until commercial banks agreed to reschedule. As Anne Krueger, former research director of the Bank, has observed, "the Brady Plan gave official acceptance—so long denied—to the view that the existence of debt itself might be a barrier to the resumption of growth in heavily indebted countries. In that way it officially sanctioned debt reduction, whereas earlier U.S. policy had vigorously rejected that alternative."[92]

The idea that World Bank resources might be used to support debt reduction measures was discussed with senior Bank management before being announced. In those discussions the Bank agreed to make a statement that welcomed the new ideas on debt strategy and agreed that a broader menu of options, including measures to reduce the stock of debt and service payments, was important support for countries that performed well. The Bank also indicated preliminary support, pending review of the legal feasibility and costs, for a U.S. idea to use Bank funds to help countries cover interest payments. As stated in a letter from a senior Bank official to the U.S. Treasury, "assuming there are no legal impediments, the formulation of us making a loan, beyond our normal country program limits, seems a very attractive way to cover interest payments. . . . *If* we can guarantee interest, we should also be able to lend for it and the loan approach would avoid a lot of balance-sheet and perceptual problems [with which] we have been concerned."[93] But this time the U.S. initiative met with strong opposition among some members of the Bank, particularly the United Kingdom and Germany, who argued that financing debt reduction was not an appropriate use of World Bank resources. Only after intense debate, which limited the measures that the Bank could take, did the executive board approve a program for implementing the Bank's part of the Brady initiative.

In the implementation of both the Baker and the Brady plans, the U.S. Treasury and the Federal Reserve Board (whose concern was the stability of the banking system) were active participants in IMF, World Bank, and commercial bank negotiations with debtor countries. They also urged commercial banks to continue lending in the first half of the 1980s and to accept some debt reduction in the second half. Finally, according to former chairman of the Federal Reserve Paul

92. Anne O. Krueger, *Economic Policies at Cross-Purposes* (Brookings, 1993), p. 97.
93. Letter from Ernest Stern, World Bank senior vice president for finance, to Charles Dallara, assistant secretary of the Treasury for Policy Development, March 7, 1989.

Volcker, they "directed" the lending of the Bank.[94] Within the Bank this direction at times raised concerns about the viability of the arrangements being put together for individual countries and the possible effect on the Bank's own portfolio. Two Bank documents, worth quoting at length, disagree with the United States over the adequacy of financing packages and the role of the Bank in securing them. The first is a note prepared for President Barber Conable before a luncheon with Treasury Undersecretary David Mulford.

> I want to follow up on the comment made to you by David Mulford to the effect that the difference between the Bank's approach to the Brady Initiative and that of the Fund is a matter of "activism" on the part of the Operations Complex. Naturally, I resent the allegation that the Bank is behaving irresponsibly. But more importantly, this comment indicates a lack of understanding on the part of the U.S. Treasury as to the real reasons why the two institutions have taken somewhat different approaches to a common concern.
>
> In the case of the Fund, the Brady Initiative is being implemented by increasing access to Fund resources, with a specific though legally indirect link to debt and debt service reduction. While this may be a somewhat artificial activity for the Fund, the resources being provided are like all other IMF resources, namely additions to the country's reserves, which the country then uses to effect debt reduction. In the case of the Bank, we are making specific loans that are explicitly for the purpose of debt and debt service reduction. Since this is not an activity that normally falls under the specific investment projects clause of the Articles, we have to justify such lending under the exceptional circumstances provisions, hence we have to satisfy ourselves about the materiality of benefits in terms of growth and increased investment.
>
> This has two important implications. First, the Bank more than the Fund has to be concerned with the adequacy of the financing package over the medium term. If the financing is not adequate, growth may not take place and the material benefits for investment will not be realized. The IMF need not be as concerned with medium term effects; if debt reduction is part of a one-year program, the only thing that would prevent the Fund from supporting it (apart from conditionality) is the Fund's own policy objective of tying debt reduction support to the EFF—something that the Board of the Fund can deal with on a case by case basis.
>
> Second, if the financing package negotiated by the country is inadequate, the Fund can insist on a change in the program, including further adjustment on the part of the country. If financing is too tight to permit growth, that alone would not prevent the IMF from supporting the program of debt reduction. But it could prevent the Bank from doing so, again because of the materiality criteria.
>
> In other words, it is significantly more difficult for the Bank to make loans for debt and debt service reduction than it is for the Fund to increase access for this purpose. This is not a matter of management style. It is anchored in the legal differences in the two institutions. For this reason also our approach to the review of progress under the Brady Initiative was different from that of the Fund. In dealing with financing assurances, the Fund was able to throw the problem back onto the country. In our case, we need to stress

94. Catherine Gwin, interview with Paul Volcker, May 27, 1992.

up-front the importance of adequate financing. This has a tendency to come across as more interventionist than the Fund, but the alternative is either to let ourselves be 'rolled' on lending standards or block transactions that are already negotiated on grounds that they do not meet the materiality test. We do not have the alternative of simply lending for debt reduction operations as though they were isolated investment projects, detached from the overall medium term adjustment program and financing plan.

. . . This is a matter both of the Articles and of credit risk management, not 'activism.' It is ironic that the Treasury perceives the Fund to be more supportive of the Brady Initiative than is the Bank. A close look would show that the Fund management is actually more reserved about the program and—if asked—probably grateful that they do not need to . . . expend as much management energy defending their support for the Initiative on an ongoing basis.[95]

The second document, which expresses many of the same points of disagreement, is an internal Bank memorandum reporting on a meeting with the U.S. Treasury to discuss papers reviewing the Brady debt strategy. After noting that the "tone of the meeting was informal, friendly and constructive," the memorandum went on to outline points in disagreement between the United States and the Bank on the handling of both official and commercial debt.

The discussion covered a number of topics but two points seemed to be of particular concern: first, Treasury staff are upset at the lack of prior consultation on "proposals" for official debt; second, they have serious reservations about a more pro-active role for the Bank and the Fund in commercial bank debt negotiations. . . . On commercial bank negotiations, Treasury staff criticized the papers as being unbalanced and failing to give adequate recognition to what had been achieved. They seemed most concerned about the suggestion that the Fund and the Bank would get more directly involved in the negotiations, perhaps imposing restraints on the terms of transactions, seeking to shape the modalities of debt and debt service reduction and/or intervening to get the financing gap closed. [A senior official of the department] reiterated the Treasury's view that the "strengthened debt strategy" involves a change in the gap process, and a need on the part of the official institutions to live with more uncertainty and financing risk. He argued that the previous approach produced a false sense of comfort about financing packages and that the new approach could not be launched without the official institutions adopting a different approach on financing assurances.

[The Bank and Fund representatives] stressed that the key issue is how to strike the right balance between the old critical mass approach and the completely hands-off acceptance of whatever financing could be raised on a voluntary basis. In our view, the pendulum has swung too far away from a disciplined and preagreed financing plan based on fair burden sharing of all parties. Instead, the commercial banks take the amount of Bank and Fund financing as a given and expect the two institutions to support whatever package they have negotiated with the countries concerned. We do not regard a hands-off approach as acceptable but acknowledge that the degree of intervention required is a matter of judgment.[96]

95. World Bank internal memorandum, May 2, 1990.
96. World Bank internal memorandum, March 29, 1990 (confidential).

In sum, in response to the debt crisis the United States turned—belatedly and reluctantly—to the international financial institutions. Consistent with the tilt toward the Fund and Bank, the United States supported an IMF quota increase in 1983, a $12 billion replenishment for IDA in 1987, and a doubling of Bank capital in 1988. It did not support the debt strategy with other policy initiatives in such areas as aid and trade.[97] But it displayed an unprecedented assertiveness within the Bank in the implementation of the debt strategy and in regard to other policy matters that arose in the second half of the 1980s and the early 1990s.

A New Assertiveness

In the 1987 IDA 8 negotiations, which were completed relatively quickly, the United States agreed to a replenishment that brought IDA lending back to its 1981–83 level in nominal terms and that increased the U.S. annual payment in current dollars to $958 million while holding its share to 25 percent. At the same time, the United States achieved agreement on four policy changes. Two of them— a larger proportion of the total IDA lending dedicated to policy-based lending and a larger IDA share for Sub-Saharan Africa—met with little disagreement from other donors. More controversial were U.S. demands for reducing the maturity of IDA credits (which the Treasury claimed it sought to help win passage of the IDA bill once it went to Congress) and a limit of 30 percent of annual IDA funding that would be available to India and China combined.

In the fall of 1987 in a reversal of its previous opposition, the Reagan administration agreed to a general capital increase of $74.8 billion, but it delayed making a request to Congress until after IDA 8 was approved. As part of the negotiations the United States agreed to release a portion of its Bank shares to other countries, including Japan, but only after obtaining agreement on a change in the Articles of Agreement of the Bank that protected the U.S. veto power.[98] In presenting its request for the capital increase to Congress, the administration emphasized three points: that the Bank, in having taken on a broader responsibility in the debt crisis, had increased its disbursements by more than 40 percent since 1985 and needed additional capital; that the Bank was acting as an important catalyst for economic

97. Krueger, *Economic Policies at Cross-Purposes,* chap. 5.

98. The veto applies to matters requiring more than a simple majority, notably decisions regarding the Articles, not specific loans. Japan's willingness to provide more of the IDA 8 replenishment had been made contingent on substantial expansion of its Bank share, which would make its share significantly greater than that of Germany and signal that it stood second only to the United States. A major improvement in Japan's position could only occur, however, if the United States agreed to let its own share slip below 20 percent (which was the percentage that ensured its veto). During the IDA 8 negotiations the United States indicated its intention to seek a change in the Articles to enable it to retain its veto with only 15 percent of total share and thereby accommodate an increase for Japan without sacrificing its own position.

reforms; and that under its new president, Barber Conable, it had completed a swift and significant reorganization intended to be responsive to matters of high administrative costs that had been raised by the United States for many years. After a year of wrangling with a coalition of liberal congressmen, who objected to a Bank bailout of commercial banks, and conservative congressmen, who continued to condemn the Bank for shoring up socialist regimes, the administration won solid support for the capital increase. The outcome was in part a vote of confidence for Conable, a former member of Congress, and in greater part the result of a renewed executive branch effort to gain support for the Bank.

Three years later in the IDA 9 replenishment talks, the United States again agreed to maintain lending levels in real terms, but it insisted on a ceiling for its own contribution, which led to a further decrease in its share to 21.6 percent. It again demanded the adoption of a number of its policy positions, including continued emphasis on Africa, efforts to improve IDA-IMF collaboration, and greater attention to poverty alleviation as a criterion for IDA allocations, as well as new measures to protect the environment. In contrast to the general policy demands the United States had made in previous replenishment talks, its environmental demands included specific policy and operational reforms: environmental impact assessments of proposed projects, environmental action plans for borrower countries, and disclosure of assessments and plans to local nongovernmental organizations and other concerned groups in advance of loan approvals by the Bank board.[99]

The demands were devised, developed, and successfully advanced in a skillful campaign by nongovernmental organizations. They worked through Congress to force the administration to take up environmental protection and allied themselves with like-minded groups in other countries to build an international consensus on the greening of the World Bank. In early 1983, environmentalists in the United States had begun actively to investigate the environmental impact of Bank project lending and persuaded the House Subcommittee on International Development Institutions and Finance to hold the first oversight hearings on the MDBs and the environment. As one of the leading environmental activists commented in recounting the development of the green campaign against the Bank, witnesses at the hearing described "case after case of environmental and social disasters financed by the Bank, and its sister institutions: huge dams that displaced indigenous peoples, botched irrigation schemes that contributed to the spread of waterborne diseases such as malaria and schistosomiasis . . . cattle ranching schemes that destroyed tropical forests, and massive resettlement projects." Representatives of indigenous peoples' human rights organizations testified on the harm being done to tribal peoples by such projects as the Polonoroeste loan in the Amazon of Brazil.

99. The discussion of environmental policy issues from early 1983 through mid-1987 draws heavily on Bruce Rich, "Greens Lay Siege to the Crystal Palace," a chapter in a forthcoming book on the World Bank and the environmental movement.

Several months later the U.S. Treasury forwarded the rebuttals of the MDBs to the House Subcommittee on International Development Institutions and Finance —more than 1,000 pages—that the environmental groups called "evasive and misleading."[100] Following a review of the MDBs' responses, the subcommittee, in consultation with nongovernmental organizations, issued recommendations for reform of the World Bank's environmental protection procedures, many of which Congress passed into law (P.L. 99-190) in late 1985. The law called on the Treasury Department "to monitor environmental aspects of Bank activities, to facilitate constructive U.S. involvement in assuring that sound environmental policies are implemented by multilateral agencies supported by the U.S., and to expedite the flow of information between the Banks and the U.S. Congress, other relevant federal agencies and the public regarding environmental considerations."[101] But the environmental campaign of the nongovernmental organizations did not end there.

In 1984, U.S. environmental activists working together with groups in Brazil developed an extensive research dossier on the Bank's by-then controversial Polonoroeste project, which became the basis of further congressional hearings. A letter was signed by leading individuals and groups that urged the Bank to cease disbursements for Polonoroeste and take steps to improve the ecological design and review of its projects. Dossier and letter were then sent by a representative of Congress to the Bank. A month later the Bank sent a brief response, indicating that Polonoroeste was a carefully planned regional development program and that the Bank would continue to monitor the situation closely and consider concerns raised as the project continued. Senator Robert Kasten of Wisconsin, to whom the environmentalists next turned, sent a letter to Bank President A. W. Clausen, describing the response as a "brush off" and an "insult," and another letter to Secretary of the Treasury Donald Regan, calling it "outrageous." In March 1985, Clausen aides told Kasten that the environmentalists would get a credible response in a meeting with Clausen and senior management of the Bank. In that meeting, held on May 22, 1985, the Bank acknowledged what had been known for two months—that it had decided to halt funding for Polonoroeste to prevent environmental damage. The Polonoroeste campaign became, in a real sense, the beginning of effective action by like-minded groups around the world. They used modern communications technology to inform one another of crises and to mount in a matter of hours international letter-writing and lobbying campaigns to protest other objectionable projects.

In June 1986 the United States cast its first vote against a Bank loan out of concern for the environment. By late 1986 several other countries, including Germany, Sweden, the Netherlands, and Australia, were instructing their executive

100. Ibid., msp. 98.
101. *Department of Defense Appropriations Act, 1986* (H.J. Res. 465).

directors to demand environmental reforms that echoed those urged by the United States. And in May 1987 Bank President Barber Conable announced a series of organizational and operational reforms. To the environmental action groups, the Conable reforms were a marked improvement over previous practices, but they did not go far enough in ensuring that the Bank would regularly take effects on the environment into account in its project and program lending. Therefore, as a result of continued pressure from nongovernmental organizations, U.S. legislation in 1989 (P.L. 101-240) further enjoined U.S. executive directors to the Bank and the other MDBs to propose procedures "for systematic environmental assessment of development projects for which the respective Bank provides financial assistance, taking into consideration the guidelines and principles for Environmental Impact Assessment promulgated by the United Nations Environment Program."[102] The act further required the multilateral banks to make environmental assessments or comprehensive summaries of the assessments available to affected groups and local nongovernmental organizations.

While nongovernmental organizations working through Congress mobilized U.S. pressure for change in Bank environmental policies and practices, it was the U.S. Treasury that took the initiative and promoted examination of the other major U.S. policy issue involving the World Bank: the role of the Bank in the development of the private sector. In marked contrast to the NGO environmental campaign, the promotion of this issue by the Treasury Department involved far less effort to seek international consensus on changes to be sought in Bank policies and less analysis of the challenges and implications for the Bank. The 1981 Treasury assessment of the multilateral development banks had clearly signaled the Reagan administration's intention to move MDB lending policy away from support for state-led growth and toward direct support for development by private enterprise. This effort continued under the Bush administration. But frustrated by its ability to instigate marked change in Bank support for private sector development, the administration brought the issue to a head in the 1990–91 negotiations for an International Finance Corporation capital increase.

Initially, the United States, along with Japan, opposed an IFC capital increase. But when the Japanese government dropped its opposition, the United States, as a condition for its support of the increase, sought to extract concessions on policies it had been promoting for several years. In particular, it sought to tie reforms in the Bank to the IFC negotiations. What it proposed were internal reforms intended to strengthen the Bank's capacity to aid private sector development, a study to explore changes in the Articles of Agreement to remove the prohibition against direct lending to private enterprises (a provision the United States had demanded when the Articles were written), and agreement on a target of 50 percent of total Bank lending in support of the private sector by 1995.

102. *International Development and Finance Act of 1989* (H.R. 2494).

Although other donor countries agreed with the United States that help in developing a country's private sector had become a central challenge for the Bank in light of marked change in development strategies throughout the developing world and the collapse of communism throughout the crumbling Soviet empire, they resented the manner and rejected the content of the U.S. demands. They opposed the demand for a change in the charter and the related lending target. As a fallback position, the United States pressed to get a commitment for a study of Charter reform and for organizational changes within the Bank, but it continued to withhold support for the IFC capital increase while these points were being debated.

In the meantime, in late May 1991 the Foreign Operations Subcommittee of the House Appropriations Committee recommended in a funding bill the $40.3 million U.S. share of the negotiated capital increase, in spite of the fact that the Treasury had not asked for the IFC funds. The subcommittee also chastised the Treasury Department for failure to consult with Congress on its agenda for change in the Bank. The subcommittee report registered regret that the IFC negotiations were being used as a lever to change the Bank and disagreed with the administration's proposals for change. In addition, the subcommittee made its approval of $100 million for the Enterprise for the Americas Initiative (a high priority of the Bush administration) conditional on U.S. support for the IFC.

Several weeks later, at a board meeting scheduled to address the IFC capital increase, the U.S. executive director announced that the United States was prepared to support the increase and called for discussion of papers prepared by the U.S. Treasury on changes proposed in the IFC and the Bank. The board expressed strong opposition to many of the points. The U.S. executive director, on instructions from Treasury official David Mulford, said that under the circumstances the United States would withdraw its support. The meeting was then adjourned on a technicality, the issue was left unresolved, and a week later the United States reversed its position again and agreed to the IFC capital increase, leaving a bitter taste in the mouths of all involved. Overall, the U.S. lack of analytic rigor and highhanded manner hindered its effectiveness in advancing what was, in fact, a timely and important issue for the Bank. Many serious questions about how the World Bank responds to the fundamental changes in the development strategies being pursued by both its long-standing and its new borrowers were glossed over by the U.S. démarche and remain to be answered.

Ironically, the Reagan and Bush administrations, which had wanted to cut back on U.S. participation in the World Bank and other international financial institutions, wound up relying heavily on those institutions to handle problems that the United States could not (for budgetary and other reasons) manage bilaterally. They also pressured the Bank to expand its role in debt relief, macroeconomic policy reforms, environmental protection, private sector development, and the transformation of eastern Europe and the former Soviet Union. Similar U.S. pressure has had great influence on the evolution of Bank activities during its fifty-year history. However, the United States can now no longer exercise the kind of unilateral influence over Bank policies and practices that it once did. There has been a waning of U.S. power in the Bank, due only in part to its steadily declining share of both Bank and IDA funding, and a corresponding change in the way it has sought to exercise its influence in recent years.

Influence on the Bank

Over the years there have been two conflicting opinions of U.S. influence on the Bank. One, held by many members of Congress, argues that the United States has too little influence on what the Bank does. The Bank, it continues, is run by highly paid, aloof bureaucrats, unresponsive to U.S. concerns and accountable only to themselves. The opposite opinion, held by considerable numbers of the Bank staff, nongovernmental groups in borrower countries, and other member countries, maintains that the Bank is run by and under the thumb of the United States. Analysis of the record supports neither position. U.S. influence on the Bank has been important but not absolute.

From the outset the United States considered the Bank an instrument of U.S. foreign policy and used its influence to try to ensure that Bank practices promoted development in ways that complemented U.S. long-term goals and short-term political and economic interests. Although the United States is not the only donor country to use its influence to pursue national interests, the wide scope, frequency, and intensity of its pressure distinguishes it from other donor countries. Its position on specific issues has not always prevailed, but where it has defined an issue as a matter of priority, it has usually had its way. Still, various factors limit the exercise of U.S. influence: the importance to financial markets of nonpoliticized lending decisions; the centrality of burden sharing as a U.S. policy goal; the foreign policy advantage for a donor country to be insulated from tough loan decisions, a protection lost if it is seen as dominating decisions; the clear understanding of all World Bank presidents that the role of the institution depends on its being independent and being seen as independent; and more prevalent opposing views of other donor countries.

The Sources and Strength of U.S. Influence

The basis of U.S. influence derives, on the most fundamental level, from the origins of the Bank and the fact that its Charter and guiding principles have a distinctly American cast. Over the years the United States has used its influence to ensure that those principles are not disregarded.

Other sources of U.S. influence include its position as the largest shareholder in the Bank, the importance of its financial market as a source of capital for the Bank

Table 6-3. *U.S. Contributions and Voting Shares, World Bank and International Development Association, Selected Years, 1946–90*[a]
Millions of U.S. dollars unless otherwise specified

Contributions and shares	1946	1950	1960	1970	1980	1990
World Bank						
Subscription	3,175.0	3,175.0	6,350.0	6,350.0	9,347.9	19,606.0
Paid in	158.8	635.0	635.0	635.0	934.8	1,627.6
Percent of total	41.4	38.0	32.9	27.4	23.4	15.7
Voting share (percent)	. . .	34.1	30.3	24.5	21.1	15.1
IDA[b]						
Contribution[c]	. . .	. . .	320.3[d]	1,112.3[e]	6,405.6[f]	14,764.9[g]
Percent of total	. . .	. . .	35.4	31.6	32.9	27.0
Voting share (percent)	. . .	. . .	31.3	25.3	21.5	17.2

Source: World Bank annual reports.

a. For World Bank, expressed in U.S. dollars as of July 1, 1994; for IDA, expressed in U.S. dollars as of January 1, 1960.

b. IDA was established in 1960.

c. Cumulative subscriptions and supplementary resources.

d. Figures are as of June 30, 1961, the date of publication of its first annual report.

e. Expressed in U.S. dollars as of January 1, 1960. Cumulative contribution through IDA 2.

f. Cumulative contribution through IDA 5.

g. Cumulative contribution through IDA 8.

(and in the early days the only source), its hold on the position of Bank president and other senior management positions, and the close attention the United States has paid to Bank activities, reinforced by the Bank's location in Washington, D.C. Although its relative importance in many of these dimensions has declined, the United States remains the dominant member of the Bank, in large part because no other country or group of countries has chosen to challenge it.

THE U.S. POSITION AS LEAD SHAREHOLDER. The United States has always had dominant influence on the Executive Board and management of the Bank by virtue of being the largest shareholder and largest contributor to IDA. This is a position it maintains, although the relative size of its Bank shareholding, its share of IDA replenishments, and its corresponding share of votes have decreased (table 6-3). As a result, Bank management may listen to the views of other donor countries more than it once did, but as in any corporation, it cannot afford to run afoul of its largest shareholder.

The United States is also the dominant member on the Bank's board—but only in part because it is lead shareholder. Formally, most Bank decisions, including those affecting lending levels and loan allocations, require a simple majority vote of the board. This means that the United States, as a major but not majority shareholder, can be outvoted and must marshal support for its views to be decisive. Decisions are, however, often worked out between the United States and Bank management before they ever get to the board, or among members of the board before they get to a vote. And most board decisions are taken by consensus. It is the weight of its voice, therefore, more than the exercise of its vote that gives the United States effective power on the board. And the weight of its voice has been determined by its influence over other major donor countries, especially Germany and Japan.

THE IMPORTANCE OF THE U.S. CAPITAL MARKET. As table 6-1 shows, U.S. capital no longer plays so dominant a role in total borrowing as it did in the Bank's early years. With the globalization of capital markets and the diversification of the Bank's portfolio, the importance of the U.S. market and U.S. dollar have fluctuated relative to those of other countries. Nonetheless, the United States still accounted for 20 percent of Bank medium- and long-term borrowing by country (before swaps) between 1980 and 1990.

The requirement that the Bank obtain the permission of any country to borrow in its currency has meant that the United States could influence its policies and practices by threatening to deny it access to the U.S. market. That possibility was one of the reasons why Robert McNamara moved quickly after becoming Bank president to diversify the Bank's portfolio and dilute its dollar dependence. The United States has, however, not often denied the Bank access to its market.[103] Even less frequently has it used this authority to put pressure on the Bank. In one instance in the mid-1970s, the United States postponed granting permission to borrow as a means of signaling its displeasure over the Bank's rate of growth. And in 1984 a Treasury official told the Bank's vice president, Ernest Stern, that since it had consistently ignored U.S. concerns about lending to the energy sector, the United States was "reviewing whether the Bank should continue to have access to the U.S. capital markets."[104] In the end, accommodation on energy sector lending was reached and the seriousness of the threat never tested.

For the most part, the imperatives of U.S. monetary policy, not concerns about Bank activities, have been behind the occasional denials or postponements. In the early 1980s, for example, the Reagan administration denied permission to borrow because it said that it wanted to avoid pressure on interest rates. Apparently, it also meant this action to send other members of the Group of Seven advanced industrialized nations a message. The other G-7 countries were concerned that the United States was not managing its fiscal and monetary affairs effectively. The United States told the Bank to raise the funds it sought elsewhere and maintained that this would show the other G-7 countries just how committed it was to prudent economic policy. At the same time, however, the Reagan administration took the lead in getting member countries to agree to liberalize consent procedures for Bank borrowing. The authority to grant or deny access to its market has been, in other words, more an implied than an applied source of power.

103. Catherine Gwin, interview with Eugene Rotberg, Washington, D.C., August 14, 1991.
104. Bank memorandum, April 6, 1984.

Far more significant a source of influence is that were the United States to express serious disinterest in the Bank or serious concern over its financial state of affairs, the effect on the financial markets would likely be immediate.[105] It is this perhaps more than anything else that makes the Bank take particular note of U.S. views. This influence has gradually been tempered by the Bank's leverage over the United States as a result of the large stake that U.S. bondholders have come to have in it and the size of the claim on U.S. callable capital that could be made should Bank lending run into serious trouble. These mitigate interference on political grounds in either the Bank's borrowing or lending operations.

THE U.S. HOLD ON THE BANK PRESIDENCY AND STAFF. By tradition rather than formal rule, the United States has the prerogative to name the president of the World Bank. It has always nominated a U.S. citizen. This prerogative was initially granted not only because the United States was the Bank's largest shareholder but also because it was the key guarantor and principal capital market for Bank bonds. The market's view was important, for example, in the appointment of John McCloy instead of Graham Towers of Canada. But as U.S. support for the Bank has waned and the relative importance of the U.S. market has declined, this privilege has been called into question. Had the United States not nominated McNamara to a second term, it is likely that other countries would have usurped the privilege. And when it came time to select his successors, concern that conservative influences in the Reagan and Bush administrations would put forward candidates unacceptable to the international community led to talk of finding non-American alternatives. For example, having decided to resign, Barber Conable worried that Treasury Secretary Nicholas Brady had no serious interest in the appointment of his successor and therefore appealed directly to President Bush. Noting that there was a lot of dissatisfaction with U.S. leadership in the Bank, Conable warned the president that unless he nominated a person of stature, the Europeans and Japanese would take the privilege away from the United States.[106] In each instance, however, an acceptable U.S. candidate was identified and the American prerogative sustained.

The history of the World Bank shows that the choice has been critical to the life of the institution, although the impact of the person selected has not always been foreseeable. The United States has a record of nominating people who have Wall Street or Washington, not development, experience but who end up fervently championing both the institution and the need to tackle global poverty. This was as true of George Woods as of Robert McNamara, whose appointment reflected more a way for McNamara to escape the stigma of U.S. Vietnam War policy than a commitment on President Johnson's part to strong Bank leadership. Not surprisingly, there was much international consternation over the appointment. Each

105. Catherine Gwin, interview with Eugene Rotberg.
106. John Lewis and Richard Webb, interview with Barber Conable, Washington, D.C., May 8, 1991.

Bank president has also asserted independence from the United States. Even Conable, who of all the recent presidents was criticized for being too much under the thumb of the U.S. government, sought in the later years of his term to assert the Bank's independence. In 1990, for example, he pushed the executive board to support renewed lending to China despite congressional and administration opposition. Nonetheless, the privilege of selecting the Bank's president has ensured, at a minimum, a general policy orientation compatible with that of the United States.

The high proportion of Americans on the Bank staff has also been said to provide the United States with reinforcing influence. This claim has become moot as the proportion of U.S. nationals on the professional staff has contracted from 60 percent in 1951 to 26 percent in 1991.[107] Nonetheless, the United States has regularly urged that U.S. citizens be put in key management positions. For a time, it insisted on having U.S. directors in charge of the Latin American, Central American, and Caribbean regions (though this has not been true since the mid-1970s). And in many years Americans have held one or more vice presidential positions. Perhaps more significant, many staff members have been trained in the United States. But the U.S. economics profession is not itself of one mind, so the nature of the selection from within the profession is what seems to reinforce and sustain an institutional mind-set. Many on the outside view this inbreeding as extending not only to those brought onto the staff but also to the circle of consultants used to referee or participate in research efforts.

U.S. ATTENTION TO THE BANK. The United States has paid closer attention to the Bank than has any other major shareholder and has frequently flexed its muscle. As a result, even with its relative loss of power in the Bank, the United States still dominates largely by default. Neither Japan nor the western European nations as a group have yet shown sufficient interest to challenge U.S. leadership.

The United States is the only country that carries out detailed reviews of every Bank loan proposal and the only one to maintain constant contact with the Bank through government officials in addition to its representative to the board. Often, the United States will question a prospective loan early in the preparation process. And during final deliberation of a loan proposal by the Bank's executive board, it will make comments designed to draw attention to general matters of concern in order to influence future lending. Bank policy papers, evaluation reports, and special studies are also closely monitored. Executive branch officials have often emphasized that these procedures provide the United States with a substantial measure of influence and have repeatedly offered examples to illustrate the extent

107. For the 1951 figure see Mason and Asher, *World Bank since Bretton Woods*, table 4-3; for the 1991 figure see *World Bank, Human Resources Data, Annual Review, FY 1993* (Washington, 1993), p. B-1.

to which the Bank has been willing to make changes in loan and policy proposals on U.S. recommendations.[108]

Formal responsibility for conveying U.S. views and carrying out U.S. policy in the Bank rests with the U.S. executive director, who with other directors has the authority (under Article V, sections 1 and 2) over all Bank decisions. Far more important than the executive director, however, is the direct and constant interaction between the Bank and the U.S. Treasury. This interaction occurs daily at the staff level in regard to the detailed reviews of loan proposals and other routine matters. It occurs frequently at higher levels at the initiative of both the Bank and the U.S. government, especially, but not only, in regard to countries of importance to the United States.

The intensity of Bank-Treasury interaction is a unique feature of U.S. relations with the Bank, obviously facilitated by the Bank's location in Washington. As Bank files indicate, the U.S. government has privileged access to it that differs significantly from that of other member countries. The United States is sometimes consulted on a matter before other members are. It has regularly received early drafts of papers and studies, (they are now also circulated to other members in draft). And the top management of the Bank spends much more time meeting with, consulting, and responding to the United States than it does any other member country.

Although this intense interaction has changed little over the years, the way the United States mobilizes other member countries in support of its views has changed considerably. Initially, it was so predominant that its positions and the decisions of the board were virtually indistinguishable. For the most part, other member countries simply followed its lead, not only because of the strength of its support of the Bank but also because of the quality of its leadership.[109] But as the strength and quality declined, the United States could not count on automatic support. It began, therefore, to go outside the board with increasing frequency. Since the late 1970s it has made démarches to G-7 counterparts in national capitals as well as to executives on the Bank board. Building a working relationship with G-7 counterparts in capitals was a deliberate strategy of the Carter administration and was largely aimed at counteracting the mounting opposition to the Bank in

108. See Sanford, *U.S. Foreign Policy.* See also statement by C. Fred Bergsten, *Hearings before the Subcommittee on International Development Institutions and Finance of the Committee on Banking, Finance and Urban Affairs,* 96th Cong. 1st sess. (GPO, April 24, 1979); and statement, *Hearings before the Subcommittee on Foreign Operations of the Committee on Appropriations,* 96th Cong. 1st sess. (GPO, March 27, 1979).

109. This included for a time the U.S. executive director, but as interest in the Bank waned so too did the quality of the appointees. After the first few appointments, the executive director has been selected by the Treasury and has been on its staff. The most notable decline in quality and stature came not surprisingly in the first half of the 1980s when the Treasury itself was openly critical of the Bank.

Congress. Although this strategy broke down during the Reagan retrenchment, the Treasury returned to it in the second half of the 1980s in an effort to mobilize support for policy initiatives on debt in less developed countries, on China, and on the environment.

The Treasury has exerted decisive pressure by threatening to withhold its support from replenishment and capital increase negotiations. Although in earlier years the aim was to pressure others to a larger share of IDA funding, the tactic came to be used for other purposes. In the late 1970s, in response to repeated congressional delays in the passage of IDA funding bills, the United States and the other donor countries developed procedures or triggers that defined the level of commitment required for replenishment to go into effect. These triggers were set at a level of 85 percent of IDA voting stock so as to require U.S. participation. While the intention of the triggers was to hold U.S. feet to the fire, they gave the United States a de facto veto over IDA refunding because a threat to withhold its contribution could put not just the U.S. share but an entire replenishment negotiation in jeopardy. And this is a power the United States has come to use to assert its views on major issues of policy. That is, it has made major decisions on policy issues conditions of its participation in IDA replenishments and Bank and IFC capital increases. In this way it has furthered positions for which it may not have had majority support on the executive board.

The Exercise of U.S. Influence

Over the years the United States has used multiple sources of influence pervasively, episodically, and often inconsistently in pursuit of both long-term foreign policy goals and short-term political and economic interests. In so doing it has been driven by contradictory but simultaneously held attitudes toward the Bank. On the one hand it has looked to the Bank to promote development and an open world economy. On the other hand it has considered the Bank but one of its many instruments of foreign policy—a source of funds to be offered or denied to reward friends, punish enemies, or advance any number of other objectives defined by domestic constituency groups or immediate foreign policy aims.

To a considerable extent the United States has used its influence in ways that have strengthened and supported the dominant mission of the Bank. One of the major longer-term U.S. aims has been to increase the resources available for reconstruction and development while containing the burden on its own budget of providing that financing. In this effort it has been more than moderately successful. As its annual reports show, total Bank lending increased from $250 million in 1947 to $21 billion in 1992 (including IDA but not IFC loans), but the U.S. share of the amount shrank significantly. Thus a dollar of U.S. budgetary outlays leverages considerably more development resources now than it did at the start-up of the Bank. A second U.S. objective has been to develop the Bank's capacity to promote development—in ways consistent with U.S. political and economic interests. The United States has brought considerable influence to bear on matters of broad policy, specific country and sector lending decisions, and Bank administration and management.

DEVELOPMENT POLICY. The United States generally endorsed expanding both the geographic and substantive scope of the Bank's lending program. This support has not precluded it from using its influence at times to block or water down proposals to change Bank policies and practices. For example, during the drafting of the Bank's Charter, the United States argued against allowing direct lending to private enterprises. It resisted proposals for substantial increases in program lending in the 1950s and 1960s and fought proposals to increase local currency costs of projects. In the late 1970s it opposed the idea of structural adjustment lending proposed by the Bank's management. Among the reasons given were that the initiative contravened the Articles of Agreement of the Bank and that limited program lending had already been tried and had failed. It took Bank management three years to sell structural adjustment lending to the United States and other skeptical member countries. Not until confronted with the debt crisis and the need to find a way to avoid a collapse of the international financial system did the United States revise its position.

For the most part, however, on the broad issues of development policy and strategies, U.S. and World Bank views have evolved together, at least until disputes in the 1980s over specific policy issues, notably the increased support of private enterprise. Major changes in Bank development policy, especially changes in the sector allocation of Bank lending, were actively if at times belatedly supported by the United States. In the 1950s and early 1960s the United States initiated and encouraged major changes in development assistance policy, especially the increased focus on agricultural production. The Bank followed the U.S. lead and worked in concert with the U.S. bilateral aid program in the field. This interaction was particularly intense when the United States was providing large amounts of aid to India and Latin America at the time of the Alliance for Progress. In the 1970s the McNamara Bank and the United States shifted simultaneously toward more poverty-oriented development policies. Thus the United States supported the Bank's reorientation from infrastructure projects to agriculture and rural development and later to education, health care, and population control projects. These changes were advocated by members of the development profession in the United States, viewed as shared goals of member countries, and considered generally noncontentious.[110] But in the 1980s this close coincidence of views broke apart.

110. Former Treasury official C. Fred Bergsten in testimony before a subcommittee of the House in April 1979 made this point, although, for domestic political reasons, he overstated the strength of U.S. influence. According to Bergsten, starting in 1972 the World Bank began to alter the nature of its lending to reach the poorest populations in borrowing countries more directly. "The U.S. Government strongly influenced this change in direction,

The United States, the Bank, and most member countries came to broad agreement on the importance of crucial economic policy reforms to be advanced through Bank lending for structural adjustment. Indeed, this approach was labeled "the Washington consensus" in recognition of the convergence of views on reforms advocated by Washington-based institutions, the Bank, and the IMF. But beyond agreement on a core of reforms needed to bring about macroeconomic equilibrium, the consensus did not hold. And the United States, whose positions on some issues conveyed a strong ideological orientation favoring the private sector, was often sharply at odds with both Bank management and other member countries.

For instance, the United States expressed concern that the Bank was not serving, as it should have, as a lender of last resort. In opposition to the Bank's view that adjustment often required substantial financing, the U.S. pushed for reductions in lending levels while urging the Bank to increase pressure on countries to reform. Disputes between the United States and the Bank on this matter emerged in regard to lending to countries such as India that the United States believed ought to be relying more on private finance, lending for oil and gas exploration, and more generally in discussions about replenishments and capital increases for IDA and the Bank. Also, although the United States and the Bank agreed on the need to promote market-based reforms, they differed on the importance to be attached to private ownership and, more generally, the role of the state in the economy. This difference was particularly marked in the U.S. response to Bank lending in the energy sector. Although neither the Bank management nor other member countries agreed, the United States sought to prohibit loans to national oil companies.

The handling of the debt crisis was another major policy matter on which U.S. and Bank views diverged. Through most of the 1980s the Bank followed the U.S. lead on handling the crisis and did not venture proposals for new actions. Before the announcement of the Brady proposal, the Bank was widely criticized for not taking more initiative and for being reluctant to cross the U.S. Treasury. In early 1988, for example, commercial bank lenders to Brazil tried to get the Bank to insure a portion of a new loan package under negotiation, but the Treasury opposed the idea on the grounds that it was unnecessary and might foster the impression that such guarantees should be common.[111] Later in the spring, Conable sent to the board a Bank debt study suggesting the need for an expanded Bank role in facilitating new money packages and other forms of financial relief, including debt-reduction schemes. The report also noted that consensual debt relief, including outright forgiveness, might be the only workable solution for some debtors. In

and the Congress played a major part in so doing. The United States was able to attract wide support within the Bank and among member countries for the reaching-the-poor thrust, and the progress made is unarguable." Statement, *Hearings before the Subcommittee on Foreign Operations of the Committee on Appropriations,* 96th Cong. 1st sess. (GPO, April 3, 1979).

111. Walter S. Mossberg, "World Bank's Conable Runs into Criticism on Poor Nations' Debt," *Wall Street Journal,* June 21, 1988, pp. 1, 25.

its annual world debt report released early the following year, the Bank noted again that the debtor countries' position had stubbornly failed to improve and that "imagination and resolve" were needed. But absent from this public document were any recommendations of its own. Only after the Brady proposals were made did the Bank publicly endorse debt reduction and an expanded Bank function. In implementing the Brady initiative, however, the Bank was at times at odds with the United States, especially on the size of the financial packages that needed to be put together for some countries.

The most visible dispute, however, was over the U.S. effort to tie the 1991 IFC capital increase to major reforms in the Bank's private sector development activities. In a sense this marked the culmination of a decade-long effort to force the Bank to take direct actions to promote development of the private sector in borrowing countries. Although other member countries—both developed and developing—generally concurred that the Bank needed to support private sector development more strongly, they did not accept the ideological tenor of the U.S. pressure nor many of the specific reform notions the U.S. sought to impose. In 1992 the Japanese government requested that the Bank review the Asian development experience, which represented an alternative market-based development approach distinct from the U.S. model and prescriptions.

COUNTRY AND SECTOR ALLOCATIONS. The country and sector allocations of Bank lending have also experienced U.S. influence, though less heavily than is often assumed. Bank lending and U.S. policy interests have usually converged, and the United States has not often interfered directly in specific loan decisions. Along with other donor countries, it has accepted Bank lending to countries with which it was not on good terms. And, more often than not, it has accepted the sectoral composition of Bank lending in individual countries. But the United States has repeatedly used its influence, directly and controversially, to affect decisions relating to both particular countries and certain commodity areas. The record is mixed on the actual impact of this pressure. In many cases the Bank resisted the interference. In the early 1970s, for example, it made loans to India and Egypt despite U.S. objections; in the midst of the Vietnam War, it resisted U.S. pressure to lend to South Vietnam; and despite congressional opposition, the Bank has made loans to various developing countries to expand production of palm oil and other commodities competitive with U.S. products. Yet a heavy U.S. hand has been laid on some loan decisions, and although instances of strong U.S. interference do not account for the direction of most Bank lending, they have been a source of tension between the United States and both the Bank management and Bank board.

In the main, the United States has been willing to have money put where it is most needed or could be used most effectively. And it has been willing to vote against a loan to a friendly country on economic or technical grounds, sometimes to the dismay of the State Department. Nonetheless, like some other donor countries, the United States has regularly encouraged the Bank to lend to favored countries. As a former Bank official said in 1970, "the French are always pressing us to slant

IDA funds toward French Africa. Similarly, the Japanese, whose interest is in Southeast Asia, are persuading us to put more assistance into that area. And the United States, I need scarcely add, is always telling us that more funds should be channeled into Latin America."[112]

More than other donor countries, the United States has also tried to block loans to "problem" countries. In those instances in which lending has been reduced or denied, the Bank has always had reasoned economic arguments for its decision. Strictly speaking, therefore, it has often concurred with rather than conceded to U.S. pressures. But throughout the Bank's history there have been particular cases of strong pressure from high-level U.S. officials either to lend or not to lend to specific countries.

This pressure has been in evidence since the Bank's earliest days. In 1947, for example, John McCloy, with the encouragement of the U.S. Department of State, decided that the Bank's first loan would go to France. The Communist party had won a minor position in the coalition government, and the U.S. government feared that it might increase its mandate in the next election. The loan carried tough terms, which the French government protested but accepted. The Bank would lend only half of the $500 million the French requested, and it would closely supervise the French economy to ensure that the government took steps to balance its budget, increase taxes, and cut consumption of certain luxury imports. In addition, the State Department "informed the French that they would have to 'correct the present situation' by removing any communist representatives in the Cabinet. The Communist party was pushed out of the coalition government in early May 1947, and within hours, as if to underscore the linkage, McCloy announced that the loan would go through."[113]

Also in the spring of 1947 the Bank entered into negotiations with Poland for a $128.5 million loan for coal-mining equipment—much scaled down from Poland's request for $600 million. The *New York Times* reported that although the Polish loan was considered a sound investment, the United States objected, fearing "the political effect of such a credit to Poland's Communist-led government."[114] Nonetheless, the Bank sent a team to Poland in mid-1947 to evaluate the project. The resulting favorable staff report was followed in the fall by a visit to Poland by Bank President McCloy and the subsequent start of formal negotiations of a loan for some $50 million. But the Department of State made clear that it would oppose even a small loan, and McCloy "privately made it known" to interested Bank members "that he now thought his Wall Street investors would not approve."

112. J. Burke Knapp, "Determination of Priorities and the Allocation of Resources," in John P. Lewis and Ishan Kapur, eds., *The World Bank Group, Multilateral Aid and the 1970s* (Lexington, Mass.: Lexington Books, 1973), p. 50.

113. Bird, *The Chairman*, p. 291.

114. "World Bank Loan to Poland Stymied," *New York Times*, November 5, 1947, p. 43. See also Robert W. Oliver, *International Economic Co-operation and the World Bank* (Macmillan, 1975), pp. 241, 244–45.

Instead, in their negotiations with the Poles, McCloy and Garner now began to raise conditions that they knew to be unacceptable. They demanded that Poland first stabilize its currency according to guidelines issued by the International Monetary Fund. Instead of $45 million, the Bank's loan committee suggested $25 million, and even that was to be contingent on the Poles' agreeing to sell their coal to Western Europe and use the hard-currency proceeds to make payments on the Bank's loan. Poland's executive director at the Bank and its ambassador in Washington—both anticommunists—tried to persuade their government to accept these unusually tough terms. But, since they had originally sought $600 million, the $25 million the Bank offered now was hardly incentive enough for the Polish Communists to agree to such concessions also. Simultaneously, a firm consensus developed within the Truman administration rejecting the notion that Western aid might help preserve the coalition government in Warsaw. . . . So, finally, in mid-1948, Eugene Black told McCloy that he had been formally instructed by the Truman administration to vote against any loan for Poland. McCloy then suspended all further negotiations with the Poles.[115]

The rejection of a loan to Czechoslovakia at roughly this same time underscored the U.S. position against World Bank lending to Eastern Europe. In both the Czech and Polish cases the World Bank justified its refusal on the grounds that political uncertainty undermined each country's status as a good credit risk. As stated in the Bank's 1948 Annual Report,

> the Bank is not unmindful of the importance of the economic development of its member countries in Europe which are not participants in the ERP.
>
> It is unfortunate but nonetheless true that the existing political difficulties and uncertainties in Europe present special problems which have thus far prevented the Bank from making loans in those countries. The Bank is fully cognizant of the injunction in its Articles of Agreement that its decisions shall be based only on economic considerations. Political tensions and uncertainties in or among its member countries, however, have a direct effect on economic and financial conditions in those countries and upon their credit position.[116]

The political situation did not change in ways that opened prospects for Bank lending, and Poland and Czechoslovakia withdrew from Bank membership in the 1950s.

There are additional examples in each decade of decisions not to lend following strong U.S. pressure. For the most part the cold war provided the reason through the end of the 1980s. The effort in the 1950s to negotiate financing for the construction of the Aswan Dam in Egypt provides an illustration.[117] In July 1956 the withdrawals of American and then British offers to join the Bank in financing

115. Bird, *The Chairman*, pp. 295–96.

116. International Bank for Reconstruction and Development, Second Annual Report, (Washington, 1947), p. 17, quoted in Brown, *United States and Politicization*, pp. 128–29.

117. This summary account draws on Mason and Asher, *World Bank since Bretton Woods*, pp. 627–42.

the dam were followed within a week by President Gamal Abdel Nasser's decision to nationalize the properties of the foreign-owned Suez Canal Company. In response, France, Britain, and Israel initiated military action against Egypt.

The Bank's relation to the Aswan Dam project had been a long and complicated one. Suffice it to say here that despite the staff's support for the project, which would have carried with it stiff conditions agreed to after difficult negotiations with Egypt, the United States and Britain were deterred from joint financing largely by Nasser's expression of Arab nationalism and support for discontented elements in several Arab countries. As Bank negotiations were nearing closure, support in the U.S. Department of State for a resolution of the affair began to diminish, in part in response to growing congressional opposition. "In March 1956, when the foreign aid bill for the fiscal year 1957 was presented to a House Subcommittee on Appropriations, no congressman defended the Aswan Dam financing against attack."[118] In mid-May, Nasser gave diplomatic recognition to Communist China, which further dissipated State Department support. Although Bank president Eugene Black and the Egyptian ambassador in Washington continued to promote the project, Secretary of State John Foster Dulles indicated on July 19, 1956, that the United States had decided not to participate. The following day the British financing offer was withdrawn. Ultimately, the Bank's offer lapsed, since it no longer had any financial partners.

During the 1960s and into the 1970s the United States sought to block Bank lending in a number of cases involving disputes over the expropriation of U.S. private property, especially in Latin America. Under pressure from the United States, the Bank had developed a formal policy, explained in a 1969 publication:

> The Bank is charged, under its articles of agreement, to encourage international investment. It has, therefore, a direct interest in the creation and maintenance of satisfactory relations between member countries and their external creditors. Accordingly, the normal practice is to inform governments who are involved in such disputes that the Bank or IDA will not assist them unless and until they make appropriate efforts to reach a fair and equitable settlement.[119]

Thus a settlement need not have been reached as long as "appropriate efforts" to this end were made by a prospective borrower. This left room for interpretation of the facts and disagreement with the United States, which generally urged a strict ruling but did not always get its way. Strong U.S. pressure was followed by reduced Bank lending to Peru after its nationalization of the International Petroleum Company in 1969. In contrast, the Bank made a loan to Guyana in 1971 despite U.S. opposition. Although the U.S. government did not consider that Guyana was doing enough to resolve an expropriation dispute, Bank management and a majority of the Bank board did.

118. Ibid., p. 638.
119. International Bank for Reconstruction and Development, *Policies and Operations* (Washington, 1969), cited in Brown, *United States and Politicization*, pp. 162–63.

The Bank suspended lending to Chile from 1970 to 1973 following the election of Salvador Allende and his nationalization of the Chilean copper mines. Although the suspension is often cited (even by the U.S. government) as an instance in which U.S. pressure was decisive, the actual record is complex. Indeed, the details provide a particularly interesting picture of the interface between U.S. pressure and World Bank decisionmaking.

The United States pressured the Bank not to lend to the Allende government after nationalization of Chile's copper mines. Despite the pressure, the Bank sent a mission to Santiago (having determined that Chile was in compliance with Bank rules requiring that for lending to resume after a nationalization, procedures for compensation had to be under way). Robert McNamara subsequently met with Allende to indicate that the Bank was prepared to make new loans contingent upon government commitments to reform the economy. But the Bank and the Allende regime could not come to terms on the conditions for a loan. Throughout the period of the Allende regime, Chile received no new loans.[120]

Shortly after Allende's assassination in 1973 during a coup that brought General Pinochet's military junta to power, the Bank resumed lending, providing a fifteen-year credit for copper mine development. A retrospective internal Bank memorandum concluded that the Bank had made errors of both professional and tactical judgment in this sequence of decisions. It had failed to support the underlying social objectives of the Allende regime and therefore did not position itself to make the legitimate point that the economic costs of the government's program were unnecessarily high and could be reduced by proper economic management. Conversely, in lending to the junta the Bank ignored the retreat from long-term social objectives and the high social costs of the economic reforms. Moreover, the memorandum argued, the Bank made the mistake of not bringing the decision to suspend lending to Allende's government to the executive board so that it would be seen as a board action. Nowhere did the memorandum refer to pressure from the United States.[121] In an interview in 1991 McNamara said that U.S. pressure was not the cause of the Bank's decision to refuse to lend. Rather, he explained, the Bank simply could not justify lending under the economic conditions that prevailed.[122] Still, the sequence of decisions on Chile was clearly consistent with U.S. policy objectives. The suspension of lending in 1970–73 was cited in the 1982 U.S. Treasury report as a significant example of the successful exercise of U.S. influence

120. In its statement before the 1972 World Bank's annual meeting, the Chilean government protested that its rationalization policy was the reason for the country's having received no new loans during the twenty-two months of the Allende administration, despite having submitted elaborate project proposals. International Bank for Reconstruction and Development, *Summary Proceedings of the 1972 Annual Meetings of the Boards of Governors* (Washington, 1972), p. 55.

121. Confidential memorandum from Mahbub ul Haq to Robert McNamara, April 1976.

122. Jonathan Sanford, "The MDBs and the Suspension of Lending to Allende's Chile," Congressional Research Service, December 13, 1974, supports McNamara's claim.

on the Bank. And although the Bank reached an agreement in principle on new lending in June 1973, the loan proposals were not formally considered by the board until after the September coup that brought General Pinochet to power. As a Bank white paper explained, preliminary reactions to the proposals by several executive directors "raised a serious question as to whether the proposals would command a favorable vote at that time. Hence, after consultation with the Government of Chile, the management postponed indefinitely the placing of this item on the agenda of the Executive Directors, and this is how matters stood at the time that the Allende government was deposed."[123]

Ironically, in the later years of the Pinochet regime the U.S. government asked the Bank to postpone board discussion of a structural adjustment loan to Chile to avoid congressional opposition on human rights grounds at a time when the administration was seeking support for Bank refunding. But in a letter to James Baker, the assistant secretary of the Treasury, on October 29, 1986, Barber Conable rejected the U.S. request.

The Bank's decision not to lend to Vietnam in the late 1970s was another instance in which strong U.S. pressure was exerted. Although McNamara said at the time and maintained in later interviews that the decision was made by the Bank on economic considerations, at least some of the staff servicing Asian countries felt otherwise. A memo to McNamara and a long "private note" written in August and September of 1979 by a senior Bank official for East Asia and the Pacific region summarize the views of two economic missions to Vietnam.[124] The first mission in 1978 led to the beginnings of project preparation work on a modest scale. The level of funding earmarked for Vietnam was held by McNamara to $150 million, far below the $400 million the allocative norms would have subscribed to the country.

The Bank's mission reported that economic conditions were not favorable, that economic management left much to be desired, but that there was no case for suspending the Bank's meager engagement there. Indeed, Shahid Husain, the head of the mission, reported in a memo to McNamara that it was the judgment of the mission that Vietnam's economic performance could not be rated lower than that of some other IDA borrowers in the region, including Bangladesh and Pakistan, and that experience on project implementation in Vietnam was actually better. Although in the wake of massive refugee flows Vietnam faced serious international criticism and it would therefore be inappropriate to take a project to the board, "there are reasonable prospects that in due course we should be able to build a meaningful dialogue on economic and development issues. So, while being responsive to the environment, we should try to keep our channels open to the Viet-

123. World Bank, "Chile and the World Bank," white paper, cited in Brown, *United States and Politicization*, p. 167.

124. "A Private Note on Internal Bank Deliberations on Vietnam," September 21, 1979; and confidential memorandum from Shahid Husain to Robert McNamara, August 31, 1979.

namese."[125] The mission's contention, in contrast to what McNamara said publicly in *Newsweek,* was that on substantive grounds there was no basis for stopping all lending to Vietnam. The Bank should wait until it could get sufficient support for lending from the board. Thus the staff in charge of the region did not support a suspension of lending on economic grounds; but whether McNamara was driven by strong U.S. and other donor pressure or his own determination remains open to debate.

A more recent example in which the Bank's refusal to lend clearly coincided with U.S. policy is that of Nicaragua in the 1980s. The reason for the suspension of lending was the accumulation of arrears. However, in September 1984 the Nicaraguan government formally proposed a solution to its arrearages problem. The proposal encompassed three actions: a freeze until the end of 1984 on disbursements and repayments, preparation and appraisal by the World Bank of an economic adjustment program for presentation to the board before the end of June 1985, and a loan rescheduling or loan repayment in local currency. The third measure, the Nicaraguan government noted, was consistent with Article IV, section 4(c) of the Articles of Agreement, which provides, "if a member suffers from an acute exchange stringency, so that the service of any loan contracted by that member or guaranteed by it or by one of its agencies cannot be provided in the stipulated manner, the member concerned may apply to the Bank for a relaxation of the conditions of payment." In the view of senior Bank staff, such actions would have entailed substantial danger for the Bank's "market image" and "shareholder relations."[126] Its response, which in Nicaragua's view showed "an absence of a constructive attitude on the part of the Bank," was to insist that the country settle its overdue payments in full and negotiate a stabilization program with the IMF.[127] Only when those two conditions were met would the Bank be in a position to help with the preparation of a medium-term program. No concerted effort was made, however, to help the Sandinista regime meet these conditions, as was done, for example, in response to Zambia's arrearage problems later in the 1980s.

Although one need not dispute the Bank's economic policy assessments of Allende's Chile, Vietnam, and Nicaragua under the Sandinistas, it is worth noting that equally harsh assessments could have been made, but were not, of Somoza's Nicaragua, Marcos's Philippines, and Mobutu's Zaire, regimes that were all important cold war allies of the United States.

Instances in which the United States successfully influenced increases or more rapid lending to a particular country are even harder to pin down unequivocally because of the broad concurrence of U.S. geopolitical interests and Bank country

125. Husain, memorandum, August 31, 1979; and Susan Drake, "Vietnam's Troubles," *Newsweek,* August 20, 1979.

126. Internal memorandum, December 21, 1984 (confidential).

127. Cable from Joaquin Cuadra Chamorro, Nicaraguan minister of finance, to David Knox, December 19, 1984.

allocations. But examples exist in each of the Bank's decades. For instance, the United States influenced increased lending to Japan in the 1950s despite the Bank's reluctance because of the country's inadequate creditworthiness.[128] It is ironic that the United States pushed the Bank to finance steel projects in Japan, given that country's managed approach to industrialization and later U.S. opposition to lending to the steel sector in many other countries.

Two more recent examples of seemingly favorable treatment of countries important to the United States involve Bank decisions to release structural adjustment financing despite assessments by staff that conditions did not warrant lending. In 1988 the Bank provided the first tranch of a sectoral adjustment loan to the government of Argentina despite the fact that an IMF stabilization program had been held up because of differences between the Fund and the government, including differences over the size of the country's deficit.[129] Treasury and World Bank officials have since said that the United States was interested in helping Argentine President Raul Alfonsín and had indicated to the Bank that it would support a decision to release funding to Argentina even in the absence of an IMF program. Despite opposition by some of its staff, the Bank released the funds. The United States, under a change of leadership at the Treasury, then reversed itself and openly criticized the Bank's action.[130]

During the Persian Gulf crisis, Secretary of State James Baker offered Turkey support for increased Bank lending in appreciation for the country's assistance against Iraq. After Baker's visit, the World Bank released the second tranch of a sector adjustment loan that had previously been held up because of Turkey's failure to satisfy the Bank's loan conditions even though the IMF judged the country's macroeconomic performance unsatisfactory.[131] According to one study of World Bank policy-based lending, a large number of country cases reveal this same phenomenon—that although alliance with the United States does not earn a recipient country gentler loan conditions, it does yield "a more forgiving treatment of slippage on conditions."[132]

U.S. pressures on the Bank in regard to loans for the production of certain commodities intensified in the 1970s. In the Bank's early days the United States did not want it to lend directly to private companies nor act as a substitute for private lending. In the 1970s pressure was applied, some of it mandated by Congress, in an

128. "The Ironies That Built Japan, Inc.," *Washington Post*, July 18, 1993, p. H12.
129. See chapter 11 of this volume.
130. This sequence of events was confirmed in interviews, including Catherine Gwin, interview with Charles Dallara, New York, October 2, 1991, and is corroborated in Polak, op. cit.
131. Ibid.
132. Paul Mosley, Jane Harrigan, and John Toye, *Aid and Power: The World Bank and Policy-Based Lending*, vol. 1 (London: Routledge, 1991), p. 128.

attempt to prevent Bank support for increasing production of commodities that competed with those of producers in the United States. In most instances of congressionally mandated opposition to commodity loans—for palm oil or citrus products, for example—Bank management stood up to the United States and successfully gained executive board approval. This was the case with a loan for palm oil production to Papua New Guinea, which the United States tried to block in the late 1970s. But U.S. opposition was not without effect. U.S. legislation and U.S. position in the Bank were cast in terms of opposition to loans for commodities that were in surplus on the world market. The impact of this position was to make the Bank especially careful in its consideration of rates of return in these commodity areas. From the staff's point of view there was quite simply a higher burden of proof for products singled out by the United States.[133]

For certain other commodities, notably steel, mined products, oil, and gas, it was the U.S. administration even more than Congress that strongly opposed Bank lending. The Bank's decision in March 1987 to limit support for steel projects to providing technical assistance, thereby stopping loan requests from India and Pakistan, was the result, at least in part, of strong U.S. opposition over a number of years. In 1985 the United States had voted against an IFC equity investment in a steel project in Brazil and later opposed a Bank steel sector restructuring loan to Mexico (which was approved in 1988). The case of Mexico provides, however, an interesting example of conflicting American objectives and the nuances of U.S. opposition votes. The matter arose at a time when Bank and Mexico debt management and policy reform efforts were beginning to work well. For the Bank to retreat on a project that was well advanced would have seriously undermined the efforts. Besides, the United States had a keen interest in seeing a successful resolution to Mexico's debt crisis. It therefore voted against the loan, but it did not try to change the views of other members of the board, which it knew would support the loan. Congressional requirements were thus satisfied, although all parties were fully aware that the loan approval was never in doubt.

The United States also voted against but did not oppose with much vehemence a steel sector loan to China at a time in the 1980s of warm U.S.-China relations. Yet in other cases where U.S. interests were not strong, opposition to steel sector lending was more forceful and projects were shelved.[134] According to former Bank Vice President Burke Knapp, U.S. opposition to steel production loans in the 1980s had as much to do with opposition to the Bank's lending to large state enterprises as to its lending for steel production per se. The United States had not objected to

133. Catherine Gwin, interview with Burke Knapp, Washington, D.C., September 25, 1992.

134. Internal Bank documents from the period show that Barber Conable rejected the recommendations of Ernest Stern that the Bank provide loans to assist steel sector restructuring in cases other than China and Mexico. Conable was presumably influenced by his knowledge of the strength of opposition on this issue in Congress and the administration.

earlier steel sector loans to Japan, where production was in the hands of private companies, but consistently opposed support for state-owned steel enterprises in developing countries as more and more producers came into the market.

In mining, the United States argued against Bank lending both on grounds of oversupply in the world market and the availability of private finance for worthy investments. For instance, the United States blocked consideration of a request by a Brazilian joint venture mining company for an IFC loan that was intended to boost Brazil's export of iron ore.[135] It also opposed a major IFC investment in the Escondida copper project in Chile. Escondida is one of the world's largest and richest copper ore bodies. U.S. copper producers were clearly concerned about the added competition and the potential for the new mine to drive low world copper prices even lower. However, the IFC estimated the impact of Escondida on copper prices to be "modest and transitory." And both Japan and Germany, which viewed Escondida as a stable long-term source of supply, were expected to provide the bulk of the loan financing in exchange for long-term service contracts. As a result, U.S. objections were not sustained and the investment went ahead.

After the oil price shock of 1973–74 the United States supported increased Bank lending in the energy sector. Much of what the Bank undertook was then noncontroversial. However, lending for oil and gas exploration and development became a matter of serious dispute between the United States and the Bank, especially after the change from the Carter administration to the Reagan administration. In the opinion of Edward Fried, U.S. executive director at the Bank during part of the Carter years, a serious effort should have been made to increase oil production and conserve use in developing countries because they were going to be big users as well as potential sources of supply.[136] The question was what the role of the Bank should be.

From the U.S. point of view, it was a bad idea for the Bank to spend money on oil drilling, but the institution could be influential in promoting exploration and development. Toward the end of the 1970s Sheikh Ahmed Zaki Yamani of Saudi Arabia proposed in a speech that the World Bank and oil surplus economies cooperate to boost energy sector development in the developing world. The idea was picked up by Fried and after discussion with the Bank put forward as a proposal for an energy affiliate that would provide a way of enlarging and concentrating the Bank's work in the whole energy field. The proposal moved ahead until the Reagan administration withdrew U.S. support. The new administration not only considered the affiliate another window for increasing the lending of the Bank, which it opposed, but also argued that financing for oil and gas production should come from the private sector. The World Bank could foster policies that

135. Jonathan Friedland, "Inside Job at the World Bank," *South*, no. 83 (September 1987), pp. 9–10.

136. Catherine Gwin, interview with Edward Fried, Washington, D.C., July 16, 1992.

encouraged private sector investment, but it should not make loans to governments or state-owned oil and gas companies.[137] A U.S. note to World Bank directors explaining the new administration's opposition to the energy affiliate said that the United States would not approve development bank action that borrowed from private capital markets to make long-term loans to governments of developing countries for energy development.[138]

Following its defeat of the energy affiliate proposal, the United States continued to oppose the Bank's energy lending policy and specific loan proposals not consistent with an emphasis on private sector financing and investment. A series of internal Bank memos reporting on conversations with the Treasury and the U.S. executive director in April and May 1984 make clear the nature and intensity of the dispute between the United States and the Bank (including both management and members of the board). In the conversations a Treasury official expressed concern over the Bank's "undue enthusiasm" for oil and gas lending that, he stated, could and should have been left to the private sector. Referring in one conversation to a specific Nigerian gas engineering loan as a scandal, he argued that Nigeria was a rich country and could easily secure the financing for itself. In response to the assessment that Nigeria could not get commercial bank financing at that time, he stated, "that was their own fault." They had "messed up" and could in due course restore their creditworthiness. Although a Bank representative made the point that the Bank was not like other lenders because it sought to improve the policy framework, establish appropriate prices, and improve production incentives, the Treasury official emphasized that the United States would continue to oppose loans to national oil companies and loans where it deemed private financing to be attainable.[139]

In subsequent Board discussions and votes the United States insisted that Bank lending not displace private equity and lending. To this end, it proposed two lending guidelines: there should be no Bank oil and gas lending to creditworthy countries and no Bank lending to established national oil companies. From the Bank's perspective this proposal discounted its technical contribution to the design and physical aspects of an investment or exploration program and the value of its policy advice. The inevitable conclusion, if the U.S. position prevailed, was that the Bank would then not lend at all "since we ourselves would not advance a case that we would be financing a hydrocarbon project simply to transfer resources."[140] Neither Bank management nor other member countries disagreed with the principle that the Bank's function should be residual and its lending not replace other financing available on reasonable terms; but there was considerable disagreement

137. Clyde H. Farnsworth, "U.S. Rejects Proposal to Form World Bank Energy Affiliate," *New York Times*, August 13, 1981, "Sunday Week in Review," p. 15.

138. World Bank internal memorandum, April 6, 1984.

139. Ibid.; and World Bank internal memorandum, May 9, 1984.

140. World Bank internal memorandum, April 6, 1984.

on the proposed U.S. guidelines. As a compromise, new energy policy guidelines were formulated that provided clearer limits on Bank lending for oil and gas exploration and development but allowed loans to national oil companies, emphasized policy leverage, and held Bank financing to a minimum necessary to achieve policy impact.

What then, is the conclusion to be drawn about U.S. influence on specific loan decisions? The record confirms that with both management and the board, U.S. views have carried great weight on loan decisions. This is not the case when the United States is required by congressional legislation to vote a specific way on designated categories of loans, because the United States acting alone can always be outvoted. But it is the case when the government has chosen to apply heavy pressure on the management and other members of the board in regard to a specific loan. Loans made despite strong opposition by the Bank's largest shareholder are the exception. However, U.S. pressure affecting the Bank's decision to make a loan to a specific country or for a specific project is also the exception. The more pervasive influence is at the level of lending policy or in the details of a loan.

ADMINISTRATION AND FINANCE. The United States has also applied strong pressure in matters of Bank administration and finance. Although instances of major disagreements between the United States and the Bank on matters of lending policy have been limited, at least before the 1980s, administrative matters have been a constant source of dispute. Four of them have been the focus of greatest attention and debate: the size of the Bank's administrative budget, increases in staff salaries and benefits, maintaining the value of Bank capital, and the evaluation and transparency of Bank activities. On all four the United States has had major influence.

The United States has not been the only member country to express strong and continuous concern about the growth of the Bank's administrative budget (most of which has occurred since the late 1970s), but it has been one of the most vocal. Concern came to a head in June 1986 when the budget proposed by management was opposed by the United States, Japan, and France, with Germany and the United Kingdom abstaining. This vote of no confidence occurred two days before Barber Conable assumed office, which led him to ask Treasury Secretary Baker, who had prevailed on him to accept the presidency, "what are you doing to me?"[141] The outcome was a major reorganization carried out in the early months of his presidency.

Conable was told by the government that there was too much fat in the system. In consultation with him McNamara agreed that reorganization was needed. But, again according to Conable, the Bank had to put together such a rich personnel separation package that he lost the support of the U.S. government for the re-

141. John Lewis and Richard Webb, interview with Barber Conable, Washington, D.C., May 8, 1991.

organization. The Bank staff considered the reorganization disruptive and, more seriously, without clear purpose or apparent benefit to programs. Indeed, many inside and outside the Bank claimed at the time that the reorganization led to a serious mismatch between the new tasks the Bank was being pressured to take on (in environmental sensitivity, in eastern Europe and the former Soviet Union, and in private sector development) and the inadequate size and composition of the staff. Another problem, observers believed, was too little sector-specific technical expertise as a result of the reorganization. A reorganization in 1992, instigated not by the board but by Bank President Lewis T. Preston, responded to some of the concerns raised by the Conable reorganization and to the findings of an internal evaluation, commissioned by Preston in 1991, on the Bank's portfolio management.[142] That evaluation, which documented a serious deterioration in the Bank's portfolio performance, challenged the Bank's management as well as its board to institute major operational changes that incorporate but go beyond the kind of changes the United States has been demanding for many years.

The United States also criticized the high salaries of senior Bank staff as early as the 1960s. Salaries, it believed, should be compatible with U.S. civil service pay scales. But the issue did not become seriously divisive until the mid-1970s. It has since remained a point of tension, even though salary levels are now determined on the basis of a formula advanced by the United States.

In 1976 the United States successfully achieved a reduction in proposed Bank salary increases, which it regarded as excessive. This was a time when salary increases for U.S. public officials were being held down as part of a deficit-reduction, anti-inflation campaign. To win support for its position, the United States made a series of high-level representations to other member country governments. That same year, Congress linked the U.S. contribution to the Bank and IDA to the condition that the U.S. executive director not receive compensation in excess of that paid a U.S. government official at the level of assistant secretary.

In response to the U.S. pressure, member governments agreed to form a Joint Committee on Compensation of the Bank and the Fund. The committee was made up of executive directors from each institution and outside experts and was charged with recommending principles and levels of compensation. The United States further proposed that the G-5 countries commission a separate but similar study by an independent management consulting firm. Based on the recommendation of the two studies, the Bank board agreed to a compensation framework in 1979.

Underpinning the agreement was a formula proposed by the United States that would base future compensation levels and adjustments on compensation paid by "comparator organizations" in U.S. public and private sectors and similar organizations in a few selected high-income member countries (which were taken into

142. Portfolio Management Task Force, *Effective Implementation: Key to Development Impact* (Washington: World Bank, 1992).

account to ensure that the Fund and Bank would remain competitive employers in the international as well as the U.S. market). Following the adoption of its formula, the U.S. position was that the principles and mechanism were in place but questions of interpretation remained that would require watching.[143]

In subsequent years the United States made clear through high-level representations to other governments that its concerns about salary levels had not yet been resolved. In April 1986 Treasury Secretary Baker sent a letter to all governors of the Bank stating that the work of the Joint Committee on Compensation "suggests that there are serious problems in the current compensation system." The letter continues that although it is "not possible at this stage to determine precisely how much Fund and Bank salaries and benefits are out of line, or exactly what changes in the compensation system are needed," he urged governments to join the United States "in supporting a delay in any salary increase until . . . a revised compensation system has been installed."[144] In July 1989 Assistant Secretary of the Treasury Charles Dallara, in a letter to Barber Conable, strongly opposed management's recommendations on a revised system. The recommendations of the Fund and Bank management, Dallara said, were at odds in important respects with Joint Committee recommendations that the United States supported but that were "already a compromise among all participants in the Committee." Dallara concluded,

> Because the compensation issue has not been resolved satisfactorily, I fear that it could undermine our efforts to obtain funding from the Congress for both the Bank and IMF. For our part, we cannot and will not defend the new "system," which in our view does not represent a system, but rather a disparate and unwieldy collection of JCC and staff inspired elements. Both managements were fully aware of our concerns before their proposals were adopted, so I can assume you are confident of your ability to explain and defend the decisions taken and their implications.[145]

Thus after a decade and a half of contention, compensation remains a serious source of controversy. The United States is insistent on holding down excessive salaries and perks; others counter that the effect of U.S. pressure is to undermine the Bank's ability to attract high-quality staff from other countries.

The role of the dollar in the valuation of Bank capital is another matter on which the United States and the Bank (including all other members of the board) have been in dispute for many years. Although valuation is not a matter of major significance for the operations of the Bank, the U.S. refusal to abandon what is

143. See National Advisory Council on International Monetary and Financial Policies, *Annual Report, Fiscal Year 1981* (Washington, 1981), pp. 41–42.

144. Letter from Secretary of the Treasury James A. Baker to each of the governors of the Bank, April 25, 1986.

145. Letter from Assistant Secretary of the Treasury Charles H. Dallara to Barber Conable, July 10, 1989.

perceived as special treatment has posed financial difficulties for the Bank and antagonized other member countries. In effect, by insisting on maintaining the value of Bank capital in terms of a fixed rate of exchange between special drawing rights (SDRs) and the dollar, the United States has kept itself in the unique position among member countries of having to assume no exchange risk in its capital contributions to the Bank.

The valuation of Bank capital became an issue between the United States and the Bank when the second amendment of the Articles of Agreement of the IMF, which created the SDR, came into force. The Bank's Articles had stipulated that the standard of value for Bank capital was the U.S. dollar "of the weight and fitness in effect on July 1, 1944." This weight and fitness referred to the amount of gold for which one dollar could freely be exchanged. The Bretton Woods exchange system set the value of every other currency in terms of the dollar, which, as long as a fixed dollar price of gold prevailed, meant that every other currency also had a fixed gold value. But once the dollar was delinked from the price of gold, the executive directors of the Bank were faced with having to decide whether the successor to the 1944 gold dollar should be the SDR or the current U.S. dollar (at a rate of exchange of 1.20635, the last par value of the dollar), and whether the question should be decided through the executive directors' powers of interpretation of the Articles of Agreement or through an amendment to them. The opinion of the Bank's general counsel, and the preference of all member countries except the United States, was that the SDR should be substituted for the 1944 gold dollar on the basis of the directors' powers. The United States argued, and still argues, that a change would require an amendment because it would impose a different, flexible obligation on member governments. As a result, the United States and other countries would have to pass legislation whenever their currencies depreciated to fulfill obligations to maintain value on paid-in capital. And the United States opposed such an amendment for the same reason—that a change in SDR valuation would require legislative authorizations and appropriations for each maintenance-of-value payment the United States might be obliged to make.

For the United States the problem is more political than financial. The likely effect on the U.S. budget (positive or negative) would be minuscule. However, to accept a new maintenance-of-value obligation in the Bank would be to accept (as all other countries have had to do) an open-ended obligation to make such payments as would be required should the dollar decline against an agreed standard of value. No a priori ceiling could be set on such an obligation. Therefore, to fulfill it would require open-ended authorization and periodic appropriation legislation, which successive administrations have argued would be politically impractical even though financially trivial.

The unequal treatment that has resulted from the U.S. refusal to accept a maintenance-of-value obligation is a source of irritation among member countries. It has also posed financial headaches for the Bank from time to time. In the fall of

1987 a considerable depreciation in the U.S. dollar caused a decrease in the Bank's headroom—the difference between the amount of loans outstanding and the Bank's legal lending limit—from $18.2 billion at the end of September to $8 billion at the end of December.[146] The problem was exacerbated because negotiations for a general capital increase for the Bank had been blocked for several years by the United States. To avoid a temporary suspension of disbursements on all outstanding loans and a loss of credit standing in the markets, the Bank discussed the possibility of a special bridging operation with central banks. The aim would have been to cover further substantial dollar depreciation before Bank receipt of new subscriptions under a capital increase (not agreed to until the late 1980s). But the need for such an agreement was averted.

Over the years the United States has also persistently tried to strengthen Bank audit and evaluation procedures and has pressured the Bank to make more information on its activities available to the public.

Serious U.S. attention to audit and evaluation procedures began in Congress in the late 1960s. In June 1970 a bill authorizing the next installment of IDA funding proposed a GAO audit of the Bank. In September, Robert McNamara issued an administrative circular within the Bank, noting that since 1968 budgetary and financial controls had been strengthened by creation of the Programming and Budgeting Department, establishment of the Audit Committee of the executive directors, and strengthening the Office of Internal Auditor. In addition, the circular called for establishing an Operations Evaluation Unit whose task would be "to review past lending operations with the central objective of establishing whether the actual benefits of the completed projects are in accordance with those expected at the time of appraisal and, in the case of divergence, the reason."[147] In mid-1971 this unit was converted into the Operations Evaluation Department. But for several years thereafter the United States urged independence from management of both the audit and evaluation operations. The OED, it argued, should be closely related to, if not directly under, the board.

In 1973 a GAO report once again recommended independent evaluations of Bank operations and activities. Legislation was proposed that would require the U.S. government to seek establishment of an independent evaluation unit in the World Bank (as Congress had previously mandated in 1967 for the International Development Bank) that would separate the postproject review system from the regular project implementation process. This step was taken by the Bank in July. The OED, along with the Internal Auditing Department, was made a separate department under a vice president who had no other direct operational responsibilities. But the matter did not end there.

146. At that time, each 1 percent depreciation of the dollar vis-à-vis other G-7 currencies eroded the Bank's headroom by $800 million.

147. Robert S. McNamara, administrative circular, September 2, 1970, p. 1.

In December 1973, legislation was approved requiring that the United States actively seek to establish an independent review and evaluation system under the Bank's governing body. The law also required that a statement of auditing and reporting standards be prepared by the U.S. comptroller-general to assist the Bank's board in devising terms of reference for an independent review system. The comptroller-general's statement, released in June 1974, proposed that the findings and related recommendations of the OED be reported to the Bank board. In response, McNamara proposed that the OED be formally linked to the board as well as to the president and that the head of the department be selected by the executive directors from a list of names put forward by the president. But the United States continued to urge even greater independence. It sought and achieved the establishment of the OED as a department that reported to the board. In addition, the staffing and design of the work program was to be the responsibility of the director-general of the OED, subject to review and approval of the board on which the president, as chair, would have a significant role. After that, McNamara lost interest in the operations of the OED. And for a time it was insignificant and not a source of much internal learning. Although the United States takes credit (as in the 1982 Treasury assessment) for fostering stronger audit and evaluation procedures, one might wonder how serious it ever was about project evaluation and impact and whether the poor record on project implementation, documented in the Bank-initiated 1992 Wapenhans report, would have occurred if the United States had reached a compromise with McNamara in the mid-1970s and addressed the issue of impact consistently.[148]

Since the early 1970s the United States has also pressured the Bank to make more of its analysis available to the public. Congress first focused on the idea largely out of frustration with the Treasury's lack of Hill consultation on Bank policy issues. Although the Treasury supported Congress's efforts to institute stricter audit and evaluation procedures, it did not endorse demands for greater disclosure of Bank country papers and loan documentation, claiming that greater transparency would undermine Bank operations. Both Treasury and Bank management took the position that it was up to the borrower government to decide what documents to release. With little movement on the issue having occurred, greater transparency was again pushed aggressively in the late 1980s and early 1990s by environmental nongovernmental organizations outraged by their inability to get documentation on Bank activities deemed environmentally detrimental. The Bank is now devising a change in practice, but the new procedures are certain to remain a matter of congressional scrutiny in the early years of implementation.

Overall, U.S. influence in the Bank in matters of administration, lending, and development policy appears to have had a mix of strongly favorable and seriously

---

148. Portfolio Management Task Force, "Effective Implementation: Key to Development Impact," World Bank, September 1992.

detrimental effects. On the positive side, the United States has used its influence to broaden the Bank's base of donor support; it has encouraged expansion of development focus and scope of lending; and it has achieved improvements in procedures of accountability and transparency of Bank operations.

On the negative side, however, the constant U.S. pursuit of narrow objectives, driven more by short-term foreign policy aims or domestic political imperatives than by concern for the effectiveness of Bank operations, has taken an inordinate amount of the time of the Bank's high-level management and has undermined staff morale. U.S. reluctance and delay in meeting its funding commitments have obliged senior management to devote large amounts of time in replenishment negotiations and in securing bridging arrangements.

U.S. pressure has also obliged the Bank to wage a constant fight for its autonomy. As a result, its leadership and staff have "developed a 'protective shell' of beliefs and practices" that, while insulating the Bank from U.S. pressures, has hindered its effective functioning.[149] It has spent far too much time, attention, and caution in developing loan proposals and has given inadequate consideration to potential risks and alternative approaches. At the same time, the United States along with other countries has pushed the Bank, especially in recent years, into more and more areas of activity without adequate assessment of existing institutional strengths and weaknesses and without sufficient questioning of how far the institutional capabilities could be stretched. This has caused a serious deterioration in the quality of the Bank's operations. The matter of loan quality has now been starkly illuminated by the Wapenhans report, and any discussion of the sources of the problem would be incomplete without attention to the role played by the members of the board, including the United States.[150]

Furthermore, the history of the World Bank shows that the choice of its president is crucial to the life of the institution. The past three appointments have not been strong. Even McNamara's dynamic tenure could not have been anticipated—at least there was nothing to suggest that he would be a leading development figure or that he was appointed with that in mind. The United States more than any other member country can be held accountable for the leadership the Bank has enjoyed from its birth to its approaching half-century mark.

Finally, and perhaps most seriously for the future of the Bank, the combination in the 1980s of U.S. policy inconsistencies, increased assertiveness on selected issues, and dwindling support has strained relations between the United States and other member countries. There is a growing sense among them that the United States has been overplaying its hand and causing unnecessary politicization and

149. William Ascher, "The World Bank and U.S. Control," in Margaret Karns and Karen Mingst, eds., *The United States and Multilateral Institutions* (Boston: Unwin Hyman, 1990), p. 116.
150. Portfolio Management Task Force, "Effective Implementation."

polarization of the Bank board. This resentment has been aggravated by the increase in the 1980s of congressional micromanagement of U.S. participation in the Bank. Generally, the United States has been more successful in advancing particular issues when it has worked to build consensus than when it has been mandated by Congress to vote a particular way. One result of the growing resentment is that Japan and the major donors of Europe are focusing more on other institutions in which they exercise greater control: the European Community's development fund, the newly launched European Bank for Reconstruction and Development, and the Asian Development Bank. Yet any weakening of the World Bank would seem to run counter to the interests of the United States, which have generally been well served by Bank policies and operations and at a remarkably low cost.

A Tally of Costs and Benefits

Over the past half century the United States has not only contributed to but has significantly benefited from the activities of the World Bank. The most comprehensive assessment to date of the costs and benefits of participation in the Bank was the 1982 Treasury report, which concluded unequivocally that the World Bank and the other multilateral development banks had been effective instruments of U.S. objectives. Referring specifically to the Bank, the report stated:

> On the whole, the policies and programs of the World Bank Group have been consistent with U.S. interests. This is particularly true in terms of general country allocation questions and sensitive policy issues. The international character of the World Bank, its corporate structure, the strength of the management team, and the Bank's weighted voting structure have ensured broad consistency between its policies and practices and the long term economic and political objectives of the United States.[151]

Referring to all the multilateral development banks together, it noted that they had been "most effective in contributing to the achievement of our *global economic and financial objectives* and thereby also helping us in our long term political/strategic interests." They were less effective instruments, however, for achieving short-term policy objectives, where identification of the assistance with the United States was important and, it emphasized, there was "room for improvement in terms of encouraging more effective economic policy reform in individual [less developed countries]."[152]

One of the main ways U.S. interests have been served is by Bank lending—far beyond an amount the United States was willing to provide bilaterally—to

---

151. Department of the Treasury, *United States Participation in Multilateral Development Banks*, p. 59.
    152. Ibid., p. 4.

countries of strategic or economic importance to the United States. Indeed, as has been frequently noted in executive branch testimony before Congress in defense of World Bank funding requests and reiterated in the Treasury assessment, most Bank lending has gone to those countries. The point is made, for example, in a letter from President Reagan to Robert Michel, the Republican leader in the House, urging support for the 1988 general capital increase: "The Bank commits the vast majority of its funds in support of specific investment projects in the middle income developing nations. These are mostly nations (such as the Philippines, Egypt, Pakistan, Turkey, Morocco, Tunisia, Mexico, Argentina, Indonesia and Brazil) that are strategically and economically important to the United States."[153]

Bank lending has also served broad U.S. economic interests in the building of a free, open, and stable international economic system. According to the Treasury assessment, "by promoting economic and social development in the Third World, fostering market-oriented economic policies, and preserving a reputation for impartiality and competence, the MDBs encourage developing countries to participate more fully in an international system based on liberalized trade and capital flows. . . . This means expanding opportunities for U.S. exports, investment, and finance." In addition, the ability of the multilateral banks to design and implement high-quality development loans has contributed to a more efficient process of development assistance. Their "capability to administer programs productively and efficiently ensures cost effectiveness and can maximize the use of scarce development resources."[154]

The United States has achieved these benefits for a remarkably low financial expenditure. Two points are relevant here. First, U.S. investment in the Bank and its contributions to IDA have been highly leveraged. In the case of the Bank the United States had paid in $1,857,100,000 of the $218,209,900,000 provided in loans as of mid-1992. In the case of IDA it has contributed a relatively larger share of the funds over the years, and the leveraging effect has been less but by no means insignificant. As of mid-1992 it had contributed $18,081,500,000 of the total $71,065,000,000 lent.[155]

Second, the net effect of the World Bank Group on the U.S. balance of payments has been positive (table 6-4). One reason is that the United States has received substantial procurement benefits: World Bank procurements have totaled $26,060,700,000. In addition, interest payments to U.S. bondholders living in the United States have been $20,169,700,000 and administrative expenses incurred in U.S. dollars in the United States, $10,948,700,000. These amounts have been the major factors contributing to a total net balance of payments effect (in real terms)

153. Letter from President Ronald Reagan to Representative Robert Michel, June 10, 1988, p. 1.
154. Department of the Treasury, *United States Participation in Multilateral Development Banks,* pp. 48, 52.
155. World Bank data.

Table 6-4. *World Bank and International Development Association Operations and U.S. Balance of Payments, Cumulative, 1946–91*
Millions of constant 1990 dollars

Operations	Total
World Bank	
Current account	
Procurement of goods[a]	26,060.7
Interest to bondholders[b]	20,169.7
Interest to loan holders	626.5
Administrative expenses including issuance cost of bonds[c]	10,948.7
Currency swap activity	−4,357.4
Investment income	16,916.7
Balance on current account	36,531.4
Capital account	
Assets	
U.S payment of 1 percent subscription	66.4
U.S. payment of 9 percent subscription	597.3
U.S. payments[d]	126.0
Local currency releases[e]	1,071.2
Net bond sales[f]	13,623.4
Net loan sales	−696.9
Total assets	14,787.4
Liabilities	
Investments with maturities over one year	20,645.3
Investments with maturities of one year or less	−110.2
Total liabilities	20,535.1
Balance of capital account	5,747.7
Net change	42,279.1
IDA	
Current account	
Procurement of goods[g]	5,112.3
Administrative expenses	4,612.6
Investment income[h]	−642.4
Balance on current acount	9,082.8
Capital account	
Assets	
Subscriptions and contributions[i]	18,634.4
Total assets	18,634.4
Liabilities	
Investments with maturities over one year	104.9
Investments with maturities of one year or less	117.8
Total liabilities	−12.9
Balance of capital account	−18,647.3
Net change	−9,564.6

Source: World Bank Treasury Department.

a. Includes procurements specifically identified as originating in the United States and the same proportion of procurement not identifiable by country of origin.

b. Interest payments to U.S. bondholders living in the United States.

c. Administrative expenses incurred in U.S. dollars in the United States, including the issuance cost of bonds.

d. Capital subscription paid by the United States.

e. Capital subscription in 18 percent national currencies released in U.S. dollars and used for loan disbursements.

f. Bonds sold for delayed delivery are included in the year in which settlement is made.

g. Includes procurements specifically identified as originating in the United States and the same proportion of procurement not identifiable by country of origin.

h. For years from inception through June 30, 1964, the ratio of average of U.S. investments to average total investments was applied to total investment income. For fiscal 1965 and subsequent years, the amount shown is the actual amount as computed for the statement "Statistical Summary of Funds Received by Source."

i. Excludes notes not encashed.

of \$42,279,000,000, which more than compensates for the net negative effect of support for IDA of some \$9,564,500,000. Obviously, U.S. contributions to the Bank entail an opportunity cost, but taking into account the political and economic interests served, the conclusion about U.S.-World Bank relations is one of shared benefit.

Conclusion

A number of broad observations can be drawn from this review of the history of the U.S. relations with the World Bank from 1945 to the early 1990s.

More than any other country, the United States has shaped and directed the institutional evolution, policies, and activities of the World Bank. And for the most part, U.S. participation has supported the institution's rise to prominence in development cooperation. The United States has applied pressure both to stop and to encourage particular loan agreements, but the greater influence has been at the level of policy and institutional evolution and growth. Much, though not all, of what the United States has promoted has helped foster constructive changes in the Bank, including the increase in agriculture and poverty-oriented lending, the increasing concentration of IDA lending on the poorest countries, the introduction, after some reluctance, of structural adjustment lending, and the recent attention to environmental sustainability and transparency of transactions.

Although U.S. support for the World Bank has shown some ups and downs, it has been more stable than other elements of U.S. economic assistance. This stability has largely been due to the value to the United States of the leveraging effect of contributions to the Bank, perceptions of the Bank's relative effectiveness as a provider of both development financing and policy advice, and the view held by most administrations and members of Congress that the Bank contributes to the broad interest of the United States in a growing and open world economy. With the exception of Reagan's first administration, all administrations since the Bank's founding have advanced these views and, with only few exceptions, leading Republicans and Democrats in Congress have concurred.

Criticisms of the World Bank from various voices in the United States have, however, greatly intensified since the mid-1970s. These opinions have come from all points on the political spectrum, including churches and other NGOs, the traditional bulwarks of support for development assistance. In part the criticism reflects the increased prominence of the Bank in development and the closer scrutiny it receives. In part it reflects changing ideas about development, not all of which suit Bank lending operations as easily as the earlier preoccupations with infrastructure development. And in part the criticism reflects the loss of a clear sense of purpose and direction in U.S. development policy, for which the Bank is but one instrument.

U.S. policy toward the World Bank has always reflected an underlying ambivalence toward both development assistance and multilateral cooperation. Recognizing the long-term benefits of the relatively efficient and relatively depoliticized development financing the Bank offers, the United States has also looked upon it as an instrument of foreign policy that was expected to be responsive to short-term U.S. positions. As a result, U.S. policy toward the Bank and the positions it has taken within the Bank have been erratic, often reflecting more the ebb and flow of U.S. politics and foreign policy than a coherent view of the Bank's development financing and a steadfast concern for the effectiveness of its operations.

Two features of the policy process have strongly influenced the character of U.S. World Bank policy. On the one hand the dominant role of the Treasury has limited the development content of U.S. policy and participation in the Bank. On the other hand Congress and, indirectly, NGOs have been instrumental in designing U.S. Bank policy. This involvement has influenced Treasury's dominant role, keeping development concerns in sharper focus in the formation of U.S. policy than might otherwise have been the case. But Congress has also been a conduit for particularistic views on Bank lending and has been responsible for the proliferation of restrictions and demands on the Bank that have been unilaterally promoted by the United States. Debates in Congress have also led to frequent failures on the part of the United States to deliver its share of negotiated replenishments within an internationally agreed time frame and have forced other countries to make up for temporary U.S. shortfalls to avoid a break in IDA lending. Both kinds of actions have eroded U.S. influence on the board of the Bank and on the Bank's efficiency.

Finally, the United States has also pressed successfully for ever greater burden sharing by other developed country members of the Bank. But it has resisted the power sharing that ought to go along with their growing financial contributions. If the United States wants to see the Bank continue to function and evolve in ways consistent with U.S. interests, it will have to dedicate effective personnel to its Bank policy positions (including the position of U.S. executive director), arrive at an understanding with Congress on the major priorities of U.S. policy toward the Bank, structure development policy expertise into its Bank policymaking process, and engage actively with other member countries in consensus building. It must shed the ideological strictures of the past decade of U.S. Bank policy and develop with other countries, notably Japan, the policy guidance for and oversight of the challenging new era of the World Bank's second half century.

SEVEN

Japan and the World Bank

Toyoo Gyohten

JAPAN'S POSTWAR "miracle" was the result of many factors, including abundant and diligent human resources, the socioeconomic structure inherited from before the war, export drives, and government industrial policies. These are the self-help efforts on which the philosophy of today's Japanese development assistance is based. In addition, Japan relied on external assistance until the early 1960s, mainly from the United States and the World Bank. Indeed, during the early 1960s the size of Japan's loan outstanding from the Bank was second only to India's, but the Bank believed it was safe to lend to Japan. In the thirteen years that Japan borrowed from the Bank, the loans brought many things, including new and rebuilt physical infrastructure and knowledge of software and technologies. Because of its rapid economic growth, Japan graduated from borrowing from the Bank in 1966. In 1971, as the Bank's funding in the Tokyo market increased, Japan became a net creditor to it. In 1990, repayment was completed and Japan genuinely graduated from the Bank. The first part of the World Bank–Japan relationship is thus a history of graduation.

The most recent relationship is based on increasing interaction. Since the late 1970s Japan's positions at international financial institutions (IFIs) have become important because of its increasing economic presence. It became the second-largest shareholder (the United States is the largest) at the Bank in 1984. Financial contributions have been made and positions taken, but Japan's human and intellectual contributions to these institutions are still somewhat delayed. Now, the country is more than ever expected to play an important role in the IFIs, among them the World Bank.

The objectives of this chapter are threefold. First, it tells the history of the World Bank and Japan, a story of graduation, emphasizing the experiences of individual projects and their implications. Second, the section titled "The Asian Perspective" reviews the recent discussions between the World Bank and Japan on how to understand economic development with respect to experiences in East Asia. The third section contemplates the present and future perspectives of the World Bank and Japan and gives some comments on both.

Overview of the World Bank–Japan Relationship

From 1945 until 1952 Japan was occupied by the Allied powers. Throughout the country defeatism prevailed. Economic hardship overshadowed future prospects. Postwar inflation occurred because of money-financed wartime expenditures and was followed by a sharp decline in production, mainly in iron and coal. Fearing total destruction of the economy, the government introduced the Priority Production System (PPS), which allocated resources heavily to priority sectors. As a result, industrial output climbed to more than 70 percent of its prewar level.[1] But the PPS created credit-line expansion financed by the Bank of Japan as well as fiscal expansion through increased government subsidies and not only exacerbated inflation but also introduced huge distortions into the economy.

In 1949, to alleviate the situation, Joseph Dodge, an economic advisor to the Allied powers, imposed fiscal and monetary austerity. Under the Dodge stabilization policy, a single exchange rate of $1 = ¥360, to be maintained until 1971, replaced the multiple exchange rates and prepared the ground for Japan's comeback in the world economy. Although the deflationary effects of the stabilization policy were so acute that the number of bankruptcies skyrocketed and unemployment increased, it is certain that the policy initiated the normalization of the economy.

In the early 1950s the Korean War brought windfall gains to the Japanese economy through increased consumer demand and export opportunities and paved the way to the rapid growth that followed. As the economy started to normalize, it became increasingly clear that infrastructure was the main bottleneck for further reconstruction and development. In this regard, it is worth noting that Japan had an advanced economy even before the war: it experienced takeoff from 1878 to 1900.[2] Thus the initial stages of the postwar economic evolution can be seen as reconstruction rather than new development. Although domestic savings were relatively high compared with that in today's less developed countries, they were insufficient

1. Fusae Ota, Hiroya Tanikawa, and Tasuke Otani, *Russia's Economic Reform and Japan's Industrial Policy* (Tokyo: Research Institute of International Trade and Industry, Ministry of International Trade and Industry [MITI/RI], 1992).

2. Walt W. Rostow, *The Stages of Economic Growth: A Non-Communist Manifesto* (Cambridge University Press, 1960).

to accommodate the huge demand. Thus Japan started seeking possible sources of capital abroad.[3]

In response to the emergence of communist regimes in Asia as well as a surge of leftists in Japan, the United States granted a large sum of aid, mainly the Government and Relief in Occupied Areas (GARIOA) and the Economic Rehabilitation in Occupied Areas (EROA) assistance to Japan in parallel with the Marshall Plan in Europe. The GARIOA and EROA supported vital imports of food and materials for industrial production, some $2.1 billion worth from 1946 to 1952.[4] The U.S. government's intention was to reduce assistance to Japan gradually and to achieve balance of payments equilibrium by about 1952. When the assistance was actually terminated in 1952, the Japanese economy was bolstered by the Korean War and the balance of payments situation was improved. Through his stabilization policy, Dodge introduced a counterpart fund system under which revenues in local currency from resales of aid-financed import goods were kept in a government fund, separate from fiscal budget. These were used to improve infrastructure and provided part of the original capital of the Japan Development Bank.[5]

On the political front the supreme commander of the Allied powers was transcendent and controlled almost all government activities, including diplomatic undertakings. The peace treaty signed in San Francisco became effective on April 28, 1952, which meant that Japan was restored to full sovereignty in the international community. Against this background, the Japanese government started negotiations to join the Bretton Woods institutions.

Japan and the Bretton Woods Institutions

Although economic assistance from the United States was terminated in 1952, the shortage of capital in Japan was obvious, and it appears that the U.S. government intended to switch sources of economic assistance from its own budget to the World Bank to lessen the burden on American taxpayers. But assistance to West Germany was continued by the newly established U.S. Economic Assistance Agency (ECA), and World Bank lending was never granted to West Germany. It is arguable that the NATO framework made Americans more attached to Germany than to Japan, which worked in West Germany's favor.

Given the termination of aid, Japanese authorities were eager to join the Bretton Woods institutions as a key step toward international recognition, even though the

3. Because of the shortage of domestic savings, the introduction of foreign capital was given policy priority by the Yoshida cabinet.

4. According to Ministry of Finance, *Showa Zaisei Shi: Shusen kara Kowa made,* vol. 3 [The History of Fiscal Policies in the Showa Period: From Surrender to the Peace Treaty] (Tokyo: Toyo Keizai Shimpo-sha, 1976), p. 272. Total U.S. overseas assistance from 1945 to 1958 was $72 billion.

5. Based on such experience, Overseas Economic Cooperation Fund (OECF) program loans require borrowing countries to establish counterpart funds.

peace treaty was yet to be signed.[6] In April 1950 Minister of Finance Hayato Ikeda visited Washington and expressed the Japanese government's informal intention to join the International Monetary Fund (IMF).[7] The Fund welcomed the statement and requested the government to provide data on Japan's balance of payments, fiscal budget, inflation, and so forth. The newspapers applauded the intention as a significant step toward Japan's return to the international community.

Japanese officials examined the pros and cons of membership in the Bretton Woods institutions. The benefits included the psychological effects on the Japanese of asserting the country's international standing, the increased credibility of the yen, credits from the IMF, loans from the World Bank, and the pump-priming effects of promoting private financial inflows through increased creditworthiness. The costs and burden of joining included the discontinuation of foreign exchange controls, IMF approval before altering exchange rates, and that the benefits of membership might not be large—that is, credits and loans from the institutions might not be available immediately.

Through such considerations, government officials concluded that while direct benefits might not be immediately tangible, at least the psychological and diplomatic implication that Japan had taken a significant step was important. They assumed that benefits from World Bank loans would be more direct and substantial than those of the IMF credits, although they did not have a clear plan of how much to borrow or to what sector or project to allocate the loans.[8]

Diet Discussions and Public Response

Soon after the peace treaty had become effective, the Japanese government began formal consideration of the Bretton Woods issues. In May 1952 the Diet started discussion on the IMF–World Bank Articles of Agreement and associated domestic legislation. The government's explanations on the necessity for membership were that direct benefits might not be immediate and tangible, but they would bring increased creditworthiness and thus give the country access to foreign capital. Legislators asked Hayato Ikeda how much the country might be able to borrow

6. Italy joined the International Monetary Fund before it resumed international sovereignty, and Japanese authorities saw that as a precedent. However, after examining the pros and cons it was concluded that membership in the Bretton Woods institutions was not of urgent concern.

7. At the time, Japan was occupied, and such international deals had to be endorsed by the Allied powers to become effective. Indeed, the supreme commander of the Allies, General Douglas MacArthur, did not approve the official request for membership in the IMF and the World Bank. Finally the request was made on August 9, 1952, after the departure of General MacArthur.

8. They were preoccupied by the problem of how to pay the IMF quota and the World Bank subscription, because they believed that Japan's gold and foreign currency reserves were insufficient.

from the Bank. The finance minister did not give exact figures but again stressed the importance of creditworthiness that membership in the Bretton Woods institutions would bring. There was also a question of whether the government had a specific borrowing plan. An official answered that although there were no concrete plans, infrastructure, especially hydroelectric power development, was expected to be the major beneficiary of the Bank loans. Legislation approving membership passed both the lower and upper houses of the Diet by mid-June, and the Japanese ambassador in Washington signed the Articles of Agreement on August 13, 1952.[9] Japan had become the fifty-second member of the IMF and the Bank. It was the ninth largest shareholder, and was raised to eighth and then seventh by capital increases in 1959 and 1965.

The Japanese public welcomed IMF and Bank membership, which was remarkable considering that there was substantial anti-American feeling and the Bretton Woods institutions were regarded as American agents.[10] But it is important to remember that Japan achieved the membership well before joining the United Nations in 1956. This fact symbolizes the significance of the event as a step toward full-fledged participation in the international community and future economic power.

After the seventh IMF and Bank annual meeting, though it was the first for Japan, an election was held for the IMF–World Bank Board of Governors and Japan was elected one of the executive directors.[11] It was to represent the constituency of Japan, Thailand, Burma, and Ceylon (Sri Lanka).[12]

The World Bank Mission to Japan

In July 1952 Eugene Black, president of the World Bank, indicated that the first Bank mission to Japan would be sent once the country became a member. The purpose of the mission was not to appraise individual projects but to identify

9. West Germany joined the IMF and the Bank the next day.

10. Newspapers reported the signing with headlines such as "Japan Returns to the International Economic Community: It Joins the IMF and the World Bank." See "Kokusai keizai shakai ni fukki: Tsuuka kekin, Sekai ginko e seishiki kamei," *Asahi Shimbun*, August 14, 1952, p. 1. Anti-American resentment, mainly caused by harsh U.S. economic policy toward Japan and reinforced by leftist influence, was widely felt among Japanese during and immediately after the Dodge stabilization period.

11. In the process of membership negotiations, the Japanese government insisted that the IMF quota as well as Bank subscription be $300 million to $350 million rather than the $250 million indicated for member countries of the IMF, because the amount should be "appropriate to Japan's international standing." An official of the Ministry of Finance has written, "We were quite disappointed to know how the world saw Japan after the defeat." Shichiro Murai, "Kokusai Tsuuka Kikin ni Kamei Surumade" [The Way to IMF Membership], *Gaikoku Kawase*, vol. 57 (1952), pp. 1–4. In the same spirit, Japanese officials thought that Japan deserved seats on the boards of the IMF and the Bank.

12. Nepal, Singapore, Laos, and Malaysia joined the constituency later.

Japan's general economic condition as well as potential projects for Bank financing. Before the mission, a Bank staff member suggested that the mission's priority would be potential projects rather than a general economic survey because basic data were readily available.[13] Such a reversal was unusual for a first mission to a new recipient country: in other developing countries, where basic soft infrastructure was lacking, the first mission would spend much of its time and resources to collect and process basic data.

The government had held a number of vice ministerial meetings to discuss the projects proposed to the Bank, and on October 18, 1952, it published a report, "Projects for Which Loans from the International Bank for Reconstruction and Development Are Desired." The report included seven projects that were expected to cost about $900 million.[14] When the proposals were disclosed, an ardent petition was issued by the Japan Electric Machinery Manufacturers Association, headed by Taizo Ishizaka, demanding that the loans for power development not be used to import foreign generators.[15] The reasons the association gave were that Japanese manufacturers had enough capability to meet domestic demand and were now seeking export opportunities; they were making efforts to upgrade their products through licensing from foreign firms; and imported generators would not only damage domestic manufacturers, but also affect the international reputation of Japanese products, thus impeding export possibilities. It is not clear how or whether the government and the Bank reacted at the time, but at least the petition shows that Japanese manufacturers were determined to achieve self-reliance and intended to expand exports.[16]

The mission arrived in Tokyo in October and stayed until January 1953. Robert Garner, vice president of the Bank, joined the mission in December and participated in a great many sessions with government officials, prefectural officials, and private sector entrepreneurs. During these road shows, some prefectural governors and entrepreneurs requested Bank loans for projects not listed on the government proposals. This was a reflection of the high expectations they had for the loans, but such unorganized lobbying as well as excessive geisha entertainment

13. IMF staff had been involved in making laws on foreign exchange control before Japan became a member of the IMF.

14. The projects were hydroelectric power development, highway construction, electrification of the Japan National Railway, industrial port construction, development of a new air transport system, modernization of the iron and steel industry, and coal shaft development. Some of these proposals were later funded by the Bank and some were not. Government of Japan, "Projects for Which Loans from the International Bank for Reconstruction and Development Are Desired" (Tokyo, October 18, 1952).

15. Ishizaka was president of Tokyo Shibaura Denki (Toshiba). In 1952 he was elected president of Keidanren, the most powerful business lobby in Japan.

16. When the hydroelectric power project was financed by the Bank, it was done with a so-called impact loan, which did not exclude local cost financing. However, it is difficult to establish a relationship between this fact and the petition.

seemed to have irritated the Bank officials.[17] Upon his departure, Garner held a news briefing at which he expressed his stern views on the Japanese economy and the state of affairs in the country.[18] First, he said, the government was trying to borrow more than Japan could afford, and therefore the proposed projects should be very carefully scrutinized. Second, he said that officials should have a more concrete plan of how they wanted to develop the economy. Third, he pointed out that because its balance of payments situation was still unstable, Japan should try to capture export markets in Southeast Asia. Bank assistance to Southeast Asian countries would then be a roundabout but effective way to assist Japanese economic development. He was even reported as saying that before it would deserve Bank loans, Japan needed Scottish chartered accountants to rectify what he saw as a messy state of affairs.

In Washington, Garner reported the results of the mission to the World Bank Board. Again he expressed skepticism about Japan's borrowing capability. He added that he had suggested to Prime Minister Yoshida that a government body for coordinating an overall borrowing plan be established, and he understood that the prime minister mentioned the suggestion in the Diet. Although such a coordinating entity was not established, coordination among the ministries was strengthened and no similar complaints were heard from the Bank again.

The First Loan: Thermal Power Plants

In November 1952 the Kansai Electric Power Company made a request for an exporter's credit to the Export-Import Bank of Washington to import two 66,000-kW steam generators from an American manufacturer.[19] Groundwork for the credit had been commissioned in autumn 1952 by Kansai Electric and the Japan Development Bank as the on-lender to the company. The Eximbank's response was favorable, and the Japanese government listed the project on the national power development program in March 1953. The listing was followed by the approval of the project by the bank's board in May. However, in June 1953 the U.S. Congress passed legislation that reduced the terms of reference of the Eximbank to short-term credits only and switched longer-term financing to the World Bank.[20]

17. It was said that Ministry of Finance officials had tried to arrange a geisha entertainment, allegedly at Garner's request. Reports went on to say, however, that Minister of Finance Tadaharu Mukai rejected the idea because he thought it was inappropriate for a country asking for assistance from the Bank to indulge in such extravagance. I do not know whether the story is true.

18. Press statement issued by Robert L. Garner, vice president, International Bank for Reconstruction and Development, Tokyo, December 19, 1952.

19. Similar arrangements were being made by the Chubu Electric Power Company and the Kyushu Electric Power Company. Eventually, all three projects were financed by the first loan.

20. There was a struggle between World Bank President Eugene Black and Eximbank Chairman Herbert Gaston. Black tried to persuade the Japanese ambassador in Washington

Following the change in U.S. policy, the Japanese government reluctantly submitted an application for a Bank loan in June 1953.[21] The Bank proposed conditions to the loan, mainly:

—Three beneficiary power companies should raise their power supply prices to strengthen their financial positions. Therefore, it was recommended that the government commit itself to a prompt increase in power supply prices.

—The proposed five-year power development plan was too ambitious and needed to be scrutinized further. Moreover, it was recommended that the government commit itself to improve debt-equity ratios of the power companies.

—Along with power development, reducing system losses was also important and effective. So the government should commit itself to efforts to reduce the losses.

In principle the government accepted the conditions, but the proposal to raise power prices triggered considerable debate among Japanese bureaucrats and politicians. It was astonishing to the Japanese that the World Bank should demand such a sensitive alteration in policy: keeping power prices low was regarded as a fundamental benefit for much of the Japanese population. As a compromise the government agreed that it would approve price increases "with reasonable promptness." This episode has a significance beyond surface events: through negotiations, Japanese officials had learned that the Bank was not a mere moneylender but an institution that cared very much for the details and outcomes of its projects.

Another issue was guarantee conditions. In the beginning the government considered that as a government agency the Japan Development Bank did not need official guarantees. However, the World Bank insisted that a government guarantee was required even if the JOB was the borrower and on-lender to the power companies, and that this condition was to be customary for all other loans. Finally, the government had to accept the Bank's argument, and three types of draft agreements were prepared—a World Bank–Japanese government guarantee agreement, a Bank-JOB loan agreement, and project agreements between the Bank and power companies.[22]

Yet another problem was the negative pledge clause. The Bank demanded that its position as creditor to Japan should be no less favorable than that of other

---

that the financing for the steam power generator should come from the World Bank rather than Eximbank. He implied that the amount of the already proposed loans for hydroelectric power development ($120 million) would be reduced should Japan get financing from the Eximbank for the steam power generator. For competition in lending to Japan in general, see Edward S. Mason and Robert E. Asher, *The World Bank Since Bretton Woods* (Brookings, 1973), pp. 500–01.

21. The proposed terms of Eximbank loans were more favorable than those of the World Bank. Moreover, the Japanese government's intention was to finance hydroelectric development with a World Bank *impact* loan. The World Bank loan for the steam power projects was a *tied* loan—that is, the proceeds of the loan were for imports of specific items.

22. The government needed special legislation to enable it to enter into the guarantee arrangement.

creditors. This meant that even assets of the Bank of Japan could be collateralized for loans from the World Bank. The Japanese government opposed the condition, but the Bank, being skeptical about Japan's borrowing capacity, took a stern stance, and at last the government had to accept the condition. When the agreement was disclosed in September 1953, Japanese media assailed the government's negotiation position as "traitorous" and "an act of shame."

However disputable, these conditions were finally settled, and officials were looking forward to signing the agreements. But just before they were to be signed, there was a snag: negative pledge clauses were found in loan agreements between the power companies and Japanese commercial banks. This reawakened the dispute, and the signing was postponed. The World Bank demanded that all the loan agreements with the commercial banks be translated into English and submitted for its scrutiny. It further demanded that the loan agreements be altered so as not to compromise its position as the superior creditor. These done, it still delayed the signing. But at last, on October 15, 1953, the first loan agreement for $40.2 million between the Bank and the JOB, the guarantee agreement between the Bank and the Japanese government, and the project agreements between the Bank and the power companies were signed in Washington.

In these early negotiations there were significant culture shocks experienced by both the Bank and Japanese officials. To the Japanese the conditions stipulated in the agreements seemed much too detailed and exhaustive of the possible scenarios. Such a contractual form was quite foreign to a society in which implicit long-term confidence among parties had been of the utmost importance and strict legal contracts were rare. By the same token, it could be argued that during the negotiations, Bank officials were unusually alert and suspicious. Supposedly this was the result of the skepticism the Garner mission had brought back. As dealings between Japan and the Bank deepened, however, such cultural gaps were narrowed and the Bank came to regard Japan as a model borrower.

The Era of Rapid Growth

From 1955 to 1966, the year of the last World Bank loan, Japan borrowed thirty times for a total of more than $800 million. The loans were used to develop basic industries, power, roads and railways, and agriculture. The following are some experiences of the Bank loans during this period of rapid growth.

IRON AND STEEL SECTOR. The World Bank's skepticism about Japan's ability to repay its debts persisted, and the second Bank loan was made two years after the first. When the Priority Production System ended in 1949, it was clear that Japan's iron and steel industry could not compete internationally. The first modernization plan was carried out from 1950 to 1954, financed mainly by domestic resources. After 1954 a second plan totaling ¥120,000 million (about $330 million) for further modernization was outlined. However, to keep the country's budget balanced, domestic finance was restricted. So the government of Japan sought Bank loans to carry out the plan. Along with other modernization programs the plan was explained to a Bank mission, headed by Russel Dorr, that visited Japan in October 1953. The mission's objective was threefold: to identify and discuss Japan's macroeconomic and sectoral policies, to examine the Bank's overall lending plan for Japan, and to conclude legalities involving the first loan. The mission pointed out that the government needed prudent macroeconomic policies to curb inflationary pressure and sincere efforts to promote exports, especially to Southeast Asia. It concluded that agriculture, iron and steel, and coal mining would be the focus of the Bank's interest. As for the government's request for so-called impact loans, the mission's answer was that such loans were exceptional and should not be applied to Japan.[23]

Following the mission, Bank President Eugene Black, still doubtful of Japan's borrowing capacity, sent a letter in July 1954 to Minister of Finance Sankuro Ogasawara stating that it was understood that the borrowing Japan could afford would be $100 million a year. The mission identified agriculture, iron and steel, and coal mining as priority sectors for Bank financing. The Bank was willing to finance the proposed hydroelectric project if technical aspects were worked out satisfactorily.[24]

Appraisal work was carried out, and the loan agreement for the modernization project of Yawata Iron and Steel Co., Ltd., was signed in October 1955. The agreement included a condition allowing loans to strengthen the financial position of the company, which was novel both to Yawata and the Japan Development Bank. The Yawata loan was the inception of Bank financing in the manufacturing sector. Following the loan, the Bank financed a package of four industrial projects for a total of $8.1 million in Japanese fiscal year 1955. The loan covered the iron and steel, automobile, and shipbuilding industries. The notable feature of this package was that the Bank did not demand agreements with individual companies, which added flexibility to project implementation.

In 1956 the Japanese government's economic white paper stated, "the postwar economic rush is over," signaling that the Japanese economy had entered another stage of stable growth. In December 1956 a loan agreement for modernization and expansion of the Kawasaki Steel Chiba factory was signed. Two years of painful efforts had finally been rewarded.

When the project was first announced, there was considerable criticism of it. The plan envisaged the first integrated steel mill in Japan, with an annual capacity of 500,000 tons of crude steel, 10 percent of the nation's production at the time.

23. The government's perception was that the local cost part rather than foreign currency portion of the project was underfunded; as a result, officials wanted to introduce untied impact loans. Impact loans were defined as exceptional in article IV, sections 3(b) and (c) of the Articles of Agreement.

24. Nihon Kaihatsu Ginko, *Kokusai Fukkou Kaihatsu Ginko Karyoku Shakkan* [The IBRD Loan for Steam Power Plants] (Tokyo: Japan Development Bank, 1955), p. 321.

The project was regarded as too risky. It ran contrary to the government's policy of scaling down investment in the sector. The Bank loan would not cover all of the cost, and the associated demand for enormous local matching funds would crowd out borrowing by other industries. Any expected cost reductions in the price of iron were doubtful because of the large interest payments and depreciation costs. Finally, the market for sheet steel would stumble as a result of the increased capacity. However, Kawasaki, determined to introduce a Bank loan, convinced both the government and the Bank that growing demand for sheet steel and export possibilities could be gained by cost reductions.[25]

Along with other steel manufacturers, Kawasaki got two more Bank loans.[26] But having been assured of Japan's creditworthiness and ability to borrow from the private sector, the Bank set conditions for these loans, such as strengthening the companies' financial positions. Moreover, in the 1960s the Bank extended loans only when a joint market-based offering, that is, bond finance, was made. In summary, the Bank's main contributions to the Japanese iron and steel sector were enabling the introduction of new processes and reminding companies of the importance of a healthy financial position.

POWER DEVELOPMENT. Although the first World Bank loan to Japan was to develop thermal power generation, the power companies, having experienced what they considered needlessly tedious procedures associated with the loans, became increasingly reluctant to borrow from the Bank and turned to the Export-Import Bank.[27] In view of such circumstances, President Black visited Japan in May 1957. Upon arrival, he issued a statement in which he indicated that impact loans could be provided to Japan and that the terms were flexible, subject to the condition of the national economy and the types of projects. Black held a meeting with Finance Minister Hayato Ikeda, and they basically agreed that the Bank loans were to be used for power development, road construction, and industry, especially the iron and steel sector, and the terms of the loans were to be flexible. Both parties were keen to see economic development in Southeast Asia. During his visit, Black saw the realities of the Japanese economy and altered his earlier view of Japan's

25. Kawasaki applied for the loan as early as May 1954. However, the Bank pointed out the company's financial weakness and demanded that it show improvements in this regard. To meet the Bank's demand, Kawasaki suspended dividend payments for one and a half years and increased internal reserves. It also scaled back a part of the project in line with the Bank's recommendation.

26. The second loan for the Kawasaki project, signed on January 29, 1958, was the first impact loan to Japan.

27. By this time, Eximbank had resumed its provision of long-term financing. In November 1960 a staff member of the World Bank told the Japan Development Bank that if power companies tried to introduce Eximbank loans tied to American products, it would be difficult for World Bank staff to persuade the board to approve impact loans to Japan. Nihon Kaihatsu Ginko, *Nihon Kaihatsu Ginko Juu-nen-Shi* [Ten Years of JOB] (Tokyo: Japan Development Bank, 1963), p. 327.

borrowing capacity.[28] After his visit, Bank operations in Japan became more active than ever. Consequently, a rush on loans ensued: eight projects totaling $174 million, including power projects, were approved by the Bank in just thirteen months.

Following the Black mission, the Bank financed six power development projects, five of them hydroelectric. The most notable was the Kurobe No. 4 (258,000-kW) project, for which the Bank granted an impact loan of $37 million. Kurobe Valley is located in the middle of a mountainous area, and power development had been considered since the early 1900s. Before the war five middle-size power stations were built, but their output was not enough to accommodate postwar increases in demand. In September 1957 the Japanese government applied for impact loans, including the one for Kurobe No. 4.

When appraisal work had been finished and loan negotiations were ready to wind up, Japanese newspapers reported that the power companies were to be reorganized.[29] This news made the Bank doubtful of the government's policy integrity as well as the viability of the project because reorganization appeared to make power companies financially even weaker through the merger of efficient companies with less efficient ones. So the Bank once more raised the question of the pricing of power. For clarification it demanded a letter from the Ministry for International Trade and Industry (MITI) stating that the government did not intend to merge power companies and that necessary actions to improve the financial positions of the power companies would be taken.

This demand ignited fierce debates among politicians and bureaucrats, and the matter was brought before the cabinet. After two months of debate, the cabinet approved the MITI letter, although it had watered down the commitment to price increases. Thus even after five years of dealings, the government was still quite uncomfortable with Bank demands that involved touchy political matters. The loan agreement for the Kurobe project was signed on June 13, 1958, and "the dam project of the century" entered into full-fledged construction. The construction took seven years and introduced frontier technologies, which were employed later by other Bank-financed projects such as motorways and the bullet train.

MOTORWAY PROJECTS. Plans for a motorway in the industrial belt stretching from Tokyo through Nagoya to Osaka had been on the table since the 1930s. Because of the war and postwar turbulence, the plan had been postponed, but as the economy grew, it became clear that the motorway was badly needed. In 1956 a team of American consultants headed by Ralph J. Watkins came to Japan and carried out extensive survey work on the state of the roads and issued a report, "Kobe-Nagoya Expressway Survey for the Ministry of Construction." The conclusion of the report states concisely, "The roads of Japan are incredibly bad. No

28. In 1956 the annual growth rate of GDP was 6.4 percent and of manufacturing output 23.1 percent. See Shigeo Ohara, *Nempyo de miru Nihon keizai no ashi dori,* 2d ed. [The History of Japan with a Chronological Table] (Tokyo: Zaikei Shyouhou-sha, 1994), pp. 56–57.

29. After the war the national power company had been divided into nine companies.

other industrial nation has so completely neglected its highway system." And it adds that neglect of the system "is imposing a heavy cost burden on the Japanese economy."[30] The Nihon Doro Kodan (Japan Highway Public Corporation) reviewed the recommendations of the Watkins report and published its own report, which formed the foundation of the Bank appraisal work that followed.

From the beginning the Nihon Doro Kodan contemplated bond financing for the project, but because of the poor performance of American toll road projects, the market for road construction bonds was unpromising. But the World Bank, following the Black mission, indicated that it was willing to extend impact loans, and the Japanese government made a request in September 1957. A Bank fact-finding mission came to Japan in February 1958 and recommended that the Doro Kodan employ foreign consultants. The company requested its German counterpart to nominate an appropriate expert for the project. Xaner Dorsch, a veteran engineer of the German autobahn, visited Japan and gave detailed recommendations on the design of the motorway. His recommendation included application of clothoid curve designing, which had become an international standard but had yet to be introduced in Japan.[31]

Because of the "complete neglect," the basic know-how of motorway construction was lacking in Japan, and construction companies had to rely heavily on foreign consultants. But Japanese road engineers mastered new technologies quickly by working closely with the consultants.[32] The concept and importance of independent consultants was new to Japan, where in-house engineers dealt with technical matters, which limited technical spillover as well as objective evaluation of technologies. Through their experiences with consultants, in-house engineers in road construction, plant engineering, power, telecommunications, and other industries started to become independent, and some have now achieved international reputations.

On March 17, 1960, almost four years after the Watkins report, the $40 million first loan for the Doro Kodan project was approved by the Bank. Five more loans, including the last Bank loan to Japan, followed, covering the cost of most of the motorway between Tokyo and Kobe.

Although the loans to the Doro Kodan were impact loans, certain portions of the construction work were open to international competitive bidding. In the third loan an American construction company submitted the cheapest bid and was awarded

30. Kobe-Nagoya Expressway Survey Team, "Kobe-Nagoya Expressway Survey for the Ministry of Construction," August 1956, p. 14.

31. A clothoid is a curve such that the rate of changes in the direction of a car driving at constant speed is fixed; the driver need only turn the wheel at a constant speed. World Bank Tokyo Office, *Segin shakkan kaisou* [Memoir of the World Bank Loans to Japan] (Tokyo, 1991a), p. 69.

32. Xaner Dorsch and Paul Sonderegger, an American soil specialist, visited Japan every year until 1964. A group of engineers who worked closely with Dorsch called themselves the "Dorsch School." Nihon Doro Kodan, *Sekai ginko shakkan keii*, vol. 1 [The World Bank Loan] (Tokyo, 1969).

the contract.[33] This was the first foreign company to win a contract in a Bank project in Japan, and the Bank was pleased to know that international competitive bidding had proven effective. However, because the company could not establish cooperative relationships with local subcontractors and engineers, the progress of its work was slow and it finally canceled the contract. According to Doro Kodan records, there appeared to be two main reasons for the cancellation. First, because of an economic boom at the time, good local civil engineers were attracted by larger construction companies. Second, there had been a *keiretsu* relationship among Japanese contractors and subcontractors, and it was very difficult for a foreign company to get acceptance.

In March 1961 Burke Knapp, vice president of the Bank, had a meeting with the finance minister and indicated that the proposed second loan to the Doro Kodan would be the Bank's last public sector loan to Japan. Loans to the private sector would also be gradually reduced. This was the first suggestion of Japan's graduation from World Bank loans.[34] At the Bank board, the matter of graduation was raised by developing countries whenever loans to Japan were discussed. On such occasions Japan claimed that although industrialization had progressed, the government was experiencing shortages of capital to improve the long-standing inadequacy of basic infrastructure. Officials also asserted that Japan was increasing its assistance to developing countries through International Development Association contributions as well as bilateral assistance.[35]

THE BULLET TRAIN. Today, the 500-kilometer trip from Tokyo to Osaka takes only two and one-half hours by *Shinkansen* bullet train. At the foot of the *Shinkansen* platform in Tokyo station there is a plaque with the inscription, "This railway was accomplished by the wisdom and toil of the nation." Indeed, as was the Tokyo-Kobe motorway, the bullet train was a long-standing project. It was first suggested to the Bank by Minister of Finance Eisaku Sato at the Bank-IMF annual meeting in 1958. Examination of the project and of Japan National Railways (JNR), the prospective borrower, started soon after. In the initial stages the Bank was

33. According to a Bank official, this company was not a first-rate one in the United States, and the Bank was rather surprised to learn that it had been selected. Nihon Doro Kodan, *Sekai ginko shakkan keii*, vol. 3, p. 139.

34. Following Knapp's statement, Eugene Black also suggested Japan's graduation at a Bank board meeting, although he added he was prepared to consider additional loans if economic conditions changed. Consequently, Doro Kodan became pessimistic about additional loans from the Bank and sought to sell a bond issue in the U.S. market to finance the remaining part of the Tokyo-Kobe project. See the section "Graduation from the Bank Loans: What Japan Gained" later in this chapter.

35. Japan was an original member and the sixth largest contributor to IDA. Japanese bilateral assistance has its roots in 1950s and 1960s reparation payments to Asian countries that it formerly occupied. Japan's first attempt at development assistance was its participation in the Colombo Plan in 1954. The first yen loan to a developing country was made to India in 1958 by the Export-Import Bank of Japan. The Overseas Economic Cooperation Fund, which deals with yen soft loans, was established in 1961.

cautious because the concepts presented by the Japanese government and the JNR appeared "experimental" and "glamorous."[36] Bank staff insisted that, as a policy, the Bank could not extend loans for projects that included experimental elements. Their impression was that although a maximum speed of 150 kilometers per hour on international narrow gauge was acceptable, 250 kilometers per hour on standard gauge was too fast. The JNR explained that 250 kilometers per hour was an approximate figure decided politically and that new technologies employed for the project were already satisfactorily tested.[37] The Bank remained unconvinced, but at least it was satisfied with the financial viability of the project and the financial health of the JNR.[38] The economic impact of the project was understood to be an overall efficiency gain: speeding up passenger transport would allow additional cargo capacity on the existing parallel line.[39]

Finally the Bank agreed to send an appraisal mission, which visited Japan in May 1960. For a month it carried out detailed examinations focusing on everything from the management structure of the JNR to the project's design and its implementation schedule. Its findings were favorable, and in May 1961 an agreement for an $80 million loan was signed by Bank President Black and Chairman Shinji Sogou of the JNR.

The loan was an impact loan, but like those for motorway projects, it included a portion open to international competitive bidding. Although some foreign companies were prequalified, they finally withdrew their bids. Land acquisition, implemented simultaneously with construction work, was one of the most difficult elements of the project and took nearly five years to complete. The *Shinkansen* bullet train started commercial operations on October 1, 1964, ten days before the opening ceremony of the Olympic games in Tokyo. It is ironic that although the bullet train itself was quite profitable, the JNR fell into deficit in 1964. Its financial position worsened, and finally it was liquidated and divided into six regional companies.

36. The proposal was to construct a railway with a maximum speed of 250 kilometers per hour, thus enabling a one-day return trip between the two metropolitan areas. The plan also envisaged introducing international standard-gauge tracks (the Japanese standard was international narrow gauge).

37. These technologies included seamless superlong rails, a new type of rail bed, electricity supply, specially designed trains, and an automatic train control system. Most had been developed domestically. Nihon Kokukyuu Tetsudou [Japan National Railways], *Nihon kokuyuu tetsudou hyaku-nen-shi,* vol. 12 [Centenary of JNR] (Tokyo: Dainihon Insatsu, 1973).

38. The Bank demanded that train fares be increased enough to secure the financial health of the JNR. The fare increase was carried out, although it was politically very difficult. This episode suggests how badly the government needed the Bank loan.

39. There was a tricky part in this explanation. In the initial plan, cargo transport was included in the project, and it appears that the JNR took this line with the Bank. Ministry of Finance, "Okura-shou no rekishi tokoro dokoro" [A History of the Ministry of Finance], *Finance,* January 1994, p. 84.

Graduation from the Bank Loans: What Japan Gained

As mentioned earlier, the first time Japan's graduation from World Bank loans was officially suggested was in 1961 by Knapp and Black. For a time no loans to Japan were approved by the board after the second motorway project in 1961. Following their announced intentions, the Japanese government expanded bond financing in the private market.[40] However, in 1963 the interest equalization tax introduced by the U.S. government made Japan's bond issues in the New York market difficult to sell. In view of the situation, Minister of Finance Kakuei Tanaka met Bank President George Woods at the 1963 World Bank–IMF annual meeting in Washington and persuaded him to extend $300 million over three years. The first of the new loans, for the third motorway project, was approved by the board in September 1963 and six more in the next two years.

At every Board meeting, however, it was suggested that Japan had developed enough to graduate from Bank loans. Indeed, it joined the Organization for Economic Cooperation and Development (OECD) in 1964 and also became an IMF Article 8 country that year. The Olympic games and the Bank-IMF annual meeting were held in Tokyo in 1964, thus exhibiting Japan's economic power. At the annual meeting, Prime Minister Ikeda concluded his statement by saying, "My country, let me say, is prepared to contribute even more positively than before to international cooperative endeavors."[41]

When George Woods visited Japan in October 1965, he told Minister of Finance Takeo Fukuda that the Bank-Japan relationship should go back to the 1961 status, meaning a loan to continue work on the Tokyo-Kobe motorway would be the last Bank lending operation in Japan. He said that the lending had been continued on condition that the Japanese government make every effort to raise the maximum amount possible in private markets, and Japan had become able to raise enough funds for its needs. Although Fukuda argued that there were limits to the financing available in private markets and Japan needed Bank loans, which would also endorse its creditworthiness, Woods's stance was adamant.[42] Following the meeting, Japanese government officials were informally prepared to give up further loans from the Bank and were mainly concerned with limiting the psychological damage to the Japanese economy.

The last loan for the Tokyo-Kobe motorway was approved by the board on July 29, 1966, and Japan graduated from thirteen years of Bank lending. The Asian Development Bank, in which Japan and the United States were the largest share-

40. The first foreign currency bond was issued in the New York market in 1959 for a hydroelectric project. This was part of a parallel loan from the Bank.

41. Hayato Ikeda, "Address by the Prime Minister of Japan," *Summary Proceedings, Annual Meeting 1964* (Washington: International Monetary Fund, 1964), p. 4.

42. Ministry of Finance officials had examined a possible buy-back operation of Japan's debt to the Bank, thus raising the ceilings on the fresh loans to Japan. However, the idea was finally abandoned and was not presented to Woods.

holders and the president was Japanese, had its inaugural meeting in Tokyo, gathering representatives from more than thirty countries. Thus, as former prime minister Ikeda had declared, Japan embarked on its way to becoming the world's largest provider of economic assistance to developing countries.

The thirty-one Bank loans to Japan totaled $857 million net of cancellations. What did the loans bring to the nation? Quantitatively, the share of borrowing from the Bank amounted to 18.7 percent of total borrowing from 1959 to 1964; borrowing from the United States amounted to 67.4 percent of total borrowing in the same period. Borrowing from the Bank was thus helpful but quantitatively not decisive. However, the qualitative impact of the Bank loans appears to be more important. New construction technologies were brought in, developed, and learned with the Bank projects, as in the Kurobe No. 4 and motorway projects. The Bank's loan conditions had a side effect akin to technology transfer. The Bank often imposed conditions of financial soundness on executing agencies and had them change their pricing policies. Such actions provoked debates and friction among the Japanese, but it is undeniable that they realized the importance of the conditions and made efforts to improve the financial positions of steel and other companies.

For their part, the Bank staff learned that the Japanese way of doing business was different from the American or European way. Initially, the disparity caused some difficulties, but as dealings became more common, Bank officials established a cordial relationship with their Japanese counterparts. In the later stages, Bank officials learned a mixed approach to dealing with the Japanese: sometimes they used coercive methods; in other cases they nurtured. When Japanese officials faced coercive demands, they, though superficially annoyed, sometimes exploited the demands as external leverage (*gaiatsu*) to launch difficult policy alterations.

On July 16, 1990, the Doro Kodan repaid the last of its debt obligation, and Japan genuinely graduated from a Bank borrower to a large shareholder.

Becoming the Second-Largest Shareholder

Once they were convinced that there would be no further loans from the Bank, Japanese government officials started to seek genuine graduation from the Bank— that is, for Japan to become a net creditor to the Bank. Initially, a debt buyback operation, such that credits to Japan on the Bank balance sheet would be reduced, was considered. However, the Bank rejected the idea on the grounds that it needed to keep creditworthy borrowers like Japan on its balance sheet to maintain its AAA status.[43] So the Japanese government decided to participate in the Bank's borrowing operations, thus becoming a net creditor to it. In 1969 the Bank of Japan

43. During the 1980s when the debt crisis in Latin America cast a pall over American bond markets, a Bank financing officer successfully convinced some West Coast security houses to buy Bank bonds by pointing out that the Bank had a good portfolio, including loans to Japan and European countries.

purchased $162.5 million of Bank loans in prepayment of Bank loans to Japan. The Bank's first borrowing in Japan was in 1970 when two issues of serial bonds of ¥36 billion each ($100 million) were sold to the Bank of Japan. In 1971 the Bank of Japan purchased two more issues of serial bonds (¥36 billion). These purchases totaled more than $500 million, which exceeded the $450 million of Japanese debt outstanding to the Bank. Hence, Japan became a net creditor to the Bank only five years after the last loan. In addition, as a result of the 1970 general capital increase, which lifted it from the seventh largest shareholder to the fifth, Japan obtained an appointed seat on the board of executive directors in 1971, thus increasing its influence on Bank operations.

TOKYO OFFICE: HARBINGER IN THE TOKYO MARKET. When Japan joined the OECD, commitments were made to liberalize the country's current account and to achieve greater capital mobility. Liberalization measures were announced in June 1966, and Japan gradually opened its capital markets. Following these actions, the Bank opened its office in Tokyo in November 1970. The objectives of the Tokyo office were liaison with the Japanese government, assisting Bank borrowing operations in Japan, public relations, and recruitment of Japanese nationals to work in the Bank. However, borrowing operations were emphasized, and the office has been reporting to the Office of the Vice President (Treasurer) ever since. Aritoshi Soejima was appointed director of the office on the recommendation of the Ministry of Finance: such an arrangement has continued to this day. This was because Robert McNamara, then Bank president, was convinced of the future prospects of the Tokyo market.

The first Bank samurai bond (a nonresident yen bond issued in Tokyo) of ¥11 billion ($30.6 million) was issued in the Tokyo market on June 30, 1971.[44] Thereafter, the Bank enhanced its samurai bond operations until 1986, except for the period from 1973 to 1977 when an interest rate surge made issuing bonds difficult. In 1984, after U.S.-Japan talks, liberalization of the Japanese capital markets and the internationalization of the yen were announced. The Bank, having issued a modest amount of Euroyen bonds, promptly reacted to the announcement, and the number of Euroyen bond issues greatly increased. In view of such developments, the Bank introduced a Euro-linked Daimyo bond (a ¥40 billion, or $286.7 million, nonresident yen bond issued in Tokyo and settled in the Euromarket) in 1987, thus enabling more efficient borrowing operations. In 1985 the Bank introduced the first Shogun bond (a nonresident foreign currency bond issued in Tokyo) in the Tokyo market. As a result of less favorable conditions in the Tokyo market because of heavy regulation and unique business customs, only six Shogun bonds were issued by the Bank before 1989. This raised a question about the unique characteristics of the Tokyo market. Since 1991 the Bank has shifted its

44. The very first samurai bond, for ¥6 billion ($16.7 million), was issued by the Asian Development Bank in November 1970.

yen borrowing program to global yen bonds, which was another of its innovations, and the efficiency of the borrowing operations was further improved through full integration of the Tokyo, New York, and Euromarkets.

The Bank has been a harbinger in the yen capital markets. In each operation the Tokyo office has functioned as liaison with the government of Japan and with the Tokyo capital market community. Its relationship with the Ministry of Finance has been especially important: it would have been difficult to persuade the ministry to permit such innovative funding methods had the director been sent from Bank headquarters and unfamiliar with Japanese business customs and with the ins and outs of government functions.

THE SELECTED CAPITAL INCREASE OF 1984. In the early 1970s Japan recorded a huge balance of payments surplus annually and, in the wake of foreign pressure that arose from trade imbalances, reduction of its trade surplus became an important policy matter. Moreover, the 1973 oil shock, which hampered the Japanese economy, revealed the importance of multilateral aid as a means of economic diplomacy. Consequently, in 1977 the government announced that Japan would double its overseas direct aid in five years; in 1978 a revised target was announced as the first medium-term aid goal—a doubling of aid by 1980. The first target was more than achieved, and since then, in line with its increasing economic power, Japan has announced five medium-term targets.[45] In addition, the first surplus recycling scheme, which included non-aid resources, was announced in 1986, followed by the second and the third, and developed into the Fund for Development Initiative, announced in 1993.[46] These initiatives contributed to mitigating developing countries' debt problems in the 1980s.

Although the amount of economic assistance expanded rapidly, the lack of a coherent philosophy about it caused criticisms that the aid was faceless. So in 1992 the concept of Japan's economic assistance was stated as the Overseas Development Aid Charter and was authenticated by the cabinet. This delay in conceptualization does not mean that Japan's assistance before the charter lacked coherence, but it comes from the very nature of the Japanese: they are too practical to conceptualize their deed.

Against this background, Japan increased contributions through the international financial institutions, among them the Bank group. The contributions were spurred by political as well as economic reasons. In view of the country's increasing impor-

45. Those are the second (doubling overseas direct aid from 1981 to 1985, which fell short of the target); the third (more than $40 billion from 1986 to 1992, which was achieved in 1987); the fourth (doubling aid from 1988 to 1992, which was nearly achieved); and the fifth ($70 billion to $75 billion from 1993 to 1997, which was announced in 1993.

46. These were the first (1986; $10 billion contributions to the IMF, subscriptions to multilateral development banks, participation in the banks' borrowing programs, and establishment of the Japan Special Fund in the Bank); the second (1987; $20 billion in five years); and the third (1989; $65 billion from 1987 to 1992). All have been achieved. The Fund for Development Initiative is expected to provide $70 billion of untied aid funds and $50 billion of non-aid funds.

tance in the global economy (Japan's GNP had become second only to that of the United States in 1968), public opinion demanded that Japan's position at the financial institutions be in line with its international economic standing.[47] Japan is an original member of the International Finance Corporation (IFC) and the International Development Association (IDA), and its original rankings were the seventh and sixth largest contributor, respectively.

During the IDA 5 negotiations (1975–77), Japan first demanded that its shares at IDA and the International Bank for Reconstruction and Development (IBRD) be harmonized. Its cumulative contribution to IDA was proportionally twice as much as its subscription to IBRD capital. However, Japan's claim was not heard by other countries.

The Bank, basically welcoming Japan's intention to increase its shareholding at the IBRD, proposed a selective capital increase that would have raised the country to the equivalent of the German position.[48] After debates among major shareholders, it was decided that a simultaneous selective capital increase, which would keep France in a slightly higher position than Japan, be proposed. Finally as a compromise, Japan got 4,000 unallocated shares while France received 1,900, and Japan, Germany, and France were almost equally placed. However, Japan still remained the fifth largest shareholder of the IBRD. Concurrently, a general capital increase was put on the table as early as 1977 by Bank President McNamara, and discussions were held. The capital increase was needed because of a predicted shortage of capital and was deemed urgent. Therefore, no fundamental reshuffling of share ranking was discussed. Finally, it was concluded in 1980 by a proportional increase of capital from post-1979 selective capital increase shareholding: Japan again remained the fifth.

In 1983 at the IMF's eighth general quota review, Japan was allocated 10 percent of the selective quota increase, which meant that its position at the IBRD would be automatically raised by an associated selective capital increase. Although there were again extensive discussions among other shareholders, they led to a conclusion favorable to Japan. Therefore the 1984 selective capital increase finally raised Japan to the position of second largest shareholder of the IBRD. At the same time, IDA 7 replenishment was being discussed, and Japan's contribution to IDA was increased considerably.

There are several factors behind this story of Japan's "getting the right place." First, Japan's persistent trade surplus and the emerging debt problems of developing countries placed international pressure on the country to increase its contribution to poorer countries. Second, the United States, suffering from a huge fiscal

47. In 1977 the Diet, upon passing laws related to the IDA 5 replenishment, resolved that Japan's "de facto economic power" be reflected in the coming IMF fifth general review of quota. Japan's position at the IMF was fifth after IMF 5, as it was at the International Bank for Reconstruction and Development. Such resolutions had been customary until Japan became the second largest shareholder of the Bank.

48. At the same time, IDA 6 replenishment was under discussion.

deficit, was unable to maintain the traditional high burden sharing, especially in IDA. As long as its dominant position was unaffected, it had every reason to support Japan's increasing contribution to the Bank as a whole. Third, the other industrial countries had problems similar to those of the United States, and the impossibility of increasing their contributions overcame political pressure to maintain their positions. Fourth, by enhancing contributions to IDA, Japan was able to obtain enthusiastic support from developing countries.

Japan as Second-Largest Shareholder

THE JAPAN SPECIAL FUND AND THE POLICY AND HUMAN RESOURCES DEVELOPMENT FUND. In the context of surplus recycling, Japan established the Japan Special Fund along with a scholarship fund and a consultant trust fund with the Bank in 1987. The JSF was counted as part of the surplus recycling scheme, and the initial endowment was ¥30 billion of untied grants in three years. The purpose of the JSF was to help the Bank prepare projects and at the same time to alleviate the financial burden on developing countries that was associated with preparation. In view of urgent needs for human resource development and sound economic policies in developing countries, an announcement was made at the 1990 World Bank–IMF annual meeting by Ryutaro Hashimoto, Japanese minister of finance, that these funds were to be added to and integrated into the Policy and Human Resources Development (PHRD) Fund.[49]

The PHRD includes technical assistance grants that include funds for environmental protection activities, women-in-development activities, and private sector development activities, thus focusing on the crosscutting issues. The fund also includes training grants through the Economic Development Institute, a training wing of the Bank; a consultant trust fund; and a scholarship fund. The initial PHRD endowment was ¥14.2 billion in 1990, and the amount has been expanding in line with the increasing demand for such technical assistance, notably assistance to former planned economies. The main feature of the PHRD is that, although the endowment is a Japanese grant fund, its procurement is basically untied and management of the fund is completely delegated to the Bank. Compared with other bilateral grant funds with the Bank, which are normally tied to donor countries and their use controlled by donor discretion, the amount of the PHRD is far bigger and more flexible. Therefore, according to a recent survey by the Bank, task managers responded that the PHRD is by far the best means available for project preparation. Indeed, it appears that there are internal competitions to capture the lion's share of the fund. As a result, its geographical distribution is more or less in line with the Bank's operations.

With the traditional UN Development Program (UNDP) funding for project preparation declining, the PHRD is now the main source for Bank project prepara-

---

49. World Bank, Cofinancing Services, "Policy and Human Resources Development Fund: Japanese Grant Facility: Operational Review" (1993).

tion and welcomed in and outside the Bank. Some might argue that the fund is a means for Japan to influence the Bank beyond the country's voting power there.[50] The argument is intriguing, but it does not capture the true nature of the PHRD. The management of the PHRD is largely delegated to the Bank, and the government of Japan's say is limited to the overall ceiling of the grant and, if any, its inclination toward project preparation rather than implementation support, thus leaving the geographical distribution and choice of individual projects to the Bank. This is the key reason for the PHRD's wide appreciation among the Bank's managers.

COFINANCING OPERATIONS. Japan was one of the original members of the Consultative Group meetings when the Aid-India consortium launched them in 1958, but cofinancing with the Bank rapidly increased during the late 1970s along with the successive overseas direct aid targets and surplus recycling initiatives. Japan's cofinancing in fiscal years 1984 to 1993 was $16.4 billion, or 46.5 percent of the Bank's total cofinancing operations. Japan is by far the largest cofinancier, followed by Germany, whose share remains 7 percent.

There are several reasons why Japan's cofinancing effort increased. First, having made various commitments, Japan needed to increase its financial contributions to developing countries. Second, Japan did not have enough institutional capacity for project formulation because of a lack of expertise in aid-providing agencies as well as a scarcity of internationally qualified consultants. Third, because of this deficiency, Japan needed certain know-how from the Bank: indeed Japan's aid agencies have assimilated the Bank's procedures and organizational structure.

During the 1980s, cofinancing with the Bank was distributed to almost all the world's regions. In the wake of debt problems, cofinancing of structural adjustment lending increased. In the 1990s, as the Japanese government and its aid agencies have accumulated extensive experience in Southeast Asia, they have obtained their own capacity for project formulation; thus cofinancing operations in Southeast Asia are on the decline. Also, the share of adjustment lending in cofinancing is decreasing, reflecting the declining needs for balance of payments finance in many countries. However, in regions with which Japan is not familiar, such as Latin America, Africa, and to a lesser degree South Asia, aid agencies are still learning and need the Bank's expertise. So in 1993, the idea of the Accelerated Cofinancing Facilities was proposed. An ACF is intended to streamline procedures associated with cofinancing, thus drawing on the Bank's expertise as much as possible. Through such a facility, the Japanese government and its aid agencies are expected to acquire more know-how.

It appears that some within the Bank are not satisfied with increased cofinancing operations, as can be seen from the so-called Wapenhans report.[51] The report

50. See, for example, Edward J. Lincoln, *Japan's New Global Role* (Brookings, 1993).

51. World Bank, "Effective Implementation: Key to Development Impact," Portfolio Management Task Force Report ("The Wapenhans Report") (Washington, September 1992), R92-195.

implies that cofinancing increases the probability of poor project performance through complicated procedures associated with the financing, although on average the report appreciates cofinancing as a critical means of filling funding gaps. Criticisms aim mainly at tied cofinancing, which entails extra loan conditions and special rules on procurement. However, this was not the case for Japan; its cofinancing loans are all untied. Indeed, a task force on cofinancing gave a positive assessment of Japan's cofinancing operations with the Bank. Yet most of the operations work in one way: the Bank prepares the projects and Japan follows. Thus it is now all the more desirable that the Bank-Japan relationship centered on cofinancing be raised to an equal partnership.

The Asian Perspective

Japan's Experience

Japan's economic development is often called a miracle, but economic development is a historical product and by no means a miraculous phenomenon. For Japan the miracle hypothesis focuses on postwar development. However, the postwar period does not tell the whole story. From the Meiji Restoration in 1868 until World War II, Japan acquired most of what constitutes the foundation of a modern society—legal system, bureaucracy, military system, banking system, and so on. In the early stages, basic knowledge was acquired from foreign experts employed by the government. Learning was fast, and soon the government initiated state-led economic development with a slogan, "progress toward wealth and might": this period can genuinely be called the state development phase. At the same time, a universal education system was introduced; this broadened the human resource base, which also contributed to postwar development. After the turn of the century, industrialization, mainly by financial cliques, gained momentum, and Japan was equipped with most of the heavy industries, bolstered by imported natural resources from Asia. A bank-centered financial system, along with the postal savings system, evolved and mobilized funds for industrialization.

In view of the lack of human resources and basic economic frameworks in today's developing countries, lessons from Japan's prewar experience have no less relevance to the developing countries than its postwar experience. These experiences are the broadening of the human resource base, technology transfer and acquisition through learning by doing, and the bank-centered financial system. In looking into postwar development, the important point is that those bases were inherited from before the war. Although they were considerably damaged by World War II, the fundamentals for rapid growth were already there. As such, it is recommended that much greater attention be paid to, and lessons be drawn from, Japan's prewar experience.

Japan's postwar development is well known and described in various publications, including *The East Asian Miracle* by the World Bank, and need not be repeated here.[52] The main features of postwar development are maintenance of a stable macroeconomy, except for the periods after the oil shocks; the role played by the Fiscal Investment and Loan Program (FILP); export development; bank-oriented finance; and good corporate governance and management. Most of these points are elaborated on in *The East Asian Miracle,* but some are discussed below.

The Way to The East Asian Miracle *Study*

In 1989 the government of Japan received a request from a member of the Association of Southeast Asian Nations for an Overseas Economic Cooperation Fund loan from the ASEAN–Japan Development Fund (AJDF). The fund was founded in 1987 as part of the surplus recycling plan and was intended to provide concessional resources to foster private sectors in ASEAN countries. It has two components: one is for intra-ASEAN projects and the other for concessional two-step loans (on-lending) to small- and medium-scale industries that support export manufacturing in ASEAN countries. This type of loan had been extended to various Asian countries based on the Japanese perception that to support prospective private sectors it was necessary for the second-step loans to be concessional, provided the target has been identified and targeting has worked. This was a belief derived from Japan's own experience through FILP.

The World Bank, however, insisted that interest rates be on the market-clearing level because preferential rates would distort financial markets and harm economic development. Such a perception is obviously based on a neoclassical view of financial markets. The Bank's neoclassical perception has its origin in Ronald McKinnon's work and is as follows.[53] Many developing countries adopted policies of financial repression under which the government kept interest rates artificially low. As a result, credit rationing was unavoidable, and savings were further discouraged because of negative real interest rates. Credit rationing, however, tended to result in misallocation of resources due to imperfect information and institutional weakness: after all, money is fungible and targeting would not work. Thus McKinnon's (and the Bank's) prescription for developing countries was to liberalize the financial market so as to attain market-determined interest rates that would "correct" the misallocation of resources.

As far as the particular OECF loan was concerned, a compromise was reached. However, the issue did not end with just a compromise: both the Bank and OECF staffs were aware that the difference was fundamental. The Bank's attitude was based on rigorous economic theories and its experiences in Latin America and

52. See World Bank, *The East Asian Miracle: Economic Growth and Public Policy* (Oxford University Press, 1993); Ryutaro Komiya, Masahiro Okuno, and Kotaro Suzumura, *Industrial Policy of Japan* (Academic Press, 1988).

53. Ronald I. McKinnon, *Money and Capital in Economic Development* (Brookings, 1973).

Africa, where most such schemes had failed. The OECF's ideas relied more on experiences in Japan and in other Asian countries, where many successful cases had been observed. Both parties shared the view that developing countries had a lot of market malfunctioning and failures. But as for the remedies, their views differed. The Bank, having experienced ample examples of failed attempts of government interventions (some of them had been advised and supported by the Bank during the 1950s and 1960s) and their aftermaths, concluded that the market failures were much less costly than "government failures," thus more or less rejecting government interventions.[54] The Bank's position was that, where appropriate, subsidies should be provided out of fiscal budgets rather than in the form of subsidized interest rates so as to maintain the transparency and directness of the subsidies.

Japanese officials, priding themselves on their successful economic policies, believed that the extensive market failures in developing countries justified government interventions; and as long as targeting worked, such subsidized loans were an effective means to foster economic development.[55] They argued that economic theory did not say that fiscal subsidies were preferable to subsidized interest rates. Moreover, they claimed that subsidized interest rates did not encourage corruption and misallocation of resources, although such tendencies did exist in certain sectors of the economy. They concluded that as long as there was no theoretical reason to deny subsidized interest rates, the problems raised by the Bank could be controlled through adequate supervision by the recipient countries and the donors.

Following these discussions, the OECF issued an occasional paper, the first in its thirty-year history, discussing not only the two-step loans but also the Bank's approach to structural adjustment.[56] The fact that the organization issued its first occasional paper after thirty years, whereas the Bank had issued numerous discussion papers and working papers, reflects the difference in working styles between the OECF (or the Japanese government) and the Bank.[57] The Bank is paper oriented or reasoning oriented, while the Japanese are more experience oriented.[58]

The OECF paper raises several points on the need for investment promotion, infant industry protection and export promotion, financial market policy, and a slower privatization process. The main points of the paper are as follows:

54. See, for example, Anne O. Krueger, "Government Failures in Development," *Journal of Economic Perspectives*, vol. 4, no. 3 (summer 1991), pp. 9–23; World Bank, *World Development Report* (Washington, 1991).

55. See Isao Kubota, "The Case for Two Step Loans," paper prepared for the World Bank–Overseas Economic Cooperation Fund biannual consultation meeting, May 1991.

56. Overseas Economic Cooperation Fund, "Issues Related to the World Bank's Approach to Structural Adjustment: Proposal from a Major Partner," *OECF Research Quarterly*, no. 73 (1991), pp. 4–18.

57. The OECF so far has issued just a few occasional papers.

58. This might be a bit of an exaggeration. The Japanese government and its affiliated institutions are increasingly voicing their views on economic policies in the form of papers. See note 60, for example.

1. Streamlining procedures and liberalizing markets may not be sufficient to induce continuous waves of investment. In such cases, investment promotion aiming directly at prospective industries is required.

2. The costs associated with hasty trade liberalization are large. Rapid liberalization tends to result in static comparative advantage, which does not reflect dynamic aspects of economic development. Thus due attention should be paid to the liberalization process and some infant industries need time-bound protection from international competition. At the same time, efforts to promote prospective export sectors are necessary.

3. The financial markets in developing countries are incomplete and the signaling function of interest rates does not work. Also, due to various market failures, market mechanism has its limitations and does not necessarily bring the optimal allocation of resources.

4. Although needs for privatization are understandable, the Bank's rather universal approach is not sufficient: situations are different among countries and a more country- and situation-specific approach should be sought. Moreover, privatization through foreign participation is politically not always sustainable, though it could be efficient.

5. Japanese fiscal and monetary policies in the postwar era may be worthy of consideration. These are centered on preferential tax treatment and development finance institutions lending.

The paper, although offering nothing new theoretically, was reported as the government's rebuttal to the Bank's approach and attracted considerable attention.[59] However, the Japanese in principle understood the importance of market-based development and by no means intended to supplant the market-oriented views held by the Bank: they just pointed out the limits of the textbook approach to development.

In 1991 the Bank issued the World Development Report subtitled *The Challenge of Development* in which a "market-friendly approach" was proposed. The approach, although based on the neoclassical framework, acknowledges some areas such as education, health, and other basic human needs in which government has comparative advantage and is encouraged to act aggressively. At the same time, the report endorses the neoclassical perception that government should not be the main actor in manufacturing and certain service sectors where the private sector has the advantage. Many development practitioners appreciated the approach as a step forward from the textbook approach, but some were not satisfied and the government-versus-market debates continued.

59. For comments from British academics and policymakers, see Kazumi Goto, *Nemureru paatonaa no chiteki mezame: Kouzou Chousei ni kansuru OECF ronbun ni yoserareta Eikoku karano messeiji o chushin to shite* [The Intellectual Awakening of a Sleeping Partner: Some Comments from the U.K. on OECF's View of Structural Adjustment], *OECF Research Quarterly*, no. 76 (1993), pp. 151–83.

These debates were strongly influenced by trends in economic literature. During the late 1970s and early 1980s, a new "classical" revolution occurred that almost supplanted Keynesian-oriented views. The new classicists believed in laissez faire and through rigorous mathematical deduction showed that any government attempts to alter an economy would be nullified by superrational, farsighted economic agents. The thesis was attractive for policymakers who had experienced huge fiscal and external imbalances as a result of the oil shocks, and the new classicists prevailed, particularly in the United States. The Japanese, especially government officials, though somewhat attracted by the thesis, in principle remained under Keynesian influence because the thesis seemed too abstract and incompatible with reality. They also doubted the value of complete laissez faire.[60]

Since the early 1980s, new Keynesians have emerged, emphasizing the importance of market failures such as coordination failures and increasing returns to scale in explaining the real economy. Now in the 1990s the two parties coexist: the new classicists have made their models more sophisticated, and the new Keynesians have broadened their areas of analysis.

Against such a background, the Bank's inclination toward the neoclassical view may be partly due to the fact that most Bank economists were trained in or influenced by the new classical dominance during the 1970s and 1980s. Indeed, during the 1950s and 1960s, when the Keynesian view prevailed, the Bank supported state-led projects in many countries. Or, the inclination could be explained in another way: as a borrower from the international financial markets, where laissez faire has been sacrosanct, the Bank needs to satisfy the institutional investors who buy its bonds by maintaining an AAA rating.

East Asian Miracle *Study*

Such was the prelude to the *East Asian Miracle* study. At the Bank-IMF annual meeting in 1991, Yasushi Mieno, governor of the Bank of Japan and World Bank alternate governor for Japan, said, "Experience[s] in Asia have shown that although development strategies require a healthy respect for market mechanisms, the role of the government cannot be forgotten. I would like to see the World Bank and the IMF take the lead in a wide-ranging study that would define the theoretical

---

60. The Ministry of International Trade and Industry published policy recommendations in 1992 for Russia's economic reform based on Japan's postwar experience. The paper argued that Russia should apply gradualism, not "shock therapy," and recommended an industrial policy similar to Japan's PPS and selective interventions. The papers were taken up by various media including the *Financial Times,* July 20, 1992, and the *Far Eastern Economic Review,* August 13, 1992. However, such policy measures should not be applied in view of Russia's political situation—too many opportunists and a weak central government.

underpinnings of this approach and clarify the areas in which it can be successfully applied to other parts of the globe."[61]

It is true that the Japanese government encouraged the Bank to conduct a study of the experiences of East Asian countries in view of their successful economic development and economic policies. But it appears that it was Lawrence Summers, then vice president for policy, research, and external affairs at the Bank, who initiated the study. The study was officially launched in the spring of 1992 when the study team headed by John Page was formed. The Japanese government did not intervene in the research or the writing of the report, except for asking the Bank to ensure that the draft report should be commented on by Asian researchers and former government officials, a rare occurrence in Bank studies. The researchers were mainly American-trained Asian economists. The Japan Development Bank participated in the study and prepared a report on Japan's policy-based finance.

As drafts came up for review, considerable discussion was induced among Bank staff on the report's evaluation of the role of government policies in economic growth. Some of the staff were not satisfied with the approval of active government intervention, and the discussions in the report seemed to have been somewhat watered down. Finally, the report was released at the IMF-Bank annual meeting in 1993, and attracted much media attention. The major findings are:

—The East Asian countries have been unusually successful in sharing the benefits of growth, while achieving a remarkable record of economic growth.

—It is confirmed that "getting fundamentals right," including stable macroeconomic management, investment in people, establishment of secure financial systems, and unbiased agricultural policies, was imperative for sustained economic growth.

—The East Asian countries applied selective policy measures, including industrial policies, directed credit schemes, and export promotion, of which export promotion particularly seems to have contributed to the economic growth in those countries.

—As for applicability of those experiences to today's developing countries, "getting fundamentals right" can be applied in any country without reservation, and selective intervention policies are generally not recommendable to the developing countries where institutional capacity is not sufficient. However, the scope for export promotion remains substantial even in today's international economic environment.

It would be fair to say that the report's conclusion is a subtle mixture (and compromise) of the neoclassical and interventionist views. It could also be said to be inconclusive and equivocal. Indeed, when the report was made public, some critics argued that the Bank had finally admitted that interventionist policies

61. Yasushi Mieno, "Statement by the Alternate Governor of the Bank and Fund for Japan," *Summary Proceedings, Forty-Sixth Annual Meeting of the Board of Governors, 1991* (Washington: International Monetary Fund, 1991), p. 67.

worked while others observed that the Bank's neoclassical stance did not change at all. The media highlighted the *East Asian Miracle* affair as a dispute between the Bank and Japanese experts. However, such an observation does not do justice to the Japanese government. The government's critique of the Bank's view, if any, was intended to contribute to improving development policies; it was not intended to become part of academic disputes. In this regard, it is all the more welcome that the report attracted much attention and that a lot of discussion has been induced around the globe. These discussions in and out of the Bank should further deepen the study's influence, which would add more choices to development policy measures.

In this connection, it is worthwhile to raise some points that were not well articulated in the report. First, links between the East Asian countries should be studied more fully in view of the recent horizontal division of labor among countries through direct investment and other means. This division of labor was first raised by Kaname Akamatsu as the "flying geese theory" in the 1930s and has now been analyzed in more rigorous frameworks.[62] Second, the microstructures of management and corporate governance in the East Asian countries should be more thoroughly explored, although they may not be separable from the cultural background. It seems that the Japanese style of management, under which staff members work together in a large room, facilitates close coordination and information sharing, thus avoiding possible coordination failures.[63] Finally, the applicability of East Asian lessons to other developing countries should be carefully examined in light of the socioeconomic situations in the countries concerned.

Comparison with the Asian Development Bank

The Asian Development Bank was established in 1966. The regional development banks, that is, the Inter-American Development Bank (1960) and the African Development Bank (1964), were already in existence. The idea of creating a similar institution in Asia had popped up at various forums in Asia. In Japan, as early as 1963, a group of private experts chaired by Takeshi Watanabe, who later became the first president of the ADB, produced a rough outline of the new regional bank. According to the outline, the bank should be capitalized with $3 billion, of which the United States and Japan would subscribe 30 percent each. Membership would be extended to nonregional industrial countries with the aim of exploiting a wider resource base. The bank's headquarters were planned to be set up in Tokyo.

In 1964 at the UN Economic Commission for Asia and the Far East (ECAFE) meeting in Manila, a motion was adopted to convene the Experts Meeting for the

62. Kaname Akamatsu, "Shinkoku Kogyokoku no Sangyou Hatten," *Ueda Teijiro Hakushi Kinen Ronbunshu*, vol. 4 (July 1937); Gene M. Grossman and Elhanan Helpman, *Innovation and Growth in the Global Economy* (MIT Press, 1991).

63. Masahiko Aoki, *Information, Incentives, and Bargaining in the Japanese Economy* (Cambridge University Press, 1988).

Establishment of the Asian Development Bank. The most controversial issue discussed at the meeting was whether to invite non-Asian developed countries to join the bank. Representatives of developing Asian countries expressed a strong preference for limiting the membership to Asian countries, following the formula adopted by the African Development Bank. In the end, however, the Japanese argument in favor of non-Asian membership prevailed.

At the ECAFE meeting in New Zealand in March 1965, an intergovernmental conference was established to finalize the plan. In the early stages the United States remained noncommittal. Eugene Black, former president of the World Bank, was most instrumental in persuading the U.S. government of the importance of membership in the bank. The United States decided to join the ADB with an equal share with Japan of 20 percent of total capital. The inaugural meeting of the bank was held in Tokyo in 1966. The bank's headquarters were established in Manila, and Takeshi Watanabe, former executive director of the World Bank and senior officer of the Japanese Ministry of Finance was elected the first president.

In many respects Watanabe molded the corporate philosophy and corporate culture of the Asian Development bank. During his presidency Watanabe insisted on two principles. The first was that the organization was a bank and not an aid-giving agency. His first job as president was to visit major international capital markets and creditor governments with the aim of convincing them of the bank's sound operational policy. In spite of strong political pressure from wishful developing members, the bank took more than a year to make its first loan.

The second principle Watanabe insisted on was that the bank's role should be similar to that of a family doctor: it should be fully familiar with the condition of each member of the family, and it should be ready to rush to the patient to provide first aid. Since the Asian Development Bank is a modest institution, a patient in critical condition who requires a big operation needs to be transferred to a big hospital—the World Bank.

Watanabe's gospel has been inherited by the five Japanese presidents who succeeded him. The organization has managed to maintain its status as the soundest regional bank. It has also preserved certain regional characteristics such as its strong emphasis on agricultural development and the improvement of public infrastructure. It cannot be denied that its activity as the family doctor contributed to nurturing the developmental dynamism in the region that was unleashed in the 1980s.

The economic situation in East Asia has changed dramatically over the past two decades. The achievement of self-sufficiency in food production is no longer a major economic issue in the region. And a wave of privatization has been spreading. Large amounts of foreign private capital have flown into the region in various forms. As a result, the Asian Development Bank's role needs to be adapted accordingly.

The bank was the first international institution in which Japan shared equal leadership with the United States. Accordingly, the U.S.-Japan relationship has been the critical factor in the management of the bank. On the whole, the two largest shareholders have succeeded in working together productively. There have been times when their views on the bank's operational strategy and the issue of capital replenishment have differed, but the rifts have been ironed out before they paralyzed the bank's operations. The United States has supported the continued Japanese presidency and refrained from making overt demonstrations of power. Japan has also made the utmost effort to reach a compromise with U.S. positions and has not dared to form a regional alliance to resist the nonregional influence. From the very inception of the bank, it has been obvious that U.S.-Japan cooperation was truly vital to the successful development of the institution. Fortunately, all parties concerned seem to be fully aware of the situation.

The relation between the Asian Development Bank and the World Bank has also been a cooperative one, although with certain elements of healthy competition. Around the time of the establishment of the Asian Development Bank in 1966, President Watanabe paid his respects to George Woods, president of the World Bank, in Woods's office in Washington and asked if the World Bank could spare a few experienced staff members to train the new recruits at the ADB. Woods turned down the request, reminding Watanabe that they were competitors. The idea of creating a relationship of "family doctor versus big hospital" between the ADB and the World Bank did not materialize due probably to the rapid growth of the former. However, the two institutions have learned from experience how best to cooperate. They have sometimes joined in cofinancing schemes and sometimes agreed to a division of labor. In response to the rapidly changing global economy, particularly in the Asia-Pacific region, both the World Bank and the ADB have had to redefine their roles, and the relation between them will be an inseparable item to be addressed in the process of redefinition.

For Japan the Asian Development Bank is certainly a special institution. Japan was actively involved in its creation and has provided the largest share of the institution's human and financial resources. There is no question that Japan considers itself the most responsible shareholder for the successful management of the bank. However, it is not correct to argue that Japan controls the bank as if it were Japan's own. Other creditor members, particularly the United States and the European countries, have not hesitated to oppose policies proposed by the president or the Japanese government. Although there have been accusations that Japan is domineering and self-interested, they have not gained the support of the majority of other members. The fact that the institution is viewed as the most successful regional bank speaks for itself that members as a whole support the way it is run.

Japan's position in the World Bank is quite different. There Japan does not consider itself the most responsible shareholder. Its request for a larger share of the voting rights and a greater role in management is motivated by three considerations. The first is that Japan's role as one of the largest providers of global aid should be better reflected in its role in the Bank. Second, Japan's overall financial contribution to the Bank should be better matched by its voting share. Third, Japan can and should contribute more to the activities of the World Bank with the benefit of the knowledge and experience it has gained in the developmental effort at home and in East Asia.

It should not be forgotten that Japan has always been a country where a greater contribution to multilateral development banks was unanimously supported by the government, by taxpayers, and by all political parties.

Advice to the Bank

The Future World Bank: Diversification of Means

The Bretton Woods institutions have passed their first fifty years, and the global economic and political environment has changed. The Bank, as the leading provider of funds, has contributed greatly to economic development, and that role should not change in years to come. However, in view of changes taking place, the role should be modified.

Looking at the post–cold war world, one finds some successful economies, mainly in Asia, where private funds are flowing in, economies in transition that will need continuous support from the international financial institutions for the foreseeable future, and impoverished and stagnant countries, especially in Africa, where there is even greater and probably insatiable demand for development finance. All these exist in the context of an increasingly tight fiscal position for all industrialized countries that will make the expansion of development assistance more difficult.

The Bank has reacted to these situations, and in recent years it seems to be switching its regional distribution of resources from Asia and to a degree from Latin America to the economies in transition and to Africa. It would be an overstatement to say that someday the Bank will become the Bank for Africa and Economies in Transition, but the need is there and the Bank should serve it. Still, there remains a huge demand for Bank involvement in Asia as well as in Latin America, although the forms of involvement should be different from the ones in Africa or the economies in transition.

Privatization, a movement to which the Bank has contributed much, has become popular in Asia and Latin America. However, these countries are yet to be able to attract enough private funds on their own. The rationale for continuous Bank support to Asia and Latin America is there: given the increasing importance of the private sectors in those regions, the Bank can and should play a catalytic role. In this regard, it needs to reconsider its means to assist the private sector. So far, it has been inclined to lend to the public sector, which poses a mismatch with such needs.

Several options, not mutually exclusive, have been proposed. Some argue that the IBRD should transfer a much larger share of its net income to the IFC and

IDA. Bank (not IFC) lending to the private sector without sovereign guarantee has also been suggested. Although these suggestions merit serious examination, they bear certain risks of damaging the Bank's financial position through reduced reserve funds and increased risks, thus affecting its AAA investment rating, which should be preserved as an international asset.

Compared with these options, the guarantee function of the Bank is less likely to affect its financial position while the pump-priming effects of the function are very great. The guarantee function, which is clearly stipulated in the Articles of Agreement, had been put somewhat on the sidelines until the late 1980s: the Bank had had the B-loan scheme whose guarantee ratio was just 25 percent. In 1989 the Expanded Cofinancing Operations (ECO) program was introduced to replace the B-loans as a three-year trial operation. A review of the ECO in 1992 confirmed its effectiveness and made the following modifications: the ECO can be applied to purely private sector operations (previously it needed to be accompanied with Bank loans to public sector–affiliated projects), and when appropriate, the guarantee ratio can be raised to 100 percent (previously 50 percent). This modification further reinforced the ECO program, which is expected to be enhanced even more.

The Bank's role as the organizer and coordinator of the Consultative Group meetings is also financially important. As the most experienced development organization, the Bank can analyze and discuss economies of the developing countries in an authoritative way, thereby assuring the bilateral and multilateral donors of the economic situations and financial needs of these countries. The Bank's analysis usually forms the basis of the discussions at the Consultative Group because in many cases the Bank has established a monopoly position in this field. Bilateral donors, in the wake of their weakening fiscal positions, increasingly need to scrutinize their aid strategies and allocations. Given this background, the Bank's high-quality economic analysis and policy recommendations are much sought after. Bank reports serve as a useful yardstick and can influence bilateral donors' decisionmaking. Therefore, the Consultative Group's meetings, along with associated Bank analysis, are an area in which the Bank should further strengthen its capability of analyzing economies and formulating policy recommendations from an objective viewpoint. In so doing the Bank should be cautious not to be too authoritative: this is the point at which the checks and balances between the Bank and other donors should work.

Thus, the guarantee function being an example, the Bank needs to diversify its financial means to meet varying needs. Certainly, where appropriate, it needs to provide traditional IBRD-IDA loans and credits, which will remain the main vehicle of finance. Especially in poorer countries, IDA credits are still much in demand, and support from donor countries is needed.

In terms of coordination, the Consultative Group meetings remain critical. In addition, the growing development agenda calls for more extensive technical assistance from the Bank as complementary to mainly financial activities. Therefore, the Bank must be flexible in adjusting to these changing needs for its financial and development know-how. The Bank Group as a whole should reconsider its optimal synergetic role, taking into account the comparative advantage of each sub-organization.

Development Policies and the Bank

Post–cold war developments and the increasing attention to the health of the environment have raised a renewed and long agenda for development. The Bank is more than ever expected to act aggressively to achieve development goals that include sustainable development, poverty reduction, private sector development, environmental conservation, transition from planned to market economies, and democracy and good governance. The importance of these objectives is beyond doubt, and now they are accompanied by the concept of sustainable development, which was fully endorsed by the Earth Summit in Rio de Janeiro in 1992. The Bank has been working to adapt itself to the new environment and needs to continue doing so.

As for the environment, the Bank established a new Vice Presidency for Environmentally Sustainable Development in 1993. The office is expected to formulate Bank strategies for the environment and to disseminate the best practices. The importance of dissemination outside the Bank is well recognized. At the same time, it is recommended that the vice presidency actively carry out training and dissemination inside the Bank; otherwise the regions may pay insufficient attention to such crosscutting matters.

Lewis Preston, president of the Bank, put poverty reduction as its central objective, an action that has gained broad consensus. Indeed, except for a few countries in Asia, poverty in developing countries is worsening. But no panacea has been found, and even the *East Asian Miracle* study, while applauding the region's success in shared growth based on right fundamental policies, was unable to provide a quick remedy for other developing countries. Against this background, the Bank is reinforcing its poverty-targeted operations, such as health, primary education, social safety nets, and urban infrastructure.

In the wake of the collapse of planned economies and the lingering problems of overgrown public sectors in developing countries, the Bank also emphasizes private sector development. Indeed the private sector has been and will remain the primary participant in the free market economy, and efforts to foster its health are needed more than ever. In this respect the Bank has established the Vice Presidency for Finance and Private Sector Development, which is expected to function in much the same way as the one for environmentally sustainable development.

Thus various efforts have been made, and the Bank should continue to review its policy priorities and direction. Poverty reduction, environmental conservation, and private sector development are not unchangeable creeds. They are subject to continuous review and modification. For example, assisting the private sector alone does not bring fruitful results: the private sector and the government should go hand in hand. There remains ample room for the government to prepare a favorable environment for fostering the private sector, as can be seen from the *East Asian Miracle* study: this can be done only by the government. So there is still considerable scope for the Bank to support governments by advising on effective public sector management, appropriate regulatory frameworks, and human resource development that facilitate emerging entrepreneurship.

The Bank also needs to review its policies on poverty reduction. Although reducing poverty is imperative and targeting an impoverished population is most effective, if policies go to extremes, they may not help the overall economy of a poor country catch up with the economies of industrial countries, allowing global inequality to persist. Excessive targeting on the poor may also trigger resentment from well-off populations, which would make poverty reduction politically unsustainable. The same may apply to environmental conservation, although in this instance win-win policies do not apply in the long run. Thus the problems are not straightforward, and the Bank must act flexibly in tackling them.

Along with these relatively new priorities, the Bank needs to continue to support infrastructure projects, not only in poor countries but also in middle-income countries where there is still a lot of demand. In some middle-income countries the lack of infrastructure has become a major barrier for further development, and the imbalances between metropolitan and rural areas are being exacerbated. To rectify the imbalances the Bank needs to play a catalytic role, such as using its guarantee function to attract private sector funds in the case of middle-income countries and providing traditional IBRD and IDA financing for poorer countries. Given the fact that the private sector capital flows to middle-income countries in the form of direct and portfolio investments are expanding, the Expanded Cofinancing Operations program, which provides "partial Bank guarantees to support borrowers in gaining access to syndicated bank loans and international capital markets," is best suited to infrastructure needs.[64] The ECO program, launched in 1989 to replace the previous B-loan scheme, has so far provided guarantees to one project each in Hungary, India, Pakistan, and Jamaica; several others are being considered. In view of its flexibility and ability to mobilize relatively large sums of private capital flows compared with the traditional IBRD loans, the ECO has added a new dimension to Bank operations and is expected to be improved.

Human resource development is another important function. Rapid accumulation of human resources has been one of the key factors of East Asia's success. There are two components in human resource development. First, a broad human resource base is of the utmost importance. Japan's postwar success in manufactur-

---

64. On capital flows to middle-income countries see, for example, World Bank, *World Debt Tables: 1993–94*, vol. 1 (Washington, 1993), p. 72.

ing owes much to the availability of relatively cheap, abundant, and educated labor, which enabled companies to adapt to new technologies and achieve rapid productivity growth. Much attention has been paid to higher education in developing countries, the effects of which have barely trickled down to vast undereducated populations and have led to brain drain overseas (including to the Bank). This does not help developing countries achieve their development goals, especially poverty reduction. The Bank has been and must continue to play a leading role in this regard, including education, population control, health, nutrition, and women in development.

Second, while basic education will lift up the human resource base, human resource development within government is also crucial. At the very least, government needs to prepare an environment in which private entrepreneurship can flourish, but in most developing countries the governments are not up to such performance: they are simply incapable or they lack good governance. The need for the government to function properly is emphasized in the *East Asian Miracle* study and elsewhere, and the Bank has been contributing to good governance by providing technical assistance associated with structural adjustment operations and through policy dialogues with borrowing countries. But such assistance tends to be neglected once a country graduates from structural adjustment operations because of an improved balance of payments position. It is in this way that huge structural impediments within the government are left intact. To avoid this outcome, the Bank needs to improve its technical assistance to borrower governments, including ones that no longer need structural adjustment lending.

Structural adjustment has been questioned by the Japanese. From a different point of view, Tony Killick of the Overseas Development Institute in London points out that although the policy thrust of the adjustment programs is generally sound, there is little evidence of strong program results in low-income countries.[65] Killick contends that this is in part because conditionality has a modest capability for achieving improved economic policies, and international financial institutions have similar constraints of their own, such as limited knowledge of a country and mismatch of time horizons between the adjusting countries and the institutions. He concludes that imposed policy change rarely works and emphasizes the importance of policy ownership of developing countries. His points seem complementary to the Japanese critique. The Bank and borrowing countries, in the process of adjustment operations, need to pay more attention to policy ownership, which should be the central element of much needed self-help efforts by the developing countries.

The Bank has been the intellectual leader in development matters. It is certainly important that it continue to develop new ideas and directions in development policies. Collection and dissemination of the best practices is no less important.

65. Tony Killick, "Improving the Effectiveness of Financial Assistance for Policy Reform," paper prepared for the 47th meeting of the Development Committee, Overseas Development Institute, London, September 27, 1993.

The East Asian experience suggests that each country owes much to learning and adopting good practices from elsewhere in the region. Although it is arguable that the East Asian interaction was possible only because of similar cultural and historical backgrounds of the countries in the region, the region's experience gives many lessons that can be adopted by countries in other regions. The Bank is endowed with abundant experience, both successes and failures, and must construct development policies and strategies based on such unique assets in combination with its innovative research work. In so doing, the Bank and policymakers in developing countries need to be patient: learning by doing, which facilitates policy ownership of developing countries, takes time, usually more than a generation.

The Bank as Bureaucratic Organization

The Bank as an organization has many faces: its well-known highly qualified staff (often with doctorates), its bureaucracy and inflexibility, and its secrecy, just to mention a few. In any case, as an organization the Bank has not only strengths but also weaknesses. In this section, I would like to raise some questions on the institution's organization.

WISE MEN'S COMPLACENCY? The Bank and the IMF staff members are highly qualified: most of the professional staff, especially economists, hold doctorates or master's degrees from top-ranked universities.

Such an intellectual environment enables the Bank to bridge the distance between academics and practitioners: the Bank is *the* intellectual leader in the field of development. Indeed, it has initiated a lot of new ideas and practices such as structural adjustment frameworks, outward-oriented policies, win-win policies of environmental protection, and so on, as can be seen from the annual World Development Reports and other Bank publications. Most bilateral and multilateral aid agencies have assimilated its policies and procedures. The Bank also chairs Consultative Group meetings for which it prepares policy framework and country papers in collaboration with the IMF and borrower governments.

But this intellectual environment or institutional culture seems to have some drawbacks, although it is beyond doubt that the Bank's output on average is of high quality and it is expected to display intellectual leadership. The dominance of economists in the institution may make it too sensitive to the trends of mainstream economic literature, especially in the United States. The problem is that the trends are likely to be driven by socioeconomic changes in the industrial countries, whereas the situations in developing countries remain unchanged. Also, economists tend to pursue sophisticated models that may have little relevance for the real world. This may create gaps between development practice and the policy prescriptions the Bank has established as a virtual monopoly in developing countries.

Moreover, the dominance of economists entails the danger of making the Bank's policy recommendations misleading to developing countries, whose situation needs a more interdisciplinary approach and a mix of skills: economists with scant experience in government and business administration may not be the people best suited to making recommendations to governments in developing countries. The post–cold war developments and the situations in these countries have raised multifaceted challenges, including economies in transition, poverty targeting, environmental protection, good governance, and ownership of development policies. These issues are not separable from wider social and political situations in the countries. In this respect, the practitioners most needed are interdisciplinary rather than individuals with specialized doctorates. Thus it is recommended that the Bank seriously reconsider the appropriateness of its staff's mix of skills. The Bank should also seek ways to cooperate more effectively with other organizations to draw upon their expertise.

AN OVERGROWN ORGANIZATION? With more than 6,000 permanent staff members, the Bank is a large institution by any standard. Given the expanding operations and constant need for quality improvement, the amount of associated work justifies the number to some extent. However, some argue that the Bank is overgrown. For example, the loan commitment per staff member at the OECF (with about 320 staff members in 1994) is three times that of the Bank. Although this does not mean that the OECF is more efficient than the Bank nor that the quality of OECF loans is comparable with those of the Bank, this fact may partly confirm the critics' view.[66]

It could be argued that the Bank has embraced too many roles. For example, some of the Bank's functions overlap with those of other international financial institutions, especially the IMF, and redefinition of demarcations may conclude that some of the Bank's roles, for example, macroeconomic analysis and some regional initiatives, could be given to the IMF and regional development banks, which have comparative advantages in these fields. Some suggest that the IMF and the Bank will eventually merge.[67] It is certainly true that there are many overlapping responsibilities at the two institutions, and they need much closer coordination. But merging seems farfetched. The roles of the IMF and the Bank are in principle different, though some elements such as transition issues overlap: one deals with macroeconomic matters, while the other specializes in developmental issues. Merging them into a mega-institution may do more harm than good: it will bring mega-bureaucracy and cannot be cost effective.

66. I have by no means intended to say that the OECF's performance is superior to the Bank's. The request system of the Japanese ODA means that the OECF does not to have to prepare its own projects, whereas the Bank is involved in the project preparation from the initial stages. Likewise, the depth of project appraisal and economic and sector work of the OECF could be said to be less than that of the Bank.

67. "Sisters in the Wood: A Survey of the IMF and the World Bank," *Economist*, October 12, 1991, p. 5–48.

The size of the Bank also means difficulties in maintaining institutional identity, thus making it a bureaucratic machine. For example, it is widely observed that tasks of officers are divided in a piecemeal fashion, which often leaves an impression that the Bank is not working as an organization but as a collection of individuals. Of course, highly specific skills and expertise are often needed, and as long as piecemeal decisions are made, such an organization is most effective. However, such an organization makes interdepartmental coordination difficult and thus creating an institutional identity difficult. As a result, different parts of the institution tend to act in different ways. More important, when the Bank faces drastic changes in the external environment, readjustment can only be initiated by top management, an institutional weakness; such centralization of management was the trademark of the centrally controlled economies, which have collapsed.

Compartmentalization of day-to-day business and centralization of decision-making have other drawbacks. Because lower entities of the institutions are highly specialized, they tend to pay much less attention to overall administrative issues, portfolio management, and managerial discipline. Although I would not argue for a fundamental reshuffling, I would like to see the Bank make efforts to modify and streamline its business conduct. This is also important to improve the Bank's reputation.

It might be worthwhile to reconsider the career path of the young professionals who constitute the mainstream of the Bank staff. Before they are promoted to managers, they experience only narrow fields of the operation. This means that they tend to climb narrowly defined ladders in Washington, thus facilitating organizational inflexibility, which is not compatible with the interdisciplinary demands of the Bank's constituent countries. As a remedy, it is recommended that these staff members, especially when they are junior, be posted to field offices in developing countries and acquire experiences in the realities of development. To avoid organizational inflexibility and to bring in fresh management perspectives, the Bank should also appoint more outsiders to managerial posts.

BANK INITIATIVES FOR IMPROVEMENT: CONTINUOUS MOMENTUM NEEDED. Although I have raised a number of criticisms, I by no means wish to denounce the Bank as a white elephant. As a former civil servant, I know the complexity associated with the reorganization of large institutions, and so I do appreciate recent Bank initiatives for improving development effectiveness and organizational transparency as a courageous step forward.

As a preferred creditor as well as the leader in the development field, the Bank needs to maintain its reputation and the good performance of its portfolio. The Bank itself is quite aware of the needs, and the Wapenhans report, which was initiated by Lewis Preston, pointed out various problems.[68] The report attracted much attention, and was followed by an action plan to improve Bank-borrower

68. World Bank, "Effective Implementation: Key to Development Impact."

dialogue, development policy ownership of borrowers, participation of affected people, project design, supervision of ongoing projects, operations evaluation, and internal changes. The scope of the plan is thus wide, and if fully implemented it will immensely improve the effectiveness of Bank operations.

The Bank is facing an increasing number of criticisms from nongovernmental organizations. Although there are legitimate criticisms, there could also be unsubstantiated or misleading statements. It is understandable that the Bank, as an organization, needs to protect itself from unnecessary and sometimes misleading allegations by misunderstanding and misinformation. This led the Bank to adopt a broad information disclosure policy, and an inspection panel system, which are expected to increase the organization's transparency and accountability, though information disclosure should be carefully operated in order not to violate borrowing countries' sovereignty and cofinancers' need to safeguard their own interests.

In the face of pressures from nongovernmental organizations, the Bank's shareholder governments are increasingly cautious about portfolio performance. Although there are further criticisms that those efforts are not sufficient, changes take time and they should be implemented step by step. The shareholders thus need to provide full moral support to the Bank's initiatives while remaining vigilant on the progress of implementation. When necessary, they should whip the Bank to expedite the progress, and they are duly expected to do so. Furthermore, the shareholders can contribute to the improvement of portfolio performance by, for example, insisting on allocating a larger share of the budget to operation evaluation.

Advice to Japan

Having raised a number of demanding points about the Bank, it is fair to pose some to Japan.

Human Contributions

Japanese representation on the staff of the Bank is far from being in line with its financial contributions.[69] The share of Japanese staff at the Bank was 1.8 percent in fiscal year 1994 and 2.1 percent among professional staff.[70] Japan's financial contributions are far larger: its share of the Bank is more than 6 percent, for example, and

69. This section owes much to Hirono and Stern's comment to Ryokichi Hirono, "Japan's Leadership Role in the Multilateral Development Institutions," in Safiqul Islam, ed., *Yen for Development: Japanese Foreign Aid and the Politics of Burden-Sharing* (Washington: Council on Foreign Relations, 1991), pp. 171–81. See also Masaki Shiratori, *Sekai Ginko Gurupu: Tojyoukoku enjyo to Nihon no yakuwari* [The World Bank Group] (Tokyo: Kokusai Kaihatsu Journal-sha, 1993); Ministry of Finance, *Kokusai Kin-yuu Kikan ni okeru Nihon-jin Shokuin no Katsudou Sokushin ni Tsuite* [On Promotion of Japanese Staff Members at International Financial Institutions] (Tokyo, 1987).

70. Figures are for the World Bank Group, including IBRD, IFC, and MIGA. Professional staff includes higher-level staff in grades 18–30.

contributions to IDA make up more than 17 percent of the organization's budget. Japan is determined to enhance its human contributions to the international community and the Bank is not an exception. Although the Japanese government has been trying to contribute intellectually to the Bank's policy formulation, its influence is naturally limited as long as the Japanese staff representation remains so low (the management and staff play a central role at the Bank). The problem is well recognized and it has become customary for the Diet, when Bank capital increases are brought up, to pass a resolution demanding an increase in the number of Japanese on the staff.

There are several causes of the low representation: language barriers, the lack of job security compared with Japanese industry's practice of lifelong employment, and the increasingly unattractive Bank pay because of the appreciating yen. In addition, there seems to be a mismatch of the qualifications required by the Bank and the ones Japanese candidates can offer. The Bank usually demands postgraduate degrees and work experience in specialized fields. Although there are a number of Japanese experienced in various fields, they usually do not hold graduate degrees because Japanese companies, where most of the candidates gain work experience, normally recruit recent graduates and provide in-house training.

There are many interrelated factors, and the difference in working styles is one: as noted earlier, the Bank is paper oriented whereas Japan is far more experience oriented. The difference is difficult to overcome, and no quick remedy can be found. However, if we change our viewpoint, such a difference could be a source of benefit both to the Bank and to Japan: they can learn good practices from each other. So there is a compelling need to create a critical mass of Japanese staff in the Bank to transfer Japanese practical know-how.

What, then, can the government of Japan and the Bank do? First, the government should provide incentives for potential candidates to work at the Bank. The government needs to create an atmosphere that working with the Bank is meritorious through, for example, increased exposure and public relation efforts of the Bank's activities. Second, a targeting approach is also needed. Younger Japanese are increasingly studying abroad, and if the government concentrates its efforts on this population, the probability of getting candidates is much higher. The government can also target returnees from abroad, especially women, who historically find it difficult to get senior positions in Japan. Third, the government should improve the exchange of personnel between the Bank and its Japanese counterparts, such as the Eximbank in Japan and the OECF, which would enable networking among these institutions. Finally, both the Bank and the Japanese government need to be patient; there is no quick remedy.

Financial Contributions

Japan is committed to increasing its financial contribution and is expected to do so, but the contribution has been called faceless or purposeless. The contribution is changing: in the case of international assistance to Cambodia, Vietnam, and Mongolia, Japan clearly played a leading role in collaboration with the Bank. Likewise,

Japan contributed to the establishment of sectoral investment programs under the third phase of the Special Program of Assistance (SPA-3) to Sub-Saharan Africa. These attempts are certainly welcome and should be enhanced.

However, the fiscal position is increasingly tight even in Japan, and it is more and more essential that aid monies be used effectively. In this regard Japan needs to strengthen its agencies for bilateral aid. Likewise, Japan needs to be vigilant about the efficiency and effectiveness of the multilateral development banks, to which it has contributed so much. The U.S. administration, facing budgetary and congressional pressure, is using carrot-and-stick tactics toward the multilateral development banks. Although such a coercive approach is not absolutely recommendable for Japan, it may provide a reference point.

Intellectual Contributions

As noted earlier, the difference in working styles and ways of thinking encourages the exchange of views between the Bank and Japan. Apparently, the *East Asian Miracle* study has been conducted as an initial attempt, and the fact that many seminars and workshops followed the report is certainly favorable. Japan needs to continue its efforts. Japanese policymakers and aid practitioners need to learn more about how the Bank has reached its present policy prescriptions in structural adjustment, trade liberalization, and financial markets. At the same time, they need to look more deeply into themselves, because the Japanese miracle has long become a historical phenomenon and some of the facts may have different interpretations in today's context.

Conclusion

The relationship between the Bank and Japan is often referred to as a successful graduation story. Indeed, Japan, whose borrowing capacity the Bank initially treated with doubt, is now the largest provider of aid to developing countries. Needless to say, Japan gained many valuable things from the Bank. These included new ways of thinking and novel technologies, not to mention infrastructure financed by the Bank. It is beyond doubt that the Bank contributed greatly to Japan's postwar development.

Now not only has Japan graduated financially from the Bank, it is the second largest shareholder. However, there are still many areas in which Japan needs the Bank. Take project formulation. Japanese aid agencies still do not have the expertise that agencies in the Bank have, and the Japanese agencies need to rely on cofinancing with the Bank. But in economic policy, management, and other fields, Japanese experiences remain to be exploited by the Bank.

Therefore, it is necessary and desirable that such a mutually beneficial relationship be explored and strengthened. I would like to see the Bank and Japan establish an ever closer and more constructive relationship in this respect.   .

EIGHT

The World Bank's Lending in South Asia

S. Guhan

FROM THEIR founding through the end of fiscal year 1990 the World Bank and its affiliate the International Development Association (IDA) funded 719 project operations in the seven countries of South Asia, for a total of more than $50 billion, spread over more than twenty sectors and subsectors.[1] The region contains some of the oldest and largest borrowers of the World Bank Group and includes India, its largest single borrower. Containing a fifth of the world's population and perhaps three-quarters of its absolute poor, South Asia has been, and will continue to be, a prime theater of involvement for the Bank.[2]

1. South Asia, for the purposes of this paper, includes India, Pakistan, Bangladesh, Sri Lanka, Nepal, Bhutan, and Maldives. The Bank's classification of South Asia has reflected, over the years, growth in its membership and changes consequent on internal administrative reorganizations. India was an original signatory to the Bretton Woods agreements. Pakistan joined the Bank in 1950, to be followed by Sri Lanka (then Ceylon) in the same year. Nepal became a member in 1961. These four countries along with Afghanistan, Iran, and Burma constituted the Bank's "South Asia" before 1973. The region was merged into "Asia" during 1973–75, when Bangladesh joined the Bank (1973) upon its emergence as a separate country. Between 1975 and 1987, when South Asia again came to be treated as a separate region, it included India, Pakistan, Bangladesh, Myanmar, Nepal, Sri Lanka, Maldives (which became a member in 1978), and Bhutan (in 1981). In the reorganization of the Bank in 1987, Pakistan was included in the Europe, Middle East, and North Africa (EMENA) region, and the other seven countries were merged in Asia. The reorganization of 1991 revived South Asia as a separate region comprising the seven countries covered in this chapter.

2. Except where the International Bank for Reconstruction and Development (IBRD) and the International Development Association (IDA) are distinguished in the text or in context, references to "the Bank" include IDA, and loan amounts include credits.

317

The scope of this chapter is confined to the project lending operations of the Bank in South Asia and needs to be situated in the wider context of Bank-borrower relationships that will be discussed in a forthcoming history of the World Bank. It must also be selective in its treatment of major topics, given the volume, scope, and diversity of the Bank's project lending. Moreover, whereas this review is confined to a window of time, the Bank is a continually evolving organization, and therefore some of the judgments made here are likely to have only a transient validity. Despite these limitations, a study of what the Bank has attempted, achieved, and failed to achieve in the 1970s and 1980s should be of special interest for at least two reasons. First, these two decades witnessed a phenomenal growth and diversification in project lending, making them a particularly active and interesting period. Second, the 1970s and 1980s may also prove to have been a watershed, since the coming decades in South Asia are likely to see a slowdown in the growth of overall lending levels as well as a shift toward nonproject, adjustment lending.

The chapter is organized as follows. The first section sets out the development context in South Asia by way of background. The second discusses the important characteristics of project lending in the region. The third reviews lending strategies, the policy dialogue, and project impact in terms of major sectors and borrowers. The concluding section puts together an overall assessment of the Bank's project lending experience over the two decades.

South Asia: The Development Context

The countries of South Asia, despite important differences, share several characteristics that distinguish them as a region. The main land mass of South Asia is marked off from the rest of the continent by the deserts of Balochistan in the northwest, the Himalayan ranges in the wide middle, and the thick jungles of northeastern India and Myanmar in the east. The Indus River basin straddles Pakistan and India, while the Ganges and the Brahmaputra flow through India and Bangladesh.

The South Asian countries are reasonably well endowed with minerals and with fuel resources for energy development. Hydroelectric resources are important for power generation in India, Pakistan, and Sri Lanka, and there is massive untapped potential in Nepal. There is considerable scope for irrigation in all the major countries of the region. Except from the rivers fed by Himalayan snowmelt, irrigation depends directly on rain or on rain-fed rivers or on groundwater recharged by rain and river flows. The combination of snowmelt and rain in the summer months often leads to heavy flooding in the north and northeast of the subcontinent, Bangladesh being particularly vulnerable. Droughts are equally common, and it is not unusual for different parts of the region to be in the grip of floods and drought at the same time. Cyclonic storms in the Bay of Bengal

Table 8-1. *Population Characteristics for Seven South Asian Countries, Selected Periods, 1980–91*

Indicator	India	Pakistan	Bangla-desh	Sri Lanka	Nepal	Bhutan	Maldives
Population, 1990 (millions)	850.0	112.0	107.0	17.0	18.9	1.4	0.2
Population density, 1991 (persons per square kilometer)	253.0	137.0	725.0	256.0	131.0	30.0	693.0
Average annual growth of population, 1980–90 (percent)	2.1	3.1	2.1	1.4	2.6	2.2	3.2
Urban share of total population, 1990 (percent)	27.0	32.0	16.4	21.4	9.6	5.2	29.4
Average annual growth of urban population, 1980–90 (percent)	3.6	4.5	5.6	1.7	6.6	5.2	5.8
Hypothetical stationary population (millions)[a]	1,862.0	399.0	257.0	28.4	58.8	5.3	1.0

Source: World Bank, *Social Indicators of Development 1991–92* (Johns Hopkins University Press, 1992), pp. 142, 234, 22, 286, 216, 34, 192.

a. A stationary population is one in which age- and sex-specific mortality rates have not changed over a long period and fertility rates have remained at the replacement level; that is, the net reproduction rate equals 1.

periodically cause heavy damage to lives, crops, homes, and property in Bangladesh and along the eastern coast of India. Although seismic activity is not frequent, serious earthquakes have occurred in Nepal, in northern India and Pakistan, and most recently in central India. Soil waterlogging and salinity caused by the formation of alkaline pans are major problems in Pakistan.

Demographics

The South Asian population of nearly 1.1 billion as of mid-1991 is shared very unequally among the countries in the region (table 8-1). India, the second most populous country in the world, accounts for more than three-quarters of the region's total, with a current population of about 850 million. Far behind but next in size come Bangladesh and Pakistan, with populations of around 110 million each, while Nepal and Sri Lanka each have populations of a little less than 20 million. Bhutan (1.4 million) and Maldives (0.2 million) are tiny. Since 1960 annual population growth in the region has been around 2.3 percent, with a marginal slackening to 2.2 percent in the 1980s. There is considerable variation among the major South Asian countries in population growth rates and their determinants. India, growing by 2.1 percent per year between 1980 and 1990, is still adding about 18 million every year to its numbers. Current annual growth rates are also high in three of the other countries: 3.1 percent in Pakistan, 2.1 percent in Bangladesh, and 2.6 percent in Nepal. Sri Lanka has, in contrast, achieved an impressive demographic transition, bringing down birth and death rates to 20 and 6 per 1,000, respectively, and its current growth rate to 1.4 percent per year.

With one-fifth of the world's population, South Asia occupies barely 4 percent of global land area; accordingly, population densities are very high. The level and growth of urbanization, however, have so far remained low. Even in India and Pakistan, which are the most urbanized, about 70 percent of the people live in rural areas. City sizes have grown in absolute numbers, however, and increasingly the provision of urban services has emerged as a major problem and an expensive one. The large absolute sizes and high densities of population in South Asia have many consequences and implications for development: there is intense pressure on the environment; agricultural holdings are small and fragmented; the cost of providing education, health, and other basic services is high; and urban congestion is a serious problem.

Gross National Product

The South Asian countries are all classified by the World Bank as low income, and four of them—Bangladesh, Nepal, Bhutan, and Maldives—are classified as least developed. The region as a whole recorded an average annual real GNP growth of 4.3 percent in the 1960s, which declined to 3.5 percent in the 1970s but accelerated to over 5 percent in the 1980s. South Asia's growth performance is doubtless modest, but it has been sustained and there are some hopeful signs of acceleration. Also, the region's recent performance is impressive in that it represents a break from that of the colonial period before the 1950s, when long-term growth was barely 1 percent per year, agricultural growth stagnated, and per capita real incomes were stationary despite low (around 1 percent) population growth.[3]

There are fairly wide variations in growth performance, overall and per capita, among the major South Asian countries (table 8-2). Pakistan has shown the best long-run record of GNP growth, in the range of 5 to 6 percent over the last three decades, followed by India and Sri Lanka with growth rates close to 4 percent. Bangladesh's long-run growth rate has been only around 3 percent, while that of Nepal has been close to 3.3 percent. Within each country there have also been large fluctuations in growth from one year to the next as a result of internal factors (weather, natural calamities, civil unrest) and changes in the external environment (terms of trade, global recession, and aid flows). In the medium term, policy changes have also played their part in improving or dampening economic performance.

3. The growth rates given here are official U.S. dollar–denominated GNP growth rates as reported by the World Bank; that is, they are generally official national estimates converted to real dollars at official exchange rates. For growth rates in the colonial period see A. Heston, "National Income," in Dharma Kumar, ed., *The Cambridge Economic History of India*, vol. 2 (Cambridge University Press, 1983), pp. 376–462.

Table 8-2. *Output Indicators for Seven South Asian Countries,*
Selected Years and Periods, 1965–90

Indicator	India	Pakistan	Bangla-desh	Sri Lanka	Nepal	Bhutan	Maldives
GNP per capita, 1990 (dollars)	350.0	380.0	210.0	470.0	170.0	190.0	450.0
Average annual growth rate of GDP (percent)							
1965–80	3.6	5.2	1.7	4.0	1.9	n.a.	n.a.
1980–90	5.3	6.3	4.3	4.0	4.6	7.5	n.a.
Average annual growth rate of per capita GNP, 1965–90 (percent)	1.9	2.5	0.7	2.9	0.5	n.a	2.8
GDP structure, 1990 (percent of total)							
Agriculture	31.0	26.0	38.0	26.0	60.0	43.0	n.a.
Industry	29.0	25.0	15.0	26.0	14.0	27.0	n.a.
Services	40.0	49.0	46.0	48.0	26.0	29.0	n.a.

Source: World Bank, *World Development Report 1992: Development and the Environment* (Oxford University Press, 1992), pp. 218, 220, 222, 285.

n.a. Not available.

Sectoral growth rates have varied over time and among countries. At the end of the 1980s agriculture accounted for 26 percent of GDP in Sri Lanka and Pakistan, about 30 percent in India, and nearly 40 percent in Bangladesh; industry contributed 20 to 30 percent of GDP in India, Pakistan, and Sri Lanka and only 15 percent in Bangladesh; services accounted for about 40 or 50 percent of GDP in most of the countries. The declining contribution of agriculture to GDP with no corresponding decline in its employment share has widened rural-urban income inequalities and dampened increases in real wages in agriculture. Industrial growth, besides being inadequate, has not been sufficiently labor intensive.

Investment and Saving

Gross domestic investment as a proportion of GDP in South Asia has risen significantly, to more than 20 percent by the end of the 1970s from levels of 10 to 15 percent three decades ago. At the end of the 1980s India, with the highest investment ratio in the region (about 23 percent), had the lowest dependence on foreign saving (about 10 percent of investment). Pakistan's investment ratio was lower (about 18 percent), but external dependence was higher (about 30 percent), while Sri Lanka and Nepal with investment ratios around 20 percent relied on foreign saving for financing 35 to 55 percent of investment. Bangladesh, with the lowest investment ratio (about 12 percent), depended most on external saving (about 80 percent of investment).

Industry

The manufacturing sector in the South Asian countries encompasses a wide spectrum ranging from large, modern factory establishments to small-scale units, modern and traditional, and a large component of dispersed household activities such as handlooms, crafts, and artisanal occupations. In the last four decades industrial structures have considerably broadened and diversified, particularly in India and Pakistan, extending to the chemical, fertilizer, machinery, transportation, electrical, and electronics industries. Initially, import substitution rather than exports or domestic demand was relied upon to provide the impetus for industrialization. Industry was sheltered behind high tariffs as well as quantitative import restrictions. The pessimistic policy stance toward export promotion was confirmed by high-cost, excessively protected, noncompetitive manufactures, which could not compete in world markets. Consequently, South Asia fell behind the newly industrializing countries of East Asia in exploiting exports as an engine of growth in the formative decades of the 1960s and 1970s.

Another feature of industrialization in South Asia has been extensive public sector ownership of key industries. Besides owning enterprises directly, the state has played a major role in the regulation and promotion of private enterprise in the principal South Asian countries. Industrial regulation has been pervasive, affecting the location, capacity, and technology of new units and their expansion or diversification; regulations relating to imports, foreign technology, and capital markets have also been widespread. The 1980s, however, witnessed a perceptible trend toward deregulation, export-oriented trade policy reform, some degree of privatization, and financial sector reforms in most of the region, including Pakistan, Bangladesh, Sri Lanka, Nepal, and, most recently, India.

Infrastructure

There has been considerable progress since decolonization in the development of infrastructure, although it continues to be overstretched and under pressure. From very low initial levels, power generation capacity by the end of the 1980s had risen to about 71,000 megawatts (MW), including some nuclear capacity in India (1,800 MW) and Pakistan (70 MW). However, commercial energy consumption levels are still low, only about two-thirds of the average for low-income economies even in India and Pakistan, which are the most advanced. In many rural areas of South Asia, especially in Nepal, energy needs are still met from fuel wood, the traditional source, at the cost of steady deforestation. In the last three decades transportation, particularly roads, has seen much improvement, and India has one of the largest railway systems in the world. However, there are wide variations between countries and between urban and rural areas within countries. There has been good progress in developing telecommunications, although numbers of telephone lines per thousand residents are still very low, especially in rural areas.

Trade Structures

In general, external trade structures in the South Asian countries are characterized by relatively low ratios of exports to GDP, a large proportion of traditional exports in the total, and very low shares in world trade. It is encouraging that the South Asian countries have, in the last three decades, significantly reduced their dependency on importation of food and fuel. India, Pakistan, and Sri Lanka are more or less self-sufficient in foodgrains, although grain imports occur in years of shortfall and for replenishing stocks. Bangladesh, however, continues to depend on substantial food importation, most of which is financed by food aid. Nepal is an exporter of rice. Typically, crude oil and petroleum products accounted for about 15 to 20 percent of the import bill in the late 1980s; this proportion would have been much higher but for increases in the domestic production of oil, gas, and coal since the late 1970s, a development that has received considerable support from the World Bank.

Macroeconomic Adjustment

By and large, South Asia adjusted well to the first oil shock in the early 1970s, helped by emigrant remittances and aid flows, energy import substitution, and domestic macroeconomic policies that kept inflation and fiscal deficits under reasonable control. But the decade of the 1980s, following the second oil shock, plunged the major South Asian countries into serious and continuing balance of payments problems for a variety of reasons: remittances by South Asians working abroad plateaued; aid flows registered low real increases in volume while their concessionality significantly declined as a result of changes in the composition of aid; commercial borrowings and resort to the International Monetary Fund increased, entailing heavy repayment burdens; widening fiscal deficits resulted in excessive domestic absorption spilling over into the balance of payments; large quantities of defense goods were imported (in India, Pakistan, and Sri Lanka); drought, floods (particularly in Bangladesh), civil strife (Sri Lanka), and political uncertainties toward the end of the 1980s (India, Pakistan, Bangladesh) had disruptive effects; and, most recently, the sharp although temporary impact of the 1990–91 Gulf crisis gave the economies of the region a severe jolt. These factors resulted in sizable debt accumulation in the 1980s: from a total of about $35 billion in debt outstanding and disbursed for India, Pakistan, and Bangladesh in 1980 to over $90 billion in 1989. Debt service rose by the end of the 1980s to over 20 percent of exports in India, Pakistan, and Bangladesh.

In the 1980s fiscal deficits burgeoned in India, Pakistan, and Bangladesh to around 7 to 9 percent of GDP. Sri Lanka, despite having reduced its very large fiscal imbalance around 1980, still ran a deficit of nearly 12 percent of GDP in 1989. In the context of worsening fiscal deficits and balance of payments problems, most of the South Asian countries—Pakistan, Bangladesh, Sri Lanka, Nepal, and most recently India (in 1991)—have embarked on macroeconomic stabilization

Table 8-3. *Human Development Indicators for Seven South Asian Countries*

Indicator	India	Pakistan	Bangla-desh	Sri Lanka	Nepal	Bhutan	Maldives
Life expectancy at birth (years)	59	56	52	71	52	49	62
Crude death rate (deaths per 1,000 population)	11	12	14	6	14	17	9
Infant mortality rate (infant deaths per 1,000 live births)	92	103	105	19	121	123	70
Total fertility rate[a]	3.9	5.8	4.6	2.4	5.7	5.5	6.2
Crude birth rate (births per 1,000 population)	30	42	35	20	40	39	43
Adult illiteracy (percent)[b]							
Total	52	65	65	12	74	62	n.a.
Female	66	79	78	17	87	75	n.a.
Primary school enrollment (percent of eligible population)							
Total	98	38	70	107	86	26	n.a.
Female	82	27	64	106	57	20	n.a.
Secondary school enrollment (percent of eligible population)							
Total	43	20	17	74	30	5	n.a.
Female	31	12	11	76	17	2	n.a.

Source: World Bank, *Social Indicators of Development 1991–92* (Johns Hopkins University Press, 1992), pp. 142–43, 234–35, 22–23, 286–87, 216–17, 34–35, 192–93.

a. Number of children that would be born to a woman if she were to live to the end of her childbearing years and bear children at each age in accordance with prevailing age-specific fertility rates.

b. Among persons older than 15 years of age.

n.a. Not available.

and structural adjustment reforms in fiscal, trade, investment, balance of payments, and financial sector policies and in sectors such as agriculture, industry, and energy; the Bank has played a major role in stimulating and supporting these reforms.

Human Development

Four decades ago, at the time of independence from colonial rule, all the South Asian countries with the notable exception of Sri Lanka had very low literacy rates and short life expectancies and fared poorly on other educational, health, and human development indicators. Progress since then has been steady but slow (table 8-3). Sri Lanka, which got an early start in human development, has achieved an adult literacy rate of 88 percent, a life expectancy of 71 years, an infant mortality rate of 19 per thousand live births, and a total fertility rate of 2.4, close to the replacement ratio. On the other hand, adult literacy is still only about 48 percent in India, 35 percent in Pakistan and Bangladesh, and 26 percent in Nepal. Life expectancies are less than 60 years in India and Pakistan and around 50 in Bangladesh, Nepal, and Bhutan. Infant mortality rates are as high as 120 per thousand in Nepal and Bhutan, and marginally below or above 100 in India, Pakistan, and Bangladesh. In each country there are wide differentials between males and females, between rural and urban populations, and across regions on principal social indicators such as literacy, female literacy, school enrollment, access to preventive and curative health facilities, and availability of safe water. Of direct concern are continuing high total fertility rates operating on large absolute population sizes alongside falling death rates. Total fertility rates are between 5 and 6 in Pakistan and Nepal and in the range of 4 to 5 in India and Bangladesh.

Poverty and Inequality

Consistent, reliable, and comparable data on poverty and inequality are not available for the major South Asian countries.[4] The best available estimates suggest that the poverty proportion (defined as the proportion of households whose income or consumption falls below nationally stipulated poverty levels) in the late 1980s was as high as 70 to 80 percent in Bangladesh, about 60 percent in Nepal, 30 to 40 percent in India and Pakistan, and about 20 percent in Sri Lanka. These estimates would imply that the number of absolute poor in South Asia is on the order of 450 million, of whom about 70 percent are in India and nearly 15 percent in Bangladesh. About 80 percent of the poor are in rural areas, and in the main, urban poverty is a spillover of rural immiseration. Available evidence suggests some decline in the poverty proportion in both India and Bangladesh between the late 1970s and the mid-1980s.

The distribution of income and of land and other assets is highly skewed in all countries of the region: in India, Pakistan, and Bangladesh the income share of the poorest 20 percent of the population is typically about 8 to 9 percent, while that of the top 10 percent of the population is 25 to 30 percent. In each country the regional dimensions of poverty are important, the poorest regions being the eastern states in India, the northwest frontier and Balochistan in Pakistan, the hilly tribal areas in eastern Bangladesh, the mountainous part of Nepal, and the dry zone in northern Sri Lanka.

---

4. There is a large literature on rural poverty in South Asia. T. N. Srinivasan and Pranab K. Bardhan, eds., *Rural Poverty in South Asia* (Columbia University Press, 1988); and Inderjit Singh, *The Great Ascent: The Rural Poor in South Asia* (Johns Hopkins University Press, 1990) are two recent contributions.

Politics and Governance

India and Sri Lanka have remained vigorous, open democracies, although the Indian record was blotted by the regime's resort to emergency powers in 1975–77. Pakistan and Bangladesh have gone through prolonged periods of military or authoritarian civilian rule, but democracy was restored in the late 1980s; Nepal has moved from an absolute to a constitutional monarchy. All the South Asian countries except Nepal and Bhutan retain the bureaucratic legacy of the British colonial administration, which for all its shortcomings has provided the region with development-oriented administrative structures and capabilities. These have been sustained by a series of five-year development plans and growth in capacities for project planning and implementation.

The region has, however, been bedeviled by conflicts and tensions between and within countries. The Kashmir issue has been a major irritant in Indo-Pakistani relations, erupting into wars in 1948–49 and in 1965. The birth of Bangladesh (the former East Pakistan) as an independent state in 1971 resulted from a civil war in undivided Pakistan, followed by hostilities between India and Pakistan. Problems have arisen between landlocked Nepal and India on trade and transit, between Bangladesh and India on the use of eastern river waters, and between India and Sri Lanka over the latter's Tamil problem (Sri Lanka has been facing serious internal ethnic conflict in its north and east with its Tamil minority since 1983). Militancy has been a problem at a regional level in India and Pakistan as well. In the late 1970s Pakistan had to cope with a massive influx of refugees from Afghanistan. All this has taken its toll on current economic management, project implementation, and long-term development. Equally important, intraregional tensions have gotten in the way of closer cooperation in trade, investment, energy, irrigation and flood control, and environmental protection, in all of which there is much potential for regional coordination and cooperation.[5]

The Development Agenda

This overview has tended to concentrate on the principal development problems of South Asia, especially as they have emerged in the last two decades. At the same time, however, the very considerable achievements of the postcolonial period should not be overlooked. Starting from very low levels of income, the countries in the region have nearly trebled their saving rates and have registered sustained

---

5. On regional cooperation possibilities in South Asia see B. G. Verghese, *Waters of Hope: Integrated Water Resource Development and Regional Cooperation within the Himalayan-Ganga-Brahmaputra-Barak Basin* (New Delhi: Oxford University Press and IBH Publishing House, 1990); and A. A. Waqif, ed., *Regional Cooperation in Industry and Energy: Prospects for South Asia* (New Delhi: Sage Publications, 1991). A number of studies relating to possibilities for regional cooperation have been undertaken for and under the auspices of the South Asian Association for Regional Cooperation (SAARC).

growth. Much progress has been made toward food security, and famines have been prevented. Industrial structures have gained in depth and diversity. Social indicators have improved. In all this, aid has made a useful contribution.

The continuing development priorities for South Asia are also quite clear: adequate and sustained growth in per capita incomes; agricultural development to provide the basis for food security, poverty alleviation, reduction of imports and expansion of exports, and the creation of demand and supply in the large home markets; preventive and promotional measures for population control in a wider framework of human development, particularly literacy, female literacy, primary health, access to drinking water, sanitation, and nutrition; urban services oriented to the poor; domestic energy development combined with efficient and economic energy use; infrastructural development; and macroeconomic policy reforms that can contain inflation and avoid recurring fiscal and balance of payments crises. The Bank's lending operations in South Asia have been and are being addressed to this many-sided and complex agenda, and it is with reference to that agenda that the size, salience, and success of the Bank's contribution have to be assessed.

The Bank's Lending Operations in South Asia: An Overview

South Asia includes some of the IBRD's and IDA's largest and oldest borrowers; India, Pakistan, and Sri Lanka have been borrowers since the 1950s. India, with total commitments of $35.3 billion as of the end of fiscal 1990, was in absolute terms the largest single borrower from both the IBRD and IDA. Pakistan ($7.4 billion, the seventh largest) and Bangladesh ($5.3 billion, the thirteenth largest) have also been substantial borrowers. At the end of fiscal 1990 the IBRD and IDA had cumulatively undertaken 719 lending operations in the seven South Asian countries, for a total amount of about $51 billion, of which about $23 billion or 45 percent was lent by the IBRD and about $28 billion or 55 percent by IDA (see table 8-4).[6]

The Bank has been an important source of external financing to the major South Asian countries (table 8-5), accounting for about two-fifths of all long-term debt outstanding and disbursed as of 1990 in Nepal, for about a third in India and Bangladesh, and for about a fifth in Pakistan and Sri Lanka. The Bank has a large share of official debt outstanding and disbursed in India (close to 60 percent), around 40 percent in Bangladesh and Nepal, and between 20 and 25 percent in Pakistan and Sri Lanka. India has depended almost entirely on the Bank and IDA for its multilateral borrowing, while the Asian Development Bank (ADB) and Arab multilateral funds have been important sources in the multilateral portfolios of Pakistan, Bangladesh, Sri Lanka, and Nepal.

6. All figures for lending refer to initial commitments at the time of approval. They do not take into account cancellations or loans and credits not declared effective.

Table 8-4. *Cumulative World Bank Lending to Seven South Asian Countries, Fiscal Year 1990*

	IBRD		IDA		Total	
	Number of loans	Millions of dollars	Number of loans	Millions of dollars	Number of loans	Millions of dollars
India	134	18,319.2	178	16,955.7	312	35,274.9
Pakistan	71	4,175.1	82	3,237.0	153	7,412.1
Bangladesh	1	46.1	126	5,248.6	127	5,294.7
Sri Lanka	12	210.7	50	1,323.8	62	1,534.5
Nepal	...	...	56	1,058.3	56	1,058.3
Bhutan	...	...	5	22.8	5	22.8
Maldives	...	...	4	23.9	4	23.9
Total South Asia	218	22,751.1	501	27,870.1	719	50,621.2
Memorandums						
All borrowers	3,176	186,661.7	2,005	58,222.0	5,181	244,883.7
All borrowers excluding China	3,126	181,381.5	1,972	54,294.7	5,098	235,676.2
South Asia's share in total (percent)	...	12.2	...	47.9	...	20.7
South Asia's share in total, excluding China (percent)	...	12.5	...	51.3	...	21.5

Source: World Bank, "IBRD and IDA Cumulative Lending Operations, by Borrower or Guarantor, June 30, 1990," *The World Bank Annual Report 1990* (1990), pp. 178–81.

Table 8-5. *Long-Term Debt Outstanding and Disbursed, Five South Asian Countries, 1990*
Percent

Source of lending	India	Pakistan	Bangladesh	Sri Lanka	Nepal	All five countries
	All long-term debt					
Official	58.5	94.6	98.7	84.5	93.2	71.2
IBRD	12.5	10.3	0.6	1.7	...	10.0
IDA	21.7	12.7	36.5	17.9	43.2	22.1
Private	41.5	5.4	1.3	15.5	6.8	28.8
Total long-term	100.0	100.0	100.0	100.0	100.0	100.0
	Official debt					
Multilateral	59.4	41.9	54.7	36.0	85.1	53.9
IBRD	21.4	10.9	0.6	2.0	...	14.0
IDA	37.1	13.3	37.0	21.1	46.4	31.1
Other	0.9	17.7	17.1	12.9	38.7	8.8
Bilateral	40.6	58.1	45.3	64.0	14.9	46.1
Total official	100.0	100.0	100.0	100.0	100.0	100.0
	Multilateral debt					
IBRD	36.1	26.0	1.0	5.6	...	26.0
IDA	62.5	31.9	67.6	58.7	54.5	57.7
Other	1.4	42.1	31.4	35.7	45.5	16.3
Total multilateral	100.0	100.0	100.0	100.0	100.0	100.0

Source: World Bank, *World Debt Tables 1990*.

Table 8-6. *Share in Total IDA Lending, and IDA Share in Total World Bank Lending, Seven South Asian Countries, by Decade, 1961–90*
Percent

Country	Share in total IDA lending				IDA lending as a share of total World Bank lending			
	1961–70	1971–80	1981–90	1961–90	1961–70	1971–80	1981–90	1961–90
India	46.1	39.4	23.0	29.1	70.4	81.2	35.8	48.1
Pakistan	12.3	5.1	5.3	5.6	43.6	75.4	37.7	43.7
Bangladesh	5.5	7.3	10.1	9.0	76.6	100.0	100.0	99.1
Sri Lanka	0.9	1.9	2.5	2.3	26.2	100.0	89.1	86.3
Nepal	0.1	1.3	2.2	1.8	100.0	100.0	100.0	100.0
Bhutan	0.0	0.0	0.1	0.0	40.0	0.0	100.0	100.0
Maldives	0.0	0.0	20.1	0.0	40.0	100.0	100.0	100.0
Total South Asia	64.9	55.0	43.2	47.9	62.2	83.6	46.2	55.9

Source: Author's calculations based on World Bank data.

Through fiscal 1990 South Asia received 12.5 percent of the Bank's global commitments, 50.8 percent of IDA's, and 21.4 percent of those of the Bank and IDA taken together, if lending to China is excluded, as would seem appropriate since China became a borrower only in the 1980s. South Asia's share in cumulative IDA commitments (excluding China and again through fiscal 1990), at about 51 percent, has been distinctly less than the region's share of the combined population of all low-income countries (excluding China) of 59 percent. It has also steadily declined in the last three decades: from 63.3 percent in 1961–70, to 55.3 percent in 1971–80, and to 43.2 percent in 1981–90 (table 8-6). This is a reflection of progressive increases in the proportion of IDA lending going to Africa in the 1970s and 1980s, and to other eligible borrowers in the 1970s (mainly Indonesia) and of the entry of China in the 1980s, claiming about a 10 percent share in IDA lending in that decade. India, IDA's largest borrower, and to a lesser extent Pakistan have had to bear the brunt of reductions over time in shares of IDA lending to South Asia.[7] It has been possible in the last decade to substantially supplement IDA credits with Bank loans to these two countries, since they have been considered creditworthy for the latter. Although this has both enabled and compensated for reductions in IDA lending to them while increasing the volume of overall lending from the Bank Group, there has been a significant loss of concessionality.

Trends from decade to decade in the nominal volume of total lending and its distribution between the Bank and IDA are shown in table 8-7. Total lending to South Asia in the 1970s was four times the amount lent during the 1960s, with the increase largely accounted for by IDA. Lending in the 1980s was three times that

7. India's share in IDA lending has declined steeply from 45 percent in the 1960s to 39.5 percent in the 1970s and 23 percent in the 1980s. In recent IDA replenishments a ceiling of 30 percent has been placed on lending to India and China combined.

Table 8-7. *IBRD and IDA Lending to South Asia, by Decade, 1960–69*
Millions of U.S. Dollars

Period	IBRD	IDA	Total	IDA share in total (percent)
Through 1960	787.9	0.0	787.9	0.0
1961–70	1,086.7	1,786.6	2,873.3	62.2
1971–80	1,920.0	9,806.2	11,726.2	83.6
1981–90	18,956.5	16,277.3	35,233.8	46.2
Through 1990	22,751.1	27,870.1	50,621.2	55.1

Source: Author's calculations based on World Bank data.

in the 1970s; this time the increase was substantially due to a step-up in IBRD lending to India and Pakistan. Reflecting these changes, IDA's proportion in total lending went up from 62 percent in 1961–70 to 84 percent in 1971–80, but dropped thereafter to 46 percent in 1981–90.

India received 70 percent of cumulative lending to South Asia up to fiscal 1990, followed by Pakistan (15 percent) and Bangladesh (10 percent). The other four countries received a combined share of 5 percent. India's share of IDA lending to South Asia (61 percent) has been significantly less than its population share in South Asia (77 percent). Pakistan's share (12 percent) has been somewhat higher than its population share (10 percent), while Bangladesh's share (19 percent) has been distinctly higher than its population share (10 percent).

MODES AND PROFILE OF LENDING. Table 8-8 shows that project loans have been the predominant mode of resource transfer in South Asia, accounting for 93 percent of cumulative Bank and IDA lending through fiscal 1990. Nonproject lending accounted for 6.8 percent. Specific technical assistance loans accounted for the remaining 0.2 percent and have been confined to five countries, with Bangladesh, Pakistan, and Nepal the main recipients. Within South Asia, Bangladesh has received the largest proportion of nonproject lending (28.2 percent), followed by Nepal (10.4 percent), Sri Lanka (7.1 percent), and Pakistan (5.7 percent); India's proportion is the lowest (3.8 percent).

Lending to individual countries has been subject to fluctuations and interruptions from one period to another. Apart from variations in IDA lending related to replenishment delays at various junctures, policy considerations (or "implied conditionality") have operated in determining lending levels from time to time. The 1970s witnessed a decline in the share of lending to Pakistan because of problems that persisted almost throughout that decade, such as the uncertainty consequent on Pakistan's unilateral declaration of a moratorium on repayments following the emergence of Bangladesh and, subsequently, the nationalization policies of the administration of Zulfikar Ali Bhutto (1972–77), which met with the Bank's disapproval.[8]

8. See World Bank, *World Bank in Pakistan—Review of a Relationship 1960–1984* (2 vols.), Operations Evaluation Department (OED) report 6048 (Washington, January 1986), vol. 1, pp. 12–17.

Table 8-8. *Cumulative World Bank Lending to South Asia, by Country and Type of Loan, as of Fiscal Year 1990*
Millions of U.S. Dollars

Country or region	Project lending	Nonproject lending	Technical assistance	Total
India	33,944.9	1,330.0	0.0	35,274.9
	(96.2)	(3.8)	(0.0)	
Pakistan	6,971.1	420.0	21.0	7,412.1
	(94.0)	(5.7)	(0.3)	
Bangladesh	3,737.7	1,492.5	64.5	5,294.7
	(70.6)	(28.2)	(1.2)	
Sri Lanka	1,422.1	109.4	3.0	1,534.5
	(92.7)	(7.1)	(0.2)	
Nepal	939.3	110.0	9.0	1,058.3
	(88.7)	(10.4)	(0.9)	
Bhutan	19.8	0.0	3.0	22.8
	(86.8)	(0.0)	(13.2)	
Maldives	23.9	0.0	0.0	23.9
	(100.0)	(0.0)	(0.0)	
Total South Asia	47,058.8	3,461.9	100.5	50,621.2
	(93.0)	(6.8)	(0.2)	
Asia	46,264.4	3,600.9	100.7	49,966.0
(other than South Asia)	(92.6)	(7.2)	(0.2)	
Africa	30,203.7	4,238.5	809.7	35,251.9
	(85.7)	(12.0)	(2.3)	
LAC[a]	57,476.3	5,080.7	256.5	62,813.5
	(91.5)	(8.6)	(0.4)	
EMENA	41,398.8	4,750.9	81.4	46,231.1
(excluding Pakistan)[a]	(89.5)	(10.3)	(0.2)	
Total	222,402.0	21,132.9	1,348.8	244,883.7
	(90.8)	(8.6)	(0.6)	

Source: Author's calculations based on World Bank data. Figures in parentheses are percentages of country or regional totals.
a. LAC = Latin America and the Caribbean; EMENA = Europe, Middle East, and North Africa.

Lending to Bangladesh in the initial years (1971–74) was confined to a few non-project and reconstruction loans because of the Bank's insistence on Bangladesh's assuming its share of the liabilities of undivided Pakistan, and because of the country's early nationalization policies.[9] In Sri Lanka, policy differences with governments of the left-oriented Sri Lanka Freedom Party (SLFP) were reflected in reduced lending in 1961–65 and again in 1970–77.[10] In India, however, lending from the Bank and IDA taken together has followed an upward trend.

9. The early years of Bank-Bangladesh relationships are the subject of Just Faaland, ed., *Aid and Influence: The Case of Bangladesh* (St. Martin's Press, 1981).
10. See World Bank, *The World Bank and Sri Lanka: A Review of a Relationship,* OED report 6074 (Washington, 1986); see also Edward S. Mason and Robert E. Asher, *The World Bank since Bretton Woods* (Brookings, 1973), pp. 438–41.

Table 8-9. *Project Lending in South Asia, by Sector and Decade, Fiscal Years 1970–90*

Sector	Up to FY 1970			FY 1971–FY 1980			FY 1981–FY 1990			Up to FY 1990		
	Number of loans	Millions of dollars	Percent of total	Number of loans	Millions of dollars	Percent of total	Number of loans	Millions of dollars	Percent of total	Number of loans	Millions of dollars	Percent of total
Infrastructure	69	1,706.3	56.8	46	3,508.0	34.6	89	15,741.6	46.4	204	20,955.9	44.5
Energy	22	455.4	14.8	21	2,249.3	22.2	60	11,955.1	35.3	103	14,649.8	31.1
Oil, gas, and coal	3	73.7	2.4	3	240.0	2.4	17	2,958.0	8.7	23	3,271.7	6.9
Power	19	371.7	12.4	18	2,009.3	19.8	43	8,997.1	26.5	80	11,378.1	24.2
Transportation	41	1,098.2	36.6	16	794.7	7.8	23	2,930.5	8.6	80	4,823.4	10.3
Telecommunications	6	162.7	5.4	9	464.0	4.6	6	856.0	2.5	21	1,482.7	3.1
Industry	28	655.9	21.8	33	1,637.7	16.1	47	5,056.0	14.9	108	7,349.6	15.6
Agriculture and rural development	31	556.2	18.5	109	3,923.9	38.7	119	8,936.5	26.4	259	13,416.6	28.5
Social sectors	7	85.8	2.9	30	1,077.5	10.6	57	4,166.8	12.3	94	5,330.1	11.4
Total project lending	135	3,004.2	100.0	218	10,153.7[a]	100.0	312	33,900.9	100.0	665	47,058.8[a]	100.0
Memorandums												
Nonproject lending	8	655.0	...	20	1,545.0	...	13	1,261.9	...	41	3,461.9	...
Technical assistance	1	2.0	...	5	27.5	...	7	71.0	...	13	100.5	...
Total lending	144	3,661.2	...	243	11,726.2	...	332	35,233.8	...	719	50,621.2	...

Source: Author's calculations based on World Bank data.

a. Includes $6.6 million in supplementary commitments to a number of reactivated projects in Bangladesh.

SECTORAL LENDING. Table 8-9 shows the sectoral distribution of project lending to South Asia in three periods: up to fiscal 1970, fiscal 1971 to fiscal 1980, and fiscal 1981–90. The 1970s witnessed large proportionate increases compared with the pre-1970 period in lending for agriculture and the social sectors, principally offset by a very steep reduction in the share of transportation. In the 1980s there was a sharp increase in lending for energy, substantially offset by a reduction in the share for agriculture. In sum, compared with the previous period, the main thrust of lending in the 1970s was for agriculture, along with continued emphasis on energy and the emergence of the social sectors as a major category. In the 1980s there was a marked shift from agriculture to energy, including a strong component of lending for the development of oil, gas, and coal.

PROJECT LENDING. The shift in the Bank's sectoral pattern of project lending in the 1970s and 1980s toward agriculture and the social sectors, which are less import intensive than infrastructure or industrial investments, carried with it a substantial element of local procurement in goods and services earmarked for domestic bidding under loan agreements. There has also been scope for local procurement in transportation and in lending for energy, telecommunications, and industry, in which some South Asian countries, notably India with its large domestic manufacturing capacities, have been able to supply goods and services under international competitive bidding (ICB) or domestic bidding. In the late 1980s disbursements for local procurement in India were about 50 to 60 percent of total disbursements.[11] To this extent the project lending of the Bank provided "free foreign exchange" to the borrower, that is, foreign exchange usable for the indirect external costs of Bank projects, for project and nonproject imports other than those financed by the Bank (developmental or otherwise) or debt servicing, or for augmenting reserves. Also, the counterpart funds arising from such foreign exchange provided budget support.

The loosening of the format of project lending in the last two decades has also tended to blur the distinction between project and program lending. In the major South Asian countries there has been substantial intermediation through development financing institutions (DFIs), agricultural credit institutions, and other intermediaries. Financing of outlays in specific periods of time in an ongoing project or program (time-slice financing) has been undertaken in the railways, telecommunications, and irrigation for medium-term projects and programs of sectors, entities, or states (in India). Sector loans have permitted the use of funds for a variety of projects and activities in agriculture, industry, and transport. Similarly, industrial restructuring loans have permitted capital investment, modernization, and rehabilitation covering multiple units in various industries. Some loans, especially in irrigation and transportation, have been in the nature of lines of credit available for numerous small-scale individual projects such as tubewells, minor

11. These figures are based on data compiled from the Bank's annual reports.

irrigation schemes, tanks, rural roads, and so on. Notably in India, single-project loans have covered investments and activities in a number of states and localities.

The average loan in South Asia has been about 50 percent larger than the average for all borrowers from the Bank Group. In nominal terms, for the region as a whole, the average project loan increased from $22 million in the pre-1970 period to $47 million in 1971–80 and $109 million in 1981–90. Apart from inflation, several factors contributed to this trend. Large investments in infrastructure, industry, and irrigation were both necessary and possible because of the geographic and economic size of the principal South Asian countries, notably India. Lending through financial intermediation and by multistate and multicomponent loans in recent years has increased loan sizes, especially of loans for agricultural credit and irrigation, which have been of a substantial order. Growth in the proportion of lending for energy in the 1970s and 1980s was another major factor. Large, loosely structured, and complex projects in recent years have had an impact on staff requirements for project preparation, appraisal, and supervision, and on project performance. They have also added to the problems of monitoring and evaluation.

AID COORDINATION. The Bank has played an important role in South Asia in mobilizing and coordinating aid through consortiums and consultative groups under its chairmanship. The earliest consortium was for India in 1958, followed by the Pakistan consortium in 1960. The Sri Lanka aid group came into being in 1965. After some initial hesitancy on the part of Bangladesh, a consultative group was set up for that country in 1973. There is also an aid group for Nepal. Participants in Bank-sponsored consortia and consultative groups include, apart from the Bank and IDA, Development Assistance Committee member bilateral donors and the ADB, Arab funds, European Economic Community, and the International Fund for Agricultural Development among multilateral donors. The Bank has also catalyzed aid from other sources. In 1975–87 about a third of Bank projects in South Asia attracted cofinancing, mainly from official bilateral sources, amounting in those projects to about two-fifths of total lending from external sources.

IMPLEMENTATION EXPERIENCE. The Bank's performance indicators relating to project implementation in the South Asian countries have been somewhat above the average for all borrowers from the Bank and IDA during most of the last two decades.[12] Basically, three types of factors have affected project performance in South Asia. The first are force majeure disruptions such as those caused by wars, civil strife, and natural calamities, which have affected a number of South Asian countries during various periods in the last two decades. The second are factors specific to projects; the Bank classifies these as managerial, technical, financial, and

---

12. This is brought out by various indicators of performance in issues of the Bank's *Annual Reviews of Project Implementation and Supervision* (ARIS).

political.[13] Political and financial commitments to Bank projects have been relatively satisfactory in South Asia. Technical problems have varied from project to project, depending in part on the adequacy and quality of project preparation and appraisal. Managerial efficiency in project implementation has, however, been a matter of serious concern in most countries. The third set of factors comprises countrywide macroeconomic, sectoral, and intersectoral problems (for example, inflation, balance of payments constraints, and shortages of commodities and infrastructural inputs), which affect projects but over which project executing agencies may have little or no control. Such factors have affected all projects, whether financed by the Bank or by other sources.

Repayment covenants have been honored in South Asia without default, even in times of grave balance of payments difficulties, except for a brief interregnum in Pakistan pending the assumption of liabilities by Bangladesh upon its independence. In a number of cases other covenants, such as those relating to audit, staffing, and institutional matters, have not been fulfilled adequately or on schedule. But in the main these have not jeopardized implementation. There have been delays and difficulties in the funding of domestic resources, particularly in projects executed by the state and provincial governments of India and Pakistan, respectively. Budgetary resources at these levels are more constrained and under greater pressure than at the central level. Furthermore, whereas the central government has a direct incentive in speeding the utilization of aid to augment foreign exchange availability, states and provinces are primarily concerned with their domestic budgetary problems.

Part of the domestic funding problem in the 1980s relates to currency depreciation, which has entailed increases in project scope and required increased local currency funding for absorbing loan amounts in full. Procedural delays in enlarging projects and nonavailability of domestic funds in the short run have both contributed to lags in utilization. Covenants on which compliance has been least satisfactory in South Asia, as elsewhere, are those whereby the Bank has sought to influence sectorwide or economywide reforms through its lending for individual projects or for groups of repeat projects. Such cases have mostly related to revenue covenants and to the imposition or revision of rates and tariffs in energy, transport, irrigation, and urban water supply projects. Covenants relating to prompt loan recoveries and recoveries of receivables by financial and other intermediaries have also encountered difficulties in compliance.

Enforcement of procurement procedures is an important aspect of project lending operations. While South Asian borrowers are by now quite familiar with the Bank's procurement and bidding procedures, difficulties have arisen in many

13. Managerial problems include staffing, land acquisition, contractual, and procurement problems; in the main, financial problems relate to compliance with financial covenants and underfunding of domestic resources; political problems are identified as those arising from policy differences between the Bank and the borrower.

projects for a variety of administrative reasons, such as delays in finalizing bid specifications, evaluation of offers, and placing of contracts. Disputes have also arisen at a substantive level, particularly in India, about the scope for domestic bidding, short-listing of foreign sources, and choice of technology.

Many of these problems have their roots in India's strong desire to maximize the utilization of domestic manufacturing capabilities. In a number of sectors and subsectors (for example, power, railways, telecommunications, agricultural credit, and fertilizer projects) procurement issues in India have led to substantial implementation delays as well. However, the Bank's strict enforcement of fair and open procurement procedures has gone a long way toward preventing corruption, arbitrariness, and malpractice in the placement and enforcement of contracts, in which the countries of South Asia, as others elsewhere, have not been otherwise blemishless. One can, however, never be sure that there has been no corruption at all at any level or in any form in Bank projects. Kickbacks, for instance, can be sought and received even from a properly chosen supplier, and malpractice at the stage of execution is a possibility.

Disbursement ratios (the proportion of disbursements to cumulative commitments at the beginning of the year) are a summary indicator of progress in project implementation. The slowdown of disbursement ratios and the buildup of project pipelines were matters of concern in the late 1980s, especially in India and Bangladesh. In India, undisbursed balances at the end of the 1980s in Bank loans and IDA credits amounted to nearly $12 billion, equivalent to about four years of current commitment levels. Overall project aid in the pipeline in Bangladesh rose from about $2 billion in 1981 to about $5 billion at the end of the decade, while disbursement ratios steeply declined, from 28 percent to 19 percent. Performance in individual projects aside, the capacity of the system as a whole to absorb project lending is showing clear signs of stress in these countries. The sectoral and structural adjustment lending operations of the Bank in the major South Asian countries in the 1980s and early 1990s are a response to this phase in South Asia, in which, in the words of one of the Bank's annual reviews (ARIS, 1982), "the interaction between project lending and other lending instruments available to the Bank (sector and program lending, SALs) becomes particularly important if further progress is to be achieved."

The Lending Experience in South Asia: 1971–90

With the preceding sections as background, we proceed to examine the Bank's project lending experience in the 1970s and 1980s at the sectoral level and with special reference to major South Asian borrowers.[14] The 1970s and 1980s account

14. This section relies on extensive material generated by the OED, especially its project performance audit reports. Out of 530 projects funded in South Asia in the 1971–90 period, PPARs are available for 156—a reasonable sample size. In addition, country economic

Table 8-10. *Project Lending for Four Countries in South Asia, by Sector,*
Fiscal Years 1971–90

Sector	India Number of loans	India Millions of dollars	Pakistan Number of loans	Pakistan Millions of dollars	Bangladesh Number of loans	Bangladesh Millions of dollars	Sri Lanka Number of loans	Sri Lanka Millions of dollars
Energy	42	11,288.5 (35.2)	17	1,654.5 (27.1)	11	882.3 (25.0)	6	196.7 (15.1)
Transportation	13	2,463.3 (7.7)	17	530.0 (8.7)	9	437.6 (12.4)	4	171.5 (13.1)
Telecommunications	6	1,017.0 (3.2)	3	176.0 (2.9)	2	55.0 (1.6)	1	30.0 (2.3)
Industry	31	4,663.8 (14.5)	20	1,216.5 (20.0)	15	604.9 (17.1)	8	167.3 (12.8)
Agriculture and rural development	111	9,202.2 (28.6)	35	1,745.2 (28.6)	33	941.6 (26.6)	22	554.6 (42.5)
Education	3	552.0 (1.7)	7	400.2 (6.6)	8	370.1 (10.5)	2	77.5 (5.9)
Population, health, and nutrition	9	594.3 (1.8)	1	18.0 (0.3)	3	125.0 (3.5)	1	17.5 (1.3)
Urbanization	14	1,365.3 (4.2)	3	176.0 (2.9)	1	47.6 (1.3)	2	13.0 (1.0)
Water supply and sewerage	12	986.9 (3.1)	3	176.6 (2.9)	3	72.0 (2.0)	3	76.2 (6.0)
Total	241	32,133.3 (100.0)	96	6,093.0 (100.0)	85	3,542.7[a] (100.0)	49	1,304.3 (100.0)

Source: Author's calculations based on World Bank data. Figures in parentheses are percentages of column totals.
a. Includes $6.6 million for a number of reactivated projects.

for 80 percent by number and 94 percent by value of all project lending by the
Bank up to 1990 in South Asia. The four major borrowers we have concentrated
on—India, Pakistan, Bangladesh, and Sri Lanka—account for 89 percent of numbers of projects and 98 percent of lending money in the 1971–90 period.
Table 8-10, which gives a breakdown of project lending operations for the four
countries during this period by major sector, provides the framework in terms of
dimensions and relative priorities for the discussion of individual sectors that
follows.

---

memorandums, country studies, sector studies, and country-specific sector studies have
been useful. Independent academic studies have been valuable in supplying the pinch of salt
to be taken with these Bank documents; we cite in particular the two excellent "relationship"
studies dealing with Pakistan and Sri Lanka, undertaken for the OED by academic teams led
by John Lewis and Gustav Papanek, respectively. In this category also belongs R. H. Cassen
and others, *The Effectiveness of Aid to Pakistan: A Report to UNDP/Government of Pakistan*
(Oxford: International Development Centre, 1990).

Table 8-11. *World Bank Energy Lending for Four South Asian Countries, Fiscal Years 1971–90*
Millions of U.S. dollars

Subsector	India	Pakistan	Bangladesh	Sri Lanka
Electric power	8,594.2	1,378.0	664.3	196.7
Generation	6,412.0	183.0	92.0	42.7
Thermal	4,134.2	183.0	92.0	42.7
Hydroelectric	2,277.8	0.0	0.0	0.0
Transmission and distribution	1,295.7	457.0	211.0	154.0
Rural electrification	536.5	160.0	184.0	0.0
Sectoral and multipurpose	350.0	578.0	177.3	0.0
Technical assistance	0.0	0.0	0.0	0.0
Oil, gas, and coal	2,694.3	276.5	218.0	0.0
Oil and gas exploration and development	1,615.3	166.5	218.0	0.0
Pipelines	340.0	103.0	0.0	0.0
Coal exploration and development	739.0	7.0	0.0	0.0
Total	11,288.5	1,654.5	882.3	196.7

Source: Author's calculations based on World Bank, *Annual Report*, various years.

Energy

Energy has been the leading sector for Bank activity, claiming nearly a third ($14.6 billion) of the Bank's cumulative project lending. The share of lending to the sector increased significantly, from about 15 percent of project lending before 1970 to about 22 percent in the 1970s and 35 percent in the 1980s. Table 8-11 shows the pattern of lending in the energy sector in the 1971–90 period. Resource endowments in South Asia for energy development have made possible the growth and diversification of the Bank's project lending in this sector. Sharply increased lending for oil, natural gas, and coal in the 1970s and 1980s has greatly aided balance of payments adjustment. The Bank's long familiarity with the sector, its ability to extend large loans that are open to worldwide procurement, its flexible approach in lending to different types of investments, and its analytical work in the area of sector studies have all been of great value to borrowers. Bank loans have also utilized domestic capacities (for generation equipment in India, for example, and for pipeline construction in India and Pakistan).

INDIA. In India, transmission and distribution (T&D), including rural electrification, was the main emphasis in power sector lending in the 1970s and early 1980s. Many of the loans catered to individual states in different regions of India and provided for strengthening of regional grids for energy transfers. Starting in the late 1970s, the Bank turned to financing large generation and allied transmission facilities through superthermal stations (units of 500 MW capacity or greater) close to sources of coal and built by the National Thermal Power Corporation (NTPC), a central-government entity set up for the purpose. This shift was influenced in part by increased domestic capability in India to produce generating equipment and in part by the Bank's preference for centralized generation on grounds of economy and efficiency. In this period, apart from a few loans routed through central-level intermediaries such as the Rural Electrification Corporation and the Power Finance Corporation, the Bank's exposure to state electricity boards (SEBs) was limited, although it was shifting toward them in the later 1980s; so far there have been no sectoral adjustment loans.

Since the Bank overcame its ideological inhibition against lending for oil and gas development, it has kept up a steady stream of project financing in this area. This has been a significant contribution to technology transfer from sources other than the Soviet Union, on which India's Oil and Natural Gas Commission had been entirely dependent, and to reducing dependence on oil imports. One of the early loans of the Bank was to private sector coal mines in India, but following the nationalization of the coal mines in 1973, the Bank opted out of coal development until 1984 when it made a loan to Coal India, the public sector entity in this field, to be followed by further lending in subsequent years.

PAKISTAN. Three distinct phases are apparent in the history of Bank lending for the energy sector in Pakistan. During the 1960s the Bank was heavily involved in hydroelectric projects arising from the Indus Waters treaty, the hydropower stations at Mangla and Tarbela being the major investments. The first loan to Pakistan's Water and Power Development Authority (WAPDA) was made in 1970, but during 1972–74 a hiatus in lending for the energy sector followed, a consequence of the slowing down of the Bank's overall lending to Pakistan in the 1970s. Between the mid-1970s and the mid-1980s there were a series of loans for T&D. In the second half of the 1980s there were a couple of loans each for generation and for T&D, including one for rural electrification. This period also saw two loans for energy sector adjustment and one for stimulating private investment in energy development. One of the earliest loans to Pakistan (1954) was for the pipeline from the Sui gas field; four more loans followed for extending the pipeline to provide feedstock for fertilizer and power plants. Other loans have supported exploration assistance to the public sector Oil and Gas Development Corporation, the development of the Toot oil field, refinery improvements, and a geological survey for prospecting for coal in Balochistan. In both power and natural gas the Bank's emphasis on T&D and on pipelines has appropriately reflected the fact that hydroplants and gas fields are distant from demand centers in Pakistan.[15]

BANGLADESH. With limited hydroelectric potential and little access to coal, Bangladesh is heavily dependent on natural gas, of which the country's eastern

15. For a detailed account see World Bank, *A Review of World Bank Lending for Natural Gas: Country Case Study: Pakistan*, OED report 10828, June 30, 1992.

region has substantial reserves. The rural areas are very poorly served by electricity. Against this background, Bank lending has heavily concentrated on natural gas development, oil and gas exploration, T&D in the power sector, and a couple of loans for rural electrification through cooperatives. In 1989 Bangladesh received a sectoral adjustment loan to support resource development, institutional reforms and investment, and pricing and demand management.

SRI LANKA. The Bank's involvement in Sri Lanka's energy sector has suffered from the vicissitudes of its overall relationship with that country. In the pre-1970 period, loans for the power sector (1954, 1959, 1961, and thereafter only in 1969 and 1970) were made mostly when governments of the United National Party were in power. For almost a decade thereafter, between 1970 and 1979, there was only one small transmission loan in the Colombo area. Essentially, toward the end of the 1970s the Bank had lost contact with the power sector in Sri Lanka, leaving it to bilateral donors to finance the large hydroelectric projects of the Mahaweli development program. However, an effort to get back on track was initiated in 1982 in an energy sector assessment study conducted jointly by the Bank and the United Nations Development Programme (UNDP). Later loans, except for a diesel generating station in 1982, have been for T&D, including a time-slice loan in 1988 for the Electricity Board's five-year distribution program.

IMPLEMENTATION. Implementation in energy sector projects appears to have been generally satisfactory. Serious delays have occurred in only a few projects, and strong competition among suppliers in the 1980s has contained import costs. Available project performance audit reports (PPARs) indicate that shortcomings in project preparation have affected performance in some projects. Among the shortcomings have been optimistic demand forecasts (for the Sri Lanka IV power project and the Bakhrabad gas project in Bangladesh), insufficient risk analysis (the Second Toot oil field in Pakistan), and inadequate field investigations (the Kulekhani hydroelectric project in Nepal). Land acquisition delays have also been a factor. NTPC's Singrauli thermal project and the Bombay High oil and gas project in India, and the energy sector adjustment loan to Pakistan, are examples of successful implementation, although Singrauli has given rise to serious environmental problems.

PROBLEMS OF THE POWER SECTOR. The basic problem in the power sector in South Asia, as among other Bank borrowers, is that large investments and generally satisfactory physical execution of individual projects have not been accompanied by better system performance.[16] Investment planning has been oriented to increasing supply, to the relative neglect of efficiency and economy in operations, demand management, and energy conservation. T&D has lagged behind investments in generation. Quality of service in many utilities is poor, leading to damage

16. See World Bank, *A Review of World Bank Lending for Electric Power*, World Bank Energy Series Paper 2 (March 1988).

or unusability of equipment and to reliance on high-cost captive facilities among users.

Total network losses, technical and nontechnical (the latter include losses due to theft and inadequate billing and collection) have been very high in many South Asian countries, ranging from around 20 percent in India and Sri Lanka to between 25 and 40 percent in Pakistan and Bangladesh. The sustainability of projects is gravely threatened by poor financial performance, reflected in inadequate internal resource generation, low or negative returns on investment, and high levels of commercial receivables. Average tariffs have consistently trailed behind costs, and industrial consumers cross-subsidize underpriced electricity for agricultural and residential users.[17] Increasingly, environmental problems have also emerged, mainly in the form of emissions and fly ash accumulation in thermal plants and siltation of hydroelectric reservoirs.

THE POLICY DIALOGUE. In its long association with the power sector in India, the Bank has been involved in a continual dialogue on financial matters. In the 1970s the Bank was able to persuade the government to appoint a high-level committee to prescribe financial norms to SEBs.[18] Subsequently, in 1985, a statutory requirement was placed on them to achieve a minimum rate of return of 3 percent on assets after providing fully for depreciation and interest. In practice, most SEBs have not been able to meet the norm, largely because of subsidized power to agriculture.

Although the Bank has had a long-term direct stake in reducing agricultural power subsidies, arising from its lending both for rural electrification and for irrigation pumpsets, its leverage for upgrading financial performance has been ineffective for a number of reasons. To begin with, the Bank's direct lending to individual SEBs and its continuous involvement with any one of them have been limited; financial covenants, to the extent imposed, have been inadequately fulfilled or postponed. Faced with this situation, the Bank increasingly turned in the 1980s to financing investments in central-government-owned operations—mainly the large generating plants of the NTPC—hoping thereby to exercise policy influence directly at the central-government level and indirectly through the NTPC over state-level utilities. Although the Bank has been able to make a significant contribution to institution building in the NTPC itself, its expectation of using the NTPC to secure reforms in the SEBs has not been realized. Instead, the continued poor financial situation of the SEBs has been transmitted to the NTPC in the form

17. In fiscal 1990 the combined return on net assets of SEBs in India was negative, on the order of −10 percent; their operating losses exceeded the equivalent of $1.6 billion; financial subsidies were estimated at $1.9 billion, and economic subsidies were perhaps about four times as much, because average tariffs were only about 50 percent of long-run marginal costs. See World Bank, *India: Long Term Issues in the Power Sector,* report 9786-IN (1991).

18. For an account of the Bank's intervention in this phase see Mason and Asher, *The World Bank since Bretton Woods,* pp. 437–38.

of large arrearages for power purchases, reflected as unsupportable levels of receivables in the NTPC's accounts.

This development once again turned the Bank toward the SEBs in the later 1980s. The greatest handicap in promoting managerial and financial reforms in the SEBs arises from the fact that, under the Indian Constitution, power sector development is a responsibility assigned to the states. The central government has little leverage over the states, since the bulk of its developmental assistance to them is entitlement based and not linked to performance conditionalities. In these circumstances the Bank's options are limited: it could either reduce or suspend lending until needed reforms are implemented; or it could continue to intermediate through central entities on condition that they, in turn, exercise effective leverage over the states; or it could try to exert leverage over the SEBs directly. At the close of the 1980s the Bank was trying all three options.

The question remains whether the Bank should have tried to exercise more effective leverage earlier instead of allowing problems to accumulate to the extent they have in India's power system. As a practical matter, the Bank's only recourse would have been to withdraw from lending in an attempt to enforce financial and other covenants, but such a course, considering the size of the loans in the energy sector, would have considerably slowed achievement of its lending targets besides disrupting additions to capacity in this crucially important sector. On the other hand, given the very large investment requirements for energy development in prospect, the Bank's contribution in the future is likely to be proportionately less than in the past, and therefore so is its ability to promote reform. It could be argued then that, because of the "unquestioned funding of power needs," the Bank has acquiesced in postponing reforms to a point where they have become urgent and complicated on the one hand, while on the other the Bank's possible influence in seeing that they are effectively tackled has become diluted. There can be no easy resolution of this dilemma, especially in retrospect.

In the other major South Asian countries, which have been free from India's center-state problems, the Bank's institutional interaction has been confined to central electricity authorities. Such interaction has not been without problems, but they have been of a different kind from those posed in India. Paradoxically, whereas the pressure for continued lending at a rapid pace has inhibited the policy dialogue in India, discontinuities in lending have had the same result in Pakistan and Sri Lanka. The hiatus during the early 1970s in lending for power in Pakistan reduced the Bank's capacity to influence reforms in energy pricing and improvements in WAPDA's functioning; the Bank had to wait until the sectoral adjustment loans of the mid-1980s to acquire more comprehensive leverage. In Sri Lanka the Bank pressed for the establishment of the Ceylon Electricity Board (CEB) as early as 1958, but by the time the CEB finally came into being in 1969, the Bank had entered into its long period of hibernation, which was to last until the end of the 1970s. There was thus an effective loss of policy dialogue in Sri Lanka for nearly two decades in this sector. In Bangladesh management and financial problems in utility functioning, although noted in Bank documents throughout the 1980s, began to be comprehensively addressed only in the sectoral adjustment loan of 1989.

In South Asia current low levels of commercial energy consumption, steady demand growth at around 10 percent per year (two to three times the rate of GDP growth), and escalating unit costs of investment add up to large requirements for additional capacity and for financial resources to make them possible.[19] If the Bank is to continue to play an important role in the energy sector, it will have to complement its own lendable resources with significant cofinancing from official and private sources and use its lending to promote major reforms in the operational and financial functioning of its borrower agencies. This will require an optimal combination of project and sectoral lending instruments, effective institutional interaction at various levels, and dogged policy dialogue. The Bank has entered into this phase in Pakistan, Bangladesh, and Sri Lanka and is poised to do so in India. In Pakistan and Bangladesh sectoral adjustment loans are addressed to better planning, reduction of subsidies in power and natural gas pricing, energy conservation, rehabilitation and modernization of equipment, and improvements to system operation and maintenance. In India and Sri Lanka the detailed sector studies that the Bank has undertaken provide the basis for policy options to the borrowers and for charting the Bank's own lending modalities and priorities in the years ahead.

Transportation

Transportation was by far the leading sector in South Asia in the Bank's pre-1970 project lending portfolio, claiming a share of about 37 percent. The proportion sharply declined to 8 to 9 percent in the 1970s and 1980s. Table 8-12 provides an analysis by subsector of transportation lending in 1971–90.

RAILWAYS. The Bank has had a long-term relationship with the Indian Railways (IR) since 1949 and made sixteen loans totaling about $1.5 billion up to the end of the 1980s to this single entity. The first thirteen loans were essentially time-slice program loans for locomotives, rolling stock, line capacity, track renewal, electrification, and system additions based on successive medium-term plans of the railways. In contrast, from the fourteenth loan (1987–88) onward special attention was paid to corporate planning, technological upgrading through specific project components (such as funding for a new wheel and axle plant), production facilities for diesel and electric locomotives, workshop modernization and rationalization, and centralized unit exchange facilities for locomotive maintenance.

19. The Bank's estimate is that the power sector alone in South Asia will need about $70 billion in foreign exchange in the 1990s, which is nearly six times the Bank's total lending for power up to fiscal 1990. See Edwin A. Moore and George Smith, *Capital Expenditure for Electric Power in the Developing Countries in the 1990s,* World Bank Energy Series Paper 21 (February 1990), p. 63.

Table 8-12. *World Bank Transportation Lending for Four South Asian Countries, Fiscal Years 1971–90*
Millions of U.S. dollars

Subsector	India	Pakistan	Bangladesh	Sri Lanka
Railways	1,525.7	110.0	0.0	0.0
Roads	604.6	202.0	338.9	118.5
Highways	450.0	202.0	118.0	40.5
Rural roads	154.6	0.0	62.3	0.0
Rehabilitation	0.0	0.0	158.6	78.0
Sector loan	0.0	184.0	0.0	0.0
Ports	250.0	34.0	85.0	0.0
Tankers	83.0	0.0	0.0	0.0
Inland water transport	0.0	0.0	13.7	0.0
Bus transport	0.0	0.0	0.0	0.0
Total	2,463.3	530.0	437.6	171.5

Source: Author's calculations based on World Bank, *Annual Report,* various years.

In general, loans to the IR have been successfully implemented, although delays have occurred in some cases because freight demand has been below projections. In the second-generation loans the main problem area has been the establishment of modern centralized maintenance facilities for locomotives. The IR has resisted this component, largely because of the significant staff redundancy it would have entailed. As a result the Bank's evaluators came to recognize that in the IR any component that is likely to have a substantial impact on the level or deployment of labor is going to experience serious difficulties.[20] As regards financial performance, the IR has been able to meet its statutory dividend requirement of about 5 percent on capital to the government, taking one year with another, but depreciation provisions have been underfunded—a matter of concern in the context of heavy replacement requirements for aging track and rolling stock. Freight traffic subsidizes passenger traffic, in which demand growth and public pressure are strong; subsidies to commuter traffic and losses on uneconomic lines are large. Overstaffing is significant in the IR's labor force of nearly 2 million. The Bank has been well aware of these problems, but its policy dialogue on these issues has not been particularly sustained or successful despite its long association with the IR.

Railway loans to Pakistan have been much smaller, aggregating to $110 million spread over eleven loans. Implementation was not satisfactory in some of the earlier loans; operational and financial problems have been of the same kind as in India, only perhaps worse. A review carried out after the eleventh railway project in Pakistan noted that "the borrower did little or nothing of what the Bank asked,

20. World Bank, *India: Railway Modernization and Maintenance Project* (Credit 844-N), Project Performance Audit Report 7020, (November 30, 1987).

and yet rather than ask why, the Bank simply repeated the same conditionality, adding more specifics and more targets."[21]

ROADS. Three broad types of investments have been financed in the roads subsector: important national highways (including bridges) or segments thereof in all major South Asian countries; rural roads in India and Bangladesh; and rehabilitation of roads damaged in floods in Bangladesh and damaged as a result of ethnic conflict in the late 1980s in Sri Lanka. In addition, a sectoral loan combining rail and road inputs has been made to Pakistan ($184 million). The Bank's thrust in this subsector has been to introduce modern standards of design, construction, and maintenance; to encourage institution building at the governmental level by supporting the creation and strengthening of highway departments (especially in Pakistan, Bangladesh, and Sri Lanka); and to strengthen the local construction industry by providing equipment and training (Pakistan, Bangladesh, and Sri Lanka).

A number of road projects have encountered serious delays and cost overruns, especially in Pakistan and Bangladesh. The main problems have been delays in land acquisition, fragmentation of contracts, technical and financial inadequacies of the local construction industry, and poor coordination on the part of executing agencies. Yet economic rates of return have been high, in part explained by rising fuel costs in the last two decades. Although a number of agricultural and irrigation projects have included components for rural roads, specific lending for this purpose, despite its importance, has been limited: only 15 percent of lending for roads in 1971–90 and mainly confined to Bangladesh and to two states in India. The reason is that the Bank has been reluctant to face problems in design, appraisal, intermediation, and supervision inherent in financing large numbers of dispersed individual works.

As part of its lending to the transport sector, the Bank has been instrumental in promoting transport coordination studies in India and Pakistan. The studies have produced useful recommendations relating to intermodal coordination of traffic, especially with a view to fuel conservation, but their impact on policy has been limited, and no serious dialogue to follow up on these studies has taken place.

Transportation lending had to accept a sharp downturn in its share in Bank lending in the 1970s and 1980s. The broad issue that arises in this context is whether the Bank's interventions could have been more sharply focused in terms of subsectoral priorities, possible alternative types of projects within them, and policy dialogue. Prima facie, it would seem that the Bank's concentration on and well-established relationship with the Indian Railways has blunted the Bank's influence on wider policy matters: transport policy and coordination, financial performance of railways and ports, and maintenance standards for roads. This is not, however, due

21. Alice Galenson and Louis Thompson, "The Bank's Evolving Policy Toward Railway Lending," World Bank, Infrastructure and Urban Development Department, August 1991, p. 5.

Table 8-13. *World Bank Industry Lending for Four South Asian Countries,*
by Purpose of Loan, Fiscal Years 1971–90
Millions of U.S. dollars

Purpose of loan	India	Pakistan	Bangladesh	Sri Lanka
Specific project loans	2,198.8	216.5	181.5	0.0
Fertilizers	1,598.8	183.5	106.0	0.0
Petrochemicals and refineries	500.0	33.0	75.5	0.0
Paper and pulp	100.0	0.0	0.0	0.0
Rehabilitation and restructuring	500.0	96.0	95.0	0.0
Cement	500.0	96.0	0.0	0.0
Textiles	0.0	0.0	75.0	0.0
Jute	0.0	0.0	20.0	0.0
DFIs:[a] general purpose	585.0	400.0	75.0	112.8
DFIs:[a] specific purpose	1,380.0	204.0	78.4	54.5
SSEs[a]	65.0	134.0	42.0	50.0
Export development	545.0	70.0	25.0	4.5
Technology development	560.0	0.0	0.0	0.0
Electronics	210.0	0.0	0.0	0.0
Energy conservation	0.0	0.0	11.4	0.0
Sectoral reform	0.0	300.0	175.0	0.0
Financial sector	0.0	150.0	175.0	0.0
Industrial sector	0.0	150.0	0.0	0.0
Total	4,663.8	1,183.5	529.4	167.3

Source: Author's calculations based on World Bank, *Annual Report,* various years.
a. DFI = development financing institution; SSE = small-scale enterprise.

entirely to the Bank's passivity but is also to be explained by political problems (for example, overmanning and social burdens at the IR) and the diffuseness, in space and over time, of the lending pattern in this sector.

Industry

Apart from project lending, the Bank Group's support to industry includes IFC's operations and program lending to sustain and increase industrial output. Project lending to industry itself has been highly diversified, and this diversity is not adequately captured in the Bank's threefold classification of lending for this sector into industry, development financing institutions (DFIs), and small-scale enterprises (SSEs). Table 8-13 presents a more specific analysis of industrial lending during 1971–90 by country. The bulk of it has been for fertilizer and petrochemical projects (41 percent) and for on-lending through DFIs (48 percent).

FERTILIZERS AND PETROCHEMICALS. The Bank's rationale and motivation for financing fertilizer production in South Asia stem from several factors. Fertilizer use has become a sine qua non for increasing agricultural output with the introduction in the mid-1960s of new technology based on high-yielding seeds. Consumption of chemical fertilizers has been rapidly increasing in the major South Asian countries, which are also endowed with domestic feedstock resources to support local manufacture. Given the demand, supply, and price fluctuations in world fertilizer markets, in which their own needs are a large factor, it makes sense for the major South Asian countries to create a domestic manufacturing base in order to create cost-effective substitutes for imports and reduce their exposure to the vagaries of the world market.

Until the late 1960s the Bank was unwilling to lend for public sector enterprises in this field, and the Indian government took a restrictive approach to allowing private investment in the sector. As part of the Bank's policy dialogue with India, an understanding was reached around the mid-1960s: the Bank would lend for fertilizer units in the public sector, while India would open the field for private investment. Between 1971 and 1986 the Bank made twelve loans in India for fertilizer projects, for a total of $1,598.8 million: eight operations in the public sector ($788 million) and four ($811 million) for plants implemented by the Indian Farmers Fertilizers Cooperative (IFFCO) in the cooperative sector.[22] Earlier loans, during the years 1972–75, were for plants based on fuel oil or naphtha as feedstock, whereas those in the late 1980s included loans for natural gas–based plants fed by pipeline from the Bombay High field. Inasmuch as the Bank has also assisted gas development and conveyance from Bombay High, its overall support to India's fertilizer development has been substantial; the Bank has, indeed, played a major role in India's becoming the fourth-largest producer of fertilizers in the world.

In the earlier loans, delays ranging between one and two years and substantial cost overruns resulted from delays on the part of both suppliers and executing agencies. In some cases teething problems have also been serious. Problems such as equipment failures, power shortages, poor quality and erratic supply of feedstock, and managerial and labor problems have occurred from time to time. However, a detailed study by the Bank found that all except one of the projects had achieved capacity utilization of around 80 percent in the mid-1980s and were economically viable.[23] Many of the implementation problems in the fertilizer sector in India could be traced to India's insistence on maximizing domestic supplies and engineering services, a policy that has not been without its dividends: in the words of a Bank study, "this strategy of learning to cope with a multitude of operational as well as design problems led to the formation of a highly skilled cadre of technical

22. The loan for the public sector Thal Vaishet Fertilizer project (1979, $250 million), included in these figures, never became effective. This project is discussed later in the text.

23. World Bank, *Sustainability of Projects: Review of Experience in the Fertilizer Subsector*, OED Report 6073 (1986).

and operational staff which provides the basis for a rapid expansion of the subsector" and in turn "has created numerous opportunities to use domestic capabilities."

The Bank has not always seen eye-to-eye with India in choosing technology. Differences on this score came to a head in the Thal Vaishet project, where the government revised an earlier choice (which had been objectively arrived at) to favor an equipment supplier (Snamprogetti) that had not been on the original short list. The government claimed standardization of technology as the justification, but the Bank was not convinced and decided not to render the loan effective.[24] In the longer run this technological tie-up has resulted in high-cost contractual arrangements for process know-how and equipment in Indian fertilizer projects.

In the late 1980s the Bank took a pause in what had been its continued lending for individual projects and turned its attention to the sectoral problems of the Indian fertilizer industry. An important Bank study in 1987 found that, apart from a small group of public sector plants of earlier vintage, which were noncompetitive because of very high energy costs and low capacity utilization, capital costs were so high in second-generation gas-based plants as to undermine economic viability despite very favorable energy and conversion factors.[25] The reasons were mainly threefold: technological tie-ups, which limited competitive contractual arrangements for design, technology, and equipment; high costs of domestic equipment and supplies used in projects; and a retention price scheme (RPS) that encouraged overcapitalization by failing to provide incentives for cost optimization.

Based on this analysis, the Bank's policy reform package consists of two main elements. One is to mothball and, if necessary, retire the unviable plants, and the other is to replace the RPS with a pricing regime calculated to bring investment and operating costs, in the longer run, in line with or at least closer to international parameters. Since high prices for fertilizers in India are largely a reflection of high production costs, this strategy, if implemented, will also help to reduce fertilizer subsidies to farmers and will make an important contribution to reducing the government's budget deficit. The Bank has been able to press its dialogue on pricing reform along similar lines in Pakistan and Bangladesh, where, however, domestic production is of a much smaller proportion. It remains to be seen whether it will succeed in India, where the reforms envisaged will entail high political costs as a result of layoffs as well as short-run disincentives for new investment and expansion.

In Pakistan an early Bank loan (1968) was for a joint venture between the Dawood Industrial Group and Hercules, Inc., a U.S. company. This was successful at implementation and in subsequent stages. Later loans were for the Multan fertilizer project (a joint venture of the government and Abu Dhabi National Oil

---

24. This and other contracts to Snamprogetti have come in for considerable criticism in India, where it is alleged that the contracts were granted as favors to the local representative of the firm, a family friend of the late Prime Minister Rajiv Gandhi.

25. World Bank, *India: Fertilizer Industry Strategy Study,* Report 6805-IN (1987).

Company) and for the Fauji project (implemented by a private charitable trust for ex-servicemen). The Multan project experienced a large cost overrun due to a sharp escalation in imported and domestic costs and force majeure circumstances such as flooding, shipping accidents, and political disturbances. Production in this plant has, however, stabilized, and good capacity utilization has been achieved. Both implementation and production performance have been satisfactory in the Fauji project. There the Bank made an important contribution by identifying a second technical partner to replace the first one, who withdrew soon after project approval, and to restitute the initial loan. In Bangladesh the Bank has financed the gas-based project in Ashuganj and the rehabilitation of three other major plants.

The Bank has made a significant contribution to the development of the petrochemical industry in India in lending to the public sector Indian Petrochemical Corporation ($500 million in two loans). Refinery improvement loans in India, Pakistan, and Bangladesh have contributed to better capacity utilization, rationalization of production, and energy conservation.

DEVELOPMENT FINANCING INSTITUTIONS. In India the principal DFI through which the Bank has operated is the Industrial Credit and Investment Corporation of India (ICICI).[26] Up to 1981 the Bank had made thirteen general-purpose loans to the ICICI to meet the equipment import requirements of large and medium-size industries. Since then the Bank's approach has been, on the one hand, to target its lines of credit more closely to specific industries and purposes (SSEs, exports, technology development, electronics, energy conservation) and, on the other, to diversify on-lending through multiple intermediaries including commercial banks, to ensure better coverage in terms of regions, industries, and types of entrepreneurs and to facilitate the negotiation of comprehensive financial packages. In this phase as well, the ICICI has been a major participant in on-lending.

The ICICI has been consistently commended in the Bank's evaluations as a "sound, mature, and efficiently managed institution."[27] Through the years the ICICI has progressed on many fronts. Whereas its portfolio originally tended to be concentrated in western India, it is now more regionally diversified, with special attention being given to backward areas. Rates of return, repayment ratios, and disbursement profiles have been satisfactory. Good capability has been built up in project identification and in loan appraisals, monitoring, and evaluation. The institution has succeeded in diversifying its foreign exchange sources by tapping commercial loans in international markets at low spreads. Government ownership since 1969 has not impaired the ICICI's autonomy. To all this the Bank's close and cordial interaction with the ICICI has contributed a great deal.

26. The ICICI was founded in 1955 in the private sector with the active involvement of the Bank. It came under government ownership (52 percent) in 1969 after the major commercial banks, which were its shareholders, were nationalized.

27. World Bank, *India: Industrial Credit and Investment Corporation of India, Limited (Loans 789-IN and 902-IN)*, Project Performance Audit Report 3428 (April 1981), p. iv.

The Bank's involvement in the Industrial Development Bank of India (IDBI), a public sector institution, has been much more limited, dating only from the 1970s; previously the Bank had lent only to private sector DFIs. In recent years the IDBI has participated, along with the ICICI and other participating financial institutions, in lines of credit for electronics and export industries and for technology development. It has also provided a channel for on-lending to state financial corporations (SFCs) in India for small and medium-size industries and for public sector and joint ventures in the states. Because of policy differences with the government regarding subsidies and levels of protection, the Bank has not extended any specific lines of credit to SSEs in India. Nor has its second-best approach of supporting SSEs through SFCs been sustained or successful; SFCs have had high arrearage ratios, and their management, never very strong, has been subject to frequent political interference.

In Pakistan, the PICIC (Pakistan Industrial Credit and Investment Corporation) corresponds to the ICICI in being the Bank's chosen vehicle for intermediation. The PICIC's portfolio underwent major shocks in the 1970s, which witnessed such disruptive political and economic developments as the civil war, the external hostilities of 1971, and the nationalization of major industries. Very large arrears from its borrowers have been a major problem for the PICIC. Beginning in about the mid-1980s, the Bank has diversified its intermediaries in Pakistan, relying much more on the commercial banking sector for general-purpose lending and for supporting reforms in the financial and industrial sectors. To a limited extent the Bank has also used public sector DFIs in Pakistan, namely, the Industrial Development Bank of Pakistan (IDBP) and the National Development Finance Corporation (NDFC), which finances public enterprises. The IDBP's portfolio has been adversely affected by sizable arrears in repayment, besides a serious loss in its portfolio and professional staff consequent on the separation of Bangladesh. Political interference has also been a problem.

The Bank's experience with the Bangladesh Shilpa Bank (BSB) has been bedeviled with problems right from the beginning. Over a long period, arrears have affected 90 percent or more of the portfolio, management has been subject to political interference both in lending and in effecting recoveries, and loans have been heavily concentrated in Dhaka and Chittagong. By the mid-1980s the Bank had decided to discontinue further lending to the BSB until it made tangible progress in restructuring its portfolio and improving its creditworthiness. An action plan toward this end was prepared, and the Bank's financial sector loan to Bangladesh in 1990 was addressed, inter alia, to promoting the needed changes. The question has been raised in the Bank's PPARs whether in retrospect it would not have been advisable for the Bank to have "conditioned support for BSB to actual institutional and policy reforms and not to mere assurances of prospective initiatives and actions."[28]

28. World Bank, *Bangladesh: Bangladesh Shilpa Bank (BSB) (Credit 632-BD)*, Project Performance Audit Report 6413 (September 24, 1986), p. vi.

In Sri Lanka all the Bank's lending for the industrial sector has been in the form of loans intermediated through the Development Finance Corporation of Ceylon (DFCC) and other public financing institutions. Although the bulk has been for medium-size and large industries in the private sector, loans to SSEs have also been significant. The DFCC has been rated as a successful institution overall, and the Bank has been generally satisfied with its competence in loan management and in mobilizing external and domestic resources.

Agriculture

Agriculture has been, along with energy, a leading sector in the Bank's project lending operations in South Asia, claiming about 29 percent of cumulative lending up to fiscal year 1990. There was a sharp increase in the sector's share from about 19 percent in the pre-1970 period to nearly 39 percent in the 1970s, followed by a decline to about 26 percent in the 1980s. In broad terms, Bank projects in the last two decades have sought to support the spread of new technology (the so-called Green Revolution) through the provision of irrigation, credit, and extension services; to diversify crop husbandry with allied activities (agro-industries, dairying, fisheries, and perennial or tree crops); and to pay heed to problems of resource management (of forests and watersheds, for instance) and regional balance (area development).

The subsectoral pattern of lending during the 1971–90 period to the major South Asian borrowers is shown in table 8-14. In all countries irrigation accounts for the single largest share within the agricultural portfolio: about 47 percent in the region as a whole and about 40 to 50 percent in the major countries. Among other subsectors, agricultural credit dominates (19 percent) but is almost entirely concentrated in India and Pakistan. Area development is significant in Bangladesh and Sri Lanka and tree crops in Sri Lanka. Research and extension have received attention in all countries. The only sector loan has gone to Pakistan. The discussion that follows is confined to the important subsectors of concentration in the four major borrowers.

IRRIGATION. Although irrigation has had a long history in India, it is only since independence that its development has been striking and sustained. Net irrigated area has doubled from 21 million hectares in 1950 to 42 million hectares by the mid-1980s, with gross irrigated area rising from 23 million to 54 million hectares in the same period. Concurrently there has been a considerable regional diversification, especially into previously unirrigated parts of central (Rajasthan and Madhya Pradesh) and eastern (Bihar and Orissa) India; an enormous increase in private well irrigation, which has trebled and now accounts for nearly half of total net irrigated area; and a reorientation of irrigation from extensive water use for drought protection toward intensive application to achieve productivity increases.

The development of irrigation since the 1950s has thrown up a number of priorities and interrelated problems. There have been competing claims on overall

Table 8-14. *World Bank Agriculture Lending for Four South Asian Countries, by Purpose of Loan, Fiscal Years 1970–91*
Millions of U.S. dollars

Purpose of loan	India	Pakistan	Bangladesh	Sri Lanka
Irrigation, flood control, and	4,324.0	778.1	499.9	203.1
drainage	(47.0)	(44.6)	(53.0)	(36.6)
Agricultural credit	1,887.4	457.8	40.0	0.0
	(20.5)	(26.2)	(4.2)	(0.0)
Agricultural sector lending	0.0	200.0	0.0	0.0
	(0.0)	(11.5)	(0.0)	(0.0)
Agro-industry	898.0	106.4	52.5	0.0
	(9.8)	(6.1)	(5.6)	(0.0)
Area development	539.2	17.0	141.0	76.5
	(5.9)	(1.0)	(15.0)	(13.8)
Fisheries	55.5	1.7	72.6	0.0
	(0.6)	(0.1)	(7.7)	(0.0)
Forestry	349.8	21.0	39.0	28.9
	(3.8)	(1.2)	(4.1)	(5.2)
Livestock	584.1	10.0	0.0	47.0
	(6.3)	(0.6)	(0.0)	(8.5)
Perennial crops	84.0	0.0	21.0	165.0
	(0.9)	(0.0)	(2.2)	(29.8)
Research and extension	480.2	153.2	75.6	34.1
	(5.2)	(8.7)	(8.2)	(6.1)
Total	9,202.2	1,745.2	941.6	554.6
	(100.0)	(100.0)	(100.0)	(100.0)

Source: Author's calculations based on World Bank, *Annual Report*, various years. Figures in parentheses are percentages of column totals.

resources between capital investments and maintenance outlays, and within the investment budget between new starts and completion of ongoing projects. There is a need to close the gap between creation of potential and its utilization and to increase efficiency and equity through reliable supply and better water management by users. Distribution of water between different types of users, crops, and seasons should be more equitable. Dams should be of better construction quality and built to higher standards of safety. Public sector capabilities in project identification and preparation, construction, supervision, operation, and maintenance require improvement. There should be more effective response to environmental issues, especially the resettlement and rehabilitation of displaced persons. Adequate attention should be paid to economic rates of return in the choice of projects and to better cost recovery to ensure the financial sustainability of investments.[29]

29. World Bank, *India: Irrigation Sector Review*, 2 vols., report 9518-IN (December 20, 1991); see also World Bank, *India: 1991 Country Economic Memorandum*, vol. 2, "Agriculture, Challenges and Opportunities," report 9412-IN (August 23, 1991), pp. 74–83, 99–101.

The Bank has attempted to respond to this gamut of problems in the choice and structuring of its projects and through its technical assistance and policy dialogue. The latter have been addressed mainly to issues such as command area development, canal lining, on-farm development, structures and practices to facilitate better water management, dam safety, resettlement and rehabilitation, training, and cost recovery. Success in achieving these objectives has, however, been below expectations. The most commonly noticed implementation deficiencies in Bank projects are delays and cost overruns, reduced command areas, and lower productivity impact.

There is much evidence in supervision reports, project completion reports (PCRs), PPARs, and sector reviews to indicate that project design has often been based on incomplete data and field investigations. In a number of cases appraisal preceded the completion of detailed designs. In some, more cost-effective alternatives were not explored in project choice or design. In others, inappropriate sequencing of works has been the problem. Funding for time-slice and sectoral investments, while promoting flexible and fast disbursement, has paid insufficient attention to technical soundness and economic viability.[30] Inadequate budgetary allocations and delayed releases of funds on the part of executing agencies have been a major cause of delays and cost overruns. Managerial problems have included shortages and high turnover of key staff, inadequate coordination, and poor supervision of contractors. Shortages of cement, steel, and equipment have also been fairly common.

On the environmental aspects of irrigation projects, the two major areas in which the Bank has concentrated are dam safety and resettlement and rehabilitation of displaced families. The Bank's efforts have resulted in greater awareness of and improved procedures for dam safety, and in the funding of a few specific projects. The record in resettlement and rehabilitation has been much less satisfactory. A review of twenty-two projects funded between 1978 and 1990 that entailed resettlement concluded that "in several key projects, despite legal covenants, the resettlement component has yet to be prepared, or is being implemented either inadequately or not at all."[31]

Resettlement and environmental issues became a cause célèbre in the Narmada project in Gujarat, for which the Bank made two loans totaling $450 million in 1985.[32] Widespread opposition to the project from environmental groups in India and in the United States prevailed upon the Bank to appoint an independent review of the resettlement and environmental aspects of the project in June 1991 by a team under Bradford Morse, former head of the UNDP. The

30. See World Bank, Project Performance Audit Report 9716 (June 1991).

31. Quoted in *Sardar Sarovar: Report of the Independent Review* (Ottawa: Resource Futures International, 1992), p. 53.

32. The Sardar Sarovar dam on the Narmada River and its 75,000 kilometers of canals are intended to irrigate 1.8 million hectares, provide drinking water to 40 million people, and to generate electricity. Ibid., pp. 5, 242.

review, published in June 1992, was the first independent assessment of a major project. It concluded that the Bank and India both failed to carry out adequate assessments of the human impacts and environmental consequences of the projects and that the measures instituted or implemented to mitigate them were far from adequate.

The report documented several specific failures. There was inadequate assessment of the human impact before funding in 1985. Planners failed to consult the affected population, resulting in hostility to the project, which created serious obstacles to implementation. The claims of several categories of affected families, such as members of indigenous tribes, squatters, landless families, canal-displaced marginal farmers, and elder sons in affected households, were ignored. Relief efforts in the states of Maharashtra and Madhya Pradesh, where the bulk of the affected people live, were inadequate in scale and poorly implemented. There was a lack of data and programs for tackling the environmental impact—upstream, downstream, and in the command area—particularly in regard to catchment treatment, health hazards, and the impact on fisheries.

According to the review, the failure of the Bank was a consequence of its incremental strategy: "The Bank has been aware of major resettlement problems . . . but has failed to act firmly to address them. Violations of legal covenants are flagged and then forgotten; conditions are imposed and when the borrower fails to meet them, the conditions are relaxed or their deadlines are postponed." Since this strategy has not yielded results and has been counterproductive in provoking the intense hostility of the affected population (supported by activists), the review recommended that the Bank "take a step back" from the projects and consider them afresh.

In response to the review, the Bank admitted "that past efforts—including efforts by the Bank—to resolve" the long-standing problems identified in the Narmada project "have not been adequate."[33] A detailed action plan was formulated in collaboration with the Indian government to remedy the various deficiencies. On this basis the Bank decided to continue its support for the project. However, this incremental step also failed to help. The Indian government was unable to meet the requirements of the action plan and eventually withdrew the project from Bank funding.

As in the case of environmental issues, the incremental strategy of the Bank has not succeeded in upgrading cost recovery. Cost recovery covenants in individual project agreements have been "seldom enforced, often relaxed and sometimes ignored," and the Bank's standard response has been to provide for further studies, which has enabled an "easy way out."[34] Despite its substantial lending for irrigation, rural electrification, and tubewells (the latter being the main component in its

33. Memorandum from the president to the executive directors of the Bank on *India: Sardar Sarovar (Narmada) Projects*, R92-168 (September 11, 1992), p. 2.

34. World Bank, *World Bank Lending Conditionality: A Review of Cost Recovery in Irrigation Projects*, OED report 6283 (June 25, 1986), p. i.

agricultural credit portfolio), the Bank has been unable or unwilling, or both, to pursue effectively the issue of large and mounting subsidies—for surface irrigation and groundwater exploitation through electrified pumpsets—which now add up to about two-thirds of all farm subsidies in India.

In Pakistan the Bank's involvement in irrigation falls into three distinct phases. In the 1950s the Bank was preoccupied with the negotiation of the Indus Waters Treaty between India and Pakistan.[35] Investments beginning in the 1960s related to the large Indus Basin works arising from the treaty, namely, the Mangla and Tarbela dams and major barrages and canals connected with them. It was only in the 1970s and 1980s that the Bank was able to concentrate on the long-standing problems of waterlogging and salinity in Pakistan's irrigation system.[36] In doing so it was greatly influenced by approaches evolved by the U.S. Agency for International Development (USAID) in earlier decades, when the Bank itself was preoccupied with Indus Basin works.

Beginning with the first USAID-initiated SCARP (salinity control and reclamation project) in 1958, the preferred technical option was vertical drainage (the use of tubewells to pump excess water into canals) based on public tubewells rather than horizontal drainage (lining of canals to reduce seepage, surface-tiled drains, and subsurface drains) and private tubewell development. The Bank went along with this approach and made three SCARP-type loans during the 1970s. Although these projects led to investments in a large number of public tubewells, they had no appreciable impact on the incidence and extent of waterlogging and salinity. A number of technical and managerial problems relating to SCARP tubewells also began to assert themselves, such as mismanagement, frequent pump breakdowns, electricity failures, and high recurring costs, with declining ratios of cost recovery.

It was only during the late 1970s that the Bank began to entertain serious reservations about this model. The change of course finally came in its revised action program (RAP) of 1979, which emphasized smaller system rehabilitation and water management projects and reliance on private tubewells, especially in nonsaline areas. Bank lending in the 1980s, following this approach, has been for a series of rehabilitation, drainage, and on-farm management projects emphasizing horizontal drainage and water conservation in the field. A major individual drainage project has been funded in Sind (the Left Bank Canal).

35. For a summary of the Bank's contribution to the Indus Waters Treaty see Mason and Asher, *The World Bank since Bretton Woods,* pp. 610–27; N. D. Gulhati, *Indus Waters Treaty: An Exercise in International Mediation* (New Delhi: Allied Publishers, 1973) provides a more detailed account.

36. The framework for the Bank's activities in this phase was provided by P. Lieftinck, A. R. Sadove, and T. C. Creyke, *Water and Power Resources of West Pakistan: A Study in Sector Planning* (Johns Hopkins University Press, 1968). Canal flows in Pakistan have led to so much seepage that the water table has risen alarmingly over the years in areas without adequate drainage. This is compounded by salinity affecting 15 to 40 percent of canal command areas during various parts of the year.

A part of the irrigation portfolio has included loans from time to time (1977, 1987, and 1988) for the repair and rehabilitation of flood-damaged irrigation works. The Bank has also provided technical assistance and institutional inputs to the Water and Power Development Authority (WAPDA). In the late 1980s a project was undertaken to phase out public tubewells by transferring them to private ownership. In effect, the technical philosophy of the Bank's irrigation lending to Pakistan in the 1980s represents a complete reversal of that followed during most of the 1970s.

The Bank has been more successful in Pakistan than in India in improving cost recovery in irrigation. Water charges have been raised on successive occasions during the 1980s, and the government has accepted the objective of full cost recovery in principle. However, maintenance outlays continue to be underfunded by the provincial governments, which are the ones responsible for it, with the consequence that considerable new funding is periodically required for repair and restoration. The drain on resources entailed by public tubewells has been another factor in exacerbating the resource problem.

Overall, waterlogging and salinity continue to be serious problems in Pakistan, and their solution will depend much on microlevel research, technology, and management. In this context the Bank has been criticized for tending to rely far too much on the shifting predilections of external consultants and for having failed to promote domestic capacity in WAPDA and elsewhere for location-specific, problem-oriented action research in tackling Pakistan's persistent problems of waterlogging, drainage, and salinity.[37]

Irrigation projects in Bangladesh have faced different problems. Bangladesh is blessed with massive water resources and burdened with massive problems of water control. Annual flows in the Brahmaputra-Ganges river system are about double those of the Mississippi and six times those of the Indus. In July and August, the peak of the wet season (April–November), flooding usually occurs when snowmelt runoff and monsoon rains coincide, submerging about two-thirds of cultivated land to varying depths. During the dry season (December–March) there is little rainfall, and about 60 percent of cultivable land remains fallow. This is particularly unfortunate because dry-season irrigation for the Boro rice crop has proved to be the more important contributor to incremental grain production. At the same time, Bangladesh is endowed with enormous groundwater aquifers, sustained by a highly dependable natural recharge cycle, which have been only partially exploited for dry-season cultivation.

Complex issues relating to technical and economic options and trade-offs and priorities for flood control and irrigation in Bangladesh have been debated over the years.[38] In the early 1960s a master plan prepared by the UNDP emphasized what

37. World Bank, *World Bank in Pakistan,* vol. 2, p. 67.

38. For concise summaries see World Bank, *Bangladesh: Drainage and Flood Control Project (Credit 864-BD),* Project Performance Audit Report 8805 (June 29, 1990); and World Bank, *Bangladesh: Promoting Higher Growth and Human Development* (Country Study, 1987), pp. 54–57.

it saw as long-term solutions to the flooding problem through constructing embankments and polders to prevent inundation. As these projects were implemented, the validity of this approach came to be questioned from a number of angles. The structural works were difficult to engineer, extremely costly, susceptible to damage from the changing course of the river, and expensive to maintain, and they utilized scarce arable land. Nor was it easy to combine wet-season irrigation objectives with flood control measures. It proved infeasible to link cost recoveries to flood control, while the limited recoveries from irrigation were inadequate in relation to the large outlays required to ensure against floods.

A major Land and Water Resources (LWR) Sector Study undertaken by the Bank in 1972 represented a shift from the approach of the UNDP master plan and essentially came out in favor of larger-scale surface irrigation requiring primary pumping, minor surface irrigation from natural drains using low-lift pumps, and groundwater utilization by means of a variety of tubewells: deep, shallow, and hand-operated. Flood control and drainage works were to be limited to relatively modest and localized investments that could be expected to be cost effective. These broad priorities have influenced the Bank's lending strategies in the 1970s and 1980s.

Lending for minor irrigation has been accomplished through the Bangladesh Agricultural Development Corporation (BADC). The BADC had been renting out irrigation equipment, mostly low-lift pumps and deep tubewells, to farmers' irrigation groups or cooperatives before 1981; since then it has moved to outright sales and to a greater emphasis on shallow tubewells. Although minor irrigation has, in principle, sought to promote more equitable water use, the operations of the BADC have raised a number of problems, to which the Bank's and the government's responses have been neither clear nor consistent. The problems include how to reduce subsidies in the pricing and rentals of equipment; determining the appropriate pace of transition from rentals to sales; improving the maintenance and utilization of equipment; and establishing a greater role for the private sector in the manufacture, supply, and servicing of equipment.[39] Critics, within and outside the Bank, have pointed out that benefits from minor irrigation projects have been highly skewed in favor of larger landowners, who have dominated irrigation groups and cooperatives. These landowners have preempted supplies and services to themselves and acted as "waterlords," selling water at high prices to small and marginal farmers and tenants.[40] Although the shift to privatization-cum-sales has enlarged the clientele for pumpsets and tubewells, it has also had the effect of restricting the access of smaller cultivators to them. Groundwater regulation, which the Bank sought to promote in its earlier lending operations, has had perverse

39. World Bank, *Bangladesh: Review of the Experience with Policy Reforms in the 1980s*, OED report 8874 (1990), pp. 41–75.

40. Ibid., pp. 57–80; B. Hartmann and J. K. Boyce, *Quiet Violence: A View from a Bangladesh Village* (London: Oxford University Press, 1983), chap. 19.

effects on equity: large farmers, who were early entrants and major beneficiaries from lending, have installed deep tubewells, but regulation has discouraged small farmers seeking to install shallow tubewells. The Bank has come, somewhat belatedly, to the conclusion that groundwater regulation is neither feasible nor desirable.

Meanwhile the catastrophic floods that affected Bangladesh in 1987 and in 1988, displacing some 30 million people from their homes, once again brought the unresolved problem of flood control to the fore. Following these floods as many as four major studies were sponsored by the UNDP, USAID, and the governments of France and Japan in the late 1980s. At the request of the Bangladesh aid group the Bank has tried to sift through, prioritize, and phase in the proposals that emerged from those studies, arbitrating between large structures on the one hand and more affordable measures on the other. The Action Plan for Flood Control that was under consideration in 1989 included nonstructural measures (flood forecasting, warning, preparedness, and disaster management); structural protection (embankments, drainage, water control), with special emphasis on protecting urban concentrations; and regionwide project-oriented studies. An agenda is thus being evolved in Bangladesh for flood control and irrigation, largely as a result of trial and error over a period of nearly three decades. The action plan can be expected to generate a portfolio of domestic projects for flood control, but regional projects to tame and utilize the eastern waters of the Ganges, the Brahmaputra, and their tributaries and branches are also a major challenge. If the Bank is someday able to promote a basinwide approach in this matter among India, Nepal, and Bangladesh, it could once again play a historic role, recalling its signal contribution to the Indus Basin settlement in the 1950s.[41]

From an irrigation perspective, Sri Lanka is divided distinctly into wet and dry zones. The wet zone, located in the southwestern part of the island, occupies about 30 percent of its land area but accounts for more than 80 percent of cultivated land. Extension of irrigation in the dry zone is, accordingly, a major priority. The Mahaweli Development Master Plan developed in 1965–68 seeks to provide irrigation to about 365,000 hectares of land in the dry zone through fifteen reservoirs located on the Mahaweli Ganga River and its tributaries and on the Madura Oya River, and to generate 500 MW of power. The original plan was divided in three phases to be implemented over thirty years. Although the Bank showed some initial interest in the project, it did not play an active role in the studies leading to the master plan because of the deterioration in its relations with the Sri Lanka Freedom Party (SLFP) government of 1961–65. The studies were then carried out by UNDP and the Food and Agriculture Organization (FAO). The Bank's first loan to the project was for the initial stage of the first phase. It included components for a power station and for downstream development of irrigation. Despite a delay of two years in completion, this project was judged successful on the whole, the main problems

41. Verghese, *Waters of Hope*; and the USAID study on Eastern Waters.

that remained being cost recovery, effective water management, and illegal occupation of land.

Late in 1977 the United National Party (UNP) government then in power decided to accelerate the Mahaweli development program. At this stage the Bank was much more forthcoming—indeed, uncharacteristically so—and in fact willing to offer a loan even before the completion of an implementation strategy study it had earlier insisted upon. The main reasons for this were strong pressure from bilateral lenders, the Bank's own desire not to be left out of a prestigious project, and its interest in supporting the right-of-center UNP government, which saw acceleration of the Mahaweli program as a compensation for the sociopolitical costs of the food subsidy reductions, devaluation, and liberalization. Starting again in 1977, the Bank by 1984 had made three more project loans and a technical assistance loan for Mahaweli. Total lending for Mahaweli in the four project loans (1970–84) amounted to $183.6 million, and the project has dominated Bank lending for irrigation in Sri Lanka.

At the macroeconomic level the accelerated Mahaweli program has inflicted severe costs on the Sri Lankan economy. The high and escalating cost of the program (from 12 billion to 40 billion rupees by the mid-1980s) led to substantial budget deficits in the early 1980s and consequent domestic inflation and balance of payments problems. Mahaweli has also diverted construction materials and capacity from other projects. Through its initial hesitancy (in the late 1960s) and its subsequent enthusiasm (since 1977), the Bank has not put itself in a position to moderate the destabilizing effects of this mammoth project on the rest of Sri Lanka's economy.[42]

The Bank's dialogue with the Sri Lanka government over cost recovery in irrigation projects has had a checkered course. Cost recovery covenants in earlier projects, including the one in the first Mahaweli loan, had to be renegotiated when the SLFP came to power in 1970 because the free delivery of water to farmers was one of its election promises. At that point the Bank settled for promises of "future" cost recoveries based on further studies. In fact, no water charges were levied from 1970 to 1977. The UNP government, which came to power in 1977, tried to introduce water charges in 1978, but collections ceased in 1981. Following the negotiations for the third Mahaweli loan, collections began again in 1984. They are reported to have reached reasonable levels in the Mahaweli system but have remained negligible elsewhere.

AGRICULTURAL CREDIT. Following the report of a joint reconnaissance mission with the FAO in 1968, the Bank energetically entered into indirect "wholesale" lending for provision of agricultural credits to farmers in India, with individual

42. On the Mahaweli project see World Bank, *The World Bank and Sri Lanka*, pp. 89–96; and World Bank, *Sri Lanka: A Break with the Past: The 1987–90 Program of Economic Reforms and Adjustment*, 2 vols., Report 7220-CE (May 27, 1988), vol. 2, pp. 74–88. In subsequent years expenditures on the Mahaweli project declined substantially; the major problem that remains is to reduce the large institutional structure created for it.

loans during 1970–73 to ten major states for a total amount of $637 million. Thereafter, on the basis of its experience at the state level, the Bank moved to mediate its lending through the Agricultural Refinance and Development Corporation (ARDC, later to become NABARD, the National Bank for Agriculture and Rural Development). Between 1975 and 1986 five lines of credit for a total of $1,250 million were extended to the ARDC and NABARD, which in turn have used cooperative credit institutions at the state and substate levels for on-lending. Minor irrigation projects (open dug wells, tubewells, and electric pumpsets) have been the main component in agricultural credit financing. Earlier loans also allowed some measure of financing for land leveling and tractors, whereas later loans routed through the ARDC and NABARD covered supplementary activities such as livestock, fisheries, poultry, tree crops, and horticulture.

Besides providing a useful conduit for substantial resource transfers through large loans, the Bank's decision in the mid-1970s to channel its lending for agricultural credit through a "wholesaling" institution at the national level has had several advantages. The ARDC and later NABARD have been able to reach out to less developed states and regions (whose share has improved over time to 50 percent) and to small farmers (who account for nearly half of all borrowers) and to allocate funds to different states according to their needs and performance. Bank loans have contributed to improved procedures and standards within the on-lending agencies. Working with these institutions, the Bank has been able to strengthen state groundwater directorates and to suggest regulations to prevent excessive groundwater exploitation. Commercial banks have been induced to supplement the cooperative credits.

Although the objectives and the modality of lending in this subsector have thus been sound, severe institutional problems have emerged over time in India's agricultural credit system. These relate primarily to overdues and to inadequate lending margins, which in combination have begun to gravely threaten the viability of the cooperative credit system. At the close of the 1980s, 40 to 50 percent of agricultural loans had fallen overdue, and a sizable proportion of these were in default for over three years. Apart from the standard reasons that explain low recovery (such as variable incomes of borrowers, poor project selection, and inadequate follow-up), political interference in the form of promises to write off loans or to waive interest dues have encouraged willful default, mainly on the part of larger farmers.

NABARD has sought to deal with the problem of mounting overdues by cutting off refinancing to cooperative banks or their branches with high proportions of defaulted loans in their portfolios; this, however, has only limited the availability of credit, mainly to small and first-time borrowers. The second major problem is that lending margins, the spread between on-lending and refinance rates of interest, have been kept at levels (about 3 percent) that are only about half of what is required to cover the costs of administration and normal risks. In effect, therefore, there is a significant interest subsidy to the ultimate borrowers in addition to the subsidy implied when borrowers default or have their debt-servicing obligations waived.[43]

Successive PPARs relating to the second (1977), third (1980), and fourth (1982) ARDC loans drew attention to the unsustainable level of arrearages. Performance of the third ARDC loan was actually classified as unsatisfactory because of the large and growing volume of arrears. The PPAR for that loan, issued in 1989, wondered "whether meeting the short-run disbursement targets of the Bank and the government's need for foreign exchange . . . was adequate justification for continuing to support a deteriorating institutional credit system in India."[44] The alarm bell was sounded too late, however, for meanwhile, in 1986, the Bank had made one more loan, on this occasion to NABARD. All that was done to address the problem of arrearages was to provide that a comprehensive study would be undertaken to formulate measures to rectify the situation. There has been no further lending to NABARD while the study is being completed. When, on what scale, and subject to what reforms—actual or promised—lending for agricultural credit will resume remains to be seen. The Bank, of course, cannot be blamed for poor recoveries. But it can be reasonably criticized for not trying hard enough to see that credit discipline is enforced in a timely manner, and it can certainly be faulted for continuing to lend in the face of a deteriorating situation, allowing resource transfer considerations to prevail over concerns for institutional sustainability.

Certain other issues related to agricultural lending are also important. There has been an intense debate on the labor displacement effects of lending for the purchase of tractors (see the discussion with reference to Pakistan below).[45] In practical terms, however, this is not a major issue in India because of the relatively small proportion of lending for mechanization. Another concern relates to the

43. World Bank, *Agricultural Credit Projects: A Review of Recent Experience in India*, report 3415 (1981); also M. Lipton and J. Toye, *Does Aid Work in India? A Country Study of the Impact of Official Development Assistance* (London: Routledge, 1990), pp. 170–73.

44. World Bank, *India: Fourth Agricultural Refinance and Development Corporation Credit Project (ARDC IV)(Loan 2095-IN/Credit 1209-IN)*, Project Performance Audit Report 7925 (June 30, 1989), p. vi. The Bank's OED had this to say four years later about the 1986 loan to NABARD: "Since the project, starting in 1986, did not achieve significantly better results than its predecessor . . . and since the recommendations of the study team, released in 1989, have still to be implemented, the whole decision process leading up to loan approval is viewed by the Bank in retrospect to have been misguided and controlled by disbursement pressures rather than common sense." *Review of Bank Lending for Agricultural Credit and Rural Finance (1948–1992)*, report 12143 (World Bank, 1993), p. 85, para. 6.13.

45. See World Bank, *Operations Evaluation Report: Agricultural Credit Programs*, (1976); Hans P. Binswanger, *The Economics of Tractors in South Asia: An Analytic Review* (New York: Agricultural Development Council, 1978); Bina Agarwal, "Tractorisation, Productivity and Employment, A Reassessment," *Journal of Development Studies*, vol. 16 (April 1980), pp. 375–86.

overuse of groundwater and the need for groundwater regulation. The Bank has tried to promote groundwater discipline through spacing and density criteria for wells, but no state in India has been able or willing, for political reasons, to bring forward comprehensive legislation in this respect. Highly subsidized agricultural power tariffs are an added factor in the wasteful use of water (and electricity). The Bank has provided substantial support to both power and well irrigation and could have attempted a cross-sectoral aggregation of leverage on the subsidy issue. That the opportunity was missed is regrettable for several reasons: cheap power has mainly benefited larger farmers and has led to ecologically undesirable levels and patterns of groundwater use, and it is the single most important factor responsible for the poor financial position of the state electricity boards.

In Pakistan lending for agricultural credit has all along been routed through the Agricultural Development Bank of Pakistan (ADBP). Three loans in this area were made from 1965 through the end of the 1960s, but a long lull in operations followed until 1980. This interruption was due to the poor management and recovery performance of ADBP, for which political interference was partly responsible. ADBP improved recoveries in the 1970s, enabling the Bank to make a new series of loans, for larger amounts, in the 1980s. Unlike NABARD in India, ADBP has continued to maintain a reasonably good recovery record.

A substantial part of agricultural lending in Pakistan has gone into financing of farm mechanization, principally tractors. Tractors have resulted in increased production, mainly through expansion of cultivated area rather than higher cropping intensities, shifts in cropping patterns, or yield increases. Large farmers have been the primary beneficiaries from access to finance as well as subsidized interest rates, which ADBP has been able to ensure because of its low-interest borrowing from the State Bank of Pakistan. On the other hand, tractors have led to displacement of tenants, casualization of farm labor, and an increase in disguised, if not in open, unemployment. As noted above, there has been a debate within the Bank and outside on these socially regressive effects of tractors, but the Bank has tended to underplay the issue and to go along with the government and ADBP in their continued support for tractorization.[46]

A much smaller proportion of agricultural lending through ADBP has been for groundwater irrigation. This is surprising because the irrigation strategies of the Bank have emphasized the role of private tubewells in the control of waterlogging, and tubewells, unlike tractors, have a positive effect on labor absorption. The main criticisms of the Bank's agricultural lending in Pakistan thus relate to both commission and omission: tractor loans have run counter to professed equity objectives of employment promotion in rural areas, while inadequate lending for tubewells

---

46. John P. McInerney and Graham F. Donaldson, *The Consequences of Farm Tractors in Pakistan*, Working Paper 210 (World Bank, February 1975); *Operations Evaluation Report: Agricultural Credit Programs*, vol. 2, pp. 53–55; Godfrey J. Tyler, "Poverty, Income Distribution and the Analysis of Agricultural Projects," *International Labour Review*, vol. 118 (July–August 1979), pp. 459–72.

points to lack of coordination in lending strategies between the irrigation and agricultural credit subsectors.

AGRICULTURAL EXTENSION. The agricultural extension projects of the Bank represent an ambitious effort at reforming grass-roots agricultural administration in India, a country of vast size, diversity, and complexity of farming conditions. At the time of the Bank's initial involvement in the mid-1970s, agricultural extension services in India suffered from several shortcomings: poorly trained and inadequate staff fragmented among different crops, channels of command, and types of duties; weak linkages between extension and research; and inadequate allocations of finance and manpower for extension. Basing its strategy on pilot projects in the Chambal and Rajasthan command areas, the Bank made fifteen loans for agricultural extension in India between 1977 and 1987, covering as many as seventeen states. Earlier loans were for individual states, but those since 1985 have each covered a number of states.

The Bank's blueprint for extension is based on what is called the training-and-visit (T&V) approach.[47] Although eminently sensible in its conception, this approach has suffered much distortion in both design and implementation across the several states of India. The problems include high turnover, poor training, and low motivation of staff; diversion of extension staff to nonextension duties; inadequate tuning of extension messages to local cropping conditions and farmers' resources; poor links with research, inadequate research inputs, and feeble reciprocal feedback between field and research; deficient selection of contact farmers and lack of interest on their part in dissemination; and inadequate coordination between extension and availability of inputs. The Bank itself has been criticized for taking on too much at too rapid a pace and for replicating a single model over states and regions with very different administrative and agroeconomic conditions instead of stabilizing implementation in a few states and systematically incorporating lessons from earlier phases into subsequent ones.

There has been a vigorous debate between the Bank and its critics regarding the extent of these problems and the degree to which they have continued in different states.[48] The Bank has tried to effect improvements in its repeat projects in some of the states and has carried out detailed reviews, resulting in a number of specific

47. The T&V approach is to appoint full-time village extension workers (VEWs) to work exclusively on extension; establish a single line of command between VEWs and extension headquarters; select contact farmers to disseminate information; establish a fixed and regular cycle of fortnightly visits by VEWs; use simple, practical, relevant messages concentrating on the most important crops; provide regular in-service training to staff at all levels; initiate a system of feedback from farmers via extension staff to researchers; and develop monitoring and evaluation procedures.

48. See National Institute of Rural Development (NIRD), *Training and Visit System of Agricultural Extension: The Indian Experience* (Hyderabad, 1983); Mick Moore, "Institutional Development, The World Bank, and India's New Agricultural Extension Programme," *Journal of Development Studies*, vol. 20 (July 1984), pp. 303–17; Gershon Feder and Roger Slade, "A Comparative Analysis of Some Aspects of Training and Visit System of Agricultural Extension in India," *Journal of Development Studies*, vol. 22 (January 1986), pp. 407–27; World Bank, *India: Agricultural Extension Sector Review Report*, report 9383-IN (1988); M. Macklin, "Agriculture Extension in India: Past, Present and Future" (World Bank, 1991).

recommendations to strengthen the functioning of the system. The limited number of studies evaluating the T&V approach are not conclusive, for it is difficult to disaggregate the impact of extension on agricultural productivity from changes in other factors such as irrigation, credit availability, fertilizer use, and prices.

In Pakistan, Bangladesh, and Sri Lanka T&V has been promoted on a much smaller scale. In Pakistan, beginning with smaller operations between 1978 and 1985, a substantial loan was made for the introduction of T&V in Punjab and Sind in 1987. Initial experience has been more or less the same as in India, with high staff turnover and other managerial problems. It is too soon to say whether the Punjab-Sind project will be able to overcome these problems. In Sri Lanka as well, the problems encountered in India and Pakistan have repeated themselves.

AREA DEVELOPMENT. An early project, approved in 1974, provided five-year time-slice financing for India's Drought Prone Areas Program (DPAP), which at that time covered seventy-two districts in thirteen states. This was conceived as a pilot project through which project components could be tested and the successful ones introduced in larger-scale subsequent operations. The project scope was wide ranging, including water resources, dry land farming, fodder and livestock, forestry, fisheries, sericulture, horticulture, and technical assistance. Although the project itself was a reasonable success, it did not fulfill its function as a pilot because the monitoring and evaluation component was not implemented; thus no systematic lessons could be learned for the future. More important, the government did not request further Bank participation in the DPAP.

Other area development projects in India in the 1970s were mostly directed toward the utilization of irrigation in specified command areas (Chambal command in Madhya Pradesh, for example) by providing supplementary investments (field channels, roads) and inputs (credit, extension services). In the 1980s the orientation of area development projects shifted from irrigation utilization to resource management. A project was undertaken to prevent environmental degradation in the Himalayan regions of two northern states (Himachal Pradesh and Haryana).

Of special interest is the development of a portfolio of national watershed management projects. Two such projects, each covering a number of states, were funded in the late 1980s and aimed at improving yields in rain-fed areas through in situ moisture conservation practices along with vegetative bunding (vetiver grass) for slope stabilization. Another type of area development project formulated at the end of the 1980s consisted of state-specific integrated agricultural development projects containing components for irrigation, extension, various activities allied to agriculture, and elements of institution building. Yet another project is addressed to the development of a tribal area in the economically backward state of Bihar.

Regional imbalances are wide in India, there is evidence that they have worsened over time, and backward regions are an important aspect of the poverty problem. In this context it is a pity that the Bank has not been able so far to assist area-specific, broad-based rural development in India through investments, lending, and other programs for income generation, employment creation, provision of rural infrastructure, facilities to meet basic needs, and so on. India has a number of central and state-level programs in this area, and the Bank's involvement in them would have been of great value in many ways. Apart from increased funding, a fruitful dialogue might have taken place over how to improve the concepts, design, institutions, implementation, and cost-effectiveness of area development projects, with both partners benefiting from the lessons learned. These opportunities have been missed primarily because of the government's reluctance to entertain the Bank's involvement, but perhaps also because the Bank has not shown much eagerness to get into this thorny area.[49]

Rural development on an area-specific basis has been one of the Bank's continuing concerns in Bangladesh. In 1976, soon after the country was formed, a pilot loan for rural development was made drawing inspiration from the experiment undertaken in the Comilla region in the 1960s under the leadership of Akhter Hamid Khan. On the whole, project performance was not satisfactory, and the design turned out to be too complex and expensive to implement effectively. Monitoring and evaluation were not adequate to provide lessons for future lending.[50]

Further lending in this subsector has consisted of an employment-oriented project in 1980 to complete earthworks (roads and minor irrigation) undertaken in the food-for-work program, and a second and much larger ($100 million) rural development project in 1983. The latter is a countrywide project with provision for credit, irrigation, institution building, and assistance to the Bangladesh Rural Development Board. In the absence so far of audited project performance reports, it is hard to assess the impact of these projects.

Sri Lanka initiated a rural development scheme in 1979 as part of a package to balance economic liberalization with social justice and as a follow-up to an earlier decision to decentralize development efforts at the district, division, and village levels. The Bank has involved itself in this program and during 1979–83 financed three projects covering five districts. Bank projects have supported productive activities such as tree crop planting, economic infrastructure (tanks and roads), agricultural services and credit, basic needs (education, health, and water supply), and rural electrification. The first two projects (Kurunegala, started in 1979, and Matale and Puttalam, 1981) have performed well, but the third, in the northern

49. At the analytical level, however, the Bank has been interested in antipoverty and rural employment programs. See Robert V. Pulley, *Making the Poor Creditworthy: A Case Study of the Integrated Rural Development Program in India,* Discussion Paper 58 (World Bank, 1989); Martin Ravallion, "Reaching the Rural Poor through Public Employment: Arguments, Evidence, and Lessons from South Asia," *World Bank Research Observer,* vol. 6 (July 1991), pp. 153–75.

50. World Bank, *Bangladesh,* Project Performance Audit Report 6521 (November 1986); Michael Bamberger and Shabbir Cheema, *Case Studies of Project Sustainability: Implications for Policy and Operations from Asian Experience* (World Bank, Economic Development Institute, 1990), pp. 47–62.

districts (Vavuniya and Mannar, 1983), has been set back by ethnic unrest. In contrast to similar projects financed by other donors, Bank projects are implemented by line officials in Sri Lanka's administrative structure without any expatriate participation. The Bank's willingness to mesh its lending with the contents and delivery structures of an ongoing government program has been an important factor in the smooth, cost-effective, institution-strengthening implementation of these projects. The criticism has been made, however, that the Bank has been reluctant to deviate from its project blueprint, unlike sponsors of other projects, which have provided more flexibility; it is also asserted that beneficiaries under Bank projects tend to be small farmers rather than more disadvantaged groups such as landless households.[51]

TREE CROP DEVELOPMENT IN SRI LANKA. Tree crops—tea, rubber, and coconut—are vital to the Sri Lankan economy. They contribute about half of merchandise exports, with tea alone accounting for about 40 percent, and provide a significant proportion of revenues and employment. The major tea and rubber estates in Sri Lanka were nationalized in the early 1970s under land reform legislation. There has been a sharp secular decline since the early 1960s in the production and export of tree crops because of international competition, declines in export prices, poor public sector management, and excessive domestic taxation.

Since 1978 the Bank has assisted six tree crop projects. The first tree crop diversification project (1978), which aimed to diversify unsuitable estate tea lands into mixed tree crops and to resettle estate labor, was a failure largely because of intense social and political opposition, which the Bank had failed to anticipate. The other projects have been reasonably successful, despite delays and cost increases, in realizing the objectives of rehabilitation, diversification, new planting, and institutional development. To improve the profitability of the tea and rubber plantations, the Bank has engaged in a protracted dialogue with the government on the reduction of export taxes and has achieved some progress in this regard.

It is commendable that the Bank has contributed to the development of Sri Lanka's tree crop sector, overcoming its inhibition against lending for public sector enterprises. However, one criticism that has been made is that the smallholder component in the tea and smallholder rubber projects has not had much impact.[52] This is a shortcoming from the point of view of both equity and growth, because smallholders in Sri Lanka account for a third of tea, two-thirds of rubber, and almost all of coconut production.

The Social Sectors

The share of the social sectors—education, population control, health and nutrition, urban development, and water supply and sewerage—in total Bank

---

51. World Bank, *Rural Development: World Bank Experience 1965–86* (1988), pp. 72–74, profile 3.

52. World Bank, *The World Bank and Sri Lanka*, p. 82.

lending to South Asia sharply increased in the 1970s and 1980s, from barely 3 percent before 1970 to 10 to 12 percent. All Bank lending to the region for population control, nutrition, and urban development has come in these two decades. Table 8-10 provides data on the pattern of lending for the social sectors in South Asia over this period.

EDUCATION. Except for a small loan of $12 million for two agricultural universities, lending in the educational sector in India has consisted of two large loans for vocational training and education of technicians in 1989 ($280 million) and in 1990 ($260 million). These loans are too recent for their results to be assessed. Although the Bank has been interested in lending for general (nontechnical) education in India, the government has not been responsive.

The Bank began lending for education in Pakistan in 1964 but did not seriously involve itself in this sector until 1977, despite Pakistan's strikingly low levels of educational development. Operations in the 1960s were for small amounts, directed to vocational training. During 1977–86 three loans for general education (for a total of $77.5 million) and two for vocational training ($65.2 million) were made. Substantially larger loans for primary education were made only at the close of the 1980s: $145 million in 1987 and $112.5 million in 1990. Audited performance reports for the first three loans in Pakistan provide a largely negative picture of performance, with two of these projects being rated as unsatisfactory. Assessments are not yet available for the more recent primary education projects funded in 1984, 1987, and 1990.

In Bangladesh it took the Bank nearly a decade to make its first loan for primary education. The loan of $40 million in 1980 was, however, a substantial one. It extended to parts of eight districts and covered about 10 percent of the country. There were shortfalls in a number of project objectives, and outcome indicators relating to enrollment and dropout ratios in the project area did not indicate any clear improvement. Questions were raised about the sustainability of the project and whether the project implementation unit created for it was the appropriate institutional option.[53] Bangladesh has also received loans for vocational (including agricultural) training, technical education, and business management and civil service training. In Sri Lanka two loans have been made for training in the construction industry and a large one in 1990 ($49 million) for general education aimed at quality improvement and institutional strengthening.

Several issues concern the Bank's lending strategy in the education sector and the impact, sustainability, and replicability of Bank-financed projects. The evaluation literature, in the form of PPARs and sector studies, for South Asia is quite limited, however, because substantial lending has taken place only since the mid-1980s, and educational loans have been slow in disbursement.[54]

---

53. Bamberger and Cheema, *Case Studies of Project Sustainability*, chap. 4.
54. The OED sector study of educational projects predates the main period of lending for education in South Asia. World Bank, *Review of Bank Operations in the Education Sector*, OED report 2321 (December 29, 1978).

POPULATION. More than 95 percent of the Bank's lending in the area of population control in South Asia is concentrated in India and Bangladesh.[55] India has had a strong, well-articulated commitment to population control, especially since the mid-1960s. The Bank's first loan to India in this area was made in 1972, the year it began lending for population-related projects, but the second operation came a full eight years later, in 1980. The Bank's reluctance to be associated with population control in this interregnum may have been influenced by public reaction to forced stabilization during the emergency period (1975–77) in India.

Up to 1988 the Bank had funded five projects in all, for a total of $245.7 million; this represents a small fraction (less than 4 percent) of India's outlays on family welfare. Four of the projects were for provision of infrastructure (buildings and vehicles), staff, training, and services (such as IEC, or information, education, and communication) in selected districts of various states, and the fifth was for urban services in Bombay and Madras.

Outcome indicators in the first two projects did not reveal any improvement in contraceptive prevalence or in maternal and child health indicators in project areas over nonproject ones in the same region. Project components relating to monitoring and evaluation, operations research, and IEC have also failed to perform up to expectations. Altogether, neither the scale and continuity of the Bank's lending nor the design and impact of its projects have had much influence on India's population program in terms of policy, improvements to implementation, or lessons learned. Essentially their main contribution has been to provide infrastructural support to ongoing programs.

The Indian population program has been criticized on a number of counts, mainly the following. It is charged that there is an excessive concentration on population control, based chiefly on sterilization, to the relative neglect of maternal and child health and allied programs such as female literacy, water supply, and sanitation. Wide regional disparities in the provision and acceptance of services are also noted, with the populous, high-fertility northern Indian states faring worse than the rest. Finally, the program is criticized for excessive emphasis on the supply side and not enough on demand generation through IEC.

It is widely acknowledged that future reductions in fertility will depend largely on methods of birth spacing for younger mothers and on efforts to improve maternal and child health and female literacy, with necessary improvements in the delivery of services, including greater involvement of community and nonofficial groups. The sixth (in 1989, for $124.6 million) and seventh (in 1990, for $96.7 million) Bank-sponsored projects at the close of the 1980s addressed some of these priorities. They were also larger in loan amount and scope. The Bank has secured a

55. For assessments of Bank lending for population management in India and Bangladesh see World Bank, *Population and the World Bank: A Review of Activities and Impacts from Eight Case Studies,* OED report 10021 (October 22, 1991), pp. 12–33.

foothold at the national policy level only in the seventh project. If this had happened earlier, the Bank could have gained greater leverage in this program, which in India is entirely supported by central funds.

In contrast, the Bank's involvement in population matters in Bangladesh has been much more venturesome. The first project (in 1975) was nationwide and multisectoral, involving eight different ministries and including a number of components. Subsequent projects in 1979 and in 1986 have doubled the amounts lent in previous projects and have been equally wide in scope. All these projects were cofinanced by a number of bilateral donors, who contributed considerable grant funds, thereby providing flexibility. The Bank has played a leading and catalytic role in mobilizing and coordinating foreign assistance in this field.

The main criticism of Bank projects in Bangladesh is that their magnitude, complexity, and momentum have overwhelmed the capacity of the Bangladesh government's administrative apparatus to absorb them, leading to serious shortcomings in coordination at the middle levels of administration and in quality of services in the field. However, the "big push" approach followed in Bangladesh, although wasteful, was perhaps crucial in reducing total fertility from 7 percent to below 5 percent and in increasing the prevalence of contraceptive use from 3 to 32 percent between 1970 and 1989, in a country with very low and almost stagnant levels of socioeconomic development. The Bank has recognized, however, that its future strategy in Bangladesh cannot be a mere continuation of the past: the approach will have to be intensive and fine-tuned rather than extensive and eclectic.

The Bank's only loan in Pakistan is a small one ($18 million in 1983) to support promotional efforts. Despite its great need, Pakistan has not adopted active measures for population control. After years of indecision caused mainly by political and religious opposition, the Population Welfare Plan (PWP) in Pakistan was introduced in 1980. It is a low-key, phased approach designed to promote demand for, and acceptability of, contraceptive services through maternal and child health services, functional education, and programs for women's welfare.[56] The Bank's only other loan in the population policy area was one to Sri Lanka ($17.5 million in 1988); that loan has a large health component stressing maternal and child health and birth spacing methods. It is ironic that Pakistan, with more than a threefold higher fertility rate and a sixfold larger population than Sri Lanka, has received the same amount of lending in this sector, although of course the Bank cannot be blamed for this.

NUTRITION. The Bank's interventions in nutrition have been confined to two projects in the southern state of Tamil Nadu in India. The first Tamil Nadu Integrated Nutrition Project (TINP-1) of 1980 has been adjudged a successful

56. On the evolution of population policy in Pakistan see Samuel S. Lieberman, "Accommodation and Control of Population Growth," in Shahid Javed Burki and Robert Laporte Jr., eds., *Pakistan's Development Priorities: Choices for the Future* (Oxford University Press, 1984), pp. 139–200.

model of cost-effective targeting in tackling malnutrition among children in the vulnerable age group of 6 to 36 months. During the project period severe malnutrition (grades 3 and 4) in the target group has been reduced by a third to a half through selective food supplementation based on periodic weight and growth monitoring. The second project (1990) covers those districts in the state not covered in the first one and incorporates the lessons learned in it. Valuable and innovative as the project has been, its replication in other states in India is in some doubt, mainly because the Bank's highly selective approach to nutrition supplementation is politically unpalatable. The Bank has recently assisted the centrally supported Integrated Child Development Services (ICDS) program, which is less selective in its feeding program and includes preschool education as one of its components; in the process the Bank's influence has led to necessary modifications in the ICDS.

URBAN DEVELOPMENT. The Bank has given substantial support to urban projects in the major South Asian countries. A number of the principal cities in the subcontinent—Calcutta, Bombay, Madras, and Kanpur (in India), Lahore (Pakistan), Dhaka and Chittagong (Bangladesh), and Colombo (Sri Lanka)—have received urban development loans. In India the portfolio includes repeat loans to major cities such as Calcutta, Bombay, and Madras; separate loans for public (bus) transport in some of them (including Bombay and Calcutta); and projects for major towns besides the main metropolis in a number of states (Madhya Pradesh, Gujarat, Uttar Pradesh, Tamil Nadu). In 1988 the Bank also made a substantial loan ($250 million) to the Housing Development Finance Corporation, the major Indian private sector institution engaged in mortgage financing. In Sri Lanka the Bank's urban sector study of 1984 was welcomed by the government as very useful and was followed by a loan in 1986 to support a number of sectoral programs in Colombo and other urban areas.

Typically, urban projects have straddled a number of sectors and implementing agencies. The Calcutta project (1974), for instance, contained forty-four subprojects in six sectors, and the Madras project (1977) involved ten agencies dealing with six sectors. As might be expected in such wide-ranging projects, coordination has turned out to be a major problem in the short term, while the longer-term financial and institutional sustainability of many projects is not assured. Other problems have included land acquisition delays, underfunding of local costs, and poor cost recovery, especially in the bus transport and settlement components. A valuable contribution of the Bank is the introduction of the concepts of "sites and services" and slum improvement. These have proved to be affordable, low-cost, replicable solutions to urban housing. The Bank's assistance is only a small part of what is needed to tackle urban problems in South Asia, but its contribution in demonstrating workable options has been appreciated.

WATER SUPPLY AND SEWERAGE. The Bank has been very active in the area of water supply and sewerage, largely as an adjunct to its support for urban development. It has financed major urban water supply projects in India (in Bombay, Madras, Hyderabad, and major towns in several states, including Uttar Pradesh, Maharashtra, Punjab, Rajasthan, and Tamil Nadu), Pakistan (Lahore and Karachi), Bangladesh (Dhaka and Chittagong), and Sri Lanka (Greater Colombo and other important towns). Support to rural water supply has been limited to a single project in India (in Kerala state). Many water supply and sewerage projects have encountered delays and cost overruns. In a number of cases inadequate initial investigations, design changes, and poor performance by consultants have been responsible for delays and cost escalation. By and large, however, project objectives have been achieved. Cost recovery has remained the major problem in most projects.

The Lending Experience: A Critical Assessment

The Bank's contributions in the last two decades to economic development in South Asia have been substantial and many sided. In nominal terms, the volume of lending in the 1970s increased to as much as four times that of the 1960s and grew threefold again in the 1980s. Resource transfers in these two decades have included a substantial element of local cost financing, providing both external and counterpart domestic resources in freely usable forms. In all South Asian countries Bank lending has played a critically important role in supplementing the foreign exchange required for development; concurrently, it has substantially supplemented domestic saving in countries where it is relatively low such as Pakistan, Bangladesh, and Nepal.

Coming predominantly in the form of project lending, the Bank's resource transfers have resulted in investments in many sectors of crucial importance to South Asia's growth, self-reliance, and welfare. As a development lender, the Bank has been interested in extending the benefits of its project lending beyond the successful completion of the project itself to improvements in implementation capacity, long-term sustainability of projects, and diffusion and replication of the learning experience in project execution, institution building, and sectoral policy reforms.

This concluding section turns to a summary assessment of the impact of the principal characteristics of the Bank's project lending in South Asia, as they have emerged in actual practice in the last two decades, on the realization of the Bank's larger developmental objectives. The assessment is critical and concentrates on what the Bank could or might have done differently to realize a greater measure of success in achieving its stated objectives. This selective focus is heuristic and should not be misunderstood as partial or prejudiced: it is not meant to underestimate the Bank's considerable positive contributions, all of which have been duly noted in the earlier sections, or the considerable problems that the Bank has encountered with its South Asian borrowers.

Lending Strategies

There can be no question that the broad lending strategies of the Bank in South Asia, in terms of sectoral and subsectoral involvement, have been appropriate to the developmental priorities and resource endowments of the borrowers in the region. Support for agriculture, with special emphasis on irrigation, agricultural credit, and extension services, along with financing of fertilizer manufacture, has reinforced the adoption of new technology that can achieve higher yields. Energy investments have been of crucial importance, and their diversification into oil, gas, and coal has helped to reduce the region's hydrocarbon imports. Lending to development financing institutions has provided a wide spectrum of support to medium-sized industries in the private sector. In the social sectors, lending for urban development, water supply, and population control have been especially worthwhile.

It can be argued that the Bank might have paid more attention to certain subsectors (small-scale enterprises, rural roads, rural water supply) than it has; that it could have involved itself earlier in some important activities (general education in Pakistan and Bangladesh, for example); and that there could have been a greater continuity in lending in some cases (in power in Sri Lanka, for example). However, one cannot come to definitive judgments on such issues because many factors—the Bank's own familiarity and comparative advantage, borrowers' preferences, and the availability and terms of other sources of finance—determine the pattern of sectoral involvement.

Project Features

To proceed from the broad sectoral to the project level, valid criticisms of project designs and other modalities of the lending process may be raised. The very substantial increases in lending in South Asia that occurred in the 1970s and 1980s have both enabled and entailed—especially in India—relatively large loans for individual projects or for lending through intermediary institutions. Large and repeat projects have facilitated resource transfer targets, helped in institution building (for instance, the National Thermal Power Corporation and the training-and-visit approach to agricultural extension in India), and economized on transaction costs such as staff time involved in preparation, appraisal, and negotiation.

However, these projects have not been without their disadvantages. First, there have been important diseconomies of scale. Often, large projects have involved multiple components or multiple executing agencies and locations. They have been difficult to coordinate, implement, and monitor, entailing a higher intensity of supervision. This, in turn, has reduced staff time available for preparation and appraisal, diluting their quality and exacerbating the burden on supervision. Second, large investments and repeat projects have discouraged experimentation, lesson learning, and institution building, all of which would call for a more relaxed and reflective pace of lending. Third, it has been difficult to postpone lending for large projects when that might be called for, because of the disruption it would cause to annual lending programs based on resource transfer targets. This inflexibility has reduced the Bank's leverage in the policy dialogue, as exemplified by several cases in India involving energy, agricultural credit, and irrigation.

The structural, technical, and institutional aspects of Bank projects have also come in for criticism. In India the Bank's own evaluations have wondered whether time-slice and sectoral approaches have not resulted in inadequate attention to project preparation, appraisal, and sequencing. The Bank has also been criticized for seeking to introduce uniform water management regimens in different parts of a large country like India without due regard for local conditions.[57] In Pakistan the Bank had to reverse its approach to waterlogging and salinity from SCARP-type vertical drainage relying on public tubewells to horizontal drainage and private tubewells. In Bangladesh, despite much trial and error over the years, flood control has remained intractable, and major problems connected with tubewell irrigation have remained unresolved. In Sri Lanka the Bank has had to acquiesce in the accelerated Mahaweli program instead of being able to steer its composition and phasing by optimal cost-effectiveness considerations. In agricultural extension the Bank has replicated the standard training-and-visit blueprint without taking pause to learn from experience. As the independent review of the Narmada project has shown, investigations of environmental aspects have not been timely, adequate, or thorough. Educational lending has lacked critical mass or continuity. Lending for population management in Bangladesh has involved excessive cost, both financial and institutional; in India it has concentrated too much on civil construction.

Implementation

Implementation is primarily the responsibility of the borrower. Performance here has varied across sectors, countries, states in India, and time periods, depending on both macroeconomic and project-specific factors and subject to disruptions caused by unpredictable natural events. No data are available to assess how Bank-financed projects have fared compared with those financed by other donors or by borrowers on their own. However, interregional comparisons among the Bank's borrowers broadly indicate that project performance in South Asia was, if anything, somewhat better than the global average during most of 1970–90.

For its part, the Bank has striven through its supervisory missions to promote concern for time, cost, and quality at all stages of project execution. Considerable technical assistance has also been provided in the course of supervision. Supervision coefficients (staff weeks spent on supervision per project in a year) have been

57. Robert Chambers, *Managing Canal Irrigation: Practical Analysis from South Asia* (Cambridge University Press, 1988); and Robert Wade, "The World Bank and India's Irrigation Reform," *Journal of Development Studies,* vol. 18 (January 1982), pp. 171–84.

relatively high in South Asia, in part because of the high proportion of agricultural projects, which have entailed detailed monitoring and technical assistance. Other factors are the size and complexity of projects and problems arising from center-state relations in India. Furthermore, supervision intensity is explained by the fact that in complex projects not all components get prepared or appraised to the same degree of adequacy or readiness; the load on supervision in these circumstances is a reflection of "deferred preparation and appraisal."

Resident missions have been given a role in supervision, principally in agricultural projects in India and in the social sectors in Pakistan and Bangladesh. Being nearer to the field, they have been able to monitor implementation problems closely and respond to them quickly. The other side of the coin is that proximity breeds intrusiveness; resident staff have sometimes been perceived as breathing down the neck of executing agencies. But on the whole, if Indian experience is any guide, the Bank's supervision inputs have been considered helpful, and its assistance in solving field-level problems has been appreciated.[58]

Problems relating to management of projects by the borrowing country have been a matter of serious and frequent concern in project execution in South Asia. Most such deficiencies have had their roots and ramifications in country-wide problems—political, economic, and administrative. When this is the case, the lack of success in implementation reflects generic problems in the borrower's entire project portfolio. It is clear, by the same token, that better performance of the Bank's portfolio can be achieved in the longer run only by strengthening borrowers' overall institutional capabilities to prepare, execute, monitor, and supervise projects.

In principle, the Bank has been interested in strengthening such capabilities in the apex ministries and technical agencies of its borrowers, but in practice it has not invested enough effort and time in a generalized effort to strengthen project-related capacities across the board in ministries and technical agencies at the national and subnational levels. Essentially, the imperative of meeting lending targets has not allowed projects to proceed at a pace patient enough to secure a larger involvement of borrower agencies at various stages of the project cycle. (Interestingly, on the other hand, the same consideration has made the Bank quite patient with failures to comply with covenants.)

In some ways Bank projects also appear to have had negative effects on the general portfolio management of borrowers. The Bank's insistence on staffing, funding, and other specific commitments on the projects for which it lends has diverted manpower as well as material and financial resources from non-Bank-financed projects, affecting complementary investments and overall development. This has been the case particularly in staff-intensive activities (training-and-visit

58. On the Indian experience see S. Guhan and A. Mozoomdar, *Bank Project Supervision Activities in India* (World Bank, Consultants' Report, 1989).

extension services, education, population control) and in projects entailing lumpy outlays (irrigation, urban development, water supply).

Evaluation

Monitoring and evaluation during project execution has been a weak area. In a number of projects, appropriate mechanisms either were not put in place soon enough or did not produce useful lessons for future operations.[59] This has had especially adverse implications in projects envisaged as pilot operations, meant to provide a basis for wider replication. The contribution of ex-post evaluation to operations has also been limited. In the case of repeat projects based on more or less standard blueprints, such evaluations have not been able to contribute to midcourse modifications because the pace of lending has been too fast to be steadied or steered by PCRs and PPARs finalized several years after project initiation. On the other hand, in one-of-a-kind projects, insights from PPARs have not had a wider application.

The usefulness of PPARs is further limited because they are confined to comparing results at or around the time of project completion with estimates and objectives at the time of appraisal. There are several problems in relying on economic rates of return reestimated in PCRs or PPARs as indicators of project performance. First, variations can be quite large between the initial estimates made at appraisal and those made at project completion, because of windfall increases or calamitous declines in output prices. Second, in many cases project benefits are estimated with reference to what would have obtained in the absence of the investment. This involves counterfactual judgments that may not always be reliable. Third, in some cases economic rates of return depend on assumed returns on subsystems (agricultural extension, for example), whose performance cannot be separated from that of related investments and activities (credit, irrigation) that impinge on the project but are outside of its scope. Fourth, rates of return reestimated immediately after project completion do not give any idea of what they are likely to be through the life of the project—thus they do not throw light on the sustainability of the project.

Many "new style" projects in agriculture and the social sectors, unlike the traditional ones, do not relate to fixed installations such as power plants or fertilizer factories, whose performance can be more or less guaranteed on completion, but instead entail continuing activities that are more fragile because they involve "software" and a human dimension: examples are on-farm water use and the delivery of agricultural extension, educational, population, and nutrition services. In such cases it is necessary to return to the project once a reasonable period has elapsed since its completion, to find out whether planned inputs and expected

59. Vigar Ahmed and Michael Bamberger, *Monitoring and Evaluating Development Projects: The South Asian Experience* (World Bank, EDI, 1989).

outcomes have been sustained on a durable basis. The Bank has undertaken some impact evaluations and sustainability studies of its projects, but not on a sufficient scale or on a systematic basis. This is, indeed, a serious gap.

Policy Dialogue

In the course of financing single projects, repeat projects, and clusters of projects, the Bank's technical assistance and policy dialogue have extended upstream to issues of general application at the subsectoral and sectoral levels. There have been numerous examples. The emphasis on on-farm development and user-level water management has provided a much-needed corrective to irrigation practices in all of South Asia. The insistence on groundwater discipline, dam safety, and resettlement and rehabilitation of displaced families has focused attention on important issues that tend to be neglected.

Despite its continuing problems, the training-and-visit approach represents a major contribution to the reform of agricultural administration. Project designs in India for watershed management and nutrition have been innovative. Tree crop projects in Sri Lanka have enabled the Bank to secure changes in export taxes. Financing of fertilizer projects has provided a nexus for price reform in Pakistan and Bangladesh. General-purpose lending through DFIs has been better focused. Energy conservation and productivity improvements have been promoted in refineries, fertilizer plants, power plants, and the cement industry. Technology has been modernized in railways and telecommunications. Needless to say, the Bank has not been successful in all that it has attempted, but it has succeeded in charting initiatives of much relevance for its borrowers.

By and large, the Bank's efforts to enforce financial covenants of various kinds—relating to cost recovery, tariffs, self-financing, receivables, and repayments—have not been successful. In India and Sri Lanka, which have continued to hold regular elections, populist politics has been a serious obstacle to liberalizing tariffs, reducing subsidies, and ensuring loan repayments, even to the extent to which governments have been interested in doing these things. Basically, it has not been possible for the Bank to gain enough leverage on such issues at the sectoral level from individual project operations, however large and continuous they have been. Ironically, in fact, the size and continuity of lending operations have blunted the pressure for reform.

In practical terms, the only option available to the Bank has been the "exit" option—to discontinue lending pending the demonstration of serious intent for reforms. Indeed, that is the option that the Bank has taken, later rather than sooner, in the cases of NABARD and NTPC in India, for example. In Pakistan and Bangladesh as well, it has not always been easy to enforce financial and revenue covenants, although the situation has been somewhat more encouraging than in India: cost recovery in irrigation, power, and gas steadily improved in the 1980s, and progress has been made in fertilizer pricing reform. Adjustment lending in Pakistan and Bangladesh has no doubt been a factor in inducing progress in these directions.

The Bank's policy dialogue has not been confined to the project or to project-related sectors. Annual country economic memorandums (CEMs), sector- and issue-related studies prepared as part of CEMs, and other economic and sectoral studies have all provided opportunities for the Bank to interact with borrowers at the policy level and with line ministries and executing agencies. They have also provided an agenda for lending operations, especially for adjustment lending. In the 1980s the Bank issued a number of economic and sectoral reviews of high quality.[60]

There has not, however, been much sharing of the Bank's policy analyses and prescriptions with the media, nongovernmental organizations, and academia as part of a wider effort to mold opinion among the public at large, even in a country like India which offers good opportunities for doing so. Bank studies more often get leaked than published, with the consequence that the Bank tends to be charac-terized as an agent of external pressure rather than as a partner in development. In good measure, borrower governments are responsible for creating a conspiratorial ambience around the policy dialogue between them and the Bank; in doing so they have only added to their own problems in securing understanding and support in the public domain for reforms.

Within governments, the Bank's policy interaction has been closest with mini-stries of finance and relatively less with planning commissions, line ministries, and technical agencies. Ministries of finance have tended to centralize the aid relation-ship and have been reluctant to allow Bank staff to "run around." On the other hand, sector ministries, apex agencies, and state and provincial governments in India and Pakistan, lacking direct interest in aid mobilization, have not been eager to entertain criticism of their policies and programs. Nevertheless, acting mainly at the operational level, resident missions have made a quiet contribution over time to interpreting the Bank to the borrowers and vice versa. In this background, the advice that there is a need for "more, more expert, more senior, more continuous, more project-localized Bank expertise" in resident missions is well taken.[61]

Institution Building

The institutional aspects of the policy dialogue require discussion at different levels. At the project level the Bank has faced the familiar dilemma between devising ad hoc structures for implementing its projects and strengthening existing institutions. Ad hoc institutional innovations have had a mixed record in terms of

60. These include studies relating to the agricultural sector as a whole in India, Pakistan, and Nepal; to irrigation, flood control, and drainage in India, Pakistan, and Bangladesh; and to a number of agricultural subsectors in India.

61. Lipton and Toye, *Does Aid Work in India?* p. 99.

their effectiveness and sustainability. In many urban projects they have been useful; however, in training-and-visit they have encountered serious difficulties, and the project implementation units in the Bangladesh educational and population programs have not proved appropriate. In South Asia the Bank's recourse to such "island" models has, however, been limited. By and large, the Bank has wisely opted to strengthen existing institutions in its lending operations.

Another aspect of institutional interaction relates to the public sector. In the late 1960s, when the Bank overcame its unwillingness to lend to public sector enterprises, the breakthrough had particularly beneficial results in South Asia by enabling substantial investments in oil, gas, and coal throughout most of the region; in fertilizer manufacture in India, Pakistan and Bangladesh; and in the tree crop sector in Sri Lanka. These major exceptions apart, the Bank has not been able to shed its inhibition toward public ownership at the ideological or at the practical level. Periods of nationalization in Pakistan, Bangladesh, and Sri Lanka have met with a contraction in the Bank's overall lending, and not just for industry. In India, although a Bank study of the steel sector identified opportunities for lending for rehabilitation and improvement, the Bank finally decided not to proceed.[62] In many situations, particularly in India and Sri Lanka, the Bank has tended to ignore chances to lend to state enterprises and has missed opportunities for improving their performance by getting involved. (Ironically, on the other hand, the Bank has at times stayed with the public sector long after objective factors ceased to justify doing so, tubewell irrigation in Pakistan and Bangladesh being a major example.)

Institution building, from a broader perspective, also involves strengthening domestic capabilities outside the state sector. Features of the Bank's lending such as local cost financing, domestic price preference in international competitive bidding, and earmarked local bidding have made a definite contribution in this respect. However, the Bank's use of consultants—on its own account for project preparation, appraisal, and supervision—has tended to favor expatriates in preference to domestic consultants. This has not only conflicted with the need to develop the good potential for domestic consulting expertise in major South Asian countries but has also adversely affected project performance, in some cases because of a lack of continuity (and perhaps also of commitment) in exogenous advice. For their part, South Asian governments themselves have not done enough to utilize or encourage their domestic consultancy resources.

The Bank has given substantial assistance to intermediaries such as NABARD, the National Cooperative Development Corporation (NCDC), and the Indian Dairy Corporation (IDC) in India, and BADC in Bangladesh. Its loans to the Indian Farmers Fertilizers Cooperative have provided valuable support to the cooperative sector in India's fertilizer industry. Many components in the Bank's urban development and water supply projects have been implemented through

62. *India: Steel Sector Strategy Report,* report 6599-IN (World Bank, July 1987).

urban local authorities, and rural development projects in Sri Lanka have utilized decentralized entities with good success. However, despite many opportunities for doing so, the Bank has not ventured to work through rural local (*panchayati raj*) authorities in India. This has been both a cause and a consequence of the Bank's limited involvement in India in area development, rural roads, and rural water supply. Despite their presence in many fields of development—particularly in India, Bangladesh, and Sri Lanka—the Bank's active involvement with non-governmental organizations has been relatively recent.

Alleviation of Poverty

Since the 1970s poverty alleviation has been a major objective of the Bank's lending operations, besides being the subject of a great deal of its rhetoric. In the 1970s the thrust of the Bank's policy was to target urban and agricultural (especially rural development) projects to poverty groups in terms of quantified proportions of outlays or benefits. In the early 1980s the focus was widened to countrywide programming for poverty reduction.[63]

To what extent poverty alleviation has taken place at all in recent decades in major South Asian countries remains a topic of inconclusive debate. What is indisputable is that South Asian poverty is massive and deeply rooted in several structural factors. It is clearly impossible to assess at a macroeconomic level the Bank's contribution to poverty alleviation in South Asia, except to say that given the nature and dimensions of the problem, the impact of aid from all sources, let alone from the Bank, is likely to have been only marginal. This is especially the case since aid has operated through discrete projects and programs and has not addressed itself, directly or through policy dialogue, to structural changes such as land reform. We can therefore only discuss to what extent and in what ways the Bank has attempted to orient its projects toward helping the poor, and review the evidence on the success or failure of such efforts.

The Bank's agricultural portfolio can claim to be poverty oriented in three ways: by contributing to increases in output, lending for agriculture has indirectly benefited the poor; there has been an effort to skew direct benefits to landholders toward smaller farmers; and subsectors where lending can directly benefit the landless poor (such as dairying) have been supported.

The Bank itself has not undertaken benchmark-cum-impact studies to assess the indirect (or "trickle-down") effects that its production-oriented projects may have had on sustained poverty reduction where they have been implemented. In irrigation, the emphasis at the project design stage has been on benefiting a substantial proportion of small farmers, but in practice it has been impossible to ensure any

---

63. See "Poverty Monitoring and Progress Reports," in *Poverty Reduction Handbook* (World Bank, 1992), chapter 9-I.

such earmarking of water use. All that has been possible is to promote greater equity among farmers—whether large, medium size, or small—in different reaches of canal irrigation. In agricultural credit, Bank projects have attempted to channel progressively larger proportions of loans to small farmers, but this has not altered the fact that tubewells in most parts of India, Pakistan, and Bangladesh are predominantly owned by large farmers. Tractors provided through agricultural credits in Pakistan have not only favored larger farmers but have displaced employment for the rural poor. Extension projects emphasize reaching out to small farmers, but it is difficult to ensure that this is being done—the farmers contacted first by training-and-visit programs have often been the larger and more influential ones, who enjoy better access to complementary inputs such as water, credit, and fertilizers.

In the dairy cooperatives, which the Bank has substantially supported in India through the IDC, available evidence indicates that the beneficiaries have been mainly medium-size farmers rather than small farmers or landless peasants. The social forestry projects have not, contrary to original expectations, provided the village poor with fuelwood and may have even reduced their access to traditional grazing and fuel from village commons. Bank projects in tree crop agriculture in Sri Lanka have not paid sufficient attention to smallholder plantations in rubber or tea. Broad-based rural development through area projects has been successful in Sri Lanka, but even there benefits have not percolated down to the most disadvantaged segments of the rural population. Early efforts at rural development in Bangladesh have not been a success, and the recent countrywide project has yet to show results. In India the Bank has not been able or willing to get involved in the government's antipoverty programs, such as those for drought-prone area development, asset distribution to poor rural households, and employment generation for rural unskilled labor.

In sum, it may not be unfair to conclude that thus far the Bank's contributions to poverty alleviation through its agricultural and area development operations have been neither significant nor particularly successful. Certainly, they have fallen far short of an "assault on poverty."[64]

This leaves out population, nutrition, education, urban, and water supply projects, which include several elements of poverty alleviation. In Bangladesh the Bank's population programs have aided the decline in fertility. The emphasis on rural, primary, and girls' education in Pakistan and Bangladesh has been useful, but

---

64. For independent assessments see Graham Donaldson, "Government-Sponsored Rural Development: Experience of the World Bank," in C. Peter Timmer, ed., *Agriculture and the State, Growth, Employment and Poverty in Developing Countries* (Cornell University Press, 1991), pp. 156–90; S. Guhan, "Aid for the Poor: Performance and Possibilities in India," in John P. Lewis, ed., *Strengthening the Poor: What Have We Learned?* (New Brunswick, Transaction Books, 1988); Hartmann and Boyce, *Quiet Violence;* and Lipton and Toye, *Does Aid Work in India?*

neither the continuity and scale of Bank assistance to general education nor project performance has been such as to make any tangible impact. The nutrition project in India has demonstrated a cost-effective approach for tackling malnourishment in children, to which those of the poor are most exposed, but it has been confined so far to parts of a single state. The settlement and water supply projects have undoubtedly benefited the poorer, although not the poorest, sections of urban and semiurban populations in a number of major cities and towns.

By the beginning of the 1990s the Bank had once again reformulated its approach to poverty reduction. "Sustainable poverty reduction" has been described as "the Bank's overarching objective." The new, two-pronged strategy relies, on the one hand, on economic growth to generate income-earning opportunities for the poor, and, on the other, on improved access to education, health care, and other social services to help the poor take advantage of these opportunities. The consequent core poverty lending program (1990–93) envisages a number of projects in India, Pakistan, Bangladesh, and Sri Lanka that will seek to translate this strategy into lending operations.[65]

Conclusion

One cannot but conclude that, in actual practice, the Bank's project lending in South Asia has fallen short of the expectations, and often the claims, placed on it by the Bank. Although, to be sure, several factors relating to the borrowers are responsible for this outcome, the Bank's own actions have contributed to less than optimal benefits from project lending. Three interrelated approaches predominate.

First, resource transfer considerations—however valid in their own right—have had an adverse impact on various stages of the project cycle. Based on balance of payments needs on the demand side and lending targets on the supply side— arrived at annually in meetings of consortia and consultative groups—the Bank has proceeded to program its project operations, subjecting them to tightly administered lending schedules. Targeted lending of this kind has had wide-ranging implications for lending strategies, project preparation, appraisal, implementation and supervision, and the policy dialogue.

Second, the Bank has followed what might be called an incremental strategy in the pursuit of its policy dialogue. Basically, this strategy would appear to have been impelled by three concerns: the Bank's desire to adhere to its lending targets, its reluctance to jeopardize its relationships with its large and important South Asian borrowers, and its desire to maintain the continuity of its involvement in priority sectors of their development. In the circumstances that have prevailed in South Asia in the last two decades, this strategy of continued lending linked to promises

65. See World Bank, *World Development Report 1990: Poverty Reduction and World Bank Operations*, report 8491 (1990); and *Poverty Reduction Handbook*.

rather than performance has had its inevitable consequences. The enforcement of basic covenants, whether related to financial performance, environmental standards, or institutional reform, has had to be soft pedaled. Lending has had to proceed despite clear indications of systemic sectoral problems. In several cases where reforms continued to be postponed, problems eventually accumulated to a point where the Bank was forced to suspend operations, making it all the more difficult to secure them as a basis for the subsequent resumption of lending. Given these contradictions, inherent in any attempt to reconcile resource transfer targets with project-mediated developmental objectives, the only other logically valid option would have been to strike a better balance between project and nonproject lending, so that the burden on projects for resource transfers could be eased. This would have allowed the pace and pattern of project lending to be better tuned to the realization of the Bank's objectives. Concurrently, a greater measure of nonproject lending might have been able to stimulate and support reforms, so as to render project lending more efficacious.

This brings us to the third factor, which is that the Bank attempted to blend project and nonproject lending in some sort of orchestrated fashion only toward the end of the period covered in this account. Earlier, in the mid-1960s, program lending to India, while providing much-needed balance of payments support, had been aimed at persuading India to devalue, liberalize imports, and give higher priority to agriculture.[66] Program credits for industrial imports continued until the mid-1970s as a measure of support for fuller utilization of capacity. From then until 1991, when India received its first structural adjustment loan, all lending to India was through projects.

In Pakistan, program loans between the mid-1960s and the mid-1970s were basically general-purpose lending for industrial imports, without being tuned in any very specific manner to promoting or supporting macroeconomic reforms. Lending to Pakistan in nonproject form was revived only with the structural adjustment loan of 1982, the first such lending in South Asia. This was followed by sectoral adjustment lending later in the 1980s.

Program lending to Bangladesh has continued steadily since the beginning of operations in 1971 on the grounds that the very difficult conditions of economic management in that country justified flexible, fast-disbursing balance of payments and budgetary support to sustain minimum levels of essential imports and to generate counterpart funds for development. The Bank's evaluation of the entire series of program credits until 1986 to Bangladesh was that they did not succeed in achieving adequate or sustained reforms at the macroeconomic or the sectoral

66. This phase has been described by Mason and Asher, *The World Bank since Bretton Woods*, pp. 677–83, as "the Bank's most significant attempt to use the leverage of its lending to modify macroeconomic policies in a major member country." See also John P. Lewis, *Governance and Reform: Essays in Indian Political Economy* (Oxford University Press, forthcoming).

level.[67] With this experience, the Bank has turned to sectoral adjustment lending in Bangladesh since 1987. Both Sri Lanka and Nepal received structural adjustment loans at the end of the 1980s (1990 in Sri Lanka and 1987 and 1989 in Nepal); until then there had been only one small program loan for Sri Lanka and none at all for Nepal.

Thus, in the 1960s and 1970s, the use of program lending as an instrument of policy dialogue was fitful and not particularly effective; no deliberate attempt was made until the adjustment loans, mostly in the late 1980s, to coordinate nonproject and project lending with further macroeconomic and sectoral reforms. The fact that, effectively, project lending has been the only available mode for the policy dialogue—entirely so in India and for the most part in other South Asian countries—has meant that several objectives of the Bank as a development lender have had to be pursued through a single instrumentality. The result has been that achievement of these objectives has been less than optimal.

The 1990s may well prove to be a watershed in terms of both the quantum and the nature of the Bank's lending operations in South Asia. In varying degrees, all South Asian borrowers will remain dependent on aid in the proximate future, and within the Bank Group they will be critically dependent on lending from the International Development Association (IDA). It has been possible to compensate for the decline in South Asia's share in IDA resources in the 1980s through substantial increases in IBRD lending to India and Pakistan. In the 1990s the current attenuated creditworthiness of India and Pakistan will not permit anything like the increment in Bank loans that occurred in the previous decade. Objectively, a strong case can be made for increasing IDA allocations to South Asia, particularly to India.[68] However, there is no escaping the fact that IDA resources will continue to be scarce because of the pressure on them from Sub-Saharan Africa and from new Central Asian borrowers. In this context, efficiency in resource use rather than ready resource transfers will have to be the dominant note of lending operations. Alongside and related to this is the phase of Bank-supported adjustment—macroeconomic and sectoral—in which all South Asian countries, including India, now find themselves. This will entail a much larger share in total lending (increasing at a slower pace) for nonproject adjustment lending, leaving fewer resources for project lending. The major challenge that the Bank and its borrowers will face in these circumstances will be, on the one hand, to get much more out of project lending in terms of execution and impact and, on the other, to deploy adjustment lending for macroeconomic and sectoral reforms that can maximize the effectiveness of discrete project investments. The decade ahead is thus likely to be both lean and hard for the Bank and its borrowers in South Asia.

67. World Bank, *Bangladesh: Review of the Experience,* points out that external assistance "by providing a cushion inadvertently created a desensitizing effect on the recipient's behaviour by alleviating the pressure on the political authorities to be more resolute in addressing pressing economic problems" (p. x).
68. See Robert Cassen, Vijay Joshi, and Michael Lipton, "Stabilization, Structural Reform and IDA Assistance to India" (1992).

NINE

The World Bank as a Project Lender: Experience from Eastern Africa

Alex Duncan

FOR MOST of its life and in most of the countries in which it works, the World Bank's business has focused on projects: loans or credits for specified purposes, to be disbursed within a finite period, often for an identified group of beneficiaries at defined locations. Most, but not all, projects are mechanisms for investment to raise productive capacity or to relieve bottlenecks in production. Some, though, have the explicit aim of expanding consumption—food aid projects, for instance—while increasingly projects in some countries, including those under review in this chapter, are blurring the distinction between capital and recurrent expenditure and are providing for the latter.

Introduction

Project lending is at the center of the relationship between the Bank and its borrowing member countries, and over time has both dominated and been

The author is grateful to the many people within and outside the World Bank who were generous with their time and with their opinions. Two characteristics of the organization have made this study a particular pleasure: first, the Bank's persistence in making available to outsiders material that could provide ammunition to its critics, and, second, the diversity of opinion among its staff—a diversity that is not always reflected in the Bank's public face, especially when ranks close around a newly adopted approach to development. In regard to the first, my experience is not universally shared. One fierce critic, Graham Hancock, author of *Lords of Poverty: The Powers, Prestige, and Corruption of the International Aid Business* (London: Macmillan, 1989), found that the Bank closed ranks to prevent his access to inside information.

dominated by that relationship. The Bank's ability to achieve its aims of promoting growth and development was largely determined, up to the adoption of structural adjustment around 1980, by the performance of the projects it supports; project performance is in turn intimately linked to the wider economic circumstances of the borrower; and the capacity of political and civil institutions to plan and implement development is, as sometimes painful experience has shown, a principal determinant of project performance.

The Bank's experience with project lending in Sub-Saharan Africa has forced it to take a progressively wider perspective on the causes of project failure. It has moved upstream through causality, initially seeking remedies within projects at the technical or organizational level, then focusing on economic policy and on public sector management, and more recently attending to the nature of government. In going through this process, the Bank itself has had to change, developing new lending instruments to complement projects—a change that since 1980 has required internal restructuring and new skills among the Bank's own staff. But in the mid-1990s there remains an air of bafflement in the Bank about Africa. The record of project success has not on the whole been good. Fifteen years after structural adjustment began, the jury is still out on how far its aims have been achieved and the effectiveness of Africa's public institutions in responding to Bank prescriptions.[1]

The role of a project within the development process is clearest and most harmonious where the following conditions hold: growth is occurring, so that a project is an addition to the capacity of the economy; the constraints on continued growth are scarcities either of capital or of technical skills, which can be readily provided through the mechanisms of a project; and the economy is generating revenues through the public or private sectors that are sufficient to support the investments over the years after the end of project implementation. In many instances World Bank funds, disbursed through projects, have found conditions like these and have made a positive contribution to growth and development in low-income countries.[2]

Such conditions are not always found, however. Some of the most troubling cases for the Bank have arisen where the obstacles to development are complex and deeply rooted and do not lend themselves to straightforward resolution through projects. This can occur where wider policy or capacity issues hinder project implementation and cannot be addressed by the project, or where the impact of even well-implemented projects is diffused. The latter situation is captured by the "macro-micro paradox," where respectable project results accompany macroeconomic stagnation or decline. The explanations for this paradox range

---

1. The Bank's approach to structural adjustment has itself changed, as a recent critique has noted; see R. H. Green and M. Faber, eds., "The Structural Adjustment of Structural Adjustment, 1980–93," *IDS Bulletin*, vol. 25 (July 1994).

2. Evidence for the record of World Bank projects worldwide comes from its own evaluation department and from outside reviews. The former are summarized annually in the Project Performance Audit Reports, of which the seventeenth was produced in 1991.

from "the ancient problem of fungibility" to more recent analyses of the possible contribution of aid funds to persistent overvaluation of a currency.[3]

This chapter looks at the Bank's experience with project lending in a part of the world, Sub-Saharan Africa, where it has met many of these difficulties. The continent's record on development is by no means all bad. Since African countries gained independence there have been considerable widespread improvements in important social indicators, and in a few countries economic performance has been satisfactory by world standards. The World Bank has played a creditable role in those achievements. However, the record of much of Africa over the past thirty years is one of economic stagnation and even decline, and World Bank lending has neither reversed this nor been immune to its effects.

The chapter is based on case studies of four countries of eastern Africa—Kenya, Malawi, Tanzania, and Zambia—and of particular sectors within those countries: agriculture and rural development, highways, and education. These countries were selected largely because their similarities in important respects allow common lessons to emerge from the World Bank's approach to project lending. They were chosen in part because of the political continuity they show (in none of them has there been a violent overthrow of a government or a civil war) and because of their inheritance of comparable administrative systems at independence. This approach, however, is subject to the limitations inherent in taking case studies. The four countries are not intended to be representative of other African countries in a statistical sense, nor do they necessarily represent a cross section of Africa's experience. They do not include a Francophone country, for instance; nevertheless, much of the experience with project lending in these countries can be seen elsewhere in the continent, and indeed in other parts of the world. The sectors have been chosen because they account for a good proportion of the Bank's projects, are essential if the growth and equity aims of development are to be met, and provide a range of experience spanning social and engineering sectors.

The approach here is to try to understand how and why the Bank changed over the years as it gained experience with project lending in the four countries, and how and why particular strategic decisions were made. The chapter therefore relies partly on perceptions of World Bank staff expressed through interviews as well as through documents of the time, most of them internal. Interviews have also been conducted with current and former officials of the countries concerned who have been on the receiving end of Bank analyses and missions; the chapter also tries to reflect views from that perspective.[4]

---

3. On fungibility, see Paul Mosley, *Overseas Aid: Its Defense and Reform* (Brighton, Sussex, England: Wheatsheaf Books, 1987), p. 140; for a more recent analysis, see Howard White, "The Macroeconomic Impact of Development Aid: A Critical Survey," *Journal of Development Studies*, vol. 28 (January 1992), pp. 163–240.

4. Perhaps rightly for a bank, the World Bank is not regarded with much affection by many of its interlocutors, though often individual staff members are respected and liked for

One broad conclusion of the chapter is that the Bank has been steadier in its main aims than in the instruments it has chosen. The aims have been fairly consistently to promote economic growth and, where possible, equity. Arguably the main exception was the higher priority given to poverty alleviation under Robert S. McNamara; some suggest that the Bank lost sight of the poverty objective in Africa during the early years of structural adjustment in the early 1980s. In implementation, however there has been more variability in the Bank's record; like a climber confronted by unexpectedly rough ground, the Bank has from time to time set off on a giddy traverse. The switch from infrastructure to agriculture and the social sectors in the late 1960s and early 1970s was one such; policy-based lending ten years later another; and a third, more recently, has been the emphasis on institutional capacity and governance—though the impact this may have on lending programs is not yet known. Within individual countries or sectors, as this chapter suggests, the Bank's work has sometimes lacked coherence or consistency over time. Different observers give this feature of the Bank's experience a different gloss. It has certainly involved a learning process, sometimes orderly; more unkindly, one Bank staff member observed that there is "always a search for a golden bullet."

These changes have taken the Bank a long way from its earlier almost exclusive reliance on project lending as the means of promoting development. After an expansion in project lending in the years after independence, both in volume and in the range of sectors covered, project lending to many African countries peaked in the late 1970s and early 1980s, in absolute terms, but especially in relation to policy-based lending, which has moved center stage in Bank lending to the countries under review.

It has been a general finding of reviews of the effectiveness of international aid that aid is usually little better than the general economic performance of the receiving country. A policy framework, effective public and private institutions, the absence of war, and other conditions that promote economic development are also the conditions needed to make aid worthwhile. Although individual projects may perform better than the overall economy, the generality of projects will not, and the majority will in any case not be sustainable.

Four Countries

Kenya, Malawi, Tanzania, and Zambia shared certain similarities at independence in the early 1960s: they were all Anglophone, with a common colonial

---

a combination of competence and what is perceived to be traces of idealism that have survived high salaries and a competitive bureaucracy. The Bank is widely viewed as the most professional of the multilateral development agencies, but its position, along with that of the International Monetary Fund (IMF), as the effective key to almost all aid flows to aid-dependent countries also makes it feared.

experience of British rule; all had small populations (there were fewer than 10 million people in Kenya and Tanzania and fewer than 5 million in Malawi and Zambia); and all were poor, with the great majority of inhabitants living off farming (only Zambia had a large mining sector and a significant urban population). At independence the countries were faced with formidable political and economic tasks, among them nation building, which was given top priority, together with the evolution of durable, locally based political structures; increasing indigenous ownership of many modern sectors of the economy, which were largely in the hands of foreign or ethnic minorities; and building up scarce entrepreneurial and technical skills.

The postindependence experiences of the four countries were on the surface perhaps more similar politically than economically. All introduced one-party rule; by the early 1990s all of them (most recently Malawi) were showing signs of adopting more open political systems. Zambia and Malawi have changed their ruling parties through elections, and Kenya has reintroduced multiparty elections. If not notably democratic, these countries are striking for their political continuity over three decades in an unstable continent.

The apparent similarities cover considerable differences in the political experience. In comparison with its immediate neighbors, Kenya has achieved a framework of political institutions broadly sympathetic to economic growth; yet there has been mounting concern over the years about the nature of politics in Kenya. Acute inequality combined with ethnicity and factionalism have led to frequent—and hitherto usually incorrect—predictions of instability. Also growing over the years has been an increasingly noisy criticism of corruption which, by the late 1980s, had caused some aid donors to reduce their funding of some sectors.

In Malawi, domestic political stability, in a framework of autocratic rule and ownership by the president of large parts of the formal economy, contributed to rapid economic growth for fifteen years after independence, to continuity in the civil service (with a heavy use of expatriates in senior positions for some years after independence), and to a high capacity to implement development projects through the 1970s. In the early 1980s, however, external political shocks resulting from war in Mozambique led to closure of the main trade routes (with costly diversions principally through South Africa), worsening terms of trade, an influx of refugees, and increases in defense-related spending.[5] These factors combined to bring economic growth in Malawi to an almost complete halt through much of the 1980s.

In Tanzania, as in Kenya, political stability made the country in the years up to the mid-1970s a natural recipient for much Bank funding. This circumstance was reinforced by the Bank's approval of the country's development strategy, by a

5. This feature of Malawi's experience is captured by the title of an Economic Development Institute (EDI) publication: Ravi Gulhati, "Malawi: Promising Reforms, Bad Luck," EDI Development Policy Case Studies (1989).

Table 9-1. *Key Social Indicators, Four East African Countries, 1969, 1979, 1989*

Country	Infant mortality rate (deaths per thousand)	Life expectancy at birth (years)	Total fertility rate (average number of births per woman)	Food production per capita (1987 = 100)	Primary school enrollment ratio (percent)	Secondary school enrollment ratio (percent)	Population (millions)
Kenya							
1969	104.0	49.5	8.0	126.3	58.0[a]	9.0[a]	11.1
1979	84.8	54.4	8.0	109.4	108.0	18.0	16.0
1989[b]	68.7	59.0	6.8	104.4	96.0[c]	23.0[c]	23.3
Malawi							
1969	194.6	40.1	7.8	120.1	n.a.	n.a.	4.4
1979	171.4	43.8	7.6	122.9	59.0	4.0	5.9
1989[b]	147.7	47.4	7.6	103.8	66.0[c]	4.0[c]	8.2
Tanzania							
1969	133.0	44.7	6.5	103.0	34.0[a]	3.0[a]	13.1
1979	121.0	49.2	6.6	114.4	100.0	4.0	18.1
1989[b]	102.7	53.7	6.7	99.7	66.0[c]	4.0[c]	25.6
Zambia							
1969	109.0	46.1	6.7	113.1	90.0[a]	13.0[a]	4.0
1979	91.6	49.8	6.8	111.6	95.0	16.0	5.5
1989[b]	76.6	53.7	6.7	106.2	97.0[d]	17.0[e]	7.8

Source: World Bank, *World Tables 1991*.

n.a. Not available.

a. 1970.

b. Estimated.

c. 1987.

d. 1986.

e. 1985.

reportedly close personal relationship between Tanzanian president Nyerere and Bank president Robert McNamara,[6] and for some years by Tanzania's deserved reputation for financial probity in the public service. Tanzania's socialist approach and promotion of active political participation through the political party Tanganyika African National Union (TANU) (later the Chama Cha Mapinduzi, or CCM—Party of the Revolution) set it apart from the other three countries, in which the political parties rapidly withered away as effective means of broad political involvement.

Unlike the other three countries, Zambia's political and economic development was for several years after independence dominated by external events, notably the aftermath of southern Rhodesia's Unilateral Declaration of Independence (UDI) in 1965. This situation contributed to the imposition of a state of emergency in Zambia (which lasted until 1991) and led to very costly disruption of external trade, necessitating major expenditures on external infrastructure, notably an oil pipeline and a railway linking Zambia to part of Dar es Salaam in Tanzania. Domestically, Zambia's single party was ultimately unable to bring about the necessary severe internal adjustments required by a sustained fall in copper prices and by the failure over thirty years to diversify the economy.

The World Bank's involvement with the four countries began at an extremely low starting point at independence. Contrary to a widespread perception that Africa's record is in all respects dismal, the countries have all achieved improvements in key social indicators, many of them impressive (see table 9-1). At independence each of the countries was characterized by a high infant mortality rate, short life expectancy, and abysmal educational standards, all of which improved markedly over the next two decades, even during what is often called the lost decade of the 1980s. Infant mortality fell in each case between 1969 and 1989, by between 30 and 45 per thousand, although it remained high, especially in Malawi where it was at 147.7 per thousand. Life expectancy at birth rose by 7 to 10 years in each country, although it remained below 50 years in Malawi. Primary school enrollment in 1969 was lower than 60 percent of the relevant age groups in all but Zambia, where it was 90 percent; by 1979 it had risen to between 95 and 108 percent in Kenya, Tanzania, and Zambia, although only 59 percent in Malawi; by 1987 it remained high in Kenya and Zambia but had apparently fallen back in Tanzania to only 66 percent. Secondary school enrollment rose from 9 percent to 23 percent in Kenya and from 13 percent to 17 percent in Zambia, but stagnated at around 3 percent to 4 percent in Tanzania and Malawi.

Rapid population growth has been a feature of all four countries, the rate rising between 1980 and 1988 in Kenya, Malawi, and Zambia to between 3.6 percent and 4.2 percent a year and in Tanzania to 2.8 percent a year (see table 9-2). Only Kenya showed a declining fertility rate (the average number of children born to a woman) between 1979 and 1989, from an almost uniquely high level of 8.0. As a result of

6. World Bank, "Annual Review of Evaluation Results: 1989" (1990), pp. 6–15.

Table 9-2. *Annual Growth Rates of Key Economic Indicators, Four East African Countries, 1965–88*

Country	Gross domestic product	Gross domestic investment	Gross national income per capita	Population
Kenya				
1965–73	8.5	15.9	3.7	3.4
1973–80	5.1	4.4	0.6	3.8
1980–88	4.0	–1.1	–0.7	4.2
Malawi				
1965–73	5.7	16.0	4.6	2.8
1973–80	5.8	3.2	–0.5	3.0
1980–88	2.5	–6.4	–1.7	3.8
Tanzania				
1965–73	5.0	9.6	1.4	3.2
1973–80	1.9	4.2	–3.7	3.3
1980–88	2.7	0.3	–1.9	2.8
Zambia				
1965–73	2.4	6.2	–0.7	3.0
1973–80	0.3	–16.5	–9.6	3.1
1980–88	0.6	–4.5	–2.8	3.6

Source: World Bank, *Trends in Developing Economies, 1990* (1990).

these growth rates, as well as poor agricultural performance, food production per person in all four countries declined between 1969 and 1989 (table 9-1).

In their different ways the countries illustrate Africa's patchy economic record (see table 9-2). During the first decade after independence, to 1973, GDP, investment, and per capita income each grew rapidly in Kenya, Malawi, and Tanzania, but slowly in Zambia. During the period from 1973 to 1980 only Malawi and Kenya maintained satisfactory growth rates; incomes declined in Tanzania and Zambia, in the latter case extremely rapidly, by 9.6 percent a year. Between 1980 and 1988 the fall in per capita income continued in all four countries, although by the latter half of the decade Kenya and Tanzania appeared to be moving in the direction of resumed growth. By 1989, after twenty-five years of postindependence development, all four countries remained in the Bank's category of low-income countries.

Bank-Country Relationships

There have been three phases to the relationship between the World Bank and the four East African borrowing countries, phases determined primarily by the countries' overall economic performances, by the Bank's perception of the appropriateness of their development strategies, and by the Bank's more single-minded pursuit of market-based solutions during the past decade. In the first phase of the

relationship, there was a closeness of view and community of interest as—a harmony—the Bank sought to expand project lending and found governments anxious
to borrow, the Bank either actively supported the countries' strategies or was more
tolerant of alternative approaches than it was in later years, and neither the Bank
nor governments had yet been faced by the dilemmas created by Africa's economic
stagnation. The second phase, centering on the early 1980s although varying in
duration, was a period of reassessment when the relationship came under strain as
the Bank cut back and redesigned projects, focused increasingly on policy and
institutional questions, and developed new nonproject lending mechanisms. The
third phase has been a period of policy convergence resulting principally from the
introduction by governments, with varying degrees of willingness and rigor, of
policy and institutional changes, and recognition that the Bank was indispensable if
concessional resources were to be secured from foreign multilateral or bilateral
sources.[7] This policy convergence has not always brought with it an easy relationship, as there have often been differences of view and disputes over implementation; but in recent years these differences have taken place in all four countries in
the context of Bank-approved moves toward economic liberalization. Although this
broad pattern of phases has existed in all four Bank-country relationships, there
have been significant differences in timing and circumstances. These phases are
considered in turn for each country.

First Phase: Harmony

The Bank's project lending program in Kenya began well, but there were to be
sharp changes. In 1974 the Bank took the view that in the decade after independence Kenya's "economic performance has in most respects been outstanding,"
a perception that had underpinned a sharp rise in project lending over the period.[8]

In Malawi there was to be a similar sobering of the Bank's view of economic
performance and prospects after an optimistic beginning. The 1974 Country Program Paper (CPP) observed that "measured against its poor natural endowments,
progress [in Malawi] since 1964 has been remarkable."[9]

The Bank's role in Tanzania's development has been an influential one, both
through an exceptionally harmonious early stage, when the Bank provided support
and encouragement for Tanzania's policy of self-reliant socialism during the 1970s,
and later in the mid-1980s when the Bank acted as midwife to Tanzania's process of
economic liberalization. The Bank's role has also been controversial, as many
(including the present author) take the view that Tanzania was encouraged intellec-

---

7. This sequence of phases was suggested by World Bank, "Tanzania Relations, 1961–
1987," Operations Evaluation Department report 8329 (January 1990). It holds true for the
other three countries.
   8. World Bank, "Country Program Paper: Kenya" (June 17, 1975), p. 1.
   9. World Bank, "Country Program Paper: Malawi" (October 7, 1974), p. 2.

tually and assisted financially by outside agencies, including the Bank, to adopt a development strategy that—with the benefit of hindsight—turned out to be disastrous. The early years of the relationship were characterized by close cooperation and a rapidly expanding portfolio of Bank projects. A 1973 Country Program Note reflects the strength of the Bank's support:

> From a donor's point of view Tanzania comes close to being a model developing country in the sense that the Government is seriously committed to development in a climate of political and social stability. President Nyerere has given the country a clear sense of direction with the long-term perspective of a socialist society. Development policies and priorities are generally well thought-out and well conceived. The country's domestic resource mobilization effort is commendable while monetary policies are responsible. . . . We are inclined to give Tanzania an excellent performance rating and recommend a maximum Bank Group effort to assist the country in the pursuit of its development objectives.[10]

This confidence was reflected in a major expansion of Bank lending, from an average of two projects a year in the late 1960s and early 1970s to the average of six operations a year proposed in the 1976 Country Program Paper, a proposal that was approved.[11]

There was greater consistency in the Bank's understanding of and involvement in Zambia. The dominant economic questions related to mining, which in 1968 accounted for 54 percent of GDP and 98 percent of exports (95 percent of the latter coming from copper). Mining was controlled by two foreign companies in which the government held a 60.3 percent share. The agricultural sector was concomitantly less important; the inadequate statistics suggest that it fell from 11 percent to 4 percent of GDP during the 1960s as many of the 1,200 European farmers who produced most of the marketed surplus left the country, and, in contrast to other countries, were not replaced by a lively class of smallholder or African commercial farmers. The production of maize, beef, tobacco, and dairy goods in consequence declined. A policy of low producer prices after independence frustrated efforts to step up smallholder production, even though in the early 1970s the government was spending one-sixth of its capital investments in the agricultural sector.

The Bank was never optimistic about Zambia's prospects—rightly, as events turned out. The country's declining share of the world copper market, the long-term decline in copper prices, and Zambia's inability over several decades to diversify its economy led, by the late 1980s, to a decline of some 50 percent in per capita income over what it had been twenty years before. In 1970 the Bank's analysis emphasized the constraints on economic growth, both internal and external. External constraints were largely associated with Zambia's geopolitical position

10. World Bank, "Country Program Note: Tanzania" (February 12, 1973), pp. 14–15.
11. World Bank, "Country Program Paper: Tanzania" (December 2, 1976), p. 1.

and its vulnerability to fluctuations and trends in world copper price and internal constraints, particularly with the extreme shortage of skilled manpower and the extension of state ownership. The 1970 Country Program Paper noted that "Zambia's present relative affluence may not last long and it would be unrealistic to stop and re-start our lending program according to fluctuations in the price of copper."[12] As the copper price continued to decline through the 1970s (by 40 percent in 1975 alone), contrary to the expectations of the Bank and of the government, Zambia's efforts to adapt were commended by the Bank: "These measures, which have improved the short-term outlook as well as set the stage for beneficial long-run structural change, are worthy of our support."[13] Bank project lending continued.

The Second Phase: Reassessment

In Kenya, the Bank staff became concerned during the 1970s—strongly so by the end of the decade—with worsening inequality, and, by 1978, with the quality of policymaking:

> We are increasingly concerned about several critical problem areas. These relate to the current political situation and its impact on decision-making with respect to key issues such as agricultural pricing and industrial policy. . . . In the light of these concerns, this year's CPP will consider whether the present high level of Bank Group lending can be justified and sustained, given the detectable deterioration of economic policy decision-making.[14]

By the late 1970s Bank documents also began to reflect concerns about long-term structural problems, notably the perceived imbalance between population and available natural and financial resources, as well as issues of employment and equity. The 1978 Country Program Paper concluded, "We should in light of the current political and social realities lower our estimates of what can reasonably be achieved in the medium-term. A period of consolidation is therefore called for."[15] Accordingly, the proposed 1979–83 project lending program was $76 million lower than that for 1978–82, although simultaneously the Bank revised upward its estimates of the volume of aid the country would need if growth was to be maintained.[16] The Bank's growing concern about these wider realities set the scene for a shift of emphasis away from project aid and toward structural adjustment and associated policy and institutional reforms, in parallel with IMF-supported stabilization programs undertaken in the early 1980s. The latter achieved a measure of success in bringing key deficits to containable levels and prepared the ground for

12. World Bank, "Country Program Paper: Zambia" (July 13, 1970), p. 15.
13. World Bank, "Country Program Paper: Zambia" (April 7, 1976), p. 22.
14. World Bank, "Country Program Paper: Kenya" (January 1973), p. 2; and World Bank, "Country Program Paper: Kenya" (January 16, 1978), p. 1.
15. World Bank, "Country Program Paper: Kenya" (January 16, 1978), p. 20.
16. World Bank, "Country Program Paper: Kenya" (December 19, 1980), p. 8.

resumed growth from the mid-1980s, but at the expense of sharp cuts in development programs.

In regard to Malawi, from 1978 on the tone of Bank analyses reflected growing doubts about Malawi's heavy emphasis on estate agriculture at the expense of smallholders: "While we judge Malawi's overall performance to be good, we are concerned about, among other things, the relatively slow growth of small-scale agriculture" and continuing difficulties in overcoming the acute shortage of skilled local manpower.[17] These cautions were to strengthen as data collected principally by Malawian researchers and the United Nations Children's Fund (UNICEF) during the early 1980s revealed that despite rapid growth and impressive project implementation, malnutrition and poverty in Malawi remained severe. Malawi presents a dilemma for the interpretation of the Bank's project-led development strategy of the 1960s and 1970s: despite an uncommonly effective project implementation record and rapid economic growth, the majority of the population continued to live in extreme poverty.

Economic events in Malawi moved rapidly after 1978: growth slowed, and inflationary pressures rose; agricultural estates and public agencies ran into managerial and financial problems by the early 1980s, by which time budget and current account deficits were rising; and large overseas borrowing was undertaken at commercial rates. There was severe drought in 1980 and 1981, and external transport routes through Mozambique to the sea were disrupted and, by 1984, completely cut.

By 1974 Bank documents on Tanzania were already flagging worries about at least the transitional costs of Tanzania's reforms:

> It is hard to imagine that fundamental social changes can be achieved without major adjustment problems and at least a temporary deceleration of growth. . . . For some years the Government has been trying to shift the emphasis of investment toward more directly productive projects, especially in agriculture, but there is a lack of such well-prepared projects. Meanwhile, a high proportion of available resources is invested in social infrastructure of uncertain productivity. This raises serious questions about the country's future savings' capacity.[18]

For several years thereafter, however, the close relationship of the Bank with Tanzania persisted. In the 1977 Country Program Paper the Bank took the view that "while the various failures of the Government have been noted throughout this paper, judgements have been made in past CPP's that these traits have resulted in an environment conducive to long-term economic development. It is our view that these judgements remain appropriate. . . . At present there are no fundamental policy disagreements with the Government."[19]

A coffee boom in 1977–78 and war with Uganda in 1979 concealed the extent of Tanzania's economic decline, which became precipitate, however. In a dramatic

17. World Bank, "Country Program Paper: Malawi" (March 28, 1978), p. 1.
18. World Bank, "Country Program Paper: Tanzania" (March 14, 1974), p. 3.
19. World Bank, "Country Program Paper: Tanzania" (November 3, 1977), p. 11.

turnaround in 1980, linked to a break in relations between Tanzania and the IMF, the Bank brought an end to new lending until policy reforms were introduced. Similar actions were taken by other Western donors during the late 1970s and early 1980s. It became a matter of time before the government introduced basic economic reforms, which it did from 1984 on. Tanzanian officials of the period sometimes express bitterness that the Bank, having assisted the country's progress into a quagmire, could at short notice walk away, apparently unaccountable.

This experience of the Bank in Tanzania presents, albeit in extreme form, one of the dilemmas of project lending under conditions where the wider policy context is not conducive to economic growth, namely, that making available investment resources may get in the way of needed policy change. The Bank's Operations Evaluation Department (OED) summarized the situation as follows: "There was little pressure [on the Tanzanian government] to listen to the facts, thanks to the availability of resources from donors, including the Bank, until the 1980s."[20]

In Zambia, the Bank's hope in the later 1970s that improved economic management would lead to recovery in the later 1980s was disappointed. In 1979 the Bank noted, "It appears that Zambia is about to enter the sixth year of an economic and financial crisis set off by a 40 percent drop in copper prices in 1975."[21] This crisis continued through the 1980s, with Zambia's terms of trade dropping from 100 in 1970 to 26 in 1984.[22] Exacerbated by three years of drought at the start of the decade, the crisis led the government to seek relief from Paris Club creditors in 1983 and 1984. Although the Bank recognized the significance of influences outside the government's control, the Bank's confidence in the government's ability to take the necessary measures declined during this period. In 1977 Bank staff took the view that "government officials are aware of the problems and, in most instances, know the measures necessary to deal with them. Nonetheless while some steps have been taken, progress has been slow because in some cases political considerations have precluded stronger actions and in other cases long-run policies are still being formulated."[23] By 1985 the tone was more abrupt: "Zambia's attainment of these [development] objectives has been frustrated in the past by a combination of external events, domestic policies and inadequacies in administrative capacity."[24]

The Third Phase: Policy Convergence

The World Bank's structural adjustment programs in Kenya, among its earliest, were at best only partly successful and led to strained relations with the Bank, which improved only after 1986 when the government issued a paper on overall

20. World Bank, Operations Evaluation Department, "Annual Review of Evaluation Results: 1989," pp. 6–16.
21. World Bank, "Zambia: Country Strategy Paper" (November 13, 1979), p. 1.
22. World Bank, "Country Program Paper: Zambia" (1985), pp. 4–5.
23. World Bank, "Country Program Paper: Zambia" (June 24, 1977), p. 9.
24. World Bank, "Country Program Paper: Zambia" (1985), p. 6.

economic policy that "could have been written by the Bank."[25] Thereafter lending continued with projects firmly embedded in a sequence of sectoral programs.

In Malawi as in Kenya, the Bank (and other donor agencies) responded to the country's economic crisis by reducing the hitherto complete focus on project lending in favor of structural adjustment, in parallel with a series of stabilization programs. The government was apparently in broad agreement with these, though it had little room for maneuver; the government resisted, however, on specific issues, notably the removal of fertilizer subsidies, the liberalization of food-crop marketing, and the Bank's opposition to cross-subsidization within the crop marketing agency, Admarc.[26] Unfortunately, throughout the 1980s these programs were unable to bring about the desired recovery, and per capita income and food production continued to fall or stagnate in a country already among the world's poorest. At the time of writing there is still little sign of resumed and sustainable economic growth.

In Tanzania, from the mid-1980s, the Bank-government relationship and the volume of project and nonproject lending recovered; the improvement was based largely on the Economic Recovery Program of 1986, in which the Bank had a hand. In part the overall redirection of policy came about because of Tanzania's own perceptions of what was needed and in part because of the high leverage that could be applied at a time of crisis by the Bank and bilateral donors. The impact of the policy change cannot yet be known. But there are clear signs of recovery in some areas of the economy (such as food crops), although not in others (such as most export crops). The improvements have resulted in good measure from stepped-up balance of payments support that improved the supply of capital and consumer goods and from policy changes (including the unblocking of market channels), rather than from project-related investment.[27] To sustain this progress will require project lending to address the severe weaknesses in productive capacity. There is no likelihood, however, of the Bank and other outside agencies repeating their earlier emphasis on investments in production and distribution within the public sector.

In Zambia the policy convergence phase is more recent, having got under way mainly since the change of government in late 1991. The new government has a stronger market orientation than its predecessor and is receiving higher levels of support from the Bank and other sources. It is too early to judge whether the long-term decline, which has seen sharp reductions in per capita income since the 1970s, can be reversed.

25. Confidential personal communication, World Bank, 1991.

26. Elizabeth Cromwell, "Malawi," in A. Duncan and J. Howell, eds., *Structural Adjustment and the African Farmer* (London: Overseas Development Institute, James Currey and Heinemann, 1992), pp. 113–57.

27. Food Studies Group, *Agricultural Diversification and Intensification Study: Final Report*, vol. 1: *Findings and Policy Implications* (Oxford University Press, 1992).

From this overview of four countries' economic performance and their relationship with the Bank during the three phases, several features have emerged: project lending cannot overcome a wider environment that hinders growth; continued project lending can delay desirable policy change by enabling governments to avoid painful decisions; and resumed project lending—along with balance of payments support—can be an incentive, in the present cases an incentive that explains the policy reorientation of the 1980s. Project lending is thus an integral part of the totality of the Bank's relationships with governments. A later section indicates that the effectiveness of projects in contributing to growth and poverty alleviation cannot be separated from a country's wider economic and institutional performance.

Project Lending in the Context of Overall Aid Receipts

The World Bank's project lending to African countries, although important in intellectual leadership and in amounts, must be seen in the context of aid receipts as a whole. The twenty years from the late 1960s to the late 1980s were a period of growing aid dependency in the four East African countries under review, which among them accounted in 1989 for 17.5 percent of total aid to Sub-Saharan Africa (see the statistical appendix to this chapter). Over the two decades total net receipts of Official Development Assistance (ODA) in constant 1989 terms rose by between three and five times in each of the four countries.[28] In millions of U.S. dollars, aid receipts were:

	1969–71 (annual average)	1980	1989
Kenya	234.5	556.4	972.0
Malawi	125.0	201.1	399.2
Tanzania	197.2	934.9	920.2
Zambia	72.3	414.5	390.4

Between 1969–71 and 1989 there was also a sharp increase in aid dependency as measured by the rise in net ODA as a percentage of GNP: in Kenya from 3.9 percent to 12.3 percent; in Malawi from 9.4 percent to 26.3 percent; in Tanzania from 4.0 percent to around 25 percent; and in Zambia from 1.1 percent to 9.0 percent. These increases are all high by international standards, but similar to those in much of Africa. In India the comparable figure has been from 1 percent to 2 percent.

28. The text here follows the Organization for Economic Cooperation and Development (OECD) definition of ODA as aid offered by official agencies to promote the economic and welfare development of developing countries, with aid being concessional (having a grant element of at least 25 percent). Data for the three following tables are from the statistical appendix.

For the same period the increase in net ODA per capita in the four countries was also considerable; in constant 1989 U.S. dollars, increases were:

	1969–71 (annual average)	1980	1989
Kenya	20.8	33.4	41.8
Malawi	27.9	33.3	48.5
Tanzania	15.3	49.8	35.9
Zambia	16.9	73.4	49.8

The sources of the aid have been predominantly bilateral, bilateral aid typically accounting for 65 percent to 85 percent of aid receipts (although for less than 50 percent of Malawi's aid) during most recent years. Bank lending has fluctuated as a proportion of the whole; the variability of Bank lending to Zambia has been especially extreme owing to the changeable nature of the relationship. For the two decades, World Bank disbursements of ODA as a percentage of each country's total aid receipts were:

	1969–71 (annual average)	1980	1989
Kenya	10.7	18.2	22.9
Malawi	22.5	12.9	19.3
Tanzania	16.0	7.0	12.1
Zambia	0.0	0.5	1.0

Sector-specific and project lending has predominated in total ODA flows, accounting (depending on the year) for 81 percent to 94 percent of total commitments in Kenya, 61 percent to 94 percent in Malawi, and 67 percent to 86 percent in Tanzania.[29] Thus the sectoral focus has always been strong, even since 1984 when in all the countries policy-based lending has been high on the agenda. Sectoral adjustment programs, a vehicle for combining investment funding with policy and institutional reforms, have been the Bank's preferred vehicle for lending in the four countries, after a brief period in the early 1980s when the first adjustment programs tended to be economywide.

Phases in Project Lending

Just as there have been three main phases in Bank-country relationships, there have been three broad phases in the World Bank's project lending to the four East

29. Disbursements by the Bank to Zambia fluctuated wildly, rising from 0.5 percent of total aid in 1980 to 20.1 percent in 1985 before falling to 1.0 percent in 1989.

African countries. In the first, during the early years after independence (except in the case of Zambia, where Bank lending began in 1953 through projects of the Central African Federation), there was a heavy emphasis on lending for infrastructure projects. This was perceived to be a prerequisite for development, was in line with economic thinking in many developing countries (such as India during the 1950s), and encompassed capital-intensive sectors in which the Bank had a comparative advantage and a good deal of experience internationally. In both Kenya and Tanzania some of the early infrastructure projects that dominated the Bank's portfolios were channeled through the East African Community institutions that ran the harbors, railways, and a joint airline. Within a short time, however, a switch in emphasis to other sectors, as well as the later breakup of the East Africa Community (ending one of the most promising attempts at regional integration undertaken in Africa) led the Bank to become involved almost entirely with national institutions.

During the second phase, building up from the late 1960s through the 1970s, there was a growing emphasis on lending for directly productive sectors, particularly agriculture and rural development, and for social sectors. This emphasis was given impetus by Robert McNamara in a speech in Nairobi in 1973, by a change in thinking among academics and development practitioners away from a "trickle-down" orientation,[30] and later by the attention paid to "basic needs," although this term did not become part of the Bank's reformist nomenclature.

This overall change in the Bank's orientation strongly affected project lending in the four countries reviewed. In Kenya, for instance, the Bank's 1978–82 lending program provided only 20 percent for infrastructure, 63 percent for directly productive sectors, and 17 percent for social sectors. The expansion of agricultural lending in Tanzania took place from 1972, with a relative shift away from roads and power to agriculture and general rural development. Similarly, in Zambia, of the Bank's first five projects up to 1969, two were for power, two for railways, and one for roads; during that year, however, Bank projects were started for livestock, forestry, and education. Of the Bank's next eight projects in Zambia, six were for agriculture and rural development (which in the 1977–81 program accounted for 30 percent of Bank lending) and education. The Bank also supported Zambian industry, which from a small base, had grown rapidly, largely as a result of protection; 12 percent of the Bank's 1977–81 program was for industry and was mainly channeled through the Development Bank of Zambia.

In the third phase, from the end of the 1970s and the early 1980s onward, projects were placed more firmly in the context of policy and institutional reform through the mechanisms of structural adjustment, and then through sectoral adjustment programs.

30. The thinking that underpinned this reorientation was set out in Hollis Chenery and others, *Redistribution with Growth: Policies to Improve Income Distribution in Developing Countries in the Context of Economic Growth* (Oxford University Press, 1974).

Project Performance by Sector

As the World Bank and governments accumulated experience over time, there were shifts in the aims and the design of projects within sectors. The focus here, as noted earlier, is on sectors of agriculture and rural development, highways, and education. The performance in each sector for each of the four countries is considered in turn.

Agriculture and Rural Development

As with its project lending as a whole, the World Bank's lending for agriculture and rural development falls into three phases. The first, from the early 1960s to 1973, began with the financing of large-scale agriculture, although a growing number of smallholder-focused schemes were funded through the later 1960s.[31] Smallholder projects were especially emphasized in Kenya, where the adoption of a smallholder strategy under what was known as the Swynnerton plan of the 1950s had early on created a framework for broad-based growth to which the Bank usefully contributed.

During the second phase, from 1974 to 1979, there was a large expansion of overall lending, with greater emphasis placed on poverty alleviation. With the recognition that the benefits indirectly resulting from infrastructural investment and economic growth, when concentrated geographically or in a few sectors, could not be guaranteed to solve problems of poverty and inequality, the Bank from the late 1960s devised an overall strategy for rural development. This was articulated by McNamara at the World Bank's Annual Meeting in 1973 in Nairobi and subsequently issued as a sector policy paper. In a note of caution, McNamara recognized that the Bank was entering new terrain, that there would have to be experiments, and that there would be failures.

Implementation of the new approach came to be closely associated with area development projects (often called integrated rural development projects),[32] which became the Bank's main instrument for attempting to bring about directly a wider involvement in the benefits of rural development. There were apparent advantages: at a time when analyses were emphasizing the linkages among causes of poverty (low productivity, poor health and education, and inadequate water supplies, among others), multicomponent area development projects provided a mechanism whereby the Bank could address several issues simultaneously and through a single implementing unit set up for the purpose—an important consideration where weak implementing capacity was often a constraint on what could be

31. World Bank, "Rural Development: World Bank Experience, 1965–86," Operations Evaluation Department (1988), pp. xiii–xv.
32. Other interventions were minimum package programs, coordinated national programs, and sectoral or special programs. See World Bank, "Rural Development," p. xvi.

achieved. For Bank managers under pressure to expand commitments, these projects were an effective means of doing so (it was reported that "project staff recall feeling they were under pressure to produce bigger and broader projects").[33] The increase in commitments was rapid, from an average of fewer than two area projects a year, involving Bank lending of $7.9 million, in fiscal years 1968–70 to seventeen projects involving lending of $413.9 million a year in fiscal years 1974–76.

In the event, the impact of area development projects was disappointing worldwide, and especially in eastern and southern Africa.[34] By the 1980s the Bank had almost entirely abandoned them. Disappointment resulted from several causes: implementation proved difficult, in part because of overly complex design and excessive size and numbers of components; institutional development suffered, especially in the many cases where semiautonomous project units were set up and relied heavily on expatriates, rather than on line agencies; implementation schedules were unrealistic (a finding not restricted to area projects); experience with monitoring and evaluation was almost universally poor; and such benefits as existed were often not sustainable.

The strategy to reorient Bank lending toward the poor was generally highly desirable, not least because of its impact on the design of lending across several sectors. However, the disappointing results of the lending instrument most associated with that approach was a setback to the Bank—and to other development agencies that had also adopted the approach—and meant that the question of how best to attack rural poverty was still not resolved.

The third phase of Bank lending for agriculture and rural development has lasted from 1980 to the present, although the number of area development projects has declined. Such projects have been replaced by a series of projects supporting sectoral institutions nationwide, notably for research and extension; some have included tentative attempts to involve the private sector in research and extension for smallholders; and they have typically been implemented alongside efforts to liberalize output marketing and input supply systems. This approach has the merit of taking a long-term view and of not sidestepping difficult institutional questions. But the dilemma remains; where the problems of the public sector (such as low pay and motivation, conflicting aims, and debilitating corruption) are deeply rooted, the hoped-for benefits from this new approach in agriculture will not be fully realized without thorough, and necessarily long-term, political and administrative reform. The Bank's changes in approach to the agricultural and rural development sector can be seen in the countries under review.

KENYA. In the early years, the Bank supported the smallholder-oriented Kenya Tea Development Authority (with a project approved in 1964 and a second phase

33. World Bank, "Rural Development," p. 22.

34. Twelve of fifteen area development projects in this region were assessed by the Bank's OED as failures, the only exceptions being one in Mauritius and two in Malawi. See World Bank, "Rural Development," p. 25.

approved in 1968) and funded smallholder credit projects (approved in 1967, 1972, and 1977). The latter projects involved a difficult process of reorienting Kenya's Agricultural Finance Corporation toward smallholder lending.[35]

The Bank's 1974–78 lending program proposed an expanded portfolio with fifteen agriculture projects, of which four were continuations or expansions of first-phase projects; the remainder reflected proposals of an agricultural sector mission, which, in the words of a 1973 Country Program Paper, "has given considerable emphasis to methods of reaching poorer sections of the rural population of Kenya. There is no doubt that some of these projects will be difficult to identify and prepare, particularly those in new areas of lending."[36] The major agricultural projects arising from this approach included the Integrated Agricultural Development Projects I and II, which provided inputs and services through most of the agricultural areas of the country (less than 20 percent of Kenya is arable, the remainder being semiarid), using Kenya's cooperative structure as the main means for delivery. The production impact of these projects was poor, and they arguably overloaded and weakened the cooperatives. Project II was stopped early in favor of a revised approach to agricultural development, based on national extension and research programs. These reached second phases by the late 1980s, and at the time of writing remain the major donor-supported approaches to Kenyan agriculture.[37]

The Second National Livestock Project was based on a modest-sized 1968 pilot project that was ultimately (in 1981) judged unsuccessful,[38] but not before the greatly expanded multidonor second project was undertaken, with the Bank in the lead. The second project attempted throughout the drier parts of the country to promote livestock development through tenure and management changes, investments in water, and the provision of services. This experience was no exception to the finding that projects attempting to develop extensive livestock systems in eastern Africa have almost all been unsuccessful; the Bank now tends to avoid them.[39] For perhaps two sets of reasons such livestock projects have proven difficult for the Bank to deal with. In the first place, pastoralism is an integral part of complex social systems, and there is fundamental disagreement among livestock specialists, social scientists, and others as to the extent and causes of stress in pastoral systems. One influential book criticizes what it terms the mainstream view of pastoralism—a view that underlay many Bank projects—according to which a combination of rising human and animal numbers and communal grazing leads

35. World Bank, "Project Performance Audit Report: Kenya, Smallholder Agricultural Credit Project," Operations Evaluation Department report 0834 (1975).

36. World Bank, "Country Program Paper: Kenya" (January 1973), p. 12.

37. World Bank, "Project Performance Audit Report: Kenya, Integrated Agricultural Development Project," Operations Evaluation Department report 5305 (1984).

38. World Bank, "Impact Evaluation Report: Kenya, First Livestock Development Project," Operations Evaluation Department report 3622 (1981).

39. World Bank, "Rural Development," p. xiv.

inexorably to degradation; the book concludes that many livestock projects had been misconceived.[40] In the second place, there is disagreement among specialists even on basic technical concepts and on the order of magnitude of key parameters. There is debate, for instance, on whether the notion of stocking rates has any meaning in conditions of great year-to-year climatic variability, and measurement of animal numbers and range and animal productivity is extremely difficult in practice.

As a result of a reassessment of its approach to agriculture in Kenya made around 1980, the Bank has pursued two lines. First, the Bank's approach made a major switch toward policy issues during the 1980s, under the Second Structural Adjustment Loan and, after 1986, under the First and Second Agricultural Sector Adjustment projects. Second, the Bank has led multidonor projects, which continue in the mid-1990s, to support mainline government agencies responsible for services to the agriculture sector; these projects are under the National Extension Project and the National Agricultural Research Project.

TANZANIA. In Tanzania the Bank supported the country's agricultural development strategy during the 1970s through two main types of projects. Among the first type several focused on the principal commodities; these included the National Maize Project, which provided key inputs for the main food crop in selected regions of the country; two livestock projects; a cashew nut development project, which provided for crop improvement and investment in processing factories; the Flue-Cured Tobacco Project and the Tobacco Processing and Handling projects; and the Geita Cotton Project. All came to be regarded as largely unsatisfactory by Tanzanian officials, as well as by the Bank's Operations Evaluation Department, in part because of severe problems of implementation and sustainability, and in part because the production response was disappointing.[41] Among the second type, the Bank assisted in drawing up a national program of area-based Regional Integrated Development projects, in three of which the Bank was lead donor: at Kigoma in the west of the country, at Tabora in the center of the country, and at Mwanza-Shinyanga, adjoining Lake Victoria. All were rated unsuccessful. This litany of disasters reflected weak public sector implementation in Tanzania and the Bank's misreading in the early 1970s of the country's strategy and prospects.

With the resumption of Bank lending to Tanzania after the mid-1980s, the major efforts in agriculture took the form of a sector adjustment program that focused on resolving constraints imposed by government policies and shortcomings of the public sector and national programs to strengthen agricultural research and extension. These efforts were similar to those in Kenya in the 1980s.

40. Stephen Sandford, *Management of Pastoral Development in the Third World* (Chichester, England: Wiley, 1983), p. 11.
41. World Bank, "Project Performance Audit Report: Tanzania," Operations Evaluation Department report 5197 (June 19, 1984).

MALAWI. The emphasis in Malawi through the 1970s was on area-based projects. These began with the Lilongwe Land Development Project, which served as a pilot scheme to devise new approaches. It was the Bank's first agriculture project in the country, approved in 1968, with a second phase that began in 1971 and then a third phase in 1975; it attracted worldwide attention and emulation. As a result of this, a multidonor set of projects was devised, covering the whole of Malawi by supporting a structure of agricultural development districts. The Bank funded two projects. One, in the south, was the Shire Valley Development Project (with a first phase approved in 1968, a second in 1973, and a consolidation phase in 1978), which has been regarded by the Operations Evaluation Department as successfully implemented, despite its location among adverse agro-ecological conditions. The second, Karonga Rural Development Project (first phase approved in 1972, with a second phase in 1976), has been considered unsatisfactory, as most crops did not achieve production targets. Both projects combined infrastructure with research, extension, and input services, together with a comprehensive marketing network provided by the state-owned agency, Admarc. They were succeeded in the Bank's portfolio by the nationwide Rural Development Program of 1978. This program was inevitably less intensively staffed than the individual projects had been, and there was a consequent loss of momentum. It also suffered from overly complex design, in which agricultural and nonagricultural infrastructure components were to be executed through the same management structure. Recurrent cost problems also emerged more acutely than before.[42]

As in Kenya and Tanzania, during the 1980s the Bank subsequently changed its approach in Malawi from area-based projects in favor of supporting national structures (for example, through the Smallholder Fertilizer Project approved in 1983) and addressing policy and institutional issues. Sector adjustment programs moved center stage, with agricultural pricing issues and a subsidy on fertilizer proving to be hardy perennials.

ZAMBIA. In Zambia, where agriculture was not a major part of the Bank's portfolio, the pattern was similar. Between fiscal years 1966 and 1977 agriculture and forestry accounted for less than 10 percent of gross Bank loans to Zambia—$42 million out of $463 million. Early projects concentrated on large-scale agriculture. These included the Livestock Development Project (approved in 1969, later canceled), which focused on state farms; the first and second Industrial Forestry projects (approved in 1968 and 1977); and the Commercial Crops Farming Development Project (approved in 1970), which had severe implementation problems and little production impact. The emphasis on large-scale agriculture through much of the 1970s reflected the comparatively limited size of the smallholder farming sector in Zambia, compared with the same sector in the other countries

42. World Bank, "Malawi: National Rural Development Program Phase 1," Operations Evaluation Department report 6797 (1987).

under review. The Coffee Production Project (approved in 1978) contained both state farm and smallholder elements, but was only partly successful in meeting production targets. The Eastern Province and Southern Province Agricultural Development projects (both approved in 1981) emphasized smallholders, but also were rated as unsatisfactory by the Operations Evaluation Department as they had little impact on production.

Three features of the process of change in the World Bank's approach to agriculture and rural development in Africa are noteworthy. First, the Bank's strategy to involve low-income groups in the process of development was undoubtedly an improvement on earlier strategies. Implementation and project results arising from the strategy were, in many cases disappointing, however. Second, emphasis on that strategy, occurring at a time when the Bank's overall lending expanded rapidly and when Bank staff were under pressure to disburse funding, meant that rapidly increasing amounts were channeled through a form of project lending whose effectiveness had not been proven. As a result there was a tendency to seize on promising pilot schemes and magnify them earlier than either their results or the implementation capacity of the recipient warranted. Third, the strategy was based on financing projects, rather than on policy or institutional change. An Operations Evaluation Department review explains this: "Although the need for appropriate policies in support of projects was stressed at the time, it was nonetheless decided to proceed, even in unpromising circumstances, in the hope of thereby assisting some governments to change their policies."[43] If this was the hope, it was disappointed in too many instances to warrant continuing with a project-led approach.

A major review of agriculture in Africa and of Bank lending for the sector concluded that the main explanations for sectoral performance were not to be found in projects but in a wider arena, and specifically in three sets of circumstances: luck (covering initial endowments and economic shocks); macroeconomic policies (principally implicit and explicit taxation of agriculture, and public expenditure); and sectoral policies (dealing with factors, services and markets).[44] It was a growing recognition by the Bank that project lending was not an instrument that could address most of these circumstances that led in many countries to the strategy of structural adjustment.

Highways

Highway projects have been a continuing main theme in Bank lending from the earliest days of involvement in the countries under review. A working transport

43. World Bank, "Rural Development," p. xiv.

44. This was the Managing Agricultural Development in Africa (MADIA) study. Its findings are encapsulated in Uma Lele, *Agricultural Growth and Assistance to Africa: Lessons of a Quarter Century* (San Francisco: International Center for Economic Growth/ ICS Press Publications, 1990). See also Uma Lele, ed., *Aid to African Agriculture: Lessons from Two Decades of Donors' Experience* (Johns Hopkins University Press for the World Bank, 1991), especially chapters 3, 12.

system is clearly a prerequisite for sustained economic development; the Bank was seen as having a comparative advantage in the necessary technical and institutional skills from its long involvement in other developing countries. Moreover, for highways limited technological adaption for local conditions was needed; construction projects were attractive in that they involved substantial one-time expenditures (often in foreign exchange); and for a long time, in many countries at least, the assumption could be made that subsequent maintenance would be undertaken by the government, with little further Bank involvement.

In the early years of the Bank's lending to the four East African countries, lending for highways was characterized by an exclusive focus on projects, although the Bank has always had a close interest in the transport coordinating agencies in the countries involved, and many of the early projects had an institutional component. In 1975, however, the Bank announced that sector lending would become a main instrument for sectors and countries where the institutional framework was able to deal with it: thereafter, highway lending increasingly took that form. Sector lending for transport offered significant advantages to the Bank:

> It was expected to allow the commitment and fast disbursement of large sums, save staff time, broaden Bank impact by encompassing the investment program of the entire transport sector, strengthen local capabilities to plan and manage investment programs, and permit a focus on the policy issues necessary to achieve sector-wide objectives.[45]

Three major shifts occurred during the 1970s in the Bank's approach to transport project lending.[46] The first was in the context of sector lending and highlighted planning, management, and institutional issues. Thirty percent of 120 transport projects reviewed included actions of wider sectoral implications. In assessing the sector focus for projects, the Operations Evaluations Department concluded that it was valuable when sustained, but that it required a heavy input of staff time and that commitment from governments could not always be taken for granted. A major feature of the sector approach was institutional: in 17 of the 120 projects, the project was the instrument for the establishment of a new institution; in 95 projects there were institutional strengthening components.

As the weakness of road maintenance (for both organizational and financial reasons) and the high economic returns to be obtained from successful maintenance programs became clear, the focus of Bank transport projects shifted increasingly to maintenance. In some cases, such as the Kenya Highway Maintenance Project, it was even the sole focus. The Bank made major efforts to persuade

45. World Bank, "Annual Review of Project Performance Results for 1987," Operations Evaluation Department report 7404 (August 1988), p. 60.

46. A valuable overview of World Bank lending for transport is provided by World Bank, "Tenth Annual Review of Project Performance Audit Results," vol. 2, Operations Evaluation Department (August 1984), pp. 160–85. This brings together the Bank's experience with 120 transport projects approved between 1965 and 1978.

governments of the importance of putting in place effective maintenance systems. Considerable difficulties were encountered, however, in part because compared with road construction, maintenance requires careful tailoring to the local cultural milieu and is administration intensive,[47] and in part because of the political and administrative difficulties inherent in securing funds for recurrent expenditure, not just by governments but also by the Bank.[48]

In the third shift, relatively more highway investment came to be directed toward road networks that supported agriculture and rural development. In part this reflected progress during the 1960s toward completing primary road networks, the logical further step being to move to secondary and tertiary roads; and in part this shift was associated with the Bank's post-1973 rural development strategy, which emphasized decentralized investment.

KENYA. The main themes in lending for highway projects were reflected in specific country experiences. The Bank's involvement with Kenya's transport system dated back to a first highway project approved in 1964, which supported a program that in the following decade extended a network of national and regional roads. Rapid expansion of traffic in the late 1960s, however, exacerbated by uncontrolled axle weights, put many roads under strain. Measures taken with the Bank's support in a series of subsequent highway projects through the 1970s included an upward revision of road construction standards in 1970, attempts to strengthen inadequate maintenance capacity (including the largely unsuccessful Highway Maintenance Project, approved in 1970),[49] and reorganization, under which some 40,000 kilometers of roads was transferred from local authorities to the central Ministry of Works.[50] One major multidonor initiative in which the Bank played a leading role was the Rural Access Roads Program (approved in 1976), which devised labor-intensive methods regarded as having made an innovative contribution to the country's employment strategy. The Bank's principal activity during the 1980s took the form of a highways sector loan, to replace highways projects, of which there had been a sequence of five.

TANZANIA. The Bank's first involvement with Tanzania's highways dated back to a first highway project approved in 1964, which focused on stretches of the main road network. It was revised in 1968 to take account of delays caused by the mass exodus of expatriates from senior positions in the Ministry of Communications and Works. A second highway project was approved in 1969 to construct sections of the

47. World Bank, "Annual Review of Project Performance Audit Results for 1987," p. 172.

48. Peter S. Heller and Joan C. Aghevli, "The Recurrent Cost Problem: An International Overview," in John Howell, ed., *Recurrent Costs and Agricultural Development* (London: Overseas Development Institute, 1985), pp. 22–49.

49. World Bank, "Project Performance Audit Report: Kenya, Highway Maintenance Project," Operations Evaluation Department report 3659 (November 1981).

50. World Bank, "Project Performance Audit Report: Kenya, Fourth and Fifth Highway Projects," Operations Evaluation Department report 4534 (June 1983).

main road to Zambia, then under pressure because of Rhodesia's Unilateral Declaration of Independence. A third project (with a loan component approved in 1969
and a credit component approved in 1971) focused on supporting agricultural
development programs through road building, but is regarded as having failed to
generate benefits because increased agricultural production, on which the benefits
of the project depended, did not materialize.[51] The fourth and fifth highway
projects (approved in 1974 and 1979) changed the focus of the Bank's lending from
investments in highway construction to improvements in highway maintenance and
institution building.[52] Physical implementation was disappointing, but progress was
made with institutional reforms and (under the fifth and sixth highway projects) in
staff training.

Throughout the period of Bank involvement, poor maintenance has continued
to be a major problem, reducing the economic benefits of investments in highway
construction and rehabilitation. Further, the stagnation of the Tanzanian economy
and consequently of traffic has meant that expected benefits, such as those for the
third highway project, were not realized. Here again, it is seen that the impact of a
project is inseparable from the wider economic performance of a country. Currently the Bank is involved in Tanzania, with other donors, in a $650 million Integrated
Roads Project, in effect, a sectorwide initiative combining national and secondary
roads. Labor-intensive approaches to rural roads are also being tested, principally
under a U.S.-funded component.

MALAWI. In Malawi, the Bank has supported the transport sector since 1967.
The first highway project, approved in 1968, provided for the construction of key
stretches of the main north-to-south trunk road and for institutional strengthening
of the Roads Department, which at that time was heavily staffed by expatriates at
senior levels, as in Zambia. The second and third highway projects (approved in
1974 and 1977) were in support of a national strategy that combined improvements
to the primary road network with easing rural movements; but as in the other
countries, an emerging weakness was road maintenance, which deteriorated as
budgets came under pressure. The fourth project (approved in 1981) focused on
this issue, as well as on extending the rural road network and upgrading the main
north-south route. The latter component developed innovative labor-intensive
techniques that compared favorably with the costs of more capital-intensive
methods. The Bank's role in the transport strategy in Malawi combined useful
continuity with imaginative responses to changing local conditions.

ZAMBIA. Such continuity was not achieved in Zambia. The first and second
highway projects (approved in 1966 and 1968) reconstructed long stretches of

51. World Bank, "Project Performance Audit Report: Tanzania, Third Highway Project,"
Operations Evaluation Department report 4031 (1982).
52. World Bank, "Project Completion Report: Tanzania, Fourth Highway (Maintenance)
Project," Operations Evaluation Department report 6483 (1986).

Zambia's two main trunk roads, the Great North Road to Tanzania and the Great East Road to Malawi, which were crucial after Rhodesia's Unilateral Declaration of Independence. Both roads, however, subsequently suffered from the common failure to impose limits on axle weights, and deterioration of the surfaces set in.[53] It was more than ten years before the approval of the next highway project, in 1978, for which the principal aims were to improve the maintenance of the rapidly deteriorating network, to plan for future expansion, and to strengthen the Roads Department through the recruitment of expatriate technical assistance. This change in project objectives was not successful, largely, in the view of the Bank's audit report, because key local officials were not convinced of the value of redirecting spending toward maintenance.[54]

The experience with the World Bank's approach to highway projects in the four countries reviewed points up some of the Bank's comparative advantages, in particular, the scale of its operations, which permit both continuity and dialogue with government on policy and institutional questions. Continuity is crucial; one review, based on seven country studies (including one of Kenya), found that ten to fifteen years were required to bring about policy change in the transport sector: "The case studies repeatedly show the Bank staff's failure to appreciate how much time it takes to replace one set of policies with another."[55] Compared with the Bank's approach in the agriculture and rural development sector and the education sector, there has been greater consistency in its approach over time in the highway sector, in part because, with highways, there have been fewer problematic technical issues, and in part because there has been a narrower range of public institutions with which the Bank has had to deal. As in the case of the other sectors, however, problems with highway projects, and in particular with maintenance, have caused the Bank to become intimately involved with government planning, management, and financial processes.

Education

The populations of the four countries under review came to independence with very limited skills and education levels. Improvements in education were rightly seen by the new governments in all the countries as central social objectives of and means to development. Demand for education was also overwhelming among the people; it was perceived everywhere as the way out of poverty. With population growth of 3 to 4 percent a year and one-half of the population typically under the age of fifteen years, meeting this demand was a massive task.

The record of education in Africa is mixed. As table 9-1 indicates, progress has been made over the past generation in all the countries in improving literacy from

53. World Bank, Operations Evaluation Department Audit Report 0292 (December 1973).

54. World Bank, "Project Completion Report: Zambia, Third Highway Project," Operations Evaluation Department report 9187 (December 1990).

55. Ian G. Heggie, "Designing Major Policy Reform," World Bank Discussion Paper 115 (Washington, January 1991), abstract.

its earlier dismal levels. The World Bank's contribution, through education projects and through its involvement in policy questions, has been considerable. However, there are still major shortcomings. Compared with other continents, Africa remains short of skills in critical areas; educational facilities are poor and under pressure from restricted public spending; and the quality of much teaching, from primary schools to universities, is low and in some cases falling.

It is probably a fair judgment to say that in the earlier years, until about the late 1970s, much Bank lending for education in Africa was unfocused. That is the picture presented by an overview of the education projects in the four countries, and it is the conclusion of an authoritative review: "The pre-eminence of the Bank in education and training policy formulation for the developing world is not much older than ten years. Prior to that, in the 1960s and early 1970s, the Bank was certainly lending for education, but the research base for their lending strategies was not in place."[56] In good measure, the combination of the Bank's catholic approach with an emphasis by local interest groups on secondary and tertiary education goes a long way toward explaining a striking feature of Bank education projects: how little was directed in the early years toward primary education.

The Bank's first financing for education projects came in 1962. Since then its approach has gone through several broad phases, although the Bank has sometimes found it difficult to define a consistent approach in a given country. Initially the Bank restricted its financing to hardware and the sectors of education considered directly productive in economic terms. The emphasis was thus on secondary, tertiary, and technical or vocational education, and on teacher training. A progressive relaxation of these criteria meant that by the mid- to late 1970s Bank funds could be used for almost any aspect of educational development. From about that time the Bank placed increasing emphasis on improving the access of the rural and urban poor to education.[57] During the 1970s there began a "massive expansion" of analytical work on education,[58] which by the 1980s provided the base for a different agenda for the Bank, in particular, for a rebalancing of Bank lending toward primary levels and for the pursuit of low-cost quality throughout education.

Parallel with these changes, and in line with the Bank's changing approach to agriculture and rural development and to highways, the Bank paid increasing attention to the policy and institutional contexts of educational spending and came to link its projects to sector programs. The Bank went through a sustained process of developing its expertise and understanding of education, leading to a milestone 1988 paper on Africa, which encapsulated long experience and more than a decade of research.[59]

56. Kenneth King, *Aid and Education in the Developing World: The Role of the Donor Agencies in Educational Analysis* (London: Longman, 1991), p. x.

57. World Bank, "Review of Bank Operations in the Education Sector," Operations Evaluation Department report 2321 (December 1978).

58. King, *Aid and Education,* p. 210.

59. World Bank, "Education in Sub-Saharan Africa: Policies for Adjustment, Revitalization, and Expansion" (1988).

As in the other sectors, the Bank's experience in education in Kenya, Malawi, Tanzania, and Zambia reflected the trend away from project lending and toward sectoral approaches. But more than in the other sectors, project lending for education in the earlier period lacked dominant themes; in the following review of country experience it is hard to avoid an excessively dense enumeration of unrelated project details.

KENYA. In Kenya the Bank's first education project, approved in 1966, coincided with a period of rapid expansion of education, with primary school enrollment doubling from 1963 to 1973. Government commitment was strong: in 1964 the sector absorbed 24 percent of government recurrent expenditure and 30 percent of capital expenditure; by 1973 these had risen to 43 percent and 50 percent, respectively, which is high by any standards and too high in the Bank's view. Financial issues were the main recurring policy theme in the education sector dialogue between the Bank and the Kenya government for twenty years. The Bank took the view that spending for education was excessive in comparison with spending for other sectors and through the 1970s urged the government to control education expenditures and to adopt a strategy aimed "at improving the quality and efficiency of the system and at expanding education solely on the basis of identified manpower needs and the government's financial capacity."[60] In 1988 the Bank was still saying that the health and education sectors faced "serious financial problems and distortions in the pattern of public expenditures" and was continuing to urge greater efforts to recover costs from education users on an unenthusiastic government.[61]

The Bank's first education project in Kenya provided finance for expanded secondary and technical schooling and for primary teacher training. The Operations Evaluation Department judged that, although the project was successful in reaching quantitative targets, it was implemented against a background of falling quality in education. The Bank's second project (approved in 1970) principally expanded agricultural education and training and to a lesser extent teacher training and attempted to improve educational planning and management in the government. The third project (1975) focused on improving the quality of basic education and of establishing an education and training strategy. The fourth (1978) had three main objectives: manpower planning for agriculture and general public sector management, improved equity in access to basic education, and improved planning and management. Despite long delays in implementation, the projects are regarded as having achieved their basic aims.[62]

MALAWI. The Bank's first education project in Malawi, approved in 1967, focused on secondary schooling and primary teacher training and provided for construction and hardware, but gave relatively little attention to policy and educa-

60. World Bank, "Country Program Paper: Kenya" (December 19, 1980), p. 17.

61. World Bank, "Kenya: Policy Framework Paper 1988 to 1990" (January 7, 1988), p. 13; and World Bank, "Country Strategy Paper: Kenya" (February 25, 1988), p. 10.

62. World Bank, "Project Performance Audit Report: Kenya, Third and Fourth Education Projects," Operations Evaluation Department report 6712 (1987).

tional planning.[63] It was well implemented. The second project, approved eight years later, stressed primary and rural education, secondary education for girls, and the capacity for planning and management of the Ministry of Education and Culture. Inadequate maintenance of schools emerged as an issue.[64] The third, fourth, and fifth projects (approved in 1979, 1981, and 1983, respectively) had overlapping objectives; they provided for greater efficiency and greater access to primary and secondary schooling and the university, teacher training, and among other things financed the preparation of a national education plan and provided technical support for the education ministry.

The Bank by that time had become closely involved in all levels of Malawi education, an involvement that was intensified by two education sector credits (in 1987 and 1989). One study of the Bank's lending for education in Malawi took the view that it was not until the second of these sector credits that the Bank lost its predominant focus on hardware and began to pay as much attention to qualitative issues as it should have, but that even if late the Bank had played a commendable role in bringing about this change.[65]

TANZANIA. It is hard to disagree with the Operations Evaluation Department's judgment that Bank lending for education projects in Tanzania has been "eclectic" and lacking in strategic consistency.[66] The Bank has funded seven education projects in the country, the first approved in 1963. The projects had a variety of objectives, often with little identifiable connection. The first two supported secondary education, then perceived to be the priority, together with assistance to expand two primary and one secondary teacher training colleges. The third, approved in 1971, supported the Ministry of Agriculture in setting up rural training centers and institutes (the latter for subprofessional staff).

The fourth to seventh projects (in effect from 1973 onward) were classic projects of the times: they featured large amounts of hardware, focused on higher levels of education, were multicomponent, and were hard to implement and ultimately unsustainable. The fourth project, for instance, covered three secondary schools (later dropped from the project because of cost overruns), three teacher training colleges, two vocational training centers, eight community centers, one rural health center, and a medical school for the university. Largely because of the complexity of this project and general implementation difficulties, a project im-

63. World Bank, "Project Performance Audit Report: Malawi, First Education Project," Operations Evaluation Department report 2914 (1980).

64. World Bank, "Project Performance Audit Report: Malawi, Second Education Project," Operations Evaluation Department report 4572 (1983).

65. Coralie Bryant, "Investing in People: World Bank Lending for Human Resource Development in Malawi," Consultant's Report for the Operations Evaluation Department, draft (1989).

66. World Bank, "Tanzania: World Bank/Tanzania Relations, 1961–1987," Operations Evaluation Department report 8329, vol. 2 (1990), p. 228.

plementation unit was set up. The fifth project was just as multifaceted and had to be implemented by three separate agencies. A Bank review concluded that there were "no overall policy problems in education" with the government's emphasis on primary schooling, but that there was cause for concern about the execution of the four projects to date: "These projects have been subject to considerable delays in execution, in part resulting from poor overall management, problems in recruiting technical assistance, and procurement difficulties."[67]

As in other sectors in Tanzania, the Bank's involvement in education has been problematic. From an exceptionally low base at independence, educational achievements during the 1960s and 1970s were remarkable, and the Bank contributed to these. However, the country's economic crisis and subsequent pressure on public spending and other operational shortcomings of the public sector caused a sharp fall in the quality of education, and during the 1980s enrollments fell. Education in Tanzania provides another example of why the contribution of projects to national development cannot be separated from the wider performance of the economy and public institutions.

ZAMBIA. In Zambia the Bank's first and second education projects (both approved in 1969) provided support for a range of educational activities: teacher training for primary schools, expanded and improved secondary schooling, and technical education, as well as support for the schools of engineering and education at the university. The third project (approved in 1973) again provided for the construction of, or extensions to, a range of institutions: the Agricultural Science Department at the university, twelve medical training centers, sixty-one secondary schools, and four teacher training colleges and farmer training centers. This project and a fourth project (approved in 1976) ran into implementation problems; these were partly solved by a project implementation unit that relied on expatriate staffing provided by Norway, but recurrent cost funding had become a severe problem.[68]

Some general observations about Bank education projects in East Africa can be made. First, although the Bank has shown a commitment to education over a long period, the multiple aims of individual projects and the apparent lack of consistency over time among them reflect the absence of a clear sense of strategy until the 1980s. Second, Bank education projects have often been more successful in physical implementation than in maintaining or improving the quality of education. Even in physical implementation, however, the complexity of some projects has caused problems for rural area development efforts. Third, finance has been a persistent problem: there has been difficulty in providing for recurrent needs, and often a high proportion of available funds has been absorbed by salaries, compared with the proportion available for materials. The Bank's efforts to encourage greater orderliness in educational finance, including higher levels of cost recovery, have not been effective.

67. World Bank, "Country Program Paper: Tanzania" (March 14, 1974), p. 12.
68. World Bank, "Project Completion Report: Zambia, Fourth Education Project," Operations Evaluation Department report 5552 (1985).

The Bank has moved a long way in defining priority issues within education. The impact of past lending would no doubt have been greater had the Bank been able to identify a consistent approach earlier, both in general and in particular countries. But it remains true also that the benefits to be gained from even successful education programs are dependent on wider economic performance, which in the four countries under review has fallen short of expectations.

Performance Issues: Projects in the Structural Adjustment Context

The end of the 1970s and early 1980s saw a major change in the World Bank's approach to project lending in Africa. Many projects were closed or not renewed, and structural adjustment, with its focus on addressing policy and institutional constraints to development, moved center stage in the Bank's activities. Structural adjustment lending is not restricted to Africa, but it is particularly pronounced in that continent. Project lending, although it did not end, came to take place routinely only in the context of adjustment. Paralleling and supporting this change, the Bank's own internal reorganization unified program and project divisions and increased the relative weight given to policy analysts in determining Bank programs, downplaying that of project staff and technical specialists.

The Bank's concern with policy and institutional questions in borrowing countries, and the associated instrument of program loans, was not entirely new, as the preceding review of project experience in the various sectors has indicated. In Kenya the Bank provided a program loan for $30 million in 1975, linked to medium-term economic restructuring and to wide-ranging policy discussions with the Bank: "In accordance with . . . the understandings reached with the Bank during the program loan discussions, the Government has made substantial progress in increasing the priority accorded to agriculture."[69] Similarly, there was a project-policy linkage in the mid-1970s in Tanzania: "We have been discussing the problems affecting the trucking industry with the Government for some time and it is perhaps partly in response to these discussions that the Government has recently asked us (February 1974) to help them sort out the various trucking management and policy issues with a view to rationalizing the industry."[70] To many projects, moreover, policy conditions were attached as covenants, although these were often ineffective in bringing about policy change.[71]

If policy conditions and program lending were not new, what was new in the Bank's approach from around 1980 was the intensity of the policy dialogue and the

69. World Bank, "Country Program Paper: Kenya" (November 30, 1976), p. 12.
70. World Bank, "Country Program Paper: Tanzania" (March 14, 1974), p. 15.
71. See for instance, World Bank, "Conditionality in World Bank Lending: Its Relation to Agricultural Pricing Policies," Operations Evaluation Department report 7357 (1988). This report concluded that among the instruments available to the Bank for affecting price policies, projects "had the narrowest objectives" and were generally ineffective (p. v).

increasingly close coordination of the Bank's policy concerns with International Monetary Fund programs and with the disbursement of project funds (both by the Bank and by other Western donors). Structural adjustment was partly complementary to project lending—insofar as removing policy constraints would permit more successful project lending—and partly a substitute for it, as the two lending mechanisms competed for funds.

Two broad sets of reasons underlay the relative decline in project lending and the rise of structural adjustment: the need to find a means of arresting overall economic decline, and the unsatisfactory performance of projects. Interviews with World Bank staff and Bank documents have given differing views of the extent to which the change was a response to factors internal to individual countries (whether project or policy related) or to external conditions, notably unsustainable current account deficits, which were exacerbated by the 1979 oil crisis.

Africa's Economic Decline

A principal reason for the shift in Bank strategy was growing unease about Africa's seemingly inexorable economic decline at a time when the Bank and other Western development agencies were putting ever larger amounts of money into Africa. The ideal conditions for project lending—namely, sustained economic growth, with past project investments being maintained by private or public revenues in a buoyant economy, and new projects adding to the productive base— did not apply in most African economies.

The four economies reviewed here reflected a bleak general picture around 1980. Among other things, Kenya's public expenditure had become overextended after the coffee boom of 1976–77, a situation exacerbated by the oil price rise of 1979; Tanzania's economic decline had become sharply visible after 1979; Malawi's economy was unable to recover from external shocks; and Zambia had been in secular decline since the early 1970s. None of the countries appeared likely to recover unaided. Project lending did not address the causes of decline, whether internal or external, and projects were unlikely to show satisfactory rates of economic return to economies in this state. The experience of Bank staff, accumulated during project implementation and documented (often some years later) by Operations Evaluation Department studies, showed that a new approach was needed in place of almost exclusive reliance on projects.[72]

The relationship between the policy change that the Bank sought to bring about and internal growth and investment was illustrated by a 1980 analysis of the situation in Kenya by Bank staff:

72. The different explanations given for the introduction of structural adjustment vary according to the weight given to the poor performance of projects. The Bank president's memorandum of February 1980 to the Board of Directors, which introduced structural adjustment, identified it wholly as a positive response by the Bank to adverse economic conditions facing the developing countries and did not mention project performance: "The

Policy reforms are needed to change Kenya's economic structure. Inefficiency in Kenya's industrial and agricultural base (including poor performance by parastatals), has become an increasingly constraining element to growth. Economic development will inevitably slow down unless there is a rapid transition to more efficient production which could satisfy domestic demand and permit competition in overseas markets. . . . The case for extended program assistance is as follows. Without substantial program assistance from the Bank or bilateral sources, the Kenyan economy will probably stagnate until there is another upturn in the terms of trade. . . . The program of industrial policy reform, export promotion measures, and efforts to revitalize the agricultural sector, which the proposed structural adjustment credits would support, offer the best chance for Kenya to overcome the terms of [the] trade cycle to which the economy is presently bound.[73]

Project lending clearly would not bring about the changes needed, although these changes were a necessary condition for improved project performance.

Poor Project Performance

A second set of reasons for the change in strategy, stressed by many World Bank staff members, was that projects were doing badly, whether in terms of economic and institutional benefits, cost overruns, or implementation delays. In the words of one senior official, during the program review process in 1978–79, "everywhere we looked in Africa, the programs were in trouble."[74] It became more difficult to justify continued large-scale project lending, and the Bank began increasingly to look beyond project-specific issues to understand what was going wrong. The 1981 report "Accelerated Development in Sub-Saharan Africa" was a key element in this process; although sometimes criticized (and wrongly caricatured) for overstating the importance of price issues, it was influential in bringing policy issues to the fore as a matter of routine in the design of Bank lending for Africa.[75]

The perception among project staff and managers that projects were doing badly in Africa was borne out—inevitably with some delay because of the duration

---

changes in the international economy in recent years, including the increase in the price of oil, continued high levels of inflation and prolonged period of slow growth in the OECD countries, are posing increasingly acute problems for many of the developing countries. The management of their economies has become more complex. They face deteriorating terms of trade and growing current account deficits. With increasingly severe resource constraints governments must consider how they can adjust their development patterns and economic structures to the substantially changed international economic environment. This set of circumstances has led to considerable discussion of additional ways and means [by] which the Bank can assist its members, including the use of a new form of lending which we have named 'structural adjustment' lending." Memorandum, Robert S. McNamara to World Bank Board of Directors, February 5, 1980.

73. World Bank, "Country Program Paper: Kenya" (December 19, 1980), p. 12.

74. Personal interview with Pierre Landell-Mills, World Bank, June 1991.

75. World Bank, "Accelerated Development in Sub-Saharan Africa: An Agenda for Action" (1981).

of the project cycle— by more systematic ex-post evaluation data. But the interpretation of project evaluation results is subject to well-known problems, including:

—Fungibility: the process whereby financing with aid funds for a particular project releases local funds for another activity that has less value for development. At the margin, there is some truth in this argument.[76] However, in view of the large proportion of investable resources in the countries under review that is made available under aid funding, it is not plausible to argue that they wholly substitute for government funds.[77] In many African countries, including those under review, aid dependence has reached the point at which almost 100 percent of the government's capital expenditures are aid funded. The fungibility argument is not plausible under such conditions.

—Implementation that diverts resources: particular projects may be implemented at the expense of other activities when scarce resources, such as technical manpower and the time of senior managers, are diverted, often to satisfy a powerful donor such as the Bank.

—Sustainability: most evaluations occur at the end of project implementation, but the longer-term impact of a project may be significantly better or worse than appears at that time (see the section on sustainability below).

—Methodological and measurement issues: how to measure the benefits from agricultural credit projects, for instance, has long been contentious among evaluation practitioners. The counterfactual—what would have happened in the absence of a project—can perhaps never be known. Moreover, the weak base of data in many developing countries makes it difficult to know what the situation was at the start of a project and what trends there were during and after implementation.

—The qualitative nature of some project aims: it is difficult to find objective measures for some project results, including, for instance, institution building.

—The difficulty of assessing the real contribution projects make to overall growth and development: often the results of individual projects appear to be satisfactory, although the overall economy is in decline (the macro-micro paradox).

Despite these inevitable shortcomings, the Bank's evaluation material provides a unique record of a great deal of development experience and is important among the various means the Bank has for learning from its past. Partly in response to the shortcomings of project-specific evaluations, the Operations Evaluation Department's approach has shifted in recent years to put more emphasis on themes, sectors, and studies of the overall relationship between the Bank and a particular borrowing country. There is always a problem of openness and confidentiality in making such material available, and it is arguable that in the past the Bank has been

76. A Kenyan official in the Ministry of Livestock Development, when asked why agricultural projects were so aid dependent, replied: "Aid organizations will not fund police uniforms and guns. So we have to spend our money on that, while their money goes on agriculture." Personal communication, Nairobi, July 1992.

77. The issue of fungibility has received a good deal of attention. See Mosley, *Overseas Aid;* and Cassen and Associates, *Does Aid Work? Report to an Intergovernmental Task Force* (Oxford University Press, 1986).

420   THE WORLD BANK AS A PROJECT LENDER

Table 9-3. *Operations Rated Satisfactory and Unsatisfactory, by Approval Year, Africa and All Regions, 1961–89*
Number of operations unless otherwise specified

Approval year	Africa			All regions		
	Unsatisfactory	Satisfactory	Percentage satisfactory	Unsatisfactory	Satisfactory	Percentage satisfactory
1961	1	0	0.0	1	6	85.7
1962	...	...	...	0	1	100.0
1963	0	1	100.0	0	3	100.0
1964	1	3	75.0	3	11	78.6
1965	1	2	66.7	2	12	85.7
1966	0	8	100.0	1	25	96.2
1967	0	9	100.0	6	28	82.4
1968	6	19	76.0	11	58	84.1
1969	4	31	88.6	10	84	89.4
1970	9	25	73.5	21	91	81.3*
1971	9	22	72.0	19	93	83.0
1972	10	34	77.3	20	119	85.6
1973	10	40	80.0	26	141	84.4
1974	24	34	58.6	46	128	73.6
1975	22	45	67.2	42	136	76.4
1976	19	29	60.4	41	160	79.6
1977	22	35	61.4	46	153	76.9
1978	20	29	59.2	56	138	71.1
1979	14	24	63.2	37	119	76.3
1980	8	21	72.4	26	102	79.7
1981	3	20	87.0	15	66	81.5
1982	5	6	54.5	13	41	75.9
1983	2	7	77.8	8	19	70.4
1984	0	2	100.0	3	6	66.7
1985	1	0	0.0	1	4	80.0
1986	...	...	...	0	1	100.0
1987	...	...	...	0	2	100.0
1988	...	...	...	0	1	100.0
1989	...	...	...	...	...	...
Total	191	446	70.0	454	1748	79.4

Source: World Bank Operations Evaluation Department, "Annual Review of Evaluation Results, 1989" (August 1990), table 1-11.

unduly restrictive. Recently, greater efforts have been made by the department to circulate some of its reports more widely, but in view of the usefulness of such material to many practitioners in developing countries who operate in conditions of professional isolation, still more could be done to make it available to a wider public. Indeed, much the same should be done with other Bank publications that at present have restricted distribution; the Bank's moves in 1993 to widen distribution of some of these is welcome.

Table 9-4. *Operations Rated Satisfactory, by Sector, Africa and All Regions*

Sector	Africa	Average, all regions
Agriculture and rural development	51	70
Area development	49	53
Irrigation	38	80
Industry and energy	79	88
Industry	50	81
Development finance corporations	75	85
Oil and gas	100	100
Power	88	92
Telecommunications	85	95
Infrastructure and urban development	83	85
Transport	82	84
Highways	85	89
Ports	81	85
Urban	100	88
Waste supply and waste disposal	92	88
Human resources and technical assistance	75	80
Education	79	83
Population, health, and nutrition	100	60
Technical assistance	56	71
Program and policy lending	88	88
Structural adjustment loans	89	73
All sectors	70	81

Source: World Bank Operations Evaluation Department, "Annual Review of Evaluation Results" (October 1994), table 1-5.

The most general assessment of project performance is a simple determination of whether the operation is satisfactory or not. The Operations Evaluation Department's traditional method of assessing this is based on achievement of at least a 10 percent economic rate of return (ERR), or other significant benefits if the economic rate of return is lower, or an evaluator's qualitative judgment about performance if no ERR has been calculated.

According to such OED assessments, among projects approved between 1961 and 1989 African projects fared somewhat worse than projects in other regions, but not strikingly so, with 70 percent of 637 projects in Africa being rated satisfactorily, compared with 80 percent in all regions (see table 9-3). For most of the period, however, the norm for Africa was comparable with the norm in all regions at well over 70 percent; the exception was for the projects approved in Africa between 1974 and 1979, when the satisfactory proportion fell sharply. It was this generation of projects that gave Bank management such concern and prompted the shift toward policy-related lending.

Within Africa there have also been marked differences in performance among sectors (see table 9-4). For operations evaluated during 1974–88, the principal divergence between Africa and all other regions occurred in agriculture and rural

Table 9-5. *Agricultural Sector Operations Rated Satisfactory and Unsatisfactory in 1961–85, Africa and All Regions*

Number of operations unless otherwise specified

Approval year	Africa			All regions		
	Unsatisfactory	Satisfactory	Percentage satisfactory	Unsatisfactory	Satisfactory	Percentage satisfactory
1961	1	0	0.0	1	0	0.0
1962	...	...	...	0	0	n.a.
1963	...	...	...	0	0	n.a.
1964	0	1	100.0	0	1	100.0
1965	...	...	...	0	2	100.0
1966	...	...	...	0	1	100.0
1967	0	3	100.0	5	9	64.3
1968	4	4	50.0	7	8	53.3
1969	3	9	75.0	5	24	82.8
1970	3	6	66.7	7	24	77.4
1971	4	6	60.0	8	23	74.2
1972	7	9	56.3	12	26	68.4
1973	7	13	65.0	13	39	75.0
1974	15	13	46.4	21	43	67.2
1975	11	11	50.0	17	40	70.2
1976	12	6	33.3	22	45	67.2
1977	10	8	44.4	21	53	71.6
1978	13	6	31.6	30	42	58.3
1979	5	6	54.5	17	33	66.0
1980	6	4	40.0	11	24	68.6
1981	2	1	33.3	6	12	66.7
1982	...	...	...	4	3	42.9
1983	1	0	0.0	1	0	0.0
1984	...	...	...	1	0	0.0
1985	...	...	...	0	2	100.0
Total	104	106	50.5	210	458	68.6

Source: World Bank Operations Evaluation Department, "Annual Review of Evaluation Results, 1989" (August 1990), table 1-12.
n.a. Not available.

development; performance was 51 percent satisfactory in Africa, against 70 percent satisfactory in all regions. On the other hand, in other sectors in Africa as elsewhere, 75 percent or more of operations were rated satisfactory. In the agricultural sector alone a majority of earlier projects—those approved up to 1973—were satisfactory, but there was a marked decline thereafter, when only one-third to one-half of projects in Africa were rated satisfactory (see table 9-5). A valuable review of the performance of agricultural projects in Africa ascribed the difficulties they faced to three major factors: adverse macroeconomic environments, management and institutional weaknesses, and technical shortcomings, in more or less equal proportions.[78]

The Problem of Sustainability

The apparent success of project implementation at the end of five years is an almost necessary condition of benign project effects; it is far from being a sufficient condition, however. As a result of the general decline in the performance of projects after the end of the Bank-supported implementation phase, the Bank has expressed greater concern about the extent to which project benefits are sustained in the years after project closure. Among the several reasons why benefits might not be sustained are the inability of a government to continue funding existing levels of activity, institutional weakness that reemerges when project-funded technical assistance has ended and climatic, political, and market risks.

In response to this concern, the Operations Evaluation Department began in 1979 to undertake selected evaluations of longer-term project effects, typically five years after the end of Bank support for a project. The results were disturbing. Thirty-one such evaluations had been conducted by 1985, 17 of them in Africa; all were of projects judged satisfactory at audit. Of the 31 projects, 13 were assessed to have successfully achieved sustainability: that is, the net flow of benefits assessed by the impact evaluation achieved a 10 percent or higher economic rate of return; or, where no ERR was reestimated, benefits equaled or exceeded levels foreseen at audit. Eight projects were regarded as marginal or uncertain, and the remaining 10 projects failed to sustain the minimum flow of benefits needed to qualify for continued success. Of these 18 projects, 16 were in Africa. Only one African project was regarded as sustainable.[79]

Among the factors adduced to explain the difficulty in keeping up project benefits,[80] two in particular deserve emphasis, given the attention paid to them in current Bank programs. These are public financing and institutional issues.

PUBLIC FINANCING. Financial problems during and after project implementation have been a recurring theme in explaining difficulties with both project performance and sustainability after the withdrawal of donor support. A judgment passed on a program in Malawi could apply to many others: "The National Rural Development Program is not sustainable within Malawi's present budgetary resources. It has been set up almost entirely with external resources but external

---

78. Harry Walters and others, "The Performance of Agricultural Projects in Africa: A Review of Project Ratings and Risks" (World Bank, September 1990), pp. 7–8.

79. Data are from World Bank, "Sustainability of Projects: First Review of Experience," Operations Evaluation Department report 5718 (1985), pp. i–ii, 8.

80. World Bank, "Sustainability of Projects," pp. 10–25.

donors are reluctant to continue financing the recurrent costs which are needed to maintain it."[81] The Bank's response to such funding problems by the late 1970s and early 1980s was threefold: to focus more widely on the budgetary process and to rationalize public sector investment programs; to reduce the number of projects; and, during project implementation, to raise the proportion of total project costs it was prepared to fund. In the Bank's 1977 Country Program Paper for Tanzania the focus was on financial problems faced during implementation: "Local resource constraints have, in fact, affected a number of Bank Group projects. . . . In view of this situation we feel justification of local cost financing on country grounds should be retained. We expect to continue to finance approximately 75 percent of total project cost (including all co-financing) over the next five years."[82] In regard to Kenya, the 1980 Country Program Paper came to a similar view, finding a

> rapidly growing gap between the growth of public revenues and public expenditures. Efforts to strike a balance between these two components have so far been at the expense of development expenditure by delaying the implementation of some projects. As a result delays in project implementation due to lack of counterpart funds is becoming worrisome and it is likely to be some years before public savings can be restored to reasonable levels. In order to help the Government achieve this objective by carrying out its program of policy changes and at the same time avoid costly delays in project implementation, we recommend in this CPP to lend up to 80 percent, instead of 75 percent of total financing requirements (including all cofinancing) and to continue to finance local costs of projects where necessary.[83]

A similar judgment was made regarding Zambia in 1985: "The lack of counterpart funding and budgetary releases for recurrent expenditures have been the major factors delaying project execution." However, the Country Program Paper concluded (optimistically, as it turned out) that "within Zambia's overall budget constraints, the new budgeting procedures have shifted resources to the development sectors and this has significantly eased the funding problem for many Bank projects."[84]

In all countries the financial problems encountered during project implementation were exacerbated after the withdrawal of donor support, which coincided with the end of the government's formal obligation to provide counterpart funds and with a reduction in the leverage applied by or on behalf of the project's management.

INSTITUTIONAL ISSUES. A recurring theme in the Bank's project lending has been its concern with public sector institutions, a concern not matched in earlier years by the Bank's internal expertise to deal with them. Recognition of this gap led to an expansion during the 1980s in Bank staff with institutional skills, in the

81. World Bank, "Project Performance Audit Report: Malawi," Operations Evaluation Department report 9750 (June 18, 1991), p. xix.
82. World Bank, "Country Program Paper: Tanzania" (November 4, 1977), p. 14.
83. World Bank, "Country Program Paper: Kenya" (December 1980), p. 13.
84. World Bank, "Country Program Paper: Zambia" (February 25, 1985), pp. 24–25.

establishment of new divisions to deal with institutions, and in considerable research.[85] As in the case of the education sector, the Bank has considerably strengthened its ability to take a strategic approach to this critical set of issues.

In devising approaches to project implementation, the Bank has faced a dilemma between, on the one hand, the need to press ahead with project execution, and, on the other, the desire to strengthen and support the institutions of government. It is striking that this dilemma has persisted from the 1960s and early 1970s to the present. Indeed, in some respects it is now sharper than ever, as public institutions in some countries have become weaker rather than stronger. What has changed, however, is the Bank's response.

During the period up to the late 1970s, the Bank's response was commonly to encourage and finance a special project unit charged with implementation. Such units can be found in all sectors. The Bank's discomfiture with this approach was apparent in many project appraisal documents, where the intention was ritually stated that the special unit would be absorbed into the parent ministry in due course. These project units have taken various forms: at one extreme is a permanent authority, such as the Kenya Tea Development Authority; more commonly, the units have been less permanent, have been formally located within a ministry, and have reported to a senior official, although they have had their own budgets and budgeting procedures. The units often exist in an uncomfortable parallel with other technical branches. Frequently project units have offered improved terms of employment, thus facilitating staff recruitment but sometimes weakening main government agencies.

In recent years the Bank has more resolutely turned away from such units, as part of a strategic approach to institution building. The National Agricultural Research Project in Kenya (1986, and a second phase that began in 1994) is now more typical: the project is defined as the first stage of a fifteen- to twenty-year program, whose early stages have been primarily concerned with reorganization, staff training, and the introduction of improved management and finance systems.

The persistence of the Bank's concern with institutional issues can be seen in the four countries reviewed. A 1979 overview of Tanzania by Bank staff summarizes the situation:

85. Recent publications reflecting this concern include: Robert M. Lacey, "The Management of Public Expenditures: An Evolving Bank Approach," World Bank, Policy, Planning, and Research Working Paper 46 (1989); John Nellis, "Public Enterprise Reform in Adjustment Lending," World Bank, Policy, Planning, and Research Working Paper 233 (1989); Mary M. Shirley, "The Reform of State-Owned Enterprises: Lessons from World Bank Lending," Policy and Research Series 4, World Bank (1989); Cheryl W. Gray, Lynn S. Khadiagala, and Richard J. Moore, "Institutional Development Work in the World Bank: A Review of 84 Bank Projects," Policy, Research, and External Affairs Working Paper 437 (1990); and Ahmed Galal, "Public Enterprise Reform: Lessons from the Past and Issues for the Future," World Bank Discussion Paper 119 (1991).

At Independence trained manpower was almost non-existent and in spite of an early emphasis on middle level training, the deficit of skilled manpower grew throughout the sixties as the development program increased. With the accelerated expansion of the public sector in the late sixties/early seventies an already thinly stretched bureaucracy had to man a series of new parastatals and ministries were required both to oversee the operations of the new parastatals as well as provide a range of additional services.[86]

In all four countries the functions of the state expanded after independence to encompass more ambitious development aims and a wider range of production and distribution activities. Governments, and the Bank, made assumptions that later turned out to be unrealistic about public sector capacity to undertake them.

There were, however, country differences. In Kenya in the early years, the Bank shared a widespread view that the civil service was overall "a powerful and effective administrative body," and it spoke of the "impressive absorptive capacity of Kenya."[87] As the 1970s progressed, increasing concern was expressed that the development strategies adopted were administration intensive and that institutions were in some cases inadequate. Of the focus on programs to benefit low-income groups, such as those in smallholder agriculture and small-scale industry, it was reported that "this strategy will inevitably subject weak public institutions to ever-increasing pressure. Although by African standards the efficiency of Kenyan government agencies is good, it is nevertheless a matter of concern"; the same report noted that "implementation constraints of the Ministry [of Agriculture] presents perhaps the most serious challenge to our continued lending in this sector."[88] The same concern was reiterated by a high-profile, though ultimately not very influential, Kenya government report of 1982, which found that overextension of public institutions and finances had led to reduced efficiency.[89]

Of the situation in Zambia, the Bank reported in 1985 that

staffing problems, reflecting a variety of constraints, including noncompetitive public sector salaries, lack of comprehensive manpower planning and development, overloading of public sector entities, inadequate programming for staffing needs, and cumbersome design of projects, have had adverse effects on project execution. Projects involving two or more entities have suffered from coordination difficulties. These absorptive capacity constraints must be given much more attention in project design if implementation is to improve in the future.[90]

Part of the Bank's difficulty with weak institutions has been corruption and lack of financial accountability, which have played an increasingly high-profile role in them; it is a difficulty that the Bank and other development organizations have found hard to deal with satisfactorily. Only in recent years has the Bank been

86. World Bank, "Country Program Paper: Tanzania" (December 12, 1979), p. 4.
87. World Bank, "Country Program Paper: Kenya" (June 17, 1975), p. 3.
88. World Bank, "Country Program Paper: Kenya" (January 16, 1978), pp. 12, 15.
89. Kenya Government, *Report and Recommendations of the Working Party on Government Expenditures,* P. Ndegwa, chairman (Nairobi: Government Printer, 1982).
90. World Bank, "Country Program Paper: Zambia" (February 25, 1985), p. 25.

prepared to acknowledge the issue openly; the 1989 report "Sub-Saharan Africa: From Crisis to Sustainable Growth" discusses corruption in the context of the Bank's growing concern with governance.[91] Such acknowledgment would have been inconceivable ten years before, and is only possible now in the context of more robust attitudes taken by some Western governments.

The Bank responded to these obstacles to project implementation and sustainability during the 1980s by gradually taking a more comprehensive approach to government finances (principally through the mechanism of public expenditure reviews) and to public sector management and institution building. In addition, institutional development (ID) components have become more common than before within specific projects; some 90 percent of current projects have ID elements, compared with 72 percent in 1978.[92] It is too early to determine whether the new emphasis will result in more sustainable projects; but the record of the past indicated that there was no alternative but to develop new approaches to a generic problem.

Conclusions

The quarter century reviewed in this chapter has seen considerable achievement in improving the main social indicators in much of the African continent, but as a whole it has been a period of great economic and political disappointment. Both governments and the World Bank have learned a good deal and changed many of their practices, but Africa is still far from achieving sustainable economic growth and reducing its dependence on foreign aid. Indeed, many trends are worryingly in the wrong direction. In context, it has been difficult for the Bank to devise workable development instruments, and by the early 1990s there was uncertainty, perhaps bafflement, among many in the organization over how to proceed in a part of the world that arguably has the greatest need for aid funds but is apparently least able to use them effectively.

Projects alone have not proven to be the key to Africa's development, although for perhaps twenty years the Bank assumed that they were. In all sectors the Bank has found itself impelled, sometimes unwillingly, to involve itself closely with budgetary processes and with the planning and management of public institutions at the heart of government. Reflecting a view among some that its approach to Africa was fundamentally flawed because it misunderstood the nature of African society, the Bank by the late 1980s was paying attention to the nature of government and civil institutions in Africa to try to understand why it continued to find policy and institutional issues so problematic.[93] These have not been easy roles for

91. World Bank, "Sub-Saharan Africa: From Crisis to Sustainable Growth: A Long-Term Perspective Study" (1989).

92. Samuel Paul, "Institutional Development in World Bank Projects: A Cross-Sectoral Review," World Bank, Policy, Research, and External Affairs Working Paper 392 (1990).

93. For an inside view of the issues, see Pierre Landell-Mills, "Governance, Civil Society and Empowerment in Sub-Saharan Africa," paper prepared for the 1992 annual conference

the Bank to take on; different staff skills have been needed, and internal organizational structures have had to be changed to meet the challenge.

The relationships between the Bank and Kenya, Malawi, Tanzania, and Zambia have also undergone transformations, moving through three phases: harmony, reassessment (and sometimes mutual alienation), and (more recently) policy convergence. Projects have both influenced and been influenced by these changes. Initially, problems with the project portfolio were one of the main reasons for the Bank to adopt policy-based lending, whose subsequent dominance led the Bank to put projects in the back seat. Yet structural adjustment operations—the new context for project lending in these countries—hold out the promise of being able to address some policy and institutional questions, while projects are used to address the capacity constraints that remain at the heart of underdevelopment.

Sectoral differences in the Bank's experience have also emerged, and the Bank has responded in different ways. One distinction often identified, and confirmed by this review, is that between the "hard" (engineering and science) sectors and the "soft" (rural development and social) sectors. The contrast between the Bank's experience with education and with highways tends to reinforce the view that the Bank has found hard sectors easier to deal with than soft sectors. Yet the difference is one of degree only: in all three sectors reviewed, the Bank has had to adapt to local social circumstances. In the education and rural sectors, the need to adapt has been pervasive; in the highway sector, the need was to devise workable approaches to maintenance, in particular labor-intensive techniques.

Reviewing across countries and sectors underlines how much the Bank has learned and how much it has altered its lending operations in Africa. At its best in this process of change, the Bank is impressive, establishing a strong research base and defining a strategy that comes in due course to affect its lending operations. Occasionally, however, the Bank has succumbed to the temptation to seek the golden bullet, though this practice is perhaps less common now than it used to be, as the bruising experience of lending in Africa has instilled a strong sense in many staff of the need to take long views. The longer view, in combination with policy and institutional reforms and project investments, is a genuine improvement on what came before. But it requires that the Bank be more consistent in its choice and use of development instruments than it has been sometimes in the past, not least because of the confusion caused among borrowers when the Bank adopts a change of nomenclature or focus.

The power of the Bank to influence both individual governments and approaches to sectors across many countries raises difficult issues of institutional accountability. From the perspective of many aid-dependent borrowers, the Bank is predominant in defining approaches to development and, along with the IMF, in

of the Society for the Advancement of Socio-Economics, Irvine, Calif. For an outside view, see Laurence Cockcroft, *Africa's Way: A Journey from the Past* (London: I. B. Tauris, 1990).

determining the level of financial flows to sectors and to the economy as a whole from multilateral and bilateral sources. In many instances the Bank's role has been benign; where it has gone wrong, as in Tanzania, or when it promoted a generation of area development projects many of which did not work, the Bank has not always been prompt to acknowledge the fact.

In the period under review the Bank has widened its perspective on development problems and on the means by which they can be addressed. In project lending, a main lesson has been that it is not possible to divorce the performance and usefulness of development projects from the wider performance of a country's economy and of the public sector. At one time, some projects were criticized on the grounds that they were "cathedrals in the desert"; the Bank has now learned that although it is difficult enough to build in the desert, it is often impossible to keep the edifice standing after the builders depart. Accordingly, the Bank's diagnosis of why projects have not made the expected contribution to development has come to focus increasingly on issues of public policy, finance, and institutions.

To reiterate the conclusion of a senior minister in Tanzania: "We underestimated the importance of macro-economic policy, and we overestimated our ability to manage things in the public sector."[94] After the late 1970s the Bank came to a similar conclusion about the direction of much of its project lending, devised new instruments that decreased the predominance of projects, took on new skills, and reorganized itself internally to unify project and policy lending. The new approaches recognize that Africa's development will take a long time and must be based on building up domestic capacities in the public and private sectors, on policies and political systems that are consistent over time and that favor investment. Project lending will continue to have an important role in the future as a channel for investment funds, but it will not be the main determinant of whether Africa escapes its trap of underdevelopment.

94. Personal communication to author, 1992.

Statistical Appendix

Table 9-A1. *Total Aid Flows to Sub-Saharan Africa, 1984–90*
Millions of U.S. dollars unless otherwise specified

Type of disbursement	1984	1985	1986	1987	1988	1989	1990
Net ODA (current prices)	8,227	9,525	11,533	13,069	14,801	15,313	17,879
Net ODA (constant 1989 prices)	12,603	14,425	14,110	13,891	14,683	15,313	...
Bilateral (percent)	69.3	68.8	68.7	69.5	69.7	67.4	...
Multilateral (percent)	30.7	31.2	31.3	30.5	30.3	32.6	31.5
IBRD	0.1	0.1	0.0	0.0	0.0	0.0	0.0
IDA	9.2	9.0	11.9	12.5	9.6	10.1	10.6
Net ODA as percentage of GNP	4.2	4.8	6.8	8.7	n.a.	n.a.	...
Net ODA per head (current prices)	20.0	22.5	26.4	29.0	331.8	31.9	...
Net ODA per head (constant 1989 prices)	30.7	34.0	.32.2	30.8	31.5	31.9	...

Source: Organization for Economic Cooperation and Development (OECD), *Geographical Distribution of Financial Flows to Developing Countries*, various years, 1984–90.
n.a. Not available.

Table 9-A2. *Aid Flows to Kenya, 1969–90*
Millions of U.S. dollars unless otherwise specified

Types of disbursement	1969–71[a]	1974–76[b]	1980	1981	1982	1983	1984	1985	1986	1987	1988	1989	1990
Net ODA (current prices)	60	136	396	449	485	400	411	438	455	572	808	972	1,083
Net ODA (constant 1989 prices)	234	314	556	655	724	600	629	663	556	607	802	972	…
Bilateral (percent)	81.8	83.6	69.8	81.2	69.9	85.5	79.2	80.0	85.1	78.4	75.8	63.8	…
Multilateral (percent)	18.2	16.4	30.2	18.8	30.1	14.5	20.8	20.0	14.9	21.6	24.2	36.2	31.7
IBRD (percent)	0.0	0.0	0.3	0.6	0.7	0.2	0.5	0.6	0.2	0.0	0.0	0.0	…
IDA (percent)	10.7	7.6	17.9	3.1	17.1	4.7	8.4	7.6	6.2	12.2	11.7	22.9	…
Net ODA as percentage of GNP	3.9	4.7	5.8	6.9	8.2	6.9	6.9	7.4	6.5	7.5	10.0	12.3	…
Net ODA per head (current prices)	5.4	10.2	23.8	25.9	26.9	21.5	21.2	21.8	21.8	26.4	36.0	41.8	…
Net ODA per head (constant 1989 prices)	20.8	23.5	33.4	37.8	40.2	32.2	32.5	33.0	26.7	28.1	35.7	41.8	…

Source: OECD, *Geographical Distribution of Financial Flows to Developing Countries,* various years, 1969–90.
a. Average for 1969, 1970, 1971.
b. Average for 1974, 1975, 1976.

Table 9-A3. *Aid Flows to Malawi, 1969–90*
Millions of U.S. dollars unless otherwise specified

Types of disbursement	1969–71[a]	1974–76[b]	1980	1981	1982	1983	1984	1985	1986	1987	1988	1989	1990
Net ODA (current prices)	32	56	143	137	121	116	158	113	198	280	366	399	478
Net ODA (constant 1989 prices)	125	128	201	200	181	175	242	171	242	298	363	399	…
Bilateral (percent)	73.4	73.4	52.8	59.7	53.7	48.2	32.6	46.8	42.9	60.7	49.6	45.5	45.1
Multilateral (percent)	26.6	26.6	47.2	40.3	46.3	51.9	67.4	53.2	57.1	39.3	50.4	54.5	54.9
IBRD (percent)	0.0	0.1	2.9	0.4	0.0	0.0	0.0	0.0	0.0	0.0	0.0	0.0	…
IDA (percent)	22.5	18.2	10.0	14.5	21.5	25.0	47.9	28.9	39.3	15.7	16.4	19.3	…
Net ODA as percentage of GNP	9.4	7.9	13.6	12.6	11.5	10.1	13.8	10.5	17.7	23.8	27.5	26.3	…
Net ODA per head (current prices)	7.2	11.1	23.7	22.1	18.9	17.4	22.8	15.7	26.7	36.5	46.0	48.5	…
Net ODA per head (constant 1989 prices)	27.9	25.5	33.3	32.2	28.2	26.1	34.9	23.8	32.6	38.7	45.6	48.5	…

Source: OECD, *Geographical Distribution of Financial Flows to Developing Countries*, various years, 1969–90.
a. Average for 1969, 1970, 1971.
b. Average for 1974, 1975, 1976.

Table 9-A4. *Aid Flows to Tanzania, 1969–90*
Millions of U.S. dollars unless otherwise specified

Types of disbursement	1969–71[a]	1974–76[b]	1980	1981	1982	1983	1984	1985	1986	1987	1988	1989	1990
Net ODA (current prices)	51	244	666	673	684	593	557	486	680	882	981	920	1,154
Net ODA (constant 1989 prices)	197	583	934	981	1,022	889	854	737	832	937	973	920	…
Bilateral (percent)	75.6	80.2	80.2	74.3	72.6	74.8	74.8	78.6	76.3	81.5	80.0	74.8	72.8
Multilateral (percent)	24.4	19.8	19.1	25.7	27.4	25.2	25.2	21.4	23.7	18.5	20.0	25.2	27.2
IBRD (percent)	0.0	0.0	1.8	0.4	0.1	0.0	0.1	0.1	0.0	0.0	0.0	0.0	…
IDA (percent)	16.0	7.1	5.2	11.4	14.3	10.7	9.9	5.8	12.3	9.9	10.0	12.1	…
Net ODA as percentage of GNP	4.0	9.8	13.6	12.5	13.4	9.4	9.7	7.1	14.2	27.6	33.5	34.9	…
Net ODA per head (current prices)	3.9	17.4	35.5	34.7	34.1	28.6	26.0	21.9	29.5	37.0	39.7	35.9	…
Net ODA per head (constant 1989 prices)	15.3	39.6	49.8	50.6	50.9	42.9	39.8	33.2	36.1	39.3	39.4	35.9	…

Source: OECD, *Geographical Distribution of Financial Flows to Developing Countries*, various years, 1969–90.
a. Average for 1969, 1970, 1971.
b. Average for 1974, 1975, 1976.

Table 9-A5. *Aid Flows to Zambia, 1969–90*
Millions of U.S. dollars unless otherwise specified

Types of disbursement	1969–71[a]	1974–76[b]	1980	1981	1982	1983	1984	1985	1986	1987	1988	1989	1990
Net ODA (current prices)	18	70	295	230	317	216	239	328	464	429	478	390	491
Net ODA (constant 1989 prices)	72	159	414	336	473	325	366	497	567	456	474	390	…
Bilateral (percent)	81.5	82.9	79.1	78.2	83.5	84.6	75.9	65.6	75.2	80.6	85.2	80.5	83.2
Multilateral (percent)	18.5	17.1	20.9	21.8	16.5	15.4	24.1	34.4	24.8	19.4	14.8	19.5	16.8
IBRD (percent)	0.0	0.0	0.0	0.0	0.0	0.0	0.0	0.0	0.0	0.0	0.0	0.0	…
IDA (percent)	0.0	0.0	0.5	0.9	2.7	3.8	6.5	20.1	15.9	9.4	1.0	1.0	…
Net ODA as percentage of GNP	1.1	0.8	8.2	5.9	8.7	7.1	9.8	16.3	33.7	24.4	14.4	9.0	…
Net ODA per head (current prices)	4.4	14.0	52.3	39.6	52.6	34.6	36.8	48.6	66.3	59.0	63.3	49.8	…
Net ODA per head (constant 1989 prices)	16.9	32.3	73.4	57.7	78.7	51.8	56.4	73.7	81.0	62.7	62.8	49.8	…

Source: OECD, *Geographical Distribution of Financial Flows to Developing Countries*, various years, 1969–90.
a. Average for 1969, 1970, 1971.
b. Average for 1974, 1975, 1976.

TEN

The World Bank's European Funding

Hilmar Kopper

THE WORLD Bank (or, to be exact, the International Bank for Reconstruction and Development, IBRD) was founded by the leading industrial nations in an attempt to prevent economic crises such as those that occurred between World War I and World War II. In 1944 representatives of forty-four nations assembled at the Monetary and Financial Conference sponsored by the United Nations in Bretton Woods to discuss plans for a new world monetary system. This led to the establishment of the International Monetary Fund (IMF) and the IBRD. These complementary but independent institutions were formed to promote growth and to guarantee monetary stability in the international economy. The two organizations were to serve as pillars of the future world economic system.[1]

The new world monetary order was based on a system of virtually fixed exchange rates, which were adjusted occasionally under certain circumstances. The parities of the various national currencies were expressed in terms of a gold standard or fixed in relation to a currency that could be exchanged for gold, thus making these currencies either directly or indirectly convertible.[2] The IMF was responsible for surveilling these parities, defining permissible fluctuation margins for exchange rates, and recommending the necessary adjustments. After 1971, when the system

The author and the editors would like to thank Michael Fabricius for his contributions to this chapter.

1. Edward S. Mason and Robert E. Asher, *The World Bank since Bretton Woods* (Brookings, 1973), pp. 11–35.

2. Herman van der Wee, *Der gebremste Wohlstand* [Geschichte der Weltwirtschaft im 20. Jahrhundert], vol. 6 (Munich: Deutscher Taschenbuch Verlag 1984), p. 484f.

of fixed parities collapsed, it was replaced by floating exchange rates, and the IMF was given the task of monitoring the operation of the new system. From the beginning the new world monetary system was to be linked to liberal international markets for goods and capital. However, it took some time for the European economies to recover from World War II and bring their payment balances back into equilibrium. Only then could foreign exchange restrictions be lifted.[3]

The objective of the World Bank was to promote urgently needed investment projects, initially focusing on European postwar reconstruction. The Bank commenced operations in Washington in June 1946; one year later, it issued its first loan toward the reconstruction of Western Europe. It quickly became apparent, however, that the funds at the Bank's disposal were insufficient. After the Marshall Plan (the European Recovery program) was under way in 1948, the World Bank began to concentrate on supporting developing countries. However, until well into the 1960s it continued to extend long-term loans to both industrial and developing countries to finance infrastructural measures and development programs. It was not until the end of the 1970s that the Bank's role as the world's preeminent project lender was firmly established.[4]

In looking at the World Bank's operations, interest usually centers on its lending policy and the resulting economic and political implications. But most of the Bank's development lending is limited to the capital subscribed by member states and the funds it is able to borrow on national and international capital markets. Therefore the Bank's lending capacity is directly related to its ability to borrow.[5]

This chapter focuses on the role of European capital markets in the World Bank's funding, beginning with an overview of the Bank's various sources of funding, an outline of the Bank's borrowing strategy, and a chronological survey of its borrowing activities on the world's capital markets. Against this background, the characteristics of the European capital markets and their significance to the Bank's borrowing are presented in more detail. Recent developments are then interpreted with regard to their impact on the Bank's funding, including the establishment of the Euromarket as well as the introduction of financial innovations. The costs of the Bank's borrowing are presented as they developed in the course of its operations. Some concluding remarks emphasize the more salient aspects of the World Bank's European funding and address its prospects.

3. Ibid., pp. 484–89, 505–09, 523–30, 542–60.

4. Deutsche Bundesbank, *Internationale Organisationen und Abkommen in Bereich von Währung und Wirtschaft* (Frankfurt, 1986) p. 47f; and Percy S. Mistry, "The World Bank's Role as a Borrower" (1989), p. 192.

5. According to the World Bank's Articles of Agreement, the Bank's outstanding and disbursed loans must not exceed its subscribed capital and reserves. Contrary to this 1:1 ratio, the risk assets of commercial banks often exceed 15 to 20 times their equity base. Eugene H. Rotberg, "The Financial Operations of the World Bank," in *Bretton Woods Commission Background Papers* (Washington: Bretton Woods Commission, 1994), p. 198.

The World Bank's Borrowings

To finance its operations, the World Bank draws on four sources of funds: paid-in capital, retained earnings, repayment of loans, and borrowing on the world capital markets.

Since the signing of the Articles of Agreement in 1945, the World Bank's authorized capital has grown from $10 billion to roughly $184 billion in fiscal year 1992, of which $152.25 billion was subscribed. Each country's share of capital subscribed consists of a paid-in portion and a callable portion, which may be called in only to meet obligations of the Bank. Initially, member countries had to pay in 20 percent of their capital share; but in the course of three major capital increases (1959, 1980, and 1988), paid-in capital was reduced to 10 percent, 7.5 percent, and 3 percent, respectively. In fiscal year 1992 only about $10 billion of $152.25 billion was paid in. (The percentage of each capital subscription paid in differs from country to country, but this works out to an average of 6.6 percent.)

Though the importance of paid-in capital for the funding of business activities has declined over the years, funds paid in are still important as permanent cost-free equity funds that enhance the credit and profitability of the Bank. The remaining capital share is known as callable capital. It is purely liable capital and forms the basis for the World Bank's credit standing on the capital markets. (No call has ever been necessary to date.)[6] The World Bank's net income is a further source of obtaining funds for lending. Given the consistently high profitability of the Bank, this source has substantially helped finance lending.[7] The same applies to loan repayments: the World Bank has never had a loan loss.

By far the biggest part of the Bank's funding is obtained on the international capital markets. In general, the possibility of drawing on these markets is based on the trust that potential investors place in a borrower. As the first development bank and international organization of its kind, the Bank initially faced substantial difficulties in gaining a prime rating on the capital markets, simply because the existing valuation criteria for risk assessment did not apply. In the initial stage of the Bank's operations, the paid-in capital of member states, especially that of the United States, served as a measure for creditworthiness. At first, the major U.S. rating agencies—whose ratings decisively influence institutional investors' purchasing decisions in the United States—gave World Bank debt a rating of only "A." It was not until 1959 that the much-coveted "AAA" rating was awarded the Bank, and it has held onto it ever since.

On the other capital markets as well, the Bank had to work to achieve a good credit standing to enable its paper to be placed without difficulty and at a good

6. Internationale Bank für Wiederaufbau und Entwicklung, *Die Weltbank* (Frankfurt: Fritz Knapp Verlag, 1963), p. 31; Mistry, "World Bank's Role as a Borrower," p. 191; and International Bank for Reconstruction and Development, *Annual Report 1992*, p. 212.

7. S. Melvin Rines, "The World Bank," in S. Melvin Rines and Christine A. Bogdanowicz-Bindert, eds., *The Supranationals* (London: Euromoney Publications, 1986), p. 73.

price. With this goal in mind, the Bank's decision to have its bonds issued by reliable banking syndicates, which remained virtually unchanged over the years, proved to be wise. Though the Bank realized that it might be paying higher fees owing to the lack of competition, this drawback was outweighed by the fact that syndicate members could be expected to promote the Bank's securities in their own interest. This support applied to the achievement of legal eligibility in the respective capital market as well as to price supports, if necessary.[8] To a large extent, it is also the achievement of the banks in the various syndicates that on many capital markets World Bank issues are offered at conditions only minimally below those of government issues, which traditionally have the best market access. In composing the syndicates, the World Bank usually asked one bank to lead the consortium, basing its decision on the respective bank's market position and placement power. The lead manager then—in agreement with the World Bank—would recruit other banks as members of the syndicate, defining each member's quota and exploring and fixing the conditions under which bonds would be offered.[9]

A publication commemorating the twenty-fifth anniversary of the World Bank provides an illustration of the significance of the syndicate banks in the acceptance of the Bank's bonds: "As an indication of certain differences between U.S. and U.K. investment practices, when a member of the Bank staff suggested that the prospectus should carry a full description of the borrowing institution, the suggestion was waived aside with the assurance that the name of Baring was all that was needed."[10]

The World Bank traditionally obtains most of its funding by floating bond issues of its own. Because it places these funds at the borrowers' (that is, the developing countries') disposal in the long term, it prefers to take up long-term funds at fixed rates. The World Bank borrows in both public and private international capital markets as well as directly from the central banks of its member countries.

The World Bank has traditionally aimed at achieving the greatest possible flexibility by means of diversifying currencies, markets, types of placement, and maturities. This avoidance of any undue dependence has provided the Bank with the best possible terms and conditions. Not surprisingly, the Bank has been trying to borrow as inexpensively as possible, at fixed rates, and at medium- to long-term

8. Mason and Asher, *World Bank since Bretton Woods*, p. 141; Mistry, "World Bank's Role as a Borrower," p. 199; and Eugene H. Rotberg, *The World Bank's Borrowing Program: Some Questions and Answers* (World Bank, September 1979), p. 6ff.

9. For example, as to the role of the lead manager in syndicates in Germany, the Bundesbank states, "Lead management comprises the handling of all syndicate business, especially negotiations with the issuer, the invitation to underwrite the issue, transactions with the underwriters, allocation of underwriting shares, bookkeeping for the issue, monitoring payments, etc." "Erklärung der Bundesbank zu DM-Emissionen," *Monatsberichte der Deutschen Bundesbank* (July 1992), p. 39.

10. Mason and Asher, *World Bank since Bretton Woods*, p. 139. The British investment bank Baring Brothers was the lead manager of the syndicate consisting of six banking houses for the first World Bank bond issue on the U.K. market in fiscal 1951.

maturities. To minimize its borrowing costs by identifying the most favorable opportunities and the best timing, the Bank traditionally bases its borrowing decisions on the broadest possible information gathered continuously from the world's capital markets. However, the range of options it can choose from has always been subject to the restrictions it has faced regarding access to various capital markets. Given the possibility of unforeseeable restrictions to the Bank's access to capital, it has traditionally tended to demand more capital than currently needed, thus often taking the opportunities it encountered.[11]

Volume and Shift in Geographic Concentration

In the first years of the World Bank's operations in particular, undertaking widespread financial transactions was impossible; the U.S. market was the only one available for borrowing. After 1945 there were no functioning capital markets in Europe or Japan. It was only after their national economies had stabilized in the 1950s that the European governments were able to gradually lift restrictions on trade and capital movements. In late 1958 Germany and most other European countries made their currencies convertible and linked them to the gold-dollar standard. This was the cornerstone for setting up free foreign exchange and capital markets with as few restrictions and as little intervention as possible from national monetary authorities.[12]

Throughout the 1950s, the American market remained the major source of borrowing. Of the World Bank's first $1 billion of bonds issued, $835 million were in U.S. dollars and only $165 million in other currencies. That is not to say, however, that European investors were not interested: as early as 1951, substantial amounts of World Bank paper were already being sold outside the United States.[13] In fiscal year 1953 European banks took part in the syndicate for a World Bank dollar issue for the first time; of the $175 million dollar bonds offered that year, $50 million were sold to investors in Europe.[14] A year later, the World Bank placed an entire $50 million issue with private and sovereign investors outside the United States for the first time.[15]

The uneven picture the World Bank's borrowing presented in the early years is only partly explained by the difficulties and restrictions on the international capital markets at the time. It is also a result of the changes the World Bank's business

11. Rotberg, "Financial Operations of the World Bank," p. 221.

12. van der Wee, *Der gebremste Wohlstand,* pp. 484ff, 505ff.

13. In the 1950s, European commercial banks became significant and regular buyers of IBRD dollar bonds for their trust account clients. Rotberg, "Financial Operations of the World Bank," p. 201; and IBRD, *Sixth Annual Report 1950–1951,* p. 44.

14. IBRD, *Ninth Annual Report 1953–1954,* p. 40.

15. IBRD, *Tenth Annual Report 1954–1955,* p. 37.

activities underwent over the years. By the end of the 1950s the Bank had evolved
from a bank for the reconstruction of Europe to an intermediary between industrial
and developing countries. Its range of activities involved not only providing and
arranging loans but also offering comprehensive project assistance, including
economic and technical as well as political and social components. Looking back, it
is clear that the World Bank's borrowing rose steadily in the long run, but this
growth often took place in leaps and bounds.

At the end of its first decade of operation, the Bank had borrowed only
$1.014 billion and (outside of the U.S. market) had issued only in Switzerland, the
United Kingdom, Canada, and the Netherlands. This first era of World Bank
activity was greatly influenced by the Bank's third president, Eugene R. Black, who
headed the Bank from 1949 to 1962. During his tenure, Black charted a new course
for the Bank after its uncertain beginnings and shaped the fundamental structure
of its business operations. At the end of his term, the Bank's borrowing on the
American market came to a halt. Between 1962 and 1965, no long-term dollar
borrowings took place in the U.S. market, mainly because the balance of payments
situation in the United States made it increasingly difficult to obtain approval from
the monetary authorities to issue foreign bonds.[16] Even the World Bank, which
enjoyed special privileges in many respects, was affected.[17] At the same time the
Bank registered relatively high liquidity; in fiscal year 1964, for instance, it did not
have to raise any new funds to finance its operations.

With the end of U.S. predominance in funding the World Bank, the European
capital markets became increasingly important for its borrowing. The Bank's relative
inactivity on all capital markets came to an end in 1965 with issues in the United States,
Canada, Switzerland, the United Kingdom, and Germany, although the issue costs and
the borrowing volumes on the latter markets were by no means a match for U.S.
conditions. At 5.5 percent on the German market, for instance, borrowing costs were
1 percent higher than in the United States, the highest rate the World Bank had yet
paid. However, the Bank's management considered it important to establish a presence
on these financial markets as early as possible to build up good credit. The Bank
expected that these markets would steadily gain in significance in the years to come.[18]

Although the U.S. capital market with its low interest rates remained the World
Bank's preferred source of borrowing, by 1969 the Swiss and German capital

16. Rotberg, "Financial Operations of the World Bank," p. 202.

17. Internationale Bank für Wiederaufbau und Entwicklung, *Jahresbericht 1964–1965*,
p. 14; Mason and Asher, *World Bank since Bretton Woods*, p. 136; and Internationale Bank
für Wiederaufbau und Entwicklung, *Jahresbericht 1965–1966*, p. 39. "World Bank issues
were exempt on the understanding that the Bank would not sell in the U.S. market portions
of loans for on-lending to countries whose borrowing was subject to the IET" (Interest
Equalization Tax); M. S. Mendelsohn, *Money on the Move* (McGraw-Hill, 1980), p. 32.

18. Mason and Asher, *World Bank since Bretton Woods*, p. 140f.; Mistry, "World Bank's Role
as a Borrower," p. 197ff.; Internationale Bank für Wiederaufbau und Entwicklung, *Jahresbericht
1963–64*, p. 16; and IBRD, *Borrowing Operations FY 1987–91, A Retrospective*, p. 2.

markets had joined the American market as the major sources of the Bank's financial funds. By then, the World Bank had also placed five bond issues in the Netherlands (1954, 1955, 1961, 1962, 1968), one in Belgium (1959), one in Italy (1961), and one in Sweden (1967). The Bank's borrowing in Austria in 1963 had been dollar denominated; its plans for an issue in France in 1965 had failed.[19] By June 30, 1969, twenty-five years after its foundation, the World Bank had borrowed a total of $7.34 billion, nearly one-quarter ($1.73 billion) of which was in European currencies (table 10-1).

A period of reorientation in the history of the Bank began in 1968 with the presidency of Robert McNamara, who served in this capacity until 1981. He set out to redesign the Bank's lending policy, strongly expanding its lending volume. This in turn was reflected by increased borrowing, which tripled within a few years. The World Bank's annual gross borrowing figure grew from $1.2 billion in fiscal 1969 to $3.5 billion in fiscal 1975 (table 10-2). This meant that the opportunities at hand had to be analyzed much more cautiously and also called for long-term funding plans. In 1970 the World Bank launched its first yen issue, placing it with the Bank of Japan. Within a short time, Japan joined the United States and the Federal Republic of Germany as one of the three biggest suppliers of capital for the World Bank. Between fiscal years 1969 and 1971 Germany and Japan provided 55 percent of the Bank's total borrowing.[20]

In November 1973 the price of oil on world markets quadrupled, bringing on the first oil crisis. This caused balance of payments shifts not only in the developing countries but also in many industrial states, which in turn upset international capital flows. For the World Bank it meant shifting its borrowing emphasis to central banks and governments, at times relying solely on them. At the same time, the Bank turned to new capital markets in the oil-exporting countries by issuing in local currency as well as in deutsche marks, Swiss francs, and U.S. dollars. In so doing, it helped to recycle at least some of the "petrodollars" into international financial circles.[21] This shift in emphasis, though weaker, was continued in fiscal year 1975 and coincided with a doubling of borrowing compared with previous years. It was not until 1976 that the capital markets again started supplying the majority (that is, 61 percent) of borrowed capital.[22] Borrowing in the oil-exporting countries dropped sharply after 1975 and virtually ceased after 1980; meanwhile, public and private capital markets in Germany, Switzerland, and Japan emerged as the major and most reliable sources of World Bank borrowing.[23]

19. Mason and Asher, *World Bank since Bretton Woods*, p. 140f.

20. Mistry, "World Bank's Role as a Borrower," p. 205.

21. van der Wee, *Der gebremste Wohlstand*, p. 561f.; Mendelsohn, *Money on the Move*, p. 54f.; and Mistry, "World Bank's Role as a Borrower," p. 205ff.

22. Internationale Bank für Wiederaufbau und Entwicklung, *Jahresbericht 1975–76*, p. 104.

23. Rotberg, "Financial Operations of the World Bank," p. 203.

Table 10-1. Borrowings by International Bank for Reconstruction and Development, Fiscal Years 1948–71,[a] by Currency
Millions of U.S. dollar equivalents

Currency	1948	1949	1950	1951	1952	1953	1954	1955	1956	1957	1958	1959	1960	1961	1962	1963	1964	1965	1966	1967	1968	1969	1970	1971	Total/currency
U.S. dollars	250.0	...	...	50.0	150.0	50.0	175.0	50.0	...	275.0	650.0	303.0	282.5	508.0	200.0	110.0	100.0	398.4	234.7	482.0	590.4	587.0	349.5	375.0	6,270.5
Swiss francs	4.0	...	6.6	...	11.6	11.6	34.8	...	11.6	46.5	...	23.3	14.0	45.1	46.5	...	...	14.0	...	21.7	29.1	18.6	...	...	339.0
U.K. pounds	...	...	...	14.0	...	...	...	14.0	...	...	...	...	28.0	...	...	...	...	...	...	...	...	...	...	...	56.0
Canadian dollars	...	...	...	...	13.6	...	22.7	13.6	...	...	...	...	...	...	...	...	...	23.1	18.5	18.5	13.9	...	...	...	123.9
Dutch guilders	...	...	...	...	...	...	...	10.5	10.5	...	...	...	...	13.8	...	11.0	...	...	...	11.0	11.0	...	...	33.2	90.0
German deutsche marks	...	...	...	...	...	...	...	...	...	...	...	95.2	50.4	220.2	...	...	...	162.5	34.8	32.0	75.9	561.0	38.3	294.9	1,565.2
Belgian francs	...	...	...	...	...	...	...	...	...	...	...	10.0	...	...	...	...	...	...	...	...	...	...	...	...	10.0
Italian lire	...	...	...	...	...	...	...	...	...	...	...	...	...	...	24.0	...	...	...	...	...	...	...	...	...	24.0
Swedish kronor	...	...	...	...	...	...	...	...	...	...	...	...	...	...	...	...	...	...	...	...	14.5	...	...	...	14.5
Kuwaiti dinars	...	...	...	...	...	...	...	...	...	...	...	...	...	...	...	...	...	...	...	...	...	42.0	...	...	42.0
Japanese yen	...	...	...	...	...	...	...	...	...	...	...	...	...	...	...	...	...	...	...	...	...	...	200.0	219.0	419.0
Libyan dinars	...	...	...	...	...	...	...	...	...	...	...	...	...	...	...	...	...	...	...	...	...	...	...	28.0	28.0
Total borrowing	254.0	...	6.6	64.0	175.2	61.6	232.5	88.1	22.1	321.5	650.0	431.5	374.9	787.1	270.5	121.0	100.0	498.0	288.0	554.2	734.8	1,208.6	735.0[b]	1,368.0	9,447.2
Total borrowing in European currencies	4.0	...	6.6	14.0	11.6	11.6	34.8	24.5	22.1	46.5	...	128.5	92.4	279.1	70.5	11.0	...	176.5	34.8	53.7	130.5	579.6	38.3	328.1	2,098.7

Source: International Bank for Reconstruction and Development, annual reports, 1948–71.

a. Fiscal years cover period from July to June. Fiscal year 1948, for example, covers July 1, 1947, to June 30, 1948.

b. The annual report for 1969–70 does not give complete details on the breakdown of total borrowing.

Table 10-2. *Borrowings by International Bank for Reconstruction and Development, Fiscal Years 1972–92,[a] by Currency*
Millions of U.S. dollar equivalents

Currency	Fiscal year																					Total/currency
	1972	1973	1974	1975	1976	1977	1978	1979	1980	1981	1982	1983	1984	1985	1986	1987	1988	1989	1990	1991	1992	
U.S. dollars	795.9	440.0	659.3	2,515.0	2,154.5	2,787.5	1,467.8	665.8	1,202.8	1,111.0	3,459.0	5,268.1	3,181.3	3,486.8	3,342.5	3,077.9	3,545.4	3,641.7	4,157.8	9,552.2	9,357.1	65,869.4
German deutsche marks	341.4	371.4	220.3	512.2	859.3	1,394.1	1,119.5	1,172.4	2,183.2	1,437.0	1,030.5	1,195.1	1,532.7	1,659.3	1,731.3	1,392.1	1,167.0	701.2	1,706.0	909.1	478.6	23,113.7
Swiss francs	140.9	30.8	177.5	120.6	441.6	532.0	362.8	1,546.3	964.2	962.5	1,565.4	1,397.8	1,644.6	1,952.7	1,871.4	1,494.7	1,117.0	623.2	940.0	1,524.5	489.6	19,900.1
Italian lire	…	43.0	32.5	…	…	…	…	…	…	…	…	…	…	51.2	27.7	…	242.0	218.7	788.4	1,017.8	1,595.9	4,017.2
Dutch guilders	…	61.6	…	…	167.2	…	40.1	…	…	251.9	650.9	702.6	68.9	758.8	643.2	552.2	215.4	285.0	157.6	182.6	…	5,454.6
U.K. pounds	16.6	…	…	…	…	…	…	…	…	215.8	310.5	168.6	452.2	364.5	130.5	153.2	589.9	231.9	317.6	393.3	…	3,352.0
European Currency Units	24.0	…	…	…	…	…	…	…	…	…	…	…	129.9	221.0	399.6	161.6	167.3	232.2	384.4	…	923.9	2,619.9
Spanish pesetas	…	…	…	…	…	…	…	…	…	…	…	…	…	…	…	…	83.1	373.5	232.1	267.7	144.4	1,100.8
French francs	30.9	…	…	…	…	…	…	…	…	…	…	…	…	…	134.7	…	184.1	146.9	179.3	185.5	175.4	1,036.8
Belgian francs	35.0	24.5	…	…	…	…	…	…	…	…	…	42.1	73.4	50.5	113.5	165.4	132.1	…	…	…	…	636.5
Austrian schillings	…	…	…	…	…	…	…	…	81.0	…	…	61.0	…	83.6	52.1	28.5	75.3	…	84.3	…	…	465.8
Swedish kronor	…	…	17.8	…	…	…	…	…	…	…	…	…	…	…	156.2	43.1	…	…	…	71.1	86.4	374.6
Finnish markkaa	…	…	…	…	…	…	…	…	…	…	…	…	…	…	…	66.1	148.0	140.7	…	…	…	354.8
Portuguese escudos	…	…	…	…	…	…	…	…	…	…	…	…	…	…	…	…	…	…	…	…	227.8	227.8
Luxembourg francs	…	…	…	…	…	…	…	…	…	…	…	…	18.0	15.8	27.1	26.8	54.9	25.5	28.5	…	…	196.6
Danish kroner	…	…	…	…	…	…	…	…	…	…	…	…	…	17.4	53.2	…	119.6	…	…	…	…	190.2
Norwegian kroner	…	…	…	…	…	…	…	…	…	…	17.2	…	…	29.4	29.5	…	…	…	…	…	…	76.1
Japanese yen	150.1	605.1	460.6	121.0	188.6	7.0	646.0	1,700.3	742.2	1,090.6	1,381.1	1,325.9	1,700.2	2,090.4	1,854.4	1,853.9	2,364.1	2,070.8	2,140.3	1,656.7	3,618.7	27,768.0
Canadian dollars	69.4	…	…	…	…	…	…	…	…	…	…	130.7	228.5	304.4	147.0	180.3	347.0	209.6	253.1	131.1	…	2,001.1
Australian dollars	…	…	…	…	…	…	…	…	…	…	…	…	…	…	51.1	125.0	174.5	119.2	286.5	132.1	…	888.4
Kuwaiti dinars	140.0	121.6	84.4	…	…	…	…	…	…	…	105.9	…	…	…	…	…	105.3	…	…	…	…	557.2
Hong Kong dollars	…	…	…	…	…	…	…	…	…	…	…	…	…	…	…	…	…	64.0	64.1	77.4	64.5	270.0
Libyan dinars	…	…	101.3	…	…	…	…	…	…	…	…	…	101.3	…	…	…	…	…	…	…	…	202.6
N.Z. dollars	…	…	…	…	…	…	…	…	…	…	…	…	…	…	…	…	…	45.5	…	149.3	…	194.8
Saudi riyals	…	…	…	140.8	…	…	…	…	…	…	…	…	…	…	…	…	…	…	…	…	…	140.8
Venezuelan bolivars	…	…	23.3	100.0	…	…	…	…	…	…	…	…	…	…	…	…	…	…	…	…	…	123.3
U.A.E. dirhams	…	…	76.0	…	…	…	…	…	…	…	…	…	…	…	…	…	…	…	…	…	…	76.0
Lebanese livres	…	24.9	…	…	…	…	…	…	…	…	…	…	…	…	…	…	…	…	…	…	…	24.9
Total borrowing	1,744.2	1,722.9	1,853.0	3,509.6	3,811.2	4,720.6	3,636.2	5,084.6	5,173.4	5,068.8	8,520.5	10,291.9	9,831	11,085.8	10,608.8	9,320.8	10,832	9,285.8	11,720	16,250.4	17,162.3[b]	161,234.0
Total borrowing in European currencies	588.8	531.3	448.1	632.8	1,468.1	1,926.1	1,522.4	2,718.7	3,228.4	2,867.2	3,574.5	3,567.2	4,619.7	5,204.2	5,213.8	4,083.7	4,295.7	3,135.0	4,818.2	4,551.6	4,122.0	63,117.5

Source: International Bank for Reconstruction and Development, annual reports, 1972–92.
a. Fiscal years cover period from July to June. Fiscal year 1948, for example, covers July 1, 1947, to June 30, 1948.
b. The increase in total borrowing of more than $5 billion in 1991 and 1992 results from the fact that the figures in the respective annual reports do not include the difference in outstanding short-term borrowing in comparison with earlier years, but total outstanding short-term borrowing.

In the 1980s the bank's borrowing took another substantial leap, doubling from roughly $5 billion in fiscal year 1979 to $10.3 billion in 1983. This time, growth was attributable to wider activity and increased lending during the debt crisis of the 1980s, but above all it was related to a strong increase in the repayment of debt due. In those turbulent years the Bank's profile changed. It was no longer merely a financial broker that took in fixed-income funds with medium- and longer-term maturities and then lended long term. Instead, it became a financial institution still aiming for maturities of two, five, or more years for its liabilities but beginning to make use of new financing instruments to increase the profitability of the funds at its disposal. The Bank pursued this policy so successfully that by the end of the 1980s its profits from financial transactions exceeded its return on lending.[24]

Borrowing from Central Banks and Government Agencies

Because large-scale access to the capital markets was initially out of the question, the World Bank sought other funding possibilities. It approached its member states with the aim of borrowing short-term funds and issuing bonds and notes against the foreign exchange reserves of central banks or individual governments.[25] The Bank obtained its first funds from this source in 1953; with a maturity of three years, these were the first shorter-term funds ever taken up by the Bank. The first issue, aimed especially at this customer group, consisted of two-year bonds, floated in September 1956, with a volume of $75 million. It was also the second dollar bond completely sold outside the United States; sixteen central banks took up $52 million, with the rest assumed by private investors. There were six further issues up to 1958 in which private investors were also allowed to participate. Since then, however, they have no longer been eligible for these issues, because the paper can be placed without difficulty with central banks, government agencies, and international institutions. In addition, the exclusion of private lenders enables the Bank to achieve lower interest payments. These issues of two-year bonds formed the Bank's only short-term borrowings until 1982.

It did not take long for the Bank to realize that central bank borrowing was a growing and comparatively stable market and thus a relatively reliable source of capital.[26] This source was particularly important in the aftermath of the first oil crisis. Another reason for the World Bank to shift its borrowing emphasis to central banks and governments during the early 1970s was to avoid saturating private capital markets with its paper.[27] In fiscal year 1972, 32 percent of its funds were

24. Mistry, "World Bank's Role as a Borrower," p. 208.

25. IBRD, *Third Annual Report 1947–1948*, p. 28.

26. Mason and Asher, *World Bank since Bretton Woods*, p. 142; and IBRD, *Twelfth Annual Report 1956–1957*, p. 12.

27. Mistry, "World Bank's Role as a Borrower," p. 205; and Rotberg, "Financial Operations of the World Bank," p. 203.

supplied by these two sources, which increased to 59 percent in 1973 and to 80 percent in 1974. However, this proved to be only a temporary shift, and by the latter half of the 1970s the private capital markets had regained their important position in refunding the Bank's activities.

Overall, between fiscal years 1972 and 1992, the World Bank placed issues totaling $33.2 billion with central banks and government agencies, which accounted for nearly one-fifth of its borrowing in this period. The biggest single suppliers of funds were Deutsche Bundesbank and Bank of Japan. In fiscal 1992, medium- and long-term placements with central banks and governments amounted to more than $1.3 billion out of medium- and long-term borrowing of roughly $11.8 billion. Since 1984, via the so-called Central Bank Facility, these sources have also provided the Bank with short-term funds of up to one year. In 1992 outstanding borrowings under this program had reached the agreed-upon ceiling of $2.6 billion.[28] However, the borrowing under this facility constituted only a small share of the Bank's total borrowings. The bulk of the Bank's funding was borrowed on capital markets. The role of the European capital markets in this context is addressed in the next section.

Capital Markets in Europe

What are the factors determining the World Bank's funding on European capital markets? To understand the intricacies that characterized the Bank's borrowing in this field, particularly in its first decades, it is important to note that the Bank often had only restricted access to the public capital markets, or none at all. The Bank's decisions on where to borrow were based not only on its interest in minimizing costs by looking for the most favorable interest rates and maturities, but also by strategic considerations (for example, the importance of introducing World Bank paper to new markets). At the same time, in its access to national capital markets the Bank was and is subject to national legal provisions relating to nonresident issues and the respective government's approval. This latter requirement arises from the Bank's Articles of Agreement, which require it to obtain explicit permission of each government in whose currency or market it intends to borrow, regardless of whether that market is highly restricted or very liberal. In the case of Euroissues, all countries whose currency or banks are involved have to approve the issue.[29]

A government can restrict the placement of nonresident issues along several different lines of macroeconomic reasoning. For example, if there is a balance of payments deficit, the government might want to avoid the additional strain that

28. Internationale Bank für Wiederaufbau und Entwicklung, *Jahresbericht 1992*, pp. 74–77; and IBRD, *Borrowing Operations FY 1980–89, A Retrospective*, p. 2.

29. Rotberg, "Financial Operations of the World Bank," p. 204.

would result from increasing capital exports. Excessive calls on the external liquidity of the central bank and of the respective capital market can conflict with the goal of monetary stability. Therefore the possible repercussions of large-scale lending by international institutions for the financial stability of the creditor countries are often anticipated with particular care. Moreover, the government might restrict its capital market for nonresident issues to promote the investment of capital at home.

Other considerations apply to the World Bank in particular. For example, the Bank's access to individual capital markets was sometimes restricted because of political disagreements between the Bank and the respective government with regard to the Bank's lending to specific countries. In some cases, the Bank's access has been conditioned by its access to other markets or currencies out of "burden sharing" considerations. In addition, increasing competition from other borrowers (such as supranational institutions and other development banks with close ties to some governments) has led to a restriction of the Bank's funding in the respective national markets.[30]

On the other hand, the restrictions imposed on the World Bank's access to capital markets should not be overestimated. The increasing international integration has been accompanied by an overall liberalization of the world's capital markets, thus reducing the possibilities of national governments controlling the movement of capital. Therefore restrictions on the part of governments were more important in the first decades of the Bank's borrowing than in recent years.[31] In addition, a government's restrictions on the World Bank's access to borrowing were often counterbalanced by that government's general support for the World Bank as a multilateral lending institution. After all, the Bank's member countries have an interest in ensuring its ability to operate according to its Articles of Agreement. Overall, the World Bank has enjoyed unparalleled access to world capital markets. In 1993 it was twice as large a borrower in international capital markets as any other single borrower; and in every country in which it borrows, it is the largest nonresident borrower.[32]

The various European capital markets and their individual characteristics are presented in the order they emerged in the Bank's funding.

Switzerland

The World Bank launched its first borrowing operation on a capital market outside of the United States in Switzerland, which before World War II had been the third largest international capital market after London and New York. With its

---

30. Ibid., pp. 206–08.

31. Richard O'Brien, *Global Financial Integration: The End of Geography* (New York: Council on Foreign Relations Press, 1992).

32. Rotberg, "Financial Operations of the World Bank," p. 208.

policy of neutrality, a stable economy and currency, and a legal framework conducive to financial transactions, Switzerland continued to attract substantial nonresident funds after 1945. The Swiss government kept its interest rates below those of other European countries, at times even below U.S. rates. Its low interest rate structure and the Swiss banks' traditional placement strength among private and institutional investors quickly allowed the Swiss capital market to reassert its importance.[33] Although Switzerland did not become a member of the World Bank until 1992, it recognized the Bank's legal capacity and character as early as 1951, according it rights on the Swiss market similar to those on the markets of the Bank's member states.[34]

The background to this arrangement included two Swiss franc issues that were not offered officially via the capital market but were privately placed. In June 1948 the World Bank had issued 2.5 percent serial bonds with a volume of SFr 17 million, assumed by the Bank for International Settlements.[35] The second issue, in March 1950, consisted of 2.5 percent serial bonds with a volume of SFr 28.5 million, which were taken up by the three leading Swiss banks and the Bank for International Settlements.[36] The first public placement of a World Bank bond on the Swiss capital market took place in 1951, with an issue amounting to SFr 50 million at an interest rate of 3.5 percent and a twelve-year maturity. The issue was strongly oversubscribed and, like all following issues, was sold by a Swiss banking syndicate lead-managed by Swiss Bank Corporation, Crédit Suisse, and Union Bank of Switzerland.[37] This is the biggest and most important of the four Swiss banking syndicates that place issues on the tightly regulated market for foreign bonds.

Switzerland is the biggest lender in relation to the size of its national capital market, but there are certain restrictions on the issue of foreign bonds. For example, the Swiss National Bank periodically determines the "appropriate" aggregate volume of capital exports. Foreign borrowings of SFr 10 million or more are subject to formal Swiss National Bank authorization, but applications are seldom turned down. Also, in the early 1970s only one medium-sized issue was allowed per year, and before 1985 the volume of individual issues was limited; in fact, foreign bonds may be placed only if a Swiss bank is lead manager and the other

33. Charles P. Kindleberger, *A Financial History of Western Europe* (George Allen & Unwin, 1984), p. 449; Martin Körner, "Schweiz," in Hans Pohl, ed., *Europäische Bankengeschichte* (Frankfurt: Fritz Knapp Verlag, 1993), p. 556f; and Ernst Zbinden and Werner Stricker, "The Bond Markets of Switzerland," in Stuart K. McLean, ed., *The European Bond Markets*, 5th ed. (Chicago: Probus Publishing Company, 1993), pp. 1358ff, 1395.

34. Internationale Bank für Wiederaufbau und Entwicklung, *Die Weltbank*, p. 93; and IBRD, *Sixth Annual Report 1950–1951*, p. 44.

35. IBRD, *Third Annual Report 1947–1948*, p. 27.

36. IBRD, *Fifth Annual Report 1949–1950*, p. 40.

37. "Neue Weltbankanleihe in der Schweiz," *Zeitschrift für das gesamte Kreditwesen*, vol. 8.2 (December 1, 1955), p. 16.

members of the syndicate are domiciled in Switzerland.[38] As a result of resistance
on the part of the Swiss National Bank and the Swiss federal government, there is
no Euromarket for Swiss francs. But because of its strong currency and low, stable
interest rates, Switzerland is still very attractive for foreign borrowers—so much so
that since 1978 its market for foreign bonds has become the second largest source
of funds after the Eurodollar market.[39]

The Swiss capital market is one of the major sources of funding for the World
Bank, with private placements being of particular importance. Whereas private
placements usually may range from SFr 20 million to 200 million, the World Bank
is exempted from observing this ceiling. In the use of its currency for direct
placements with official sources, Switzerland has turned out to be quite liberal. A
typical feature of the Swiss bond market is that the volumes of individual issues are
comparatively small because the monetary authorities used to limit the size of
individual issues to give investors a wider selection.[40] As a result, it has been
unusual for a publicly offered Bank bond to exceed SFr 200 million. With regard to
the World Bank's swap operations, the Swiss authorities have taken a relaxed
stance.[41]

Between fiscal years 1972 and 1992, the World Bank borrowed a total of
$19.9 billion in Swiss francs, with public offerings accounting for $4.27 billion and
$9.21 billion from private placements.[42] More than $6 billion were placements with
central banks and government agencies, roughly $95 million were short-term
funds, and the rest were placements in OPEC states.

United Kingdom

The first public World Bank bonds issued outside the United States were floated
on the capital market in London in May 1951: bonds in the amount of £5 million at
an interest rate of 3.5 percent and a maturity of twenty years, which the British
capital market took up without any difficulty.[43] The bond issue also held its ground
successfully on the secondary market. When the Bank launched a second bond

38. Peter Gallant, *The Eurobond Market* (Cambridge, England: Woodhead-Faulkner,
1988), p. 104; and World Bank, *Recent Developments in Foreign and International Bond
Markets and Implications thereof for IBRD Funding* (December 1981).

39. George Ugeaux, "Supranationals in the Primary Bond Market," in Rines and Bogdanowicz-Bindert, eds., *The Supranationals*, p. 25; IBRD, *Seventh Annual Report 1951–
1952*, p. 38; and Bryan de Caires, ed., *The Guide to International Capital Markets 1989*
(London: Euromoney Publications, 1989), pp. 159–63.

40. Kindleberger, *Financial History of Western Europe*, p. 449; and "Zur Freizügigkeit im
Kapitalverkehr der Bundesrepublik mit dem Ausland," *Monatsberichte der Deutschen Bundesbank* (July 1985), p. 23f.

41. World Bank, *Recent Developments in Foreign and International Bond Markets*.

42. Based on the evaluation of data from the relevant annual reports.

43. IBRD, *Sixth Annual Report 1950–1951*, p. 43.

issue three years later in a bull market, the only difference in the terms and conditions was that the yield differential vis-à-vis British government bonds (known as gilts) had been reduced by half. The fact that, on the basis of the Bretton Woods Agreement, World Bank bonds were exempt from British withholding tax for nonresidents—an advantage that not even domestic government bonds could offer at the time—made them particularly attractive to foreign investors.[44] The third bond issue was launched in 1959, for £10 million at 5 percent interest and with a twenty-three-year maturity. This bond issue was rather expensive for the World Bank, but it was probably considered a good opportunity to strengthen the market's interest in Bank paper.[45] All three issues were managed by a syndicate of London banks led by Baring Brothers & Co., Hambros Bank, Lazard Brothers & Co., Morgan Grenfell & Co., N.M. Rothschild & Sons, and J. Henry Schroder & Co.[46]

The British authorities had allowed these bond issues despite tight regulations and continuing strict exchange controls. Thereafter, the London capital market was not accessible to the World Bank for some time. Contrary to the Bank's earlier expectation of tapping the London capital market regularly, the next issue was not launched until 1972, at 8 percent for £10 million with a five-year maturity. After 1972, the British domestic market was closed to all foreign bonds. In the same year, the Eurosterling market was introduced; however, the weakness of the pound and high interest rates prevented its full development until late 1977, when the second Eurosterling bond was placed.[47] Finally, in 1979, the British government enacted a program of reform to deregulate the U.K. financial markets. It began with the removal of exchange controls, which had hampered the domestic bond market, and led to the simplification of the Bank of England's authorization procedure. However, it was not until high interest rates had come down in 1980 that the Bank returned to the British domestic bond market (in 1981), and it approached the Eurosterling market for the first time in 1983. The World Bank has been a regular customer on both markets ever since, with the distinctions between the two gradually disappearing.[48] The Bank of England requires sterling-denominated issues to be lead-managed by a U.K.-based firm or a foreign-owned firm satisfying its

44. *The Economist,* July 17, 1954, p. 216.

45. *The Economist,* December 12, 1959, p. 1092.

46. Internationale Bank für Wiederaufbau und Entwicklung, *Die Weltbank,* p. 93f; and IBRD, *Sixth Annual Report 1950–1951,* p. 43.

47. Mason and Asher, *World Bank since Bretton Woods,* p. 139; Mendelsohn, *Money on the Move,* pp. 54, 137; de Caires, ed., *Guide to International Capital Markets 1989,* p. 165; Gallant, *Eurobond Market,* p. 95ff; Rotberg, "Financial Operations of the World Bank," p. 202; and IBRD, *Annual Report 1971–1972,* p. 70.

48. *Midland Bank Review,* September 1983, p. 24; "Zur Freizügigkeit im Kapitalverkehr der Bundesrepublik mit dem Ausland," *Monatsberichte der Deutschen Bundesbank* (July 1985), p. 23ff; and Stuart McLean and others, "The Bond Markets of the United Kingdom," in McLean, ed., *European Bond Markets,* pp. 1413f, 1432.

regulations. Out of fifteen World Bank issues launched on the Euromarket between 1982 and 1992, twelve were placed by issue syndicates lead-managed by
Baring Brothers.[49]

Between fiscal years 1972 and 1992, the World Bank borrowed $3.35 billion in
sterling issues. Of that total, $968 million consisted of public offers or other
placements on the domestic market, and funds amounting to $2.292 billion were
taken up on the Eurosterling market. A total of $92.1 million was placed in 1982
and 1983 with central banks or government agencies.[50] From the World Bank's
borrowing perspective, sterling has played a modest role, accounting for not more
than roughly 3 to 5 percent of total borrowings in each year since fiscal 1981. The
nominal cost of sterling borrowings has been similar to that for U.S. dollars.[51]

The Netherlands

The third national capital market in Europe that the World Bank approached to
meet its financing needs was the Dutch market. It was made particularly attractive
by the government's policy of low interest rates and the fact that since the conception of the bond market in the sixteenth century no withholding tax had ever been
levied there.[52] In 1954, a syndicate of fourteen banks under the management of
Nederlandsche Handel-Maatschappij offered the first World Bank bond issue for
Fl 40 million with a life of fifteen years and an interest rate of 3.5 percent. The
second issue followed only one year later, also for Fl 40 million and with a
3.5 percent coupon but a maturity of twenty years.[53] It then took until 1961 for the
next issue to be launched in the Netherlands: fixed-income securities in Dutch
guilder in the amount of Fl 50 million at 4.5 percent and with a twenty-year life.
The syndicate was again headed by Nederlandsche Handel-Maatschappij.[54] Today,
Dutch guilder bonds are issued chiefly by ABN-AMRO Bank, which succeeded
Nederlandsche Handel-Maatschappij after mergers in 1964 and 1991.[55]

Because Dutch regulations required sinking funds for all nonresident bond
issues—an unattractive feature for many foreign issuers and investors—the Dutch
central bank agreed to the establishment of a Euroguilder market in 1969, which
allowed easier access for nonresidents but was out of bounds for nationals. The
World Bank first turned to the Euroguilder market in fiscal 1981 and has been
represented there with regular issues ever since. In 1986 the domestic market was
also deregulated, and foreign investors (including the World Bank) were keen to

49. International Financing Review, Bond Base, IBRD Issues by Currency 1980—22nd
April 1993; and McLean and others, "Bond Markets of the United Kingdom," p. 1514.
50. Based on the evaluation of data from the relevant annual reports.
51. World Bank, *Recent Developments in Foreign and International Bond Markets.*
52. de Caires, ed., *Guide to International Capital Markets 1989*, pp. 133, 137.
53. Internationale Bank für Wiederaufbau und Entwicklung, *Die Weltbank*, p. 92.
54. Internationale Bank für Wiederaufbau und Entwicklung, *Jahresbericht 1962–1963*, p. 12.
55. Ugeaux, "Supranationals in the Primary Bond Market," p. 25.

make use of the new opportunities. As a result of this, the significance of the Euroguilder market has declined.[56] As the largest nonresident borrower in the Dutch capital market, the World Bank has a market share of 25 percent of total nonresident guilder borrowings.[57]

Between fiscal years 1972 and 1992 the World Bank took up guilder funds in the amount of $5.45 billion, for the most part through publicly offered bond issues. Of this figure, $1.06 billion was attributable to the Eurocapital market, $3.18 billion to the domestic market, $1.05 billion to placements with central banks and government agencies, and $162.2 million to other (that is, internationally offered) issues in 1986 and 1987.[58] After the deutsche mark and the Swiss franc, the Dutch guilder is the third most important European borrowing currency of the World Bank. All issue syndicates were managed either by ABN-AMRO Bank, its predecessors, or Rabo-Bank.[59]

Belgium

Another European country that kept its interest rates artificially low by limiting foreign borrowers' access to domestic capital markets was Belgium.[60] In 1959 the World Bank launched its first and only issue on the Belgian capital market in the 1950s and 1960s. With the help of a syndicate including Société Générale de Belgique, Banque de Bruxelles, Kredietbank, and Société Belge de Banque, the World Bank issued bonds for BFr 500 million with a 5 percent coupon and a ten-year maturity. The issue was oversubscribed by more than 100 percent.[61]

In the 1970s the World Bank returned to the Belgian capital market only twice, in 1972 and 1973. This was because of the restrictions imposed by the Belgian authorities, who wanted to reserve the bond market for the public sector and allowed access only to those international organizations of which Belgium is a member (and even then only in exceptional cases). The issue size is limited to BFr 3 billion to 6 billion.[62] The World Bank returned to the Belgian capital market in 1983 and then took up funds quite regularly, but stopped doing so after 1988.

56. de Caires, ed., *Guide to International Capital Markets 1989*, pp. 133, 137; and Peter van der Linde and others, "The Bond Markets of the Netherlands," in McLean, ed., *European Bond Markets*, p. 906f.

57. Including borrowings from official sources, this percentage increases to about 30 percent. World Bank, *Recent Developments in Foreign and International Bond Markets*.

58. Based on the evaluation of data from the relevant annual reports.

59. International Financing Review, Bond Base, IBRD Issues by Currency 1980—April 22, 1993.

60. Kindleberger, *Financial History of Western Europe*, p. 449.

61. Internationale Bank für Wiederaufbau und Entwicklung, *Die Weltbank*, p. 90; and IBRD, *Fourteenth Annual Report 1958–1959*, p. 13.

62. de Caires, ed., *Guide to International Capital Markets 1989*, pp. 27–34; "Zur Freizügigkeit im Kapitalverkehr der Bundesrepublik mit dem Ausland," *Monatsberichte der Deutschen Bundesbank* (July 1985), p. 21; and Françoise Beirens, Gilbert François, and Chris van Aeken, "The Bond Markets of Belgium," in McLean, ed., *European Bond Markets*, pp. 245f, 276, 296.

Overall, the World Bank borrowed $636.5 million through Belgian franc issues between fiscal years 1972 and 1988. Of this, $521 million were public offerings and other placements on the domestic market, and $115 million were placements with central banks and government agencies.[63] Belgian monetary authorities have not yet granted permission for the creation of a Euromarket for Belgian francs.

Federal Republic of Germany

After 1945, the German capital market was faced with a number of special problems. Apart from the general economic difficulties after World War II and the relatively slow integration of the Federal Republic of Germany into the West, West Germany was initially unable to conduct any borrowing or issuing business on an international scale. The question of Germany's foreign debts was not settled until the London Debt Agreement was signed in 1953.[64]

On the other hand, by 1952 the German economy had regained enough strength to register its first export surpluses.[65] In the same year the Federal Republic of Germany joined the World Bank with a capital share of $330 million, which at the time was the sixth largest contribution.[66] Because of the strong rise in balance of payments surpluses from the mid-1950s and Germany's resulting high liquidity, there was increasing pressure from abroad for the German federal government to revalue its currency. It was against this background that the World Bank approached Deutsche Bundesbank in 1957. This led to the Bundesbank purchasing U.S. dollar notes of the World Bank that same year, followed by deutsche mark–denominated notes a year later.

By fiscal year 1958 the Bundesbank had already advanced to being the biggest single purchaser of short-term World Bank paper, lending a total of $250 million. In the early 1960s, the Bundesbank was the biggest single bearer of Bank securities. The notes provided the World Bank with short-term and also (to a lesser degree) long-term funds. The initially short-term loans were later consolidated and extended, thus allowing the Bank to use long-term funds at intermediate-term costs.[67] The initial

63. Based on the evaluation of data from the relevant annual reports.

64. Hermann J. Abs, *Entscheidungen 1949–1953* (Mainz/Munich: v. Hase & Koehler 1991); and Christoph Buchheim, "Die Bundesrepublik in der Weltwirtschaft," in Wolfgang Benz, ed., *Die Geschichte der Bundesrepublik Deutschland*, vol. 2: *Wirtschaft* (Frankfurt: Fischer, 1989), p. 183f.

65. Gerold Ambrosius, "Das Wirtschaftssystem," in Benz, ed., *Die Geschichte der Bundesrepublik Deutschland*, vol. 2: *Wirtschaft*, p. 38.

66. In the course of subsequent capital increases, Germany's subscribed capital grew to roughly 8.73 billion in special drawing rights by mid-1992, which corresponded to a capital share of 5.74 percent. Germany today ranks third after the United States and Japan in terms of size of capital subscription. Deutsche Bundesbank, *Internationale Organisationen und Abkommen* (Frankfurt, 1986), p. 71; IBRD, *Seventh Annual Report 1952–1953*, app. D; and Internationale Bank für Wiederaufbau und Entwicklung, *Jahresbericht 1992*, p. 222f.

67. Deutsche Bundesbank, *Internationale Organisationen und Abkommen*, p. 72; IBRD, *Thirteenth Annual Report 1957–1958*, p. 10; and World Bank, *Recent Developments in Foreign and International Bond Markets*.

purchases were not only a response to the pressure to revalue, but also an expression of what the Bundesbank referred to as the "obligations of the Federal Republic of Germany toward the rest of the world."[68] In this sense, the financial contributions to international organizations were considered one form of development aid. In particular, they signaled the Bundesbank's support for the World Bank at a time when the institution was hardly known in Germany. By the early 1970s the volume of outstanding borrowings from the Bundesbank had risen to roughly DM 2.5 billion and has remained at about the same level ever since. Today, borrowings usually take the form of five-year deutsche mark notes and, to a much lesser extent, two-year U.S. dollar notes.[69]

In the 1950s the German capital market was not particularly attractive for foreign issuers not only for the reasons already noted, but also because the interest rate on the domestic capital market was much higher than on other markets. Nevertheless, as early as the summer of 1954, representatives of the Federal Ministry of Economics, the Bank deutscher Länder (the predecessor of the Deutsche Bundesbank) and Kreditanstalt für Wiederaufbau (Reconstruction Loan Corporation) convened to discuss possible deutsche mark transactions by the World Bank. Against the background of obtaining World Bank loans for reconstruction projects in Germany and for Germany's export industry, the question was how the Bank could obtain deutsche mark funding for these loans. However, the suggestion of launching a deutsche mark issue on the German capital market was turned down because of the high interest rate.[70]

Initially, the German public was not well informed about the activities of the World Bank. There were high expectations on the part of German exporters that the Bank would provide them with attractive export opportunities. In this sense, the World Bank was often confused with the Export-Import Bank of the United States (Eximbank).[71] To guarantee these export-promoting effects, an appropriate representation of German nationals on the Bank's permanent staff was considered instrumental to get access to important information. Following an invitation by the

68. "Longer-Term Claims in the Balance Sheet of the Deutsche Bundesbank," *Monthly Report of the Deutsche Bundesbank* (Frankfurt, December 1965), p. 3p.

69. Deutsche Bundesbank, *Statistische Beihefte zu den Monatsberichten der Deutschen Bundesbank, Reihe 3: Zahlungsbilanzstatistik*, Anlage 18 (November–December 1968), Anlage 17 (December 1976), Anlage 10 (December 1983), Anlage 12 (December 1992).

70. Memo dated June 16, 1954, Deutsche Bundesbank, Historisches Archiv, B 330/17557; various newspaper clippings from 1953 and 1954 in Deutsche Bank, Historisches Archiv, SE / 00 1534; Bundesverband der Deutschen Industrie, *Die Weltbank: Bericht über den Besuch einer deutschen Delegation bei der Internationalen Bank für Wiederaufbau und Entwicklung in Washington, 6. bis 8. Dezember 1954* (Bergisch-Gladbach: Heider, 1954), p. 10; and Eugene R. Black, "Deutschland und die Weltbank," *Europa-Archiv*, vol. 10 (March 20, 1955), p. 7392.

71. Otto Donner, "Die Weltbank und Deutschland," *Zeitschrift für die Gesamte Staatswissenschaft*, vol. 112 (1956), pp. 1–2.

World Bank to learn about its activities, a delegation of the Federal Association of German Industry (Bundesverband der Deutschen Industrie) visited Washington in 1954. Delegation members quickly realized that the widespread expectations of direct export benefits resulting from a stronger representation of Germany on the Bank's staff were not realistic. Against the background of these misconceptions, the then executive director (who was German) observed that the World Bank was "one of the most misunderstood institutions," with even highly specialized practitioners seeming to see the Bank in a "peculiarly mystic light."[72]

In the following years, the Ministry of Economics kept in touch with the World Bank, and in 1956 Süddeutsche Bank (one of the institutions merged in 1957 to form Deutsche Bank) received a request from the World Bank for an estimate of what costs and tax treatment to expect for a bond issue.[73] However, it needed the restoration of the deutsche mark's foreign convertability in 1958 by the government of the Federal Republic of Germany to create the monetary basis for German banks to conduct international lending business once again.[74] In the same year, plans to launch the first World Bank issue on the German capital market became more concrete. In the spring of 1958 the Bank approached Hermann J. Abs, Deutsche Bank's first board spokesman after World War II, with an offer to assume the management of a future German banking syndicate for World Bank issues in Germany. Deutsche Bank was chosen because it had the biggest placement power in Germany and because the Bundesbank had already indicated that it was not interested.[75] Deutsche Bank accepted the offer.[76]

Although the World Bank could have placed its bonds at 3 to 4.5 percent on other markets, it was apparently willing to accept an interest rate of 5.5 percent on the German capital market to gain a foothold there.[77] A number of questions still

72. Bundesverband der Deutschen Industrie, *Die Weltbank*, p. 11; and Donner, "Die Weltbank und Deutschland," p. 1. Throughout the 1950s, several articles in journals explained the activities of the Bretton Woods organizations to the German public: Hans Möller, "Die Beziehungen der Bundesrepublik zum Internationalen Währungsfonds und zur Internationalen Bank für Wiederaufbau und Entwicklung," *Europa-Archiv*, vol. 9 (October 20, 1954), pp. 6959–64; Black, "Deutschland und die Weltbank," pp. 7389–97; and Erich Achterberg, "Die übernationale Bank," *Zeitschrift für das gesamte Kreditwesen*, vol. 3.1 (January 1, 1950), pp. 31–33.

73. Drechsler to Krebs, 23.3.1956, Deutsche Bank, Historisches Archiv, SE / 00 3822.

74. Helmut Schlesinger, "Geldpolitik in der Phase des Wiederaufbaus (1950–1958)," in *Währung und Wirtschaft in Deutschland 1876–1975*, Deutsche Bundesbank (Frankfurt: Fritz Knapp Verlag 1976), p. 604; and *Geschäftsbericht Deutsche Bank AG 1958*, p. 19.

75. In 1958, Deutsche Bank participated in a World Bank loan for Cassa per il Mezzogiorno designed to promote the development of southern Italy. Emminger to Zahn, November 7, 1958, Deutsche Bundesbank, Historisches Archiv B 330/14152.

76. Excerpt from the minutes of a board meeting on April 3, 1958, Deutsche Bank, Historisches Archiv, SE / 00 3822.

needed to be clarified. These included West Germany's borrowing capacity vis-à-vis the World Bank, its eligibility for advances against collateral, and the paper's eligibility for the investment of monies held on trust. Nonetheless, initial talks were already being held with Dresdner Bank regarding its participation in this syndicate.[78] By the end of the year, Deutsche Bank presented the Bank with its proposals on volume, maturity, and other conditions for a bond issue in West Germany.[79]

In the spring of 1959 interest rates on newly issued bonds reached a postwar low of 5 percent, and the World Bank launched its first issue on the German capital market that April. It was a bond issue with a volume of DM 200 million, interest of 5 percent, and a fifteen-year life. This was then the biggest single issue ever offered by the World Bank outside the dollar region. The offer was made at par on April 9, 1959, and thus afforded the World Bank the most favorable conditions extended to any borrower on the German capital market since the currency reform in 1948. Owing to the high issue volume and the World Bank's wish to have the paper broadly distributed, the issue was launched by a syndicate consisting of seventy-three banks—a postwar record in Germany—under the lead management of Deutsche Bank and co-lead management of Dresdner Bank. The issue was initially oversubscribed, and the share of foreign purchasers (especially from Switzerland, where the World Bank had launched a Swiss franc bond issue at 4 percent earlier in the year) was estimated at 50 percent.[80]

As a result of the Bundesbank's restrictive monetary course, bond market interest rates rose again to 6 percent at the end of 1959, and many bonds with lower coupons fell to levels clearly below their issue price.[81] A poor performance of the World Bank's bonds in the secondary market would have hurt not only the Bank's own standing but also the reputation of Deutsche Bank, and it would have put an end to such bond issues for quite some time. Under these circumstances, Abs decided to launch a support operation for the World Bank issue and keep its price at 98 percent in the interest of investors and the newly developing deutsche mark

77. "Own Report" of November 11, 1958, on "The First Loan of the World Bank in the Federal Republic of Germany," Deutsche Bank, Historisches Archiv, SE / 00 3822.

78. Internal memo of March 5, 1957, Deutsche Bank, Historisches Archiv, SE / 00 3822; and memo on talks with the members of the Board of Managing Directors of Dresdner Bank, December 17, 1958, Deutsche Bank, Historisches Archiv, SE / 00 3822.

79. Martin to Abs, December 24, 1958, Deutsche Bank, Historisches Archiv, SE / 00 3822.

80. "Weltbankanleihe sofort überzeichnet," *Deutsche Zeitung*, vol. 29 (April 11, 1959); Deutsche Bank, Historisches Archiv, SE / 00 1527; IBRD, *Fourteenth Annual Report 1958–1959*, p. 13; *Geschäftsbericht Deutsche Bank AG 1960*, p. 16; and Volkswirtschaftliche Studiengruppe der Amsterdam-Rotterdam Bank N.V., Deutsche Bank AG, Midland Bank Limited, Société Générale de Banque S.A., and Generale Bankmaatschappij N.V., *Europäische Kapitalmärkte: Ein Bericht über die Märkte in Belgien, der Bundesrepublik Deutschland, Großbritannien und den Niederlanden* (March 1966), p. 43.

81. Fritz Seidenzahl, *100 Jahre Deutsche Bank* (Frankfurt, 1970), p. 398.

foreign bond market. The other banks in the syndicate, however, did not support this course of action. As a result, up to 66 percent of the issue had to be bought back into Deutsche Bank's portfolio.[82] This support operation conducted on its own initiative strengthened the lead manager's position. It marked the beginning of a long-standing relationship in which the institutions maintained close, steady contact. Deutsche Bank continuously lead-managed the syndicate for World Bank deutsche mark issues from 1959 until 1984. Initially, the syndicate was co-led with Dresdner Bank; in the late 1970s, Commerzbank and WestLB joined the syndicate's co-leadership; and after 1984, other German banks also took on the role of lead manager.[83]

With a total volume of DM 350 million, 1959 had been an exceptional year for international issues in the Federal Republic of Germany. Foreign bond issue volumes ebbed in West Germany in subsequent years because of the interest differential between the German capital market and major foreign markets. This changed in 1964 in the wake of economic policy shifts at home and abroad. In the United States the services balance was rapidly deteriorating, and the dependence of foreign issuers on the American capital market as the sole major international market available only made balance of payments problems worse. The U.S. government therefore undertook a number of measures aimed at improving the services balance. One was the introduction of an Interest Equalization Tax, as a result of which U.S. nationals or U.S. corporations purchased fewer foreign securities. At the same time this tax made borrowing on the American market more expensive for nonresident issuers, who began looking for new opportunities on the capital markets in Europe. World Bank paper, however, was exempt from this tax.[84]

While other European countries were banning or restricting access to their markets by foreign issuers owing to domestic capital requirements, the West German government was trying to promote foreign issues both to ward off the growing influx of capital from abroad and to attempt to achieve an export of capital. It did so by making nonresident issues exempt from the 25 percent capital gains tax (introduced in 1964) on fixed-income securities of German issuers held by foreign-

82. Abs to Black, September 16, 1959; Abs to Black, November 14, 1959, Deutsche Bank, Historisches Archiv, SE / 00 1523; and "Deutsche Bank's Dominant Role with Supranationals," in Rines and Bogdanowicz-Bindert, eds., *The Supranationals*, p. 180.

83. International Financing Review, Bond Base, IBRD Issue by Currency 1980—April 22, 1993. As early as 1968, when the World Bank under President Robert McNamara had set the goal of doubling its lending volume within five years, which of course entailed an enormous increase in capital market borrowing, the World Bank launched its first private placements with German central savings banks and central giro institutions. Since then, and above all between 1977 and 1988, other placements on the German capital market have played a strong part in the World Bank's borrowing in deutsche marks. Memo of June 10, 1968, Deutsche Bank, Historisches Archiv, SE / 00 3825; and information based on the evaluation of data from the relevant annual reports.

84. Internationale Bank für Wiederaufbau und Entwicklung, *Jahresbericht 1965–1966*, p. 39.

ers. This made deutsche mark–denominated foreign issues much more attractive to nonresident investors. If these bonds were purchased by German residents, that too was a means of exporting capital in times of high balance of payments surpluses. In 1964 demand for foreign deutsche mark paper grew to such an extent that the coupon began to fall in this market segment. This rendered the situation even more favorable for foreign issuers, particularly as interest rates in most other industrial countries were clearly on the rise. The issue volume of foreign bonds in 1964 came to roughly DM 900 million, thereby surpassing the aggregate total of all foreign issues from 1957 to 1963 of DM 760 million. The volume of deutsche mark foreign issues continued to soar after 1964. Capital requirements that had traditionally been covered in New York were now partly satisfied by issues of deutsche mark foreign bonds.[85]

In the initial stages, foreign borrowers could access the German market without applying for formal authorization, unless of course (like the World Bank) their Articles of Agreement required them to do so. As the number and volume of issues continued to climb, fears were expressed about undue pressure on the capital market. Consequently, in 1968 the Bundesbank and the German banks reached a gentlemen's agreement under which deutsche mark issues should be launched only at home and not abroad. To this end, only German banks were to act as lead managers. In addition, an issuing calendar was drawn up by a subcommittee of the Central Capital Market Committee, which consisted of representatives of six German banks and, as a guest, one representative of the Bundesbank, to coordinate the placements of foreign bonds on the German capital market. This procedure kept the Bundesbank informed of the volumes and the conditions for the issues and allowed it to influence the volumes agreed on by the banks acting as lead managers, thus ensuring consistency with the macroeconomic situation.[86] However, overall (and particularly in comparison with other European capital markets) the German monetary authorities took a liberal stance with regard to international capital movements.[87]

85. "Die Emission ausländischer Anleihen in der Bundesrepublik," *Monatsberichte der Deutschen Bundesbank* (December 1964), pp. 3–7; and Wilfried Guth, "Die internationale Verflechtung des deutschen Kapitalmarktes," in *30 Jahre Kapitalmarkt in der Bundesrepublik Deutschland* (Schriftenreihe des Instituts für Kapitalmarktforschung, Frankfurt: Fritz Knapp Verlag, 1981), p. 131.

86. "Freedom of Germany's Capital Transactions with Foreign Countries," *Monthly Report of the Deutsche Bundesbank* (July 1985), p. 14. For the task of the Central Capital Market Committee, see Volkswirtschaftliche Studiengruppe der Amsterdam-Rotterdam Bank N.V., Deutsche Bank AG, Midland Bank Limited, Société Générale de Banque S.A., and Generale Bankmaatschappij N.V., *Europäische Kapitalmärkte*, p. 33. On the Central Capital Market Committee, see Rüdiger Freiherr von Rosen, *Der zentrale Kapitalmarktausschuss: ein Modell freiwilliger Selbstkontrolle der Kreditinstitute*, Probleme des Kapitalmarkts: Monographien 4 (Frankfurt am Main: Fritz Knapp Verlag, 1973).

87. There is no evidence that this overall liberal position was ever questioned by disagreement of the German government with regard to policy decisions of the World Bank. Mason and Asher, *World Bank since Bretton Woods*, p. 140; and de Caires, ed., *Guide to International Capital Markets 1989*, pp. 75–83.

This broadly liberal position remained unaffected, with one exception. After three decades of consistently large surpluses, the German current account showed a deficit in the spring of 1979. Reflecting increased concern over the external payment position, the Bundesbank concluded an agreement with the issuing banks, with the objective of reducing the pressure capital exports exerted on the exchange rate.[88] From the Bundesbank's perspective, the borrowing of the multilateral institutions was hardly affected: according to the Bundesbank's monthly report, "Even at times of high current account and balance-of-payments deficits—as for example in the period 1979 to 1981—support for these institutions was never seriously reduced."[89] Nonetheless, the World Bank's funding in deutsche marks was notably reduced during the early 1980s.[90] Overall, however, the Bank took advantage of the favorable conditions on the German capital market (stemming from the stability of the deutsche mark and a declining interest rate) by regularly borrowing substantial long-term funds in West Germany.

From the mid-1980s, in response to German capital market performance, the stabilization of the dollar, and the needs of an attractive international financial center, the Bundesbank fully liberalized the capital market in Germany by lifting the coupon tax and abolishing the Central Capital Market Committee. Since then, planned issues have not needed to notify the Bundesbank in advance, subsidiaries of foreign banks based in Germany have been allowed to manage syndicates for deutsche mark bonds, and the maturity of deutsche mark bonds issued by nonresidents has been lowered from five to two years. In the course of this liberalization, the Bundesbank also suspended its reservations about emerging innovative financial instruments such as variable interest bonds, zero coupon bonds, double currency bonds, and bonds linked to currency and interest swaps. These instruments had been put on a negative list since the beginning of 1980 because the Bundesbank saw difficulties in assessing the significance of these innovations for the German capital market.[91]

With the liberalization of the German capital market, the Bundesbank's approval of new issues has become a mere formality. This has not loosened the close contacts the World Bank maintains with German authorities. It is not only with the

88. "International Monetary Developments and Policy," *Monthly Report of the Deutsche Bundesbank* (1981), p. 62.

89. "The Financing of the International Monetary Fund and Multilateral Development Banks," *Monthly Report of the Deutsche Bundesbank* (September 1983), p. 43.

90. For short periods in 1980 and 1981 the German capital market was effectively closed to all foreign borrowers including the World Bank. World Bank, *Recent Developments in Foreign and International Bond Markets;* and Rotberg, "Financial Operations of the World Bank," p. 206.

91. "Zur Freizügigkeit im Kapitalverkehr der Bundesrepublik mit dem Ausland," *Monatsberichte der Deutschen Bundesbank* (July 1985), p. 14f; "Neue Rahmenbedingungen für DM-Auslandsanleihen," *Monatsberichte der Deutschen Bundesbank* (July 1989), pp. 16–18; and "Erklärung der Bundesbank zu DM-Emissionen," p. 39.

German government and the Bundesbank that the World Bank maintains regular relations, but also with the commercial banks. From their perspective, World Bank issues have become a prestigious asset, in high demand because of the relatively low risk involved. Given the attractiveness of the World Bank's paper, the relationships many banks maintain with this important client are unusually close.

From fiscal years 1972 to 1992 the World Bank issued deutsche mark bonds worth more than $23 billion. According to Bank sources, this borrowing was divided into German market issues for $21.3 billion and international placements with central banks and government agencies for $1.8 billion. However, these figures require some explanation, because the total amount of placements with central banks was much higher. This has to do with the revolving bonds that have been placed repeatedly with Deutsche Bundesbank since the end of the 1950s and that form part of the domestic issues figure. The World Bank also does not distinguish between deutsche mark issues on the domestic and the Eurocapital market; instead, it regards all deutsche mark bonds it issues as "classical" foreign issues (that is, issues placed by a nonresident on the domestic market of any given country).[92] The distinction between deutsche mark foreign bond issues and deutsche mark Eurobonds is in fact a rather theoretical one: it is only a question of how the issue syndicate is put together. If it consists solely of German banks, the issue is considered to be a "classical" foreign issue, and as soon as foreign banks are present in the syndicate, it is considered a Eurobond.[93] Because the German monetary authorities make no distinction in terms of access to the German market, they are de facto treated equally. For World Bank issues this means that a large part of public offerings were actually placed on the Euromarket.

Between 1980 and 1991 the World Bank issued deutsche mark Eurobonds in the equivalent of just under $9.4 billion.[94] Pending a decision on the tax treatment of World Bank paper after the introduction of an interest income tax in Germany, no deutsche mark issues were launched on the Euromarket in 1992. That year also marked the World Bank's lowest level of deutsche mark borrowing since the late 1970s, amounting to only $478.6 million.[95] This may have been because of high interest rates in Germany, but the preparations for the first global bond issue in deutsche marks, which were under way at the same time, also played a significant part (see section on global bonds below). The first deutsche mark–denominated global bond was finally issued in October 1993. The issuing volume came to DM 3 billion at 5.875 percent and a ten-year maturity. The global bond was lead-managed by Deutsche Bank and Salomon Brothers and was several times

92. Figures based on the evaluation of data from the relevant annual reports.
93. Mendelsohn, *Money on the Move*, p. 139.
94. International Financing Review, Bond Base, IBRD Issues by Currency 1980—April 22, 1993.
95. See table 10-2 and figures based on the evaluation of data in the relevant annual reports.

oversubscribed. Beginning in spring 1993, the World Bank made use of the new borrowing instruments approved by the Bundesbank in 1985 by issuing its first floating rate bonds and reverse floater warrants on the deutsche mark Eurobond market, but not in any substantial volume.[96]

Italy

The World Bank undertook its first borrowing operation in Italy in 1961. Five percent lira bonds for a total of 15 billion lire were publicly offered for subscription. The bonds were sold at par and had a life of fifteen years. The issue syndicate consisted of Banca Nazionale del Lavoro, Banco di Napoli, Banco di Sicilia, Banca Commerciale Italiana, Credito Italiano, and Banco di Roma under the management of Banca d'Italia.[97] The second and third issues followed in 1972 and 1973. However, the Italian bond market did not develop fully until the 1980s. The World Bank executed its next borrowing transaction in lire in 1985, which set a number of precedents in the Italian market, including annual coupons and final pricing fixed just before the opening of subscription.[98] The Bank did not tap the Italian market regularly until a Euromarket for lire was introduced in 1985. After the World Bank's first Eurolira bond in 1988, all further borrowing was carried out through publicly offered issues on the Euromarket. Placement was always handled by a syndicate managed by a big Italian bank.[99]

Over the past twenty years, the World Bank has issued lira bonds in the amount of roughly $4 billion. The Italian capital market has thus been a minor source of funds to the World Bank.[100]

Austria

The World Bank approached the Austrian capital market for the first time in 1962 with notes denominated in U.S. dollars in the amount of $5 million, issued at 4 percent and with a five-year life, sold to the Österreichische Nationalbank, the Austrian central bank. The issue was coupled with a public offering of bonds for $5 million at 4.5 percent and fifteen-year maturity and was the first issue in foreign

96. "Zur Freizügigkeit im Kapitalverkehr der Bundesrepublik mit dem Ausland," p. 15ff; and International Financing Review, Bond Base, IBRD Issues by Currency 1980—April 22, 1993.

97. Internationale Bank für Wiederaufbau und Entwicklung, *Jahresbericht 1961–62*, p. 12.

98. World Bank, *Recent Developments in Foreign and International Bond Markets*.

99. International Financing Review, Bond Base, IBRD Issues by Currency 1980—April 22, 1993; de Caires, ed., *Guide to International Capital Markets 1989*, pp. 97–113; and Wilma Vergi, "The Bond Markets of Italy," in McLean, ed., *European Bond Markets*, pp. 842ff, 870f.

100. Figures based on data from relevant annual reports.

currency offered to the Austrian public since 1930. It was handled by a syndicate consisting of twelve Austrian banks and lead-managed by Österreichische Kontrollbank AG. The bonds were launched at an initial issue price of 102 percent.[101]

A market for nonresident bonds did not evolve in Austria until after 1968, but through the 1970s it remained insignificant owing to legal and fiscal barriers as well as investor preference for domestic paper. Before 1989 foreign issues had been limited to supranational agencies with only two or three issues per year, and the World Bank, which had tapped the Austrian schilling market for the first time in fiscal year 1980, was the largest single issuer. The small size of the market and the heavy capital outflow that followed the introduction in January 1984 of a tax on interest earned led to severe restrictions being placed by the Austrian authorities. To secure the government's consent to its transactions, the World Bank had to swap the respective net proceeds of its issues into another currency (for example, Swiss francs). There is no Euromarket for the Austrian schilling.[102]

Between fiscal years 1980 and 1990 the World Bank borrowed funds amounting to $465.8 million in Austria, of which $437.5 million were public offerings or placements on the domestic market and $28.5 million were international placements.[103]

France

The French capital market was closed to borrowers outside the franc region for years. This changed in November 1963, when French authorities declared that the French market was to be reopened to foreign participants. In the years that followed, a few supranational institutions obtained permission to launch issues. The World Bank, however, did not see a favorable opportunity.[104] The first French franc Eurobond was offered as early as 1967; but the Euromarket, reflecting the ups and downs of the French economy, was repeatedly closed for years at a time. It therefore took until 1972 for the World Bank to first approach the French franc–Euromarket with an issue for FFr 150 million at 7.25 percent and maturing in fifteen years. When the highly regulated market was finally reopened in 1985 with official permission required for all planned issues, rapid growth ensued.[105] In the same year the World Bank was the first international organization to launch an

101. Internationale Bank für Wiederaufbau und Entwicklung, *Jahresbericht 1962–1963*, p. 13.

102. Wolfgang Fast and others, "The Bond Markets of Austria," in McLean, ed., *European Bond Markets*, p. 164ff, 178, 216; International Financing Review, Bond Base, IBRD Issues by Currency 1980—April 22, 1993; and World Bank, *Recent Developments in Foreign and International Bond Markets.*

103. See table 10-2 and figures based on evalution of data from relevant annual reports.

104. Internationale Bank für Wiederaufbau und Entwicklung, *Jahresbericht 1964–1965*, p. 63; and Mason and Asher, *World Bank since Bretton Woods*, p. 140ff.

105. de Caires, ed., *Guide to International Capital Markets 1989*, pp. 69–74; and Philippe Willemetz and others, "The Bond Markets of France," in McLean, ed., *European Bond Markets*, pp. 450ff, 485, 505.

issue on the French market.[106] This issue, amounting to a modest FFr 1 billion (U.S.$107 billion), was the result of long negotiations between the Bank and the French Treasury, which led to the French government's decision to exempt the IBRD bonds from France's 10 percent withholding tax. This made the Bank the only borrower in the French market (besides the French government) to be exempted from this tax requirement. As a result, World Bank bonds are the only bonds in the French domestic market priced within the same range as government bonds.[107]

Between fiscal years 1972 and 1992, the World Bank launched franc issues for more than $1 billion through public offerings and one international placement. According to Bank sources, between 1972 and 1988 it placed issues totaling $322.1 million on the domestic market and from 1989 to 1992 launched issues for $687.1 million on the Euromarket. All issue syndicates for Bank paper in local currency were lead-managed by a French bank, in keeping with the country's regulations to this effect.[108]

Luxembourg

The Luxembourg capital market did not reach sizable proportions until the 1980s. It is supervised by the Institut Monétaire Luxembourgeois, where new issues must be registered to be included in the issue calendar. Together with the public sector and state-owned companies, the World Bank is one of the preferred issuers on this market. Since 1984 it has regularly made full use of its issuing scope, namely a maximum of LFr 1 billion per year. In so doing, together with two private placements, the Bank had launched issues for a total of $196 million by mid-1992, which were placed on the domestic market either as public offerings or as private placements.[109]

Sweden and Denmark

The Swedish capital market was subject to severe restrictions from 1940 to 1980 in an attempt to keep interest rates low for the benefit of state borrowing and housing construction. Therefore the Swedish capital market has been relatively unimportant as a source of financing for the World Bank. It was not until 1967 that

106. "Paribas—A Special Relationship with Supranationals," in Rines and Bogdanowicz-Bindert, eds., *The Supranationals,* p. 175.

107. World Bank, *Recent Developments in Foreign and International Bond Markets.*

108. See table 10-2 and information based on the evaluation of data from the relevant annual reports; International Financing Review, Bond Base, IBRD Issues by Currency 1980—April 22, 1993; and "Zur Freizügigkeit im Kapitalverkehr der Bundesrepublik mit dem Ausland," p. 21ff.

109. de Caires, ed., *Guide to International Capital Markets 1989,* pp. 125–26; Beirens and others, "Bond Markets of Belgium," pp. 317–19; and information based on the evaluation of data from the relevant annual reports.

it placed its first issue in Sweden: 6 percent paper with a volume of 75 million Swedish kronor and a maturity of twenty-five years.[110] The next issue followed seven years later, in fiscal year 1974. Beginning in 1980 the capital market was gradually deregulated, but the World Bank did not reenter the Swedish capital market until 1987. In 1988 the Eurokroner bond market opened with a World Bank issue, which was followed by several more after further liberalization.[111]

All in all, between fiscal years 1974 and 1992, the World Bank borrowed the equivalent of $374.6 million through bond issues. The greater part ($227.3 million) was taken up on the Eurobond market, and $147.3 million was placed on the domestic market.[112]

The Danish central bank had a tight grip on capital movements until well into the 1970s, given the country's permanent balance of payments deficits. What is more, the World Bank kept out of the Danish capital market principally for cost considerations, as it was one of the more expensive markets available to the Bank. Following a reduction of Denmark's deficits and its integration into the European Economic Community, in April 1985 a liberalization process led to the issue of the first Eurobond in Danish kroner, undertaken by the European Investment Bank. The World Bank followed suit that May with its first issue on the Danish capital market, a semiprivate placement lead-managed by Denmark's largest savings bank.[113] The market experienced a boom in the years that followed, underpinned by favorable interest rate developments. The World Bank, however, did not return to the Danish market until 1988.

Between 1985 and 1988, the World Bank borrowed funds in Danish kroner in the amount of $190 million, largely via the domestic market but also on the Euromarket or as an international placement. Bond issues must be notified to the Danish central bank in advance, with Danish banks acting as lead manager.[114]

Norway and Finland

The capital markets in Norway and Finland are also subject to major restrictions. However, in Finland, in the late 1980s the World Bank was granted permis-

110. Internationale Bank für Wiederaufbau und Entwicklung, *Jahresbericht 1967–1968*, pp. 26, 77.

111. de Caires, ed., *Guide to International Capital Markets 1989*, pp. 147–57; and Stefan Clevhammar and others, "The Bond Markets of Sweden," in McLean, ed., *European Bond Markets*, pp. 1256ff, 1293, 1312.

112. See table 10-2 and information based on the evaluation of data from the relevant annual reports; and International Financing Review, Bond Base, IBRD Issues by Currency 1980—April 22, 1993.

113. World Bank, *Recent Developments in Foreign and International Bond Markets*.

114. de Caires, ed., *Guide to International Capital Markets 1989*, pp. 53–57; Hasse H. Nilsson and Niels Retboll, "The Bond Markets of Denmark," in McLean, ed., *European Bond Markets*, pp. 336ff, 353, 361, 378; see table 10-2 and information based on the evaluation of data from the relevant annual reports; and International Financing Review, Bond Base, IBRD Issues by Currency 1980—April 22, 1993.

sion several times to launch issues in local currency on the domestic market. In contrast, Norway's domestic market remained closed for foreign borrowers, including the World Bank. It took until 1982 before the Bank tapped the Euro-Norwegian kroner market, which had come into existence in January 1980.[115]

As of June 1992, the World Bank had borrowed more than $350 million in Finnmark in three issues launched on the domestic market between 1987 and 1989 and $76 million in Norwegian kroner in three issues placed on the Euromarket between 1982 and 1986.[116]

Spain and Portugal

The Iberian countries witnessed major changes on their capital markets in the 1980s. The easier accessibility was enhanced further when Spain and Portugal joined the European Community in 1986. In 1987 peseta-denominated "matador bonds" were created in Spain. These are not exactly Eurobonds but form a part of the domestic market, in which issuing parties are nonresident companies or organizations. They are subject to a number of regulations by Spanish authorities and have to be lead-managed by a resident bank. In August 1987 the World Bank was given its first opportunity to start issuing in Spain, and it has been a regular customer ever since. Between fiscal years 1988 and 1992 the World Bank borrowed more than $1.1 billion in pesetas on the domestic market.

Euroissues in escudos have been a feature in Portugal since 1988. The issues of supranationals have almost no liquidity in the Portuguese domestic market because they are mainly transacted abroad. The World Bank launched two issues for a total of $227.8 million in fiscal year 1992.[117]

European Currency Unit

The World Bank's issues are denominated not only in national currency but also in European currency units (ECUs). The first ECU bonds were issued in 1981, and the World Bank entered this market in November 1983. It has since accessed this market segment regularly, raising more than $2.6 billion through 1992. The issues

---

115. World Bank, *Recent Developments in Foreign and International Bond Markets*.

116. de Caires, ed., *Guide to International Capital Markets 1989*, pp. 59–67; Baste Nepstad and others, "The Bond Markets of Norway," in McLean, ed., *European Bond Markets*, pp. 994ff, 1044; Päivi Härkönen and others, "The Bond Markets of Finland," in McLean, ed., *European Bond Markets*, pp. 416ff, 430; see table 10-2 and information based on the evaluation of data from the relevant annual reports; and International Financing Review, Bond Base, IBRD Issues by Currency 1980—April 22, 1993.

117. Rodrigo Sousa and others, "The Bond Markets of Spain," in McLean, ed., *European Bond Markets,* pp. 1176ff, 1193, 1201, 1209f, 1248ff; Miguel de Braganca and Joao Ermida, "The Bond Markets of Portugal," in McLean, ed., *European Bond Markets,* p. 1141; and see table 10-2 and information based on the evaluation of data from the relevant annual reports.

have been principally in the form of public offerings, though some have also been placed privately or with government agencies.[118]

The Establishment of the Euromarket

In the first two decades after World War II, cross-border capital movements were for the most part steered by various governments for economic and foreign policy reasons. At first, financial resources were intended for the reconstruction of Europe, and later for development aid in the third world. Some private capital transfers took place, but they were financed via national capital markets. The international capital market played only a minor role in the first two postwar decades and was limited solely to "classic" foreign bonds (that is, bonds issued on domestic capital markets by nonresidents). This is the only segment of today's complex international capital market that can look back on a long tradition: the issue of foreign bonds in Europe can be traced back to the beginning of the nineteenth century or even earlier.[119] Compared with volumes customary on the international capital market today, transactions in the first two decades after 1945 were insignificant.[120]

That was to change with the introduction of the Euromarket, which is defined as an international market for financial transactions in a currency that is not the local currency of any of the contracting partners.[121] Unlike national capital markets, it is entirely free of national regulation (such as foreign exchange controls or interest ceilings) and is not subject to supervision by national monetary authorities (including minimum reserve regulations or authorization procedures for new issues). The Euromarket is subject to less taxation and so interest margins are also lower, which generally means that lending interest is below national rates and deposit interest is above them.[122]

Ideally, free competition governs access to this market (that is, depending on capital available, the earnings achievable, and the preference for certain currencies).[123] In fact, however, the situation on the Eurobond market was for many years such that only

118. See table 10-2 and information based on the evaluation of data from the relevant annual reports.

119. Mendelsohn, *Money on the Move*, p. 54; and Karl Erich Born, *Geld und Banken im 19. und 20. Jahrhundert* (Stuttgart: Alfred Kröner Verlag, 1977), p. 64ff.

120. Mendelsohn, *Money on the Move*, p. 54.

121. *Gabler Wirtschaftslexikon*, 12th ed., vol. 1 (Wiesbaden: Gabler Verlag, 1988), p. 1639.

122. Artur Woll, ed., *Wirtschaftslexikon*, 6th ed. (Munich: R. Oldenbourg Verlag, 1992), p. 184.

123. Mendelsohn, *Money on the Move*, p. 55; *Gabler Banklexikon Handwörterbuch für das Bank- und Sparkassenwesen*, 9th ed., vol. 1 (Wiesbaden: Gabler Verlag, 1984), p. 669; and Orlin Grabbe, *International Financial Markets* (Elsevier Science Publishing, 1986), p. 272ff.

Eurobonds in U.S. dollars or currency units such as ECUs were largely free of restrictions and limited only by the market's capacities. For example, where the issue of Eurobonds in deutsche marks, Dutch guilder, and French francs was concerned, the countries' monetary authorities have always had ways and means of indirectly controlling volumes.[124] Because the Euromarket is not subject to government control and large transaction volumes are settled, the credit standing of the participants—above all, of the issuers and the intermediary banks—is a major prerequisite for its acceptance in the high-quality market segments. Consequently there are only a relatively small number of participants in these markets. Deutsche Bank has been active on the Eurobond market from the start and has contributed greatly to its development. Since the 1970s it has established itself as one of the major players in this market, along with Goldman Sachs, Morgan Stanley, and the big Swiss banks, to name only a few.[125]

Although the Eurodollar market dates back to the late 1950s, the Eurobond market began in 1963, when the first Eurobond was issued. It came into being because of a resurgence of international demand for capital from European industrial nations and a number of newly developing countries whose needs could not be satisfied on the regulated domestic capital markets in Europe or on the U.S. capital market.

Although access to the American market was free of official regulation, the scope of action allowed foreign borrowers was severely curtailed by American investors' inherent distrust of foreign bonds. This distrust dates back to losses suffered in the Great Depression, as well as to the far-reaching disclosure requirements of the Securities and Exchange Commission and the strict valuation criteria of the rating agencies. The World Bank was the only exception here.[126]

In 1963 foreign issuers' access to the New York market also became limited by the introduction of the Interest Equalization Tax and a number of subsequent measures taken by the American authorities to help reduce balance of payments problems and guarantee a stable dollar. In the 1960s, Belgium, Switzerland, and Germany also took steps to curb tax flight and regulate cross-border capital movements. This redirected international capital flows onto new markets, causing the Euromarket to boom. The first regional center to emerge was London—thanks to its decades of experience with international financial transactions and the Bank of England's liberal stance—followed later by Luxembourg, Brussels, and other financial centers both in Europe and elsewhere. These centers, however, were never able to challenge the significance of London.[127]

124. Mendelsohn, *Money on the Move*, p. 138; and "Why Deutsche Is Top at Eurobond Trading," *Euromoney* (May 1993), pp. 30–36.

125. Gallant, *Eurobond Market*, p. 124f.

126. Mendelsohn, *Money on the Move*, p. 54.

127. Geoffrey Jones, "Great Britain," in *Europäische Bankengeschichte* (Frankfurt: Fritz Knapp Verlag, 1993), p. 495f; Mendelsohn, *Money on the Move*, p. 32ff, 136f; Derek Honeygold, *International Financial Markets* (Woodhead-Faulkner, 1989), p. 164f; and "The International Capital Markets of Europe," *Bank of England: Quarterly Bulletin* (September 1970), pp. 295–99.

Eurobonds are bonds issued in a currency other than that of the country where they are offered and whose placement is usually handled by an international banking syndicate.[128] This banking syndicate usually has one or more lead managers responsible for the placement in the market (that is, in several countries at the same time). In contrast to foreign bonds, whose interest rate structure and market conditions reflect those prevailing in the country where they are placed, international bonds have greater scope for shaping their issue conditions and depend, if anything, on key factors of the issuing currency and international placement capacities. Generally speaking, they are somewhat more expensive for the borrower than classic foreign bonds. Eurobonds were initially denominated in U.S. dollars only, but other currencies, such as deutsche marks, pounds sterling, francs, and yen, followed soon after the Bretton Woods system was abandoned in the early 1970s. Initially, Eurobonds were fixed-income securities; but since the 1980s many new instruments have emerged, such as floating rate bonds, zero coupon bonds, and perpetual floating rate notes, to name only a few. These have substantially extended the possibilities and volumes of capital transfers.[129]

The World Bank was a relative latecomer to the Eurobond market, launching an issue for ¥ 20 billion ($75.4 million) in fiscal year 1978.[130] It did not access the market regularly until 1980. As late as 1979, Eugene Rotberg, treasurer of the World Bank for many years, voiced reservations about the Bank's issuing dollar-denominated Eurobonds. He wondered, among other things, whether the price fixing for Eurodollar bonds could be realistically and correctly carried out. He also doubted that the Eurobond managers' placing power would be sufficient and criticized a lack of transparency among issuers, issuing houses, syndicate members, and customers.[131] But these doubts must have been overcome before long, for in June 1980 the World Bank launched two U.S. dollar issues, one for $300 million at 10.25 percent and seven-year maturity, the other for $200 million at 9.75 percent and five-year maturity.[132] Both bonds were placed by a syndicate lead-managed by Banque Paribas.[133] The third Eurobond issue in dollars for $500 million followed in 1981, lead-managed by Deutsche Bank. Since then, Deutsche Bank has played a preeminent role in Eurodollar issues for the World Bank.[134] After issuing its first

128. *Gabler Wirtschaftslexikon,* 10th ed., vol. 2 (Wiesbaden: Gabler, 1979), p. 1350.

129. Honeygold, *International Financial Markets,* p. 166f.

130. Internationale Bank for Wiederaufbau und Entwicklung, *Jahresbericht 1977–1978,* p. 113.

131. Rotberg, *World Bank's Borrowing Program,* p. 9f.

132. Internationale Bank für Wiederaufbau und Entwicklung, *Jahresbericht 1979–1980,* p. 85.

133. "Paribas—A Special Relationship with Supranationals," p. 175.

134. Out of the fifty-six U.S. dollar bonds issued by the World Bank between 1980 and April 1992 for a total of $22.32 billion, Deutsche Bank or its London subsidiary lead-managed thirty-four issues. International Financing Review, Bond Base, IBRD Issues by Currency 1980—April 22, 1993.

U.S. dollar global bond in 1989, the Bank ceased issuing dollar-denominated Eurobonds.

New Funding Channels

To increase its borrowing at favorable conditions, the World Bank turned to new markets and market segments. After its first yen issue on the Eurobond market in 1978, the Bank transacted its first currency swaps in 1982, enabling it to cut costs for its borrowing in deutsche marks and Swiss francs. Another reason for the World Bank's introduction of currency swaps was that it was beginning to saturate the capital markets in certain currencies. The technique of swapping currencies, in which the World Bank had a pioneering role, provided it with greater access to lower-coupon currencies than would have been possible through direct borrowing. In the years that followed, swaps allowed the Bank to borrow more strongly in the traditional markets and gave it greater access to preferred currencies. At the same time, swap transactions opened up new capital markets, enabling the Bank to borrow in a wider range of currencies than would otherwise be possible based on cost considerations. This innovation enabled the Bank to acquire currencies that had been too expensive before, at rates below its direct borrowing costs in the markets for those currencies. The availability of currency swaps, for instance, played a major role in the Bank's decision to issue bonds in ECUs.[135]

In fiscal year 1982 the World Bank entered into hedging transactions for a total of $758 million, of which $198 million were in deutsche marks and $560 million in Swiss francs.[136] By 1992 currency swap transactions had more than quadrupled, reaching a total of $3.2 billion. Backed by the instrument of currency swaps, the World Bank launched issues on a number of new markets, so that from 1945 to 1992 it had taken up funds in twenty-eight currencies or currency units. Swap target currencies between 1982 and 1992 were Swiss francs, deutsche marks, yen, Dutch guilders, Austrian schillings, and U.S. dollars.[137] In 1989 the World Bank decided to institute a balanced relationship between the three big currency blocks in its loan currency pool, calling for 90 percent of the lendable funds to be in the ratio of U.S.\$1 : DM 2 (DM, SFr, Fl) : ¥ 125. This target had been reached by March 1991 by procuring appropriate funds, which explains the high U.S. dollar borrowing figure for that year.[138]

135. Rotberg, "Financial Operations of the World Bank," p. 204; and Internationale Bank für Wiederaufbau und Entwicklung, *Jahresbericht 1981–1982*, p. 53f.

136. Internationale Bank für Wiederaufbau und Entwicklung, *Jahresbericht 1981–1982*, p. 53f.

137. IBRD, annual reports, 1982 to 1992.

138. IBRD, *Borrowing Operations FY 1987–91, A Retrospective*, p. 1.

Furthermore, the executive directors in 1982 resolved to alter the Bank's lending policy to allow the Bank to undertake short-term borrowings. Up to that point the Bank had extended medium- or long-term loans at fixed interest rates. That policy was changed so the Bank could protect itself from a mismatch between the cost of borrowing and the return on lending. Since then, the Bank has been issuing loans with variable rates that are regularly readjusted in line with the cost of its borrowing. In so doing, it passes on at least part of the interest rate risk to the borrower. However, thanks to this reorientation the World Bank was able to take up its first short-term borrowings in September 1982 via a Discount Note program in the United States.[139] In the program's first year, the Bank obtained $1.5 billion. At the end of fiscal year 1992 it had total notes outstanding of $2.75 billion.

In fiscal year 1984 the World Bank introduced another short-term financing program: the Central Bank Facility in U.S. dollars, which was reserved for central banks and government agencies. By June 30, 1992, liabilities under this program amounted to $2.6 billion. In fiscal 1989 the Bank launched a short-term borrowing program in Swiss francs known as COPS, with maturities of up to one year, which are accepted on the Swiss market as a virtual equivalent to commercial paper. Liabilities under this program amounted to $24.5 million in fiscal 1992. At the end of the same year, total short-term borrowing outstanding came to nearly $5.4 billion, thus accounting for nearly one-third of total borrowing in that year.[140]

In addition to its short-term borrowing, the World Bank also extended its borrowing program in fiscal year 1984 to include issues with variable interest rates. The first two issues of this kind were placed in dollars on the U.S. and Eurobond markets. At virtually the same time, in fiscal 1985, it introduced its first interest rate swaps, which subsequently became an important liability management tool for the Bank. In fiscal 1989 the Bank combined interest and currency swaps to achieve greater flexibility in borrowing and to further cut lending costs.[141] The Bank's first zero coupon bonds were introduced in fiscal 1985.

The World Bank launched a new form of investment in 1989 known as global bonds. This international U.S. dollar–denominated paper is offered simultaneously in the major financial centers and is then traded between the centers. The idea behind global bonds is to bridge the gap between the Eurodollar bond market and the domestic U.S. dollar bond market and to balance out yield differentials between the two markets for World Bank paper, thus reducing the Bank's borrowing costs in U.S. dollars. Previously the acquisition of Eurobonds, which are bearer

139. Rotberg, *World Bank's Borrowing Program*, p. 5f; and Rines, "The World Bank," p. 68.

140. Internationale Bank für Wiederaufbau und Entwicklung, *Jahresbericht 1991–1992*, p. 76f; *Jahresbericht 1983–1984*, p. 81; and *Jahresbericht 1988–1989*, p. 68.

141. IBRD, *Borrowing Operations FY 1980–89, A Retrospective*, pp. 1–3; Rotberg, "Financial Operations of the World Bank," p. 204; Internationale Bank für Wiederaufbau und Entwicklung, *Jahresbericht 1983–1984*, p. 76f; and IBRD, *Annual Report 1985*, p. 75.

securities, had been subject to tight restrictions in the United States. On the other hand, it was assumed that many investors on the Euromarket refrained from purchasing domestic dollar bonds because of SEC registration requirements. By bringing both markets together, it was hoped that both American and European investors would benefit from lower costs and greater liquidity.

The first global bond had a volume of $1.5 billion, which was twice the size of any prior World Bank issue. The issue mandates were divided among fourteen leading international banks, with the syndicate lead-managed by Deutsche Bank and Salomon Brothers. Because the clearing and settlement systems in Europe and the United States worked together on the distribution and trading of the paper, combining international and domestic demand, global bonds virtually anticipated the development of a free international capital market.[142] The concept proved highly successful, and by fiscal 1992 the World Bank had issued six global bonds for a total of $9.5 billion. In 1992 the World Bank launched its first yen-denominated global bond for ¥ 250 billion ($1.9 billion), which increased its access to the Japanese market and helped reduce its borrowing costs for yen.[143] The first deutsche mark–denominated global bond followed in October 1993.

The World Bank's success in introducing the global bonds can be interpreted as reflecting its increasing independence from financial and political restrictions. Apparently, there was little or no constraint on its ability to fund a lending program of almost any size. The diversity of the funding channels the World Bank can draw on today has strengthened its bargaining position vis-à-vis national governments. Moreover, by the late 1980s the Bank's liquidity had risen enough that it no longer needed to respond immediately to investor or governments constraints on access to markets.[144] Furthermore, the Bank's ability to develop financial innovations reflects the expertise and the high technical capacity of its staff. Given the sophisticated character of many of the financial innovations, their assessment and evaluation is often perceived as a demanding task by governments and central banks.

Borrowing Costs

Over the decades, the World Bank's borrowing costs have risen steadily. The first dollar bonds in 1947 had coupons of 2.25 or 3 percent, and the first Swiss franc bonds in 1948 and 1950 were issued at 2.5 percent. In the 1950s the Bank's funding costs at times reached 5 percent. The early 1960s witnessed a substantial climb in

142. Internationale Bank für Wiederaufbau und Entwicklung, *Jahresbericht 1990*, p. 79f; and "Weltbank emittiert ihren ersten Global Bond," *Börsen-Zeitung*, September 19, 1989.

143. Caren Chesler-Marsh, "The Global Conundrum," *Euromoney* (January 1992); and Internationale Bank für Wiederaufbau und Entwicklung, *Jahresbericht 1992*, p. 77.

144. Rotberg, "Financial Operations of the World Bank," pp. 211, 213f.

interest rates, especially for new issues outside the United States. This rise was attributable to a growing demand for capital on the European domestic markets, particularly by local authorities, but also by U.S. corporations, who were forced by U.S. capital market restrictions to turn to the European markets to cover foreign investment borrowing needs. Owing to strict government regulations, Switzerland remained the only country with an interest rate level below 5 percent.[145]

After 1965 Canada registered the industrialized world's highest capital market interest rates; in 1967 the World Bank launched an issue there with a coupon of 6¼ percent, and the first issue at 7 percent followed in 1968. The 8 percent mark was passed in 1970 with the placement of two-year dollar bonds with central banks and government authorities. In the 1970s average funding costs remained high, fluctuating between 6.5 and 8.5 percent. In 1980 a level of more than 8 percent was reached, peaking at 10.93 percent in 1982. In the latter half of the 1980s the World Bank's average borrowing costs fell slightly, but it must be kept in mind that the figures quoted from 1986 on reflect the influence of currency swaps. A low was reached in 1987 with an average interest rate of 5.9 percent, which rose again by 1991 to 8.06 percent and then eased to 6.69 percent in 1992. However, it needs to be pointed out that these overall average figures do not reflect the sometimes highly turbulent and even counteracting interest rate developments in individual markets, which affected World Bank borrowing in various ways.[146]

At the end of fiscal year 1992 the Bank had $5.4 billion outstanding in short-term borrowing and $91.7 billion in medium- and long-term liabilities (accounting for 94 percent of its total borrowing). Fixed-income securities and variable-rate paper accounted for $91.6 billion and $0.1 billion, respectively, of medium- and long-term liabilities. The average maturity for medium- and long-term borrowing was 6.4 years. More than one-third of this borrowing ($37.4 billion) was in European currencies.[147]

Outlook

Of all the supranationals, the World Bank is by far the biggest and most prestigious borrower on the international capital markets.[148] In the 1980s the Bank at times accounted for more than 50 percent of total borrowing by supranational organizations. In terms of objectives, structure, and operations, the Bank served as

145. Internationale Bank für Wiederaufbau und Entwicklung, various annual reports, especially *Jahresbericht 1965–66*, p. 41.

146. Data taken from the respective annual reports. The figures given relate to fiscal years.

147. Internationale Bank für Wiederaufbau und Entwicklung, *Jahresbericht 1992*, pp. 77, 220.

148. S. Melvin Rines, "Supranationals and the Capital Markets: An Overview," in Rines and Bogdanowicz-Bindert, eds., *The Supranationals*, p. 15.

forerunner and model for the regional development banks that were later founded. With only the U.S. capital market accessible in the postwar years, the Bank helped to open the national and international capital markets and played a decisive role in developing the wide range of financing methods and instruments available on the capital markets today. In its fifty years of existence, the biggest markets for the Bank's borrowings have been the United States, followed by the Federal Republic of Germany and (since the 1970s) Japan. The currencies of these countries are its preferred transaction currencies. Its total outstanding medium- and long-term liabilities at the end of June 1992 totaled $91.7 billion, of which $28.8 billion were in yen, $23 billion in U.S. dollars, and $12.9 billion in deutsche marks.[149]

The World Bank today ranks among the world's leading issuers on national and international capital markets. This is true not only in terms of the issue volumes it regularly places on the markets but also in terms of the Bank's innovative potential, with which it shapes, fosters, and occasionally even rediscovers capital markets all over the world. It was the World Bank that launched the concept of global bonds— initially in U.S. dollars, followed by yen, and finally in the deutsche mark sector. Apart from these large-scale issues in the world's major capital markets with which the Bank covers most of its borrowing requirements, it also engages in numerous smaller transactions on virtually all other national and international capital markets. On the one hand, in so doing, the Bank helps to develop national markets. The recent examples of Italy, Spain, and Portugal raise the question of which market will be the next to open its doors to the Bank and subsequently to other international issuers. On the other hand, by introducing new instruments or changing institutional conditions, the Bank has always endeavored to increase the efficiency of the markets. For fifty years now, investors, banks, and other market participants have been able to rely on the World Bank as a cost-conscious and sophisticated client and a dependable, relationship-oriented, and strategically minded partner, always intent on acting in the best interests of all contracting parties.

149. Internationale Bank für Wiederaufbau und Entwicklung, *Jahresbericht 1992*, p. 220.

ELEVEN

The World Bank and the IMF: A Changing Relationship

Jacques Polak

AT THEIR birth, John Maynard Keynes baptized the International Monetary Fund (IMF) and the World Bank as the Bretton Woods twins. The epithet seemed apt: they were born at the same time and place, as offspring of the same parent countries. But even at birth they were very dissimilar twins, and over the next thirty or thirty-five years, with only limited and superficial contact, they grew increasingly apart. Many of the recent difficulties in the relations between the two institutions have occurred because conditions in the world economy have increasingly forced them, set in their ways and after the onset of middle age, to live in much closer operational proximity, in continuous awareness of each other's established rights and acquired sensitivities.

Introduction

The Bank's Articles of Agreement contain a direct link between the two institutions: in order for a country to be able to become a member of the Bank, it must be a member of the Fund. This provision reflected two considerations. First, while membership in the Fund entailed rights (access to credit) and obligations (observance of the agreed rules on exchange rates and currency restrictions), for borrowing countries membership in the Bank involved only the benefit that membership qualified a country for Bank loans. Linking of the two memberships served to reduce the risk of free ridership. Second, it was well recognized at Bretton Woods that stable monetary conditions were essential to the success of the Bank's lending,

473

and the precondition of membership in the Fund was thus seen as enhancing the quality of the Bank's loans.[1] (Many years later, a much closer relation between a country and the Fund, namely, a credit arrangement with the attendant conditionality, became the standard requirement for a country's access to the Bank's structural adjustment lending.)

The initial fields of operation of the two institutions were clearly separated. At the start, the Bank had, of course, two tasks: reconstruction and development. In the Bank's first decade, 43 percent of its lending went to industrial countries in Europe, initially as reconstruction loans, and to such countries as Australia, New Zealand, South Africa, and Japan; many of these loans were program loans. But as far as its lending to developing countries was concerned, more than three-quarters in the first two decades was devoted to infrastructural projects.[2]

The Fund, by contrast, was to be the center of the postwar international monetary system—a system based on fixed exchange rates, to be changed only in instances where they had become unsustainable, and aiming at rapidly increasing freedom for current account transactions. The Fund's credit operations were derived from its function as guardian of the international monetary system: they served to help countries, even when they encountered payment difficulties, to stick to the rules of the system—whether the difficulties were of their own making, owing to policy slippages, or imposed from the outside, for example, by a recession in the world economy. In either event, it was expected that the country should be in a position to repay Fund credit within a three- to five-year period. The Fund at an early stage introduced the practice of disbursing credit in tranches, under standby arrangements, to ensure that agreed policies were indeed being followed.

The funding of the two institutions' financial activities also diverged sharply. In the Bank, a small portion of the capital is paid in, and there is no connection between a country's shareholding and the amount of credit it can receive from the Bank. The bulk of Bank lending is funded on the world's capital markets, guaranteed by the uncalled portion of its capital. In the Fund, member countries contribute an amount equal to their quota, partly in SDRs (special drawing rights), but predominantly in their own currency. These quotas determine not only voting rights but also the amount of access to Fund credit. By using the currency contributions, the Fund finances its credit operations from the foreign exchange reserves of members' central banks.[3] When demand for Fund credit was large compared with

1. Report of the Netherlands delegation to the Bretton Woods Conference, New York, 1945, p. 72.

2. Calculated from table in John Adler, "Development Theory and the Bank's Developing Strategy—A Review," IMF/World Bank, *Finance and Development*, vol. 14 (December 1977), p. 33.

3. Willem F. Duisenberg and André Szász, "The Monetary Character of the IMF," in Jacob A. Frenkel and Morris Goldstein, eds., *International Financial Policy: Essays in Honor of Jacques J. Polak* (Washington: International Monetary Fund, 1992), pp. 254–66.

its quota resources, the Fund has also borrowed, but only from central banks or member countries, never from the market.

The 1969 amendment of its Articles of Agreement gave the Fund a wholly new function, namely, to supplement the stock of international reserves if this stock threatened to become inadequate. To perform this task, the Fund was authorized to add its own money, SDRs, to the existing stocks of gold and dollars. But the dream of a world monetary system based on the SDR has remained unfulfilled. The Fund has created SDRs only in 1970–72 and 1979–81, and the total stock of SDRs outstanding, at just over SDR 20 billion, was less than 3 percent of world nongold reserves, which, at the end of 1992, stood at SDR 693 billion.[4] Various proposals to use SDR creation to finance development in general, and perhaps lending by the International Development Association (IDA) in particular, which would have provided a financial link between the Fund and the Bank group, never found sufficient support in the industrial countries. The attempt was finally abandoned in 1986, when the Fund's Interim Committee (its ministerial policy committee) excommunicated any concept of "the link" between reserve creation and development finance, stating that "the SDR . . . should not be a means of transferring resources."[5]

The different tasks and the different sources of finance may to some extent explain the differences in character between the two institutions. For example, the need to provide information to the buyers of the Bank's bonds may have helped to make the Bank a more open institution than the Fund. To enable the Bank to float bond issues in the world's capital markets, its Articles of Agreement do not give the Bank the general immunity that the Fund has; this in turn may well have induced the Bank, long before the Fund, to establish an Administrative Tribunal. In the 1980s, concern about the possible impact on its credit standing of arrears by its debtors made the Bank more willing than the Fund to engage in "defensive lending"—new lending to protect the service on previous loans.[6]

The Fund's concern from the start with the overall economy of its member countries, and in particular balance of payments and exchange rate questions, made treasuries and central banks the natural institutions to select executive directors for the Fund, often from among their own officials, and to be the source of instructions from capitals to these directors. Treasuries also play an important role in the choice and guidance of members of the executive board of the Bank— but there they have to share this role with ministers of development or foreign affairs. By now, only two countries (France and the United Kingdom) are represented in the two boards by the same person; two others, Belgium and the Netherlands, followed the same practice for many years but gave it up. The result of this

4. IMF, *International Financial Statistics* (Washington, July 1993), p. 31.
5. Interim Committee communiqué, IMF, Washington, April 10, 1986, para. 7. IMF survey, vol. 15 (April 1986), p. 116.
6. See "Areas of Potential Conflict" later in this chapter.

separation—combined with insufficient coordination in capitals—has been that on occasion the two boards took different attitudes on matters of common concern to the institutions. Striking examples could be seen in the contrasting reactions of the two boards (positive in the Fund, widely negative in the Bank) to the 1989 agreement between the heads of the organizations on collaboration between the Fund and the Bank, and again on the same subject, in reference to the former Soviet Union, in 1992. Over the years the boards have found themselves at odds on other major and minor common problems, ranging from conditionality and country strategies to staff compensation and class of air travel. Indeed, among the causes of friction between the Fund and the Bank, insufficient attention in capitals to the resolution of conflicts stands out as a major reason.

But these conflicts arose mostly in recent years. In earlier years, the clear differences in focus between the two institutions made collaboration a low-priority issue. Budget-conscious officials in member governments would of course press from time to time for the avoidance of duplicate services or overlapping requests for statistical information. But separate organizations with their own sources of income are likely to respond to such pressures only reluctantly and in a minimal way. The most important joint feature that the two organizations came up with was a joint library. Even that was not very joint: the Fund wanted to have a library, and the Bank reluctantly agreed to bear part of the cost. There was no choice about the meetings of the two boards of governors; since these were joint meetings, they had to be run jointly.

The interest of one organization in the work of the other, such as it was, tended to be asymmetrical. The macroeconomists employed by the Fund did not have a profound interest in the irrigation systems or the electric power plants financed by the Bank. But economists in the Bank had a more than casual interest in the performance of a debtor country's economy as a whole. This interest had two strands. The first was the realization that even the best projects suffer if there are severe distortions in the general economy. Perhaps more powerful initially was the second reason: that poor economic performance bodes ill for a country's creditworthiness. From the start of its operations, "creditworthiness" was a prime preoccupation of the Bank. That it did not as such appear as a concern of the Fund (the word is not found in the indexes to the Fund's histories) reflects a fundamental difference of approach between the two institutions in their early decades. The Bank appraised a country's creditworthiness by taking into account both external conditions and the country's policies; if it found the country's creditworthiness insufficient, it refused to lend for even the best projects. The Fund, having far more explicit authority to do so, appraised policies and, if necessary, negotiated changes in policies before it became willing to lend.

The extent to which staffs in the two institutions worked together on macroeconomic policy advice in individual countries appears to have depended a great deal on the inclinations of regional managers. From all evidence, concern with macroeconomic policies was most prominent in the Bank's Latin American region, particularly by the mid-1960s.[7] Indeed, in that region prior agreement with the Fund was, for many years, a condition for Bank lending.[8] Not only staff but also management took an interest in what is now called "policy coordination with the Fund." The oral instructions that I received as head of a Fund mission to Colombia in 1955, formulated in a meeting between the vice president of the Bank and the deputy managing director of the Fund, conveyed the same notion, expressed in the heartier language of those days: "You twist their right arm and we'll twist their left arm."

With the growth of the two organizations, such informal coordination, conducted by their most senior officials, obviously became impractical.[9] In 1966, discussions held between officials of the two institutions produced for the first time agreement on their respective areas of primary responsibility. For the Bank, this area was defined as "the composition and appropriateness of development programs and project evaluation, including development priorities." For the Fund, it was "exchange rates and restrictive systems . . . adjustment of temporary balance of payments disequilibria, and . . . evaluating and assisting members to work out financial stabilization programs."[10] Taken by themselves, these guidelines could appear to exclude the Bank from all macroeconomic concerns, and the Fund from many of them, such as fiscal and monetary policies. Why would the Bank, especially, have agreed to so narrow a "turf"—a question that arose most forcefully from the perspective of the acrimonious turf battle between the two institutions in 1989? On closer inspection, however, the guidelines were indicative only of the outer regions of each organization's area of responsibility, where there was at least some hope that trespass by the other could usually be prevented. It was recognized that in between these regions there was a "large . . . area of common interest" and that no aspect of the "structure and progress" of member countries should be ignored by either institution.[11] The primary aim of the exercise was to avoid inconsistent advice to member countries, and the staff of each organization was instructed to adopt the views of the other one in its area of primary responsibility. In the course of 1969–70, there was further agreement on standard practices to implement these principles, including consultation before missions, debriefing after them, exchange of documents, and so on. A major stimulus toward this further effort had come from the Pearson commission. Its recommendation went well beyond consistent policy advice; it urged "unified country assessments."[12] For that, the organizations

7. Edward S. Mason and Robert E. Asher, *The World Bank since Bretton Woods* (Brookings, 1973), pp. 453–55.

8. Ibid., p. 554.

9. Margaret G. de Vries, *The International Monetary Fund, 1966–1971: The System under Stress*, vol. 1 (Washington: IMF, 1976), p. 611.

10. Ibid., p. 611.

11. Mason and Asher, *The World Bank since Bretton Woods*, p. 551.

12. Report of the Commission on International Development, Lester B. Pearson, chairman, *Partners in Development* (Praeger, 1969), p. 230.

would not be ready until the late 1980s, and then only for part of their developing country membership.

Changing Conditions in the World Economy

A number of impulses converged in the last two decades to intertwine what were previously the Fund's and the Bank's mostly separate lives.

Contrary to a widely held expectation at the time, the collapse of the par value system in 1971–73 did not, at least initially, greatly affect demand for credit from the Fund. Floating of currencies remained the exception, limited to half a dozen major countries. Most countries continued to peg their currencies, either on a reserve currency—such as the U.S. dollar or the French franc—or on currency baskets, either the SDR or a custom-built basket. Just as in the 1950s and 1960s, these pegs were often undermined by insufficient control over inflation in the pegging country, leading to the need for a package of policy adjustments and balance of payments credit: the two components of an arrangement with the Fund. These developments, together with the oil shocks of the 1970s, kept the Fund actively working with many members in the design of policy packages and the extension of financial support, even before the debt crisis of the next decade presented it with new, large challenges.

One factor that did reduce the demand for credit from the Fund was competition from the commercial banks. In the 1970s, as the memories of the interwar debt crisis faded and tens of billions of dollars in OPEC deposits needed to be employed somewhere, hordes of commercial banks stampeded into sovereign lending. The resulting supply of unconditional credit tended to deprive the Fund of part of its clientele. Since 1976, no industrial country has had an arrangement with the Fund, and until 1982, when the debt crisis taught them otherwise, the major developing countries also believed that they were better off taking up no-questions-asked loans from consortiums of banks than making their access to balance of payments loans subject to the scrutiny and the policy conditions of the Fund.

For the Bank, the competition from other lenders was less pervasive and more country or sector specific. Various countries in Asia found that the commercial banks offered better terms than the Bank for industrial projects. In Thailand and Malaysia the Bank lost opportunities to lend because of the competition from Japanese official credits at interest rates (in yen terms) far below those charged by the Bank. But China, Indonesia, and India continued to be large Bank borrowers through the 1980s, attracted by the longer maturities and the technical assistance associated with Bank loans.

Both institutions remained deeply involved with countries struggling with the debt problem, mainly in Latin America and Africa. And in the last few years, both saw their clientele widened with the arrival as eager borrowers and seekers of policy advice of first, the Eastern European countries, and then the constituent republics of the former Soviet Union. In the 1990s, these countries became a major area of operation for both Fund and Bank, which posed anew the issue of collaboration between the two institutions.

Both institutions also found grounds for expanding the scope of their lending operations in the deteriorating situation of their developing member countries, many of whose economies were in a weak position in spite of the financial and other services that the institutions had given them during many years. In the last quarter of the twentieth century, after the broad expansionary forces of the postwar period had run their course, the world economic climate turned less friendly to the developing countries, with less buoyant demand in the industrial world, deteriorating terms of trade, and higher real interest rates. The new climate faced the developing countries—as they increasingly realized during the 1980s—with the necessity to adopt major changes in their economic policies, including greater attention to macroeconomic stabilization and greater reliance on markets and the price mechanism. The new situation also posed important challenges for the international institutions: to assist their members in the almost revolutionary process of policy change and to support this process by enlarged lending, combined with a more determined application of both macroeconomic and structural conditionality.

The Fund and the Bank were both ready, indeed anxious, to increase their lending. If their operations had been closely integrated, the Fund would have taken on the job of enforcing intensified conditionality with respect to financial stabilization, the Bank the corresponding task on the structural side. As it was, however, both institutions interpreted the situation of their members as requiring them to tend the garden across the street as well as their own. The Fund moved some distance into structural conditionality, the Bank into macroeconomic management. During a crucial period—from late 1979 to mid-1981—the Fund actually relaxed conditionality in its own area of responsibility, in particular for exchange rate adjustment.[13] In the case of the Bank, however, it has been argued that only through its entry into the field of policy lending could it acquire the leverage to insist on a broad range of supply-side policies by its borrowers; earlier experience had shown the alternative, to tack economywide conditionality onto the financing of projects, to be unworkable.[14]

The next two sections describe the lateral moves made by the two institutions as a result of which each ended up working to some extent in the other's

13. Supporting evidence for the softening of Fund conditionality during this period is found in John Williamson, "The Lending Policies of the International Monetary Fund," in John Williamson, ed., *IMF Conditionality* (Washington: Institute for International Economics, 1983), pp. 641–49.

14. Stanley Please, *The Hobbled Giant: Essays on the World Bank* (Westview Press, 1984), chap. 3.

field.[15] Although some fears to that effect were expressed in each board at the time the moves were initiated, trespass was certainly not the institutions' driving motive. In the Fund as well as in the Bank, the widening scope of concerns was felt as a natural response to the changed circumstances of members and a deepened understanding of the problems of development. Indeed, the paramount need for the combined application of macroeconomic stabilization, structural adjustment, institutional reform (and, in the 1990s, good governance) became the accepted credo not only of the Bank and the Fund but also over time of the regional banks, the aid agencies of the industrial countries, and, most importantly, of an increasing number of developing countries.

The Fund Moves toward the Bank's Field

As it lost the clientele of its industrial countries, which had accounted for half or more of its loan portfolio, the Fund in the 1970s began to tailor its credit facilities to the specific needs of the developing countries. The Extended Fund Facility (EFF), created in 1974 (in part as a consolation prize for the failure of the reform exercise to produce additional finance for development through "the link" between SDR allocations and development aid), was aimed at financing structural adjustment in developing countries. The facility addressed itself to the problems of members whose balances of payments could be turned around only over an extended period, for example, because of "structural maladjustments in production and trade" with widespread price and cost distortions, or "slow growth and an inherently weak balance of payments position which prevents pursuit of an active development policy."[16] To countries in such situations, the Fund now offered larger financial assistance (as a percentage of quota) and longer repayment periods. Instead of the Fund's standard three to five years, EFF credits could be repaid over four to eight years, further lengthened to four to ten years in 1979.

In making its case for the EFF, the Fund for the first time focused on issues such as structural maladjustments to which it had paid less attention in the past but that were central to the operations of the Bank. In extending its lending period, the Fund (as one of the few joint Bank-Fund directors, Pieter Lieftinck of the Netherlands, remarked) bridged the gap between its own short-term balance of payments credit and the Bank's long-term development lending: it entered the field of medium-term lending.[17]

The EFF was followed in 1976 by the establishment of a "Trust Fund" (financed by profits on the sale of part of the Fund's gold), which made medium-term loans,

15. For an early description of these moves, and the problems they created, see Williamson, "The Lending Policies of the IMF," pp. 617–21.

16. IMF Decision 4377-(74/114) on Extended Fund Facility in IMF, *Selected Decisions,* 15th issue (Washington, 1990), pp. 70–73.

17. Margaret G. de Vries, *The International Monetary Fund, 1972–1978: Cooperation on Trial,* vol. 1 (Washington: International Monetary Fund, 1985), pp. 367–68.

subject to weak conditionality, to low-income countries. The Trust Fund also introduced a distinction that the Bank had pioneered twenty years earlier when it had created IDA: near-zero interest rates for the subcategory of low-income developing countries. (The Fund had made earlier steps in this direction when it arranged interest subsidies for the poorer countries.) Ten years later this distinction was consolidated in the Structural Adjustment Facility (SAF), established in 1986, and in particular the Enhanced Structural Adjustment Facility (ESAF, with stronger conditionality), established in late 1987. These new facilities in the Fund replicated to a large extent the Bank-IDA structure, with a similar list of countries eligible for near-zero interest rates—although the lending period of SAF and ESAF remains at the ten-year limit that also applies to the EFF.

ESAF has another similarity to—and potential source of conflict with—IDA: its sources of funds.[18] In order to assemble quickly a large amount (about SDR 6 billion) that could be lent out at highly concessional interest rates, contributions for ESAF were solicited in a highly eclectic manner. Depending on legislative or administrative convenience, some countries made loans to the Fund at market interest rates, some countries (or their central banks) lent at concessional interest rates, and some gave budgetary grants to be used for interest subsidies. Although that (relatively small) part of ESAF's funding that derives from aid budgets potentially competes with the funding of IDA, ESAF has not proved to be an obstacle in the negotiation of the tenth IDA replenishment exercise.[19]

The Bank Moves toward the Fund's Field

By the late 1970s, the Bank took an initiative that moved part of its lending closer to that of the Fund. The Bank had increasingly become convinced that sound individual projects contributed little to development in a setting of poor macroeconomic policies, and around 1980, as the international economic environ-

18. The problem was signaled in the Bank as early as October 1986, in a memorandum dated October 29, 1986, from Ernest Stern to Barber Conable in preparation for a luncheon meeting with de Larosière: "The Fund has now told us of their intention to send missions to European capitals and to Tokyo to try and raise concessional financing in support of their SAF programs. This short-circuits the Consultative Group and Round Table processes; interferes with IDA fund raising and that of ADB; ignores our mandate to mobilize aid resources and runs contrary to the intention expressed by every donor that we should seek to improve aid coordination. While the Fund has asked us to join these trips, participation is not relevant and does not solve the problem of conflicting basic objectives." (In the end, Bank staff did join in the Fund's trips.)

19. Unlike IDA in the Bank, ESAF is not a permanent facility in the Fund, but agreement was reached on its continuation beyond 1993. At the Munich summit of July 7–8, 1992, the Group of Seven (G-7) stated that the "IMF should continue to provide concessional financing to support the reform programmes for the poorest countries" and that the IMF should proceed to a full examination of the options beyond 1993, "including a renewal of the facility." (Para. 20 of the G-7 Munich summit communiqué of July 8, 1992.)

ment became more hostile to development, it began to see the need for correct macropolicies as overwhelming. At the same time, the deteriorating economic situations in many, especially the heavily indebted, developing countries cut into the supply of qualifying projects and thus tended to slow down the flow of Bank lending based on projects. This situation in turn provoked fears of the emergence of "negative net lending" (or, allowing also for interest payments, "negative resource transfers"), which might undermine the willingness of hard-pressed countries to keep their debt service to the Bank current. These various considerations induced the Bank to revive a lending approach it had used with some countries, such as India and Pakistan, in the 1960s and 1970s, consisting of balance of payments (rather than project-related) loans linked with broad understandings on the borrowing country's general economic policies. The new term introduced for such loans was "structural adjustment" lending. (A few years later the Fund selected the same label for its lateral expansion.) The identity of label is not inappropriate: although structural adjustment lending by the Bank and the credit activities of the Fund maintain their distinguishing characteristics, there is much that they have in common.

Under the Bank's structural adjustment lending, which by now accounts for more than one-fourth of its total lending, relatively large sums of money (judged large enough to draw the interest of the borrowing country's highest policy-makers)[20] are made available in quickly disbursing loans in exchange for broad policy commitments with respect to the economy in general (SALs) or a major sector (SECALs).

In the early stages of structural adjustment lending, Bank officials tended to play down its financial aspects—whether in deference to the limitations that the Bank's Articles of Agreement impose on nonproject lending (allowed only "in exceptional circumstances," according to Article III, Section 4[vii]) or to deflect criticism (for example, in the Bank board) that by giving balance of payments financing, the Bank trespassed on the Fund's field of operations. In a 1982 conference, Ernest Stern insisted that "the primary purpose of a SAL is not to fill a current account deficit but to support a medium-term program of changes necessary to reorient the economy and to bring its current account deficit to a more sustainable level over a number of years."[21] Stanley Please makes the same point with even greater emphasis, adding that "the Bank considers the provision of emergency balance of payments assistance as entirely an IMF responsibility."[22]

But by the end of the decade, adjustment lending—with its double aim of covering a balance of payments gap and bringing about needed structural change

20. Elliot Berg and Alan Batchelder, "Structural Adjustment Lending: A Critical View," World Bank CPD Discussion Paper 1985-21 (Washington, 1985), p. 27.

21. Ernest Stern, "World Bank Financing of Structural Adjustment," in Williamson, *IMF Conditionality*, p. 103.

22. Please, *The Hobbled Giant*, p. 30.

—had generally been accepted as one of the Bank's important and permanent activities. In the second report on structural adjustment lending the rationale for such lending is given as follows:

> 1.1. In the typical country initiating a structural adjustment program, the government has realized that major policy reforms offer the best hope for restoring sustainable growth. Balance of payments financing facilitates the phased reduction of the financing gap over a period of time, while structural reforms are being implemented and their effects start to emerge.[23]

There is no clear distinction between this rationale and that of lending by the IMF, as currently interpreted. Such lending is justified by the Fund's fifth purpose:

> (v) To give confidence to members by making the general resources of the Fund temporarily available to them under adequate safeguards, thus providing them with opportunity to correct maladjustments in their balance of payments without resorting to measures destructive of national or international prosperity.[24]

This purpose lacks the reference to sustainable growth as a component of the Fund's rationale. But in the past few years, the Fund has moved in the direction of elevating growth to one of its explicit purposes, indeed to its quintessential objective. The managing director told the Economic and Social Council of the United Nations (ECOSOC) in its July 1990 meeting: "Our prime objective is growth. . . . It is with a view toward growth that we carry out our special responsibility of helping to correct balance of payments disequilibria."[25]

As will be discussed below, the conditionality applied by the two institutions in these lending operations, while not becoming identical, has converged into a large common area, and in general the countries borrowing under these conditions have been the same. Against this background, it is surprising that the first two Bank reports on SAL operations claim virtually sole credit for the Bank for the improvement in economic performance in countries that have had extended Bank adjustment programs. Thus, in its 1990 study on the effect of the Bank's adjustment lending policies, the Bank observed that "Bank involvement in a country's adjustment program has, on average, been associated with better growth performance." Specifically, it found that between 1981–84 and 1985–88, adjustment programs were estimated to have added close to 2 percentage points to the rate of GDP growth.[26] The possibility that simultaneous Fund programs might also deserve

23. World Bank, *Adjustment Lending Policies for Sustainable Growth,* Policy and Research Series, no. 14 (Washington, 1990), p. 1.

24. International Monetary Fund, *Articles of Agreement* (Washington, 1976), Article I, Purpose (v), p. 2.

25. Jacques J. Polak, *The Changing Nature of IMF Conditionality,* Essays in International Finance, no. 184 (Princeton University), pp. 18–19.

26. World Bank, *Adjustment Lending Policies,* pp. 11, 18. It is an ironic comment on Fund-Bank collaboration in the research field that an almost simultaneous and in many

some credit for the good performance observed is disposed of by a throwaway comment: "The IMF was also supporting most of these programs."[27] In the third report on adjustment lending, the inseparability of the effects of Fund and Bank adjustment programs is duly recorded in the introductory chapter, the reader apparently being trusted to recall this admonition when he reads the body of the report on the effects of Bank adjustment lending.[28]

The Debt Crisis

As mentioned earlier in this section, the developments in world financial markets in the late 1970s and early 1980s had largely narrowed down the clientele of the Fund to countries that experienced difficulties in servicing previously contracted debt; such countries were also responsible for an important part of the portfolio of the Bank. As a consequence, both institutions became, in the course of the 1980s, deeply involved in the debt crisis.

In the first phase of this crisis, from August 1982 to late 1985, when the primary concern of the major industrial countries was the protection of the international banking system, the Fund, under the spirited guidance of its managing director, Jacques de Larosière, carried the main load for the international institutions. It was the Fund that negotiated policy packages with debtor countries, starting with Mexico, and assembled the quid pro quo financial packages. The Fund put up large amounts of credit; it persuaded governments to extend export credits and commercial banks to restructure loans falling due, provide "new money" (additional credit),

---

respects similar Fund study found that the growth rate of countries with Fund programs was significantly reduced compared with the growth rate in countries without such programs. Mohsin S. Khan, "The Macroeconomic Effects of Fund-Supported Adjustment Programs," *International Monetary Fund Staff Papers*, vol. 37 (June 1990), p. 215, cited in Polak, *The Changing Nature*, p. 42. There are sufficient differences in the techniques used in the two studies to account for the differences in findings, but these questions are not explored in the sources mentioned.

27. World Bank, *Adjustment Lending Policies*, p. 18.

28. World Bank, *Adjustment Lending and Mobilization of Private and Public Resources for Growth* (Washington, 1992), p. 7. "Bank adjustment lending is usually undertaken in parallel with IMF programs—almost always for SALs and in most cases for SECALs. The Fund has primary responsibility for supporting policy changes to tackle the immediate sources of inflation or balance of payments difficulty and the Bank for supporting measures that get a new pattern of growth going. Macroeconomic and structural reform are intimately linked, however, and their effects cannot be sensibly separated. The analysis is thus, to a large extent, equivalent to an assessment of the joint effects of Bank- and Fund-supported programs."

A similar view is expressed in a Bank research paper. See Patrick Conway, *How Successful Is World Bank Lending for Structural Adjustment?* World Bank Country Economics Department, Policy, Research, and External Affairs Working Papers, WPS 581 (Washington, January 1991), p. 22.

and maintain interbank lines of credit. Although the Bank participated in the financial packages, in this phase of the debt crisis, in which the emphasis was still primarily on stabilization rather than deepgoing structural adjustment, its role and financial contribution were modest.[29] In the three calendar years 1983–85, the Fund lent $12.7 billion to the six largest problem debtors (Argentina, Brazil, Chile, Mexico, the Philippines, and Yugoslavia), compared with $2.3 billion in adjustment loans to the same countries from the Bank.[30]

The Baker initiative, unveiled at the Fund-Bank annual meetings in Seoul in October 1985, in response to the unexpected persistence of the debt crisis, envisaged greatly expanded structural adjustment lending by the Bank as well as a more modest lending role for the Fund. In the next two years (1986–87) gross lending to the same six countries by the two institutions were about the same (about $4.5 billion), but as the Fund's repurchase provisions started to kick in, net lending by the Fund in this period became negative. With the increase in the Bank's financial role, its policy role also became more important; in several cases (Colombia, Mexico) commercial banks began to rely on disbursement decisions of the Bank, rather than the Fund, as triggers for the release of successive tranches of commercial bank credit.

In March 1989, the debt crisis entered upon a third phase, in which the two institutions were called upon to make parallel efforts. In response to an initiative by U.S. Secretary of the Treasury Nicholas F. Brady, the Fund and the Bank adopted substantially similar guidelines to govern the access to additional credit by heavily indebted countries that were willing to undertake satisfactory policy packages. In this phase, the negotiation of stabilization packages fell again clearly to the Fund; the Bank, at the same time, continued to play its major role in the design of structural reforms in such areas as tax policy and administration (a field in which the Fund was also active), the reform of public enterprises, social security, trade, financial sectors, and, in more recent years, privatization.

Areas of Potential Conflict

As the two institutions moved their fields of operation increasingly toward a common area, many facets of their activities tended to converge: the list of client countries, conditionality, and, finally, the specific policy areas in which both institutions had major, but not always compatible, interests.

29. During this period, the Bank did actively pursue a wide range of studies on the debt problem as evidenced, for example, by the symposium on debt that it organized in April 1984. See Gordon W. Smith and John T. Cuddington, eds., *International Debt and the Developing Countries* (Washington: World Bank, 1985).

30. Jacques J. Polak, *Financial Policies and Development* (Paris: Organization for Economic Cooperation and Development, 1989), p. 170, table 8.4.

Converging Clientele

Once the Bank had phased out its lending to industrial countries, the Fund and the Bank had quite divergent lists of client countries. The Fund of course had major financial dealings with many developed countries, including the United Kingdom, France, Italy, and Japan. With most of these, as well as with the larger developing countries, its financial relations were episodic in character—related to relatively brief payments crises, with credits reversed as soon as the payments position had been straightened out. Some major developing countries that were consistent borrowers from the Bank did not need the Fund for decades (Mexico did not draw between 1962 and 1976; Venezuela drew for the first time in 1989; and so, except for some minor amounts, did Nigeria).[31] With the onset of the debt crisis, however, all pressures worked to steer countries that borrowed from one institution to also turn to the other for credit. From the start of its structural lending activity, the Bank operated on the general principle that eligibility for adjustment lending required a concurrent stabilization program supported by the Fund. Although there were a few notable exceptions to this rule (which are discussed later in this chapter), it became universal after the Fund-Bank accord of March 1989.[32] In particular since the start of the debt crisis, the Fund has actively promoted "financing packages" for countries whose policies it supported, and the World Bank was always an obvious candidate to seek out in this connection. And, lastly, the borrowing country itself, once it had taken the often very hard decision to adopt the kind of policies that the Fund and the Bank espoused, had every reason to start negotiations with both in order to obtain maximum financial support for these policies. It is not surprising then to find that most countries that the Bank classified as "intensive adjustment lending" countries had arrangements with the Fund in five, six, seven, or even eight years of the period 1980 to 1988.[33]

Converging Conditionality

"Conditionality" is a term of art (or perhaps less generously, a bit of jargon) that refers to the conditions of economic policy a lender stipulates as a basis for concluding a loan arrangement and for allowing subsequent drawings under such an arrangement. Writing in the early 1970s, Edward Mason and Robert Asher used the term exclusively to describe the conditions imposed by the Fund, although by that time the Bank had already been experimenting in a few countries (Peru, Chile) with loan conditions affecting the conduct of macroeconomic policy.[34] In the

31. IMF, *International Financial Statistics* (Washington), various issues.

32. World Bank, *Adjustment Lending Policies,* para. 4.22.

33. Based on a comparison of the data in World Bank, *Adjustment Lending and Mobilization of Private and Public Resources for Growth* (Washington, 1992), p. 15, table 1.1, and Khan, "Macroeconomic Effects," p. 226, table 7.

34. Mason and Asher, *The World Bank since Bretton Woods,* pp. 895, 452–54.

context of structural adjustment lending, however, conditionality in broad economic policies became an integral part of Bank-member relationships.

Although some convergence has occurred over the years, the Bank's practices on conditionality differ considerably from those of the Fund. In its pure form, Fund conditionality stipulates a limited number (rarely more than ten) of monitorable indicators of performance. If at the end of a specified period (typically a quarter) all performance criteria are met, the member's access to the next tranche is ensured; if only a single performance criterion is not met, drawings are automatically interrupted. The Bank's conditions are far more numerous, averaging fifty-six per SAL in a recent year (1989).[35] Many of them are in general terms and not monitorable, thus leaving the release of a second (or in some SALs a third) tranche a subject of negotiation or judgment. Although the Bank has increased reliance on numerical indicators, their function is still only to guide the Bank in making judgments about whether the country is proceeding along a satisfactory macroeconomic path.[36]

The difference in the conditionality practices of the two institutions is, however, less stark than the preceding description might suggest. Fund conditionality is not applied in its pure form. First, the Fund may grant waivers for minor deviations from the agreed criteria, or accept program revisions in the case of major ones. In both cases, disbursements still occur, though not on the dates originally envisaged. Second, the Fund nowadays normally includes a midterm "review" of conditionality in a standby arrangement, which amounts to a fresh consideration between the Fund and the member of the conditions that will apply to the remaining drawings under arrangement.[37] Nevertheless, the outcome for disbursements under a given arrangement differs considerably between the two institutions. In the Fund, a considerable proportion of standby arrangements is canceled before all contemplated drawings are made. In the Bank, while delays in tranche releases under SALs and SECALs are common, the second and third tranches are in the end almost without exception released,[38] and hard bargaining is reserved for the time when the next SAL is negotiated.[39] A factor contributing to the Bank's approach is the staff's "perceived bias toward disbursement," which probably explains in the

35. World Bank, *Adjustment Lending Policies*, p. 55, table 4.6.

36. Polak, *The Changing Nature*, p. 57.

37. The effect of the review is "that one advantage of conditionality for the member country is lost, namely, assured access as long as those clauses are met." Alexandre Kafka, "Some IMF Problems after the Committee of Twenty," in Frenkel and Goldstein, *International Financial Policy*, p. 121.

38. World Bank, Operations Evaluation Department, *Effectiveness of SAL Supervision and Monitoring* (Washington, June 1991), p. 36.

39. The approach to conditionality is in some respects similar to that followed by the Fund for three-year SAF credits. There is no midyear review, and the full annual amount is released as soon as an annual program is agreed upon. Serious policy negotiation takes place before the next annual program, which may be delayed for many months or indeed fail to go into effect.

first place why the staff feels comfortable with a multiplicity of imprecise conditions.[40] Curiously, pressure from the IMF also receives some credit (if that is the correct term) for the ease with which SAL tranches are released. The calculations underlying the Fund's financial programs normally allow for any expected SAL disbursements; if these do not occur on time, the country may miss a Fund performance criterion, thus cutting off Fund credit as well.[41]

Despite the differences in the techniques of conditionality practiced by the two institutions, the convergence on many of the same indicators opens up wide areas for mutually reinforcing conditionality and for potential conflict.[42]

"No Cross-Conditionality!"

One of the trickiest issues arising in this connection relates to cross-conditionality.

The term itself is presumably an offshoot of the long-standing provision of cross-default: an understanding among creditors of the same debtor that default toward one creditor will be considered default toward all. Similarly, cross-conditionality between the Fund and the Bank (usually conceived of in one direction only—from Fund to Bank—given that only the Fund applies its conditionality in an automatic manner) would mean that failure by a debtor country to meet the conditions of the Fund would entail inability to draw the initial or subsequent tranches of a Bank SAL or SECAL. The developing countries, which consider such a provision as a "ganging up" by the two institutions against them, have sought to establish a taboo on cross-conditionality. In a formal sense they have succeeded; both institutions adhere to the slogan "No cross-conditionality!" as an article of faith.[43] The practical significance of this achievement is perhaps less clear cut.

To begin with, one may wonder how two institutions that both extend balance of payments credit subject to macroeconomic conditionality, and that put great store in the harmonization of the views expressed by their respective staffs (as expressed by that other slogan: "Avoid inconsistent advice"), can fail to end up with packages of policy conditions that must be very much the same in substance if not procedure. There is some logic in the position taken by one executive director in the Bank's Committee of the Whole when it discussed the March 1989 agreement, who stated

40. World Bank, *Effectiveness of SAL Supervision and Monitoring,* pp. 31, 34, 46.
41. Ibid., pp. 27, 28.
42. On a procedural level, one can note a convergence between the disbursement cycles of SALs and Fund ESAF credits. SAL tranching has tended to move from two to three (that is, to an approximately six-month cycle), and ESAF has proceeded from quarterly to half-yearly disbursement.
43. See World Bank, "Bank-Fund Collaboration in Assisting Member Countries," R89-45 (Washington, March 31, 1989), para. 24. "The Executive Directors of the Bank and the Fund have stressed repeatedly the need to avoid cross-conditionality: each institution must continue to proceed with its own financial assistance according to the standards laid down in its Articles of Agreement and the policies adopted by its Executive Board."

that he was against regular meetings between senior staff of the Bank and the Fund as well as all the provisions for strengthening collaboration.[44]

One large step toward de facto cross-conditionality consists in the Bank's practice—usual before, and universal since, March 1989—to limit adjustment lending to countries having concurrent stabilization programs with the IMF. That practice does not ensure that the country in question is still observing the Fund's conditionality when it comes to the release of subsequent tranches. "The absence of cross-conditionality means that, after approval of a loan by the Board, failure to meet the Fund targets is not grounds to hold up effectiveness and tranche releases of a Bank loan. *Therefore, the loan agreements also need to contain a clear definition of expected progress in the macroeconomic program.*"[45] Interestingly, this arrangement, ostensibly to avoid cross-conditionality, conforms exactly to what the Fund's former general counsel had warned against as constituting "double jeopardy or cross-conditionality," namely, "the application by each organization of the criteria of both."[46] And the present general counsel of the Bank comes to substantively the same conclusion: while the Bank and the Fund avoid "cross-conditionality in the legal sense," any meaningful discussion of this subject should not, he warns, ignore the reality that the Bank does not normally provide adjustment loans to countries without a Fund program.[47]

Converging Areas of Policy Concern

With both institutions active in the structural adjustment business, the old demarcation lines—short term and macro for the Fund, long term and micro (or structural) for the Bank—have tended to fade. The exchange rate, the local currency prices paid for producers of major exports, such as coffee or cocoa, the prices for major consumer goods, such as rice or petroleum, the fiscal situation—to name only a few typical variables—are equally crucial to the success of a Fund arrangement as to that of a Bank structural credit.

But overlapping areas of policy concern do not readily ensure identities of view. There are, in the first place, the essentially personal differences of view on the extent that certain policy variables in a given country need to be changed. With

44. "Summary of Discussion of the Meeting of the Executive Directors of the Bank and IDA, in a Committee of the Whole," SD 89-21, May 9, 1989 (Washington, June 1, 1989), para. 43. (Hereafter "Committee of the Whole.")

45. World Bank, *Adjustment Lending Policies*, para. 4.22. Emphasis added.

46. Joseph Gold, "The Relationship between the International Monetary Fund and the World Bank," *Creighton Law Review*, vol. 15 (1981–82), pp. 499–521, reprinted in Joseph Gold, *Legal and Institutional Aspects of the International Monetary System: Selected Essays*, vol. II (Washington: IMF, 1984), p. 474.

47. "Bank-Fund Coordination—Questions in Respect of the Recent Note on Collaboration regarding the States of the Former Soviet Union," memorandum of the vice president and general counsel, SecM92-640, Washington, May 14, 1992, p. 9.

their broadly common economic training and developing-country experience, all Fund and Bank economists may agree on the need for a shift in a certain policy variable—say, the exchange rate or the budget deficit. But the magnitude of the change needed does not have a precise scientific answer. In any organization, differences of view on such questions are ultimately decided hierarchically. Between organizations, there is no higher authority to decide. The procedural steps agreed between the two managements provide for the upward movement of contentious questions. When differences of view are indeed random and personal, this process is likely to lead rather easily to an agreed answer, as officials further away from the individual case will be more inclined to see the other's point of view and have less to lose by compromising.

Typically, however, the differences that come into the open between Bank and Fund staff are not random or personal, but institutional. Indeed, many of the conflicts between the two institutions in the 1980s can be seen as part of a long—too long—mutual learning process on the design of consistent short- and medium-term Fund-Bank programs, in which the short-term stabilization expertise of the Fund is married to the medium-term growth frameworks and the institution-building expertise of the Bank.

A Bank staff report to the board, of which considerable use is made in the remainder of this section, presents a balanced view of these institutionally determined differences of view on three critical aspects of adjustment programs.[48]

GOVERNMENT REVENUE AND EXPENDITURE. Bank and Fund staffs are of course aware of the need to reduce the government deficit as an essential element in any stabilization policy. But they tend to conceive of this objective in light of different institutional priorities. For the Fund, the achievement of a deficit target by cutting expenditure and raising revenue is seen as extremely important. This action may entail some compromises on what are in themselves desirable expenditures (such as local currency counterpart funds for Bank-sponsored investment projects or social expenditures on poverty reduction) or on less than desirable taxes (for example, temporary taxes on certain exports to which the Bank wants to give the maximum incentive). These differences of view on fiscal priorities, combined with different premises as to what can realistically be achieved, may lead the Bank staff to accept a higher target for the budget deficit than does the Fund staff—the Bank tending to question the realism of the assumption that structural deficits could quickly be turned around by attempts to increase taxes and compress government wages and investment, and the Fund, the realism of counting on additional foreign financing to cover the larger deficit.

THE BALANCE OF PAYMENTS GAP. In making medium-term projections of the balance of payments and financing gaps, the Fund typically uses an "availa-

48. World Bank, Country Policy Department, *Progress Report on Bank-Fund Collaboration,* RD 86-112 (Washington, May 29, 1986), pp. 4–5.

bility" approach (how large a deficit will the country be able to finance?) and the Bank, a "requirements" approach (how much foreign financing does the country need to meet a specified target?). The Fund's approach reflects concern over the achievement of macroeconomic balance and a viable payments position within available resources; the Bank's traditional emphasis is on the financing and imports required to achieve a specified rate of consumption or growth.

EXCHANGE RATES. In no area of conditionality are the motivations and the interests of the two institutions as complicated as in that of the exchange rate. Until the early 1980s, the Bank staff was generally prepared to leave exchange rate matters to the Fund. This was in line with the agreed distribution of primary responsibility. It was also the most comfortable position to adopt. To battle the minister of finance on an issue on which he had staked his and the government's prestige was perhaps not the choicest way for the Bank's mission or its resident representative to make friends or win influence. If the Fund mission were willing to assume the role of the "bad guy," the Bank's representative could afford to stand aside as the "good guy" who delivered the politically attractive goodies.[49]

But work in the Bank's Economics Department since the early 1980s tended to shift at least some of the Bank staff from being gentler to being more hawkish than the Fund staff on exchange rates as they increasingly sought long-run changes in countries' economic structure, including in particular the development of new export industries.[50] This objective might require a more depreciated real exchange rate than the Fund economists would contemplate, leading some Bank economists to the conclusion that even though a country had a Fund program, the Bank might consider it necessary to include exchange rate conditions in its loan "because the Fund has different exchange rate objectives than the Bank."[51] Differences on exchange rate policy were particularly pronounced in the countries that form the West African Monetary Union, where the Bank favored devaluation of the CFA franc—even insisting on a quasi-devaluation by means of export subsidies and

49. Oral information from Alassane D. Ouattara, who was then the director of the Fund's African Department, around 1985. A somewhat similar view from the Bank's side is given by Stanley Please, who worries why the Bank has a more favorable image than the Fund. "Is it possible," he asks, "that the Bank has 'bought' its relatively good image too dearly" by avoiding putting major policy issues in the center of its operations? See Please, *The Hobbled Giant*, pp. 96–97.

50. See, for example, Constantine Michalopoulos, "World Bank Programs for Adjustment and Growth," in Vittorio Corbo, Morris Goldstein, and Mohsin Khan, *Growth-Oriented Adjustment Programs* (Washington: IMF/World Bank, 1987): "The Bank has tended to place greater reliance on exchange rate adjustment relative to fiscal or monetary contraction as a means of demand-side adjustment because of the potential benefit that exchange rate adjustment could have to medium-term restructuring of the economy" (pp. 52–53).

51. Fred Jaspersen and Karim Shariff, *The Macroeconomic Underpinnings of Adjustment Lending*, World Bank Policy, Research, and External Affairs Working Papers, WPS 511 (Washington, October 1990), p. 11.

import duties in Côte d'Ivoire—while the Fund supported alternative adjustment measures to preserve the stabilizing effects of the CFA system. For both CFA countries and other countries, Fund economists, though sharing the developmental objectives of their Bank colleagues, might be more inclined to question whether nominal devaluation would achieve a durable real depreciation of the magnitude desired—that is to say, whether in many countries the main effect of nominal devaluation might not be continuous inflation. (It so happened that roughly at that same time [in the mid-1980s] at least part of the Fund's board and staff were having second thoughts about the Fund's experience with targeting sharply devalued real exchange rates and showed an increasing interest in the use of the exchange rate as an anchor for price stability.)[52]

Arrears

Until the debt crisis of the 1980s, the Fund and the Bank operated on the assumption that they enjoyed the status of "preferred creditors" and that no borrowing country, however severe its difficulties, would risk its reputation by failing to pay interest and amortization to the institutions when due. The decade of the 1980s proved that this assumption was not necessarily valid, which produced a new source of potential conflict between the institutions.

As the debt crisis unfolded, both the Fund's and the Bank's portfolios proved vulnerable to the problem of arrears. Any comparison is admittedly open to qualifications; the classification of countries in serious arrears ("nonaccrual status" in the Bank, "ineligibility" in the Fund) is not fully comparable between the two institutions, the number of countries involved is small, and the considerable movement in and out of the arrears category affects the comparison as of any one date. As of the end of their respective 1991 fiscal years (the Fund's ending in April, the Bank's in June), the Fund listed nine and the Bank listed eight countries in serious arrears, but only four of them appeared on both lists. The absolute amounts of credit outstanding to the countries in serious arrears were also similar (around $2.5 billion in the Bank, around $3.1 billion in the Fund). But these amounts were a much smaller proportion of total loans outstanding in the Bank (less than 3 percent) than in the Fund (more than 10 percent).[53]

Although specific factors were frequently responsible for a country falling into arrears with one or the other organization, or for working itself out of an arrears situation, at least one systematic factor explains why the Fund's arrears problem has

52. Polak, *The Changing Nature*, pp. 37–38.

53. Data from *World Bank Annual Report 1991*, pp. 193, 203; and IMF *Annual Report 1991*, pp. 67–68, 147. (The figures differ from those for "amounts in arrears," which include overdue interest but exclude amounts owed by countries in arrears but that have not yet fallen due.) Liberia, Panama, Sierra Leone, and Peru were in arrears to both institutions. Guatemala, Nicaragua, Iraq, and the Syrian Arab Republic appear on the Bank list only; of these, the latter two had no debt to the Fund. Cambodia, Somalia, Sudan, Vietnam, and Zambia appear on the Fund list only; the latter country, after having cleared its Bank arrears during fiscal 1991, was in a workout process aimed at clearing its Fund arrears.

been proportionally more serious than the Bank's: the nature of its lending operations gives the Bank opportunities to stave off impending arrears that the Fund
lacks. A country that has slipped into a position where its policies no longer qualify
it for Fund credit may still continue to receive a stream of money from Bank
project loans, which makes default vis-à-vis the Bank an unattractive option.[54]

The two institutions' different flow patterns of new credits versus interest and
amortization on old loans have made it difficult for the Fund and the Bank to agree
on a common line toward countries in arrears to one of them. The Fund's inclination has been to ask for a cessation of any new lending or disbursement on the part
of both organizations to any country in default on its obligations to one of them. But
a strict rule of this nature would run against the interest of the Bank, which might
in some cases want to maintain some net disbursement to minimize the default risk.
The ambiguous provisions on the response to arrears that were agreed in the 1989
concordat reflect these conflicts of interest (see below).

Institutional Differences

The many years of living almost entirely separate lives had ill prepared the
Bretton Woods twins for the involuntary cohabitation that the experience of the
1980s forced upon them. In their dealings with developing-country members, the
Fund and the Bank found themselves in what was very much the same business:
structural adjustment lending subject to policy conditionality to countries struggling with persistent balance of payments difficulties. It was a situation that cried
out for the closest possible collaboration, perhaps with an agreed assignment of
tasks if serious conflicts were to be avoided. Cooperation, which had appeared as
merely desirable over the preceding decades, became imperative at short notice.

This task was not easy for two institutions that had over time acquired such
different personalities (or "cultures," to use the term frequently applied as a
capsule description of their different identities). For one thing, the Fund had for a
long time managed to remain relatively small; even after recent increases, its staff
in 1992 numbered about 2,500. The corresponding figure for the Bank group
(which includes the International Finance Corporation [IFC]) is about 9,000.[55]

54. In addition, the Bank introduced in 1988 a facility to assist certain countries that had
both Bank loans and IDA credits outstanding with the payment of interest on their loans.
Under what was called the "Fifth Dimension" scheme, IDA-only countries with outstanding
Bank loans could receive supplementary annual IDA allocations for approximately 90 percent of the amount they owed the Bank as interest, provided (a) they were current in their
debt service payments to both the Bank and IDA and (b) they had IDA-supported adjustment programs. *The Use of IDA Reflows*, IDA/R88-106 (Washington, September 16, 1988).

55. Calculations provided by Fund staff. Figures for both institutions include consultants
and temporary contractuals and exclude executive directors' offices and their staffs. Memorandum from Hartmut Wiesner to Paul Wright re comparison of IMF and World Bank
staffing for FY 1992–93, Washington, August 25, 1992.

Most of the Fund's professionals are economists; the functions of the Bank required the integration of many other professions—engineers, agriculturalists, financial planners, education specialists, and many others. Size and diversity have brought forth a heavier bureaucratic structure in the Bank than in the Fund. In the Bank more time is spent on budgeting, many-year planning, internal coordination, reporting, and large meetings than in the Fund. Until a few years ago, the term "management" in the Fund referred to two persons, the managing director and the deputy managing director; in the Bank, some 500 persons (division chiefs and up) carry the title of "manager."[56] As a result, the Bank's decisionmaking is slower, more ponderous than that of the Fund. At the same time, the Fund staff is more disciplined; "policy positions and relations with members are firmly controlled from the top."[57] Bank staff members are less constrained than Fund staff in making statements about countries' policies, knowing the Bank will, if necessary, disown such statements as "personal views."[58] Consultants, which the Bank uses much more extensively than the Fund and who have only a limited loyalty to the organization, would in any event be more difficult than staff members to keep in line.

The difference in culture is evident also in the way one organization tends to respond to a draft policy paper of the other that it receives for comment. If the Fund receives such a request from the Bank, views from various departments or divisions will be consolidated into a single memorandum signed by a senior official. But if the Fund asks the Bank for its views, it is more likely to receive in response a bundle of memorandums written by a variety of staff members throughout the Bank, expressing their personal views.

In a recent conversation with the author, a British observer (Clyde Crook, the economics editor of *The Economist*) likened the Fund's coherence, discipline, and esprit de corps (combined perhaps with a certain arrogance?) to the characteristics of the U.K. Treasury. Arrogance indeed was what some senior Bank officials felt characterized the attitude of the Fund staff. As one put it: "It has proved difficult to get collaboration in substance because of the difference in responsibilities, but it has been made far more difficult by the nature of the Fund as a human institution which is

56. The 1991 figure was 534, World Bank Personnel Department, Washington, prepared by Bill Silverman.

57. Richard Goode and Andrew M. Kamarck, "The International Monetary Fund and the World Bank," in Joseph A. Pechman, ed., *The Role of the Economist in Government, an International Perspective* (New York, London: Harvester-Wheatsheaf, 1989), p. 233.

58. The mutual exasperation on the subject of staff freedom of speech in the two institutions is well reflected in a passage from an observation by Ernest Stern in the course of the negotiation of the concordat: "It is the Fund's favorite activity to claim that every time a Bank staff member says something in the field with which the Fund disagrees, we have made a policy recommendation. Policy recommendations are only those negotiating conditions approved by the Regional Vice President and the Senior Vice President, Operations." ("Comments on the Bank-Fund Collaboration in Financial Assistance Paper," attached memorandum, Ernest Stern to Barber Conable and Stanley Fischer, January 19, 1989.)

secretive, which is arrogant, which is very patronizing in terms of what the Bank does as opposed to what they do, this whole superior attitude of the Fund in always treating the Bank as a second-class citizen."⁵⁹ By contrast, the Bank's more free-wheeling style would rather remind one of the larger departments of the U.S. administration.

One of the major differences in operation between the two institutions is found in the process through which operations in the Bank ("transactions" in the Fund) are prepared. Some of these differences are inherent in the different functions that the two institutions perform. Even with the widening of the Fund's interests into structural aspects, poverty issues, even the environment, the bread and butter of Fund missions remains the crucially important issues of macroeconomic management, such as monetary policy, overall fiscal policy, and the exchange rate. Over the years, the Fund has built up, and instilled into its staff, a well-programmed approach to these issues. The mission's counterparts in the receiving country are primarily finance ministries and central banks. The subjects with which the Bank has to deal are not so neatly concentrated. It has to pay attention to a much wider array of issues, stretching over many sectors and institutions; it also has a longer planning horizon and its contacts in the government need to be much more widely dispersed than the Fund's. The separate pursuit by the two institutions of these different tasks has over time led to widely divergent practices in their relations with member countries. These differences can perhaps best be illustrated by a comparison of Bank and Fund operational missions—in both institutions a major instrument in the design of financial transactions.

As a result of the Fund's practice of holding, normally annually, intensive consultations with all its member countries and other contacts, its staff is generally quite familiar with the financial situation in a country that makes a preliminary request for a standby arrangement. This makes it possible for the mission to prepare, before departing, a brief that sets out broadly the amount and the policy conditions of a Fund credit on which the mission is authorized to agree with the country it is going to visit. The brief is cleared by the head of the regional department and other interested departments and approved by the managing director. As a result of this brief, the mission is in a position to negotiate a letter of intent on behalf of the Fund's management. If unexpected developments seem to make it necessary to deviate from the brief, the mission is in contact with headquarters to ensure that whatever it agrees to is backed by Washington. Although formally the mission chief agrees *ad referendum* to the letter of intent, it is usually possible for him to confirm management agreement within a few days after the mission's return to headquarters. It then takes a few weeks (in urgent cases a long

59. Stanley Please, "Oral History," August 26, 1986, p. 6. Please also acknowledges instances of arrogance in the Bank, but as the misbehavior of a "very small minority" rather than as a pervasive cultural trait. See Please, *The Hobbled Giant*, pp. 98–99.

weekend) to prepare the mission's report to the executive board. Board approval within three or four weeks after submission of the report is then a practical certainty; only on the rarest occasion has the Fund board found it necessary to overrule the managing director on an agreement that he had authorized his staff to negotiate with a member country.[60] In the Bank, too, management approval virtually ensures passage of a loan proposal through the executive board.

The Bank, dealing with a much broader range of issues, for many of which ready-made solutions may not be at hand, generally cannot send out a mission with a well-defined mandate on how to solve the country's problems. Before negotiations about a SAL or a SECAL are undertaken, an "appraisal mission" visits the country with the task of exploring options. That mission is guided by instructions from the (interdepartmental) Loan Committee on the basis of an "initiating memorandum" prepared by the region. The process of negotiation with the country starts only after the appraisal mission has reached agreement with the authorities on the broad design of the program. In the event of major changes from the original proposal, this agreement is again reviewed by the Loan Committee.

Although the scope of the Bank's interests may have made this two-step process of reaching agreement with a borrowing country unavoidable, it nevertheless has several drawbacks. To begin with, it takes more time (see below), which makes coordination with Fund financial support more difficult. Also, since the appraisal mission (unlike a Fund operational mission) has no authority to commit the Bank, it is handicapped in obtaining far-reaching agreements from the authorities of the borrowing country. Problems not resolved at this stage may reemerge in the process of negotiation (which is usually held in Washington).

The complexity of the Bank's operations is also reflected in a number of other differences from the Fund. Bank missions tend to be larger than Fund missions (say, eight to ten persons rather than four to six). They also last longer (say, three to four weeks rather than two). Unlike Fund missions, Bank appraisal missions are typically headed by someone below the rank of division chief. One reason is that the Bank has fewer regional division chiefs than the Fund—about half as many to

---

60. One such occasion (perhaps the only one in the Fund's history) occurred in November 1979, when the board considered a standby arrangement of SDR 17 million for Sierra Leone. Almost all directors from the industrial countries considered the program too weak to qualify for drawings in the upper credit tranches without the further measures that were promised to be implemented by the time of the first review only. They therefore suggested that the initial drawing, proposed at SDR 9 million in the staff paper, be scaled back to the balance remaining in the country's first credit tranche (the first 25 percent of quota), which was SDR 6.9 million. Even in this case, however, the view of the managing director on the issue of principle prevailed: while there was some reduction in the amount of the first drawing, the compromise agreed was SDR 7.5 million, which included at least a symbolic amount in the second credit tranche. Executive Board Minutes (EBM) 79/168 and 79/169, November 2, 1979. (After two satisfactory reviews, Sierra Leone was allowed to draw the full SDR 17 million.)

cover the same number of developing countries. Second, the heavy bureaucratic structure of the Bank compels division chiefs to spend a large proportion of their time "managing" their divisions, leaving little time for work in the field. Most important, the process of negotiating financial assistance to a country takes much longer in the Bank than in the Fund. Reports underlying Bank loans "rarely take less (and typically considerably more) than six months to progress through their various drafts."[61] While the Fund is geared to respond quickly to requests for financial assistance and negotiates agreements within months or even weeks, the Bank usually requires a lead time of up to a year or more to put a structural adjustment loan in place. The Bank considers this time well spent if it has the intended effect of ensuring better policy management in the future as a result of governments taking "deep remedial action."[62] There is, indeed, a widely held view in the Bank that its procedures, time consuming as they may be, have a better chance of leading to an adjustment program that the government "owns" and therefore fully supports than the less flexible programs that countries agree to with the Fund under severe time pressure.[63]

These different operating modes, which have grown up over the years in the two institutions, put practical difficulties in the way of collaboration between them. Reasons of timing make it difficult for the Bank to become associated with an external financing package in support of a Fund adjustment program. The Fund has also at times found it impossible to wait for the Bank to provide it with a judgment on a country's investment program, perhaps not always realizing that it is much simpler to set a ceiling on public expenditure than to perform the laborious task of deciding the least harmful way of applying individual cuts.[64]

A 1988 Bank report notes the difficulties in achieving full synchronization of the cycles of SAF operations in the Fund and adjustment lending in the Bank, which could only be done "at appreciable cost . . . which may well outweigh the benefits that would derive from it." Perhaps so, but sometimes an air of complacency seems to permeate the Bank's plea not to be disturbed in the periodicity of its operations:

61. George B. Baldwin, "Economics and Economists in the World Bank," in A. W. Coats, ed., *Economists in International Agencies* (Praeger, 1986), p. 79.

62. Please, "Oral History," August 26, 1986, p. 18.

63. From a conference paper by two Bank staff members: "A key aspect [of Bank program-type aid] is the element of consensus in the policy adjustment. Unlike programmes which are initiated in crisis conditions [read: Fund programs] and allow limited input and flexibility for the recipient, adjustment programmes are, for the most part, initiated outside of crisis conditions. . . . The acceptance of the conditions in the finance agreement by the member country ought to reflect an agreement on their appropriateness on the part of the policy-makers." V. Thomas and K. Meyers, "Development Lending and Conditionality," in C. J. Jepma, ed., *North-South Cooperation in Retrospect and Prospect* (London and New York, Routledge, 1988), p. 146.

64. World Bank, "Bank-Fund Collaboration," R85-30 (Washington, February 4, 1985), para. 67.

Bank lending, of both the adjustment and non-adjustment type, is quite diversified in form and content and is processed and presented to the Board on a continuing basis during the year. The dialogue with country authorities that lies behind it is also multifaceted and takes place at various levels. The programming and management of Bank lending are, therefore, quite complex. This also applies to Bank adjustment lending, which has different components that are structured around different cycles and specific instrumentation.[65]

If the Fund, which is set to perform on cycles of much shorter amplitude, cannot always wait for the Bank, the Bank has also sometimes been handicapped by the set timing of the Fund's consultation cycles—normally only once a year. This question arises especially for countries where there is no Fund program, and where the economic situation or the country's policies may have changed significantly since the last consultations. "In these cases"—it was agreed in 1989—"the Bank will ask the Fund's views, leaving time for consultations with the country authorities as needed."[66] In other words, the Fund commits itself henceforth to conduct such supplementary consultations promptly to produce a view that can serve as a basis for the Bank's structural adjustment operations.

Uneasy Cooperation, 1980–88

In the course of the 1980s the staffs of the Bank and the Fund periodically submitted reports to their executive boards on the status of Fund-Bank collaboration. These were informative documents that went into considerable detail about the difficulties that had been encountered. They invariably concluded that the two institutions had, in one way or another, resolved the differences of view. In broad terms and in elegant prose the message delivered was that cooperation was essential, that it was working better and better, and that there was a need for further improvement. One sentence taken from a Fund report conveys, in carefully chosen words, satisfaction with the partial success and no more than a hint at the corresponding partial failure:

> In several countries, lending activities of the two institutions were closely coordinated in support of the policy advice given by each other. In such instances, Fund-supported programs incorporated essential elements of the structural reforms supported by the Bank, which helped strengthen the program design. By and large, such coordination was achieved without impairing the timely response to members' requests for financial assistance.[67]

---

65. World Bank, "Policy Framework Papers: A First Review of Experience in the World Bank," R88-68 (Washington, March 17, 1988), p. 18.

66. World Bank, "Bank-Fund Collaboration," R89-45, para. 20.

67. "Fund-Bank Collaboration—Developments in 1985," IMF Board document SM/86/40 (Washington, February 25, 1986), circulated to Bank board under the same title as SecM86-610, May 29, 1986, p. 19.

Staff Reports

Beneath their smooth surfaces, staff reports showed fundamentally different attitudes toward coordination in the two institutions. The Bank tended to emphasize that the severity of members' economic problems in the 1980s had increasingly intertwined the scope of Fund and Bank activities, which made attempts at demarcation of their respective responsibilities less and less relevant. Instead, it urged, the Bank and the Fund should "cooperate in developing a more integrated perspective of the adjustment process so that the medium-term implications of the policy measures undertaken for stabilization, including the resources to support them, are more explicitly recognized and a shared view on these implications emerges."[68] The sentence quoted implied that the Fund was insufficiently aware of the trade-off between adjustment and growth, and the Bank's experience was offered for the design of alternative policy packages with the same stabilization impact but better medium-term growth implications.[69]

The Fund's position on these issues is rather more reticent. It does not accept the trade-off between adjustment and growth. And it insists that the overlapping areas of concern make a clear demarcation of responsibilities more rather than less important.[70]

Meanwhile, many small procedural steps were taken to acquaint and associate each organization more closely with the work of the other. Staff transfers for a period of two or three years were encouraged. Fund staff papers to the board began to contain an annex about the relations with the Bank of the country discussed. When the Bank board discussed a country that also had a Fund program, Fund staff members were invited to observe and, as a further step, authorized to answer questions that directors might want to put to it. Correspondingly, the Fund invited Bank participation in reverse situations. More information was exchanged on mission plans, more simultaneous missions were conducted (but few joint missions, which raised difficult questions of chain of command), and more frequently staff members were attached to a mission from the sister organization. Draft papers, briefing papers, and debriefing papers were more generally (but not without exception) exchanged.[71] More channels were agreed for the resolution of

68. World Bank, "Bank-Fund Collaboration," R85-30, para. 71.

69. Ibid., para. 30.

70. World Bank, Managing Committee, minutes of meeting of January 22, 1985, p. 1. In an earlier Managing Committee meeting, it was noted that the industrial countries supported this position of the Fund and were disinclined to welcome "any Bank involvement that would clutter up the focus on short-term balance of payments problems." World Bank, Managing Committee, minutes of meeting of October 15, 1984, p. 3.

71. A 1980 agreement on the exchange of documents excluded those that Fund area departments considered too sensitive. When a practice developed in some areas of making such papers available informally at staff level, the Fund clamped down with tighter security procedures. World Bank, "Bank-Fund Collaboration," R85-30, para. 41.

conflicts that could not be handled at lower levels; a monthly luncheon between the president of the Bank and the managing director of the Fund, each accompanied by a few senior officials, was instituted as the highest level of arbitration, where remaining conflicts were, in one way or another, disposed of.

An attempt was also made to explore in greater depth several aspects of collaboration by the organization of a joint conference of the Fund and the Bank on "Growth-Oriented Adjustment Programs." The conference was held in February 1987.[72] Participation in the conference was carefully balanced between outsiders and insiders, Fund and Bank, staff and executive directors, and speakers from developed and developing countries.[73] The conference produced a number of good papers and good discussions; it also produced, on the whole, the harmony that it had been designed to demonstrate, perhaps because for the most part, the discussion "coasted on generalizations."[74]

All in all, it appeared that the two organizations had found a workable modus vivendi on the question of collaboration. In general, the picture was one of fruitful and harmonious day-to-day contacts between the staffs, going well beyond any-thing existing elsewhere among international institutions. For the most part, the activities of the two staffs were complementary rather than duplicative. Collabora-tion was particularly close for many of the IDA-ESAF countries.

The structure of formal and informal arrangements between the two institutions did not, however, deal adequately with the underlying problems of overlap and potential conflict, and these problems also seemed impervious to systemic im-provement. Dissatisfaction with this state of affairs on the part of a few of the leading member governments led to several initiatives for change during the 1980s.

Member Government Initiatives

A first stab in this direction was made by the U.K. director on the occasion of a Fund board discussion of Fund-Bank collaboration in 1984. Nigel Wicks proposed a long list of steps to deepen collaboration, including "the preparation of a consis-tent country economic analysis," informal joint meetings or seminars of the two boards, closer coordination of training and research, joint missions, and cross-attendance of staff at board meetings.[75] Although he received support from the two other joint directors (from France and Belgium), the board's reaction to Wicks's more radical proposals was, at best, lukewarm, and his intervention did not lead to important changes in the practices of the two organizations.[76]

72. See published proceedings by Vittorio Corbo, Morris Goldstein, and Mohsin Khan, eds., *Growth-Oriented Adjustment Programs* (Washington: IMF and World Bank, 1987).

73. At the last moment, something was even done on the question of gender balance by including one woman (compared with fifty men) among the speakers.

74. Richard N. Cooper, one of the conference's two moderators, at the final session. See Corbo and others, *Growth-Oriented Adjustment Programs*, p. 523.

75. EBM/84/180, November 21, 1984.

76. EBM/84/171, November 28, 1984.

The next initiative, taken by the United States in September 1985, had a greater impact. It came when the Fund started to discuss the modalities of relending the repayments that began to flow in from the Trust Fund loans that the Fund had made from 1976 to 1980. On this occasion, Charles Dallara (the U.S. executive director) put forward a "U.S. Proposal for an IMF/World Bank Program to Promote Economic Adjustment and Growth."[77] Under this program, eligible low-income countries would have access to Trust Fund reflows and various sources from the World Bank under a series of two-year macroeconomic and structural economic programs. Although each board would approve any use of the funds coming from its institution, the approach envisaged was a highly integrated one. "A joint Fund/ Bank team would negotiate with a member [of] each program, and ideally prepare a single document for consideration and approval by both the Fund and Bank Executive Boards." These two boards should act "at roughly the same time, or certainly within a short consecutive time-frame," to protect the member from "bureaucratic and institutional difficulties." The plan was advocated as providing "a comprehensive and coordinated approach to macroeconomic and structural reform programs" and as an "excellent means of strengthening Fund/Bank collaboration."[78]

Policy Framework Papers

This proposal led to an intensive discussion in both boards, and while it was not adopted in full, it gave rise to a major collaborative innovation in connection with the lending by the two institutions to low-income countries. On March 26, 1986, the executive board of the Fund approved the Structural Adjustment Facility (SAF) that would be based, in the case of each country, on a policy framework paper (PFP) to be developed in close collaboration of the applicant country and the staffs of the Fund and the Bank. The PFP would describe the country's major problems; the objectives of a three-year program; the priorities and the broad thrust of macroeconomic and structural policies; and the need for and sources of external financing. So far, the decision followed closely the U.S. proposal, but the same did not apply to decisionmaking. Instead of the proposed closely linked lending action by the two institutions, the agreed outcome was that the Bank board (sitting as a Committee of the Whole, to safeguard the fiction that the board did not discuss countries' general economic programs) would be the first to discuss a PFP, which would then—together with a report on these discussions—go to the Fund

---

77. A U.S. document under this title, dated September 12, which formed the basis for Charles Dallara's statement in the Fund board the next day, was circulated for information to the Bank board on September 20, 1985, as SecM85-1083. The description of the plan in the text is based on the minutes of the Fund Board meeting (EBM/85/141, September 13, 1985).

78. World Bank, "U.S. Proposal for an IMF/World Bank Program to Promote Economic Adjustment and Growth," SecM85-1083 (Washington, September 20, 1985).

board for its approval. In the Fund, approval of a PFP was a requirement for, and often coincided with, approval of a SAF credit for the first year of the three-year period; the PFP thus became one of the three documents underlying the Fund's SAF operations, the other two being the letter of intent that specified the policy intentions for the first year and the appraisal by the Fund staff.

In the Bank, a similarly close association between the PFPs and IDA (or other concessional) lending was not established, in spite of a further push in that direction by the United States. At the 1987 annual meeting, U.S. Secretary of the Treasury James A. Baker III urged that "IDA loans should also be integrated into policy frameworks as closely as loans from the SAF" (in the same breath, Baker also proposed the formation of "a joint committee of the two Executive Boards to review policy framework papers").[79] The Bank, however, successfully resisted such close linkage of IDA lending to the PFPs.[80] Its staff argued that PFPs lacked the required "specificity, monitorability and depth" and that it would be too difficult to remodel them for this purpose. It also invoked the specter of cross-conditionality[81] as well as that of "asymmetry of treatment" between borrowers subjected to PFPs and others that would have access without them, which, it was argued, would be "very hard, if not impossible, to justify"—although it has caused hardly a ripple in the Fund. But the decisive argument against a major role for PFPs in Bank lending remained the difficulty of synchronization between the two institutions. The cycle of Bank lending simply takes too long for it to be closely linked to a document that had to be negotiated immediately before a SAF operation of the Fund.

As PFPs were more closely linked to Fund than to Bank operations, they were sometimes seen in the Bank as too much addressed to the Fund's preoccupations (short term and stabilization) and too little to those of the Bank (growth).[82] On the Fund side, there were complaints that Fund-Bank negotiations on the treatment of structural issues in PFPs caused delays in reaching agreement with a prospective borrower on a SAF program. On both sides it was realized that, at least in the early years, the contribution that the borrower made to the PFP was limited, so that the PFP process did not serve as much as had been hoped in the generation of internal consensus on needed policies. The reasons for this were set out in the 1988 Bank review on PFPs:

> Progress in involving country authorities in the PFP process has instead been quite slow. Government participation has so far remained generally limited in scope and uneven in quality. This state of affairs has many reasons. First, the PFP process was a novel one. It

79. IMF, *Summary Proceedings of the Forty-Second Annual Meeting of the Board of Governors, September 29–October 1, 1987* (Washington), p. 111.

80. World Bank, *Policy Framework Papers: A First Review of Experience in the World Bank*, R88-68 (Washington, March 1988), pp. 15–18.

81. "Directly tying . . . IDA credits to a document that would require some form of joint Bank-Fund official approval would raise again the fear of cross-conditionality." Ibid., p. 17.

82. See, for example, minutes of the Operations Committee meeting, March 7, 1988.

required a break-in period not only for the Bank and the Fund, but for country authorities as well. Second, in many low-income countries the capacity of government authorities to deal with additional demands of the type envisaged by the design and preparation of PFPs is rather limited. These tasks are often quite willingly delegated to Fund and Bank staff. Third, access to SAF resources was often urgently needed, and these needs further encouraged delegation of responsibilities to the staff of the two institutions for the sake of speed and continuity of action. Fourth, Fund-Bank procedures, which reflected in part the preoccupations of many country authorities with speed of access to SAF and the scarcity of domestic resources usable in the PFP process, tended to consolidate the practice of preparation and clearance of the main body of PFPs in Washington and of subsequent field discussion with country authorities of semifinished drafts.[83]

Even with limited country participation, the PFP process has served one of its intended purposes: it has strengthened Bank-Fund cooperation. If the need to agree on a joint document has taken considerable time and effort, it also has provided the vehicle for the achievement of common views by the two staffs on issues of adjustment with growth that are crucial to the borrowing country. And PFPs came to be recognized, in both the Fund and the Bank, as valuable documentation for the guidance of donor countries.

Argentina

The initiatives toward closer coordination taken by major members described in the previous section had their modest effects in taking off some of the rough edges in Fund-Bank relationships. They led to more contacts, more information, and more meetings at all levels. But they could not eliminate the tensions caused by two organizations operating competitively in the same field with different perspectives, and they did not offer a remedy for these tensions in the event that conciliation broke down. That, of course, was an unlikely event. Despite some close calls, it did not materialize from 1980 to 1987. But it did in 1988, in the Argentina case.

In the full glare of the publicity of the Berlin annual meeting, the president of the Bank announced a massive $1.25 billion package of new loans for Argentina. The package consisted of two quick-disbursing structural adjustment loans ($700 million) together with two large project loans. Yet Argentina had failed to observe the performance criteria of its latest Fund standby arrangement, and, in the Fund's view, its current and prospective policies did not justify yet another attempt to revive that arrangement or to conclude a new one.

The result was a very public blowup—between the Fund and the Bank as well as between Bank President Barber Conable and several major members of the

83. World Bank, *Policy Framework Papers: A First Review of Experience in the World Bank*, R88-68 (Washington, March 17, 1988), p. 7.

Bank. In a subsequent meeting of the Bank board the package was subjected to exceptionally sharp criticism from a number of executive directors from industrial countries, leading to one negative vote and two abstentions (plus a third one on the Banking Sector Loan).

Press reports from Berlin have portrayed the Argentine case as an instance of political pressure overriding the judgment of economists. There is no question that in the summer of 1988 President Conable was urged by U.S. Secretary of the Treasury James A. Baker III to conclude an arrangement with Argentina. But political pressure is only part, and not the most interesting part, of the explanation of the Argentina operation. As early as 1985, in response to the favorable expectations created by the Plan-Austral, the Bank had undertaken a major effort for Argentina. It initiated adjustment lending to the country and—unusual for a country of that size—established a special "Argentine Program Division." Following these initiatives, the Latin American and Caribbean (LAC) region, with the knowledge and support of senior Bank management, had since early 1988 been working on a medium-term Argentine adjustment plan—first in close cooperation with the Fund and thereafter mostly on its own—to underpin the Bank's structural lending program. Toward the summer of that year, however, others in the Bank—among them the Bank's chief economist, Stanley Fischer—questioned the wisdom of large-scale Bank lending without a simultaneous attempt to tackle Argentina's crushing debt problem.[84] It is quite possible, therefore, that without strong pressure from the United States, President Conable would still have put on the brakes and thus avoided a predictable clash with the Fund. But even if a final collision had been prevented, the collision course on which the two staffs were engaged since early 1988 deserves close attention. Beyond some features specific to the Argentine case, that course shows two interesting characteristics: it was fueled by some of the persistent differences in approach between the two institutions that had been evident throughout the 1980s (discussed above); and it proceeded in spite of unusually far-going attempts at integrating the work of the two staffs.

The Fund's experience with Argentina through the 1980s had been far from satisfactory. By early 1988, Argentina had had twenty quarters of IMF programs and had got through only three of them without waivers, some of only technical importance but others clearly indicative of a substantive lack of performance. Of a fifteen-month standby arrangement for SDR 1,500 million, concluded in January 1983, Argentina was able to draw only the first two installments, of SDR 300 million each. Almost two years elapsed before agreement could be reached on a new program, in support of which the Fund offered a credit of SDR 1,419 million in six tranches of SDR 236.5 million. That program was approved by the Fund board on December 28, 1984; within the week, Argentina failed to observe the end-December performance criteria. Five of the six tranches were, in the end, drawn

84. Memorandum, Fischer to Conable and Qureshi, August 8, 1988.

after new letters of intent had been submitted in June and July 1985 and in February and June 1986; in March 1986, the Fund decided to reduce the amount of the arrangement by one tranch, to SDR 1,182.5 million. A third program (for SDR 1,113 million) was "approved in principle" (subject to "satisfactory arrangements [having] been made for the financing of Argentina's balance of payments needs in 1987") in February 1987 but did not become effective until July of that year. This arrangement too became stuck a number of times as performance criteria were missed; its amount was reduced to SDR 947.5 million in March 1988, and when it expired in September 1988, less than two-thirds of the reduced amount had been drawn.[85]

Undaunted by this experience, the Fund in February 1988 started discussions with Argentina for an ambitious three-year EFF which, since it would extend beyond the term of the Alfonsín government, would require certain understandings with the opposition. In the board discussion in March 1988, Argentina's willingness to negotiate an EFF was cited by the staff as an argument for the board to grant Argentina yet another waiver under the 1987 program. (As discussed below, these negotiations between Argentina and the Fund came to nought later in 1988.) At the same board meeting, the alternate executive director from Argentina, Ernesto Feldman, conveyed a government promise to reduce the fiscal deficit for 1988 to 2 percent of GDP (as against the 2.9 percent contained in the supplementary letter of intent that the board had under consideration), and the deficit for 1989 to zero.[86]

The new targets were in sharp contrast to the ongoing fiscal performance, but they had been agreed in a meeting between Argentine President Raul Alfonsín and Managing Director Michel Camdessus in Madrid—a meeting in which Alfonsín had received the impression that Argentina might obtain substantial debt relief.[87]

The Bank, meanwhile, was actively engaged in the development and execution of a large lending program for Argentina. In fiscal 1987 it approved five loans, for a total of $965 million. Lending for the next three fiscal years was planned on a similar scale. Although these loans were intended to facilitate reforms and strengthen the productive base of Argentina, it was also realized in the Bank that, without a comprehensive approach to the debt problem, their main effect might be that Argentina would continue a little longer to meet the interest burden of its commercial bank debt and to postpone a crisis that was due to come.[88] This feeling was shared by the Argentineans, the Fund, and the U.S. Treasury, but no clear solution emerged on how to avoid an ultimate crisis. The Bank staff, in close contact with

85. International Monetary Fund, *International Financial Statistics—Transactions of the Fund, 1991* (Washington), pp. 3, 22; EBM/86/43 (March 10, 1986), p. 64; EBM/86/102 (June 23, 1986), p. 20; EBM/87/29 (February 18, 1987), p. 38; EBM/87/107 (July 23, 1987), p. 9; EBM/88/41 (March 18, 1988), p. 3.

86. EBM/88/40/R-2, March 18, 1988, p. 2.

87. Conversation with Raul Alfonsín, Washington, April 9, 1992.

88. Memorandum, Pieter Bottelier to Marianne Haug, January 13, 1988.

the Argentine authorities, created its own task force for the purpose of developing a financial program (including debt reduction) for the five-year period ahead. The exercise was nothing if not ambitious; it was hoped the Bank's task force "would eventually comprise the secretariat for a multi-agency group organized to raise broad-scale awareness of Argentina's problems and create a constituency for an international effort."[89]

In early 1988, the staffs of the two organizations were thus actively engaged in the design of a medium-term solution to Argentina's financial problems. At a Conable-Camdessus meeting on February 25, 1988, arranged to combine these efforts, the managing director proposed the joint preparation of a "medium-term outline," patterned in substance on the PFPs prepared for SAF-IDA countries. He expressed the intention that he and the president would jointly review the paper to be prepared in a few weeks.[90]

The Fund staff quickly produced a draft paper, in which it incorporated the ambitious fiscal targets to which President Alfonsín had agreed in Madrid. The Bank staff took exception to this approach. It had felt for some time that the Fund's approach to Argentina could not succeed and that the Bank should not tie its programs to it. Specifically, the Bank staff believed that the Fund arrangements with Argentina concentrated unduly on aggregate macroeconomic targets to be achieved in a rather narrow time frame. In view of the profound structural problems of the Argentine economy, the Bank staff questioned whether these targets were attainable without radical structural changes, and they were concerned about the Fund's willingness to accept new fiscal measures without adequate regard for their impact on the efficiency of the economy. Concern on these matters in the Bank ran so high that Conable addressed a letter to Camdessus, in which he referred to "skepticism in Argentina about the realism of the fiscal targets" and urged that "in the area of structural and institutional reform, we should move more deliberately, and ensure that our analysis and recommendations are soundly based." If the Fund could not wait, he suggested that structural reform be dealt with separately from stabilization.[91] In a confrontational follow-up meeting with Richard Erb, the deputy managing director of the Fund, senior Bank officials, including Moeen Qureshi, Stanley Fischer, and Shahid Husain, pressed the Fund to relax its position on the budget but found the Fund adamant on that issue.

From there on, the two organizations went their separate ways. An alternative draft plan prepared by the Bank became the basis for an aide-mémoire left by the

89. Memorandum to files, H. Nissenbaum, LA4CO, February 4, 1988. Argentina had indicated that it hoped to establish a task force with the World Bank, the IMF, and the U.S. government in which, because of the structural nature of the policy program, the Bank would play a leading role. (Note by Pieter Bottelier, January 14, 1988, reporting on a meeting of an Argentine delegation with Qureshi.)

90. Author's recollection of a handwritten note by Michel Camdessus, February 25, 1988.

91. Letter from Barber Conable to Michel Camdessus, March 18, 1988.

Bank's economic mission in Buenos Aires on March 22, 1988, and for the draft of a medium-term economic program given to Argentina on April 22. In April, too, the vice president in charge of LAC could report to the president that the Bank was "working with the Government on an adjustment program and we expect the outlines of it to be ready in May."[92]

In the Argentina case, the Fund's traditional hurry proved unnecessary. By the spring of 1988, its effort (though never abandoned) had run out of steam. In May, the precondition for a three-year EFF—cooperation from the opposition—proved, not surprisingly, beyond reach. An attempt to negotiate a standby arrangement for the remainder of the Alfonsín term was also unsuccessful, as the authorities were unable to bring up the necessary effort. And the Fund's management, after having been attacked with unusual sharpness by directors in December 1987 and March 1988 for its readiness to accept repeated Argentine promises, had come to realize that its credibility could not stand yet another Argentine program of questionable quality.

For the Bank it would have been much less obvious to decide, in effect, to sit out the Argentine elections. The Bank's experience with its sector loans to Argentina had, on the whole, been gratifying. In June 1988, the staff gave the board a warm appraisal of Argentina's reform efforts, which, moreover, on one major issue, privatization, presented the staff's expectations as if they were facts:

> Albeit a little late and slower than most had wished, Argentina has embarked on a broad medium-term program of structural economic adjustment . . . while simultaneously consolidating a democratic system of government. . . . The economy has been made more internationally competitive with an aggressive exchange rate, new export promotion policies, a reduction in the coverage of QRs [quantitative import restrictions], and, as President Alfonsín announced yesterday, the reduction in the average tariff level to 30 percent; moreover, the Congress is now completing legislation that will rationalize and curb inefficient and costly subsidies to promote domestic industry. The Government has also improved efficiency through price deregulation, demonopolization *and privatization of public enterprises including the state company for oil and gas, YPF, the national airline, the national telecommunications company, and a state-owned shipping company.* A plan for the reorganization of the heavily subsidized state railway company is expected to be announced in the near future. At the same time, the banking system and the role of the central bank are being reorganized and subjected to strict financial and monetary discipline. The Federal Government has established new incentives for Provincial Governments to exert fiscal discipline by eliminating routine Central Bank financing for provincial bank deficits and establishing a clear revenue sharing formula. Major reforms for the social sector, including public housing, health, and education are under active preparation. Most of these efforts are being supported by the World Bank. Apart from improving long-term growth prospects, the structural reforms currently under way or under preparation should also yield significant improvement on the fiscal side.

92. Shahid Husain to Conable, *Argentina: Meeting* [of Conable] *with the Minister of Economy,* April 13, 1988.

Now is precisely the moment when international creditors should be encouraging Argentina's program for economic reform. Without continuing strong World Bank support, the entire structural adjustment program may suffer.[93]

Following its own call to arms, the Bank staff intensified its Argentine work. The vice president in charge of LAC (Shahid Husain) led a mission designed to assess the new Argentine stabilization plan (the *Primavera Plan*), in order to develop "an independent World Bank perspective on the structural factors underlying Argentina's public finance problems" and to specify the conditions for two sectoral loans—the Banking Sector Loan and the second Trade Policy Loan.[94] These negotiations produced a draft letter of development policy as well as an understanding that the amount to be released in October would be limited to $150 million, after further agreement with the government on its fiscal, monetary, and balance of payments program. Subsequent releases would be dependent on reviews by the Bank of the "exchange rate, fiscal and domestic credit developments." A further staff mission prepared the ground for the completion of the package, agreement on which was announced at a press conference in Berlin on September 25.

The Bank's action in August–September was unusual in two respects. Not only did the Bank engage in a major structural lending program with full awareness of the fact that the Fund considered the macroeconomic conditions lacking, it also set out to negotiate such conditions on its own, and made future disbursements under its sectoral loans conditional upon Argentina's macroeconomic performance being satisfactory to the Bank. The effect of this was not only to make the Bank's operations independent of the Fund's judgment of a country's macroeconomic policies, but also to put the Bank in the Fund's shoes as macroeconomic policy lender. This inference is underlined by a recommendation in the Bank's 1988 report on adjustment lending, to the effect that all future adjustment loans be supported by a macroeconomic policy statement that would become the basis for subsequent tranche releases.[95] In the case of Argentina, however, the action taken by the Bank was based on the assumption of early support from the Fund: without accompanying Fund lending plus a debt agreement with the commercial banks that a Fund program might unlock, the Bank was well aware that its program was critically underfinanced.

The primary weakness of the government's financial program was not the level of its fiscal targets (4.6 percent of GDP for 1988 and 2.4 percent for 1989), as

93. *Argentina—Agricultural Sector Loan* (Ln. 2675-AR), *Waiver of Conditions*, board presentation, June 2, 1988. Emphasis added. At the time of this statement, none of the public enterprises had been privatized, although negotiations to that end were under way for the airline and the telecommunications company.

94. "Argentina: Principal Findings and Proposed Strategy," memorandum from Husain to Qureshi and Qureshi to Conable, Washington, September 2, 1988.

95. World Bank, *Report on Adjustment Lending*, R88-199 (Washington, August 8, 1988), p. 20.

against the (almost certainly unrealistic) targets of 2 percent and 0 percent respectively announced in the Fund board half a year earlier.[96] But the letter of development policy lacked credible evidence on how these targets were expected to be reached. It referred to future action in the areas of tax administration and collection, and tax reform (intended to take effect by July 1, 1989), as well as to expenditure cuts by the national administration and public enterprises.[97] As had been widely expected from the start, the government, facing a steadily eroding political situation, proved unable to deliver on its fiscal promises. As a result there were no further releases under the two policy loans. The Bank's most prominent entry into the field of monitoring macroeconomic policy met, within months, the same fate as the three preceding programs of the Fund.

The case of Argentina was not an isolated incident where the normal collaborative procedures of the two institutions had, by some unfortunate accident, been derailed. The case of Turkey, which played at almost the same time as that of Argentina, in many respects duplicates that experience.

Turkey had five successive standby arrangements with the Fund: in 1978, 1979, 1980 (a three-year arrangement), 1983, and 1984.[98] By 1985 Turkey had restored access to credit markets and was no longer interested in arrangements with the Fund. After five SALs, it had also exhausted that form of access to balance of payments loans, which was then replaced by SECALs. In the course of 1988, the Bank was negotiating a Financial Sector Adjustment Loan with Turkey. That loan was designed to encompass a statement of macroeconomic policy that the Bank staff would periodically monitor, and release of the second tranche was made conditional on a finding by the Bank of satisfactory macroeconomic performance. The Fund was in close consultation with the Bank and gave its opinion, based on Article IV consultations, that Turkey's macroeconomic performance was less than satisfactory. The Bank went ahead with the loan. When the Fund's appraisal (which had found wide agreement in the Bank) was confirmed by events, release of the second tranche in early 1989 was held up; in fact, that release did not occur until October 1990 in the context of the Gulf War.

It cannot be assumed from the discussion of these two cases that the Fund always took the more conservative view. For Côte d'Ivoire the relative positions of the Fund and the Bank were the reverse of what they were on Argentina and Turkey. On several occasions since the mid-1980s, the Fund accepted the adjustment efforts of Côte d'Ivoire as sufficient to justify the extension of Fund credit,

---

96. When the Fund reached an agreement with the Menem government in the autumn of 1989, it contained a figure for the 1990 fiscal deficit of 1.25 percent of GDP, following an estimated actual deficit of 16 percent in 1989 (EBS/89/194, p. 2).

97. Argentina, letter of development policy, World Bank, Washington, September 22, 1988, para. 6.

98. IMF, *International Financial Statistics, Transactions of the Fund* (Washington, 1991), p. 11.

while the Bank's technicians considered these efforts inadequate in anything but the short run. Again, interagency feelings ran high; in preparation for a Conable-Camdessus meeting in the fall of 1989, the Bank staff described the case as clearly one of "Argentina in reverse." In the end, the differences of view did not lead to a parting of the ways; the Bank overcame its reservations and continued structural adjustment lending, if only to safeguard the repayment of earlier loans.

Toward a Fund-Bank Concordat

The Argentine experience, together with several other cases where Fund and Bank approaches had conflicted, reawakened a strong interest in the Fund in a more formal delineation of the respective areas of responsibility—a subject that, as already noted, the Bank had been trying to avoid. In the process toward this end, a major role was played by the executive directors from the industrial countries and their superiors, the deputy finance ministers, and deputy central bank governors, meeting as the deputies of the Group of Ten (G-10).

In mid-1988 (before the Argentine crisis had surfaced), the managing director had suggested that a new review of Fund-Bank collaboration might be useful. In his proposed work program for the period ahead, he had included a low-key paragraph on Fund-Bank collaboration:

> The principles guiding the division of labor between the Fund and the World Bank are well established. Thus, problems that occasionally may arise relate to the practice of implementing them, particularly when dealing with individual country cases. The policy framework paper process has proved a useful vehicle for sorting out potential problems at an early stage with regard to many countries. If the Board wishes, we could take stock of the evolution of Fund/Bank collaboration since the 1985 review before the 1989 Annual Meetings.[99]

There is no indication that at that time anything more radical than the earlier reports on this topic was envisaged. The approach proposed also appeared generally acceptable to the board; only the directors for the United Kingdom and the United States suggested that the less than satisfactory application of the agreed principles called for an earlier deadline for the study than September 1989.

The open conflict at the Berlin annual meeting gave a new impetus to the consideration of relations between the Fund and the Bank. At a Fund board meeting on November 4, 1988, at which the staff's work program was considered, many directors urged acceleration of the submission of a staff paper, so that the board could consider the matter before the next meeting of the Interim Committee scheduled for April 3, 1989. At about the same time, the G-10 deputies also began to focus attention on the subject. In April 1988, they had received a mandate to

99. EBM/88/109 (July 20, 1988), p. 11.

study the "role of the IMF and the World Bank in the context of the debt strategy." This study had also initially been approached at a rather leisurely pace, for completion by September 1989. Unable to do much about the debt strategy, the deputies applied themselves increasingly, after Berlin, to the question of collaboration between the Fund and the Bank—a subject on which they had also reported three years earlier.[100]

Argentina had shown how much there was potentially at stake for the Fund in the collaboration issue. Its "Good-Housekeeping seal" threatened to be devalued if the Bank made it a practice to make policy loans irrespective of the Fund's judgment of a country's general policies. And the demand for the Fund's arrangements might evaporate if the Bank succeeded in marketing SECALs with macroeconomic monitoring, but with conditionality softer than that of the Fund. The feelings on the subject of Fund management and staff were widely shared in the treasuries and central banks of the industrial countries, which, being often critical of the Fund's conditionality, saw that of the Bank as even less demanding.

For the immediate future, the Fund's position had been saved by the failure of the Bank's Argentina affair. In Turkey, too, the attempt of the Bank to substitute itself for the Fund as the macroeconomic policy lender had proved unsuccessful. But there was no reason to assume that things would always work out this way.

These concerns—together with the difference in culture discussed earlier—go far to explain the hard negotiating position that the Fund adopted. Throughout the discussions, it laid claim to primary responsibility for all that was macroeconomics. As Bank staff members continued to point out, that broad term, which had not been used in the 1966 understanding, includes not only stabilization but also such obvious concerns of the Bank as growth models or judgments about a country's creditworthiness.

Receipt by the Bank, in January 1989, of a Fund staff draft on future collaboration and similarly attuned draft sections for the G-10 deputies' report thus provoked widespread resentment. It was felt that these documents slighted the Bank's macroeconomic responsibilities and subjugated its decisionmaking process to the Fund. Fischer delivered a forceful protest at the next G-10 deputies meeting and, in an atmosphere of tension, negotiations started between Bank and Fund staffs and, increasingly, between Camdessus and Conable, to prepare a joint paper to supersede the 1966 understandings. Because of its formal character, this paper is referred to here as a Fund-Bank concordat.

By March 9, these negotiations had greatly narrowed the differences, but Camdessus and Conable took different views on how far this process had gone. The former took the line that agreement had been reached. He instructed the Fund

---

100. Group of Ten, *The Functioning of the International Monetary System, A Report to the Ministers and Governors by the Group of Deputies* (Basle, Switzerland, June 1985), pp. 45–47.

staff to issue a joint memorandum to the two boards from himself and the president of the Bank, "Bank-Fund Collaboration in Assisting Member Countries." In the covering memorandum, the Fund board was asked to discuss, and presumably to endorse, the proposed arrangements immediately after the weekend, on Monday, March 13.[101]

If agreement had indeed been reached, the position of the two staffs at a meeting of the G-10, to be held in Paris the next day (March 10), would have been facilitated, and it would have demonstrated to the G-10 that the two organizations could resolve disputes without further outside coaxing. As it turned out, however, Conable did not agree to all aspects of the new text. In a memorandum dated March 10 (sent to the Bank's executive directors on March 13) he asked for the deletion of a two-paragraph section in the draft, entitled "Role of the Institutions in Areas of Primary Responsibility." The deletion was intended to make clear that the understanding between the institutions on areas of "primary responsibility," which had been substantially expanded from the narrow scope of the 1966 wording, did not mean that "one institution ha[d] a veto power over the other."[102]

The planned discussion in the Fund board was canceled and new rounds of discussion ensued, in which the Bank pursued two objectives: to drop the concept of primary responsibility (or at least to get a fair share for the Bank in the "macro" area), or to delete (or at least weaken) the enforcement provisions contained in the contested section.

A compromise was reached first on the second objective. The two contested paragraphs were kept (their contents were distributed over paragraphs 11 and 12 of the final text), but one crucial passage was weakened. The March 9 draft had stated that "in the event differences of view persisted even after a thorough common examination of them, the institution which does not have the primary responsibility *would need to yield* to the judgment of the other institution." The new text proposed by the Bank omitted the severe words "need to" and added a qualifier: "except in exceptional circumstances." To reduce the likelihood of open conflict in cases of this nature, a sentence was added that "in those cases, which are expected to be extremely rare, the managements will wish to consult their respective Executive Boards before proceeding."[103] The change in wording thus had the double effect of removing from the document the one clause that established an absolute separation of jurisdiction and adding an extra safeguard, the involvement of the executive boards.

But, as the managing director reported to an informal board session on March 24, this slight weakening in the enforcement provisions did not suffice to

101. IMF, "Bank-Fund Collaboration in Assisting Member Countries," SM/89/54 (Washington, March 9, 1989).

102. World Bank, "Bank-Fund Collaboration," R89-35 (Washington, March 13, 1989), para. 1; and IMF, "Bank-Fund Collaboration," SM/89/54, para. 9.

103. Ibid., para. 13, emphasis added; and new text in World Bank, "Bank-Fund Collaboration," R89-45, para. 12.

eliminate the Bank's opposition to the description in paragraph 9 of the institutions' respective areas of competence. Since the managing director knew that elimination of the macroeconomic prerogative of the Fund was unacceptable to the Fund board, he acknowledged that a stalemate had been reached; he would, therefore, fall back on instructing the staff to improve the quality of cooperation under the existing rules by better procedures and implementation.[104]

The board's response was as expected. It made it clear that the impasse could not be allowed to continue. It supported the managing director's position on the need for an explicit recognition of the primary responsibility of the Fund in the macroeconomic area. Some directors pointed to the embarrassment that would arise if, by the time of the meeting of the Interim Committee, the dispute remained unresolved and would become the subject of even wider speculation in the press than had already occurred. Given the directors' broad support, the managing director undertook to renew discussions with the Bank in order to come up with "a clear paper without sacrificing principles."[105] The president of the Bank also told his directors that he would make a further effort to reach agreement. Thus the negotiations resumed. In the next few days, two sets of drafting changes were introduced to reach an agreed text. The first of these expanded the description of the Bank's area of responsibility. The document of March 9 had described the Bank's focus briefly: "specific projects, sector programs, development strategies, and related considerations of creditworthiness of its members." In the new version, this was broadened to: "development strategies; sector and project investments; structural adjustment programs; policies which deal with the efficient allocation of resources in both public and private sectors; priorities in government expenditures; reforms of administrative systems, production, trade and financial sectors; the restructuring of state enterprises and sector policies. Moreover, as a market-based institution, the Bank also concerns itself with issues relating to the creditworthiness of its members."[106]

The second change was designed to acknowledge some role for the Bank in the "macro" area. But since the drafters were unable to agree on a functional (horizontal) allocation of macroeconomic responsibilities between the two institutions, they (unlike the contestants in King Solomon's court) settled for a vertical slicing of the baby. The Fund's responsibilities remained defined in broad terms ("surveillance, exchange rate matters, balance of payments, growth-oriented stabilization policies and their related instruments").[107] But the Fund agreed to narrow its focus to "the

104. IS[Informal Session]/89/3, March 24, 1989, pp. 3–4. This document attaches Bank redrafts of paragraphs 12 and 13. With one trivial change, these two paragraphs entered into the final text as paragraphs 11 and 12.

105 Ibid., p. 14. In the Bank, too, the opinion was that the negotiations had broken down. (Stanley Fischer, "Notes on Fund-Bank Collaboration," March 26, 1989.)

106. World Bank, "Bank-Fund Collaboration," R89-45.

107. Ibid., para. 9.

aggregate aspects" of macroeconomic policies and their related instruments. This formulation left room for the Bank to claim that it, too, had a recognized responsibility in the macroeconomic area. Of course, the modifiers "aggregate" and "macro" have approximately the same meaning and the expression "the aggregate aspects of" has no established meaning in economics. When asked in an informal discussion of executive directors to define "aggregate macroeconomic policies," Jacob Frenkel, the Fund's economic counselor and director of the research department, was initially stumped for an answer. At a later board meeting, he was reported to have addressed the question as follows:

> A detailed answer was not possible, but the relevant point was the Fund's obligation to discharge its responsibilities under Article IV of the Articles of Agreement. The Board's Article IV consultation discussions involved statistics on macroeconomic policies, but Board members had queried why the discussion should focus on aggregate macroeconomic policies if the intention was to consider macroeconomic variables. Adding to the confusion was the concept that every microeconomic policy had macroeconomic implications and vice versa. To resolve that dilemma, it would be necessary to understand the definition of aggregate. However, there was no way to have a meaningful macroeconomic analysis with reference to a single-value macroeconomic variable or aggregate. It was important to recognize that for the Fund to discharge its responsibilities in the various areas of surveillance—growth-oriented stabilization policies and related instruments —the proper level of aggregation was necessary.[108]

After this effort at agreement on language to describe, with due ambivalence, the areas of primary responsibility of the two institutions, the document devotes another 2,000 words or so to procedures for enhanced collaboration. These procedures are, in the first instance, directed at the resolution of conflicts by setting various layers of consultation, culminating in monthly meetings of the managing director and the president. They also include improved flows of information, exchanges of staff members, joint "task forces," and, in some cases, joint missions. There is a reference to the existing practice that adjustment lending is "not normally undertaken unless an appropriate Fund arrangement is in place"; absent such an arrangement, the Bank will seek the Fund's views, giving the Fund enough time to conduct special consultations.[109]

A subject that had given rise to some recent difficulties between the organizations was the question of lending by one of them to a country that had arrears to the other. Although the document invokes "the full spirit of solidarity," it stops short of adopting the principle (favored by the Fund) that one organization will not lend to countries in arrears to the other. Or rather, it first enunciates this principle, but then adds the qualifying proviso "if the overdue obligations to the Fund [Bank]

---

108. EBM/89/51 (May 3, 1989), p. 18. Fund etiquette does not allow the minutes to reveal whether this explanation was received with "[hilarity]."

109. World Bank, "Bank-Fund Collaboration," R89-45, paras. 19, 20.

were an indication that the resources of the Bank [Fund] would not be safe-guarded" (para. 23), thus leaving it to each institution to decide what it considers safe to do. This approach is confirmed in the next section (appropriately called "Independence of Institutional Decisions"), where a procedure is set out in the event that the management of one institution does decide to propose lending to a country that has arrears to the other: in such cases, management will informally consult its board before telling the member in question of its decision (para. 25).

The reaction of the two boards to the finally agreed text was notably different.[110] The Fund board in general welcomed the agreement, although some directors showed some unhappiness about the concessions made to the Bank.[111] The reception by the Bank's directors was less positive. In a discussion of the agreement in the Committee of the Whole (a venue chosen because directors were not asked to approve the document), several speakers saw no need for a new agreement and objected to specific provisions. Among the directors who welcomed the agreement, some stressed the need for flexibility in implementation.[112] To allay some legal questions that were raised, the general counsel submitted a paper after the meeting that elaborated several points he had made during the meeting. He pointed out that the agreement between the president of the Bank and the managing director of the Fund reflected "only the understanding reached between the two managements," was not "a binding agreement between the two institutions," and could not "limit the authority of the Executive Directors in interpreting the Articles in future."[113]

Three years later it became evident, however, that these extensive discussions and explanations still had not cleared the air as far as the Bank board was concerned. In April 1992, the heads of the two organizations sent a supplementary note to their respective boards, outlining guidance for staff collaboration in their work with the new members from the former Soviet Union. On the issue of country assessments, this note was more explicit and (intentionally or not) broader than paragraph 19 of the concordat on the role of the Fund in connection with Bank lending: "Prior to lending . . . the Bank expects to receive a policy letter that sets out the Government's program for structural adjustment, set in a macroeconomic framework which would be based on understandings reached with the Fund (as spelled out in the Letter of Intent for Fund arrangements)."[114]

While the discussion of this note in the Fund board was uneventful, many members of the Bank board expressed concern over the statement cited, as the

110. World Bank, "Bank-Fund Collaboration," R89-45, contains the text.

111. EBM/89/51, May 3, 1989.

112. "Committee of the Whole," p. 2.

113. "Note on Meetings of the Executive Directors—The Implications of Discussing the Memorandum on Bank-Fund Collaboration in the Committee of the Whole," SecM89-619 (Washington, May 16, 1989).

114. World Bank and IMF, "Bank-Fund Collaboration on the States of the Former Soviet Union," R92-76 (Washington, April 28, 1992), p. 1.

president acknowledged in his summing up, "since this would amount to explicit de facto cross conditionality." In response, the president made two substantive concessions and one procedural one. He noted the prevailing view in the board that Bank investment lending (unlike structural adjustment lending) should not require a Fund letter of intent if the Bank itself was satisfied with the direction of the country's economic policies. He specified that the new wording referred only to the special circumstances of the countries of the former Soviet Union and would not affect the existing arrangements for other countries as set out in the March 1989 memorandum. And he promised to discuss future papers on Bank-Fund collaboration with the board "as a normal procedure."[115]

Beyond the Concordat

Two institutions operating to a large extent in common territory run many risks, some more serious than others, of stepping on each other's toes. The concordat addressed some, but not all, of the issues that had made for Bank-Fund controversy; of those that it addressed, it solved some but not all. The post-concordat situation—which admittedly has lasted less than four years at the time of writing—can be analyzed under four headings.

—1. To begin with, there was no attempt to come to grips with the overt cause of the difficulties: that both institutions now give medium-term balance of payments credit to the same countries. Even if the Bank had decided to give up SALs altogether (a suggestion apparently made in the Bank), this might have done little to reduce the area of overlap, since SECALs too are essentially balance of payments loans and had indeed been the source of recent conflicts. There was no evident support in the institutions for a suggestion that the Fund should take the lead in organizing assistance in countries where stabilization was the dominant problem, and the Bank in countries whose most pressing need was a sustained revamping of their economic structure (mostly poor countries in Sub-Saharan Africa, but also certain oil exporters).[116] Nor were various suggestions for closer integration of the credit activities of the two institutions, such as those made by the United States (see above), accepted.

—2. To avoid differing policy advice—singled out as "the objective of the enhanced collaboration procedures"—the concordat created further procedures besides those already in existence.[117] It appears to be the view of the two staffs that

115. "Chairman's Summing Up, Bank-Fund Coordination," World Bank board discussion on May 29, 1992, Washington.

116. Please, *The Hobbled Giant,* pp. 74–80; and Richard E. Feinberg and Catherine Gwin, "Reforming the Fund," in Catherine Gwin, Richard E. Feinberg, and others, *The International Monetary Fund in a Multipolar World: Pulling Together* (Washington: Overseas Development Council, 1989), p. 23.

117. World Bank, "Bank-Fund Collaboration," R89-45, para. 12.

these procedures have on the whole worked well. Problems have been resolved below the top level; the monthly luncheons of the managing director and the president have tended to address issues that appeared (or might have appeared) on the horizon rather than actual conflicts left unresolved at lower levels. In the end, moreover, occasional instances of inconsistent advice are not a disaster: perhaps, as one executive director once suggested in the Fund board, the country in question might be trusted to choose which advice to heed. More generally, by demonstrating the grave consequences for both organizations of noncooperation, the Argentine crisis appears to have had a healthy cathartic effect on the collaborative process.

—3. It is clear from the concordat itself (for example, paragraphs 11 and 12) that no serious effort was made to avoid duplication of staff work between the two organizations. (Duplication is of course not unknown to flourish within organizations as well.) Subsequent experience does not, in any event, show striking success in this area. In 1990, the Bank concluded that it "should conduct its own assessment of macroeconomic developments for decision making about loans and tranche releases and for better risk management on the ground that, even when there is a Fund agreement at the time a SAL or SECAL is concluded, that agreement may have lapsed by the time the Bank has to decide on a tranche release."[118] A Bank staff working paper puts forward an even broader case for the Bank making its own judgments. First, "the Bank and the Fund differ with regard to objectives and priorities"; and second, "given that the Fund has an increasingly mixed record to its programs achieving their objectives, it is also not sufficient for the Bank to rely on a Fund program to ensure that stabilization policies are adequately implemented."[119] A recent example: in early 1992, the Bank decided that it would not approve sectoral loans for Brazil even though the country had just concluded a standby arrangement with the Fund; in the opinion of the Bank the fiscal policy component of that program was not sufficiently credible to expect the program to succeed.

In a somewhat similar way, the Fund has found it necessary to fill in gaps in areas that are traditionally covered by the Bank. In principle, the Bank is responsible for reviews of public expenditure; in practice, however, the Fund sometimes finds that the Bank cannot provide a review that is reasonably current; in those cases the Fund may make its own analysis.

Again, some stir was caused in the Fund when the Bank started, in 1991, a new annual publication, *Global Economic Prospects and the Developing Countries*, which covers some of the same ground as the Fund's *World Economic Outlook*. Particular concern was felt by some about the fact that, for their consideration of the world economy for 1991 and 1992, Bank directors were presented with one sophisticated forecast of oil prices and Fund directors and the Interim Committee

118. World Bank, *Adjustment Lending Policies*, pp. 68, 47–48.
119. Jaspersen and Shariff, *The Macroeconomic Underpinnings of Adjustment Lending*, pp. 34–36.

with a different, equally sophisticated, forecast.[120] Instances of this nature tend to provoke quite different reactions in the two institutions. The "open" culture of the Bank will stress that forecasting oil prices is an inherently risky undertaking and that governments are thus well served by receiving two independent, and different, attempts at the same objective. The more "bureaucratic" culture of the Fund would expect the staff (of either one or the other organization) to put forward its best efforts, together with all the qualifications that the material required. Going beyond that within the Fund/Bank family would be seen as confusing to the recipients of the information and as needless duplication.

Clearly, while duplication may often not be cost effective, neither are all attempts at eradicating it. And although duplication may prove irritating to whoever covered a particular area first, it need not, if practiced in moderation, become a major cause of interagency conflict.

—4. What is such a cause—and what was historically the primary reason why the concordat had to be concluded—is a decision of one organization to give a policy loan to a country when the other has made it known to the country that its policies do not qualify for such a loan.[121] It is grounds for satisfaction that this event has not occurred in the past three years. But it is a legitimate question whether this is the result of the concordat or, as one senior Bank staff member put it to me, of the "inoculation" that the Bank received from the Argentine disaster. Note that paragraph 19 of the concordat does not explicitly bar Bank policy lending in cases such as Argentina or Turkey in 1988. But the consultation procedures that it mandates ensure that such action would not take place inadvertently; and the recollection of the Argentina case would—as long as it lasts—almost certainly deter the Bank from proceeding against the known views of the Fund.

But it needs to be stressed that the counterpart is not true. While the Bank may be well advised to heed the Fund's negative advice, it cannot, as an independent organization responsible to its shareholders and its bondholders, agree to lend to a country merely on the basis of a favorable macroeconomic judgment by the Fund. The analysis done by the Fund, if freely shared with the Bank, will no doubt facilitate the latter's work in coming to its macroeconomic judgment; but to be able to make such a judgment, the Bank must insist on having the analytical capacity.

The conclusion would seem justified that, in the aftermath of the concordat, the subject of coordination has returned to the untidy, but controlled, mixture of cooperation in general and mutual irritation on occasion that characterized the situation in the mid-1980s.

120. World Bank, *Global Economic Prospects and the Developing Countries,* 1991, pp. 40–41; and IMF, *World Economic Outlook* (Washington, May 1991), p. 22.
121. Modest project loans by the Bank to a country that the Fund considers unqualified to receive credit because of its policies or of arrears to the Fund do not necessarily raise a conflict; such lending has continued to occur.

Against this background it is curious to note that some recent statements by the United States seem to minimize the distinction between the two institutions, portraying them as essentially fungible sources of talent and money. In his March 1989 speech announcing a new approach to the debt strategy, U.S. Secretary of the Treasury Nicholas F. Brady

> called on the international financial institutions to continue to play central roles through their efforts to promote sound policies in debtor countries by giving advice and financial support. He suggested that the Fund and the World Bank could also provide funding, as part of their policy-based lending programs, for debt or debt service reduction purposes.[122]

The U.S. speech at the 1991 annual meeting in Bangkok went one step further, being cast wholly in the mode of "the-Fund-and-the-Bank." Secretary Brady used that expression and its mirror image over twenty times in a short speech, even where it was obviously out of place.[123] But perhaps this portrayal of the Bretton Woods twins as joined in Siamese fashion should be dismissed as a mere rhetorical tribute to the host country?

In fact, however, developments following from the disintegration of the Soviet Union offered a wide range of different tasks to the two institutions, thus restoring a clearer differentiation of their respective images. The enormous problems of integration in the world economy, transition, macroeconomic stabilization, and fundamental restructuring in fifteen new member countries presented the Fund and the Bank with more challenges than their present staffs could handle. The Fund in particular threw itself at the new opportunities with notable zeal. At the 1991 annual meeting, the managing director expressed himself with an emotional commitment not witnessed at such meetings since Robert McNamara's sermons against "absolute poverty" in the 1970s:

> Last, but by no means least, the historic changes under way in the *Baltic states* and the *Soviet Union* present a major and most welcome challenge to us all. They have opened a "new frontier" for our spirit of initiative and cooperation. For the Bretton Woods institutions, a long-awaited opportunity for them to become truly universal, and to serve the entire family of nations with a renewed sense of commitment, is drawing close. . . . On October 5, I had the honor of signing with President Gorbachev an agreement on a special association. This will enable us to work with the Union and the Republics to help them design and implement their reforms, and to provide wide-ranging technical assistance. . . . We look forward to being able to help this great country realize its enormous

---

122. *IMF Survey,* vol. 18 (March 1989), p. 90.

123. "The time has come for the Fund and the Bank to strengthen their support for the private sector"; "Fund and Bank staff will have to advise and educate individuals in the private sector and in local government." International Monetary Fund, *Summary Proceedings of the Forty-Sixth Annual Meeting of the Board of Governors, October 15–17, 1991,* Washington, pp. 41–45.

economic potential, to working with this community of peoples who have contributed so much over the centuries to the arts, to technology, indeed to all areas of intellectual and spiritual life, to our civilization at its highest.[124]

When the G-7 at their 1990 Houston summit asked the Bretton Woods institutions, the Organization for Economic Cooperation and Development, and the European Bank for Reconstruction and Development to study jointly the economy of the Soviet Union, they gave the Fund the de facto lead role by asking it to act as the "convener" for the study. Since then, the Fund has held onto this position of prominence—which also involves the greatest risk in the event of failure—in the work on the former Soviet Union.

Experience since 1946, but especially since about 1980, suggests that certain organizational difficulties are inherent in the forced cohabitation of two separate financial organizations with at least partially overlapping fields of activity. Up to now, the member governments have (implicitly rather than explicitly) accepted these difficulties rather than attempt to integrate the resources and manpower of the two institutions.

Nevertheless, the suggestion of merger is clearly in the air. It has recently been raised by Stanley Fischer. Though noting some obvious advantages of a single agency, including the saving from having only one board of executive directors, he concludes against merger "as long as the agencies continue to operate with as much secrecy as they do."[125] The economics editor of the *Economist* concludes a long survey article on the "Bretton Woods sisters" with the observation that "a merger makes sense, and in time it will happen."[126]

That seems natural from the viewpoint of the Bank, once the Bank's structural adjustment lending is accepted as a permanent feature with policy priority over project lending. Why should there be two very similar international organizations providing balance of payments credits under similar macroeconomic conditionality to the same developing countries?

If the question is put that way, the preprogrammed answer is of course merger; and not merger of the Fund and the Bank but merger of the Fund into the Bank, the latter being the recognized development institution.

But to put the question in this way is also to ignore a major—indeed historically the major—raison d'être of the Fund. The Fund was established because the health of the international monetary system was a dominant preoccupation of the nations meeting at Bretton Woods. The Fund's responsibilities for the system provide the justification for its credit activities, including its power to allocate

124. Ibid., p. 20. Emphasis in original.

125. Stanley Fischer, "Panel Session II: Implications for International Monetary Reform," in Michael D. Bordo and Barry Eichengreen, eds., *A Retrospective on the Bretton Woods System* (University of Chicago Press, 1993), p. 594.

126. Clive Crook, "The IMF and the World Bank," *The Economist,* October 12, 1991, p. 48.

SDRs. In the past fifteen years—indeed since the negotiation of its second amendment in the mid-1970s—the Fund cannot be said to have contributed much to the functioning of the international monetary system. That system has evolved in many directions—floating rates under various regimes of management, the European Monetary System, now perhaps on the road toward European Monetary Union, "monetary anchors," "crawling pegs," and so on—without major Fund involvement at most critical junctures. The SDR mechanism has been dormant for more than a decade. But the experience since the collapse of the Bretton Woods system in 1971 certainly does not lead one to conclude that the problems of the international monetary system have been solved. Nor is there reason to believe that the G-5 or the G-7—after the promising steps of the Plaza and the Louvre agreements—are ready to take over the Fund's systemic responsibilities. This then is not the time to abolish (by merger or otherwise) the one international organization whose task it remains to be concerned about that system.

TWELVE

The World Bank as "Intellectual Actor"

Nicholas Stern with Francisco Ferreira

THE SUBJECT of this chapter is the contribution of the World Bank to the understanding of the economics of development. In looking at the Bank's intellectual role it must be kept in mind that the Bank is not primarily an institution for the creation

In preparing this chapter we have benefited greatly from the guidance of our colleagues at the Suntory and Toyota International Centres for Economics and Related Disciplines at the London School of Economics: Beatriz Armendariz, Robin Burgess, David Coady, Haris Gazdar, and Samarjit Shankar. In Washington Laura Powell and Karen Semkow provided most helpful research advice and support. Devesh Kapur has been a constant source of help, guidance, and insight.

More than thirty long interviews were conducted with key World Bank participants; see the section "Perceptions from Within." A number of interviewees provided most valuable help outside the interviews. Special mention should be made of Benjamin King. The authors also learned much from discussions with Montek Singh Ahluwalia, Dennis de Tray, Johannes Linn, Mary Morgan, Manmohan Singh, Richard Stern, and Lawrence Summers, and from a seminar at the U.S. Agency for International Development in February 1992. Dennis de Tray provided special help and guidance in his liaison role. Early versions of the chapter were presented at seminars at the Brookings Institution in June 1992 and at the Bank in April 1993. We are grateful to the editors of the volume, other participants at the seminar, and the following for helpful comments on that draft: Nancy Birdsall, Angus Deaton, Jaime de Melo, Stanley Fischer, Jeffrey Hammer, Gerry Helleiner, David Henderson, Greg Ingram, Andrew Kamarck, Jochen Kraske, Anne Krueger, Peter Lanjouw, Robert Laslett, Michael Lipton, Costas Michalopoulos, David Newbery, Michael Petit, Robert Picciotto, Stanley Please, George Psacharopoulos, Graham Pyatt, Anandarup Ray, Ernest Stern, Vinod Thomas, Jacques van der Gaag, and John Williamson.

We are grateful for the kindness shown by all those mentioned above. The interpretations and views in what follows are our own. We would like to thank the Suntory and Toyota International Centres for Economics and Related Disciplines for their support.

and dissemination of ideas. The Bank from its inception, and explicitly and prominently since Robert S. McNamara's presidency, has seen itself as a development
agency. Its primary work is in its operations departments, dealing with project- and
policy-based lending. But advice and lending, be they for projects or economywide
policies, need an intellectual framework, and in the Bank's case that comes for the
most part from economics as applied to the problems of developing countries. The
primary concern of this analysis is how the Bank has interacted with, drawn on, and
contributed to development economics.

In analyzing the Bank's influence on development economics it must be recognized that the Bank's size gives it a unique position. The Bank employs around 800
professional economists and has a research budget of around U.S.$25 million a
year. These resources dwarf those of any university department or research institution working on development economics. There are more than 3,000 additional
professionals in the Bank. The size of the Bank's lending program (of the order of
$15 billion to $20 billion a year) allows it to exert considerable influence on the
thinking and policies of borrowing countries. The weight of the number of development economists, the research budget, and the leverage from lending means that
the Bank's potential influence is profound, and that the Bank cannot be seen as just
one of a number of fairly equal actors in the world of development economics.

Other chapters provide perceptions of the Bank from different parts of the
world; this chapter offers views of the Bank from academic life and in terms of the
Bank's intellectual activities and contributions. It must be emphasized that our
perception of these activities and contributions does not coincide with the views of
the Bank's research departments or of its employees' published research. Much of
the Bank's intellectual role has been driven and performed by the operations side,
and the production of publishable research is only one, and arguably not the most
important, activity of the research departments.

The analysis here is confined largely to the Bank's contributions to economics
rather than to other social sciences. In development economics, however, as in
other aspects of economics, one cannot but realize the significance of other disciplines. The Bank has been involved in political science, demography, statistics,
and sociology, among other disciplines. But given the predominance of economists
among the social scientists on the Bank's staff, it is likely that the roles of noneconomists have been small, at least relative to that of economists. Whether that is
as it should be is another question.

This chapter is based in part on Nicholas Stern's interaction with the Bank over
twenty years in Asia, Africa, Latin America, North America, and Europe, and in
both operations and research, although never as a staff member of the Bank. That
experience allows an outside view, but at the same time limits knowledge of the
internal workings of the Bank. The chapter also draws on the literature on development economics as found in university libraries and lecture courses, and on more
than thirty hour-long interviews with major actors in the Bank's intellectual history,

including Robert S. McNamara, all the vice presidents for research, and many individual researchers carrying out their own programs. This chapter does not set out to provide a comprehensive assessment or appraisal of publications. This would require resources beyond those available for this study. The attempt here is to provide a view of the Bank from outside, from academic economics; it must, however, be a personal view, and it embodies our perceptions of what is important in development economics and the Bank's role in it.

"Acting Intellectually" and the Role of Research in the Bank

What does "acting intellectually" mean, as far as the World Bank is concerned? How are its intellectual activities performed? Where in the Bank are they carried out, and by whom? In answering these questions one must be concerned with the intellectual contributions of both the operations and research sides of the Bank. Our view from outside the Bank, however, leads us to a focus on only one part, which is the intellectual contribution of the research side (not necessarily the most important part).

Four different, but overlapping, ways of acting intellectually may be distinguished. Ideas can be created, stimulated, disseminated or promoted, and applied. The research side of the Bank has been involved in all four, but so too has operations. The research side does much more than pursue research projects and programs; it also contributes directly to policy work and operations, and it promotes debate on policy among relevant agencies and governments. Many inside and outside the Bank would argue that the latter two purposes are of even greater importance than the production of good research and interaction with the academic world. On the whole, the research side has been rather effective in fulfilling the roles that these two purposes embody, but they are neither our main concern nor areas where an outsider has a comparative advantage.

The Bank can participate in the creation of ideas in a number of ways—in setting an agenda, in the course of its operational work in producing research studies, in providing, assembling, and assessing data and other research material, and in drawing lessons from its own practices. Ideas were generated, for example, from the Bank's agenda for structural adjustment. Ideas of significance in the academic world have been generated through the Bank's operations, as when the Bank played a leading role in analyzing the Chinese economy following the opening up of information sources during China's reforms of the 1980s. In the area of research studies, the Bank's work on agriculture and on the functioning of rural markets and social services has been of particular significance in producing ideas. The provision, assembly, and assessment of data can have a substantial creative influence in most of the social sciences; for example, the availability of survey data at the household level has had a fundamental effect on the ability of the profession to do policy work on the distributional impact of different activities—an area in which the Bank, through its Living Standards Measurement Study program, has been productive. In other areas the Bank has also had a major impact through its work on data. In particular, the tables at the back of the Bank's World Development Reports have been profoundly influential as data sources for the profession.[1] The drawing of lessons from the Bank's own practices has, in part, been conducted through the Operations Evaluation Department, the Economic Development Institute, the World Development Reports, and a number of the Bank's publications.

The Bank can stimulate activity and ideas among those outside the Bank and learn from them, by interacting with and in various ways facilitating outside work. This can take place through meetings and through providing materials, organizing conferences, and commissioning research. The Bank has been involved in many academic conferences, and an important fraction of its research budget goes to research outside the Bank. Many of the best Bank studies have been done with the collaboration of outside researchers.

The Bank may disseminate and promote ideas, whether or not they have been generated inside the Bank, to the world of development practitioners and researchers in a number of ways. The Bank has stressed institution building in connection with its research activities, in the sense that it attempts not only to make ideas available, but also to help establish domestic centers in developing countries that might be capable of assimilating, applying, and advancing them. The Bank's Economic Development Institute (established in 1956) has played an important role in the training of senior government servants and others. The Country Economic Reports (produced in the Bank's country divisions and resident missions) are intensely studied by the countries concerned and provide a vehicle for advancing analyses and perspectives of the Bank. The World Development Reports are not oriented toward original research, but do play a major role in drawing together the results of basic research of relevance to policy in important areas. The Bank also publishes the journals *World Bank Economic Review* and *World Bank Research Observer.* The movement of individuals within the Bank, in particular from research to operations, plays a part in the internal dissemination of ideas.

The Bank's major intellectual contribution may be regarded as in the application of ideas. This is in large part what the operations side of the Bank tries to do; it exercises considerable intellectual influence in its dialogue on policy as a whole and on projects. Through lending leverage, policy dialogue, and technical assistance on projects, the Bank's operations provide valuable experience in the application of ideas.

Having defined the Bank's intellectual activities, it can be asked whether these activities should constitute a prominent pursuit or objective of the Bank. Some

---

1. Whether these data have always been produced and used in appropriate ways and with due discretion is another question.

intellectual activities, such as policy dialogue, should now be clearly recognized as an appropriate part of the Bank's role. However, there is a need for explicit discussion of whether or not the Bank should be doing research, be publishing World Development Reports, or have an Economic Development Institute. Our own judgment is that these activities are properly part of the Bank's work and that, given its central significance as a development agency and focus for policy formation, the Bank has an obligation to play a part in the generation of the ideas that it uses. And it must ensure that there is careful thought on how those ideas should be used, for it is in the application of ideas that the Bank exercises particular intellectual influence.

Economic Phases and Intellectual Fashions

The half century since the Second World War has seen various phases of economic growth, economic problems, and international economic relations. Different parts of the developing world have performed, and have been affected, in different ways. The preoccupations of the economics profession, its orthodoxies, idiosyncrasies, and debates, have shifted during this time in various patterns and directions. The concerns of the World Bank also changed over that time, in large part in response to the economic environment and the ideas of the economics profession, but also with prevailing political pressures and as a result of changing personalities inside and outside the Bank. In this section changes in the world, in the economics profession, and in the Bank are set side by side to help form a perspective on how the Bank has responded to ideas and to problems. A diagrammatic representation of these relationships is provided in table 12-1, which is clearly schematic, subjective, and somewhat superficial, but does give some structure to the temporal and intellectual relationships under study.[2]

World Economic Developments

In table 12-1 the second column provides a sketch, of heroic simplicity, of international economic history since the Second World War. During the 1950s and 1960s many developing countries achieved independence. Growth rates of income per capita in Asia and Latin America were moderately high. International trade expanded rapidly (by 6.1 percent a year between 1953 and 1963 and by 8.9 percent

2. Such "potted" history is always subjective, and that provided here may be compared, for example, with that by Hollis B. Chenery in H. B. Chenery, M. S. Ahluwalia, C. L. G. Bell, J. H. Duloy, and R. Jolly, *Redistribution with Growth* (London: Oxford University Press for the World Bank and the Institute of Development Studies, 1974); H. B. Chenery, "From Engineering to Economics," *Banco Nazionale del Lavoro Quarterly Review*, no. 183 (December 1992), p. 371.

Table 12-1. *Economic Phases and Intellectual Concerns inside and outside the World Bank*

Time period	World economic developments	Economists' concerns	World Bank priorities
1950s and 1960s	Rapid growth in incomes Rapid expansion of trade Trade liberalization in OECD Popularity of import-substitution industrialization Rising commodity prices Independence of many developing countries	Planning and government intervention Balanced and unbalanced growth Two-gap model Import-substitution industrialization Growth theories and dualism	Project analysis and lending Infrastructural investment Industrialization Focus shifts from Latin America in the 1950s to India and Pakistan in the 1960s Growing concern in the 1960s for an economy-wide policy framework and balanced growth
1970s	Oil price increases in 1973 and 1979 Balance of payments problems; collapse of Bretton Woods exchange regime Rising external debt and fiscal deficits Deceleration of income growth and trade expansion	Attraction of outward orientation and costs of protection: effective protection, domestic resource costs, shadow prices Cost-benefit analysis and project appraisal Incomplete information and markets, incentives, risks, and institutions Poverty and income distribution Rational expectations and macroeconomic policy Computable general equilibrium models	Poverty Income distribution Rural development and agriculture Human development—education, health, nutrition, population Infrastructure Urban problems
1980s	Mixed growth experience in early 1980s (continued strength in Asia, stagnation in Africa and Latin America) Fall in commodity prices Debt crisis Inflation in developing countries Transition from socialism Worldwide recession in late 1980s	Structural adjustment Debt New growth theory Household behavior Imperfect competition and new industrial organization, trade, and industrialization theories	Structural adjustment and stabilization Trade liberalization "Getting prices right" Public finance, capital markets Privatization Population, environment

Source: Nicholas Stern and Francisco Ferreira.

a year between 1963 and 1973), and there was a steady reduction in trade restrictions through the General Agreement on Tariffs and Trade (GATT).[3] As infant mortality rates declined and life expectancy grew, there was a substantial expansion in population. A number of East Asian countries were laying the foundations for subsequent very rapid growth.

In a number of countries, notably India and China, physical planning played a central role in economic affairs. In both India and China, however, planning saw major crises: in China, the terrible famines around 1960 following the sharp policy changes associated with the Great Leap Forward and in 1966 the beginning of the Cultural Revolution; in India, crises in the mid-1960s following wars, the death of Jawaharlal Nehru, India's first prime minister under independence, and very poor harvests. Many countries followed trade and industrial policies based on import substitution behind high tariff or quota barriers.

In the 1970s the growth of developing countries in Asia and Latin America continued. So too did the growth of world trade, though at a lower rate than before (between 1973 and 1983 world trade grew at 2.8 percent a year).[4] The rapid growth of a number of newly industrialized countries (Korea, Brazil) was becoming marked. Much of Sub-Saharan Africa saw slower growth, stagnation, or decline in the 1970s. The sharp oil price increases of 1973 and 1979 had substantial effects on a number of economies, bringing large boosts in incomes to oil exporters and balance of payments problems to oil importers. Balance of payments difficulties associated with the oil crises were layered on top of those that were emerging from rising protectionism in both developed and developing countries.[5] Notwithstanding increases in the fraction of national income taken in taxation around the world, public expenditure was increasing still more rapidly (as a fraction of national income) in a number of countries. The major problems of public finance and inflation became more acute.

The 1980s saw some sharp changes. The problem of debt became intense and reached crisis proportions with Mexico's suspension of debt servicing in 1982. Structural adjustment became the order of the day from the early 1980s, although several countries (Peru and Brazil, for example) failed to adopt associated liberalization measures. In terms of economic growth, much of Latin America saw stagnation, as did most of Africa south of the Sahara. The newly industrializing countries of East Asia maintained their rapid growth, with Indonesia and Thailand, for example, showing striking performances of the kind expected of—and continued by—Korea, Taiwan, Singapore, and Hong Kong. The 1980s also saw remarkable growth in China, following the economic reforms begun in 1979. India, too, produced a modest acceleration in growth rates in the early part of the 1980s. But

3. J. N. Bhagwati, *Protectionism* (MIT Press, 1988).
4. Ibid.
5. Ibid.

in both India and China problems of inflation and public finances started to appear in the later 1980s. Through the 1980s China's international trade showed a remarkable expansion, with exports rising to 14 or 15 percent of national income by the end of the decade, up from around 5 percent at the beginning of the 1980s.[6]

Economists' Changing Concerns

An equally heroic account of some of the prominent ideas and debates in the economics profession is presented in the third column of table 12-1. Many economists in the 1950s and 1960s were arguing, from a number of perspectives, that markets and incentives worked inadequately in developing countries and that government should play a major role in determining the allocation of resources, particularly of investment. Economists differed over strategies for government direction, for example, in the debates on balanced versus unbalanced growth, but the desirability of government intervention in the economies of developing countries commanded broad agreement. (There were clear voices raised against this apparent consensus, however—in development economics, for example, those of Peter Bauer and Gottfried Haberler.)[7] Many economists from both industrialized and developing countries were studying and advising on the techniques of planning. The predilection for planning and direct controls in the profession was in many cases accompanied by pessimism concerning the prospects for exports from developing countries—a pessimism associated particularly with Hans Singer and Raúl Prebisch.[8] Thus import-substitution industrialization was recommended by many, even though the issues concerning planning and import substitution were logically distinct.

The macroeconomics of development was strongly influenced by two-gap models, in which Hollis Chenery played a leading role.[9] The two gaps concerned savings-investment and the balance of trade. Export pessimism was embodied in a perceived constraint on exports; domestic inflexibilities were incorporated through fixed import requirements for investment. Foreign aid, seen through the optics of these models, could be particularly productive in allowing investment to expand by

6. A. Hussain and N. H. Stern, "Effective Demand, Enterprise Reforms and Public Finance," China Programme Discussion Paper 10 (Suntory and Toyota International Centres for Economics and Related Disciplines [hereafter STICERD], London School of Economics, 1991), table 2.4.

7. P. T. Bauer, *Dissent on Development* (Harvard University Press, 1972); G. Haberler and A. Y. C. Koo, *Selected Essays of Gottfried Haberler* (MIT Press, 1985).

8. R. Prebisch, *The Economic Development of Latin America and its Principal Problems* (New York: UN Economic Commission for Latin America, 1950); H. W. Singer, "The Distribution of Gains between Investing and Borrowing Countries," *American Economic Review*, vol. 40 (May 1950), pp. 473–85.

9. M. Bruno and H. B. Chenery, "Development Alternatives in an Open Economy," *Economic Journal*, vol. 72, no. 285 (1962), pp. 79–103.

overcoming the constraint on its foreign exchange component. In both the planning and two-gap models prices played a minimal role and production techniques offered little choice, with fixed coefficients being a fairly universal assumption.

The 1950s and 1960s brought intense work on aggregate models of economic growth for both developed and developing countries. Although those for developed countries were predominantly for only one sector, those for developing countries gave dualism a prominent role. Particularly influential was Lewis's model of economic growth with unlimited supplies of labor.[10] In this model the process of development was depicted as a transfer of resources out of a traditional sector into an advanced sector, with the growth of the advanced sector being driven by the investment of profits generated in that sector. Taking these various strands together, economic debate in the 1950s and 1960s can be seen as focused on growth through industrialization and import substitution, with the government playing a central role in the process.

The late 1960s and 1970s brought greater emphasis on the application of basic microeconomic principles. Concern about dubious industrial and project decisions taken in the face of distorted domestic prices, or without reference to prices at all, led many economists to work on the measurement of price distortion and on characterization of the consequences of some of the industrial and trade policies that had been followed during the previous decades. Many studies emerged, including those on effective protection, domestic resource cost, and shadow prices. In economic theory academics became much more concerned than previously about problems of economic information and incentives and the way in which institutions developed to take into account or alleviate some of these problems. From this perspective there was particularly intense study during the 1970s and into the 1980s on rural factor markets and institutions (particularly in regard to labor, land, and credit).

Both the 1960s and 1970s saw concern with the conceptual basis for the measurement of poverty and income inequality, and a desire to track in models what income distribution effects might be. The same concern was reflected in empirical studies of poverty and income distribution. There was considerable discussion of the influence of income distribution on savings and growth, and of how growth itself would influence income distribution (much of this discussion built on the work of Arthur Lewis and Simon Kuznets).[11] Also actively studied was human development and its role (as both an input and output) in economic development and income distribution.

Computational advances, both in theory and through more powerful technology, began to exert an influence in economic concerns in the 1970s. Equilibrium prices

---

10. W. A. Lewis, "Economic Development with Unlimited Supplies of Labour," *Manchester School of Economics and Social Studies,* vol. 22 (May 1954), pp. 139–91.

11. Ibid.; W. A. Lewis, *The Theory of Economic Growth* (Homewood, Ill.: Irwin, 1955); S. Kuznets, *Economic Growth of Nations: Total Output and Production Structure* (Harvard University Press, 1971).

and allocations could be calculated in economic models incorporating a substantial number of actors, sectors, and parameters—calculations that produced a literature on so-called computable general equilibrium models. The 1970s saw many applications of the models to both developed and developing countries, and these continue.

The 1980s brought a shift of concerns, driven in part by availability of data and by computing technology, and in part by the acute problems of structural adjustment and debt. There was much empirical work on structural adjustment, and debt was intensively studied, particularly in theory. Toward the mid-1980s an increasing concern with theories of growth resurfaced, in part as a result of developments in the theory of industrial organization and in part from empirical work that made use of large, newly available bodies of cross-country data, in particular the Penn studies of Kravis, Summers, and Heston.[12] New theories of industrial organization were also influential in the transformation of international trade theory, to take into account imperfect competition and increasing returns to scale. Data, computing, and econometric advances allowed for the development of empirical studies using household survey data. These data sets were multipurpose and were applied in national income accounting, in models of individual and household behavior, as well as in the evaluation of income-distributional and standard-of-living consequences of different policies.

World Bank Priorities

As the fourth column of table 12-1 suggests, during its first twenty years the World Bank saw itself primarily as a project-lending institution, with a particular emphasis on infrastructural activities. This did not mean, however, that there was no view on processes of development and policies designed to stimulate them. Indeed, the focus on infrastructure was predicated on the view that such investment is critical to industrialization and development and represents an area where government action has some comparative advantage. Mason and Asher, in their review of the Bank's first twenty-five years,[13] suggest that the Bank recognized that the public and private sectors had different roles to play. They felt that "a primary condition" for development was "an adequate complement of public overhead capital: railways, roads, power plants, port installations, and communications

---

12. See I. B. Kravis, A. W. Heston, and R. Summers, *World Product and Income: International Comparisons of Real Gross Product* (Johns Hopkins University Press, 1983); R. Summers and A. Heston, "A New Set of International Comparisons of Real Product and Price Levels Estimates for 130 Countries, 1950–1985," *Review of Income and Wealth,* (1988), pp. 1–25; R. Summers and A. Heston, "The Penn World Table (Mark 5): An Expanded Set of International Comparisons, 1950–1988," *Quarterly Journal of Economics,* vol. 106, no. 2 (May 1991).

13. E. S. Mason and R. E. Asher, *The World Bank since Bretton Woods* (Brookings, 1973).

facilities," adding that "this capital is customarily provided by the public sector, which must be developed systematically, with due attention to the progressive elimination of bottlenecks. Hence the need for planning and programming public sector investment."[14]

Although planning—in the sense of determining priorities and sequencing, and ensuring the integration and coordination of various projects—was thus envisaged for the activities that should fall under the natural jurisdiction of the state, Mason and Asher thought that in "the areas of agriculture, industry, commerce, and financial and personal services" the private sector could perform better.[15] In 1949, in fact, the Bank criticized a UN Economic and Employment Commission report which advocated heavy industrial projects in the public sector. The Bank suggested that governments of less developed countries had enough to do in trying to provide adequate infrastructure, and that domestic and foreign savings, channeled through the private sector, should take care of these other areas.

Furthermore, as the Bank's *Fifth Annual Report, 1949–50*, stressed, the Bank was bound by the Articles of Agreement, which stated that "loans made or guaranteed by the Bank shall, except in special circumstances, be for the purpose of specific projects. . . ." Defending this policy, the report went on to argue that: "criticism of the specific project approach has almost always been based on the assumption that the Bank examines the merit of particular projects in isolation. In fact the Bank does the opposite. The Bank seeks to determine what are the appropriate investment priorities. Consistently with this approach the Bank has encouraged its members to formulate long-term development programs. The existence of such a program greatly facilitates the task of determining which projects are of the highest priority."[16]

Although these quotations indicate the Bank's approach to development issues and lending policy during the 1940s and 1950s, those views were not founded on internal research. Indeed, until the mid-1960s the Economics Department was small and undermanned (on the history of the Economics Department, see the next section).

The period during which the Bank held firm views on the nature of the development process but did little research into it extended roughly up to the late 1950s, and coincided with a phase in Bank lending in which most lending was still made to developed countries (by 1957, 52.7 percent of financing still went to such countries). During the same period the main recipients of Bank loans to less developed countries (LDCs) were in Latin America. This led to an awareness of the importance of stabilization and sensible fiscal and monetary policies to provide a macroeconomic environment in which the private sector could thrive. However, as Mason and Asher put it, "if Latin America had focused the Bank's attention on

14. Ibid., p. 458.
15. Ibid., p. 459.
16. World Bank, *Fifth Annual Report, 1949–50* (Washington: 1950), p. 7.

development problems in the early 1950s, it was India and to a lesser extent Pakistan that came to the center of the stage in the late 1950s and early 1960s."[17] The new prominence of the subcontinent appears to have been one factor behind a change in the economywide views held within the Bank—notably, the conceptual division between areas suitable for the public and the private sectors progressively lost its sharpness. Public sector loans for agricultural projects began to be made, and the distinction between foreign exchange components and local expenditure components of projects also diminished in importance.[18]

Although some acceptance of both an economywide policy perspective and planning was evident during the 1950s and 1960s, the former was of greater consistency and importance and was the one which was to grow in strength. Many people within the Bank remained skeptical of the advantages of tampering with the price mechanism. The tone of the "Report of the Country Mission to Spain" of 1961, for example, was unashamedly promarket throughout, placing the responsibility for efficient use and allocation of resources in development squarely on the shoulders of the price mechanism: "In the market economy, economic discipline should be enforced by a freely functioning price mechanism that brings about the best allocation of resources through the force of competition."[19] Practical recommendations were generally to remove restrictive or monopolistic practices, encourage competition, phase out most subsidies and price controls, replace quotas by tariffs, and expose the economy to foreign competition.

A further important influence during this period was that of Bela Balassa, who first joined the Bank in 1966 as a consultant. In time he came to be seen as one of the leading defenders of the price mechanism, as well as a prominent proponent of outward orientation. But he himself stated that those ideas were not dominant in the Bank at the time of his arrival,[20] and he must thus be counted among those who resisted any drift toward planning in the 1960s. (For further discussion of Balassa's role and contributions, see the section "Perspectives from Within.")

With the arrival of McNamara in 1968 the Bank became explicitly and prominently a development agency. This focus brought with it a still greater stress on the economywide view, a broadening of perspectives on what constituted development, and generally an openness concerning the kinds of tools and policies to be

17. Mason and Asher, World Bank since Bretton Woods, p. 471.

18. J. Tinbergen, in an interview, saw it as "completely natural that the United States thought that the Bank had to finance the infrastructure, but that the superstructure would have to come from private initiatives." After quoting counterexamples, Tinbergen referred to the opposition of the Bank's president to publication of a book he had written for the Bank in 1955 and noted that "of course, an American could not understand this [viewpoint]." See J. R. Magnus and M. S. Morgan, "The ET Interview: Professor J. Tinbergen," Economic Theory, vol. 3 (1987), pp. 134–35.

19. World Bank, "Report of the Country Mission to Spain" (1963), p. 57.

20. M. Fanwar-George, "Bela Balassa's Life Philosophy," The Bank's World (March 1990), pp. 10–11.

examined and supported. Indeed, by the time of McNamara's arrival the fundamental purpose of the Economics Department was seen as the provision of a well-documented and researched economywide view, which would bridge the gap between projects and area aggregates. As McNamara wrote in 1968: "I would like to explain *why* the World Bank Group does research work, and why it publishes it. We feel an obligation to look beyond the projects we help to finance towards the whole resource allocation of an economy, and the effectiveness of the use of those resources."[21] The rise of the economists continued, and at the turn of the decade the Bank created a vice-presidency for research, under the direction of Hollis Chenery.

Poverty and human development became prominent issues, with McNamara making a conscious attempt to use and respond to the leading ideas of the times. McNamara's speech to the Bank's Board of Governors in Nairobi on September 24, 1973, placed poverty at the top of the policy agenda and signaled a major shift in Bank thinking. Although growth remained a central concern, increasing attention was paid to its distributional impact. In addition, concern with direct measures to reach the poor was embodied in the establishment of the Agriculture and Rural Development Department in 1973, the Urban Development Department in 1975, and the Population, Health, and Nutrition Department in 1979.

The spirit of research in the 1970s was that of problem solving—a spirit reflected in McNamara's speeches and strategies and in the kinds of models used. There was stress on targets and means to achieve the targets, and thus on an input-output approach to policy and to modeling. Such an approach could at times be rather mechanical, and left little scope for concern with institutions and with prices. Indeed, many of the models used contained no prices other than those that were Lagrange multipliers on constraints in optimization problems.

The 1980s in the Bank were dominated by the problems of structural adjustment and debt. Direct concern with poverty and income distribution declined, and it was not uncommon to hear Reaganite denigrations of those concerned with the poor—terms such as "bleeding hearts," "social planners," and the "flaunting of compassion" were used.[22] Toward the end of the 1980s there was a late response to political pressures regarding the environment. After McNamara left, the Bank's 1981–82 population policies acquired a lower profile. Taking these developments

21. Robert S. McNamara, foreword to A. A. Walters, "The Economics of Road User Charges," World Bank Staff Occasional Papers (Washington: International Bank for Research and Development, 1968), p. v.

22. Nicholas Stern quotes here from experience as a participant-observer. There are those in the Bank who, when challenged with this evidence, would accept the existence within the Bank at that time of the outlook embodied in such remarks, but who would argue that it is good policies rather than fine expressions of concern that matter. Others would say that the casting of epithets was confined to a small minority (and some would embrace both responses).

together, it can be said that in the 1980s the Bank showed a greater preoccupation with macroeconomic issues and with the price aspects of microeconomics. In contrast, sectoral modeling and planning played a less important role.

The history of both the development economics profession and the Bank does show responses to changing world conditions. For a period in the 1970s, on certain issues, the Bank's research was at the frontiers of the subject. Nevertheless, it was during that period that the Bank could be charged with responding only slowly to the profession's increasing emphasis on and analysis of the problems associated with planning, protection, and distorted economic signals. Although the presidential leadership of the Bank during the 1980s was considerably less forceful than in the 1970s, economic events, the central position of the Bank among world economic institutions, and the actions of the Bank's operations departments combined to place the Bank in a position of substantial leadership. In a sense, the World Bank's role as leader was heightening just at the time when it lost its most dominant personality.[23]

Research and the Intellectual Agenda

In discussing the World Bank's role in setting the intellectual agenda and carrying out research, we pay particular attention to the last twenty years but first provide some background on the evolution of the Bank's research facilities and research agenda. The perspective is that of two individuals standing outside the Bank.

The Bank produced papers and research documents almost from its inception. The Economic Development Institute, established in 1956, provided material for the education of government servants. The Staff Occasional Paper Series, founded by Kamarck as a vehicle to publish the research findings of the new Economics Department, began in 1966 with a paper on choices between hydroelectric and thermal power by Herman van der Tak, which included a foreword by President George Woods on the value of research. The series included papers by Alan Walters on road user charges and by Benjamin King on growth and debt. A substantial research facility was first introduced at the Bank by President George D. Woods in 1964–65, with Irving S. Friedman as economic adviser to the president and chair of the Economic Committee, and Andrew M. Kamarck as director of the Economics Department. At their departure in 1970, staff in the department had increased sixfold and a number of occasional and discussion papers had been published. With the major reorganization of the Bank in 1972, research came under the aegis of the Development Policy Staff, also known as the Economics

---

23. It will be noted that this history of changing ideas within the Bank and the profession does not coincide with a Kuhnian view of the way in which ideas change in the sciences. See T. S. Kuhn, *The Structure of Scientific Revolutions* (University of Chicago Press, 1962).

Department, headed by Hollis Chenery, who succeeded Kamarck and was also designated vice president for research.[24] Under McNamara and Chenery the profile of research within the Bank grew rapidly.

The Bank was reorganized again in 1982, creating the Economics Research Staff to replace the Development Policy Staff, with Anne Krueger as vice president in charge. There was a shift toward macroeconomic and trade issues, with poverty moving down on the agenda, and a shift in the size of research projects, with research funds now being concentrated on a few very large cross-country programs. When the Bank was reorganized once more in 1987, Krueger left,[25] and Stanley Fischer became vice president for development economics and the Bank's chief economist. The research agenda was broadened again and the portfolio of projects was rebalanced to include fewer very small and very large projects and more medium-sized projects. Fischer was succeeded in 1991 by Lawrence Summers,[26] who resigned to join the Clinton administration in January 1993. An outline of research department history is given in table 12-2. The history of the Bank's research component stands in interesting contrast to the history of the IMF, which had a research department from the beginning.

In considering next the Bank's role in structural adjustment, it is important to keep in mind that it was a leader in terms of agenda setting rather than research: its leadership came in large part from the operations side. A number of examples of research areas where the Bank has made successful contributions (the agricultural and social services sectors, urban problems, and China, for example) are then described, as are areas where the intellectual performance of the Bank has been less than impressive (debt analysis and cost-benefit analysis).

Structural Adjustment

In two respects the World Bank might be regarded as an intellectual leader in the understanding of structural adjustment and stabilization.[27] First, from 1980 to 1982, the Bank helped set the topic firmly among the most urgent issues then facing developing countries. The launching of Structural Adjustment Lending (SAL) programs in February 1980, McNamara's speech to the Board of Governors in September 1980, and the choice of adjustment as the main topic of the 1981 World Development Report were fundamental in drawing the attention of many in the development community—policymakers and academics alike—to the mag-

24. Chenery held the post from 1972 to 1982, when he returned to Harvard University.
25. Krueger left to join Duke University.
26. Fischer resigned to return to the Massachusetts Institute of Technology.
27. Comments in this section have been substantially influenced by F. H. G. Ferreira, "The World Bank and the Study of Stabilization and Structural Adjustment in LDCs," Development Economics Research Programme Discussion Paper 41, STICERD, London School of Economics, 1992.

Table 12-2. *World Bank President and Officers Responsible for Research and Economics*

Term	President	Term	Title	Officeholder
			Senior research positions	
1946 (June–Dec)	Eugene Meyer	1946–52	Director, Research Department	Leonard B. Rist
1947–49	John J. McCloy	1952–61	Director, Economic Staff	Leonard B. Rist
		1962–63	Acting director, Economic Staff	John C. de Wilde
1949–62	Eugene R. Black	1963–64	Acting director, Economic Staff	Dragoslav Avramovic
		1964–70	Economic advisor to the president. Chairman, Economic Committee	Irving S. Friedman
1963–68	George D. Woods	1965–70	Director, Economics Department	Andrew M. Kamarek
1968–81	Robert S. McNamara	1970–72	Economic advisor to the president. Chairman, Economic Committee	Hollis B. Chenery
		1972–82	Vice president, Research	Hollis B. Chenery
1982–87	A. W. Clausen	1982–87	Vice president, Economics Research Staff	Anne Krueger
1987–91	Barber Conable	1987–89	Vice president, Operations Policy Staff	Shahid Husain
		1987–91	Senior vice president, Policy Research and External Affairs	David Hopper
		1987–90	Vice president, Development Economics, and chief economist	Stanley Fischer
		1987–92	Vice president, Policy Research and External Affairs (now Operations Policy Staff)	Visvanatan Rajagopalan
		1989–91	Senior vice president, Policy Research and External Affairs	Wilfred Thalwitz
1991–present	Lewis Preston	1991–92	Vice president, Development Economics, and chief economist	Lawrence Summers

Sources: F. Ferreira, "The World Bank and the Study of Stabilization and Structural Adjustment in LDCs," Development Economics Research Programme DP no.41, STICERD, LSE. (1992); E. S. Mason and R. E. Asher, *The World Bank since Bretton Woods* (Brookings, 1973); World Bank, "Setting Research Priorities at the World Bank: An Historical Review," PRE mimeo, 1990.

nitude of the challenge of adjustment. Although it must be stressed that these actions by the Bank were very different from any recognition of an imminent debt crisis, they nonetheless constituted recommendations for strategy changes some two years before Mexico's crisis of August 1982. But an understanding of what would later be meant by structural adjustment was far from clear at the Bank in that early period, and no claim can be made that the analyses and recommendations proposed at that time were pathbreaking.

The second respect in which the Bank may be seen as an intellectual leader on structural adjustment refers to its (post-1982) analyses of and perspectives on appropriate policies, and in particular to the application of basic microeconomic principles to reforms of the supply side of adjusting economies (with a focus on prices). These theories and views were not new; indeed, in many respects an emphasis on the importance of prices, trade, and incentives in efficiency and growth had long lain at the heart of economics. They had been stressed by many prominent commentators, both in the profession and in the Bank.[28] But in the mid-1980s and in discussions of adjustment the Bank, notwithstanding its slow response in the 1970s to the changing views in the profession, became a prominent champion of many of the central tenets of the neoclassical resurgence. The World Development Reports of 1983, 1985, 1986, and 1987 all focus on the importance of careful price, trade, tax, and institutional reforms for increasing the efficiency of resource allocation (crucially, domestic investment) as a necessary element of structural adjustment. It was during the 1980s and on this topic that the Bank was seen to be leading the charge of the neoclassical resurgence.

The early World Development Reports, and most contemporaneous literature, saw structural adjustment as a process by which not only individual countries but also the international financial system as a whole should respond to the balance of payments disequilibria set in motion by the oil price shocks of 1973–74 and 1979–80. The reports had a strong demand-side flavor and emphasized macroeconomic policies, notably real depreciations to induce a flow of resources toward the production of tradables, and broad aggregate targets, such as low inflation and (more prominently) balance of payments equilibrium. This emphasis came with a global outlook, which favored capital flows, on the then-current scale, from the surplus countries to the deficit countries in order to facilitate the sectoral adjustment of the latter from nontradables to tradables. Subsequent notions of structural adjustment would continue to feature macroeconomic policies intended to restore an economy to internal and external balance (with stable prices, full employment, and a current account balance), but would also stress microeconomic attempts to increase the efficiency of the supply side of the economy. The supply-side focus

28. B. Balassa, *The Structure of Protection in Developing Countries* (John Hopkins University Press, 1971); B. Balassa, "Exports and Economic Growth," *Journal of Development Economics*, vol. 5 (1978), pp. 181–89; B. Balassa, *Development Strategies in Semi-Industrial Economies* (John Hopkins University Press, 1982).

included particularly issues such as the boundary between the public and private
sectors, the structure of the tax system, trade and protection policy, property rights,
development of capital markets, and institution building, in addition to those basic
aspects of balance of payments associated with shifts in output patterns towards
tradable sectors. Hence supply-side aspects of structural adjustment would now be
seen as embodying two broad thrusts—first, the structure of incentives and
markets, the role of government, and ownership patterns, and second, sectoral
restructuring with a move toward tradable sectors.

Whether terms such as stabilization, macroeconomic adjustment, and structural
adjustment refer to a part or the whole of this package, or how overlapping they
are, does not seem to be the subject of a wide consensus. But by structural
adjustment we mean the combination of supply- and demand-side policies just
described, directed toward the transformation of the structure of an economy in
response to serious disequilibria, aiming both to restore macroeconomic equilibrium and to improve microeconomic efficiency. The Bank's two claims to leadership in structural adjustment, as well as weaknesses in the different phases of the
Bank's continuing stress on adjustment in the 1980s, are examined below.

In McNamara's September 1980 speech to the Board of Governors, he drew
attention to the current account deficits of oil-importing countries and argued that
they required a program of structural adjustment to expand exports and reduce
imports. This argument was in contrast to the emphasis on the notion of recycling
of surpluses that had been prominent after the first oil price shock. The 1980
speech was given in the wake of the oil price increase of 1979 and a (mistaken)
prediction that the real price of oil would go on rising through the 1980s. The oil
price increase was seen as permanent and it was suggested that adjustment to it
should begin sooner rather than later. Such a required adjustment was emphasized
more firmly by the Bank in the late 1970s than it had been for the earlier oil price
increase in 1973.[29] The 1970s had seen continued growth, helped by extensive
borrowing after the first oil price shock and a gradual decline in oil prices over the
later 1970s.

McNamara, however, also emphasized that those deficits had been growing
through the 1970s so that the oil price increase was aggravating a problem that had
already been emerging. Thus he argued that the problem was not simply one of
external finance or of recycling surpluses from oil-exporting countries. Such
finance and recycling were indeed important because they would make the adjustment less socially damaging, but they could not substitute for the adjustment
process itself. In this process special emphasis was laid on domestic energy production. At the same time, McNamara rejected the idea that poverty could wait but
that deficits could not. He argued strongly that the attack on poverty should be

29. But see H. B. Chenery and others, *Redistribution with Growth* (London: Oxford
University Press for the World Bank and the Institute of Development Studies, 1974).

sustained throughout the adjustment process. In his 1974 preface to *Redistribution with Growth,* Chenery emphasized the same point with reference to adjustments that might follow the oil price increase of 1973.[30]

McNamara's speech marked one public manifestation of arguments that had been going on within the Bank during the latter part of the 1970s (and earlier), to the effect that the Bank should concentrate less on projects and more on the overall policy environment. (Stanley Please was a prominent exponent of this view within the Bank.) The speech itself focused on shifting resources toward traded sectors and left open the process by which that shift could come about. McNamara suggested that whether this process should be export promotion or import substitution would depend on the circumstances of the country under study. The spirit of the speech was still macroeconomic and sectoral, and did not pay special attention to the problems of distorted incentives and prices that may have generated the difficulties in the balance of payments. These distortions were being strongly emphasized in the profession throughout the 1970s, but only later came to be seen as part of structural adjustment.

The World Development Report of 1981 was dedicated chiefly to adjustment and it had an important impact on the development economics profession. Attention to the topic in academic circles had up to then been limited, and the World Bank was the first to give it a high profile in the development community. Basic elements of structural adjustment recommended in the 1981 World Development Report were outward orientation (and real exchange rate depreciation), increased savings, and increased share of investment without detriment to its efficiency. Mention had also been made of "adjustment" in the World Development Report for 1980, the year in which the Bank's new structural adjustment loans (SALs) were launched. Thus through the two World Development Reports, McNamara's 1980 speech, and the launching of the SAL program, the Bank had made a major change in both its actions and words—a change followed by change in the profession.

There were nevertheless some serious shortcomings in the Bank's analyses of that early period. Most noteworthy, perhaps, was an insistence on seeing the adjustment process as essentially global in nature, in combination with wildly optimistic predictions about the sustainability of external financing of deficits in most less developed countries. Hence McNamara told his Board, "There will have to be major adjustments in both national and international policies, and a sustained, collective effort on the part of the world community,"[31] and the 1981 World Development Report predicted that aggregate net transfers to all developing countries in 1985 would be between U.S.$36.3 billion and U.S.$54.3 billion, when in the event they were U.S.$0.7 billion *in the reverse direction.* For 1990, the 1981

30. Ibid.
31. Robert S. McNamara, *The McNamara Years at the World Bank* (Johns Hopkins University Press, 1981), p. 621.

World Development Report expected things to edge up still further, with transfers lying somewhere in the range from U.S.$56.7 billion to U.S.$96 billion; in the event, transfers again went *in the reverse direction* (by some U.S.$9.8 billion in 1988, for example).[32]

Such wishful thinking as regards the willingness of the world community (both private institutions and official donors) to finance adjustment in most developing countries in the 1980s, and the accompanying global view of the process, led to some poor advice—notably, the early emphasis on the benefits of recycling funds from current-account surplus countries to those with large deficits, often through the international financial system. The World Development Report of 1981 stated, "There is nothing inherently undesirable about external deficits, since deficits imply resource transfer. . . . These effects . . . provide a rationale for external borrowing to contribute to structural adjustment."[33] Although there is nothing strictly incorrect in this passage, interpreted as policy advice from the World Bank in mid-1981 it sent decidedly the wrong message to adjusting countries.

In the structural adjustment context as in others, the Bank is not a monolith, and significant differences of emphasis exist even among major documents. Thus, although a reading of the 1981 World Development Report must have encouraged optimism about the availability and the desirability of borrowing to finance a high investment mode of adjustment, McNamara's 1980 address to the Board was more cautious: "The point I want to stress here is the necessity of using external finance in support of structural adjustments, and not as a substitute for them."[34] Nevertheless, shortly afterward, in late 1982, many countries were faced with an international climate in which no new external finance was available whatsoever. Perhaps even more irritatingly for developing countries, the Bank itself had (somewhat abruptly) changed its mind: whereas in 1982 the Bank held that "the developing countries, despite the rise in their current account deficits from U.S.$40 billion in 1979 to U.S.$115 billion in 1981, have been much more successful than the industrialized countries in adjusting to the new situation," in 1986 the Bank thought that "at the root of the poor performance and debt problems of developing countries lies their failure to adjust to the external developments that have taken place since the early 1970s, coupled with the magnitude of the external shocks."[35]

An overall assessment of the Bank's analyses and policy recommendations regarding structural adjustment in 1979–82 must therefore conclude that, although the Bank is to be commended for substantially raising the profile of the issue in the development community, there were serious shortcomings in its understanding of

32. For further discussion and for sources, see Ferreira, "World Bank and the Study of Stabilization."

33. World Bank, *World Development Report* (Oxford University Press, 1981), p. 54.

34. McNamara, *The McNamara Years at the World Bank*, p. 620.

35. World Bank, *World Development Report* (Oxford University Press, 1982), p. 7; World Bank, *World Development Report* (Oxford University Press, 1986), p. 33.

the nature and severity of the experience soon to be that of many developing countries.

In the aftermath of Mexico's problems in August 1982, however, and possibly as a result of new priorities at the Bank itself (after the appointments of Clausen and Krueger to replace McNamara and Chenery), the nature of analysis and policy pronouncements at the Bank concerning adjustment changed significantly. Structural adjustment soon came to be associated not only with macroeconomic stabilization but also with reducing price distortions, the role of the government, and making markets work more effectively. A particular problem here was the perceived need to bring relative domestic producer prices into closer harmony with world prices, so that production decisions were more firmly based on the opportunity costs facing the country.

The policies involved in structural adjustment had been advocated by many in the profession through the 1970s, following the disillusionment with planning that became widespread in the 1960s.[36] However, in its formulation and discussion of structural adjustment and surrounding policies the Bank was attempting something which had not been closely analyzed in the profession, namely the coordination of the various macroeconomic, sectoral, and microeconomic elements into a single program with a view to immediate applications.[37] From the academic perspective it was this economywide approach, together with emphasis on the process of change itself and asking how a country was to move from an earlier set of policies to the new set of policies, that constituted the innovative aspects of structural adjustment.

This emphasis on coordination of macroeconomic, microeconomic, and sectoral policies, which comes to light in the Bank's official and research documents from 1982 onward, seems to have originated in part from evaluations of the performances of the first structural adjustment loan recipients. Such reflection on the experiences of the operations side exemplifies one of the mechanisms by which dominant ideas or approaches change in the Bank. Between 1980 and 1983, fourteen SALs were made to nine countries—Turkey, Kenya, Bolivia, the Philippines, Senegal, Guyana, the Ivory Coast, Thailand, and Jamaica. The loans were designed around four key components: trade reform, resource mobilization (a euphemism for fiscal reform), reforms aimed at increasing the effectiveness of resource use, and institution building.[38] Not only were the last two components

36. Balassa, *Structure of Protection in Developing Countries;* Balassa, "Exports and Economic Growth"; Balassa, *Development Strategies in Semi-Industrial Economies.* On the extent to which the basic ideas had been anticipated in the profession, see D. P. Coady, "The Raising and Allocation of Public Revenues in LDC's: The Contribution of the World Bank," Development Economics Research Programme Discussion Paper 46, STICERD, London School of Economics, August 1993.

37. However, Little, Scitovsky, and Scott, in *Industry and Trade,* did devote careful attention to the process of change.

38. Some, both within and outside the Bank, have suggested that the actual success of institution building, in the sense of developing sustainable indigenous capacities for research, policymaking, and policy implementation, has been very limited in a number of

entirely directed toward increasing allocative and productive efficiency throughout the economy, but even the first two embodied concerns that were not evident in the intellectual output of the Bank in relation to adjustment until later, such as detailed examination of public sector pricing and public enterprise efficiency as integral aspects of reducing budget deficits.

In fact, an Operations Evaluation Department (OED) draft report on these loans concluded that some of the most successful aspects of the programs were on the more microeconomic and sectoral fronts.[39] Agriculture and energy were often targeted for price reforms, intended to raise the effectiveness of resource use. In Turkey and Senegal significant increases in producer prices of food brought them in line with international prices and compensated suppliers for the abolition of subsidies for fertilizers and other inputs. Although the draft report was somewhat ambiguous on the distributional impact of some of the reforms, it seems that Bank personnel were sufficiently impressed by such applied experiences of adjustment to raise the profile of such allocative issues in official publications; until 1982–83, publications did not emphasize the role of these issues in the adjustment process.[40]

The Bank had a comparative advantage here relative to the academic economics profession. It was faced firmly with the issues in an applied context and had to give policy advice beyond the macroeconomic (advice to cut budget deficits and switch resources toward tradable sectors was not in itself sufficient counsel). In addition, the Bank had a collection of skills—microeconomic, sectoral, and macroeconomic —and had expertise on particular countries that was not matched elsewhere, at least not outside the countries concerned, and sometimes not inside. It has been in the Bank's collection of competence across the board, rather than its outstanding talent in any particular dimension, that the Bank has been strong, as was well demonstrated in its work on structural adjustment.

The Bank's record on structural adjustment since 1982 is not one of unrelieved glory, however. Its attention to equity issues from 1982 to the end of the decade appears to have been somewhat token, at least relative to its record in the 1970s. The costs of adjustment for the poor can be very high,[41] and McNamara's warnings in his 1980 speech on the need to take account of the poor in the adjustment process do not seem to have been consistently heeded within the Bank. Speaking of programs to reduce infant mortality, he maintained that "the economic returns

developing countries, particularly in Africa. The Operations Evaulation Department recognizes that the time lags for successful institutional work are very large, but questions about the Bank's seriousness in committing the necessary resources to this area have been raised.

39. It must be remembered, however, that the IMF's distaste for the Bank's articulation of the term "macroeconomic" sometimes leads the Bank to express itself elliptically. World Bank, "Experience with Structural Adjustment Lending," Operations Evaluation Department Draft (February 1986).

40. See below, section "Research Publications," especially table 12-9.

41. See G. Cornia, R. Jolly, and F. Stewart, eds., *Adjustment with a Human Face* (Oxford: Clarendon Press, 1987).

will be huge. And the same is true of other investments in the immense untapped human potential of the absolute poor. Even in a period of austerity—indeed, especially in a period of austerity—those investments must be accelerated."[42] He mentioned, in 1980, ongoing research at the Bank aimed at redesigning and reorganizing social services so as to explore complementarities among programs, which might enable governments to expand coverage within tight budgetary conditions. The two priority areas singled out were primary education (especially for girls) and basic health care.

Under the new direction given to the research department from 1982 to 1987, the concern with the effects of adjustment on inequality and poverty does seem to have been deemphasized, however. This is apparent in the little attention dedicated to that concern in the World Development Reports of the time; that the Bank was for a while a lagging follower in this issue is admitted quite plainly in the World Development Report of 1990, which marks the full restoration of the issue to prominence: "It was UNICEF that first brought the issue [the effects of adjustment on the poor] into the center of the debate on the design and effects of adjustment."[43] Even the attention that the issue was accorded did not always take account of progress made elsewhere in the profession. For example, despite significant advances in the conceptualization and measurement of poverty proposed in the 1980s,[44] World Development Reports before 1990 still used the head count almost exclusively.

It is not suggested that there was no support at all for inquiry into the equity aspects of adjustment at all during the 1982–87 period. But most of the support that existed facilitated external research rather than work inside the Bank's research department; two important examples were papers by Feder and colleagues in 1986 and by Demery and Addison in 1987, both issued by the Bank.[45] Even in such cases, however, the original interest and impetus for research often predated Bank support. In a 1985 paper Addison and Demery provided a comprehensive preview of their 1987 paper, and their early research was supported by the Overseas Development Institute.[46] One view in the Bank seems to have associated demotion of interest in poverty in this period with a belief that adjustment could be

42. McNamara, *The McNamara Years,* p. 639.

43. World Bank, "Women in Development: Progress Report on the Implementation of the World Bank's Operational Strategy," Development Committee Pamphlet 28 (1991), p. 45.

44. See A. K. Sen, "Poor, Relatively Speaking," *Oxford Economic Papers,* vol. 35 (July 1983), pp. 153–69.

45. G. Feder, "Land Ownership Security, Farm Productivity and Land Policies in Rural Thailand," Working Paper (World Bank, 1986); L. Demery and T. Addison, "The Alleviation of Poverty under Structural Adjustment," Working Paper (World Bank, 1987).

46. T. Addison and L. Demery, "Macro-Economic Stabilization, Income Distribution and Poverty: A Preliminary Survey," ODI Working Paper 15 (London: Overseas Development Institute, 1985).

quick enough so that poverty would be on the back burner only for a short time. Even allowing for the benefits of hindsight, such a view seems curiously optimistic.

Barber Conable's presidency (1987–91) saw a greater emphasis on poverty, and in 1987—with Fischer's appointment as chief economist and the publication of Cornia, Jolly, and Stewart's *Adjustment with a Human Face* by UNICEF, several research papers for the Bank's Living Standards Measurement Study, and Demery and Addison's 1987 paper by the Bank—marked a revival of interest in the subject within the institution. This interest has continued to the present, and the 1990 World Development Report was dedicated to poverty; a whole chapter was related to the effects of adjustment on the poorest. This may well be seen as another example of a response by researchers and writers to discoveries that originate in the monitoring of Bank programs and experiences in specific countries. Much of the evidence marshaled by Demery and Addison, for instance, came from evaluations of the structural development loans (SALs) to Thailand of 1982–84, the Chilean SAL of October 1985, and assistance to employment and training programs in Senegal in 1986–87, among others.[47]

Such feedback is part of a two-way process, and the growing emphasis on monitoring and alleviating poverty during adjustment, in research and official publications, led to the creation in 1987 of the Social Dimension of Adjustment (SDA) program, in partnership with the UN Development Program (UNDP) and the African Development Bank. The SDA program had a strong emphasis on survey monitoring of social, poverty, and inequality indicators during adjustment in Sub-Saharan Africa. Although an offshoot of LSMS, the SDA program has its own independent standing, which reflects a continuing rise in the profile of distributional and welfare issues in the Bank's study of adjustment since the late 1980s. This study has been formalized in the Bank's 1992 *Poverty Reduction Handbook,* which opens with President Preston's declaration that "sustainable poverty reduction is the overarching objective of the World Bank."[48] One can be forgiven for being reminded of the language of the McNamara days. The *Handbook* has specific sections on policy strategies in the context of structural adjustment, and incorporates analytical advances in many areas. An example is Martin Ravallion's discussion of different poverty measures and concepts, which retains the head count as only one among a larger armory of indicators.[49]

The view of the World Bank as causal or as an animator in the process of adjustment should not be assumed from its central role. One should ask whether the process would have happened anyway, without the Bank. If a country is about to be forced to make radical changes as a result of severe deterioration in its payments position, should the Bank really be given great credit for putting structural adjustment firmly on the agenda? Mexico's inability to service debt in August

47. Demery and Addison, "Alleviation of Poverty."
48. World Bank, *Poverty Reduction Handbook* (Washington, 1992), introduction.
49. Martin Ravallion, *Poverty Reduction Handbook,* chapter 1.

1982 was by then a fact of life, and some change was essential. Further, not only was the need for change obvious, but the Mexican view has been that the changes were substantially homegrown.[50] Many in the Bank, on the other hand, would challenge that view and claim to have exercised a major influence on the shape of the reforms. And it must be recognized that there have been homegrown attempts at adjustment that were disastrous (as in Peru and Brazil in the 1980s), so it cannot be assumed that favorable reforms would emerge automatically. Indeed, there is a common tendency to use direct (as opposed to market-friendly) control measures in difficult times, and the evidence suggests that those Latin American countries which followed Bank programs have shown more successful recoveries than those which did not. Thus, although care should be taken not to overstress the Bank's role as an agenda-setter, the second of the reasons set out at the beginning of this subsection for suggesting that the Bank deserves credit in the adjustment area is not so clearly subject to the same criticism. There were a number of ways to react to the crises, and the Bank's influence in important aspects pointed clearly in particular—and in our view positive—directions.

In concluding this discussion of structural adjustment, it should be recognized again that the Bank's leading role in the crucial period of the first half of the 1980s was not driven by its own research. The events under discussion saw the Bank take an operational lead in embracing policies that had been suggested by research done largely outside the Bank in the 1960s and 1970s—research associated with, for example, Bhagwati, Corden, Krueger, and Little,[51] and, within the Bank, by Balassa.

Some Successes

As a success, structural adjustment has been discussed separately above because of its breadth as a subject, its centrality to the recent history of the Bank, and its importance as an example of Bank leadership. Other important examples of intellectual leadership at the Bank—some of which are also broad but more long term in nature, others of which are more sectoral or regional—can be briefly reviewed: work on the determinants of growth and mechanisms for the alleviation of poverty in specific regions (China) and in specific sectors (urban problems, agriculture, transport, and electricity). We also comment on examples of the Bank's use of such techniques as programming models and computable general equilibrium models. It must be emphasized that the list is subjective and not exhaustive.

DETERMINANTS AND PATTERNS OF GROWTH. From the early days at the Bank, and certainly from the establishment of the research sections in the early 1970s, it was recognized that one of the Bank's strongest comparative advantages lay in its ability to assemble data and experience from many countries. This has

---

50. P. Aspe, "Stabilization and Structural Change: The Mexican Experience," Robbins Lectures, London School of Economics, January 1992.

51. A. O. Krueger, *Foreign Trade Regimes and Economic Development: Liberalization Attempts and Consequences* (New York: National Bureau of Economic Research, 1978); W. M. Corden, *Trade Policy and Economic Welfare* (Oxford University Press, 1974).

been exploited in a number of ways over the years, for example in the work by Chenery and his collaborators on patterns of growth. Chenery's work built on earlier studies outside the Bank by Colin Clark and Simon Kuznets,[52] and had the advantage of a longer run of data and a much broader set of countries. Chenery's *Structural Change and Development Policy* of 1979 and Chenery, Robinson, and Syrquin's *Industrialization and Growth* of 1986 are standard reference books on cross-country analyses of growth and would be present on most reading lists on development economics.[53] The earlier work had a primary focus on cross-country regressions; the later work supplemented these regressions with in-depth studies of different countries that allowed one to look behind the aggregate statistics. As would be expected in an area of active research, work was going on outside the Bank at the same time, for example by Adelman and Morris and by Reynolds,[54] but there is no doubt that Chenery's work occupied a leading position.

Together these studies constitute a valuable attempt to organize cross-country data in a way that allows one to use different experiences to comment on the determinants and consequences of growth. However, a fundamental problem in this area is the scarcity of variables which can properly be described as exogenous. This means that most studies are of relationships that are only dubiously identified. Further, the data used in such studies are often weakly based and subject to large margins of error—problems rarely acknowledged and perhaps not always fully appreciated by those who use these studies. The same reservations must apply to the many more recent examples of cross-country regressions such as those in the May 1991 issue of the *Quarterly Journal of Economics* that have been stimulated to some extent by the availability of the Kravis, Summers, and Heston data on purchasing power parity comparisons of national incomes.[55] The Bank has recently been participating in such work, as in the growth conferences in Lisbon and Washington in early 1993.[56] To point to the problems in this type of work is not to argue that it should be abandoned. The analysis of the determinants of growth must be at the heart of development economics, and it is important to try to understand

52. S. Kuznets, *Economic Growth of Nations: Total Output and Production Structure* (Harvard University Press, 1971); C. Clark, *The Conditions of Economic Progress* (London: Macmillan, 1940).

53. See H. B. Chenery, *Structural Change and Development Policy* (Oxford University Press, 1979); H. B. Chenery, S. Robinson, and M. Syrquin, *Industrialization and Growth: A Comparative Study* (Washington: World Bank, 1986).

54. See I. Adelman and C. Morris, *Economic Growth and Social Equity in Developing Countries* (Stanford University Press, 1973); J. Reynolds, "The Spread of Economic Growth to the Third World: 1850–1980," *Journal of Economic Literature*, vol. 21 (1983), pp. 941–80.

55. See Summers and Heston, "New Set of International Comparisons"; and Summers and Heston, "Penn World Table."

56. Ben King has pointed out that records of Bank interest in the International Comparison Project (ICP) date back as far as November 1971. We are grateful to Ben King for pointing this out.

how different policies can and do influence economic growth. Recent examples of comparative case studies include those on trade liberalization in the World Bank volume edited by Papageorgiou, Choksi, and Michaely and those by Little, Cooper, Corden, and Rajapatirana.[57]

POVERTY. Poverty was catapulted into the center of the Bank's activities by McNamara's speeches to the Board of Directors in 1972 and 1973.[58] The 1973 speech given in Nairobi was a particular landmark, with its emphasis on the 40 percent of the world population in so-called absolute poverty, the concentration of that population in rural areas, and the promotion of rural development. An important facet of the Bank's work on poverty in the early years was its link with human development, emphasized rather later in the World Development Report on Poverty in 1980 (the series began only in 1978), which picked up ideas that had been central to much of the Bank's work during the later part of the 1970s. The facets of human development highlighted during the McNamara years—namely education, health, nutrition, food security, and population—have continued to be important themes. Although less prominent in the 1980s than they were in the 1970s, they resumed a higher profile in the late 1980s with the resurgence of an emphasis on human development and poverty reduction.

It is interesting that the McNamara years at the Bank were characterized by his strong desire to stay independent of the U.S. government (see the section "Perspectives from Within"). Although causation is hard to establish, those were the years when poverty was on the front burner at the Bank. For six or seven years after McNamara's departure, coinciding in the main with the Reagan presidency in the United States, poverty, although still acknowledged as important, was moved to the back burner. Action on poverty requires not only growth, but also measures by public bodies to protect the poor (a safety net) and to provide education and health support (the so-called social sectors in human development). That public measures of this type and population control were ideologically out of fashion in the United States in the 1980s coincided with reduced prominence of these issues within the Bank.

The broad changes that appear to have taken place in the early 1980s are reflected in the Bank's statements on whether policies designed to stimulate growth alone are sufficient to eradicate or substantially reduce poverty. Whereas McNamara told his Board that "the pursuit of growth without a reasonable concern for equity is ultimately socially destabilizing,"[59] the 1984 World Development

57. See D. Papageorgiou, A. M. Choksi, and M. Michaely, *Liberalizing Foreign Trade in Developing Countries: The Lessons of Experience* (Washington: World Bank, 1990); I. M. D. Little and others, "Boom, Crisis and Adjustment: The Macroeconomic Experience of Developing Countries," 1992, mimeographed.

58. The discussion in this section has been substantially influenced by R. S. L. Burgess, "The World Bank and Poverty," STICERD, London School of Economics, 1992, mimeographed.

59. McNamara, *The McNamara Years*, p. 656.

Report stated that "with a continuation of slow growth, millions of people in many developing countries will become progressively poorer; with faster growth, almost everybody in the world will enjoy some increase in real income."[60] And this was stated despite some paragraphs warning of the dangers to long-term growth of cuts in social expenditure that had been carried out within adjustment packages in countries like Brazil and Mexico. By the end of the 1980s the pendulum had swung back somewhat, with the World Development Report of 1990 arguing that both growth and safety nets were necessary if poverty were to be alleviated. The emphasis remained decidedly on growth, however, and between the World Development Reports of 1980 and 1990 there is a substantial difference in stress as regards direct poverty alleviation measures.

One of the most important contributions of the McNamara-Chenery years was the 1974 book *Redistribution and Growth* by Chenery and his coauthors, which looked directly at the possible conflicts between growth and equity and was influential both within the Bank and in the literature. An important program initiated in these years was the Living Standards Measurement Study (LSMS), in which Graham Pyatt had an influential role in the early years. This program has been multipurpose, contributing to the study of national income and other statistics, the analysis of household behavior, and the study of distributional issues. The first LSMS research paper was distributed in 1980, and in the following ten or so years around ninety papers were produced in the LSMS Working Paper Series. The program appears to have been under some threat in the mid-1980s, and interpretations of events differ as to the sources and solutions of the problems. However, under Dennis de Tray it survived the hiatus and has gone on to make important contributions (as it did in its early stages) both to the analysis of poverty and to household behavior.[61] It has also shown important guidance and leadership on methods of rapid checking and collection to provide clean data sets in a short space of time. It has drawn in many leading scholars of consumer behavior from outside the Bank, such as Angus Deaton.

The high profile given to poverty by McNamara and the research achievements exemplified by *Redistribution with Growth* and the LSMS program do add up to an important leadership role on poverty issues. Nevertheless, six or seven years in the later 1970s and four or five years at the end of the 1980s and early 1990s is not a high proportion of the Bank's fifty years, because it can be argued—and we think should be—that poverty alleviation should never have slipped from prominence.

CHINA. China joined the World Bank in 1980, and McNamara, in his interview for this book, regarded this as one of his great political achievements. The Bank also showed originality and initiative in its economic work on China. Anyone

60. World Bank, *World Development Report* (Washington, 1980), p. 38.

61. It has been suggested by some that the apparent hiatus from 1982 to 1987 was a result of intensive attention given to pilot surveys, which actually laid the groundwork for the subsequent collection of timely and high-quality data and the surge in output of LSMS studies.

working in the region must look to the World Bank's China Department as a major source of knowledge and expertise on the Chinese economy. Such excellence relative to that of the economics profession has probably not been matched in any other substantial geographical region.[62] It arose from an unusual opportunity—the sudden opening up of Chinese data sources and China's seeking of outside advice from the Bank—but it was one that the Bank grasped impressively.

A crude measure of the importance of the Bank's Chinese research is provided by the subject matter of recent World Bank discussion papers. Taking the fifty papers (numbers 129 through 178, the last distributed in 1992), no fewer than twelve were on China. Most were supraregional, but of those on regional topics three were on Poland, two on Latin America, two on Japan, and one each on Vietnam, India, Asia, and Africa. Most of the China papers represent work to which scholars of China from outside the Bank would wish to refer. Special mention should be made of the study of the Chinese economy, carried out largely in 1984, directed by Edwin Lim and Adrian Wood,[63] which constituted a substantial and original contribution to the understanding of the Chinese economy.

SECTORAL STUDIES. The World Bank's work on sectors has often been strong. Much of it has been done outside the research departments. We choose just four examples and comment on these only briefly: agriculture, urban issues, transport, and electricity.

Agricultural sector work at the Bank has long been of a high standard. We discuss three examples with which we are most familiar; they are in no sense exhaustive. The first concerns work by Avishay Braverman, Jeffrey Hammer, Inderjit J. Singh, Lyn Squire, and others on agricultural price reform in which simple modeling techniques were used to provide insights into the revenue, output, and welfare aspects of price reform.[64] This kind of simple and transparent modeling is helpful to policymakers, and it was developed at the Bank as a result of its obligation to advise on policy in several markets simultaneously. In such a context cross-market effects are important.

The second example in the agricultural sector concerns Bank participation in intensive microeconomic studies where economic theory was brought to bear in some detail to understand the behavior of individual farmers and markets. Of

62. Recently the Bank has played an important role in the development of policy toward Eastern Europe and the former Soviet Union, but there has not been quite the same opportunity for leadership and for scholarship in research as that presented in China in the 1980s.

63. See E. Lim and A. Wood, *China: Long-Term Development Issues and Options* (Johns Hopkins University Press, 1985). In addition to this summary volume, there were six annex volumes and nine background papers distributed as staff working papers.

64. See A. Braverman, J. Hammer, and C. Y. Ahn, "Multimarket Analysis of Agricultural Pricing Policies in Korea," in D. M. G. Newbery and N. H. Stern, eds., *The Theory of Taxation for Developing Countries* (Oxford University Press for the World Bank, 1987); I. J. Singh, L. Squire, and J. Strauss, "Agricultural Household Models: A Survey of Recent Findings and Their Policy Implications," *World Bank Economic Review*, vol. 1, no. 1 (September 1986), pp. 149–80.

particular relevance is the work of Hans Binswanger, Thomas Walker, James Ryan, and Inderjit Singh on the International Crops Research Institute for the Semi-Arid Tropics (ICRISAT) data on economic activities in sample households.[65]

In a third example, and in a similar spirit, theories of risk, information, and incentives were extensively used to gain a better understanding of rural credit, land and factor markets, and rural institutions. This work was associated mainly with the Bank's Agriculture and Rural Development Department under the direction of Avishay Braverman, and drawing on the expertise of outside academics.[66]

The Bank's sectoral contributions in urban studies resulted from work that grew in part from the emphasis on poverty in the McNamara years.[67] Initial concerns included increasing urbanization, the consequent pressures on economic and social infrastructure, and the deteriorating living conditions of urban migrants from rural areas. Whereas the Bank first became involved in urban development in the early 1970s, other multilateral agencies (especially the UN Development Program) had been active since the 1960s. Although the Bank was a laggard, its programs did eventually provide important lessons for future policies,[68] for example, through its demonstration projects on slum upgrading. By the 1980s it was recognized that,

---

65. See H. Binswanger and M. Rosenzweig, "Behavioural and Material Determinants of Production Relations in Agriculture," *Journal of Development Studies*, vol. 20 (1986), pp. 503–39; T. Walker and J. Ryan, *Village and Household Economies in India's Semi-Arid Tropics* (Johns Hopkins University Press, 1991); H. P. Binswanger, S. R. Khandker, and M. R. Rosenzweig, "How Infrastructure and Financial Institutions Affect Agricultural Output and Investment in India," *Journal of Development Economics*, vol. 41, no. 2 (August 1993), pp. 337–67; see also Singh, Squire, and Strauss, "Agricultural Household Models." It is interesting that Tinbergen (see Magnus and Morgan, "The ET Interview," pp. 134–35) saw it as "completely natural that the United States thought that the Bank had to finance the infrastructure, but that the superstructure would have to come from private initiatives." After quoting some counterexamples he says, in referring to the opposition of the Bank's president to publication of a book he had written for the Bank in 1955, "But, of course, an American could not understand this. . . ."

ICRISAT (in Hyderabad in southern India) collected detailed information on the economic activities of sample households over a period of time in several villages. These were used in a number of important studies, among them studies of behavior toward risk, credit, and income mobility. ICRISAT is one of the institutes of the Consultative Group on International Agricultural Research (CGIAR), discussed in the section "Perceptions from Within."

66. For important collections of papers, see K. Hoff, A. Braverman, and J. E. Stiglitz, *The Economics of Rural Organization: Theory, Practice and Policy* (Oxford University Press for the World Bank, 1993); and the *World Bank Economic Review* for September 1990.

67. This subsection has drawn on D. P. Coady, "Urban Development and the World Bank," STICERD, London School of Economics, 1992, mimeographed. We have benefited from conversations with him.

68. See L. Rodwin, "Some Lessons and Implications of the World Bank's Experience in Urban Development," in B. Higgins and D. J. Savoie, eds., *Regional Economic Development* (Boston: Unwin Hyman, 1988); M. P. van Dijk, "Employment in World Bank Urban Development Projects in Africa," in M. Raj and P. Nienfield, eds., *Housing and Income in Third World Urban Development* (London: Aspect Publishing, 1990).

although Bank-financed projects did improve over time and provide a workable model for the expansion of urban projects, lack of indigenous administrative skills and of the appropriate institutional support were major constraints on their widespread adoption. Strong fiscal pressures and consequent constraints on the public sector in the 1980s led to greater emphasis on improving local resource mobilization and increasing private sector participation, as well as on improving management and institutional support. Within the Bank there is a belief that it "should move towards a broader view of urban issues, a view that moves beyond housing and residential infrastructure, and that emphasizes the productivity of the urban economy and the need to alleviate the constraints on productivity."[69]

Together with developing its urban projects and its approach to them, the Bank also mounted a number of research programs that have made important contributions to urban economics. We point briefly to just two, which were launched in the 1970s and have produced or led to a number of publications in the 1980s and 1990s: the study on urban public finances associated with Roy Bahl and Johannes Linn, and the city study in which Gregory Ingram and Rakesh Mohan played a prominent role.[70]

These projects involved a comparative case study of ten cities in several countries. It found that although, on average, local or regional finance was less important quantitatively in developing than developed countries, there were many cases where local taxes were very important. It compared pricing, user charges, and taxes in practice with those that might be desirable in theory. It provided a number of interesting policy examples for revenue raising and guidance on efficient structuring of price and tax mechanisms. The study was extended to include a second, but closely related, project on the pricing and financing of urban public services. Many results from the urban public finance study have recently become available under the same covers.[71]

The city study was concerned with understanding the development and locational and functional organization of cities. Its approach was to look closely at the behavior of different actors and the development of different functions rather than to use a large-scale, all-embracing city model. It focused on labor markets and income distribution as well as on the more standard infrastructural transport and housing issues—which was an unusual focus for urban studies at that time. The examples in the initial case were Bogotá and Cali in Colombia.[72] The studies found that there were strong regularities in urban growth patterns in cities in developing

69. M. A. Cohen, "Urban Policy and Economic Development: An Agenda for the 1990's," Urban Development Division, World Bank, 1991, mimeographed.

70. See G. K. Ingram, "Housing Demand in the Developing Metropolis," World Bank Staff Working Paper 663 (1984).

71. See R. W. Bahl and J. F. Linn, *Urban Public Finance in Developing Countries* (Oxford University Press for the World Bank, 1992).

72. See R. Mohan, "'The City Study': Understanding the Developing Metropolis," *World Bank Research News*, vol. 5 (fall/winter 1984).

countries around the world. For example, demand for housing and transport showed strong consistencies across cities. The strongest transport links to growth were highways, with buses and trucks having greater importance than private cars (in contrast to the importance of railways and private cars in the development of many cities in richer countries). These and other studies resulted in a series of books.[73]

In the urban sector the Bank's project commitment to urban development led its research from the early 1970s. The research itself has shown the Bank exploiting its advantages in the use of comparative case studies to produce valuable contributions both for immediate policy and for the longer-term understanding of development.

Work in the Bank on transport—the third sector on which we comment—arose naturally in the early years with the emphasis on infrastructure.[74] Although this work was initially dominated by engineers, economists came to play a role, and important analytical work on transport pricing took place at the Bank. Alan Walters's work on the economics of road user charges was an early and important contribution; it exerted a considerable influence on subsequent work, both inside and outside the Bank, as did de Weille's 1966 paper on the same subject.[75] The major (and expensive) research project on Highway Design and Maintenance Standards has provided valuable inputs (through publication and software) for countries designing roadbuilding and maintenance programs. This was primarily an engineering project, but had important components bridging engineering and economics. The project led to the important theoretical paper by David Newbery, which was followed by more applied papers by Reuben Gronau and Ian Heggie.[76] It also gave rise to interesting econometric work by Chesher and Harrison in 1987 and by Chesher in 1990 on vehicle operating costs.[77]

Many of the major economics contributions in the area of transport have come from economists who were either in the Bank for only a short period or were consultants, rather than from those making their careers in the Bank. A key longer-term player at the Bank in the interaction between Bank concerns and

73. See, for example, K. S. Lee, *The Location of Jobs in a Developing Metropolis* (Oxford University Press, 1989); R. Mohan, *Work, Wages, and Welfare in a Developing Metropolis* (Oxford University Press, 1986); and E. S. Mills and C. M. Becker, *Studies in Indian Urban Development* (Oxford University Press, 1986).

74. We are grateful to David Newbery for his advice on this subject.

75. See A. A. Walters, "The Economics of Road User Charges," World Bank Staff Occasional Paper 5 (Washington: IBRD, 1968); J. de Weille, "Quantification of Road User Savings," World Bank Staff Occasional Paper 2 (Washington, 1966).

76. D. M. Newbery, "Road Damage Externalities and Road User Charges," *Econommetrica*, vol. 56 (March 1988), pp. 295–316; R. Gronau, "Are Ghana's Roads Paying Their Way? Assessing Road Use Cost and User Charges in Ghana," Policy, Research, and External Affairs Working Papers: Transport, WPS 773 (Washington: World Bank, 1991); and I. Heggie, "Optimal User Charges and Cost Recovery for Roads in Developing Countries," Policy, Research, and External Affairs Working Papers: Transport, WPS 780 (Washington: World Bank, 1991).

77. See A. D. Chesher and R. Harrison, *Vehicle Operating Costs: Evidence from Developing Countries*, vol. 1 in the Highway Design and Maintenance Standards Series (Johns

outside academics has been Esra Bennathan.[78] Recent work by Bank staff and others on deregulation and reform in the transport sector appears in a 1979 report on a Bank symposium edited by José Carbajo.[79] In this subject area the Bank has shown leadership not only in the creative application of theory, which has exerted a strong influence on empirical work, but also in getting theorists to think further about basic questions.

We examine the Bank's work in the electricity sector as an example of its infrastructure activities and of related public sector pricing. As an agency for which infrastructural investment has always been a central (at times an exclusive) activity, the Bank has gained considerable expertise in the design, selection, and management of public sector projects. In the 1950s and 1960s the Bank's preoccupation on the pricing side was with the financial viability of projects.[80] It was more concerned with a level of prices that would allow adequate financial returns than with devising a structure of prices that in addition might reflect appropriate economic incentives. In the 1970s it adopted a two-step technique in which marginal costs were calculated, for different times and types of supply, and then adjustments were made to reflect implementation difficulties, distributional objectives, fiscal objectives, and financial objectives.[81]

This procedure does not fully reflect the existing economic theories of public sector pricing, where marginal costs and revenue requirements are explicitly blended to produce pricing rules.[82] In this sense the Bank was not sufficiently well acquainted with the available economic theory's emphasis on marginal cost as the appropriate basis for pricing.[83] On the other hand, a charitable interpretation of the second step would see it as incorporating the revenue requirements that are central to the modern theory, and

Hopkins University Press for the World Bank, 1987); A. D. Chesher, "Optimal Scrapping, Vehicle Operating Costs and the Estimation of the Benefits to Highway Improvements," in J. P. Florens and others, eds., *Microeconometrics: Surveys and Applications* (Oxford: Basil Blackwell, 1990).

78. See E. Bennathan and A. A. Walters, *Port Pricing and Investment Policy for Developing Countries* (Oxford University Press for the World Bank, 1979).

79. See José Carbajo, ed., *Regulatory Reform in Transport: Some Recent Experiences* (Washington: World Bank, 1993).

80. For details, see D. Julius and A. P. Alicbusan, "Public Sector Pricing Policies—A Review of Bank Policy and Practice," Projects Policy Department, World Bank, 1986; and Coady, "Raising and Allocation of Public Revenues."

81. World Bank, "OMS 2.25: Cost Recovery Policies for Public Sector Projects," World Bank, 1977.

82. For example, see W. J. Baumol and D. F. Bradford, "Optimal Departures from Marginal Cost Pricing," *American Economic Review*, vol. 60 (June 1970); P. A. Diamond and J. A. Mirrlees, "Optimal Taxation and Public Production, Part I: Production Efficiency," and "Part II: Tax Rules," *American Economic Review*, vol. 61, no. 1 (March 1971), pp. 8–27, and no. 3 (June 1971), pp. 261–81; D. M. G. Newbery and N. H. Stern, eds., *The Theory of Taxation for Developing Countries* (Oxford University Press for the World Bank, 1987); and Coady, "Raising and Allocation of Public Revenues."

83. Some within the Bank suggest that the team was fully conversant with existing theory but adopted the two-step technique in the Operational Manual Statement purely for ease of exposition.

which generally point to prices above marginal cost for revenue reasons. There would be further contributions for pollution or other types of externality. The calculation of marginal costs is, however, common and crucial to all these approaches, and it is here that the Bank has been a leader. The importance of the calculations is emphasized by the discovery that actual prices are often well below marginal costs.

The calculation of marginal cost in an electricity power system is a challenging and often subtle task. It must blend knowledge and understanding of the basic idea with a whole array of conceptual and practical difficulties concerning the long run and the short run, peak and off-peak loads, switching between different sources of generation, the probability of supply and the costs of outages, and so on. The Bank's encouragement of, and assistance in, this kind of calculation is of great practical and educational usefulness in helping power authorities to appreciate the economics of a crucially important sector—particularly in regard to opportunity costs and incentives.[84]

TECHNIQUES: ECONOMYWIDE MODELING. The World Bank has been prominent in the development and application of techniques for economywide modeling. In the 1970s these techniques were largely of the input-output and linear programming variety, and the Bank built some of the largest programming models of developing countries that were available. At one point it seemed as if the solutions to the problems of the world were perceived as lying in ever more disaggregated linear programming models. Although a great deal of ingenuity was shown, probably by the end of the Chenery years these approaches were running into diminishing returns. However, a number of important contributions were made within this framework, including social accounting matrices (SAMs), on which much of the work of Pyatt and his colleagues was carried out at the World Bank.[85] SAMs remain a valuable tool for understanding interrelationships within economies.

During the late 1970s and early 1980s the Bank saw intensive development of computable general equilibrium models. This was another technique developed outside the Bank that came to be applied intensively within the Bank. The 1991 Report on Research in the Bank cites a book published by the Bank on computable general equilibrium models—de Melo and Sapir's *Trade Theory and Economic Reform*—as one of the most widely quoted, and it has become a standard reference in the subject.[86] Such models are no doubt useful tools, although due to their large appetite for assumptions and data and their lack of transparency, their usefulness

---

84. For further references on the electricity sector, see R. Turvey and D. Anderson, *Electricity Economics: Essays and Case Studies* (Johns Hopkins University Press for the World Bank, 1977); and M. Munasinghe and J. J. Warford, *Electricity Pricing: Theory and Case Studies* (Johns Hopkins University Press for the World Bank, 1982). On this and other public sector pricing questions, see Julius and Alicbuson, "Public Sector Pricing Policies," and Coady, "Raising and Allocation of Public Revenues."

85. See, for example, F. G. Pyatt and J. Round, *Social Accounting Matrices: A Basis for Planning* (Washington: World Bank, 1985).

86. See J. de Melo and A. Sapir, eds., *Trade Theory and Economic Reform: Essays in Honor of Bela Balassa* (Oxford: Basil Blackwell, 1991).

should not be exaggerated. Again, much work on similar lines was going on outside the Bank—the Bank was a participant in an ongoing academic process. Recently, for example, the OECD Development Center has been taking a lead in promoting this type of research.[87]

Some Less Impressive Performances

In some subjects the Bank has followed the profession only slowly, among them debt, the environment, the role of women in the development process, and cost-benefit analysis. The reasons for, and the manner of, the Bank's slow responses vary across these examples as discussed below.

DEBT. In its role as the leading international development agency the World Bank might reasonably have been expected to fulfill two major tasks in relation to the debt crisis facing less developed countries in the 1980s.[88] The first would have been to monitor international macroeconomic conditions before the onset of the crisis in 1982 and to issue policy advice or counsel on the potential dangers of heavy borrowing so as to avoid—or at least alleviate the severity of—the belated adjustment process that followed. The second would have been to respond more acutely after 1982 when, given the severity of the crisis, the search for mechanisms to resolve it became crucial in determining how and when growth, poverty alleviation, and development might resume in a large number of developing countries. The evidence suggests that the Bank was overly optimistic before 1982, sometimes disseminating assessments and advice that it would directly contradict later with the benefit of hindsight. Evidence also seems that during the crisis, after 1982, the Bank was a slow follower in the debate on possible remedies. This pace may have reflected political pressures brought to bear on the institution by its major shareholders, and the evidence may underestimate the extent of internal Bank discussions; one senior member of staff referred to the existence of "secret reports"—but an assessment of the intellectual effect of the Bank on public discussion, analysis, and perceptions of the debt crisis cannot be based on internal secret documents, which might or might not become available many years later.

Between 1974 and 1982 the Bank's view of borrowing by developing countries was influenced by the need of the global economy to respond to the large current

87. See F. Bourguignon, J. de Melo, and C. Morrisson, "Poverty and Income Distribution During Adjustment: Issues and Evidence from the OECD Project," *World Development*, vol. 19 (1991), pp. 1485–1508, on "Adjustment with Growth and Equity," where computable general equilibrium (CGE) models are used with some success to illuminate the distributional consequences of structural adjustment.

88. This section draws heavily on B. Armendariz, "Analytical Issues on LDC Debt: A Survey," *World Economy*, vol. 16, no. 4 (July 1993), pp. 467–82; and B. Armendariz and F. H. G. Ferreira, "The World Bank and the Analysis of the International Debt Crisis," in J. Harris, J. Hunter, and C. Lewis, eds., *The New Institutional Economics and Third World Development* (London: Routledge, 1995).

account imbalances that originated with the vast terms of trade changes of the oil price shock of 1973–74, and which were exacerbated by the second shock in 1979. In this context, although the growth in debt indicators for many countries was recognized, borrowing was seen as an essentially beneficial component of the global adjustment process. In his 1975 presidential address, McNamara regarded the need of middle-income countries for greater access to external capital as the "most immediate and pressing problem in the global development scene. . . ."[89] In 1977 he felt that "the major lending banks and major borrowing countries are operating on assumptions which are broadly consistent with one another . . . " and concluded that "we are even more confident today than we were a year ago that the debt problem is indeed manageable, and need not stand in the way of desirable rates of growth for the developing countries. . . ."[90]

Although the shock in 1979 caused some changes in the Bank's position, these were not sufficient to reverse the Bank's pro-recycling emphasis (see the section on structural adjustment above). The most significant change in position was indeed a greater focus on the need for countries to use external finance to adjust to what was now seen as a permanent change in the world economy. This shift was coupled with an understanding that such internal adjustments would require significant changes in the way these economies operated.

The main factors conspiring to make many borrowers' positions unsustainable by 1982 were clearly identified by the World Development Report of 1981: the tightening of monetary conditions globally in 1979 (high positive real interest rates), the contemporaneous fall in terms of trade for less developed countries, the worldwide recession, the rising proportion of loans contracted in variable interest rate (VIR) agreements, and the rise in the fraction of outstanding debt of less developed countries to commercial banks (from 49.6 percent in 1975 to 61.5 percent in 1978). In light of the Bank's awareness of these phenomena, it is remarkable that it continued to make optimistic predictions about the availability of voluntary capital flows in the 1980s. The Bank's unwillingness to read the signs it had just laid out is made quite plain in the same World Development Report: "While [these] trends indicate that the developing countries will face more serious debt-management difficulties in the future, *they do not signal a generalized debt problem for the developing countries.*"[91]

The importance of external finance in enabling most less developed countries to manage the high-growth mode of adjustment advocated in the 1981 World Development Report—and generally by the Bank at this stage—was obvious, so any doubt as regards its availability was uncomfortable. The report stated that "given the profitability of lending to developing countries, their exemplary records (with

89. McNamara, *The McNamara Years,* p. 287.

90. Ibid., p. 456. See also H. Gazdar, "The Bretton Woods Institutions and the Debt Crisis," University of Sussex (IDS), 1990, mimeographed.

91. World Bank, *World Development Report* (1981), p. 61; emphasis added.

few exceptions) in meeting their obligations and their continuing need for foreign finance, it seems unlikely that financial intermediaries will discriminate against developing countries as a group"; hence, "Summing up these various influences on commercial banks, it seems highly probable that both borrowers and lenders will adapt to changing conditions without precipitating any general crisis of confidence."[92]

It was not just inside the Bank that views of the situation were sanguine, and it is remarkable that, notwithstanding the rapid increase in indebtedness, the world banking system continued to pour money into developing countries. It has been observed that "in a mere two years, 1980 and 1981, total bank exposure nearly doubled over the level of 1979 in the major debtor countries."[93] That soon stopped, and the debt crisis broke on the world in August 1982 when Mexico found it impossible to produce the necessary foreign exchange to make its debt service payments on time.

It is not clear how much awareness there was outside the Bank of the forthcoming collapse. Nevertheless, papers such as "Debt with Potential Repudiation: Theoretical and Empirical Analysis" by Eaton and Gersovitz,[94] which would have circulated as a discussion paper before that year, should have sent some warning lights flashing. Although those authors did not explicitly predict a sharp increase in default risk or a sudden decline in the supply of voluntary lending, a number of interesting theoretical and empirical conclusions have been derived in their study. Their empirical analysis suggested that, as early as 1974, sixty-five countries out of their sample of eighty-one were more likely to have their total borrowing from private international markets determined by a supply constraint (that is, by rationing) imposed by lenders to reduce risk of default than by their own demand at ruling interest rates. In light of their conclusions, the sudden and marked deterioration in international conditions in 1979–82 pointed to a real possibility of default by many countries.

The Bank was in a unique position in its access to data on developing country performance and on capital flows, and as regards its responsibility to provide technical advice and assistance to policymakers in the interests of long-term growth and development. In this context, the Bank's endorsement of and emphasis on increased borrowing to facilitate adjustment and create resource transfers—as late as 1981—cannot be seen in a positive light in retrospect.

After 1982 a curious situation developed, in which the management of sovereign debt and possible remedies that would take into account the interests of both lenders and borrowers became a popular subject with academic economists.[95]

92. Ibid.

93. J. Sachs, "Introduction," in J. Sachs, ed., *Developing Country Debt and the World Economy* (University of Chicago Press, 1989), p. 9.

94. J. Eaton and M. Gersovitz, "Debt with Potential Repudiation: Theoretical and Empirical Analysis," *Review of Economic Studies,* vol. 48 (April 1981), pp. 289–309.

95. See Armendariz, "Analytical Issues on LDC Debt," for a survey.

Naturally the subject must have occupied professionals in governments, private banks, and international financial institutions (IFIs) just as much. Nevertheless, the tone of discussion and the nature of approaches proposed in these different quarters varied significantly. The Bank, now under A. W. Clausen as president, took a cautious line, changing the focus from macroeconomic concerns with the availability of foreign finance (so prominent under McNamara) to microeconomic advice on "getting prices right." External causes were deemphasized, and blame for the crisis was laid predominantly on domestic policy errors, notably the use of borrowed funds for consumption or for investment purposes that were badly directed, partly due to distorted prices. In 1986 a report from the Operations Evaluation Department of the Bank stated that "the flexibility provided by access to foreign borrowing will have been lost because of past policy errors."[96]

The Bank adhered closely to the view—espoused publicly by the governments of its major shareholders—that a "solution" to the crisis must be based on a "restoration of creditworthiness," and that the way for countries to achieve this was to maintain debt service up to date, avoid the need to reschedule loans for as long as possible, and lower their debt-export and debt service–export ratios. These objectives could best be secured through prompt efforts at internal adjustment aimed at reorienting production toward tradables, through the familiar combination of expenditure reduction and expenditure switching policies. As the World Development Report of 1985 put it, "Despite the many problems they have had recently, developing countries need a continuing flow of bank lending to regain their growth momentum. For this to happen, however, developing countries must restore their creditworthiness—and that depends on their own policies and on the strength and stability of world economic growth."[97] The role envisaged for the international financial system was merely to provide some rescheduling when there was absolutely no other alternative.

In contrast, some early proposals addressed the "debt overhang" problem in a more radical manner. In 1983 Peter Kenen of Princeton University had suggested that a new international institution, an international debt discount corporation, could be created to buy developing country debt from the banks at a 10 percent discount. It would then be able, because of the discount from which it benefited on purchase, to lower the interest rate charged to debtors. Kenen further envisaged an extension of loan maturities, in another concessional element. Felix Rohatyn proposed to the U.S. Senate that developing country debt could be stretched out to longer maturities (of fifteen to thirty years), and interest reduced to something like 6 percent. Norman Bailey, of the U.S. National Security Council, suggested that debt be swapped for a form of equity asset that would entitle the holder to a fraction of the country's export earnings.[98]

96. World Bank, "Experience with Structural Adjustment Lending."
97. World Bank, *World Development Report* (Oxford University Press, 1985), p. 124.
98. For a more complete survey of these early proposals, see W. Cline, *International Debt and the Stability of the World Economy* (Washington, Institute for International Economics, 1983).

Later in the 1980s, the thrust, if not the specific details, of these suggestions—namely, the need to reduce the debt burden as a prerequisite for the resumption of growth in debtor countries, which in turn would enable them to service the remaining obligations in a less strenuous and more reliable manner—became widely accepted in academic circles.[99] At the early stage of the crisis, however, many thought that it was merely one of liquidity, and that the potential moral hazard induced by forgiveness, coupled with the risk to the financial health of some major banks, made an approach based on rescheduling without reducing present values a more sensible idea than debt reduction. This view was prevalent at the International Debt and the Developing Countries Conference held by the Economic Research Staff of the World Bank in April 1984. The papers presented there were compiled in a volume edited by Smith and Cuddington.[100] Taken together, these papers constitute a meritorious effort toward an understanding of the debt crisis, although concrete proposals to deal with the problem were cautious if compared to those of Kenen and others. Generally, participants emphasized two shortcomings of the current strategy. One was that the public good/externality nature of involuntary sovereign lending by a private bank (in that it improved the potential value of debts to other banks) and the ensuing free-rider problem provided scope for greater coordination of the process by the IMF, the Bank, and even creditor governments than then existed. The other was that short-term reschedulings (generally of one year), which were the rule at the time, were seen as collectively inefficient, even if a single lender had an incentive to keep a problem debtor on a short leash. A number of the authors, and notably Krugman, suggested expanding the scope of rescheduling to provide multiyear restructuring of a country's foreign debt. This suggestion had already been made by Cline, among others.[101]

The balance of opinion seemed to be that in most countries the ultimate ability to generate the necessary stream of foreign exchange—that is, solvency—existed. Although there were indeed suggestions that some due interest should be capitalized and loan maturities extended, and that banks ought perhaps to charge interest rates below market rates on some of their loans, debt relief was, however, suggested only on a modest scale (sufficiently to justify the conference organizers' claim). Again, this was in contrast to the more radical proposals mentioned earlier, as well as to the tone of the academic debate a few years down the road and to the views expressed in the Bank's own subsequent conference in 1989.

To some extent the Baker strategy, proposed by U.S. Treasury Secretary James A. Baker III in 1985, was intended to address precisely those issues that were most prominent at the 1984 conference. It tackled the free-rider problem among commercial banks involved in concerted lending by providing third-party backing and

99. See Sachs, *Developing Country Debt,* for a collection of papers.
100. See G. W. Smith and J. T. Cuddington, *International Debt and the Developing Countries* (Washington: World Bank, 1985).
101. See Cline, *International Debt.*

coordination by international financial institutions such as the IMF and the Bank. This was meant to increase the volume of "new money" available for rescheduling. Longer periods for rescheduling also became more common, starting with a U.S.$49 billion multiyear package for Mexico. We make no claim, however, that the main driving force behind the Baker strategy was the 1984 conference. All one can say is that the prevalent issues and tone at that occasion were broadly in line with the subsequent U.S. initiative in 1985, except for any mention of the appropriateness of partial debt forgiveness.

But if the Bank's positions were not radical or innovative in the 1982–85 period, from 1986 to 1988 they appear to have lagged even further behind the rapidly evolving debate. In a paper written before joining the Bank, Fischer emphasized the severe decline in income per capita in the fifteen heavily indebted countries identified by Baker, the massive resource transfers from those countries, and the resulting collapse in their domestic investment rates.[102] The focus in the debate had changed substantially from the solvency-versus-liquidity issue toward the seriousness of the effects of the crisis on debtor countries. Proposed solutions reflected that change. In Fischer's paper, as well as in most other papers devoted to possible solutions that were gathered in Sachs's *Developing Country Debt and the World Economy,* the possible desirability of debt relief, and a wealth of different mechanisms through which to achieve it efficiently, were discussed; there is no contention to Sachs's claim that "partial debt relief can therefore be Pareto improving (i.e., to the benefit of both creditors and debtors)."[103] In contrast, the role of the Bank at this stage was that of a supporter of the Baker strategy, with its response to the concerns so widely voiced in 1984–85 still based on concerted lending and loan rescheduling.

An indictment of this role appears in the paper by Diwan and Husain that introduces their volume *Dealing with the Debt Crisis,* a report on the Bank's 1989 conference on debt.[104] There they acknowledged that the strategy was unsuccessful, that it had modest targets for new money ($13 billion annually), that even those targets were never achieved (net annual flow was only about $4 billion), that "the official sector had only moral suasion to ensure that the private sector met the plan's targets," and, fundamentally, that "controversies, even of a few billion dollars, miss the point: the transfer of resources from the highly indebted countries to the industrial countries for external debt was more than $100 billion during 1986–88."[105]

An unusually frank admission of the reasons behind the Bank's behavior at that time was given by its chief economist, Stanley Fischer:

102. S. Fischer, "Resolving the International Debt Crisis," in Sachs, ed., *Developing Country Debt,* chap. 17.
103. Sachs, ed., *Developing Country Debt,* p. 28.
104. I. Diwan and I. Husain, *Dealing with the Debt Crisis* (Washington: World Bank, 1989).
105. Ibid., p. 4.

The record shows that frank and open debate does not take place in official and banking circles. It was clear to the participants in this conference at the beginning of 1989, as it had been clear to many much earlier, that growth in the debtor countries would not return without debt relief. But the official agencies operate on the basis of an agreed upon strategy, and none of them could openly confront the existing strategy without having an alternative to put in place. And to propose such an alternative would have required agreement among the major shareholders of these institutions. So long as the United States was not willing to move, the IFIs were not free to speak.[106]

In 1988 a willingness to contemplate some element of debt reduction began to manifest itself among those major shareholders. K. Miyazawa, then Japan's finance minister, used the IMF–World Bank meetings in Berlin that year to propose officially sponsored debt reduction schemes. François Mitterrand of France followed suit later that year in Toronto, where official creditors agreed on a set of guidelines for concessional relief for low-income, severely indebted countries; these guidelines were thereafter known as the Toronto terms. The World Development Report of 1988, the first entirely under Fischer as chief economist, marked the Bank's official jump from the Baker bandwagon by including suggestions that some debt relief and a reduction of the debt overhang could be important elements in facilitating the transition from adjustment to growth. The report was just in time to claim precedence to the change in the official U.S. position, which came with the Brady plan in 1989. That plan was aimed at middle-income, severely indebted countries. From then on there appears to have been an increase in the liveliness of the debate on debt at the Bank, as well as in the Bank's sponsorship of research on the topic. The Debt and International Finance Department frequently issued papers that often focused on issues related to voluntary, market-based debt reduction schemes and the associated incentive problems.[107]

This improvement in the Bank's record in the theoretical debate after 1988 came in addition to the Bank's significant contribution to the study of developing-country debt, begun much earlier, through the publication of comprehensive data on the direction, magnitude, and effects of the debt flows. This contribution was made mostly through the World Debt Tables, which, when complemented by the World Development Indicators, provided the basis for much academic and policy work on the subject. Furthermore, within the framework of the Brady initiative, the Bank's role in helping countries to design and negotiate menus for debt reduction with their creditors provided a new scope for application of the ideas being researched and debated throughout the profession. By the end of 1990 Brady deals had been concluded with Costa Rica, Mexico, and the Philippines, and other countries were negotiating their own packages.

106. Stanley Fischer, in Diwan and Husain, *Dealing with the Debt Crisis*, p. v.
107. See, for example, S. Claessens, "The Debt Laffer Curve: Some Estimates," World Bank, Debt and International Finance Department, July 1988, mimeographed.

The Mexican example, besides being the earliest, is also probably the most studied. The deal covered some $49 billion in commercial loans and, according to some estimates, involved $12 billion for relief. Net external transfers were reduced by $4 billion a year for some six years from 1989.[108] This was accomplished by allowing participating commercial creditors to choose from a menu of facilities, including exchange of debt for a discount bond (at 65 percent of par), or for a par bond with fixed interest at 6.25 percent, all with thirty-year maturities. The Bank and the IMF were involved in financing the required collateral for these bonds, and creditor banks were also given the option to swap debt for equity in a privatization program.

Available evidence indicates that debt relief successfully contributed to reducing fiscal pressure on the Mexican government, hence lowering inflation and expectations of peso devaluations. Restored confidence in the peso caused a substantial fall in domestic interest rates and initiated some return of flight capital. The Mexican adjustment experience of the late 1980s was seen as one of the most successful in Latin America, and the debt relief component involved was seen as instrumental in that success.[109] This perception was justified notwithstanding any subsequent problems related to the appreciation of the Mexican peso.

On the whole, however, it is not possible to claim that the Bank has so far displayed intellectual leadership on issues relating to the debt crisis of the 1980s. As Fischer quite plainly admits from the Bank, "academic research, writing and opinion have been far more influential on the debt issue than the academics may believe, or than officials like to pretend, for the academics are unencumbered by the official need to support the official strategy. It was academics who were first to point out that the stabilization focus of the programs imposed on debtors to deal with the debt crisis from 1982 to 1985, while necessary, was not sufficient for growth."[110]

THE ENVIRONMENT. An environment department was not established at the World Bank until 1987, long after the environment had become a major issue both politically and in the academic world. The Bank also has often appeared to respond to environmental issues only reluctantly, seeing them as political irritants that get in the way of making the project loans that managers view as their prime commitment. Nevertheless, since 1987 the Bank has seen more activity on the environment, and it has at least become more sensitive to criticism of support for projects seen to be environmentally damaging. It has not, however, been a major actor as regards research in this area.

Some simple indications of the extent to which the world outside the Bank had become involved in environmental economics before the Bank became seriously

108. World Bank, *World Development Report* (Oxford University Press, 1990, 1991).

109. World Bank, *World Development Report* (1990), p. 21; *World Development Report* (1991), pp. 125–27.

110. Fischer, in Diwan and Husain, *Dealing with the Debt Crisis,* p. v.

interested can be outlined. Resources for the Future, an organization of long standing devoted to the study of resource and environmental issues,[111] had been responsible for the publication of an important theoretical text on environmental economics by Karl-Göran Mäler in 1974.[112] In the late 1980s Mäler became an adviser on environmental issues for the Bank, as did Partha Dasgupta, whose *Control of Resources* was published in 1982.[113] The *Journal of Environmental Economics and Management* was founded in the mid-1970s. Less academic landmarks were "Limits of Growth," published by the Club of Rome in 1972, and the rise of the Green parties in Europe during the 1970s. Hence the subject was one of intense interest both academically and politically for a decade or two before the Bank became involved. The Bank was also slow to respond to environmental concerns compared with other international organizations. For example, the Organization for Economic Cooperation and Development produced a series of major publications on environmental issues in the mid-1980s, presenting work that had begun considerably earlier.

It must be acknowledged that environmental issues were slower to be raised in regard to developing countries than for developed countries. Nevertheless, by the mid-1980s the Bank was being criticized heavily for the environmental effects of its projects—for example, the effect of dams on local water systems and of roads in the exploitation and reduction of rain forests. The World Commission on Environment and Development (known as the Brundtland Commission) in 1987 published the report *Our Common Future*, which sharply raised the world profile of the subject (and, for better or for worse, planted the term "sustainable development" firmly in the vocabulary).[114] The establishment of the Bank's Environment Department was therefore, a laggardly response to external pressure, although it must be recognized that the environment was of strong interest to the newly arrived president of the Bank, Barber Conable.

Since its establishment the Environment Department has played an important role in advancing the application of environmental economics in developing countries. This was indicated in the World Development Report of 1992, on development and the environment, which expressed strongly the important argument that "economic development and sound environmental management are complementary aspects of the same agenda. Without adequate environmental protection, development will be undermined; without development, environmental protection will fail."[115] It further stated that "humanity's stake in environmental protection is

111. Resources for the Future was established in 1952 with help from the Ford Foundation.

112. See K. G. Mäler, *Environmental Economics: A Theoretical Inquiry* (Johns Hopkins University Press for Resources for the Future, 1974).

113. P. Dasgupta, *The Control of Resources* (Oxford: Basil Blackwell, 1982).

114. World Commission on Environment and Development, *Our Common Future* (Oxford University Press, 1987).

115. World Bank, *World Development Report* (1992), p. 25. An example of a "win-win" (to use the report's jargon) improvement would be the raising of electricity prices closer to

enormous, and [that] environmental values have been neglected too often in the past."[116] A second indication of the Bank's recent environmental interest was the publication edited by Low on international trade and the environment, which emphasized the point that because environmental externalities do not usually originate in international trade itself, policies focusing on the restriction of trade are only second-best instruments, and probably poor ones at that.[117]

The Bank's commitment to environmental issues was questioned by some as a result of a leak to the *Economist* magazine, in late 1991, of extracts from an internal memorandum of Lawrence Summers, then chief economist. The memorandum suggested the possibility that environmental issues were being overemphasized in relation to developing countries, and that those countries might actually have lower marginal costs in dealing with or tolerating pollutants. Although the Bank had to distance itself vigorously from these remarks, faith in its seriousness about environmental matters was shaken. It should be recognized that because environmental problems usually have their origins in the absence of markets for environmental services (an absence that in turn often reflects nonexistent, ambiguous, or disputed property rights, or the high costs of enforcing such rights), structural adjustment programs that focus on the reform of free markets and institutions are a natural framework in which environmental problems should be addressed.[118] Given the failure of the Bank to systematically undertake rigorous cost-benefit analyses of projects (and policies) that do not involve externalities, it is not surprising that the identification and incorporation of the environmental externalities often associated with some (especially rural) projects have been prioritized by the Bank only recently. The identification and valuation of such externalities are substantially more difficult exercises. Greater emphasis on the need for more rigorous cost-benefit analyses of projects (and policies) is a prerequisite for addressing environmental problems.[119]

WOMEN IN DEVELOPMENT. Another area where the World Bank has been a relatively slow follower concerns the role of women in the economic development process. Although the gender issue had elicited academic attention as early as the 1970s,[120] the Bank started to give the subject serious consideration only in the late

---

marginal cost (in many cases they are far below), which would both improve resource allocation (or development from a narrow focus) and reduce externalities from pollution in power generation. Thus the external diseconomy of the pollution would be reduced at a negative cost. The price reform would be beneficial from both viewpoints.

116. Ibid., p. 1.

117. P. Low, ed., "International Trade and the Environment," World Bank Discussion Paper 159, 1992.

118. For further discussion, see D. Reed, *Structural Adjustment and the Environment* (London: Earthscan Publications for World Wide Fund for Nature, 1992).

119. We are grateful to David Coady for a helpful discussion of these issues.

120. For a seminal study, see E. Boserup, *Women's Role in Economic Development* (London: Gower, 1970).

1980s. A table on women in development, listing data on health and welfare, education, and maternal mortality, was added to the Bank's World Development Indicators only in 1988. In fiscal year 1989 only 25 percent of all Bank economic and sector reports included "substantive discussions or recommendations on women in development"; two years later the figure was 62 percent.[121]

These and other data provided in a progress report prepared by the Central Operations Department suggest that, since those timid beginnings in the late 1980s there has been substantial effort by various departments at the Bank to pay attention to gender issues throughout their mainstream programs and projects.[122] Country assessment papers, legal studies, and policy guidelines dealing with gender issues have all been prepared. Regional offices have been asked to integrate and monitor general aspects of gender issues into operations as fully as possible. Within the Policy Research and Extension Affairs complex a women-in-development division had nine full-time staff members in 1991; in the Economic Development Institute a full-time women-in-development coordinator was appointed in fiscal year 1991. The Operations Evaluation Department has assigned a staff member to monitor gender-related issues in the context of evaluation. Nevertheless, despite this rapid transformation in the level of institutional awareness of gender issues in economic development, the 1991 progress report acknowledges that "the Bank's experience with gender-related concerns is still relatively new, and the sample of country and sectoral strategies and of projects with specific women-in-development actions is fairly limited."[123]

COST-BENEFIT ANALYSIS. The Bank's work on cost-benefit analysis presents a number of paradoxes.[124] Bank activity was for many years primarily focused on infrastructural projects, and that type of project remains its central activity. Given such activity, and the Bank's economic and international influence, it might be supposed that the Bank would have become a world leader in cost-benefit analysis. Further, as development economists became increasingly concerned in the 1960s and 1970s with the problem of distorted prices resulting from misguided development policies, techniques were developed in the cost-benefit literature to measure those distortions; and the Bank was itself becoming increasingly worried about the policy environment (often embodied in price distortions) surrounding its projects. Again, it might be supposed that the Bank would have led, or at least embraced, the development of these techniques. In fact, it was other institutions, such as the OECD and the United Nations Idustrial Development Organization (UNIDO),

121. World Bank, "Women in Development: Progress Report on the Implementation of the World Bank's Operational Strategy," Development Committee Pamphlet 28 (1991), p. 45.
122. Ibid.
123. Ibid., p. 47.
124. See Coady, "Raising and Allocation of Public Revenues," for further discussion of some of these issues.

that led in their development.[125] The Bank, notwithstanding there being many present who could understand, develop, and apply the techniques, never really incorporated these later developments into its decisionmaking.[126]

From an early period there was an understanding within the Bank of the importance of evaluating projects by using cost-benefit techniques. One example is the 1961 publication *Investment Criteria and Project Appraisal*, in which discounted cash flow methods were discussed in detail (in particular, the contribution by Benjamin King).[127] Another is Squire and van der Tak's *Economic Analysis of Projects*,[128] which incorporated the central principles of the procedure developed by Little and Mirrlees—a procedure that uses as shadow prices world prices for traded goods and the marginal social cost of production for nontraded goods.[129] The need to take account of project effects on the distribution of income, primarily through the shadow wage rate, was recognized.[130] Notwithstanding an apparently strong interest within the Bank (coordinated by the now-defunct Central Projects Division), it has been argued by Little and Mirrlees that these relatively simple rules and procedures were never seriously implemented at the Bank and that the inclusion of distributional issues in project analysis has never been prominent.[131] They suggest that the only relevant change in Bank policy since the 1960s has been some movement in the direction of using world prices for traded goods. The 1980s saw a decline in interest in cost-benefit analysis within the Bank in spite of the emphasis placed on structural adjustment and getting the prices right (which would appear to require some notion of what the "right prices" are).[132]

125. See I. M. D. Little and J. A. Mirrlees, *Manual of Industrial Project Analysis in Developing Countries*, vol. 2: *Social Cost-Benefit Analysis* (Paris: OECD Development Center, 1969); I. M. D. Little and J. A. Mirrlees, *Project Appraisal and Planning for Developing Countries* (London: Heinemann, 1974); and P. S. Dasgupta, S. Marglin, and A. Sen, *Guidelines for Project Evaluation*, E.78.II.B.3. (New York: United Nations, 1972).

126. See I. M. D. Little and J. A. Mirrlees, "Project Appraisal and Planning Twenty Years On," *Proceedings of the World Bank Annual Conference on Development Economics* (Washington: World Bank, 1991), pp. 351–82.

127. See Economic Development Institute, *Investment Criteria and Project Appraisal* (Washington: International Bank for Reconstruction and Development, 1961).

128. L. Squire and H. G. van der Tak, *Economic Analysis of Projects* (Johns Hopkins University Press, 1975).

129. See Little and Mirrlees, *Manual of Industrial Project Analysis*, vol. 2; and I. M. D. Little and J. A. Mirrlees, "A Reply to Some Criticisms of the OECD Manual," *Bulletin of the Oxford University Institute of Economics and Statistics*, vol. 34 (1972), pp. 153–68.

130. See A. Ray, *Cost-Benefit Analysis: Issues and Methodologies* (Johns Hopkins University Press for the World Bank, 1984).

131. Little and Mirrlees, "Project Appraisal and Planning."

132. Some at the Bank would argue that cost-benefit techniques were fully understood but rejected on intellectual grounds. Discussions with the staff of the Bank over twenty years make us highly skeptical of this view. The explanation is more operational; see the next paragraph in the text below. For another discussion of the use of cost-benefit analysis in the

One possible reason for the absence of serious practice of social cost-benefit analysis may be the pressure to disburse loans that has always been present at the Bank, but which was intense in the 1970s and 1980s. Managers have generally been regarded as successful to the extent that they could get their loans approved. In these circumstances careful appraisal has been regarded as a distracting inter-ference rather than as a crucial and productive input. Serious cost-benefit analysis takes time and high-quality analytical resources, and has therefore been seen as managerially irritating and costly. The balance of pressure in the Bank has been perceived to lean toward getting projects out. Whether or not a project turns out to be of good quality is often revealed only after the manager backing it has already been promoted or otherwise moved on. On the other hand it is fair to guess that promotion for stopping bad projects in attempts to increase quality may have been rare. In the get-things-done atmosphere of the McNamara years the environment for careful project selection was perhaps less positive than it might have been.

The Bank's Comparative Advantage and an Assessment

The example of World Bank leadership in the agenda setting associated with structural adjustment illustrates an important comparative advantage of the Bank. Structural adjustment requires an economywide view; macroeconomic, sectoral, microeconomic, and country expertise; and involvement in the policy process across the economy. This package of skills is in many circumstances unique to the Bank. In a major university department someone may be found who is a world figure in macroeconomics, but one is unlikely to find a group of people with particular knowledge of a given country,[133] and, among them, competence in macroeconomic, sectoral, and microeconomic work. This the Bank can provide. And although academics have been arguing about and proposing strategies for economic development since the dawn of the subject, they have been much less concerned than the Bank with the issue of how to move from one strategy to another.

A second respect in which the Bank has a comparative advantage is in its assembly and analysis of cross-country data. As we observed earlier, this was effectively exploited by Chenery and his colleagues in the 1970s, both in the use of cross-country regression analyses and the use of case studies of country experience

---

World Bank, see N. Leff, "The Use of Policy Science Tools in Public-Sector Decision Making: Social Cost-Benefit Analysis in the World Bank," *Kyklos*, vol. 38 (1985), pp. 60–76; and N. Leff, "Policy Research for Improved Organizational Performance: A Case from the World Bank," *Journal of Economic Behavior and Organization*, vol. 9 (1988), pp. 393–403.

133. Such knowledge is more likely to be available inside the country, but there are unfortunately few developing countries with a high level of technical expertise in economics of sufficient breadth and depth. Many of the better economists are hired by international institutions such as the Bank.

in making comparative development analyses. The latter was an important feature of Bank work in the 1980s. Another major influence of the cross-country comparisons has been the data sets—the World Development Indicators at the back of the World Development Reports. These data constitute an important reason why the reports have such a wide circulation. But this wide circulation places a special responsibility on the Bank to present the data in a careful and scholarly manner. These statistics have become a prime source for all those working on development economics.

The presentation of World Bank cross-country statistics, including particularly those in the World Development Reports, has been heavily criticized, by Srinivasan among others.[134] Many of the numbers come from highly dubious sources or have been constructed in ways that leave one skeptical as to whether they can be helpfully used. Srinivasan cites a number of cases where detailed population figures and growth rates were produced without support from censuses and from poor surveys. Income figures may be plagued by definitional and measurement problems, especially if they are to be used for cross-country comparisons. Given its unusual position, the Bank could have been a much stronger leader in exercising appropriate caution, in discussing the presentation of data, in the development of superior systems, and in cross-country analysis. It has been a long way behind the Penn project of Kravis, Summers, and Heston,[135] as well as the OECD, where Angus Maddison, with a small group, has made major contributions in the understanding of cross-country comparative data.[136]

A third area in which the Bank has a comparative advantage is in dealing with infrastructural and sectoral issues. Here it can, for example, accumulate expertise from the experience of different countries in tackling problems concerning road, electricity, or water systems. The Bank's contribution in these sectors has on the whole been of considerable value, and would not have been replicated by an academic establishment or by the relevant industry or sector of a particular country. Perhaps its contribution would have been improved still further if the Bank had been better at maintaining a corporate memory. Frequent administrative upheaval does not make for careful accumulation of experience. In this respect the Bank compares unfavorably with the International Monetary Fund, where the careful maintenance of records in the Fiscal Affairs Department (for example) has made its library and personnel outstanding repositories of knowledge and experience on tax reform in developing countries.

A fourth area in which the Bank has a potential comparative advantage, but where it has not performed as well as that advantage might have permitted,

---

134. See T. N. Srinivasan, "Database for Development Analysis: An Overview," *Journal of Development Economics,* vol. 44, no. 1 (June 1994), pp. 3–27. Srinivasan also includes other international organizations among his targets.

135. Summers and Heston, "The Penn World Table (Mark 5)."

136. See A. Maddison, *The World Economy in the 20th Century* (Paris: OECD, 1989).

concerns international capital markets, financial relations, and debt. As an international financial institution the Bank (with the Fund) is powerfully placed to be an intellectual leader in a way not open to researchers in a single country. As we have indicated, however, the constraints placed on the Bank precisely because it is an international financial institution can prevent that potential from being realized.

World Development Reports

The World Development Reports are probably the most widely read of all World Bank documents.[137] Indeed, they are probably the most widely read publications in development economics. They are important intellectual contributions from at least four perspectives. First, they allow the World Bank to work out its views on a subject of importance, the theme for a given year. Second, they offer a commentary on the world economic situation, as seen by the Bank at a particular point in time. Third, they provide a perspective on the chosen subject which is accessible to practitioners. And, fourth, they provide a useful assembly of data on different countries.

The Bank has been careful to make the World Development Reports easily available to the layperson, through both language and worldwide distribution. Thus the reports provide a crucial bridge between the Bank and the outside world. Since 1983 they have had a professional editor, who has played a major role in keeping the reports readable and intelligible. At times, however, accessibility appears to have been achieved at a considerable cost. In particular, documentation has fallen far short of that which would be acceptable in a scholarly publication; given that the reports are widely quoted in support of particular positions, this is a serious drawback. The reports have also suffered from an enforced reticence on political matters. Generally, anything that might offend politicians of particular countries has been avoided, so there is a pervasive weakness in the reports on matters of political economy. In effect, each member country has veto power over material referring to it.

The World Development Reports were initiated by Robert McNamara. The first was prepared under the direction of Ernest Stern, with D. C. Rao as the team leader; it broadly set the pattern for those that followed, although the first two development reports were not explicitly categorized by a particular theme—a hallmark of subsequent World Development Reports. The reports are usually assembled over a period of between twelve and eighteen months, by a team of around ten people working under a team leader, and with substantial research

137. This section draws heavily on H. Gazdar, "The World Development Reports: A Survey and Assessment," Development Economics Research Programme Discussion Paper, STICERD, London School of Economics, 1992, and has benefited from conversations with him.

support. They have budgets of a size that allows the commissioning of many background papers. The research input is very large relative to the resources available to most academic studies. The statistical series at the end of the report are assembled on a regular basis by statistical divisions within the Bank. As of February 1993 there had been fifteen World Development Reports issued.

The World Development Indicators, presented in tables, appear as an annex to each main report. They have undergone improvements both in coverage and in organization over the years. The tables have been responsive to changes in the development agenda through the inclusion of new data and the reorganization of existing data. An outline of main issues covered in all World Development Reports from 1978 to 1991 is provided in table 12-3. In the first World Development Report, the table of Basic Indicators included, among other indicators, energy consumption and production, food production, population, area, GNP per capita, and the annual rate of inflation. Literacy rates and life expectancy were added in 1979, and energy was moved to a separate table. In 1983 food production was also taken out of the Basic Indicators table and placed in a new table on agriculture and food. It is perhaps symbolic that literacy rates were removed from the Basic Indicators in 1984, to be brought back in 1990 in the World Development Report focused on poverty. Recent notable innovations have been indicators on women in development (in 1988) and on forests, protected areas, and water (in 1991), perhaps as a result of the Bank's rising concern with gender issues and with the environment.

Medium- and long-term projections of key economic variables are reported every year for groups of countries. These are derived from the Bank's models of the global economy and from various scenarios under different assumptions about policy and other exogenous variables. An assessment of the accuracy of projections presented in earlier World Development Reports, which was published in the report for 1991, found them to have been almost universally overoptimistic. Although the authors of the reports have been at pains to point out that these projections should not be interpreted as forecasts, persistence of errors lends support to charges that the Bank's outlook on the international economic environment has suffered from costly blind spots or biases. An example might be the Bank's slowness to appreciate the problems of debt accumulation in the late 1970s.[138]

A summary of World Development Report themes and some commentary on that content is provided in table 12-4.

None of the World Development Reports have been innovative intellectual statements in their own right; that is not what they have set out to achieve. They

---

138. A cynical insider has expressed the view that the method of construction of the projections, together with their purpose, meant that they were bound to be overly optimistic. It has also been suggested that the Bank take a medium-term forecast, add something for policy improvement, and then use the results to argue that things would look even better if the Bank spent more money.

Table 12-3. *Main World Development Indicators, 1978–91*

Indicator	Years reported[a]
Basic indicators	1978–91
Growth of production	1978–91
Structure of production	1978–91
Growth of consumption and investment	1978–91
Structure of demand	1978–91
Structure of consumption	1988–91
Agriculture and food	1983–91
Structure of manufacturing	1987–91
Manufacturing earnings and output	1987–91
Industry	1979–86
Commercial energy	1979–91
Growth of merchandise trade	1978–91
Structure of merchandise exports	1978–91
Structure of merchandise imports	1978–91
Origin and destination of merchandise exports	1978–87
Origin and destination of manufactured exports	1982–88
OECD imports of manufactures; origin and composition	1989–91
Trade in manufactured goods	1979–81
Balance of payments and debt service ratios	1978–82
Balance of payments and international reserves	1984–91
Total external debt	1985–91
Flows of external capital	1978–83
Flows of publicly guaranteed external capital	1984–86
Flow of public and private external capital	1987–91
External public debt and international reserves	1978–83
Public and private external debt and debt service ratios	1986–91
External public debt and debt service ratios	1984–91
Terms of public borrowing	1983–91
ODA from OECD and OPEC members	1978–91
ODA receipts	1986–91
Demographic and fertility indicators	1978–91
Labor force	1978–88
Urbanization	1978–91
Indicators related to life expectancy	1979–91
Women in development	1988–91
Population projections	1978–91
Health-related indicators	1978–87
Health and nutrition	1988–91
Education	1978–91
Forests, protected areas, and water	1991–
Defense and social expenditure	1981–83
Central government expenditure	1984–91
Central government current revenue	1984–91
Money and interest rates	1987–91
Income distribution and International Comparison Project estimates of GDP	1984–91
Income distribution	1979–88

Sources: World Development Reports (1978–91).

a. There was one table for each indicator in years when present.

Table 12-4. *Themes of World Development Reports, 1978–92*

Year	Main themes	Comments
1978	Development experience, the international environment, growth and poverty	Emphasized relatively favorable international economic environment over past twenty-five years and raised worries about the rise of protectionism. Fairly descriptive. Introduced important themes that recur, such as human capital and the growth-equity-poverty relationship. Dissented from trickle-down economics. Action urged on poverty as well as growth. Stressed need for long-term adjustment.
1979	Employment and urbanization	Noted rising debt but was fairly sanguine on prospects (written before the 1979 oil price rise). Foresaw adjustment with growth as possible in face of oil price rise of 1973. Problems of population, employment, and urban bias emphasized. Promoted small farms and labor-intensive industrialization as poverty alleviation strategies. Extra focus allowed greater depth and scholarship.
1980	Human development and poverty	Emphasized importance of education, training, nutrition, and health in promoting growth and relieving poverty. Rural development theme recurred. Cautious on link from growth to poverty reduction. Promoted cause of poor, both as an end in itself and as a means to faster growth. Raised problems of policy's falling victim to vested interests.
1981	Adjustment, trade, and capital flows	Returned to worries about the international economic environment. Stressed need to expand financial flows to LDCs with little apparent concern for debt problems. Useful country studies on adjustment, but macroeconomic in orientation. Some repetition of 1980 discussion on human development.
1982	Agricultural development	Offered a rosy view of growth and adjustment of LDCs in 1970s— "good use of additional borrowing." Published three months before the Mexican debt crisis broke. Saw China's and India's self-sufficiency as providing insulation from international economic changes. Some mention of problems of debt burdens and higher interest rates. Emphasized link between rapid growth and rapid agricultural growth, but was short on evidence. Advocated reform of agricultural policy and reiterated support for small farmers. Agricultural and rural development seen as key to alleviation of rural poverty.
1983	Management in development	First mention of debt crisis; association with high interest rates. Spoke of "illiquidity" and need for more capital inflows. Again mention of China's and India's resilience as being associated with low trade involvements. Warnings on protectionism. Beginning of emphasis on markets and outward orientation. Associated price distortions with poor performance. Provided a working guide to issues in the management of the macroeconomy, state-owned enterprises, projects and programs, and public service.
1984	Population	Some pessimism about longer-term world growth appeared. Linked earlier benign recycling of the 1970s with debt crisis. Importance of adjustment and coordinated international action stressed. Externality and information arguments for population policy advanced. Consequences of high population growth argued to be damaging, but empirical and theoretical support fairly weak.
1985	International financial flows	Those countries that avoided debt crisis had growth before world market entry, expanded the traded sector, and diversified exports. Looks like ex-post wisdom given earlier recycling emphasis. Emphasis on costs of protection and price distortions. Provided useful guide to international financial system and some interesting simulations. Less strong on analysis.

Year	Topic	Description
1986	Pricing and trade in world agriculture	Lower interest rates and success at bringing down inflation seen as positive developments. Noted importance of growth in agriculture, both to combat poverty and to lead economic growth. Optimistic about potential for technological advance. Saw need for better pricing, infrastructure, trading regimes, and research. Progress noted in dealing with famines outside Africa. Distortions in trade seen as leading to food exports being mostly from industrialized countries.
1987	Industrialization and foreign trade	External payments imbalances of industrial countries seen as a threat to stability. Continued worry about protectionism. Advantages of outward orientation argued strongly. Much made of experience of the East Asian countries. Conclusions from empirical work incautious.
1988	Public finance	Emphasis continued on reducing external imbalances for industrial countries, restructuring for developing countries, reducing resource transfers from developing countries. For public finance in developing countries, recommendations were: prudent macroeconomics, simplified tax systems to increase revenue and reduce distortions, and more control and quality in spending. Association between fiscal deficits and debtors noted. Useful guide to public finance for developing countries.
1989	Financial systems	Problems of financial institutions seen as arising from excessive government intervention and external shocks. Main policy recommendation was liberalization of financial institutions. An unambitious but useful manual on its subject, as in 1988.
1990	Poverty	Two-part strategy recommended—labor-intensive growth plus provision of social services, particularly primary education, primary health care, and family planning. Cross-country comparison (of limited usefulness) of poverty using universal poverty line. Little support found for Kuznets inverted U curve. Some discussion of safety nets, also of adjustment and poverty. Presented coherent assimilation of various themes around poverty reduction.
1991	Development experience and the role of the state	Assembled experience from development economics and growth over past few decades. A competent survey. Presented modern consensus with role for state in infrastructure, human development, and promotion of more efficient markets with private sector dominating elsewhere. Integrated picture of the benefits of policy reform in different areas. Discussed political economy of development and reform.
1992	Environment and development	Report proposed to set the agenda (along with 1990 and 1991 reports) for development policy for the 1990s. Probably little here, even taking the three together, that would change the research strategy of development economists, for whom there would be little new; a useful assemblage, however. The linkage among environmental protection, poverty reduction, and economic growth seen as valuable, as was the focus on those aspects of the environment of immediate relevance to developing countries—water sanitation, urban pollution. Report continued the trend of improvement in the quantity and quality of information.

Source: World Development Reports, 1978–92.

have tried to bring to the reader an understanding of available contributions to a particular topic. Although each of the reports after the first two has had a particular theme, a number of issues have recurred from the beginning: tensions between growth and poverty alleviation; rural development and urban bias; human capital; employment generation; trade policy; and structural adjustment and macro-economic policy. In presenting such topics the reports have generally succeeded rather well. A number of them—among them the 1983 report on management, the 1985 report on international finance, the 1988 report on public finance, and the 1989 report on financial systems—have been valuable users' guides for the un-initiated. Many of the case studies presented in the sidebars in the reports have been illuminating to both development practitioner and academic. However, al-though a collection of available work on a subject can show real bite, insight, perspective, and judgment, the World Development Reports have rarely risen to that level. Perhaps one reason for this is that they are written by a large team over a short period of time, rather than by a small team over a longer period. The latter method might be more likely to allow thought processes to reach some kind of maturity and to provide more incisive insights and greater structure.

Using table 12-4 as a reference, we now examine the reports as a time series, tracing the development of Bank thinking and contributions on a number of issues, and observing some contradictions and defects over the years.

The Bank's role as an international development agency endows it with a natural advantage in and indeed a responsibility for addressing international aspects of domestic policies. Two key issues in this regard are trade policy and safeguarding the natural environment. Although the latter issue has been neglected by the Bank until comparatively recently, the former has received a great deal of attention over the years. Through the World Development Reports the Bank has taken a consis-tent and strong line on the dangers of protectionism. It has been a champion of the cause of developing countries against the protectionism of industrialized countries, and it has (fairly) consistently warned of the dangers of distortions of markets resulting from excessive protection in developing countries themselves. On inter-national capital flows and the problems of debt the Bank has been less consistent, as discussed earlier.

After the debt crisis broke in the early 1980s, the resilience of India and China in the face of international trade shocks, arising from their self-sufficiency and low involvement in international trade, was remarked upon in moderately positive terms in the World Development Reports. In contrast, strong attacks on protec-tionism in developing countries were to come later in the 1980s. Even in the report for 1985 there appears to be some praise for countries that opted for domestic growth before entry into world markets—that is, they provided some protection for industrial sectors in order to establish those sectors. In the later 1980s the reports continued to chastise industrial countries for their payment imbalances, seeing these as in part responsible for high interest rates and threats to the stability of the trading and financial system. Over the years there is also some inconsistency in the Bank's position on the relationship between growth and poverty alleviation, as discussed earlier.

In the foreword to the World Development Report of 1991 Barber Conable suggested that together the World Development Reports of 1990, 1991, and 1992 would set an agenda for the 1990s. The report for 1991 presents a useful summary of an emerging school of thought—perhaps a consensus—on the appropriate role for state activity in human development, infrastructure development, and the promotion of an active and competitive private sector unhindered by bureaucratic intervention. It also shows a bolder foray into political economy than has been seen in earlier World Development Reports.

In the reports there has been an impressive consistency in stressing human development and the importance of education and health as both inputs and outputs to the growth process, and as determinants of poverty. This emphasis is quite striking in looking at the World Development Reports as a whole, particularly in the light of the launching of the *Human Development Report* in 1990 by the United Nations Development Program, which was seen in part as a publication that might restore the balance of the World Bank's alleged preoccupation with economic growth.[139]

Taken together, the World Development Reports should be seen as central to the World Bank's intellectual contribution. The reports have not generally set the agenda, but they have discharged effectively their task of communicating major themes and disseminating major ideas in development economics.

Policy Dialogue and Projects

It was emphasized early in this chapter that a central aspect of the Bank's intellectual contribution has come through its dialogues and interaction with policymakers and others in developing countries. To a great extent this has arisen through the operational departments of the Bank, in the interchanges of their daily operations, but the research departments have also played a role, both in their inputs to policy and in training. Examples of such interactions can be seen in looking briefly at the Bank's country reports and some influential reports on the African continent, some aspects of the Bank's project experience, and the role of its Economic Development Institute (EDI).

Further examples of ways in which the Bank is directly helpful to practitioners outside the Bank lie in the guides and handbooks the Bank produces, such as the *Poverty Reduction Handbook* and *Historically Planned Economies: A Guide to the*

139. United Nations Development Program, *Human Development Report* (Oxford University Press, 1990).

Data, both published in 1992.[140] These have different purposes. The *Handbook* helps in the design and selection of projects and policies that contribute to the alleviation of poverty. The *Guide* provides help in understanding data generated in formerly centrally planned economies so that economists and statisticians outside the Bank are better able to understand the meaning of past data and assist with new data, and those inside the Bank are guided on procedures that are consistent with concepts and practices in capitalist economies. In both cases the Bank makes a direct and practical intellectual contribution.

Country Reports

An important part of the Bank's intellectual influence in its policy dialogue with countries is achieved through negotiations on structural adjustment loans, where these are relevant, but more continuously through the economic reports that come out periodically from the Bank's country desks. Many of those in developing countries have argued that the Bank's commentary on the state of the country's economy and its assemblage of economic assessments have provided useful input into their thinking. In our experience the quality of the country reports is higher than that of other World Bank internal and published documents. It is clear that the priority attached to these reports, both inside and outside the Bank, is high. To say that they are generally of high quality and eagerly read is not to say that they are influential. The measurement of influence in this context is neither conceptually nor practically easy. The country reports are voluminous, and the judgments we seek are not straightforward.

The Bank produces a variety of reports on specific countries, with different circulation criteria. The most widely circulated are the Country Economic Reports, which are discussed with country officials, and some of which are subsequently made public. Country Economic Reports generally reflect the economic analysis contained in another, more restricted category of papers, the Country Program Papers and their successors, the Country Strategy Papers. Because of their greater confidentiality, the latter provide greater insight into some of the Bank's views, particularly those of a more political nature. As their number is very large, only a few examples of the reports can be discussed here; we look at examples from Kenya, India, and Mexico, where Nicholas Stern has worked professionally. Some of the political analysis in these reports is relevant only to an understanding of the formation of the Bank's medium-term lending programs, but the economic themes are broadly those developed in dialogue with the countries through the Country Economic Reports.

The structure of the Country Program Papers examined is similar for those of all three countries. An introduction giving basic indicators for the country is followed by a survey of the political panorama, then by a more detailed analysis of the

---

140. See World Bank, *Poverty Reduction Handbook;* World Bank, *Historically Planned Economies: A Guide to the Data* (Washington, 1992).

economic situation. This analysis contains a general assessment of the recent macroeconomic performance of the economy, a structural discussion of the comparative performance of different sectors (for example, industry, agriculture, energy, and basic infrastructure), and statements on the distribution of income and the progress—or lack thereof—in reducing poverty. That analysis is followed by statements on the economic and sector work of the Bank in the country and on its proposed assistance and lending strategy. Included are breakdowns of Bank loans by sectors and their evolution over time. Obvious efforts are made to ensure that strategy takes into account those areas where the greatest needs are identified in the preceding analytical sections, but attached internal memoranda suggest that sometimes those sections are written (or rewritten) to provide support for a lending portfolio previously agreed to.[141]

KENYA. For this discussion, the Kenya Country Program Papers examined were those for 1973, 1975, 1976, 1978 through 1981, 1984, and 1985; and the Country Strategy Paper for 1988 was also examined. The most notable persistent objectives seen in these reports are the reduction of poverty and income inequality, policies to generate employment opportunities, and population control. Sporadic concerns can be grouped under stabilization and structural adjustment policies, designed to deal with balance of payments and fiscal crises, as well as to help achieve a resumption of growth at pre-1973 rates. There is an incisive concern with political considerations throughout.

The more even distribution of the benefits of development was a key objective throughout the period spanned by the reports. This is generally associated with a concern with growing unemployment and underemployment in Kenya, and naturally also with policies to slow the rate of population growth (still 4 percent in 1988). In the Country Strategy Paper of 1988 these issues still received prominent attention.

The Country Program Papers are understandably not immune to general changes of emphasis and direction in the Bank as a whole; the rise to prominence of structural adjustment concerns in the early to mid-1980s is evident in the Kenyan material. The Country Program Paper for 1984 considered that far-reaching measures to correct structural problems were essential for the resumption of sustained growth. The measures in question included agricultural pricing and marketing reform, exchange rate devaluations, fiscal discipline, price reform and reorganization of public sector enterprises, and replacement of quotas by tariffs. Making lending levels conditional on appropriate implementation of the package of adjustment measures was proposed more than once.

---

141. The following comment in an office memo from the International Finance Corporation (IFC) to the Country Division Chief regarding the 1984 Country Program Paper (CPP) for Kenya is instructive: "I have reviewed the draft CPP and my main comment is that it does not support the proposed lending for transport. Although the proposed allocation for transport lending [is] of U.S.$200 million . . . , the first 23 pages of the CPP contain only two references to transportation in Kenya." IFC office memo, July 17, 1984.

As to political considerations, the introductory paragraphs of the Kenyan reports are invariably dedicated to a review of recent political events and to an analysis of how the president is dealing with opposition, tribal tension, and occasional coup attempts and political assassinations. The transition from the presidency of Jomo Kenyatta to that of Daniel Arap Moi was the subject of intense speculation. Political constraints, once identified as such, are taken as essentially given.

INDIA. Country Program Papers for India for 1970, 1972, 1974, 1976, 1978, 1980, and 1983, as well as Country Strategy Papers for 1985 and 1988, were examined. The general tone of most of the reports for India is positive, in that policy initiatives taken by the government are endorsed. In the 1970s the three objectives that appeared most pressing to the Bank were to continue the drive to reduce extreme poverty in rural areas (part of Prime Minister Indira Gandhi's program when she was first elected); to increase the domestic savings and investment rates so as to spur faster growth; and to manage the balance of payments with appropriate caution so as to avoid foreign exchange shortages that could harm imports of inputs and thus create supply-side bottlenecks and slow growth of industrial output.

In the earlier reports on India the approach to the balance of payments was essentially in tacit agreement with the dominant import substitution strategy and a two-gap view of the world. The discussion is couched in terms of import "requirements" for industrialization, and finding ways to finance them. Only later—and particularly from 1978 onward—does the emphasis begin to change toward increasing exports, specializing in accordance with comparative advantage, and reducing import barriers to ease input bottlenecks for industry. Also from the mid-1970s onward the usual emphasis on raising domestic savings and investment is generally accompanied by discussion of the need to increase the efficiency of investment. Note is taken of the upward trend in the capital-output ratio, and this is identified as a signal that resources are not being used effectively.

In the 1980s there was moderate praise for India's structural adjustment policies, which were aimed at reducing the high rates of effective protection for many industries, lowering inflation (successfully done),[142] and channeling investment to the energy and basic infrastructure sectors. The emphasis on fighting poverty remained an important cornerstone of the Bank's activities. The 1988 Country Strategy Paper suggests that growth alone would not be sufficient to achieve India's poverty alleviation goals, and that increased and better-allocated expenditures on human resource development would be necessary to support growth and directly alleviate poverty. This is quite close to the view expressed in

---

142. Inadequate attention to public finances during the 1980s was later to result in the inflationary, budgetary, and foreign exchange difficulties that became severe at the end of the decade.

1972 that poverty should be tackled directly and that time had run out for relying on economic growth to bring about the necessary improvements. There is in the India papers a stronger and more consistent emphasis on direct measures, as opposed to a go-for-growth strategy, in pursuit of poverty alleviation than is found in the Bank's more prominent policy pronouncements.

Generally, Indian policymakers have prided themselves on the notion that the Bank has never had the upper hand. This view could be seen as having some support in the Bank's Country Program Papers and Country Strategy Papers for the 1970s and 1980s. On the other hand, it could be argued that those Bank economists engaged in work in a particular country under study absorb some sense of its priorities, and that this is no bad thing. It is not always easy to strike a balance between absorption and the provision of dispassionate description and advice.

MEXICO. The sample of Country Program Papers examined for Mexico included those for 1971, 1973, 1976, 1978, 1980, and 1984. Again, the two main themes running through the analyses are the fight against poverty (particularly rural poverty) and macroeconomic soundness in pursuit of high growth. The first is consistent with McNamara's priorities, and the second with a caution that contrasts with the tone of the World Development Reports. The 1973 and 1976 reports did indeed sound strong notes of fiscal prudence. However, these appropriately careful sentiments fade somewhat in the later reports of 1978 and 1980, when awareness of the potentially disastrous consequences of delaying action to redress the trend toward growing economic imbalance was not evident.

There is throughout these reports a directness that is unusual in public Bank documents, and which involves an unabashed political economy approach. This is often evident in the language in some passages (because of their confidential nature, however, Country Program Papers and Country Strategy Papers cannot be quoted here). Mexican presidents are mentioned by name, the undemocratic shortcomings of the dominant Institutional Revolutionary Party (PRI) are discussed, and political constraints on policy are openly acknowledged. Even the fact that the government chose not to accept Bank loans for education because of sensitivity to foreign influences over the curriculum is calmly accepted and understood. This is entirely sensible, but quite distinct from the tone of other Bank publications. It strikes the reader that such frankness and good sense are a result of confidentiality.

AN OVERVIEW OF COUNTRY REPORTS. The Country Program Papers and their more public counterparts, the Country Economic Reports, are an important part of both the Bank's intellectual interaction with a country and the formulation of its own lending policies. But they are not without faults. There do seem to be signs of rewriting around precommitted loan plans. And at times the reports can appear too accepting of a government's own perception and articulation of where it stands and where it is going—a latter feature more likely in the case of reports on bigger countries such as India and Mexico that also have confident and accomplished public servants and economists. Such faults sometimes led to a hesitancy in pointing out the misguided nature of policies, as happened with Mexico's fiscal position in the late 1970s.

On balance, however, and acknowledging that the quality is variable, the country reports consistently show the Bank in a positive light as assessor, commentator, and adviser. The reports are generally well researched and articulated and show a refreshing frankness and directness. Often they provide an overall assessment of the current position of a kind unlikely to be available anywhere else. Public servants and policymakers in developing countries study the public versions of the reports carefully. Even in India, where it has been politically imperative for public figures to show strong independence from the Bank and where economists are numerous, the Bank's Country Economic Reports are read avidly. The reports are a very important part of a largely unseen aspect of the Bank as intellectual actor.

AFRICA REPORTS. In addition to policy dialogue carried out through country reports, the 1980s saw a series of important World Bank reports on the problems of Sub-Saharan Africa as a whole.[143] That of 1981, often known as the Berg report, represented a turning point in the perception of policy by the countries themselves and by donor countries and agencies. The movement toward more market-oriented policies advocated in that report was reflected in subsequent lending programs and was in stark contrast to such approaches to development as that associated with the African socialism of the late 1960s and early 1970s in Tanzania. The four later Sub-Saharan Africa reports also exerted strong policy influences, with that of 1989 moving the issue of governance to center stage.[144] The 1989 report was also marked by substantial participation by economists from Africa itself—participation that was partly responsible for the emphasis on governance.[145]

Project Experience

Projects are the most basic and frequent source of World Bank intellectual interaction with developing countries. The expertise that the Bank has acquired, or is able to assemble, is to a great extent transmitted through the development of projects. It is in respect to advice and technical skills, among other factors, that the Bank as a lender is different from a commercial bank.

143. See World Bank, *Accelerated Development in Sub-Saharan Africa: An Agenda for Action* (Washington, 1981); World Bank, *Progress Report on Development Prospects and Programs* (Washington, 1983); World Bank, *Towards Sustained Development Prospects in Sub-Saharan Africa* (Washington, 1984); World Bank, *Financing Adjustment with Growth in Sub-Saharan Africa, 1986–90* (Washington, 1986); and World Bank, *Sub-Saharan Africa: From Crisis to Sustainable Growth* (Washington, 1989).

144. By governance here is meant the manner of governing, or the way in which government and related social and economic institutions function.

145. We are grateful to Stanley Please for guidance and discussion on this subject.

Detailed work on projects accounts for what is sometimes seen as high staffing levels at the Bank. The Bank stays in close touch with a project to which it lends, from the early days of project formulation, through to the development of the project on the ground as loans are disbursed. Many from developing countries who work on projects suggest that they have learned a great deal from this participation.

The Operations Evaluation Department has attempted to examine the Bank's project experience as a whole and to learn from it in a systematic way. It has found, for example, that the Bank has generally been successful in its traditional infrastructural area, but less successful outside that area, as measured by standard evaluation techniques such as social cost-benefit analysis and internal rates of return.[146]

For the World Development Report of 1991 a large set of projects was used to link projects with the overall policy environment.[147] The exercise is in many respects the most original aspect of that report, although discussion of it covers only 6 of nearly 300 pages in the report. The exercise made use of what must be a unique data source, comprising data on 1,200 projects over twenty years on which cost-benefit calculations have been performed. Such a database is a potential gold mine for research and is the type of resource which the Bank is specially positioned to produce and to use. The resource is within the Operations Evaluation Department. Given the richness of the source, it is regrettable that it has not been greatly used in research and policy formation. However, within the Bank high status is given to and excitement and interest are generated by new projects, so it is perhaps unsurprising from an institutional point of view that the Operations Evaluation Department has had a low profile.

The 1991 World Development Report and other reports showed that nondistortionary pricing systems and stable macroeconomic environment have been important to the success of projects, as measured by social rates of return. Thus the Bank's systematic analysis of projects, both in dialogue with borrowing countries and in drawing general lessons from the wealth of experience that projects provide, has been an important part of its intellectual contribution. The importance of projects in intellectual interchange points to the potential value of exploiting its historical project data in research on development.

The Economic Development Institute

A third means by which the World Bank interacts with policymakers in developing countries is the training programs run through its Economic Development Institute (EDI). The institute was founded in 1955 and was initially headed by

146. See Operations Evaluation Department, "Annual Review of Evaluation Results 1990," World Bank, 1991.
147. See World Bank, *World Development Report* (1991).

Alexander Cairncross. Its original objective was to provide training for government servants from developing countries, the first intake of which took place in 1956. The original motivation for the institute was "an increasing awareness by the World Bank of the need for more efficient economic management within its developing member countries and of the then almost nonexistent opportunities for mid-career training in this field."[148]

Speaking in 1966, Cairncross recalled that: "the first thing that those who attended courses at the EDI ten years ago wanted to hear about was how to set about preparing a development program. Their interest lay not in economic theory nor even in specific problems in applied economics, but in an area of discussion where there are few good textbooks—the administration of economic policy."[149] This the Bank saw as an opportunity to influence the level and quality of the development policy debate—and indeed of decisionmaking—in many member countries. Accordingly, for seven years the institute's course menu consisted of a single offering, the General Development Course, taught to just over twenty people each year.

In the early 1960s, it became clear that, at that rate, the objective of raising the quality of economic decisionmaking in member countries through training would not be significantly furthered. As the Bank's operations grew, it was also felt that project analysis might deserve greater attention in the institute's courses, as "this gap was especially evident to staff of the World Bank Group since the scarcity of well-prepared projects directly affected lending operations."[150] This view triggered a move toward project training and away from general development that would last for some twenty years, until a reversal was engineered in 1984. In 1963 the General Projects course was inaugurated; and sector-specific courses on industrial and agricultural projects followed in the late 1960s. In the early 1970s these were joined by courses on education, transportation, urban growth, water supply, and waste disposal projects, among others. The pedagogical approach adopted was firmly practical in nature. Roughly 60 percent of participants had had no previous training in economics, and the courses were designed around case studies and problem solving. From 1972, when Andrew Kamarck took over as institute director, institutional channels were created to ensure a flow of ideas and concerns between the institute and the operations side of the Bank, and a concern with "preserving the staff from scholasticism" was expressed.[151]

The late 1970s were a period of uncertainty for the Economic Development Institute. Significant changes in the world economy, a continuing lack of satisfac-

148. Economic Development Institute, *Training for Development—A Report of the World Bank's Economic Development Institute* (Washington: World Bank, June 1975), p. 4.

149. A. K. Cairncross, "The Short Term and the Long in Economic Planning," Tenth Anniversary Lecture, Economic Development Institute, Washington, 1966, p. 2.

150. Economic Development Institute, *Training for Development*, p. 5.

151. Ibid., p. 11.

tory integration with the operations side of the Bank, and the small scale of its own program all contributed to a sense of discomfort within the institute—a discomfort that was captured in the report of a task force established in 1982 to review institute objectives and activities. The task force was chaired by Shahid Husain. Its report, entitled *The Future of the Economic Development Institute*, stated that "mobilization of Bank staff, particularly economists with experience in economic analysis and policy, is difficult. Very few senior staff have participated in teaching at EDI and staff participation overall has been modest. EDI has also been largely excluded from the Bank's internal discussions on development concerns. . . . The morale of EDI staff has suffered because of their perception that the Bank's management is not concerned about the Institute's role and future."[152]

Largely as a result of the recommendations in that report, the institute nowadays defines itself as acting in four distinct areas. The first is still training for policymakers from developing countries. The other three are institutional assistance, the preparation and publication of training materials, and the administration of scholarship programs. In training for policymakers there has been a move in the direction of emphasizing the exchange of ideas and experiences among participants, rather than relying excessively on a lecture mode. There are four broad types of training courses: senior policy seminars (of short duration and for a very high level of staff), economic and sector management seminars (for senior-level staff and of longer duration), project analysis and management seminars, and the training of trainers.

These training activities constitute the institute's most important output. In fiscal year 1992, some 115 courses were given, 72 percent of which were policy related, as opposed to project related or for teacher training.[153] They reached some 2,500 participants, up from 1,500 in 1988, when they already accounted for more than 56 percent of all institute staff time and more than 65 percent of institute funds.[154]

Inputs, Outputs, Organization, and Strategy in Research

In looking at the Bank's intellectual interactions from one perspective, the only relevant feature of research is the output—its contribution in terms of quality and quantity. However, the Bank may also be concerned with the productivity of its

152. World Bank Task Force on the Economic Development Institute, *The Future of the Economic Development Institute* (Washington: Economic Development Institute, April 1983), pp. v–vi.

153. Economic Development Institute, *The Economic Development Institute: FY92 Review and FY93 Program* (Washington: World Bank, April 1992).

154. Economic Development Institute, *EDI Strategic Plan, 1990–1994* (Washington: World Bank, April 1984).

Table 12-5. *Educational Levels Attained by Policy, Research, and External Affairs Professional Staff, as of 1991*

Discipline	Number of individuals[a]	
	Undergraduate degree in	Highest degree (doctoral, master's, bachelor's; certificates and diplomas) in[b]
Social sciences		
Management, law, accounting	9	26
Economics, finance	136	252
Public administration	4	5
Politics	14	12
Other	52	93
Physical sciences		
Engineering	42	43
Physics, chemistry, mathematics	21	15
Agricultural sciences, biology	16	19
Total	294	465

Source: Authors' own research, using Bank records.

a. In all, 532 individuals were surveyed; of these, 91 were women. No data were available on 67 individuals, including 9 women. Data on 6 individuals were incomplete.

b. Of the survey respondents, 210 held degrees at the doctoral level, 153 at the master's level, and 57 at the bachelor's level; 37 held certificates or diplomas. Many holding higher degrees do not have bachelor's degrees.

resources, so an understanding of the nature of the inputs may help in assessing the output that emerges. Our purpose here is to examine who does research in the Bank, what is produced, and how it is organized; our concern is with the process of production rather than the intellectual content of the output. The focus is on standard forms of research output rather than on other dimensions such as interaction with operations, countries, or agencies.

Personnel

Research at the World Bank in 1992 was located in the Policy, Research, and External Affairs section (known as PRE). To provide an overview of the educational background of professional members of the PRE staff (those ranking at level 18 or above), 532 high-level staff members were surveyed in 1991.[155] Results of the data analysis are presented in tables 12-5 (educational levels attained) and 12-6 (institutions attended). By far the largest number of individuals held degrees in economics or finance, at both the undergraduate level (46 percent of the sample of 294) and at higher levels (55 percent of the sample of 465); see table 12-5. Among the 465 for whom data were available, 210 (46 percent) held degrees at the doctoral level (table 12-5). Of 465 individuals for whom data on graduate schools were available, 290 attended American schools and 74 attended British institutions, together

155. We are grateful to Karen Semkow for carrying out this work.

Table 12-6. *Institutions Attended by Policy, Research, and External Affairs Professional Staff, as of 1991*

Location of school	Number of individuals[a]	
	Undergraduate degree	Graduate degree
United States	127	. . .
Ivy League	. . .	46
MIT, Stanford, University of Chicago	. . .	34
State universities	. . .	90
District of Columbia area	. . .	72
Other	. . .	48
United Kingdom	. . .	. . .
Oxford	6	13
Cambridge	9	13
London School of Economics	3	13
Other	24	35
Western Europe	22	41
Canada	9	10
Africa, Latin America, Asia	66	27
Japan	3	0
Other	25	23[b]
Total	294	465

Source: Authors' own research, using Bank records.
a. See notes to table 12-5.

composing nearly 80 percent of the sample (see table 12-6). Similarly, among those attending undergraduate schools, 127, or 43 percent, attended U.S. institutions. The picture that emerges, then, is of a staff primarily educated in the United States with doctoral degrees in economics, though there is also a strong educational showing by the United Kingdom.

The predominance of economics and U.S. graduate schools is understandable because the subject matter of the Bank work involved is in large part economics and the best graduate schools are in the United States. It must be emphasized that the nationalities involved are diverse. But these numbers should raise the question of whether the professional search staff may not be excessively homogeneous and be looking at the world in one particular way. A recent study of graduate education in the United States has indeed expressed concern over the uniformity within the U.S. graduate economics system.[156] U.S. graduate schools, not surprisingly, tend to concentrate on U.S. examples, and the United States is in many ways a rather peculiar country. For example, it has a tax system and a constitution that are very different from those found in other countries, and a strand in political philosophy

156. See A. O. Krueger, "Report of the Commission on Graduate Education in Economics," *Journal of Economic Literature*, vol. 28 (1991), pp. 1035–53.

Table 12-7. *Pre-Bank Experience of Policy, Research, and External Affairs Professional Staff, as of 1991*

Data category	Number of individuals[a]	Percentage of individuals	Cumulative years of experience
Number of jobs held			
1	56	12.9	. . .
2	79	18.2	. . .
3	86	19.9	. . .
4	92	21.2	. . .
5	45	10.4	. . .
More than 5	75	17.3	. . .
Location of previous jobs			
United States	220	50.8	. . .
Canada	13	3.0	. . .
Europe	70	16.2	. . .
Japan	1	0.2	. . .
Latin America, Africa, Asia	105	24.2	. . .
Other[b]	24	5.5	. . .
Type of work experience			
Government	78	18.0	1,005
Academic	128	29.6	1,335
Public international	72	16.6	413
Private	126	29.1	1,115
Other public authority	29	6.7	317

Source: Authors' own research, using Bank records.

a. The total sample was 433 individuals out of 532 staff members surveyed; data were not available for 99 individuals.

b. Includes the Middle East, Australia, and New Zealand.

oriented toward individualism and against the state that is much more dominant than is the case in other countries. U.S. graduate schools, for example, have shown less interest in applied welfare economics, poverty, and income distribution than their counterparts elsewhere. When the pre-Bank work experience of the professional staff is examined, domination by the United States is again found; more than 50 percent of the staff members have had previous jobs in the United States (see table 12-7). Looking at cumulative years of experience, it is clear that there is a broad spread between academic, government, public international, and private institutions.

We have the strong impression, although we have not been able to find data to substantiate it, that the Bank's outside research contracts are also awarded predominantly in the United States. Again, it could be argued that because most of the research is in economics and the best graduate schools and research establishments are in the United States, this is perfectly natural. But again, if borne out by the data, this circumstance would reinforce the rather undifferentiated intellectual perspective found in the World Bank. It is not always easy for those at the Bank's headquarters in Washington, D.C., to understand that a Washington perspective on the world is far from universally shared. It is worrying that there often appears to be a conviction in the Bank of a monopoly on good sense. Opposition can be regarded as misguided, uneducated, or malevolent (notwithstanding that what is regarded as good sense often can undergo dramatic change). The Bank is, of course, not the only bureaucratic institution in which uniformity of view or outlook may be found.[157]

Some uniformity is desirable. Just as one would expect members of a mathematical or physics institute to agree on the rules of arithmetic, so too one would hope for some substantial common ground among economists working in an international organization. However, it would be desirable to see that coupled with a broad perspective on institutions—an understanding that there are many possible ways for incentive structures and economic organizations to arise and to be designed, and that some institutional structures that have evolved, although they may be unfamiliar in the United States and western Europe, may well be functional in important respects. Other institutional structures, traditional or otherwise, may be serious obstacles to economic advance. What one is looking for is a combination of breadth of vision and effectiveness in analysis and judgment that allows discrimination, and which is not formula driven. It is not easy to educate for that, but the experience offered in the work of the World Bank could provide a more ecumenical outlook than perhaps it does. Robert McNamara himself expressed concern with what he regarded as the "somewhat extreme market ideology" in the United States (see the section "Perspectives from Within").

There is no suggestion here that high standards of education and quality of students should be abandoned in the search for a holy grail called breadth of perspective or outlook. As long as U.S. graduate schools maintain their dominance in economics, it is likely they will produce the best material for the Bank. But change in those institutions can be encouraged, and graduate students can be encouraged to think about exposure to more than one educational environment. Further, the advance of institutions in developing countries can be encouraged, as the Bank attempts to do through the Economic Development Institute. Finally, it is important for those at the Bank to be aware of and to guard against potential narrowness of perspective.

Research Publications

The World Bank's research output is voluminous, and it is beyond the scope of this chapter to attempt any detailed assessment of its quality. But the Bank has itself recently compiled some numerical indicators on quantity and quality of Bank

---

157. The suggestion of uniformity may come as a surprise to those within the Bank who see vigorous internal argument, but it is striking to those from outside who come into contact with the Bank.

output in its annual report on the Bank research program.[158] Examining Tower's 1990 compendium of development economics reading lists,[159] the Bank found that one-sixth of the reading assignments were drawn from World Bank research publications and journal articles. Readings on macroeconomic and trade topics were found to draw particularly heavily on Bank publications, and the World Development Reports appeared prominently on most of the reading lists.[160] In assessing quality, the Bank's annual report used the Social Science Citation Index to measure citations to Bank-authored journal articles relative to a baseline average for economics and business journal articles over the 1980s. It found that Bank-authored publications are cited 20 to 40 percent more often than the average article and that this was a trend that seemed to be rising in the late 1980s. On these two measures of quality, reading lists and citations, Bank publications would seem to do well.

There are a number of reasons for caution, however. One is that the Bank is such a prominent organization in development economics that citation of publications is likely to be relevant whether or not they are regarded as having high quality. Another is that the importance of the Bank's statistical database means that others frequently refer to its publications. Still another is that in their writings Bank personnel may feel an obligation to refer to publications of the Bank. Moreover, the World Development Reports constitute a special publication that is of far greater importance than anything else the Bank publishes (more than 120,000 copies are distributed each year; the *World Bank Economic Review* and the World Debt Tables trail in the distance, with 12,000 and 11,000 copies a year, respectively). And it should be kept in mind that the compendium of reading lists produced by Tower, which is very useful, was not intended to provide an unbiased sample of reading lists on development economics.

Judging quality by citation is therefore, in the context of Bank research publications as in others, to use a narrow and possibly misleading index. If academic development economists were asked to list the thirty most important books or articles on development published in the years since the Bank's research department was established—very different from the compilation of a reading list for students—we suspect that few would list many articles by Bank researchers. No doubt some of the work led by Chenery in the 1970s would be included by many, but it is not easy to cite other cases.

Notwithstanding these reservations, it is clear that in terms of readership Bank publications have a higher profile than the average publication in the economics

158. See World Bank, "Report on the World Bank Research Program," Report 10153, December 1991.

159. E. Tower, *Development Economics Reading Lists* (Durham, N.C.: Eno River Press, 1990).

160. Ibid. A breakdown of Bank publications (in the reading lists) by general subject would seem to provide some confirmation of our assessments of Bank priorities in the earlier section on agenda setting and research. Although stabilization and adjustment (with debt) head the list with 83 readings, project analysis comes at the bottom with 12.

Table 12-8. *Distribution of Bank Publications by Publication Type*

Publication type	Average number distributed[a]
World Development Reports	120,000
World Bank Economic Review	12,000
World Debt Tables	11,000
World Bank Research Observer	5,000
World Tables	5,000
Books	2,500
Facsimiles (such as discussion papers)	1,500

Source: World Bank, "Report on the World Bank Research Program," Report 10153, December 1991.

a. Average of the number of copies of a single item or category member shipped to readers since its first publication. In 1992 the two journals had circulation on the order of 15,000 each.

profession. The distribution of Bank publications by publication type is outlined in table 12-8, and a list of the Bank's best-sellers since 1980 is given in table 12-9. In looking at table 12-8, it should be borne in mind that the circulation of a specialist journal in economics might be 1,000 to 2,000, and that of a scholarly treatise might be 2,000 or so. The Bank's marketing, pricing, and translation policies deserve

Table 12-9. *World Bank Best-Sellers since 1980*

Author	Title	Year published	Copies distributed[a]
W. Baum	*Investing in Development*	1985	21,500
J. P. Gittinger	*Economic Analysis of Agricultural Projects*	1982	15,600
C. Timmer, W. Falcon, and S. Pearson	*Food Policy Analysis*	1983	15,500
J. Austin	*Agroindustrial Project Analysis*	1981	14,300
P. Streeten	*First Things First*	1981	12,000
D. J. Casley and K. Kumar	*Project Monitoring and Evaluation*	1987	11,500
R. Dornbusch and F. L. Helmers	*The Open Economy: Tools for Policymakers in Developing Countries*	1988	9,300
G. Psacharopoulos and M. Woodhall	*Education for Development: An Analysis of Investment Choices*	1985	8,800
D. J. Casley and K. Kumar	*Collection, Analysis and Use of Monitoring and Evaluation Data*	1988	7,600
G. Meier	*Pricing Policy for Development Management*	1983	6,700

Source: World Bank, "Report on the World Bank Research Program," Report 10153, December 1991.

a. Many copies of Bank books have been given away by Bank staff; the number includes both sales and complimentary copies. The number of copies distributed is shown to the nearest hundred.

congratulations, for they ensure that Bank publications do get into developing countries—which cannot be said of commercial publishers' books on development economics.

We must be less congratulatory about speed of publication at the Bank. Discussions with Bank personnel and experience with the Bank suggest that Bank production of books is slower and more cumbersome than production by commercial publishers, often to the frustration of authors. For example, it took five years from the convening of a conference for papers on that conference to appear in *The Economics of Rural Organization*,[161] the Hoff, Braverman, and Stiglitz volume, and many further embarrassing examples of delay could be cited. Such delays diminish the enthusiasm of researchers for participating in Bank activities.

The quantity of articles by World Bank staff in journals rose from around 100 in 1981 to around 170 at the end of the decade.[162] These numbers include articles by more than just the research staff, although the research staff probably accounted for 75 to 80 percent of them. It is not easy to decide how many members of the Bank staff should be classified as researchers. Roughly 3.5 percent of the Bank's administrative (nonlending) budget is devoted to research;[163] high-level staff in the Policy, Research, and Extension Affairs section number more than 600. Taken together, these numbers suggest that the Bank's research staff might number several hundred. To the Bank's formal journal publications must be added a large number of working papers that the Bank makes available. The Bank lists its publications in its publications index; in the late 1980s this was running at around 400 a year, the bulk of which were reports or papers. Many Bank documents that resemble research working papers are not published. There is no doubt that the Bank produces a great deal of research and that its reports are widely read and cited.

Reports on Bank Research

Research groups existed in the World Bank from 1946 on, under various guises (see table 12-2).[164] As discussed earlier, substantial expansion of research activities took place in 1964–65, and the Bank's reorganization of 1972, which placed research under Chenery, marked the ascent of research to prominence during the McNamara years. The Bank's research work was first externally reviewed by the General Research Advisory Panel, under Sir Arthur Lewis; the panel's report went to the Bank's Board in 1979. It contained a number of recommendations, including

161. See Hoff and others, *Economics of Rural Organization* (1993).
162. World Bank, "Report on the World Bank Research Program."
163. "Review of World Bank Programs and Fiscal Year Budgets," internal document of World Bank, 1992.
164. We have drawn here on a useful note by Dennis de Tray of September 19, 1990, "Setting Research Priorities at the World Bank: An Historical Review" (World Bank, 1990).

more active exploitation of the Bank's comparative advantage in conducting multi-country comparative studies. It also recommended more collaborative research with member countries and a more active research dissemination strategy. A second review was carried out by Assar Lindbeck in the early 1980s; his report was presented to the Board as part of the 1984 "Report on the World Bank Research Program." Lindbeck recommended a move away from what he characterized as engineering economics (that is, forecasting and planning models) toward an economics more firmly based on behavior. This was accepted within the Bank, and it has been argued that research priorities were reallocated accordingly.

The Bank prepares its own annual report on the research program for the Board each year, and Bank research projects are externally reviewed. The annual report on the World Bank research program also provides a list of research priorities for the Bank, which serve as guidelines for research managers and the research committee.

The Bank also plays an important role in stimulating the production and ex-change of ideas through its various conferences. In addition to the two conferences on debt (in 1984 and 1989) already cited, mention should be made of the more recently inaugurated annual World Bank Conference on Development Economics, launched under Stanley Fischer. These conferences play a useful role in keeping Bank personnel abreast of the activity elsewhere in development economics.

Research Resources and Strategy

It is clear that research at the World Bank is a large-scale activity involving substantial inputs and outputs. It is more directed than is the case at other aca-demic institutions, and lines of hierarchy in the Bank are much stronger than elsewhere. There are several hundred researchers in the departments at the Bank, and many others in the Bank spend a substantial part of their time on research. In a big economics department like that at the London School of Economics (with a teaching staff of fifty), five people might spend part of their time on research in development economics, and even these five would also teach development economics and other subjects, do research on other subjects, and do administration. In universities research support would not, on average, be superior to that at the Bank. Hence the resources devoted to research on development economics at the Bank are huge by academic standards, even allowing for the fact that researchers at the Bank, like academics, have substantial nonresearch commitments. It is thus important to the profession, as well as to the Bank, to ask about the allocation and quality of these resources at the Bank.

In examining the quality of the Bank's research resources, it must be recognized that the Bank does not hire the best academics. It does indeed hire graduate students from the likes of MIT, the University of Chicago, and the London School of Economics, but our general impression (we cannot provide statistical evidence) is that those hired are not among the top graduating students. It is also rare for anyone to be hired away from the Bank to join the faculty of a top-rated university. There are exceptions to both of these statements, of course, but we believe that they are fair assessments. In that regard, it is interesting to find the following remarks by Edward Mason in a letter to George Woods (then World Bank president) dated December 16, 1964: "The Bank is not getting top quality candidates from leading graduate schools in the United States. . . . Economists in the Bank for the most part quickly lose contact with and standing in the profession."[165] The situation has probably improved since then, but we suspect that the problem remains, albeit to a lesser extent.

The reasons for the best graduate students going into non-Bank activities lie partly on the demand side and partly on the supply side. The Bank, when it recruits at the young professional level, looks for a whole mix of talents, not only superior academic performance. The very best graduate students look either for an academic career, to which they would attach special satisfaction, or perhaps for employment more lucrative than that at the Bank.

The Bank nevertheless has a long history of attracting good academics as consultants, or on secondment, for short periods. Many or most of the best development economists over the last twenty or more years will have had links of this kind with the Bank at some stage. Such an internal-external arrangement may well constitute an appropriate organizational strategy, but it does leave open the question of whether the Bank has got the balance right.

At the Bank limitations on staff quality are compounded by the understandable constraints associated with research in an operations-oriented institution. Researchers are not free to follow intellectual inspiration. They are under constraints of designated priorities and of an apparent need to be immediately useful to operations. Further, there is the strong hierarchy and an atmosphere much more deferential than would be found in universities. Among researchers there is considerable concern with what superiors will think of conclusions reached, to the occasional detriment of concentration on whether an analysis is sound.

We are not well positioned to compare research at the World Bank with that in private operations-oriented institutions, but a note from the late 1970s by Douglass Carmichael may be pertinent.[166] Carmichael argued that in firms in innovation-intensive industries, research and development (R&D) is seen as a major policy-making part of the institution, with a correspondingly high status, and that an industry's R&D section is partly staffed by entrepreneurs who are closely related to practical application of the firm's products. The section is organized internally in such a way that there is a maximum of collegial relations and open, frank discussions; managers are coworkers rather than headmasters. Carmichael described a

165. We are grateful to Ben King for calling this letter to our attention.
166. We are grateful to Devesh Kapur for conveying this internal note to us.

sense of fun and inquiry in these research and development institutions that can be recognized in university life, but which does not, according to our impressions, so often appear in research at the Bank.[167]

The research activities of the Bank might be compared with those of the much smaller research department at the International Monetary Fund. As noted earlier, even though research at the IMF has a fairly low profile, the Fund has had a research department since its inception. And the Fund's research had a leading role to play in one of the most important developments in macroeconomics since the Second World War—the monetary approach to the balance of payments. Jagdish Bhagwati, in the Radhakrishnan lectures at Oxford University in 1992, reflected on the research role of the Bank and the Fund, observing that the World Bank and the IMF "are distinguished for the absorption and diffusion of new and important ideas rather than for their creation. This is, of course, as it should be. The universities are naturally the major source of innovation in economics. The evolution of the monetarist approach to the balance of payments by Jacques Polak, and the influential theoretical work by Marcus Fleming and Robert Mundell, at the IMF nearly a quarter-century ago, are among the exceptions that underline this rule."[168] This perception of the Bank's role in intellectual history is one that many, including ourselves, would share, but Robert McNamara probably had greater ambitions in mind when he restructured the research department at the Bank in 1972.[169]

What should be concluded from these observations? There is the possibility that the Bank has not organized its research in a way that allows it to be as effective as it might be. One possible alternative strategy, which has been discussed from time to time within the Bank, would be to have a smaller high-quality research staff and to contract out more research. A case can even be made for going beyond contracted research to the use of some Bank research funds to establish a research foundation that would receive research applications from outside the Bank. We would guess that the output from, say, U.S. National Science Foundation research grants would be very much higher than the output to be expected from a Bank researcher. Another possible strategy, as planned by McNamara toward the end of his term as Bank president, would be a concerted attempt to get many of the very best people to the Bank for an intense and high-powered research assault on the problems of development.

It is not our purpose to recommend any of these strategies. Care must be taken not to discuss them in the abstract sense of "what makes a good research outfit."

167. This view has been challenged by a number of participants in the Bank's research activities, who would argue that we have missed or underplayed much of the excitement in Bank research.

168. J. R. Bhagwati, *India in Transition: Freeing the Economy* (Oxford University Press, 1993), p. 69.

169. Some within the Bank have suggested to us that the Bank has produced much more high-quality research than other UN agencies. Although this may seem plausible, an assessment would take us far beyond the scope of this chapter.

The World Bank does have distinctive comparative advantages, and its research strategy should be designed to build on them. These advantages lie to a great extent in the characteristics of the Bank's operational activities, so whatever strategy is adopted, if it is to exploit these advantages, must be closely knit into operations. That is consistent, however, with devoting an important part of research activities to fundamental issues. Basic research in development economics should not be divorced from experience, examples, and policy.

Perceptions from Within

This section reports on perceptions of the Bank as expressed in interviews conducted by Nicholas Stern in the period from December 1990 to September 1992 with more than thirty key figures in the Bank's intellectual life over the past fifty years. (The account of the interviews and the interpretation of them are Stern's own, as are comments in the first person.) Interviews were held with all the Bank vice presidents who have had responsibility for research, all three senior vice presidents in office in 1991, and Robert McNamara. All except McNamara were economists. This selection was based in part on the identification of the important figures in Bank intellectual life, but also in part on Stern's personal acquaintance with key figures; in addition, advantage was taken of opportunities for interviews that happened to arise. Formal interviews were conducted with the following persons on the dates given:

Shankar Acharya	May 16, 1991	Deepak Lal	May 7, June 7, 1991
Bilsel Alisbah	May 15, 1991	Michael Lipton	January 8, 1991
Bernard Bell	June 3, 1992	Robert McNamara	February 14, 1992
Clive Bell	February 17, 1992	I. G. Patel	May 9, 1991
Hollis Chenery	May 13, 1991	Guy Pfeffermann	May 16, 1991
Armeane Choksi	May 15, 1991	Stanley Please	December 18, 1990
Richard Eckaus	May 13, 1991	Graham Pyatt	February 21, 1991
Stanley Fischer	May 15, 1991	Moeen Qureshi	May 17, 1991
David Hopper	May 17, 1991	Lyn Squire	October 2, 1991
Shahid Husain	May 14, 1991	Ernest Stern	February 14, June 3, 1992
Greg Ingram	May 17, 1991	Ardy Stoutjesdijk	May 14, 1991
DeAnne Julius	July 12, 1991	Vito Tanzi	May 15, 1991
Basil Kavalsky	May 14, 1991	Wilfried Thalwitz	May 16, 1991
Benjamin King	May 17, 1991	Herman van der Tak	May 15, 1991
Timothy King	May 16, 1991	Bevan Waide	December 18, 1990
Anne Krueger	November 20, 1991		

A number of less formal interviews, as well as guidance, were provided by Montek Singh Ahluwalia, Angus Deaton, Dennis de Tray, David Henderson, Robert Laslett, Johannes Linn, Manmohan Singh, Richard Stern, and Lawrence Summers.

The formal interviews were generally about an hour in length and were fairly unstructured. A number of topics recurred in many interviews, and there were clearly some differences of opinion, as would be expected among this number of economists. Nevertheless, there was considerable concordance of views on many subjects. In the account that follows I distill my own perception of the picture that arises from these interviews, referring only occasionally to the comments of particular individuals. The report is organized around the topics that occurred most frequently; not surprisingly, many are the topics that have been the focus of this chapter. I had wished to interview Bela Balassa as well, but he died after a long illness in early 1991. I give some reflections on his contribution at the Bank and elsewhere, based on his writings and discussions with others.

Given the importance of Robert McNamara in the history of the Bank and my perceptions of his role, an account of my interview with him is treated in a discrete subsection. Most of the interviews are not so treated, although there are subsections on the interview with Bernard Bell on the Bank's role in, and his view of, economywide policymaking.

On the Intellectual Contribution of the Bank

Very few of the interviewees saw the Bank as having a major role in intellectual leadership in the economics profession. Many, however, saw that the Bank fulfilled an important role in distilling the more useful ideas and concepts in the profession into a form that could be useful for policymakers. There was a general feeling that policy at the Bank had to proceed whether or not detailed and sound intellectual analysis of the problem at hand was available. On the other hand, it was also felt that the Bank should not rush to follow intellectual developments before they had been properly digested. Many stressed the importance of policy dialogue in shaping the views of policymakers in borrowing countries, and the importance of the Bank's contribution in leading intellectual discussion among development agencies.

On the Environment for Research

Finding the right environment for research in the Bank would involve a balance among the three competing pulls: a sense of direction, tolerance and encouragement of ideas, and the demands of operations. A number of those interviewed regarded that balance as almost impossible to provide in any satisfactory way. Many from operations saw researchers as luxuriating in self-indulgent independence unless sharply checked, and being of tangential importance to the Bank. Many from research and from operations saw the research side as having only marginal influence on what the Bank actually did. The operational pressures for loan pushing were seen as intense and too powerful for research to challenge (although Anne

Krueger did emphasize the potential for influence of the chief economist in the loan committee). However, examples were offered by interviewees of shifts in strategy that arose from initiatives that came, at least in part, from the research side. One of these was the change in the profile of poverty in the mid-1970s.

Different periods at the Bank were seen quite differently. In the 1950s and most of the 1960s, before there was any substantial research, research did not have a high profile. Nevertheless, those twenty years were not viewed as a blank period from the intellectual point of view. Discussions of projects versus plans, pricing, cost-benefit analysis, and other subjects, for example, were fairly vigorous at that time, and many research papers were produced within the Economics Department. The 1970s were seen as a period of some excitement on the research front. Many spoke of Chenery's tolerance and encouragement of others while at the same time plowing his own particular furrow. His close relationship with McNamara meant that ideas could get to the top. McNamara's use of his annual speech to the Bank's governors, and his use of the research side of the Bank in working up the draft of the speech, were seen as genuine avenues for influence. However, there was also a feeling that toward the end of the 1970s it was running out of steam, and that the particular kind of economics that was being pursued, with its emphasis on input-output and planning models, had probably yielded most of the insights that it could at that time.

The early 1980s was considered to be full of the excitement of structural adjustment, but it was not here that the research side of the Bank was seen to lead the way. A switch of interest toward markets and prices was welcomed by many. However, some spoke of a decline in the research atmosphere, of a degree of intolerance, and of a requirement to toe the "party line." Others saw a rescue from intellectual tiredness and dead ends.

Projects, Policies, and Planning

It would seem that lively discussion of projects and the policy environment, and the role of the state in that policy environment, have been a feature of the Bank throughout its history. It would be wrong to picture the Bank as an institution focused only on projects before the arrival of McNamara. Those interviewees who were active in the pre-McNamara years stressed strongly that the policy environment had always been an issue. The economywide approach was indicated particularly by Bernard Bell's visit to India in the early 1960s, which was cited many times as an example. Interest in the policy environment rose through the 1950s and 1960s, associated in part with the rise of the economists in the Bank, relative to the engineers. Many saw the dominance of the economists as being essentially established by the late 1960s.

The emphasis on infrastructure of the Bank's early years required some overall view of an economy, because activities concerning transport and ports cannot be seen in isolation from other sectors. That is not to embrace economywide planning, however. Many interviewees stressed the Bank's involvement with planning in India, the importance of India in the Bank's thinking, and its eventual disillusionment with large-scale government intervention. It was argued by some that the early attractiveness of economic planning was a perception shared by the Bank's Board, among others. Wilfried Thalwitz even cited the example of a Kennedy administration response to a request for the U.S. view of a lending program for Peru: "If they have a five-year plan, then that's OK" was the apparent reply. Thalwitz also cited the Bank's Colombia report of 1959 and its India Report of 1964 as examples of the prominence of the economywide approach (including important elements of planning) in the Bank in the late 1950s and early 1960s.

Under McNamara it was clear that the economywide view was still present and that government planning was still seen as important. The importance of the market was recognized throughout the McNamara years, but it is probably fair to say that the Bank was not seen as a leader in the general movement away from planning that took place in the academic profession and in some agencies and governments in the 1970s.

THE BELL MISSION TO INDIA. Given the importance attached by many Bank figures to Bernard Bell's mission to India, it is pertinent to give his account of the mission as he related it in his interview. George Woods, then president of the World Bank, had asked Bell in mid-1964 to lead a major study on India in connection with an aid consortium headed by the Bank. A number of members of the consortium were becoming negatively disposed to further aid. The Indian Ministry of Finance had agreed to a mission to India as part of the study, on the understanding that the mission's reports would be for the Bank president and the Indian Ministry of Finance only. Woods, who evidently had a poor view of Bank employees, told Bell not to include on his team anyone from "the lousy Bank staff," as Woods, according to Bell, referred to them. However, Bell did include on his team some younger staff members whom Woods did not know and to whom he did not object. Work for the study took from five to six months, and the study was completed by May or June 1965. The result was a fourteen-volume report, with different volumes contributed by different participants and a summary volume by Bell.

The study on India did not focus on the issue of economic planning versus nonplanning. But it did recommend the elimination of many bureaucratic regulatory devices in both industry and agriculture. In so doing, it had in Bell's view run into opposition from the Indian upper castes and cadres who, as he interpreted it, had joined with the British colonial service in taking the arrogant view that they knew better than any alternative group or mechanisms where scarce resources should be allocated. The mission also took a fairly comprehensive economywide view, and in so doing constituted a major and influential landmark for the Bank. Like the Indian economy, the mission had a strong focus on agriculture, and Bell emphasized the importance and quality of the report's agricultural volumes written by Sir John Crawford and David Hopper.

The mission also recommended currency devaluation, and the Ministry of Finance objected strongly that devaluation might be regarded as failure. The Indian press mounted a personalized campaign against both Woods ("a Wall Street tycoon") and Bell (one headline reading "To Hell with Bell"). When the devaluation came in 1966 it was not only seen by those close to the government of Prime Minister Indira Gandhi as a defeat but as a result of World Bank pressure.[170]

BELL'S WORK IN INDONESIA. In the interview, Bell also emphasized the importance of his work and that of the Bank in Indonesia. Under pressure from McNamara to accept the job, following a request from the Indonesian planning minister relayed through Bell, Bell went to Indonesia to set up the World Bank resident office in Jakarta. Bell had had considerable experience in Indonesia in the early 1960s through a U.S. Agency for International Development program. The years after September 1968 saw a major and influential relationship between the Bank and Indonesian economic ministers, which had the strong support of President Suharto (who had come to power in 1966). Bell stayed in Indonesia until October 1972. The turnaround and subsequent impressive performance of the Indonesian economy can be linked to the 1968–72 period and is an example of where the Bank's influence, intellectual and otherwise, has been of great importance. Bell argued that the Bank has never had that kind of influence on Indian economic policy.

On Structural Adjustment and Debt

The Bank was generally agreed by interviewees to be a leader on structural adjustment, but there was recognition that this leadership was brought on by events and by the operations side, rather than the research side, of the Bank. McNamara was seen as a leader in some aspects of structural adjustment, although not in regard to the liberalization of the supply side, which came to be a prominent feature of the Bank in the later 1980s.

There was also fairly universal agreement that the Bank had been slow to respond to the debt issue. Some saw this as a result of pressure from the United States and U.S. fear of undermining its own banks.

On Poverty and Human Development

Many saw the Bank as being a leader on issues of poverty in the 1970s and were proud that the Bank had raised the human development issues that were stressed then. Although it was recognized that these were ideas that had not originated in the Bank, some leadership role for the Bank was seen among development agencies and through publications such as the 1974 book *Redistribution with Growth*, by Chenery and his coauthors.

170. See R. Thapar, *All These Years* (New Delhi: Seminar Publications, 1991), pp. 262–63.

On CGIAR

A number of interviewees mentioned the importance of the Bank in the development of the Consultative Group on International Agricultural Research (CGIAR). Although the initial impetus came from the Rockefeller and Ford foundations, the group has had substantial leadership from the World Bank. CGIAR (and hence the Bank) was perceived as playing a major role in the green revolution and in the expansion of agricultural technology in food production throughout the world. Mentioned with pride were the international research centers that have been involved in developing new agricultural technology and, in particular, new seeds (for example, CIMMYT in Mexico and IRRI in the Philippines, whose work on wheat and rice has been of fundamental importance). The Bank has been the coordinator of the funding for CGIAR, which provides umbrella funding for the group. Its role in supporting CGIAR was generally seen as a major intellectual contribution.

On World Development Reports

Those from both the operations and the research sides of the Bank underscored the importance of the World Development Reports. This is one publication from the research side that appears to be embraced warmly in all corners of the Bank, and it is clearly one of the few that is read by the rest of the Bank. Although the quality of the reports was seen to be variable, the average standard was perceived to be high, and generally there was some satisfaction in its centrality on the development stage.

On Bela Balassa

Bela Balassa was associated with the World Bank for twenty-five years, from the time he joined as a consultant to the Economics Department in 1966. For most of the period he was part-time with the Bank and part-time with Johns Hopkins University. His preferences were for, and his expertise was in, a subject and style that was rather different from the input-output modeling that dominated the Bank during many of the Chenery years. His emphasis was always on prices and trade and the damaging effects, both static and dynamic, of distorting either.

It is an example of Chenery's openness and encouragement of different ideas that Balassa was seen as a valued adviser and given scope to develop and present his ideas within the Bank. It is striking, however, that during the McNamara-Chenery years Balassa's perceptions and priorities were not predominant either in Bank research or its policy pronouncements. His basic ideas came to be mainstream in the Bank only in the 1980s, more than fifteen years after he joined, notwithstanding his consistency and articulateness in expressing them.

His work was voluminous, but many of his main themes are captured in his two books (both with collaborators), *The Structure of Protection in Developing Coun-*

tries of 1971 *and Development Strategies in Semi-Industrial Economies* of 1982.[171] In the first of these volumes, early calculations of effective rates of protection were provided for a number of developing countries in Latin America and Asia. Balassa charted how the rates had often grown in a haphazard way as a result of permissive responses to pressures. He laid great emphasis on the dynamic costs of restrictions of trade, markets, and competition. He recognized clearly his contemporaries who were writing in the same vein and repeatedly referred to the work of Harberger, Johnson, Bhagwati, and Little, Scitovsky, and Scott, among others.[172]

Balassa was an early participant in what Little (1981) called the "neoclassical resurgence" and was one of the earliest advocates in the Bank of outward orientation in trade. He did not, however, advocate unfettered free markets. He was behind the view that manufacturing industries generate significant positive externalities that justify permanent government incentives, and he saw budgetary pressures as often entailing tariffs rather than (first-best) subsidies to promote manufacturing. He observed that "one may argue that manufacturing offers some advantages over primary production in the form of labor training and in encouraging the expansion of related industries that do not enter into the profit calculations of the firm, but benefit the national economy."[173] However, he saw considerable difficulty in quantifying these benefits and argued for homogeneous rates within the manufacturing sector, warning repeatedly against tailor-made protection for specific firms. As an order of magnitude he suggested "effective protection rates on manufactured activities in excess of about 10% impose costs that are not commensurate with the expected benefits."[174] It is interesting that these "virtues of manufacturing," argued in the 1960s by Kaldor and others, have reemerged with the popularity of human capital approaches to growth theory in the late 1980s and early 1990s.

Balassa also acknowledged the possible justification of extra temporary protection when learning is important, and embraced in addition the optimal tariff argument, suggesting that, in the context of export taxes, "to maximize welfare the marginal revenue from exports must be equated to the long-run marginal cost of the industry, with allowance for the use of exhaustible resources in exporting."[175]

171. B. Balassa, *The Structure of Protection in Developing Countries* (Johns Hopkins University Press, 1971); B. Balassa, *Development Strategies in Semi-Industrial Economies* (Johns Hopkins University Press, 1982).

172. See A. C. Harberger, "Using Resources at Hand More Effectively," *American Economic Review* (*Papers and Proceedings*, May 1958), pp. 134–55; H. G. Johnson, "Optimal Trade Intervention in the Presence of Domestic Distortions," in R. E. Baldwin and others, eds., *Trade, Growth and the Balance of Payments: Essays in Honor of Gottfried Harbeler* (Amsterdam: North-Holland, 1965), pp. 3–35; J. N. Bhagwati, "The Theory and Practice of Commercial Policy: Departures from Unified Exchange Rates," Special Papers in International Economics 8 (Princeton University International Finance Section, January 1968); and Little and others, *Industry and Trade*.

173. Balassa, *Structure of Protection*, pp. 95–96.

174. Balassa, *Development Strategies*, p. 69.

175. Ibid., p. 66.

Generally, Balassa's 1982 volume reflects many of the same themes as the 1971 volume, but focuses further on both factor markets and the problems of sequencing and pacing a transition. He stressed themes that would come to dominate the profession in the 1980s in discussions of the supply side and structural adjustment. He saw a need for a gradual approach to tariff reduction, because, he argues, rigidities in factor markets might threaten entire sectors under very sharp movements in effective protective rates. Here again he shows himself a number of years ahead of the bulk of the profession. The esteem in which he was held, at the Bank and elsewhere, is apparent in the 1991 collection of essays in his honor, edited by Jaime de Melo and André Sapir, on subjects in trade theory and economic reform.[176]

On Robert McNamara

The McNamara years are seen by many in the World Bank as its great epoch and a time of intellectual excitement. Nevertheless, some exhaustion seems to have been evident at the Bank at the end of thirteen years of his high energy. McNamara was universally seen as a man open to ideas. On the other hand, his numerical and programming approach to management and analysis was seen as diverting by some and as leading to spurious manipulation of data within the Bank. McNamara's independence from the United States was also much admired and valued. Many compared him favorably in this respect with his successors. But many argued as well that U.S. hostility to international institutions in general, and to the Bank in particular, had reached levels in the late 1970s and early 1980s that required close attention.

McNamara was seen as a manager who worked through targets. The targets of particular importance were the lending programs. As a result, it was argued by some, the loan officers were seen as the vanguard and loans were pumped out with inadequate regard for quality. Some of those with whom he did not get on described McNamara as a person who classified people as "useful" and "unuseful," and who ignored the latter (including, it was suggested, his chief economic adviser before Chenery). McNamara's dominance made many afraid to speak up, leading some to argue that at least some discussions at the Bank during the McNamara years were stultified.

The Interview with Robert McNamara

McNamara saw his first ninety days as president of the World Bank as the period when he established his view that the Bank's role should change from being an institution for infrastructural project lending to being a development agency. This change he saw as both basic and necessary. He argued that the academic profession

176. See de Melo and Sapir, eds., *Trade Theory and Economic Reform.*

could not then provide theories and tools that could be directly applied to solving the problems he perceived, so the Bank had to work out much for itself. He felt, and feels, strongly that a broad view of human development is fundamental, emphasizing in particular education and health. Both his strength of feeling and his predilection for quantification came through in his discussion of the basic human right to health. In that regard, China and Cuba were way ahead of many developing countries; one could show, as a measure of deprivation of human rights, that the infant mortality rate in the black community in the Washington, D.C., area was much higher than that in Cuba. Although human rights had many dimensions, it was crucial to recognize the achievements of some countries, in particular China, as regards health. McNamara also compared China favorably with Pakistan in terms of literacy, arguing that Pakistan's position on female literacy, for example, was poor.

Although McNamara saw his presidency as having achieved major advances in emphasizing health and education, he thought now that he had not gone far enough. He felt he should have stressed more the importance of political, human, and economic structures in the process of development. For example, he cited the work of the Bank in connection with lending to Zaire, which he saw as probably wasted because the political, economic, and human environment to use the funds was not present. He was also skeptical as to whether the appropriate environment exists now in the former Soviet republics. He suggested that the academic economics profession has had a poor understanding of the economics of transition. And he argued that Deng Xiaoping and the Chinese had "got it right" in the sense that first one should go for liberalization of agriculture and then of industry, and that economic transformation should proceed before political reform. He was proud of his introduction of China into the World Bank.

McNamara stressed that his sources of ideas were the people around him within the Bank, as well as his extensive intellectual contacts outside. Among those within the Bank he pointed particularly to Hollis Chenery, Mahbub ul Haq, Shahid Husain, and Ernest Stern. Outside the Bank he drew on his many friendships in the academic world, including those of David Bell, Edward Mason, and Barbara Ward, among others. He made every effort to be open and to be in contact with people from many different backgrounds. He was interested in the best and the brightest from wherever they came.

McNamara regarded his rejection of trickle-down economics and his emphasis on the problems of absolutely poor people as of paramount importance and also as revolutionary. He was convinced that investing in poor people could have very high returns although, for such investment to be fruitful, some social infrastructure was necessary. Such infrastructure was probably absent in Sub-Saharan Africa; in this suggestion McNamara reflected the governance theme of the Bank's Africa reports of the late 1980s.

He rejected any notion that markets and price mechanisms had been given insufficient attention under his leadership, arguing that he had been in charge of a major private sector company and did not need lessons on the importance of the price mechanism. He was concerned with the problems of making economies work. He tried, for example, to move President Anwar Sadat away from providing food subsidies in Egypt, but was hindered by political problems, which were severe (the IMF wanted to proceed more quickly than did McNamara). The problems as he saw them were those of transition—how to move from one system to another. Emphasizing again that he did not need education in the market, he stressed that the question was how to introduce the price mechanism and competitive markets without destroying order. In this respect he regarded the United States as having a somewhat extreme market ideology and as often showing little understanding of the problems facing developing countries.

In McNamara's thirteen years at the Bank the United States was frequently late in agreeing and contributing to replenishment of International Development Association funds, and many times he had to shame the country into it. McNamara emphasized that the United States had had little influence on the Bank during his leadership there, and he felt that such influence would have been negative had he allowed it to be exercised. He cited as an example attempts by the U.S. secretary of state to take loans to India off the agenda of the Bank's Board at a time when the United States was particularly interested in cultivating relationships with Pakistan. McNamara challenged the secretary on this and won the votes of the Board. He cited as another example the occasion in the late 1970s when the U.S. administration had tried to prevent him from going to Beijing to negotiate the entry of China into the World Bank. In all his thirteen years at the Bank McNamara had only once entered a U.S. embassy.

As a further example of his intellectual leadership, McNamara cited his 1980 speech on structural adjustment, which was about lending for transition. He had started to raise these issues with the Board in the late 1970s. He stressed the importance of his speeches to the Board in setting the Bank's agenda and prepared for these speeches in the preceding months. He saw his 1973 Nairobi speech on poverty as particularly significant. Toward the end of the 1970s McNamara was working on the idea of institutionalizing the intellectual leadership of the Bank; he wanted to make the 1980s years of stronger intellectual advance. He had thought of establishing a subsidiary of the Bank, financed by the Bank, to buy brains and thinking power for problem solving and understanding economic development. At that time he envisioned a budget of $50 million a year, with $100,000 allocated for each brain (including support services), and a total of five hundred brains.

Commentary by Nicholas Stern

Much of the perspective gained from the interviews is embodied in my own summary of them. I should stress that I have quoted little verbatim and that my summary may betray a greater concordance of view than was in fact present. I did

gain a strong impression of very able people dedicated to the cause of development. There was little in the way of intellectual pretentiousness (in this regard the
interviewees compared favorably with academics) and great concern to apply ideas
in a sensible way. There is no doubt that many found the Bank frustrating in the
intellectual sense, and many raised serious doubts about its ability in the past, apart
from a few short periods, to provide the best atmosphere for serious research.

Although the Bank has not been consistently an intellectual leader in originating
ideas, there have been periods—the early McNamara years with the focus on
human development and the early 1980s with the focus on structural adjustment—
when it was at the intellectual forefront. There can be little doubt about the
importance of McNamara's personality and energy in the Bank's history. At the
same time, it must be recognized that important intellectual contributions were
made at the Bank both before and after McNamara, and that the development of a
fairly balanced consensus (as embodied, for example, in the World Development
Report of 1991) was to a substantial extent distilled after, rather than during, his
tenure. Nevertheless, it was clearly in the McNamara period that the Bank came to
realize its role as a development agency and took a wider view of economic
development. That breadth of vision, which was to some extent lost in the early
1980s, now appears to be in the process of restoration.

Conclusions

Like other chapters in this volume, this chapter about the World Bank's relationship with the world of ideas, primarily those of development economics, has
presented a view of the Bank from outside, in this case from academic life. This
does not mean that we have seen the Bank's relations with ideas, or its role as
intellectual actor, in terms of the production of scholarly books or articles alone; we
have emphasized its roles in setting agendas and in policy dialogue, for example. In
accordance with the view from outside we have not investigated in detail the crucial
activities of the research department in its interactions with the operations departments. Thus our subject matter has included much from outside the research
department and excludes much from within it.

The focus has been on the past twenty-five years, although the account has often
gone back further. This is for three reasons: the rise of the economists dates from
the late 1960s, the research department was restructured in 1972, and the Mason-
Asher history covers the earlier period. Our research method has been a mixture of
a number of things. First, since this is about intellectual activities, we have used the
literature itself. Second, we have used a series of interviews with key participants;
third, we have drawn on Stern's own interactions with the Bank, which have
covered the last twenty years. The upshot is part history, part reportage, and part
evaluation.

The World Bank has occupied a central position in the study of the economics of development. One reason for this is that its influence on the policy choices of developing countries through its lending programs has led academics and others to examine the Bank's behavior as a subject of interest in its own right. A second reason is that the combined weight of numbers of economists engaged in, and funds allocated for, the analysis of economic development at the Bank means that it cannot be other than a major player.

As an agenda setter, the Bank clearly was a leader in structural adjustment in the 1980s. This came about in part from McNamara's emphasis on the subject in the last years of his presidency, but more particularly from the beginnings of structural adjustment loans themselves. The study of structural adjustment both inside and outside the Bank largely followed the Bank's operational actions. These started with an emphasis on the macroeconomic demand side and the requirement for shifts in the balance of payments, but soon came to include the now familiar stress on freeing the supply side of the economy through price liberalization, privatization, tax and expenditure reforms, and the like. The Bank also moved to the forefront on poverty and human development in the early years of McNamara's presidency. In these areas it was less clearly a leader because it was picking up threads that were prominent outside the Bank, but it did join the vanguard with great vigor. The Bank has also made serious contributions to research on economic development on a number of other fronts, including its work on comparative economic growth under Chenery; on China in the 1980s; on agriculture, urban affairs, and transport; and on poverty and income distribution.

We have argued that in other aspects of the Bank's work its contribution has been rather small and that it had been slow in reacting to some world events and to some ideas. Of particular importance, it was slow to recognize the debt crisis of the 1980s and to assimilate academic and other contributions to resolving the crisis.

In some of its intellectual activities the Bank has shown a comparative advantage—particularly those that require an examination of an economy as a whole and that can usefully draw on comparative experience, and those that require collective expertise of people with microeconomic, sectoral, macroeconomic, and country knowledge that can be applied to solving pressing practical problems. Some of these advantages are manifest in the World Development Reports, which have been of great value in distilling and disseminating knowledge of particular important areas in development economics. Use of the statistics in the reports has been so extensive in the profession that a great responsibility is associated with their production and presentation—a responsibility which, in our judgment, requires greater care, caution, and qualification than has generally been shown.

An important part of the Bank's intellectual contribution has been its leadership in policy dialogue with governments and among development agencies, as demonstrated through its country papers, project loans, and the Economic Development Institute. Thus it has made other decision makers more strongly aware of the contributions of economic analysis and has added analytical rigor to policy discussions that might otherwise have been less well informed and argued.

The Bank can now be viewed as having joined in a fairly broad consensus on development. That consensus sees the state as an important actor in human development and infrastructure, in social protection, and in the promotion and regulation of the market; but it does not see the state as a major producer in sectors outside the infrastructure, and it argues for keeping down bureaucratic intervention (through such forms as licenses and quotas) in the production process. The World Bank's arrival at participating in this consensus has been in some respects slower than that of the rest of the profession,[177] but the Bank has played an important part in promulgating the consensus to policymakers.

Clearly the Bank has made an effort over the years to learn from experience, but it does give the appearance from time to time of reacting too slowly and too strongly. Thus, for example, on the research side, the Bank is seen as retaining a commitment to input-output modeling rather longer than those outside the Bank, but then indulging, in the early 1980s, in perhaps an excessive rejection of state activity in its single-minded pursuit of getting the prices right. In the process some emphasis on human development and poverty was lost, although the balance was somewhat restored toward the end of the 1980s.

The process of change within the World Bank has been more spasmodic and episodic than in the profession outside, notwithstanding that the profession itself has displayed some immaturity in swinging back and forth in its enthusiasms. However, the Bank has often had to react to events in a less leisurely manner than have academics. Although responsibility for any action might understandably lead to caution, it could, in principle, require a decisiveness that gives the impression of sharp change. And occasionally pressures build up within the Bank (such as those associated with the emergence of program lending) which, combined with changing events outside the Bank (such as the oil price increases of the 1970s and the debt crisis of the early 1980s), lead to a decision that looks like an abrupt change of course. It must also be recognized that the "profession" represents a kind of average of observations, whereas the Bank represents but one observation (albeit a large one) that, in a crude statistical sense, can be expected to show more variance.

Some of the irregularity of change at the Bank may have arisen from the changing presidencies of the Bank and of its vice presidencies for research. There have been problems with continuity. The strong leadership of McNamara and much of the research work under Chenery was associated with a target-oriented, input-output, problem-solving approach. The research atmosphere was enthusiastic and ecumenical, however. Further, much of Chenery's own work on compara-

---

177. See N. H. Stern, "The Economics of Development: A Survey," *Economic Journal*, vol. 99 (1989), pp. 597–685, for a discussion of the state of development economics. It should be noted that the Bank's commitment to social protection can often seem less than wholehearted.

tive development was distinct from this problem-solving perspective. The end of the McNamara era coincided with the aftermath of the second oil price increase, the beginning of structural adjustment, and the debt crisis. The Bank was pitched into a leadership role just at the moment when its strongest leader departed as president.

Following the departure of McNamara and Chenery, research was under some threat, but it did survive. Under Anne Krueger the more "engineering" approach to economics was overtaken by an emphasis on smaller government and better price signals. Some have argued that at the same time the research atmosphere became less tolerant and the concern with poverty less marked. The status of research under the Bank presidents of the 1980s was never what it had been in the 1970s. In the second half of the 1980s the survival of the research activities and the change of leadership led to a calmer environment, although the research side continued to experience some problems of uncertainty associated with the two short vice presidencies of Stanley Fischer and Lawrence Summers.

As we suggested in our discussions of structural adjustment and policy dialogue, the Bank's operational side has occasionally played a major intellectual role in setting agendas, but its predominant role has been more continuously its interaction with policymakers and other agencies. That is not a role that arises in isolation from the research departments. The ideas, and indeed the personnel, involved in these interchanges are often rooted in Bank research. As we have noted, it has not been our central concern to examine the research-operations links within the Bank.

In concluding our discussion of the intellectual role of the World Bank, or the Bank as intellectual actor, it must be recognized that the Bank has rarely seen itself as primarily an intellectual or academic institution. It sees its job as promoting development. It can use and disseminate ideas and encourage an analytical approach in carrying out its task, but the generation of research ideas is not, in itself, its first priority. We would argue, however, that the Bank cannot put responsibility for the development of ideas entirely outside its boundaries. It should discharge this responsibility in a direct and creative way. This it has often tried to do, with some success, but after more than twenty years with a research establishment its role as an intellectual creator has been a modest one. In taking due account of the World Bank's objectives, internal structures, and external pressures, we cannot suppress the feeling that rather more might have been achieved.

THIRTEEN

Greening the Bank:
The Struggle over the
Environment, 1970–1995

Robert Wade

NO OTHER field of Bank operations has grown as fast as its environmental activities. Starting with just five environmental specialists in the mid-1980s, the Bank employed three hundred a decade later, complete with a vice presidency for "environmentally sustainable development."[1] In the same period the budgetary resources devoted to explicitly designated environmental work (including project preparation and research) grew at 90 percent a year from a very low base, while agriculture and forestry resources shrank at 1 percent a year from a high base. Before 1987 project officers had wide discretion as to how much attention they paid to environmental aspects of their projects, and the Bank's work on countrywide policies made only occasional reference to environmental problems. After 1987, the Bank established

This chapter draws on nine months of fieldwork inside the Bank between late 1994 and mid-1996 and also on my experience as a World Bank economist in 1984–88. The research was financed by grants from the Ford Foundation, the U.K. Overseas Development Administration, the U.K. Economic and Social Research Council's "Global Institutions" program, and the Brookings Institution. I am grateful to Frances Korten, David Stanton, and David Vines for help with the financing; to Devesh Kapur, Maritta Koch-Weser, Heidi Silver, and John Briscoe for help with administrative arrangements inside the Bank; and to the Institute of Development Studies, Sussex University, and Brown University for research support. Among the more than one hundred people interviewed, I am especially indebted to Devesh Kapur, Barbara Bramble, John Briscoe, Cindy Collins, Herman Daly, Jonathan Fox, Maritta Koch-Weser, Antonia Macedo, Jane Pratt, Bruce Rich, Jeremy Warford, and to several more Bank staff who wish to remain anonymous.

1. World Bank, *The World Bank Group and the Environment, Fiscal 1994: Making Development Sustainable*, 1994, p. 157.

Table 13-1. *Indicators of the Bank's Environmental Work, 1975–95*

Indicator	1975	1980	1985	1990	1995
Staff	2	3	5	106[a] (270)[c]	162[b] (300)[d]
Lending (U.S.$ millions)[e]	n.s.	n.s.	15	180	990
Bank reports[f]					
Environment	13	46	57	196	408
Poverty	16	57	16	95	210
Total	635	968	1,238	1,593	1,760

a. Higher-level staff of Environment Department plus four REDs. World Bank, *The World Bank and the Environment* (World Bank, 1991), p. 3.

b. Fiscal 1994. Regular staff plus long-term consultants in Environment Department, four REDs, plus Social Policy divisions. World Bank, *Making Development Sustainable* (World Bank, 1994), p. 157.

c. "Overall, based on time recorded by staff, some 270 staff years (regular staff plus consultants) were devoted to environment this year. This corresponds to about 6 percent of total Bank time." World Bank, *World Bank and the Environment*, p. 3.

d. "Taken together, more than 300 higher-level staff and long-term consultants are now working on environmental matters in the Bank." *World Bank and the Environment*, p. 157.

e. The size of the active portfolio of loans whose primary objective is to strengthen environmental management. See World Bank, *The World Bank Group and the Environment since the Rio Earth Summit: Mainstreaming the Environment* (World Bank, 1995), fig. 1, p. 5, and appx. B.

f. Number of reports listed in Bank Reports Database with "environment" and "poverty," respectively, in abstract; and total number of reports in each calendar year.

n.s. Not significant.

mandatory procedures for subjecting projects to environmental review and clearance and began a portfolio of "environmental" projects, the primary objective of which was to improve or rehabilitate parts of the environment. That portfolio grew by twelve to twenty-five new projects a year over the first half of the 1990s and amounted to $1 billion to $2 billion in new lending commitments and 5 to 10 percent of total new commitments. At the macro level, the Bank by the mid-1990s had helped virtually all its borrowers prepare National Environmental Action Plans (NEAPs), and it began integrating environmental criteria into countrywide policies so as to link advice about instruments of economic policy such as exchange rates, subsidies, and taxes to their effects on environmental sustainability.

At least in principle, environmental sustainability joined economic growth and poverty reduction to form the core objectives for Bank work. All this activity was accompanied by an outpouring of high-quality research reports on environment-development interactions, making the Bank arguably the largest center for such research in the world. Environmental legitimacy reached the point where the two managing directors for operations informed their staff in 1996: "Environmental issues are now central to our Country Assistance Strategies."[2] Indicators of the Bank's environmental work since 1975 are summarized in table 13-1.

2. Letter, Gautam Kaji and Caio Koch-Weser to all operational staff, "Social Development and Results on the Ground," March 1, 1996.

On the surface, the history of the Bank's environmental activities appears to be a case of new insights leading an institution rapidly to integrate new objectives and criteria into its operational routines. According to the Bank, the change is the result of the staff's and management's own "increasing understanding of the relationship between environmental protection and development."[3] But its many environmental critics say that the change has been driven largely by environmental non-governmental organizations (NGOs) mounting high-pressure campaigns to force the Bank to change its ways. Certainly the Bank's environmental activities stand out not only as the fastest growing of its operations but also as those that have attracted the most criticism. From the mid-1980s to the present, a spiraling coalition of environmental NGOs has attacked the Bank for sponsoring projects that cause large-scale environmental damage and for failing to comply with its own environmental and resettlement policies. Despite the Bank's efforts to expand its environmental staff and procedures, NGOs complain that the staff are isolated from operations, that the procedures are readily bypassed, and thus that not much real learning has taken place. Each side in this debate uses rhetorical excess to win public support, portraying itself as virtuous and the other as villainous. The high stakes render their own accounts inherently suspect.

This chapter tells two stories. One is about the factors that led the Bank to pay attention to environmental criteria. The other is about the effects of its organizational structure and incentive system on what it has and has not done to advance environmental objectives. The way in which "environmental" concerns were handled by the Bank certainly changed drastically after the 1987 reorganization. This change was spearheaded by NGOs in the mid-1980s who used the Polonoroeste project in the Brazilian Amazon as ammunition in their attack on the Bank's environmental record. In response, during the 1987 reorganization the Bank began to integrate a distinct set of environmental objectives into its project work, notably by creating the Environment Department and four regional environment divisions and by establishing environmental assessment procedures soon afterward. But this failed to quell the NGO attacks, which arrived in a second wave in the late 1980s and early 1990s, in connection with the Narmada dam-and-canal project in India. Again, the Bank moved to remedy its failings: from about 1992 to 1995 it tried to achieve a higher level of integration of a still more distinct set of objectives, under the banner of "mainstreaming the environment." This action was also related to governance reforms of the mid-1990s, intended to make the Bank more transparent and publicly accountable, reforms that were once again prompted mainly by environmental NGOs. As a result of these organizational and political pressures, environmental considerations have been defined and encoded in Bank routines;

3. Ibrahim Shihata, "The World Bank and the Environment: Legal Instruments for Achieving Environmental Objectives," in Shihata, *The World Bank in a Changing World*, vol. 2 (The Hague: Martin Nijhoff, 1995), chap. 5, p. 184.

but in between the procedures and the operational practice is the "slipping clutch" of the Bank's incentive system.[4]

Frontier Economics with "Environment" Added, 1970–87

The environmental NGOs that pressed the Bank to pay more attention to the environment in the 1980s claimed that some Bank-financed projects were causing large-scale environmental damage, and that these environmental costs were not being sufficiently weighted in the Bank's cost-benefit calculations. They gave the impression that "some" projects meant too many to be treated as exceptions. The Bank simply did not have the capacity to subject its projects to environmental criteria, they said, as indicated by the absence of environmental specialists on the staff and of procedures for environmental assessment. Without some major organizational changes, the Bank would continue to promote projects that caused environmental damage and would fail to realize its potential as a lever for country-wide upgrading of environmental practices.

The Bank replied that the NGOs were talking about only a very small proportion of its total projects, and that environmental skills were in fact widely diffused through the organization. Though not called "environmental," these skills were encoded in the good professional practices of engineering, agronomy, and the other technical disciplines. "Good agriculture *is* good environment, good engineering *is* good environment," said the Bank. Right up to 1986, management claimed to be satisfied with the staff and procedures it used for environmental review.

Environment before "Environment"

Infrastructure lending—much of it having a direct and possibly damaging effect on the "natural environment"—accounted for as much as two-thirds of Bank lending in the 1950s and 1960s, compared with about one-third in the next two decades. And yet, despite the absence of environmental specialists and environmental assessment procedures, there were few reports of significant environmental damage. A statistical analysis of more than three hundred project completion reports covering lending over the period 1961–80 showed little evidence of gross environmental negligence or damage.[5]

It is quite possible that the damage was in fact rather small. In the 1950s and 1960s, compared with subsequent decades, the Bank was dealing with a smaller set of borrowers with stronger implementation capacities and lower population den-

4. No attempt is made here to provide a comprehensive inventory of the Bank's environmental actions, or to weigh up the net impact of Bank work on environmental conditions in borrowing countries. For inventories and evaluations of effectiveness on the ground, see the Bank's annual reports on the environment, and ibid. Also see the critical works cited below.

5. See World Bank, "Renewable Resource Management in Agriculture," Operations Evaluation Department (OED) Report 7345, June 24, 1988, para. ix.

sities. It could be more selective about project sites because fewer projects were already in place. And the sectors receiving its support were usually less environmentally sensitive ones, such as standard infrastructure (ports, railways, bridges), than the agriculture and irrigation projects that became more important in the 1970s. Bank staff consisted mainly of technically trained people who were later to be eclipsed by generalist economists and young professionals. Furthermore, although no one in the 1950s and 1960s showed open concern for the environment agenda as such, some parts of that agenda were already well established within the Bank, especially by the 1970s. Bank reports on environmentally sensitive sectors such as livestock and jungle settlement showed an awareness of ecological hazards.[6] The Forestry Policy Paper of 1978 (the first of its kind) highlighted the ecological values of forests, making it a milestone in thinking about forestry in a development context.[7] Some mining projects had explicit environmental protection covenants in the loan agreement, requiring the borrower to prepare plans for the protection of affected coastal waters, for example, or to enact pollution control legislation.[8]

These remarks present only one side of the case, however. It is likely that the reporting regime then in place (inside and outside the Bank) was too weak to pick up more than egregious cases of damage, and perhaps not all of those. A 1988 Operations Evaluation Department (OED) report on the Bank's resource management in agriculture points out that the statistical analysis of three hundred project completion reports mentioned earlier does not tell the full story: "Environmental issues frequently were not given much attention when the projects were designed. Such issues, therefore, often got little attention in the supervision reports, PCRs and PPARs [Project Completion Reports and Project Performance Audit Reports] prepared later."[9] Also, long-term environmental effects may not have been in evidence at the time of project completion when the reports were written, but may show up later. One OED review of more than one hundred household and industrial water supply projects approved between 1967 and 1989 found that environmental protection "was not the subject of any significant issues identified in PCRs and PPARs," yet almost all of the projects added large volumes of water into the urban areas they were designed to serve. The review commented, "Appropriate environmental responses would have been ex-

6. World Bank, "Livestock Projects," SecM74-738, October 29, 1974; World Bank, "The Settlement of Agricultural Lands: An Issues Paper," Agriculture and Rural Development Department Report 1670, June 1977; World Bank, "The Experience of the World Bank with Government-Sponsored Land Settlement," OED Report 5625, SecM85-560, May 1, 1985. Between 1972 and 1979, twenty project reports had "soil erosion" in the project abstract; this figure rose to twenty-nine in 1980–89, which suggests some attention to soil erosion, though not a great deal.

7. World Bank, "Forestry," Sector Policy Paper, 1978, chart 1, p. 16.

8. See Shihata, "The World Bank and the Environment," pp. 201–02.

9. World Bank, "Renewable Resource Management in Agriculture," para. ix.

pected for each project," including the methods of collecting and disposing of waste water.[10]

Aside from the Bank's own reporting system, which obviously had its problems, few other means existed for spotlighting environmental costs on the ground in the 1950s and 1960s. Citizen groups or international NGOs were still in their infancy. Later, when some of them launched the Bank campaign, they found many more cases of significant environmental damage than—for reasons of tactics—they actually used in the campaign: projects that promoted cattle ranching in rain forests, pesticide-intensive agriculture, irrigation projects without drainage, and dam projects without resettlement.

Right up to the late 1980s, the Bank paid attention to only a few specific aspects of what would later be called environmental problems, and then mainly within rather than beyond the boundaries of specific projects. The project staff tended to discount the value of environmental objectives that went beyond good professional practice, and that sometimes were well within those limits. In the late 1970s, for example, a staff member, newly recruited after working for several years near a Bank-supported Federal Land Development Authority (FELDA) settlement project in Malaysia, gave the project officer photographic evidence showing that FELDA was not complying with a loan condition that required it to leave a band of 200–300 meters of forest on either side of the river ("riparian forest buffers"). The loan condition reflected the general view that riparian buffers help protect wildlife and the riverine ecology. The project officer, however, told him to mind his own business: "FELDA is a very effective agency, it's doing a good job, the loan is disbursing well, we should be careful not to offend it." Yet the evidence showed that FELDA was breaking a loan condition. This is just the sort of behavior the NGOs were later to complain about: even when the Bank had environmentally sound loan conditions, project officers not infrequently ignored them in the absence of any systematic checking procedures or internal champions. One can infer that the project officer in this case was unwilling to hinder the lending program for the sake of a few forest buffers, the value of which did not rank highly in relation to his own understanding of the mission of economic development or to the cost to his own performance evaluation.[11]

When the Bank revised its key statement on project appraisal (OPM 2.20) in 1971, it mentioned for the first time the environmental aspects of projects and suggested without elaboration that impact on the environment should be considered in such appraisals, as appropriate. In 1975 the Bank issued its project officers with "Guidelines on Environmental Dimensions of Projects." But a com-

10. World Bank, "Water Supply and Sanitation Projects: The World Bank's Experience, 1967–1989," OED Report 10789, SecM92-950, June 19, 1992, p. 57.

11. The new recruit was David Williams. Interview with the author, March 13, 1996.

parison by the OED of projects initiated before and after OPM 2.20 showed no discernible increase in attention to environmental matters.[12]

In the 1970s and 1980s the Bank was also doing economic and sectoral work that might have provided a suitable framework for analyzing and mitigating environmental problems at the level of whole sectors or countries. However, it was not until the early 1990s that the Bank extended its environmental activities beyond just mitigating the damage caused by projects that were chosen without regard to environmental consequences. According to the 1988 OED study of renewable resource management in agriculture, "ESW [economic and sector work] did not provide the strategic framework for deciding specifically what the main resource management issues in a country were, and the options for dealing with them."[13] It cites Nepal as an example of a missed opportunity. The Bank fully understood the seriousness of the resource degradation that had taken place in both the hills and the plains of Nepal but did little to address the problem in its lending. Indeed, its lending program in agriculture was dominated by irrigation in the plains, which was, as the OED report says, "virtually irrelevant to the catastrophe that was predicted unless there were massive shifts in policy and investment to change the use of forest lands in the Terai [plains] and all lands in the hills."[14] Brazil is another case in point. In the early 1970s policy changes in favor of agricultural mechanization plus widespread frost damage to coffee plantations in the south brought large changes in land use, causing massive migration to the forest frontier in the northwest. The process was not picked up in the Bank's economic and sector work until 1981, well after the Bank had become deeply involved in the northwest.

Speaking of projects completed between 1961 and 1980, the OED study concludes, "Environmental considerations have had little influence on the selection or design of projects. For all practical purposes, they have been added as an afterthought, through a paragraph in the [Staff Appraisal Report] composed primarily to comply with a [policy directive]."[15] Yet some ecological awareness was manifest in policy papers about land settlement projects, livestock projects, and forestry, for example. But it played almost no role in the selection and design of projects (although a few factors such as soil erosion were certainly taken into account), or in the formal operational frameworks for specific countries; and it was not called "ecological" or "environmental" awareness, just "good agronomy" or "good engineering."[16]

12. World Bank, "Renewable Resource Management in Agriculture," para. viii.
13. Ibid., para. v.
14. Ibid., para. xiii.
15. Ibid., para. xviii.
16. The low level of explicit environmental awareness before the early 1970s is reflected in the Mason and Asher history of the first twenty-five years of the Bank. It contains just three references to "IBRD concern with ecology" in a volume that exceeds 750 pages.

Adding Environment

When in the early 1970s, in response to burgeoning public concern with "environment" in the West, the word entered into the Bank's lexicon, the staff were both skeptical and perplexed. They were skeptical because some environmental concerns seemed to be nothing new; perplexed because some sounded fuzzy, complex, and unquantifiable, and a threat to the familiar routine of project work. At the least, repairing the results of and setting limits to environmentally harmful activities might inflate immediate project costs (for example, adding drainage to irrigation canals) and bring few tangible benefits within a time frame that would allow them to be picked up by standard discounting procedures. Besides, the borrowers were on the whole hostile to Bank talk about environment.

In 1970 Robert McNamara took the occasion of his annual address to the United Nations Economic and Social Council to speak about the need to help developing countries mitigate environmental damage caused by economic growth. "The problem facing development finance institutions, including the World Bank," he said, "is whether and how we can help the developing countries to avoid or mitigate some of the damage economic development can do to the environment, without at the same time slowing down the pace of economic progress."[17] McNamara told his audience that the Bank had just created the post of environmental adviser to direct the Bank's environment work. This made the Bank the first multilateral or bilateral agency to have an environmental adviser. Because the Bank was later to become the target of savage environmental criticism, its early leadership in this area deserves emphasis.

Why did McNamara take this initiative? The broader context provides some clues. The late 1960s was a time of growing concern about environmental issues in the West, especially in the United States. The number of articles on the environment in the *New York Times* rose from 150 in 1960 to 1,700 in 1970.[18] Several schools of thought on the subject began to form and jostle for support, sharing an explicit regard for the value of "the environment" and a disbelief that economic decisions based on market prices could safeguard that worth. They were reacting against what Kenneth Boulding usefully called "frontier economics," the reigning

---

Mason and Asher comment that "the IBRD has not, at least until recently, paid enough attention to the ecological or environmental effects of the projects it has financed." Edward S. Mason and Robert E. Asher, *The World Bank since Bretton Woods* (Brookings, 1973), p. 259.

17. Robert McNamara, "Speech to the United Nations Conference on the Human Environment," Stockholm, Sweden, June 8, 1972, in *The McNamara Years at the World Bank: Major Policy Addresses of Robert S. McNamara, 1968–1981* (Johns Hopkins University Press, 1981).

18. Wolfgang Sachs, "Environment," in *The Development Dictionary: A Guide to Knowledge as Power* (London: Zed Books, 1992), p. 27.

assumption that economic growth and material prosperity were limitless, unconstrained by either "sources" (the supply of natural resources) or "sinks" (the waste-absorbing systems of the biosphere).[19] Indeed, there was no need to manage the biophysical environment since it was irrelevant to the functioning of the economy. The most moderate reaction, beginning around the middle to late 1960s, came to be known as the "environmental protection" approach. It sought to apply an environmental version of the Hippocratic oath: "First do no harm." Threats to endangered species and the health effects of pollution and toxic wastes were considered the prime targets of public action, and legislation was sought to prevent unpriced environmental services from being overexploited. Smokestacks should be made taller, factory wastes should be given "end-of-pipe" treatment, and polluters should be made to pay pollution taxes. Investment projects should receive environmental impact assessment. The U.S. government, responding to pressures from U.S. environmental groups, passed the National Environmental Policy Act in late 1969, which required U.S. government agencies to undertake environmental assessments designed to mitigate or avoid the environmental damage caused by public investment projects.

At the other extreme of environmentalism's spectrum was the "deep ecology" school. Pressures created by the more than twofold increase in the world's population in the twentieth century up to 1970 and the more than tenfold increase in the size of the world economy, it argued, were threatening the sustainability of the biophysical processes that support all life on the planet, human and otherwise. Instead of seeking infinite economic growth, societies should try to meet simple material needs and create "harmony with nature." The dominant threat was not poverty, disease, and "natural" disasters, but ecosystem collapse and man-made disasters. Societies should abandon capital intensity and economies of scale and in their place adopt decentralized decisionmaking and small-scale endeavors. The Club of Rome's *The Limits to Growth* (1972) seemed to give credence to this viewpoint with its computer-based scenarios showing how future economic growth might be checked by resource constraints, in the absence of a radical restructuring of world economic priorities. The subject was hotly debated.

As the recognized lead agency in the work on development issues, the Bank could not remain oblivious to this rising tide of concern, particularly because many in the new environmental movement were saying that economic growth should be stopped, an idea fundamentally opposed to the Bank's mission. In addition, the Bank had to consider what position it would take at the United Nations Conference

19. Kenneth Boulding, "The Economics of the Coming Spaceship Earth," in Herman Daly, ed., *Economics, Ecology and Ethics: Towards a Steady-State Economy* (San Francisco: W. H. Freeman, 1980), pp. 253–63. The following discussion of schools, or paradigms, draws on Michael E. Colby, "The Evolution of Paradigms of Environmental Management in Development," World Bank, PPR Working Paper WPS 313, November, 1989.

on the Human Environment scheduled for 1972 in Stockholm. Sweden, worried about acid rain, pollution in the Baltic, and the levels of pesticides and heavy metals in fish and birds, had first proposed the conference. The prospect of having to stand up and explain what the Bank had been doing to protect the environment forced McNamara to think about what the Bank should be doing. Stockholm was the first in a series of large UN meetings through the 1970s on "global issues"—on population, food, human settlements, water, desertification, science and technology, and renewable energy—that helped change the public's perception of the environment. It was no longer seen as an unconstrained global space in which countries could individually maximize economic growth ("frontier economics") but as an interrelated world system.

McNamara was sympathetic to environmental concerns. In his 1972 speech to the Stockholm conference he said with passion, "The evidence is now overwhelming that roughly a century of rapid economic expansion has gradually contributed to a *cumulatively monstrous assault on the quality of life* in the developed countries."[20] In later years, he admitted to having been "a green for over sixty years, a member of the Sierra Club since 1933. My wife was a green, my kids too, my daughter is a forester."[21] But theirs was an unsophisticated kind of environmentalism by today's standards; and he—like most others working on development issues—did not at first think of "environmental" problems as an important consideration for poor countries. He credits Barbara Ward with having convinced him otherwise. Ward was a leading figure in the preparation for the Stockholm conference and was then writing what became an influential book on development and the environment.[22] "To him, as to so many other people, she gave the extra nudge, the touch of rhetoric that he needed."[23] Of the members of the Bank's Board, the executive directors from the United States, Scandinavia, and Canada supported the move to screen Bank projects for their environmental impacts.

With the Stockholm conference in prospect, McNamara established the post of environmental adviser, to which he appointed James Lee. Lee was an American expert in *public health and epidemiology,* with earlier experience as a game warden in the United States. He remained the Bank's chief adviser on environmental matters until he retired in 1987.

On his second day at the Bank, in late 1970, Lee had his first meeting with McNamara, who promised "his full support and the full support of the Board in carrying out what he felt was going to be a very difficult assignment." By way of example, McNamara described a problem that had arisen in a game park in

20. Robert McNamara, speech to the United Nations Conference on the Human Environment, in *The McNamara Years at the World Bank,* p. 196, emphasis added.

21. Robert S. McNamara, interview with the author, February 20, 1995.

22. Barbara Ward and René Dubois, *Only One Earth: The Care and Maintenance of a Small Planet* (New York: Norton, 1972).

23. Roland Bird, "Barbara Ward," *Economist,* June 6, 1981, p. 38.

Tanzania, where a Bank project proposed to run a power transmission line close to the game lodge and thus spoil its view. No less a personage than Prince Bernhard of the Netherlands, a leader of the world conservation movement, had told Mc-Namara that conservation groups were very upset and that "this just couldn't be." McNamara looked at Lee and said: "I want you to turn this around."

> Then he reached over to the other side of his desk where he had a pile of letters that was probably about six or seven inches high. These were all letters of criticism and condemnation that had been levelled against the Bank by the *health* community saying that the Bank was not acting in a very responsible way in terms of the impact of its projects on the public's health and well-being. . . . And so, with a little smile on his face he said, "Oh, I also have these. I want you to read them and turn this around too." And that was the end of our discussion.

Later the same day, Lee continued, "I found myself in a bloody adversarial relationship with . . . the responsible officer for Tanzania. He had already made up his mind that this transmission line was going to go the way that they had selected, planned, and worked out, and he wasn't about to make those changes just because of some damn animals some place. So we had quite a confrontation that first day." Soon afterward Lee visited the game park with a Bank power engineer. "We did find a route that was much better from the standpoint of its impact on the wildlife and on the game reserve, and when the cost-benefit analysis was done, it turned out to be a cheaper route—much to everyone's surprise."[24]

Three points stand out in this account. First, from the start the Bank's environmental staff had an important public relations function: to "turn around" external criticisms. Second, from the start the environmental staff were involved in "bloody adversarial" relationships with the rest of the Bank. The story about Lee's show-down with the project officer for Tanzania, and of the successful review of the cost-benefit analysis, became known throughout the Bank and helped to establish Lee as someone to be reckoned with. Third, what the Bank did under the label "environment" included residual matters such as relocating a power line so that it would not spoil the view from a game lodge, matters that no one else wanted to deal with. Otherwise the Bank's environmental activities at that time focused more on public health than on the biophysical system, in part because health groups had been the most critical of the Bank and because Lee's own expertise was in public health and occupational health and safety.

The main theme of this early environment work was *disease prevention*. Lee explained: "I saw my role as trying to identify those health problems that were going to be associated with any of our development activities," such as hydro-electric projects and irrigation projects.[25] "Wherever you manipulate surface waters

24. James Lee, interview, World Bank Oral History Program, April 4, 1985, pp. 3–4, emphasis added.
25. Ibid., p. 10–11.

on the land in countries where [waterborne] diseases are present, you are going to exacerbate . . . the incidence of the diseases." This was quite a new focus in the Bank. Indeed, Lee later recalled that when, upon his appointment, he went to the Joint Library to explore its holdings in environment and health, "I found nothing."[26]

The United Nations Conference on the Human Environment, 1972

The Stockholm conference put the "environment" on the international agenda. What was the Bank's role? Soon after Lee arrived, at the end of 1970, Maurice Strong, the chief organizer, came to see him and McNamara. Strong said that "the World Bank was the first of the development finance institutions to take an interest in the [environmental] field and that the Bank had a rich history in terms of the economics of development. . . . He said my own position was something of a pioneering effort . . . and so therefore he and his staff would be calling on the Bank to help them with the preparations for the conference, for defining the issues. . . . I remember him saying to [a senior Bank manager who was at the meeting], 'This fellow is going to do a lot of travelling . . . , because we need the input of the Bank.'. . . I found myself . . . virtually commuting to Geneva. . . . I'd be in Geneva on a host of committees in which we were doing the preparatory work."[27]

Late in 1971 it looked as though the whole conference might founder before it began.[28] The developing-country representatives claimed that the conference was being strong-armed into adopting a rich-country view of environmental problems, seeking to impose on them mitigation measures that would only add to the costs of economic development and slow it down. "The only view rich and poor countries seemed to share," wrote one observer, "was the conviction that environmental conservation and economic development are in conflict with each other."[29] As Lee recalled, the developing countries "threatened to pull out of it. . . . So [Maurice Strong] called upon the Bank and said, 'Well, after all, you are the closest to the developing countries. . . . The developing countries will listen to you if you can make a case for us, that is, a case for the environment and its importance to the developing countries.' The Bank then assigned the responsibility for that to two of us. One was Mahbub ul Haq, who was going to look at it from the standpoint of the developing countries and economics. . . . I was going to look at it . . . from the point of view of identifying the environmental problems, the linkages, the relationship to people, and so on."[30]

26. Ibid., p. 5.

27. Ibid., p. 6.

28. Philippe Le Prestre, *The World Bank and the Environmental Challenge* (Selinsgrove, Pa.: Susquehanna University Press, 1989), chap. 1.

29. Peter Bartelmus, *Environment and Development* (Boston: Allen & Unwin, 1986), p. 11.

30. Ul Haq had been secretary for planning in Pakistan and had written *The Poverty Curtain: Choices for the Third World* (Columbia University Press, 1976). At this time he had just joined the Bank as a senior economics adviser, recruited directly by McNamara. Lee, Oral History, April 4, 1985, p. 8.

The critical meeting was held in the village of Founex, Switzerland. The Founex meeting of 1971 is where the first steps were taken toward the marriage between "development" and "environment." Some twenty-seven specialists and delegates "sat down for what was going to be a sort of head-to-head, eye-to-eye, nose-to-nose discussion on these matters." In the event, Mahbub ul Haq persuaded the developing-country delegates that "there really was good cause, both then and in the future, for them to be concerned about these matters. . . . [T]hey promised that they would . . . support the conference, that they would enter into it with good, full faith."[31] The Bank helped gain their support by agreeing to provide funds to cover any additional costs directly attributable to its environmental standards. The Founex report became the basis of the Declaration, Principles, and Recommendations issued by the Stockholm conference. It was largely drafted inside the World Bank, by Mahbub ul Haq and his team.[32]

At the conference, McNamara delivered a keynote address announcing the first formal commitment to environmental soundness in development from any of the multilateral development banks. "The question," McNamara urged his audience to consider, "is not whether there should be continued economic growth. There must be. Nor is the question whether the impact on the environment must be respected. It has to be. Nor—least of all—is it a question of whether these two considerations are interlocked. They are. The solution of the dilemma revolves clearly not about whether, but about how."[33]

Clearly, the Bank played a leading role in the Stockholm conference. The environmental adviser was a principal figure in the preparatory work; senior Bank official Mahbub ul Haq was the key person in persuading the developing countries not to withdraw; and McNamara's speech established the Bank as the leading agency in dealing with the environmental problems of developing countries.

Loss of Momentum after 1972

All through the 1970s and into the 1980s the Bank was considered a leading advocate of environmental protection among those concerned with such issues. Yet having acquired the mantle of leadership, the Bank downplayed environmental issues in the years that followed, both to the outside world and still more to itself. Only three months after the Stockholm conference, McNamara made no mention of environmental issues in his annual report to the Board of Governors, neither in his review of Bank activities during the previous year nor in his outline of the

31. Ibid.

32. Le Prestre, *The World Bank and the Environmental Challenge,* p. 83; and "Development and the Environment: The Founex Report," in *In Defence of the Earth: The Basic Texts on Environment—Founex, Stockholm, Cocoyoc,* UNEP Executive Series 1 (1989).

33. Robert McNamara, "Speech to the UN Conference on the Human Environment," June 8, in *The McNamara Years at the World Bank,* p. 196.

program for the next five years. His report the following year was also silent on the issue except for a passing mention of the Office of Environmental Affairs as one of a number of new offices. The *Annual Report* for 1973 did have a short and anodyne section on "environmental impact"; but six years elapsed before another environmental heading appeared (in 1979), and another six years before the next one appeared (in 1985). So of the eleven annual reports between 1974 and 1985, only one had a separate section on the Bank's environmental work. Why? The answer has to do with McNamara's understanding, a change in the U.S. role, the wishes of borrowing countries, the inclinations of staff, and the nature of the environmental debate.

MCNAMARA'S UNDERSTANDING. McNamara himself, though committed to minimizing the environmental damage caused by Bank projects, thought that the Bank could do what was needed with a minor initiative, worthy of no more than occasional advertising. He told Lee, "Take each project, identify whether it is likely to have adverse environmental consequences. Most will not, these can be put aside. Some will, and they can be fairly easily identified. Concentrate on these, and identify how to reduce or offset the damage." Years later he recognized that "then we were in the Stone Age of environmental awareness, we were very ignorant of what we were doing. We knew so little that we were sure that the number of projects with significant environmental implications would be very small and that for those it would be easy to identify how to reduce the environmental damage to tolerable levels at tolerable cost—two percent to four percent of project cost at a maximum and generally less."[34] He drew a contrast with the poverty work. "We saw the direct attack on absolute poverty as very complex. We did not see the requirement of avoiding significant environmental damage as very complex. This reflected a lack of understanding on our part."

THE U.S. GOVERNMENT'S RETREAT AND ABSENCE OF NGO PRESSURE. At the start of the 1970s the U.S. government had taken a leadership role in multilateral environmental issues, but then it suddenly retreated. This move coincided with a wider sputtering out of its leadership across the whole of the UN system as it became preoccupied with the 1973 oil crisis.[35] None of the other Part I countries attempted to fill the role.

For their part, the U.S. Congress and Treasury did not push environmental issues in their dealings with the Bank, and their overall relations with the Bank were cordial and unassertive compared with what was to come. Furthermore, NGOs by and large ignored the Bank and its environmental record. The lineup of forces—or rather the absence of forces—can be seen in a small incident from the

34. McNamara, interview, February 20, 1995.
35. Harold Jacobson and David Kay, "The Environmental Protection Activities of International Organizations: An Appraisal and Some Suggestions," paper presented at annual meeting of American Political Science Association, Washington D.C., August 31–September 3, 1979.

early 1970s. A prominent member of Congress, Henry Reuss (Democrat of Wisconsin), criticized the Bank's forestry projects and asked the U.S. General Accounting Office to make an investigation. A year later, in 1974, the report was released and Reuss's office issued a press statement drawing attention to its findings, which were critical of the Bank. (The report concluded that the World Bank in three of its tropical forestry projects—in Malaysia, Kenya, and Zambia—failed to prescribe "any specific measures to insure the environmental integrity" of the forests.) A senior Bank official, who had received a copy of the press release in advance, contacted Reuss's office to protest about an inaccuracy. He spoke to a staffer who conceded that the press release gave a false impression but it "was already in the mails and could not be changed. . . . He added that *he was sure no damage was done since he did not expect anybody to pay much attention to the release.* He also expounded at length upon the very friendly relations that existed between Rep. Reuss and Mr. McNamara and said they had no intention of doing the Bank's work any harm."[36] The tone of those members of Congress who in the mid-1980s called for reports on the Bank's environmental work would be very different.

DEVELOPING-COUNTRY SKEPTICISM. Developing countries (especially big and important ones such as India and Brazil) reasserted their doubts about the Bank's role. This reflected their disagreement with the North's pressure for environmental protection measures at the expense, as they saw it, of economic growth. The central development strategy of that time was based on the frontier economics assumption that most developing countries had vast stocks of underexploited land, forest, and water resources that had to be brought into production as soon as possible. The stocks seemed so great that few were concerned about perpetuating them over time, except in special cases. The capacity of the atmosphere, rivers, and seas to absorb the wastes of economic activity also seemed to be limitless, except, again, in special cases.

The developing countries took the line: "You chopped down your forests and used them for consumption and exports. Why shouldn't we?" It is a safe guess that 95 percent of government officials and politicians took the view—in regard to harvesting rain forest, dumping untreated sewerage into rivers, or welcoming pollution-intensive factories—"Yes, there are risks, but we have to take them, our people are starving, first we have to grow and then we can clean up." When U.S. congressional panels insisted that U.S. environmental standards be applied to the rest of the world, developing countries heard protectionist lobbyists seeking grounds to exclude their exports. When the North said they must halt the destruction of rain forests, they heard the voice of the North's pulp and paper industry threatened by cheap southern imports.

---

36. Memorandum, J. Burke Knapp to files, April 16, 1974, emphasis added. A copy of the press release that contains the first quotation is attached to this file.

What few recognized was that temperate and tropical habitats differ in their vulnerability to ecological degradation and in the kinds of environmental problems they face. In temperate environments the main environmental concerns are air and water pollution, which (except perhaps for ozone depletion and global warming) can be reversed within decades. In tropical environments pollution is but one of many other more intransigent problems such as deforestation, soil erosion, and species extinction. Developing countries did not come to this realization until the 1980s and 1990s. Indeed, the more they thought about their "sovereignty" in such matters, the more resistant they became to the idea of being told that they must introduce ecological controls. As one senior Brazilian official remarked in 1972: "Each country must evolve its own development plans, exploit its own resources as it thinks suitable, and define its own environmental standards. The idea of having such priorities and standards imposed on individual countries or groups of countries, on either a multilateral or a bilateral basis, is very hard to accept."[37] These views were upheld in the Charter of Economic Rights and Duties of States, a set of principles promulgated in 1974 by the UN General Assembly that declared in Article 2, "Every State has and shall freely exercise full permanent sovereignty, including possession, use and disposal, over all its wealth, natural resources and economic activities."[38]

Compounding this resistance was the political sensitivity of many environmental problems. Upstream polluters damage downstream fisheries; mining and logging operations threaten indigenous peoples; emission of pollutants into the atmosphere threatens the health of local peoples and may disturb the global climate; urgent present-day needs threaten the well-being of future generations. In most cases the people who gain are the politically powerful, those who lose are those with no say in the decisionmaking.[39] Governments tend to shrink from environmental actions that, apart from the costs they entail, direct attention to these conflicts of interest and may deter powerful constituencies from continuing to support them.

BANK STAFF'S SKEPTICISM. Inside the Bank the large majority of the staff was also skeptical about McNamara's idea of subjecting Bank projects to scrutiny by self-styled "environmentalist specialists" using different standards from their own "good professional practice." And like the developing countries, they equated "environmental" problems largely with pollution (rather than, say, deforestation,

37. João Augusto de Araujo Castro, "Environment and Development: The Case of the Developing Countries," in David A. Kay and Eugene B. Skolnikoff, eds., *World Eco-crisis* (University of Wisconsin Press, 1972), quoted in Le Prestre, *The World Bank and the Environmental Challenge*, p. 79.

38. UN, "Charter of Economic Rights and Duties of States," General Assembly Resolution 3281 (XXIX) of December 12, 1974.

39. This draws on World Bank, *World Bank Support to the Environment; A Progress Report, Fiscal 1990.*

desertification, or soil erosion), and saw pollution as a problem connected with affluence and therefore one that developing countries could afford to ignore. If these countries added to their costs by adopting less polluting technologies, and if they reduced their exploitation of natural resources such as minerals and forests, they would merely slow the rate of economic growth. Even if there were some serious environmental problems in some developing countries, why should the Bank, as a *development* institution, have to deal with them except where they had such an adverse impact on project returns that it changed the cost-benefit calculation for that particular project?

Staff skepticism was fueled by the gap between the generalities of environmental goals and the incentives of the organization. Under McNamara's command and control system of management, Bank staff were under intense pressure to find more projects and get them through the Board on time. Their public service ethic to make the world a better place was refracted through this central imperative. In this light, environment appeared as a new source of complication and delay.

EXTREMISM OF ENVIRONMENTAL DEBATE. In response to the burgeoning environmental movement, mainstream economists, political conservatives, and industrialists in the West began to harbor *anti*-environmental sentiments. Some commentators portrayed the environmental movement as a Trojan horse for socialism. Much of what the Bank said about the environment in the several years after Stockholm seemed intent on demolishing the idea of limits to growth. Little effort was made to set out a more positive agenda based on analysis of the environmental problems of developing countries.[40]

In short, the Bank's borrowers and most of its staff were skeptical about introducing explicit environmental considerations and self-styled environmental professionals. The Stockholm conference provided them with an excuse: it set up a new UN agency, the United Nations Environmental Program (UNEP), to carry forward the Stockholm agenda. Its members could now say: let the Bank take care of development, let UNEP take care of environment.

Centralized and Small

Yet McNamara did pledge to the Stockholm conference that the Bank would take environmental matters into account. The Bank could have attempted to introduce environmental criteria into project work in a decentralized manner, making the entire organization aware of environmental concerns through training courses and new operating procedures, and placing environmental coordinators in each region. Instead it chose a more centralized route, creating a central office and changing operating procedures by just enough to give that office some oversight. In

---

40. See Mahbub ul Haq, "The Limits to Growth: A Critique," *Finance and Development*, vol. 9, no. 4 (December 1972), pp. 2–8.

this respect, the Bank responded just as many American government agencies did at this time upon being asked to incorporate environmental concerns in their operations. As one analyst remarked, adding an office is a "structural response that most agencies could make with the least amount of disruptions over the shortest period of time."[41]

The centralized approach was consistent with the *prophylactic* role assigned to the Bank's environment office. Its job was not to worry about the wise management of natural resources, but to screen projects chosen elsewhere in the Bank. It was not to question whether a factory should be built, but only to propose how to reduce the environmental "externalities."

In practice, the Office of Environmental Affairs was usually involved in project design only at a *late* stage of the project cycle, "at the 'eleventh hour,'" too late to modify the design.[42] Its few staff were only rarely taken on project identification or even project appraisal missions. And as noted earlier, work on the Bank's overall lending strategy for a country (as in Country Program Papers) did not integrate ecological limits into the definition of the borrower's development problems.

Through the 1970s the Bank's Office of Environmental Affairs (OEA) remained tiny in terms of personnel, budget, and powers, quite marginal to the organization. For two years James Lee worked on his own. A second staff member joined in 1973. Then Robert Goodland arrived in 1978, leaving the New York Botanical Garden to join the Bank as its tropical ecologist; he was to feature prominently in the Bank's subsequent environmental work. Early on Lee established an elaborate filing system to keep track of Bank projects of interest to his office, employing a full-time archivist to maintain the system. The staff struggled to keep abreast of the flow. A study of the Bank's environmental work in 1977 reported, "The workload is awesome—one staff member [of the Office of Environmental Affairs] said he had reviewed over one hundred projects in forty-five days and had made recommendations on sixty-five of them."[43] The study commented that "this heavy workload inevitably leads to occasional hurried and superficial judgements."

By 1983 the office had three regular specialists.[44] The Bank was then approving about 250 new lending operations totaling $15 billion a year, in addition to super-

41. Lynton Caldwell, "Alabama Lectures," Indiana University, 1981, p. 38, processed, quoted in Le Prestre, *The World Bank and the Environmental Challenge*, p. 60.

42. World Bank, *Environment and Development* (World Bank, 1975), p. 8.

43. Robert E. Stein and Brian Johnson, *Banking on the Biosphere? Environmental Procedures and Practices of Nine Multilateral Development Agencies* (Lexington, Mass.: Lexington Books, 1979), p. 13.

44. In 1983 the former Office of Environmental Affairs was renamed Office of Environmental and Scientific Affairs, because the science and technology adviser and his staff of one had been folded into it, his own office having been abolished. See Bruce Rich, *Mortgaging the Earth: The World Bank, Environmental Impoverishment and the Crisis of Development* (Boston: Beacon Press, 1994), pp. 111–12.

vising hundreds of ongoing projects, and had a professional staff of about 2,800.[45] By 1984–87 the office had five environmental specialists.[46] Consultants came and went. For most of the period from 1970 to 1987 the OEA had virtually no travel budget of its own; its staff could not visit projects unless invited and paid for by the project officer. And its staff had less authority over the project divisions than other offices or departments within the central advisory staff; unlike the other advisers (for irrigation, tree crops, and so on), the environmental advisor had no sign-off powers that would have allowed him to block a project going forward for Board approval.

Scope

Lee defined environmental issues as an "environmental stool" with three legs: the first leg was the naturally occurring environment and the urban environment; the second, public health and occupational health and safety; the third, the "social" dimension. In the first several years, he emphasized disease prevention, occupational health and safety inside large factories, and the reduction of air and water pollution from large factories. This agenda—which focused mainly on the "brown" issues of industrial activity, energy utilization, and urban concentrations—reflected Lee's own expertise in public health and was amenable enough to technical solution that it was able to moderate opposition from inside the Bank and from the borrowing countries.

On the other hand, the office gave little attention to the "naturally occurring environment" or life-support systems: to the protection, rehabilitation, or enhancement of the self-regulating capacities of natural ecosystems, as in water pollution projects (other than those tied to specific industrial projects), air pollution projects (with the same qualification), drainage projects, soil conservation and antidesertification projects, protective forestry projects, solid waste disposal projects, range-management projects, and wildlife protection projects. Such endeavors, to the extent that the Bank launched any, were the preserve of technical experts who considered that they knew quite enough about environmental stewardship. When later the environmental NGOs began to attack the Bank, they did so especially for its neglect of these "green" or natural resource issues, which had been driving the growth of environmental consciousness in the West for the previous two decades.

Tribal Peoples and Forced Resettlement

At the end of the 1970s the Bank's environment agenda began to include the rights of tribal (or indigenous) peoples. Lee explained:

45. World Bank, *Annual Report, 1983*, p. 12.
46. James Lee (public health specialist and environmental adviser), Robert Goodland (tropical ecologist), Bernard Baratz (chemical engineer), Roger Batstone (chemical engineer), and Ragnar Obervee (environmental scientist).

I was concerned about the impact of the Bank's projects on people. After all, we have
projects where people . . . who are living in an area that's going to be flooded for a
hydroelectric power project are going to be removed, are going to be resettled. I found
out they often weren't being resettled in a very humane way. People were sort of looked
upon as objects or economic entities. . . . We began finding that the development that we
were promoting . . . had some very traumatic effects on these people. It introduced new
diseases. The acculturation process which goes on when mainstream society comes up
against these people was very unsavory, was very traumatic. There clearly was a need for
the Bank to get out in front of this and to adopt a policy . . . that said that the Bank was
concerned about the future of these people and was going to do something about it.

Lee went on to say that outside pressure was critical in getting the Bank to take
action: "There were a number of outside groups who were quite vociferous . . . in
bringing this to our attention . . . groups like Amnesty International, the Harvard
group of Cultural Survival . . . and others. They were quick to chastise us and rightly
so. And so . . . my office moved out in front on this and . . . began to fashion . . . a
tribal policy for the Bank."

Lee continued, "Well, you can imagine that when you begin to trespass on the
sovereign rights of countries regarding their people, that becomes a very, very
delicate affair, to put it mildly. So we had to walk a very, very fine line. The end
result was . . . that we stepped over that line quite far. We just said in essence,
'Look, the World Bank is being asked to provide financing for development
projects that are going to impact upon tribal peoples. We're not going to do it
unless all the following conditions are observed.' Our covenants, those measures
. . . were hard for some of our member countries to swallow. They found it very,
very difficult."[47]

The particular impetus for framing a tribal people's policy came from the
preparation of the Amazon program called Polonoroeste, appraised by the Bank in
1980. In order to protect Indians from the incursions of settlers and loggers, Robert
Goodland sought to include the creation of Indian reserves in the project design.
Similar issues had arisen in the Indonesian Transmigration project going on at
about the same time. The respective division chiefs for these projects resisted this
suggestion, saying that the Bank had no policy calling for the protection of tribal
peoples. Goodland took the lead in writing and then persuading the Bank to adopt
a general set of policy principles regarding indigenous peoples, with which to lasso
the recalcitrant division chiefs.[48]

Linked to this push, the Bank forged a policy for involuntary resettlement at
about the same time. Guidelines for involuntary resettlement were incorporated
into the Bank's Operational Manual in 1980.[49] Like the tribal policy, the Bank's

47. Lee, Oral History, April 4, 1985, pp. 15–16.
48. "Tribal People in Bank-Financed Projects," OMS 2.34, February 1982.
49. "Social Issues Associated with Involuntary Resettlement in Bank-Financed Projects,"
OMS 2.33, February 1980.

policy on forced resettlement was a response to outside pressure, particularly from church groups concerned about events in a few Bank-supported projects that sent letters directly to McNamara. Like the tribal policy, resettlement had a dedicated champion inside the Bank (Michael Cernea), who used McNamara's support to force the Bank to address the issue.

Why were "tribal people" and "involuntary resettlement" treated as "environmental" issues? One reason is that the label "environment" has tended to be applied to issues (such as the health effects of projects) that the Bank was forced to deal with, whether in response to outside pressures or because of internal conviction, but that do not clearly fit elsewhere. Another reason is that much of the Bank's definition of what constitutes "environment" has come from the U.S. environmental movement. The environmental movement has become the champion of "tribals" and "oustees" (people forced to move) because the same projects that damage the green environment often harm their welfare. Furthermore, the way people respond to these projects may further damage the environment (resettlement may cause deforestation). Finally, by integrating "human rights" with the "environment," the environmental movement could appeal to a wider constituency and reinforce its claim to the moral high ground; it gave a defense against the charge, "You are more concerned for the fish than for the humans." With its critics defining environment in this way, the Bank felt compelled to do the same.

Syndrome of Mistrust

The relationship between the Office of Environmental Affairs and the rest of the Bank was often characterized by the sort of "bloody adversarial relationship" Lee found himself in on his second day. Some confrontation between the environmental staff and the projects people was to be expected, since they were to screen projects at a late stage in the cycle and identify ways to reduce environmental damage, and perhaps as a result they delayed the project and added to its costs. These interventions often ran against the wishes of the project officer and his or her division chief, for reasons already explained. Whatever the level of confrontation in this regard, Lee added to it. According to observers, he saw his office as a band of valiant warriors going up against the big bad Bank. "He got the backs up of practically everyone in the Bank," said one. "He went around claiming that nobody had paid any attention to the environmental effects of projects before he arrived. This was such nonsense that people said, 'To hell with you.'"[50] Lee did little to build up coalitions of support with other units of the Bank, so as to add leverage to his own slight staff, budget, and authority. He was openly disdainful of economics and economists, refusing even to employ an environmental economist in his office. This attitude suggested that he was unwilling to learn the lingua franca of the Bank.

50. Retired vice president, interview with the author, 18 March 1995.

But Lee could not be ignored too openly. He had, it was believed, direct access to McNamara. This made him feared while McNamara remained president. Project staff developed the art of avoiding his scrutiny; omitting the office from circulation lists was the simplest way to do so. Senior managers sought to avoid meeting staff from the environment office even when there were clear grounds for doing so. In one case the deputy director of the central Agriculture Department consistently declined to meet with the environmental officer preparing environmental guidelines for the Bank's agricultural work. Stories abounded intimating that the environmental specialists could not be trusted to keep their word: they would tell the project officer that they would no longer oppose a project if certain changes were made, and then continue to do so. Lee and others in his office were suspected of actively encouraging the environmental NGOs to criticize the Bank. They were said to be betraying the organization by leaking documents to outside interest groups, a serious offence in an organization as gripped by secrecy as the Bank before the 1990s.

This sort of delegitimizing response only made matters worse. Looking back from 1985, Lee recalled: "Not so much now but in the early days . . . there wasn't a day or almost an hour that we weren't in some sort of an adversarial position with somebody who didn't want to do what we wanted them to do or were doing something we didn't want them to do. Or the outside people were telling us we weren't doing enough."[51] Even in 1985 he still overheard Bank staff saying that "the environmental staff can be very antagonistic!"

There developed, in short, a syndrome of mistrust between (most of) the environmental office and the rest of the Bank. It was a syndrome in the sense that the behavior of each side served to confirm the negative expectations of the other. It eroded the effectiveness of the environmental staff and discredited the idea of "environment" as a proper subject of Bank concern.

The Bank's External Image

Although "environment" had become a bad name inside the Bank, the concerned public continued to view the Bank as the leader in addressing country environmental issues. The environmental adviser was besieged with invitations to conferences. "The interest was incredible. And all coming to the Bank for information, for assistance. Everybody in those days wanted to study the Bank."[52] Lee went to the conferences and reported on the many good things the Bank was doing to protect the environment in developing countries. It was easy to sustain a reputation for environmental responsibility in development activities in the 1970s, for the other multilateral or bilateral agencies (apart from the U.S. Agency for International Development after the late 1970s) were doing little.

51. Lee, Oral History, 1985, p. 28.
52. Ibid., pp. 19–20.

Indeed, in 1981 the National Wildlife Federation awarded the World Bank a Special Environmental Achievement Award for its leadership in environmentally sound development among both multilateral and bilateral development finance organizations. For many years the Federation had given awards for "best environmental legislator of the year," "best environmental reporter of the year," and the like. But this was the first time the Federation had given an award for "international" environmental activities. The award—a sculpted white whooping crane—went to the Bank as a way to highlight the fact that the Bank was then the *only* development finance organization with an environment office. The Bank put it on display in the lobby of the main entrance, where it stood for several years.

The International Institute for Environment and Development (IIED), in a study published in 1979, also praised the Bank. It said, "The World Bank has the most advanced environmental policy and practices of any aid organization included in this study [eight other development agencies, including the five regional multilateral development banks] and undoubtedly exerts intellectual leadership on environmental matters in the entire international development community."[53] This sounds generous, but the text makes clear that the Bank was the only one of the eight agencies included in the study to make *any* systematic attempt to include environmental considerations in its lending procedures. The text goes on to point out that even the Bank's guidelines allowed many gaps and loopholes.

The Environmental Assessment Procedures of 1984

The "Guidelines on Environmental Dimensions of Projects" issued by the Office of Environmental Affairs in 1975 were no more than checklists of things to watch out for in different kinds of projects, and their use by project staff was entirely voluntary. Outside the Bank, beginning in the late 1960s in the United States, a methodology was developed for systematically assessing the environmental impacts of investment projects. By 1979 USAID was routinely using the "environmental assessment" (EA) methodology for all its major investment projects overseas. Over the 1980s other bilateral aid organizations established their own procedural framework for EAs.[54] The Development Assistance Committee (DAC) of the Organization for Economic Cooperation and Development (OECD) arranged meetings of aid donors to share their experience with environmental analysis and coordinate their own EA guidelines. The Asian Development Bank

53. Stein and Johnson, *Banking on the Biosphere?* p. 11.

54. Such as the Canadian International Development Agency (CIDA) in 1986, the Finnish International Development Agency in 1987, and the German Federal Ministry for Economic Cooperation in 1987. The International Union for the Conservation of Nature established a technical advisory service called Service for the Initiation of EIA [Environmental Impact Assessment] Procedures in 1984. The United Nations Environment Program also developed principles and guidelines for environmental assessment.

(ADB) also developed a set of EA guidelines, drawing on the USAID model, though it did not require that they be used.[55] By the mid-1980s EAs had become a routine technique in the development agencies of many OECD countries, but not in the World Bank or in the regional development banks with the partial exception of the ADB. *This gap was what U.S.-based environmental NGOs targeted in their campaign to pressure the Bank to boost its environmental capabilities.*

In 1984, in response to the gap and to NGO pressure, the Bank introduced a new Operational Manual Statement (which was considered more imperative than any other type of Bank policy) setting out Bank guidelines on the environmental review of projects.[56] The Bank, it said, *would endeavor* to ensure that

1. each project affecting renewable natural resources does not exceed the regenerative capacities of the environment;

2. projects with unavoidable adverse consequences for the environment are sited in areas where the environmental damage is minimized, even at somewhat greater costs.

The Bank *would not* finance any projects that

1. would severely harm or create irreversible environmental deterioration, including species extinction, without mitigatory measures acceptable to the Bank;

2. unduly compromise the public's health and safety;

3. displace people or seriously disadvantage certain vulnerable groups without undertaking mitigatory measures acceptable to the Bank;

4. contravene any international environmental agreement to which the member country concerned is a party.

The environmental directive *stated* that

1. short-term development gains must often be balanced against the creation of longer-term environmental or resource impairment;

2. prevention in environmental work is preferable and usually less costly than remedial actions;

3. the Bank's approach is tailored to local circumstances and respects the vast differences among its developing member countries;

4. project preparation missions should routinely review environmental aspects with the borrower;

5. results of environmental measures are to be reported in the Project Completion Report.[57]

55. See Asian Development Bank, "Review of the Bank's Environmental Policies and Procedures," board paper, November 5, 1985; and Asian Development Bank, *Environmental Planning and Management and the Project Cycle*, ADB Environment Paper 1, September 1987.

56. "Environmental Aspects of Bank Work," OMS 2.36, May 1984, written largely by Robert Goodland.

57. This is a nearly complete list of the main points of OMS 2.36.

But the directive had no teeth. Its requirements were difficult to monitor, because it was difficult to determine whether they had been followed. The people who had an organizational interest in doing the monitoring numbered less than half a dozen. Those people had little budget of their own with which to review projects, and their role was only advisory. In effect, compliance was left to the discretion of the project officers and their superiors, to those who had a direct interest in making sure that environmental considerations did not slow down a project or add materially to its costs.

The 1984 directive was silent on most of the concrete issues of environmental assessments: What types of projects required EAs? How comprehensive did they need to be? Who was to decide when one was needed? What level of sophistication was required? What was the method of preparation? Who was to prepare it? Who was to review it? Who was to finance it? When in the project cycle must it be ready? And so on. The senior management wanted these details left to individual project officers.[58]

Conclusions

The Bank made the first move toward developing an explicit environmental capacity—by appointing an environmental adviser in 1970—for a variety of reasons: the impending UN conference on the environment, McNamara's personal sympathy with environmental issues, support from a few rich-country governments (notably the United States), and the growing criticism of Bank projects by NGOs (though mild compared with what was to come). At this time, the relevant NGOs were public health and poverty rather than environmental ones. The appointment of an environmental adviser established the Bank as the pioneer in the new field of environment and development.

Throughout the 1970s and well into the 1980s, borrowing countries and some of the rich countries failed to see why the Bank should subject its projects to scrutiny by in-house environmentalists. Most of the staff agreed. Even those who thought that the Bank should endeavor to mitigate environmental damage in its own projects did not think the *Bank* should go beyond this. The Bank's country economic papers paid little or no attention to natural resource and ecological problems. Nowhere in the Bank were people asking what could be done to improve the environment in developing countries or to reduce the damage from development in general (not necessarily in Bank-supported projects) and then frame an agenda for lending.

The marginal role of environmental criteria and environmental specialists in the Bank's work over the 1970s and on into the 1980s can be understood as the result of not only McNamara's conviction that this was an adequate response (given the understanding of environmental issues at the time), but also a compromise be-

58. Management of the Operational Policy Staff, in which the Office of Environmental Affairs was located; its senior management included Vice President Warren Baum and Director V. Rajagopalan.

tween the pro- and the anti-environment forces. Against such strong opposition, no greater commitment of resources to environmental protection could be made. The Bank's approach to environmental work was limited to prophylaxis applied to the Bank's own projects, in the spirit of an environmental Hippocratic oath.

Yet the Bank continued to make magnificent claims about its environmental work, as McNamara himself did when describing the Bank's internal environmental practices to the Stockholm conference of 1972: "Each project processed in the Bank is now reviewed by the Environmental Office, and a careful in-house study is made of the ecological components," he said. At the time of the speech there was just one professional in the office, with a second due to join. McNamara went on to say: "In cooperation with other development agencies, we have designed a careful set of guidelines, and have built into our whole economic assistance strategy a feasible method for correlating ecological protection with effective and cost-conscious development." There were only fragments of such guidelines in existence at the time of the speech, and nothing that could be described as a feasible method for correlating ecological protection with effective development. Although McNamara claimed that "the environmental criteria we have established in the Bank encompass the entire spectrum of development," the guidelines that were later produced, in 1975, dealt mainly with industrial pollution and occupational health and safety, with only back-of-the-envelope checklists of things to bear in mind for other sectors; and in any case they were little known inside the Bank.

McNamara also said: "Our project officers are thoroughly briefed in our environmental criteria, and in their early discussions with potential borrowers draw these considerations to their attention. Far from being resented, the considerations are welcomed."[59] Project officers had virtually no training in the Bank's rudimentary criteria; they often resisted raising environmental issues with borrowers—the strong career incentives to move money not infrequently conflicted with the norms of good professional practice; and borrowers usually resented talk of having to add environmental mitigation measures.

One interpretation of McNamara's Stockholm speech is that he was expressing his hopes for the future in the guise of statements about the present, to garner support for the idea of closing the gap. Another is that he believed these claims to be accurate enough descriptions in relation to the then much greater scientific uncertainties about the components of a proper environmental assessment.

In any case, the Bank continued to make the same claims in the same words even as it did little to bring the reality closer into line. The 1977 *Annual Report* said: "Every project is now routinely examined for its environmental implications (including health), and any protective measures, identified as necessary, are incorporated into its design and execution."[60] President A. W. Clausen reiterated in

59. McNamara, "Speech to the UN Conference on the Human Environment," pp. 198–99.
60. World Bank, *Annual Report, 1977,* p. 9.

1981, "For a decade now, the Bank has required, as part of project evaluation, that every project it finances be reviewed by a special environmental unit. . . . I'm pleased to say that it has been possible to incorporate adequate protective measures in all the projects we have financed during the past decade."[61] Yet only about half of the Staff Appraisal Reports for agriculture and forestry projects prepared after 1971 included a statement on the project's environmental impacts.[62] Not until 1984 was such a statement required.

By the early 1980s the Bank was being closely scrutinized by environmental NGOs. Its claims to environmental awareness and consideration were increasingly questioned. Even though the Bank had been among the first to take into account the environmental costs of development projects, it was now accused of being a foot-dragger. "For all the murmurings about ecology that had begun to emanate from its Washington portals, the Bank too often still seemed willing to wink at environmental consequences in its eagerness to dole out big loans."[63] The first project to come under sustained scrutiny was Polonoroeste.

Pressures for Change: Polonoroeste (Brazil), 1979–89

The principal objective of the Polonoroeste ("northwest pole") project was to pave a 1,500-kilometer highway from Brazil's densely populated south-central region into the sparsely populated northwest Amazon, in the states of Rondônia and adjoining Mato Grosso. In addition, it was to construct feeder roads at the frontier end of the highway, rehabilitate existing agricultural settlements, establish new settlements, provide health care, and create ecological and Amerindian reserves. The affected area was the size of Ecuador (or California or Great Britain). Between 1981 and 1983, the Bank approved five loans in support of Polonoroeste, totaling $457 million. Well over half went for the highway and feeder roads. The Bank was the only non-Brazilian source of finance.[64]

Polonoroeste is important in the history of the Bank's environmental work for two reasons. First, it was conceived in the Bank as an innovation, which was to give unprecedented attention in the institution to mitigating the adverse effects of a development project on the environment and on indigenous peoples. In the Bank's

61. A. W. Clausen, "Sustainable Development: The Global Imperative," Fairfield Osborn Memorial Lecture in Environmental Science, Washington, D.C., November 12, 1981, in World Bank, *The Development Challenge of the Eighties, A. W. Clausen at the World Bank, Major Policy Addresses 1981–1986* (World Bank, 1986), pp. 29–30.

62. World Bank, "Renewable Resource Management in Agriculture," para. viii.

63. Roger D. Stone, *The Nature of Development: A Report from the Rural Tropics on the Quest for Sustainable Economic Growth* (Alfred A. Knopf, 1992), p. 72.

64. World Bank, "World Bank Approaches to the Environment in Brazil: A Review of Selected Projects," vol. 5, "The Polonoroeste Program," OED Report 10039, SecM92-64, April 30, 1992.

eyes it was to be a model of comprehensive regional development planning. Whereas the Brazilian government was interested in getting the Bank to help finance the highway, the Bank used its money to induce the government to agree to things that would show the world how to do sustainable development in rain forest areas.

Second, and ironically, this same Polonoroeste became the spearhead for the environmental NGOs' attack on the Bank. In a crescendo of articles, television documentaries, and hearings before the U.S. congressional committees during 1983 to 1987, the Bank's environmental critics held up Polonoroeste as "the Bank's biggest . . . and most disastrous involvement in forest colonization in the tropics," the quintessential example of its wider pursuit of misguided development strategies.[65] Polonoroeste offered powerful images—of palls of smoke, bulldozed trees, blackened stumps—and a saga of victims (immiserized peasants and Amerindians) and villains (military governments, rapacious loggers, and multilateral banks). The Sierra Club's indictment of the World Bank and other multilateral development banks, in a publication called *Bankrolling Disasters,* featured on its cover a color photograph of a newly cleared forest in the Polonoroeste area with the caption, "A typical scene of destruction as development advances in the Amazon."[66] The *Ecologist* published a special issue called *The World Bank: Global Financing of Impoverishment and Famine,* with articles on Polonoroeste.[67] *Sixty Minutes,* the most widely watched U.S. television newsweekly, featured Polonoroeste in a 1987 documentary that sharply criticized the World Bank for wasting U.S. taxpayers' dollars. Following these and other denunciations, dozens of protest letters poured into the Bank president's office every day.

Why Did the Bank Become Involved?

From the beginning some people in the Bank warned that the risks in this project were too high and that better alternatives for agricultural development existed elsewhere in the northern half of Brazil. But the Bank decided not to stay away for several reasons.

1. Being the *World* Bank, it believed it had a responsibility to help in the great task of "conquering" (the verb of choice) the Amazon, widely described at the time as "The World's Last Land Frontier."[68] The "conquest" would occur whether the Bank became involved or not. The Bank's help in one corner of the Amazon would

65. Bruce Rich, "Multi-lateral Development Banks: Their Role in Destroying the Global Environment," *Ecologist,* vol. 15, no. 1/2 (1985), p. 59.

66. Sierra Club, *Bankrolling Disasters: International Development Banks and the Global Environment* (Sierra Club, 1986).

67. "The World Bank: Global Financing of Impoverishment and Famine," *Ecologist,* vol. 15, no. 1/2 (1985).

68. See, for example, Devbrat Dutt, "Brazil's Conquest of Amazonia," *Bank Notes,* vol. 1, no. 7 (June 1972), pp. 1, 8.

produce more effective results in that corner than otherwise and would have a demonstration effect on development elsewhere in the Amazon and in other tropical rain forests.

2. The Bank assumed that the Brazilian government would pave the highway, whether it helped or not. Migration would inevitably increase; the region could not be walled off. The Bank's help in financing what the Brazilians wanted—the highway—would give it leverage in promoting other components that the government was less interested in—agriculture, forest protection, Amerindian protection, and health—and thereby turn it into a model of integrated rural development.

3. The Bank presented Polonoroeste as a *poverty* program. Sizable numbers of settlers—would-be small farmers—were already in the area following earlier waves of migration, but they had been more or less abandoned since the government had failed to provide the expected infrastructure and services. A *Washington Post* article in 1979 described Rondônia as "a land of absolute and total desperation," adding: "Elected officials, church leaders and technicians here charge that Brazil's Amazon's pioneers are victims not so much of the frontier's inevitable ruggedness as the Brazilian government's lack of planning and the constant zig-zags in its Amazon development policy."[69] The Bank calculated that the rate of return to getting the existing settlers established would be high. Indeed, the initial thrust of the project, after the road, was "consolidation" of the existing agriculture in the region rather than "new settlement"; the idea of financing new settlement came later. Without the Bank (said the Bank), the Brazilian government would continue its mistaken, geometrical-grid settlement practices and do little to make the small farmers viable. The government would do still less to mitigate the environmental and social costs. Therefore Bank involvement would help reduce poverty and reduce the environmental and Amerindian damage.

4. The champion of the project in the Bank was convinced that the governor of Rondônia "had his heart in the right place," that he was genuinely intent on alleviating the poverty of the settlers, as indicated by his commitment to upgrade slums during his tenure as mayor of a regional city.[70] This confidence in the commitment of the governor translated into confidence in the ability of the government apparatus to carry out its commitments.

5. Brazil was a large, self-confident country, hailed as a "miracle" grower in the 1970s. Equally important, it had a competent bureaucracy at the top levels. It was a big borrower from the Bank and therefore a most valued customer. The Bank could not easily say to the Brazilian government, "We don't believe you can be relied on to carry out your commitments; therefore, we will not support the project."

6. The Bank wished to increase lending to an important borrower at a time when Brazil's foreign exchange requirements were rapidly increasing. Polonoroeste

69. Larry Rohter, "Hopes of Amazon Pioneers Dashed in Nightmare of Misery," *Washington Post,* January 28, 1979, pp. A24–25.

70. Robert Skillings, interview with the author, June 24, 1996.

presented *"the possibility of making a large loan, or more precisely set of loans, to an important client country at a time when the latter was in increasing need of foreign exchange,"* and "when the continued flow of Bank resources was considered essential to maintain the confidence of other international lenders in the latter's medium and long-run development prospects."[71] These are the words of a project review published by the Bank's Operations Evaluation Department in 1992. Or in the words of a Bank participant in the project, "The Bank money machine was looking for big projects in the late 1970s, there was a lot of pressure to lend, *any argument for not lending was very unpopular,* people's careers were being made or not made by the size of their lending."[72] The road component was especially attractive because it promised to disburse about $250 million dollars quickly at a time when other ways to disburse to Brazil were limited.[73]

7. The force of these various reasons, especially those having to do with Polonoroeste as a model for the development of "the world's last land frontier," came from the fact that they had a powerful champion in the Bank. This was Robert Skillings, who had become chief of the Brazil country programs division in 1971 and stayed in that position until late 1982. He had joined the Bank in 1947, by the time of his retirement in the late 1980s being the longest-serving Bank staff member ever. He had the reputation, in the words of an observer, of being "an extremely forceful personality." By the late 1970s the Amazon had become his passion. During a sabbatical year in 1978–79 at the nearby Johns Hopkins School of Advanced International Studies, he spent much of the time researching and teaching about the Amazon, visiting the region several times and coauthoring a book about it.[74] Market exploitation of the Amazon was inevitable, he said; the only question was whether it happened wisely or in the free-for-all anarchy of the American West. The Bank could help ensure that this global asset was developed wisely.

From the top of the Bank, McNamara strongly supported the project. He was eager to see the Bank do more to reduce poverty in northeast and northwest Brazil. Polonoroeste also matched his love of heroic goals.

Internal Opposition

An eight-person fact-finding mission went out in late 1979. The members disagreed about what the Bank should do. Robert Goodland, the tropical ecologist,

71. World Bank, "World Bank Approaches to the Environment in Brazil," pp. 245, 27.

72. John Malone, interview with the author, October 30, 1995.

73. For example, the Bank would not lend to Brazil for agricultural credit—a favorite way to disburse large amounts quickly—because of Brazil's policies for subsidized agricultural credit.

74. Robert Skillings and Nils Tcheyan, *Economic Development Prospects of the Amazon Region of Brazil,* Johns Hopkins University Center for Brazil Studies, School of Advanced International Studies, Washington, D.C., 1979. See also Robert Skillings, "Economic Development of the Brazilian Amazon: Opportunities and Constraints," *Geographical Journal,* vol. 150, no. 1 (1984), pp. 48–54.

argued that the risks of jungle settlement were simply too high. The Bank should instead focus on the development of the savannah (*cerrado*) of central Brazil, an area nearly as big as the Amazon, relatively empty of people, one in which development would not destroy forests and expose fragile soils, whose climate was more suitable to agriculture, and whose location was nearer to major markets. He was then excluded from the later work on the project, except that he used the Office of Environmental Affairs' budget to send his own consultant to the area from time to time in the ensuing years and passed the consultant's reports on to the project team. Other members of the mission argued that the Bank should move slowly on the highway project for two or three years while efforts were made to help the Brazilians build the foundations for the agriculture, environment, Amerindian, and health components, through proper soil surveys and cadastral surveys. Skillings, supported by the chief of the Latin American Highways Division, decided to go ahead with the road as planned, on the grounds that the government would not be interested in borrowing for an altered sequence and that agricultural improvement without the road—without good access to markets—was infeasible.

On this reconnaissance mission, Bank staff realized, as they had not before, that the road would go through the lands of vulnerable Amerindian tribes. The mission leader brought up the issue with Brazilian officials. A shouting match ensued, the officials insisting that there was "no way the Bank will be involved in Amerindian protection." The Brazilians regarded Amerindian protection as a national security issue, no more appropriate for the Bank than it would be for the Brazilian government to tell the U.S. Central Intelligence Agency how to conduct its business.

The agricultural component of project preparation was entrusted to a group of five people (one of them half-time), and the transport and health components were assigned to several others. Together the staff spanned five divisions. There was no overall project leader in a substantive sense (only a loan officer who provided administrative coordination). Skillings came as close to playing the role of project leader as anyone, but he was in charge of all the Bank's dealings with Brazil, in addition to Polonoroeste. The transport and health components were carried out quite separately, with little connection to the agriculture/ecological/Amerindian component.

Most of the people working on the core of the project were idealistic and young (in their late twenties and early thirties). They saw themselves as innovators, charged with taking the Bank into the unknown problem areas of environmental protection, indigenous people, and appropriate agricultural methods in tropical rain forests. They had lively debates among themselves.

As project preparation proceeded, many people expressed reservations about Bank involvement. The transport economist (Renato Schulz) responsible for the economic analysis of the highway continued to urge that the Bank delay the highway until more of the other components were in place. To Skillings's argument that agricultural improvement without the highway was infeasible, he responded that the delay would be only for a few years, that it would help restrain the flood of migrants, and that some agricultural crops (cocoa in particular) were already being marketed along the existing unpaved road. At the time of project appraisal he made this argument particularly forcibly and was dismissed from the team, then dispatched to one of the Bank's dumping grounds, the Operations Evaluation Department.[75] Most of the other outspoken critics were located outside the Latin America region, in the Central Projects Staff, which contained the advisory staff on technical subjects (including the Agriculture and Rural Development Department and the Office of Environmental Affairs). To cite one of many examples, the assistant director of the Agriculture and Rural Development Department joined with the environmental adviser to write several strong critiques. They argued that the draft project proposal grossly exaggerated the agricultural potential of the northwest Amazon. Not only was there hardly any evidence on the condition of the soils (yet the whole project rested on assumptions about soils), but the little evidence that did exist suggested that the soils were highly variable, and "it would be unwise at the present time to assume that most of such lands would be suitable for development of agriculture." They concluded: "Certainly there would seem to be better opportunities to increase agricultural productivity elsewhere, but there is no consideration of such alternatives in the report. . . . This seems to be a serious gap in the logic for the development of agriculture in the northwest."[76] Meanwhile, one of the main protagonists in favor of the project himself concluded, after examining the capabilities of the Amerindian protection agency on which the Bank was relying to implement key safeguards, "FUNAI is presently a weak institution, demoralized by the ongoing dissension between administrators and technical staff. This conclusion is more or less universally accepted in Brazil, as is the feeling that a thorough restructuring of FUNAI is urgently needed. Such a restructuring . . . will be a long-term proposition and, thus, the Bank should be prepared to accept considerable risk in the interim if it decides to continue its association with FUNAI."[77]

Loan Approval, 1981

Despite the persistent criticisms leveled at the project by the Central Projects Staff, Division Chief Skillings remained unmoved. Privately he felt that these opponents "were second guessing us from on high, without having an intimate knowledge of the area."[78] Publicly (inside the Bank) he reiterated what he had said

75. The chief of the Brazil Highways Division was promoted to assistant director of the Latin America Projects Department soon after Polonoroeste was approved.

76. D. C. Pickering, assistant director AGR/CPS, and J. Lee, OEA, to D. J. Mahar, economist LC2, May 20, 1980.

77. Dennis Mahar, economist LC2DA, to Robert Skillings, division chief LC2DA, July 7, 1980.

78. Robert Skillings, interview with the author, June 24, 1996.

all along. First, the development of the savannah, Goodland's preferred alternative, would have required a forced migration program, since the savannah had few people. Second, at a meeting with a few of the critics in November 1980, "Mr. Skillings was of the opinion that the Bank's presence in the proposed development scheme was important to obtaining consideration of the environmental and tribal peoples issues. He admitted that it was not likely that all the recommendations made with regard to both issues would be implemented, but felt that even partial consideration and implementation were sufficient to warrant the Bank's participation."[79] Much of what the Bank was doing, he said, was simply designed to get the Brazilian government to follow its own legislation on the protection of peoples and areas adversely affected by development projects, in a political situation in which no powerful interests within Brazil wished the legislation to be enforced. He described how at a meeting with the head of the main coordinating body for Polonoroeste within the Brazilian government he had tried to bring up the need for Amerindian safeguards. As he spoke, the head of the coordinating agency reared back in his chair, clasped his hands over his ears, and said, "Please, *please,* don't bring up Indians." This individual went on to explain that the Bank's involvement in the protection of Indians would just invite trouble from the array of Brazilian interests that had no wish to protect them.

In April 1981 the Loan Committee (of the operational vice presidents) met to discuss the decision to proceed to negotiations with the Brazilians (negotiations about phase I, the biggest component of the three-phase program). This was the last point in the process that the project could, in practice, be turned back or modified. According to the minutes, the representatives from the Latin America region "explained that existing information confirms that *adequate soils and appropriate cultivation techniques are available for agricultural development* of the Northwest Region."[80] They also said that the Bank could be reasonably confident that the new settlements would be confined to areas with soils that could support them, because "areas of unsuitable soils have in the past normally been shunned even by spontaneous migrants." The minutes record that members of the Central Projects Staff "expressed concern" that, "in the absence of land use planning and *enforcement,*" unsuitable soil areas would "increasingly be invaded for shifting cultivation of food crops leading to rapid environmental degradation." But the Agriculture and Rural Development (AGR) Department had already signed off on the project, fundamental objections notwithstanding. By this time the project had too much momentum behind it for it to be redesigned; and the project statement had indeed been modified to take into account some AGR concerns—the text said more forcefully than before that the sites of new settlement would *only* be in areas

79. Memorandum, James Lee to files, November 25, 1980.

80. "Minutes of Loan Committee Meeting to Consider the Northwest Region Development Program and First-Stage Project held on April 15, 1981," May 7, 1981; all emphases added.

of good soil—but left unanswered the AGR points that no one knew where and how extensive the good soils were and that no enforcement mechanism existed to ensure that people were channeled toward them.

On the issue of Indian protection, the chairman, Ernest Stern, "inquired whether any participant in the meeting felt that the Bank was not doing anything it should be doing. The general view," the minutes continue, "was that the proposed measures were satisfactory but that *close monitoring of their implementation* would be required, especially given the fact that the issue was controversial and that the Bank would undoubtedly continue to be subject to criticism."

The environment adviser suggested that the Bank should meet with critics of the project "in order to fully share facts and views on the steps being taken . . . to protect the interests of the Amerindian population, in an effort to defuse what is a highly charged emotional issue." The Latin American region said no. "The Region observed that some of the positive results obtained on this matter were made possible by the atmosphere of mutual confidence that prevailed in our discussions of the matter with the Government, and . . . caution was required in making public the results of these discussions." In reply, "the Environmental Advisor said that the critics could be expected to take their case to the governments of several of the Bank's important donor countries." Stern offered a modest proposal: that the region should respond by placing an article on the whole program, including the Indian issue, in *Finance and Development* (the Bank/Fund monthly publication); and arrange "appropriate discussions on the topic with the members of the Board in due course."

At the end of the meeting, the chairman noted that "results achieved to date indicate that the Bank has had more influence with the proposed program and project than with many other projects it has financed in Brazil. A lot of progress has been made on the Amerindian issue and on devising a more balanced and integrated program. *Control would be difficult and bad publicity unavoidable. This would remain a high-risk project, but one worth doing.*"

Though not recorded in the minutes, Stern several times asked whether the Brazilian federal and state governments had the capacity to carry out the plans. He had been warned by his office's project reviewer, Jane Pratt, that several of the vice presidents had privately stated they had serious doubts in this regard, as in several others. At the meeting, however, they refused to respond to Stern's invitation to express them. Late in the one-and-a-half-hour discussion a vice president asked for the floor, sat back in his chair, folded his arms, and said: "What we are really saying is, 'The Government of Brazil is willing to sign its name to a legal contract that it will undertake certain obligations. Do we believe it, or do we not? If all the provisions are in the legal contract, then the only basis for not going ahead is that we don't believe that the government is credible when it signs an internationally-binding agreement.'" He implied that the Bank could not take such a position. "We have," he continued, "all the leverage of suspension. If Brazil does not meet the covenants, we can suspend." A guffaw greeted this remark. Someone said, "Since when have we suspended? The threat is not credible." Stern came in sharply: "I have agreed to suspensions every time they have been recommended by the regions, without exception." He went on with a twinkle, "That's the trouble with you guys. You are always trying to second-guess me. You are not sending recommendations [for suspension] up. *I* am not the block."[81]

In December 1981 the phase I project went to the Board. The staff (from the Latin America region) gave a glowing presentation. As well as the many benefits that would flow from the removal of infrastructural bottlenecks, the project included, according to the minutes, "specific environmental protection measures, including an ecological research component designed to help monitor the impact of developmental activities on the natural environment." In addition, "the health project would support efforts to control malaria and to improve basic health infrastructure in Rondônia. In conjunction with these projects, the Government was carrying out a special project to safeguard the health and lands of the region's Amerindian population." Then came the one caution from the staff: "Despite the mitigating efforts included in the projects, the effort to attempt to guide a spontaneous movement already under way carried many risks [left unspecified]. However, *the risks were considerably lower than those which would have existed in the absence of the program.*"[82]

The Board resoundingly endorsed the project. Several Board representatives complemented the Bank and the Brazilian government for the excellence of the conception and design. They pointed to the "truly integrated nature and the comprehensive approach to development" demonstrated in the project and "cited the balance among infrastructure, agriculture, health and even ecology and Amerindian welfare." Said one, "The strategy for harmonious development of the region and opening it to productive settlement was a bold attempt which deserved admiration and substantial external support." The subsequent discussion concerned such issues as the admirable structural adjustment efforts being made by the Brazilian government, the extent of local cost financing in the agricultural development part of the project, the need to coordinate the construction of the feeder roads with the farm access roads, whether there was an excessive number of prequalified construction firms preparing bids, cofinancing issues, and so on. Only one speaker raised worries about the core of the project: "He stressed the risk that if the project were not successful, it could harm the image of the Bank. . . . He stressed the necessity of the Bank monitoring the project closely, with periodic progress reports to the Board." Another speaker seconded his remarks. The staff assured them that monitoring and evaluation had been built in.

81. Jane Pratt, interview with the author, March 15, 1995. Pratt participated in the meeting as one of Stern's two project reviewers. Being one of the few people in the Bank trained in environmental assessments, she took a particular interest in Polonoroeste.

82. IBRD/IDA/IFC, summary of discussions at the meeting of the executive directors, "Loans to Brazil for Integrated Development of the Northwest Region," meeting of December 1, 1981, SD81-52, dated December 15, 1981, emphasis added.

Unmentioned were the questions that had been raised at the working levels about the basic economic viability of the project, about the potential for agriculture in the region, about alternative transport modes or alternative regions for agricultural development; and there was only glancing reference to the fundamental question of the implementation capacity of the government agencies in the region. Indeed, even at the working levels this latter question had not been raised in other than a piecemeal way.

The Bank did not go into Polonoroeste inadvertently, ignorant of the dangers. It was convinced that the dangers could be and would be offset by appropriate safeguards; and that come what may, the results would *inevitably* be worse if the Bank were not involved. Yet *the Bank made no serious assessment of the probability that those "adequate safeguards" would be carried out on the ground.*

Performance on the Ground

The ex-ante descriptions of the disorder that the project would help to avoid turned out to be reasonably accurate ex-post descriptions of what happened on the ground as a result, to some extent, of its partial implementation. The roadworks raced ahead (the paving of the highway was completed within three years) whereas everything else lagged far behind. With most of the funds disbursed for the road building, the Bank had relatively little leverage left for getting the other things done.

The paved highway and the Bank's endorsement of the whole project brought a flood of migrants. (The Bank did not make any estimates of the effects of the highway on migration, nor did it work out alternative scenarios based on different migration assumptions.) A "golden west" fever took hold. The population in the project-affected area surged from an estimated 620,000 in 1982 to 1.6 million in 1988.[83] The assumptions on which the Polonoroeste development strategy had been based turned out to be wildly inaccurate, and the performance indicators veered far from their expected path.

The infrastructure of public support for small farmers began to materialize only years later. The concerned government agencies proved largely unable or unwilling to implement what the Brazilian government had agreed with the Bank they would do. The national land agency, INCRA—the most powerful agency in the area, and the de facto government because of its jurisdiction over a land corridor 100 kilometers wide on either side of the highway—was ostentatiously corrupt. The other federal agencies operating in the region were so centralized that they could scarcely purchase even a tankful of gasoline without authorization from Brazilia, this in the days before fax machines and e-mail. The territorial agencies scarcely functioned at all.[84]

83. World Bank, "World Bank Approaches to the Environment in Brazil," p. 59, n. 21.

84. Rondônia was a federal territory, not a state, when Polonoroeste began. Indeed, the governor of Rondônia strongly supported Polonoroeste as part of his campaign to make Rondônia a state.

Consequently, neither the state government nor the national government did much to enforce the boundaries of the Amerindian reserves, or to limit the logging, or to provide the agricultural credit and the agricultural extension necessary to make the jungle settlements viable. Deforestation and spontaneous settlement occurred outside the demarcated areas, helped by the feeder roads. "In Rondônia there is not even a parody of forest management," reported a forester consultant to the Bank in 1985.[85] The forestry agency was not able to count the logs coming out, let alone check the logging. Logging trucks came to be known as "ants," because of their numbers and incessant activity. The Amerindian protection agency proved not only ineffectual but contemptuous of Amerindians at its top levels. In the sites of new agricultural settlements, the land agency often performed soil surveys and allowed settlement to begin in precisely the wrong sequence: first it settled the people and then it began to do (limited) soil surveys.

Brazil's fiscal crisis and inflation in excess of 100 percent wreaked havoc on implementation planning. Government agencies did not receive their operating budgets until halfway through the year, which in the Amazon meant not until the start of the rainy season. Because much of the project work had to be done in the dry season, it was delayed until the rains had passed. By then the budget allocation had lost much of its purchasing power. In one case, a member of the project team, Maritta Koch-Weser, asked to see a health center shown in the project accounts to have been finished. She was taken to the spot and shown a rotting pile of timber. Project officials explained that by the time they received authorization to spend the budgeted funds, the money had been substantially devalued by inflation, and then the rainy season began; by the next dry season the money would pay for no more than the wood. This is what Koch-Weser referred to as the "one-legged cow" problem; the budgeted amounts, given these financial conditions, would suffice only for the equivalent of one-legged cows. The problem was especially serious in the health component: almost nowhere in the whole project area did the three necessary ingredients all exist together: a health clinic, a trained person, and essential supplies. Political bosses used their control of one or another of the ingredients to win political support. Malaria raged like a monster out of control. Many thousands died.

There were unanticipated legal problems, too (the project missions had not included a legal expert). Several of the ecological and Amerindian reserves, once demarcated, had uncertain legal validity, because there were counter-claims to the same land, and Brazilian law had no way to reconcile the competing claims.

85. Marc Dourojeanni, "An Example of the Complexity of the Development in the Humid Tropics: The Northwest Region Development Program in Brazil," cited in Graham Searle, *Major World Bank Projects: Their Impact on People, Society and the Environment* (Camelford, Cornwall: Wadebridge Ecological Centre, 1987), p. 99.

The highway and feeder roads opened the area not only to the intended bene-ficiaries, small farmers, but also to loggers, miners, and cattle ranchers (who received large state subsidies). These latter categories had been more or less ignored in the planning, for the program was for "small farmers," even though it was also billed as an integrated *regional* development program. Their activities formed a flourishing extractive economy. The combination of poor soils, lack of farming skills, and lack of farm services induced many small farmers to join the extractive economy.

Underlying many of the implementation problems was the "carpetbagging" nature of frontier society (in the North American sense), with predatory elites easily able to suborn the local offices of government agencies.[86] Almost everyone who benefited from the extractive economy in the region was opposed to the ecological and Amerindian components; and by the implementation stage of Polonoroeste, under the impact of new mining discoveries, the extractive economy began to swamp the agricultural economy. Even with more political support, it would still have been difficult to strengthen implementing capacity on the ground in the face of the fiscal crisis, high inflation, and, above all, the flood of migrants that the upgrading of the highway itself helped to bring.

Feedback and Response

Although the Bank undertook no political analysis of Polonoroeste (nor of any other project), everyone recognized that the project was risky and in need of careful supervision. During loan negotiations the Bank insisted that a non-governmental Brazilian agency be given the task of monitoring, a step the Brazilian side resisted. Eventually the Brazilians appointed a university-based consulting group with no environmental expertise; when the Bank pressed them on this point, the consulting group linked up with a marine and oceanographic institute that had no "green" expertise; when the Bank pressed them again, a year went by before the consulting group found an organization with green credentials.

"In practice," said the OED report on Polonoroeste, "the Bank appears to have been slow to perceive the various distortions associated with the early execution of the program. Furthermore, at least until disbursements were suspended in early 1985, the Bank appears to have been largely ineffective in dealing with or correct-ing these problems."[87] Another Bank report, examining the Bank's worldwide monitoring and evaluation efforts, commented: "Project management [in Brazil] at times tried all its tools—vetoing access to information, claiming that evaluations

86. Margaret Keck, "Planafloro in Rondônia, Brazil: The Limits of Leverage," in Jonathan Fox and David Brown, eds., *The Struggle for Accountability: The World Bank, NGOs, and Grassroots Movements* (MIT Press, 1998 [1994]).

87. World Bank, "World Bank Approaches to the Environment in Brazil," vol. 5, p. 94.

were not carried out to the letter of the contract or competently, or not releasing travel funds or salaries . . . to make sure the process was as difficult as possible."[88]

The OED report goes on to say that the Bank's supervision inputs fell far short of what everyone said would be essential. "The extensive participation of Bank staff. . . , in addition to FAO personnel, in the planning and design of POLONO-ROESTE . . . stands in sharp contrast to its more limited and, apparently, poorly coordinated role in the supervision of program execution between 1982 and 1984." In the whole of 1984, for example, there was only one supervision mission, totaling 13 staff weeks.[89] Bank staff were not stationed near the region. Not surprisingly, the Brazilians concluded that the Bank was not entirely committed to the nonroad objectives of the project.

Nevertheless, the growing imbalance between the road work and the rest of the project became well known inside the Bank. But the Brazilians' failure to meet core conditions notwithstanding and in disregard of the terms of the loan agreement, the Board approved the phase III loan for Polonoroeste in October 1983 for the purpose of creating *new* agricultural settlements.[90] In their presentation of the phase III project to the Board, the Latin America region's staff said nothing about the difficulties encountered on the ground, merely that the project had "built upon and extended to new settlement areas the strategy of development used in the prior phases, *which were being implemented in line with forecasts.*" With respect to the special project for the protection of Amerindian communities, the staff said that "the Bank had monitored the progress of this special project closely and would continue to do so," without revealing the results of its "close monitoring" other than, "the Bank would not have gone ahead with any project in the region if it had not been convinced that the government was implementing the Amerindian component *to its fullest capacity*" (it did not say whether "its fullest capacity" was sufficient).

By this time, two years after they had approved phase I, some Board members expressed concern about Polonoroeste. To each the staff gave reassuring replies that concealed much contrary information.[91] And the staff misled not only the Board but also the president. In a briefing paper on Polonoroeste to Clausen in December 1983, the staff wrote, "The Bank maintains the right to supervise the

88. World Bank, "An Overview of Monitoring and Evaluation in the World Bank," OED Report 13247, June 30, 1994, p. 31.

89. World Bank, "World Bank Approaches to the Environment in Brazil," vol. 5, p. 94. However, members of the core team say that they piggybacked supervision work on top of project preparation work for later projects in the three-phase package, so that actual supervision was more than the "supervision" figures show.

90. Phase II had been for the extension of Phase I into the next-door state of Mato Grosso.

91. IBRD/IDA/IFC, summary of discussions at the meeting of the executive directors, October 25, 1983, SD83-51, dated December 16, 1983.

Special Project [for Amerindian protection] and no obstacles in this respect have been encountered. Bank staff contact with FUNAI is easy. . . . *Implementation of the Special Project is now satisfactory.* . . . We have, and will continue to monitor the Special Project closely given its sensitivity and visibility in the international scene."[92] Evidence from the files shows that the division chief was busy telling the Brazilian government that implementation was very unsatisfactory.[93] Few of the thirty-seven Indian reserves had been demarcated and registered, and many had been invaded by squatters, loggers, and others.

Suspension of Disbursements

At the working levels alarm bells continued to ring. A nine-member midterm review mission went out in November 1984 and presented its report in late February 1985. The report documented at length the many failings.[94] The whole program's "mitigating" measures had been "stunted by weak program coordination, institutional inefficiencies and an undisguised lack of political support for environmental and Amerindian protection." In addition, the program's agricultural strategy "remained largely unimplemented" because the government had failed to comply with its contractual obligation to provide credit to small farmers in the region (contradicting what the staff had told the Board in the approval meeting for the phase III loan a year or so earlier). The midterm review continued, "The Rondônia state government [took] a course in clear violation of the spirit of the Northwest loan agreements by allowing settlement in low potential areas." On the other hand, it also said that for all its failings, the Amerindian Special Project had raised "the quality of assistance provided to [the Indians] to levels unrivaled elsewhere in Brazil."[95]

The whole Northwest program had arrived at a critical juncture, the midterm review concluded. If the program were "to stem [the] adverse and growing trend towards transgressions into reserve lands and failures in small-farmer colonization," it needed to be strengthened with "far more effective coordination and implementation instruments."[96] The review calld for the Bank to suspend disbursements and laid out an action plan to which the Brazilians would have to commit themselves in order for disbursements to be resumed. It concluded, "The above proposals . . . are

92. Briefing paper to A. W. Clausen from Suitbertus van der Meer (acting regional vice president) through Ernest Stern, "Brazil—Northwest Region Integrated Development Program—Briefing on Amerindians," dated December 28, 1983, emphasis added.

93. For example, telegram from Hendrick van der Heijden to Minister Mario Andreazza, Ministry of Interior, dated March 17, 1983. Van der Heijden replaced Skillings as division chief for Brazil Programs.

94. World Bank, midterm review, internal memorandum of February 25, 1985, cited in World Bank, "World Bank Approaches to the Environment in Brazil," vol. 5, pp. 64–75.

95. Ibid., p. 75.

96. Ibid., pp. 65–66.

made with the firm belief that past Bank involvement in the Northwest program has, overall, helped to prevent even worse outcomes, and that, however unrewarding and thankless the defense of the small farmers, Indians and environment of the region may be, . . . the Bank should do its utmost to help overcome the present difficulties and remain involved in the orderly development of the Amazon."[97]

How did such a midterm review come to be written, one that contradicted much of what the earlier reports on the project had been saying? In large part, it was an accident of personnel. John Malone had been the deputy resident representative in the Bank's largest overseas office, in Indonesia. In that capacity he had been a strong internal critic of the Bank's support for the Indonesian Transmigration project, which involved moving hundreds of thousands of people from the densely populated inner islands to agricultural settlements on the outer islands, many of them in rain forests. He had later been a division chief in OED for six years, in charge of OED's Agriculture Division. In that capacity he had seen at close quarters the propensity of the Bank to proclaim victory in a project and sweep the contrary evidence under the carpet. His job, OED's job, was to lift the carpet. He acquired a reputation as an outspoken critic of poor-quality projects. This reputation accounted in part for his difficulties in getting out of OED and back into operational work. He had earlier worked closely with Donald Martinusen, who by that time had replaced the division chief of agricultural projects in Brazil under whose charge Polonoroeste had been started. Martinusen proposed that he recruit Malone as his *deputy* division chief, which would at least get him out of OED even at the cost of dropping a rank. Martinusen himself was critical of the agricultural assumptions of Polonoroeste but had no stomach for fighting. He put his newly arrived and forthright friend John Malone in charge of the midterm review of Polonoroeste. Malone was not impressed by what he saw and was determined to say so, in the face of opposition from the chief of the Brazil Programs Division but with the support of the new vice president for Latin America, David Knox.

Soon after the midterm review was presented in March 1985, the decision was made to suspend disbursements until a "Corrective Action Program" could be agreed upon and certain specific measures taken for Amerindian protection. The decision to suspend owed much to the fact that by the start of 1985 a completely new line of command on Polonoroeste was in place, comprising people who had no special interest in the project because they had not been involved in its initiation. It included a new project officer (Maritta Koch-Weser), who had been responsible for "social" aspects of the project since 1981 and who had just been put in charge of the whole project, including the transport and health components (recall that until this time no one was responsible for integrating the whole). The new line of command also included the new division chief and the new deputy division chief for Brazil agricultural projects; Skillings's successor as chief of the Brazil Country Programs

97. Ibid., p. 66.

Division, who considered Polonoroeste an embarrassing nuisance that he did not wish to deal with; and a new vice president for Latin America.

With this radical change in personnel, Maritta Koch-Weser, who had long ago concluded that only suspension might induce the Brazilians to take their commitments seriously, was able to act. Several other things happened at about this time that facilitated action. The midterm review had just been finalized, setting out the grounds for suspension (though it did not say anything that was not already well known to those involved). Ernest Stern, who had to see the midterm review, could not be kept in the dark. And there was a specific pretext: the Bank learned in early 1985 that yet another of the Indian reserves had recently been invaded by settlers.

Then came two changes in the larger context. First, the Bank was hit with intense public criticism over what U.S. and Brazilian environmental groups were calling the Polonoroeste "debacle." The NGOs were demanding suspension, and powerful figures in the U.S. Congress were insisting that the United States cut its contributions to the Bank. Second, Brazil's first civilian government in twenty years had just taken office and accepted the suspension as an indictment of its predecessors rather than itself. Five months later, in August 1985, when the Brazilian government presented to the Bank an action plan to deal with the problems and showed evidence that the settlers had been removed from the recently invaded Indian reserve, the Bank resumed disbursements.

After 1985

Maritta Koch-Weser, project officer from early 1985, was moved off Polonoroeste in 1987, upon the arrival of a new director of the Brazil Department. He could not understand all the fuss about Indians, he remarked; they wear T-shirts and sneakers just like everyone else. The director appointed his own project officer, who began his tenure by agreeing to the Brazilian government's request to terminate the contract with the university-based monitoring and evaluation unit. The unit had begun to produce some critical reports about Polonoroeste; and it was inconvenient to have such reports still arriving when he was beginning to prepare a big follow-on project to Polonoroeste. In any case, the new project officer was a general economist more interested in agricultural production than in social and environmental issues. John Malone, meanwhile, had left the division in 1986, tired of working in Brazil. "It was tough sledding," he said later, "like pushing on a rubber diaphragm—it gives when you push, but as soon as you stop it snaps back to its original shape."[98]

Suspension did have an effect. In the period from 1985 to the effective end of the Polonoroeste project in 1989, the Brazilian government somewhat strengthened the implementing capacities of the state agencies, roughly demarcated

98. John Malone, interview with the author, October 30, 1995.

most of the reserves, and provided some of the infrastructure of the settlement projects (the health centers, water supply systems, schools, and storage facilities). Gradually the government on the ground began to make some progress in doing some of the things it had agreed to do years before.

Yet the OED study found that "despite the government's formal compliance with most of the recommendations made by the Bank at the time of the mid-term review [late 1984–early 1985], in general the situation in September-October 1989 was not very different from that encountered in late 1984. . . . Polonoroeste appears to have been largely unable to implement and/or sustain many of its environmental protection measures or to avoid the continuing invasion of reserve areas by loggers, prospectors, and spontaneous settlers."[99] In retrospect, the outcome could hardly have been different, for all the fine, innovative plans about where the forest and Amerindian reserves should go and about what sort of crop patterns the new settlers should follow. It was not just that the Bank and Brazil had few data on such fundamentals as soils and their distribution, as the specialists in AGR kept saying. It was, more basically still, that the Bank hardly addressed the question of the ability and willingness of the federal and territorial agencies to do what the plans required them to do. The Bank's desire to lend to Brazil and at the same time show the world how to conduct rain forest settlement well, coupled with its general avoidance of political analysis, led the relevant people to make assumptions about Polonoroeste that the Latin American vice president described, looking back, as "almost deliberately naive."[100] The fact that the Bank was intimately associated with a project that could plausibly be blamed for accelerating the destruction of Brazil's rain forest and Amerindian ways of life gave environmental NGOs ammunition against the Bank once they began to target it in the early to mid-1980s.

Pressures for Change: The NGO Campaign and the U.S. Treasury's Push for Environmental Reforms

In May 1987 the Bank's new president, Barber Conable, announced plans for a big expansion of environmental capacity, just what the Bank had been saying for years it did not need.[101] He was speaking to a gathering of environmentalists from

---

99. World Bank, "World Bank Approaches to the Environment in Brazil," p. 108. For more on the wider political context of Amazonian destruction, see Andrew Hurrell, "Brazil and the International Politics of Amazonian Destruction," in A. Hurrell and B. Kingsbury, eds., *The International Politics of the Environment* (Oxford: Clarendon Press, 1992).

100. David Knox, who became vice president for Latin America in time for the midterm review of Polonoroeste, interview with the author, May 15, 1995.

101. For example, in 1984, at the first-ever meeting between President Clausen and representatives of some environmental NGOs, Clausen declared that "he was not going to increase the Bank's environmental staff," as they had been urging. Rich, *Mortgaging the Earth*, p. 125.

many organizations at the World Resources Institute, among them some of the Bank's fiercest critics. The Bank admitted that its plans owed much to the critics: "There's no question that the monitoring by the non-governmental organizations in the U.S. was an important factor [in the Bank's decision to create the new environmental department and divisions]," said David Hopper, the senior vice president in charge of this part of the Bank.[102] The point was echoed in press reports. One commented that "the World Bank has finally conceded to its critics," another that "the changes culminate four years of congressional hearings and constant badgering by environmentalists."[103]

Undoubtedly the campaign led by U.S. environmental NGOs was a major factor in driving the Bank to change its ways. But the causes were a good deal more complex. The campaign was but the "seed" injected into the appropriate crystalline solution, namely, the wider "zeitgeist" or spirit of concern expressed in scientific circles and the media. But this metaphor, too, fails to tell the whole story. There were other forces at play. The U.S. Congress was one. It had to approve U.S. contributions to IDA and could be swayed by lobbyists. The U.S. Treasury was another. The role of the Treasury helps to explain why the Bank held off the campaign for four long years.

The Zeitgeist

In the late 1970s and early 1980s the environment was at the crest of a new wave of scientific and public concern in the West. The push was no longer for "environmental protection" in a piecemeal fashion, but for comprehensive "environmental management." The underlying assumption was that resource degradation due to poverty and population growth was the central threat requiring public action, and that environmental "sustainability" was a necessary constraint on development.[104] Consequently, sustainability must be a criterion for selecting whole patterns of economic activity. This meant that investment projects would no longer be selected on the basis of economic criteria and then adjusted to reduce their environmental damage; environmental standards had to enter into the selection process from the start. The aim was less to make polluters pay than to remove the need to pollute, less to build taller smokestacks than to find alternatives to such factories, including different ways to supply the same goods and services and ways to reduce the demand. The aim was to value and conserve not just stocks of physical resources but also ecosystem processes, to see forests as the source of not only commercial

102. Quoted in Linda Hossie, "World Bank Seeks to Clean Up a Host of Destructive Projects," *Globe and Mail* (Toronto), July 23, 1987.

103. Alun Anderson, "World Bank Policy to Add Ecology to Economics," *Nature,* vol. 327 (May 14, 1987); Constance Holden, "World Bank Launches New Environment Policy," *Science,* May 15, p. 769.

104. See Colby, "The Evolution of Environmental Management."

and fuelwood timber but also other nonpriced nontimber products, including soil protection, biodiversity, and carbon sequestration. Inasmuch as the environmental assessment was the operational instrument of the "environmental protection" paradigm, the instrument of "environmental management" was the national environmental action plan.

The new wave of concern also had a stronger crossborder accent than before, focusing in part on the large-scale destruction of tropical rain forests. The media publicized some of the most egregious cases, for example, in Indonesia's outer islands and Brazil's Amazon, often in highly charged language. Nicholas Guppy, a professional forester, wrote an article, "Tropical Deforestation," describing his visits to Indonesia's transmigration sites and Brazil's Polonoroeste:

> Visiting such areas it is hard to view without emotion the miles of devastated trees, of felled, broken and burned trunks, of branches, mud and bark crisscrossed with tractor trails—especially when one realizes that in most cases nothing of comparable value will grow again on the area. *Such sights are reminiscent of photographs of Hiroshima, and Brazil and Indonesia might be regarded as waging the equivalent of thermonuclear war upon their own territories.*[105]

None of the rhetorical excesses of the NGO campaign ever quite matched Guppy's charge that the governments of Brazil and Indonesia (both backed by the World Bank) were waging the equivalent of nuclear war upon their territories. It was published not in a wild-eyed environmental broadsheet but in the conservative journal *Foreign Affairs*.

These scientific and public policy concerns sustained the growth of environmental NGOs, green political parties, and environmental agencies in many Part I countries. People in these countries began to see for the first time that the welfare of *their* children could be affected by something that happened in developing countries: by the destruction of rain forests, in particular. And during the 1980s, as problems of air and water pollution worsened throughout the developing countries in ways that their elites could not escape, it became increasingly difficult for their governments to brush aside environmental concerns with the notion that "environmental problems are problems of affluence." They began to admit that they faced some serious environmental issues that could not be postponed until affluence had arrived.

Within developing countries, deterioration on the ground triggered the growth of local and national groups dedicated to stopping the destruction. In Brazil various groups protested the forced resettlement of people under the Sobradhino dam in the late 1970s, sending their message not only to the Brazilian government but also to the World Bank, which was helping to finance the project. In India's Narmada Valley, local NGOs loudly complained about the lack of attention to resettlement

105. Nicholas Guppy, "Tropical Deforestation: A Global View," *Foreign Affairs*, vol. 62, no. 4 (spring 1984), p. 943, emphasis added.

under the Bank-supported Sardar Sarovar project from the early 1980s onward, and international NGOs such as Oxfam and the Natural Resources Defense Council linked up with them to amplify their voice.

A series of headline-grabbing environmental disasters over the 1980s galvanized public awareness of environmental dangers both locally and internationally. In late 1984 a leak of cyanide gas at a pesticide plant in Bhopal, India, caused the death of more than 3,000 people and injured many more. (The Bank was not involved in the plant.) Brazilian church groups and NGOs brought to international attention the disaster of Cubatao, a chemical complex near São Paulo whose neighborhood population had the world's highest rate of certain kinds of fetus deformations (such as babies born without a brain). In the mid-1980s the Brazilian government came to the Bank for help in cleaning it up. This was one of a number of events in Brazil that persuaded the government to abandon its old attitudes and take steps to make private firms reduce pollution.

Also in the mid-1980s the United Nations created a world commission, the Bruntland Commission, to investigate the effects of development on the environment. The Commission held hearings around the world through 1986 and into 1987, even in some of the countries whose governments had been most antipathetic to environmental issues. The hearings attracted a great deal of publicity, and, partly because sponsored by the United Nations, they added legitimacy to the idea that environmental values should be injected into economic development policies. The Commission and its report helped to popularize the notion of environmentally sustainable development.[106]

The NGO Campaign, 1983–87

Between 1983 and 1987 more than twenty hearings on the environmental and social performance of the multilateral banks were held before six subcommittees of the U.S. Congress. The center of attention was the World Bank. Congress had to approve U.S. contributions to the Bank's lending resources and decided at this time to base its approval on some new conditions. Among other conditions, the U.S. executive director of the Bank would be required to press the Bank's management to undertake stipulated environmental reforms, the implication being that if the Bank's management did not act, Congress would look less favorably upon the next request.

Despite having a public relations department several times bigger than the Office of Environmental Affairs, the Bank for the first two years (1983 and 1984) ignored the campaign, treating it as a passing irritation. The fact that there had been few actual *reports* of major environmental damage in its projects over the

106. The World Commission on Environment and Development, *Our Common Future* (Oxford University Press, 1987).

previous several decades made the Bank confident of its existing arrangements. Besides, had it not just received the National Wildlife Federation's Special Environmental Achievement Award in 1981? In any case, it had no fora of consultation with NGOs.[107] Direct contact with NGOs seemed to contradict two of the Bank's constitutional principles: that it would deal with citizens and legislators of member governments through the designated representatives of those governments on the Board of the Bank; and that it would maintain a fiduciary relationship with member governments, a relationship of confidentiality in which the responsibility for releasing information pertaining to a borrower lay with the borrowing government. Besides, how was the Bank to decide which NGOs to consult and which to avoid?

When the Bank did respond to the NGO campaign it appeared to do so in an arrogant and dismissive manner, which merely brought the critics out in full force. The NGOs kept pressing, the hearings on the Hill kept coming, the Congress kept insisting that the Treasury persuade the Bank to strengthen its environmental capacity, the threats to its funding grew louder, and the public (mainly in North America and Europe) wrote more and more letters protesting its policies. Many people who had never heard of the Bank came to know of it as "the bank that destroys rain forests."

First Steps, 1983–84

Three U.S. environmental NGOs led the campaign to change the Bank:[108] the Natural Resources Defense Council (NRDC), the Environmental Policy Institute, and the National Wildlife Federation (NWF).[109] The first two were small organizations created in response to the first wave of public concern about the environment in the late 1960s and early 1970s. Advocacy was their primary business, which they

107. This is not literally true. The Bank had long had contact with foundations such as Ford and Rockefeller, drawing on their expertise in policymaking and in particular projects. It also established an NGO–World Bank Committee in 1982, a committee that included mostly northern and poverty-oriented NGOs such as Care, the Red Cross, the World Council of Churches, and no environmental NGOs. It was window dressing, without practical significance, until the late 1980s, when it began to include southern NGOs and more radical northern ones (such as Development Gap).

108. This section on the early years of the campaign draws on Gordon Lee Foer, "Mutual Interests: The Evolution of the U.S. Environmental Movement and the Campaign to Reform the Environmental Policies of the World Bank," master's thesis in Urban and Environmental Planning, Tufts University, 1988; Bruce Rich, *Mortgaging the Earth*; Barbara Bramble and Gareth Porter, "Non-governmental Organizations and the Making of US International Environmental Policy," in Andrew Hurrell and B. Kingsbury, eds., *The International Politics of the Environment* (Oxford: Clarendon Press, 1992); and interviews with participants.

109. The Environmental Policy Institute later merged with Friends of the Earth, taking the latter's name.

pursued through the legislatures of the state and federal governments, through the courts, and through the media. For this purpose they built up able staffs of lawyers, scientists, and lobbyists. In contrast, the National Wildlife Federation had four million members distributed across the United States, a wide array of publications, and a vast direct-mail machine; it brought grass roots activism and electoral weight to the advocacy arena.

Through the 1970s these organizations concentrated on domestic environmental issues in the United States. They deployed lawyers and scientists to lobby for changes in U.S. policies and to bring lawsuits against noncompliers. By the early 1980s they had honed their lobbying and legal skills to a fine point, winning victories against prominent U.S. companies. The companies finally adopted a less confrontational, more cooperative stance toward them.[110]

At the NRDC, a young lawyer and new recruit, Bruce Rich, wanted to focus on international environmental issues. At the same time that Rich was wondering how to pursue an international agenda at NRDC, the NWF hired another young lawyer, Barbara Bramble, to initiate its international program. The two of them linked up, bringing together the complementary skills of their respective organizations. Brent Blackwelder of the Environmental Policy Institute joined them.

Early in 1983 they began to consider the World Bank as a target for an international environment campaign. They chose the Bank for several reasons. First, they did not want to attack foreign governments directly, because such a move could easily backfire. Second, they wanted to target organizations that both wielded real influence and received contributions from the U.S. government over the spending of which they, as taxpayers, had some right to comment. Here they played on a peculiarity of the U.S. political system that allows advocacy NGOs to have much more influence over the U.S. government than NGOs in any other member country. Under the Constitution, the U.S. Congress is required to appropriate money for the federal government *each year.* Lobby groups thus have ample opportunity to attach conditions to the spending of U.S. funds. This strategy—to go for organizations that wield real influence and receive funds from the U.S. government—put the NGOs on the trail of the multilateral development banks. Third, the NGOs chose the World Bank as the primary target rather than another of the multilateral development banks because it was more politically salient than the others. Finally, the Bank also happened to be right next door, in Washington, D.C. They did not choose the Bank because they thought its environmental and social record was worse than that of other multilateral development banks. Initially, they thought of focusing on the Inter-American Development Bank's financing of cattle ranching in Central American rain forests as the centerpiece of the campaign but dropped the idea when they discovered that hardly anyone in Congress or in the

110. Andrew Hoffman, "A History of Environmental Coverage in *Chemical Week*," *Chemical Week*, August 24, 1994, pp. 27–44.

administration knew anything about the Inter-American Development Bank, whereas everyone knew of the World Bank.

The trio's basic strategy was to work with environmental and indigenous rights groups in the United States and in a few other countries having the largest share of voting rights in the Bank. They would publicize a small number of large projects against which it would be easy to mobilize opposition. (Focusing on the myriad of resource users in developing countries whose aggregate decisions account for more environmental degradation than large projects would not be nearly as effective.) Using these few projects as levers, they would build pressure on member governments to move the Bank, through the executive directors, to institute environmental reforms. They also gave high priority to finding covert allies inside the Bank. They fully recognized that it was equally important to work with NGOs in developing countries, but progress on this front turned out to be slow.

Soon after the idea of a campaign had crystallized, Rich, Bramble, and Blackwelder put their heads together to draft some legislation for the U.S. Congress. The trio invited some mass-membership organizations to sign on, including the Sierra Club, Friends of the Earth, and the National Audubon Society.

Then they persuaded the chairman of a House committee dealing with international development issues (the House Banking, Finance, and Urban Affairs Subcommittee on International Development Institutions and Finance) to hold hearings before going to legislation. The hearings would generate useful publicity. At the hearings, held during two days at the end of June 1983, representatives of the environmental organizations joined with representatives of indigenous rights organizations to present a picture of the environmental and social damage wrought by some Bank-supported projects.[111]

Referring to the Polonoroeste project in northwest Brazil, they held up satellite photographs of the rain forest and pointed to the crucial feature: dozens of smoke plumes rising up and mingling with the clouds, the result of fires lit deliberately to clear the forest. They presented several more photographs from lower altitudes, showing a crosshatch pattern of feeder roads and blotches of land cleared by colonists. Had the Bank not helped to finance the 1,500-kilometer highway, the witnesses argued, considerably fewer colonists would have come into the area and the environmental and social damage would have been much less.

Polonoroeste was only one of a string of environmental and social "disasters" financed by the Bank and its counterpart institutions, said the witnesses. They went on to describe the Indonesian Transmigration Program, which caused great

111. House Committee on Banking, Finance, and Urban Affairs, Subcommittee on International Development Institutions and Finance, *Environmental Impact of Multilateral Development Bank-Funded Projects*, 98th Cong., 1st sess., June 28 and 29, 1983. See Foer, *Mutual Interests*; and Rich, *Mortgaging the Earth*.

damage to the rain forest and native peoples there; then a livestock project in Botswana that had allegedly contributed to desertification and the destruction of wildlife; and then a mega-irrigation and hydro project on India's Narmada River, which would turn a hundred thousand people out of their homes and lands to make way for the reservoir and canals.[112]

They also talked about the Bank's internal environmental organization, describing the Office of Environmental Affairs as a public relations sham (adding that the other multilateral development banks had no environmental staff whatsoever). On the second day representatives of indigenous peoples' rights organizations spoke. They charged that many projects financed by the Bank and the other lending institutions were a catastrophe for tribal peoples, verging in some cases on genocide.

The hearings closed with a question period, followed by the chairman's summary: the testimony, he said, had been "shocking" and "eye-opening."[113] The subcommittee decided that the issues raised by the hearings were unusually important and had to be explored further. It requested that the Treasury forward the testimony to the multilateral banks for their response.

This was at the end of June 1983. In January 1984 the multilateral banks sent their responses to the Treasury and thence to the House Subcommittee on International Development Institutions and Finance. The Bank was terse and defensive in its reply to the charge that it and the other multilateral banks "do a poor job of assessing the social and environmental consequences of large development projects, in part because they devote inadequate staff and budget to the review": "This may apply to some development banks since some of them have yet to develop the capability to deal with these elements of the development process. However, the World Bank, with its Office of Environmental Affairs, is the oldest, largest, and most experienced institution dealing with these issues." It took pains to point out that "every project proposed for financing comes to the attention of OEA early in the project cycle," and that by the time of project appraisal (the last stage before the project goes for approval) "the environmental assessment will have been largely completed."[114]

The House subcommittee employed a special assistant to evaluate the responses from the multilateral banks and to prepare a series of recommendations for environmental reform. The assistant relied heavily on the environmental NGOs. Many of the original recommendations made by Rich, Bramble, and Blackwelder in April 1983 went into the list of "congressional recommendations." More hearings were held on the draft recommendations in September 1984, and further recom-

112. See Sierra Club, *Bankrolling Disasters.*

113. Quoted in Rich, *Mortgaging the Earth,* p. 115.

114. World Bank response to the House Banking Subcommittee on International Development Institutions and Finance, titled "Bank Environmental Policy," from James A. Lee to Thomas Blinkhorn (through V. Rajagopalan), January 11, 1984.

mendations were added to the list. In the end, nineteen recommendations, concentrating on actions that could be monitored by Congress and the public, were issued by the House subcommittee in December 1984. These recommendations called on the Bank and its counterpart institutions to increase their environmental staffs by a substantial number, to consult with environmental and health ministries when preparing projects, to consult with and share information with nongovernmental organizations, to finance a higher proportion of small-scale, less ecologically disruptive projects, and to expand the Economic Development Institute's training courses in natural resource management. The Treasury agreed with most of the recommendations and assigned a full-time staff person in its Office of Multilateral Banks to monitor the environmental aspects of multilateral bank loan proposals.

As the campaign gathered momentum through 1984 in the wake of the hearings, other people and organizations became more actively involved. (Many had earlier held back, being prepared to take the Bank's own statements at face value.) With its original three animateurs, the campaign held regular meetings with the full coalition at least bimonthly, and subgroups met more often to plan a strategy and coordinate the activities of each participant. The movement remained loosely articulated, without any central command, and certainly could not have reached such a wide range of organizations and viewpoints otherwise. The advocacy organizations—those concerned with environmental issues, such as the NRDC, and those promoting indigenous peoples' rights, such as Survival International—tended to take an adversarial position toward the Bank, believing that the Bank would only change under head-on confrontation. Rhetorical excess being inherent in their mode of operation, they were prone to attribute all problems in Bank-supported projects to the Bank. Some even argued that the world would be better off without it. The campaign obtained many confidential World Bank documents from a small number of sympathetic World Bank staff, and at times smuggled one of their members into the buildings late at night to go through files with an internal sympathizer. The movement prided itself on the thoroughness of its documentation.[115]

The Bank's seeming numbness to environmental concerns only strengthened the resolve of its leaders. When the trio finally met directly with a senior official, David Hopper, vice president for South Asia, he told them matter-of-factly that in South Asian conditions the rate-of-return criterion would generally not allow the

115. Information on environmental and resettlement problems associated with Bank and other multilateral development bank projects came to them from such sources as Edward Goldsmith and Nicholas Hildyard, *The Social and Environmental Effects of Large Dams* (Camelford, Cornwall: Waybridge Ecological Centre, 1984); Stein and Johnson, *Banking on the Biosphere?*; the in-house review by Michael Cernea of the record of resettlement in Bank-supported projects, on which he had based the writing of OMS 2.33, "Social Issues Associated with Involuntary Resettlement in Bank-Financed Projects," February 1980; and from internal leaks.

Bank to support an irrigation project with adequate drainage because the drainage added too much to present costs in relation to its discounted long-term benefits. Rather, the Bank had to put in the irrigation system and wait for salinity and waterlogging to take land out of production. Then it could justify a drainage project. This, to the campaign members, sounded preposterous: it would obviously take many years for land made unfit for cultivation by salinity and waterlogging to become productive again once drainage is put in, and it costs five times as much to construct adequate drainage as it does to irrigate in the first place.[116]

Showdown over Polonoroeste, 1984–85

Polonoroeste had featured in the June 1983 hearings. During the summer of 1984 Bruce Rich and anthropologist Steve Schwartzman, recently returned from Brazil, gathered detailed information on the project and the Bank's role. Polono-roeste was to provide the central "image" required to attract attention; they would use it to test their strategy, which was to direct public and legislative concern to a small number of dramatic cases and use them to push for bigger changes in Bank policies. In September 1984 Polonoroeste was the subject of a special hearing before the House Science and Technology Subcommittee on Natural Resources, Agricultural Research, and Environment. The star witness was agronomist José Lutzenberger, Brazil's leading environmental activist. In an eloquent denunciation of the project, he also criticized the Bank not only for ignoring the Brazilian government's flouting of Bank loan conditions but also for abetting the underlying agricultural strategy of the project. He concluded, "On behalf of the environmental groups of Brazil, I call on the Bank to stop the [Highway 364] road and re-think its policy on Rondônia."[117]

Lutzenberger's testimony to the U.S. Congress was shown on Brazilian and American television. After the hearings the chairman of the House committee wrote to Treasury Secretary Donald Regan urging the Treasury to press the Bank to take urgent steps to check the deforestation and threats to Amerindians that Polonoroeste had unleashed. At the same time, in October 1984, Bruce Rich organized the sending of a letter to President Clausen about Polonoroeste. The letter called on the Bank to enforce its loan covenants with the Brazilian govern-ment by immediately suspending disbursements. It listed eight specific steps that the Brazilian government should carry out and asked how the Bank would ensure that the steps were taken. It continued, "The prompt implementation of these

116. As recalled and interpreted by Barbara Bramble, interview with the author, June 20, 1996.

117. House Committee on Science and Technology, Subcommittee on Natural Resour-ces, Agricultural Research, and Environment, Tropical Forest Development Projects: Status of Environmental and Agricultural Research, 98th Cong., 2d sess., September 19, 1984, p. 22.

measures would help to forestall increasing concern in the U.S. Congress and the West German Bundestag over evidence of the Bank's inadequate attention to sustainable management of natural resources and to the indigenous people who depend on those resources."

The letter used Polonoroeste as an example of why the Bank needed to "undertake concrete measures and commit real resources, such as more professionally trained staff, to improve the ecological design and review of its projects. Further neglect and delay of the Bank in addressing these environmental management issues will not only inflict grave long-term damage on the Bank's image, but could ultimately undermine public and legislative support for funding of the Bank in its most important donor countries." The letter was signed by thirty-two non-governmental organizations from eleven countries, including the presidents of the American and Brazilian anthropological associations; environmental groups in the United States, Europe, and Brazil; and eleven members of the West German parliament.[118] It was accompanied by the extensive research dossiers on Polonoroeste prepared by Rich and Schwartzman. The letter and accompanying dossier were featured in a *New York Times* article shortly afterward.[119]

The Bank's letter of reply, cleared by Clausen and by the vice president for Latin America but signed by the chief of the Brazil programs division (the appropriate person to reply to an outside enquiry about the Bank's work in Brazil), was brief and formal. It said, in part,

> As you are aware, POLONOROESTE is a carefully planned regional development program, which seeks to stabilize and maximize the economic development of the region, while minimizing the risks to the regional ecology and Amerindian populations. We very much share the concerns you have noted in your letter. We have discussed them in detail with the Brazilian authorities and are encouraged by those discussions to believe that effective action will be taken. We recognize, however, that close monitoring will be necessary and we will therefore continue to follow the situation very closely.[120]

Outraged, Rich showed the correspondence to Senator Robert W. Kasten, Jr., and his staff. Kasten, a conservative Republican from Wisconsin, was chair of the key Senate Appropriations Subcommittee on Foreign Operations and therefore had the power to set the subcommittee's agenda and to initiate legislation governing U.S. participation in the Bank. His position made him, for the Bank, the most powerful senator of the most powerful member state. Earlier, when in February 1984 Kasten's subcommittee had held hearings on the World Bank and Bruce Rich

118. The Green Party had been active in mobilizing opposition to Polonoroeste in Germany.

119. Eric Eckholm, "World Bank Urged to Halt Aid to Brazil for Amazon Development," *New York Times,* October 17, 1984, p. A17.

120. Roberto Gonzalez Cofino, chief, Brazil Division, to Bruce Rich, NRDC, November 7, 1984.

had testified on behalf of seven environmental organizations, Kasten had indicated his personal sympathy with what the environmental NGOs were trying to do. Later, in November 1984, when Kasten and his staff saw the Bank's response to Rich's letter, they "hit the roof. [The Bank's reply] seemed to confirm their worst suspicions about the arrogance and lack of accountability of multilateral institutions."[121]

Senator Kasten Intervenes, 1984–85

Then the environmental campaign took a new and ominous turn from the Bank's point of view: Senator Kasten agreed to intervene. Kasten was not only the most powerful person in the U.S. Senate as far as the Bank was concerned, but also a well-known critic of foreign aid. Kasten might use the Polonoroeste project in particular and environmental issues in general as yet another pretext for opposing U.S. contributions to the Bank. He had already made known his view that if the multilateral development banks did not follow the nineteen-point congressional recommendations he would be inclined to work for funding cuts. Leading the fight to reform the *Bank's* environmental performance would also earn him electoral credit from the strong environmental movement back home in Wisconsin without incurring the wrath of *Wisconsin's* environmentally unfriendly industries.

In January 1985, Senator Kasten sent a letter to Clausen, describing the Bank's letter to Rich as "at best a brush-off, but frankly, more correctly described as an insult":

> As you know better than anyone else, securing support for U.S. contributions to multi-lateral development institutions is difficult at best. That the World Bank would respond in such a cavalier fashion to groups and individuals who would otherwise support their programs is most difficult to understand. The questions and concerns raised in the October 12th letter to you are legitimate and deserve a credible and responsive answer. I, therefore, put these questions and concerns to you and ask that you respond to me as Chairman of the Foreign Operations Appropriations Subcommittee.[122]

Kasten also wrote a letter to Don Regan, Treasury secretary. "Dear Don," it began,

> As you can see from the letter [the October 12th letter sent to Clausen by the environmentalists] these groups have outlined a number of specific concerns, as well as making what I believe are sound suggestions, only to be answered by a one paragraph letter which can only be described as outrageous. The response to these groups is an insult. . . . As you well know, securing appropriations for international financial institutions is not an easy proposition under the best of circumstances, and for the World Bank to treat organizations and individuals which are otherwise supportive of their types of programs obviously compounds our difficulties.

121. Rich, *Mortgaging the Earth*, p. 123.
122. Letter, Senator Robert Kasten to A. W. Clausen, January 24, 1985.

I am taking this matter up with you personally because I believe it requires attention at the highest levels, and hopefully as a result the World Bank will be more responsive to legitimate concerns about the environment in the future.

Kasten sent copies of the correspondence to Regan's designated successor, James Baker.

After many draft replies had been discussed with the U.S. Treasury and the U.S. executive director, and after Kasten's office had angrily returned a reply that proposed a meeting between Kasten and the U.S. executive director, Clausen invited Kasten to meet with him and his staff directly.[123] The concessions to Senator Kasten greatly worried some people at the top of the Bank. Ernest Stern wrote on his copy of Clausen's revised letter to Kasten: "Tom—I think this offer of a meeting is unfortunate. I believe we will not be able to satisfy the group and will lose some flexibility in dealing with the Brazilians. But even if I am wrong about this particular case, at best it reinforces undesirable precedents. Our meetings with the population lobby are not proving productive. We run great risks in opening, and maintaining, these direct lines of communications." He underlined the sentence in Clausen's letter that read, "As Chairman of the Senate Foreign Relations Appropriations Subcommittee, you are certainly entitled to a full and complete answer," and wrote in the margin, "Yes, but not from us directly, which is the unfortunate implication." The Bank's general counsel, Ibrahim Shihata, also wrote Clausen a memo, headed "Provision of Information to Senator Kasten." He emphasized that the Bank's Articles of Agreement required the Bank to deal with national legislatures and individual legislators only through the finance ministry, through the Treasury in the case of the United States. "The Bank's policy in regard to requests from national legislatures or individual legislators has been generally to decline directly to provide sensitive information or formally to deal directly with these entities or persons." He went on to urge that a reply to a letter from any legislator (including Kasten) should be limited to "cordial assurances that the matter would receive the full attention of the Bank's management and that the Executive Director concerned would be informed of all relevant findings."[124] But for all the qualms, Clausen's invitation to a meeting was sent. Soon afterward the president's office was informed that letters from the protesting public were coming in at the rate of thirty to forty a day, generated by an article titled "Debacle in the Amazon," by Pat Aufderheide and Bruce Rich.[125]

The meeting, on May 22, 1985, was civil. It was more in the nature of a political ballet than a meeting; Kasten and the environmentalists already knew everything

123. A. W. Clausen to Senator Robert Kasten, March 1, 1985.
124. Ibrahim Shihata to A. W. Clausen, March 5, 1985.
125. Letter, Peter Riddleberger (D.C., PIO) to Roy Southworth (assistant to president), dated March 26, 1985, about public response to Pat Aufderheide and Bruce Rich, "Debacle in the Amazon," *Defenders,* March/April 1985, pp. 20–32.

the Bank officials were about to tell them. But the symbolism was important: Senator Kasten had persuaded the president of the World Bank, as well as three other top managers whose attendance Kasten had requested, to meet with him and representatives of several knowledgeable NGOs and explain to them the current state of the Polonoroeste project. This, to Kasten and the environmentalists, looked like a breakthrough in accountability to a member government.

The Bank Responds

At about the same time that the Bank, through the president, was making the concessions to Kasten and the campaign, Ernest Stern was preparing a memorandum for the U.S. executive director (James Burnham). The memorandum set out the Bank's response to suggestions from the U.S. Treasury Department as to how the Bank should improve its environmental capabilities. These suggestions were based on those from the NGOs. Stern's reply indicates that the Bank's number two was still assuming that the Bank was doing quite enough.

Stern stated that the Treasury's suggestions were all familiar to the Bank, which had considered them "along with other variants" in the past. To the first suggestion—increase the number of professional environmental specialists—he replied that "the staff of the Environment Unit does not adequately reflect the depth of environmental expertise in the Bank, because we expect these issues to be of concern to all project officers, and hold them accountable for it." The implication is that the Bank already had enough environmental expertise. The fact that "we *expect* these issues to be of concern to all project officers" was used to support the conclusion that the Bank had a greater depth of (*actual*) environmental expertise than the size of the Environment Unit would lead one to suppose. He gave no evidence to back it up—no personnel figures, for example—and made no reference to procedures by which project officers were held accountable for environmental issues. In fact, the Bank had *never* attempted to conduct a review of its environmental work and its environmental skills, so much did it take for granted that its environmental expertise was sufficient.

To the second suggestion—reorient the environmental unit to pay particular attention to agriculture, energy, and transport, because these are the sectors where the greatest environmental damage is being caused by Bank-financed projects—Stern replied that the Treasury Department's note did not give enough credit to the environmental unit "for its current responsibilities in project review . . . , and *it is not entirely clear how further responsibilities relating to these sectors could be effectively shared with the regional projects staff.*"

To the third suggestion—assign full-time responsibility for environmental issues to a specific staff person in each of the six regional offices—Stern replied that it raised the question of how to ensure *uniformity* of project review across regions. Project staff might use the excuse of a regional environmental expert not to pay attention to environmental problems themselves. The only real solution, he said, was for "senior regional office management [to] *continue* to reiterate its firm commitment to the environmental policies and practices of the Bank"—just as it had been doing in the past. Stern rejected two other suggestions in the same unyielding spirit.[126]

Although the Bank said this to outsiders, senior management saw the situation differently. In early 1984 a senior management subcommittee at the Bank discussed "environmental aspects of Bank work." The chairman, Ernest Stern, asked those present

> whether Bank staff know that they have a responsibility to consider environmental issues on every project, whether they do so, and whether management looks at these issues. The view was, *as a matter of routine, environmental issues are not considered, but that they are taken into account in specific instances when environmental consequences are pointed out by the Bank's environment advisor, the press, or special interest groups in host countries.*[127]

The U.S. Treasury Becomes Serious, 1986–87

As 1986 approached, the campaign broadened and intensified: more NGOs became involved; denser networks formed between U.S., European, and developing country NGOs; the NGOs began to target the regional multilateral banks as well as the World Bank; thousands of letters poured in to aid and environmental agencies in the Part I countries; and the second Reagan administration began to press the World Bank and the other multilateral banks more determinedly to undertake environmental reforms.

The NGOs had concentrated on the Congress, because the first Reagan administration (January 1981 to January 1985) had been openly hostile both to the multilateral development banks and to the environmental movement. With the arrival of James Baker as Treasury secretary early in the second Reagan administration, Treasury began to apply direct pressure on the Bank to "clean up" its environmental act—even as the administration remained skeptical on most domestic and international environmental issues. The reason was the role assigned to the Bank in handling the debt crisis of developing countries (see volume 1, chapter 11).

The change of stance at the Treasury helps to explain why the Bank changed its mind. What is striking about the first several years of the campaign is how little the Bank moved in response to all the pressure. For one thing, the top management

126. Ernest Stern, senior vice president of operations, to James Burnham, U.S. executive director, April 3, 1985, emphasis added. See further, World Bank, "Environmental Aspects of World Bank Projects: Some Commonly Asked Questions and Answers," July 17, 1986, processed.

127. Memorandum, Luis de Azcarate to files, "Meeting of the Operational Policy Subcommittee, March 9, 1984," March 30, 1984; emphasis added.

was preoccupied with short-term issues of the debt crisis. And it considered that the Articles of Agreement precluded any direct bargaining-type dealings with NGOs or national legislatures.[128] Ernest Stern, in particular, vigorously resisted the idea that the Bank should dance to the tune of the major shareholder. Besides, the tune was coming mainly from the Congress, not from the Treasury, and it was the Treasury, as the Bank's official interlocutor, to which the Bank had to give serious attention. The Treasury for the first several years (in the first Reagan administration) did not believe that the Bank or other multilateral financial institutions had any business with the "environment," nor did the finance ministries of other Part I countries. True, it assigned a person to monitor the environmental activities of the multilateral banks, but this was largely theater. Treasury's chief concern was with the Latin American debt crisis, which required IBRD money, not IDA money (for which Latin America was not eligible). Congress could hold up IDA money, but it could not hold up IBRD money (almost all of which was borrowed); or rather, Congress could not hold up IBRD money until the Bank requested a capital increase.

The so-called Baker plan, formulated in September 1985, proposed to give the World Bank a more prominent role in lending to debt-ridden developing countries; in return for more lending, those countries would undertake structural reforms to ensure repayment and long-term growth, and to pay off debts to private U.S. banks. However, it began to be clear in 1986 that the Bank required a capital increase for it to be able to undertake this expanded role (see volume 1, chapters 11 and 16). The Congress had to approve an increase in the U.S. capital contribution to the IBRD. It was at this point that the Treasury had to take seriously what the Congress, and Senator Kasten in particular, had been saying about the Bank's environmental record. Hence the Treasury put weight behind the environmentalists' recommendations. It wanted the Bank to do what was necessary to diffuse the environmentalists' criticisms, and so remove the grounds on which Congress might hold up an IBRD capital increase. Baker began to make it known that the Reagan administration indeed "is committed to press for these [increased World Bank] funds," but it recognized that "this will not be an easy issue to present to Congress"[129]—partly because the Congress had such a vote-winning pretext for saying no in the Bank's environmental record.

The Campaign Intensifies, 1986–87

In 1987 Congress was scheduled to approve both an increase in the U.S. contribution to the IBRD's capital base and an IDA replenishment (IDA 8). The environmental NGOs recognized that 1987 would be "a crucial year for the cam-

---

128. IBRD, *Articles of Agreement,* Article III, Section 2.

129. Tom Raum, "World Bank Fund Increase Faces Tough Fight, Baker Says," *Boston Globe,* September 29, 1987, p. 47. The capital increase was approved by a majority of shareholders in April 1988 and by the U.S. Congress in September 1988.

paign to influence the MDBs," because "considerable opportunity exists for organizations to influence the direction of foreign assistance."[130]

With these two windows of opportunity in view, the environmental organizations energized themselves through 1986. Some new international environmental NGOs came into existence around this time, including the Rainforest Action Network and the International Rivers Network. Some existing ones of radical bent, such as Greenpeace and Earth First! became more involved in the NGO campaign. In the developing countries, environmental NGOs continued to proliferate, many forming links with northern NGOs. And many of them focused on the World Bank or its counterparts. Criticizing those organizations and *their* projects, and merging their criticisms with foreign-based ones, was politically safer than criticizing their own governments.

In 1986 the Sierra Club published *Bankrolling Disasters,* a manual showing how ordinary citizens could link up with the campaign and influence the multilateral development banks.[131] It was subtitled *The Citizen's Environmental Guide to the World Bank and the Regional Multilateral Development Banks.* The manual explained how the banks worked, what happened in the "debacle" projects, the reasons for the campaign, and some of the campaign's successes. It also gave the names and addresses of other environmental organizations involved in the campaign. Fifteen thousand copies were distributed to USAID missions, World Bank executive directors and staff, regional multilateral bank counterparts, government officials, and NGOs throughout the world.

The American press gave the campaign influential coverage. The *New York Times* and other prominent newspapers ran articles on it, and leading scientific journals such as *Nature* and *Science* carried articles critical of the Bank.[132] Because they came out of the United States, these stories about the campaign were picked up by media in developing countries, notably in Brazil, and helped foster networks between the northern and southern NGOs.

The NGOs scored a significant if partial victory in June 1986, when Secretary Baker directed the U.S. executive director of the Bank to vote against an Electric

130. *Interaction Newsletter,* February 1986, Global Tomorrow Coalition, cited in Foer, *Mutual Interests,* p. 63.

131. Written by Bruce Rich and Steven Swartzman, published by Sierra Club because the Environmental Defense Fund, where Rich was by then based, had insufficient funds to publish it.

132. For example, Eric Eckholm, "World Bank Urged to Halt Aid to Brazil for Amazon Development," *New York Times,* October 17, 1984, p. A17; Philip Shabecoff, "World Lenders Facing Pressure from Ecologists," *New York Times,* October 30, 1986; John Walsh, "World Bank Pressed on Environmental Reforms," *Science,* vol. 234, November 14, 1986, pp. 813–15; Frederic Krupp, "New Environmentalism Factors in Economic Needs," *Wall Street Journal,* November 20, 1986; Linda Hossie, "World Bank Seeks to Clean up a Host of Destructive Projects," *Globe and Mail* (Toronto), July 23, 1987; Diane Dumanoski, "Environmental Concerns Derail Brazilian Road Loan," *Boston Globe,* August 6, 1987; Timothy Aeppel, "Rainforest Misuse Prompts Ultimatum," *Christian Science Monitor,* August 14, 1987.

Power Sector Loan to Brazil. The loan was to finance the construction or completion of 25 dams; these 25 dams would be the first step in a program to build 136 dams by the year 2010. Environmentalists lobbied hard against the loan. At the Board meeting, several executive directors spoke against approval, drawing on material supplied to them by NGOs such as Oxfam and the Environmental Defense Fund. The U.S. alternate executive director said,

> The Bank has been involved in regional planning in Rondônia for at least six years. One would hope at least that planning for the Indian protection aspects of projects in that state would have benefitted from the Bank's tribal people's policy and from the unfortunate experience of the Polonoroeste project.
>
> We find instead a proposal that includes financing of the Gi-Parana Dam in Rondônia where there has been virtually no planning to address the needs of the Amerindian population or the need for protection of the environment in the immediate area of the dam. . . . This is pure folly.[133]

The loan was approved. But the U.S. "nay" represented the first time any member of the Bank had voted not to approve a loan on environmental grounds. (In the earlier Polonoroeste case, in which the Bank took sanctions against a borrower on environmental grounds for the first time, the issue was suspension, not loan approval, and it did not involve the Board.) Environmental concerns were not the only drivers, however. The tough stance of the United States also reflected its response to Brazil's threats of debt default at this time. The Electric Power Sector Loan gave a convenient context for the United States to send yet another signal about the costs to Brazil should it default.

By this time Bank management was trying to take a different tack in its relations with environmental NGOs. Having previously treated them as illegitimate interlocutors, it now accepted that too much was at stake for this strategy to be worth continuing. In a letter to Bruce Rich at this time, Clausen took issue with some of their concerns about the Brazil Electric Power Sector Loan to Brazil. He repeated the standard claim, "It would be easier for us to pull out of these activities and concentrate our assistance in projects unrelated to critical environmental or socio-cultural issues. We would thus avoid being subject to *so much unwarranted criticism.* But, if we were to do that, the situation concerning these issues would become progressively worse."

He went on to strike a new, almost solicitous tone:

> I would like to hope that your institution will find it possible to maintain, in the future, a constructive approach to Bank activities related to the protection of the environment and of indigenous populations. If that were the case, you can be sure that *the Management and staff of the Bank would be ready to maintain a fruitful dialogue* in which we could

---

133. Hugh W. Foster, U.S. alternate executive director, statement to the Board of Executive Directors regarding the Brazil Electric Power Sector Loan, June 1986, quoted in Rich, *Mortgaging the Earth,* p. 137.

take advantage of the expertise on these critical policy areas accumulated over the years by your organizations.[134]

In September 1986, environmental, development, and human rights NGOs held the first "alternative" Annual Meeting, at the time of the Annual Meeting of the Bank and the Fund in Washington D.C. It was during this meeting that activist rock climbers scaled a World Bank building and bedecked it with the slogan, "World Bank destroys tropical rain forests," in sight of the main entrances of both the Bank and the Fund. The Alternative Meeting was organized by Chad Dobson, who would go on to found the Bank Information Center in 1987. The Bank Information Center specialized in making confidential World Bank documents publicly available.

Late in 1986, some twenty-five groups of varying size and strength sent representatives to a meeting arranged by the Environmental Policy Institute to coordinate strategy. At the meeting a letter was written to the multilateral development banks, setting out a by-now familiar list of demands (expand environmental staff, and so on), giving them six months to initiate action in response to the demands and a year to implement them fully, or else face a concerted campaign to persuade governments to cut off all funding.[135]

By this time the executive directors of several major Part I countries, such as Canada, the Netherlands, Australia, the Nordic countries, and the United Kingdom, were also actively pressing for environmental reforms in the Bank similar to those that the U.S. executive director had been urging for a long time. But they continued to do so more quietly than the United States and were more inclined to accept the Bank's argument that its involvement in environmentally damaging projects would make the projects less bad. Indeed, several of them—and still more the executive directors from the borrowing countries—were critical of what they saw as the U.S. government's double game, of criticizing the Bank on environmental grounds in order to play to the domestic environmental gallery while doing little to hold up the flow of lending (which Treasury Secretary Baker wanted to maintain as part of his debt-reduction plan).

The public complaints of U.S. politicians and officials about the Bank's lack of progress continued to swell: "When people find out what's been going on," Kasten exclaimed in late 1986, "you're going to see people out in the street saying, 'My God, did you read this information. Why are our dollars being used to fund this kind of destruction?'" The official in charge of the Treasury's Office of Multilateral Development Banks said, apropos of the Bank's failure to consult those affected by its development projects, "I think it's a disaster, it's a mistake, and it's been going on for years."[136]

134. A. W. Clausen to Bruce Rich, June 26, 1986, emphasis added.

135. Meeting on November 5, 1986. Cited in Foer, *Mutual Interests*, p. 64.

136. Robert W. Kasten and James Conrow, interview with Nicholas Claxton, producer and director, *The Price of Progress*, documentary film (London: Central Independent Television, 1987), cited in Rich, *Mortgaging the Earth*, p. 145.

Leaders of seven environmental groups wrote a letter to *Science* in April 1987 to clarify where they stood on the issue of "zeroing out" funding for the Bank and its counterparts:

> We publicly endorse the Administration's budget request for the multilateral develop-
> ment banks for fiscal year 1987. . . . We do, however, believe that improvements in the
> quality of World Bank lending should not be left to chance. U.S. contributions to the
> World Bank should be accompanied by explicit expectations that the Bank will make
> rapid, measurable progress toward the goal of environmentally sound, sustainable de-
> velopment. Despite four years of heightened scrutiny by Congress, the Reagan Ad-
> ministration, and the public, the World Bank has yet to make the needed reforms.

The letter warned,

> Unless the Bank can demonstrate that it has taken major steps to improve the environ-
> mental soundness of its lending, there will very likely be difficulties similar to those of
> past years in obtaining appropriations that total almost $1 billion per year. . . . By rapidly
> implementing reforms, World Bank President Conable can ensure that environmental
> concerns no longer cast doubt on the quality of the Bank's performance.[137]

The Bank Responds, Despite Opposition

Former U.S. Representative Barber Conable, veteran of twenty years in Congress, knew when he became president in 1986 that he had no choice but to defuse
the environmental issue, the Bank's prickliest public relations problem at the time.
He knew that the second Reagan administration wanted him for president because
of his presumed abilities in defusing congressional opposition to U.S. contributions
to the Bank's lending resources. As a long-standing environmental sympathizer he
was in any case keen to push in this direction. The senior management, too, came
to accept that the NGOs had succeeded in making the costs of not acting too high.
Issues of far more immediate importance to the Bank than environmental ones—
IDA and the capital increase—were being put at risk by the NGOs' environmental
attacks.

Many of the borrowing governments, however, especially the big and important
ones like Brazil and India, remained strongly opposed to the Bank's assertion of
environmental criteria, still considering (as they had at the 1972 Stockholm conference) that this infringed on their sovereignty over their own natural resources.
They deeply resented the U.S. pressure, regarding the U.S. executive director as
little more than the mouthpiece of U.S. NGOs. To whom were those NGOs
accountable, they kept asking? By what right could those U.S.-based NGOs claim
to speak for the citizens of their own countries, as though they had more legitimacy
than the governments themselves? (The Brazilian executive director voiced these

137. Letter signed by leaders of seven environmental organizations, *Science,* April 3,
1987.

objections particularly strongly, reflecting the strident environmental nationalism of the Sarney government of 1985–90.)[138]

To these questions the U.S. NGOs admitted that they had no right to tell the governments of developing countries what to do. But they claimed every right to lobby the U.S. government on what instructions should be given to the U.S. executive director about how Bank lending resources, which included U.S. tax dollars, should be used. And they claimed every right to help NGOs in developing countries raise their voice in the organization whose decisions were helping to cause, they said, the damage they were protesting about. When the Bank claimed that project X would bring great material benefits to local people, the U.S. NGOs were able to produce not only reports to the contrary from the local area, but even local people themselves. This constituted persuasive testimony. On one occasion two Brazilian Kaiapo Indian chiefs, in full ceremonial regalia, descended on the Congress, the State Department, and the World Bank, brought by leaders of the NGO campaign to protest the Bank's power sector loan to Brazil. A dam financed by the loan would flood their lands and destroy their way of life, they said. Their visit generated valuable media publicity for the argument that this was a damaging loan.

The Bank's shift on the environment, this account suggests, was largely *tactical,* a response to the need to reduce the threat to its lending resources. The circumstances that made it move were to shape the content of its environmental work.

Institutionalizing "Environmental Protection," 1987–93

"The World Bank has been part of the [environmental] problem in the past," and it had "stumbled" in Polonoroeste, declared Barber Conable to the World Resources Institute on May 5, 1987.[139] He went on,

> We are creating a top-level Environment Department to help set the direction of Bank policy, planning and research work. It will take the lead in developing strategies to integrate environmental considerations into our overall lending and policy activities.
>
> At the same time, new offices in each of the four regional technical departments will take on a dual role. They will function both as environmental watchdogs over Bank-supported projects and as scouts and advocates for promising advances in resource management.

"These organizational changes," he assured his audience, "do not just add layers of interference to head off errors of commission. The added staff will help define

138. Hurrell, "Brazil and the International Politics of Amazonian Destruction."

139. His admission upset members of the Polonoroeste project team, who continued to think that the project was much better than it would have been without the Bank.

policy and develop initiatives *to promote growth and environmental protection together.* They will work to ensure that environmental awareness is integral to all the Bank's activities."[140] The president of the World Resources Institute called Conable's speech "a charter for a new day at the World Bank."[141]

The structure outlined by Conable was soon created. It included a central Environment Department, plus four Regional Environment Divisions (REDs), each one servicing one or two of the regions. The central Environment Department, itself divided into several divisions, would provide the Bank-wide policy work, the conceptualizations, the research, the public relations, as well as specific assistance to country departments. The four REDs were part of the newly created Technical Departments, located within the regional (or lending) vice presidencies. The REDs' primary job was to provide support on environmental aspects of project design to the lending divisions within the region. In addition, they were to "review and clear" projects being prepared in the region; they had "sign-off authority." This greatly enhanced their ability to influence lending.

The significance of environmental review and clearance should be seen in the context of the wider reorganization. Before 1987 the disciplinary or subject matter advisers (the irrigation adviser, the forestry adviser, for example) had to be sent project documents in their area of expertise and could make "lots of trouble" when they saw a project that failed to meet certain standards. The Central Policy Staff, where these advisers were based, constituted, in a sense, the Bank's "curia," which prevented the operatives from sinning after supping with the borrowers (though Polonoroeste illustrates how easy it was for a determined division chief and project officer to override or ignore them). The 1987 reorganization greatly curtailed the ability of the disciplinary advisers located in the center to exercise influence over the design of projects in the regions, because of the overriding importance attached to vesting accountability in the director of each country department, making him or her responsible for everything that the Bank did in that country or set of countries. This required, it was argued, that authority for clearing projects be vested entirely in the country department and regional vice president.[142]

Although project officers were given new discretion to ignore the advice of the technical specialists, their previous discretion to ignore "environmental" aspects was curtailed by the creation of the REDs, semi-independent environment cham-

140. Barber B. Conable, "Address to the World Resources Institute," Washington, D.C., May 5, 1987, pp. 5–6; emphasis added. The speech was written largely by Jeremy Warford.

141. Gus Speth, president of the World Resources Institute, quoted in Philip Shabecoff, "World Bank Offers Environmental Projects," *New York Times,* May 6, 1987.

142. Hence the old Loan Committee, on which had sat all the regional vice presidents and to which went all projects for approval, was abolished in the 1987 reorganization and replaced by a committee of senior managers to which projects went for approval only in exceptional circumstances, plus regional loan committees on which the regional vice president was the senior figure.

pions with sign-off authority. A project could not go forward for approval by the vice president until it had been cleared by the RED division chief. After 1987 this was the only locus of subject-matter sign-off outside the country department (though Legal and Procurement continued to have independent sign-off authority, as before). Hence the organizational design met a quality control desideratum, that the people responsible for passing a project on inevitably somewhat subjective environmental *quality* criteria should be partly independent of those who have a vested interest in getting the project approved and the money committed, that they should not be traveling on the same battleship at full speed ahead. The REDs were still under the authority of the regional vice president, however, who had to balance environmental criteria against economic rates of return and lending targets.

Having created a complex of in-house environmental champions, the Bank also had to establish a set of procedures by which projects would be environmentally assessed. These two developments—environmental staffing and environmental assessment procedures—constituted the first serious attempt to move from "environment as exception" to "environment as routine." At the risk of oversimplification, it can be said that the moves were intended to inject the ideas and practices of the "environmental protection" paradigm firmly into the Bank's project-level work, and the ideas of the "environmental management" paradigm into its countrywide work. The REDs were to do the former, the central Environment Department was to do the latter.

Establishing the Environment Department, 1987–91

The early press statements about the reorganization announced "100 new environmental posts," but by the end of 1987 the figure was closer to 50 environmental posts (as compared with about five in 1986). Of these, the central Environment Department had about two dozen positions, the four REDs each had between five and ten.[143] In this structure the Environment Department was to be the flagship. Yet from the beginning the department malfunctioned for several years and was discredited in the rest of the Bank.

As the department was being created, a search began for a director. Many names were considered, but none seemed to fit the bill. Months went by. Meanwhile the Environment Department was organizing itself without a director. Nominally, Senior Vice President David Hopper was in charge. He had no plan for how the

---

143. By fiscal 1990 (July 1989–June 1990) the Environment Department comprised twenty-four higher-level staff and about eight consultants; the four regional Environment Divisions together contained thirty higher-level staff and about fifteen consultants. The expenditures of the whole complex amounted to $11.7 million (Central Department, $3.9 million; Africa RED, $2.4 million; Asia, $2.3 million; EMENA, $2.1 million; Latin America, $0.9 million). World Bank, *The World Bank and the Environment*, first Annual Report, Fiscal 1990, Washington, D.C., 1990, p. 72, annex 2.

department should be organized, but he did talk to NGOs who gave suggestions, and he did consult with a few internal staff who were obvious candidates for division chief positions. At first, two divisions were formed, then the same staff were reassigned to three divisions on the return from a long mission of a man with a strong claim to a division chief position, who had been overlooked in his absence. From senior management came confused and changing signals as to whether the central vice presidencies should do mainly policy or mainly operational support. In the first eight months there were at least three changes of direction: first, the senior management said that the central departments had to justify their existence by helping the operational departments on projects or programs; then they said that the central departments should concentrate on policy formulation, cross-regional learning, and research, and let operations do operations; then they hit on a compromise, with the idea that people in central departments should aim to spend 40 percent of their time in operational support, the rest on policy. All the central departments were affected by the churning and the zigzagging, but Environment as the smallest had the least capacity to shift and no director to make a case one way or the other.

The division chiefs of the Environment Department could not agree among themselves on priorities and territory and lacked the staff and budgets to implement both the serious policy work and the operational support being called for. With no director, they had no authority to turn to for guidance and arbitration. Vice President V. Rajagopalan was no help, barely concealing his view that the Bank's venture into (explicitly designated) environmental matters was a mistake. All the while the NGOs barraged the department with criticism. The acting director had a special table in his room piled high with letters, like a volcano. For the first several months an edict was in force from the top of the Bank saying that all letters had to be answered. The acting director felt overwhelmed as the volcano grew by the day. Eventually he received a quiet word to the effect that not all letters had to answered, and with relief swept the pile into the rubbish bin. In the meantime, the operational parts of the Bank were raked by uncertainty over how to operate the new organizational structure, while being under great pressure to deliver lending programs. The last thing they wanted to hear about was new environmental requirements.

The larger reorganization was partly about cutting staff numbers, and many people suddenly found themselves on the internal job market, their previous position gone. They scrambled for somewhere to go. Having heard his managers say that they could not manage because they did not have a free hand in the choice of who worked for them, Conable determined to allow his new senior managers to pick their subordinates, and so on down the hierarchy, in the interests of accountability. People scrambled to use their personal contacts to find a post, creating a perception that managers were employing their friends rather than selecting the best match for the post. "Cascading cronyism," it came to be called, and it compounded the cynicism and anxiety.

Environment was the only expanding area. Some who had an environmental qualification or track record got positions there, as did several anthropologists (since "social" issues of resettlement and tribal concerns were placed under environment, as before 1987). But a sizable number of those who ended up in the environment complex had no training or experience in environmental issues; they went there on cascading cronyism networks, or in order to get onto other promotion ladders after their own had been blocked. Exclaimed one observer, looking back from 1995, "We took guys who were standing about the hallways, called them environmentalists, and stuck them in the environment divisions. Overnight they hatched as environmentalists!" In the words of another, "A lot of dead wood that would not leave the Bank got kicked into environment." Over the first two years the environmental complex experienced a staff shakeout; those who had gone there as a refuge left for jobs elsewhere, allowing the complex to recruit people with more environmental experience. At the same time, some of the best people also left, fed up with what they saw as the Bank's lack of seriousness.

Of those with an environmental qualification or track record, most were "greens," reflecting the origins of the complex as a response to NGOs pushing a mainly "green" agenda. "Brown" specialists were few. But the operational departments typically saw "brown" issues looming larger than "green" ones and were frustrated by the lack of capacity in the environment complex to help on the brown side. Moreover, few of the environmental staff had qualifications in environmental economics, yet economists were firmly in control in the rest of the Bank. This, too, limited the demand from—and legitimacy in the eyes of—the lending departments.

As the search for a director continued, Hopper was still bent on finding a good scientist with environmental credentials. Name after name looked promising and then dropped away; at least one offer was made and declined. The pressure to make an appointment mounted. Hopper decided to change course and look for a generalist manager with some environmental experience. Eventually Kenneth Piddington was nominated. He looked attractive. He was a New Zealand civil servant who had been working on New Zealand and South Pacific environmental issues since the mid 1970s and had recently been appointed director of the New Zealand Conservation Department. He was an outsider to the Bank, which gave him credibility in the eyes of some environmental organizations, and being unknown to the concerned NGOs carried no negatives in their eyes. At an interview lunch in Washington, Hopper asked him what he thought about NGOs and the Bank's relations with them. Piddington replied, "When you deal with NGOs you can predict the script but you can't amend it." Hopper—having worried that Piddington might be too close to NGOs—slapped him on the back and said, "Boy, you've got yourself a job." With relief, the Bank rushed to make him an offer. Conable made him a special plea: "I need your help."[144]

144. Kenneth Piddington, interview with the author, June 27, 1996.

Piddington served as director of the Environment Department from his arrival in late April 1988 (nearly a year after the department had been created) to mid-1991. His tenure was turbulent. Most directors coming in from the outside have had difficulty getting the measure of the place—particularly in building the "social capital" of trust and obligation with their own staff and with the vice presidents and other directors on whom they depend for guidance and cooperation. A distinguished Canadian medical administrator, brought in as first director of the new Population, Health, and Nutrition (PHN) Department in 1979, quit in frustration after a year, saying he could not understand the Bank's mentality. Yet the PHN job was much simpler than that of environment director, not least because it did not involve the same fire fighting and arm wrestling with NGOs. If someone so qualified could not do the PHN job well, it is no surprise that the first environment director should have struggled. In his judgment, it would have helped if he had had prior experience of the Bank and knowledge of the unusually powerful role of the U.S. Treasury and Congress in shaping the Bank's decisions; and if he had been supported by his senior management.[145]

Piddington was not impressed with the quality of most of the staff in the department (whom he had no hand in recruiting). However, he made a point of meeting frequently with the division chiefs of the four REDs, just the five of them over lunch, without the division chiefs of his own department. These meetings matched his philosophy of internalizing environmental functions by moving them closer to operations, and hence building up the REDs.[146] But they contributed to the perception that Piddington was not being the champion of the Environment *Department* that the staff expected him to be, a role that his philosophy of internalization led him to downplay.

Meanwhile, the operational departments steered clear to the extent they could. The department did "nothing" for them, they complained. Even if it had been fully functioning it would have attracted this criticism, in view of the resistance to environment in general and the fact that its two dozen people dealt with five regions.[147] Consequently, most of the Bank's nineteen country departments saw little of it. When the department did promise support to the regions the support often could not accommodate the normally volatile schedule of operational missions, thus compounding the criticism that nothing was forthcoming. And when central staff were made available for operational support, they tended—it was said—to be less than competent.[148] Hence the operational departments tended to

145. Ibid.

146. See Kenneth Piddington, "The Role of the World Bank," in Hurrell and Kingsbury, eds., *The International Politics of the Environment*.

147. At this time, in the late 1980s, Asia constituted one vice presidential region; in late 1991 it was to be divided into South and East Asia.

148. This was a common perception, yet operational staff would also agree that quite a number of individuals in the department, name by name, were exceptionally able.

look elsewhere for environmental help: to the REDs or to off-the-street consultants. When the task manager responsible for preparing the China Environment Sector Study organized a sizable (eight-person) mission in 1991, he selected no one from the Environment Department and only one person from the Asia RED. The few people in the environment complex whose competence he trusted were tied up with work elsewhere.

The early work on what became the Global Environmental Facility (GEF) was hobbled by the wider confusion. Piddington's arrival coincided with vigorous debate outside the Bank about how to finance actions to deal with global environmental problems.[149] He and some of his staff became strong proponents of a Bank initiative, but senior managers showed little enthusiasm.[150] Hence the Bank took little part in the outside debate at first, and again the organization received attention in the media as a footdragger. Said the *New York Times*, "As the World Bank considers how to use its considerable leverage to help reduce the threat to global warming, environmentalists and politicians are complaining that it is not exerting strong leadership."[151] The stance of senior management was based partly on the fear that donors would substitute contributions to a global environmental fund for their contributions to IDA, then being renegotiated. But the general sense that the department was malfunctioning contributed to the resistance of senior management. Then in the fall of 1989, when the discussions about a financial mechanism were accelerating, Piddington went on long leave to New Zealand for family reasons. The acting director began to forge a more positive Bank response, together with two senior officials elsewhere in the Bank.[152] On Piddington's return in early 1990, he as director took charge of the GEF discussions. But by then Ernest Stern, with the IDA negotiations out of the way, swung the finance complex's apparatus for raising IDA replenishment behind the task of raising serious money for the GEF. He entrusted the work to two senior officials unconnected with Environment, one of whom was closely related to the French Ministry of Finance, which was playing the lead role among the donors.[153] These two helped to structure the Bank's proposals in a way consistent with what the French and Germans were wanting.

149. Helen Sjöberg, "From Idea to Reality: The Creation of the Global Environment Facility," UNDP/UNEP/World Bank, Global Environment Facility Working Paper 10, Washington, D.C., 1994.

150. Stein Hansen, Maritta Koch-Weser, and Ernst Lutz, "Environmental Funding Options," internal draft working paper, June and November versions, 1988.

151. "Pressure on World Bank to Save the World," *New York Times*, September 11, 1989.

152. Jane Pratt, acting director, Environment Department; Alex Shakow, External Affairs; and David Bock, Finance.

153. It is said by insiders that Stern initiated the idea of a French initiative. The two officials were Thierry Baudon, then chief of the regional Environment Division for Europe, the Middle East, and North Africa, working with Heinz Vergin, then chef de cabinet to Qureshi. See Sjöberg, "From Idea to Reality." The former did not conceal his view of the low quality of 90 percent of the Environment Department's staff.

In late 1990 a task force of directors from across the Bank met to help formulate a strategy for the department—an unprecedented opening up of a department to outside scrutiny. In early 1991, with rumors of a departmental reorganization in the air, a sizable delegation of staff went to see the Bank's ombudsman about the department's problems, a rare event in Bank history. In the reorganization of mid-1991 Piddington stepped into an advisory role.

In short, the first several years after 1987 were a time of lost opportunity in the Bank's environment work. The Bank did much less by way of integrating ideas of environmental management into its work than the mandate of the Environment Department indicated. To a point, it could hardly have been otherwise, for the whole environment complex faced something close to a "lose-lose" situation. On the one hand, the Bank could not satisfy the NGOs, who were not about to demobilize just because the Bank had created an environment complex. Indeed, some of the more active of them had been misled by their access to Barber Conable into believing that they could influence the staffing of the new complex, including the choice of director and division chiefs. When they realized their influence was slight, they became disenchanted with the whole process and became, again, strident critics. But the environment complex did not satisfy the operational staff, either. The earlier "syndrome of mistrust" between the Office of Environmental Affairs and the operational staff, well entrenched after seventeen years, could not easily be erased. Indeed, the situation was worse than before from the point of view of the operational staff, because the environment complex was now much larger and had real power. Yet it had no *monitorable* objectives, and neither it nor anyone else had sufficient data to permit rational decisionmaking on what to do about the environment (in the eyes of the operational staff). Worse, the environment complex was considered somewhat incompetent in the first several years after 1987, staffed with "retreads," "greens," and "noneconomists" unable to meet the operational departments' demand for environmental advice.

Furthermore, the Environment Department was caught up in the general uncertainty about the role of all of the central departments after the 1987 reorganization (Agriculture, Infrastructure, and Energy, as well as Environment) in the new, more decentralized and country-focused Bank, and caught up, too, in the general administrative confusion that resulted in delays in some other senior appointments. On top of all this, senior managers were reluctant to facilitate and lead; in the name of not micromanaging they declined to take control of events within their domain that were clearly out of control.

Yet through the confusion the Environment Department began to integrate environmental criteria into regular Bank work, as promised in the IDA negotiations. It helped to recruit environmental specialists into the Bank, to launch training courses in environmental analysis, to prepare national environmental action plans, and to prepare environmental projects. That this much was done in the face of the organizational confusion is testimony to the conviction of some of the staff that this was the opportunity of a lifetime. But the most important step after 1987—the operational directive on environmental assessments—was mainly the work of the REDs.

Making Environmental Assessment Procedures, 1988–91

As already mentioned, the 1984 directive on environmental aspects of projects was vague on all the key questions of environmental assessments: Which types of projects required full or partial EAs? Who should decide? Who should prepare? Who should review, and when in the project cycle must an EA be ready? After 1987 two forces—one external and one internal—combined to make the Bank establish environmental assessment procedures that answered these questions and that matched the procedures already formulated for various bilateral aid agencies.

The external pressure arose from Bank and U.S. Treasury negotiations regarding how much the United States would subscribe to the IDA 9 replenishment. The Treasury asked the Bank for a copy of its "EA directive." It did so because Congress was in the middle of passing a law that enjoined U.S. executive directors of multilateral development banks, including the World Bank, first, to propose procedures "for systematic environmental assessment of development projects for which the respective Bank provides financial assistance, taking into consideration the guidelines and principles for Environmental Impact Assessment promulgated by the United Nations Environment Program," and second, to make the assessments available to "affected groups" and "local nongovernmental organizations."[154] Congress, of course, was acting not on its own initiative but on that of environmental NGOs. Having succeeded in getting the Bank to create a cadre of internal environmental champions, they wished to ensure that those champions had rules with which to discipline the operational staff.

At the top of the hierarchy, President Conable and Senior Vice President Ernest Stern were well aware of Congress's demands. Stern faced them through the IDA negotiations, for which he, by this time head of the financial complex, was responsible. His problem was that the Bank did not have what the Treasury was asking for: an EA directive that would meet Congress's standards. He and Conable informed their subordinates that they expected the Bank to devise Bank-wide EA procedures forthwith. According to the minutes of a senior management meeting, "Mr. Stern . . . was concerned that the Bank has been needlessly conveying the impression that it is a reluctant and recalcitrant participant in the environmental effort."[155]

The internal pressure came from the REDs. The 1987 reforms had given REDs review and clearance powers, but offered no clear guidelines on how those powers were to be used. The Environment Department was in no shape to take responsibility for producing an EA directive. In the meantime, two of the REDs, frus-

---

154. US Public Law 101-240 in 1989. See volume 1, chapter 6.
155. Minutes of the President's Council meeting, August 31, 1989, p. 3.

trated by the lack of anything coming from the department, had been preparing environmental assessment guidelines for use within their own regions. These were the REDs that had recruited two experts in environmental assessment, one from USAID, the other from the Asian Development Bank. They began in mid-1988 to draw up EA procedures for their regions. They then sent the statement of procedures to the operational divisions within their regions, saying that these procedures would guide the RED in exercising its sign-off authority. The fact of having such procedures in two of the regions and not in the others drew complaints from task managers such as: "If my project was in Latin America or Africa an EA would not be necessary [because the REDs for those regions had formulated no environmental assessment guidelines]. Why should I have to do one just because the project is in Asia or Europe/Middle East/North Africa?"

The two who were drafting EA procedures for their regions asked the division chief of the largest RED (for Asia) to establish an "EA Steering Committee" under whose auspices they would cooperate in producing Bank-wide procedures. The committee included, in addition to the two of them and the Asia RED division chief, six others, drawn from other REDs, operational divisions, the Legal Department, and the Environment Department. The organizers included two operational division chiefs known to be hostile to regularizing the use of EAs.[156] They wanted to use the Steering Committee not only for feedback but also to generate a sense of "ownership" of the result, especially among the critics.

The original two teamed up with an old Bank hand, an American who had worked in the small Office of Environmental Affairs before 1987, who knew the Bank well, and who had earlier also worked on EAs for domestic projects in the United States.[157] These three had known each other for a long time and were almost the only people in the Bank with hands-on experience with environmental assessments as defined by the profession of environmental assessors. They started work in late 1988. They aimed to produce an Operational Manual Statement—by then rechristened Operational Directive (OD)—which would set out the procedures and conditions of use of EAs throughout the Bank. The OD format would make them as close to obligatory as any Bank procedures.

The three knew they were writing for an audience of the topmost executives, especially Stern and Conable. They also expected opposition from the staff. They worked on the draft for several months, sharing it for comment among just a few people. The process was protracted by the frequent absence of team members on

156. This was not a high-status committee. Only three of its nine members were division chiefs, including the cochair, Gloria Davis, chief of the Asia RED.

157. The team included Stephen Lintner, formerly of USAID and then in the Europe/Middle East/North Africa RED; Colin Rees, former head of the ADB's environmental unit and then in the Asia RED; and Bernard Baratz, the old Bank hand who had earlier worked in the Office of Environmental Affairs and was then in the Environment Department.

mission. At the end of April 1989 they sent the draft out through the rounds of successively higher-level reviews required for all draft ODs. By then they had a tight deadline for final approval; the final OD had to be approved by late August so that it could be presented to the governors at the World Bank Annual Meeting in September. President Conable stated in a letter to his senior vice presidents in May of 1989, widely circulated to staff, "Priority should be given to the completion of the Operational Directive on Environmental Impact Assessment. This Directive should be reviewed by the President's Council as soon as possible, before the summer break."[158] This would help to clinch the IDA 9 negotiations.

The timetable allowed only a short time for review. It called for the first consultation to be with the division chiefs in all of the Bank's technical departments and sector operations divisions (about 110 in number), who were to send back comments within two weeks. Then directors would receive a revised draft and would comment within twelve days; then the new draft would go to the vice presidents, and so on up to the Board in August, in time for presentation to the Annual Meeting in September.

The responses from the operating levels of the Bank were anything but enthusiastic. Many reviewers doubted the need for formal guidelines. One said, "After reading it [the draft], I wondered why we need yet another set of guidelines in this area." He likened the procedures to "applying lipstick to mosquitoes."[159] Another said, "The OD reminds us of the approach adopted by one of our member countries, the United States, in the late sixties and early seventies, which required lengthy and somewhat mindless bureaucratic environmental assessments for schemes both large and small which then frequently became bogged down as a result of both over-enthusiastic activism (at forums) and lack of time to complete an assessment to bureaucratically acceptable standards."[160] Many protested the abbreviated timetable for considering such an important document.

The clauses that attracted the most criticism were those for consultation and project classification. The consultation clause in the May 1989 version said: "If screening determines that an EA is required, a 'scoping session' is normally conducted to identify the key environmental issues to be analyzed in the EA report. . . . It is a forum of selected knowledgeable persons from national, municipal, and local governments; nongovernmental organizations (NGOs); institutions of higher learning; and affected groups" (paragraph 14).

This caused a firestorm of criticism across the Bank. Many people said that it entered "political" territory that the Bank had no business to be in. The drafters of

158. Letter, Barber B. Conable to W. D. Hopper and M. A. Qureshi, May 11, 1989.
159. Comment, Thomas Blinkhorn, AS4CO, May 5, 1989.
160. Comment, Maurice Dickerson, EM4IN, May 16, 1989.

the OD flagged consultation as one of the issues to be decided by senior management. Senior management supported a strong consultation requirement, considering that the OD would lack credibility in the eyes of the U.S. government and U.S. environmental NGOs if the consultation clause were to be diluted.

The second main criticism of the draft OD, after consultation, had to do with the classification of projects according to the likely significance of their environmental impact, and hence according to the requirement for a full-scale EA. The draft OD classified projects into category A (those that could be expected to have "significant" environmental impacts for which full-scale EAs are required); category B (those that may have "specific environmental impacts," for which more limited environmental analysis is normally appropriate); category C (those that normally do not result in significant environmental impact, for which environmental analysis is normally unnecessary); and category D (those called "environmental projects" but not requiring a separate EA because environmental assessment would be a major part of project preparation itself). The list of category A projects included large-scale aquaculture, river basin development, large-scale electrical transmission, forestry, large-scale industrial plants, and industrial estates. These projects may all lead to substantial changes in the use of renewable resources (for example, the conversion of land to agricultural production, timber production); substantial changes in farming and fishing practices (for example, the introduction of new crops); substantial changes in the exploitation of water; and so on. Category B included small-scale agroindustries, small-scale irrigation, small-scale electrical transmission, and so on. Category C included projects in education, nutrition, and institutional development. This procedure, requiring that the depth of analysis be proportional to the potential environmental impacts, is derived from the USAID scheme, from which the Asian Development Bank had earlier taken its own procedures and list.

Many critics said that category A should be drastically reduced or eliminated altogether, on the grounds that no general type of project should be subject to mandatory EA; the judgment should be left to Bank officials in the concerned region. These critics stressed that USAID's EA procedures were a bad model; many of its EAs were pro forma exercises not worth the paper they were written on. On the other hand, a few vociferous environmental specialists wanted to eliminate category B on the grounds that it provided a loophole for what should be category A projects. They also wanted to eliminate category D on the grounds that it, too, might be used as a loophole. (They pointed to the way that the sanitation engineers, for example, sought to call all sanitation projects category D, by definition, and therefore make them exempt from EAs.) The EA team sought a compromise, retaining B and D categories while simplifying what they saw as overcomplex USAID procedures.

When the EA draft reached the President's Council in late August 1989, another hot issue came up. When should the EA be released to the executive directors, and to others? Senior Vice President Stern reported that U.S. Treasury Secretary Nicholas F. Brady had recently sent a letter to the Bank asking for substantial advanced notice—for the EA to be delivered to the U.S. executive director well before the project came to the Board. Stern also reported that NGOs were pressing hard for the EA to be disclosed long before the project design was set. Stern suggested as a solution that the Bank could release the EA to the executive directors two to three weeks before the distribution of the gray-cover version of the report, with the understanding that this early release was specifically to help the executive directors obtain input from their *public* institutions. "Early release would not be intended or designed to get NGO input"[161]—meaning "international" or "Washington-based NGOs." (The principle of disclosure to "affected peoples," who might include *local* NGOs, had already been accepted as a condition of consultation.) But this solution would be left at the level of an understanding rather than written into the OD.

Some twenty-six drafts later, the final OD was ready by the time of the Annual Meetings of 1989.[162] It was announced with fanfare. The vice president for central operations, the director of the Environment Department, and members of the writing team gave a presentation to an invited audience of some three hundred government officials. They later did the same at a meeting of a hundred or more NGO representatives and others.

The NGOs were disgruntled, however, because they had not been consulted at any point in the drafting of the OD, and for reasons to do with the Narmada campaign (explained later in the chapter) were especially powerful at this time. In response, the Bank committed itself to an early revision to take account of NGO reactions. The revised version, OD 4.01, October 1991, said, "The purpose of EA is to ensure that the development options under consideration are environmentally sound and sustainable." This made clearer than had the earlier version that "sustainability" was not a value to be traded off in an economic analysis. Rather, it implied that *all* the options under consideration should meet sustainability criteria. The new OD also dropped the D project category altogether, in line with its drafter's view of the D category as a loophole by which too many projects could avoid scrutiny.[163]

Other important changes were made to the clauses on consultation and information disclosure, as the NGOs wanted.[164] The earlier OD had said no more about information disclosure than "The Bank encourages the borrower to release relevant information to appropriate interested parties."[165] The revised version of 1991 spelled this out in detail:

161. Minutes of President's Council meeting, August 28, 1989, p. 2.

162. "Environmental Assessments" is formally presented as "Annex A" to OD 4.00, the OD itself remaining unwritten.

163. The revised OD was drafted by Robert Goodland, who had been more or less excluded from the drafting of the original version.

164. OD 4.01, paras. 19–21.

165. OD 4.00, para. 25.

In order for meaningful consultations to take place between the borrower and affected groups and local NGOs, it is necessary that the borrower provide relevant information prior to consultations. The information should be provided in a timely manner and in a form that is meaningful for, and accessible to, the groups being consulted. Such information normally includes (a) for the initial consultation, a summary of the project description and objectives, and potential adverse effects of the proposed project; and (b) once the EA report has been prepared, a summary of its conclusions in a form and language meaningful to the groups being consulted. . . . The borrower should make the EA report available at some public place accessible to affected groups and local NGOs for their review and comment.[166]

The revised OD also requires the borrower to release the EA to the executive directors. It does not say so in just these words, because formally the EA is the borrower's property, not the Bank's, and property rights must be respected. Rather, it says, "Bank policy is to request the borrower's advance permission to release the EA report to the executive directors (EDs) because the report is the borrower's property. . . . If the borrower indicates at any time that it is not in a position to release such a report to the EDs, the Bank should not proceed with further work on the project."[167] So the borrower is free not to release the EA to the executive directors, in which case the Bank stops the project. This is freedom of a limited kind. The decision to take a tough position on EA disclosure was made at the top of the Bank. The people drafting the revision were astonished, for it was much tougher than they thought they could get away with. It was one thing to persuade the Bank to accept EA disclosure to local people, for once the Bank had agreed to a consultation requirement, disclosure was clearly implied; it was quite another to get the Bank to accept EA disclosure to the executive directors. Disclosure to executive directors seemed to breach a cardinal principle of Bank governance, the presumption of the confidentiality of borrower-country documents.

Again, U.S. pressure through the U.S. executive director was critical in crossing this line. U.S. law says that federal decision makers must have access to environmental assessments so that they can make well-informed decisions, all the better informed because they in turn release the EAs to experts outside the government and elicit their feedback. The U.S. administration treats the U.S. executive directors of multilateral institutions as "federal decision makers" and therefore as subject to the U.S. law that says federal decision makers must have access to EAs. This raises difficult issues of extraterritoriality, which can be defined as the extent to which a multilateral organization is bound by the national laws of any one of its members. Without entering upon that subject, one might note here that the Bank

166. OD 4.01, para. 21.
167. The text continues with a qualification: "Unless the Senior Vice President, Operations . . . , decides otherwise on the recommendation of the Regional vice president concerned, and for objective reasons unrelated to the environmental soundness of the project" (OD 4.01, para. 22). Such reasons may be geopolitical.

has to accommodate to some degree the demands of the U.S. executive director especially because of IDA, but it tries to do so without admitting the extraterritorial reach of U.S. law. Although the demand was driven by the U.S. executive director, some other directors from Part I countries were supportive. The procedure would give them a legitimate way to get their hands on the documents and then to release them to various parties, partly to obtain their technical advice and partly to notify those with commercial interests in, for example, environmental consulting. (Several executive directors' offices have one or more staff responsible for identifying procurement implications of project documents and making the knowledge available to their national firms.)

The EA procedures set the framework of much of the Bank's environment work up to the mid-1990s. By 1996 more than 100 projects had been subject to a comprehensive (category A) EA, and some 450 projects had been subject to limited (category B) environmental analysis, in a total of about 1,000 projects.[168] Much of the time of the REDs was spent advising task managers on how to do EAs (or how to get the borrower to do EAs), and then in reviewing and clearing the result.

But the EA work was project specific and piecemeal, consistent with the narrow focus of the "environmental protection" paradigm. In itself it did not involve or require the formulation of a comprehensive view of development-environment interactions. That was to be the job of the central Environment Department, but, as pointed out earlier, the department was stuck in low gear for the first several years after 1987. By the late 1980s the Bank came under a second wave of attack for its environmental and social record, this time mounted by an international coalition of NGOs and eventually joined by several Part I governments. What sparked this second attack were the Narmada projects in Northwest India. This time the Bank was pressured to go further in integrating environmental and social criteria into its lending and advice, in the direction of the "environmental management" paradigm.

Pressures for Change: The Narmada Projects (India), 1978–93

The Narmada Valley Projects constitute a basinwide, interstate development scheme to harness the Narmada River, one of India's last "unexploited" resources for hydropower and irrigation. As envisaged by Indian planners, four big dams and thousands of smaller ones would be built along the Narmada River during the next half century or so, making it one of the biggest water resource schemes in the world. The reservoir of the first of the big dams, Sardar Sarovar, would be 200 kilometers long and displace some 40,000 households. The canal, 100 meters

168. World Bank, Environment Department, "The Impact of Environmental Assessment: Second Environmental Assessment Review of Projects Financed by the World Bank (July 1992–June 1995)," draft, March 20.

across the water at the head, would be one of the biggest in the world. The canal network would extend for 75,000 kilometers and irrigate almost two million hectares of arid land. Its construction would remove some portion of the land of 68,000 households.

The swelling international campaign against Narmada and against the Bank that took off around 1987 helped stiffen the management's commitment to internal environmental reforms of the kind described earlier, notably the creation and expansion of an environmental establishment and the institutionalization of EA procedures. But the main effects came later. In response to years of concerted outside pressure, in 1993 the Bank and the government of India canceled the Bank's disbursements for Sardar Sarovar. This was the first time the Bank had taken such a step anywhere in the world on environmental or social grounds (as distinct from financial or procurement grounds). Earlier it had appointed an independent panel to review the Sardar Sarovar project and the Bank's role in it, and the independent review had reached conclusions highly critical of the Bank.[169] The momentum of criticism led the Bank to accede to the demands of NGOs and some executive directors that the Bank establish, in 1993–94, a permanent "independent inspection panel" to which affected parties could complain that they had been harmed by the Bank's noncompliance with its own operational policies. It also led the Bank to agree on a policy of freer disclosure of information about projects under preparation. And it helped to change the Bank's stance toward NGOs from illegitimate to legitimate interlocutors.[170] These important changes in the Bank's governance—making features new to the governance of *any* multilateral financial organization—were driven by the constantly boiling pot of Narmada.

Entry Conditions

The government of India approached the Bank for help with the Narmada scheme in 1978, and in the same year the Bank sent a reconnaissance mission to determine an appropriate means for Bank involvement. The Bank prepared the first-stage project (Sardar Sarovar dam and canals) in 1979–83 and appraised it in 1983–84; the Board approved a loan and credit in March 1985 for $450 million.

On the Indian side, several initial conditions set the stage for what happened later. First, the costs and benefits of Sardar Sarovar were spread unequally between the three riparian states. Gujarat, where the dam was located, got the irrigation benefits. Madhya Pradesh (MP), where most of the reservoir was located, had most

---

169. Bradford W. Morse, *Sardar Sarovar: Report of the Independent Review* (Ottawa: Resource Futures International Inc., 1992), also known as the Morse Commission Report.

170. World Bank, "The World Bank's Partnership with Nongovernmental Organizations," Participation and NGO Group, Poverty and Social Policy Department, World Bank, Washington, D.C., May 1996.

of the people to be forcibly resettled (80 percent of the 245 villages to be flooded were in MP). The third state, Maharashtra, had a small share of the costs and a smaller share of the benefits.[171] Gujarat strongly wanted the project; MP did not and only agreed to cooperate in the expectation that this would encourage the Bank to help fund a large upstream dam in MP from which it would derive most of the benefits; and Maharashtra had little interest in Sardar Sarovar whatsoever. Second, there was no superordinate agency above the state governments to take authoritative decisions. Third, Gujarat was well advanced in planning the scheme by 1978 (while work on the ground had been halted by an interstate water dispute, resolved in 1979 by a federal tribunal after ten years of deliberation). When the Bank reconnaissance mission arrived, the chief engineer for Gujarat placed on the table eighteen volumes of plans and said, "Here are our plans. We start tomorrow."[172]

On the Bank side, the new vice president for South Asia, David Hopper, an expert in Indian irrigation and agriculture, remained vice president during the critical first two-thirds of the Bank's involvement, from 1979 to 1987. The chief of the India irrigation division was Gabriel ("Gabby") Tibor, one of the Bank's long-serving and most charismatic division chiefs, an irrigation engineer regarded by colleagues as innovative and hard charging.

Hopper and Tibor agreed—as did the secretary of irrigation for the government of India—that the Bank had for too long been helping Indian engineers to perfect nineteenth-century British engineering design instead of upgrading to late-twentieth-century standards. Sardar Sarovar would be, if Gujarat's plans were not changed, a canal that reflected a late-nineteenth-century solution to a problem that no longer existed: the design would make water flow at a speed that was neither so slow as to deposit silt nor so fast as to cause erosion. In the twentieth century these constraints could be removed by the use of reservoirs to handle the silt problem and canal lining to handle the erosion problem. With reservoir and lining in place, it was possible to design a canal that gave the higher levels of water control required for the more intensive and variegated agriculture of the late twentieth century. Hopper and Tibor wanted to seize the rare opportunity of Sardar Sarovar to make a beachhead of change in India's conservative irrigation establishment. Conversely, they thought Gujarat's existing plans would be a disaster in the making: the resulting canal would have insufficient water control to avoid extensive waterlogging and salinity. Hence issues of seepage, drainage, and water control became central to the project's definition. In this limited sense the Bank, supported by the irrigation secretary, gave great weight to "environmental" issues, though not described as such.

171. The distribution of power was meant to compensate. Under the terms of the tribunal award (clause VII) MP was to get 57 percent of the net power, Maharashtra 27 percent, and Gujarat 16 percent. But power is less valuable to politicians than irrigation in an economy of this type. Besides, the power plant being in Gujarat, the other states could not be sure that Gujarat would comply with the stipulated shares.

172. Per Ljung, project officer, interview with the author, March 12, 1996.

People both in the Bank and in India took for granted that, provided the water-logging/salinity problems were taken care of and the engineering brought up to late-twentieth-century standards, the benefits would be so large relative to the costs that the nonmonetary costs did not have to be examined carefully. This assumption had a pervasive effect on what the planners paid attention to. It is seen, for example, in the response to a Bank resettlement specialist who at a meeting with project staff in the late 1980s asked about the effect of the project on the drinking water supply of villages downstream of the dam. "We are bringing drinking water to X hundred villages in Gujarat that have never had reliable supplies before," they responded impatiently, as though the benefits to the new villages were so obviously greater than any possible losses to the downstream villages that the calculation did not have to be made.[173]

Resettlement

The national and international campaign against Narmada focused on resettlement more than environment. The resettlement problems that in the end prompted the Bank to pull out were inherent in the situation from the beginning, as long as the project was held either to the resettlement standards contained in the interstate water tribunal's decision or to the standards of the Bank's own resettlement directive (which said the Bank required a resettlement plan whose "main objective is to ensure that settlers are afforded opportunities to become established and economically self-sustaining in the shortest possible period, *at living standards that at least match those before resettlement*").[174]

All three states worried about the consequences of complying with the tribunal's award and the Bank's directive. Compensation in the Sardar Sarovar project, they thought, would set precedents that the courts might then apply retrospectively to the many hundreds of thousands of people already displaced by infrastructure projects, and to those to be displaced by future projects, including the many more Narmada projects. The federal government had limited leverage over the states on resettlement matters because resettlement, like water, was a state subject. The states therefore began to play a game akin to "chicken," each aiming to do as little as possible for their own "oustees" in the hope that others would bear the costs. In particular, MP did little for those being displaced (the great majority of the total) in the hope that they would go to Gujarat. Under the terms of the tribunal award, Gujarat was meant to reimburse MP for resettlement costs, but the MP government had no confidence that Gujarat would actually do so. Maharashtra, too, sat on its hands until 1988–89. Gujarat, although it had to offer to accommodate migrants from the other states as part of the tribunal award, did almost nothing (also until the

173. William Partridge, interview with the author, March 10, 1995.
174. OMS 2.33, "Social Issues Associated with Involuntary Resettlement in Bank-Financed Projects," February 1980, para. 18.

late 1980s) in the hope of dissuading them from coming. While playing this game, all three states calculated that the Bank knew that if it (the Bank) insisted on applying its guidelines to Narmada, people resettled from other Bank-financed projects in India, who got little compensation, would start insisting on the same. This would open a Pandora's box from which the Bank would surely shrink.

The India Irrigation Division, meanwhile, its attention focused on helping to redesign the infrastructure to late-twentieth-century standards, ignored resettlement completely. Not until 1983, as Sardar Sarovar was being appraised, did the Bank's sociologist and resettlement champion, Michael Cernea, discover that the appraisal mission's terms of reference contained no mention of resettlement. Yet the resettlement implications were huge. Cernea launched his own crusade to get the India Irrigation Division to pay attention to resettlement. Using his own Agriculture and Rural Development Department's budget, he hired a well-known resettlement expert, Thayer Scudder, to investigate the resettlement situation. Scudder was "appalled" by what he found.[175] Nothing had been done to inform villagers about resettlement options and rehabilitation packages. Scudder eventually recommended that the Bank pressure the state governments to agree on an "annual rolling plan" for resettlement instead of insisting on a comprehensive plan covering several years into the future.

By the time of Board presentation in March 1985, enough had been done by way of planning for the staff to assure the Board, with some truth, that "the measures embodied in the plan for resettlement and rehabilitation represented a significant advance over the practices of the past in India."[176] What the staff did not say—nor did the supporting documents—was that the "plan" was no more than a diluted version of the resettlement principles enunciated in the interstate water tribunal's award of 1979. But the tribunal's award was mainly about water sharing and did not claim to set out comprehensive resettlement principles. Some of the most difficult issues were not even mentioned in the award.[177] It fell far short of what constituted a "plan" in the Bank's own resettlement directive. The staff also did not say that India's practices of the past generally were disastrous, and fell far short of India's own legal requirements. Hence, for all that Sardar Sarovar was intended in the Bank to be the spearhead of a whole new paradigm in Indian irrigation, the new paradigm did not, apparently, include resettlement. That was a "social" issue.

The Bank declared the Sardar Sarovar loan effective in early 1986. But then the government of India itself refused to declare the project effective for environmen-

175. Thayer Scudder, interview with the author, November 3, 1995.

176. Summary of discussions at the meeting of the executive directors of the Bank and IDA, March 7, 1985.

177. The award was nevertheless important in resettlement thinking. It established for the first time in India the principle of land for land (as distinct from cash for land) and indirectly shifted thinking in the Bank toward the same principle.

tal reasons. This caused a hiatus in the project until the government cleared up the problem in 1987. In 1987 a resettlement mission went out to see what progress had been made in the meantime. It found that those villagers who had already been moved to make way for the dam were still languishing in resettlement villages on sterile land without even rudimentary infrastructure. On its return it recommended that the Bank threaten India with cancellation for noncompliance with the resettlement agreement.[178] Weeks later the Bank's reorganization of June 1987 hit, and the main proponent of the cancellation threat, the project's lawyer, Carlos Escudero, by then a resettlement champion, was moved, against his wishes, to work on banking in Indonesia.

Yet by this time the wider resettlement climate in the Bank was changing. The Bank's senior management, Ernest Stern in particular, signaled that the Bank had to take resettlement seriously, thanks both to an internal review by Michael Cernea of the Bank's poor resettlement record worldwide, and to the escalating anti-Narmada campaign focused on resettlement.[179] Like it or not, the India Department therefore began to formulate what it called an "incremental" approach to Narmada resettlement, one that would avoid the need for a comprehensive (and time-consuming) plan. Several years remained before large numbers of people would have to be moved, which gave time for steady pressure on the state governments to yield actions that would *in the end* constitute compliance with the Bank's directive. The incremental approach had drawbacks, however. First, it gave an excuse for never collecting data necessary to get a clear overview of the scale of the resettlement problem. Second, as news of the compensation possibilities spread, adult sons and anyone else who might make a claim raced back from across India; not only were there no good numbers at the start, but the numbers kept growing. Third, from the Indian standpoint, the incremental approach looked like a constant shifting of goalposts, a continual imposition of new targets. On the other hand, the Bank's own resettlement experts—by now several in number—tended to see the incremental approach as an unscrupulous way of always being able to declare "progress."

Nevertheless, by the late 1980s the Bank did devote serious resources to resettlement, and first in Gujarat and then in Maharashtra some real progress began to be made on the ground, though it was hardly enough to dent the international NGO campaign. The nature of the resistance in the state governments, even in Gujarat, can be seen in a submission by the Gujarat government to the independent review panel in 1992 on the subject of the canal oustees (those whose land had to be acquired as right-of-way for the canal). The submission said that the

178. Formally, the recommendation was for suspension followed by cancellation, since Bank procedures require that suspension precede cancellation.

179. World Bank, Agriculture and Rural Development Department, "Involuntary Resettlement in Bank-Assisted Projects: A Review of the Applications of Bank Policies and Procedures in FY1979–85 Projects," February 1986.

Bank's requirements (land for land) were excessively stringent, that the Land Acquisition Act of 1894 gave adequate protection, and that in any case, "For such a large irrigation project, which is to benefit the community at large, the farmers have always been ready for slight sacrifices."[180]

Environment

The whole thrust of the Bank in the first several years was to redesign Gujarat's plans so as to make the dam and canal less likely to cause waterlogging and salinity. In that limited sense, environmental details had a central place. Everything else that might be called environmental was neglected up to and beyond project approval. At the time of approval in 1985 there was virtually no knowledge of the state of forest cover in the valley, the environmental impact of forest loss (for example, on siltation in the reservoir), the impact of the project on downstream communities (for example, drinking water and fisheries), the effects on runoff into the sea and the risk of saltwater intrusion, the impact on groundwater, or the impact of resettlement on the environment (for example, on the demand and supply of fuelwood, vital to the success of resettlement).

A dated covenant went into the loan agreement with each of the states saying that an environmental workplan would be prepared by December 1985 (after approval but before effectiveness). But none of the documentation indicated what might constitute an "environmental workplan." Nor did the documentation (for example, the Staff Appraisal Report) mention that the project had not yet received clearance from the Ministry of Environment and Forests, required by both Bank and government of India rules of project approval. Earlier, in 1983, India's environment agency (then located within the Ministry of Science and Technology) had refused to clear the project because of a lack of information about environmental aspects, and the refusal still stood when the Board approved the loan.

At the Board approval meeting in 1985 only one executive director worried about potential environmental problems. The staff replied that "although a full environmental impact assessment had not been completed, a *comprehensive first-stage assessment* had been conducted by the University of Baroda and then examined by members of the World Bank appraisal team. That study covered public health, flora and fauna, fisheries, wildlife, and archaeology and had determined that *there were no endangered species in the area.*"[181] This "comprehensive first-stage assessment" was a short, general document dating from the early 1980s, that could not remotely qualify as an environmental assessment. By describing it as "first-stage" the staff covered themselves; and by reporting only the finding that there were no endangered species in the area the staff gave the impression that the environmental situation was better than it was.

---

180. Cited in Morse, *Sardar Sarovar,* p. 206.

181. IBRD/IDA/IFC, summary of discussions at the meeting of the executive directors of the Bank and IDA, March 7, 1985, SD85-10, March 21, 1985, para. 14, emphasis added.

Why was the project declared effective when the dated covenant requiring an environmental workplan had apparently not been met? The answer, at one level, is that what constituted an "environmental workplan" was unclear. The project's lawyer, with no guidance, decided that the Indian side's short list of studies to be made constituted a "plan." He signed off.

The India Department's position on environmental questions was based not only on the wish to avoid delays. It said that the likely environmental impacts simply could not be estimated so long in advance. What was needed was a mechanism to monitor environmental effects as the project developed and take mitigating actions as the effects showed up. It considered as mistaken the whole idea of requiring an environmental action *plan* of the kind that the Bank's recently introduced (1984) OMS on environmental aspects of projects (see above) could be taken to call for. Its interpretation of the phrase "environmental workplan" as meaning no more than a list of studies to be done constituted the triumph of substance over process, in its eyes.

In 1987 India's recently formed Ministry of Environment and Forests granted a provisional clearance on the condition that the three state governments complete several studies of environmental impacts by 1989. These studies were tied to the construction schedule, so the compromise became known as the pari passu principle: environmental impacts were to be determined and mitigation measures put in place in concert with construction.

Also in 1987 the Bank took the first step toward a proper environmental assessment. The India Department hired as a consultant a California water expert with a great deal of experience in preparing environmental assessments. He worked for a year and a half. But in the meantime the person who had commissioned him moved out of the project team, leaving him without an internal champion. When he presented the draft in 1988, the project officer said, "We don't have a budget to deal with these things." Of the many people sent copies, only two replied, one of them being the person who had originally commissioned him, the other being the postreorganization task manager for whom he was working. His report, running to three hundred pages, died. His task manager sent him a note of thanks saying, "The important thing is that we *have* such a report, and can point to it. It will also be a very valuable source of facts and references."[182]

Once the REDs were formed after the 1987 reorganization, one person in the Asia RED became the "contact person" for Narmada. He was a professional biologist who, before joining the Bank shortly before, had headed the Asian Development Bank's small environmental unit.[183] He set about persuading the India Department to help the state governments prepare an environmental workplan. The Canadian aid organization, CIDA, promised money. In the end,

182. Christoph Diewald to Don Levenhagen, December 12, 1988. Don Levenhagen, interviews with the author, November 6 and 8, 1995.

183. Colin Rees, one of the team of three that drew up the Bank's environmental assessment OD.

though, nothing happened. The Canadians backed away in the face of the political heat enveloping the project. The project authorities and state governments remained unsympathetic, claiming that quite enough was known about the environment; and in addition the state governments refused to cooperate with each other even over such obvious matters as a common fisheries protection plan. The India Department thought that the Asia RED contact person should himself solve the problem of the missing environmental workplan. He instead told the department that hardly anything had been done at the Indian end, that every piece of environmental data was suspect, and that recommendations about mitigation could not be made until detailed (and time-consuming) studies had been made. Worse, he began to call for changes in the dam so as to reduce the damage to estuary fisheries, and even to echo demands from Indian and international NGOs that the environment plan should examine *alternatives* to the basic design of the Narmada projects. This made the India Department apoplectic.

By 1990 everyone was at everyone else's throat. The India Department blamed the Asia RED, the environment people blamed the project people, Bank staff blamed the Indians, the central government blamed the states, the states blamed the central government, and everyone blamed the Bank. In early 1992 the consultant who in 1987–88 had written the first preliminary environmental assessment was asked to make a short report on recent developments. He found the whole project disintegrating, with very bad relations all around. Most dispiriting of all, he found that almost none of the follow-up work that the states' environmental agencies had agreed to do in discussions with him in 1987–88 had actually been done; nor had the Bank put them under any pressure to do it.

In 1992, while the independent review panel was at work, the Bank's India staff ranked Sardar Sarovar as having "moderate" environmental problems. In the covering memorandum for the report environmental problems were not mentioned as possible obstacles to the planned acceleration in the construction schedule (though resettlement and health problems were so identified). Yet the provisional clearance granted by India's Ministry of Environment and Forests in 1987 had been conditional upon the completion of eight specific environmental studies by 1989. None had been completed by that time, and virtually none had been completed by 1992 when the Bank rated the project's environmental aspects as having "moderate problems." A plausible environmental workplan was still not ready five years after the start of construction of the dam above the foundations.

External Pressure

In the late 1970s a community health organization called ARCH was working in the tribal belt of Gujarāt. When construction work on the foundations of the Sardar Sarovar dam began (initiated by the Gujarat government even before the interstate tribunal award) ARCH discovered that villagers had not been informed about the

project. Those who were going to be evicted only learned about it when government surveyors came in to mark out the future waterline of the reservoir, below
which loggers could strip the timber. When ARCH heard that the World Bank was
involved, it asked its main foreign funder, U.K.-based Oxfam, for help. The head of
Oxfam's campaign programs, John Clark, visited the Narmada Valley in 1982 and
decided to take up the project. Oxfam began to organize a letter-writing campaign
to the Bank and to U.K. members of Parliament that yielded hundreds of letters. In
1985 Oxfam orchestrated the creation of an international Narmada campaign,
involving NGOs from many countries, to press for better resettlement.

Meanwhile, another local NGO had come to prominence in the Narmada
Valley, later called the Narmada Bachao Andolan (NBA), translated as Save the
Narmada Movement. It was led by a fiery, charismatic social worker named Medha
Patkar. The NBA by 1987 had linked up with the U.S.-based Environmental
Defense Fund (EDF). There a new recruit, Lori Udall, took up the Narmada cause
full-time, encouraged by EDF's seasoned Bank campaigner, Bruce Rich (moved
from the Natural Resources Defense Council). Leadership in the international
Narmada campaign shifted from gentle Oxfam in Britain to high-octane Udall in
Washington, D.C. On the ground, the NBA came to eclipse ARCH, and by early
1988 it changed gears. Instead of pushing for better resettlement it launched a
"Stop the Dam" campaign. To many international NGOs Stop the Dam was more
attractive than Better Resettlement.

Udall coordinated the international campaign in the period from 1988 to 1992.
First, she identified groups within the more important Part I countries that might
support an anti-Narmada/anti-Bank campaign. Second, she prepared menus of
actions they might take in the circumstances of their own countries: parliamentary
or congressional hearings, public forums, press conferences, lobbying key officials,
letter-writing campaigns. She especially encouraged them to contact their country's
executive director and to go to legislators. Third, she prepared information packs
for them, drawing on materials sent by NBA and other Indian activists. Throughout
she was in frequent touch with the U.S. executive director's office. The U.S.
executive director, Patrick Coady, gave her full support.

In 1989 the U.S.-based NGOs in the campaign persuaded a congressional
subcommittee to hold hearings specifically on Narmada. These hearings mark a
watershed in the international criticism of the Bank. Thereafter the international
anti-Narmada/anti-Bank campaign took off. In May 1990 the Japanese government
announced it was withdrawing its aid for turbines and generators, under pressure
from Japanese NGOs that had mobilized against Narmada, the first time they had
taken a concerted position on international environmental/human rights issues. At
the time of the Annual Meeting in 1992 some 250 organizations from thirty-seven
countries signed a full-page open letter in the *Financial Times* (London), the *New
York Times*, and the *Washington Post*, which said, "The World Bank must withdraw
from Sardar Sarovar immediately." It went on to warn that if the Bank continued

funding the project in the face of the Independent Review (which had presented its report in June 1992) then "NGOs and activists would put their weight behind a campaign to cut off funding to the Bank."[184]

Internal Organization

Inside the Bank, project management was from the beginning centralized in Washington, as was true for just about all Bank project work. The Bank's Delhi office had no one responsible for the project until 1986. The first project officer, beginning in 1979, was an economist with training in engineering, a young professional. A new project officer took over in 1984, a long-experienced irrigation engineer who had already been working on the project. In 1986 he moved to the Delhi office. But even then all correspondence between him and the government of India had to be signed off by the chief of the India Agricultural Operations Division back in Washington, until 1989. The project officer found himself wrestling more than full-time with problems of procurement, design, and construction. He and others in the project team devoted intense efforts helping to bring the dam up to international standards. They also struggled to persuade the Indian engineers to adopt more modern techniques of canal lining, fearing that the existing techniques would yield a lining unable to withstand the force of the water. Looking back from 1995, they see that great improvements were made on the infrastructure side, which makes them all the more bitter that the Bank walked away.

Preoccupied with engineering problems, the core people (including several irrigation engineers and a couple of economists) had little time for other things. But they were also convinced that the benefits of the project were so enormous as to render nonengineering problems relatively minor. Moreover, they had no intention of pressuring the state governments to comply with the Bank's resettlement policy any more than they had to, believing the policy to be a mistake.

Their definition of priorities prevailed all the more because for much of the second half of the 1980s they were unmanaged. Just as serious implementation began on the ground, when the project should have been intensively supervised, the Bank descended into the chaos of the 1987 reorganization, when for more than two years many people were preoccupied chiefly with protecting their own necks. Partly for this reason, the project division with responsibility for the project had six division chiefs between 1984 and 1993, averaging about eighteen months each; and in the critical period from 1987 to 1989 three came and went in eighteen months. The parent department had four directors between 1984 and 1990. This high turnover of managers meant that for long stretches in the project's history, at a time when it was the spearhead of an international campaign against the Bank, the average time that the same two people were division chief and director was less

184. For example, *Financial Times* (London), September 21, 1992, p. 6.

than twelve months. This is important because incoming division chiefs and directors each took time to find out about the project (just one of many things they had to attend to). They encountered it as well established and took it as the project staff presented it.

Not until 1988 was there any form of "crisis management," and even then the response was minimal. In that year, with the anti-Narmada/anti-Bank campaign rising, one person in the Indian Agricultural Operations Division, Thomas Blinkhorn, was asked to take charge of *all* resettlement and environmental issues in Bank work in India. He worked directly with the director of the India Department. Blinkhorn believed that Sardar Sarovar and the proposed upstream dam, Narmada Sagar, were good investments that were in danger of being blown away by ill-informed critics. He shared the project staff's skepticism of the motives and competence of the Bank's own resettlement and environmental staff, who were, said the man who was project officer during the second half of the 1980s, "in a unique position of being able to communicate the non-optional, critical life-supporting need for development of the Narmada's water and power resources but . . . chose to work tirelessly to criticize the SSP [Sardar Sarovar Project] planning and implementation processes, and thereby contribute to delays while remaining ever mindful of setting up detailed criteria requiring bureaucratic manipulation—empire building—for which they were well suited."[185]

Not surprisingly, relations between the project people and the environmental and resettlement people deteriorated. And since the two sides were not in the same division or department, the antagonism could flourish as each dug in. Relations between the Bank and the concerned NGOs were even worse, with the Bank attributing to them the worst possible motives. The project officer referred to "the extreme intellectual dishonesty and related pressure tactics of the NGOs" and described their concerns about resettlement and environment as mere "tools of delay needed to organize the world net of anti-large-dam believers into a formidable political block."[186] The Bank must not cave in to such dishonest people, the project staff said.

India's Crisis

Just as the Bank began to settle down after the 1987 reorganization, India suffered a severe macroeconomic and political crisis. This caused, among other things, a high turnover in the top administrative and political positions of the Indian government. By 1991 the crisis was so serious that the country came close to defaulting on its commercial debt. The central government was anxious to involve the Bank in finding a way out of the crisis, promising in return drastic economic liberalization. For the Bank, this was the opportunity it had long been waiting for.

185. Gerry Fauss, personal communication, January 1996.
186. Ibid.

For several years the macroeconomic and political crisis and then the opportunity for far-reaching liberalization crowded out senior management attention to such relatively small things as Narmada, both in the Indian government and in the Bank.

The Independent Review

In 1988 the Dutch executive director, Paul Arlman, began to take a particular interest in Narmada and convened a small group of Part I country executive directors to follow it. Some of them met with Oxfam's John Clark and EDF's Lori Udall, and with the NBA's Medha Patkar. After the meeting with Patkar, one executive director commented, "When I hear what NGOs say about this project and then what the operations people say, it sounds like they are talking about two different projects."[187] In mid-1990 the U.S. executive director began to sound out the director-general of the Bank's Operations Evaluation Department about undertaking a special review of Sardar Sarovar. There was general uneasiness about the idea all around. Then at the end of 1990 Medha Patkar and the NBA led a "Long March" to the dam site, where they planned to stop construction by means of a sit-in. They were stopped at the Gujarat border by police. Medha Patkar and several others began a fast to the death. The fast injected new urgency. What would persuade Patkar to stop? She was demanding that the whole project be comprehensively reviewed, but the Bank would not agree. As she grew weaker and the Bank still said nothing, John Clark, Lori Udall, and others made desperate attempts to persuade the senior operational vice president, Moeen Qureshi, to announce a review. He did so just in time, and in the spring of 1991 a small number of executive directors, led by the new Dutch executive director, Evelyn Herfkins, began to consider the membership and terms of reference of an independent review panel.

There were no precedents to draw on. Herfkins used her by then well-established contacts with people like Udall and Clark to get ideas. But since the independent review would be established by the Bank, the India Department's environment and resettlement coordinator was given the responsibility of organizing the panel. He approached a number of prominent persons to see whether they would be willing to head such a body. All refused. Meanwhile Conable, in the waning months of his presidency, was growing desperate; he needed someone fast. With support from Herfkins and the other interested executive directors, he approached his former congressional colleague, Bradford Morse, who since leaving the U.S. Congress had been head of the United Nations Development Program (UNDP). Morse was in poor health. But Conable prevailed on him to chair the commission while others did the work. In June 1991 Conable announced that an independent review panel would be established and headed by Morse.

187. Quoted in Lori Udall, "The International Narmada Campaign: A Case of Sustained Advocacy," in William Fischer, ed., *Toward Sustainable Development? Struggling over India's Narmada River* (Armonk: M. E. Sharpe, 1995).

The environmental coordinator, Blinkhorn, started to look for someone to head up the real work. By this time the Environmental Defense Fund was, as he said, "practically camping in the living room," getting so many leaks out of the Bank that it was better informed than he was.[188] Udall started a letter-writing campaign aimed at the Dutch executive director Herfkins, to persuade her to push for the appointment of Thomas Berger as the principal investigator. Berger was a well-known Canadian jurist and advocate of Native American rights. He was also a friend of Udall's uncle, former U.S. Secretary of the Interior Stuart Udall, who had subsequently worked closely with Berger in a major legal case on Native American rights. Barbara Bramble, one of the original trio who led the earlier NGO campaign against the Bank and now was working behind the scenes on this one, had also worked with, admired, and advocated Berger. Herfkins proposed Berger. Blinkhorn interviewed Berger and recommended him—even knowing his reputation as a defender of indigenous peoples' rights and knowing that there were a lot of "tribals" in the Narmada area—to show that the Bank was bending over backwards to be impartial. Morse agreed. Berger, however, said he would only do it on certain conditions: that he receive a fee of $1,500 per day (an unheard of rate in the Bank, to which the head of consultants' services in the personnel department made the strongest objection), and that he pick his own team (whom he named). By this time it was August 1991. Conable and Senior Vice President Sven Sandstrom were anxious to end the long delays. They agreed with Berger's conditions. He was appointed deputy chairman.

In the NGO community, personnel selected for the review had high credibility. Inside the Bank people were worried. It was observed that the review members had little knowledge of development (Morse apart), no knowledge of India, and the fact that the chairman had been head of UNDP was regarded as ominous. "Of course, anyone related to UNDP (Mr. Morse) would not miss an opportunity to embarrass the Bank," said one.[189] Conable himself warned Morse that Berger and his team might, on the basis of their track record in handling Native American issues, prejudge this one. Morse reminded Conable that he had obtained a pledge of absolute independence. Conable backed off.

Once the core members of the review panel were appointed, they had frequent contact by phone with Udall and on their first visit to the Bank met with her at their hotel for three hours. It was true, as their critics alleged, that they knew little about the Bank and less about India. She briefed them on such issues as how they could retain their credibility in the NGO world, which NGOs were fighting which, which were trustworthy, who was doing what in the Bank, and what rules of operation to insist upon in regard to the Bank. Berger also spent a day with Clark and others at Oxfam. The team formally started work in September 1991.

188. Thomas Blinkhorn, interview with the author, April 3, 1996.
189. Senior legal official to a subordinate, comment in the margin of a copy of the Terms of Reference of the Independent Review.

Its independence from the Bank was ensured by several rules that the review panel (after briefings from Udall and Clark) had insisted upon as a condition of acceptance:

1. Complete access to all project files from the Bank and from the government of India, and to Indian NGOs and the Narmada Valley.

2. An extended period of time (originally seven months, extended to nine).

3. An independent budget, initially of $400,000 that grew to about $1 million. (The budget came from the president's contingency fund.)

4. Independent publication of the results, without the Bank's editorial control.

5. No postreview Bank employment of panel members.

Its terms of reference were limited to resettlement and environment, its task being to assess the Bank's performance in these two domains in relation to the Bank's own policies and loan agreements. The NBA initially opposed such narrow terms of reference on the grounds that many other aspects of the project had also been questioned. The Bank stood firm, and there was an indication that the Indian government had agreed to the review on condition that it be confined to resettlement and environment.[190] All the Indian governments were angry that the Bank had created such a body. Gujarat, in particular, wanted nothing to do with it. The Bank had to use maximum leverage with the chief minister of Gujarat to get him to allow the panel to enter the state.

Ten months later, on June 18, 1992, the panel issued a 363-page report.[191] The report concluded, first, that the Bank had been seriously out of compliance with its own directives on resettlement and on environmental analysis of projects; second, that "there is good reason to believe that the project will not perform as planned," that is, perform in the hydrological sense of getting the water to the expected areas; third, that adequate resettlement was unlikely to occur on the ground "under prevailing circumstances," because "a further application of the same [incremental] strategy, albeit in a more determined or aggressive fashion, would fail." Finally, it recommended that the Bank "step back" from the project. Essentially, it confirmed much of what the NGO campaign had been saying.

The review also found that "the richest source of material about the problems with resettlement in India are in the Bank's own internal documents," making it all the more "perplexing [that] there appears to be so little effort to develop a remedial *strategy* rather than confront one resettlement problem after another."[192] One review member commented that if key people in the India Department had listened to their own mission members and consultants the whole review exercise would have been unnecessary.[193]

190. Udall, "The International Narmada Campaign."

191. This was four days *after* the World Bank rose from the United Nations Conference on Environment and Development (the Earth Summit) as the key agency to implement "Agenda 21," an informal intergovernmental agreement on global environmental priorities and actions. A draft had been discussed over two days in May by a group of eleven staff and three panel members.

192. Morse, *Sardar Sarovar*, p. 53, emphasis added.

193. Quoted in Udall, "The International Narmada Campaign," p. 210.

The Decision to Continue, and Then to Cancel

In July 1992 the Bank sent a large (fourteen-person) mission to review the status of the Sardar Sarovar project, with the implicit goal of assessing whether the review was right.[194] It was received with hostility wherever it went. The mission leaders concluded that the Bank should suspend disbursements and recommended this in their Back-to-Office report: instead of saying, "You have six more months to do things x, y, z," the Bank should say, "We'll suspend now and resume when you have done x, y, and z." None of the mission members, including those resettlement experts who had not hesitated to criticize the Bank's performance, wanted *cancellation,* because they were convinced that without the Bank being involved, resettlement and environmental protection would be worse. The senior managers, however, decided that the Bank would neither suspend nor cancel but continue for another six months, or more precisely, that the Bank would recommend this to the Board, for the Board had already, very unusually, asked to reconsider the Bank's involvement in the project. Their argument was essentially, "After a rocky start we have finally got a good partner in the government of Gujarat, the Bank is demonstrably helping to improve the project, the project is potentially a very good one, of great importance to India as a whole, why cut off the branch we are sitting on, why abandon it in mid stream, what good would it do to anyone (most of all the oustees) to stop now?" And they repeated: "We mustn't cave in [to the NGOs]." The senior managers also had in mind the impact of suspension on India's foreign exchange position.

For the September 1992 Annual Meeting, the international NGOs ran the earlier-noted full-page advertisements in the three newspapers most widely read among the Annual Meeting delegates, warning that if the Bank continued funding Sardar Sarovar against the advice of the independent review, then "NGOs and activists would put their weight behind a campaign to cut off funding to the Bank."

Also in September 1992 the Bank presented to the Board a document titled "Sardar Sarovar Projects, Review of Current Status and Next Steps."[195] This interwove the Bank's reply to the independent review's report with its "action plan" for dealing with resettlement and the environment. It was to have been the work of a task force set up to reply to the independent review's report, with membership drawn from both the India Department and the environment and resettlement complex, the *first* time in the whole of the project's history that such a task force had been attempted. The result was failure. The task force was paralyzed with disagreement, and in the end the India Department environmental coordinator wrote it himself, working directly with the vice president and Managing Director Stern. The "Next Steps" document satisfied virtually no one. Operational people in

194. Known as the Cox Mission, after its leader, Pamela Cox, a member of the India Department who had not previously worked on Narmada.

195. Dated September 11, 1992.

the India Department resented the fact that the people working on the project were not allowed to reply to the review's report themselves, as a consequence of which the reply was not as convincing a rebuttal as it could have been, they said. The lawyer for the project was also unhappy because the action plan was "neither precise nor monitorable." He went on to say, "We seem to be moving away from a situation where compliance or non-compliance of GOI [government of India] and the states are measured against the legal documents, to a situation where it is unclear exactly what is being agreed upon and what commitments are being made by GOI and the states under the action plan."[196] Other internal critics observed that the document flew in the face of the Bank's ostensible objective of getting the government of India to take more ownership of the project: the action plan had been drawn up by the Bank with no input from the government of India.

The review members were even more unhappy with the Bank's reply. They claimed that the Bank had seriously distorted their findings—even though their report was in the public domain for all to see. In October the chairman and deputy chairman of the review, Bradford Morse and Thomas Berger, wrote to the president of the Bank saying that the Bank's reply *"ignores or misrepresents the main findings of our Review. . . .* [W]e do want to ensure that the senior decision-makers at the Bank are not left with an account of our findings that is at variance with what we wrote."[197] They went on to say that the Bank's presentation of its findings gave the impression that their report found the problems with the project to be much smaller, more tractable, than the report actually suggests. Review members subsequently flew to Washington to meet with the Board.

The vice president for South Asia signed a two-and-a-half-page response to the Morse and Berger letter (copied for the Board), rejecting virtually all its claims.[198]

On October 23, 1992, a few days after South Asia's response to the Morse/Berger letter, the Board met to vote on the fate of the project, with the president, the South Asia vice president, and other high-ranking Bank officials in attendance. The South Asia vice presidency had prepared a series of "benchmarks" of what should be achieved on the ground over the following six months, to strengthen the case for extending the Bank's involvement by at least another six months. These benchmarks tied the rate of construction of the dam and canal to the rate of (improved) resettlement. Failure to meet the benchmarks would provide grounds for the Bank to pull out. Bank staff present at the meeting remember it for the sheer vindictiveness of the executive directors. The Dutch executive director, who had taken a coordinating role for the project within the Board and between the Board and the Bank, reminded the meeting that the Board had asked for an

196. Salman Salman, LEGSA, to Andres Rigo, assistant general council, Operations, September 15, 1992.

197. Bradford Morse and Thomas Berger to Lewis Preston, October 13, 1992, emphasis added.

198. Joseph Wood to Bradford Morse, October 20, 1992.

independent review because it felt it could not trust Bank management. The Austrian executive director criticized Bank management for its strong-arm lobbying of the executive directors to keep the project going. The U.S. executive director, Patrick Coady, accused management of a "coverup," noting that "what is at stake is the credibility of the Board." He went on to say that if the Board allowed the project to continue, "it will signal that no matter how egregious the situation, no matter how flawed the project, no matter how many policies have been violated, and no matter how clear the remedies prescribed, the Bank will go forward on its own terms."[199]

The Bank's management gave as its core argument one that had by then become its standard justification for involvement in all difficult projects. Using language almost identical to its earlier justification for Polonoroeste it said, "While it would be safe to restrict Bank involvement to those situations in which the Borrower had already established an exemplary track record, this would in practice mean foregoing opportunities for potentially more important change. A decision by the Bank not to get involved could well mean that the project in question will still proceed but under much less favorable circumstances."[200] It did not say, though this was in its mind, that cancellation would have severe consequences for the Bank's reputation as an infrastructure lender in India and elsewhere, and perhaps for India's economic liberalization.

Much of the discussion concerned the benchmarks against which progress would be monitored. Some executive directors raised the worry—already raised by many NGO critics—that the benchmarks depended on the governments of MP and Maharashtra doing things they were disinclined to do, while the government of India patently had little influence over them. Therefore, said the critics, the benchmark exercise was dishonest because it was based on an assumption that everyone knew to be false: that the government of India, which had agreed to implement the benchmarks, had influence over MP and Maharashtra and therefore that its sign-on meant something on the ground. At the Board meeting a prominent Part I country executive director asked the key question: had the "relevant authorities" agreed to the benchmarks (meaning, had the state governments agreed)? The management said yes. On the strength of this assurance, the executive director voted with the Part II countries, tipping the balance in favor of continuing subject to review against benchmarks six months later. The majority "wished to give the benefit of the doubt to the new Government of India [at the federal level] and to acknowledge the recent efforts made by the Indian authorities."[201]

199. Quoted in Rich, *Mortgaging the Earth,* p. 301.
200. The quotation comes from the first draft of the Bank management's response to the independent review, dated June 23, 1992, p. 12.
201. Chairman's summary, "India: Sardar Sarovar Projects," executive director's meeting, October 23, 1992.

The fact that the Bank acted against the advice of the independent review—helped by the ambiguity in the review's recommendation to "step back"—reenergized the international opposition to the project and to the Bank at large. On the ground construction progressed while resettlement lagged far behind. On the other hand, environmental analysis suddenly took off. In the six months following the independent review, more progress was made toward the formulation of a regional environmental work plan than in the previous six years. Both the director of the India Department and key people in India finally accepted that the issue could not be fudged.

A senior Bank manager admitted in 1993 that suspension in 1989 would have been a healthy "shock" that might have speeded up action on the ground to fix resettlement and environmental problems.[202] But the "shock" thesis was consistently rejected, right up to 1993, in favor of the argument that incremental progress should be rewarded even if it was not sufficient to reach agreed deadlines.

At the end of March 1993, the Board was scheduled to decide whether to continue. By then India's macroeconomic position had greatly improved. On the other hand, it was clear that the benchmarks set six months before, especially those to do with resettlement, would again not be met. The South Asia vice president, Joseph Wood, who had resisted suspension or cancellation since taking charge in 1991, became persuaded there was no alternative to cancellation. The government of India and the government of Gujarat had indicated they would *not* say, "We will stop building the dam until these other matters are in hand." On the contrary, their attitude was, "Damn the NGOs, we are not going to submit to crybabies, we will continue to build the dam." They did not wish to accommodate the Bank's attempts to respond to world outrage. In any case, the lack of unified decisionmaking between the federal government and the states, plus the difficulties of cooperation between the states, meant the Bank could not count on Indian assurances. This argued against mere suspension, leaving cancellation as the only option. And cancellation looked to be necessary in order to protect IDA from the continuing storm of criticism around the Bank. A majority of the Board agreed. In the end, President Preston informed the prime minister that Narmada was jeopardizing IDA, which would hurt India.[203] The vice president for South Asia told the Indian government, "Either we cancel or you tell us you will not submit requests for disbursements."

A few days before the Board meeting, the government of India announced that it would not ask the Bank for more disbursements. The central government was not unhappy to cancel. The project was generating too many headaches, and the benefits of Bank involvement went largely to Gujarat, not to the center. A senior

202. Quoted in Hans Wyss, "Bankwide Lessons Learned from the Experience with the India Sardar Sarovar (Narmada) Project," May 19, 1993, p. 5.

203. In the paraphrase of a close participant.

Indian official said, "The project had become a cancerous tumor on the country's overall portfolio with the Bank."[204] Needing Bank help in publicizing India's market reforms, the government wanted embarrassing distractions like Narmada removed from the spotlight. Indeed, taking the moral high ground, the government explained that its decision reflected determination to uphold the quality of the planning and consultation processes even at the cost of not meeting the arbitrary deadlines agreed with the Bank six months before.[205] In private, Indian officials said that what the Bank had been doing was "not in keeping with the country's self-respect."[206] They claimed the Bank had been exercising inordinate influence given that it was contributing only 15 to 20 percent of the funds. And they recognized that the gap between Bank resettlement requirements and what India was able to deliver would almost certainly persist and be the source of constant frictions.

The leader of the main opposition movement, Medha Patkar, sent a message from a remote Narmada village saying the loss of World Bank funds was "a victory for thousands of struggling tribals and farmers in the Narmada valley."[207] The NBA then succeeded in getting the Supreme Court to halt dam construction at the beginning of 1995, until resettlement was carried out in line with India's and the Bank's policies. The halt continues, as of early 1997. Meanwhile critics allege that much of the existing resettlement is unraveling, as many of those already resettled have gone back to their original villages in the inundation zone. The Gujarat government is raising bonds to finance the project (including canal construction, which continues) at interest rates of 17 percent or more but is having trouble selling them even at these rates; all other items in the state's budget are being squeezed. NGOs, including the NBA, are calling on the World Bank to remain involved to the point of honoring its legal responsibility to see that the conditions attached to the already disbursed money are met.

Why Narmada?

Narmada became the second great focus of NGO mobilization against the Bank not because Sardar Sarovar was a bad project next to other Bank projects, or because mistakes were made that were not made elsewhere. On the contrary.

204. Quoted in "A Tactical Retreat to Save Face?" *Pioneer* (India), March 31, 1993. The Indian government also calculated that the cutoff in disbursements would not be very costly, because the IDA (zero interest) component had already been disbursed, leaving the (almost commercial rate) IBRD funds to be canceled.

205. In "Sarovar Project: India Forgoes World Bank Aid," *Statesman* (India), March 31, 1993.

206. Reported in "India Not to Seek Further WB Loan," *National Herald* (India), March 31, 1993.

207. Quoted in "The World Bank Cuts Funds to a Dam Project in India," *Independent* (United Kingdom), April 1, 1993.

Sardar Sarovar was prepared by people who were idealists and innovators, who believed they were helping to make fundamental improvements in Indian irrigation. It became the second focus of attack because it had several characteristics that lent itself to the organization of opposition: it involved the forced displacement of large numbers of people, many of whom could be presented as sympathy-deserving "tribals"; forced relocation could support a radical campaign to stop the dam; local opposition was well organized, led by a charismatic figure (Patkar); the international campaign benefited from unusually energetic and tenacious organizers (first Clark and Oxfam, then Udall and EDF); some Bank staff members and Bank consultants were severe critics of the way the project was being implemented and could help the external critics with information; and the local opposition to Narmada began to crescendo around 1986, just as Polonoroeste was losing its appeal to the NGOs. Finally, location in India also helped, because international NGOs had good access to English-language information and because India's democratic policy and free press allowed opposition. If Narmada had been in China, Indonesia, or Turkey, it could not have been used in this way.

The question, then, is not, "What did the Bank do wrong in Narmada that it did not do wrong in other projects?" According to the Bank's own analysis, Narmada suffered from serious "entry mistakes," such as poor resettlement planning or environmental assessments, the implication being that other Bank projects had better resettlement planning or environmental assessments.[208] They did not.

What did make Narmada unusual was its timing, which put it in a set of "hinge" projects. It was prepared, appraised, and approved at about the same time that the Bank introduced quite new directives on "noneconomic" criteria—resettlement and environment. These "noneconomic" criteria and directives were stoutly resisted inside the Bank by the operational people, including South Asia Vice President David Hopper. Their resistance, combined with ambiguity about the status of "directives" (as analogous to national laws or as guidelines for what would be nice to achieve), allowed the busy project people to continue to prepare the project as they had prepared projects before the resettlement and environmental directives were introduced. And, of course, "consultation" with people of the valley was entirely neglected, for the Bank did not have any directives enjoining consultation, let alone experience of it. India's federal structure made the Bank's implementation of these new directives all the more difficult because resettlement and water fell under the heading of "state" subjects, not central or joint subjects; but the Bank could lend only to the central government, and could approach the state governments only via the central government, which had only limited influence over the states. The same point applies to all federal structures, including Brazil's.

The Bank's own quality-control mechanism—review by "central" departments such as Agriculture and the Office of Environmental Affairs—was easily kept aside.

208. Wyss, "Bankwide Lessons Learned."

However, Narmada differed from Polonoroeste in that the central departments were much less involved in opposing it than they had been in Polonoroeste. The agricultural staff of the central Agriculture Department did not raise alarms about it as they had about Polonoroeste, being predisposed to be sympathetic to large-scale irrigation projects. The one exception was the person in the center whose job it was to look after resettlement, Michael Cernea. That resettlement was the single axis of center-region conflict owes much to the combination of Cernea's bulldog presence in the center, a strong local resettlement movement on the ground, and later, a powerful international anti-Narmada movement focused on resettlement. Cernea decided in 1983 to draw a line at Narmada and force the South Asia Projects Department to implement what he—with the backing of McNamara and his own Agriculture director—had only recently persuaded the Bank to adopt as a general resettlement policy.

Although at project approval in 1985 and project effectiveness in 1986 there were resettlement and environmental conditions in the loan agreements, few people on the Bank side or the India side thought they were to be taken seriously. Only later, once NGOs began to train their spotlights on resettlement, did operational people inside the Bank begin to worry about these things, and then the concern was resettlement more than the environment.

The problem then became: "How does the Bank 'retrofit' a project?" A project is in a sense no more than an agreement over the conditions for the use of borrowed funds. Once the agreement has been reached it is deeply problematic for the Bank then to say, "Sorry, but our requirements have now changed, so we must change the agreement," or even to say, "Sorry, but we now have to observe these conditions that we all thought we didn't have to, so you must observe them too." Projects are path dependent; the way they are started continues to impart a direction that continues for years.

Retrofitting is difficult. The effort to do so in Narmada as NGO pressure built up then began to produce apparently deceitful behavior on the part of the operational staff. Their logic went like this.

1. We know things are not going well in the project.

2. But do we want to pull out or suspend?

3. No, it is potentially a damn fine project, and things will go better if we are in. (Anyway, management will not allow a pullout, for "country relations" reasons.)

4. Therefore we need to justify staying in. We do so by sending up reports that things are going well or at least improving, making sure that if anything is said about things that are not going well the phrasing implies that they are minor or on the way to being fixed.

The trick is to make the aroma of words do the work that the evidence cannot. It is unlikely that anyone connected with Narmada ever said, "India needs this foreign exchange and we need India to borrow; therefore Narmada must go ahead; therefore we have to find ways to justify going ahead." Rarely, if ever, would people admit even to themselves, "This is wrong but we have to say it anyway." Rather, the bias to optimism comes in the "atmospherics." The staff could report, "The government has committed itself in this period to finish preparing ten resettlement sites but only two have been completed; and the government has failed to implement its policies on compensation"; or it could say, "The government has committed itself to prepare ten resettlement sites, two have now been completed, another four are being actively planned, and the government is initiating major improvements in the policy framework." The second version justifies staying in.

From "Environmental Protection" to "Environmental Management," 1992 to the Present

For the first several years after 1987, the history of environmental affairs in the Bank is one of grudging acceptance on the part of most of the senior management and many of the operational staff. Like it or not, they would have to pay more attention to internalizing environmental costs in projects—more attention to the "environmental protection" paradigm. They would have to do so even in the face of continuing resistance from the developing countries. As recently as 1990 Ernest Stern, the number two official in the Bank for most of the period from 1981 to 1995, warned, "I don't think you can underestimate the political explosiveness of this issue [environmental conditions on Bank loans] in many of these quite important developing countries." He added that these countries felt a profound sense of unfairness and viewed environmental conditions as "another impediment that foreigners have put on them to keep them from growing."[209] However, around 1992 and 1993 the more comprehensive ideas of the "environmental management" paradigm began to take hold at senior management and operational levels. The conversion came partly from love and partly from fear.

Narmada was the fear factor. By the early 1990s staff throughout the Bank were aware of the NGOs' anti-Bank campaign. As a division chief in the Africa region put it, Narmada had become a "four-letter word." In the wake of the independent review's report and the Bank's cancellation, managers in other parts of the Bank reinforced their signals to staff that environment and resettlement should not be ignored or fudged. One country director, hitherto not known for environmental sympathy, ordered several B projects reclassified as A (and hence made them subject to comprehensive environmental assessment), *against* the advice of the environmental specialists, saying, "This is a changed Bank. We cannot cut corners on the environment."

The Global Environmental Facility, on the other hand, helped promote conversion through love. From 1989 to late 1990 the Bank was involved in negotiating a

209. Ernest Stern, quoted in "New Environment Fund Proposed for World Bank," in *World Bank Watch*, February 26, 1990.

pilot phase, which was approved for a period of three years with funds of $1.3 billion, pledged by participating countries.[210] This experience suggested that a Bank aggressively sensitive to the environment could position itself to be the steward of much additional funding for cross-border environmental projects, especially because its weighted voting system allowed the main donors to have the preponderant say in how the funds were used (in contrast to UN agencies). This might partly offset the continued squeeze on IDA lending resources.

The preparations for the United Nations Conference on Environment and Development (UNCED) of 1992, often called the Earth Summit, or the Rio Summit, also helped to "seed" the environmental idea inside the Bank by providing it with the opportunity to demonstrate world leadership in environment-development matters and to refurbish its battered image. Like the United Nations Conference on the Human Environment of 1972 (the Stockholm conference), UNCED acted as a thought- and decision-forcing device. But whereas preparations for the Stockholm conference were confined to a handful of Bank staff for the rest of whom the conference was irrelevant, much larger numbers were involved in the preparations for Rio. The Bank's UNCED coordination office established some twenty-three forces throughout the Bank and the IFC to work on particular subjects, including sustainable agriculture, women, and private sector development.[211] These task forces, consisting mostly of people from outside the environment "ghetto," wrote reports for other groups in other organizations working on similar themes, and in turn they received reports from these other groups. Many of these other groups were NGOs filled with their learning and experience gained during the previous decade, with whom many Bank staff came into contact for the first time in the search for common positions. The Bank's coordination office published a newsletter keeping track of the preparations; by the time of the conference it was printing 7,000 copies per issue.

By this time, too, the environmental complex was well established and pushing to expand its mandate. And many task managers, as well as environmental specialists, had become aware of the limitations of project-specific EAs. Many environmental problems, they pointed out, are best handled not by inserting mitigation measures into each project as it comes along, but by operating with a wider view of the main environmental problems of a given country and taking actions directed specifically at those problems. Partly because the external critics who forced the Bank to change its environmental stance focused on particular projects, the Bank's environmental thinking after the 1987 reforms was dominated by the *project* as the unit of environmental action. Projects were where the Bank could get into trouble: noncompliance could be shown on television and held up

210. Sjöberg, "From Idea to Reality"; Olav Kjorven, *Facing the Challenge of Change: The World Bank and the Global Environmental Facility*, EED Publication 3 (Lysaker [Norway]: Fridtjof Nansen Institute, 1992).

211. A small office headed by Jane Pratt and Carlston Boucher.

before the U.S. Congress. The environmental impact of fiscal policy is much less tangible and less susceptible to the pinning of blame. Hence the more abstract issues—such as the relationship between the wider policy framework and environmental degradation—have tended to be eclipsed in the Bank's work because they were not what the critics were concerned with, and also because the obvious locus for such work inside the Bank, the central Environment Department, was malfunctioning. By 1992–93, with the Environment Department operating in higher gear, pressure began to build from inside the Bank to make macro and sectoral policies "environmentally friendly."[212]

Finally, a substantial segment of public opinion in the developing countries came around to the view that environmentalism was not just a western plot to halt growth in the South and thereby enable those most responsible for creating global environmental problems to avoid making real sacrifices. These countries eventually saw that environmental degradation was threatening the welfare benefits of growth, and even growth itself, and that investment today in environmental protection could be more productive than "grow now, clean up later."

For these reasons the phrase "mainstreaming the environment" became a "buzz-word" in Bank circles and even made its way into the title of the Bank's annual report on the environment for fiscal 1995.[213] The phrase was generally used to refer to the need for "a significant shift in emphasis from 'development' and 'environment' as two separate perspectives to a fully integrated approach toward 'environmentally sustainable development.'"[214] The Bank now gave more sustained attention to policy configurations that would benefit growth, poverty reduction, and the environment simultaneously, and to integrating these configurations into its countrywide policy work. It became a hotbed of research on the relationship between development and the environment. It helped produce National Environment Action Plans (NEAPs) for virtually all of its borrowers. Meanwhile, the portfolio of stand-alone environment projects continued to grow rapidly (table 13-1), and the REDs kept up the pace in producing environmental assessments for the Bank's A and B category projects. Organizationally, a new central vice presidency of Environmentally Sustainable Development was created to help integrate and

212. Piddington was replaced as director of the Environmental Department by Mohamed El-Ashry in 1991. Andrew Steer became deputy director after the completion of *World Development Report 1992* (see below). El-Ashry brought a rare combination of broad technical knowledge (he was trained as a geologist), management skill, and a vast network of environmental contacts (he had earlier worked for the Environmental Defense Fund and the World Resources Institute). Under El-Ashry and Steer, the department consolidated itself and began to play a larger leadership role, intellectually and organizationally. El-Ashry was simultaneously chairman of the pilot stage of the Global Environmental Facility (GEF). When the GEF was made permanent in 1994, El-Ashry became its chief executive officer, and Steer became director of the department in his place.

213. World Bank, *The World Bank Group and the Environment since the Rio Earth Summit: Mainstreaming the Environment* (World Bank, 1995).

214. World Bank, *The World Bank and the Environment* (World Bank, 1993), p. 134.

direct the burgeoning environmental work. And environmental specialists were transferred from REDs into country departments, in order to be more fully integrated in operations.[215]

There is no doubt "the environment" now has greater legitimacy than it did in, say, 1991. Right up to then a task manager could get away with saying at a project review meeting, "This power plant will have some serious effects on air quality in Shanghai, but there is no choice—we have to go ahead, China desperately needs power." Or, "This irrigation system will have no effect on the riverine ecology, because the river has no fish." Such statements would not be made in the Bank of the mid-1990s. As a prominent Bank research economist put it, "You can't write anything about development these days without mentioning the environment."[216]

The publication of *Development and the Environment,* the title of the *World Development Report 1992,* was a milestone in this shift. The report helped move the process forward in several ways. First, it presented environmental issues in a language that economists (inside and outside the Bank) could understand, as economic problems entailing costs and benefits. Second, it imparted a strong bias toward thinking that the scope for policies that benefited growth, poverty reduction, and environmental protection simultaneously was large, encouraging economists to hunt out such opportunities in their own particular countries. Third, it redirected attention toward the "brown" agenda. Much of the environment debate in the development context had been about green issues, in response to the dominant concerns of northern NGOs. *World Development Report 1992* made the case that brown issues were more important in terms of the effects on health and productivity in the South and were easier to treat with policy instruments. Fourth,

215. The trajectory of integration is seen in miniature in the case of the Legal Department. It hired its first environmental lawyer in 1988, a junior appointee shared half-time with the Environment Department, whose salary the Legal Department declined to pay any part of. She joined the Environment Department full-time in 1991. When eventually the Legal Department replaced her, in 1993, it was with a senior environmental lawyer employed full-time. By 1996 the department had an environmental affairs and international law unit with two regular staff and three long-term consultants, and the vice president and chief counsel, legal, had converted to the idea that the department needed specialized environmental capacity.

216. Lant Pritchett, interview with the author, December 10, 1996. There is a fine irony in Pritchett's remark. Pritchett was the real author of what became known, infamously, as the Summers pollution memo of 1991. Pritchett wrote a long memo on a draft of the Bank's annual publication, *Global Economic Prospects,* which included: "Just between you and me, shouldn't the World Bank be encouraging *more* migration of the dirty industries to the LDCs? . . . I think the economic logic behind dumping a load of toxic waste in the lowest-wage country is impeccable" (Lawrence Summers to distribution [GEP], December 12, 1991). Pritchett worked for Summers, vice president for Economics and Research. Summers signed the memo. The memo leaked and was published in newspapers around the world (*Financial Times,* February 10, 1992; *The Economist,* February 8, 1992). The memo became, for the Bank's environmental critics, internal and external, a ringing confirmation of their criticisms of Bank economists: they took it as an accurate statement of economists' views (whereas Pritchett wrote it in a spirit of sardonic counterpoint).

the report was written under the direction of a well-respected Bank economist, Andrew Steer. He had no previous involvement with environmental issues, and his conversion helped other economists change their minds.

The report is unflaggingly optimistic. Its argument, summarized as a "win-win" view, posits that economic growth and poverty reduction are good for the environment in both the North and in the South. It rests on technological optimism, in the sense that resource shortages create a demand for additional resources for research on how to avoid the bottlenecks, and this in turn leads societies to substitute abundant resources for scarce resources. It hardly mentions *trade-offs* between environmental protection, on the one hand, and efficiency, growth, and poverty reduction, on the other. The removal of subsidies on chemical fertilizer is a win-win move because it stimulates growth by increasing the efficiency of resource allocation and protects the environment by discouraging the use of chemical fertilizer, thereby implicitly encouraging the use of organic manure. But farmers faced with more expensive chemical fertilizer may go further up the hillside to practice erosion-accelerating slash-and-burn agriculture instead. Furthermore, the win-win view glosses over the political question of *who* wins. In most projects, some people gain when the environment is damaged whereas others pay the costs, and often the gainers have more power than those who pay. Again, the report emphasizes the scope for substituting man-made capital for natural capital, but it does not ask about the capacity of political institutions to make these substitutions happen.

But criticisms of the report as a contribution to knowledge and guide to action are, in a sense, beside the point. All *World Development Reports* are advocacy documents, and the report for 1992 was more so than most. If it had been more nuanced, more concerned with trade-offs, if it had admitted that on many questions the evidence is not clear, it would have made less impact inside and outside the Bank.[217] Yet for all the talk about the desirability of integrating an environmental problematique into all Bank thinking, and for all the output of high-quality studies on development and the environment, the actual level of integration has fallen far short of the declared intentions. This is true even in the case of project-level work, and still more so in country-level work.

Integration of Environmental Assessments

Through 1995 and into 1996 a pair of analysts from the Bank's Operations Evaluation Department carried out an evaluation of the effectiveness of the Bank's

217. The Bank's first annual report on the environment, written largely by Jeremy Warford, was frank about the uncertainties and the need for government intervention: "The studies highlight both the importance and the difficulty of establishing cause and effect relationships. Whereas poverty, population growth, legal and institutional factors, and economic policies might be expected to influence the ways in which resources are used—and therefore the way the environment is managed—the precise character of these relationships is rarely understood. . . . [For example], while liberalized trade and a free market system will often contribute to realizing both efficiency and environmental goals, this is not always the case. Free markets are not a panacea for environmental ills, and market failure will often have to [be] remedied by government intervention." World Bank, *The World Bank and the Environment, First Annual Report, Fiscal 1990*, p. 26.

environmental assessments since 1989. They found that the Bank's guidelines are among the most comprehensive in the world, and that other similar organizations have been modeling their own procedures on the Bank's. They also found that EAs are generally in compliance with the Bank's Operational Directives for EAs (4.00 and 4.01), meaning that the procedures for environmentally classifying projects, preparing Terms of Reference for the EA with the borrower, reviewing the EA after it is submitted by the borrower, and integrating the findings of the EA into the Staff Appraisal Report (which goes to the Board for project approval) are routinely done. They also found that all was not well with EAs. Four findings are particularly striking.

COMPREHENSIVENESS. The EA documents tended to emphasize comprehensiveness at the expense of major risk factors and hence tended to be unproductively bulky and expensive. This was especially so for A projects, which "often generated massive documents that are of little use in project design and during implementation."[218] One Bank staff member observed: "It is often unclear from the EA what the implications are for project activities—i.e., there is often a lot of technical data collected (species data, etc.) but it is often unclear how serious an impact it will have on the project area."[219]

ALTERNATIVES. The EAs fail to give serious attention to alternative designs—despite the call in the Operational Directive for "the systematic comparison of the proposed investment design, site, technology and operational alternatives in terms of their potential environmental impacts, capital and recurrent costs, suitability under local conditions, and institutional, training and monitoring requirements."[220] Of thirty-two EAs examined by the OED study, only thirteen (40 percent) included some discussion of alternatives, and some of these alternatives were "weak, superficial or easily dismissed options."[221] Note that the definition of "alternatives" for this purpose was modest: even a discussion of whether the trees should be fruit trees or pine trees would have been enough to qualify as "discussion of alternatives."

IMPACT ON PROJECT DESIGN. "Very few EAs actually influence project design." Out of fifty-three projects examined for this part of the study, only nine (17 percent) "had been modified to some degree because of EA findings."[222] The apparently weak impact on project design was partly due to the fact that almost half of the projects examined in the study did not meet the Operational Directive requirement that the EA must be ready before appraisal begins (of the nine A projects examined, five did not meet the requirement). More than three-quarters of Bank staff who were interviewed said that by the time the EAs are ready it is too late to use them.[223]

218. World Bank, "Effectiveness of Environmental Assessments and National Environmental Action Plans: A Process Study," OED Report 15835, June 28, 1996, p. 6.
219. Ibid., p. 24.
220. Operational Directive 4.01, Annex B, para. 2.
221. World Bank, "Effectiveness of Environmental Assessments," p. 29.
222. Ibid., p. 24.
223. Ibid., para. 2.19, p. 26. Note, however, that an EA that has no impact on project design may still usefully identify ways to mitigate damage caused by a *given* design.

SUPERVISION. Once a project has been approved there is typically little fol-low-up on the ground to see to what extent the environmental components or safeguards have been implemented. The OED study examined almost one thou-sand project supervision reports, and found that only 1 percent of them rated environmental aspects as "less than satisfactory." This suggests either that environ-mental supervision is pro forma, or that the people doing the supervising are unqualified, or both. OED field visits found that *at least* another 15 percent should have been put in the category of less than satisfactory.[224] Project designs typically call for supervision plans and monitoring and evaluation systems for other project components, but not, generally, for the environmental components. A separate OED review of the quality of the economic analysis of projects found that environ-mental performance indicators were only infrequently identified and described in the project design. This made environmental supervision that much more dif-ficult.[225] Moreover, OED visits to project sites revealed that the EAs were "often" not available at the site. For example, none of fourteen projects under implemen-tation in China had copies of the EA available, although the quality of the EA *documents* produced by the Chinese government is generally very high.[226]

A review of EAs by the Environment Department broadly concurs with the findings of the OED team, particularly with respect to the weakness of environ-mental supervision: "The principal finding of this Review when it comes to im-plementation is that the Bank's supervision, even of category A projects, is generally insufficient to determine environmental performance and may limit the Bank's ability to detect and address environment-related problems in a timely fashion as projects evolve. Knowledge of the actual environmental impacts and the performance of mitigation, monitoring and management plans is often incomplete. This deficiency could become more serious as increasing number of category A projects are implemented over the next few years."[227]

If EAs are having little impact on project design, if alternatives often are not being considered, and if the environmental aspects of projects are not being monitored when the projects are under implementation, there must be a question about the value of the process and the product. Indeed, *three-quarters* of the staff interviewed for the Operations Evaluation Department study said that EAs were not having the desired impact on the ground; and about *half* said that EAs were not being conducted effectively.[228] The weakness of supervision is especially worrying

224. Ibid., p. 6.

225. World Bank, Operations Evaluation Department, "A Review of the Quality of Economic Analysis in Staff Appraisal Reports for Projects Approved in 1993," July 5, 1995.

226. World Bank, "Effectiveness of Environmental Assessments," p. 33; and interviews with Bank staff.

227. World Bank, Environment Department, "The Impact of Environmental Assess-ment: Second Environmental Assessment Review of Projects Financed by the World Bank (July 1992–June 1995)," March 20, 1995, pp. iii–iv.

228. World Bank, "Effectiveness of Environmental Assessments," p. 20, fig. 2.1. The proportions reported in the text add up the percentage responses from 6 to 10 on a ten-point

because the project-executing agency may not perceive the environmental loan conditions to be in its *own* interest (since some of these loan conditions will be designed to deal with the "externalities" or spillovers between sectors that tend to be a distinguishing characteristic of environmental problems); full implementation is likely to require time-consuming coordination between sectoral agencies, which may well not happen in the absence of external supervision. Hence the Bank's failure to supervise may erode the shift in emphasis toward environmental goals in project preparation.[229]

That so many of the staff question the value or effectiveness of the EA process is striking. The doubts are spelled out in a memo from the chief of a water supply and sanitation division summarizing for his vice president the way his staff saw the Bank's environmental establishment (as of 1993):

> 1. The environmental establishment at the Bank (obviously with many individual exceptions) is increasingly seen as a policeman, not as a unit assisting our staff and borrowers to do better.
>
> 2. The competence and good judgement of the environmental establishment at the Bank is (again with many exceptions) perceived by our sector professionals to be low.
>
> 3. This causes much resentment among the borrowers. They are obliged to jump through incredible hoops constructed by what they perceive as first-world zealots (both staff and Board) who do not have the development interests of the country at heart.
>
> 4. Borrowers therefore legitimately think twice about getting the Bank to fund, say, sewerage projects, relying on other sources which probably demand much less than is required.[230]

A road engineer with decades of experience as a Bank project officer commented that the EA procedures had given "the power of life and death [over us] to an army of bureaucrats," but the procedures were an almost complete waste of time and resources in terms of improving the substance of road projects.

> They are all about administration, about making us jump through hoops, and only in exceptional cases—big dams or graveyards of ancestors—do they make any difference to the substance. From all the attention to EAs you would think that we [civil engineers] had

scale, from 1 = strongly disagree to 10 = strongly agree, to "EAs are conducted effectively" and "The outcome of EAs has the desired overall impact." The figures are based on a (too small) sample of twenty-six participants in focus groups. However, the same broad results come from the study's interviews with many more Bank staff. Alcira Kreimer, chief author, interview with the author, March 1, 1996. The study received trenchant criticism from the environment complex, on grounds that the samples of countries, borrower staff, and Bank staff are too small and not representative; some of the A projects included for close study were approved before the introduction of the EA OD of 1991; the study made no allowance for the strong learning effects between the Environment Department's first review of EAs and its second (for EAs dating from 1993 and after). Aidan Davy, interview with the author, September 29, 1996.

229. A point made in World Bank, *The World Bank and the Environment: First Annual Report, Fiscal 1990*, p. 70.

230. John Briscoe to Ismail Serageldin, March 25, 1993.

not done anything to mitigate environmental damage. As a civil engineer I feel strongly that we are a responsive profession—we can and do take account of society's evolving concerns and put them into the specifications. We don't have to be forced to do it by some PhD in biology. Why is it only the mitigation that *they* insist on that counts? Whatever we do the environmentalists think they have to insist on something more in order to justify their existence.[231]

Task managers often resent the power of the environmental specialists in the REDs to force them to undertake environmental studies and modifications to the design that add to costs and delays. They operate, still today, in an incentive system that rewards them hardly at all for the results of their work on the ground and mostly for moving projects toward Board approval. They will not be held accountable for poor results when, years later, long after they have moved to other positions, those results become known. On the other hand, they receive no automatic budget for EA preparation, as they do for core components of a project. The EA is meant to be the responsibility of the borrower to undertake and fund, but borrowers are, in many but not all cases, reluctant either to fund the EA from a local budget or to *borrow* from the Bank in order to do it. Often (especially in the wake of the 12 percent cut in the Bank's operational budget begun in 1994 and implemented over two years) the task manager has to take the initiative to find external *grant* funding. This is often not a straightforward matter. When an environment contact person in a regional environment division asks for an A classification of a project (requiring a full-scale EA) or for additional work on the EA, the task manager may take this to mean that yet more time will have to be spent searching, cap in hand, for money with which to pay expensive environmental consultants. (EAs may cost up to $1 million, more commonly $100,000 to $200,000.) Hence the task manager is squeezed between the wishes of the borrowing government agency, the constraints of the project timetable and preparation budget, and the need to get the environmental contact person in the RED to sign off on the EA.

The environmental specialist, on the other hand, has the power to sign off but needs to "sell" most of his or her forty-two staff weeks a year to the country departments in the form of help with handling the environmental aspects of projects, whose EAs he or she may later be asked to approve. An environmental specialist who fails to sell his or her services in this way for more than a year or two will be invited to seek employment elsewhere. A reputation for being "tough" or "unreasonable" can greatly reduce a person's marketability, and such a reputation is readily acquired by one who raises serious objections *after* a project has passed the earliest "concept" phase and resources have been invested in its preparation. On the other hand, environmental specialists are also likely to be steered by professional norms, and not only by their career line in the Bank. This incentive system produces complicated and sometimes acrimonious bargaining between task managers in country departments and environmental specialists in the regional environment divisions.

231. Jeremy Lane, interview with the author, September 20, 1996.

The EA reflects this bargaining.[232] The course of least resistance for both sides is often to make it very comprehensive (as a defense against "spot-the-gap" critics), but to suggest only a few modifications in the project design or alternative ways of providing the same benefits. And then, at implementation, when the environmental specialist no longer has a role to play, the task manager can cut corners in supervising the often difficult to supervise components that the environmental contact person had insisted on.

Planafloro (Rondônia, Northwest Brazil)

The case of the follow-on project to Polonoroeste is interesting in this regard. Known as Planafloro, it was intended to do the ecological and Amerindian zoning work that Polonoroeste had left undone, and to offer enhanced agricultural production possibilities to those who would be prevented by the zoning from

232. Take as an example a massive (1,000-megawatt) power project in a rural state of an Asian nation. The RED contact person, an engineer, argued to the task manager that the project should not be judged on its own because it was so large in comparison with the economy of the state. It would itself give a powerful impetus to industrialization. Hence it needed to be set in the context of a development plan for the regional economy and for the power sector of the whole state. There is at present, he pointed out, hardly any infrastructure in the project region. As people poured in and made shantytowns, another Singrauli (India) disaster was in prospect. Also, the contact person was alarmed by the plan to bring naphtha by rail rather than by sea, rail being more dangerous (but more productive of rake-offs). The task manager took him aside and said, "You are close to retiring from the Bank. But I still have to secure my career here. I can't afford to worry about this stuff." His objective was to get the project through—not to address wider issues of the project's sustainability and its external effects on the rest of the region. Yet he was a dedicated and much praised task manager.

The environmental contact person visited the secretary of the Ministry of Planning and Economic Affairs, and asked him whether the state had a plan for infrastructure, industry, and education. "What for?" asked the secretary, adding that *any* kind of industry would be appropriate in his eyes. The environmental contact person then approached the national power agency about whether it would prepare a regional plan on behalf of the state government. It said no, it was not responsible for what the state government did. The contact person spoke to the environment minister about the project and asked what would be done to ensure safety in transporting naphtha across long distances by rail. "Safety is not our responsibility," said the environment minister.

In the end, the task manager agreed to commission an international consulting firm to assess the risks of transporting naphtha by rail. The firm concluded that the risks were on the threshold between acceptable and unacceptable. Meanwhile the national power agency agreed to help the state government prepare a modest plan. With these two conditions met, the contact person approved the project reluctantly. "I've given up," he explained to a friend. "There's a limit to what we [in the Asia RED] can do when both the task manager and the borrower are opposed." He remains anxious about the risks of transporting naphtha by rail. And he hopes that the first step of preparing a modest plan will itself generate momentum to take the larger development planning problems more seriously.

exploiting natural resources. Both to underwrite the agriculture and to offer a "carrot" to the Rondônia state government to do the zoning, the project, like Polonoroeste, also included a large paving-of-existing-roads component (almost 4,000 kilometers). The environmental contact person in the Latin American RED had serious doubts that the project would be any more successful than its predecessor, because none of the "fundamentals" had changed.[233] He had earlier written a major report about environmental problems in the Amazon that set out his analysis of those fundamentals, in particular, the lack of both political will and institutional capacity to carry through agreements of the kind entailed by agroecological zoning.[234] He had voiced strong objections to Planafloro at the concept stage, but his objections had been overruled by the director of the Brazil Department, without explanation. When, later, the environment division was asked to clear the environmental assessment for the project, he felt he could do no more than check whether the document took care of the Bank's formal requirements, rather than fight again the argument he had earlier lost. By that time it was too late: the project had too much momentum, too much had been invested in it; the task manager could point to clauses in the agreement that would take care of all objections.

The project went ahead. It was approved by the Board in March 1992, with both the Bank and Brazil anxious to provide a tangible demonstration of their concern about the environment in the months before the Rio Earth Summit in June 1992. The OED evaluation of Polonoroeste, which contained detailed lessons from the Polonoroeste experience and which had been available to staff since 1990, was circulated to the Board only in April 1992, nearly two months *after* approval of Planafloro, and was not released for wider circulation until after the summit. The environmental contact person's own analysis of the problems of such projects, cited earlier, was released by the Brazil country department only in May 1992, though written much earlier.

As in Polonoroeste, the road-paving component, the only one that was wanted by the Rondônia state government, has been carried out on schedule. The agriculture and zoning components have hardly disbursed (as of the end of 1996). Critics claim, among other things, that the declaration of impending zoning and then its nonimplementation have *accelerated* rain forest destruction in that loggers have rushed to chop down the forest and colonists rushed to settle on the land before it is prohibited. They also note an internal feedback failure, namely, that supervision reports consistently rated project implementation as "unsatisfactory" without triggering urgent measures to enforce loan covenants. Defenders say that the project has not harmed the environment and may have done some good—though even defenders admit the cost probably exceeded the gain. (The Bank's loan was for

233. Interview with the author, February 17, 1997.
234. World Bank, "Analysis of Environmental Problems in the Amazon," Brazil Country Department Report 9104-BR, May 21, 1992.

$167 million, a welcome addition to the impecunious budget of the resource-rich state.) These arguments came to a head when some local NGOs asked the Bank's Inspection Panel to conduct an investigation into the Bank's alleged failure to carry out its commitments, in June 1995.[235]

The environmental contact person claims that only the director of the Brazil country department and the vice president for Latin America could make the judgment about whether the Brazilian authorities could be trusted to do what they had agreed to do. They, however, had a distinct interest in getting the project through the Board and in protecting Bank-Brazil relations, all the more so with the Rio Summit in view. This is how a project that everyone knew to be very risky after the experience of Polonoroeste—an almost identical project in the same region—came to reach the Board for approval. The Bank's environmental assessment procedures counted for little, as did the OED's role of learning from experience.

Integrating Environmental Sustainability in Macro and Sector Work

By 1993 Bank economists sympathetic to an environmental agenda had come to agree that much greater environmental improvements could be achieved by integrating environmental criteria into the Bank's policy work at the country level (into "economic and sector work," in Bank parlance) than by improving individual projects. This integration would cause all policy work—on fiscal policy, trade policy, land policy, public enterprise pricing policy, transportation policy, and the like—to take into account the impact of policy choices on environmental sustainability. Yet this integration up to the mid-1990s was noticeable by its absence.

It is true that National Environmental Action Plans (NEAPs) have been or are in the process of being prepared for Bank borrowers, initially for IDA countries as a condition of the IDA 9 negotiations of the late 1980s but continuing for non-IDA countries, too.[236] Formally, NEAPs were meant to be prepared by the government of each country, but the rush to prepare them in time to meet the IDA condition that no money should go to a country without a NEAP meant that the Bank took a large hand in preparing most of them. This had the merit of kick-starting a good deal of environmental work in the Bank. But at least up to the mid-1990s the plans were often "ritualistic and second-rate," in the words of the director of the Environment Department.[237] There has been a chronic tension between seeing the NEAPs as reports on "the environment" prepared by environmental specialists, and as

235. See Inspection Panel, "Request for Inspection: Brazil: Rondônia Natural Resources Management Project (Loan 3444-BR), Report on Additional Review," December 12, 1995.

236. World Bank, "Summary Proceedings, 1990 Annual Meetings of the Board of Governors," Washington, D.C., September 25–27, 1990, report of the executive directors of IDA, para. 17, p. 304. Operational Directive 4.02 (1992) formalizes Bank support for Environmental Action Plans (better known as National Environmental Action Plans).

237. Andrew Steer, interview with the author, October 28, 1994.

reports on "the environmental sustainability of development" prepared by country economists.

The NEAP was meant to feed into, and do the environmental homework for, the Country Assistance Strategy (CAS) document. The CAS is the most important document that the Bank produces for each of its borrowers; it distills what the Bank thinks its assistance and that of bilateral donors should be used for in the next three years. In practice, the CASs pay little attention to environmental issues. An internal review of twenty-five CASs (most of them written in 1995), covering some of the Bank's major borrowers, concluded: "The linkage between environment and the macro situation was not articulated. Most CAS did not assess alternative development strategies in terms of welfare improvement or sustainability related to sound management of environment and natural resources. . . . While certain 'big-tag' items are identified, such as water shortage and contamination, land erosion, and deforestation, judgements on their scope and nature are often missing, in terms of either horizontal comparison (compared with the international standards or the situation in comparable countries) or vertical comparison (worsening off or better off)."[238] Another study of how environmental issues have been reflected in eight CASs for Sub-Saharan Africa found, in 1995, that the NEAP would be referenced, but that the priorities identified in the NEAPs had little influence on priorities set in the CASs.[239] Often, the integration of environmental matters was mechanical, in the form of a paragraph added at the end. The study reports: "There are no examples of a systematic integration, or any explicit treatment at all of the impacts of macroeconomic policies on NRM [natural resource management] and the environment. . . . [With one exception] we were unable to find substantive discussion about pricing of natural resources, such as stumpage timber, scarce water, energy, and so on."

The CAS must be short (no more than fifteen to twenty pages) and must identify only four or five priorities. From the point of view of the country officer charged with writing the CAS, environmental issues are especially problematic as competitors for space. They generally do not threaten an immediate crisis, in contrast to some macroeconomic issues. They may well not have strong proponents within the borrowing country. And they are also often difficult to analyze. For all the optimism of the *World Development Report 1992* and for all the exhortation from senior managers to incorporate environmental processes and criteria, it remains unclear *how* to do this in any comprehensive way. There are not even any rules of thumb analogous to the rule that a government budget deficit of 10 percent of GDP needs urgent attention whereas a deficit of 2 percent can be lived with, rules

238. Office of the senior vice president, Development Economics, "Integrating Environmental Issues into Country Assistance Strategy," February 1, 1996, pp. v, 14.
239. Memorandum, Jan Bojo, senior environmental economist, to distribution, "Environmental Concerns in Country Assistance Strategies," April 11, 1995.

that could be used by a Ministry of Finance or a central bank to judge how to shape their policies by environmental impacts. There is great uncertainty about causal relationships. Something is known about the effects of poor air quality on health and it is possible to quantify the financial costs of the required health treatment, for example. But little is known about many ecological processes, their impacts on human health, productivity and growth, and their reversibility. And there is no methodology for assessing trade-offs where government action in favor of environmental protection must compete for limited public resources with other important purposes, such as education.[240]

In this situation, the country officer may well say, "If an environmental specialist gets involved [in the process of CAS writing], who knows what the agenda will be, he may sabotage the process by asking fuzzy questions about sustainability. The lifeboat is already full, and one more person may sink it." As the review of environmental matters in twenty-five CASs delicately put it, "Constructive exchanges in policy discussion and strategy formulation between country macroeconomists and environmental specialists are not yet a common phenomenon. . . . Some improvement in the Bank's organizational and incentive structure is needed to encourage wider and more effective consultation among experts, to reward team spirit, and to ensure collective accountability, so that a CAS can concisely state, for a country with multiple development goals, what are the key environmental challenges and how to design appropriate strategies, policies and action plans."[241] But this, it seems, is a long way off.[242]

In 1992 the World Resources Institute published a study on the environmental effects of IMF stabilization and World Bank structural adjustment programs, using

240. The official Bank position is set out in World Bank, *Economywide Policies and the Environment: Emerging Lessons from Experience* (World Bank, 1994). See also Jeremy J. Warford, Mohan Munasinghe, and Wilfredo Cruz, *The Greening of Economic Policy Reform: Principles and Case Studies* (World Bank, 1996).

241. Office of the senior vice president, Development Economics, "Integrating Environmental Issues into Country Assistance Strategy," p. 20.

242. The Indonesia country department has been at the forefront of efforts to integrate environmental issues into countrywide development strategy. This is the result of an unusual concatenation: the salience of Indonesia in the eyes of international environmental NGOs, the unusual commitment of the first two country directors after 1987, and the even more unusual fact that the country officer responsible for the CAS was also the head of the country department's three-person environment unit (having such a unit in the country department was itself unusual). The latter, moreover, was a generalist economist (Richard Calkins) who had spent many years working on Indonesia and who was himself interested, as an economist, in environmental issues. For examples of the department's strategy work on environmental issues, see the 200-page study, *Indonesia: Sustainable Development of Forests, Land, and Water* (1990), and the 300-page study, *Indonesia: Environment and Development* (1994). The CAS of 1991 identified "sustainable development" as one of five pillars of Bank support for Indonesia, after growth with stability, wider participation, human resource development, and poverty reduction (Country Assistance Strategy, Indonesia, 1991).

the Philippines as a case study.[243] This study traced the links from the stabilization and structural adjustment programs to poverty, and from poverty to deforestation, the depletion of artisanal fisheries, and the like. It demonstrated how measures to increase the substainability of country debt levels could undermine the substainability of the asset base. It urged that these links be integrated into the calculations behind the programs. But when a coauthor of the study approached the Bank's task manager for the Philippines structural adjustment program and suggested such integration, the latter said, "No, this program is already too complex without adding in the environment." And when the coauthor approached the country economist for a West African country with the same idea, the country economist replied, "We are already having enough trouble with poverty and sustainability. How can you expect us to cope with the *environment* as well?"

Between 1992 and 1994 the Asia RED completed seven studies of environmental degradation and its implications for long-term growth in East and Southeast Asia, which were intended to set the framework for a stream of investment projects or project components. But outside of China, the follow-through did not occur. In the face of government resistance to borrowing for environmental purposes and resistance to raising pollution taxes and stumpage fees, the Bank's country departments were unwilling to press the issues. The incentives for sustainable interest within the Bank were not there.

Even the many high-quality studies produced by the Bank on various aspects of development-environment integration mean less than they appear to. A high proportion of them are done not by staff members but by consultants, and therefore they expand the Bank's intellectual capital by less than would be the case if they had been written by staff. Even in the central Environment Department, whose role is intended to include a large measure of intellectual leadership, staff are tightly constrained in the time available for things other than operational support. They now have 50 percent of a forty-two-staff-week year for such nonoperational purposes, or twenty-one weeks.[244] But with operational task managers

---

While work on empirical methodologies for "green" national income accounts and physical environmental indicators has gone on outside the Bank since the late 1980s, the Bank has, for the most part, put itself in the audience. A small band of enthusiasts inside the Bank, including Saleh el Serafy, John Dixon, Ernst Lutz, Jeremy Warford, John O'Connor, and Robert Goodland, has tried to push this agenda, without much success. But see Yusuf J. Ahmad, Saleh el Serafy, and Ernst Lutz, eds., *Environmental Accounting for Sustainable Development* (World Bank, 1989); Ernst Lutz, ed., *Toward Improved Accounting for the Environment* (World Bank, 1993); World Bank, Environment Department, "Monitoring Environmental Progress: A Report on Work in Progress," March 1995.

243. Wilfredo Cruz and Robert C. Repetto, *The Environmental Effects of Stabilization and Structural Adjustment Programs: The Philippines Case* (Washington, D.C.: World Resources Institute, 1992).

244. Fifty percent for nonoperational work represents a fall from the notional 60 percent established after the 1987 reorganization, a fall driven by budget pressure.

averse to paying for operational support to be done in Washington, D.C., virtually all of it must be spent away on mission. The necessary time between missions—a week to catch up on the "In" tray, a week to prepare for the next mission—must be taken out of the twenty-one weeks for nonoperational purposes; or twelve weeks for six four-week missions. In the end, only nine weeks a year remain for substantial intellectual work, and this is scattered throughout the year rather than concentrated in one block. This regime cribs the intellectual role of the department by much more than the 50:50 split would suggest. On the other hand, it applies only to staff, not to consultants, who can be hired with country trust funds. Hence consultants do much of the thinking.

In reviewing the Bank's efforts to integrate environmental considerations, one finds that the organization has handled them best when it has organized environment as a separate *sector*, alongside agriculture, energy, forestry, and so on—a sector bounded, moreover, by *national borders*. Hence the fast growth of special (subnational) environment projects. These are fully consistent with the Bank's long-established mode of organization: they can be given to a task manager located in a country department and handled just like any other project. But conflicts of interest and difficulties of budgeting arise when environment is organized *cross-sectorally*, as a perspective to be injected into all Bank work.

These conflicts of interest have been endemic to the relations between the REDs and the country departments, as county department task managers seek to avoid having outsiders in the REDs interfere with their projects. And the organizational format encourages the assumption that the environmental specialists can be left to take care of all things environmental. For example, the agricultural divisions are now much warier than they were before about embarking upon projects in which unsafe pesticide use may be alleged, but they have done little to promote safer pesticide use. Such projects lie outside the standard production or marketing-oriented projects of the agriculture sector divisions, and also outside the mandate of the REDs.[245] Likewise, the organizational structure encourages task managers to assume that the environmental specialists should deal *only* with the environmental agency of the borrower, not, for example, with the agriculture or the industry ministry, which is the job of the agricultural or industrial specialist.

These consequences of the current organization have helped generate support for the idea of moving environmental specialists from the REDs into the operating divisions, and for downgrading the status of the REDs.[246] Though justified by "mainstreaming," the move may actually *weaken* the Bank's capacity to subject its projects to environmental scrutiny. Once in an operating division, the environmen-

245. Robert Paarlberg, "Managing Pesticide Use in Developing Countries," in Peter Haass, Robert Keohane, and Marc Levy, eds., *Institutions for the Earth* (MIT Press, 1993).

246. By 1995 both the Africa RED and the Latin American/Caribbean RED had been downgraded from divisions to "units" and had greatly shrunk in size.

tal specialist has the incentive to become a task manager for environmental projects rather than to become involved in helping other task managers with the environmental aspects of theirs. The Bank's budgetary and personnel evaluation systems strongly encourage this behavior. But as a task manager, one's technical skills will atrophy, because task managing consists mostly of administration. Insofar as the environmental specialist does work on the projects of others, the tendency is to compromise standards by more than if the environmental specialist had been in a separate division, owing to both peer pressure from the other members of the project team and authoritative pressure from the division chief.

One sees the same limited cross-sectoral reach in the mandate of the Environmentally Sustainable Development vice presidency, which does *not* include energy or population, two fields most implicated in environmental degradation. Likewise, the Bank has found it difficult to organize concerted environment work *across* country departments. The Metropolitan Environmental Improvement Program (MEIP) illustrates the problem.

Started in 1990, the MEIP aimed to devise strategies for urban management in Asia, to build up the on-the-ground capacity to implement such strategies, and to undertake preliminary project preparation for transfer to the country departments. Six Asian cities in six countries were included (Bombay, Katmandu, Colombo, Bangkok, Jakarta, and Manila). Bank professional staff numbered a maximum of four and a half, and each city had a small field office. Cutting across four country departments and aiming to foster the transfer of lessons from one city to another, the MEIP was located in the Asia RED, within the Asia Technical Department. The program flourished while UNDP provided the finance, for its work could be presented to each country department as "free of charge." When UNDP cut its funding in 1993 (as part of a general shrinkage), the MEIP director went to the two Asia vice presidents separately. He showed them different scenarios of how the MEIP program might evolve. Arguing that it was essentially a regional rather than country-specific program, he asked them to draw on vice presidential funds to provide $50,000 for each of the six countries. They declined. The country department directors also declined, saying that it should be up to the vice presidents to fund a *regional* program. They had little interest in a program whose thrust was mainly outside their own department. And they were looking for specific, yearly outputs that a program of institution building over the long term could not always promise. Yet an independent team commissioned by UNDP had rated MEIP performance very favorably.[247] Since 1993 the MEIP has continued to operate on a shoestring budget, funded by bilateral trust funds. Not only have the country

247. "Evaluation Report for the Joint UNDP/World Bank Evaluation Mission of Project RAS/89/010—Metropolitan Environmental Improvement Program (MEIP)," report prepared by Richard Ludwig and Armando Balloffet, received in MEIP office, January 9, 1992, for example, pp. 40, 44.

departments not contributed financially, but none of them has tried to bring to their urban lending programs the organizational model that MEIP developed and tested in the field. This is the model of a local steering committee and a local coordinator, linking up with local citizen groups or NGOs and having real autonomy, backed up by headquarters' expertise.

The same gravitational pull of sectors and countries as the units for Bank environmental work has hindered the drive for Bank initiatives in finding solutions to *regional* environmental problems, such as deforestation and flooding in northwest India, Nepal, and Bangladesh. There is no other organization as well placed to take this role. But the Bank has done little, not even in the Caribbean where well-established organizations of cooperation between the statelets exist. There is simply no reward structure for regional work. A project that depends on the cooperation of three states can be stymied by any one of them. Safer to go for projects under the control of a single government and a single country department.[248]

The Governance Reforms

In October 1992, just as the Board voted to continue Sardar Sarovar for another six months, negotiations for the tenth replenishment of IDA (for 1993–96) were entering their final phase. Galvanized by the Board decision to continue funding Sardar Sarovar and interpreting Sardar Sarovar as symptomatic of continuing institutional problems and policy violations inside the Bank, the NGOs that had been most active in opposing Narmada swung into a campaign to obtain two fundamental accountability reforms. They wanted a radical revision in the Bank's information policy so as to make information about projects more freely available. And they wanted an independent appeal panel that would give directly affected people access to a body empowered to investigate complaints that the Bank was violating its policy procedures and loan agreements. The NGOs announced that they would oppose pledges to IDA 10 by the United States and other governments unless these reforms were carried out. In testimony before the U.S. Congress in spring 1993, they proposed that the Congress redirect its IDA money to other organizations that were more accountable and democratic than the Bank should it not make the two reforms by June 1994.[249]

248. Indeed, the Bank has tended to channel multicountry projects for enclosed seas through the single biggest stakeholding country, which has been convenient for the Bank but unproductive of cooperation between the riparian countries. The reasons for little regional work are by no means only organizational. Loans for such purposes are messy from a legal standpoint, because the participating countries must commit themselves to cross-default clauses, which they may well be unwilling to do. Grants are easier.
249. Lori Udall, "The World Bank and Public Accountability: Has Anything Changed?" in Fox and Brown, eds., *The Struggle for Accountability*. See also the testimony of Barbara

The accountability campaign focused on the subcommittee of the U.S. Congress in charge of authorizing U.S. contributions to IDA. The chairman of the subcommittee, Representative Barney Frank, informed Ernest Stern in private that the Bank had a simple choice: either it adopted an acceptable information policy and independent appeals panel, or it got no U.S. money for IDA 10. The Bank took the threat seriously. It secretly sent drafts of the new information policy and a resolution creating an independent "inspection panel" to Frank and his subcommittee for comments before presenting them formally to the Board. Over the summer of 1993 several of the U.S. NGOs in the Narmada Action Committee commented on several drafts of the inspection panel resolution and the revised information policy, indicating provisions that were unacceptable.[250] European and Japanese NGOs also sent comments to their own executive directors.

The new information policy approved by the Board in August 1993 fell short of what the NGOs and Frank were demanding, though it also represented a substantial change from the old policy.[251] The shortfall gave the U.S. Congress an excuse to authorize its IDA payments for only two years rather than the normal three and to

---

Bramble on behalf of the National Wildlife Federation and testimony of Lori Udall on behalf of the Environmental Defense Fund before the Subcommittee on International Development, Trade, Finance, and Monetary Policy on May 5, 1993. The campaign to win the governance reforms was separate from the later Fifty Years Are Enough campaign, though the two had overlapping memberships. The latter began in the fall of 1993, with the aim of providing an organization and a program to capitalize on the publicity surrounding the 1994 anniversary of the Bretton Woods institutions. The Bank would put out lots of "propaganda," and the media would search for a contrary view in order to give the story more interest. The Fifty Years Are Enough campaign would oblige. Its initial members came from seven environmental and poverty NGOs, led by Doug Hellinger of the Development Group for Alternative Policies (Development GAP) and Bruce Rich of the Environmental Defense Fund. They raised foundation money for two full-time campaign staffers. Throughout they differed among themselves on the issue of abolition of the Bank versus reform, and in particular on whether to argue for cuts in IDA. The agonizingly negotiated platform called for cuts in Part I countries' contributions to the IBRD and the IFC, but not for cuts in IDA. The group garnered much media attention at the Annual Meeting of 1994 in Madrid. It has continued in existence more as a network than as a campaign.

250. Lori Udall, "Comments on World Bank Draft Paper on 'Functions and Operations of an Inspection Function,'" August 23, 1993, submitted to the Clinton administration by Environmental Defense Fund, Friends of the Earth, Sierra Club, National Wildlife Federation, Bank Information Center, and Council for International Environmental Law.

251. "Bank Procedures, Disclosure of Operational Information, BP 17.50," September 1993. It says that the EA for category A projects must be made available in the borrowing country at some public place accessible to affected groups and local NGOs (in this it echoes the existing provisions under OD 4.01). It also says that the same procedure applies to environmental "analysis" for IDA-funded category B projects, as had been agreed in the IDA 10 negotiations. Finally, it says that once the EA or environment report is released locally, it is to be sent to the Bank's Public Information Center, which would make it available to any interested party.

GREENING THE BANK

cut the U.S. Treasury's pledge to IDA 10 by $200 million out of $3.7 billion. During 1994 Congress continued to withhold the third year of IDA authorization and conditioned further support on the implementation of the new reforms. By 1995 the ease of access to Bank information had changed considerably. Ironically, some NGOs noticed the change in the form of *less* willingness on the part of Bank staff to leak them documents, the staff now thinking that the NGOs would be likely to see through public channels most of what they wanted to see. That the NGOs have been less than enthusiastic to do the sifting for themselves is suggested by their use of the Bank's Public Information Center (established in 1994), to which are channeled requests for Bank documents. Of the more than 30,000 direct requests for documents in fiscal 1996, about 70 percent came from commercial firms, 15 percent from public agencies, and only 3 percent from NGOs.[252]

The Board approved a resolution creating an independent inspection panel in September 1993.[253] This, too, fell well short of what the NGOs had envisioned. Its basic principles of operation as approved by the Board give it much less independence than the independent review for Sardar Sarovar had. The latter was appointed by the Board to conduct an investigation. The panel, in contrast, is restricted to recommending to the Board, on the basis of a "preliminary assessment," whether it should do an investigation, and the Board decides.[254] Neverthe-

252. These figures are consistent with the day-by-day experience of the manager of the Public Information Center (Kathleen DiTullio), who reports that business users represent the "overwhelming" majority of all users. Di Tullio, interview with the author, September 5, 1996. The figures are based on a breakdown of requests made by visitors and telephone callers, which account for about two-thirds of all direct requests (via visits, telephone, faxes, and electronic mail); the proportions among visitors and callers were generalized for the whole number of direct requests. Indirect requests cover Internet requests to see a file, of which there were almost two million in 1996. See Public Information Center, *Annual Report, 1996*. NGO staff say the PIC figures understate NGO use, first because some NGOs do not wish to identify themselves as NGOs (whereas business firms have no such hesitation), and second because once one NGO gets hold of a document, it tends to spread it, whereas firms do not.

253. World Bank, "The World Bank Inspection Panel, Resolution 93-10, Resolution IDA 93-6," September 22, 1993; and Ibrahim Shihata, *The World Bank Inspection Panel* (Oxford University Press, 1994).

254. Of the four major cases brought to the panel from its inception in 1994 to the end of 1996, the panel recommended investigations in three cases: Arun hydro project in Nepal, Rondônia Natural Resource Management ("Planafloro") project in Brazil, and Yacyreta hydro project in Argentina/Paraguay. In the Arun case, the Board agreed to an investigation; in the Rondônia case, it asked for "additional information" about the damage but not a full investigation; and in Yacyreta, it has delayed making a decision (as of February 1997). In the fourth case, Jamuna Bridge in Bangladesh, the panel was satisfied with the management's action plan for dealing with the requesters' complaints and did not call for an investigation. Calls for investigations have triggered intense politicking within the Board, the Part II countries opposing and most of the Part I countries in favor. The panel exercises a discipline on the Bank even when it does not do an investigation, because a request for an investigation galvanizes management attention to remedial measures in order to provide the Board with justification for not conducting an investigation. In the case of Rondônia the panel has been

less, the creation of the inspection panel does represent a major departure from previous practice, and its existence owes much to the precedent of the independent review for Sardar Sarovar.

Critics of the panel say that its existence pushes the Bank in the wrong direction: it encourages the Bank, rather than the country, to take "ownership" of projects.[255] Instead of establishing a panel itself, the Bank should have helped the relevant borrowers establish their own panels for the same purpose. But, politically, such an undertaking would not have reduced the threat to IDA.

It can be argued, though, that the panel does help to correct a root problem at the Bank, a pervasive assumption that half-truths can be made to look like whole truths, that external critics can be held off by assurances that the Bank is giving full attention to their concerns, that one can get away with saying one thing and doing another.

Critics of the panel, including many Bank managers, also say that under its present rules the panel discourages staff from seeking imaginative and risky solutions and causes management to steer away from projects that are inherently difficult to "panel-proof," such as dams. It imparts a legalistic thrust to Bank work, eclipsing substance (as in the injunction, "Make your projects panel-proof"), and strengthens an existing tendency toward "OD absolutism," with ODs being interpreted by outsiders as legally binding, like the laws of nation-states. As the drive to codify procedures intensified in the late 1980s and early 1990s, task managers complained of being "OD'ed [overdosed] on ODs." A study of ODs covering Bank projects showed that as of 1992 they specified a total of about two hundred separate tasks for task managers to carry out, and ODs then in the pipeline were expected to double that number.[256] Inevitably, task managers have to be selective in deciding to which of these hundreds of "requirements" to pay attention, but that leaves them and the Bank open to charges of noncompliance, now with the panel ever ready to investigate.[257] The counterargument is that the larger the organization, the greater the need for rules. The Narmada experience suggests that if something is not put into the rules (the ODs), it will typically be overlooked.

Conclusions

The history of the Bank's attempts to come to grips with the "environment" can be read as a great battle over values, attitudes, and images. As in religious wars, the

---

asked to "review" the progress of the management's action plan, giving the Board a source of information about events on the ground independent of management.

255. Elliot Berg and Don Sherk, "The World Bank and Its Environmentalist Critics," in Bretton Woods Commission, *Bretton Woods: Looking to the Future*, Washington, D.C., July 1994, pp. C305–21.

256. Memorandum, Daniel Ritchie, director, Asia Technical Department, to Gautam Kaji and Joseph Wood, vice presidents, East Asia and South Asia, respectively, July 31, 1992.

257. Critics of the panel also say that it is a vehicle for a small number of Washington-based NGOs to gain funding and prominence by initiating and preparing cases to go to the

(environmental) facts have often ended up as relatively unimportant details compared with the symbols and postures and the struggle for power. Rhetoric has flourished on all sides, for the stakes are high and supporters must be won. Yet there are no "objective" standards of value and no consensus about causal relationships.

This chapter has traced the process by which the Bank's dominant conception of the "environment" has shifted from something that needed to be taken into account only exceptionally and then by the mainline technical professionals in agronomy, engineering, and the like, to something that, at least in principle, needs to be examined as part of all project and countrywide work, and with environmental specialists on hand to help. In principle, *all* Bank work should now be assessed for its effects on economic growth, poverty reduction, and environmental sustainability. The change has consisted of a paradigmatic shift from "frontier economics" before 1987, to "environmental protection" up to the early 1990s, and on to the more comprehensive "environmental management" thereafter. Throughout it has been accompanied by changes in staffing, organization, and procedures.

The process by which one paradigm shifted to another was anything but a deliberative response to new knowledge and new opportunities. It was more akin to the grinding of tectonic plates, as people of radically different worldviews were forced by the pressures of environmental disruption and the political responses to deal with one another again and again. Or perhaps it was more akin to learning through angst, as Bank task managers, Bank senior managers, Bank economists, Bank environmental specialists, borrowing-government officials, U.S. NGO representatives, borrowing-country NGO representatives, villagers, and city dwellers tried in overlapping fora to find a common language and common ground, all calling upon powerful normative reasons for doing what they wished to do and not doing what others wished to do. That most environmental services have no market-determined prices compounded the difficulties, making the determination of the (economic) value of environmental services all the more overtly political.

The new environmental values were championed by a spiraling international concert of environmental NGOs and agencies of some Part I governments. They were for the most part resisted by developing-country governments and by many economists and engineers working on development issues. The new environmental values, said the resisters, were based on criteria—such as "ecosystem functioning," "ecosystem damage," and (especially) "environmental sustainability"—that had no clear empirical referents. Yet these kinds of fuzzy notions were being used to pose fundamental challenges to professional identities ("we only deal with hard numbers"), to question the role of "experts" in relation to citizens, and to disparage the very concept of development as we know it.

---

panel. The Center for International Environmental Law, linked to American University in Washington, D.C., has been especially active in this way, bringing activists to Washington from case countries to help prepare cases and encouraging students to work for the same end.

The Bank moved to embrace the self-consciously named environment in 1987 in large part because the NGO campaign and the U.S. Treasury made the costs of not moving too high. In this respect, what happened in the environment field is similar to what has happened elsewhere when the Bank has changed its mind: in most cases, the Bank has not moved without outside pressure from the major donors/owners of the Bank or from NGOs.[258] The "logic of discovery" of new facts has played only a minor role. And perhaps this is as it should be: the Bank operates across such a broad front of issues and has such a diverse set of stakeholders that it would be unwise to change direction except in response to *sustained* external pressure. No doubt the Bank would eventually have moved on the environment anyway because of the larger tide of ideas, despite the legacy of more than twenty years of internal resistance. But the fact that the other multilateral development banks made virtually no moves to integrate environmental considerations until well into the 1990s (with the example of the World Bank to prod them into action) does support the argument that the NGO campaign was crucial. The NGOs paid much less attention to the other multilateral banks than to the World Bank, not because they thought it worse than the others but because it had a much higher political profile.

That the Bank moved largely for tactical reasons has shaped the legitimacy and content of its environmentalism. Even by 1995 a majority of operational staff, in all probability, still believed there was no strong business case for many of the Bank's world-class standards and procedures. Even now some still see them as being imposed by the Board and NGOs, and as interfering in the task for which they are most rewarded: getting projects to the Board on time. That is the reason for the quasi-policing behavior of the REDs, and hence for the difficulties of getting beyond the idea that if all the environmental *procedures* have been complied with, the result must be all right. Also, the tactical nature of the change (combined with the basic organizational structure) tended to lock the Bank into the "environmental protection" mode. In response to the outside pressure, it has focused on doing things that could be held up to NGOs and parliaments as tangible proof of its new environmental commitment: environmental divisions, environmental assessments, environmental projects, and national environmental action plans. This represented an intensification of what the small Office of Environmental Affairs had been trying to do since 1970. The Bank went no further since the NGOs were concerned more with stopping the Bank from doing certain things than encouraging it to grapple with the major causes of environmental degradation, and since there was little *internal* impetus.

By 1992–93, however, the legitimacy of "environment" inside the Bank began to turn strongly positive. Not only in *World Development Report 1992* but in all its

---

258. Mason and Asher, *World Bank since Bretton Woods*; Le Prestre, *The World Bank and the Environmental Challenge.*

publications, it began to promote itself, evangelically, as a champion of environmental sustainability. In principle, "environmental sustainability" imparts a still more distinctive and comprehensive set of objectives to the Bank's work. But the integration of these new concerns has been severely constrained by the Bank's established organization, incentives, and knowledge.

Even environmental assessments, a well-tested methodology of the "environmental protection" paradigm, have had much less impact in modifying environmentally damaging projects and in encouraging the Bank to avoid environmentally sensitive types of projects altogether than one would expect, according to the Bank's own evaluations. The Planafloro project in the Brazilian Amazon, intended to put right what Polonoroeste did not do, illustrates to an egregious degree the weakness of the environmental assessment procedures in the face of a task manager and country director determined to get a project approved. The striking fact is that no one from outside the line of those who had a vested interest in the project was involved in its approval for submission to the Board, even though everyone knew that this project, of all projects, was both risky and exposed to intense NGO scrutiny. Yet this is standard practice rather than something unusual. One sees it also in the Narmada case, where no attempt was made to bring in wise elders from outside the India Department even as the whole Bank was engulfed by the anti-Narmada campaign. On the contrary, the response was to hunker down and exclude as many staff as possible, even within the India Department. These examples show the hazards of making "accountability" a dominant criterion of organizational design when decisionmaking is concentrated in a single individual's hands and when the measures of performance are procedural rather than related to outcomes. Such a structure can be the death of learning.

The shortfall is still more marked in nonproject work, where, for all the managing directors' remarks about environmental issues now being "central" to Country Assistance Strategies, the Bank's own studies of the role of environmental issues in these strategies show that the degree of integration is low to nonexistent. The Bank's basic organizational template—sectoral divisions within country departments—encourages "environment" to be operationalized as a sector parallel to agriculture, forestry, energy, and so on. Anything that requires "environment" to be handled other than as a subnational sector is difficult to organize and sustain, for it runs against established budgetary and reward systems. This organizational feature makes it extremely difficult to integrate the "environmental management" paradigm into the system.

Ultimately, the important question does not concern integration as such, but whether the Bank, with its sizable environmental staff and panoply of environmental procedures, now does a "better" job than it did earlier. Has its environmental work become more serious, better focused, better integrated with its wider policy work, so that the organization now makes different decisions about projects and policies that translate into better "real" impact on aspects of the environment?

Or has the Bank's environment work invented problems in order to have something to show for it, or suppressed problems in order not to delay loans? And if the Bank makes better decisions about the environment, does it thereby do "development" better? The positions of the three hundred Bank people doing environmental work as of the mid-1990s could, after all, be used to help expand agricultural or education lending, or the savings could be passed on in lower loan costs. Indeed, "real" agricultural specialists, foresters, and industrial engineers have been increasingly replaced by green and brown environmental specialists. In the process, technical skills needed to prepare and review agricultural, forestry, and energy projects have been lost.[259] Does this meet any effectiveness-of-resource-use test?

Other questions arise about the cost of the environmental assessment activity relative to its benefits. The Bank's internal procedures are expensive in staff time, as are the environmental procedures, studies, and plans that the borrower should make in order to meet the Bank's requirements. Does the lower risk of environmental damage in Bank projects—and the demonstration effects of environmentally sounder Bank projects on non-Bank projects—outweigh the additional cost of the investments? The question is almost impossible to answer in the absence of clear standards for valuing the environment and the lack of quantitative information on the environmental impact of Bank projects. What is clear is that many task managers continue to think the answer is, broadly speaking, no; they think that EAs add appreciably to project costs without appreciably improving the environmental outcomes. At the same time, the task managers have a distinct incentive to embrace this conclusion because they often experience EAs as complications to their central goal of getting projects through the Board.

Yet another question should be raised, concerning the Bank's environmental (and resettlement) standards. Do these standards create such a cost burden that they significantly impair the Bank's ability to compete against other sources of funds that are less stringent (the Japan Import-Export Bank or the regional multilateral banks, for example)? Should the standards be varied by country groupings rather than made uniform for all? The Bank's environmental critics have tended to forget that it is, at base, a lending institution; its ability to carry out its development-within-the-limits-of-sustainability function rests on its ability to lend, and hence on finding governments willing to pay its prices.

The Bank has moved from Old Testament harshness ("environment versus growth") to New Testament reconciliation (environmentally sustainable development). But it has yet to engage in an open internal debate about what it should be doing in the environment field, a debate in which the sort of questions raised in this

259. Agriculture and rural development have been squeezed not only by environment but also by human resource lending (education, health, nutrition). See Lynne Darling Sherburne-Benz, *Poverty Reduction and the World Bank: Progress and Challenges in the 1990s* (World Bank, 1996), table C-1.

chapter can be tackled—and disagreements honestly aired—with a view to finding answers that command some consensus and are operationally meaningful. This would be difficult, however, without reforming the command and control style of management and introducing ways to evaluate staff by the effectiveness of their projects more than by their reliability in moving them to the Board. Failing some change in the system of internal incentives, there is a danger that New Testament reconciliation may remain at the level of images and values and bring little improvement in what happens on the ground.

Contributors

Alex Duncan is Program Director of the Food Studies Group, Oxford University.

Francisco Ferreira is an Economist with the East Asia and Pacific Region of the World Bank.

S. Guhan is an Emeritus Fellow of the Madras Institute for Development Studies, India.

Catherine Gwin is Vice President of Studies at the Overseas Development Council.

Toyoo Gyohten is former Chairman of the Board of Directors, Bank of Tokyo Ltd., and former Vice Minister of Finance for International Affairs, Japan.

Jonas Haralz is former Executive Director of the World Bank for Nordic Countries.

Devesh Kapur is Assistant Professor of Government at Harvard University.

Mahn-Je Kim is Chairman of POSCO and former Deputy Prime Minister and Minister of Economic Planning of Korea.

Hilmar Kopper is at Deutsche Bank AG.

Carol Lancaster is a Professor at Georgetown University.

John P. Lewis is Professor of Economics and International Affairs Emeritus, Princeton University.

Bakary Ouayogode is Director of Research Programs, MRSEPT.

Jacques Pégatiénan is at the Université Nationale de Côte d'Ivoire.

Jacques Polak is President of the Per Jacobbsen Foundation and former Director of Research and former member of the Executive Board of the International Monetary Fund.

Nicholas Stern is a Professor at the London School of Economics and Chief Economist at the European Bank for Reconstruction and Development.

Carlos M. Urzúa is at El Colegio de Mexico.

Robert Wade is Professor of Political Science at the Watson Institute for International Studies at Brown University.

Richard Webb is Chairman of Cuanto S.A., Lima, Peru, and Governor, Central Reserve Bank of Peru, 1980–85.

Index

Page numbers for entries occurring in notes are followed by an n and those for entries in tables, by a t.

751

49; Mexican debt crises and, 53, 55,
102–03, 105–06, 108, 233, 564; Mexican oil boom and, 69; orientation
toward developing countries, 479, 480–
81; Pearson Commission and, 477–478;
peso devaluation and, 53, 55; potential
areas of conflict with the IBRD, 485–
93; proposed merger with the IBRD,
312, 520–21; relations with Tanzania,
396–97; research activities of, 595;
South Asian operations of, 323; special
drawing rights of, 474, 475; stabilization
programs, environmental effects of,
722–23; Structural Adjustment Facility
of, 481; Sub-Saharan Africa structural
adjustment lending by, 181, 182, 191–
92; tax reform data of, 570; Trust Fund
of, 480–81; U.S. Congress and, 222
International Monetary Fund, relations
with the IBRD, 473–521; concordat for,
510–26; during debt crisis, 478–79, 484–
85; effect of changing world economy
on, 478–85; lending conditionality issue
in, 483, 485–89; member government
initiatives and, 500–01; policy framework papers and, 501–03; postconcordat,
516–21; staff reports and, 499–500
International Petroleum Company, 255
International Rice Research Institute
(IRRI), 601
International Rivers Network, 669
"International Trade and the Environ-
ment" (Low, ed.), 566
Investment Criteria and Project Appraisal,
568
IR. *See* Indian Railways
Iranian hostage crisis, 224
IRRI. *See* International Rice Research Institute
Irrigation project loans, to South Asia,
351–59, 352t, 361–62
Ishizaka, Taizo, 280
Italy, as IBRD bond market, 441, 460
Ivory Coast. *See* Côte d'Ivoire
Ixtapa-Zihuatanejo, 65

Jamaica: Expanded Cofinancing Operations loans to, 309; structural adjustment loans to, 543
Japan, 7–8, 275–316; African structural adjustment support by, 178; Allied occupa-

tion of, 276; as Asian Development
Bank shareholder, 290–91; Bretton
Woods institutions and, 277–78; bullet
train loans to, 288–89; Dodge stabilization policy for, 276, 277; economic loans
and grants to Korea, 23; Economic Rehabilitation in Occupied Areas aid to,
277; first IBRD loan to, 281–83;
Government and Relief in Occupied
Areas aid to, 18, 277; graduation from
IBRD loans, 288, 290–91; human
resource development in, 309–10; as
IBRD cofinancier, 296–97; IBRD financial contributions by, 315, 316; IBRD
first mission to, 279–81; IBRD intellectual contributions by, 316; as IBRD
lender, 203t, 472; IBRD loan policy
toward (*1950–55*), 278–83; IBRD loan
policy toward (*1955–66*), 283–91; as
IBRD shareholder, 275, 291–92, 295–
97; IDA share harmonization and, 294;
IFC capital increase opposition by, 241;
IMF membership of, 278–79; international financial institutions and, 275,
293–94; iron and steel sector loans to,
283–85; Kurobe power plant project in,
286, 291; management style in, 303;
Meiji Restoration in, 297; motorway
project loans to, 286–88, 290, 291; Narmada Valley Project opposition by, 696;
Nihon Doro Kodan of, 287–88, 291;
OECD membership of, 290; post–
World War II economic development
of, 275, 297–98; power development
loans to, 285–86; Priority Production
System in, 276, 283; relationship with
IBRD, 276–81; selected capital increase
of *1984* and, 293–95; steel sector loans
to, 260–61; thermal power plant loan to,
281–83; U.S. aid to, 277; U.S.-
supported loans to, 259
Japan Development Bank, 277, 282, 284, 302
Japan Electric Machinery Manufacturers
Association, 280
Japanese, as IBRD staff members, 314–15
Japan National Railways (JNR), 288
Japan Special Fund, 295
Jasperson, Fred, 85
Jaycox, Edward (Kim), 177; CFA franc
devaluation and, 181; Global Coalition